AMERICA'S TOP JOBS

for People Without a Four-Year Degree

Detailed Information on 190 Good Jobs in All Major Fields and Industries

Sixth Edition

- ★ **Thorough, up-to-date descriptions of 190 top jobs for people without a four-year degree**

- ★ **Information on skills needed, education and training required, salaries, growth potential, and much more**

- ★ **Special section on how to find a job fast**

- ★ **Resume examples by professional resume writers for top jobs that do not require a four-year college degree**

- ★ **Helpful information on labor market trends**

Part of America's Top Jobs® Series

Michael Farr

jist Works

America's Top Jobs for People Without a Four-Year Degree, *Sixth Edition*
Detailed Information on 190 Good Jobs in All Major Fields and Industries

© 2003 by JIST Publishing, Inc.

Published by JIST Works, an imprint of JIST Publishing, Inc.
8902 Otis Avenue
Indianapolis, IN 46216-1033
Phone: 800-648-JIST   Fax: 800-JIST-FAX
E-mail: info@jist.com   Web site: www.jist.com

Visit our Web site for more details on JIST, free job search information, book excerpts, and ordering information on our many products!

Some other books by Michael Farr:
The Very Quick Job Search
The Quick Resume & Cover Letter Book
America's Top Resumes for America's Top Jobs
Getting the Job You Really Want
Best Jobs for the 21st Century
    (LaVerne L. Ludden, coauthor)

Other books in the America's Top Jobs® series:
America's Top 300 Jobs
America's Fastest Growing Jobs
America's Top Computer and Technical Jobs
America's Top Jobs for College Graduates
America's Top Military Careers
Career Guide to America's Top Industries

For other career-related materials, turn to the back of this book.

Quantity discounts are available for JIST books. Please call our Sales Department at 1-800-648-JIST for more information and a free catalog.

Editors: Susan Pines, Veda Dickerson, Mary Ellen Stephenson
Cover and Interior Designer: Aleata Howard
Interior Layout: Carolyn J. Newland

Printed in the United States of America
05 04 03 02   9 8 7 6 5 4 3 2 1

ISBN 1-56370-882-5

Relax—You Don't Have to Read This Whole Book!

This is a big book, but you don't need to read it all. I've organized it into easy-to-use sections so you can browse just the information you want. To get started, simply scan the table of contents, where you'll find brief explanations of the major sections plus a list of the jobs described in this book. Really, this book is easy to use, and I hope it helps you.

Who Should Use This Book?

This is more than a book of job descriptions. I've spent quite a bit of time thinking about how to make its contents useful for a variety of situations, including

★ **Exploring career options.** The job descriptions in Section One give a wealth of information on many of the most desirable jobs in the labor market.

★ **Considering more education or training.** The information helps you avoid costly mistakes in choosing a career or deciding on additional training or education—and it increases your chances of planning a bright future.

★ **Job seeking.** This book helps you identify new job targets, prepare for interviews, and write targeted resumes. The career planning and job search advice in Section Two has been proven to cut job search time in half!

★ **Career planning.** The job descriptions help you explore your options, and Sections Two and Three provide career planning advice and other useful information.

Source of Information

The occupational descriptions in this book come from the good people at the U.S. Department of Labor, as published in the most recent edition of the *Occupational Outlook Handbook*. The *OOH* is the best source of career information available, and the descriptions include the latest data on earnings and other details. Other sections also present solid information from various sources at the U.S. Department of Labor. So, thank you to all the people at the Labor Department who gather, compile, analyze, and make sense of this information. It's good stuff, and I hope you can make good use of it.

Mike Farr

Mike Farr

Table of Contents

Summary of Major Sections

Introduction. The introduction explains each job description element, gives tips on using the book for career exploration and job seeking, and provides other details. *The introduction begins on page 1.*

Section One: Descriptions of 190 Top Jobs for People Without a Four-Year Degree. This section presents thorough descriptions of 190 jobs that do not require a four-year college degree. Each description gives information on significant points, nature of the work, working conditions, employment, training, other qualifications, advancement, job outlook, earnings, related occupations, and sources of additional information. The jobs are presented in alphabetical order. The page numbers where specific descriptions begin are listed here in the table of contents. *Section One begins on page 9.*

Section Two: *The Quick Job Search—Seven Steps to Getting a Good Job in Less Time.* This brief but important section offers results-oriented career planning and job search techniques. It includes tips on identifying your key skills, defining your ideal job, using effective job search methods, writing resumes, organizing your time, improving your interviewing skills, and following up on leads. The second part of this section features professionally written and designed resumes for some of America's top jobs for people without a four-year college degree. *Section Two begins on page 425.*

Section Three: Important Trends in Jobs and Industries. This section includes two well-written articles on labor market trends. The articles are short and worth your time. *Section Three begins on page 485.*

Titles of the articles in Section Three are

★ "Tomorrow's Jobs"

★ "Employment Trends in Major Industries"

The 190 Jobs Described in Section One

The titles for the 190 jobs described in Section One are listed below, in alphabetical order. The page number where each description begins is also listed. Simply find jobs that interest you, and then read those descriptions. An introduction to Section One begins on page 3 and provides additional information on how to interpret the descriptions.

v

INTRODUCTION

This book is about improving your life, not just about selecting a job. The career you choose will have an enormous impact on how you live your life.

While a huge amount of information is available on occupations, most people don't know where to find accurate, reliable facts to help them make good career decisions—or they don't take the time to look. Important choices such as what to do with your career or whether to get additional training or education deserve your time.

If you are considering a job change, this book will help with solid information. Typically, a higher level of training and education is needed to get better jobs, but some jobs that offer high pay do not require a four-year degree. The education, training, skills, and experience needed for the jobs described in *America's Top Jobs for People Without a Four-Year Degree* vary enormously. This book gives you the facts you need for exploring your options.

A certain type of work or workplace may interest you as much as a certain type of job. If your interests and values are to work with children, for example, you can do this in a variety of work environments, in a variety of industries, and in a variety of jobs. For this reason, I suggest you begin exploring alternatives by following your interests and finding a career path that allows you to use your talents doing something you enjoy.

Also, remember that money is not everything. The time you spend in career planning can pay off in more than higher earnings. Being satisfied with your work—and your life—is often more important than how much you earn. This book can help you find the work that suits you best.

Keep in Mind That Your Situation Is *Not* "Average"

While projected employment growth and earnings trends are quite positive for many occupations and industries, keep in mind that the averages in this book will not be true for many individuals. Within any field, some people earn more and some less.

My point is this: Your situation is probably not average. Some people do better than others, and some are willing to accept less pay for a more desirable work environment or for other reasons. Earnings vary enormously in different parts of the country, in different occupations, in different industries, and with different employers. But this book's solid information is a great place to start. Reliable information will give you a strong foundation for good decisions.

Four Important Labor Market Trends That Will Affect Your Career

Our economy has changed in dramatic ways over the past 10 years, with profound effects on how we work and live. Section Three of this book provides more information on labor market trends but, in case you don't read it, here are four trends that you simply *must* consider.

I. Education and Earnings Are Related

I'm sure you won't be surprised to learn that people with higher levels of education and training have higher average earnings. The data that follows comes from the Department of Labor's Internet site. The site presents the median earnings for people with various levels of education. (The median is the point where half earn more and half earn less.) The site also indicates the average percentage of people at that educational level who are unemployed. Based on this information, I computed the earnings advantage of people at various education levels compared to people with a high school degree.

Earnings for Year-Round, Full-Time Workers Age 25 and Over, by Educational Attainment

Level of Education	Median Annual Earnings	Premium Over High School Grads	Unemployment Rate
Professional degree	$80,230	$51,423 (179%)	1.3%
Doctoral degree	$70,476	$41,669 (145%)	1.4%
Master's degree	$55,302	$26,495 (92%)	1.6%
Bachelor's degree	$46,276	$17,469 (61%)	1.9%
Associate degree	$35,389	$6,582 (23%)	2.5%
Some college, no degree	$32,400	$3,593 (12%)	3.2%
High school graduate	$28,807	——	4.0%
Less than a high school diploma	$21,400	$–7,407 (–25%)	7.1%

Source: Earnings—U.S. Census Bureau, Current Population Survey, PINC-3, updated 12/2001; Unemployment rate—Bureau of Labor Statistics, 1998 data; Earnings—Bureau of the Census, 1997 data.

The earnings gap between a college graduate and someone with a high school education is growing wider and is now $17,469 a year. That's enough to buy a nice car, make a down payment on a house, or even take a month's vacation for two to Europe. As you see, over a lifetime, these additional earnings can make an enormous difference in the college graduate's lifestyle.

And there is more. Jobs that require a four-year college degree are projected to grow about twice as fast as jobs that do not. Research shows that people with higher educational levels are less likely to be unemployed and that they remain unemployed for shorter periods of time. Overall, the data on earnings and other criteria indicate that people with more education and training do better than those with less. There are exceptions, of course, but for most people, more education and training results in higher earnings and lower rates of unemployment.

Many jobs can be obtained without a college degree, and some workers without college degrees earn more than those with degrees. However, most better-paying jobs require either training beyond high school or substantial work experience.

2. Knowledge of Computer and Other Technologies Is Increasingly Important

As you look over the list of jobs in the table of contents, you may notice that many jobs require computer or technical skills. Even jobs that do not appear to be technical often call for computer literacy. Managers, for example, are often expected to understand and use spreadsheet, word-processing, and database software.

In all fields, people without job-related technical and computer skills will have a more difficult time finding good opportunities than people who have these skills. Older workers, by the way, often do not have the computer skills that younger workers do. Employers tend to hire the skills they need, and people without these abilities won't get the best jobs. So consider upgrading your job-related computer and technology skills if you need to—and plan to stay up-to-date on your current and future jobs.

3. Ongoing Education and Training Are Essential

School and work once were separate activities, and most people did not go back to school after they began working. But with rapid changes in technology, most people are now required to learn throughout their work lives. Jobs are constantly upgraded, and today's jobs often cannot be handled by people who have only the knowledge and skills that were adequate for workers a few years ago. To remain competitive, people without technical or computer skills must get them. Those who do not will face increasingly limited job options.

What this means is that you should plan to upgrade your job skills throughout your working life. This can include taking formal courses, or it can mean reading work-related magazines at home, signing up for on-the-job training, and participating in other forms of education. Upgrading your work-related skills on an ongoing basis is no longer optional for most jobs, and you ignore doing so at your peril.

4. Good Career Planning Has Increased in Importance

Most people spend more time watching TV in a week than they spend on career planning during an entire year. Yet most people will change their jobs many times and make major career changes five to seven times.

While you probably picked up this book for its information on jobs, it also provides a great deal of information on career planning. For example, Section Two gives good career and job search advice, and Section Three has useful information on labor market trends. I urge you to read these and related materials, because career-planning and job-seeking skills are the keys to surviving in this new economy.

Information on the Major Sections of This Book

I want this book to be easy to use. In the table of contents, I provide brief comments on each section, and that may be all you need. If not, here are some additional details you may find useful in getting the most out of this book.

Section One: Descriptions of 190 Top Jobs for People Without a Four-Year Degree

Section One is the main part of this book and probably the reason you picked it up. It contains brief, well-written descriptions for 190 major jobs typically held by people without four-year college degrees. The content for these job descriptions comes from the U.S. Department of Labor and is considered by many people to be the most accurate and up-to-date data available. The jobs are presented in alphabetical order.

Together, the jobs in Section One provide enormous variety at all levels of earnings and training. One way to explore career options is to go through the table of contents and identify jobs that seem interesting. If you are interested in medical jobs, for example, you can quickly spot those you want to learn more about. You may also see other jobs that look interesting, and you should consider those as well.

Next, read the descriptions for the jobs that interest you and, based on what you learn, identify those that *most* interest you. Those are the jobs you should consider. Sections Two and Three give you additional information on how best to do so.

Each occupational description in this book follows a standard format, making it easier for you to compare jobs. The following overview describes the kinds of information found in each part of a description and offers tips on how to interpret the information.

Job Title

This is the title used for the job in the *Occupational Outlook Handbook,* published by the U.S. Department of Labor.

Numbers

The numbers following the job title refer to closely related job titles from the Occupational Information Network (O*NET). The O*NET was developed by the U.S. Department of Labor to replace the older *Dictionary of Occupational Titles* (*DOT*). Like the *DOT* in the past, the O*NET is used by state employment service offices to classify applicants and job openings, and by a variety of career information systems. You can get additional information on the related O*NET titles on the Internet at www.onetcenter.org or at www.careerOINK.com. Reference books that provide O*NET descriptions include the *O*NET Dictionary of Occupational Titles* and the *Enhanced Occupational Outlook Handbook,* both published by JIST Publishing. Your librarian can help you find these books.

Significant Points

The bullet points in this part of a description highlight key characteristics for each job, such as recent trends or education and training requirements.

Nature of the Work

This part of the description discusses what workers typically do in a particular job. Individual job duties may vary by industry or employer. For instance, workers in larger firms tend to be more specialized, whereas those in smaller firms often have a wider variety of duties. Most occupations have several levels of skills and responsibilities through which workers may progress. Beginners may start as trainees performing routine tasks under close supervision. Experienced workers usually undertake more difficult tasks and are expected to perform with less supervision.

In this part of a description, you will also find information about the influence of technological advancements on the way work is done. For example, the Internet allows purchasing agents to acquire supplies with a click of the mouse, saving time and money.

This part also discusses emerging specialties. For instance, webmasters—who are responsible for all the technical aspects involved in operating a website—comprise a specialty within systems analysts, computer scientists, and database administrators.

Working Conditions

This part of the description identifies the typical hours worked, the workplace environment, physical activities, risk of injury, special equipment, and the extent of travel required. For example, police and detectives are susceptible to injury, while paralegals and legal assistants have high job-related stress. Radiologic technologists and technicians may wear protective clothing or equipment; construction laborers do physically demanding work; and flight attendants travel regularly.

In many occupations, people work regular business hours— 40 hours a week, Monday through Friday. In other occupations, they do not. For example, sales worker supervisors often work evenings and weekends. Work settings can range from a hospital, to a mall, to an off-shore oil rig.

Employment

This section reports the number of jobs the occupation recently provided and the key industries where these jobs are found. When significant, the geographic distribution of jobs and the proportion of part-time (less than 35 hours a week) and self-employed workers in the occupation are mentioned. Self-employed workers accounted for nearly eight percent of the work force but were concentrated in a small number of occupations, such as carpenters, photographers, and farmers.

Training, Other Qualifications, and Advancement

After you know what a job is all about, you need to understand how to train for it. This section describes the most significant sources of training, including the training preferred by employers, the typical length of training, and advancement possibilities. Job skills are sometimes acquired through high school, informal on-the-job training, formal training (including apprenticeships), the armed forces, home study, hobbies, or previous work experience. For example, experience is particularly important for many sales jobs. Many professional and technical jobs, on the other hand, require formal postsecondary education—postsecondary vocational or technical training, or college, postgraduate, or professional education.

This section of the job description also mentions desirable skills, aptitudes, and personal characteristics. For some entry-level jobs, personal characteristics are more important than formal training. Employers generally seek people who communicate well, compute accurately, think logically, learn quickly, get along with others, and demonstrate dependability.

Some occupations require certification or licensing to enter the field, to advance, or to practice independently. Certification or licensing generally involves completing courses and passing examinations. More and more occupations require continuing education or skill improvement to keep up with the changing economy or to improve advancement opportunities.

Job Outlook

In planning for the future, you must consider potential job opportunities. This section of a job description indicates what factors will result in growth or decline in the number of jobs. In some cases, the description mentions that an occupation is likely to provide numerous job openings or relatively few openings. Occupations which are large and have high turnover, such as insurance sales agents, generally provide the most job openings, reflecting the need to replace workers who transfer to other occupations or who stop working.

Some statements discuss the relationship between the number of jobseekers and the number of job openings. In some occupations, there is a rough balance between jobseekers and openings, whereas other occupations are characterized by shortages or surpluses. Limited training facilities, salary regulations, or undesirable aspects of the work—as in the case of social and human service assistants—can cause shortages of entrants. On the other hand, glamorous or potentially high-paying occupations, such as actors or musicians, generally have surpluses of jobseekers. Variation in job opportunities by industry, size of firm, or geographic location also may be discussed. Even in crowded fields, job openings do exist. Good students or well qualified individuals should not be deterred from undertaking training or seeking entry.

Susceptibility to layoffs due to imports, slowdowns in economic activity, technological advancements, or budget cuts are also addressed in this section. For example, employment of real estate brokers and sales agents is sensitive to slowdowns in the economy, while employment of tool and die makers is sensitive to technological advancements.

Key Phrases Used in the Descriptions
This box explains how to interpret the key phrases that describe projected changes in employment. It also explains the terms for the relationship between the number of job openings and the number of job seekers. The descriptions of this relationship in a particular occupation reflect the knowledge and judgment of economists in the Bureau's Office of Occupational Statistics and Employment Projections.

Changing Employment Between 2000 and 2010

If the statement reads:	Employment is projected to:
Grow much faster than average	Increase 36 percent or more
Grow faster than average	Increase 21 to 35 percent
Grow about as fast as average	Increase 10 to 20 percent
Grow more slowly than average	Increase 3 to 9 percent
Little or no change	Increase 0 to 2 percent
Decline	Decrease 1 percent or more

Opportunities and Competition for Jobs

If the statement reads:	Job openings compared to job seekers may be:
Very good to excellent opportunities	More numerous
Good or favorable opportunities	In rough balance
May face keen competition or can expect keen competition	Fewer

Earnings

This section discusses typical earnings and how workers are compensated—annual salaries, hourly wages, commissions, piece rates, tips, or bonuses. Within every occupation, earnings vary by experience, responsibility, performance, tenure, and geographic area. Earnings data from the Bureau of Labor Statistics and, in some cases, from outside sources are included. Data may cover the entire occupation or a specific group within the occupation.

Benefits account for a significant portion of total compensation costs to employers. Benefits such as paid vacation, health insurance, and sick leave may not be mentioned because they are so widespread. Employers may offer other, less-traditional benefits, such as flexible hours and profit-sharing plans to attract and retain highly qualified workers. Less-common benefits also include childcare, tuition for dependents, housing assistance, summers off, and free or discounted merchandise or services.

Related Occupations

Occupations involving similar duties, skills, interests, education, and training are listed here. This allows you to look up these jobs, if they interest you.

Sources of Additional Information

No single publication can completely describe all aspects of an occupation. Thus, this section lists mailing addresses for associations, government agencies, unions, and other organizations that can provide occupational information. In some cases, toll-free phone numbers and Internet addresses also are listed. These are provided for your convenience and do not constitute an endorsement. Free or relatively inexpensive publications offering more information may be mentioned. Some of these are available in libraries, school career centers, guidance offices, or on the Internet.

Section Two: *The Quick Job Search*—Seven Steps to Getting a Good Job in Less Time

For more than 20 years now, I've been interested in helping people find better jobs in less time. If you have ever experienced unemployment, you know it is not pleasant. Unemployment is something most people want to get over quickly—in fact, the quicker the better. Section Two will give you some techniques to help.

I know that most of you who read this book want to improve yourselves. You want to consider career and training options that lead to a better job and life in whatever way you define this—better pay, more flexibility, more-enjoyable or more-meaningful work, proving to your mom that you really can do anything you set your mind to, and so on. That is why I include advice on career planning and job search in the first part of Section Two. It's a short section, but it includes the basics that are most important in planning your career and in reducing the time it takes to get a job. I hope it will make you think about what is important to you in the long run.

The second part of Section Two showcases professionally written resumes for some of America's top jobs for people without a four-year degree. Use these as examples when creating your resume.

I know you will resist completing the activities in Section Two, but consider this: It is often not the best person who gets the job, but the best job seeker. People who do their career planning and job search homework often get jobs over those with better credentials, because they have these distinct advantages:

1. **They get more interviews,** including many for jobs that will never be advertised.

2. **They do better in interviews.**

People who understand what they want and what they can offer employers present their skills more convincingly and are much better at answering problem questions. And, because they have learned more about job search techniques, they are likely to get more interviews with employers who need the skills they have.

Doing better in interviews often makes the difference between getting a job offer or sitting at home. And spending time planning your career can make an enormous difference to your happiness and lifestyle over time. So please consider reading Section Two and completing its activities. I suggest you schedule a time right now to at least read Section Two. An hour or so spent there can help you do just enough better in your career planning, job seeking, and interviewing to make the difference. Go ahead—get out your schedule book and get it over with (nag, nag, nag).

One other thing: If you work through Section Two, and it helps you in some significant way, I'd like to hear from you. Please write or e-mail me via the publisher, whose contact information appears elsewhere in this book.

Section Three: Important Trends in Jobs and Industries

This section is made up of two very good articles on labor market trends. These articles come directly from U.S. Department of Labor sources and are interesting, well written, and short. One is on overall trends, with an emphasis on occupational groups; the other is on trends in major industry groups. I know this sounds boring, but both articles are quick reads and will give you a good idea of factors that will impact your career in the years to come.

The first article is titled "Tomorrow's Jobs." It highlights many important trends in employment and includes information on the fastest growing jobs, jobs with high pay at various levels of education, and other details.

The second article is titled "Employment Trends in Major Industries." I included this information because you may find that you can use your skills or training in industries you have not considered. The article provides a good review of major trends with an emphasis on helping you make good employment decisions. This information can help you seek jobs in industries that offer higher pay or that are more likely to interest you. Many people overlook one important fact—the industry you work in is as important as the occupation you choose.

Tips on Using This Book

This book is based on information from government sources and includes the most up-to-date and accurate data available anywhere. The entries are well written and pack a lot of information into short descriptions. *America's Top Jobs for People Without a Four-Year Degree* can be used in many ways. The following discussion provides tips on the four most-frequent uses:

● For people exploring career, education, or training alternatives

● For job seekers

● For employers and business people

● For counselors, instructors, and other career specialists

Tips for People Exploring Career, Education, or Training Alternatives

America's Top Jobs for People Without a Four-Year Degree is an excellent resource for anyone exploring career, education, or training alternatives. Many people take career interest tests to identify career options. This book can be used for the same purpose.

Many people do not have a good idea of what they want to do in their careers. They may be considering additional training or education but may not know what sort they should get. If you are one of these people, *America's Top Jobs for People Without a Four-Year Degree* can help in several ways. Here are a few pointers.

Review the list of jobs. Trust yourself. Research studies indicate that most people have a good sense of their interests. Your interests can be used to guide you to career options you should consider in more detail.

Begin by looking over the occupations listed in the table of contents. Look at all the jobs, because you may identify previously overlooked possibilities. If other people will be using this book, please don't mark in it. Instead, on a separate sheet of paper, list the jobs that interest you. Or make a photocopy of the table of contents and mark the jobs that interest you.

Next, carefully read the descriptions of the jobs that most interest you. A quick review will often eliminate one or more of these jobs based on pay, working conditions, education required, or other considerations. After you have identified the three or four jobs that seem most interesting, research each one more thoroughly before making any important decisions.

Study the jobs and their training and education requirements. Too many people decide to obtain additional training or education without knowing much about the jobs the training will lead to. Reviewing the descriptions in this book is one way to learn more about an occupation before you enroll in an education or training program. If you are currently a student, the job descriptions in this book can also help you decide on a major course of study or learn more about the jobs for which your studies are preparing you.

Do not be too quick to eliminate a job that interests you. If a job requires more education or training than you currently have, you can obtain this training in many ways.

Don't abandon your past experience and education too quickly. If you have significant work experience, training, or education, these should not be abandoned too quickly. Many skills you have learned and used in previous jobs or other settings can apply to related jobs. Many times, after people carefully consider what they want to do, they change careers and find that the skills they have can still be used.

America's Top Jobs for People Without a Four-Year Degree can help you explore career options in several ways. First, carefully review descriptions for jobs you have held in the past. On a separate sheet of paper, list the skills needed in those jobs. Then do the same for jobs that interest you now. By comparing the lists, you will be able to identify skills you used in previous jobs that you could also use in jobs that interest you for the future. These "transferable" skills form the basis for moving to a new career.

You can also identify skills you have developed or used in nonwork activities, such as hobbies, family responsibilities, volunteer work, school, military, and extracurricular interests.

The descriptions can be used even if you want to stay with the same employer. For example, you may identify jobs within your organization that offer more rewarding work, higher pay, or other advantages over your present job. Read the descriptions related to these jobs, and you may be able to transfer into another job rather than leave the organization.

Tips for Job Seekers

You can use the descriptions in this book to give you an edge in finding job openings and in getting job offers—even when you are competing with people who have better credentials. Here are some ways *America's Top Jobs for People Without a Four-Year Degree* can help you in the job search.

Identify related job targets. You may be limiting your job search to a small number of jobs for which you feel qualified, but by doing so you eliminate many jobs you could do and enjoy. Your search for a new job should be broadened to include more possibilities.

Go through the entire list of jobs in the table of contents and check any that require skills similar to those you have. Look at all the jobs, since doing so sometimes helps you identify targets you would otherwise overlook.

Many people are not aware of the many specialized jobs related to their training or experience. The descriptions in *America's Top Jobs for People Without a Four-Year Degree* are for major job titles, but a variety of more specialized jobs may require similar skills. Reference books that list more specialized job titles include the *Enhanced Occupational Outlook Handbook* and the *O*NET Dictionary of Occupational Titles*. Both are published by JIST.

The descriptions can also point out jobs that interest you but that have higher responsibility or compensation levels. While you may not consider yourself qualified for such jobs now, you should think about seeking jobs that are above your previous levels but within your ability to handle.

Prepare for interviews. This book's job descriptions are an essential source of information to help you prepare for interviews. If you carefully review the description of a job before an interview, you will be much better prepared to emphasize your key skills. You should also review descriptions for past jobs and identify skills needed in the new job.

Negotiate pay. The job descriptions in this book will help you know what pay range to expect. Note that local pay and other details can differ substantially from the national averages in the descriptions.

Tips for Employers and Business People

If you are an employer, a human resource professional, or other business person, you can use this book's information to write job descriptions, study pay ranges, and set criteria for new employees. The information can also help you conduct more-effective interviews by providing a list of key skills needed by new hires.

Tips for Counselors, Instructors, and Other Career Specialists

Counselors, instructors, and other career specialists will find suggestions in the previous tips for using this book to help people explore career options or find jobs. My best suggestion to professionals is to get this book off the shelf and into the hands of the people who need it. Leave it on a table or desk and show people how the information can help them. Wear this book out—its real value is as a tool used often and well.

Additional Information About the Projections

Readers interested in more information about projections and details on the labor force, economic growth, industry and occupational employment, or the methods and assumptions used in this book's projections should consult the November 2001 edition of the *Monthly Labor Review,* published by the Bureau of Labor Statistics. It provides information on the limitations inherent in economic and employment projections.

For more information about employment change, job openings, earnings, unemployment rates, and training requirements by occupation, consult *Occupational Projections and Training Data* published by the Bureau of Labor Statistics.

For occupational information from an industry perspective, including some occupations and career paths that *America's Top Jobs for People Without a Four-Year Degree* does not cover, consult another BLS publication, the *Career Guide to Industries*. This book is also available from JIST, under the title *Career Guide to America's Top Industries*.

DESCRIPTIONS OF 190 TOP JOBS FOR PEOPLE WITHOUT A FOUR-YEAR DEGREE

This is the book's major section. It contains descriptions for 190 major occupations that typically do not require a four-year college degree. The jobs are arranged in alphabetical order. Refer to the table of contents for a list of the jobs and the page numbers where their descriptions begin.

The table of contents can also help you identify jobs you want to explore. If you are interested in technical jobs, for example, you can go through the list and quickly find those you want to learn more about. Also, you may spot other jobs that might be interesting, and you should consider those as well. Read the descriptions for any jobs that sound interesting.

While the descriptions in this section are easy to understand, the introduction to this book provides additional information for interpreting them. When reading the descriptions, keep in mind that they present information that is the average for the country. Conditions in your area and with specific employers may be quite different.

Also, you may come across jobs that sound interesting but require additional training or education. Don't eliminate them too soon. There are many ways to obtain training and education, and most people change jobs and careers many times. You probably have more skills than you realize that can transfer to new jobs, so consider taking some chances. Get out of your rut. Do what it takes to fulfill your dreams. Be creative. You often have more opportunities than barriers, but you have to go out and find the opportunities.

Actors, Producers, and Directors

O*NET 27-2011.00, 27-2012.01, 27-2012.02, 27-2012.03, 27-2012.04, 27-2012.05

Significant Points

- Actors endure long periods of unemployment, intense competition for roles, and frequent rejections in auditions.

- Formal training through a university or acting conservatory is typical; however, many actors, producers, and directors find work based on experience and talent alone.

- Because earnings for actors are erratic, many supplement their incomes by holding jobs in other fields.

Nature of the Work

Actors, producers, and directors express ideas and create images in theater, film, radio, television, and other performing arts media. They interpret a writer's script to entertain, inform, or instruct an audience. Although the most famous actors, producers, and directors work in film, network television, or theater in New York or Los Angeles, far more work in local or regional television studios, theaters, or film production companies engaged in advertising, public relations, or independent, small-scale movie productions.

Actors perform in stage, radio, television, video, or motion picture productions. They also work in cabarets, nightclubs, theme parks, and commercials, and in "industrial" films produced for training and educational purposes. Most actors struggle to find steady work; only a few ever achieve recognition as stars. Some well-known, experienced performers may be cast in supporting roles. Others work as "extras," with no lines to deliver, or make brief, cameo appearances speaking only one or two lines. Some actors also teach in high school or university drama departments, acting conservatories, or public programs.

Producers are entrepreneurs, overseeing the business and financial decisions of a production. They select scripts and approve development of script ideas, arrange financing, and determine the size and cost of stage, radio, television, video, or motion picture productions. Producers hire directors, principal cast members, and key production staff members. They also negotiate contracts with artistic and design personnel in accordance with collective bargaining agreements and guarantee payment of salaries, rent, and other expenses. Producers coordinate the activities of writers, directors, managers, and agents to ensure that each project stays on schedule and within budget.

Directors are responsible for the creative decisions of a production. They interpret scripts, express concepts to set and costume designers, audition and select cast members, conduct rehearsals, and direct the work of cast and crew. Directors approve the design elements of a production, including sets, costumes, choreography, and music.

Working Conditions

Actors, producers, and directors work under constant pressure. To succeed, they need patience and commitment to their craft. Actors strive to deliver flawless performances, often while working in undesirable and unpleasant conditions. Producers and directors experience stress from the need to adhere to budgets, union work rules, and production schedules; organize rehearsals; and meet with designers, financial backers, and production executives.

Acting assignments typically are short term (ranging from 1 day to a few months), which means that there often are long periods of unemployment between jobs. The uncertain nature of the work results in unpredictable earnings and intense competition for even the lowest paid jobs. Often, actors, producers, and directors must hold other jobs to sustain a living.

When performing, actors typically work long, irregular hours. For example, stage actors may perform one show at night while rehearsing another during the day. They also might travel with a show when it tours the country. Movie actors may work on location, sometimes under adverse weather conditions, and may spend considerable time in their trailers or dressing rooms waiting to perform their scenes. Actors who perform in television often appear on camera with little preparation time because scripts tend to be revised frequently or written moments before taping.

Evening and weekend work is a regular part of a stage actor's life. On weekends, more than one performance may be held per day. Actors and directors working on movies or television programs, especially those who shoot on location, may work in the early morning or late evening hours to do nighttime filming or to tape scenes inside public facilities outside of normal business hours.

Actors should be in good physical condition and have the necessary stamina and coordination to move about theater stages and large movie and television studio lots. They also need to maneuver about complex technical sets while staying in character and projecting their voices audibly. Actors must be fit to endure heat from stage or studio lights and the weight of heavy costumes. Producers and directors should anticipate such hazards and ensure the safety of actors by conducting extra rehearsals on the set so that actors can learn the layout of set pieces and props, allowing time for warm-ups and stretching exercises to guard against physical and vocal injuries, and providing adequate breaks to prevent heat exhaustion and dehydration.

Employment

In 2000, actors, producers, and directors held about 158,000 jobs, primarily in motion pictures, theater, television, and radio. Because many others were between jobs, the total number of actors, producers, and directors available for work was higher. Employment in the theater is cyclical—higher in the fall and spring seasons—and concentrated in New York and other major cities with large commercial houses for musicals and touring productions. Also, many cities support established professional regional theaters that operate on a seasonal or year-round basis.

In summer, stock companies in suburban and resort areas also provide employment opportunities. Actors, producers, and directors may find work on cruise lines and in theme parks. Many smaller nonprofit professional companies, such as repertory companies, dinner theaters, and theaters affiliated with drama schools, acting conservatories, and universities provide employment opportunities for local amateur talent and professional entertainers. Auditions typically are held in New York for many productions across the country and for shows that go on the road.

Employment in motion pictures and films for television is centered in New York and in Hollywood. However, small studios are located throughout the country. Many films are shot on location and may employ local professional and nonprofessional actors. In television, opportunities are concentrated in the network centers of New York and Los Angeles, but cable television services and local television stations around the country also employ many actors, producers, and directors.

Training, Other Qualifications, and Advancement

Persons who become actors, producers, and directors follow many paths. Employers generally look for people with the creative instincts, innate talent, and intellectual capacity to perform. Actors should possess a passion for performing and enjoy entertaining others. Most aspiring actors participate in high school and college plays, work in college radio stations, or perform with local community theater groups. Local and regional theater experience and work in summer stock, on cruise lines, or in theme parks help many young actors hone their skills and earn qualifying credits towards membership in one of the actors' unions. Union membership and work experience in smaller communities may lead to work in larger cities, notably New York or Los Angeles. In television and film, actors and directors typically start in smaller television markets or with independent movie production companies, then work their way up to larger media markets and major studio productions. Intense competition, however, ensures that only a few actors reach star billing.

Formal dramatic training, either through an acting conservatory or a university program, generally is necessary; however, some people successfully enter the field without it. Most people studying for a bachelor's degree take courses in radio and television broadcasting, communications, film, theater, drama, or dramatic literature. Many continue their academic training and receive a Master of Fine Arts (MFA) degree. Advanced curriculums may include courses in stage speech and movement, directing, playwriting, and design, as well as intensive acting workshops.

Actors at all experience levels may pursue workshop training through acting conservatories or by being mentored by a drama coach. Actors also research roles so that they can grasp concepts quickly during rehearsals and understand the story's setting and background. Sometimes actors learn a foreign language or train with a dialect coach to develop an accent to make their characters more realistic.

Actors need talent, creative ability, and training that will enable them to portray different characters. Because competition for parts is fierce, versatility and a wide range of related performance skills, such as singing, dancing, skating, juggling, and miming are especially useful in lifting actors above the average and getting them noticed by producers and directors. Actors must have poise, stage presence, the capability to affect an audience, and the ability to follow direction. Modeling experience also may be helpful. Physical appearance often is a deciding factor in being selected for particular roles.

Many professional actors rely on agents or managers to find work, negotiate contracts, and plan their careers. Agents generally earn a percentage of the pay specified in an actor's contract. Other actors rely solely on attending open auditions for parts. Trade publications list the time, date, and location of these auditions.

To become a movie extra, one must usually be listed by a casting agency, such as Central Casting, a no-fee agency that supplies extras to the major movie studios in Hollywood. Applicants are accepted only when the number of persons of a particular type on the list—for example, athletic young women, old men, or small children—falls below the foreseeable need. In recent years, only a very small proportion of applicants has succeeded in being listed.

There are no specific training requirements for producers. They come from many different backgrounds. Talent, experience, and business acumen are very important determinants of success for producers. Actors, writers, film editors, and business managers commonly enter the field. Also, many people who start out as actors move into directing, while some directors might try their hand at acting. Producers often start in a theatrical management office, working for a press agent, managing director, or business manager. Some start in a performing arts union or service organization. Others work behind the scenes with successful directors, serve on boards of directors, or promote their own projects. No formal training exists for producers; however, a growing number of colleges and universities now offer degree programs in arts management and managing nonprofits.

As the reputations and box-office draw of actors, producers, and directors grow, they might work on bigger budget productions, on network or syndicated broadcasts, or in more prestigious theaters. Actors may advance to lead roles and receive star billing. A few actors move into acting-related jobs, such as drama coaches or directors of stage, television, radio, or motion picture productions. Some teach drama privately or in colleges and universities.

Job Outlook

Employment of actors, producers, and directors is expected to grow faster than the average for all occupations through 2010. Although a growing number of people will aspire to enter these professions, many will leave the field early because the work, when it is available, is hard, the hours are long, and the pay is low. Despite faster-than-average employment growth, competition for jobs will be stiff, in part because of the large number of highly trained and talented actors auditioning for roles. Only performers with the most stamina and talent will regularly find employment.

Expanding cable and satellite television operations, increasing production and distribution of major studio and independent films, and continued growth and development of interactive media, such as direct-for-web movies and videos, should increase demand for actors, producers, and directors. A strong Broadway and off-Broadway community and vibrant regional theater network are expected to offer many job opportunities.

Earnings

Median annual earnings of actors were $25,920 in 2000. The middle 50 percent earned between $16,950 and $59,769. The lowest 10 percent earned less than $12,700, and the highest 10 percent earned more than $93,620. Median annual earnings in the industries employing the largest numbers of actors were as follows:

Motion picture production and services $54,440
Producers, orchestras, and entertainers 28,310
Miscellaneous amusement and recreation services 13,500

Minimum salaries, hours of work, and other conditions of employment are covered in collective bargaining agreements between show producers and the unions representing workers. Actors' Equity Association (Equity) represents stage actors; Screen Actors Guild (SAG) covers actors in motion pictures, including television, commercials, and films; and the American Federation of Television and Radio Artists (AFTRA) represents television and radio studio performers. While these unions generally determine minimum salaries, any actor or director may negotiate for a salary higher than the minimum.

On July 1, 2001, the members of SAG and AFTRA negotiated a new joint contract covering all unionized employment. Under the contract, motion picture and television actors with speaking parts earned a minimum daily rate of $636 or $2,206 for a 5-day week. Actors also receive contributions to their health and pension plans and additional compensation for reruns and foreign telecasts of the productions in which they appear.

According to Equity, the minimum weekly salary for actors in Broadway productions as of June 25, 2001, was $1,252. Actors in off-Broadway theaters received minimums ranging from $440 to $551 a week as of October 30, 2000, depending on the seating capacity of the theater. Regional theaters that operate under an Equity agreement pay actors $500 to $728 per week. For touring productions, actors receive an additional $106 per day for living expenses ($112 per day in larger, higher-cost cities). According to Equity, fewer than 15 percent of its dues-paying members actually worked during any given week during 2000. Median earnings for those able to find employment in 2000 were less than $10,000.

Some well-known actors—stars—earn well above the minimum; their salaries are many times the figures cited, creating the false impression that all actors are highly paid. For example, of the nearly 100,000 SAG members, only about 50 might be considered stars. The average income that SAG members earn from acting, less than $5,000 a year, is low because employment is erratic. Therefore, most actors must supplement their incomes by holding jobs in other fields.

Many actors who work more than a set number of weeks per year are covered by a union health, welfare, and pension fund, which includes hospitalization insurance and to which employers contribute. Under some employment conditions, Equity and AFTRA members receive paid vacations and sick leave.

Median annual earnings of producers and directors were $41,030 in 2000. The middle 50 percent earned between $29,000 and $60,330. The lowest 10 percent earned less than $21,050, and the highest 10 percent earned more than $87,770. Median annual earnings in the industries employing the largest numbers of producers and directors were as follows:

Motion picture production and services	$50,280
Producers, orchestras, and entertainers	38,820
Radio and television broadcasting	34,630

Many stage directors belong to the Society of Stage Directors and Choreographers (SSDC), and film and television directors belong to the Directors Guild of America (DGA). Earnings of stage directors vary greatly. According to the SSDC, summer theaters offer compensation, including "royalties" (based on the number of performances), usually ranging from $2,500 to $8,000 for a 3- to 4-week run. Directing a production at a dinner theater usually will pay less than directing one at a summer the-

ater, but has more potential for income from royalties. Regional theaters may hire directors for longer periods, increasing compensation accordingly. The highest paid directors work on Broadway and commonly earn $50,000 per show. However, they also receive payment in the form of royalties—a negotiated percentage of gross box office receipts—that can exceed their contract fee for long-running box office successes.

Producers seldom get a set fee; instead, they get a percentage of a show's earnings or ticket sales.

Related Occupations

People who work in performing arts occupations that may require acting skills include announcers; dancers and choreographers; and musicians, singers, and related workers. Others working in theater-related occupations are hairdressers, hairstylists, and cosmetologists; fashion designers; set and exhibit designers; sound engineering technicians; and writers and authors.

Sources of Additional Information

For general information about theater arts and a list of accredited college-level programs, contact:

● National Association of Schools of Theater, 11250 Roger Bacon Dr., Suite 21, Reston, VA 20190. Internet: http://www.arts-accredit.org/nast/default.htm

For general information on actors, producers, and directors, contact:

● Actors Equity Association, 165 West 46th St., New York, NY 10036. Internet: http://www.actorsequity.org

● Screen Actors Guild, 5757 Wilshire Blvd., Los Angeles, CA 90036-3600. Internet: http://www.sag.org

● American Federation of Television and Radio Artists—Screen Actors Guild, 4340 East-West Hwy., Suite 204, Bethesda, MD 20814-4411

Administrative Services Managers

O*NET 11-3011.00

Significant Points

● Administrative services managers work in private industry and government and have varied responsibilities, experience, earnings, and education.

● Competition should remain keen due to the substantial supply of competent, experienced workers seeking managerial jobs; however, demand should be strong for facility managers and for administrative services managers in management consulting.

Nature of the Work

Administrative services managers perform a broad range of duties in virtually every sector of the economy. They coordinate and direct support services to organizations as diverse as insurance companies, computer manufacturers, and government offices. These workers manage the many services that allow organizations to operate efficiently, such as secretarial and reception, administration, payroll, conference planning and travel, information and data processing, mail, materials scheduling and distribution, printing and reproduction, records management, telecommunications management, security, parking, and personal property procurement, supply, and disposal.

Specific duties for these managers vary by degree of responsibility and authority. First-line administrative services managers directly supervise a staff that performs various support services. Mid-level managers, on the other hand, develop departmental plans, set goals and deadlines, implement procedures to improve productivity and customer service, and define the responsibilities of supervisory-level managers. Some mid-level administrative services managers oversee first-line supervisors from various departments, including the clerical staff. Mid-level managers also may be involved in the hiring and dismissal of employees, but they generally have no role in the formulation of personnel policy. Some of these managers advance to upper level positions, such as vice president of administrative services.

In small organizations, a single administrative services manager may oversee all support services. In larger ones, however, first-line administrative services managers often report to mid-level managers who, in turn, report to owners or top-level managers. As the size of the firm increases, administrative services managers are more likely to specialize in specific support activities. For example, some administrative services managers work primarily as office managers, contract administrators, or unclaimed property officers. In many cases, the duties of these administrative services managers are similar to those of other managers and supervisors.

Because of the range of administrative services required by organizations, the nature of these managerial jobs also varies significantly. Administrative services managers who work as contract administrators, for instance, oversee the preparation, analysis, negotiation, and review of contracts related to the purchase or sale of equipment, materials, supplies, products, or services. In addition, some administrative services managers acquire, distribute, and store supplies, while others dispose of surplus property or oversee the disposal of unclaimed property.

Facility managers have duties similar to those of administrative services managers, but also plan, design, and manage buildings and grounds in addition to people. They are responsible for coordinating the aspects of the physical workplace with the people and work of an organization. This task requires integrating the principles of business administration, architecture, and behavioral and engineering science. Although the specific tasks assigned to facility managers vary substantially depending on the organization, the duties fall into several categories, relating to operations and maintenance, real estate, project planning and management, communication, finance, quality assessment, facility function, and management of human and environmental factors. Tasks within these broad categories may include space and workplace planning, budgeting, purchase and sale of real estate, lease management, renovations, or architectural planning and design. Facility managers may suggest and oversee renovation projects for a variety of reasons, ranging from improving efficiency to ensuring that facilities meet government regulations and environmental, health, and security standards. Additionally, facility managers continually monitor the facility to ensure that it remains safe, secure, and well maintained. Often, the facility manager is responsible for directing staff, including maintenance, grounds, and custodial workers.

Working Conditions

Administrative services managers generally work in comfortable offices. Managers involved in contract administration and personal property procurement, use, and disposal may travel between their home office, branch offices, vendors' offices, and property sales sites. Also, facility managers who are responsible for the design of workspaces may spend time at construction sites and may travel between different facilities while monitoring the work of maintenance, grounds, and custodial staffs. However, new technology has increased the number of managers who telecommute from home or other offices, and teleconferencing has reduced the need for travel.

Most administrative services managers work a standard 40-hour week. However, uncompensated overtime frequently is required to resolve problems and meet deadlines. Facility managers often are on call to address a variety of problems that can arise in a facility during non-work hours. Because of frequent deadlines and the challenges of managing staff and resources, the work of administrative services and facility managers can be stressful.

Employment

Administrative services managers held about 362,000 jobs in 2000. About half worked in service industries, including engineering and management, business, educational, social, and health services. The remaining workers were widely dispersed throughout the economy.

Training, Other Qualifications, and Advancement

Educational requirements for these managers vary widely, depending on the size and complexity of the organization. In small organizations, experience may be the only requirement needed to enter a position as office manager. When an opening in administrative services management occurs, the office manager may be promoted to the position based on past performance. In large organizations, however, administrative services managers normally are hired from outside, and each position has formal education and experience requirements. Some administrative services managers have advanced degrees.

Specific requirements vary by job responsibility. For first-line administrative services managers of secretarial, mailroom, and related support activities, many employers prefer an associate degree in business or management, although a high school diploma may suffice when combined with appropriate experience. For managers of audiovisual, graphics, and other technical activities, postsecondary technical school training is preferred. Managers of highly complex services, such as contract administration, generally need at least a bachelor's degree in business, human resources, or finance. Regardless of major, the curriculum should include courses in office technology, accounting, business mathematics, computer applications, human resources, and business law. Most facility managers have an undergraduate or graduate degree in engineering, architecture, construction management, business administration, or facility management. Many have a background in real estate, construction, or interior design, in addition to managerial experience. Whatever the manager's educational background, it must be accompanied by related work experience reflecting demonstrated ability. For this reason, many administrative services managers have advanced through the ranks of their organization, acquiring work experience in various administrative positions before assuming first-line supervisory duties. All managers who oversee departmental supervisors should be familiar with office procedures and equipment. Managers of personal property acquisition and disposal need experience in purchasing and sales, and knowledge of a variety of supplies, machinery, and equipment. Managers concerned with supply, inventory, and distribution should be experienced in receiving, warehousing, packaging, shipping, transportation, and related operations. Contract administrators may have worked as contract specialists, cost analysts, or procurement specialists. Managers of unclaimed property often have experience in insurance claims analysis and records management.

Persons interested in becoming administrative services or facility managers should have good communication skills and be able to establish effective working relationships with many different people, ranging from managers, supervisors, and professionals, to clerks and blue-collar workers. They should be analytical, detail-oriented, flexible, and decisive. They must also be able to coordinate several activities at once, quickly analyze and resolve specific problems, and cope with deadlines.

Most administrative services managers in small organizations advance by moving to other management positions or to a larger organization. Advancement is easier in large firms that employ several levels of administrative services managers. Attainment of the Certified Administrative Manager (CAM) designation offered by the Institute of Certified Professional Managers through work experience and successful completion of examinations can increase a manager's advancement potential. In addition, a master's degree in business administration or related field enhances a first-level manager's opportunities to advance to a mid-level management position, such as director of administrative services, and eventually to a top-level management position, such as executive vice president for administrative services. Those with the required capital and experience can establish their own management consulting firm.

Advancement of facility managers is based on the practices and size of individual companies. Some facility managers transfer from other departments within the organization or work their way up from technical positions. Others advance through a progression of facility management positions that offer additional responsibilities. Completion of the competency-based professional certification program offered by the International Facility Management Association can give prospective candidates an advantage. In order to qualify for this Certified Facility Manager (CFM) designation, applicants must meet certain educational and experience requirements.

Job Outlook

Employment of administrative services managers is expected to grow about as fast as the average for all occupations through 2010. Like other managerial positions, there are more competent, experienced workers seeking jobs than there are positions available. However, demand should be strong for facility managers because businesses increasingly are realizing the importance of maintaining and efficiently operating their facilities, which are very large investments for most organizations. Administrative services managers employed in management services and management consulting also should be in demand, as public and private organizations continue to contract out and streamline their administrative services functions in an effort to cut costs. Many additional job openings will stem from the need to replace workers who transfer to other jobs, retire, or stop working for other reasons.

Continuing corporate restructuring and increasing utilization of office technology should result in a flatter organizational structure with fewer levels of management, reducing the need for some middle management positions. This should adversely affect administrative services managers who oversee first-line managers. Because many administrative managers have a variety of functions, however, the effects of these changes on their employment should be less severe than for other middle managers who specialize in only certain functions.

Earnings

Earnings of administrative services managers vary greatly depending on the employer, the specialty, and the geographic area. In general, however, median annual earnings of administrative services managers in 2000 were $47,080. The middle 50 percent earned between $32,550 and $67,630. The lowest 10 percent earned less than $23,800, and the highest 10 percent earned more than $90,120. Median annual earnings in the industries employing the largest numbers of these workers in 2000 follow:

Computer and data processing services	$54,700
Colleges and universities	51,470
Local government	48,470
Management and public relations	44,420
State government	43,710

In the federal government, contract specialists in nonsupervisory, supervisory, and managerial positions earned an average of $60,310 a year in 2000. Corresponding averages were $58,050 for facilities managers, $57,360 for industrial property managers, $53,830 for property disposal specialists, $57,400 for administrative officers, and $48,410 for support services administrators.

Related Occupations

Administrative services managers direct and coordinate support services and oversee the purchase, use, and disposal of personal property. Occupations with similar functions include office and administrative support worker supervisors and managers; cost estimators; property, real estate, and community association managers; purchasing managers, buyers, and purchasing agents; and top executives.

Sources of Additional Information

For information about careers in facility management, facility management education and degree programs, and the Certified Facility Manager designation, contact:

- International Facility Management Association, 1 East Greenway Plaza, Suite 1100, Houston, TX 77046-0194. Internet: http://www.ifma.org

General information regarding facility management and a list of facility management educational and degree programs may be obtained from:

- The Association of Higher Education Facilities Officers, 1643 Prince St., Alexandria, VA 22314-2818. Internet: http://www.appa.org

For information about the Certified Administrative Manager designation, contact:

- Institute of Certified Professional Managers, James Madison University, College of Business, Harrisonburg, VA 22807. Internet: http://cob.jmu.edu/icpm

Agricultural Workers

O*NET 45-2011.00, 45-2041.00, 45-2092.01, 45-2092.02, 45-2093.00

Significant Points

● Farm workers comprise 9 out of 10 agricultural workers.

● Duties and working conditions vary widely, from working in nurseries, to producing crops and raising livestock outdoors, to inspecting agricultural products in plants.

● Most workers learn through short-term on-the-job training; agricultural inspectors need work experience or a college degree in a related field.

● Employment is projected to grow more slowly than average.

Nature of the Work

Agricultural workers have a range of responsibilities, from planting, cultivating, grading, and sorting agricultural products to inspecting agricultural commodities and facilities. They may work with food crops, animals, or trees, shrubs, and plants. Depending on their jobs, they may work outdoors or indoors.

Agricultural inspectors are employed by federal and state governments to inspect agricultural commodities, processing equipment and facilities, and fish and logging operations for compliance with laws and regulations governing health, quality, and safety. They inspect horticultural products or livestock to detect harmful disease or infestations. To assist in eradicating disease, they also inspect livestock to help determine the effectiveness of medication and feeding programs. They may collect samples of pests, or of suspected diseased animals or materials, and send such samples to a laboratory for identification and analysis.

Graders and sorters, agricultural products work to ensure the quality of the agricultural commodities that reach the market. They grade, sort, or classify unprocessed food and other agricultural products by size, weight, color, or condition.

Farmworkers and laborers, crop, nursery, and greenhouse manually plant, maintain, and harvest food crops; apply pesticides, herbicides, and fertilizers to crops; and cultivate the plants used to beautify landscapes. They prepare nursery acreage or greenhouse beds for planting; water, weed, and spray trees, shrubs, and plants; cut, roll, and stack sod; stake trees; tie, wrap, and pack flowers, plants, shrubs, and trees to fill orders; and dig up or move field-grown and containerized shrubs and trees. Additional duties include planting seedlings, transplanting saplings, and watering and trimming plants.

Farmworkers, farm and ranch animals care for live farm, ranch, or aquacultural animals that may include cattle, sheep, swine, goats, horses and other equines, poultry, finfish, shellfish, and bees. They also tend to animals raised for animal products, such as meat, fur, skins, feathers, eggs, milk, and honey. Duties may include feeding, watering, herding, grazing, castrating, branding, de-beaking, weighing, catching, and loading animals. They also may maintain records on animals, examine animals to detect diseases and injuries, and assist in birth deliveries and administer medications, vaccinations, or insecticides as appropriate. Daily duties include cleaning and maintaining animal housing areas.

Farmworkers, agricultural production may have a wide range of duties, some of which overlap duties of other farmworkers described above. They tend to livestock and poultry; plant and harvest crops; and apply pesticides, herbicides, and fertilizers to crops. These farmworkers also repair farm buildings and fences. Other duties may include operating milking machines and other dairy processing equipment, supervising seasonal help, irrigating crops, and hauling livestock products to market. Some farmworkers operate tractors, fertilizer spreaders, hay bins, raking equipment, balers, combines, threshers, and other equipment used for plowing, sowing, and harvesting. They also may help with the sorting, storage, and working in post-harvest treatment of crops.

Working Conditions

Working conditions vary widely. For example, some inspectors do field work, and may travel frequently. Federal food inspectors may work in highly mechanized plants or with poultry or livestock in confined areas with extremely cold temperatures and slippery floors. The duties often require working with sharp knives, moderate lifting, and walking or standing for long periods. Many inspectors work long and often irregular hours. Inspectors may find themselves in adversarial roles when the organization or individual being inspected objects to the inspection process or its potential consequences.

Graders and sorters may work with similar products for an entire shift, or may be assigned a variety of items. They may be on their feet all day and may have to lift heavy objects, whereas others may sit during most of their shift and do little strenuous work. Some graders work in clean, air-conditioned environments, suitable for carrying out controlled tests. Some may work evenings or weekends because of the perishable nature of the products. Overtime may be required to meet production goals.

For farm workers in nurseries, work is seasonal; spring and summer are the busier times of the year and hours in the cold weather tend to be fewer. These workers enjoy relatively comfortable working conditions while tending to plants indoors. However, during the busy seasons when landscape contractors need plants, work schedules may be more demanding, requiring weekend work. Moreover, the transition from warm weather to cold weather means that nursery workers might have to work overtime with little notice in order to move plants indoors in case of a frost.

Farm workers enjoy a somewhat independent lifestyle working with animals or on the land. Benefits include the wide-open physical expanse, the variability of day-to-day work, and the rural setting. However, hours are generally uneven and often long; work cannot be delayed when crops must be planted and harvested, or when animals must be sheltered and fed. Weekend work is common, and farm workers may work a 6- or 7-day week during planting and harvesting seasons. About 1 out of 5 agricultural workers had variable schedules, compared with fewer than 1 in 10 workers in all occupations combined. As much of the work is seasonal in nature, many workers also obtain other employment. Migrant farm workers, who move from location to location as crops ripen, live an unsettled lifestyle, which can be stressful.

Much farm and ranch work takes place outdoors in all kinds of weather and is physical in nature. Harvesting fruits and vegetables, for example, may require much bending, stooping, and lifting. Some field workers may lack adequate sanitation facilities, and their drinking water may be limited. The year-round nature of much livestock production work means that ranch workers must be out in the heat of summer, as well as the cold of winter. Those who work directly with animals risk being bitten or kicked.

Farm workers in crop production risk exposure to pesticides and other potentially hazardous chemicals that are sprayed on crops or plants. However, exposure is relatively minimal if safety procedures are followed. Those who work on mechanized farms must take precautions when working with tools and heavy equipment to avoid injury.

Employment

Agricultural workers held 987,000 jobs in 2000. Farm workers held 909,000 jobs, graders and sorters 63,000 jobs, and agricultural inspectors 15,000 jobs. More than 60 percent of all agricultural workers held jobs in crop and livestock production and almost 21 percent held jobs in agricultural services, mostly for farm labor contractors. About 15 percent of farm workers were part-time employees, about the same proportion as for workers overall.

Training, Other Qualifications, and Advancement

Becoming an agricultural inspector requires relevant work experience, or a college degree in a field such as biology or agricultural science. Inspectors are trained in the applicable laws or inspection procedures through some combination of classroom and on-the-job training. In general, people who want to enter this occupation should be responsible, like detailed work, and be able to communicate well. Federal government inspectors whose job performance is satisfactory advance through a career ladder to a specified full-performance level. For positions above this level, usually supervisory positions, advancement is competitive and based on agency needs and individual merit. Advancement opportunities in state and local governments and in the private sector are often similar to those in the federal government.

For graders and sorters, training requirements vary on the basis of their responsibilities. For those who perform tests on various agricultural products, a high school diploma is preferred and may be required. Beginners provided with short-term on-the-job training may fill simple jobs.

Farm workers learn through short-term on-the-job training. Fifty-six percent of these workers do not have a high school diploma, compared with only about 13 percent of all workers in the economy. The proportion of workers without a high school diploma is particularly high in the crop production sector, where there are more labor-intensive establishments employing migrant farm workers.

In nurseries, entry-level workers must be able to follow directions and learn proper planting procedures. If driving is an essential part of a job, employers look for applicants with a good driving record and some experience driving a truck. Workers who deal directly with customers must get along well with people. Employers also look for responsible, self-motivated individuals, because nursery workers sometimes work with little supervision.

Advancement depends on motivation and experience. Farm workers who work hard and quickly, have good communication skills, and take an interest in the business may advance to crew leader or other supervisory positions. Some agricultural workers may aspire to become farm, ranch, and other agricultural managers, or farmers or ranchers themselves. In addition, their knowledge of raising and harvesting produce may provide an excellent background for becoming purchasing agents and buyers of farm products. Knowledge of working a farm as a business can help agricultural workers become farm and home management advisors. Those who earn a college degree in agricultural science could become agricultural and food scientists.

Job Outlook

Overall employment of agricultural workers is projected to grow more slowly than the average for all occupations over the 2000–2010 period—primarily reflecting the outlook for farm workers, who constitute 9 out of 10 agricultural workers. Low wages, the physical demands of the work, and high job turnover should result in abundant job opportunities.

Continued consolidation of farms and technological advancements in farm equipment will dampen employment growth. Nevertheless, farms remaining in operation will still need workers to help with farms' operations, and farm labor contractors' employment of farm workers is expected to increase rapidly. Farm workers in landscape and horticultural services should have among the most rapid job growth, reflecting the demand for agricultural services such as landscaping.

Slower-than-average employment growth also is expected for agricultural inspectors, as governments at all levels are not expected to hire significant numbers of new inspectors and regulators. Similarly, slow growth is expected for graders and sorters, reflecting projections for the industries in which they work.

Earnings

Median weekly earnings of farm workers were $309 in 2000. The middle 50 percent earned between $250 and $404. The lowest 10 percent earned less than $205, and the highest 10 percent earned more than $526.

Median hourly earnings of graders and sorters, agricultural products were $7.11 in 2000. The middle 50 percent earned between $6.34 and $8.78. The lowest 10 percent earned less than $5.87, and the highest 10 percent earned more than $11.18.

Median hourly earnings of agricultural inspectors were $13.75 in 2000. The middle 50 percent earned between $10.61 and $17.85. The lowest 10 percent earned less than $8.79, and the highest 10 percent earned more than $21.91.

Few agricultural workers are members of a unions.

Related Occupations

The duties of farm workers who perform outdoor labor are related to the work of fishers and fishing vessel operators; forest, conservation, and logging workers; and grounds maintenance workers. Farm workers who work with farm and ranch animals perform work related to that of animal care and service workers. The work of agricultural inspectors and graders and sorters is related to work performed by inspectors, testers, sorters, samplers, and weighers in manufacturing industries.

Sources of Additional Information

Information on jobs as agricultural workers is available from:

- National FFA Organization, The National FFA Center, Career Information Requests, P.O. Box 68690, Indianapolis, IN, 46268-0960. Internet: http://www.ffa.org

Information on farm worker jobs is available from:

- The New England Small Farm Institute, 275 Jackson St., Belchertown, MA 01007. Internet: http://www.smallfarm.org/newoof/companions.html

Information on obtaining a position as an agricultural inspector with the federal government is available from the Office of Personnel Management (OPM) through a telephone-based system. Consult your telephone directory under U.S. Government for a local number or call (912) 757-3000; Federal Relay Service: (800) 877-8339. The first number is not toll free, and charges may result. Information also is available from the OPM Internet site: http://www.usajobs.opm.gov

Aircraft and Avionics Equipment Mechanics and Service Technicians

O*NET 49-2091.00, 49-3011.01, 49-3011.02, 49-3011.03

Significant Points

- The majority of these workers learn their job in 1 of about 200 trade schools certified by the Federal Aviation Administration.

- Opportunities should be favorable, but keen competition is likely for the best paying airline jobs.

Nature of the Work

To keep aircraft in peak operating condition, aircraft and avionics equipment mechanics and service technicians perform scheduled maintenance, make repairs, and complete inspections required by the Federal Aviation Administration (FAA).

Many aircraft mechanics, also called airframe, powerplant, and avionics aviation maintenance technicians, specialize in preventive maintenance. They inspect engines, landing gear, instruments, pressurized sections, accessories—brakes, valves, pumps, and air-conditioning systems, for example—and other parts of the aircraft, and do the necessary maintenance and replacement of parts. Inspections take place following a schedule based on the number of hours the aircraft has flown, calendar days since the last inspection, cycles of operation, or a combination of these factors. Large, sophisticated planes are equipped with aircraft monitoring systems, consisting of electronic boxes and consoles that monitor the aircraft's basic operations and provide valuable diagnostic information to the mechanic. To examine an engine, aircraft mechanics work through specially designed openings while standing on ladders or scaffolds, or use hoists or lifts to remove the entire engine from the craft. After taking an engine apart, mechanics use precision instruments to measure parts for wear and use X-ray and magnetic inspection equipment to check for invisible cracks. Worn or defective parts are repaired or replaced. Mechanics may also repair sheet metal or composite surfaces, measure the tension of control cables, and check for corrosion, distortion, and cracks in the fuselage, wings, and tail. After completing all repairs, they must test the equipment to ensure that it works properly.

Mechanics specializing in repairwork rely on the pilot's description of a problem to find and fix faulty equipment. For example, during a pre-flight check, a pilot may discover that the aircraft's fuel gauge does not work. To solve the problem, mechanics may troubleshoot the electrical system, using electrical test equipment to make sure that no wires are broken or shorted out, and replace any defective electrical or electronic components. Mechanics work as fast as safety permits so that the aircraft can be put back into service quickly.

Some mechanics work on one or many different types of aircraft, such as jets, propeller-driven airplanes, and helicopters. Others specialize in one section of a particular type of aircraft, such as the engine, hydraulics, or electrical system. *Powerplant mechanics* are authorized to work on engines and do limited work on propellers. *Airframe mechanics* are authorized to work on any part of the aircraft except the instruments, powerplants, and propellers. *Combination airframe-and-powerplant mechanics*—called A & P mechanics—work on all parts of the plane, except instruments. The majority of mechanics working on civilian aircraft today are A & P mechanics. In small, independent repairshops, mechanics usually inspect and repair many different types of aircraft.

Avionics systems are now an integral part of aircraft design and have vastly increased aircraft capability. *Avionics technicians* repair and maintain components used for aircraft navigation and radio communications, weather radar systems, and other instruments and computers that control flight, engine, and other primary functions. These duties may require additional licenses, such as a radiotelephone license issued by the U.S. Federal Communications Commission (FCC). Because of technological advances, an increasing amount of time is spent repairing electronic systems, such as computerized controls. Technicians also may be required to analyze and develop solutions to complex electronic problems.

Working Conditions

Mechanics usually work in hangars or in other indoor areas, although they can work outdoors—sometimes in unpleasant weather—when hangars are full or when repairs must be made quickly. Mechanics often work under time pressure to maintain flight schedules or, in general aviation, to keep from inconveniencing customers. At the same time, mechanics have a tremendous responsibility to maintain safety standards, and this can cause the job to be stressful.

Frequently, mechanics must lift or pull objects weighing as much as 70 pounds. They often stand, lie, or kneel in awkward positions and occasionally must work in precarious positions on scaffolds or ladders. Noise and vibration are common when engines are being tested, so ear protection is necessary. Aircraft mechanics usually work 40 hours a week on 8-hour shifts around the clock. Overtime work is frequent.

Employment

Aircraft mechanics and service technicians held about 173,000 jobs in 2000; fewer than 10 percent were avionic technicians. About two-thirds of all salaried mechanics worked for airlines or airports and flying fields, about 12 percent worked for the federal government, and about 9 percent worked for aircraft assembly firms. Most of the rest were general aviation mechanics, the majority of whom worked for independent repairshops or for companies that operate their own planes to transport executives and cargo. Few mechanics were self-employed.

Most airline mechanics work at major airports near large cities. Civilian mechanics employed by the armed forces work at military installations. Large proportions of mechanics who work for aircraft assembly firms are located in California or in Washington state. Others work for the FAA, many at the facilities in Oklahoma City, Atlantic City, Wichita, or Washington, DC. Mechanics for independent repairshops work at airports in every part of the country.

Training, Other Qualifications, and Advancement

The majority of mechanics who work on civilian aircraft are certified by the FAA as "airframe mechanic," "powerplant mechanic," or "avionics repair specialist." Mechanics who also have an inspector's authorization can certify work completed by other mechanics and perform required inspections. Uncertified mechanics are supervised by those with certificates.

The FAA requires at least 18 months of work experience for an airframe, powerplant, or avionics repairer's certificate. For a combined A & P certificate, at least 30 months of experience working with both engines and airframes is required. Completion of a program at an FAA-certified mechanic school can substitute for the work experience requirement. Applicants for all certificates also must pass written and oral tests and demonstrate that they can do the work authorized by the certificate. To obtain an inspector's authorization, a mechanic must have held an A & P certificate for at least 3 years. Most airlines require that mechanics have a high school diploma and an A & P certificate.

Although a few people become mechanics through on-the-job training, most learn their job in 1 of about 200 trade schools certified by the FAA. About one-third of these schools award 2- and 4-year degrees in avionics, aviation technology, or aviation maintenance management.

FAA standards established by law require that certified mechanic schools offer students a minimum of 1,900 actual class hours. Courses in these trade schools normally last from 24 to 30 months and provide training with the tools and equipment used on the job. Aircraft trade schools are placing more emphasis on technologies such as turbine engines, composite materials—including graphite, fiberglass, and boron—and aviation electronics, which are increasingly being used in the construction of new aircraft. Less emphasis is being placed on old technologies, such as woodworking and welding. Additionally, employers prefer mechanics who can perform a variety of tasks.

Some aircraft mechanics in the armed forces acquire enough general experience to satisfy the work experience requirements for the FAA certificate. With additional study, they may pass the certifying exam. In general, however, jobs in the military services are too specialized to provide the broad experience required by the FAA. Most armed forces mechanics have to complete the entire training program at a trade school, although a few receive some credit for the material they learned in the service. In any case, military experience is a great advantage when seeking employment; employers consider trade school graduates who have this experience to be the most desirable applicants.

Courses in mathematics, physics, chemistry, electronics, computer science, and mechanical drawing are helpful, because they demonstrate many of the principles involved in the operation of aircraft, and knowledge of these principles is often necessary to make repairs. Courses that develop writing skills also are important because mechanics often are required to submit reports.

FAA regulations require current experience to keep the A & P certificate valid. Applicants must have at least 1,000 hours of work experience in the previous 24 months or take a refresher course. As new and more complex aircraft are designed, more employers are requiring mechanics to take ongoing training to update their skills. Recent technological advances in aircraft maintenance necessitate a strong background in electronics—both for acquiring and retaining jobs in this field. FAA certification standards also make ongoing training mandatory. Every 24 months, mechanics are required to take at least 16 hours of training to keep their certificate. Many mechanics take courses offered by manufacturers or employers, usually through outside contractors.

Aircraft mechanics must do careful and thorough work that requires a high degree of mechanical aptitude. Employers seek applicants who are self-motivated, hard-working, enthusiastic, and able to diagnose and solve complex mechanical problems. Agility is important for the reaching and climbing necessary to do the job. Because they may work on the tops of wings and fuselages on large jet planes, aircraft mechanics must not be afraid of heights.

As aircraft mechanics gain experience, they may advance to lead mechanic (or crew chief), inspector, lead inspector, or shop supervisor positions. Opportunities are best for those who have an aircraft inspector's authorization. In the airlines, where promotion often is determined by examination, supervisors sometimes advance to executive positions. Those with broad experience in maintenance and overhaul might become inspectors with the FAA. With additional business and management training, some open their own aircraft maintenance facilities. Mechanics learn many different skills in their training that can be applied to other jobs, and some transfer to other skilled repairer occupations or electronics technician jobs.

Job Outlook

The outlook for aircraft and avionics equipment mechanics and service technicians should be favorable over the next 10 years. The likelihood of fewer entrants from the military and a large number of retirements, point to good employment conditions for students just beginning training.

Job opportunities are likely to be the best at small commuter and regional airlines, at FAA repair stations, and in general aviation. Wages in these companies tend to be relatively low, so there are fewer applicants for these jobs than for those with the major airlines. Also, some jobs will become available as experienced mechanics leave for higher paying jobs with airlines or transfer to another occupation. At the same time, aircraft are becoming increasingly sophisticated in general aviation and in regional carriers, boosting the demand for qualified mechanics. Mechanics will face competition for jobs with large airlines because the high wages and travel benefits that these jobs offer attract more qualified applicants than there are openings. Prospects will be best for applicants with significant experience. Mechanics who keep abreast of technological advances in electronics, composite materials, and other areas will be in greatest demand. The number of job openings for aircraft mechanics in the federal government should decline as the size of the U.S. Armed Forces is reduced.

Employment of aircraft mechanics is expected to increase about as fast as the average for all occupations through the year 2010. A growing population and rising incomes are expected to stimulate the demand for airline transportation, and the number of aircraft is expected to grow. However, employment growth will be somewhat restricted as consolidation within the air carrier industry continues and as productivity increases due to greater use of automated inventory control and modular systems, which speeds repairs and parts replacement.

Most job openings for aircraft mechanics through the year 2010 will stem from replacement needs. Each year, as mechanics transfer to other occupations or retire, several thousand job openings will arise. Aircraft mechanics have a comparatively strong attachment to the occupation, reflecting their significant investment in training and a love for aviation. However, because aircraft mechanics' skills are transferable to other occupations, some mechanics leave for work in related fields.

During recessions, declines in air travel force airlines to curtail the number of flights, which results in less aircraft maintenance and, consequently, layoffs for aircraft mechanics.

Earnings

Median hourly earnings of aircraft mechanics and service technicians were about $19.50 in 2000. The middle 50 percent earned between $15.65 and $23.65. The lowest 10 percent earned less than $12.06, and the highest 10 percent earned more than $26.97. Median hourly earnings in the industries employing the largest numbers of aircraft mechanics and service technicians in 2000 are shown in the following table:

Air transportation, scheduled	$21.57
Aircraft and parts	19.77
Air transportation, nonscheduled	19.16
Federal government	19.11
Airports, flying fields, and services	16.26

Median hourly earnings of avionics technicians were about $19.86 in 2000. The middle 50 percent earned between $16.31 and $24.01. The lowest 10 percent earned less than $13.22, and the highest 10 percent earned more than $27.02.

Mechanics who work on jets for the major airlines generally earn more than those working on other aircraft. Airline mechanics and their immediate families receive reduced-fare transportation on their own and most other airlines.

Almost one-half of all aircraft mechanics, including those employed by some major airlines, are covered by union agreements. The principal unions are the International Association of Machinists and Aerospace Workers and the Transport Workers Union of America. Some mechanics are represented by the International Brotherhood of Teamsters.

Related Occupations

Workers in some other occupations that involve similar mechanical and electrical work are electricians, electrical and electronics installers and repairers, and elevator installers and repairers.

Sources of Additional Information

Information about jobs with a particular airline can be obtained by writing to the personnel manager of the company.

For general information about aircraft and avionics equipment mechanics and service technicians, write to:

- Professional Aviation Maintenance Association, 1707 H St. NW., Suite 700, Washington, DC 20006

For information on jobs in a particular area, contact employers at local airports or local offices of the state employment service.

Aircraft Pilots and Flight Engineers

O*NET 53-2011.00, 53-2012.00

Significant Points

- Strong competition is expected for jobs because aircraft pilots have very high earnings, especially those employed by national airlines.

- Pilots usually start with smaller commuter and regional airlines to acquire the experience needed to qualify for higher paying jobs with national airlines.

- Most pilots traditionally have learned to fly in the military, but growing numbers have college degrees with flight training from civilian flying schools that are certified by the Federal Aviation Administration (FAA).

Nature of the Work

Pilots are highly trained professionals who fly airplanes and helicopters to carry out a wide variety of tasks. Four out of five are *airline pilots, copilots, and flight engineers* who transport passengers and cargo. Others are *commercial pilots* involved in more unusual tasks, such as dusting crops, spreading seed for reforestation, testing aircraft, flying passengers and cargo to areas not service by regular airlines, directing firefighting efforts, tracking criminals, monitoring traffic, and rescuing and evacuating injured persons.

Except on small aircraft, two pilots usually make up the cockpit crew. Generally, the most experienced pilot, the *captain*, is in command and supervises all other crew members. The pilot and copilot share flying and other duties, such as communicating with air traffic controllers and monitoring the instruments. Some large aircraft have a third pilot—the *flight engineer*—who assists the other pilots by monitoring and operating many of the instruments and systems, making minor in-flight repairs, and watching for other aircraft. New technology can perform many flight tasks, however, and virtually all new aircraft now fly with only two pilots, who rely more heavily on computerized controls. As older, less technologically sophisticated aircraft continue to be retired from airline fleets, the number of flight engineer jobs will decrease.

Before departure, pilots plan their flights carefully. They thoroughly check their aircraft to make sure that the engines, controls, instruments, and other systems are functioning properly. They also make sure that baggage or cargo has been loaded correctly. They confer with flight dispatchers and aviation weather forecasters to find out about weather conditions en route and at their destination. Based on this information, they choose a route, altitude, and speed that will provide the fastest, safest, and smoothest flight. When flying under instrument flight rules—procedures governing the operation of the aircraft when there is poor visibility—the pilot in command, or the company dispatcher, normally files an instrument flight plan with air traffic control so that the flight can be coordinated with other air traffic.

Takeoff and landing are the most difficult parts of the flight, and require close coordination between the pilot and first officer. For example, as the plane accelerates for takeoff, the pilot concentrates on the runway while the first officer scans the instrument panel. To calculate the speed they must attain to become airborne, pilots consider the altitude of the airport, outside temperature, weight of the plane, and speed and direction of the wind. The moment the plane reaches takeoff speed, the first officer informs the pilot, who then pulls back on the controls to raise the nose of the plane.

Unless the weather is bad, the actual flight is relatively easy. Airplane pilots, with the assistance of autopilot and the flight management computer, steer the plane along their planned route and are monitored by the air traffic control stations they pass along the way. They regularly scan the instrument panel to check their fuel supply, the condition of their engines, and the air-conditioning, hydraulic, and other systems. Pilots may request a change in altitude or route if circumstances dictate. For example, if the ride is rougher than expected, they may ask air traffic control if pilots flying at other altitudes have reported better conditions. If so, they may request an altitude change. This procedure also may be used to find a stronger tailwind or a weaker headwind to save fuel and increase speed.

In contrast, helicopters are used for short trips at relatively low altitude, so pilots must be constantly on the lookout for trees, bridges, power lines, transmission towers, and other dangerous obstacles. Regardless of the type of aircraft, all pilots must monitor warning devices designed to help detect sudden shifts in wind conditions that can cause crashes.

Pilots must rely completely on their instruments when visibility is poor. On the basis of altimeter readings, they know how high above ground they are and whether they can fly safely over mountains and other obstacles. Special navigation radios give pilots precise information that, with the help of special maps, tells them their exact position. Other very sophisticated equipment provides directions to a point just above the end of a runway and enables pilots to land completely "blind." Once on the ground, pilots must complete records on their flight for their organization and the FAA report.

The number of nonflying duties that pilots have depends on the employment setting. Airline pilots have the services of large support staffs, and consequently, perform few nonflying duties. Pilots employed by other organizations such as charter operators or businesses have many other duties. They may load the aircraft, handle all passenger luggage to ensure a balanced load, and supervise refueling; other nonflying responsibilities include keeping records, scheduling flights, arranging for major maintenance, and performing minor aircraft maintenance and repairwork.

Some pilots are instructors. They teach their students the principles of flight in ground-school classes and demonstrate how to operate aircraft in dual-controlled planes and helicopters. A few specially trained pilots are "examiners" or "check pilots." They periodically fly with other pilots or pilot's license applicants to make sure that they are proficient.

Working Conditions

By law, airline pilots cannot fly more than 100 hours a month or more than 1,000 hours a year. Most airline pilots fly an average of 75 hours a month and work an additional 75 hours a month performing nonflying

duties. About one-fourth of all pilots work more than 40 hours a week. Most spend a considerable amount of time away from home because the majority of flights involve overnight layovers. When pilots are away from home, the airlines provide hotel accommodations, transportation between the hotel and airport, and an allowance for meals and other expenses. Airlines operate flights at all hours of the day and night, so work schedules often are irregular. Flight assignments are based on seniority.

Those pilots not employed by the airlines often have irregular schedules as well; they may fly 30 hours one month and 90 hours the next. Because these pilots frequently have many nonflying responsibilities, they have much less free time than do airline pilots. Except for business pilots, most do not remain away from home overnight. They may work odd hours. Flight instructors may have irregular and seasonal work schedules, depending on their students' available time and the weather. Instructors frequently work at night or on weekends.

Airline pilots, especially those on international routes, often suffer jet lag—fatigue caused by many hours of flying through different time zones. To guard against excessive pilot fatigue that could result in unsafe flying conditions, the FAA requires airlines to allow pilots at least 8 hours of uninterrupted rest in the 24 hours before finishing their flight duty. The work of test pilots, who check the flight performance of new and experimental planes, may be dangerous. Pilots who are crop dusters may be exposed to toxic chemicals and seldom have the benefit of a regular landing strip. Helicopter pilots involved in police work may be subject to personal injury.

Although flying does not involve much physical effort, the mental stress of being responsible for a safe flight, no matter what the weather, can be tiring. Pilots must be alert and quick to react if something goes wrong, particularly during takeoff and landing.

Employment

Civilian aircraft pilots and flight engineers commercial held about 117,000 jobs in 2000. About 84 percent worked as airline pilots, copilots, and flight engineers. The remainder were commercial pilots who worked as flight instructors at local airports or for large businesses that fly company cargo and executives in their own airplanes or helicopters. Some commercial pilots flew small planes for air taxi companies, usually to or from lightly traveled airports not served by major airlines. Others worked for a variety of businesses, performing tasks such as crop dusting, inspecting pipelines, or conducting sightseeing trips. Federal, state, and local governments also employed pilots. A few pilots were self-employed.

The employment of airplane pilots is not distributed like the population. Pilots are more concentrated in California, New York, Illinois, Washington, Michigan, Georgia, New Jersey, Florida, the District of Columbia, and Texas, which have a high amount of flying activity relative to their population.

Training, Other Qualifications, and Advancement

All pilots who are paid to transport passengers or cargo must have a commercial pilot's license with an instrument rating issued by the FAA. Helicopter pilots must hold a commercial pilot's certificate with a helicopter rating. To qualify for these licenses, applicants must be at least 18 years old and have at least 250 hours of flight experience. The experience required can be reduced through participation in certain flight school curricula approved by the FAA. Applicants also must pass a strict physical examination to make sure that they are in good health and have 20/20 vision with or without glasses, good hearing, and no physical handicaps that could impair their performance. They must pass a written test that includes questions on the principles of safe flight, navigation techniques, and FAA regulations and must demonstrate their flying ability to FAA or designated examiners.

To fly in periods of low visibility, pilots must be rated by the FAA to fly by instruments. Pilots may qualify for this rating by having 105 hours of flight experience, including 40 hours of experience in flying by instruments; they also must pass a written examination on procedures and FAA regulations covering instrument flying and demonstrate to an examiner their ability to fly by instruments.

Airline pilots must fulfill additional requirements. Pilots must have an airline transport pilot's license. Applicants for this license must be at least 23 years old and have a minimum of 1,500 hours of flying experience, including night and instrument flying, and must pass FAA written and flight examinations. Usually, they also have one or more advanced ratings, such as multi-engine aircraft or aircraft type ratings dependent upon the requirements of their particular flying jobs. Because pilots must be able to make quick decisions and accurate judgments under pressure, many airline companies reject applicants who do not pass required psychological and aptitude tests. All licenses are valid so long as a pilot can pass the periodic physical examinations and tests of flying skills required by federal government and company regulations. Depending on their physical condition, a pilot license may have a Class I, II, and III Medical certificate. A Class I Medical Certificate requires the highest standards for vision, hearing, equilibrium, and general physical condition. Requirements for a Class II Medical Certificate are less rigid, but still require a high degree of physical health and an excellent medical history. A Class III Medical Certificate has the least stringent physical requirements. All three classes of medical certificates allow the pilot to wear glasses provided the correction is within the prescribed limits of vision.

The armed forces have always been an important source of trained pilots for civilian jobs. Military pilots gain valuable experience on jet aircraft and helicopters, and persons with this experience usually are preferred for civilian pilot jobs. This primarily reflects the extensive flying time military pilots receive. Persons without armed forces training may become pilots by attending flight schools. The FAA has certified about 600 civilian flying schools, including some colleges and universities that offer degree credit for pilot training. Over the projection period, federal budget reductions are expected to reduce military pilot training. As a result, FAA-certified schools will train a larger share of pilots than in the past. Prospective pilots also may learn to fly by taking lessons from individual FAA-certified flight instructors.

Although some small airlines will hire high school graduates, most airlines require at least 2 years of college and prefer to hire college graduates. In fact, most entrants to this occupation have a college degree. Because the number of college educated applicants continues to increase, many employers are making a college degree an educational requirement.

Depending on the type of aircraft, new airline pilots start as first officers or flight engineers. Although some airlines favor applicants who already have a flight engineer's license, they may provide flight engineer training for those who have only the commercial license. Many pilots begin

with smaller regional or commuter airlines, where they obtain experience flying passengers on scheduled flights into busy airports in all weather conditions. These jobs often lead to higher paying jobs with bigger, national airlines.

Initial training for airline pilots includes a week of company indoctrination, 3 to 6 weeks of ground school and simulator training, and 25 hours of initial operating experience, including a check ride with an FAA aviation safety inspector. Once trained and "on the line," pilots are required to attend recurrent training and simulator checks twice a year throughout their career.

Organizations other than airlines usually require less flying experience. However, a commercial pilot's license is a minimum requirement, and employers prefer applicants who have experience in the type of craft they will be flying. New employees usually start as first officers, or fly less sophisticated equipment. Test pilots often are required to have an engineering degree.

Advancement for all pilots usually is limited to other flying jobs. Many pilots start as flight instructors, building up their flying hours while they earn money teaching. As they become more experienced, these pilots occasionally fly charter planes or perhaps get jobs with small air transportation firms, such as air taxi companies. Some advance to business flying jobs. A small number get flight engineer jobs with the airlines.

In the airlines, advancement usually depends on seniority provisions of union contracts. After 1 to 5 years, flight engineers advance according to seniority to first officer and, after 5 to 15 years, to captain. Seniority also determines which pilots get the more desirable routes. In a nonairline job, a first officer may advance to pilot and, in large companies, to chief pilot or director of aviation in charge of aircraft scheduling, maintenance, and flight procedures.

Job Outlook

Pilots are expected to face strong competition for jobs through the year 2010. Many qualified persons seek jobs in this occupation because it offers very high earnings, glamour, prestige, and free or low-cost travel benefits. As time passes, some pilots will fail to maintain their qualifications, and the number of applicants competing for each opening should decline. Factors affecting demand, however, are not expected to ease that competition.

Relatively few jobs will be created from rising demand for pilots, even though employment is expected to increase about as fast as the average for all occupations through 2010. Expected growth in domestic and international airline passenger and cargo traffic will create a need for more airliners, pilots, and flight instructors. However, computerized flight management systems on new aircraft will continue to eliminate the need for flight engineers on those planes, thus restricting the growth of pilot employment. In addition, the trend toward using larger planes in the airline industry will increase pilot productivity. Future business travel could also be adversely affected by the growing use of teleconferencing, facsimile mail, and electronic communications—such as e-mail—as well as by the elimination of middle management positions in corporate downsizing. Employment of business pilots is expected to grow more slowly than in the past as more businesses opt to fly with regional and smaller airlines serving their area rather than to buy and operate their own aircraft. The number of job openings resulting from the need to replace pilots who retire or leave the occupation traditionally has been very low. Aircraft pilots usually have a strong attachment to their occupation because it requires a substantial investment in specialized training that is not transferable to other fields, and it commonly offers very high earnings. However, many of the pilots who were hired in the late 1960s are approaching the age for mandatory retirement and, thus, several thousand job openings are expected to be generated each year.

Pilots who have logged the greatest number of flying hours in the more sophisticated equipment typically have the best prospects. For this reason, military pilots often have an advantage over other applicants. Job seekers with the most FAA licenses also will have a competitive advantage. Opportunities for pilots in the regional commuter airlines and international service are expected to be more favorable, as these segments are expected to grow faster than other segments of the industry.

Employment of pilots is sensitive to cyclical swings in the economy. During recessions, when a decline in the demand for air travel forces airlines to curtail the number of flights, airlines may temporarily furlough some pilots. Commercial and corporate flying, flight instruction, and testing of new aircraft also decline during recessions, adversely affecting the employment of pilots in those areas.

Earnings

Earnings of aircraft pilots and flight engineers vary greatly depending whether they work as airline or commercial pilots. Earnings of airline pilots are among the highest in the nation, and depend on factors such as the type, size, and maximum speed of the plane and the number of hours and miles flown. For example, pilots who fly jet aircraft usually earn higher salaries than do pilots who fly turboprops. Airline pilots and flight engineers may earn extra pay for night and international flights. In 2000, median annual earnings of airline pilots, copilots, and flight engineers were $110,940. The lowest 10 percent earned less than $36,110. Over 25 percent earned more than $145,000.

Median annual earnings of commercial pilots were $43,300 in 2000. The middle 50 percent earned between $31,500 and $61,230. The lowest 10 percent earned less than $24,290, and the highest 10 percent earned more than $92,000.

Airline pilots usually are eligible for life and health insurance plans financed by the airlines. They also receive retirement benefits and, if they fail the FAA physical examination at some point in their careers, they get disability payments. In addition, pilots receive an expense allowance, or "per diem," for every hour they are away from home. Per diem can represent up to $500 each month in addition to their salary. Some airlines also provide allowances to pilots for purchasing and cleaning their uniforms. As an additional benefit, pilots and their immediate families usually are entitled to free or reduced fare transportation on their own and other airlines.

More than one-half of all aircraft pilots are members of unions. Most of the pilots who fly for the major airlines are members of the Airline Pilots Association, International, but those employed by one major airline are members of the Allied Pilots Association. Some flight engineers are members of the Flight Engineers' International Association.

Related Occupations

Although they are not in the cockpit, air traffic controllers and airfield operation specialists also play an important role in making sure flights are safe and on schedule, and participate in many of the decisions that pilots must make.

Sources of Additional Information

Information about job opportunities, salaries for a particular airline, and qualifications required may be obtained by writing to the personnel manager of the airline.

For information on airline pilots, contact:

- Airline Pilots Association, 1625 Massachusetts Ave. NW., Washington, DC 20036
- Air Transport Association of America, Inc., 1301 Pennsylvania Ave. NW., Suite 1100, Washington, DC 20004

For information on helicopter pilots, contact:

- Helicopter Association International, 1619 Duke St., Alexandria, VA 22314

For a copy of the List of Certificated Pilot Schools, write to:

- Superintendent of Documents, U.S. Government Printing Office, Washington, DC 20402. There is a charge for this publication.

For information about job opportunities in companies other than airlines, consult the classified section of aviation trade magazines and apply to companies that operate aircraft at local airports.

Air Traffic Controllers

O*NET 53-2021.00

Significant Points

- Nearly all air traffic controllers are employed and trained by the federal government.

- Keen competition is expected for the few job openings in this occupation.

- Aircraft controllers earn relatively high pay and have good benefits.

Nature of the Work

The air traffic control system is a vast network of people and equipment that ensures the safe operation of commercial and private aircraft. Air traffic controllers coordinate the movement of air traffic to make certain that planes stay a safe distance apart. Their immediate concern is safety, but controllers also must direct planes efficiently to minimize delays. Some regulate airport traffic; others regulate flights between airports.

Although *airport tower* or *terminal controllers* watch over all planes traveling through the airport's airspace, their main responsibility is to organize the flow of aircraft in and out of the airport. Relying on radar and visual observation, they closely monitor each plane to ensure a safe distance between all aircraft and to guide pilots between the hangar or ramp and the end of the airport's airspace. In addition, controllers keep pilots informed about changes in weather conditions such as wind shear—a sudden change in the velocity or direction of the wind that can cause the pilot to lose control of the aircraft.

During arrival or departure, several controllers direct each plane. As a plane approaches an airport, the pilot radios ahead to inform the terminal of its presence. The controller in the radar room, just beneath the control tower, has a copy of the plane's flight plan and already has observed the plane on radar. If the path is clear, the controller directs the pilot to a runway; if the airport is busy, the plane is fitted into a traffic pattern with other aircraft waiting to land. As the plane nears the runway, the pilot is asked to contact the tower. There, another controller, who also is watching the plane on radar, monitors the aircraft the last mile or so to the runway, delaying any departures that would interfere with the plane's landing. Once the plane has landed, a ground controller in the tower directs it along the taxiways to its assigned gate. The ground controller usually works entirely by sight, but may use radar if visibility is very poor.

The procedure is reversed for departures. The ground controller directs the plane to the proper runway. The local controller then informs the pilot about conditions at the airport, such as weather, speed and direction of wind, and visibility. The local controller also issues runway clearance for the pilot to take off. Once in the air, the plane is guided out of the airport's airspace by the departure controller.

After each plane departs, airport tower controllers notify *en route controllers* who will take charge next. There are 21 en route control centers located around the country, each employing 300 to 700 controllers, with more than 150 on duty during peak hours at the busier facilities. Airplanes usually fly along designated routes; each center is assigned a certain airspace containing many different routes. En route controllers work in teams of up to three members, depending on how heavy traffic is; each team is responsible for a section of the center's airspace. A team, for example, might be responsible for all planes that are between 30 to 100 miles north of an airport and flying at an altitude between 6,000 and 18,000 feet.

To prepare for planes about to enter the team's airspace, the radar associate controller organizes flight plans coming off a printer. If two planes are scheduled to enter the team's airspace at nearly the same time, location, and altitude, this controller may arrange with the preceding control unit for one plane to change its flight path. The previous unit may have been another team at the same or an adjacent center, or a departure controller at a neighboring terminal. As a plane approaches a team's airspace, the radar controller accepts responsibility for the plane from the previous controlling unit. The controller also delegates responsibility for the plane to the next controlling unit when the plane leaves the team's airspace.

The radar controller, who is the senior team member, observes the planes in the team's airspace on radar and communicates with the pilots when necessary. Radar controllers warn pilots about nearby planes, bad weather conditions, and other potential hazards. Two planes on a collision course will be directed around each other. If a pilot wants to change altitude in search of better flying conditions, the controller will check to determine that no other planes will be along the proposed path. As the flight progresses, the team responsible for the aircraft notifies the next team in charge. Through team coordination, the plane arrives safely at its destination.

Both airport tower and en route controllers usually control several planes at a time; often, they have to make quick decisions about completely different activities. For example, a controller might direct a plane on its landing approach and at the same time provide pilots entering the airport's airspace with information about conditions at the airport. While instructing these pilots, the controller also would observe other planes in the vicinity, such as those in a holding pattern waiting for permission to land, to ensure that they remain well separated.

In addition to airport towers and en route centers, air traffic controllers also work in flight service stations operated at more than 100 locations. These *flight service specialists* provide pilots with information on the station's particular area, including terrain, preflight and in-flight weather information, suggested routes, and other information important to the safety of a flight. Flight service station specialists help pilots in emergency situations and initiate and coordinate searches for missing or overdue aircraft. However, they are not involved in actively managing air traffic.

Some air traffic controllers work at the Federal Aviation Administration's (FAA) Air Traffic Control Systems Command Center in Herndon, Virginia, where they oversee the entire system. They look for situations that will create bottlenecks or other problems in the system, then respond with a management plan for traffic into and out of the troubled sector. The objective is to keep traffic levels in the trouble spots manageable for the controllers working at en route centers.

Currently, the FAA is in the midst of developing and implementing a new automated air traffic control system that will allow controllers to more efficiently deal with the demands of increased air traffic. For example, some traditional air traffic controller tasks—like determining how far apart planes should be kept—will be done by computer. Present separation standards call for a 2,000-foot vertical spacing between two aircraft operating above 29,000 feet and flying the same ground track. With the aid of new technologies, the FAA will be able to reduce this vertical separation standard to 1,000 feet. Improved communication between computers on airplanes and those on the ground also is making the controller's job a little easier.

At present controllers sit at consoles with green-glowing screens that display radar images generated by a computer. In the future, controllers will work at a modern workstation computer that depicts air routes in full-color on a 20- by 20-inch screen. The controllers will select radio channels simply by touching on-screen buttons instead of turning dials or switching switches. The new technology will also enable controllers to zoom in on selected corners of the air space that is their responsibility and get better images of moving traffic than is possible with today's machines. The new automated air traffic control system is expected to become operational in several phases over the next 8 years.

The FAA is also considering implementing a system called "free flight" which would give pilots much more freedom in operating their aircraft. The change will require new concepts of shared responsibility between controllers and pilots. Air traffic controllers will still be central to the safe operation of the system, but their responsibilities will eventually shift from controlling to monitoring flights. At present, controllers assign routes, altitudes, and speeds. Under the new system, airlines and pilots would choose them. Controllers would intervene only to ensure that aircraft remained at safe distances from one another, to prevent congestion in terminal areas and entry into closed airspace, or to otherwise ensure safety. Today's practices often result in planes zigzagging from point to point along corridors rather than flying from city to city in a straight line. This results in lost time and fuel. However, it may be several years before a free flight system is implemented, despite its potential advantages. For the system to work, new equipment must be added for pilots and controllers, and new procedures developed to accommodate both the tightly controlled and flexible aspects of free flight. Budget constraints within the federal government may delay or slow implementation.

Working Conditions

Controllers work a basic 40-hour week; however, they may work additional hours for which they receive overtime pay or equal time off. Because most control towers and centers operate 24 hours a day, 7 days a week, controllers rotate night and weekend shifts.

During busy times, controllers must work rapidly and efficiently. This requires total concentration to keep track of several planes at the same time and make certain all pilots receive correct instructions. The mental stress of being responsible for the safety of several aircraft and their passengers can be exhausting for some persons.

Employment

Air traffic controllers held about 27,000 jobs in 2000. They were employed by the federal government at airports—in towers and flight service stations—and in en route traffic control centers. The overwhelming majority worked for the FAA. Some professional controllers conduct research at the FAA's national experimental center near Atlantic City, New Jersey. Others serve as instructors at the FAA Academy in Oklahoma City, Oklahoma. A small number of civilian controllers worked for the U.S. Department of Defense. In addition to controllers employed by the federal government, some worked for private air traffic control companies providing service to non-FAA towers.

Training, Other Qualifications, and Advancement

Air traffic controller trainees are selected through the competitive Federal Civil Service system. Applicants must pass a written test that measures their ability to learn the controller's duties. Applicants with experience as a pilot, navigator, or military controller can improve their rating by scoring well on the occupational knowledge portion of the examination. Abstract reasoning and three-dimensional spatial visualization are among the aptitudes the exam measures. In addition, applicants usually must have 3 years of general work experience or 4 years of college, or a combination of both. Applicants also must survive a week of screening at the FAA Academy in Oklahoma City, which includes aptitude tests using computer simulators and physical and psychological examinations. Successful applicants receive drug screening tests. For airport tower and en route center positions, applicants must be less than 31 years old. Those 31 years old and over are eligible for positions at flight service stations.

Controllers must be articulate, because pilots must be given directions quickly and clearly. Intelligence and a good memory also are important because controllers constantly receive information that they must immediately grasp, interpret, and remember. Decisiveness also is required because controllers often have to make quick decisions. The ability to concentrate is crucial because controllers must make these decisions in the midst of noise and other distractions.

Trainees learn their jobs through a combination of formal and on-the-job training. They receive 7 months of intensive training at the FAA academy, where they learn the fundamentals of the airway system, FAA regulations, controller equipment, aircraft performance characteristics, as well as more specialized tasks. To receive a job offer, trainees must successfully complete the training and pass a series of examinations, including a controller skills test that measures speed and accuracy in recognizing and correctly solving air traffic control problems. The test requires judgments on spatial relationships and requires application of the rules and procedures contained in the Air Traffic Control Handbook. Based on aptitude and test scores, trainees are selected to work at either an en route center or a tower.

After graduation, it takes several years of progressively more responsible work experience, interspersed with considerable classroom instruction and independent study, to become a fully qualified controller. This training includes instruction in the operation of the new, more automated air traffic control system—including the automated Microwave Landing System that enables pilots to receive instructions over automated data links—that is being installed in control sites across the country.

Controllers who fail to complete either the academy or the on-the-job portion of the training are usually dismissed. Controllers must pass a physical examination each year and a job performance examination twice each year. Failure to become certified in any position at a facility within a specified time also may result in dismissal. Controllers also are subject to drug screening as a condition of continuing employment.

At airports, new controllers begin by supplying pilots with basic flight data and airport information. They then advance to ground controller, then local controller, departure controller, and finally, arrival controller. At an en route traffic control center, new controllers first deliver printed flight plans to teams, gradually advancing to radar associate controller and then radar controller.

Controllers can transfer to jobs at different locations or advance to supervisory positions, including management or staff jobs in air traffic control and top administrative jobs in the FAA. However, there are only limited opportunities for a controller to switch from a position in an en route center to a tower.

Job Outlook

Extremely keen competition is expected for air traffic controller jobs because the occupation attracts many more qualified applicants than the small number of job openings that result mostly from replacement needs. Replacement needs are very low because of the relatively high pay, liberal retirement benefits, and controllers' very strong attachment to the occupation. A new FAA hiring policy, allowing eligible retired military air traffic controllers to apply for FAA positions, will make competition even keener.

Employment of air traffic controllers is expected to grow more slowly than average through the year 2010. Employment growth is not expected to keep pace with growth in the number of aircraft flying because of the implementation of a new air traffic control system over the next several years. This computerized system will assist the controller by automatically making many of the routine decisions. Automation will allow controllers to handle more traffic, thus increasing their productivity.

Air traffic controllers who continue to meet the proficiency and medical requirements enjoy more job security than most workers do. The demand for air travel and the workloads of air traffic controllers decline during recessions, but controllers seldom are laid off.

Earnings

Median annual earnings of air traffic controllers in 2000 were $82,520. The middle 50 percent earned between $62,250 and $101,570. The lowest 10 percent earned less than $44,760, and the highest 10 percent earned more than $111,150.

The average annual salary, excluding overtime earnings, for air traffic controllers in the federal government—which employs 89 percent of the total—in nonsupervisory, supervisory, and managerial positions was $53,313 in 2001. Both the worker's job responsibilities and the complexity of the particular facility determine a controller's pay. For example, controllers who work at the FAA's busiest air traffic control facilities earn higher pay.

Depending on length of service, air traffic controllers receive 13 to 26 days of paid vacation and 13 days of paid sick leave each year, life insurance, and health benefits. In addition, controllers can retire at an earlier age and with fewer years of service than other federal employees can. Air traffic controllers are eligible to retire at age 50 with 20 years of service as an active air traffic controller or after 25 years of active service at any age. There is a mandatory retirement age of 56 for controllers who manage air traffic.

Related Occupations

Airfield operations specialists also are involved in the direction and control of traffic in air transportation.

Sources of Additional Information

Information on acquiring a job as an air traffic controller with the federal government may be obtained from the Office of Personnel Management through a telephone-based system. Consult your telephone directory under U.S. Government for a local number, or call (912) 757-3000; Federal Relay Service: (800) 877-8339. That number is not toll free and charges may result. Information also is available on the Internet: http://www.usajobs.opm.gov

Animal Care and Service Workers

O*NET 39-2011.00, 39-2021.00

Significant Points

- Animal lovers get satisfaction in this occupation, but aspects of the work can be unpleasant and physically and emotionally demanding.

- Most animal care and service workers are trained on the job, but advancement depends on experience, formal training, and continuing education.

Nature of the Work

Many people like animals. But, as pet owners can attest, taking care of them is hard work. Animal care and service workers—which include animal caretakers and animal trainers—train, feed, water, groom, bathe, and exercise animals, and clean, disinfect, and repair their cages. They also play with the animals, provide companionship, and observe behavioral changes that could indicate illness or injury. Boarding kennels, animal shelters, veterinary hospitals and clinics, stables, laboratories, aquariums, and zoological parks all house animals and employ animal care and service workers. Job titles and duties vary by employment setting.

Kennel attendants usually care for small companion animals like dogs and cats while their owners are working or traveling out of town. Beginning attendants perform basic tasks, such as cleaning cages and dog runs, filling food and water dishes, and exercising animals. Experienced attendants may provide basic animal healthcare, as well as bathe animals, trim nails, and attend to other grooming needs. Attendants who work in kennels also may sell pet food and supplies, assist in obedience training, help with breeding, or prepare animals for shipping.

Animal caretakers who specialize in grooming, or maintaining a pet's—usually a dog's or cat's—appearance are called *groomers*. Some groomers work in kennels, veterinary clinics, animal shelters, or pet-supply stores. Others operate their own grooming business. Groomers answer telephones, schedule appointments, discuss with clients their pets' grooming needs, and collect information on the pet's disposition and its veterinarian. Groomers often are the first to notice a medical problem, such as an ear or skin infection, that requires veterinary care.

Grooming the pet involves several steps: An initial brush-out is followed by a first clipping of hair or fur using electric clippers, combs, and grooming shears; the groomer then cuts the nails, cleans the ears, bathes, and blow dries the animal, and ends with a final clipping and styling.

Animal caretakers in animal shelters perform a variety of duties and work with a wide variety of animals. In addition to attending to the basic needs of the animals, caretakers also must keep records of the animals received and discharged and any tests or treatments done. Some vaccinate newly admitted animals under the direction of a veterinarian or veterinary technician, and euthanize (painlessly put to death) seriously ill, severely injured, or unwanted animals. Animal caretakers in animal shelters also interact with the public, answering telephone inquiries, screening applicants for animal adoption, or educating visitors on neutering and other animal health issues.

Caretakers in stables are called *grooms*. They saddle and unsaddle horses, give them rubdowns, and walk them to cool off after a ride. They also feed, groom, and exercise the horses; clean out stalls and replenish bedding; polish saddles; clean and organize the tack (harness, saddle, and bridle) room; and store supplies and feed. Experienced grooms may help train horses.

In zoos, animal care and service workers, called *keepers*, prepare the diets and clean the enclosures of animals, and sometimes assist in raising them when they are very young. They watch for any signs of illness or injury, monitor eating patterns or any changes in behavior, and record their observations. Keepers also may answer questions and ensure that the visiting public behaves responsibly toward the exhibited animals. Depending on the zoo, keepers may be assigned to work with a broad group of animals such as mammals, birds, or reptiles, or they may work with a limited collection of animals such as primates, large cats, or small mammals.

Animal trainers train animals for riding, security, performance, obedience, or assisting persons with disabilities. Animal trainers do this by accustoming the animal to human voice and contact, and conditioning the animal to respond to commands. Trainers use several techniques to help them train animals. One technique, known as a bridge, is a stimulus that a trainer uses to communicate the precise moment an animal does something correctly. When the animal responds correctly, the trainer gives positive reinforcement in a variety of ways: food, toys, play, rubdowns, or speaking the word "good." Animal training takes place in small steps, and often takes months and even years of repetition. During the conditioning process, trainers provide animals with mental stimulation, physical exercise, and husbandry care. In addition to their hands-on work with the animals, trainers often oversee other aspects of the animal's care, such as diet preparation. Trainers often work in competitions or shows, such as the circus or marine parks. Trainers who work in shows also may participate in educational programs for visitors and guests.

Working Conditions

People who love animals get satisfaction from working with and helping them. However, some of the work may be unpleasant, as well as physically and emotionally demanding, and sometimes dangerous. Most animal care and service workers have to clean animal cages and lift, hold, or restrain animals, risking exposure to bites or scratches. Their work often involves kneeling, crawling, repeated bending, and lifting heavy supplies like bales of hay or bags of feed. Animal caretakers must take precautions when treating animals with germicides or insecticides. The work setting can be noisy. Caretakers of show and sports animals travel to competitions.

Animal care and service workers who witness abused animals or who assist in the euthanizing of unwanted, aged, or hopelessly injured animals may experience emotional stress. Those working for private humane societies and municipal animal shelters often deal with the public, some of whom might react with hostility to any implication that the owners are neglecting or abusing their pets. Such workers must maintain a calm and professional demeanor while they enforce the laws regarding animal care.

Animal care and service workers may work outdoors in all kinds of weather. Hours are irregular: Animals have to be fed every day, so caretakers often work weekend and holiday shifts. In some animal hospitals, research facilities, and animal shelters, an attendant is on duty 24 hours a day, which means night shifts. The majority of full-time animal care and service workers work about 40 hours a week.

Employment

Animal care and service workers held a total of 145,000 jobs in 2000. Nearly 90 percent of this number worked as nonfarm animal caretakers; the remainder worked as animal trainers. Nonfarm animal caretakers worked primarily in boarding kennels, animal shelters, stables, grooming shops, animal hospitals, and veterinary offices. A significant number also worked for animal humane societies, racing stables, dog and horse racetrack operators, zoos, theme parks, circuses, and other amusement and recreations services. In 2000, more than 1 out of every 4 nonfarm animal caretakers was self-employed.

Employment of animal trainers was concentrated in animal services that specialize in training horses, pets, and other animal specialties; and in commercial sports, training racehorses and dogs. About 4 in 10 animal trainers were self-employed.

Training, Other Qualifications, and Advancement

Most animal care and service workers are trained on the job. Employers generally prefer to hire people with some experience with animals. Some training programs are available for specific types of animal caretakers, such as groomers, but formal training is usually not necessary for entry-level positions. Animal trainers often need to possess a high school diploma or GED equivalent. However, some animal training jobs may require a bachelor's degree and additional skills. For example, a marine mammal trainer usually needs a bachelor's degree in biology, marine biology, animal science, psychology, zoology, or related field, plus strong swimming skills and SCUBA certification. All animal trainers need patience, sensitivity, and experience with problem-solving and obedience. Certification is not mandatory for animal trainers, but several organizations offer training programs and certification for prospective animal trainers.

Most pet groomers learn their trade by completing an informal apprenticeship, usually lasting 6 to 10 weeks, under the guidance of an experienced groomer. Prospective groomers may also attend one of the 50 state-licensed grooming schools throughout the country, with programs varying in length from 4 to 18 weeks. The National Dog Groomers Association of America certifies groomers who pass a written examination consisting of 400 questions, with a separate part testing practical skills. Beginning groomers often start by taking on one duty, such as bathing and drying the pet. They eventually assume responsibility for the entire grooming process, from the initial brush-out to the final clipping. Groomers who work in large retail establishments or kennels may, with experience, move into supervisory or managerial positions. Experienced groomers often choose to open their own shops.

Beginning animal caretakers in kennels learn on the job, and usually start by cleaning cages and feeding and watering animals. Kennel caretakers may be promoted to kennel supervisor, assistant manager, and manager, and those with enough capital and experience may open up their own kennels. The American Boarding Kennels Association (ABKA) offers a three-stage, home-study program for individuals interested in pet care. The first two study programs address basic and advanced principles of animal care, while the third program focuses on in-depth animal care and good business procedures. Those who complete the third program and pass oral and written examinations administered by the ABKA become Certified Kennel Operators (CKO).

Some zoological parks may require their caretakers to have a bachelor's degree in biology, animal science, or a related field. Most require experience with animals, preferably as a volunteer or paid keeper in a zoo. Zookeepers may advance to senior keeper, assistant head keeper, head keeper, and assistant curator, but few openings occur, especially for the higher-level positions.

Animal caretakers in animal shelters are not required to have any specialized training, but training programs and workshops are increasingly available through the Humane Society of the United States, the American Humane Association, and the National Animal Control Association. Workshop topics include cruelty investigations, appropriate methods of euthanasia for shelter animals, and techniques for preventing problems with wildlife. With experience and additional training, caretakers in animal shelters may become adoption coordinators, animal control officers, emergency rescue drivers, assistant shelter managers, or shelter directors.

Job Outlook

Employment of animal care and service workers is expected to grow faster than the average for all occupations through 2010. The pet population—which drives employment of animal caretakers in kennels, grooming shops, animal shelters, and veterinary clinics and hospitals— is expected to remain stable or slightly increase. Pets remain popular, and pet owners—including a large number of baby boomers whose disposable income is expected to increase as they age—may increasingly take advantage of pet care services. These include grooming services, daily and overnight boarding services, training services, and veterinary services, spurring employment growth for animal caretakers, veterinary assistants, and animal trainers.

Demand for animal care and service workers in animal shelters is expected to remain steady. Communities are increasingly recognizing the connection between animal abuse and abuse toward humans, and should continue to commit funds to animal shelters, many of which are working hand-in-hand with social service agencies and law enforcement teams. Employment growth of personal and group animal trainers will stem from an increased number of animal owners seeking training services for their pets, including behavior modification and feline behavior training. The outlook for caretakers in zoos, however, is not favorable due to slow growth in zoo capacity and keen competition for the few positions.

Despite growth in demand for animal care and service workers, the overwhelming majority of jobs will result from the need to replace workers leaving the field. Many animal caretaker jobs that require little or no training have work schedules that tend to be flexible; therefore, they are attractive to people seeking their first job and for students and others looking for temporary or part-time work. Because many workers leave the occupation, the overall availability of jobs should be very good.

Earnings

Median hourly earnings of nonfarm animal caretakers were $7.67 in 2000. The middle 50 percent earned between $6.48 and $9.59. The bottom 10 percent earned less than $5.78, and the top 10 percent earned more than $12.70. Median hourly earnings in the industries employing the largest numbers of nonfarm animal caretakers in 2000 were as follows:

Local government	$11.80
Commercial sports	8.09
Animal services, except veterinary	7.78
Retail stores, not elsewhere classified	7.32
Membership organizations, not elsewhere classified	7.18
Veterinary services	7.07

Median hourly earnings of animal trainers were $10.54 in 2000. The middle 50 percent earned between $7.59 and $16.19. The lowest 10 percent earned less than $6.25, and the top 10 percent earned more than $20.85.

Related Occupations

Others who work extensively with animals include farmers, ranchers, and agricultural managers; agricultural workers; veterinarians; veterinary technologists, technicians, and assistants; and biological and medical scientists.

Sources of Additional Information

For more information on jobs in animal caretaking and control, and the animal shelter and control personnel training program, write to:

● The Humane Society of the United States, 2100 L St. NW., Washington, DC 20037-1598. Internet: http://www.hsus.org

For career information and information on training, certification, and earnings of animal control officers at federal, state, and local levels, contact:

● National Animal Control Association, P.O. Box 480851, Kansas City, MO 64148-0851. Internet: http://www.nacanet.org

To obtain a listing of state-licensed grooming schools, send a stamped, self-addressed, business size envelope to:

● National Dog Groomers Association of America, P.O. Box 101, Clark, PA 16113. Internet: http://www.nauticom.net/www/ndga

Announcers

O*NET 27-3011.00, 27-3012.00

Significant Points

● Competition for announcer jobs will continue to be keen.

● Jobs at small stations usually have low pay, but offer the best opportunities for beginners.

● Related work experience at a campus radio station or as an intern at a commercial station can be helpful in breaking into the occupation.

Nature of the Work

Announcers in radio and television perform a variety of tasks on and off the air. They announce station program information such as program schedules and station breaks for commercials or public service information, and they introduce and close programs. Announcers read prepared scripts or ad lib commentary on the air when presenting news, sports, weather, time, and commercials. If a written script is required, they may do the research and writing. Announcers also interview guests and moderate panels or discussions. Some provide commentary for the audience during sporting events, parades, and other events. Announcers are often well-known to radio and television audiences and may make promotional appearances and remote broadcasts for their stations.

Radio announcers often are called *disc jockeys*. Some disc jockeys specialize in one kind of music. They announce music selections and may decide what music to play. While on the air, they comment on the music, weather, and traffic. They may take requests from listeners, interview guests, and manage listener contests.

Newscasters or *anchors* work at large stations and specialize in news, sports, or weather. *Show hosts* may specialize in a certain area of interest such as politics, personal finance, sports, or health. They contribute to the preparation of the program content; interview guests; and discuss issues with viewers, listeners, or an in-studio audience.

Announcers at smaller stations may cover all of these areas and tend to have more off-air duties as well. They may operate the control board, monitor the transmitter, sell commercial time to advertisers, keep a log of the station's daily programming, and do production work. Consolidation and automation make it possible for announcers to do some work previously performed by broadcast technicians. Announcers use the control board to broadcast programming, commercials, and public service announcements according to schedule. Public radio and television announcers are involved with station fundraising efforts.

Announcers frequently participate in community activities. Sports announcers, for example, may serve as masters of ceremonies at sports club banquets or may greet customers at openings of sporting goods stores.

Although most announcers are employed in radio and television broadcasting, some are employed in the cable television or motion picture production industries. Other announcers may use a public address system to provide information to the audience at sporting and other events. Some disc jockeys announce and play music at clubs, dances, restaurants, and weddings.

Working Conditions

Announcers usually work in well-lighted, air-conditioned, soundproof studios. The broadcast day is long for radio and TV stations—some are on the air 24 hours a day—so announcers can expect to work unusual hours. Many present early morning shows, when most people are getting ready for work or commuting, while others do late night programs.

Announcers often work within tight schedule constraints, which can be physically and mentally stressful. For many announcers, the intangible rewards—creative work, many personal contacts, and the satisfaction of becoming widely known—far outweigh the disadvantages of irregular and often unpredictable hours, work pressures, and disrupted personal lives.

Employment

Announcers held about 71,000 jobs in 2000. Nearly all were staff announcers employed in radio and television broadcasting, but some were freelance announcers who sold their services for individual assignments to networks and stations, or to advertising agencies and other independent producers. Many announcing jobs are part-time.

Training, Other Qualifications, and Advancement

Entry into this occupation is highly competitive. Formal training in broadcasting from a college or technical school (private broadcasting school) is valuable. Station officials pay particular attention to taped auditions that show an applicant's delivery and—in television—appearance and style on commercials, news, and interviews. Those hired by television stations usually start out as production assistants, researchers, or reporters and are given a chance to move into announcing if they show an aptitude for on-air work. Newcomers to TV broadcasting also may begin as news camera operators. A beginner's chance of landing an on-air job is remote, except possibly for a small radio station. In radio, newcomers usually start out taping interviews and operating equipment.

Announcers usually begin at a station in a small community and, if qualified, may move to a better paying job in a large city. They also may advance by hosting a regular program as a disc jockey, sportscaster, or other specialist. Competition is particularly intense for employment by networks, and employers look for college graduates with at least several years of successful announcing experience.

Announcers must have a pleasant and well-controlled voice, good timing, excellent pronunciation, and must know correct grammar usage. Television announcers need a neat, pleasing appearance as well. Knowledge of theater, sports, music, business, politics, and other subjects likely to be covered in broadcasts improves chances for success. Announcers also must be computer-literate because programming is created and edited by computer. In addition, they should be able to ad lib all or part of a show and to work under tight deadlines. The most successful announcers attract a large audience by combining a pleasing personality and voice with an appealing style.

High school and college courses in English, public speaking, drama, foreign languages, and computer science are valuable, and hobbies such as sports and music are additional assets. Students may gain valuable experience at campus radio or TV facilities and at commercial stations while serving as interns. Paid or unpaid internships provide students with hands-on training and the chance to establish contacts in the industry. Unpaid interns often receive college credit and are allowed to observe and assist station employees. Although the Fair Labor Standards Act limits the work unpaid interns may perform in a station, unpaid internships are the rule; sometimes they lead to paid internships. Paid internships are valuable because interns do work ordinarily done by regular employees and may even go on the air.

Persons considering enrolling in a broadcasting school should contact personnel managers of radio and television stations as well as broadcasting trade organizations to determine the school's reputation for producing suitably trained candidates.

Job Outlook

Competition for jobs as announcers will be keen because the broadcasting field attracts many more job seekers than there are jobs. Small radio stations are more inclined to hire beginners, but the pay is low. Interns usually receive preference for available positions. Because competition for ratings is so intense in major metropolitan areas, large stations will continue to seek announcers who have proven that they can attract and retain a large audience.

Announcers who are knowledgeable in business, consumer, and health news may have an advantage over others. While specialization is more common at large stations and the networks, many small stations also encourage it.

Employment of announcers is expected to decline through 2010 due to the lack of growth of new radio and television stations. Openings in this relatively small field also will arise from the need to replace those who transfer to other kinds of work or leave the labor force. Some announcers leave the field because they cannot advance to better paying jobs. Changes in station ownership, format, and ratings frequently cause periods of unemployment for many announcers.

Increasing consolidation of radio and television stations, new technology, and the growth of alternative media sources will contribute to the expected decline in employment of announcers. Consolidation in broadcasting may lead to increased use of syndicated programming and programs originating outside a station's viewing or listening area. Digital technology will increase the productivity of announcers, reducing the time spent on off-air technical and production work. In addition, all traditional media—including radio and television—may suffer losses in audience as the American public increases its use of personal computers.

Earnings

Salaries in broadcasting vary widely but in general are relatively low, except for announcers who work for large stations in major markets or for networks. Earnings are higher in television than in radio and higher in commercial than in public broadcasting.

Median hourly earnings of announcers in 2000 were $9.52. The middle 50 percent earned between $6.84 and $14.28. The lowest 10 percent earned less than $5.94, and the highest 10 percent earned more than $24.35. Median hourly earnings of announcers in 2000 were $9.54 in the radio and television broadcasting industry.

Related Occupations

The success of announcers depends upon how well they communicate. Others who must be skilled at oral communication include news analysts, reporters, and correspondents; interpreters and translators; sales and related occupations; public relations specialists; and teachers. Many announcers also must entertain their audience, so their work is similar to other entertainment-related occupations such as actors, directors, and producers; dancers and choreographers; and musicians, singers, and related workers.

Sources of Additional Information

General information on the broadcasting industry is available from:

● National Association of Broadcasters, 1771 N St. NW., Washington, DC 20036. Internet: http://www.nab.org

Artists and Related Workers

O*NET 27-1011.00, 27-1013.01, 27-1013.02, 27-1013.03, 27-1013.04, 27-1014.00

Significant Points

● More than half are self-employed—about 7 times the proportion in all professional and related occupations.

● Artists usually develop their skills through a bachelor's degree program or other postsecondary training in art or design.

● Keen competition is expected for both salaried jobs and freelance work, because many talented people are attracted to the visual arts.

Nature of the Work

Artists create art to communicate ideas, thoughts, or feelings. They use a variety of methods—painting, sculpting, or illustration—and an assortment of materials, including oils, watercolors, acrylics, pastels, pencils, pen and ink, plaster, clay, and computers. Artists' works may be realistic, stylized, or abstract and may depict objects, people, nature, or events.

Artists generally fall into one of three categories. *Art directors* formulate design concepts and presentation approaches for visual communications media. *Fine artists, including painters, sculptors, and illustrators* create original artwork using a variety of media and techniques. *Multi-media artists and animators* create special effects, animation, or other visual images using film, video, computers or other electronic media.

Art directors develop design concepts and review the material that is to appear in periodicals, newspapers, and other printed or digital media. They decide how best to present the information visually, so it is eye catching, appealing, and organized. They decide which photographs or artwork to use and oversee the layout design and production of the printed material. They may direct workers engaged in artwork, layout design, and copy writing.

Fine artists typically display their work in museums, commercial art galleries, corporate collections, and private homes. Some of their artwork may be commissioned (done on request from clients), but most is sold by the artist or through private art galleries or dealers. The gallery and artist predetermine how much each will earn from the sale. Only the most successful fine artists are able to support themselves solely through the sale of their works. Most fine artists must work in an unrelated field to support their art careers. Some work in museums or art galleries as fine arts directors or as curators, who plan and set up art exhibits. Others work as art critics for newspapers or magazines, or as consultants to foundations or institutional collectors.

Usually, fine artists specialize in one or two art forms, such as painting, illustrating, sketching, sculpting, printmaking, and restoring. *Painters, illustrators, cartoonists, and sketch artists* work with two-dimensional art forms. These artists use shading, perspective, and color to produce realistic scenes or abstractions.

Illustrators typically create pictures for books, magazines, and other publications; and commercial products, such as textiles, wrapping paper, stationery, greeting cards and calendars. Increasingly, illustrators work in digital format, preparing work directly on a computer.

Medical and *scientific illustrators* combine drawing skills with knowledge of the biological sciences. Medical illustrators draw illustrations of human anatomy and surgical procedures. Scientific illustrators draw illustrations of animals and plants. These illustrations are used in medical and scientific publications and in audiovisual presentations for teaching purposes. Medical illustrators also work for lawyers, producing exhibits for court cases.

Cartoonists draw political, advertising, social, and sports cartoons. Some cartoonists work with others who create the idea or story and write the captions. Most cartoonists have comic, critical, or dramatic talents in addition to drawing skills.

Sketch artists create likenesses of subjects using pencil, charcoal, or pastels. Sketches are used by law enforcement agencies to assist in identifying suspects, by the news media to depict courtroom scenes, and by individual patrons for their own enjoyment.

Sculptors design three-dimensional art works—either by molding and joining materials such as clay, glass, wire, plastic, fabric, or metal or by cutting and carving forms from a block of plaster, wood, or stone. Some sculptors combine various materials to create mixed-media installations. Some incorporate light, sound, and motion into their works.

Printmakers create printed images from designs cut or etched into wood, stone, or metal. After creating the design, the artist inks the surface of the woodblock, stone, or plate and uses a printing press to roll the image onto paper or fabric. Some make prints by pressing the inked surface onto paper by hand, or by graphically encoding data and processing it, using a computer. The digitized images are printed on paper using computer printers.

Painting restorers preserve and restore damaged and faded paintings. They apply solvents and cleaning agents to clean the surfaces, reconstruct or retouch damaged areas, and apply preservatives to protect the paintings. This is very detailed work and usually is reserved for experts in the field.

Multi-media artists and animators work primarily in computer and data processing services, advertising, and the motion picture and television industries. They draw by hand and use computers to create the large series of pictures that form the animated images or special effects seen in movies, television programs, and computer games. Some draw storyboards for television commercials, movies, and animated features. Storyboards present television commercials in a series of scenes similar to a comic strip and allow an advertising agency to evaluate proposed commercials with the company doing the advertising. Storyboards also serve as guides to placing actors and cameras and to other details during the production of commercials.

Working Conditions

Most artists work in fine or commercial art studios located in office buildings, or in private studios in their homes. Some fine artists share studio space, where they also may exhibit their work. Studio surroundings usually are well lighted and ventilated; however, fine artists may be exposed to fumes from glue, paint, ink, and other materials. Artists who sit at drafting tables or use computers for extended periods may experience back pain, eyestrain, or fatigue.

Artists employed by publishing companies, advertising agencies, and design firms generally work a standard 40-hour week. During busy periods, they may work overtime to meet deadlines. Self-employed artists can set their own hours, but may spend much time and effort selling their artwork to potential customers or clients and building a reputation.

Employment

Artists held about 147,000 jobs in 2000. More than half were self-employed. Of the artists who were not self-employed, many worked in motion picture, television, computer software, printing, publishing, and public relations firms. Some self-employed artists offer their services to advertising agencies, design firms, publishing houses, and other businesses.

Training, Other Qualifications, and Advancement

Training requirements for artists vary by specialty. Although formal training is not strictly necessary for fine artists, it is very difficult to become skilled enough to make a living without some training. Many colleges and universities offer degree programs leading to the bachelor in fine arts (BFA) and master in fine arts (MFA) degrees. Coursework usually includes core subjects, such as English, social science, and natural science, in addition to art history and studio art.

Independent schools of art and design also offer postsecondary studio training in the fine arts leading to an Associate in Art (AA) or bachelor in fine arts (BFA) degree. Typically, these programs focus more intensively on studio work than the academic programs in a university setting.

Formal educational programs in art also provide training in computer techniques. Computers are used widely in the visual arts, and knowledge and training in them are critical for many jobs in these fields.

Those who want to teach fine arts at pubic elementary or secondary schools must have a teaching certificate in addition to a bachelor's degree. An advanced degree in fine arts or arts administration is necessary for management or administrative positions in government or in foundations or for teaching in colleges and universities.

Illustrators learn drawing and sketching skills through training in art programs and extensive practice. Most employers prefer candidates with a bachelor's degree; however, some illustrators are contracted based on their portfolios of past work.

Medical illustrators must have both a demonstrated artistic ability and a detailed knowledge of living organisms, surgical and medical procedures, and human and animal anatomy. A 4-year bachelor's degree combining art and premedical courses usually is preferred, followed by a master's degree in medical illustration. This degree is offered in only five accredited schools in the United States.

Evidence of appropriate talent and skill, displayed in an artist's portfolio, is an important factor used by art directors, clients, and others in deciding whether to hire or contract out work. The portfolio is a collection of hand-made, computer-generated, photographic, or printed samples of the artist's best work. Assembling a successful portfolio requires skills usually developed in a bachelor's degree program or other postsecondary training in art or visual communications. Internships also provide excellent opportunities for artists to develop and enhance their portfolios.

Artists hired by advertising agencies often start with relatively routine work. While doing this work, however, they may observe and practice their skills on the side. Many artists freelance on a part-time basis while continuing to hold a full-time job until they are established. Others freelance part-time while still in school, to develop experience and to build a portfolio of published work.

Freelance artists try to develop a set of clients who regularly contract for work. Some freelance artists are widely recognized for their skill in specialties such as magazine or children's book illustration. These artists may earn high incomes and can pick and choose the type of work they do.

Fine artists advance professionally as their work circulates and as they establish a reputation for a particular style. Many of the most successful artists continually develop new ideas, and their work often evolves over time.

Job Outlook

Employment of artists and related workers is expected to grow as fast as the average for all occupations through the year 2010. Because the arts attract many talented people with creative ability, the number of aspiring artists continues to grow. Consequently, competition for both salaried jobs and freelance work in some areas is expected to be keen.

Art directors work in a variety of industries, such as printing, publishing, motion picture production and distribution, and design. Despite an expanding number of opportunities, they should experience keen competition for the available openings.

Fine artists mostly work on a freelance, or commission, basis and may find it difficult to earn a living solely by selling their artwork. Only the most successful fine artists receive major commissions for their work. Competition among artists for the privilege of being shown in galleries is expected to remain acute. And grants from sponsors such as private foundations, state and local arts councils, and the National Endowment for the Arts, should remain competitive. Nonetheless, studios, galleries, and individual clients are always on the lookout for artists who display outstanding talent, creativity, and style. Population growth, rising incomes, and growth in the number of people who appreciate the fine arts will contribute to the demand for fine artists. Talented fine artists who have developed a mastery of artistic techniques and skills, including computer skills, will have the best job prospects.

The need for artists to illustrate and animate materials for magazines, journals, and other printed or electronic media will spur demand for illustrators and animators of all types. Growth in the entertainment industry, including cable and other pay television broadcasting and motion picture production and distribution, will provide new job opportunities for illustrators, cartoonists, and animators. Competition for most jobs, however, will be strong, because job opportunities are relatively few and the number of people interested in these positions usually exceeds the number of available openings. Employers should be able to choose from among the most qualified candidates.

Earnings

Median annual earnings of salaried art directors were $56,880 in 2000. The middle 50 percent earned between $41,290 and $80,350. The lowest 10 percent earned less than $30,130, and the highest 10 percent earned more than $109,440. Median annual earnings were $63,510 in advertising, the industry employing the largest numbers of salaried art directors.

Median annual earnings of salaried fine artists, including painters, sculptors, and illustrators were $31,190 in 2000. The middle 50 percent earned between $20,460 and $42,720. The lowest 10 percent earned less than $14,690, and the highest 10 percent earned more than $58,580.

Median annual earnings of salaried multi-media artists and animators were $41,130 in 2000. The middle 50 percent earned between $30,700 and $54,040. The lowest 10 percent earned less than $23,740, and the highest 10 percent earned more than $70,560. Median annual earnings were $44,290 in computer and data processing services, the industry employing the largest numbers of salaried multi-media artists and animators.

Earnings for self-employed artists vary widely. Some charge only a nominal fee while they gain experience and build a reputation for their work. Others, such as well-established freelance fine artists and illustrators, can earn more than salaried artists. Many, however, find it difficult to rely solely on income earned from selling paintings or other works of art. Like other self-employed workers, freelance artists must provide their own benefits.

Related Occupations

Other workers who apply art skills include architects, except landscape and naval; archivists, curators, and museum technicians; designers; land-

scape architects; and photographers. Some computer-related occupations require art skills, including computer software engineers and desktop publishers.

Sources of Additional Information

For general information about art and design and a list of accredited college-level programs, contact:

● The National Association of Schools of Art and Design, 11250 Roger Bacon Dr., Suite 21, Reston, VA 20190. Internet: http://www.arts-accredit.org/nasad/default.htm

For information on careers in medical illustration, contact:

● The Association of Medical Illustrators, 2965 Flowers Road South, Suite 105, Atlanta, GA 30341. Internet: http://medical-illustrators.org

Assemblers and Fabricators

O*NET 51-2011.01, 51-2011.02, 51-2011.03, 51-2021.00, 51-2022.00, 51-2023.00, 51-2031.00, 51-2041.01, 51-2041.02, 51-2091.00, 51-2092.00, 51-2093.00, 51-2099.99

Significant Points

● Virtually all assemblers and fabricators work in plants that manufacture durable goods, such as computers and automobile engines.

● A high school diploma is preferred for most positions; applicants need specialized training for some assembly jobs.

● Projected slower-than-average employment growth reflects increasing automation and the shift of assembly to countries with lower labor costs.

Nature of the Work

Assemblers and fabricators produce a wide range of finished goods from manufactured parts or subassemblies. They produce intricate manufactured products, such as aircraft, automobile engines, computers, and electrical and electronic components.

Assemblers may work on subassemblies or the final assembly of an array of finished products or components. For example, electrical and electronic equipment assemblers put together or modify missile control systems, radio or test equipment, computers, machine-tool numerical controls, radar, or sonar, and prototypes of these and other products. Electromechanical equipment assemblers prepare and test equipment or devices such as appliances, dynamometers, or ejection-seat mechanisms. Coil winders, tapers, and finishers wind wire coil used in resistors, transformers, generators, and electric motors. Engine and other machine assemblers construct, assemble, or rebuild engines and turbines, and office, agricultural, construction, oilfield, rolling mill, textile, woodworking, paper, and food wrapping machinery. Aircraft structure, surfaces, rigging, and systems assemblers put together and install parts of airplanes, space vehicles, or missiles, such as wings or landing gear. Structural metal fabricators and fitters align and fit structural metal parts according to detailed specifications prior to welding or riveting.

Assemblers and fabricators involved in product development read and interpret engineering specifications from text, drawings, and computer-aided drafting systems. They also may use a variety of tools and precision measuring instruments. Some experienced assemblers work with engineers and technicians, assembling prototypes or test products.

As technology changes, so too does the manufacturing process. For example, flexible manufacturing systems include the manufacturing applications of robotics, computers, programmable motion control, and various sensing technologies. These systems change the way in which goods are made, and affect the jobs of those who make them. The concept of cellular manufacturing, for example, places a greater premium on the teamwork of and communication within "cells" of workers than it does on the old assembly line process. Team assemblers perform all of the assembly tasks assigned to their teams, rotating through the different tasks, rather than specializing in a single task. They also may decide how the work is to be assigned and how different tasks are to be performed. Some aspects of team assembly, such as rotating tasks, are becoming more common to all assembly and fabrication occupations. As the U.S. manufacturing sector continues to evolve in the face of growing international competition and changing technology, the nature of assembly and fabrication will change along with it.

Working Conditions

The working conditions for assemblers and fabricators vary from plant to plant and from industry to industry. Conditions may be noisy and many assemblers may have to sit or stand for long periods. Both electronic and electromechanical equipment assemblers, for example, sit at tables in rooms that are clean, well lit, and free from dust. Some electrical and electronics assemblers come in contact with soldering fumes, but ventilation systems and fans normally minimize this problem. Aircraft assemblers, however, usually come in contact with oil and grease, and their working areas may be quite noisy. They also may have to lift and fit heavy objects. In many cases, developments in ergonomics have improved working conditions through changes in workstation design and the increased use of robots or other pneumatically powered machinery to lift heavy objects.

Most full-time assemblers work a 40-hour week, although overtime and shiftwork is fairly common in some industries. Work schedules of assemblers may vary at plants with more than one shift.

Employment

Virtually all of the 2.7 million assembler and fabricator jobs in 2000 were in plants that manufacture durable goods. Team assemblers, the largest specialty, accounted for 55 percent of assembler and fabricator jobs. The distribution of employment among the various types of assemblers was as follows:

Team assemblers	1,458,000
All other assemblers and fabricators	439,000
Electrical and electronic equipment assemblers	379,000
Structural metal fabricators and fitters	101,000
Electromechanical equipment assemblers	73,000
Engine and other machine assemblers	67,000
Coil winders, tapers, and finishers	56,000
Fiberglass laminators and fabricators	48,000
Aircraft structure, surfaces, rigging, and systems assemblers	20,000
Timing device assemblers, adjusters, and calibrators	12,000

Durable goods manufacturing industries employ 72 percent of assemblers and fabricators. Assembly of electronic and electrical equipment, including electrical switches, welding equipment, electric motors, lighting equipment, household appliances, and electronic devices accounted for 19 percent of all jobs. Assembly of transportation equipment, such as aircraft, autos, trucks, and buses accounted for 15 percent of all jobs. Other industries that employ many assemblers and fabricators are manufacturers of instruments, fabricated metal products, and industrial machinery (such as diesel engines, steam turbine generators, farm tractors, and office machines).

The following table shows the wage and salary employment of assemblers and fabricators in durable goods manufacturing in 2000 by industry.

Electronic and other electrical equipment	502,000
Transportation equipment	403,000
Industrial machinery and equipment	319,000
Fabricated metal products	197,000
Instruments and related products	165,000

Training, Other Qualifications, and Advancement

New assemblers and fabricators are normally entry-level employees. The ability to do accurate work at a rapid pace and to follow detailed instructions are key job requirements. A high school diploma is preferred for most positions.

Applicants need specialized training for some assembly jobs. For example, employers may require that applicants for electrical or electronic assembler jobs be technical school graduates or have equivalent military training. Other positions require only on-the-job training, sometimes including employer-sponsored classroom instruction, in the broad range of assembly duties that employees may be required to perform.

Good eyesight, with or without glasses, is required for assemblers and fabricators who work with small parts. Plants that make electrical and electronic products may test applicants for color vision, because many of their products contain many differently colored wires. Manual dexterity and the ability to carry out complex, repetitive tasks quickly and methodically also are important.

As assemblers and fabricators become more experienced, they may progress to jobs that require more skill and be given more responsibility. Experienced assemblers may become product repairers if they have learned the many assembly operations and understand the construction of a product. These workers fix assembled articles that operators or inspectors have identified as defective. Assemblers also can advance to quality control jobs or be promoted to supervisor. Experienced assemblers and fabricators also may become members of research and development teams, working with engineers and other project designers to design, develop, build prototypes, and test new product models. In some companies, assemblers can become trainees for one of the skilled trades. Those with a background in math, science, and computers may advance to programmers or operators of more highly automated production equipment.

Job Outlook

Employment of assemblers and fabricators is expected to grow more slowly than the average for all occupations through the year 2010, reflecting increasing automation and the shift of assembly to countries with lower labor costs. As manufacturers strive for greater precision and productivity, automated machinery increasingly will be used to perform work more economically or more efficiently. Recent advancements have made robotics more applicable and more affordable in manufacturing. Advances in automation should continue raising the productivity of assembly workers and adversely affecting their employment. In addition to those stemming from growth, many job openings will result from the need to replace workers leaving this large occupational group.

The effects of automation will be felt more acutely among some types of assemblers and fabricators than among others. Flexible manufacturing systems are expensive, and a large volume of repetitive work is required to justify their purchase. Also, where the assembly parts involved are irregular in size or location, new technology only now is beginning to make inroads. For example, much assembly in the aerospace industry is done in hard-to-reach locations unsuited for robots—inside airplane fuselages or gear boxes, for example—and replacement of aircraft assemblers by automated processes will be slower and less comprehensive than replacement of other workers such as welders and painters. On the other hand, automation increasingly will be used in the precision assembly of electronic goods, in which a significant number of electronics assemblers are employed.

Many producers send their assembly functions to countries where labor costs are lower. This trend in assembly, promoted by more liberal trade and investment policies, results in shifts in the composition of America's manufacturing workforce. Decisions by American corporations to move assembly to other nations should limit employment growth for assemblers in some industries, such as electronics assembly. However, a freer trade environment also may lead to growth in the export of goods assembled in the United States, resulting in the creation of additional jobs in other industries, such as aircraft assembly.

Earnings

Earnings vary by industry, geographic region, skill, educational level, and complexity of the machinery operated. In 2000, median hourly earnings were $19.64 for aircraft structure, surfaces, rigging, and systems assemblers; $13.47 for engine and other machine assemblers; $9.77 for coil winders, tapers, and finishers; $10.82 for fiberglass laminators and finishers; $10.11 for all other assemblers; $10.78 for timing device assemblers, calibrators, and adjusters; and $11.16 for electromechanical equipment assemblers.

Median hourly earnings of team assemblers were $10.32 in 2000. The middle 50 percent earned between $8.39 and $13.11. The lowest 10 percent earned less than $7.05, and the highest 10 percent earned $16.95. Median hourly earnings in the manufacturing industries employing the largest numbers of team assemblers in 2000 are shown in the following table:

Motor vehicles and equipment	$13.15
Medical instruments and supplies	10.30
Fabricated structural metal products	10.05
Miscellaneous plastics products, not elsewhere classified	9.49
Personnel supply services	7.93

Median hourly earnings of electrical and electronic equipment assemblers were $10.31 in 2000. The middle 50 percent earned between $8.44 and $12.97. The lowest 10 percent earned less than $7.10, and the high-

est 10 percent earned more than $16.28. Median hourly earnings in the manufacturing industries employing the largest numbers of electrical and electronic equipment assemblers in 2000 are shown in the following table:

Computer and office equipment	$11.68
Measuring and controlling devices	11.43
Electrical industrial apparatus	10.61
Communications equipment	10.23
Electronic components and accessories	9.93

Many assemblers and fabricators are members of labor unions. These unions include the International Association of Machinists and Aerospace Workers; the United Electrical, Radio and Machine Workers of America; the United Automobile, Aerospace and Agricultural Implement Workers of America; the International Brotherhood of Electrical Workers; and the United Steelworkers of America.

Related Occupations

Other occupations that involve operating machines and tools and assembling products include welding, soldering, and brazing workers; ophthalmic laboratory technicians; and machine setters, operators, and tenders—metal and plastic.

Sources of Additional Information

Information about employment opportunities for assemblers is available from local offices of the state employment service and from locals of the unions mentioned earlier.

Athletes, Coaches, Umpires, and Related Workers

O*NET 27-2021.00, 27-2022.00, 27-2023.00

Significant Points

● Work hours are often irregular; travel may be extensive.

● Very few athletes, coaches, umpires and related workers make it to professional rank; career-ending injuries are a constant danger for athletes.

● Job opportunities for coaches, sports instructors, and sports officials will be best in high school and other amateur sports.

Nature of the Work

We are a nation of sports fans and sports players. Interest in watching sports continues to grow, resulting in expanding leagues, completely new leagues, and more and larger venues in which to witness amateur and professional competitions. Recreational participation in sports is at an all-time high as the general population seeks the benefits of sport and exercise for its positive effect on overall health and well-being. Some of those who participate in amateur sports dream of becoming paid professional athletes, coaches, or sports officials, but very few beat the long odds and have the opportunity to make a living from professional athletics. Those who do find that careers are short and jobs are insecure, so having an alternative plan for a career is essential. For many, that alternative is a job in the ranks of coaches in amateur athletics, teaching and directing their sports in high schools, colleges and universities, and clubs.

Athletes and *sports competitors* compete in organized, officiated sports events to entertain spectators. When playing a game, athletes are required to understand the strategies of their game while obeying the rules and regulations of the sport. These events include both team sports—such as baseball, basketball, football, hockey, and soccer—and individual sports—such as golf, tennis, and bowling. As the type of sport varies, so does the level of play, ranging from unpaid high school athletics to professional sports in which the best from around the world compete before national television audiences.

In addition to competing in athletic events, athletes spend many hours practicing skills and teamwork under the guidance of a coach or sports instructor. Most athletes spend hours in hard practices every day. They also spend additional hours viewing films, critiquing their own performances and techniques and scouting their opponents tendencies and weaknesses. Some athletes may also be advised by *strength trainers* in an effort to gain muscle and stamina, while also preventing injury. Competition at all levels is extremely intense and job security is always precarious. As a result, many athletes train year round to maintain excellent form, technique, and peak physical condition; very little downtime from the sport exists at the professional level. Athletes also must conform to regimented diets during the height of their sports season to supplement any physical training program. Many athletes push their bodies to the limit, so career-ending injury is always a risk. Even minor injuries to an athlete may be sufficient opportunity for another athlete to play, excel, and become a permanent replacement.

Coaches organize, instruct, and teach amateur and professional athletes in fundamentals of individual and team sports. In individual sports, *instructors* may often fill this role. Coaches train athletes for competition by holding practice sessions to perform drills and improve the athlete's skills and conditioning. Using their expertise in the sport, coaches instruct the athlete on proper form and technique in beginning and later in advanced exercises attempting to maximize the players potential. Along with overseeing athletes as they refine their individual skills, coaches also are responsible for managing the team during both practice sessions and competitions. They may also select, store, issue, and inventory equipment, materials, and supplies. During competitions, for example, coaches substitutes players for optimum team chemistry and success. In addition, coaches direct team strategy and may call specific plays during competition to surprise or overpower the opponent. To choose the best plays, coaches evaluate or "scout" the opposing team prior to the competition, allowing them to determine game strategies and practice specific plays.

As coaches, advocating good sportsmanship, promoting a competitive spirit, tutoring fairness, and teaching teamwork are all important responsibilities. Many coaches in high schools are primarily teachers of academic subjects and supplement their income by coaching part-time. College coaches consider it a full-time discipline and may be away from home frequently as they travel to scout and recruit prospective players. Coaches sacrifice many hours of their free time throughout their ca-

reers, particularly full-time coaches at the professional level, whose seasons are much longer than those at the amateur level.

Sports instructors teach professional and nonprofessional athletes on an individual basis. They organize, instruct, train, and lead athletes of indoor and outdoor sports such as bowling, tennis, golf, and swimming. Because activities are as diverse as weight lifting, gymnastics, scuba diving, and may include self-defense training such as karate, instructors tend to specialize in one or a few types of activities. Like a coach, sports instructors may also hold daily practice sessions and be responsible for any needed equipment and supplies. Using their knowledge of their sport, physiology, and corrective techniques, they determine the type and level of difficulty of exercises, prescribe specific drills, and relentlessly correct individuals' techniques. Some instructors also teach and demonstrate use of training apparatus, such as trampolines or weights, while correcting athlete's weaknesses and enhancing their conditioning. Using their expertise in the sport, sports instructors evaluate the athlete and their opponents to devise a competitive game strategy.

Coaches and sports instructors sometimes differ in their approach to athletes because of the focus of their work. For example, while coaches manage the team during a game to optimize its chance for victory, sports instructors—such as those who work for professional tennis players—often are not permitted to instruct their athletes during competition. Sports instructors spend more of their time with athletes working one-on-one, allowing them to design customized training programs for each individual they train. Motivating athletes to play hard challenges most coaches and sports instructors but is vital for success. Many derive great satisfaction working with children or young adults, helping them to learn new physical and social skills, improving their physical condition, while also achieving success.

Umpires, referees, and other sports officials officiate competitive athletic and sporting events. They observe the play and detect infractions of rules and impose penalties established by the sports' regulations. Umpires, referees, and sports officials anticipate play and position themselves to best see the action, assess the situation, and determine any violations. Some sports officials, such as boxing referees, may work independently, while others such as umpires—the sports officials of baseball—work in groups. Regardless of the sport, the job is highly stressful because officials are often required to assess the play and make a decision in a matter of a split second and some competitors, coaches, and spectators are likely to disagree strenuously.

Professional *scouts* evaluate the skills of both amateur and professional athletes to determine talent and potential. As a sports intelligence agent, the scout's primary duty is to seek out top athletic candidates for the team they represent, ultimately contributing to team success. At the professional level, scouts typically work for scouting organizations, or more often as freelance scouts. In locating new talent, scouts perform their work in secrecy so as to not tip off players that interest them to their opponents. At the college level, the head scout is often an assistant coach, although freelance scouts may aid colleges by providing reports about exceptional players to coaches. Scouts at this level seek talented high school athletes by reading newspapers, contacting high school coaches and alumni, attending high school games, and studying videotapes of prospects' performances.

Working Conditions

Irregular work hours are the trademark of the athlete. They are also common for the coach, and full-time umpires, referees, and other sports officials. Athletes, coaches, and sports officials often work Saturdays, Sundays, evenings, and even holidays. They usually work more than 40 hours a week for several months during the sports season, if not most of the year. Some coaches in educational institutions may coach more than one sport, particularly at the high school level.

Athletes, coaches, and sports officials who participate in competitions that are held outdoors may be exposed to all weather conditions of the season; those involved in events that are held indoors work in more climate-controlled comfort. Athletes, coaches, and some sports officials travel frequently to sporting events by either by bus or airplane. Scouts also travel extensively in locating talent, often by automobile.

Employment

Athletes, coaches, and sports officials and related workers held about 129,000 jobs in 2000. Coaches and scouts held 99,000 jobs; athletes, 18,000; and umpires, referees, and other sports officials, 11,000. Nearly 30 percent were self-employed, earning prize money or fees for lessons, scouting or officiating assignments, or other services. Among the 70 percent employed in wage and salary jobs, nearly half held jobs in public and private education. About 29 percent worked in miscellaneous amusement and recreation services, including golf and tennis clubs, gymnasiums, health clubs, judo and karate schools, riding stables, swim clubs, and other sports and recreation related facilities. About 11 percent worked in the commercial sports industry.

Training, Other Qualifications, and Advancement

Education and training requirements for athletes, coaches, and sports officials vary greatly by the level and type of sport. Regardless of the sport or occupation, jobs require immense overall knowledge of the game, usually acquired through years of experience at lower levels. Athletes usually begin competing in their sports while in elementary or middle school and continue through high school and often college. They play in amateur tournaments and on high school and college teams, where the best attract the attention of professional scouts. Most schools require that participating athletes maintain specific academic standards to remain eligible to play. Becoming a professional athlete is the culmination of years of effort. Athletes who seek to compete professionally must have extraordinary talent, desire, and dedication to training.

For high school coach and sports instructor jobs, schools usually first look to hire existing teachers willing to take on the jobs part-time. If no one suitable is found they hire someone from outside. Some entry-level positions for coaches or instructors only require experience derived as a participant in the sport or activity. Many coaches begin their careers as assistant coaches to gain the necessary knowledge and experience needed to become a head coach. Head coach jobs at larger schools that strive to compete at the highest levels of a sport require substantial experience as a head coach at another school or as an assistant coach. To reach the ranks of professional coaching, it usually takes years of coaching experience and a winning record in the lower ranks.

Public secondary school coaches and sports instructors at all levels usually must have a bachelor's degree and meet state requirements for licensure as a teacher. Licensure may not be required for coach and sports instructor jobs in private schools. Degree programs specifically related to coaching include exercise and sports science, physiology, kinesiology, nutrition and fitness, physical education, and sports medicine.

For sports instructors, certification is highly desirable for those interested in teaching tennis, golf, karate, or any other kind of sport. Often one must be at least 18 years old and CPR certified. There are many certifying organizations specific to the various sports and their training requirements vary depending on their standards. Participation in a clinic, camp, or school usually is required for certification. Part-time workers and those in smaller facilities are less likely to need formal education or training.

Each sport has specific requirements for umpires, referees, and other sports officials. Referees, umpires, and other sports officials often begin their careers by volunteering for intramural, community, and recreational league competitions. For high school and college refereeing, candidates must be certified by an officiating school and get through a probationary period for evaluation. Some larger college conferences often require officials to have certification and other qualifications, such as residence in or near the conference boundaries along with previous experience that typically includes several years officiating high school, community college, or other college conference games.

Standards are even more stringent for officials in professional sports. For professional baseball umpire jobs, for example, a high school diploma or equivalent is usually sufficient, plus 20/20 vision and quick reflexes. To qualify for the professional ranks, however, prospective candidates must attend professional umpire training school. Currently, there are two schools whose curriculums have been approved by the Professional Baseball Umpires Corporation (PBUC) for training. Top graduates are then selected for further evaluation while officiating in a rookie minor league. Umpires then usually need 8 to 10 years of experience in various minor leagues before being considered for major league jobs.

Jobs as scouts require experience playing a sport at the college or professional level that enables them to spot young players who possess extraordinary athletic abilities and skills. Most beginning scout jobs are as part-time talent spotters in a particular area or region. Hard work and a record of success often lead to full-time jobs responsible for bigger territories. Some scouts advance to scouting director jobs or various administrative positions in sports.

Athletes, coaches, and sports officials must relate well to others and possess good communication and leadership skills. Coaches also must be resourceful and flexible to successfully instruct and motivate individuals or groups of athletes.

Job Outlook

Jobs for athletes, coaches, umpires, and related workers are expected to increase about as fast as the average for all occupations through the year 2010. Employment will grow as the public continues to increasingly participate in sports as a form of entertainment, recreation, and physical conditioning. Job growth will in part be driven by the growing numbers of baby boomers approaching retirement, where they are expected to become more active participants of leisure time activities such as golf and tennis and require instruction. The large numbers of the children of baby boomers in high schools and colleges will also be active participants in athletics and require coaches and instructors.

Opportunities will be best for coaches and instructors as employment increases about as fast as the average. A higher value is being placed upon physical fitness within our society with Americans of all ages engaging in more physical fitness activities, such as participating in amateur athletic competition, joining athletic clubs, and being encouraged to participate in physical education. Employment of coaches and instructors also will increase with expansion of school and college athletic programs and growing demand for private sports instruction. Employment growth within education will continue to be driven largely by local school boards. Population growth dictates the construction of additional schools, particularly in the expanding suburbs. However, funding for athletic programs is often one of the first areas to be cut when budgets become tight, but the popularity of team sports often enables shortfalls to be offset somewhat by assistance from booster clubs and parents. Persons seeking coach or instructor jobs who are qualified to teach academic subjects in addition to physical education are likely to have the best job prospects.

Competition for professional athlete jobs should continue to be intense. Employment will increase as new professional sports leagues are established and existing ones undergo expansion. Opportunities to make a living as a professional in individual sports such as golf, tennis, and others should grow as new tournaments are added and prize money distributed to participants grows. Most athletes' professional careers last only several years due to debilitating injuries and age, so a large proportion of the athletes in these jobs are replaced every year, creating job opportunities. However, a far greater number of talented young men and women dream of becoming a sports superstar and will be competing for limited opportunities.

Opportunities should be favorable for persons seeking part-time umpire, referee, and other sports official jobs in high school level amateur sports, but competition is expected for higher paying jobs at the college level, and even greater competition for jobs in professional sports. Competition is expected to be keen for jobs as scouts, particularly for professional teams.

Earnings

Median annual earnings of athletes were $32,700 in 2000. The lowest 10 percent earned less than $12,630, but more than 25 percent earned $145,600 or more annually.

Median annual earnings of umpires and related workers were $18,540 in 2000. The middle 50 percent earned between $14,310 and $28,110. The lowest 10 percent earned less than $12,550, and the highest 10 percent earned more than $35,830.

Median annual earnings of coaches and scouts were $28,020 in 2000. The middle 50 percent earned between $17,870 and $41,920. The lowest 10 percent earned less than $13,210, and the highest 10 percent earned more than $58,520. Median annual earnings in the industries employing the largest number of coaches and scouts in 2000 were as follows:

Colleges and universities	$32,880
Elementary and secondary schools	27,970
Miscellaneous amusement, recreation services	23,650

Earnings vary by education level, certification, and geographic region. Some instructors and coaches are paid a salary, while others may be paid by the hour, per session, or based on the number of participants.

Related Occupations

Athletes and coaches have extensive knowledge of physiology and sports, and instruct, inform, and encourage participants. Other workers with similar duties include dietitians and nutritionists; physical therapists; recreation and fitness workers; recreational therapists; and teachers—preschool, kindergarten, elementary, middle, and secondary.

Sources of Additional Information

For general information on coaching, contact:

- National High School Athletic Coaches Association, P.O. Box 4342, Hamden, CT 06514. Internet: http://www.hscoaches.org

For information about athletics at the collegiate level, contact:

- National Collegiate Athletic Association, 700 W. Washington St., P.O. Box 6222, Indianapolis, IN 46206-6222. Internet: http://www.ncaa.org

For information about sports officiating team and individual sports, contact:

- National Association of Sports Officials, 2017 Lathrop Ave., Racine, WI 53405. Internet: http://www.naso.org

Automotive Body and Related Repairers

O*NET 49-3021.00, 49-3022.00

Significant Points

- To become a fully skilled automotive body repairer, formal training is desirable in addition to on-the-job training because advances in technology have greatly changed the structure, components, and materials used in automobiles.

- A fully skilled automotive body repairer must have good reading and basic mathematics and computer skills to follow instructions and diagrams in print and computer-based technical manuals.

Nature of the Work

Thousands of motor vehicles are damaged in traffic accidents every day. Although some of these vehicles are beyond repair, others can be made to look and drive like new. Automotive body repairers straighten bent bodies, remove dents, and replace crumpled parts that cannot be fixed. They repair all types of vehicles but work mostly on cars and small trucks, although some work on large trucks, buses, or tractor-trailers.

Automotive body repairers use special equipment to restore damaged metal frames and body sections. Repairers chain or clamp frames and sections to alignment machines that use hydraulic pressure to align damaged components. "Unibody" vehicles, designs built without frames, must be restored to precise factory specifications for the vehicle to operate correctly. To do so, repairers use benchmark systems to make accurate measurements of how much each section is out of alignment and hydraulic machinery to return the vehicle to its original shape.

Body repairers remove badly damaged sections of body panels with a pneumatic metal-cutting gun or by other means, and weld in replacement sections. Repairers pull out less serious dents with a hydraulic jack or hand prying bar or knock them out with hand tools or pneumatic hammers. They smooth out small dents and creases in the metal by holding a small anvil against one side of the damaged area, while hammering the opposite side. They also remove very small pits and dimples with pick hammers and punches in a process called metal finishing.

Body repairers also repair or replace the plastic body parts increasingly used on new model vehicles. They remove damaged panels and identify the family and properties of the plastic used on the vehicle. With most types of plastic, repairers can apply heat from a hot-air welding gun or by immersion in hot water and press the softened panel back into its original shape by hand. They replace plastic parts that are badly damaged or very difficult to repair.

Body repairers use plastic or solder to fill small dents that cannot be worked out of the plastic or metal panel. On metal panels, they file or grind the hardened filler to the original shape and clean the surface with a media blaster before painting. In many shops, automotive painters do the painting. In small shops, workers often do both body repairing and painting. A few body repairers specialize in repairing fiberglass car bodies.

The advent of assembly-line repairs in large shops moves away from the one-vehicle, one-repairer method to a team approach and allows body repairers to specialize in one type of repair, such as frame straightening or door and fender repair. Some body repairers specialize in installing glass in automobiles and other vehicles. *Automotive glass installers and repairers* remove broken, cracked, or pitted windshields and window glass. Glass installers apply a moisture-proofing compound along the edges of the glass, place it in the vehicle, and install rubber strips around the sides of the windshield or window to make it secure and weatherproof.

Body repair work has variety and challenges—each damaged vehicle presents a different problem. Using their broad knowledge of automotive construction and repair techniques, repairers must develop appropriate methods for each job. They usually work alone, with only general directions from supervisors. In some shops, helpers or apprentices assist experienced repairers.

Working Conditions

Most automotive body repairers work a standard 40-hour week, although some, including the self-employed, work more than 40 hours a week. Repairers work indoors in body shops that are noisy, because of hammering against metal and the use of power tools. Most shops are well ventilated to disperse dust and paint fumes. Body repairers often work in awkward or cramped positions, and much of their work is strenuous and dirty. Hazards include cuts from sharp metal edges, burns from torches and heated metal, injuries from power tools, and fumes from paint. However, serious accidents usually are avoided when the shop is kept clean and orderly and safety practices are observed.

Employment

Automotive body and related repairers held about 221,000 jobs in 2000. Most repairers worked for automotive repair shops or motor vehicle dealers. Others worked for organizations that maintain their own motor vehicles, such as trucking companies. A small number worked for wholesalers of motor vehicles, parts, and supplies. About one automotive body repairer out of eight was self-employed.

Training, Other Qualifications, and Advancement

Most employers prefer to hire persons who have completed formal training programs in automotive body repair, but these programs supply only a portion of employers' needs. Therefore, most new repairers get primarily on-the-job training, supplemented, when available, with short-term training sessions given by vehicle, parts, and equipment manufacturers. Some degree of training is necessary because advances in technology have greatly changed the structure, components, and materials used in automobiles. As a result, these new technologies require proficiency in new repair techniques and skills. For example, bodies of many newer automobiles are a combination of materials—traditional steel, aluminum, and a growing variety of metal alloys and plastics. Each of these materials or composites requires the use of somewhat different techniques to reshape parts and smooth out dents and small pits. Many high schools, vocational schools, private trade schools, and community colleges offer automotive body repair training as part of their automotive service programs.

A fully skilled automotive body repairer must have good reading and basic mathematics and computer skills. Restoring unibody automobiles to their original form requires such precision that body repairers must follow instructions and diagrams in technical manuals to make very precise three-dimensional measurements of the position of one body section relative to another.

A new repairer begins by assisting seasoned body repairers in tasks such as removing damaged parts, sanding body panels, and installing repaired parts. They learn to remove small dents and to make other minor repairs. They then progress to more difficult tasks, such as straightening body parts and returning them to their correct alignment. Generally, to become skilled in all aspects of body repair requires 3 to 4 years of on-the-job training.

Certification by the National Institute for Automotive Service Excellence (ASE), although voluntary, is the recognized standard of achievement for automotive body repairers. ASE offers a series of four exams for collision repair professionals twice a year. Repairers may take from one to four ASE Master Collision Repair & Refinish Exams. Repairers who pass at least one exam and have 2 years of hands-on work experience earn ASE certification. Completion of a postsecondary program in automotive body repair may be substituted for 1 year of work experience. Those who pass all four exams become ASE Master Collision Repair and Refinish Technicians. Automotive body repairers must retake the examination at least every 5 years to retain certification.

Continuing education throughout a career in automotive body repair is required. Automotive parts, body materials, and electronics continue to change and to become more complex and technologically advanced. To keep up with these technological advances, repairers must continue to gain new skills, read technical manuals, and attend seminars and classes.

As beginners increase their skills, learn new techniques, and complete work more rapidly, their pay increases. An experienced automotive body repairer with supervisory ability may advance to shop supervisor. Some workers open their own body repair shops. Others become automobile damage appraisers for insurance companies.

Job Outlook

Employment of automotive body repairers is expected to increase about as fast as the average for all occupations through the year 2010. Opportunities should be best for persons with formal training in automotive body repair and mechanics.

Demand for qualified body repairers will increase, as the number of motor vehicles in operation continues to grow in line with the nation's population. With an increase in the number of motor vehicles in use, the number of vehicles damaged in accidents also will grow. New automobile designs increasingly have body parts made of steel alloys, aluminum, and plastics—materials that are more difficult to work with than traditional steel body parts. In addition, new, lighter-weight automotive designs are prone to greater collision damage than older, heavier designs and, consequently, more time is consumed in repair. The need to replace experienced repairers who transfer to other occupations, retire, or stop working for other reasons will account for the majority of job openings.

Changes in body shop management have begun to increase some shops' productivity, profits, and customer satisfaction. Employing a team approach to repairs decreases repair time, improves customer relations, and allows shops to increase their volume of work. By more efficiently managing inventory, shops also may be able to replace the large portion of their space occupied by parts inventory with additional work bays to service vehicles, requiring additional body repairers.

The automotive repair business is not very sensitive to changes in economic conditions, and experienced body repairers are rarely laid off. However, although major body damage must be repaired if a vehicle is to be restored to safe operating condition, repair of minor dents and crumpled fenders can often be deferred during an economic slowdown. During slowdowns, most employers will hire few new workers, some unprofitable body shops may go out of business, and some dealerships might consolidate body shops.

Earnings

Median hourly earnings of automotive body and related repairers, including incentive pay, were $15.00 in 2000. The middle 50 percent earned between $11.12 and $20.02 an hour. The lowest 10 percent earned less than $8.49, and the highest 10 percent earned more than $26.06 an hour. Median hourly earnings in the industries employing the largest number of automotive body and related repairers in 2000 were as follows:

New and used car dealers	$15.76
Automotive repair shops	15.05

Median hourly earnings of automotive glass installers and repairers, including incentive pay, were $12.46 in 2000. The middle 50 percent earned between $9.65 and $15.86 an hour. The lowest 10 percent earned less than $8.03, and the highest 10 percent earned more than $19.18 an hour. Median hourly earnings in 2000 in automotive repair shops, the industry employing the largest numbers of automotive glass installers and repairers, were $12.51.

The majority of body repairers employed by automotive dealers and repair shops are paid on an incentive basis. Under this method, body repairers are paid a predetermined amount for various tasks, and earnings depend on the amount of work assigned to the repairer and how fast it is completed. Employers frequently guarantee workers a minimum weekly salary. Body repairers who work for trucking companies, bus lines, and other organizations that maintain their own vehicles usually receive an hourly wage.

Helpers and trainees usually earn from 30 to 60 percent of the earnings of skilled workers. Helpers and trainees usually receive an hourly rate, until they are skilled enough to be paid on an incentive basis.

Some automotive body repairers are members of unions, including the International Association of Machinists and Aerospace Workers; the International Union, United Automobile, Aerospace and Agricultural Implement Workers of America; the Sheet Metal Workers' International Association; and the International Brotherhood of Teamsters. Most body repairers who are union members work for large automobile dealers, trucking companies, and bus lines.

Related Occupations

Repairing damaged motor vehicles often involves working on mechanical components, as well as vehicle bodies. Automotive body repairers often work closely with individuals in several related occupations, including automotive service technicians and mechanics, diesel service technicians and mechanics, auto damage insurance appraisers, and painting and coating workers, except construction and maintenance.

Sources of Additional Information

Additional details about work opportunities may be obtained from automotive body repair shops and motor vehicle dealers, locals of the unions previously mentioned, or local offices of your state employment service. State employment services also are a source of information about training programs.

For general information about automotive body repairer careers, write to:

- Automotive Service Association, Inc., 1901 Airport Freeway, Bedford, TX 76021-5732. Internet: http://www.asashop.org

- National Automobile Dealers Association, 8400 Westpark Dr., McLean, VA 22102. Internet: http://www.nada.org

- Inter-Industry Conference On Auto Collision Repair Education Foundation (I-CAR), 3701 Algonquin Rd., Suite 400, Rolling Meadow, IL 60008. Telephone (toll free): 888-722-3787

For information on how to become a certified automotive body repairer, write to:

- ASE, 101 Blue Seal Dr. S.E., Suite 101, Leesburg, VA 20175. Internet: http://www.asecert.org

For a directory of certified automotive body repairer programs, contact:

- National Automotive Technician Education Foundation, 101 Blue Seal Dr. S.E., Suite 101, Leesburg, VA 20175. Internet: http://www.natef.org

For a directory of accredited private trade and technical schools that offer training programs in automotive body repair, contact:

- Accrediting Commission of Career Schools and Colleges of Technology, 2101 Wilson Blvd., Suite 302, Arlington, VA 22201. Internet: http://www.accsct.org

For a list of public automotive body repair training programs, contact:

- SkillsUSA-VICA, P. O. Box 3000, 1401 James Monroe Hwy., Leesburg, VA 22075. Internet: http://www.skillsusa.org

Munster High School
Media Center

Automotive Service Technicians and Mechanics

O*NET 49-3023.01, 49-3023.02

Significant Points

- Formal automotive technician training is the best preparation for these challenging technology-based jobs.

- Opportunities should be very good for automotive service technicians and mechanics with good diagnostic and problem-solving skills and knowledge of electronics and mathematics.

- Automotive service technicians and mechanics must continually adapt to changing technology and repair techniques as vehicle components and systems become increasingly sophisticated.

Nature of the Work

Anyone whose car or light truck has broken down knows the importance of the jobs of automotive service technicians and mechanics. The ability to diagnose the source of a problem quickly and accurately—a most valuable skill—requires good reasoning ability and a thorough knowledge of automobiles. Many technicians consider diagnosing hard-to-find troubles one of their most challenging and satisfying duties.

The work of automotive service technicians and mechanics has evolved from simply mechanical to high technology. Today integrated electronic systems and complex computers run vehicles and measure their performance while on the road. Automotive service technicians have developed into diagnostic, high-tech problem solvers. Technicians must have an increasingly broad base of knowledge about how vehicles' complex components work and interact, as well as the ability to work with electronic diagnostic equipment and computer-based technical reference materials.

Automotive service technicians and mechanics use these high-tech skills to inspect, maintain, and repair automobiles and light trucks with gasoline engines. The increasing sophistication of automotive technology now relies on workers who can use computerized shop equipment and work with electronic components, while maintaining their skills with traditional hand tools. Because of these changes in the occupation, workers are increasingly called "automotive service technicians," and the title "mechanic" is being used less and less frequently. Diesel service technicians and mechanics work on diesel-powered trucks, buses, and equipment. Motorcycle mechanics repair and service motorcycles, motor scooters, mopeds, and, occasionally, small all-terrain vehicles.

When mechanical or electrical troubles occur, technicians first get a description of the symptoms from the owner or, if they work in a large shop, the repair service estimator who wrote the repair order. To locate the problem, technicians use a diagnostic approach. First, they test to see if components and systems are proper and secure, and then isolate those components or systems that could not logically be the cause of the problem. For example, if an air conditioner malfunctions, the technician's diagnostic approach can pinpoint a problem as simple as a low coolant level or as complex as a bad drive-train connection that has shorted out the air conditioner. Technicians may have to test drive the vehicle or use a variety of testing equipment, such as onboard and hand-held diagnostic computers or compression gauges, to identify the source of the problem. These tests may indicate whether a component is salvageable or if a new one is required to get the vehicle back in working order.

During routine service inspections, technicians test and lubricate engines and other major components. In some cases, the technician may repair or replace worn parts before they cause breakdowns that could damage critical components of the vehicle. Technicians usually follow a checklist to ensure that they examine every critical part. Belts, hoses, plugs, brake and fuel systems, and other potentially troublesome items are among those closely watched.

Service technicians use a variety of tools in their work. They use power tools, such as pneumatic wrenches to remove bolts quickly, machine tools like lathes and grinding machines to rebuild brakes, welding and flame-cutting equipment to remove and repair exhaust systems, and jacks and hoists to lift cars and engines. They also use common hand tools like screwdrivers, pliers, and wrenches to work on small parts and in hard-to-reach places.

In modern repair shops, service technicians compare the readouts from diagnostic testing devices to the benchmarked standards given by the manufacturer of the components being tested. Deviations outside of acceptable levels are an indication to the technician that further attention to an area is necessary. The testing devices diagnose problems and make precision adjustments with precise calculations downloaded from large computerized databases. The computerized systems provide automatic updates to technical manuals and unlimited access to manufacturers' service information, technical service bulletins, and other information databases, which allow technicians to keep current on trouble spots and to learn new procedures.

Automotive service technicians in large shops have increasingly become specialized. For example, *transmission technicians and rebuilders* work on gear trains, couplings, hydraulic pumps, and other parts of transmissions. Extensive knowledge of computer controls, diagnosis of electrical and hydraulic problems, and other specialized skills are needed to work on these complex components, which employ some of the most sophisticated technology used in vehicles. *Tune-up technicians* adjust the ignition timing and valves, and adjust or replace spark plugs and other parts to ensure efficient engine performance. They often use electronic test equipment to isolate and adjust malfunctions in fuel, ignition, and emissions control systems.

Automotive air-conditioning repairers install and repair air conditioners and service components, such as compressors, condensers, and controls. These workers require special training in federal and state regulations governing the handling and disposal of refrigerants. *Front-end mechanics* align and balance wheels and repair steering mechanisms and suspension systems. They frequently use special alignment equipment and wheel-balancing machines. *Brake repairers* adjust brakes, replace brake linings and pads, and make other repairs on brake systems. Some technicians and mechanics specialize in both brake and front-end work.

Working Conditions

Almost half of automotive service technicians work a standard 40-hour week, but over 30 percent work more than 40 hours a week. Many of those working extended hours are self-employed technicians. To satisfy customer service needs, some service shops offer evening and weekend

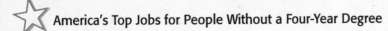

service. Generally, service technicians work indoors in well-ventilated and lighted repair shops. However, some shops are drafty and noisy. Although they fix some problems with simple computerized adjustments, technicians frequently work with dirty and greasy parts, and in awkward positions. They often lift heavy parts and tools. Minor cuts, burns, and bruises are common, but technicians usually avoid serious accidents when the shop is kept clean and orderly and safety practices are observed.

Employment

Automotive service technicians and mechanics held about 840,000 jobs in 2000. The majority worked for retail and wholesale automotive dealers, independent automotive repair shops, or automotive service facilities at department, automotive, and home supply stores. Others found employment in gasoline service stations; taxicab and automobile leasing companies; federal, state, and local governments; and other organizations. About 18 percent of service technicians were self-employed.

Training, Other Qualifications, and Advancement

Automotive technology is rapidly increasing in sophistication, and most training authorities strongly recommend that persons seeking automotive service technician and mechanic jobs complete a formal training program in high school or in a postsecondary vocational school. However, some service technicians still learn the trade solely by assisting and learning from experienced workers.

Many high schools, community colleges, and public and private vocational and technical schools offer automotive service technician training programs. The traditional postsecondary programs usually provide a thorough career preparation that expands upon the student's high school repair experience.

Postsecondary automotive technician training programs vary greatly in format, but normally provide intensive career preparation through a combination of classroom instruction and hands-on practice. Some trade and technical school programs provide concentrated training for 6 months to a year, depending on how many hours the student attends each week. Community college programs normally spread the training over 2 years; supplement the automotive training with instruction in English, basic mathematics, computers, and other subjects; and award an associate degree or certificate. Some students earn repair certificates and opt to leave the program to begin their career before graduation. Recently, some programs have added to their curriculums training on employability skills such as customer service and stress management. Employers find that these skills help technicians handle the additional responsibilities of dealing with the customers and parts vendors.

High school programs, while an asset, vary greatly in quality. The better programs, such as the Automotive Youth Education Service (AYES), with 150 participating schools and more than 300 participating dealers, conclude with the students receiving their technician's certification and high school diploma. Other programs offer only an introduction to automotive technology and service for the future consumer or hobbyist. Still others aim to equip graduates with enough skills to get a job as a mechanic's helper or trainee mechanic.

The various automobile manufacturers and their participating dealers sponsor 2-year associate degree programs at postsecondary schools across the nation. The Accrediting Commission of Career Schools and Colleges of Technology (ACCSCT) currently certifies a number of automotive and diesel technology schools. Schools update their curriculums frequently to reflect changing technology and equipment. Students in these programs typically spend alternate 6- to 12-week periods attending classes full time and working full time in the service departments of sponsoring dealers. At these dealerships, students get practical experience while assigned to an experienced worker who provides hands-on instruction and time-saving tips.

The National Automotive Technicians Education Foundation (NATEF), an affiliate of the National Institute for Automotive Service Excellence (ASE), establishes the standards by which training facilities become certified. Once the training facility achieves these minimal standards, NATEF recommends the facility to ASE for certification. The ASE certification is a nationally recognized standard for programs offered by high schools, postsecondary trade schools, technical institutes, and community colleges that train automobile service technicians, collision repair and refinish technicians, engine machinists, and medium/heavy truck technicians. Automotive manufacturers provide ASE certified instruction, service equipment, and current model cars on which students practice new skills and learn the latest automotive technology. While ASE certification is voluntary, it does signify that the program meets uniform standards for instructional facilities, equipment, staff credentials, and curriculum. To ensure that programs keep up with ever changing technology, repair techniques, and ASE standards, the certified programs are subjected to periodic compliance reviews and mandatory recertification. NATEF program experts also review and update program standards to match the level of training and skill-level achievement necessary for success in the occupation. In mid-2000, 1,491 high school and postsecondary automotive service technician training programs had been certified by ASE. Of these, 1,200 trained automobile service technicians, 224 instructed collision specialists, and 62 trained diesel and medium/heavy truck specialists.

For trainee automotive service technician jobs, employers look for people with strong communication and analytical skills. Technicians need good reading, mathematics, and computer skills to study technical manuals and to keep abreast of new technology and learn new service and repair procedures and specifications. Trainees also must possess mechanical aptitude and knowledge of how automobiles work. Most employers regard the successful completion of a vocational training program in automotive service technology as the best preparation for trainee positions. Experience working on motor vehicles in the armed forces or as a hobby also is valuable. Because of the complexity of new vehicles, a growing number of employers require completion of high school and additional postsecondary training. Courses in automotive repair, electronics, physics, chemistry, English, computers, and mathematics provide a good educational background for a career as a service technician.

There are more computers aboard a car today than aboard the first spacecraft. A new car has from 10 to 15 onboard computers, operating everything from the engine to the radio. Some of the more advanced vehicles have global positioning systems, Internet access, and other high-tech features integrated into the functions of the vehicle. Therefore, knowledge of electronics and computers has grown increasingly important for service technicians. Engine controls and dashboard instruments were among the first components to use electronics, but now, everything from brakes to transmissions and air-conditioning systems to steering systems is run primarily by computers and electronic components. In the past, a specialist usually handled any problems involving electrical systems or electronics. Now that electronics are so common, it is essential for service technicians to be familiar with at least the basic principles of electronics. Electrical components or a series of related components account for nearly all malfunctions in modern vehicles.

In addition to electronics and computers, automotive service technicians will have to learn and understand the science behind the alternate fuel vehicles that have begun to enter the market. The fuel for these vehicles will come from the dehydrogenization of water, electric fuel cells, natural gas, solar power, and other nonpetroleum-based sources. Some vehicles will even capture the energy from brakes and use it as fuel. As vehicles with these new technologies become more common, technicians will need additional training to learn the science and engineering that makes them possible.

Beginners usually start as trainee technicians, mechanics' helpers, lubrication workers, or gasoline service station attendants, and gradually acquire and practice their skills by working with experienced mechanics and technicians. With a few months' experience, beginners perform many routine service tasks and make simple repairs. It usually takes 2 to 5 years of experience to become a journey-level service technician, who is expected to quickly perform the more difficult types of routine service and repairs. However, some graduates of postsecondary automotive training programs are often able to earn promotion to the journey level after only a few months on the job. An additional 1- to 2-years' experience familiarizes mechanics and technicians with all types of repairs. Difficult specialties, such as transmission repair, require another year or two of training and experience. In contrast, brake specialists may learn their jobs in considerably less time because they do not need a complete knowledge of automotive repair.

In the past, many persons became automotive service technicians through 3- or 4-year formal apprenticeship programs. However, apprenticeships have become rare, as formal vocational training programs in automotive service technology have become more common.

At work, the most important possessions of technicians and mechanics are their hand tools. Technicians and mechanics usually provide their own tools, and many experienced workers have thousands of dollars invested in them. Employers typically furnish expensive power tools, engine analyzers, and other diagnostic equipment, but technicians accumulate hand tools with experience. Some formal training programs have alliances with tool manufacturers that help entry-level technicians accumulate tools during their training period.

Employers increasingly send experienced automotive service technicians to manufacturer training centers to learn to repair new models or to receive special training in the repair of components, such as electronic fuel injection or air-conditioners. Motor vehicle dealers also may send promising beginners to manufacturer-sponsored mechanic training programs. Employers typically furnish this additional training to maintain or upgrade employee skills and increase their value to the dealership. Factory representatives also visit many shops to conduct short training sessions.

Voluntary certification by Automotive Service Excellence (ASE) has become a standard credential for automotive service technicians. Certification is available in 1 or more of 8 different service areas, such as electrical systems, engine repair, brake systems, suspension and steering, and heating and air conditioning. For certification in each area, technicians must have at least 2 years of experience and pass a written examination. Completion of an automotive training program in high school, vocational or trade school, or community or junior college may be substituted for 1 year of experience. In some cases, graduates of ASE-certified programs achieve certification in up to three specialties. For certification as a master automotive mechanic, technicians must be certified in all eight areas. Mechanics and technicians must retake each examination at least every 5 years to maintain their certifications.

Experienced technicians who have leadership ability sometimes advance to shop supervisor or service manager. Those who work well with customers may become automotive repair service estimators. Some with sufficient funds open independent repair shops.

Job Outlook

Job opportunities in this occupation are expected to be very good for persons who complete automotive training programs in high school, vocational and technical schools, or community colleges. Persons with good diagnostic and problem-solving skills, and whose training includes basic electronics skills, should have the best opportunities. For well-prepared people with a technical background, automotive service technician careers offer an excellent opportunity for good pay and the satisfaction of highly skilled work with vehicles incorporating the latest in high technology. However, persons without formal automotive training are likely to face competition for entry-level jobs.

Employment of automotive service technicians and mechanics is expected to increase about as fast as the average through the year 2010. The growing complexity of automotive technology necessitates service by skilled workers, contributing to the growth in demand for highly trained mechanics and technicians. Employment growth will continue to be concentrated in motor vehicle dealerships and independent automotive repair shops. Many new jobs will also be created in small retail operations that offer after-warranty repairs, such as oil changes, brake repair, air conditioner service, and other minor repairs generally taking less than 4 hours to complete. Fewer national department store chains will provide auto repair services in large shops. Employment of automotive service technicians and mechanics in gasoline service stations will continue to decline, as fewer stations offer repair services.

In addition to job openings due to growth, a substantial number of openings will be created by the need to replace experienced technicians who transfer to other occupations, retire, or stop working for other reasons. Most persons who enter the occupation can expect steady work, because changes in general economic conditions and developments in other industries have little effect on the automotive repair business.

Earnings

Median hourly earnings of automotive service technicians and mechanics, including commission, were $13.70 in 2000. The middle 50 percent earned between $9.86 and $18.67 an hour. The lowest 10 percent earned less than $7.59, and the highest 10 percent earned more than $23.67 an hour. Median annual earnings in the industries employing the largest numbers of service technicians in 2000 were as follows:

Local government	$16.90
New and used car dealers	16.87
Auto and home supply stores	12.35
Automotive repair shops	12.15
Gasoline service stations	11.86

Many experienced technicians employed by automotive dealers and independent repair shops receive a commission related to the labor cost charged to the customer. Under this method, weekly earnings depend on the amount of work completed. Employers frequently guarantee commissioned mechanics and technicians a minimum weekly salary. Many master technicians earn from $70,000 to $100,000 annually.

Some automotive service technicians are members of labor unions such as the International Association of Machinists and Aerospace Workers; the International Union, United Automobile, Aerospace and Agricultural Implement Workers of America; the Sheet Metal Workers' International Association; and the International Brotherhood of Teamsters.

Related Occupations

Other workers who repair and service motor vehicles include automotive body and related repairers, diesel service technicians and mechanics, and small engine mechanics.

Sources of Additional Information

For more details about work opportunities, contact local automotive dealers and repair shops or local offices of the state employment service. The state employment service also may have information about training programs.

A list of certified automotive technician training programs can be obtained from:

- National Automotive Technicians Education Foundation, 101 Blue Seal Dr. S.E., Suite 101, Leesburg, VA 20175. Internet: http://www.natef.org

For a directory of accredited private trade and technical schools that offer programs in automotive technician training, contact:

- Accrediting Commission of Career Schools and Colleges of Technology, 2101 Wilson Blvd., Suite 302, Arlington, VA 22201 Internet: http://www.accsct.org

For a list of public automotive technician training programs, contact:

- SkillsUSA-VICA, P.O. Box 3000, 1401 James Monroe Hwy., Leesburg, VA 22075. Internet: http://www.skillsusa.org

Information on automobile manufacturer-sponsored programs in automotive service technology can be obtained from:

- Automotive Youth Educational Systems (AYES), 2701 Troy Center Dr., Suite 450, Troy, MI 48084. Internet: http://www.ayes.org

Information on how to become a certified automotive service technician is available from:

- ASE, 101 Blue Seal Dr. S.E., Suite 101, Leesburg, VA 20175. Internet: http://www.asecert.org

For general information about the work of automotive service technicians and mechanics, contact:

- National Automobile Dealers Association, 8400 Westpark Dr., McLean, VA 22102. Internet: http://www.nada.org

Barbers, Cosmetologists, and Other Personal Appearance Workers

O*NET 39-5011.00, 39-5012.00, 39-5092.00, 39-5093.00, 39-5094.00

Significant Points

- Job opportunities for cosmetologists should be favorable due to growing demand for cosmetology services.

- Barbers, cosmetologists, and most other personal appearance workers must be licensed.

- Very high numbers of personal appearance workers are self-employed; many also work flexible schedules.

Nature of the Work

Barbers and cosmetologists, also called *hairdressers* and *hairstylists*, help people look neat and well-groomed. Other personal appearance workers, such as *manicurists and pedicurists*, *shampooers*, and *skin care specialists* provide specialized services that help clients look and feel their best.

Barbers cut, trim, shampoo, and style hair. Also, they fit hairpieces, offer scalp treatments and facial massages, and shave male customers. In many states, barbers are licensed to color, bleach, or highlight hair and offer permanent wave services. A growing number of barbers are trained to provide skin care and nail treatments.

Hairdressers, hairstylists, and cosmetologists provide beauty services, such as shampooing, cutting, coloring, and styling hair. They may advise clients on how to care for their hair, straighten or permanent wave hair, or lighten or darken hair color. Additionally, cosmetologists may train to give manicures, pedicures, and scalp and facial treatments; provide makeup analysis; and clean and style wigs and hairpieces.

A growing number of workers offer specialized services. The largest and fastest growing of these are *manicurists and pedicurists*, called *nail technicians* in some states. They work exclusively on nails and provide manicures, pedicures, coloring, and nail extensions to clients. Another group of specialists is *skin care specialists*, or *estheticians*, who cleanse and beautify the skin by giving facials, full-body treatments, head and neck massages, and removing hair through waxing. *Electrologists* use an electrolysis machine to remove hair. Finally, *shampooers* specialize in shampooing and conditioning clients' hair in some larger salons.

In addition to their work with clients, personal appearance workers are expected to maintain clean work areas and sanitize all work implements. They may make appointments and keep records of hair color and permanent wave formulas used by their regular clients. A growing number actively sell hair products and other cosmetic supplies. Barbers, cosmetologists, and other personal appearance workers who operate their own salons have managerial duties that include hiring, supervising, and firing workers, as well as keeping business and inventory records, ordering supplies, and arranging for advertising.

Working Conditions

Barbers, cosmetologists, and other personal appearance workers usually work in clean, pleasant surroundings with good lighting and ventilation. Good health and stamina are important because these workers are on their feet for most of their shift. Because prolonged exposure to some hair and nail chemicals may cause irritation, special care is taken to use protective clothing, such as plastic gloves or aprons.

Most full-time barbers, cosmetologists, and other personal appearance workers put in a 40-hour week, but longer hours are common in this occupation, especially among self-employed workers. Work schedules may include evenings and weekends, when beauty salons and barbershops are busiest. Barbers and cosmetologists generally are busiest on weekends and during lunch and evening hours, therefore they arrange to take breaks during less popular times. Nearly half of all cosmetologists work part-time or have variable schedules, double the rate for barbers and for all other workers in the economy.

Employment

Barbers, cosmetologists, and other personal appearance workers held about 790,000 jobs in 2000. Nine out of 10 jobs were for barbers, hairdressers, hairstylists, and cosmetologists. Of the remaining jobs, manicurists and pedicurists held about 40,000; skin care specialists about 21,000; and shampooers about 20,000.

Most of these workers are employed in beauty salons or barber shops, but they are also found in department stores, nursing and other residential care homes, and drug and cosmetics stores. Nearly every town has a barbershop or beauty salon, but employment in this occupation is concentrated in the most populous cities and states.

Approximately half of barbers, cosmetologists, and other personal appearance workers are self-employed. Many own their own salon, but a growing number lease booth space or a chair from the salon's owner.

Training, Other Qualifications, and Advancement

All states require barbers, cosmetologists, and most other personal appearance workers to be licensed by the state in which they work. Qualifications for a license, however, vary. Generally, a person must have graduated from a state-licensed barber or cosmetology school and be at least 16 years old. A few states require applicants to pass a physical examination. Some states require graduation from high school while others require as little as an eighth grade education. In a few states, completion of an apprenticeship can substitute for graduation from a school, but very few barbers or cosmetologists learn their skills in this way. Applicants for a license usually are required to pass a written test and demonstrate an ability to perform basic barbering or cosmetology services.

Some states have reciprocity agreements that allow licensed barbers and cosmetologists to apply for and obtain a license in a different state without additional formal training. Other states do not recognize training or licenses obtained in another state; consequently, persons who wish to work in a particular state should review the laws of that state before entering a training program.

Public and private vocational schools offer daytime or evening classes in barbering and cosmetology. Full-time programs in barbering and cosmetology usually last 9 to 24 months, but training for manicurists and pedicurists, skin care specialists, and electrologists requires significantly less time. An apprenticeship program can last from 1 to 3 years. Shampooers generally do not need formal training or a license. Formal training programs include classroom study, demonstrations, and practical work. Students study the basic services—haircutting, shaving, facial massaging, and hair and scalp treatments—and, under supervision, practice on customers in school "clinics." Most schools also teach unisex hairstyling and chemical styling. Students attend lectures on the use and care of instruments, sanitation and hygiene, chemistry, anatomy, physiology, and recognition of simple skin ailments. Instruction also is provided in communication, sales, and general business practices. There are advanced courses for experienced barbers and cosmetologists in hairstyling, coloring, and the sale and service of hairpieces.

After graduating from a training program, students can take the state licensing examination. The examination consists of a written test and, in some cases, a practical test of styling skills based on established performance criteria. A few states include an oral examination in which the applicant is asked to explain the procedures he or she is following while taking the practical test. In many states, cosmetology training may be credited towards a barbering license, and vice versa. A few states combine the two licenses into one hair styling license. Many states require separate licensing examinations for manicurists, pedicurists, and skin care specialists.

For many barbers, cosmetologists, and other personal appearance workers, formal training and a license are only the first steps in a career that requires years of continuing education. Because hairstyles change, new products are developed, and services expand to meet clients' needs, personal appearance workers must keep abreast of the latest fashions and beauty techniques. They attend training at salons, cosmetology schools, or product shows. Through workshops and demonstrations of the latest techniques, industry representatives introduce cosmetologists to a wide range of products and services. As retail sales become an increasingly important part of salons' revenue, the ability to be an effective salesperson becomes vital for salon workers.

Successful personal appearance workers should have an understanding of fashion, art, and technical design. They should enjoy working with the public and be willing and able to follow clients' instructions. Communication, image, and attitude play an important role in career success. Some cosmetology schools consider "people skills" to be such an integral part of the job that they require coursework in this area. Business skills are important for those who plan to operate their own salons.

During their first months on the job, new workers are given relatively simple tasks or are assigned the simpler hairstyling patterns. Once they have demonstrated their skills, they are gradually permitted to perform more complicated tasks such as giving shaves, coloring hair, or applying a permanent. As they continue to work in the field, more training is usually required to learn the techniques used in each salon and to build on the basics learned in cosmetology school.

Advancement usually takes the form of higher earnings as barbers and cosmetologists gain experience and build a steady clientele. Some barbers and cosmetologists manage large salons or open their own after several years of experience. Others teach in barber or cosmetology schools, or provide training through vocational schools. Other options include advancing to sales representatives, image or fashion consultants, or examiners for state licensing boards.

Job Outlook

Overall employment of barbers, cosmetologists, and other personal appearance workers is projected to grow about as fast as the average for all occupations through 2010, because of increasing population, incomes, and demand for cosmetology services. Job opportunities should be favorable, especially because numerous job openings will arise from the need to replace workers who transfer to other occupations, retire, or leave the labor force for other reasons. Competition is expected for jobs and clients at higher paying salons, as applicants vie with a large pool of licensed and experienced cosmetologists for these positions. The number of self-employed, booth-renting cosmetologists should continue to grow. Opportunities will be better for those licensed to provide a broad range of services.

Employment trends are expected to vary among the different specialties within this grouping. For example, employment of barbers is expected to decline, due to a large number of retirements and the relatively small number of cosmetology school graduates opting to obtain barbering licenses. Employment of hairdressers, hairstylists, and cosmetologists should grow about as fast as average, because of continuing demand for coloring services and other hair treatments, such as perms and waves, by teens and aging baby boomers.

Rapid growth in the number of nail salons and full-service, day spas will generate numerous job openings for other personal appearance workers. Nail salons specialize in providing manicures and pedicures. Day spas typically provide a full range of services, including beauty wraps, manicures and pedicures, facials, and massages. Employment of manicurists and pedicurists is expected to grow faster than the average for all occupations, while skin care specialists and shampooers should expect average employment growth.

Earnings

Barbers, cosmetologists, and other personal appearance workers receive income from a variety of sources. They may receive commissions based on the price of the service or a salary based on number of hours worked. All receive tips and many receive commissions on the products they sell. In addition, some salons pay bonuses to employees who bring in new business.

Median annual earnings in 2000 for salaried hairdressers, hairstylists, and cosmetologists, including tips and commission, were $17,660. The middle 50 percent earned between $14,000 and $23,910. The lowest 10 percent earned less than $12,280, and the highest 10 percent earned more than $33,220. Median annual earnings were $17,620 in beauty shops and $17,570 in department stores.

Median annual earnings in 2000 for salaried barbers, including tips, were $17,740. The middle 50 percent earned between $13,580 and $24,540. The lowest 10 percent earned less than $12,030, and the highest 10 percent earned more than $33,040. Median annual earnings were $18,330 in beauty shops and $16,900 in barber shops.

Among others in this group, median annual earnings, including tips, were $20,080 for skin care specialists; $15,440 for manicurists and pedicurists; and $13,690 for shampooers.

A number of factors determine total income for barbers, cosmetologists, and other personal appearance workers, including the size and location of the salon, the number of hours worked, clients' tipping habits, and competition from other barber shops and salons. A cosmetologist's or barber's initiative and ability to attract and hold regular clients also are key factors in determining their earnings. Earnings for entry-level workers are usually low; however, for those who stay in the profession, earnings can be considerably higher.

Although some salons offer paid vacations and medical benefits, many self-employed and part-time workers in this occupation do not enjoy such common benefits.

Related Occupations

Other workers who provide a personal service to clients and usually must be professionally licensed or certified include massage therapists and fitness trainers and aerobics instructors.

Sources of Additional Information

A list of licensed training schools and licensing requirements for cosmetologists can be obtained from:

- National Accrediting Commission of Cosmetology Arts and Sciences, 901 North Stuart St., Suite 900, Arlington, VA 22203-1816. Internet: http://www.naccas.org

Information about a career in cosmetology is available from:

- National Cosmetology Association, 401 N. Michigan Ave., 22nd floor, Chicago, IL 60611. Internet: http://www.salonprofessionals.org

For details on state licensing requirements and approved barber or cosmetology schools, contact the state boards of barber or cosmetology examiners in your state capital.

Bill and Account Collectors

O*NET 43-3011.00

Significant Points

- Most jobs require only a high school diploma.

- Numerous job opportunities should arise due to high turnover.

- Slower-than-average growth is expected in overall employment, reflecting the spread of computers and other office automation as well as organizational restructuring.

Nature of the Work

Bill and account collectors, called simply *collectors*, keep track of accounts that are overdue and attempt to collect payment on them. Some are employed by third-party collection agencies, while others, known as "in-house collectors," work directly for the original creditors, such as department stores, hospitals, or banks.

The duties of bill and account collectors are similar in the many different organizations in which they are employed. First, collectors are called upon to locate and notify customers of delinquent accounts, usually over the telephone, but sometimes by letter. When customers move without leaving a forwarding address, collectors may check with the post office, telephone companies, credit bureaus, or former neighbors to obtain their new address. This is called "skiptracing."

Once collectors find the debtor, they inform them of the overdue account and solicit payment. If necessary, they review the terms of the sale, service, or credit contract with the customer. Collectors also may attempt to learn the cause of the delay in payment. Where feasible, they offer the customer advice on how to pay off the debts, such as by taking out a bill consolidation loan. However, the collector's objective is always to ensure that the customer first pays the debt in question.

If a customer agrees to pay, collectors record this commitment and check later to verify that the payment was indeed made. Collectors may have authority to grant an extension of time if customers ask for one. If a customer fails to respond, collectors prepare a statement indicating this for the credit department of the establishment. In more extreme cases, collectors may initiate repossession proceedings, service disconnections, or hand the account over to an attorney for legal action. Most collectors handle other administrative functions for the accounts assigned to them. This may include recording changes of addresses, and purging the records of the deceased.

Collectors use computers and a variety of automated systems to keep track of overdue accounts. Typically, collectors work at video display terminals that are linked to computers. In sophisticated predictive dialer systems, a computer dials the telephone automatically and the collector speaks only when a connection has been made. Such systems eliminate time spent calling busy or non-answering numbers. Many collectors use regular telephones, but others wear headsets like those used by telephone operators.

Working Conditions

Bill and account collectors typically are employed in an office environment. Bill collectors who work for third-party collection agencies may spend most of their days on the phone in a call center environment. However, a growing number work at home, and many work part-time.

Because the majority of bill and account collectors use computers on a daily basis, these workers may experience eye and muscle strain, backaches, headaches, and repetitive motion injuries. Also, those who review detailed data may have to sit for extended periods of time.

Most bill and account collectors work regular business hours. Bill collectors often have to work evenings and weekends when it is easier to reach people.

Employment

Bill and account collectors held about 400,000 jobs in 2000. About 1 in 6 collectors works for collection agencies. Many others work in banks, department stores, government, hospitals, and other institutions that lend out money and extend credit.

Training, Other Qualifications, and Advancement

Most bill and account collectors are required to have at least a high school diploma. However, having some college is becoming increasingly important. Some collectors have bachelor's degrees in business, accounting, or liberal arts. Although a degree is rarely required, many graduates accept entry-level clerical positions to get into a particular company or to enter the finance or accounting field with the hope of being promoted to professional or managerial positions. Some companies have a set plan of advancement that tracks college graduates from entry-level clerical jobs into managerial positions. Workers with bachelor's degrees are likely to start at higher salaries and advance more easily than those without degrees do.

Experience in a related job also is recommended. For example, telemarketing experience is useful for bill and account collectors. Experience working in an office environment or in customer service is always beneficial. Regardless of the type of work, most employers prefer workers with good communication skills who are computer-literate; knowledge of word processing and spreadsheet software is especially valuable.

Once hired, bill and account collectors usually receive on-the-job training. Under the guidance of a supervisor or other senior worker, new employees learn company procedures. Some formal classroom training also may be necessary, such as training in specific computer software. Bill and account collectors generally receive training in telephone techniques, negotiation skills, and the laws governing the collection of debt. Collectors must be careful, orderly, and detail-oriented in order to avoid making errors and recognize errors made by others. These workers also should be discreet and trustworthy because they frequently come in contact with confidential material. Additionally, all bill and account collectors should have a strong aptitude for numbers.

Collection agencies may require their collectors to become certified by the American Collectors Association (ACA). ACA seminars concentrate on current state and federal compliance laws. Since most states recognize these credentials, ACA-certified collectors have greater career mobility.

Bill and account collectors usually advance by taking on more duties in the same occupation for higher pay or by transferring to a closely related occupation. Most companies fill office and administrative support supervisory and managerial positions by promoting individuals from within their organization, so collectors who acquire additional skills, experience, and training improve their advancement opportunities. With appropriate experience and education, some may become accountants, human resource specialists, or buyers.

Job Outlook

Employment of bill and account collector jobs is expected to grow faster than the average for all occupations through 2010, as the level of consumer debt continues to rise and as more companies seek to improve their debt collection by contracting with third party collection agencies. Hospitals and physician's offices are two of the fastest growing areas requiring collectors. With insurance reimbursements not keeping up with cost increases, the healthcare industry is seeking to recover more money from patients. Government agencies also are using collectors more to collect on everything from parking tickets to child-support payments and past-due taxes. An increasing number of mergers between collection agencies may reduce the overall growth in the number collectors, as small, less automated agencies are bought, resulting in a bigger, more efficient firm. Contrary to the pattern in most occupations, employment of bill and account collectors tends to rise during recessions, reflecting the difficulty that many people have in meeting their financial obligations. However, success at getting people to repay their debts is better when the economy is good.

Earnings

Salaries of bill and account collectors vary considerably. The region of the country, size of city, and type and size of establishment all influence salary levels. Also, the level of expertise required and the complexity and uniqueness of a collector' responsibilities also may affect earnings.

Median hourly earnings of full-time bill and account collectors in 2000 were $12.17.

In addition to their salary, some bill and account collectors receive commissions or bonuses based on the number of cases they close.

Related Occupations

Bill and account collectors enter data into a computer, handle cash, and keep track of business and other financial transactions. Higher level collectors can generate reports and perform analysis of the financial data. Other occupations that perform these duties include brokerage clerks; cashiers; credit authorizers, checkers, and clerks; loan interviewers and clerks; new accounts clerks; order clerks; and secretaries and administrative assistants.

Sources of Additional Information

Career information on bill and account collectors is available from:

● American Collectors Association, Inc., P.O. Box 39106, Minneapolis, MN 55439-0106

Billing and Posting Clerks and Machine Operators

O*NET 43-3021.01, 43-3021.02, 43-3021.03

Significant Points

● Most jobs require only a high school diploma.

● Numerous job opportunities should arise due to high turnover.

● Slower-than-average growth is expected in overall employment, reflecting the spread of computers and other office automation as well as organizational restructuring.

Nature of the Work

Billing and posting clerks and machine operators, commonly called *billing clerks*, compile records of charges for services rendered or goods sold, calculate and record the amounts of these services and goods, and prepare invoices to be mailed to customers.

Billing clerks review purchase orders, sales tickets, hospital records, or charge slips to calculate the total amount due from a customer. They must take into account any applicable discounts, special rates, or credit terms. A billing clerk for a trucking company often needs to consult a rate book to determine shipping costs of machine parts, for example. A hospital's billing clerk may need to contact an insurance company to determine what they will reimburse. In accounting, law, consulting, and similar firms, billing clerks calculate client fees based on the actual time required to perform the task. They keep track of the accumulated hours and dollar amounts to charge to each job, the type of job performed for a customer, and the percentage of work completed.

After billing clerks review all necessary information, they compute the charges using calculators or computers. They then prepare itemized statements, bills, or invoices used for billing and record keeping purposes. In one organization, the clerk might prepare a bill containing the amount due and date and type of service; in another, the clerk would produce a detailed invoice with codes for all goods and services provided. This latter form might list items sold, credit terms, date of shipment or dates services were provided, a salesperson's or doctor's identification, if necessary, and the sales total.

Computers and specialized billing software allow many clerks to calculate charges and prepare bills in one step. Computer packages prompt clerks to enter data from hand-written forms and manipulate the necessary entries of quantities, labor, and rates to be charged. Billing clerks verify the entry of information and check for errors before the computer prints the bill. After the bills are printed, billing clerks check them again for accuracy. In offices that are not automated, *billing machine operators* run off the bill on a billing machine to send to the customer.

In addition to producing invoices, billing clerks may be asked to handle follow-up questions from customers and resolve any discrepancies or errors. And, finally, all changes must be entered in the accounting records.

Working Conditions

Billing clerks typically are employed in an office environment. However, a growing number, particularly medical billers, work at home, and many work part-time.

Because the majority of billing clerks use computers on a daily basis, these workers may experience eye and muscle strain, backaches, headaches, and repetitive motion injuries. Also, clerks who review detailed data may have to sit for extended periods of time.

Most billing clerks work regular business hours. Billing, clerks in hotels, restaurants, and stores may work overtime during peak holiday and vacation seasons.

Employment

In 2000, billing and posting clerks and machine operators held about 506,000 jobs. Although all industries employ billing clerks, the health services industry employs the most. About 1 in 3 billing clerks works in health services. Transportation and wholesale trade industries also employ a large number of billing clerks.

Training, Other Qualifications, and Advancement

Most billing clerks are required to have at least a high school diploma. However, having some college is becoming increasingly important, particularly for those occupations requiring knowledge of accounting. Some billing clerks have bachelor's degrees in business, accounting, or liberal arts. Although a degree is rarely required, many graduates accept entry-level clerical positions to get into a particular company or to enter the finance or accounting field with the hope of being promoted to professional or managerial positions. Some companies have a set plan of advancement that tracks college graduates from entry-level clerical jobs into managerial positions. Workers with bachelor's degrees are likely to start at higher salaries and advance more easily than those without degrees do.

Experience in a related job also is recommended. Experience working in an office environment or in customer service is always beneficial. Regardless of the type of work, most employers prefer workers with good communication skills who are computer-literate; knowledge of word processing and spreadsheet software is especially valuable.

Once hired, billing clerks usually receive on-the-job training. Under the guidance of a supervisor or other senior worker, new employees learn company procedures. Some formal classroom training also may be necessary, such as training in specific computer software. Billing clerks must be careful, orderly, and detail-oriented in order to avoid making errors and recognize errors made by others. These workers also should be discreet and trustworthy, because they frequently come in contact with confidential material. Additionally, all billing clerks should have a strong aptitude for numbers.

Billing clerks usually advance by taking on more duties in the same occupation for higher pay or by transferring to a closely related occupation. Most companies fill office and administrative support supervisory and managerial positions by promoting individuals from within their organization, so billing clerks who acquire additional skills, experience, and training improve their advancement opportunities. With appropriate experience and education, some clerks may become accountants, human resource specialists, or buyers.

Job Outlook

Employment of billing and posting clerks and machine operators is expected to grow more slowly than the average for all occupations through the year 2010. As computers simplify the jobs of most billing clerks, more of these jobs are being performed by other accounting or bookkeeping clerks. In addition to employment growth, many job openings will occur as workers transfer to other occupations or leave the labor force. Turnover in this occupation is relatively high, which is characteristic of an entry-level occupation requiring only a high school diploma.

Most of the employment growth will occur in the expanding health services industries and in accounting firms and other billing services companies, as a result of increased outsourcing of this service. Other areas will see declines as the billing function becomes increasingly automated and invoices and statements are automatically generated upon delivery of the service or shipment of the goods. Bills also will increasingly be delivered electronically over the Internet, eliminating the production and mailing of paper bills. The health services area will also see increasing automation. More medical billers are using electronic billing software to electronically submit insurance claims to the insurer. This speeds up the process and eliminates many of the coding errors that medical bills are prone to have. The standardization of codes in the medical field also is expected to simplify medical bills and reduce errors.

Earnings

Salaries of billing clerks vary considerably. The region of the country, size of city, and type and size of establishment all influence salary levels. Also, the level of expertise required and the complexity and uniqueness of a clerk's responsibilities also may affect earnings. Median hourly earnings of full-time billing clerks in 2000 were $11.81.

Related Occupations

Billing clerks enter data into a computer, handle cash, and keep track of business and other financial transactions. Higher level clerks can gener-

ate reports and perform analysis of the financial data. Other occupations that perform these duties include brokerage clerks; cashiers; credit authorizers, checkers, and clerks; loan interviewers and clerks; new accounts clerks; order clerks; and secretaries and administrative assistants.

Sources of Additional Information

Information on employment opportunities for billing clerks is available from local offices of the state employment service.

Boilermakers

O*NET 47-2011.00

Significant Points

- A formal apprenticeship is the best way to learn this trade.

- Due to the limited number of apprenticeships available and the relatively good wages, prospective boilermakers are likely to face competition.

Nature of the Work

Boilermakers and boilermaker mechanics make, install, and repair boilers, vats, and other large vessels that hold liquids and gases. Boilers supply steam to drive huge turbines in electric power plants and to provide heat and power in buildings, factories, and ships. Tanks and vats are used to process and store chemicals, oil, beer, and hundreds of other products.

Boilers and other high-pressure vessels usually are made in sections, by casting each piece out of molten iron or steel. Manufacturers are increasingly automating this process to increase the quality of these vessels. Boiler sections are then welded together, often using automated orbital welding machines, which make more consistent welds than are possible by hand. Small boilers may be assembled in the manufacturing plant; larger boilers usually are assembled on site.

Following blueprints, boilermakers locate and mark reference points on the boiler foundation, using straightedges, squares, transits, and tape measures. Boilermakers attach rigging and signal crane operators to lift heavy frame and plate sections and other parts into place. They align sections, using plumb bobs, levels, wedges, and turnbuckles. Boilermakers use hammers, files, grinders, and cutting torches to remove irregular edges, so that edges fit properly. They then bolt or weld edges together. Boilermakers align and attach water tubes, stacks, valves, gauges, and other parts and test complete vessels for leaks or other defects. They also install refractory brick and other heat-resistant materials in fireboxes or pressure vessels. Usually, they assemble large vessels temporarily in a fabrication shop to ensure a proper fit before final assembly on the permanent site.

Because boilers last a long time—35 years or more—boilermakers regularly maintain them and update components, such as burners and boiler tubes, to increase efficiency. Boilermaker mechanics maintain and repair boilers and similar vessels. They inspect tubes, fittings, valves, controls, and auxiliary machinery and clean or supervise the cleaning of

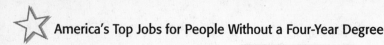

boilers using scrapers, wire brushes, and cleaning solvents. They repair or replace defective parts, using hand and power tools, gas torches, and welding equipment, and may operate metalworking machinery to repair or make parts. They also dismantle leaky boilers, patch weak spots with metal stock, replace defective sections, and strengthen joints.

Working Conditions

Boilermakers often use potentially dangerous equipment, such as acetylene torches and power grinders, handle heavy parts, and work on ladders or on top of large vessels. Work may be done in cramped quarters inside boilers, vats, or tanks that are often damp and poorly ventilated. To reduce the chance of injuries, boilermakers may wear hardhats, harnesses, protective clothing, safety glasses and shoes, and respirators. Boilermakers usually work a 40-hour week, but may experience extended periods of overtime when equipment is shut down for maintenance. Overtime work also may be necessary to meet construction or production deadlines.

Employment

Boilermakers held about 27,000 jobs in 2000. Nearly 6 out of 10 worked in the construction industry, assembling and erecting boilers and other vessels. About one-fifth worked in manufacturing, primarily in boiler manufacturing shops, iron and steel plants, petroleum refineries, chemical plants, and shipyards. Some also worked for boiler repair firms, railroads, or in Navy shipyards and federal power facilities.

Training, Other Qualifications, and Advancement

Many boilermakers learn this trade through a formal apprenticeship. Others become boilermakers through a combination of trade or technical school training and employer-provided training. Apprenticeship programs usually consist of 4 years of on-the-job training, supplemented by 144 hours of classroom instruction each year in subjects such as set-up and assembly rigging, welding of all types, blueprint reading, and layout. Experienced boilermakers often attend apprenticeship classes to keep their knowledge current. Also, the American Boiler Manufacturers Association, in conjunction with the National Board of Boiler and Pressure Vessel Operators, offers seminars on boiler equipment, operation, maintenance, and safety. When an apprenticeship becomes available, the local union publicizes the opportunity by notifying local vocational schools and high school vocational programs.

When hiring helpers, employers prefer high school or vocational school graduates. Courses in shop, mathematics, drafting, blueprint reading, welding, and machine metalworking are useful. Mechanical aptitude and the manual dexterity needed to handle tools also are important.

Some boilermakers advance to supervisory positions. Because of their broader training, apprentices usually have an advantage in promotion.

Job Outlook

Employment of boilermakers is expected to show little or no change through the year 2010. Most job openings will result from the need to replace experienced workers who leave this small occupation. Growth should be limited by the trend toward repairing and retrofitting, rather than replacing, existing boilers; the use of small boilers, which require less on-site assembly; and automation of production technologies.

Most industries that purchase boilers are sensitive to economic conditions. Therefore, during economic downturns, construction boilermakers may be laid off. However, because maintenance and repairs of boilers must continue even during economic downturns, boilermaker mechanics generally have stable employment.

Earnings

In 2000, the median hourly earnings of boilermakers were about $17.80. The middle 50 percent earned between $14.06 and $23.19. The lowest 10 percent earned less than $9.60 and the highest 10 percent earned more than $26.81. Apprentices generally start at about 60 percent of journey wages, with wages gradually increasing to the journey wage as progress is made in the apprenticeship.

Almost one-half of all boilermakers belong to labor unions. The principal union is the International Brotherhood of Boilermakers. Other boilermakers are members of the International Association of Machinists, the United Automobile Workers, or the United Steelworkers of America.

Related Occupations

Workers in a number of other occupations assemble, install, or repair metal equipment or machines. These occupations include assemblers and fabricators; machinists; industrial machinery installation, repair, and maintenance workers; pipelayers, plumbers, pipefitters, and steamfitters; sheet metal workers; tool and die makers; and welding, soldering, and brazing workers.

Sources of Additional Information

For further information regarding boilermaking apprenticeships or other training opportunities, contact local union offices, local construction companies and boiler manufacturers, or the local office of your state employment service.

For information on apprenticeships and the boilermaking occupation, contact: International Brotherhood of Boilermakers, Iron Ship Builders, Blacksmiths, Forgers, and Helpers, 753 State Ave., Suite 570, Kansas City, KS 66101. Internet: http://www.boilermakers.org

Bookbinders and Bindery Workers

O*NET 51-5011.01, 51-5011.02, 51-5012.00

Significant Points

● Most workers train on the job.

● Employment is expected to grow more slowly than average, reflecting increasingly productive bindery operations.

● Opportunities for hand bookbinders are limited because of the small number of establishments that do this highly specialized work.

Nature of the Work

The process of combining printed sheets into finished products such as books, magazines, catalogs, folders, directories, or product packaging is known as "binding." Binding involves cutting, folding, gathering, gluing, stapling, stitching, trimming, sewing, wrapping, and other finishing operations. Bindery workers operate and maintain the machines that perform these various tasks.

Job duties depend on the kind of material being bound. In firms that do *edition binding*, for example, workers bind books produced in large numbers, or "runs." *Job binding* workers bind books produced in smaller quantities. In firms specializing in *library binding*, workers repair books and provide other specialized binding services to libraries. *Pamphlet binding* workers produce leaflets and folders, and *manifold binding* workers bind business forms such as ledgers and books of sales receipts. *Blankbook binding* workers bind blank pages to produce notebooks, checkbooks, address books, diaries, calendars, and note pads.

Some types of binding and finishing consist of only one step. Preparing leaflets or newspaper inserts, for example, require only folding. Binding of books and magazines, on the other hand, requires a number of steps.

Bookbinders and bindery workers assemble books and magazines from large, flat, printed sheets of paper. Skilled workers operate machines that first fold printed sheets into "signatures," which are groups of pages arranged sequentially. Bookbinders then sew, stitch, or glue the assembled signatures together, shape the book bodies with presses and trimming machines, and reinforce them with glued fabric strips. Covers are created separately, and glued, pasted, or stitched onto the book bodies. The books then undergo a variety of finishing operations, often including wrapping in paper jackets.

A small number of bookbinders work in hand binderies. These highly skilled workers design original or special bindings for limited editions, or restore and rebind rare books. The work requires creativity, knowledge of binding materials, and a thorough background in the history of binding. Hand bookbinding gives individuals the opportunity to work in the greatest variety of jobs.

Bookbinders and bindery workers in small shops may perform many binding tasks, while those in large shops usually are assigned only one or a few operations, such as operating complicated manual or electronic guillotine paper cutters or folding machines. Others specialize in adjusting and preparing equipment, and may perform minor repairs as needed.

Working Conditions

Binderies often are noisy and jobs can be fairly strenuous, requiring considerable lifting, standing, and carrying. They also may require stooping, kneeling, and crouching. Binding often resembles an assembly line where workers perform repetitive tasks.

Employment

In 2000, bookbinders and bindery workers held about 115,000 jobs, including 9,600 working as skilled bookbinders and 105,000 working as bindery workers.

Although some large libraries and commercial book publishers have their own bindery operations, employing some bookbinders and bindery workers, the majority of jobs are in commercial printing plants. The largest employers of bindery workers are bindery trade shops—these companies specialize in providing binding services for printers without binderies or whose printing production exceeds their binding capabilities. Few publishers maintain their own manufacturing facilities, so most contract out the printing and assembly of books to commercial printing plants or bindery trade shops.

Bindery jobs are concentrated near large metropolitan areas such as New York; Chicago; Los Angeles; Philadelphia; Dallas; and Washington, DC.

Training, Other Qualifications, and Advancement

Most bookbinders and bindery workers learn the craft through on-the-job training. Inexperienced workers usually are assigned simple tasks such as moving paper from cutting machines to folding machines. They learn basic binding skills, including the characteristics of paper and how to cut large sheets of paper into different sizes with the least amount of waste. As workers gain experience, they advance to more difficult tasks and learn to operate one or more pieces of equipment. Usually, it takes one to three months to learn to operate the simpler machines but it can take up to one year to become completely familiar with more complex equipment, such as computerized binding machines.

Formal apprenticeships are not as common as they used to be, but still are offered by some employers. Apprenticeships provide a more structured program that enables workers to acquire the high levels of specialization and skill needed for some bindery jobs. For example, a 4-year apprenticeship usually is necessary to teach workers how to restore rare books and to produce valuable collectors' items.

Employers prefer to hire experienced individuals, but will train workers with some basic knowledge of binding operations. High school students interested in bindery careers should take shop courses or attend a vocational-technical high school. Occupational skill centers, usually operated by labor unions, also provide an introduction to a bindery career. To keep pace with changing technology, retraining is increasingly important for bindery workers. Students with computer skills and mechanical aptitudes are especially in demand.

Bindery workers need basic mathematics and language skills. Bindery work requires careful attention to detail so accuracy, patience, neatness, and good eyesight also are important. Manual dexterity is essential in order to count, insert, paste, and fold. Mechanical aptitude is needed to operate the newer, more automated equipment. Artistic ability and imagination are necessary for hand bookbinding.

Training in graphic arts also can be an asset. Vocational-technical institutes offer postsecondary programs in the graphic arts, as do some skill updating or retraining programs, and community colleges. Some updating and retraining programs require students to have bindery experience; other programs are available through unions for members. Four-year colleges also offer programs, but their emphasis is on preparing people for careers as graphic artists, educators, or managers in the graphic arts field.

Without additional training, advancement opportunities outside of bindery work are limited. In large binderies, experienced bookbinders or bindery workers may advance to supervisory positions.

Job Outlook

Overall employment of bookbinders and bindery workers is expected to grow more slowly than the average for all occupations through 2010 as demand for printed material grows, but productivity in bindery operations increases. Most job openings will result from the need to replace experienced workers who change jobs or leave the labor force.

Binding is increasingly mechanized as computers are attached to or associated with binding equipment. New "in-line" equipment performs a number of operations in sequence, beginning with raw stock and ending with a complete finished product. Technological advances such as automatic tabbers, counters, palletizers, and joggers reduce labor and improve the appearance of the finished product. These improvements are increasingly inducing printing companies to acquire in-house binding and finishing equipment. However, growth in demand for specialized bindery workers who assist skilled bookbinders will be slowed as binding machinery continues to become more efficient. New technology requires a considerable investment in capital expenditures and employee training; therefore, computer skills and mechanical aptitude are increasingly important.

The small number of establishments that do hand bookbinding limits opportunities for these specialists. Experienced workers will continue to have the best opportunities.

Earnings

Median hourly earnings of bookbinders were $11.42 in 2000. The middle 50 percent earned between $9.14 and $15.71 an hour. The lowest 10 percent earned less than $7.28, and the highest 10 percent earned more than $20.11.

Median hourly earnings of bindery workers were $10.05 in 2000. The middle 50 percent earned between $7.88 and $13.27 an hour. The lowest 10 percent earned less than $6.57, and the highest 10 percent earned more than $17.22. Workers covered by union contracts usually had higher earnings.

Related Occupations

Other workers who set up and operate production machinery include prepress technicians and workers; printing machine operators; machine setters, operators, and tenders—metal and plastic; and various other precision machine operators.

Sources of Additional Information

Information about apprenticeships and other training opportunities may be obtained from local printing industry associations, local bookbinding shops, local offices of the Graphic Communications International Union, or local offices of the state employment service.

For general information on bindery occupations, write to:

- Bindery Industries Association, International, 70 East Lake St., #300, Chicago, IL 60601

- Graphic Communications International Union, 1900 L St. NW., Washington, DC 20036. Internet: http://www.gciu.org

For information on careers and training programs in printing and the graphic arts, contact:

- Graphic Communications Council, 1899 Preston White Dr., Reston, VA 20191. Internet: http://www.npes.org/edcouncil/index.html

- Printing Industries of America, 100 Daingerfield Rd., Alexandria, VA 22314. Internet: http://www.gain.org/servlet/gateway/PIA_GATF/non_index.html

- Graphic Arts Technical Foundation, 200 Deer Run Rd., Sewickley, PA 15143. Internet: http://www.gatf.org

Bookkeeping, Accounting, and Auditing Clerks

O*NET 43-3031.00

Significant Points

- Most jobs require only a high school diploma.

- Numerous job opportunities should arise due to high turnover.

- Slower-than-average growth is expected in overall employment, reflecting the spread of computers and other office automation as well as organizational restructuring.

Nature of the Work

Bookkeeping, accounting, and auditing clerks are an organization's financial recordkeepers. They update and maintain one or more accounting records, including those that tabulate expenditures, receipts, accounts payable and receivable, and profit and loss. They have a wide range of skills and knowledge, from full-charge bookkeepers, who can maintain an entire company's books, to accounting clerks who handle specific accounts. All of these clerks make numerous computations each day and increasingly must be comfortable using computers to calculate and record data.

In small establishments, *bookkeeping clerks* handle all financial transactions and recordkeeping. They record all transactions, post debits and credits, produce financial statements, and prepare reports and summaries for supervisors and managers. Bookkeepers also prepare bank deposits by compiling data from cashiers, verifying and balancing receipts, and sending cash, checks, or other forms of payment to the bank. They also may handle the payroll, make purchases, prepare invoices, and keep track of overdue accounts.

In large offices and accounting departments, *accounting clerks* have more specialized tasks. Their titles often reflect the type of accounting they do, such as accounts payable clerk or accounts receivable clerk. In addition, responsibilities vary by level of experience. Entry-level accounting clerks post details of transactions, total accounts, and compute interest charges. They also may monitor loans and accounts, to ensure that payments are up to date.

More advanced accounting clerks may total, balance, and reconcile billing vouchers; ensure completeness and accuracy of data on accounts; and code documents, according to company procedures. They post transactions in journals and on computer files and update these files when needed. Senior clerks also review computer printouts against manually maintained journals and make necessary corrections. They also may review invoices and statements to ensure that all information is accurate and complete, and reconcile computer reports with operating reports.

Auditing clerks verify records of transactions posted by other workers. They check figures, postings, and documents for correct entry, mathematical accuracy, and proper codes. They also correct or note errors for accountants or other workers to adjust.

As organizations continue to computerize their financial records, many bookkeeping, accounting, and auditing clerks use specialized accounting software on personal computers. They increasingly post charges to accounts on computer spreadsheets and databases, as manual posting to general ledgers is becoming obsolete. These workers now enter information from receipts or bills into computers, which is then stored either electronically, as computer printouts, or both. Widespread use of computers also has enabled bookkeeping, accounting, and auditing clerks to take on additional responsibilities, such as payroll, procurement, and billing. Many of these functions require these clerks to write letters, make phone calls to customers or clients, and interact with colleagues. Therefore, good communication skills are becoming increasingly important.

Working Conditions

Bookkeeping, accounting, and auditing clerks typically are employed in an office environment. However, a growing number work at home, and many work part-time.

Because the majority of bookkeeping, accounting, and auditing clerks use computers on a daily basis, these workers may experience eye and muscle strain, backaches, headaches, and repetitive motion injuries. Also, clerks who review detailed data may have to sit for extended periods of time.

Most bookkeeping, accounting, and auditing clerks work regular business hours. Accounting clerks may work longer hours to meet deadlines at the end of the fiscal year, during tax time, or when monthly and yearly accounting audits are performed. Bookkeeping and accounting clerks in hotels, restaurants, and stores may work overtime during peak holiday and vacation seasons.

Employment

Bookkeeping, accounting, and auditing clerks held about 2 million jobs in 2000. Although they can be found in all industries and levels of government, a growing number work for personnel-supply firms, the result of an increase in outsourcing of this occupation. Approximately 1 out of 4 bookkeeping, accounting, and auditing clerks worked part-time in 2000.

Training, Other Qualifications, and Advancement

Most bookkeeping, accounting, and auditing clerks are required to have at least a high school diploma. However, having some college is becoming increasingly important, particularly for those occupations requiring knowledge of accounting. An associate degree in business or accounting often is required. Some clerks have bachelor's degrees in business, accounting, or liberal arts. Many graduates accept entry-level clerical positions to get into a particular company or to enter the finance or accounting field with the hope of being promoted to professional or managerial positions. Some companies have a set plan of advancement that tracks college graduates from entry-level clerical jobs into managerial positions. Workers with bachelor's degrees are likely to start at higher salaries and advance more easily than those without degrees do.

Experience in a related job also is recommended. Experience working in an office environment or in customer service is always beneficial. Regardless of the type of work, most employers prefer workers with good communication skills who are computer-literate; knowledge of word processing and spreadsheet software is especially valuable.

Once hired, bookkeeping, accounting, and auditing clerks usually receive on-the-job training. Under the guidance of a supervisor or other senior worker, new employees learn company procedures. Some formal classroom training also may be necessary, such as training in specific computer software. Bookkeeping, accounting, and auditing clerks must be careful, orderly, and detail-oriented in order to avoid making errors and recognize errors made by others. These workers also should be discreet and trustworthy because they frequently come in contact with confidential material. Additionally, they should have a strong aptitude for numbers.

Bookkeepers, particularly those who handle all the recordkeeping for companies, may find it beneficial to become certified. The Certified Bookkeeper designation, awarded by the American Institute of Professional Bookkeepers, assures employers that individuals have the skills and knowledge required to carry out all the bookkeeping and accounting functions up through the adjusted trial balance, including payroll functions. For certification, candidates must have at least 2 years bookkeeping experience, pass three tests, and adhere to a code of ethics.

Bookkeeping, accounting, and auditing clerks usually advance by taking on more duties in the same occupation for higher pay or by transferring to a closely related occupation. Most companies fill office and administrative support supervisory and managerial positions by promoting individuals from within their organization, so clerks who acquire additional skills, experience, and training improve their advancement opportunities. With appropriate experience and education, some clerks may become accountants, human resource specialists, or buyers.

Job Outlook

Little or no change is expected in the employment of bookkeeping, accounting, and auditing clerks through 2010. Virtually all job openings will stem from replacement needs. Each year, numerous jobs will become available as these clerks transfer to other occupations or leave the labor force. The large size of this occupation ensures plentiful job openings, including many opportunities for temporary and part-time work, even though turnover is lower than for other clerical jobs.

Although a growing economy will result in more financial transactions and other activities that require these clerical workers, the continuing spread of office automation will lift worker productivity and contribute to the lack of growth in employment. In addition, organizations of all sizes will continue to consolidate various record keeping functions, thus reducing the demand for these clerks. Specialized clerks will be in much less demand than those who can do a wider range of accounting activities. Demand for full-charge bookkeepers is expected to increase as they are called upon to do much of the work of accountants. Those with several years of accounting or bookkeeper certification will have the best job prospects.

Earnings

Salaries of bookkeeping, accounting, and auditing clerks vary considerably. The region of the country, size of city, and type and size of establishment all influence salary levels. Also, the level of expertise required and the complexity and uniqueness of a clerk's responsibilities also may affect earnings. Median hourly earnings of full-time bookkeeping, accounting, and auditing clerks in 2000 were $12.34.

Related Occupations

Bookkeeping, accounting, and auditing clerks enter data into a computer, handle cash, and keep track of business and other financial transactions. Higher level clerks can generate reports and perform analysis of the financial data. Other occupations that perform these duties include brokerage clerks; cashiers; credit authorizers, checkers, and clerks; loan interviewers and clerks; new accounts clerks; order clerks; and secretaries and administrative assistants.

Sources of Additional Information

For information on the Certified Bookkeeper designation, contact:

- The American Institute of Professional Bookkeepers, 6001 Montrose Rd., Rockville, MD 20852. Internet: http://www.aipb.org

Brickmasons, Blockmasons, and Stonemasons

O*NET 47-2021.00, 47-2022.00

Significant Points

- Job prospects are expected to be excellent.
- Most entrants learn informally on the job, but apprenticeship programs provide the most thorough training.
- Work is usually outdoors and involves lifting heavy bricks and blocks and working on scaffolds.
- Nearly 3 out of 10 are self-employed.

Nature of the Work

Brickmasons, blockmasons, and stonemasons work in closely related trades creating attractive, durable surfaces and structures. The work varies in complexity, from laying a simple masonry walkway to installing an ornate exterior on a high-rise building. *Brickmasons* and *blockmasons*—who often are referred to simply as bricklayers—build and repair walls, floors, partitions, fireplaces, chimneys, and other structures with brick, precast masonry panels, concrete block, and other masonry materials. Additionally, brickmasons specialize in installing firebrick linings in industrial furnaces. *Stonemasons* build stone walls, as well as set stone

exteriors and floors. They work with two types of stone: natural cut (such as marble, granite, and limestone) and artificial stone (made from concrete, marble chips, or other masonry materials). Stonemasons usually work on nonresidential structures, such as houses of worship, hotels, and office buildings.

When building a structure, brickmasons use one of two methods, the corner lead or the corner pole. Using the corner lead method, they begin by constructing a pyramid of bricks at each corner—called a lead. After the corner leads are complete, less experienced brickmasons fill in the wall between the corners, using a line from corner to corner to guide each course, or layer, of brick. Due to the precision needed, corner leads are time-consuming to erect and require the skills of experienced bricklayers.

Because of the expense associated with building corner leads, most brickmasons use corner poles, also called masonry guides, that enable them to build an entire wall at the same time. They fasten the corner poles (posts) in a plumb position to define the wall line and stretch a line between them. This line serves as a guide for each course of brick. Brickmasons then spread a bed of mortar (a cement, sand, and water mixture) with a trowel (a flat, bladed metal tool with a handle), place the brick on the mortar bed, and press and tap the brick into place. Depending on blueprint specifications, brickmasons either cut bricks with a hammer and chisel or saw them to fit around windows, doors, and other openings. Mortar joints are then finished with jointing tools for a sealed, neat, uniform appearance. Although brickmasons usually use steel supports, or lintels, at window and door openings, they sometimes build brick arches instead, which support and enhance the beauty of the brickwork.

Stonemasons often work from a set of drawings, in which each stone has been numbered for identification. Helpers may locate and carry these prenumbered stones to the masons. A derrick operator using a hoist may be needed to lift large stone pieces into place.

When building a stone wall, masons set the first course of stones into a shallow bed of mortar. They then align the stones with wedges, plumblines, and levels, and adjust them into position with a hard rubber mallet. Masons continue to build the wall by alternating layers of mortar and courses of stone. As the work progresses, masons remove the wedges, fill the joints between stones, and use a pointed metal tool, called a tuck pointer, to smooth the mortar to an attractive finish. To hold large stones in place, stonemasons attach brackets to the stone and weld or bolt these brackets to anchors in the wall. Finally, masons wash the stone with a cleansing solution to remove stains and dry mortar.

When setting stone floors, which often consist of large and heavy pieces of stone, masons first use a trowel to spread a layer of damp mortar over the surface to be covered. Using crowbars and hard rubber mallets for aligning and leveling, they then set the stone in the mortar bed. To finish, workers fill the joints and wash the stone slabs.

Masons use a special hammer and chisel to cut stone. They cut stone along the grain to make various shapes and sizes, and valuable pieces often are cut with a saw that has a diamond blade. Some masons specialize in setting marble which, in many respects, is similar to setting large pieces of stone. Brickmasons and stonemasons also repair imperfections and cracks, and replace broken or missing masonry units in walls and floors.

Most nonresidential buildings now are built with walls made of concrete block, brick veneer, stone, granite, marble, tile, or glass. In the past, brickmasons and blockmasons doing nonresidential interior work mostly built block partition walls and elevator shafts. Now, these workers must be more versatile and work with many materials. For example, some brickmasons and blockmasons now install structural insulated wall panels and masonry accessories used in many high-rise buildings.

Refractory masons are brickmasons who specialize in installing firebrick and refractory tile in high-temperature boilers, furnaces, cupolas, ladles, and soaking pits in industrial establishments. Most of these workers work in steel mills, where molten materials flow on refractory beds from furnaces to rolling machines.

Working Conditions

Brickmasons, blockmasons, and stonemasons usually work outdoors and are exposed to the elements. They stand, kneel, and bend for long periods and often have to lift heavy materials. Common hazards include injuries from tools and falls from scaffolds, but these can often be avoided when proper safety practices are followed.

Employment

Brickmasons, blockmasons, and stonemasons held about 158,000 jobs in 2000, with brickmasons accounting for the vast majority. Workers in these crafts are employed primarily by building, special trade, or general contractors. Brickmasons, blockmasons, and stonemasons work throughout the country but, like the general population, are concentrated in metropolitan areas.

Nearly 3 out of 10 brickmasons, blockmasons, and stonemasons are self-employed. Many of the self-employed specialize in contracting small jobs, such as patios, walkways, and fireplaces.

Training, Other Qualifications, and Advancement

Most brickmasons, blockmasons, and stonemasons pick up their skills informally, observing and learning from experienced workers. Many others receive training in vocational education schools or from industry-based programs that are common throughout the country. Another way to learn these skills is through an apprenticeship program, which generally provides a thorough training.

Individuals who learn the trade on the job usually start as helpers, laborers, or mason tenders. These workers carry materials, move scaffolds, and mix mortar. When the opportunity arises, they learn from experienced craftworkers how to spread mortar, lay brick and block, or set stone. As they gain experience, they make the transition to full-fledged craftworkers. The learning period on the job normally lasts longer than an apprenticeship program. Industry-based programs offered through companies usually last between 2 and 4 years.

Apprenticeships for brickmasons, blockmasons, and stonemasons usually are sponsored by local contractors or by local union-management committees. The apprenticeship program requires 3 years of on-the-job training, in addition to a minimum 144 hours of classroom instruction each year in subjects such as blueprint reading, mathematics, layout work, and sketching.

Apprentices often start by working with laborers, carrying materials, mixing mortar, and building scaffolds. This period generally lasts about a month and familiarizes the apprentice with job routines and materials. Next, they learn to lay, align, and join brick and block. Apprentices also learn to work with stone and concrete, which enables them to be certified to work with more than one masonry material.

Applicants for apprenticeships must be at least 17 years old and in good physical condition. A high school education is preferable; and courses in mathematics, mechanical drawing, and shop are helpful. The International Masonry Institute (IMI), a joint trust of the International Union of Bricklayers and Allied Craftsworkers and the contractors who employ its members, operates training centers in several large cities that help job seekers develop the skills needed to successfully complete the formal apprenticeship program. In view of the shortage of entrants, IMI has expanded these centers in recent years to recruit and train workers before they enter apprenticeship programs. In addition, the IMI has a national training and education center at Fort Ritchie, MD. The national center's programs teach basic job skills for brick, stone, tile, terrazzo, refractory, and restoration work, as well as safety and scaffolding training.

Bricklayers who work in nonresidential construction usually work for large contractors and receive well-rounded training—normally through apprenticeship in all phases of brick or stone work. Those who work in residential construction usually work primarily for small contractors and specialize in only one or two aspects of the job.

Often, experienced workers can advance to supervisory positions or become estimators. They also can open contracting businesses of their own.

Job Outlook

Job opportunities for brickmasons, blockmasons, and stonemasons are expected to be excellent through 2010—largely due to the numerous openings arising each year as experienced workers leave the occupation. In addition, many potential workers prefer to work under less strenuous, more comfortable conditions. Well-trained workers will have especially favorable opportunities.

Employment of brickmasons, blockmasons, and stonemasons is expected to increase about as fast as the average for all occupations over the 2000–2010 period as population and business growth create a need for new houses, industrial facilities, schools, hospitals, offices, and other structures. Also stimulating demand will be the need to restore a growing stock of old masonry buildings, as well as the increasing use of brick and stone for decorative work on building fronts and in lobbies and foyers. Brick exteriors should continue to be very popular, as the trend continues toward durable exterior materials requiring little maintenance. However, employment of bricklayers who specialize in refractory repair will decline, along with employment in other occupations in the primary metal industries. In addition, many openings will result from the need to replace brickmasons, blockmasons, and stonemasons who retire, transfer to other occupations, or leave these trades for other reasons.

Employment of brickmasons, blockmasons, and stonemasons, like that of many other construction workers, is sensitive to changes in the economy. When the level of construction activity falls, workers in these trades can experience periods of unemployment.

Earnings

Median hourly earnings of brickmasons and blockmasons in 2000 were $19.37. The middle 50 percent earned between $15.00 and $24.48. The lowest 10 percent earned less than $11.20, and the highest 10 percent earned more than $30.02. Median hourly earnings in the industries employing the largest number of brickmasons in 2000 are shown in the following table:

Miscellaneous special trade contractors	$22.87
Masonry, stonework, and plastering	19.55
Nonresidential building construction	19.02
Residential building construction	18.10

Median hourly earnings of stonemasons in 2000 were $14.98. The middle 50 percent earned between $10.78 and $19.24. The lowest 10 percent earned less than $9.09, and the highest 10 percent earned more than $23.03.

Earnings for workers in these trades can be reduced on occasion because poor weather and downturns in construction activity limit the time they can work.

Apprentices or helpers usually start at about 50 percent of the wage rate paid to experienced workers. Pay increases as apprentices gain experience and learn new skills.

Some brickmasons, blockmasons, and stonemasons are members of the International Union of Bricklayers and Allied Craftsworkers.

Related Occupations

Brickmasons, blockmasons, and stonemasons combine a thorough knowledge of brick, concrete block, stone, and marble with manual skill to erect attractive, yet highly durable, structures. Workers in other occupations with similar skills include carpet, floor, and tile installers and finishers; cement masons, concrete finishers, segmental pavers, and terrazzo workers; and plasterers and stucco masons.

Sources of Additional Information

For details about apprenticeships or other work opportunities in these trades, contact local bricklaying, stonemasonry, or marble-setting contractors; a local of the union listed above; a local joint union-management apprenticeship committee; or the nearest office of the state employment service or apprenticeship agency.

For general information about the work of brickmasons, blockmasons, or stonemasons, contact:

- International Union of Bricklayers and Allied Craftsworkers, 1776 I St. NW., Washington, DC. 20006. Internet: http://www.bacweb.org

- International Masonry Institute, Apprenticeship and Training, 837 Buena Vista Ave., Cascade, MD 21719. Internet: http://www.imiweb.org

Information about the work of bricklayers also can be obtained from:

- Associated General Contractors of America, Inc., 1957 E St. NW., Washington, DC 20006. Internet: http://www.agc.org

- Brick Industry Association, 11490 Commerce Park Dr., Reston, VA 22091-1525. Internet: http://www.brickinfo.org

- National Association of Home Builders, 1201 15th St. NW., Washington, DC 20005

- National Concrete Masonry Association, 2302 Horse Pen Rd., Herndon, VA 20171-3499. Internet: http://www.ncma.org

Broadcast and Sound Engineering Technicians and Radio Operators

O*NET 27-4011.00, 27-4012.00, 27-4013.00, 27-4014.00

Significant Points

- Job applicants will face strong competition for the better paying jobs at radio and television stations serving large cities.

- Television stations employ, on average, many more technicians than do radio stations.

- Evening, weekend, and holiday work is common.

Nature of the Work

Broadcast and sound engineering technicians install, test, repair, set up, and operate the electronic equipment used to record and transmit radio and television programs, cable programs, and motion pictures. They work with television cameras, microphones, tape recorders, lighting, sound effects, transmitters, antennas, and other equipment. Some broadcast and sound engineering technicians produce movie soundtracks in motion picture production studios, control the sound of live events, such as concerts, or record music in a recording studio.

In the control room of a radio or television-broadcasting studio, these technicians operate equipment that regulates the signal strength, clarity, and range of sounds and colors of recordings or broadcasts. They also operate control panels to select the source of the material. Technicians may switch from one camera or studio to another, from film to live programming, or from network to local programming. By means of hand signals and, in television, telephone headsets, they give technical directions to other studio personnel.

Audio and video equipment operators operate specialized electronic equipment to record stage productions, live programs or events, and studio recordings. They edit and reproduce tapes for compact discs, records and cassettes, for radio and television broadcasting and for motion picture productions. The duties of audio and video equipment operators can be divided into two categories: technical and production activities used in the production of sound and picture images for film or videotape from set design to camera operation and post production activities where raw images are transformed to a final print or tape.

Radio operators mainly receive and transmit communications using a variety of tools. They are also responsible for repairing equipment using such devices as electronic testing equipment, hand tools, and power tools. These help to maintain communication systems in an operative condition.

Broadcast and sound engineering technicians and radio operators perform a variety of duties in small stations. In large stations and at the networks, technicians are more specialized, although job assignments may change from day to day. The terms "operator," "engineer," and "technician" often are used interchangeably to describe these jobs. *Trans-*

mitter operators monitor and log outgoing signals and operate transmitters. *Maintenance technicians* set up, adjust, service, and repair electronic broadcasting equipment. *Audio control* Engineers regulate volume and sound quality of television broadcasts, while *video control* Engineers regulate their fidelity, brightness, and contrast. *Recording* Engineers operate and maintain video and sound recording equipment. They may operate equipment designed to produce special effects, such as the illusions of a bolt of lightning or a police siren. *Sound mixers* or *re-recording mixers* produce the sound track of a movie, television, or radio program. After filming or recording, they may use a process called dubbing to insert sounds. *Field technicians* set up and operate broadcasting portable field transmission equipment outside the studio. Television news coverage requires so much electronic equipment, and the technology is changing so rapidly, that many stations assign technicians exclusively to news.

Chief Engineers, *transmission* Engineers, and *broadcast field supervisors* supervise the technicians who operate and maintain broadcasting equipment.

Working Conditions

Broadcast, sound engineering, audio and video equipment technicians, and radio operators generally work indoors in pleasant surroundings. However, those who broadcast news and other programs from locations outside the studio may work outdoors in all types of weather. Technicians doing maintenance may climb poles or antenna towers, while those setting up equipment do heavy lifting.

Technicians in large stations and the networks usually work a 40-hour week under great pressure to meet broadcast deadlines, but may occasionally work overtime. Technicians in small stations routinely work more than 40 hours a week. Evening, weekend, and holiday work is usual, because most stations are on the air 18 to 24 hours a day, 7 days a week.

Those who work on motion pictures may be on a tight schedule to finish according to contract agreements.

Employment

Broadcast and sound engineering technicians and radio operators held about 87, 000 jobs in 2000. Their employment was distributed among the following detailed occupations:

Audio and video equipment technicians	37,000
Broadcast technicians	36,000
Sound engineering technicians	11,000
Radio operators	2,900

About 1 out of 3 worked in radio and television broadcasting. Almost 15 percent worked in the motion picture industry. About 4 percent worked for cable and other pay-television services. A few were self-employed. Television stations employ, on average, many more technicians than do radio stations. Some technicians are employed in other industries, producing employee communications, sales, and training programs. Technician jobs in television are located in virtually all cities, whereas jobs in radio are also found in many small towns. The highest paying and most specialized jobs are concentrated in New York City; Los Angeles; Chicago; and Washington, DC—the originating centers for most network programs. Motion picture production jobs are concentrated in Los Angeles and New York City.

Training, Other Qualifications, and Advancement

The best way to prepare for a broadcast and sound engineering technician job is to obtain technical school, community college, or college training in broadcast technology or in engineering or electronics. This is particularly true for those who hope to advance to supervisory positions or jobs at large stations or the networks. In the motion picture industry people are hired as apprentice editorial assistants and work their way up to more skilled jobs. Employers in the motion picture industry usually hire experienced freelance technicians on a picture-by-picture basis. Reputation and determination are important in getting jobs.

Beginners learn skills on the job from experienced technicians and supervisors. They often begin their careers in small stations and, once experienced, move on to larger ones. Large stations usually only hire technicians with experience. Many employers pay tuition and expenses for courses or seminars to help technicians keep abreast of developments in the field.

Audio and video equipment technicians generally need a high school diploma. Many recent entrants have a community college degree or various other forms of post-secondary degrees, although that is not always a requirement. They may substitute on-the-job training for formal education requirements. Experience in a recording studio, as an assistant is a great way of getting experience and knowledge simultaneously.

Radio operators do not usually require any formal training. This is an entry-level position that is generally suited with on-the-job training.

The Federal Communications Commission no longer requires the licensing of broadcast technicians, as the Telecommunications Act of 1996 eliminated this licensing requirement. Certification by the Society of Broadcast Engineers is a mark of competence and experience. The certificate is issued to experienced technicians who pass an examination. By offering the Radio Operator and the Television Operator levels of certification, the Society of Broadcast Engineers has filled the void left by the elimination of the FCC license.

Prospective technicians should take high school courses in math, physics, and electronics. Building electronic equipment from hobby kits and operating a "ham," or amateur radio, are good experience, as is work in college radio and television stations.

Broadcast and sound engineering technicians and radio operators must have manual dexterity and an aptitude for working with electrical, electronic, and mechanical systems and equipment.

Experienced technicians can become supervisory technicians or chief Engineers. A college degree in engineering is needed to become chief engineer at a large TV station.

Job Outlook

People seeking entry-level jobs as technicians in the field of radio and television broadcasting are expected to face strong competition in major metropolitan areas, where pay generally is higher and the number of qualified job seekers exceed the number of openings. There, stations seek highly experienced personnel. Prospects for entry-level positions generally are better in small cities and towns for beginners with appropriate training.

The overall employment of broadcast and sound engineering technicians and radio operators is expected to grow about as fast as the average for all occupations through the year 2010. An increase in the number of programming hours should require additional technicians. However, employment growth in radio and television broadcasting may be tempered somewhat because of slow growth in the number of new radio and television stations and laborsaving technical advances, such as computer-controlled programming and remote control of transmitters. Technicians who know how to install transmitters will be in demand as television stations replace existing analog transmitters with digital transmitters. Stations will begin broadcasting in both analog and digital formats, eventually switching entirely to digital.

Employment of broadcast and sound engineering technicians is expected to grow about as fast as average through 2010. The advancements in technology will enhance the capabilities of technicians to help produce a higher quality of programming for radio and television. Employment of audio and video equipment technicians also is expected to grow about as fast as average through 2010. Not only will these workers have to set up audio and video equipment, but it will be necessary for them to maintain and repair this machinery. Employment of radio operators, on the other hand, will grow more slowly than other areas in this field of work. Automation will negatively impact these workers as many stations now operate transmitters and control programming remotely.

Employment of broadcast and sound engineering technicians and radio operators in the cable industry should grow rapidly because of new products coming to market. Such products include cable modems, which deliver high-speed Internet access to personal computers, and digital set-top boxes, which transmit better sound and pictures, allowing cable operators to offer many more channels than in the past. These new products should cause traditional cable subscribers to sign up for additional services.

Employment in the motion picture industry also will grow fast. However, job prospects are expected to remain competitive, because of the large number of people attracted to this relatively small field.

Numerous job openings also will result from the need to replace experienced technicians who leave the occupations. Many leave these occupations for electronic jobs in other areas, such as computer technology or commercial and industrial repair.

Earnings

Television stations usually pay higher salaries than radio stations; commercial broadcasting usually pays more than public broadcasting; and stations in large markets pay more than those in small ones.

Median annual earnings of broadcast technicians in 2000 were $26,950. The middle 50 percent earned between $18,060 and $44,410. The lowest 10 percent earned less than $13,860, and the highest 10 percent earned more than $63,340.

Median annual earnings of sound engineering technicians in 2000 were $39,480. The middle 50 percent earned between $24,730 and $73,720. The lowest 10 percent earned less than $17,560, and the highest 10 percent earned more than $119,400.

Median annual earnings of audio and video equipment technicians in 2000 were $30,310. The middle 50 percent earned between $21,980 and $44,970. The lowest 10 percent earned less than $16,630, and the highest 10 percent earned more than $68,720.

Median annual earnings of radio operators in 2000 were $29,260. The middle 50 percent earned between $23,090 and $39,830. The lowest 10 percent earned less than $17,570, and the highest 10 percent earned more than $54,590.

Related Occupations

Broadcast and sound engineering technicians and radio operators need the electronics training and hand coordination necessary to operate technical equipment, and they generally complete specialized postsecondary programs. Similar occupations include engineering technicians, science technicians, health technologists and technicians, electrical and electronics installers and repairers, and communications equipment operators.

Sources of Additional Information

For information on careers for broadcast and sound engineering technicians and radio operators, write to:

- National Association of Broadcasters, 1771 N St. NW, Washington, DC 20036. Internet: http://www.nab.org

For information on certification, contact:

- Society of Broadcast Engineers, 9247 North Meridian St., Suite 305, Indianapolis, IN 46260. Internet: http://www.sbe.org

For information on careers in the motion picture and television industry, contact:

- Society of Motion Picture and Television Engineers (SMPTE), 595 West Hartsdale Ave., White Plains, NY 10607. Internet: http://www.smpte.org

Brokerage Clerks

O*NET 43-4011.00

Significant Points

- Employment of brokerage clerks is expected to decline through the year 2010, as technological advancements continue to automate many of their job duties. Some job openings will arise due to the need to replace workers who leave these occupations.

- Some of these jobs are more clerical and require only a high school diploma. Others are considered entry-level positions for which a bachelor's degree is needed.

- Because many brokerage clerks deal directly with the public, a professional appearance and pleasant personality are imperative.

Nature of the Work

Brokerage clerks perform a number of different jobs with wide ranging responsibilities, but all involve computing and recording data on securities transactions. Brokerage clerks also may contact customers, take orders, and inform clients of changes to their accounts. Some of these jobs are more clerical and require only a high school diploma, while others are considered entry-level positions for which a bachelor's degree is needed. Brokerage clerks, who work in the operations departments of securities firms, on trading floors, and in branch offices, also are called margin clerks, dividend clerks, transfer clerks, and broker's assistants.

The broker's assistant, also called sales assistant, is the most common type of brokerage clerk. These workers typically assist two brokers, for whom they take calls from clients, write up order tickets, process the paperwork for opening and closing accounts, record a client's purchases and sales, and inform clients of changes in their accounts. All broker's assistants must be knowledgeable about investment products so that they can clearly communicate with clients. Those with a "Series 7" license can make recommendations to clients at the instruction of the broker. The Series 7 license is issued to securities and commodities sales representatives by the National Association of Securities Dealers and allows them to provide advice on securities to the public.

Brokerage clerks in the operations areas of securities firms perform many duties to facilitate the sale and purchase of stocks, bonds, commodities, and other kinds of investments. These clerks produce the necessary records of all transactions that occur in their area of the business. Job titles for many of these clerks depend upon the type of work they perform. Purchase-and-sale clerks, for example, match orders to buy with orders to sell. They balance and verify stock trades by comparing the records of the selling firm with those of the buying firm. Dividend clerks ensure timely payments of stock or cash dividends to clients of a particular brokerage firm. Transfer clerks execute customer requests for changes to security registration and examine stock certificates for adherence to banking regulations. Receive-and-deliver clerks facilitate the receipt and delivery of securities among firms and institutions. Margin clerks post to and monitor activity in customers' accounts to ensure that clients make payments and stay within legal boundaries concerning stock purchases.

Technology is changing the nature of many of these workers' jobs. A significant and growing number of brokerage clerks use custom-designed software programs to process transactions more quickly. Only a few customized accounts are still handled manually. Furthermore, the rapid expansion of online trading reduces the amount of paperwork because brokerage clerks are able to make trades electronically.

Working Conditions

Most brokerage clerks work in areas that are clean, well lit, and relatively quiet. Because a number of clerks may share the same workspace, it may be crowded and noisy.

Most brokerage clerks work a standard 40-hour week.

The work performed by information clerks may be repetitious and stressful. In addition, prolonged exposure to a video display terminal may lead to eyestrain for the many brokerage clerks who work with computers.

Employment

Brokerage clerks held about 70,000 jobs in 2000. Most worked in firms that sell securities and commodities.

Training, Other Qualifications, and Advancement

Brokerage firms usually seek college graduates for brokerage clerk jobs. Increasingly, familiarity or experience with computers and good interpersonal skills is equally important to employers.

Some brokerage clerks deal directly with the public, so a professional appearance and pleasant personality are important. A clear speaking voice and fluency in the English language also are essential because these employees frequently use the telephone. Good spelling and computer literacy often are needed, particularly because most work involves considerable computer use.

Orientation and training for brokerage clerks usually take place on the job. Under the guidance of a supervisor or other senior workers, new employees learn company procedures. Some formal classroom training also may be necessary, such as training in specific computer software. Most clerks continue to receive instruction on new procedures and company policies after their initial training ends.

Brokerage clerk positions can offer good opportunities for qualified workers to get started in the business. Some brokerage and accounting firms have a set plan of advancement that tracks college graduates from entry-level clerical jobs into managerial positions.

Job Outlook

Employment of brokerage clerks is expected to decline through the year 2010, as technological advancements continue to automate many of their job duties. With people increasingly investing in securities, brokerage clerks will still be required to process larger volumes of transactions. And, some brokerage clerks will still be needed to update records, enter changes to customer's accounts, and verify securities transfers. However, due to the emergence of online trading and widespread automation in the securities and commodities industry, the demand for brokerage clerks in the coming decade will be limited. All job openings will stem from the need to replace clerks who transfer to other occupations or leave the labor force.

Earnings

In 2000, the annual earnings for the top 10 percent of brokerage clerks in 2000 were more than $51,410. Median annual earnings were $31,060.

Related Occupations

A number of other workers deal with the public, receive and provide information, or direct people to others who can assist them. Among these are dispatchers, security guards and gaming surveillance workers, tellers, and counter and rental clerks.

Sources of Additional Information

State employment service offices can provide information about employment opportunities.

Building Cleaning Workers

O*NET 37-1011.01, 37-1011.02, 37-2011.00, 37-2012.00

Significant Points

- Limited training requirements, low pay, and numerous part-time and temporary jobs should contribute to the need to replace workers who leave this very large occupation each year.

- Businesses providing janitorial and cleaning services on a contract basis are expected to be one of the fastest growing employers of these workers.

Nature of the Work

Building cleaning workers—who include janitors, executive housekeepers, and maids and housekeeping cleaners—keep office buildings, hospitals, stores, apartment houses, hotels, and other types of buildings clean and in good condition. Some only do cleaning, and others have a wide range of duties. Janitors and cleaners perform a variety of heavy cleaning duties, such as cleaning floors, shampooing rugs, washing walls and glass, and removing rubbish. They may fix leaky faucets, empty trashcans, do painting and carpentry, replenish bathroom supplies, mow lawns, and see that heating and air-conditioning equipment works properly. On a typical day, janitors may wet- or dry-mop floors, clean bathrooms, vacuum carpets, dust furniture, make minor repairs, and exterminate insects and rodents. They also notify management of the need for repairs and clean snow or debris from sidewalks in front of buildings. Maids and housekeeping cleaners perform any combination of light cleaning duties to maintain private households or commercial establishments, such as hotels, restaurants, and hospitals, in a clean and orderly manner. In hotels, aside from cleaning and maintaining the premises, they may deliver ironing boards, cribs, and rollaway beds to guests' rooms. In hospitals, they also may wash bed frames, brush mattresses, make beds, and disinfect and sterilize equipment and supplies using germicides and sterilizing equipment.

Janitors, maids, and cleaners use various equipment, tools, and cleaning materials. For one job, they may need a mop and bucket; for another, an electric polishing machine and a special cleaning solution. Improved building materials, chemical cleaners, and power equipment have made many tasks easier and less time-consuming, but cleaning workers must learn proper use of equipment and cleaners to avoid harming floors, fixtures, and themselves.

Cleaning supervisors coordinate, schedule, and supervise the activities of janitors and cleaners. They assign tasks and inspect building areas to see that work has been done properly, issue supplies and equipment, inventory stocks to ensure that adequate supplies are present; screen and hire job applicants; and recommend promotions, transfers, or dismissals. They also train new and experienced employees. Supervisors may prepare reports concerning room occupancy, hours worked, and department expenses. Some also perform cleaning duties.

Cleaners and servants in private households dust and polish furniture; sweep, mop, and wax floors; vacuum; and clean ovens, refrigerators, and bathrooms. They also may wash dishes, polish silver, and change and make beds. Some wash, fold, and iron clothes; a few wash windows. General houseworkers also may take clothes and laundry to the cleaners, buy groceries, and do many other errands.

Working Conditions

Because most office buildings are cleaned while they are empty, many cleaning workers work evening hours. Some, however, such as school and hospital custodians, work in the daytime. When there is a need for 24-hour maintenance, janitors may be assigned to shifts. Most full-time building cleaners work about 40 hours a week. Part-time cleaners usually work in the evenings and on weekends.

Building cleaning workers in large office and residential buildings often work in teams. These teams consist of workers who specialize in vacuuming, trash pickup, and restroom cleaning, among other things. Supervisors conduct inspections to ensure that the building is cleaned properly, and the team is functioning efficiently.

Building cleaning workers usually work inside heated, well-lighted buildings. However, they sometimes work outdoors sweeping walkways, mowing lawns, or shoveling snow. Working with machines can be noisy, and some tasks, such as cleaning bathrooms and trash rooms, can be dirty and unpleasant. Janitors may suffer cuts, bruises, and burns from machines, hand tools, and chemicals. They spend most of their time on their feet, sometimes lifting or pushing heavy furniture or equipment. Many tasks, such as dusting or sweeping, require constant bending, stooping, and stretching. As a result, janitors also may suffer back injuries and sprains.

Employment

Building cleaning workers held nearly 4.2 million jobs in 2000. Less than 5 percent were self-employed.

Janitors and cleaners work in nearly every type of establishment and held about 2.3 million jobs. They accounted for about 56 percent of all building cleaning workers. About 28 percent worked for firms supplying building maintenance services on a contract basis; 20 percent in educational institutions; and 3 percent in hotels. Other employers included hospitals, restaurants, religious institutions, manufacturing firms, government agencies, and operators of apartment buildings, office buildings, and other types of real estate.

First-line supervisors of housekeeping and janitorial workers held about 219,000 jobs. About 16 percent were employed in hotels; 22 percent in firms supplying building maintenance services on a contract basis; 5 percent in hospitals; and 6 percent in nursing and personal care facilities. Other employers included educational institutions, residential care establishments, and amusement and recreation facilities.

Maids and housekeepers held about 1.6 million jobs. About 25 percent were employed in hotels and other lodging places; 8 percent in hospitals; and 6 percent in nursing and personal care facilities. Other employers included religious organizations and residential care facilities.

Although cleaning jobs can be found in all cities and towns, most are located in highly populated areas where there are many office buildings, schools, apartment houses, and hospitals.

Training, Other Qualifications, and Advancement

No special education is required for most janitorial or cleaning jobs, but beginners should know simple arithmetic and be able to follow instructions. High school shop courses are helpful for jobs involving repair work.

Most building cleaners learn their skills on the job. Usually, beginners work with an experienced cleaner, doing routine cleaning. As they gain more experience, they are assigned more complicated tasks.

In some cities, programs run by unions, government agencies, or employers teach janitorial skills. Students learn how to clean buildings thoroughly and efficiently, how to select and safely use various cleansing agents, and how to operate and maintain machines, such as wet and dry vacuums, buffers, and polishers. Students learn to plan their work, to follow safety and health regulations, to interact positively with people in the buildings they clean, and to work without supervision. Instruction in minor electrical, plumbing, and other repairs also may be given. Those who come in contact with the public should have good communication skills. Employers usually look for dependable, hard-working individuals who are in good health, follow directions well, and get along with other people.

Building cleaners usually find work by answering newspaper advertisements, applying directly to organizations where they would like to work, contacting local labor unions, or contacting state employment service offices.

Advancement opportunities for workers usually are limited in organizations where they are the only maintenance worker. Where there is a large maintenance staff, however, cleaning workers can be promoted to supervisor and to area supervisor or manager. A high school diploma improves the chances for advancement. Some janitors set up their own maintenance business.

Supervisors usually move up through the ranks. In many establishments, they are required to take some in-service training to improve their housekeeping techniques and procedures, and to enhance their supervisory skills.

A small number of cleaning supervisors and managers are members of the International Executive Housekeepers Association (IEHA). IEHA offers two kinds of certification programs to cleaning supervisors and managers—Certified Executive Housekeeper (CEH) and Registered Executive Housekeeper (REH). The CEH designation is offered to those with a high school education, while the REH designation is offered to those who have a 4-year college degree. Both designations are earned by attending courses and passing exams, and must be renewed every 2 years to ensure that workers keep abreast of new cleaning methods. Those with the REH designation usually oversee the cleaning services of hotels, hospitals, casinos, and other large institutions that rely on well-trained experts for their cleaning needs.

Job Outlook

Overall employment of building cleaning workers is expected to grow about as fast as the average for all occupations through 2010, although job growth will vary depending on where they work. Average growth is expected among both janitors and cleaners and institutional cleaning supervisors, many of whom work in the services to buildings industry.

On the other hand, employment of maids and housekeeping cleaners, which includes those in private households, is expected to grow more slowly than the average. In addition to job openings due to growth, numerous openings should result from the need to replace those who leave this very large occupation each year. Limited formal education and training requirements, low pay, and numerous part-time and temporary jobs should contribute to these replacement needs.

To clean the increasing number of office complexes, apartment houses, schools, factories, hospitals, and other buildings, more workers will be assigned to teams with more efficient cleaning equipment and supplies. As many firms reduce costs by hiring independent contractors, businesses providing janitorial and cleaning services on a contract basis are expected to be one of the faster growing employers of these workers.

Earnings

Median annual earnings of janitors and cleaners, except maids and housekeeping cleaners, were $17,180 in 2000. The middle 50 percent earned between $14,030 and $22,340. The lowest 10 percent earned less than $12,280, and the highest 10 percent earned more than $29,190. Median annual earnings in the industries employing the largest numbers of janitors and cleaners, except maids and housekeeping cleaners, in 2000 are shown in the following table:

Local government	$22,900
Real estate operators and lessors	22,110
Elementary and secondary schools	21,100
Colleges and universities	20,320
Services to buildings	15,370

Median annual earnings of maids and housekeepers were $15,410 in 2000. The middle 50 percent earned between $13,230 and $18,030. The lowest 10 percent earned less than $11,910, and the highest 10 percent earned more than $22,200. Median annual earnings in the industries employing the largest numbers of maids and housekeepers in 2000 are shown in the following table:

Hospitals	$16,820
Real estate agents and managers	16,500
Nursing and personal care facilities	15,460
Services to buildings	15,150
Hotels and motels	14,760

Median annual earnings of first-line supervisors/managers of housekeeping and janitorial workers were $25,760 in 2000. The middle 50 percent earned between $19,920 and $33,740. The lowest 10 percent earned less than $16,220, and the highest 10 percent earned more than $42,850. Median annual earnings in the industries employing the largest numbers of first-line supervisors/managers of housekeeping and janitorial workers in 2000 are shown in the following table:

Elementary and secondary schools	$29,540
Hospitals	27,010
Nursing and personal care facilities	25,290
Services to buildings	23,000
Hotels and motels	21,820

Related Occupations

Workers who specialize in one of the many job functions of janitors and cleaners include pest control workers; industrial machinery installation, repair, and maintenance workers; and grounds maintenance workers.

Sources of Additional Information

Information about janitorial jobs may be obtained from state employment service offices.

For information on certification in executive housekeeping, contact:

- International Executive Housekeepers Association, Inc., 1001 Eastwind Dr., Suite 301, Westerville, OH 43081-3361. Internet: http://www.ieha.org

Busdrivers

O*NET 53-3021.00, 53-3022.00

Significant Points

- Opportunities should be good, particularly for school busdriver jobs.

- A commercial driver's license is required to operate on interstate bus routes.

- Busdrivers must posses strong customer service skills, including communication skills and the ability to manage large groups of people with varying needs.

Nature of the Work

Millions of Americans every day leave the driving to busdrivers. Busdrivers are essential in providing passengers with an alternative to their automobiles or other forms of transportation. Intercity busdrivers transport people between regions of a state or of the country; local transit busdrivers, within a metropolitan area or county; motorcoach drivers, on charter excursions and tours; and school busdrivers, to and from schools and related events.

Drivers pick up and drop off passengers at bus stops, stations, or, in the case of students, at regularly scheduled neighborhood locations based on strict time schedules. Drivers must operate vehicles safely, especially when traffic is heavier than normal. However, they cannot let light traffic put them ahead of schedule so that they miss passengers.

Local transit and intercity busdrivers report to their assigned terminal or garage, where they stock up on tickets or transfers and prepare trip report forms. In some firms, maintenance departments are responsible for keeping vehicles in good condition. In others, drivers may check their vehicle's tires, brakes, windshield wipers, lights, oil, fuel, and water supply, before beginning their routes. Drivers usually verify that the bus has safety equipment, such as fire extinguishers, first aid kits, and emergency reflectors in case of an emergency.

During the course of their shift, local transit and intercity busdrivers collect fares; answer questions about schedules, routes, and transfer points; and sometimes announce stops. Intercity busdrivers may make only a single one-way trip to a distant city or a round trip each day. They may stop at towns just a few miles apart or only at large cities hundreds of miles apart. Local transit busdrivers may make several trips each day over the same city and suburban streets, stopping as frequently as every few blocks.

Local transit busdrivers submit daily trip reports with a record of trips, significant schedule delays, and mechanical problems. Intercity drivers who drive across state or national boundaries must comply with U.S. Department of Transportation regulations. These include completing vehicle inspection reports and recording distances traveled and the periods they spend driving, performing other duties, and off duty.

Motorcoach drivers transport passengers on charter trips and sightseeing tours. Drivers routinely interact with customers and tour guides to make the trip as comfortable and informative as possible. They are directly responsible for keeping to strict schedules, adhering to the guidelines of the tours' itinerary, and the overall success of the trip. These drivers act as customer service representative, tour guide, program director, and safety guide. Trips frequently last more than one day. The driver may be away for more than a week if assigned to an extended tour. As with all drivers who drive across state or national boundaries, motorcoach drivers must comply with Department of Transportation regulations.

School busdrivers usually drive the same routes each day, stopping to pick up pupils in the morning and return them to their homes in the afternoon. Some school busdrivers also transport students and teachers on field trips or to sporting events. In addition to driving, some school busdrivers work part-time in the school system as janitors, mechanics, or classroom assistants when not driving buses.

Busdrivers must be alert to prevent accidents, especially in heavy traffic or in bad weather, and to avoid sudden stops or swerves that jar passengers. School busdrivers must exercise particular caution when children are getting on or off the bus. They must maintain order on their bus and enforce school safety standards by allowing only students to board. In addition, they must know and enforce rules regarding student conduct used throughout the school system.

School busdrivers do not always have to report to an assigned terminal or garage. In some cases, school busdrivers often have the choice of taking their bus home, or parking it in a more convenient area. School busdrivers do not collect fares. Instead, they prepare weekly reports on the number of students, trips or runs, work hours, miles, and the amount of fuel consumption. Their supervisors set time schedules and routes for the day or week.

Working Conditions

Driving a bus through heavy traffic while dealing with passengers is more stressful and fatiguing than physically strenuous. Many drivers enjoy the opportunity to work without direct supervision, with full responsibility for their bus and passengers. To improve working conditions and retain drivers, many bus lines provide ergonomically designed seats and controls for drivers.

Intercity busdrivers may work nights, weekends, and holidays and often spend nights away from home, where they stay in hotels at company expense. Senior drivers with regular routes have regular weekly work schedules, but others do not have regular schedules and must be prepared to report for work on short notice. They report for work only when called for a charter assignment or to drive extra buses on a regular route. Intercity bus travel and charter work tends to be seasonal. From May through August, drivers may work the maximum number of hours per week that regulations allow. During winter, junior drivers may work infrequently, except for busy holiday travel periods, and may be furloughed for periods.

School busdrivers work only when school is in session. Many work 20 hours a week or less, driving one or two routes in the morning and afternoon. Drivers taking field or athletic trips or who also have midday kindergarten routes may work more hours a week. As more students with a variety of physical and behavioral disabilities assimilate into mainstream schools, school busdrivers must learn how to accommodate their special needs.

Regular local transit busdrivers usually have a 5-day workweek; Saturdays and Sundays are considered regular workdays. Some drivers work evenings and after midnight. To accommodate commuters, many work "split shifts," for example, 6 a.m. to 10 a.m. and 3 p.m. to 7 p.m., with time off in between.

Tour and charter busdrivers may work any day and all hours of the day, including weekends and holidays. Their hours are dictated by the charter trips booked and the schedule and prearranged itinerary of tours. However, like all busdrivers, their weekly hours must be consistent with the Department of Transportation's rules and regulations concerning hours of service. For example, a driver may drive for 10 hours, and work up to 15 hours—including driving and non-driving duties—before having 8 hours off-duty. A driver may not drive after having worked for 70 hours in the past 8 days. Most drivers are required to document their time in a logbook.

Employment

Busdrivers held about 666,000 jobs in 2000. More than a third worked part-time. About two-thirds of all drivers worked for school systems or companies providing school bus services under contract. Most of the remainder worked for private and local government transit systems; some also worked for intercity and charter bus lines.

Training, Other Qualifications, and Advancement

Busdriver qualifications and standards are established by state and federal regulations. All drivers must comply with federal regulations and any state regulations that exceed Federal requirements. Federal regulations require drivers who operate vehicles designed to transport 16 or more passengers to hold a commercial driver's license (CDL) from the state in which they live.

To qualify for a commercial driver's license, applicants must pass a written test on rules and regulations and then demonstrate they can operate a bus safely. A national data bank permanently records all driving violations incurred by persons who hold commercial licenses. A state may not issue a commercial driver's license to a driver who already has a license suspended or revoked in another state. A driver with a CDL must accompany trainees until they get their own CDL. Information on how to apply for a commercial driver's license may be obtained from state motor vehicle administrations.

While many states allow those who are 18 years and older to drive buses within state borders, the Department of Transportation establishes minimum qualifications for busdrivers engaged in interstate commerce. Federal Motor Carrier Safety Regulations require drivers to be at least 21 years old and pass a physical examination once every 2 years. The main physical requirements include good hearing, 20/40 vision with or without glasses or corrective lenses, and a 70-degree field of vision in each eye. Drivers must not be colorblind. They must be able to hear a forced whisper in one ear at not less than 5 feet, with or without a hearing aide. Drivers must have normal use of arms and legs and normal blood pressure. They may not use any controlled substances, unless prescribed by a licensed physician. Persons with epilepsy or diabetes controlled by insulin are not permitted to be interstate busdrivers. Federal regulations also require employers to test their drivers for alcohol and drug use as a condition of employment, and require periodic random tests while on duty. In addition, a driver must not have been convicted of a felony involving the use of a motor vehicle; a crime involving drugs; driving under the influence of drugs or alcohol; or hit-and-run driving which resulted in injury or death. All drivers must be able to read and speak English well enough to read road signs, prepare reports, and communicate with law enforcement officers and the public. In addition, drivers must take a written examination on the Motor Carrier Safety Regulations of the U.S. Department of Transportation.

Many employers prefer high school graduates and require a written test of ability to follow complex bus schedules. Many intercity and public transit bus companies prefer applicants who are at least 24 years of age; some require several years of bus or truck driving experience. In some states, school busdrivers must pass a background investigation to uncover any criminal record or history of mental problems.

Because busdrivers deal with passengers, they must be courteous. They need an even temperament and emotional stability because driving in heavy, fast-moving, or stop-and-go traffic and dealing with passengers can be stressful. Drivers must have strong customer service skills, including communication skills and the ability to coordinate and manage large groups of people.

Most intercity bus companies and local transit systems give driver trainees 2 to 8 weeks of classroom and "behind-the-wheel" instruction. In the classroom, trainees learn Department of Transportation and company work rules, safety regulations, state and municipal driving regulations, and safe driving practices. They also learn to read schedules, determine fares, keep records, and deal courteously with passengers.

School busdrivers are also required to obtain a commercial driver's license from the state in which they live. Many persons who enter school busdriving have never driven any vehicle larger than an automobile. They receive between 1 and 4 weeks of driving instruction plus classroom training on state and local laws, regulations, and policies of operating school buses; safe driving practices; driver-pupil relations; first aid; special needs of disabled and emotionally troubled students; and emergency evacuation procedures. School busdrivers also must be aware of school systems rules for discipline and conduct for busdrivers and the students they transport.

During training, busdrivers practice driving on set courses. They practice turns and zigzag maneuvers, backing up, and driving in narrow lanes. Then they drive in light traffic and, eventually, on congested highways and city streets. They also make trial runs, without passengers, to improve their driving skills and learn the routes. Local transit trainees memorize and drive each of the runs operating out of their assigned garage. New drivers begin with a "break-in" period. They make regularly scheduled trips with passengers, accompanied by an experienced driver who gives helpful tips, answers questions, and evaluates the new driver's performance.

New intercity and local transit drivers are usually placed on an "extra" list to drive charter runs, extra buses on regular runs, and special runs (for example, during morning and evening rush hours and to sports events). They also substitute for regular drivers who are ill or on vacation. New drivers remain on the extra list, and may work only part-time, perhaps for several years, until they have enough seniority to receive a regular run.

Senior drivers may bid for runs they prefer, such as those with more work hours, lighter traffic, weekends off, or, in the case of intercity busdrivers, higher earnings or fewer workdays per week.

Opportunities for promotion are generally limited. However, experienced drivers may become supervisors or dispatchers, assigning buses to drivers, checking whether drivers are on schedule, rerouting buses to avoid blocked streets or other problems, and dispatching extra vehicles and service crews to scenes of accidents and breakdowns. In transit agencies with rail systems, drivers may become train operators or station attendants. A few drivers become managers. Promotion in publicly owned bus systems is often by competitive civil service examination. Some motorcoach drivers purchase their own equipment and go in to business for themselves.

Job Outlook

Persons seeking jobs as busdrivers should encounter good opportunities. Many employers have recently had difficulty finding qualified candidates to fill vacancies left by departing employees. Opportunities should be best for individuals with good driving records who are willing to start on a part-time or irregular schedule, as well as for those seeking jobs as school busdrivers in rapidly growing suburban areas. Those seeking higher paying intercity and public transit busdriver positions may encounter competition.

Employment of busdrivers is expected to increase about as fast as average for all occupations through the year 2010, primarily to meet the transportation needs of a growing school-age population and local environmental concerns. Thousands of additional job openings are expected to occur each year because of the need to replace workers who take jobs in other occupations, retire, or leave the occupation for other reasons.

School busdriving jobs should be easiest to acquire because most are part-time positions with high turnover and minimal training requirements. The number of school busdrivers is expected to increase as a result of growth in elementary and secondary school enrollments. In addition, as more of the nation's population is concentrated in suburban areas where students generally ride school buses, and less in the central cities where transportation is not provided for most pupils,more school busdrivers will be needed.

Employment of local transit and intercity drivers will grow as bus ridership increases due to population growth. There may be competition for positions with more regular hours and steady driving routes.

Competition from other modes of transportation—airplane, train, or automobile—will temper growth in the intercity bus industry. Most growth in intercity bus lines will occur in group charters to locations not served by other modes of transportation. Like automobiles, buses have a far greater number of possible travel destinations than airplanes or trains. Due to greater cost savings and convenience over automobiles, buses usually are the most economical option for tour groups heading to out-of-the-way destinations.

Full-time busdrivers are rarely laid off during recessions. However, employers might reduce hours of part-time local transit and intercity busdrivers if bus ridership decreases, because fewer extra buses would be needed. Seasonal layoffs are common. Many intercity busdrivers with little seniority, for example, are furloughed during the winter when regular schedule and charter business falls off; school busdrivers seldom work during the summer or school holidays.

Earnings

Median hourly earnings of transit and intercity busdrivers were $12.36 in 2000. The middle 50 percent earned between $9.47 and $16.78 an hour. The lowest 10 percent earned less than $7.64, and the highest 10 percent earned more than $20.03 an hour. Median hourly earnings in the industries employing the largest numbers of transit and intercity busdrivers in 2000 were as follows:

Local government	$14.68
Intercity and rural bus transportation	14.60
Local and suburban transportation	11.48
School buses	10.67
Bus charter service	10.27

Median hourly earnings of school busdrivers were $10.05 in 2000. The middle 50 percent earned between $7.28 and $12.74 an hour. The lowest 10 percent earned less than $5.99, and the highest 10 percent earned more than $15.48 an hour. Median hourly earnings in the industries employing the largest numbers of school busdrivers in 2000 were as follows:

School buses	$10.50
Elementary and secondary schools	9.97
Local and suburban transportation	9.49
Child daycare services	8.12
Individual and family services	7.84

The benefits busdrivers receive from their employers vary greatly. Most intercity and local transit busdrivers receive paid health and life insurance, sick leave, and free bus rides on any of the regular routes of their line or system. Drivers who work full time also get as much as 4 weeks of vacation annually. Most local transit busdrivers are also covered by dental insurance and pension plans. School busdrivers receive sick leave, and many are covered by health and life insurance and pension plans. Because they generally do not work when school is not in session, they do not get vacation leave. In a number of states, local transit and school busdrivers employed by local governments are covered by a statewide public employee pension system. Increasingly, school systems extend benefits to drivers who supplement their driving by working in the school system during off hours.

Most intercity and many local transit busdrivers are members of the Amalgamated Transit Union. Local transit busdrivers in New York and several other large cities belong to the Transport Workers Union of America. Some drivers belong to the United Transportation Union and the International Brotherhood of Teamsters.

Related Occupations

Other workers who drive vehicles on highways and city streets are ambulance drivers and attendants, except emergency medical technicians; taxi drivers and chauffeurs; and truckdrivers and driver/sales workers.

Sources of Additional Information

For information on employment opportunities, contact local transit systems, intercity bus lines, school systems, or the local offices of the state employment service.

General information on busdriving is available from:

- American Bus Association, 1100 New York Ave. NW., Suite 1050, Washington, DC 20005. Internet: http://www.buses.org

General information on school bus driving is available from:

- National School Transportation Association, 625 Slaters Lane, Suite 205, Alexandria, VA 22314. School Bus Fleet, 21061 S. Western Ave., Torrance, CA 90501

General information on local transit busdriving is available from:

- American Public Transportation Association, 1666 K St. NW., Suite 1100, Washington, DC 20006

General information on motorcoach driving is available from:

- United Motorcoach Association, 113 S. West St., 4th Floor, Alexandria, VA 22314. Telephone (toll free): 800-424-8262

Cardiovascular Technologists and Technicians

O*NET 29-2031.00

Significant Points

- Employment will grow faster than the average, but the number of job openings created will be low, because the occupation is small.

- Job prospects will be good due to an aging population and increased need for vascular technology and sonography as an alternative for more costly and invasive heart surgery.

- About 7 out of 10 jobs are in hospitals, in both inpatient and outpatient settings.

Nature of the Work

Cardiovascular technologists and technicians assist physicians in diagnosing and treating cardiac (heart) and peripheral vascular (blood vessel) ailments. Cardiovascular technologists may specialize in three areas of practice: invasive cardiology, echocardiography, and vascular technology. Cardiovascular technicians who specialize in electrocardiograms

(EKGs), stress testing, and Holter monitors are known as *cardiographic* or *EKG technicians.*

Cardiovascular technologists specializing in invasive procedures are called *cardiology technologists.* They assist physicians with cardiac catheterization procedures in which a small tube, or catheter, is wound through a patient's blood vessel from a spot on the patient's leg into the heart. The procedure can determine if a blockage exists in the blood vessels that supply the heart muscle and help diagnose other problems. Part of the procedure may involve balloon angioplasty, which can be used to treat blockages of blood vessels or heart valves, without the need for heart surgery. Cardiology technologists assist physicians as they insert a catheter with a balloon on the end to the point of the obstruction.

Technologists prepare patients for cardiac catheterization and balloon angioplasty by first positioning them on an examining table and then shaving, cleaning, and administering anesthesia to the top of the patient's leg near the groin. During the procedures, they monitor patients' blood pressure and heart rate using EKG equipment and notify the physician if something appears wrong. Technologists also may prepare and monitor patients during open-heart surgery and the implantation of pacemakers.

Cardiovascular technologists who specialize in echocardiography or vascular technology often run noninvasive tests using ultrasound instrumentation, such as doppler ultrasound. Tests are called "noninvasive" if they do not require the insertion of probes or other instruments into the patient's body. The ultrasound instrumentation transmits high frequency sound waves into areas of the patient's body and then processes reflected echoes of the sound waves to form an image. Technologists view the ultrasound image on a screen that may be recorded on videotape or photographed for interpretation and diagnosis by a physician. While performing the scan, technologists check the image on the screen for subtle differences between healthy and diseased areas, decide which images to include, and judge if the images are satisfactory for diagnostic purposes. They also explain the procedure to patients, record additional medical history, select appropriate equipment settings, and change the patient's position as necessary.

Those who assist physicians in the diagnosis of disorders affecting circulation are known as *vascular technologists* or *vascular sonographers.* They perform a medical history and evaluate pulses by listening to the sounds of the arteries for abnormalities. Then they perform a noninvasive procedure using ultrasound instrumentation to record vascular information, such as vascular blood flow, blood pressure, limb volume changes, oxygen saturation, cerebral circulation, peripheral circulation, and abdominal circulation. Many of these tests are performed during or immediately after surgery.

Technologists who use ultrasound to examine the heart chambers, valves, and vessels are referred to as *cardiac sonographers,* or *echocardiographers.* They use ultrasound instrumentation to create images called echocardiograms. This may be done while the patient is either resting or physically active. Technologists may administer medication to a physically active patient to assess their heart function. Cardiac sonographers may also assist physicians who perform transesophageal echocardiography, which involves placing a tube in the patient's esophagus to obtain ultrasound images.

Cardiovascular technicians who obtain EKGs are known as *electrocardiograph* (or *EKG) technicians.* To take a basic EKG, which traces electrical impulses transmitted by the heart, technicians attach electrodes to the patient's chest, arms, and legs, and then manipulate switches on an EKG machine to obtain a reading. The physician makes a printout for inter-pretation. This test is done before most kinds of surgery and as part of a routine physical examination, especially for persons who have reached middle age or have a history of cardiovascular problems.

EKG technicians with advanced training perform Holter monitor and stress testing. For Holter monitoring, technicians place electrodes on the patient's chest and attach a portable EKG monitor to the patient's belt. Following 24 or more hours of normal activity for the patient, the technician removes a tape from the monitor and places it in a scanner. After checking the quality of the recorded impulses on an electronic screen, the technician usually prints the information from the tape so that a physician can interpret it later. Physicians use the output from the scanner to diagnose heart ailments, such as heart rhythm abnor-malities or problems with pacemakers.

For a treadmill stress test, EKG technicians document the patient's medi-cal history, explain the procedure, connect the patient to an EKG moni-tor, and obtain a baseline reading and resting blood pressure. Next, they monitor the heart's performance while the patient is walking on a tread-mill, gradually increasing the treadmill's speed to observe the effect of increased exertion. Like vascular technologists and cardiac sonographers, cardiographic technicians who perform EKG, Holter monitor, and stress tests are known as "noninvasive" technicians.

Some cardiovascular technologists and technicians schedule appoint-ments, type doctor interpretations, maintain patient files, and care for equipment.

Working Conditions

Technologists and technicians generally work a 5-day, 40-hour week that may include weekends. Those in catheterization labs tend to work longer hours and may work evenings. They also may be on call during the night and on weekends.

Cardiovascular technologists and technicians spend a lot of time walk-ing and standing. Those who work in catheterization labs may face stress-ful working conditions, because they are in close contact with patients with serious heart ailments. Some patients, for example, may encounter complications from time to time that have life or death implications.

Employment

Cardiovascular technologists and technicians held about 39,000 jobs in 2000. Most worked in hospital cardiology departments, whereas some worked in offices of cardiologists or other physicians, cardiac rehabilita-tion centers, or ambulatory surgery centers.

Training, Other Qualifications, and Advancement

Although a few cardiovascular technologists, vascular technologists, and cardiac sonographers are currently trained on the job, most receive train-ing in 2- to 4-year programs. Cardiovascular technologists, vascular tech-nologists, and cardiac sonographers normally complete a 2-year junior or community college program. One year is dedicated to core courses followed by a year of specialized instruction in either invasive, noninvasive cardiovascular, or noninvasive vascular technology. Those who are qualified in a related allied health profession only need to com-plete the year of specialized instruction.

Graduates from the 23 programs accredited by the Joint Review Com-mittee on Education in Cardiovascular Technology are eligible to ob-tain professional certification through Cardiovascular Credentialing International in cardiac catheterization, echocardiography, vascular ul-trasound, and cardiographic techniques. Cardiac sonographers and vas-cular technologists may also obtain certification with the American Registry of Diagnostic Medical Sonographers.

For basic EKGs, Holter monitoring, and stress testing, 1-year certificate programs exist; but most EKG technicians are still trained on the job by an EKG supervisor or a cardiologist. On-the-job training usually lasts about 8 to 16 weeks. Most employers prefer to train people already in the healthcare field—nursing aides, for example. Some EKG technicians are students enrolled in 2-year programs to become technologists, work-ing part-time to gain experience and make contact with employers.

Cardiovascular technologists and technicians must be reliable, have mechanical aptitude, and be able to follow detailed instructions. A pleas-ant, relaxed manner for putting patients at ease is an asset.

Job Outlook

Employment of cardiovascular technologists and technicians is expected to grow faster than the average for all occupations through the year 2010. Growth will occur as the population ages, because older people have a higher incidence of heart problems. Employment of *vascular tech-nologists* and *echocardiographers* will grow as advances in vascular tech-nology and sonography reduce the need for more costly and invasive procedures. Employment of *EKG technicians* is expected to decline, as hospitals train nursing aides and others to perform basic EKG proce-dures. Individuals trained in Holter monitoring and stress testing are expected to have more favorable job prospects than those who can only perform a basic EKG.

Some job openings for cardiovascular technologists and technicians will arise from replacement needs, as individuals transfer to other jobs or leave the labor force. Relatively few job openings, due to both growth and replacement needs are expected, however, because the occupation is small.

Earnings

Median annual earnings of cardiovascular technologists and technicians were $33,350 in 2000. The middle 50 percent earned between $24,590 and $43,450. The lowest 10 percent earned less than $19,540, and the highest 10 percent earned more than $52,930. Median annual earnings of cardiovascular technologists and technicians in 2000 were $33,100 in offices and clinics of medical doctors and $32,860 in hospitals.

Related Occupations

Cardiovascular technologists and technicians operate sophisticated equipment that helps physicians and other health practitioners diag-nose and treat patients. So do diagnostic medical sonographers, nuclear medicine technologists, radiation therapists, radiologic technologists and technicians, and respiratory therapists.

Sources of Additional Information

For general information about a career in cardiovascular technology, contact:

- Alliance of Cardiovascular Professionals, 4456 Corporation Ln., Suite 165, Virginia Beach, VA 23462. Internet: http://www.acp-online.org/index.html

For a list of accredited programs in cardiovascular technology, contact:

- Joint Review Committee on Education in Cardiovascular Technology, 3525 Ellicott Mills Dr., Suite N, Ellicott City, MD 21043-4547

For information on vascular technology, contact:

- The Society of Vascular Technology, 4601 Presidents Dr., Suite 260, Lanham, MD 20706-4365. Internet: http://www.svtnet.org

For information on echocardiography, contact:

- American Society of Echocardiography, 4101 Lake Boone Trail, Suite 201, Raleigh, NC 27607. Internet: http://www.asecho.org

For information regarding registration and certification, contact:

- Cardiovascular Credentialing International, 4456 Corporation Ln., Suite 110, Virginia Beach, VA 23462. Internet: http://www.cci-online.org

- American Registry of Diagnostic Medical Sonographers, 600 Jefferson Plaza, Suite 360, Rockville, MD 20852-1150. Internet: http://www.ardms.org

Cargo and Freight Agents

O*NET 43-5011.00

Significant Points

- Many cargo and freight agent jobs are entry level and do not require more than a high school diploma.

- Workers develop the necessary skills through on-the-job training lasting from several days to a few months.

- Numerous job openings will arise each year from the need to replace workers who leave this very large occupational group.

Nature of the Work

Cargo and freight agents arrange for and track incoming and outgoing cargo and freight shipments in airline, train, or trucking terminals or on shipping docks. They expedite movement of shipments by determining the route that shipments are to take and preparing all necessary shipping documents. The agents take orders from customers and arrange for pickup of freight or cargo for delivery to loading platforms. They may keep records of the properties of the cargo, such as amount, type, weight, and dimensions. They keep a tally of missing items, record conditions of damaged items, and document any excess supplies.

Cargo and freight agents arrange cargo according to its destination. They also determine the shipping rates and other charges that can sometimes apply to the freight. For imported or exported freight, they verify that the proper customs paperwork is in order. They often track shipments using electronic data, such as bar codes, and answer customer inquiries on the status of their shipments.

Working Conditions

Cargo and freight agents work in a wide variety of businesses, institutions, and industries. Some work in warehouses, stockrooms, or shipping and receiving rooms that may not be temperature controlled. Others may spend time in cold storage rooms or outside on loading platforms, where they are exposed to the weather.

Most jobs for cargo and freight agents involve frequent standing, bending, walking, and stretching. Some lifting and carrying of smaller items also may be involved. Although automation devices have lessened the physical demands of this occupation, their use remains somewhat limited. Work still can be strenuous, even though mechanical material handling equipment is employed to move heavy items.

The typical workweek is Monday through Friday; however, evening and weekend hours are common for some jobs, and may be required when large shipments are involved or when inventory is taken.

Employment

Cargo and freight agents held about 60,000 jobs in 2000. Most jobs were in transportation. About 35 percent of cargo and freight agents worked in transportation services, 23 percent worked for air carriers, and 10 percent worked for local and long distance trucking establishments. Department stores employed 12 percent, while personnel supply services employed 3 percent.

Training, Other Qualifications, and Advancement

Many cargo and freight agents jobs are entry level and do not require more than a high school diploma. Employers, however, prefer to hire those who are familiar with computers and other electronic office and business equipment. Those who have taken business courses or have previous business, dispatching, or specific job-related experience may be preferred. Because communication with other people is an integral part of these jobs, good oral and written communications skills are essential. Typing, filing, recordkeeping, and other clerical skills also are important.

Trainees usually develop the necessary skills on the job. This informal training lasts from several days to a few months, depending on the complexity of the job.

Cargo and freight agents start out by checking items to be shipped and then attaching labels and making sure the addresses are correct. Training in the use of automated equipment usually is done informally, on the job. As these occupations become more automated, however, workers in these jobs may need longer training in order to master the use of the equipment.

Job Outlook

Employment of cargo and freight agents is expected to grow more slowly than the average for all occupations through 2010. Although cargo traffic is expected to grow faster than it has in the past, employment of cargo and freight agents will not grow as rapidly because of technological advances. For example, the increasing use of bar codes on cargo and freight allows agents and customers to track these shipments quickly over the Internet, rather than manually tracking their location. In addition, customs and insurance paperwork now can be completed over the Internet by customers, reducing the need for cargo and freight agents.

Despite these advances in technology that dampen job growth among cargo and freight agents, job openings will continue to arise due to increases in buying over the Internet, which will result in more shipments, and the importance of same-day delivery, which expands the role of agents. In addition, many job openings will be created to replace cargo and freight agents who leave the occupation.

Earnings

Median hourly earnings in 2000 for cargo and freight agents were $13.73.

Cargo and freight agents usually receive the same benefits as most other workers. If uniforms are required, employers usually provide either the uniforms or an allowance to purchase them.

Related Occupations

Cargo and freight agents plan and coordinate cargo shipments using airlines, trains, and trucks. They also arrange freight pickup with customers. Others who do similar work are couriers and messengers; shipping, receiving, and traffic clerks; weighers, measurers, checkers, and samplers; truckdrivers and driver/sales workers; and postal service workers.

Sources of Additional Information

Information about job opportunities may be obtained from local employers and local offices of the state employment service.

Carpenters

O*NET 47-2031.01, 47-2031.02, 47-2031.03, 47-2031.04, 47-2031.05, 47-2031.06

Significant Points

- More than one-fourth of all carpenters—the largest construction trade in 2000—were self-employed.

- Job opportunities should be excellent, in part because of the large number of job openings created by carpenters who leave the occupation each year.

- Many builders use specialty carpentry subcontractors who do one or two work activities, so versatile carpenters able to switch specialties should have the best opportunities for steady work.

Nature of the Work

Carpenters are involved in many different kinds of construction activity. They cut, fit, and assemble wood and other materials for the construction of buildings, highways, bridges, docks, industrial plants, boats, ships, and many other structures. Carpenters also build doors or brattices (ventilation walls or partitions) in underground passageways to control the proper circulation of air through these passageways and to

work sites. Carpenters' duties vary by type of employer. Builders increasingly are using specialty trade contractors who, in turn, hire carpenters who specialize in just one or two activities. Some of these activities are setting forms for concrete construction; erecting scaffolding; or doing finishing work, such as installing interior and exterior trim. However, a carpenter directly employed by a general building contractor often must perform a variety of the tasks associated with new construction, such as framing walls and partitions, putting in doors and windows, building stairs, laying hardwood floors, and hanging kitchen cabinets.

Because local building codes often dictate where certain materials can be used, carpenters must know these regulations. Each carpentry task is somewhat different, but most involve the same basic steps. Working from blueprints or instructions from supervisors, carpenters first do the layout—measuring, marking, and arranging materials. They cut and shape wood, plastic, fiberglass, or drywall, using hand and power tools, such as chisels, planes, saws, drills, and sanders. They then join the materials with nails, screws, staples, or adhesives. In the final step, carpenters check the accuracy of their work with levels, rules, plumb bobs, and framing squares, and make any necessary adjustments. When working with prefabricated components, such as stairs or wall panels, the carpenter's task is somewhat simpler than above, because it does not require as much layout work or the cutting and assembly of as many pieces. Prefabricated components are designed for easy and fast installation and generally can be installed in a single operation.

Carpenters who remodel homes and other structures must be able to do all aspects of a job, not just one task. Thus, individuals with good basic overall training are at a distinct advantage, because they can switch from residential building to commercial construction or remodeling work, depending on which offers the best work opportunities.

Carpenters employed outside the construction industry perform a variety of installation and maintenance work. They may replace panes of glass, ceiling tiles, and doors, as well as repair desks, cabinets, and other furniture. Depending on the employer, carpenters install partitions, doors, and windows; change locks; and repair broken furniture. In manufacturing firms, carpenters may assist in moving or installing machinery.

Working Conditions

As in other building trades, carpentry work is sometimes strenuous. Prolonged standing, climbing, bending, and kneeling often are necessary. Carpenters risk injury working with sharp or rough materials, using sharp tools and power equipment, and working in situations where they might slip or fall. Additionally, many carpenters work outdoors, which can be uncomfortable.

Some carpenters change employers each time they finish a construction job. Others alternate between working for a contractor and working as contractors themselves on small jobs.

Employment

Carpenters, the largest group of building trades workers, held about 1.2 million jobs in 2000. One-third worked for general building contractors, 20 percent worked for special trade contractors, and 12 percent worked in heavy construction. Most of the remainder worked for manufacturing firms, government agencies, wholesale and retail establishments, or schools. More than one-fourth of all carpenters were self-employed.

Carpenters are employed throughout the country in almost every community.

Training, Other Qualifications, and Advancement

Carpenters learn their trade through on-the-job training, as well as formal training programs. Most pick up skills informally by working under the supervision of experienced workers. Many acquire skills through vocational education. Others participate in employer training programs or apprenticeships.

Most employers recommend an apprenticeship as the best way to learn carpentry. Apprenticeship programs are administered by local joint union-management committees of the United Brotherhood of Carpenters and Joiners of America, the Associated General Contractors, Inc., and the National Association of Home Builders. In addition, training programs are administered by local chapters of the Associated Builders and Contractors and by local chapters of the Associated General Contractors, Inc. These programs combine on-the-job training with related classroom instruction.

On the job, apprentices learn elementary structural design and become familiar with common carpentry jobs, such as layout, form building, rough framing, and outside and inside finishing. They also learn to use the tools, machines, equipment, and materials of the trade. Apprentices receive classroom instruction in safety, first aid, blueprint reading, freehand sketching, basic mathematics, and different carpentry techniques. Both in the classroom and on the job, they learn the relationship between carpentry and the other building trades.

Usually, apprenticeship applicants must be at least 17 years old and meet local requirements. For example, some union locals test an applicant's aptitude for carpentry. The length of the program, usually about 3 to 4 years, varies with the apprentice's skill. Because the number of apprenticeship programs is limited, however, only a small proportion of carpenters learn their trade through these programs.

Informal on-the-job training is normally less thorough than an apprenticeship. The degree of training and supervision often depends on the size of the employing firm. A small contractor specializing in homebuilding may provide training only in rough framing. In contrast, a large general contractor may provide training in several carpentry skills. Although specialization is becoming increasingly common, it is important to try to acquire skills in all aspects of carpentry and to have the flexibility to perform any kind of work.

A high school education is desirable, including courses in carpentry, shop, mechanical drawing, and general mathematics. Manual dexterity, eye-hand coordination, physical fitness, and a good sense of balance are important. The ability to solve arithmetic problems quickly and accurately also is helpful. Employers and apprenticeship committees generally view favorably any training and work experience obtained in the Armed Services or Job Corps.

Carpenters may advance to carpentry supervisor or general construction supervisor positions. Carpenters usually have greater opportunities than most other construction workers to become general construction supervisors, because carpenters are exposed to the entire construction process. Some carpenters become independent contractors. To advance, these workers should be able to estimate the nature and quantity of materials needed to properly complete a job. In addition, they must be able to accurately estimate how long a job should take to complete and what it will cost.

Job Outlook

Job opportunities for carpenters are expected to be excellent over the 2000–2010 period, largely due to the numerous openings arising each year from experienced carpenters who leave this large occupation each year. In addition, many potential workers may prefer work that is less strenuous and that has more comfortable working conditions. Because there are no strict training requirements for entry, many people with limited skills take jobs as carpenters but eventually leave the occupation because they dislike the work or cannot find steady employment. Well-trained workers will have especially favorable opportunities.

Employment of carpenters is expected to increase more slowly than the average for all occupations. Construction activity should increase in response to demand for new housing and commercial and industrial plants and the need to renovate and modernize existing structures. The demand for larger homes with more amenities and for second homes will continue to rise, especially as the baby boomers reach their peak earning years and can afford to spend more on housing. At the same time, as the number of immigrants increase and as the echo boomers (the children of the baby boomers) replace the smaller baby bust generation in the young adult age groups, the demand for manufactured housing, starter homes, and rental apartments also is expected to increase.

However, some of the demand for carpenters will be offset by expected productivity gains resulting from the increasing use of prefabricated components, such as pre-hung doors and windows and prefabricated wall panels and stairs, which can be installed very quickly. Prefabricated walls, partitions, and stairs can be lifted into place in one operation; beams, and in some cases entire roof assemblies, can be lifted into place using a crane. As prefabricated components become more standardized, builders will use them more often. In addition, improved adhesives will reduce the time needed to join materials, and lightweight, cordless pneumatic and combustion tools—such as nailers and drills—all make carpenters more efficient.

Carpenters can experience periods of unemployment because of the short-term nature of many construction projects and the cyclical nature of the construction industry. Building activity depends on many factors—interest rates, availability of mortgage funds, the season, government spending, and business investment—that vary with the state of the economy. During economic downturns, the number of job openings for carpenters declines. New and improved tools, equipment, techniques, and materials have vastly increased carpenter versatility. Therefore, carpenters with all-around skills will have better opportunities than those who can do only a few, relatively simple routine tasks.

Job opportunities for carpenters also vary by geographic area. Construction activity parallels the movement of people and businesses and reflects differences in local economic conditions. Therefore, the number of job opportunities and apprenticeship opportunities in a given year may vary widely from area to area.

Earnings

In 2000, median hourly earnings of carpenters were $15.69. The middle 50 percent earned between $11.99 and $20.86. The lowest 10 percent earned less than $9.48, and the highest 10 percent earned more than

$26.73. Median hourly earnings in the industries employing the largest numbers of carpenters in 2000 are shown in the following table:

Masonry, stonework, and plastering $19.27
Nonresidential building construction 17.43
Heavy construction, except highway 16.74
Carpentry and floor work 15.51
Residential building construction 15.26

Earnings can be reduced on occasion, because carpenters lose worktime in bad weather and during recessions when jobs are unavailable.

Some carpenters are members of the United Brotherhood of Carpenters and Joiners of America.

Related Occupations

Carpenters are skilled construction workers. Workers in other skilled construction occupations include brickmasons, blockmasons, and stonemasons; cement masons, concrete finishers, segmental pavers, and terrazzo workers; electricians; pipelayers, plumbers, pipefitters, and steamfitters; and plasterers and stucco masons.

Sources of Additional Information

For information about carpentry apprenticeships or other work opportunities in this trade, contact local carpentry contractors, locals of the union mentioned above, local joint union-contractor apprenticeship committees, or the nearest office of the state employment service or apprenticeship agency.

For information on training opportunities and carpentry in general, contact:

- Associated Builders and Contractors, 1300 N. 17th St., Suite 800, Arlington, VA 22209. Internet: http://www.abc.org

- Associated General Contractors of America, Inc., 1957 E St. NW., Washington, DC 20006. Internet: http://www.agc.org

- National Association of Home Builders, 1201 15th St. NW., Washington, DC 20005

- United Brotherhood of Carpenters and Joiners of America, 101 Constitution Ave. NW., Washington, DC 20001. Internet: http://www.necarpenters.org/ubc.htm

Carpet, Floor, and Tile Installers and Finishers

O*NET 47-2041.00, 47-2042.00, 47-2043.00, 47-2044.00

Significant Points

- Almost half of all carpet, floor, and tile installers and finishers are self-employed, as compared with fewer than 1 in 5 of all construction trades and related workers.

- Most workers learn on the job.

- Carpet installers, the largest specialty, should have the best job opportunities.

- Carpet, floor, and tile installers and finishers are less sensitive to fluctuations in construction activity than are other construction trades workers.

Nature of the Work

Carpet, tile, and other types of floor coverings not only serve an important basic function in buildings, but their decorative qualities also contribute to the appeal of the buildings. Carpet, floor, and tile installers and finishers lay these floor coverings in homes, offices, hospitals, stores, restaurants, and many other types of buildings. Tile also is installed on walls and ceilings.

Before installing carpet, *carpet installers* first inspect the surface to be covered to determine its condition and, if necessary, correct any imperfections that could show through the carpet or cause the carpet to wear unevenly. They must measure the area to be carpeted and plan the layout, keeping in mind expected traffic patterns and placement of seams for best appearance and maximum wear.

When installing wall-to-wall carpet without tacks, installers first fasten a tackless strip to the floor, next to the wall. They then install the padded cushion or underlay. Next, they roll out, measure, mark, and cut the carpet, allowing for 2 to 3 inches of extra carpet for the final fitting. Using a device called a "knee kicker," they position the carpet, stretching it to fit evenly on the floor and snugly against each wall and door threshold. They then rough cut the excess carpet. Finally, using a power stretcher, they stretch the carpet, hooking it to the tackless strip to hold it in place. The installer then finishes the edges using a wall trimmer.

Because most carpet comes in 12-foot widths, wall-to-wall installations require installers to tape or sew sections together for large rooms. They join the seams by sewing them with a large needle and special thread or by using heat-taped seams—a special plastic tape made to join seams when activated by heat.

On special upholstery work, such as stairs, carpet may be held in place with staples. Also, in commercial installations, carpet often is glued directly to the floor or to padding that has been glued to the floor.

Carpet installers use handtools such as hammers, drills, staple guns, carpet knives, and rubber mallets. They also may use carpet-laying tools, such as carpet shears, knee kickers, wall trimmers, loop pile cutters, heat irons, and power stretchers.

Floor installers, or *floor layers,* apply blocks, strips, or sheets of shock-absorbing, sound-deadening, or decorative coverings to floors and cabinets using rollers, knives, trowels, sanding machines, and other tools. Some floor covering materials are designed to be purely decorative. Others have more-specialized purposes, such as to deaden sound, to absorb shocks, or to create airtight environments. Before installing the floor, floor layers inspect the surface to be covered and, if necessary, correct any imperfections in order to start with a smooth, clean foundation. They measure and cut floor covering materials, such as rubber, vinyl, linoleum, or cork, and any foundation material, such as felt, according to designated blueprints. Next, they may nail or staple a wood underlayment to the surface or may use an adhesive to cement the foundation material to the floor; the foundation helps to deaden sound and prevents the top floor covering from wearing at board joints. Finally, floor layers install the top covering. They join sections of sheet covering by overlapping adjoining edges and cutting through both layers with a knife to form a tight joint.

Floor sanders and finishers scrape and sand wooden floors to smooth surfaces using floor scrapers and floor-sanding machines. They then inspect the floor for smoothness and remove excess glue from joints using knife or scraper or wood chisel and may sand wood surfaces by hand, using sandpaper. Finally, they apply coats of finish.

Tile installers, tilesetters, and *marble setters* apply hard tile and marble to floors, walls, ceilings and roof decks. Tile is durable, impervious to water, and easy to clean, making it a popular building material in hospitals, tunnels, lobbies of buildings, bathrooms, and kitchens. To set tile, which generally ranges in size from 1 inch to 12 or more inches square, tilesetters use cement or "mastic," a very sticky paste. When using cement, tilesetters nail a support of metal mesh to the wall or ceiling to be tiled. They use a trowel to apply a cement mortar—called a "scratch coat"—onto the metal screen, and scratch the surface of the soft mortar with a small tool, similar to a rake. After the scratch coat has dried, tilesetters apply another coat of mortar to level the surface, and then apply mortar to the back of the tile and place it onto the surface.

To set tile in mastic or a cement adhesive, called "thin set," tilesetters need a flat, solid surface such as drywall, concrete, plaster, or wood. They use a tooth-edged trowel to spread mastic on the surface or apply cement adhesive, and then properly position the tile.

Because tile varies in color, shape, and size, workers sometimes prearrange tiles on a dry floor according to a specified design. This allows workers to examine the pattern and make changes. In order to cover all exposed areas, including corners, and around pipes, tubs, and wash basins, tilesetters cut tiles to fit with a machine saw or a special cutting tool. Once the tile is placed, they gently tap the surface with their trowel handle or a small block of wood to seat the tiles evenly.

When the cement or mastic has set, tilesetters fill the joints with "grout," which is very fine cement. They then scrape the surface with a rubber-edged device called a grout float or a grouting trowel to dress the joints and remove excess grout. Before the grout sets, they finish the joints with a damp sponge for a uniform appearance. *Tile finishers* help some tilesetters by supplying and mixing construction materials and doing other tasks such as applying grout and cleaning installed tile.

Marble setters cut and set marble slabs in floors and walls of buildings. They trim and cut marble to specified size using a power wet saw, other cutting equipment, or handtools. After setting the marble in place, they polish the marble to high luster using power tools or by hand.

Working Conditions

Carpet, floor, and tile installers and finishers generally work indoors and have regular daytime hours. However, when floor covering installers work in occupied stores or offices, they may work evenings and weekends to avoid disturbing customers or employees. Installers and finishers usually work under better conditions than most other construction workers. By the time workers install carpets, flooring, or tile in a new structure, most construction has been completed and the work area is relatively clean and uncluttered. Installing these materials is labor intensive; workers spend much of their time bending, kneeling, and reaching—activities that require endurance. Carpet installers frequently lift heavy rolls of carpet and may move heavy furniture. Safety regulations may require that they wear kneepads or safety goggles when using certain tools. Carpet and floor layers may be exposed to fumes from various kinds of glue and to fibers of certain types of carpet.

Although workers are subject to cuts from tools or materials, falls from ladders, and strained muscles, the occupation is not as hazardous as some other construction occupations.

Employment

Carpet, floor, and tile installers and finishers held about 167,000 jobs in 2000. Almost half of all carpet, floor, and tile installers and finishers were self-employed, as compared with fewer than 1 in 5 of all construction trades workers. The following table shows 2000 employment by specialty.

Carpet installers 76,000
Tile and marble setters 54,000
Floor layers, except carpet, wood, and hard tiles 23,000
Floor sanders and finishers 14,000

Many carpet installers worked for flooring contractors or floor covering retailers. Most salaried tilesetters were employed by tilesetting contractors who work mainly on nonresidential construction projects, such as schools, hospitals, and office buildings. Most self-employed tilesetters work on residential projects.

Although carpet, floor, and tile installers and finishers are employed throughout the nation, they tend to be concentrated in populated areas where there are high levels of construction activity.

Training, Other Qualifications, and Advancement

The vast majority of carpet, floor, and tile installers and finishers learn their trade informally, on the job, as helpers to experienced workers. Others learn through formal apprenticeship programs, which include on-the-job training as well as related classroom instruction.

Informal training for carpet installers often is sponsored by individual contractors, and generally lasts from about 1 1/2 to 2 years. Workers start as helpers, and begin with simple assignments, such as installing stripping and padding, or helping to stretch newly installed carpet. With experience, helpers take on more difficult assignments, such as measuring, cutting, and fitting.

Persons who wish to begin a career in carpet installation as a helper or apprentice should be at least 18 years old and have good manual dexterity. Many employers prefer applicants with a high school diploma; courses in general mathematics and shop are helpful. Some employers may require a driver's license and a criminal background check. Because carpet installers frequently deal directly with customers, they should be courteous and tactful.

Many tile and floor layers learn their job through on-the-job training and begin by learning about the tools of the trade. They next learn to prepare surfaces to receive flooring. As they progress, tilesetters, marble setters, and resilient floor layers learn to cut and install tile, marble, and floor coverings. Tile and marble setters also learn to apply grout and to do finishing work.

Apprenticeship programs and some contractor-sponsored programs provide comprehensive training in all phases of the tilesetting and floor layer trade. Most apprenticeship programs are union-sponsored and consist of weekly classes and on-the-job training usually lasting 3 to 4 years.

When hiring apprentices or helpers for floor layer and tilesetter jobs, employers usually prefer high school graduates who have had courses in general mathematics, mechanical drawing, and shop. Good physical condition, manual dexterity, and a good sense of color harmony also are important assets.

Carpet, floor, and tile installers and finishers may advance to positions as supervisors or become salespersons or estimators. Some carpet installers may become managers for large installation firms. Many carpet, floor, and tile installers and finishers who begin working for a large contractor eventually go into business for themselves as independent subcontractors.

Job Outlook

Employment of carpet, floor, and tile installers and finishers is expected to grow about as fast as the average for all occupations through the year 2010. Employment growth stems primarily from the continued need to renovate and refurbish existing structures. Carpet installers, the largest specialty, should have the best job opportunities.

Carpet as a floor covering continues to be popular and its use is expected to grow in structures such as schools, offices, hospitals, and industrial plants. Demand for carpet also will be stimulated by new, more durable fibers that are stain and crush resistant, and come in a wider variety of colors. More resilient carpet needs to be replaced less often, but these attractive new products may induce more people to replace their old carpeting, contributing further to the demand for carpet installers. Employment also is expected to grow because wall-to-wall carpeting is a necessity in the many houses built with plywood, rather than hardwood floors. Similarly, offices, hotels, and stores often cover concrete floors with wall-to-wall carpet, which must be periodically replaced.

Demand for tile and marble setters will stem from population and business growth, which should result in more construction of shopping malls, hospitals, schools, restaurants, and other structures in which tile is used extensively. Tile is expected to continue to increase in popularity as a building material and to be used more extensively, particularly in more expensive homes, whose construction is expected to increase. In more modestly priced homes, however, the use of tile substitutes, such as plastic or fiberglass tub and shower enclosures, is expected to increase, slowing the growth in demand for tile and marble setters. Demand for floor layers and sanders and finishers will increase as a result of an increase in construction activity, particularly of residential homes and commercial buildings, and as some people decide to replace their plywood floors with hardwood floors. Job opportunities for tile and marble setters and floor layers and sanders, relatively small specialties, will not be as plentiful as those for carpet installers.

Carpet, floor, and tile installers and finishers are less sensitive to changes in construction activity than are most other construction occupations because much of their work involves replacing carpet and other flooring in existing buildings. As a result these workers tend to be sheltered from the business fluctuations that often occur in new construction activity.

Earnings

In 2000, the median hourly earnings of carpet installers were $14.46. The middle 50 percent earned between $10.41 and $20.47. The lowest 10 percent earned less than $7.97, and the top 10 percent earned more than $26.22. Median hourly earnings of carpet installers in 2000 in carpentry and floor work were $15.25 and in furniture and home furnishings stores, $13.31.

Carpet installers are paid either on an hourly basis, or by the number of yards of carpet installed. The rates vary widely depending on the geographic location and whether the installer is affiliated with a union.

Median hourly earnings of floor layers were $14.81 in 2000. The middle 50 percent earned between $10.53 and $20.21. The lowest 10 percent earned less than $8.06, and the top 10 percent earned more than $26.01.

Median hourly earnings of floor sanders and finishers were $13.17 in 2000. The middle 50 percent earned between $10.51 and $17.80. The lowest 10 percent earned less than $8.75, and the top 10 percent earned more than $24.72.

Median hourly earnings of tile and marble setters were $16.49 in 2000. The middle 50 percent earned between $12.54 and $21.93. The lowest 10 percent earned less than $9.58, and the top 10 percent earned more than $26.61. Earnings of tile and marble setters also vary greatly by geographic location and by union membership.

Apprentices and other trainees usually start out earning about half of what an experienced worker earns, although their wage rate increases as they advance through the training program.

Some carpet, floor, and tile installers and finishers belong to the United Brotherhood of Carpenters and Joiners of America. Some tilesetters also belong to the International Union of Bricklayers and Allied Craftsmen, while some carpet installers belong to the International Brotherhood of Painters and Allied Trades.

Related Occupations

Carpet, floor, and tile installers and finishers measure, cut, and fit materials to cover a space. Workers in other occupations involving similar skills, but using different materials, include brickmasons, blockmasons, and stonemasons; carpenters; cement masons, concrete finishers, segmental pavers, and terrazzo workers; drywall installers, ceiling tile installers, and tapers; painters and paperhangers; roofers; and sheet metal workers.

Sources of Additional Information

For details about apprenticeships or work opportunities, contact local flooring or tilesetting contractors or retailers, locals of the unions previously mentioned, or the nearest office of the state apprenticeship agency or employment service.

For general information about the work of carpet installers and floor layers, contact:

- Floor Covering Installation Contractors Association, 7439 Milwood Dr., West Bloomfield, MI 48322

Additional information on training for carpet installers and floor layers is available from:

● International Union of Painters and Allied Trades, 1750 New York Ave. NW., Washington, DC 20006. Internet: http://www.iupat.org

For general information about the work of tilesetters and finishers, contact:

● International Union of Bricklayers and Allied Crafts Workers, International Masonry Institute, Apprenticeship and Training, 815 15th St. NW., Washington, DC 20005. Internet: http://www.bacweb.org

● National Association of Home Builders, 1201 15th St. NW., Washington, DC 20005

For information concerning training of carpet, floor, and tile installers and finishers contact:

● United Brotherhood of Carpenters and Joiners of America, 101 Constitution Ave. NW., Washington, DC 20001. Internet: http://www.necarpenters.org/ubc.htm

Cashiers

O*NET 41-2011.00, 41-2012.00

Significant Points

● Cashiers are trained on the job; this occupation provides opportunities for many young people with no previous work experience.

● About one-half of all cashiers work part-time.

● Good employment opportunities are expected because of the large number of workers who leave this occupation each year.

Nature of the Work

Supermarkets, department stores, gasoline service stations, movie theaters, restaurants, and many other businesses employ cashiers to register the sale of their merchandise. Most cashiers total bills, receive money, make change, fill out charge forms, and give receipts.

Although specific job duties vary by employer, cashiers usually are assigned to a register at the beginning of their shifts and given drawers containing "banks" of money. They must count their banks to ensure that they contain the correct amount of money and adequate supplies of change. At the end of their shifts, they once again count the drawers' contents and compare the totals with sales data. An occasional shortage of small amounts may be overlooked but, in many establishments, repeated shortages are grounds for dismissal.

In addition to counting the contents of their drawers at the end of their shifts, cashiers usually separate and total charge forms, return slips, coupons, and any other noncash items. Cashiers also handle returns and exchanges. They must ensure that returned merchandise is in good condition, and determine where and when it was purchased and what type of payment was used.

After entering charges for all items and subtracting the value of any coupons or special discounts, cashiers total the bill and take payment. Acceptable forms of payment include cash, personal check, charge, and debit cards. Cashiers must know the store's policies and procedures for each type of payment the store accepts. For checks and charges, they may request additional identification from the customer or call in for an authorization. They must verify the age of customers purchasing alcohol or tobacco. When the sale is complete, cashiers issue a receipt to the customer and return the appropriate change. They may also wrap or bag the purchase.

Cashiers traditionally have totaled customers' purchases using cash registers—manually entering the price of each product bought. However, most establishments now use more sophisticated equipment, such as scanners and computers. In a store with scanners, a cashier passes a product's Universal Product Code over the scanning device, which transmits the code number to a computer. The computer identifies the item and its price. In other establishments, cashiers manually enter codes into computers, and descriptions of the items and their prices appear on the screen.

Depending on the type of establishment, cashiers may have other duties as well. In many supermarkets, for example, cashiers weigh produce and bulk food, as well as return unwanted items to the shelves. In convenience stores, cashiers may be required to know how to use a variety of machines other than cash registers, and how to furnish money orders. Operating ticket-dispensing machines and answering customers' questions are common duties for cashiers who work at movie theaters and ticket agencies. In casinos, gaming change persons and booth cashiers exchange coins and tokens and may issue payoffs. They may also operate a booth in the slot-machine area and furnish change persons with a money bank at the start of the shift, or count and audit money in drawers.

Working Conditions

About one-half of all cashiers work part-time. Hours of work often vary depending on the needs of the employer. Generally, cashiers are expected to work weekends, evenings, and holidays to accommodate customers' needs. However, many employers offer flexible schedules. For example, full-time workers who work on weekends may receive time off during the week. Because the holiday season is the busiest time for most retailers, many employers restrict the use of vacation time from Thanksgiving through the beginning of January.

Most cashiers work indoors, usually standing in booths or behind counters. In addition, they often are unable to leave their workstations without supervisory approval because they are responsible for large sums of money. The work of cashiers can be very repetitious, but improvements in workstation design are being made to combat problems caused by repetitive motion. In addition, the work can sometimes be dangerous; their risk from workplace homicides is much higher than that of the total workforce.

Employment

Cashiers held about 3.4 million jobs in 2000. Although employed in almost every industry, one-third of all jobs was in supermarkets and other food stores. Restaurants, department stores, gasoline service stations, drug stores, and other retail establishments also employed large numbers of these workers. Outside of retail establishments, many cashiers worked in hotels, schools, motion picture theaters, and casinos. Because cashiers are needed in businesses and organizations of all types and sizes, job opportunities are found throughout the country.

Training, Other Qualifications, and Advancement

Cashier jobs tend to be entry-level positions requiring little or no previous work experience. Although there are no specific educational requirements, employers filling full-time jobs often prefer applicants with high school diplomas.

Nearly all cashiers are trained on the job. In small businesses, an experienced worker often trains beginners. The first day usually is spent observing the operation and becoming familiar with the store's equipment, policies, and procedures. After this, trainees are assigned to a register, frequently under the supervision of a more-experienced worker. In larger businesses, before being placed at cash registers, trainees spend several days in classes. Topics typically covered include a description of the industry and the company, store policies and procedures, equipment operation, and security.

Training for experienced workers is not common, except when new equipment is introduced or when procedures change. In these cases, the employer or a representative of the equipment manufacturer trains workers on the job.

Persons who want to become cashiers should be able to do repetitious work accurately. They also need basic mathematics skills and good manual dexterity. Because cashiers deal constantly with the public, they should be neat in appearance and able to deal tactfully and pleasantly with customers. In addition, some businesses prefer to hire persons who can operate specialized equipment or who have business experience, such as typing, selling, or handling money.

Advancement opportunities for cashiers vary. For those working part-time, promotion may be to a full-time position. Others advance to head cashier or cash-office clerk. In addition, this job offers a good opportunity to learn about an employer's business and can serve as a stepping stone to a more responsible position.

Job Outlook

As in the past, opportunities for full- and part-time cashier jobs should continue to be good, because of employment growth and the need to replace the large number of workers who transfer to other occupations or leave the labor force.

Cashier employment is expected to grow about as fast as the average for all occupations through the year 2010 because of expanding demand for goods and services by a growing population. The rising popularity of electronic commerce, which does not require a cashier to complete a transaction or accept payment, may reduce the employment growth of cashiers. However, electronic commerce will have a limited impact on this large occupation. Traditionally, workers under the age of 25 have filled many of the openings in this occupation; in 2000, more than half of all cashiers were 24 years of age or younger. Some establishments have begun hiring elderly and disabled persons as well to fill some of their job openings.

Earnings

The starting wage for many cashiers is the federal minimum wage, which was $5.15 an hour in 2001. In some states, state law sets the minimum wage higher, and establishments must pay at least that amount. Wages tend to be higher in areas where there is intense competition for workers.

Median hourly earnings of cashiers, except gaming in 2000 were $6.95. The middle 50 percent earned between $6.14 and $8.27 an hour. The lowest 10 percent earned less than $5.61, and the highest 10 percent earned more than $10.39 an hour. Median hourly earnings in the industries employing the largest numbers of cashiers in 2000 were as follows:

Department stores	$7.15
Grocery stores	6.99
Gasoline service stations	6.87
Drug stores and proprietary stores	6.63
Eating and drinking places	6.56

Benefits for full-time cashiers tend to be better than those for cashiers working part-time. In addition to typical benefits, those working in retail establishments often receive discounts on purchases, and cashiers in restaurants may receive free or low-cost meals. Some employers also offer employee stock-option plans and education-reimbursement plans.

Related Occupations

Cashiers accept payment for the purchase of goods and services. Other workers with similar duties include tellers, counter and rental clerks, food and beverage serving and related workers, gaming cage workers, postal service workers, and retail salespersons.

Sources of Additional Information

General information on retailing is available from:

● National Retail Federation, 325 7th St. NW., Suite 1100, Washington, DC 20004

For information about employment opportunities as a cashier, contact:

● National Association of Convenience Stores, 1605 King St., Alexandria, VA 22314-2792

● United Food and Commercial Workers International Union, Education Office, 1775 K St. NW., Washington, DC 20006-1502

Cement Masons, Concrete Finishers, Segmental Pavers, and Terrazzo Workers

O*NET 47-2051.00, 47-2053.00, 47-4091.00

Significant Points

● Job opportunities are expected to be excellent.

- Most learn on the job, either through formal 3-year apprenticeship programs or by working as helpers.

- As in many other construction trades, layoffs may occur during downturns in construction activity.

Nature of the Work

Cement masons, concrete finishers, and terrazzo workers all work with concrete, one of the most common and durable materials used in construction. Once set, concrete—a mixture of Portland cement, sand, gravel, and water—becomes the foundation for everything from decorative patios and floors to huge dams or miles of roadways.

Cement masons and *concrete finishers* place and finish the concrete. They also may color concrete surfaces; expose aggregate (small stones) in walls and sidewalks; or fabricate concrete beams, columns, and panels. In preparing a site for placing concrete, cement masons first set the forms for holding the concrete and properly align them. They then direct the casting of the concrete and supervise laborers who use shovels or special tools to spread it. Masons then guide a straightedge back and forth across the top of the forms to "screed," or level, the freshly placed concrete. Immediately after leveling the concrete, masons carefully smooth the concrete surface with a "bull float," a long-handled tool about 8 by 48 inches that covers the coarser materials in the concrete and brings a rich mixture of fine cement paste to the surface.

After the concrete has been leveled and floated, concrete finishers press an edger between the forms and the concrete and guide it along the edge and the surface. This produces slightly rounded edges and helps prevent chipping or cracking. They use a special tool called a "groover" to make joints or grooves at specific intervals that help control cracking. Next, finishers trowel the surface using either a powered or hand trowel, a small, smooth, rectangular metal tool.

Sometimes, cement masons perform all the steps of laying concrete, including the finishing. As the final step, masons retrowel the concrete surface back and forth with powered and hand trowels to create a smooth finish. For a coarse, nonskid finish, masons brush the surface with a broom or stiff-bristled brush. For a pebble finish, they embed small gravel chips into the surface. They then wash any excess cement from the exposed chips with a mild acid solution. For color, they use colored premixed concrete. On concrete surfaces that will remain exposed after the forms are stripped, such as columns, ceilings, and wall panels, cement masons cut away high spots and loose concrete with hammer and chisel, fill any large indentations with a Portland cement paste, and smooth the surface with a carborundum stone. Finally, they coat the exposed area with a rich Portland cement mixture, using either a special tool or a coarse cloth to rub the concrete to a uniform finish.

Throughout the entire process, cement masons must monitor how the wind, heat, or cold affects the curing of the concrete. They must have a thorough knowledge of concrete characteristics so that, by using sight and touch, they can determine what is happening to the concrete and take measures to prevent defects.

Segmental pavers lay out, cut, and install pavers, which are flat pieces of masonry usually made from compacted concrete or brick. Pavers are used to pave paths, patios, playgrounds, driveways, and steps. They are manufactured in various textures and often interlock together to form an attractive pattern. Segmental pavers first prepare the site by removing the existing pavement or existing soil. They grade the soil to the proper depth and determine the amount of base material that is needed, which depends on the local soil conditions. They then install and compact the base material, a granular material that compacts easily, and lay the pavers from the center out, so that any trimmed pieces will be on the outside rather than in the center. Then they install edging materials to prevent the pavers from shifting and fill the spaces between the pavers with dry sand.

Terrazzo workers create attractive walkways, floors, patios, and panels by exposing marble chips and other fine aggregates on the surface of finished concrete. Much of the preliminary work of terrazzo workers is similar to that of cement masons. Attractive, marble-chip terrazzo requires three layers of materials. First, cement masons or terrazzo workers build a solid, level concrete foundation that is 3 to 4 inches deep. After the forms are removed from the foundation, workers add a 1-inch layer of sandy concrete. Before this layer sets, terrazzo workers partially embed metal divider strips in the concrete wherever there is to be a joint or change of color in the terrazzo. For the final layer, terrazzo workers blend and place into each of the panels a fine marble chip mixture that may be color-pigmented. While the mixture is still wet, workers toss additional marble chips of various colors into each panel and roll a lightweight roller over the entire surface.

When the terrazzo is thoroughly dry, helpers grind it with a terrazzo grinder, which is somewhat like a floor polisher, only much heavier. Slight depressions left by the grinding are filled with a matching grout material and hand-troweled for a smooth, uniform surface. Terrazzo workers then clean, polish, and seal the dry surface for a lustrous finish.

Working Conditions

Concrete, segmental paving, or terrazzo work is fast-paced and strenuous, and requires continuous physical effort. Because most finishing is done at floor level, workers must bend and kneel often. Many jobs are outdoors, and work is generally halted during inclement weather. The work, either indoors or outdoors, may be in areas that are muddy, dusty, and dirty. To avoid chemical burns from uncured concrete and sore knees from frequent kneeling, many workers wear kneepads. Workers also usually wear water-repellent boots while working in wet concrete.

Employment

Cement masons, concrete finishers, segmental pavers, and terrazzo workers held about 166,000 jobs in 2000; segmental pavers and terrazzo workers accounted for only a small portion of the total. Most cement masons and concrete finishers worked for concrete contractors or for general contractors on projects such as highways; bridges; shopping malls; or large buildings such as factories, schools, and hospitals. A small number were employed by firms that manufacture concrete products. Most segmental pavers and terrazzo workers worked for special trade contractors who install decorative floors and wall panels.

Only about 1 out of 20 cement masons, concrete finishers, segmental pavers, and terrazzo workers was self-employed, a smaller proportion than in other building trades. Most self-employed masons specialized in small jobs, such as driveways, sidewalks, and patios.

Training, Other Qualifications, and Advancement

Most cement masons, concrete finishers, segmental pavers, and terrazzo workers learn their trades either through on-the-job training as helpers, or through 3-year apprenticeship programs. Many masons and finishers first gain experience as construction laborers.

When hiring helpers and apprentices, employers prefer high school graduates who are at least 18 years old and in good physical condition, and who have a driver's license. The ability to get along with others also is important because cement masons frequently work in teams. High school courses in general science, shop, mathematics, blueprint reading, or mechanical drawing provide a helpful background.

On-the-job training programs consist of informal instruction, in which experienced workers teach helpers to use the tools, equipment, machines, and materials of the trade. They begin with tasks such as edging, jointing and using a straightedge on freshly placed concrete. As training progresses, assignments become more complex, and trainees can usually do finishing work within a short time.

Three-year apprenticeship programs, usually jointly sponsored by local unions and contractors, provide on-the-job training in addition to a recommended minimum of 144 hours of classroom instruction each year. A written test and a physical exam may be required. In the classroom, apprentices learn applied mathematics, blueprint reading, and safety. Apprentices generally receive special instruction in layout work and cost estimation. Some workers learn their jobs by attending trade or vocational/technical schools.

Cement masons, concrete finishers, segmental pavers, and terrazzo workers should enjoy doing demanding work. They should take pride in craftsmanship and be able to work without close supervision.

Experienced cement masons, concrete finishers, segmental pavers, or terrazzo workers may advance to become supervisors or contract estimators. Some open their own concrete businesses.

Job Outlook

Despite expected slow job growth, opportunities for skilled cement masons, concrete finishers, segmental pavers, and terrazzo workers are expected to be excellent as the increase in demand outpaces the supply of workers trained in this craft. In addition, many potential workers may prefer work that is less strenuous and has more comfortable working conditions. Well-trained workers will have especially favorable opportunities.

Employment of cement masons, concrete finishers, segmental pavers, and terrazzo workers is expected to grow more slowly than the average for all occupations through 2010. These workers will be needed to build highways, bridges, subways, factories, office buildings, hotels, shopping centers, schools, hospitals, and other structures. In addition, the increasing use of concrete as a building material—particularly in nonresidential construction—will add to the demand. More cement masons also will be needed to repair and renovate existing highways, bridges, and other structures.

Employment growth, however, will not keep pace with the growth of these construction projects. Worker productivity will be increased through use of improved concrete pumping systems, continuous concrete mixers, quicker-setting cement, troweling machines, prefabricated masonry systems, and other improved materials, equipment, and tools. In addition to job growth, other openings will become available as experienced workers transfer to other occupations or leave the labor force.

Employment of cement masons, concrete finishers, segmental pavers, and terrazzo workers, like that of many other workers, is sensitive to the fluctuations of the economy. Workers in these trades may experience periods of unemployment when the level of nonresidential construction falls. On the other hand, shortages of these workers may occur in some areas during peak periods of building activity.

Earnings

In 2000, the median hourly earnings of cement masons and concrete finishers were $13.50. The middle 50 percent earned between $10.55 and $18.41. The top 10 percent earned over $24.22, and the bottom 10 percent earned less than $8.31. Median hourly earnings in the industries employing the largest numbers of cement masons and concrete finishers in 2000 are shown in the following table:

Masonry, stonework, and plastering	$15.48
Highway and street construction	14.88
Concrete work	13.90
Nonresidential building construction	13.80
Residential building construction	11.31

In 2000, the median hourly earnings of terrazzo workers and finishers were $15.06 and median annual earnings of segmental pavers were $12.46.

Like those of other construction trades workers, earnings of cement masons, concrete finishers, segmental pavers, and terrazzo workers may be reduced on occasion because poor weather and downturns in construction activity limit the time they can work. Cement masons often work overtime, with premium pay, because once concrete has been placed, the job must be completed.

Many cement masons, concrete finishers, segmental pavers, and terrazzo workers belong to the Operative Plasterers' and Cement Masons' International Association of the United States and Canada, or to the International Union of Bricklayers and Allied Craftworkers. Some terrazzo workers belong to the United Brotherhood of Carpenters and Joiners of the United States. Nonunion workers generally have lower wage rates than union workers. Apprentices usually start at 50 to 60 percent of the rate paid to experienced workers.

Related Occupations

Cement masons, concrete finishers, segmental pavers, and terrazzo workers combine skill with knowledge of building materials to construct buildings, highways, and other structures. Other occupations involving similar skills and knowledge include brickmasons, blockmasons, and stonemasons; carpet, floor, and tile installers and finishers; drywall installers, ceiling tile installers, and tapers; and plasterers and stucco masons.

Sources of Additional Information

For information about apprenticeships and work opportunities, contact local concrete or terrazzo contractors, locals of unions previously mentioned, a local joint union-management apprenticeship committee, or the nearest office of the state employment service or apprenticeship agency.

For general information about cement masons, concrete finishers, segmental pavers, and terrazzo workers, contact:

● Associated General Contractors of America, Inc., 1957 E St. NW., Washington, DC 20006. Internet: http://www.agc.org

- International Union of Bricklayers and Allied Craftworkers, International Masonry Institute, 815 15th St. NW., Suite 1001, Washington, DC 20005. Internet: http://www.bacweb.org

- Operative Plasterers' and Cement Masons' International Association of the United States and Canada, 14405 Laurel Place, Suite 300, Laurel, MD 20707

- National Terrazzo and Mosaic Association, 101 E. Market St., Suite 200 A, Leesburg, VA 20176-3122. Portland Cement Association, 5420 Old Orchard Rd., Skokie, IL 60077. Internet: http://www.portcement.org/inde.asp

- United Brotherhood of Carpenters and Joiners of America, 101 Constitution Ave. NW., Washington, DC 20001. Internet: http://www.necarpenters.org/ubc.htm

Chefs, Cooks, and Food Preparation Workers

O*NET 35-1011.00, 35-2011.00, 35-2012.00, 35-2013.00, 35-2014.00, 35-2015.00, 35-2021.00

Significant Points

- Many young people work as chefs, cooks, and food preparation workers; almost 20 percent are between 16 and 19 years old.

- Almost 1 out of 2 food preparation workers is employed part-time.

- Job openings are expected to be plentiful through 2010, primarily reflecting substantial turnover in this large occupation.

Nature of the Work

A reputation for serving good food is essential to the success of any restaurant or hotel, whether it offers exotic cuisine or hamburgers. Chefs, cooks, and food preparation workers are largely responsible for establishing and maintaining this reputation. Chefs and cooks do this by preparing meals, while other food preparation workers assist them by cleaning surfaces, peeling vegetables, and performing other duties.

In general, *chefs* and *cooks* measure, mix, and cook ingredients according to recipes. In the course of their work they use a variety of pots, pans, cutlery, and other equipment, including ovens, broilers, grills, slicers, grinders, and blenders. Chefs and head cooks often are responsible for directing the work of other kitchen workers, estimating food requirements, and ordering food supplies. Some chefs and head cooks also help plan meals and develop menus.

Large eating places tend to have varied menus and kitchen staffs often include several chefs and cooks, sometimes called assistant or apprentice chefs and cooks, along with other less skilled kitchen workers. Each chef or cook usually has a special assignment and often a special job title—*vegetable, fry, or sauce cook*, for example. Executive chefs and head cooks coordinate the work of the kitchen staff and often direct the preparation of certain foods. They decide the size of servings, plan menus, and buy food supplies. Although the terms chef and cook still are used interchangeably, chefs tend to be more highly skilled and better trained than most cooks. Due to their skillful preparation of traditional dishes and refreshing twists in creating new ones, many chefs have earned fame for both themselves and for the establishments where they work.

The specific responsibilities of most cooks are determined by a number of factors, including the type of restaurant in which they work. *Institution and cafeteria cooks*, for example, work in the kitchens of schools, cafeterias, businesses, hospitals, and other institutions. For each meal, they prepare a large quantity of a limited number of entrees, vegetables, and desserts. *Restaurant cooks* usually prepare a wider selection of dishes, cooking most orders individually. *Short-order cooks* prepare foods in restaurants and coffee shops that emphasize fast service. They grill and garnish hamburgers, prepare sandwiches, fry eggs, and cook french fries, often working on several orders at the same time. *Fast food cooks* prepare a limited selection of menu items in fast-food restaurants. They cook and package batches of food, such as hamburgers and fried chicken, which are prepared to order or kept warm until sold. *Private household cooks* plan and prepare meals, clean the kitchen, order groceries and supplies, and also may serve meals.

Other food preparation workers, under the direction of chefs and cooks, perform tasks requiring less skill. They weigh and measure ingredients, go after pots and pans, and stir and strain soups and sauces. These workers also clean, peel, and slice vegetables and fruits and make salads. They may cut and grind meats, poultry, and seafood in preparation for cooking. Their responsibilities also include cleaning work areas, equipment, utensils, dishes, and silverware.

The number and types of workers employed in kitchens depends on the type of establishment. For example, fast-food establishments offer only a few items, which are prepared by fast-food cooks. Small, full-service restaurants offering casual dining often feature a limited number of easy-to-prepare items supplemented by short-order specialties and ready-made desserts. Typically, one cook prepares all the food with the help of a short-order cook and one or two other kitchen workers.

Working Conditions

Many restaurant and institutional kitchens have modern equipment, convenient work areas, and air conditioning, but many kitchens in older and smaller eating places are not as well equipped. Working conditions depend on the type and quantity of food being prepared and the local laws governing food service operations. Workers usually must withstand the pressure and strain of working in close quarters, standing for hours at a time, lifting heavy pots and kettles, and working near hot ovens and grills. Job hazards include slips and falls, cuts, and burns, but injuries are seldom serious.

Work hours in restaurants may include early mornings, late evenings, holidays, and weekends. Work schedules of chefs, cooks and other kitchen workers in factory and school cafeterias may be more regular. Nearly 3 in 10 cooks and 1 out of 5 other kitchen and food preparation workers have part-time schedules, as compared to 1 out of 7 workers throughout the economy.

The wide range in dining hours creates work opportunities attractive to homemakers, students, and other individuals seeking supplemental income. For example, about 27 percent of kitchen and food preparation workers are 16–19 years old. Kitchen workers employed by public and private schools may work during the school year only, usually for 9 or 10 months. Similarly, establishments at vacation resorts usually only offer seasonal employment.

Employment

Chefs, cooks and food preparation workers held more than 2.8 million jobs in 2000. The distribution of jobs among the various types of chefs, cooks, and food preparation workers was as follows:

Food preparation workers 844,000
Cooks, restaurant 668,000
Cooks, fast food 522,000
Cooks, institution and cafeteria 465,000
Cooks, short order 205,000
Chefs and head cooks 139,000
Cooks, private household 5,200

Almost 60 percent of all chefs, cooks, and food preparation workers were employed in restaurants and other retail eating and drinking places. About 20 percent worked in institutions such as schools, universities, hospitals, and nursing homes. Grocery stores, hotels, and other organizations employed the remainder.

Training, Other Qualifications, and Advancement

Most chefs, cooks, and food preparation workers start as fast-food or short-order cooks, or in other lower skilled kitchen positions. These positions require little education or training, and most skills are learned on the job. After acquiring some basic food handling, preparation, and cooking skills, these workers may be able to advance to an assistant cook position.

Although a high school diploma is not required for beginning jobs, it is recommended for those planning a career as a cook or chef. High school or vocational school courses in business arithmetic and business administration are particularly helpful. Many school districts, in cooperation with state departments of education, provide on-the-job training and summer workshops for cafeteria kitchen workers with aspirations of becoming cooks. Large corporations in the food service and hotel industries also offer paid internships and summer jobs, which can provide valuable experience.

To achieve the level of skill required of an executive chef or cook in a fine restaurant, many years of training and experience are necessary. An increasing number of chefs and cooks obtain their training through high school, post-high school vocational programs, or 2- or 4-year colleges. Chefs and cooks also may be trained in apprenticeship programs offered by professional culinary institutes, industry associations, and trade unions. An example is the 3-year apprenticeship program administered by local chapters of the American Culinary Federation in cooperation with local employers and junior colleges or vocational education institutions. In addition, some large hotels and restaurants operate their own training programs for cooks and chefs.

People who have had courses in commercial food preparation may be able to start in a cook or chef job without having to spend time in a lower skilled kitchen job. Their education may give them an advantage when looking for jobs in better restaurants and hotels, where hiring standards often are high. Although some vocational programs in high schools offer training, employers usually prefer training given by trade schools, vocational centers, colleges, professional associations, or trade unions. Postsecondary courses range from a few months to 2 years or more and are open, in some cases, only to high school graduates. About

8 to 15 years as a cook is required to become a fully qualified chef. Those who gain experience, including in a supervisory capacity, may become executive chefs with responsibility for more than one kitchen. The U.S. Armed Forces also are a good source of training and experience.

Although curricula may vary, students in these programs usually spend most of their time learning to prepare food through actual practice. They learn to bake, broil, and otherwise prepare food, and to use and care for kitchen equipment. Training programs often include courses in menu planning, determination of portion size, food cost control, purchasing food supplies in quantity, selection and storage of food, and use of left-over food to minimize waste. Students also learn hotel and restaurant sanitation and public health rules for handling food. Training in supervisory and management skills sometimes is emphasized in courses offered by private vocational schools, professional associations, and university programs.

Across the nation, a number of schools offer culinary courses. The American Culinary Federation has accredited over 100 training programs and offers a number of apprenticeship programs around the country. Typical apprenticeships last three years and combine classroom and work experience. Accreditation is an indication that a culinary program meets recognized standards regarding course content, facilities, and quality of instruction. The American Culinary Federation also certifies pastry professionals, culinary educators, and chefs and cooks at the levels of cook, working chef, executive chef, and master chef. Certification standards are based primarily on experience and formal training.

Important characteristics for chefs, cooks, and food preparation workers include the ability to work as part of a team, a keen sense of taste and smell, and personal cleanliness. Most states require health certificates indicating that workers are free from communicable diseases.

Advancement opportunities for chefs and cooks are better than for most other food and beverage preparation and service occupations. Many chefs and cooks acquire high-paying positions and new cooking skills by moving from one job to another. Besides culinary skills, advancement also depends on ability to supervise less skilled workers and limit food costs by minimizing waste and accurately anticipating the amount of perishable supplies needed. Some chefs and cooks go into business as caterers or restaurant owners, while others become instructors in vocational programs in high schools, community colleges, or other academic institutions. A number of cooks and chefs advance to executive chef positions or supervisory or management positions, particularly in hotels, clubs, and larger, more elegant restaurants.

Job Outlook

Job openings for chefs, cooks, and food preparation workers are expected to be plentiful through 2010. While job growth will create new positions, the overwhelming majority of job openings will stem from the need to replace workers who leave this large occupational group. Minimal educational and training requirements, combined with a large number of part-time positions, make employment as chefs, cooks, and food preparation workers attractive to people seeking a short-term source of income and a flexible schedule. In coming years, these workers will continue to transfer to other occupations or stop working to assume household responsibilities or to attend school full time, creating numerous openings for those entering the field.

Job openings stemming from replacement needs will be supplemented by new openings resulting from employment growth, as overall employment of chefs, cooks, and food preparation workers is expected to increase about as fast as the average for all occupations over the 2000–2010 period. Employment growth will be spurred by increases in population, household income, and leisure time that will allow people to dine out and take vacations more often. In addition, growth in the number of two-income households will lead more families to opt for the convenience of dining out.

Projected employment growth, however, varies by specialty. Increases in the number of families and the more affluent, 55-and-older population will lead to more restaurants that offer table service and more varied menus—resulting in faster-than-average growth among higher-skilled restaurant cooks. As more Americans choose more full-service restaurants, employment of fast-food cooks is expected to decline and employment of short-order cooks, most of whom work in fast-food restaurants, is expected to grow more slowly than average. Duties of cooks in fast-food restaurants are limited; most workers are likely to be combined food preparation and serving workers, rather than fast-food cooks. In addition, fast-food restaurants increasingly offer healthier prepared foods, further reducing the need for cooks.

Employment of institution and cafeteria chefs and cooks also will grow more slowly than the average for all occupations. Their employment will not keep pace with the rapid growth in the educational and health services industries, where their employment is concentrated. In an effort to make "institutional food" more attractive to students, staff, visitors, and patients, high schools and hospitals increasingly contract out their food services. Many of the contracted food service companies emphasize simple menu items and employ short-order cooks, instead of institution and cafeteria cooks, reducing the demand for these workers.

Earnings

Wages of chefs, cooks, and food preparation workers depend greatly on the part of the country and the type of establishment in which they are employed. Wages usually are highest in elegant restaurants and hotels, where many executive chefs are employed.

Median hourly earnings of head cooks and chefs were $12.07 in 2000. The middle 50 percent earned between $8.98 and $16.75. The lowest 10 percent earned less than $7.39, and the highest 10 percent earned more than $22.77 per hour. Median hourly earnings in the industries employing the largest number of head cooks and chefs in 2000 were:

Miscellaneous amusement and recreation services	$16.50
Hotels and motels	15.78
Eating and drinking places	11.03

Median hourly earnings of restaurant cooks were $8.72 in 2000. The middle 50 percent earned between $7.35 and $10.33. The lowest 10 percent earned less than $6.30, and the highest 10 percent earned more than $12.43 per hour. Median hourly earnings in the industries employing the largest number of restaurant cooks in 2000 were:

Hotels and motels	$9.97
Miscellaneous amusement and recreation services	9.68
Eating and drinking places	8.57

Median hourly earnings of cooks in fast-food restaurants were $6.53 in 2000. The middle 50 percent earned between $5.90 and $7.53. The low-

est 10 percent earned less than $5.49, and the highest 10 percent earned more than $8.43 per hour. Median hourly earnings in eating and drinking places, the industry employing the largest number of fast-food cooks, were $6.52 in 2000.

Median hourly earnings of short-order cooks were $7.55 in 2000. The middle 50 percent earned between $6.32 and $9.20. The lowest 10 percent earned less than $5.67, and the highest 10 percent earned more than $10.83 per hour. Median hourly earnings in the industries employing the largest number of short-order cooks in 2000 were:

Hotels and motels	$8.66
Miscellaneous amusement and recreation services	7.94
Eating and drinking places	7.57
Gasoline service stations	6.87
Grocery stores	6.60

Median hourly earnings of institution and cafeteria cooks were $8.22 in 2000. The middle 50 percent earned between $6.70 and $10.24. The lowest 10 percent earned less than $5.84, and the highest 10 percent earned more than $12.53 per hour. Median hourly earnings in the industries employing the largest number of institution and cafeteria cooks in 2000 were:

Hospitals	$9.37
Nursing and personal care facilities	8.50
Eating and drinking places	8.29
Elementary and secondary schools	7.65
Child day care services	7.52

Median hourly earnings of food preparation workers were $7.38 in 2000. The middle 50 percent earned between $6.28 and $8.81. The lowest 10 percent earned less than $5.67, and the highest 10 percent earned more than $10.65 per hour. Median hourly earnings in the industries employing the largest number of food preparation workers in 2000 were:

Elementary and secondary schools	$8.14
Hospitals	8.12
Grocery stores	7.90
Nursing and personal care facilities	7.56
Eating and drinking places	6.88

Some employers provide employees with uniforms and free meals, but federal law permits employers to deduct from their employees' wages the cost or fair value of any meals or lodging provided, and some employers do so. Chefs, cooks, and food preparation workers who work full time often receive typical benefits, but part-time workers usually do not.

In some large hotels and restaurants, kitchen workers belong to unions. The principal unions are the Hotel Employees and Restaurant Employees International Union and the Service Employees International Union.

Related Occupations

Workers who perform tasks similar to those of chefs, cooks, and food preparation workers include food processing occupations such as butchers and meat cutters, and bakers.

Sources of Additional Information

Information about job opportunities may be obtained from local employers and local offices of the state employment service.

Career information about chefs, cooks, and other kitchen workers, as well as a directory of 2- and 4-year colleges that offer courses or programs that prepare persons for food service careers, is available from:

- National Restaurant Association, 1200 17th St. NW., Washington, DC 20036-3097. Internet: http://www.restaurant.org

For information on the American Culinary Federation's apprenticeship and certification programs for cooks, as well as a list of accredited culinary programs, send a self-addressed, stamped envelope to:

- American Culinary Federation, 10 San Bartola Dr., St. Augustine, FL 32085. Internet: http://www.acfchefs.org

For general information on hospitality careers, contact:

- International Council on Hotel, Restaurant, and Institutional Education, 3205 Skipwith Rd., Richmond, VA 23294-4442. Internet: http://www.chrie.org

Childcare Workers

O*NET 39-9011.00

Significant Points

- About 2 out of 5 childcare workers are self-employed; most of these are family childcare providers.

- A high school diploma and little or no experience are adequate for many jobs, but training requirements vary from a high school diploma to a college degree.

- High turnover should create good job opportunities.

Nature of the Work

Childcare workers nurture and teach children of all ages in childcare centers, nursery schools, preschools, public schools, private households, family childcare homes, and before- and after-school programs. These workers play an important role in a child's development by caring for the child when parents are at work or away for other reasons. Some parents enroll their children in nursery schools or childcare centers primarily to provide them with the opportunity to interact with other children. In addition to attending to children's basic needs, these workers organize activities that stimulate the children's physical, emotional, intellectual, and social growth. They help children explore their interests, develop their talents and independence, build self-esteem, and learn how to behave with others.

Private household workers who are employed on an hourly basis usually are called babysitters. These childcare workers bathe, dress, and feed children; supervise their play; wash their clothes; and clean their rooms. They also may put them to sleep and waken them, read to them, involve them in educational games, take them for doctors' visits, and dis-

cipline them. Those who are in charge of infants, sometimes called infant nurses, also prepare bottles and change diapers.

Nannies generally take care of children from birth to age 10 or 12, tending to the child's early education, nutrition, health, and other needs. They also may perform the duties of a general housekeeper, including general cleaning and laundry duties.

Childcare workers spend most of their day working with children. However, they do maintain contact with parents or guardians through informal meetings or scheduled conferences to discuss each child's progress and needs. Many childcare workers keep records of each child's progress and suggest ways that parents can increase their child's learning and development at home. Some preschools, childcare centers, and before- and after-school programs actively recruit parent volunteers to work with the children and participate in administrative decisions and program planning.

Most childcare workers perform a combination of basic care and teaching duties. Through many basic care activities, childcare workers provide opportunities for children to learn. For example, a worker who shows a child how to tie a shoelace teaches the child while also providing for that child's basic care needs. Childcare programs help children learn about trust and gain a sense of security.

Young children learn mainly through play. Recognizing the importance of play, childcare workers build their program around it. They capitalize on children's play to further language development (storytelling and acting games), improve social skills (working together to build a neighborhood in a sandbox), and introduce scientific and mathematical concepts (balancing and counting blocks when building a bridge or mixing colors when painting). Thus, a less structured approach is used to teach preschool children, including small group lessons, one-on-one instruction, and learning through creative activities, such as art, dance, and music.

Interaction with peers is an important part of a child's early development. Preschool children are given an opportunity to engage in conversation and discussions, and learn to play and work cooperatively with their classmates. Childcare workers play a vital role in preparing children to build the skills they will need in school.

Childcare workers in preschools greet young children as they arrive, help them remove outer garments, and select an activity of interest. When caring for infants, they feed and change them. To ensure a well-balanced program, childcare workers prepare daily and long-term schedules of activities. Each day's activities balance individual and group play and quiet and active time. Children are given some freedom to participate in activities in which they are interested.

Workers in before- and after-school programs may help students with their homework or engage them in other extracurricular activities. These activities may include field trips, learning about computers, painting, photography, and participating in sports. Some childcare workers may be responsible for taking children to school in the morning and picking them up from school in the afternoon. Concern over school-age children being home alone before and after school has spurred many parents to seek alternative ways for their children to constructively spend their time. The purpose of before- and after-school programs is to watch over school-age children during the gap between school hours and their parents' work hours. These programs also may operate during the summer and on weekends. Before- and after-school programs may be operated by public school systems, local community centers, or other private organizations.

Helping to keep young children healthy is an important part of the job. Childcare workers serve nutritious meals and snacks and teach good eating habits and personal hygiene. They ensure that children have proper rest periods. They identify children who may not feel well or who show signs of emotional or developmental problems and discuss these matters with their supervisor and the child's parents. In some cases, childcare workers help parents identify programs that will provide basic health services.

Early identification of children with special needs, such as those with behavioral, emotional, physical, or learning disabilities, is important to improve their future learning ability. Special education teachers often work with these preschool children to provide the individual attention they need.

Working Conditions

Preschool or childcare facilities include private homes, schools, religious institutions, workplaces in which employers provide care for employees' children, and private buildings. Individuals who provide care in their own homes generally are called family childcare providers.

Nannies and babysitters usually work in the pleasant and comfortable homes or apartments of their employers. Most are day workers who live in their own homes and travel to work. Some live in the home of their employer, generally with their own room and bath. They often become part of their employer's family, and may derive satisfaction from caring for them.

Watching children grow, learn, and gain new skills can be very rewarding. While working with children, childcare workers often improve the child's communication, learning, and other personal skills. The work is never routine; new activities and challenges mark each day. However, childcare can be physically and emotionally taxing, as workers constantly stand, walk, bend, stoop, and lift to attend to each child's interests and problems.

To ensure that children receive proper supervision, state or local regulations may require certain ratios of workers to children. The ratio varies with the age of the children. Child development experts generally recommend that a single caregiver be responsible for no more than 3 or 4 infants (less than 1 year old), 5 or 6 toddlers (1 to 2 years old), or 10 preschool-age children (between 2 and 5 years old). In before- and after-school programs, workers may be responsible for many school-age children at one time.

The working hours of childcare workers vary widely. Childcare centers usually are open year round, with long hours so that parents can drop off and pick up their children before and after work. Some centers employ full-time and part-time staff with staggered shifts to cover the entire day. Some workers are unable to take regular breaks during the day due to limited staffing. Public and many private preschool programs operate during the typical 9- or 10-month school year, employing both full-time and part-time workers. Family childcare providers have flexible hours and daily routines, but may work long or unusual hours to fit parents' work schedules. Live-in nannies usually work longer hours than those who have their own homes. However, if they work evenings or weekends, they may get other time off.

Turnover in this occupation is high. Many childcare workers leave the occupation temporarily to fulfill family responsibilities or to study, or for other reasons. Some workers leave permanently because they are interested in pursuing another occupation or because of dissatisfaction with long hours, low pay and benefits, and stressful conditions.

Employment

Childcare workers held about 1.2 million jobs in 2000. Many worked part-time. About 2 out of 5 childcare workers are self-employed; most of these are family childcare providers.

Twelve percent of all childcare workers are found in childcare centers and preschools, and about 3 percent work for religious institutions. The remainder work in other community organizations, state and local government, and private households. Some childcare programs are for-profit centers; some of these are affiliated with a local or national chain. Religious institutions, community agencies, school systems, and state and local governments operate nonprofit programs. Only a very small percentage of private industry establishments operate onsite childcare centers for the children of their employees.

Training, Other Qualifications, and Advancement

The training and qualifications required of childcare workers vary widely. Each state has its own licensing requirements that regulate caregiver training, ranging from a high school diploma, to community college courses, to a college degree in child development or early-childhood education. Many states require continuing education for workers in this field. However, state requirements often are minimal. Childcare workers generally can obtain employment with a high school diploma and little or no experience. Local governments, private firms, and publicly funded programs may have more demanding training and education requirements.

Some employers prefer to hire childcare workers with a nationally recognized childcare development credential, secondary or postsecondary courses in child development and early childhood education, or work experience in a childcare setting. Other employers require their own specialized training. An increasing number of employers require an associate degree in early childhood education. Schools for nannies teach early childhood education, nutrition, and childcare.

Childcare workers must be enthusiastic and constantly alert, anticipate and prevent problems, deal with disruptive children, and provide fair but firm discipline. They must communicate effectively with the children and their parents, as well as other teachers and childcare workers. Workers should be mature, patient, understanding, and articulate, and have energy and physical stamina. Skills in music, art, drama, and storytelling also are important. Those who work for themselves must have business sense and management abilities.

Opportunities for advancement are limited. However, as childcare workers gain experience, some may advance to supervisory or administrative positions in large childcare centers or preschools. Often, these positions require additional training, such as a bachelor's or master's degree. Other workers move on to work in resource and referral agencies, consulting with parents on available child services. A few workers become involved in policy or advocacy work related to childcare and early childhood education. With a bachelor's degree, workers may become preschool teachers or become certified to teach in public or private schools at the kindergarten, elementary, and secondary school levels. Some workers set up their own childcare businesses.

Job Outlook

High turnover should create good job opportunities for childcare workers. Many childcare workers leave the occupation each year to take other jobs, to meet family responsibilities, or for other reasons. Qualified persons who are interested in this work should have little trouble finding and keeping a job. Opportunities for nannies should be especially good, as many workers prefer not to work in other people's homes.

Employment of childcare workers is projected to increase about as fast as the average for all occupations through the year 2010. Employment growth of childcare workers should be considerably slower than in the last two decades because demographic changes that fueled much of the past enrollment growth are projected to slow. Labor force participation of women of childbearing age will increase very little, and this group of women will decline as a percentage of the total labor force. However, the number of children under 5 years of age is expected to rise gradually over the projected 2000–2010 period. The proportion of youngsters enrolled full- or part-time in childcare and preschool programs is likely to continue to increase, spurring demand for additional childcare workers.

Changes in perceptions of preprimary education may lead to increased public and private spending on childcare. If more parents believe that some experience in center-based care and preschool is beneficial to children, enrollment will increase. Concern about the behavior of school-age children during nonschool hours should increase demand for before- and after-school programs. The difficulty of finding suitable nannies or private household workers also may force many families to seek out alternative childcare arrangements in centers and family childcare programs. Government policy often favors increased funding of early childhood education programs, and that trend should continue. Government funding for before- and after-school programs also is expected to increase over the projection period. The growing availability of government-funded programs may induce some parents who otherwise would not enroll their children in center-based care and preschool to do so. Some states also are increasing subsidization of the childcare services industry in response to welfare reform legislation. This reform may cause some mothers to enter the workforce during the projection period as their welfare benefits are reduced or eliminated.

Earnings

Pay depends on the educational attainment of the worker and the type of establishment. Although the pay generally is very low, more education usually means higher earnings. Median hourly earnings of wage and salary childcare workers were $7.43 in 2000. The middle 50 percent earned between $6.30 and $9.09. The lowest 10 percent earned less than $5.68, and the highest 10 percent earned more than $10.71. Median hourly earnings in the industries employing the largest numbers of childcare workers in 2000 were as follows:

Residential care	$8.71
Elementary and secondary schools	8.52
Civic and social associations	6.98
Child daycare services	6.74
Miscellaneous amusement and recreation services	6.65

Earnings of self-employed childcare workers vary depending on the hours worked, the number and ages of the children, and the location.

Benefits vary, but are minimal for most childcare workers. Many employers offer free or discounted childcare to employees. Some offer a full benefits package, including health insurance and paid vacations, but others offer no benefits at all. Some employers offer seminars and workshops to help workers learn new skills. A few are willing to cover the cost of courses taken at community colleges or technical schools. Live-in nannies get free room and board.

Related Occupations

Childcare work requires patience; creativity; an ability to nurture, motivate, teach, and influence children; and leadership, organizational, and administrative skills. Others who work with children and need these qualities and skills include teacher assistants; teachers—preschool, kindergarten, elementary, middle, and secondary; and special education teachers.

Sources of Additional Information

For eligibility requirements and a description of the Child Development Associate credential, contact:

- Council for Professional Recognition, 2460 16th St. NW., Washington, DC 20009-3575. Internet: http://www.cdacouncil.org

For eligibility requirements and a description of the Certified Childcare Professional designation, contact:

- National Childcare Association, 1016 Rosser St., Conyers, GA 30012. Internet: http://www.nccanet.org

For information about a career as a nanny, contact:

- International Nanny Association, 900 Haddon Ave., Suite 438, Collingswood, NJ 08108. Internet: http://www.nanny.org

State departments of human services or social services can supply state regulations and training requirements for childcare workers.

Claims Adjusters, Appraisers, Examiners, and Investigators

O*NET 13-1031.01, 13-1031.02, 13-1032.00

Significant Points

- Adjusters and examiners investigate claims, negotiate settlements, and authorize payments, while investigators deal with claims in which fraud or criminal activity is suspected.

- Most employers prefer to hire college graduates.

- The greatest demand for adjusters will be in health insurance and property and casualty insurance; competition will remain keen for jobs as investigators because this occupation attracts many qualified people.

Nature of the Work

Claims adjusters, appraisers, examiners and investigators perform a wide range of functions, but their most important role is acting as intermediaries with the public. Insurance companies and independent adjusting firms employ adjusters, appraisers, examiners, and investigators to deal with the challenges they face, such as handling claims, interpreting and explaining policies or regulations, and resolving billing disputes.

Within insurance companies, claims representatives investigate claims, negotiate settlements, and authorize payments to claimants. When a policyholder files a claim for property damage or a hospital stay, for example, a claim representative must initially determine whether the customer's insurance policy covers the loss and the amount of the loss covered. They then must determine the amount to pay the claimant.

In life and health insurance companies, claim representatives typically are called claims examiners. Claims examiners usually specialize in group or individual insurance plans and in hospital, dental, or prescription drug claims. Examiners review health-related claims to see if the costs are reasonable based on the diagnosis. They check with guides that provide information on the average period of disability for various causes, expected treatments, and average hospital stay. Examiners will then either authorize the appropriate payment or refer the claim to an investigator for a more thorough review.

Claims examiners working in life insurance review the causes of death, particularly in the case of an accident, as most life insurance companies pay additional benefits if the death is due to an accident. Claims examiners also may review new applications for life insurance to make sure applicants have no serious illnesses that would prevent them from qualifying for insurance.

In property and casualty insurance, claims adjusters handle minor claims filed by automobile or homeowner policyholders. These workers contact claimants by telephone or mail to obtain information on repair costs, medical expenses, or other details the company requires. Many companies centralize this operation through a claims center, where the cost of repair is determined and a check is issued immediately. More complex cases, usually involving bodily injury, are referred to senior adjusters. Some adjusters work with multiple types of insurance; however, most specialize in homeowner claims, business losses, automotive damage, product liability, or workers' compensation.

Some clients may choose to hire a public adjuster. They perform the same services as adjusters who work directly for companies. Public adjusters assist clients in preparing and presenting claims to insurance companies and try to negotiate a fair settlement. They work in the best interests of the client, rather than the insurance company.

Claims adjusters primarily plan and schedule the work required to process a claim. They investigate claims by interviewing the claimant and witnesses, consulting police and hospital records, and inspecting property damage to determine the extent of the company's liability. Claims adjusters and examiners may also consult with other professionals, who can offer a more expert evaluation of a claim. Some of these professionals include accountants, architects, construction workers, engineers, lawyers, and physicians. The information gathered, including photographs and written or taped statements, is included in a report that is then used to evaluate a claim. When the policyholder's claim is legitimate, the claims adjuster negotiates with the claimant and settles the claim. When claims are contested, adjusters may testify in court and refer claims to an investigator.

Insurance companies and independent adjusting firms usually hire auto damage appraisers to inspect auto damage after an accident and provide repair cost estimates. Insurance companies value auto damage appraisers because they can provide an unbiased judgment of repair costs. Otherwise, the companies would have to rely on auto mechanic estimates, which might be unreasonably high.

Many claims adjusters and auto damage appraisers are equipped with laptop computers, from which they can download the necessary forms and files from insurance company databases. Many adjusters and appraisers are equipped with digital cameras, which allow photographs of the damage to be sent to the company via the Internet or satellite. There also are new software programs that can give estimates of damage based on the information input directly into the computer. These new technologies allow for faster and more efficient processing of claims.

Many insurance companies are emphasizing better customer service. One way they are achieving this is by offering access to claims services at any time. Larger companies use call centers, staffed with Customer Service Representatives. These workers obtain information from policyholders regarding claims resulting from fire damage, personal injury or illness, or an automobile accident, for example. They primarily are responsible for getting the necessary information on a claim, such as specific details of an accident. Once the information is entered, the customer service representative forwards the claim to a claims adjuster or examiner. This allows the adjusters or examiners to concentrate on investigating the claim. However, claims adjusters and examiners working for small insurance companies may still answer phones, take claims information, and then handle the claims themselves.

When adjusters or examiners suspect a case might involve fraud, they refer the claim to an investigator. Insurance investigators work in an insurance company's Special Investigative Unit and handle claims in which a company suspects there might be fraudulent or criminal activity, such as arson cases, false workers' disability claims, staged accidents, or unnecessary medical treatments. The severity of insurance fraud cases can vary greatly, from claimants simply overstating damage on a vehicle, to complicated fraud rings, often involving many claimants, fraudulent doctors and lawyers, and even insurance personnel.

Investigators usually start with a database search to obtain background information on claimants and witnesses. Investigators can access personal information and identify Social Security numbers, aliases, driver license numbers, addresses, phone numbers, criminal records, and past claims histories to establish if a claimant has ever attempted insurance fraud. Then, investigators may visit claimants and witnesses to obtain a recorded statement; take photographs; and inspect facilities, such as a doctor's office, to determine whether it has a proper license. Investigators often consult with legal counsel and can be expert witnesses in court cases.

Often, investigators also will perform surveillance work. For example, in a case involving fraudulent workers' compensation claims, an investigator may carry out long-term covert observation of the subject. If the investigator observes the subject performing an activity that contradicts injuries stated in a workers' compensation claim, the investigator would take video or still photographs to document the activity and report it to the insurance company.

Working Conditions

Working environments of claims adjusters, appraisers, examiners, and investigators vary greatly. Most claims examiners working for life and health insurance companies work a standard 5-day, 40-hour week and work in a typical office environment. Claims adjusters and auto damage appraisers, on the other hand, often work outside the office, inspecting damaged buildings and automobiles.

Damaged buildings provide potential hazards such as collapsed roofs and floors and weakened structures of which adjusters must be wary. Occasionally, experienced adjusters are away from home for days when they travel to the scene of a disaster—such as a tornado, hurricane, or flood—to work with local adjusters and government officials. Some adjusters are on emergency call in the case of such incidents. In general, adjusters are able to arrange their work schedule to accommodate evening and weekend appointments with clients. This accommodation may result in adjusters working 50 or 60 hours a week. Some report to the office every morning to get their assignments; others simply call from home and spend their days traveling to claim sites. New technology, such as laptop computers and cell phones, is making telecommuting easier for claims adjusters and auto damage appraisers. Many adjusters work inside their offices only a few hours a week. Some adjusters' businesses are based entirely out of their homes.

Insurance investigators often work irregular hours because of the need to conduct surveillance and contact people who are not available during normal working hours. Early morning, evening, and weekend work is common. Some days investigators will spend all day in the office doing database searches and making phone calls. Other times, they may be away doing surveillance or interviewing witnesses. Some of the work can involve confrontation with claimants and others involved in a case, so the job can be stressful and dangerous.

Employment

Claims adjusters, appraisers, examiners, and investigators held about 207,000 jobs in 2000. Of these, almost 13,000 were auto damage insurance appraisers. Two percent of adjusters, appraisers, examiners, and investigators were self-employed.

Insurance companies employ the vast majority of claims adjusters, appraisers, examiners, and investigators. Insurance Sales Agents and brokers and independent adjusting and claims processing firms employ them as well.

Training, Other Qualifications, and Advancement

Training and entry requirements vary widely for claims adjusters, appraisers, examiners, and investigators. However, most companies prefer to hire college graduates. No specific college major is recommended. A claims adjuster, although, who has a business or an accounting background might specialize in claims of financial loss due to strikes, equipment breakdowns, or merchandise damage. College training in architecture or engineering is helpful in adjusting industrial claims, such as damage from fires and other accidents. Some claims adjusters and examiners who are professionals in their field might decide to use their expertise to adjust claims. A legal background can be beneficial to someone handling workers' compensation and product liability cases. A medical background is useful for those examiners working on medical and life insurance claims.

Because they often work closely with claimants, witnesses, and other insurance professionals, claims adjusters and examiners must be able to

communicate effectively with others. Knowledge of computer applications also is extremely important. Some companies require applicants to pass a series of written aptitude tests designed to measure communication, analytical, and general mathematical skills. About one-third of the states require independent, or public, adjusters to be licensed. Applicants in these states usually must pass a licensing examination covering the fundamentals of adjusting; complete an approved course in insurance or loss adjusting; furnish character references; be at least 20 or 21 years of age and a resident of the state; and file a surety bond. Claims adjusters working for companies usually can work under the company license and do not need to be licensed.

It is very important for claims adjusters and examiners to receive continuing education in claims. Frequently new federal and state laws and court decisions affect how claims are handled or who is covered by insurance policies. Also, claims examiners working on life and health claims must be familiar with new medical procedures and prescription drugs. Some states that require adjusters to be licensed also require a certain number of continuing education (CE) credits per year in order to renew the license. These credits can be obtained from a number of sources. Many companies offer training sessions to inform their employees of industry changes. Many schools and adjuster associations offer courses and seminars in various claims topics. Correspondence courses via the Internet are making long-distance learning possible. Adjusters also can earn CE credits by writing articles for claims publications or giving lectures and presentations.

Many adjusters and examiners choose to pursue certain certifications and designations to distinguish themselves. The Insurance Institute of America offers an Associate in Claims (AIC) designation upon successful completion of four essay examinations. Adjusters can prepare for the examination through independent home study or company and public classes. The Institute also offers a certificate upon successful completion of the Introduction to Claims program and an examination. The Registered Professional Adjusters, Inc., offers the Registered Professional Adjuster (RPA) designation. For public adjusters specifically, The National Association of Public Insurance Adjusters offers both the Certified Professional Public Adjuster (CPPA) and Senior Professional Public Adjuster (SPPA) designations. For claims examiners in the life and health insurance industries, the International Claim Association offers the Associate, Life and Health Claims (ALHC) and the Fellow, Life and Health Claims (FLHC). Most designations require at least 5 to 10 years' experience in the claims field, passing examinations, and earning a certain number of CE credits a year.

Auto damage appraisers typically begin as auto-body repair workers, and then get hired by insurance companies or independent adjusting firms. While auto-body workers do not require a college education, most companies require at least a bachelor's degree. Only four states require auto damage appraisers to be licensed. Like adjusters and examiners, continuing education is very important because of the introduction of new car models and repair techniques. The Independent Automotive Damage Appraisers Association provides seminars and training sessions in different aspects of auto damage appraising.

Most insurance companies prefer to hire former law enforcement officers or private investigators as insurance investigators. Many experienced claims adjusters or examiners also can become investigators. Licensing requirements vary among states. Most employers look for individuals with ingenuity, who are persistent and assertive. Investigators must not be afraid of confrontation, should communicate well, and should be able to think on their feet. Good interviewing and interrogation skills also are important and usually are acquired in earlier careers in law enforcement.

Beginning claims adjusters, appraisers, examiners, and investigators work on small claims under the supervision of an experienced worker. As they learn more about claims investigation and settlement, they are assigned larger, more complex claims. Trainees are promoted as they demonstrate competence in handling assignments and progress in their coursework. Employees who demonstrate competence in claims work or administrative skills may be promoted to claims approver or claims manager. Similarly, claims investigators may rise to supervisor or manager of the investigations department. Once they achieve a certain level of expertise, many choose to start their own independent adjusting or auto-damage appraising firms.

Job Outlook

Employment of claims adjusters, appraisers, examiners, and investigators is expected to grow about as fast as the average for all occupations over the 2000–2010 period. Opportunities will be best in the areas of property and casualty insurance, and health insurance. Many job openings also will result from the need to replace workers who transfer to other occupations or leave the labor force.

Many insurance carriers are downsizing their claims staff in an effort to contain costs. Larger companies are relying more on Customer Service Representatives in call centers to handle the recording of the necessary details of the claim, allowing adjusters to spend more of their time investigating claims. New technology also is reducing the amount of time it takes for an adjuster to complete a claim, therefore increasing the number of claims one adjuster can handle. However, so long as insurance policies are being sold, there will be a need for adjusters, appraisers, examiners, and investigators. Despite recent gains in productivity resulting from technological advances, these jobs are not easily automated.

Adjusters still are needed to contact policyholders, inspect damaged property, and consult with experts. The greatest demand for adjusters will be in the property and casualty field, as well as in health insurance. An increase in the number of auto and homeowners policies sold eventually will result in more claims. As federal and state laws require health insurers to accept more applicants for insurance coverage, the number of policies sold will increase. And as the population ages, there will be a greater need for healthcare, resulting in more claims.

Demand for insurance investigators should grow along with the number of claims in litigation and the number and complexity of insurance fraud cases. Competition for investigator jobs will remain keen, however, because this occupation attracts many qualified people, including retirees from law enforcement and military careers. Many claims adjusters and examiners also choose to get their investigator license.

Like that of claims adjusters, examiners, and investigators, employment of auto damage appraisers should grow about as fast as the average for all occupations. Insurance companies and agents are selling more auto insurance policies, which eventually will lead to more claims being filed that will require the attention of an auto damage appraiser. This occupation is not easily automated, because most appraisal jobs require an onsite inspection. However, industry downsizing and the implementation of new technology that increases the efficiency of auto-damage appraisers will limit employment growth.

Earnings

Earnings of claims adjusters, examiners, and investigators vary significantly. Median annual earnings were $41,080 in 2000. The middle 50 percent earned between $31,960 and $54,300. The lowest 10 percent earned less than $25,860, and the highest 10 percent earned more than $68,130.

Claims adjusters and appraisers working for insurance companies tend to earn slightly higher average earnings than independent adjusters do because the former have a steady income. Independent adjusters receive a percentage of the insurance company's settlement with its clients. This can result in irregular income. Many claims adjusters receive additional bonuses or benefits as part of their job. Adjusters often are furnished a laptop computer, a cellular telephone, and a company car or are reimbursed for use of their own vehicle for business purposes.

Median annual earnings of auto damage insurance appraisers were $40,000 in 2000. The middle 50 percent earned between $31,900 and $49,170. The lowest 10 percent earned less than $25,030, and the highest 10 percent earned more than $56,330.

Related Occupations

Insurance adjusters and examiners must determine the validity of a claim and negotiate a settlement. They also are responsible for determining how much to reimburse the client. Similar occupations include cost estimators, bill and account collectors, medical records and health information technicians, billing and posting clerks, and bookkeeping, accounting, and auditing clerks.

When determining the validity of a claim, insurance adjusters must inspect the damage in order to assess the magnitude of the loss. Workers who perform similar duties include fire inspectors and investigators, and construction and building inspectors.

Insurance investigators detect and investigate fraudulent claims and criminal activity. Their work is similar to that of detective and criminal investigators and of private detectives and investigators.

Like automotive body and related repairers and automotive service technicians and mechanics, auto damage appraisers must be familiar with the structure and functions of different automobiles and parts.

Other insurance-related occupations include insurance sales agents and insurance underwriters.

Sources of Additional Information

General information about a career as a claims adjuster, appraiser, examiner, or investigator is available from the home offices of many life, health, and property and casualty insurance companies.

Information about licensing requirements for claim adjusters may be obtained from the department of insurance in each state.

For information about the Associate in Claims (AIC) designation, or the Introduction to Claims program, contact:

- Insurance Institute of America, 720 Providence Rd., P.O. Box 3016, Malvern, PA 19355-0716. Internet: http://www.aicpcu.org

For information on the Certified Professional Public Adjuster (CPPA) and the Senior Professional Public Adjuster (SPPA) programs, contact:

● National Association of Public Insurance Adjusters, 112-J Elden St., Herndon, VA 20170. Internet: http://www.napia.com

For information on the Registered Professional Adjuster (RPA) designation, contact:

● Registered Professional Adjusters, Inc., P.O. Box 3239, Napa, CA 94558. Internet: http://www.rpa-adjuster.com

For information on the Associate, Life and Health Claims (ALHC) and the Fellow, Life and Health Claims (FLHC) programs, contact:

● International Claim Association, 1255 23rd St. NW, Washington, DC 20037. Internet: http://www.claim.org

Information on careers in auto damage appraising can be obtained from:

● Independent Automotive Damage Appraisers Association, P.O. Box 1166, Nixa, MO 65714. Internet: http://www.iada.org

Clinical Laboratory Technologists and Technicians

O*NET 29-2011.00, 29-2012.00

Significant Points

● Clinical laboratory technologists usually have a bachelor's degree with a major in medical technology or in one of the life sciences; clinical laboratory technicians need either an associate degree or a certificate.

● Employment is expected to grow as fast as average as the volume of laboratory tests increases with population growth and the development of new types of tests.

Nature of the Work

Clinical laboratory testing plays a crucial role in the detection, diagnosis, and treatment of disease. Clinical laboratory technologists, also referred to as *clinical laboratory scientists* or *medical technologists*, and clinical laboratory technicians, also known as *medical technicians* or *medical laboratory technicians*, perform most of these tests.

Clinical laboratory personnel examine and analyze body fluids, tissues, and cells. They look for bacteria, parasites, and other microorganisms; analyze the chemical content of fluids; match blood for transfusions; and test for drug levels in the blood to show how a patient is responding to treatment. These technologists also prepare specimens for examination, count cells, and look for abnormal cells. They use automated equipment and instruments capable of performing a number of tests simultaneously, as well as microscopes, cell counters, and other sophisticated laboratory equipment. Then, they analyze the results and relay them to physicians. With increasing automation and the use of computer technology, the work of technologists and technicians has become less hands-on and more analytical.

The complexity of tests performed, the level of judgment needed, and the amount of responsibility workers assume depend largely on the amount of education and experience they have.

Medical and clinical laboratory technologists generally have a bachelor's degree in medical technology or in one of the life sciences, or they have a combination of formal training and work experience. They perform complex chemical, biological, hematological, immunologic, microscopic, and bacteriological tests. Technologists microscopically examine blood, tissue, and other body substances. They make cultures of body fluid and tissue samples, to determine the presence of bacteria, fungi, parasites, or other microorganisms. They analyze samples for chemical content or reaction and determine blood glucose and cholesterol levels. They also type and cross match blood samples for transfusions.

Medical and clinical laboratory technologists evaluate test results, develop and modify procedures, and establish and monitor programs, to ensure the accuracy of tests. Some medical and clinical laboratory technologists supervise medical and clinical laboratory technicians.

Technologists in small laboratories perform many types of tests, whereas those in large laboratories generally specialize. Technologists who prepare specimens and analyze the chemical and hormonal contents of body fluids are *clinical chemistry technologists*. Those who examine and identify bacteria and other microorganisms are *microbiology technologists*. *Blood bank technologists*, or *immunohematology technologists*, collect, type, and prepare blood and its components for transfusions. *Immunology technologists* examine elements and responses of the human immune system to foreign bodies. *Cytotechnologists* prepare slides of body cells and microscopically examine these cells for abnormalities that may signal the beginning of a cancerous growth. *Molecular biology technologists* perform complex genetic testing on cell samples.

Medical and clinical laboratory technicians perform less complex tests and laboratory procedures than technologists. Technicians may prepare specimens and operate automated analyzers, for example, or they may perform manual tests following detailed instructions. Like technologists, they may work in several areas of the clinical laboratory or specialize in just one. *Histology technicians* cut and stain tissue specimens for microscopic examination by pathologists, and *phlebotomists* collect blood samples. They usually work under the supervision of medical and clinical laboratory technologists or laboratory managers.

Working Conditions

Hours and other working conditions of clinical laboratory technologists and technicians vary, according to the size and type of employment setting. In large hospitals or in independent laboratories that operate continuously, personnel usually work the day, evening, or night shift and may work weekends and holidays. Laboratory personnel in small facilities may work on rotating shifts, rather than on a regular shift. In some facilities, laboratory personnel are on call several nights a week or on weekends, in case of an emergency.

Clinical laboratory personnel are trained to work with infectious specimens. When proper methods of infection control and sterilization are followed, few hazards exist. Protective masks, gloves, and goggles are often necessary to ensure the safety of laboratory personnel.

Laboratories usually are well lighted and clean; however, specimens, solutions, and reagents used in the laboratory sometimes produce fumes. Laboratory workers may spend a great deal of time on their feet.

Employment

Clinical laboratory technologists and technicians held about 295,000 jobs in 2000. About half worked in hospitals. Most of the remaining jobs were found in medical laboratories or offices and clinics of physicians. A small number were in blood banks, research and testing laboratories, and in the federal government at U.S. Department of Veterans Affairs hospitals and U.S. Public Health Service facilities.

Training, Other Qualifications, and Advancement

The usual requirement for an entry-level position as a medical or clinical laboratory technologist is a bachelor's degree with a major in medical technology or in one of the life sciences. Universities and hospitals offer medical technology programs. It also is possible to qualify through a combination of education, on-the-job, and specialized training.

Bachelor's degree programs in medical technology include courses in chemistry, biological sciences, microbiology, mathematics, statistics, and specialized courses devoted to knowledge and skills used in the clinical laboratory. Many programs also offer or require courses in management, business, and computer applications. The Clinical Laboratory Improvement Act (CLIA) requires technologists who perform certain highly complex tests to have at least an associate degree.

Medical and clinical laboratory technicians generally have either an associate degree from a community or junior college or a certificate from a hospital, vocational or technical school, or from one of the U.S. Armed Forces. A few technicians learn their skills on the job.

The National Accrediting Agency for Clinical Laboratory Sciences (NAACLS) fully accredits 503 programs for medical and clinical laboratory technologists, medical and clinical laboratory technicians, histologic technologists and technicians, and pathologists' assistants. NAACLS also approves 70 programs in phlebotomy, cytogenetic technology, molecular biology, and clinical assisting. Other nationally recognized accrediting agencies include the Commission on Accreditation of Allied Health Education Programs (CAAHEP) and the Accrediting Bureau of Health Education Schools (ABHES).

Some states require laboratory personnel to be licensed or registered. Information on licensure is available from state departments of health or boards of occupational licensing. Certification is a voluntary process by which a nongovernmental organization, such as a professional society or certifying agency, grants recognition to an individual whose professional competence meets prescribed standards. Widely accepted by employers in the health industry, certification is a prerequisite for most jobs and often is necessary for advancement. Agencies certifying medical and clinical laboratory technologists and technicians include the Board of Registry of the American Society for Clinical Pathology, the American Medical Technologists, the National Credentialing Agency for Laboratory Personnel, and the Board of Registry of the American Association of Bioanalysts. These agencies have different requirements for certification and different organizational sponsors.

Clinical laboratory personnel need good analytical judgment and the ability to work under pressure. Close attention to detail is essential, because small differences or changes in test substances or numerical readouts can be crucial for patient care. Manual dexterity and normal color vision are highly desirable. With the widespread use of automated laboratory equipment, computer skills are important. In addition, technologists in particular are expected to be good at problem solving.

Technologists may advance to supervisory positions in laboratory work or become chief medical or clinical laboratory technologists or laboratory managers in hospitals. Manufacturers of home diagnostic testing kits and laboratory equipment and supplies seek experienced technologists to work in product development, marketing, and sales. Graduate education in medical technology, one of the biological sciences, chemistry, management, or education usually speeds advancement. A doctorate is needed to become a laboratory director. However, federal regulation allows directors of moderate complexity laboratories to have either a master's degree or a bachelor's degree combined with the appropriate amount of training and experience. Technicians can become technologists through additional education and experience.

Job Outlook

Employment of clinical laboratory workers is expected to grow about as fast as the average for all occupations through the year 2010, as the volume of laboratory tests increases with population growth and the development of new types of tests.

Technological advances will continue to have two opposing effects on employment through 2010. New, increasingly powerful diagnostic tests will encourage additional testing and spur employment. On the other hand, research and development efforts targeted at simplifying routine testing procedures may enhance the ability of nonlaboratory personnel, physicians and patients, in particular, to perform tests now done in laboratories.

Although significant, growth will not be the only source of opportunities. As in most occupations, many openings will result from the need to replace workers who transfer to other occupations, retire, or stop working for some other reason.

Earnings

Median annual earnings of medical and clinical laboratory technologists were $40,510 in 2000. The middle 50 percent earned between $34,220 and $47,460. The lowest 10 percent earned less than $29,240, and the highest 10 percent earned more than $55,560. Median annual earnings in the industries employing the largest numbers of medical and clinical laboratory technologists in 2000 were as follows:

Hospitals	$40,840
Medical and dental laboratories	39,780
Offices and clinics of medical doctors	38,850

Median annual earnings of medical and clinical laboratory technicians were $27,540 in 2000. The middle 50 percent earned between $22,260 and $34,320. The lowest 10 percent earned less than $18,550, and the highest 10 percent earned more than $42,370. Median annual earnings in the industries employing the largest numbers of medical and clinical laboratory technicians in 2000 were as follows:

Hospitals	$28,860
Colleges and universities	27,810
Offices and clinics of medical doctors	27,180
Medical and dental laboratories	25,250
Health and allied health services, not elsewhere classified	24,370

Related Occupations

Clinical laboratory technologists and technicians analyze body fluids, tissue, and other substances using a variety of tests. Similar or related procedures are performed by chemists and material scientists, science technicians, and veterinary technologists, technicians, and assistants.

Sources of Additional Information

For a list of accredited and approved educational programs for clinical laboratory personnel, contact:

- National Accrediting Agency for Clinical Laboratory Sciences, 8410 W. Bryn Mawr Ave., Suite 670, Chicago, IL 60631. Internet: http://www.naacls.org

Information on certification is available from:

- American Association of Bioanalysts, 917 Locust St., Suite 1100, St. Louis, MO 63101. Internet: http://www.aab.org

- American Medical Technologists, 710 Higgins Rd., Park Ridge, IL 60068

- American Society for Clinical Pathology, Board of Registry, 2100 West Harrison St., Chicago, IL 60612. Internet: http://www.ascp.org/bor

- National Credentialing Agency for Laboratory Personnel, P.O. Box 15945-289, Lenexa, KS 66285-5935. Internet: http://www.nca-info.org

Additional career information is available from:

- American Association of Blood Banks, 8101 Glenbrook Rd., Bethesda, MD 20814-2749. Internet: http://www.aabb.org

- American Society for Clinical Laboratory Science, 7910 Woodmont Ave., Suite 530, Bethesda, MD 20814. Internet: http://www.ascls.org

- American Society for Clinical Pathology, 2100 West Harrison St., Chicago, IL 60612. Internet: http://www.ascp.org

Coin, Vending, and Amusement Machine Servicers and Repairers

O*NET 49-9091.00

Significant Points

- Most workers learn their skills on the job.

- Opportunities should be good for persons with some knowledge of electronics.

Nature of the Work

Coin, vending, and amusement machines are a familiar sight in offices, convenience stores, arcades, or casinos. These coin-operated machines give out change, dispense refreshments, test our senses, and spit out lottery tickets nearly everywhere we turn. Coin, vending, and amuse-ment machine servicers and repairers install, service, and stock these machines and keep them in good working order.

Vending machine servicers, often called route drivers, visit machines that dispense soft drinks, candy and snacks, and other items. They collect money from the machines, restock merchandise, and change labels to indicate new selections. They also keep the machines clean and appealing.

Vending machine repairers, often called mechanics or technicians, make sure machines operate correctly. When checking complicated electrical and electronic machines, such as beverage dispensers, they make sure that the machines mix drinks properly and that refrigeration and heat-ing units work correctly. On the relatively simple gravity-operated ma-chines, servicers check keypads, motors, and merchandise chutes. They also test coin, bill, and change-making mechanisms.

When installing machines, vending machine repairers make the neces-sary water and electrical connections and check the machines for proper operation. They also make sure installation complies with local plumb-ing and electrical codes. Because many vending machines dispense food, these workers, along with vending machine servicers, must comply with state and local public health and sanitation standards.

Amusement machine servicers and repairers work on jukeboxes, video games, pinball machines, and slot machines. They make sure that the various levers, joysticks, and mechanisms function properly, so that the games remain fair and the jukebox selections are accurate. They update selec-tions, repair or replace malfunctioning parts, and rebuild existing equip-ment. Those who work in the gaming industry must adhere to strict guidelines, because federal and state agencies regulate many gaming machines.

Preventive maintenance—avoiding trouble before it starts—is a major job of repairers. For example, they periodically clean refrigeration con-densers, lubricate mechanical parts, and adjust machines to perform properly.

If a machine breaks down, vending and amusement machine repairers inspect it for obvious problems, such as loose electrical wires, malfunc-tions of the coin mechanism or bill validator, and leaks. When servicing electronic machines, repairers test them with hand-held diagnostic com-puters that determine the extent and location of any problem. Repairers may only have to replace a circuit board or other component to fix the problem. However, if the problem cannot be readily located, these work-ers refer to technical manuals and wiring diagrams and use testing de-vices, such as electrical circuit testers, to find defective parts. Repairers decide if they must replace a part and whether they can fix the malfunc-tion onsite, or if they have to send the machine to the repair shop.

In the repair shop, vending and amusement machine repairers use power tools, such as grinding wheels, saws, and drills, as well as voltmeters, ohmmeters, oscilloscopes, and other testing equipment. They also use ordinary repair tools, such as screwdrivers, pliers, and wrenches.

Vending machine servicers and repairers employed by small companies may both fill and fix machines on a regular basis. These combination servicers-repairers stock machines, collect money, fill coin and currency changers, and repair machines when necessary.

Servicers and repairers also do some paperwork, such as filing reports, preparing repair cost estimates, ordering parts, and keeping daily records of merchandise distributed and money collected. However, new ma-chines with computerized inventory controls reduce the paperwork that a servicer must complete.

Working Conditions

Some vending and amusement machine repairers work primarily in company repair shops, but many spend substantial time on the road visiting machines wherever they have been placed. Repairers generally work a total of 40 hours a week. However, vending and amusement machines operate around the clock, so repairers may be on call to work at night and on weekends and holidays.

Vending and amusement machine repair shops generally are quiet, well-lighted, and have adequate workspace. However, when servicing machines on location, the work may be done where pedestrian traffic is heavy, such as in busy supermarkets, industrial complexes, offices, casinos, or arcades. Repair work is relatively safe, although servicers and repairers must take care to avoid hazards such as electrical shocks and cuts from sharp tools and other metal objects. They also must follow safe work procedures, especially when moving heavy vending and amusement machines.

Employment

Coin, vending, and amusement machine servicers and repairers held about 37,000 jobs in 2000. Most repairers work for vending companies that sell food and other items through machines. Others work for soft drink bottling companies that have their own coin-operated machines. A growing number of servicers and repairers work for amusement establishments that own video games, pinball machines, jukeboxes, slot machines, and similar types of amusement equipment. Although vending and amusement machine servicers and repairers are employed throughout the country, most are located in areas with large populations and, thus, many vending and amusement machines.

Training, Other Qualifications, and Advancement

Most workers learn their skills on the job. New workers are trained to fill and fix machines informally on the job by observing, working with, and receiving instruction from experienced repairers. Employers normally prefer to hire high school graduates; high school or vocational school courses in electricity, refrigeration, and machine repair are an advantage in qualifying for entry-level jobs. Employers usually require applicants to demonstrate mechanical ability, either through work experience or by scoring well on mechanical aptitude tests.

Because coin, vending, and amusement machine servicers and repairers sometimes handle thousands of dollars in merchandise and cash, employers hire persons who seem to have a record of honesty. Also, the ability to deal tactfully with people is important because the servicers and repairers play a significant role in relaying customer requests and concerns. A driver's license and a good driving record are essential for most vending and amusement machine servicer and repairer jobs. Some employers require their servicers to be bonded.

As electronics become more prevalent in vending and amusement machines, employers will increasingly prefer applicants who have some training in electronics. Technologically advanced machines with features such as multilevel pricing, inventory control, and scrolling messages use electronics and microchip computers extensively. Some vocational high schools and junior colleges offer 1- to 2-year training programs in basic electronics.

Beginners start training with simple jobs, such as cleaning or stocking machines. They then learn to rebuild machines by removing defective parts, and repairing, adjusting, and testing the machines. Next, they accompany an experienced repairer on service calls, and finally make visits on their own. This learning process takes from 6 months to 2 years, depending on the individual's abilities, previous education, types of machines serviced, and quality of instruction.

The National Automatic Merchandising Association has a self-study technicians training program for vending machine repairers. Repairers use manuals for instruction in subjects such as customer relations, safety, electronics, and schematic reading. Upon completion of the program, repairers must pass a written test to become certified as a technician or journeyman.

To learn about new machines, repairers and servicers sometimes attend training sessions sponsored by manufacturers and machine distributors that may last from a few days to several weeks. Both trainees and experienced workers sometimes take evening courses in basic electricity, electronics, microwave ovens, refrigeration, and other related subjects to stay on top of new techniques and equipment. Skilled servicers and repairers may be promoted to supervisory jobs or go into business for themselves.

Job Outlook

Job openings for coin, vending, and amusement machine servicers and repairers will arise from employment growth and from the need to replace experienced workers who transfer to other occupations or leave the labor force. Opportunities should be good for persons with some knowledge of electronics, because electronic circuitry is an important component of vending and amusement machines. If firms cannot find trained or experienced workers for these jobs, they are likely to train qualified route drivers or hire inexperienced people who have acquired some mechanical, electrical, or electronics training by taking high school or vocational courses.

Employment of coin, vending, and amusement machine servicers and repairers is expected to grow about as fast as the average for all occupations through the year 2010 because of the increasing number of vending and amusement machines in operation. Establishments are likely to install additional vending machines in industrial plants, hospitals, stores, and schools to meet the public demand for inexpensive snacks and other food items. Also, there is an increased need for vending machines in businesses with few employees. The range of products dispensed by the machines is expected to increase, as vending machines continue to become increasingly automated and begin to incorporate microwave ovens, mini refrigerators, and freezers. In addition, casinos, arcades, and other amusement establishments are an increasing source of entertainment. Also, state and multistate lotteries are increasingly using coin-operated machines to sell scratch-off tickets in grocery stores and other public places. Furthermore, circuit boards in many vending machines must be either replaced or reprogrammed so that the machines can accept the new $5 and $10 bills, increasing the need for servicers and repairers.

Improved technology in newer machines will moderate employment growth because these machines require maintenance less frequently than do older ones. These new machines will need repairing and restocking less often, and contain computers that record sales and inventory data, reducing the amount of time-consuming paperwork. The Internet is beginning to play a large role in the monitoring of vending machines from remote locations. Additionally, some new machines use wireless data transmitters to signal the vending machine company when the machine needs restocking or repairing. This allows servicers and repairers to be dispatched only when needed, instead of having to check each machine on a regular schedule.

Earnings

Median hourly earnings of coin, vending, and amusement machine servicers and repairers were $12.33 in 2000. The middle 50 percent earned between $9.18 and $15.78 an hour. The lowest 10 percent earned less than $7.06 an hour, and the highest 10 percent earned more than $19.51 an hour. Median hourly earnings of coin, vending, and amusement machine servicers and repairers were $11.24 and $10.49 in miscellaneous amusement and recreation services and nonstore retailers, respectively, in 2000. Typically, states with some form of legalized gaming have the highest wages.

Most coin, vending, and amusement machine servicers and repairers work 8 hours a day, 5 days a week, and receive premium pay for overtime. Some union contracts stipulate higher pay for night work and for emergency repair jobs on weekends and holidays than for regular hours. Some vending machine repairers and servicers are members of the International Brotherhood of Teamsters.

Related Occupations

Other workers who repair equipment with electrical and electronic components include electrical and electronics installers and repairers; electronic home-entertainment equipment installers and repairers; heating, air-conditioning, and refrigeration mechanics and installers; and home appliance repairers.

Sources of Additional Information

Information on job opportunities in this field can be obtained from local vending machine firms and local offices of your state employment service. For general information on vending machine repair, write to:

- National Automatic Merchandising Association, 20 N. Wacker Dr., Suite 3500, Chicago, IL 60606-3102. Internet: http://www.vending.org

- Automatic Merchandiser Vending Group, Cygnus Business Media, P.O. Box 803, 1233 Janesville Ave., Fort Atkinson, WI 53538-0803

Communications Equipment Operators

O*NET 43-2011.00, 43-2021.01, 43-2021.02, 43-2099.99

Significant Points

- Switchboard operators constitute 3 out of 4 of these workers.

- Workers train on the job.

- Employment is expected to decline due to new laborsaving communications technologies and consolidation of jobs.

Nature of the Work

Most communications equipment operators work as *switchboard operators* for a wide variety of businesses, such as hospitals, hotels, and personnel-supply services. Switchboard operators operate private branch exchange (PBX) switchboards to relay incoming, outgoing, and interoffice calls, usually for a single organization. They also may handle other clerical duties, such as supplying information, taking messages, and announcing visitors. Technological improvements have automated many of the tasks handled by switchboard operators. New systems automatically connect outside calls to the correct destination, and voice mail systems take messages without the assistance of an operator.

Some communications equipment operators work as *telephone operators*, assisting customers in making telephone calls. Although most calls are connected automatically, callers sometimes require the assistance of an operator. *Central office operators* help customers complete local and long-distance calls. *Directory assistance operators* provide customers with information such as phone numbers or area codes.

When callers dial "0," they usually reach a central office operator, also known as a *local*, *long distance*, or *call completion operator*. Most of these operators work for telephone companies, and many of their responsibilities have been automated. For example, callers can make international, collect, and credit card calls without the assistance of a central office operator. Other tasks previously handled by these operators, such as billing calls to third parties or monitoring the cost of a call, also have been automated.

Callers still need a central office operator for a limited number of tasks. These include placing person-to-person calls or interrupting busy lines if an emergency warrants the disruption. When natural disasters occur, such as storms or earthquakes, central office operators provide callers with emergency phone contacts. They also assist callers having difficulty with automated phone systems. An operator monitoring an automated system for placing collect calls, for example, may intervene if a caller needs assistance with the system.

Directory assistance operators provide callers with information such as telephone numbers or area codes. Most directory assistance operators work for telephone companies; increasingly, they also work for companies that provide business services. Automated systems now handle many of the responsibilities once performed by directory assistance operators. The systems prompt callers for a listing, and may even connect the call after providing the phone number. However, directory assistance operators monitor many of the calls received by automated systems. The operators listen to recordings of the customer's request, and then key information into electronic directories to access the correct phone numbers. Directory assistance operators also provide personal assistance to customers having difficulty using the automated system.

Other communications equipment operators include workers who operate telegraphic typewriter, telegraph key, facsimile machine, and related equipment to transmit and receive signals and messages. They prepare messages according to prescribed formats, and verify and correct errors in messages. As part of their job, they also may adjust equipment for proper operation.

Working Conditions

Most communications equipment operators work in pleasant, well-lighted surroundings. Because telephone operators spend much time seated at keyboards and video monitors, employers often provide work-stations designed to decrease glare and other physical discomforts. Such improvements reduce the incidence of eyestrain, back discomfort, and injury due to repetitive motion.

Switchboard operators generally work the same hours as other clerical employees at their company. In most organizations, full-time operators work regular business hours over a 5-day workweek. Work schedules are more irregular in hotels, hospitals, and other organizations that require round-the-clock operator services. In these companies, switchboard operators may work in the evenings and on holidays and weekends.

Central office and directory assistance operators must be accessible to customers 24 hours a day and, therefore, work a variety of shifts. Some operators work split shifts; that is, they are on duty during peak calling periods in the late morning and early evening and off duty during the intervening hours. Telephone companies normally assign shifts by seniority, allowing the most experienced operators first choice of schedules. As a result, entry-level operators may have less desirable schedules, including late evening, split-shift, and weekend work. Telephone company operators may work overtime during emergencies.

Approximately 1 in 5 communications equipment operators works part-time. Because of the irregular nature of telephone operator schedules, many employers seek part-time workers for those shifts that are difficult to fill.

An operator's work may be quite repetitive and the pace hectic during peak calling periods. To maintain operator efficiency, supervisors at telephone companies often monitor operator performance, including the amount of time spent on each call. The rapid pace of the job and frequent monitoring may cause stress. To reduce job-related stress, some workplaces attempt to create a more stimulating and less rigid work environment.

Employment

Communications equipment operators held about 339,000 jobs in 2000. About 3 out of 4 worked as switchboard operators. Employment was distributed as follows:

Switchboard operators	259,000
Telephone operators	54,000
All other communications equipment operators	26,000

Most switchboard operators worked for services establishments, such as personnel-supply services, hospitals, and hotels and motels.

Training, Other Qualifications, and Advancement

Communications equipment operators receive their training on the job. At large telephone companies, entry-level central office and directory assistance operators may receive both classroom and on-the-job instruction that can last several weeks. At small telephone companies, operators usually receive shorter, less formal training. These operators may be paired with experienced personnel who provide hands-on instruction. Switchboard operators also may receive short-term, informal training, sometimes provided by the manufacturer of their switchboard equipment.

New employees train in equipment operation and procedures designed to maximize efficiency. They are familiarized with company policies, including the expected level of customer service. Instructors monitor both the time and quality of trainees' responses to customer requests. Supervisors may continue to closely monitor new employees after their initial training session is complete.

Employers generally require a high school diploma for operator positions. Applicants should have strong reading, spelling, and numerical skills; clear speech; and good hearing. Computer literacy and typing skills also are important, and familiarity with a foreign language is helpful because of the increasing diversity of the population. Most companies emphasize customer service skills. They seek operators who will remain courteous to customers while working at a fast pace.

After 1 or 2 years on the job, communications equipment operators may advance to other positions within a company. Many enter clerical occupations in which their operator experience is valuable, such as customer service representatives, dispatchers, and receptionists. Operators with a more technical background may advance into positions installing and repairing equipment. Promotion to supervisory positions also is possible.

Job Outlook

Employment of communications equipment operators is projected to decline through 2010, largely due to new laborsaving communications technologies and to consolidation of telephone operator jobs into fewer locations, often staffed by personnel-supply services firms. Virtually all job openings will result from the need to replace communications equipment operators who transfer to other occupations or leave the labor force.

Developments in communications technologies, specifically the ease and accessibility of voice recognition systems, will continue to have a significant impact on the demand for communications equipment operators. The decline in employment will be sharpest among directory assistance operators; smaller decreases will occur for switchboard operators. Voice recognition technology allows automated phone systems to recognize human speech. Callers speak directly to the system, which interprets the speech and then connects the call. Because voice recognition systems do not require callers to input data on a telephone keypad, they are easier to use than touch-tone systems. The systems also can understand increasingly sophisticated vocabulary and grammatical structures; however, many companies will continue to employ operators so that those callers having problems can access a "live" employee, if desired.

Electronic communications through the Internet or e-mail, for example, provides alternatives to telephone communications and requires no operators. Internet directory assistance services are reducing the need for directory assistance operators. Local phone companies currently have the most reliable phone directory data; however, Internet services provide information such as addresses and maps, in addition to phone numbers. As telephones and computers converge, the convenience of Internet directory assistance is expected to attract many customers, reducing the need for telephone operators to provide this service.

Consolidations among telephone companies also will reduce the need for operators. As communications technologies improve and long-distance prices fall, telephone companies will contract out and consolidate telephone operator jobs. Operators will be employed at fewer locations and will serve larger customer populations.

Earnings

Median hourly earnings of switchboard operators, including answering service, were $9.71 in 2000. The middle 50 percent earned between $8.02 and $11.71. The lowest 10 percent earned less than $6.87, and the highest 10 percent earned more than $13.76. Median hourly earnings in the industries employing the largest numbers of switchboard operators in 2000 are shown in the following:

Offices and clinics of medical doctors	$9.74
Hospitals	9.54
Hotels and motels	9.16
Personnel supply services	9.02
Miscellaneous business services	8.66

Median hourly earnings of telephone operators in 2000 were $13.46. The middle 50 percent earned between $9.40 and $16.76. The lowest 10 percent earned less than $7.23, and the highest 10 percent earned more than $19.57.

Some telephone operators working at telephone companies are members of the Communications Workers of America (CWA) or the International Brotherhood of Electrical Workers (IBEW). For these operators, union contracts govern wage rates, wage increases, and the time required to advance from one pay step to the next. (It normally takes 4 years to rise from the lowest paying, nonsupervisory operator position to the highest.) Contracts also call for extra pay for work beyond the normal 6 1/2 to 7 1/2 hours a day or 5 days a week, for Sunday and holiday work, and for a pay differential for night work and split shifts. Many contracts provide for a 1-week vacation after 6 months of service; 2 weeks after 1 year; 3 weeks after 7 years; 4 weeks after 15 years; and 5 weeks after 25 years. Holidays range from 9 to 11 days a year.

Related Occupations

Other workers who provide information to the general public include dispatchers; hotel, motel, and resort desk clerks; information and record clerks; and reservation and transportation ticket agents and travel clerks.

Sources of Additional Information

For more details about employment opportunities, contact a telephone company, temporary-help agency, or write to:

- Communications Workers of America, 501 3rd St. NW., Washington, DC 20001. Internet: http://www.cwa-union.org

- International Brotherhood of Electrical Workers, Telecommunications Department, 1125 15th St. NW., Room 807, Washington, DC 20005

Computer and Information Systems Managers

O*NET 11-3021.00

Significant Points

- Projected job growth stems primarily from rapid growth among computer-related occupations.

- Employers prefer managers with advanced technical knowledge acquired through computer-related work experience and formal education.

- Job opportunities should be best for applicants with a master's degree in business administration with technology as a core component.

Nature of the Work

The need for organizations to incorporate existing and future technologies in order to remain competitive has become a more pressing issue over the last several years. As electronic commerce becomes more common, how and when companies use technology are critical issues. Computer and information systems managers play a vital role in the technological direction of their organizations. They do everything from constructing the business plan to overseeing network and Internet operations.

Computer and information systems managers plan, coordinate, and direct research and design the computer-related activities of firms. They determine technical goals in consultation with top management, and make detailed plans for the accomplishment of these goals. For example, working with their staff, they may develop the overall concepts of a new product or identify computer-related problems standing in the way of project completion.

Computer and information systems managers direct the work of systems analysts, computer programmers, support specialists, and other computer-related workers. These managers plan and coordinate activities such as the installation and upgrading of hardware and software, programming and systems design, the development of computer networks, and the implementation of Internet and intranet sites. They are increasingly involved with the upkeep and maintenance of networks. They analyze the computer and information needs of their organization and determine personnel and equipment requirements. They assign and review the work of their subordinates, and stay abreast of the latest technology in order to purchase necessary equipment.

The duties of computer and information systems managers vary with their specific titles. Chief technology officers, for example, evaluate the newest and most innovative technologies and determine how these can help their organization. The chief technology officer, who often reports to the organization's chief information officer, manages and plans technical standards and tends to the daily information technology issues of their firm. Because of the rapid pace of technological change, chief technology officers must constantly be on the lookout for developments that could benefit their organization. They are responsible for demonstrating to a company how information technology can be used as a competitive weapon that not only cuts costs, but also increases revenue.

Management of information systems (MIS) directors manage information systems and computing resources for entire organizations. They also work under the chief information officer and deal directly with lower-level information technology employees. These managers oversee a variety of user services such as an organization's help desk, which employees can call with questions or problems. MIS directors may also make hardware and software upgrade recommendations based on their experience with an organization's technology.

Computer and information system managers need strong communication skills. They coordinate the activities of their unit with those of other units or organizations. They confer with top executives; financial, production, marketing, and other managers; and contractors and equipment and materials suppliers.

Working Conditions

Computer and information systems managers spend most of their time in an office. Most work at least 40 hours a week and may have to work evenings and weekends to meet deadlines or solve unexpected problems. Some computer and information systems managers may experience considerable pressure in meeting technical goals within short timeframes or tight budgets. As networks continue to expand and more work is done remotely, computer and information system managers have to communicate with and oversee offsite employees using modems, laptops, e-mail, and the Internet.

Like other workers who sit continuously in front of a keyboard, computer and information system managers are susceptible to eyestrain, back discomfort, and hand and wrist problems such as carpal tunnel syndrome.

Employment

Computer and information systems managers held about 313,000 jobs in 2000. About 2 in 5 works in services industries, primarily for firms providing computer and data processing services. Other large employers include insurance and financial services firms, government agencies, and manufacturers.

Training, Other Qualifications, and Advancement

Strong technical knowledge is essential for computer and information systems managers, who must understand and guide the work of their subordinates, yet also explain the work in nontechnical terms to senior management and potential customers. Therefore, these management positions usually require work experience and formal education similar to that of other computer occupations.

Many computer and information systems managers have experience as systems analysts; others may have experience as computer support specialists, programmers, or other information technology professionals. A bachelor's degree is usually required for management positions, although employers often prefer a graduate degree, especially a master's degree in business administration (MBA) with technology as a core component. This degree differs from a traditional MBA in that there is a heavy emphasis on information technology in addition to the standard business curriculum. This becomes important because more computer and information systems managers make not only important technology decisions but also important business decisions for their organizations. A few computer and information systems managers may have only an associate degree, provided they have sufficient experience and were able to learn additional skills on the job.

Computer and information systems managers need a broad range of skills. In addition to technical skills, employers also seek managers with strong business skills. Employers want managers who have experience with the specific software or technology to be used on the job, as well as a background in either consulting or business management. The expansion of electronic commerce has elevated the importance of business insight, because many managers are called upon to make important business decisions. Managers need a keen understanding of people, processes, and customer's needs.

Computer and information systems managers must possess strong interpersonal, communication, and leadership skills because they are required to interact not only with their employees, but also with people inside and outside their organization. They must also possess great team skills to work on group projects and other collaborative efforts. Computer and information systems managers increasingly interact with persons outside their organization, reflecting their emerging role as vital parts of their firm's executive team.

Computer and information systems managers may advance to progressively higher leadership positions in their field. Some may become managers in nontechnical areas such as marketing, human resources, or sales. In high technology firms, managers in nontechnical areas often must possess the same specialized knowledge as do managers in technical areas.

Job Outlook

Employment of computer and information systems managers is expected to increase much faster than the average for all occupations through the year 2010. Technological advancements will increase the employment of computer-related workers; as a result, the demand for managers to direct these workers also will increase. In addition, job openings will result from the need to replace managers who retire or move into other occupations. Opportunities for obtaining a management position will be best for workers possessing an MBA with technology as a core component, advanced technical knowledge, and strong communication and administrative skills.

Rapid growth in employment can be attributed to the explosion in information technology and the fast-paced expansion of the computer and data processing services industry. In order to remain competitive, firms will continue to install sophisticated computer networks and set up more complex Internet and intranet sites. Keeping a computer network running smoothly is essential to almost every organization. Firms will be more willing to hire managers who can accomplish that.

The security of computer networks will continue to increase in importance as more business is conducted over the Internet. Organizations need to understand how their systems are vulnerable and how to protect their infrastructure and Internet sites from hackers, viruses, and other acts of cyber-terrorism. As a result, there will be a high demand for managers proficient in computer security issues.

Due to the explosive growth of electronic commerce and the ability of the Internet to create new relationships with customers, the role of computer and information systems managers will continue to evolve in the future. They will continue to become more vital to their companies and the environments in which they work. The expansion of e-commerce will spur the need for computer and information systems managers with both business savvy and technical proficiency.

Opportunities for those who wish to become computer and information systems managers should be closely related to the growth of the occupations they supervise and the industries in which they are found.

Earnings

Earnings for computer and information systems managers vary by specialty and level of responsibility. Median annual earnings of these managers in 2000 were $78,830. The middle 50 percent earned between $59,640 and $100,820. The lowest 10 percent earned less than $44,090, and the highest 10 percent earned more than $127,460.

According to Robert Half International Consulting, average starting salaries in 2001 for information technology managers ranged from $92,250 to $152,500, depending on the area of specialization. According to a 2001 survey by the National Association of Colleges and Employers, starting salary offers for those with an MBA and a technical undergraduate degree averaged $61,196; for those with a master's degree in management information systems/business data processing, $57,225.

In addition, computer and information systems managers, especially those at higher levels, often receive more benefits—such as expense accounts, stock option plans, and bonuses—than do nonmanagerial workers in their organizations.

Related Occupations

The work of computer and information systems managers is closely related to that of computer programmers, computer software engineers; systems analysts, computer scientists, and database administrators; and computer support specialists and systems administrators. Computer and information systems managers also have some high-level responsibilities similar to those of top executives.

Sources of Additional Information

For information about certification as a computing professional, contact:

- Institute for Certification of Computing Professionals (ICCP), 2350 East Devon Ave., Suite 115, Des Plaines, IL 60018. Internet: http://www.iccp.org

Further information about computer careers is available from:

- Association for Computing Machinery (ACM), 1515 Broadway, New York, NY 10036. Internet: http://www.acm.org

- IEEE Computer Society, Headquarters Office, 1730 Massachusetts Ave. NW., Washington, DC 20036-1992. Internet: http://www.computer.org

- National Workforce Center for Emerging Technologies, 3000 Landerholm Circle SE., Bellevue, WA 98007. Internet: http://www.nwcet.org

- IEEE Computer Society, 1730 Massachusetts Ave. NW., Washington, DC 20036-1992. Internet: http://www.computer.org

Computer, Automated Teller, and Office Machine Repairers

O*NET 49-2011.01, 49-2011.02, 49-2011.03

Significant Points

- Workers receive training in electronics from associate degree programs, the military, vocational schools, equipment manufacturers, or employers.

- Job growth reflects the increasing dependence of business and residential customers on computers and other sophisticated office machines.

- Job prospects will be best for applicants with knowledge of electronics, as well as repair experience; opportunities for computer repairers should be excellent, as employers report difficulty finding qualified applicants.

Nature of the Work

Computer repairers, also known as *data processing equipment repairers*, service mainframe, server, and personal computers; printers; and disc drives. These repairers primarily perform hands-on repair, maintenance, and installation of computers and related equipment. Workers who provide technical assistance, in person or by telephone, to computer system users are known as computer support specialists.

Automated teller machines (ATMs) allow customers to carry out bank transactions without the assistance of a teller. ATMs now provide a growing variety of other services, including stamp, phone card, and ticket sales. *Automated teller machine servicers* repair and service these machines.

Office machine and cash register servicers work on photocopiers, cash registers, mail processing equipment, and fax machines. Newer models of office machinery increasingly include computerized components that allow them to function more effectively than earlier models.

To install large equipment, such as mainframe computers and ATMs, repairers connect the equipment to power sources and communication lines. These lines allow the transmission of information over computer networks. For example, when an ATM dispenses cash, it also transmits the withdrawal information to the customer's bank. Workers also may install operating software and peripheral equipment, checking that all components are configured to correctly function together. The installation of personal computers and other small office machines is less complex and may be handled by the purchaser.

When equipment breaks down, many repairers travel to customers' workplaces or other locations to make the necessary repairs. These workers, known as *field technicians*, often have assigned areas in which they perform preventive maintenance on a regular basis. *Bench technicians* work in repair shops located in stores, factories, or service centers. In small companies, repairers may work in both repair shops and at customer locations.

Computer repairers usually replace defective components instead of repairing them. Replacement is common because components are inexpensive and businesses are reluctant to shut down their computers for time-consuming repairs. Components commonly replaced by computer repairers include video cards, which transmit signals from the computer to the monitor; hard drives, which store data; and network cards, which allow communication over the network. Defective components may be given to bench technicians, who use software programs to diagnose the problem and who may repair the components, if possible.

When ATMs malfunction, computer networks recognize the problem and alert repairers. Common problems include worn magnetic heads on card readers, which prevent the equipment from recognizing customer bankcards; and "pick failures," which prevent the equipment from dispensing the correct amount of cash. Field technicians travel to the locations of ATMs and usually repair equipment by removing and replacing defective components. Broken components are brought to a repair shop where bench technicians perform the necessary repairs. Field technicians perform routine maintenance on a regular basis, replacing worn parts and running diagnostic tests to ensure that the equipment functions properly.

Office machine repairers usually work on machinery at the customer's workplace; customers also may bring small equipment to a repair shop for maintenance. Common malfunctions include paper misfeeds due to worn or dirty parts, and poor copy quality due to problems with lamps, lenses, or mirrors. These malfunctions usually can be resolved simply by cleaning components. Breakdowns also may result from failure of commonly used parts. For example, heavy usage of a photocopier may wear down the printhead, which applies ink to the final copy. In such cases, the repairer usually replaces the part, instead of repairing it.

Workers use a variety of tools for diagnostic tests and repair. To diagnose malfunctions, they use multimeters to measure voltage, current, resistance, and other electrical properties; signal generators to provide test signals; and oscilloscopes to monitor equipment signals. When diagnosing computerized equipment, repairers also use software programs. To repair or adjust equipment, workers use handtools, such as pliers, screwdrivers, soldering irons, and wrenches.

Working Conditions

Repairers usually work in clean, well-lighted surroundings. Because computers and office machines are sensitive to extreme temperatures and to humidity, repair shops usually are air-conditioned and well-ventilated. Field repairers must travel frequently to various locations to install, maintain, or repair customer equipment. ATM repairers may have to perform their jobs in small, confined spaces that house the equipment.

Because computers and ATMs are critical for many organizations to function efficiently, data processing equipment repairers and ATM field technicians often work around the clock. Their schedules may include evening, weekend, and holiday shifts; shifts may be assigned on the basis of seniority. Office machine and cash register servicers usually work regular business hours because the equipment they repair is not as critical.

Although their job is not strenuous, repairers must lift equipment and work in a variety of postures. Repairers of computer monitors need to discharge voltage from the equipment to avoid electrocution. Workers may have to wear protective goggles.

Employment

Computer, automated teller, and office machine repairers held about 172,000 jobs in 2000. Wholesale trade establishments employed slightly less than one-half of the workers in this occupation; most of these establishments were wholesalers of professional and commercial equipment. Many workers were employed in computer and data processing services, as well as in appliance, radio, TV, and music stores. More than 1 in 7 computer, automated teller, and office machine repairers was self-employed.

Training, Other Qualifications, and Advancement

Knowledge of electronics is necessary for employment as a computer, automated teller, or office machine repairer. Employers prefer workers who are certified as repairers or who have training in electronics from associate degree programs, the military, vocational schools, or equipment manufacturers. Employers generally provide some training to new repairers on specific equipment; however, workers are expected to arrive on the job with a basic understanding of equipment repair. Employers may send experienced workers to training sessions to keep up with changes in technology and service procedures.

Most office machine and ATM repairer positions require an associate degree in electronics. A basic understanding of mechanical equipment also is important, as many of the parts that fail in office machines and ATMs are mechanical, such as paper loaders. Entry-level employees at large companies normally receive on-the-job training lasting several months. This may include a week of classroom instruction followed by a period of 2 weeks to several months assisting an experienced repairer.

Field technicians work closely with customers and must have good communications skills and a neat appearance. Employers normally require that field technicians have a driver's license.

Several organizations administer certification programs for electronic or computer equipment repairers. Numerous certifications, including A+, Net+, and Server+, are available through the Computing Technology Industry Association (CompTIA). To receive the certifications, candidates must pass several tests that assess computer repair skills. The International Society of Certified Electronics Technicians (ISCET) and the Electronics Technicians Association (ETA) also administer certification programs. Repairers may specialize in computer repair or a variety of other skills. To receive certification, repairers must pass qualifying exams corresponding to their level of training and experience. Both programs offer associate certifications to entry-level repairers.

Newly hired computer repairers may work on personal computers or peripheral equipment. With experience, they can advance to positions maintaining more sophisticated systems, such as networking equipment and servers. Field repairers of ATMs may advance to bench-technician positions responsible for more complex repairs. Experienced workers may become specialists who help other repairers diagnose difficult problems or work with engineers in designing equipment and developing maintenance procedures. Experienced workers also may move into management positions responsible for supervising other repairers.

Because of their familiarity with equipment, experienced repairers also may move into customer service or sales positions. Some experienced workers open their own repair shops or become wholesalers or retailers of electronic equipment.

Job Outlook

Employment of computer, automated teller, and office machine repairers is expected to grow about as fast as the average for all occupations through 2010. Job growth will be driven by the increasing dependence of business and residential customers on computers and other sophisticated office machines. The need to maintain this equipment in working order will create new jobs for repairers. In addition, openings will result from the need to replace repairers who retire or move into new occupations.

Job prospects will be best for applicants with knowledge of electronics as well as repair experience; opportunities for computer repairers should be excellent, as employers report difficulty finding qualified applicants and as reliance on computers continues to increase. Although computer equipment continues to become less expensive and more reliable, malfunctions still occur and can cause severe problems for users, most of whom lack the knowledge to make repairs. Computers are critical to most businesses today and will become even more so to companies that do business on the Internet and to households that make purchases online.

People also are becoming increasingly reliant on ATMs. Besides bank and retail transactions, ATMs provide an increasing number of other services, such as employee information processing and distribution of government payments. ATM design improvements have increased reliability and simplified repair tasks, reducing the number and extent of repairs. Opportunities for ATM repairers should be available, primarily arising from the need to replace workers who leave the specialty, rather than from employment growth.

Conventional office machines, such as calculators, are inexpensive, and often are replaced instead of repaired. However, digital copiers and other newer office machines are more costly and complex. This equipment often is computerized, designed to work on a network, and able to perform multiple functions. The growing need for repairers to service such sophisticated equipment should result in job opportunities for office machine repairers.

Earnings

Median hourly earnings of computer, automated teller, and office machine repairers were $15.08 in 2000. The middle 50 percent earned between $11.80 and $19.20. The lowest 10 percent earned less than $9.50, and the highest 10 percent earned more than $23.42. Median hourly earnings in the industries employing the largest numbers of computer, automated teller, and office machine repairers in 2000 are shown in the following table:

Professional and commercial equipment $15.28
Computer and data processing services 15.05
Radio, television, and computer stores 13.16

Related Occupations

Workers in other occupations who repair and maintain electronic equipment include broadcast and sound engineering technicians and radio operators; electronic home entertainment equipment installers and repairers; electrical and electronics installers and repairers; industrial machinery installation, repair, and maintenance workers; and radio and telecommunications equipment installers and repairers.

Sources of Additional Information

For information on certification programs, contact:

- Computing Technology Industry Association, 450 East 22nd St., Suite 230, Lombard, IL 60148-6158. Internet: http://www.comptia.org

- International Society of Certified Electronics Technicians, 3608 Pershing Ave., Fort Worth, TX 76107. Internet: http://www.iscet.org

- Electronics Technicians Association, 502 North Jackson, Greencastle, IN 46135

Computer-Control Programmers and Operators

O*NET 51-4011.01, 51-4012.00

Significant Points

- Workers learn in apprenticeship programs, informally on the job, and in secondary, vocational, or postsecondary schools; many entrants have previously worked as machinists or machine setters, operators, and tenders.

- Job opportunities will be excellent, as employers are expected to continue to have difficulty finding qualified workers.

Nature of the Work

Computer-control programmers and operators use computer numerically controlled (CNC) machines to cut and shape precision products, such as automobile parts, machine parts, and compressors. CNC machines include metal-machining tools such as lathes, multi-axis spindles, and milling machines, but the functions formerly performed by human operators are performed by a computer-control module. CNC machines cut away material from a solid block of metal, plastic, or glass—known as a workpiece—to form a finished part. Computer-control programmers and operators normally produce large quantities of one part, although they may produce small batches or one-of-a-kind items. They use their knowledge of the working properties of metals and their skill with CNC programming to design and carry out the operations needed to make machined products that meet precise specifications.

Before CNC programmers—also referred to as numerical tool and process control programmers—machine a part, they must carefully plan and prepare the operation. First, these workers review three-dimensional computerized engineering diagrams (blueprints) of the part. Next, they calculate where to cut or bore into the workpiece, how fast to feed the metal into the machine, and how much metal to remove. They then select tools and materials for the job and plan the sequence of cutting and finishing operations.

Next, computer-control programmers turn the planned machining operations into a set of instructions. These instructions are translated into a computer program containing a set of commands for the machine to follow. The program is then saved onto a computer, which functions as a server. Computer-control programmers and operators check new programs to ensure that the machinery will function properly and that the output will meet specifications. Because a problem with the program could damage costly machinery and cutting tools, computer simulations may be used to check the program instead of a trial run. If errors are found, the program must be changed and retested until the problem is resolved. In addition, growing connectivity between computer-aided design (CAD) software and CNC machine tools is raising productivity by automatically translating designs into instructions for the computer controller on the machine tool. These new computer-automated manufacturing (CAM) technologies enable programs to be easily modified for use on other jobs with similar specifications, thereby reducing time and effort.

After the programming work is completed, computer-controlled machine tool operators, metal and plastic (CNC operators), perform the necessary machining operations. The CNC operators transfer the commands from the server to the CNC control module using a computer network link. Many advanced control modules are conversational, meaning they ask the operator a series of questions about the nature of the task. Computer-control operators position the metal stock on the CNC machine tool—spindle, lathe, milling machine, or other—set the controls, and let the computer make the cuts. Heavier objects may be loaded with the assistance of other workers, a crane, or a forklift. During the machining process, computer-control operators constantly monitor the readouts from the CNC control module, checking to see if any problems exist. Machine tools have unique characteristics, which can be problematic. During a machining operation, the operator modifies the cutting program to account for any problems encountered. Unique, modified CNC programs are saved for every different machine that performs a task.

CNC operators detect some problems by listening for specific sounds—for example, a dull cutting tool or excessive vibration. Dull cutting tools are removed and replaced. Machine tools rotate at high speeds, which can create problems with harmonic vibrations in the workpiece. Vibrations cause the machine tools to make minor cutting errors, hurting the quality of the product. Computer-control operators listen for vibrations and then adjust the cutting speed to compensate. In older, slower machine tools, the cutting speed would be reduced to eliminate the vibrations, but the amount of time needed to finish the product would increase as a result. In newer, high-speed CNC machines, increasing the cutting speed normally eliminates the vibrations and reduces production time. CNC operators also ensure that the workpiece is being properly lubricated and cooled, because the machining of metal products generates a significant amount of heat.

Working Conditions

Most machine shops are clean, well lit, and ventilated. Many computer-controlled machines are totally enclosed, minimizing the exposure of workers to noise, dust, and the lubricants used to cool workpieces during machining. Nevertheless, working around high-speed machine tools presents certain dangers, and workers must follow safety precautions. Computer-controlled machine tool operators, metal and plastic, wear protective equipment such as safety glasses to shield against bits of flying metal and earplugs to dampen machinery noise. They also must exercise caution when handling hazardous coolants and lubricants. The job requires stamina because operators stand most of the day and, at times, may need to lift moderately heavy workpieces.

Numerical tool and process control programmers work in offices that typically are near, but separate from, the shop floor. These work areas usually are clean, well lit, and free of machine noise. Numerical tool and process control programmers occasionally need to enter the shop floor to monitor CNC machining operations. On the shop floor, CNC programmers encounter the same hazards and exercise the same safety precautions as CNC operators.

Most computer-control programmers and operators work a 40-hour week. CNC operators increasingly work evening and weekend shifts as companies justify investments in more expensive machinery by extending hours of operation. Overtime is common during peak production periods.

Employment

Computer-control programmers and operators held about 186,000 jobs in 2000, mostly working in small machining shops or in manufacturing firms that produce durable goods, such as metalworking and industrial machinery, aircraft, or motor vehicles. Although computer-control programmers and operators work in all parts of the country, jobs are most plentiful in the northeast, midwest, and west, where manufacturing is concentrated.

Training, Other Qualifications, and Advancement

Computer-control programmers and operators train in various ways—in apprenticeship programs, informally on the job, and in secondary, vocational, or postsecondary schools. Due to a shortage of qualified applicants, many employers teach introductory courses, which provide a basic understanding of metalworking machines, safety, and blueprint reading. A basic knowledge of computers and electronics also is helpful. Experience with machine tools is extremely important. In fact, many entrants to these occupations have previously worked as machinists or machine setters, operators, and tenders. Persons interested in becoming computer-control programmers or operators should be mechanically inclined and able to work independently and do highly accurate work.

High school or vocational school courses in mathematics, blueprint reading, computer programming, metalworking, and drafting are recommended. Apprenticeship programs consist of shop training and related classroom instruction. In shop training, apprentices learn filing, handtapping, and dowel fitting, as well as the operation of various machine tools. Classroom instruction includes math, physics, programming, blueprint reading, CAD software, safety, and shop practices. Skilled computer-control programmers and operators need an understanding of the machining process, including the complex physics that occur at the cutting point. Thus, most training programs teach CNC operators and programmers to perform operations on manual machines prior to operating CNC machines. A growing number of computer-control programmers and operators receive most of their formal training from community or technical colleges. Less skilled CNC operators may have only 12 weeks of classroom training prior to working on the shop floor.

To boost the skill level of all metalworkers and to create a more uniform standard of competency, a number of training facilities and colleges have recently begun implementing curriculums incorporating national skills standards developed by the National Institute of Metalworking Skills (NIMS). After completing such a curriculum and passing a performance requirement and written exam, a NIMS credential is granted to trainees, providing formal recognition of competency in a metalworking field. Completion of a formal certification program provides expanded career opportunities.

Qualifications for computer-control programmers vary widely depending upon the complexity of the job. Employers often prefer skilled machinists or those with technical school training. For some specialized types of programming, such as that needed to produce complex parts for the aerospace or shipbuilding industries, employers may prefer individuals with a degree in engineering.

For those entering CNC programming directly, a basic knowledge of computers and electronics is necessary, and experience with machine tools is extremely helpful. Classroom training includes an introduction to computer numerical control, the basics of programming, and more complex topics, such as computer-aided manufacturing. Trainees start writing simple programs under the direction of an experienced programmer. Although machinery manufacturers are trying to standardize programming languages, there are numerous languages in use. Because of this, computer-control programmers and operators should be able to learn new programming languages.

As new automation is introduced, computer-control programmers and operators normally receive additional training to update their skills. This training usually is provided by a representative of the equipment manufacturer or a local technical school. Many employers offer tuition reimbursement for job-related courses.

Computer-control programmers and operators can advance in several ways. Experienced CNC operators may become CNC programmers, and some are promoted to supervisory or administrative positions in their firms. A few open their own shops.

Job Outlook

Computer-control programmers and operators should have excellent job opportunities. Due to the limited number of people entering training programs, employers are expected to continue to have difficulty finding workers with the necessary skills and knowledge. Employment of computer-control programmers and operators is projected to grow about as fast as the average for all occupations through 2010. Job growth will be driven by the increasing use of CNC machine tools, but advances in CNC machine tool technology will further simplify minor adjustments, enabling machinists and tool and die makers to perform tasks that previously required computer-control operators. In addition, the demand for computer-control programmers will be negatively affected by the increasing use of software that automatically translates part and product designs into CNC machine tool instructions.

Employment levels of computer-control programmers and operators are influenced by economic cycles; as the demand for machined goods falls, programmers and operators involved in production may be laid off or forced to work fewer hours.

Earnings

Median hourly earnings of computer-controlled machine tool operators, metal and plastic, were about $13.17 in 2000. The middle 50 percent earned between $10.48 and $16.55. The lowest 10 percent earned less than $8.80, whereas the top 10 percent earned more than $20.25. Median hourly earnings in the manufacturing industries employing the largest number of computer-controlled machine tool operators, metal and plastic, in 2000 were as follows:

Metalworking machinery	$15.20
General industrial machinery	15.06
Industrial machinery, not elsewhere classified	13.05
Motor vehicles and equipment	12.05
Miscellaneous plastics products, not elsewhere classified	11.35

Median hourly earnings of numerical tool and process control programmers were $17.70 in 2000. The middle 50 percent earned between $13.81 and $21.74. The lowest 10 percent earned less than $10.39, while the top 10 percent earned more than $26.66.

Related Occupations

Occupations most closely related to computer-control programmers and operators are other metal worker occupations. These include machinists; tool and die makers; machine setters, operators, and tenders—metal and plastic; and welding, soldering, and brazing workers.

Numerical tool and process control programmers apply their knowledge of machining operations, metals, blueprints, and machine programming to write programs that run machine tools. Computer programmers also write detailed programs to meet precise specifications.

Sources of Additional Information

For general information about computer-control programmers and operators, contact:

- Precision Machine Products Association, 6700 West Snowville Rd., Brecksville, OH 44141-3292. Internet: http://www.pmpa.org

For a list of training centers and apprenticeship programs, contact:

- National Tooling and Metalworking Association, 9300 Livingston Rd., Fort Washington, MD 20744. Internet: http://www.ntma.org

For general occupational information, including a list of training programs, contact:

- PMA Educational Foundation, 6363 Oak Tree Blvd., Independence, OH 44131-2500. Internet: http://www.pmaef.org

Computer Operators

O*NET 43-9011.00

Significant Points

- Employment is expected to decline sharply due to advances in technology.

- Opportunities will be best for operators who have formal computer-related education, are familiar with a variety of operating systems, and keep up-to-date with the latest technology.

Nature of the Work

Computer operators oversee the operation of computer hardware systems, ensuring that these machines are used as efficiently as possible. They may work with mainframes, minicomputers, or networks of personal computers. Computer operators must anticipate problems and take preventive action, as well as solve problems that occur during operations.

The duties of computer operators vary with the size of the installation, the type of equipment used, and the policies of the employer. Generally, operators control the console of either a mainframe digital computer or a group of minicomputers. Working from operating instructions prepared by programmers, users, or operations managers, computer operators set controls on the computer and on peripheral devices required to run a particular job.

Computer operators load equipment with tapes, disks, and paper, as needed. While the computer is running—which may be 24 hours a day for large computers—computer operators monitor the control console and respond to operating and computer messages. Messages indicate the individual specifications of each job being run. If an error message occurs, operators must locate and solve the problem or terminate the program. Operators also maintain logbooks or operating records, listing each job that is run and events, such as machine malfunctions, that occur during their shift. In addition, computer operators may help programmers and systems analysts test and debug new programs.

As the trend toward networking computers accelerates, a growing number of computer operators are working on personal computers (PCs) and minicomputers. In many offices, factories, and other work settings, PCs and minicomputers are connected in networks, often referred to as local area networks (LANs) or multi-user systems. Whereas users in the area operate some of these computers, many require the services of full-time operators. The tasks performed on PCs and minicomputers are very similar to those performed on large computers.

As organizations continue to look for opportunities to increase productivity, automation is expanding into additional areas of computer operations. Sophisticated software, coupled with robotics, enables a computer to perform many routine tasks formerly done by computer operators. Scheduling, loading and downloading programs, mounting tapes, rerouting messages, and running periodic reports can be done without the intervention of an operator. Consequently, these improvements will change what computer operators do in the future. As technology advances, the responsibilities of many computer operators are shifting to areas such as network operations, user support, and database maintenance.

Working Conditions

Computer operators generally work in well-lighted, well-ventilated, comfortable rooms. Because many organizations use their computers 24 hours a day, 7 days a week, computer operators may be required to work evening or night shifts and weekends. Shift assignments usually are made based on seniority. However, increasingly automated operations will lessen the need for shift work, because many companies let the computer take over operations during less desirable working hours. In addition, advances in telecommuting technologies (such as faxes, modems, and e-mail) and data center automation (such as automated tape libraries) enable some operators to monitor batch processes, check systems performance, and record problems for the next shift.

Because computer operators generally spend a lot of time in front of a computer monitor, as well as performing repetitive tasks such as loading and unloading printers, they may be susceptible to eyestrain, back discomfort, and hand and wrist problems.

Employment

Computer operators held about 194,000 jobs in 2000. Most jobs are found in organizations such as wholesale trade establishments, manufacturing companies, business services firms, financial institutions, and government agencies that have data-processing needs requiring large computer installations. A large number of computer operators are employed by service firms in the computer and data-processing services industry, as more companies contract out the operation of their data-processing centers.

Training, Other Qualifications, and Advancement

Computer operators usually receive on-the-job training in order to become acquainted with their employer's equipment and routines. The length of training varies with the job and the experience of the worker. However, previous work experience is the key to obtaining an operator job in many large establishments. Employers generally look for specific, hands-on experience with the type of equipment and related operating systems they use. Additionally, formal computer-related training, perhaps through a community college or technical school, is recommended. Related training also can be obtained through the armed forces and from some computer manufacturers. As computer technology changes and data processing centers become more automated, employers will increasingly require candidates to have formal training and experience for operator jobs. And although not required, a bachelor's degree in a computer-related field can be helpful when one is seeking employment as a computer operator.

Because computer technology changes so rapidly, operators must be adaptable and willing to learn. Analytical and technical expertise also are needed, particularly by operators who work in automated data centers, to deal with unique or high-level problems that a computer is not programmed to handle. Operators must be able to communicate well, and to work effectively with programmers, users, and other operators. Computer operators also must be able to work independently because they may have little or no direct supervision.

A few computer operators may advance to supervisory jobs, although most management positions within data-processing or computer-operations centers require advanced formal education, such as a bachelor's or higher degree. Through on-the-job experience and additional formal education, some computer operators may advance to jobs in areas such as network operations or support. As they gain experience in programming, some operators may advance to jobs as programmers or analysts. A move into these types of jobs is becoming much more difficult, as employers increasingly require candidates for more-skilled computer jobs to possess at least a bachelor's degree.

Job Outlook

Employment of computer operators is expected to decline sharply through the year 2010. Experienced operators are expected to compete for the small number of openings that will arise each year to replace workers who transfer to other occupations or leave the labor force. Opportunities will be best for operators who have formal computer-related education, are familiar with a variety of operating systems, and keep up-to-date with the latest technology.

Advances in technology have reduced both the size and cost of computer equipment, while increasing the capacity for data storage and processing automation. Sophisticated computer hardware and software are now used in practically every industry, in such areas as factory and office automation, telecommunications, medicine, education, and administration. The expanding use of software that automates computer operations gives companies the option of making systems user friendly, greatly reducing the need for operators. Such improvements require operators to monitor a greater number of operations at the same time and be capable of solving a broader range of problems that may arise. The result is that fewer operators will be needed to perform more highly skilled work.

Computer operators who are displaced by automation may be reassigned to support staffs that maintain personal computer networks or assist other members of the organization. Operators who keep up with changing technology, by updating their skills and enhancing their training, should have the best prospects of moving into other areas such as network administration and technical support. Others may be retrained to perform different job duties, such as supervising an operations center, maintaining automation packages, or analyzing computer operations to recommend ways to increase productivity. In the future, operators who wish to work in the computer field will need to know more about programming, automation software, graphics interface, client/server environments, and open systems, in order to take advantage of changing opportunities.

Earnings

Median annual earnings of computer operators were $27,670 in 2000. The middle 50 percent earned between about $21,280 and $35,320 a year. The top 10 percent earned more than $43,950, and the bottom 10 percent earned less than $17,350. Median annual earnings in the industries employing the largest numbers of computer operators in 2000 are shown in the following:

Computer and data processing services	$28,530
Hospitals	26,550
Commercial banks	22,840
Personnel supply services	22,130
Miscellaneous business services	21,980

The average salary for computer operators employed by the federal government was $37,574 in early 2001.

According to Robert Half International, the average starting salaries for console operators ranged from $28,250 to $40,500 in 2001. Salaries generally are higher in large organizations than in small ones.

Related Occupations

Other occupations involving work with computers include computer software engineers; computer programmers; computer support specialists and systems administrators; and systems analysts, computer scientists, and database administrators. Other occupations in which workers operate electronic office equipment include data entry and information-processing workers, as well as secretaries and administrative assistants.

Sources of Additional Information

For information about work opportunities in computer operations, contact establishments with large computer centers, such as banks, manufacturing and insurance firms, colleges and universities, and data processing service organizations. The local office of the state employment service can supply information about employment and training opportunities.

Computer Programmers

O*NET 15-1021.00

Significant Points

● Employment growth will be considerably slower than that of other computer specialists, due to the spread of pre-packaged software solutions. Three out of 5 computer programmers held at least a bachelor's degree in 2000.

● Prospects should be best for college graduates with knowledge of a variety of programming languages and tools; those with less formal education or its equivalent in work experience should face strong competition for programming jobs.

Nature of the Work

Computer programmers write, test, and maintain the detailed instructions, called programs, that computers must follow to perform their functions. They also conceive, design, and test logical structures for solving problems by computer. Many technical innovations in programming—advanced computing technologies and sophisticated new languages and programming tools—have redefined the role of a programmer and elevated much of the programming work done today. Job titles and descriptions may vary, depending on the organization. In this occupational statement, *computer programmer* refers to individuals whose main job function is programming; this group has a wide range of responsibilities and educational backgrounds.

Computer programs tell the computer what to do, such as which information to identify and access, how to process it, and what equipment to use. Programs vary widely depending upon the type of information to be accessed or generated. For example, the instructions involved in updating financial records are very different from those required to duplicate conditions on board an aircraft for pilots training in a flight simulator. Although simple programs can be written in a few hours, programs that use complex mathematical formulas, whose solutions can only be approximated, or that draw data from many existing systems, may require more than a year of work. In most cases, several programmers work together as a team under a senior programmer's supervision.

Programmers write programs according to the specifications determined primarily by computer software Engineers and system analysts. After the design process is complete, it is the job of the programmer to convert that design into a logical series of instructions that the computer can follow. They then code these instructions in a conventional programming language, such as COBOL; an artificial intelligence language, such as Prolog; or one of the most advanced object-oriented languages such as Java, C++, or Smalltalk. Different programming languages are used depending on the purpose of the program. COBOL, for example, is commonly used for business applications, whereas Fortran (short for "formula translation") is used in science and engineering. C++ is widely used for both scientific and business applications. Programmers generally know more than one programming language; and since many languages are similar, they often can learn new languages relatively easily. In practice, programmers often are referred to by the language they know, such as Java programmers, or the type of function they perform or environment in which they work, such as database programmers, mainframe programmers, or Internet programmers.

Many programmers update, repair, modify, and expand existing programs. When making changes to a section of code, called a *routine*, programmers need to make other users aware of the task the routine is to perform. They do this by inserting comments in the coded instructions, so others can understand the program. Many programmers use computer-assisted software engineering (CASE) tools to automate much of the coding process. These tools enable a programmer to concentrate on writing the unique parts of the program, because the tools automate various pieces of the program being built. CASE tools generate whole sections of code automatically, rather than line by line. This also yields more reliable and consistent programs and increases programmers' productivity by eliminating some routine steps.

Programmers test a program by running it, to ensure the instructions are correct and it produces the desired information. If errors do occur, the programmer must make the appropriate change and recheck the program until it produces the correct results. This process is called debugging. Programmers may continue to fix these problems throughout the life of a program. Programmers working in a mainframe environment may prepare instructions for a computer operator who will run the program. They also may contribute to a manual for users.

Programmers often are grouped into two broad types—applications programmers and systems programmers. *Applications programmers* write programs to handle a specific job, such as a program to track inventory, within an organization. They may also revise existing packaged software. *Systems programmers*, on the other hand, write programs to maintain and control computer systems software, such as operating systems, networked systems, and database systems. These workers make changes in the sets of instructions that determine how the network, workstations, and central processing unit of the system handle the various jobs they have been given and how they communicate with peripheral equipment, such as terminals, printers, and disk drives. Because of their knowledge of the entire computer system, systems programmers often help applications programmers determine the source of problems that may occur with their programs.

Programmers in software development companies may work directly with experts from various fields to create software—either programs designed for specific clients or packaged software for general use—ranging from games and educational software to programs for desktop publishing, financial planning, and spreadsheets. Much of this type of programming is in the preparation of packaged software, which comprises one of the most rapidly growing segments of the computer services industry.

In some organizations, particularly small ones, workers commonly known as *programmer-analysts* are responsible for both the systems analysis and the actual programming work. Advanced programming languages and new object-oriented programming capabilities are increasing the efficiency and productivity of both programmers and users. The transition from a mainframe environment to one that is primarily personal computer (PC) based has blurred the once rigid distinction between the programmer and the user. Increasingly, adept end-users are taking over many of the tasks previously performed by programmers. For example, the growing use of packaged software, like spreadsheet and database management software packages, allows users to write simple programs to access data and perform calculations.

Working Conditions

Programmers generally work in offices in comfortable surroundings. Many programmers may work long hours or weekends, to meet deadlines or fix critical problems that occur during off hours. Given the technology available, telecommuting is becoming common for a wide range of computer professionals, including computer programmers. As computer networks expand, more programmers are able to connect to a customer's computer system remotely to make corrections or fix problems, using modems, e-mail, and the Internet.

Like other workers who spend long periods of time in front of a computer terminal typing at a keyboard, programmers are susceptible to eyestrain, back discomfort, and hand and wrist problems, such as carpal tunnel syndrome.

Employment

Computer programmers held about 585,000 jobs in 2000. Programmers are employed in almost every industry, but the largest concentration is in the computer and data processing services industry, which includes firms that write and sell software. Large numbers of programmers can also be found working for firms that provide engineering and management services, telecommunications companies, manufacturers of computer and office equipment, financial institutions, insurance carriers, educational institutions, and government agencies.

A large number of computer programmers are employed on a temporary or contract basis or work as independent consultants, as companies demand expertise with new programming languages or specialized areas of application. Rather than hiring programmers as permanent employees and then laying them off after a job is completed, employers can contract with temporary help agencies, consulting firms, or directly with programmers themselves. A marketing firm, for example, may only require the services of several programmers to write and debug the software necessary to get a new customer resource management system running. This practice also enables companies to bring in people with a specific set of skills—usually in one of the latest technologies—as it applies to their business needs. Bringing in an independent contractor or consultant with a certain level of experience in a new or advanced programming language, for example, enables an establishment to complete a particular job without having to retrain existing workers. Such jobs may last anywhere from several weeks to a year or longer. There were 22,000 self-employed computer programmers in 2000.

Training, Other Qualifications, and Advancement

While there are many training paths available for programmers, mainly because employers' needs are so varied, the level of education and experience employers seek has been rising, due to the growing number of qualified applicants and the specialization involved with most programming tasks. Bachelor's degrees are commonly required, although some programmers may qualify for certain jobs with 2-year degrees or certificates. Employers are primarily interested in programming knowledge, and computer programmers are able to get certified in a language such as C++ or Java. College graduates who are interested in changing careers or developing an area of expertise also may return to a 2-year community college or technical school for additional training. In the absence of a degree, substantial specialized experience or expertise may be needed.

Even with a degree, employers appear to be placing more emphasis on previous experience, for all types of programmers.

About 3 out of 5 computer programmers had a bachelor's degree or higher in 2000 (Table 1). Of these, some hold a degree in computer science, mathematics, or information systems, whereas others have taken special courses in computer programming to supplement their study in fields such as accounting, inventory control, or other areas of business. As the level of education and training required by employers continues to rise, this proportion should increase in the future.

TABLE 1

Highest level of school completed or degree received, computer programmers, 2000	
	Percent
High school graduate or equivalent or less	11.8
Some college, no degree	17.2
Associate degree	11.0
Bachelor's degree	47.4
Graduate degree	12.8

Required skills vary from job to job, but the demand for various skills generally is driven by changes in technology. Employers using computers for scientific or engineering applications usually prefer college graduates who have degrees in computer or information science, mathematics, engineering, or the physical sciences. Graduate degrees in related fields are required for some jobs. Employers who use computers for business applications prefer to hire people who have had college courses in management information systems (MIS) and business and who possess strong programming skills. Although knowledge of traditional languages still is important, increasing emphasis is placed on newer, object-oriented programming languages and tools, such as C++ and Java. Additionally, employers are seeking persons familiar with fourth and fifth generation languages that involve graphic user interface (GUI) and systems programming. Employers also prefer applicants who have general business skills and experience related to the operations of the firm. Students can improve their employment prospects by participating in a college work-study program or by undertaking an internship.

Most systems programmers hold a 4-year degree in computer science. Extensive knowledge of a variety of operating systems is essential. This includes being able to configure an operating system to work with different types of hardware and adapting the operating system to best meet the needs of a particular organization. Systems programmers also must be able to work with database systems, such as DB2, Oracle, or Sybase, for example.

When hiring programmers, employers look for people with the necessary programming skills who can think logically and pay close attention to detail. The job calls for patience, persistence, and the ability to work on exacting analytical work, especially under pressure. Ingenuity and imagination also are particularly important, when programmers design solutions and test their work for potential failures. The ability to work with abstract concepts and to do technical analysis is especially important for systems programmers, because they work with the software that controls the computer's operation. Because programmers are expected to work in teams and interact directly with users, employers want programmers who are able to communicate with nontechnical personnel.

Entry-level or junior programmers may work alone on simple assignments after some initial instruction or on a team with more experienced programmers. Either way, beginning programmers generally must work under close supervision. Because technology changes so rapidly, programmers must continuously update their training by taking courses sponsored by their employer or software vendors.

For skilled workers who keep up to date with the latest technology, the prospects for advancement are good. In large organizations, programmers may be promoted to lead programmer and be given supervisory responsibilities. Some applications programmers may move into systems programming after they gain experience and take courses in systems software. With general business experience, programmers may become programmer analysts or systems analysts or be promoted to a managerial position. Other programmers, with specialized knowledge and experience with a language or operating system, may work in research and development areas, such as multimedia or Internet technology. As employers increasingly contract out programming jobs, more opportunities should arise for experienced programmers with expertise in a specific area to work as consultants.

Technical or professional certification is a way to demonstrate a level of competency or quality. In addition to language-specific certificates that a programmer can obtain, product vendors or software firms also offer certification and may require professionals who work with their products to be certified. Voluntary certification also is available through other organizations. Professional certification may provide a job seeker a competitive advantage.

Job Outlook

Employment of programmers is expected to grow about as fast as the average for all occupations through 2010. Jobs for both systems and applications programmers should be most plentiful in data processing service firms, software houses, and computer consulting businesses. These types of establishments are part of computer and data processing services, which is projected to be the fastest growing industry in the economy over the 2000–2010 period. As organizations attempt to control costs and keep up with changing technology, they will need programmers to assist in conversions to new computer languages and systems. In addition, numerous job openings will result from the need to replace programmers who leave the labor force or transfer to other occupations such as manager or systems analyst.

Employment of programmers, however, is expected to grow much slower than that of other computer specialists. With the rapid gains in technology, sophisticated computer software now has the capability to write basic code, eliminating the need for more programmers to do this routine work. The consolidation and centralization of systems and applications, developments in packaged software, advanced programming languages and tools, and the growing ability of users to design, write, and implement more of their own programs means more of the programming functions can be transferred to other types of workers. As the level of technological innovation and sophistication increases, programmers should continue to face increasing competition from programming businesses overseas where much routine work can be contracted out at a lower cost.

Nevertheless, employers will continue to need programmers who have strong technical skills and who understand an employer's business and its programming needs. This will mean that programmers will need to keep up with changing programming languages and techniques. Given the importance of networking and the expansion of client/server environments and web-based environments, organizations will look for programmers who can support data communications and help implement electronic commerce and intranet strategies. Demand for programmers with strong object-oriented programming capabilities and technical specialization in areas such as client/server programming, multimedia technology, and graphic user interface (GUI), should arise from the expansion of intranets, extranets, and Internet applications. Programmers also will be needed to create and maintain expert systems and embed these technologies in more and more products.

As programming tasks become increasingly sophisticated and an additional level of skill and experience is demanded by employers, graduates of 2-year programs and people with less than a 2-year degree or its equivalent in work experience should face strong competition for programming jobs. Competition for entry-level positions, however, also can affect applicants with a bachelor's degree. Prospects should be best for college graduates with knowledge of, and experience working with, a variety of programming languages and tools—including C++ and other object-oriented languages like Java, as well as newer, domain-specific languages that apply to computer networking, data base management, and Internet application development. Obtaining vendor or language specific certification also can provide a competitive edge. Because demand fluctuates with employers' needs, job seekers should keep up to date with the latest skills and technologies. Individuals who want to become programmers can enhance their prospects by combining the appropriate formal training with practical work experience.

Earnings

Median annual earnings of computer programmers were $57,590 in 2000. The middle 50 percent earned between $44,850 and $74,500 a year. The lowest 10 percent earned less than $35,020; the highest 10 percent earned more than $93,210. Median annual earnings in the industries employing the largest numbers of computer programmers in 2000 were:

Personnel supply services	$65,780
Professional and commercial equipment	63,780
Computer and data processing services	61,010
Commercial banks	60,180
Management and public relations	57,120

According to the National Association of Colleges and Employers, starting salary offers for graduates with a bachelor's degree in computer programming averaged $48,602 a year in 2001.

According to Robert Half International, average annual starting salaries in 2001 ranged from $58,500 to $90,000 for applications development programmers/developers, and from $54,000 to $77,750 for software development programmers/analysts. Average starting salaries for Internet programmers/analysts ranged from $56,500 to $84,000.

Related Occupations

Other professional workers who deal with data and detail include computer software engineers; systems analysts, computer scientists, and database administrators; statisticians; mathematicians; engineers; financial analysts and personal financial advisors; accountants and auditors; actuaries; and operations research analysts.

Sources of Additional Information

State employment service offices can provide information about job openings for computer programmers. Municipal chambers of commerce are other sources of additional information on an area's largest employers.

For information about certification as a computing professional, contact:

● Institute for Certification of Computing Professionals (ICCP), 2350 East Devon Ave., Suite 115, Des Plaines, IL 60018. Internet: http://www.iccp.org

Further information about computer careers is available from:

● Association for Computing Machinery (ACM), 1515 Broadway, New York, NY 10036. Internet: http://www.acm.org

● IEEE Computer Society, Headquarters Office, 1730 Massachusetts Ave. NW., Washington, DC 20036-1992. Internet: http://www.computer.org

● National Workforce Center for Emerging Technologies, 3000 Landerholm Circle SE., Bellevue, WA 98007. Internet: http://www.nwcet.org

Computer Support Specialists and Systems Administrators

O*NET 15-1041.00, 15-1071.00

Significant Points

● Computer support specialists and systems administrators are projected to be among the fastest growing occupations over the 2000–2010 period.

● Job prospects should best for college graduates who are up to date with the latest skills and technologies; certifications and practical experience are essential for persons without degrees.

Nature of the Work

In the last decade, computers have become an integral part of everyday life, used for a variety of reasons at home, in the workplace, and at schools. And almost every computer user encounters a problem occasionally, whether it is the disaster of a crashing hard drive or the annoyance of a forgotten password. The explosion of computer use has created a high demand for specialists to provide advice to users, as well as day-to-day administration, maintenance, and support of computer systems and networks.

Computer support specialists provide technical assistance, support, and advice to customers and other users. This group includes *technical sup-*

port specialists and *help-desk technicians*. These troubleshooters interpret problems and provide technical support for hardware, software, and systems. They answer phone calls, analyze problems using automated diagnostic programs, and resolve recurrent difficulties. Support specialists may work either within a company that uses computer systems or directly for a computer hardware or software vendor. Increasingly, these specialists work for help-desk or support services firms, where they provide computer support on a contract basis to clients.

Technical support specialists are troubleshooters, providing valuable assistance to their organization's computer users. Because many non-technical employees are not computer experts, they often run into computer problems they cannot resolve on their own. Technical support specialists install, modify, clean, and repair computer hardware and software. They also may work on monitors, keyboards, printers, and mice.

Technical support specialists answer phone calls from their organizations' computer users and may run automatic diagnostics programs to resolve problems. They also may write training manuals and train computer users how to properly use the new computer hardware and software. In addition, technical support specialists oversee the daily performance of their company's computer systems and evaluate software programs for usefulness.

Help-desk technicians assist computer users with the inevitable hardware and software questions not addressed in a product's instruction manual. Help-desk technicians field telephone calls and e-mail messages from customers seeking guidance on technical problems. In responding to these requests for guidance, help-desk technicians must listen carefully to the customer, ask questions to diagnose the nature of the problem, and then patiently walk the customer through the problem-solving steps.

Help-desk technicians deal directly with customer issues, and companies value them as a source of feedback on their products. These technicians are consulted for information about what gives customers the most trouble as well as their concerns. Most computer support specialists start out at the help desk.

Network or *computer systems administrators* design, install, and support an organization's LAN, WAN, network segment, Internet, or Intranet system. They provide day-to-day onsite administrative support for software users in a variety of work environments, including professional offices, small businesses, government, and large corporations. They maintain network hardware and software, analyze problems, and monitor the network to ensure availability to system users. These workers gather data to identify customer needs and then use that information to identify, interpret, and evaluate system and network requirements. Administrators also may plan, coordinate, and implement network security measures.

Systems administrators are the information technology employees responsible for the efficient use of networks by organizations. They ensure that the design of an organization's computer site allows all the components, including computers, the network, and software, to fit together and work properly. Furthermore, they monitor and adjust performance of existing networks and continually survey the current computer site to determine future network needs. Administrators also troubleshoot problems as reported by users and automated network monitoring systems and make recommendations for enhancements in the construction of future servers and networks.

In some organizations, *computer security specialists* may plan, coordinate, and implement the organization's information security. These and other growing specialty occupations reflect the increasing emphasis on client-server applications, the expansion of Internet and Intranet applications, and the demand for more end-user support.

Working Conditions

Computer support specialists and systems administrators normally work in well lit, comfortable offices or computer laboratories. They usually work about 40 hours a week, but that may include evening or weekend work if the employer requires computer support over extended hours. Overtime may be necessary when unexpected technical problems arise. Like other workers who type on a keyboard for long periods, computer support specialists and systems administrators are susceptible to eyestrain, back discomfort, and hand and wrist problems such as carpal tunnel syndrome.

Due to the heavy emphasis on helping all types of computer users, computer support specialists and systems administrators constantly interact with customers and fellow employees as they answer questions and give valuable advice. Those who work as consultants are away from their offices much of the time, sometimes spending months working in a client's office.

As computer networks expand, more computer support specialists and systems administrators may be able to connect to a customer's computer remotely using modems, laptops, e-mail, and the Internet to provide technical support to computer users. This capability would reduce or eliminate travel to the customer's workplace. Systems administrators also can administer and configure networks and servers remotely, although it not as common as with computer support specialists.

Employment

Computer support specialists and systems administrators held about 734,000 jobs in 2000. Of these, about 506,000 were computer support specialists and about 229,000 were network and computer systems administrators. Although they worked in a wide range of industries, about one-third of all computer support specialists and systems administrators were employed in business services industries, principally computer and data processing services. Other industries that employed substantial numbers of these workers include banks, government agencies, insurance companies, educational institutions, and wholesale and retail vendors of computers, office equipment, appliances, and home electronic equipment. Many computer support specialists also worked for manufacturers of computers and other office equipment and for firms making electronic components and other accessories.

Employers of computer support specialists and systems administrators range from start-up companies to established industry leaders. With the continued development of the Internet, telecommunications, and e-mail, industries not typically associated with computers—such as construction—increasingly need computer-related workers. Small and large firms across all industries are expanding or developing computer systems, creating an immediate need for computer support specialists and systems administrators.

Training, Other Qualifications, and Advancement

Due to the wide range of skills required, there are a multitude of ways workers can become a computer support specialist or a systems administrator. While there is no universally accepted way to prepare for a job as a computer support specialist, many employers prefer to hire persons with some formal college education. A bachelor's degree in computer science or information systems is a prerequisite for some jobs; however, other jobs may require only a computer-related associate degree. For systems administrators, many employers seek applicants with bachelor's degrees, although not necessarily in a computer-related field.

Many companies are becoming more flexible about requiring a college degree for support positions because of the explosive demand for specialists. However, certification and practical experience demonstrating these skills will be essential for applicants without a degree. Completion of a certification training program, offered by a variety of vendors and product makers, may help some people to qualify for entry-level positions. Relevant computer experience may substitute for formal education.

Beginning computer support specialist start out at an organization dealing directly with customers or in-house users. Then, they may advance into more responsible positions in which they use what they learn from customers to improve the design and efficiency of future products. Job promotions usually depend more on performance than on formal education. Eventually, some computer support specialists become programmers, designing products rather than assisting users. Computer support specialists at hardware and software companies often enjoy great upward mobility; advancement sometimes comes within months of initial employment.

Entry-level network and computer systems administrators are involved in routine maintenance and monitoring of computer systems, typically working behind the scenes in an organization. After gaining experience and expertise, they often are able to advance into more senior-level positions in which they take on more responsibilities. For example, senior network and computer systems administrators may present recommendations to management on matters related to a company's network. They also may translate the needs of an organization into a set of technical requirements, based on the available technology. As with support specialists, administrators may become software Engineers, actually involved in the designing of the system or network, not just the day-to-day administration.

Persons interested in becoming a computer support specialist or systems administrator must have strong problem-solving, analytical, and communication skills because troubleshooting and helping others are a vital part of the job. The constant interaction with other computer personnel, customers, and employees require computer support specialists and systems administrators to communicate effectively on paper, via e-mail, or in person. Strong writing skills are useful when preparing manuals for employees and customers.

As technology continues to improve, computer support specialists and systems administrators must keep their skills current and acquire new ones. Many employers, hardware and software vendors, colleges and universities, and private training institutions offer continuing education programs. Professional development seminars offered by computing services firms also can enhance one's skills.

Job Outlook

Computer support specialists and systems administrators are projected to be among the fastest growing occupations over the 2000–2010 period. Employment is expected to increase much faster than the average

for all occupations as organizations continue to adopt and integrate increasingly sophisticated technology. Job growth will continue to be driven by rapid gains in computer and data processing services, which is projected to be the fastest growing industry in the U.S. economy.

The falling prices of computer hardware and software should help businesses expand their computing applications and integrate new technology into their operations. To maintain a competitive edge and operate more efficiently, firms will continue to demand computer specialists who are knowledgeable about the latest technologies and able to apply them to meet the needs of the organization.

Demand for computer support specialists is expected to increase because of the rapid pace of improved technology. As computers and software become more complex, support specialists will be needed to provide technical assistance to customers and other users. Consulting opportunities for computer support specialists also should continue to grow as businesses increasingly need help managing, upgrading, and customizing more complex computer systems.

Demand for systems administrators will grow as a result of the upsurge in electronic commerce and as computer applications continue to expand. Companies are looking for workers knowledgeable in the function and administration of networks. Such employees have become increasingly hard to find as systems administration has moved from being a separate function within corporations to one which forms a crucial element of business in an increasingly high-technology economy.

The growth of electronic commerce means more establishments use the Internet to conduct their business online. This translates into a need for information technology specialists who can help organizations use technology to communicate with employees, clients, and consumers. Explosive growth in these areas also is expected to fuel demand for specialists knowledgeable about network, data, and communications security.

Job prospects should be best for college graduates who are up to date with the latest skills and technologies, particularly if they have supplemented their formal education with some relevant work experience. Employers will continue to seek computer specialists who possess a strong background in fundamental computer skills combined with good interpersonal and communication skills. Due to the rapid growth in demand for computer support specialists and systems administrators, those who have strong computer skills but do not have a bachelor's degree should continue to qualify for some entry-level positions. However, certifications and practical experience are essential for persons without degrees.

Earnings

Median annual earnings of computer support specialists were $36,460 in 2000. The middle 50 percent earned between $27,680 and $48,440. The lowest 10 percent earned less than $21,260, and the highest 10 percent earned more than $63,480. Median annual earnings in the industries employing the largest numbers of computer support specialists in 2000 were:

Professional and commercial equipment $42,970
Computer and data processing services 37,860
Personnel supply services 34,080
Colleges and universities 32,830
Miscellaneous business services 21,070

Median annual earnings of network and computer systems administrators were $51,280 in 2000. The middle 50 percent earned between $40,450 and $65,140. The lowest 10 percent earned less than $32,450, and the highest 10 percent earned more than $81,150. Median annual earnings in the industries employing the largest number of network and computer systems administrators in 2000 were:

Computer and data processing services	$54,400
Telephone communication	52,620
Management and public relations	51,340
Elementary and secondary schools	45,450
Colleges and universities	44,010

According to Robert Half International, starting salaries in 2001 ranged from $30,500 to $56,000 for help-desk support staff, and from $48,000 to $61,000 for more senior computer support specialists. For systems administrators, starting salaries in 2001 ranged from $50,250 to $70,750.

Related Occupations

Other computer-related occupations include computer programmers; computer software engineers; systems analysts, computer scientists, and database administrators; and operations research analysts.

Sources of Additional Information

For additional information about a career as a computer support specialist, contact:

- Association of Computer Support Specialists, 218 Huntington Rd., Bridgeport, CT 06608. Internet: http://www.acss.org

- Association of Support Professionals, 66 Mt. Auburn St., Watertown, MA 02472

For additional information about a career as a systems administrator, contact:

- System Administrators Guild, 2560 9th St., Suite 215, Berkeley, CA 94710. Internet: http://www.sage.org

Further information about computer careers is available from:

- National Workforce Center for Emerging Technologies, 3000 Landerholm Circle SE., Bellevue, WA 98007. Internet: http://www.nwcet.org

Construction and Building Inspectors

O*NET 47-4011.00

Significant Points

- About half of all inspectors worked for local governments, primarily municipal or county building departments.

- Opportunities should be best for experienced construction supervisors and craftworkers who have some college education, engineering or architectural training, or certification as construction inspectors or plan examiners.

Nature of the Work

Construction and building inspectors examine the construction, alteration, or repair of buildings, highways and streets, sewer and water systems, dams, bridges, and other structures to ensure compliance with building codes and ordinances, zoning regulations, and contract specifications. Building codes and standards are the primary means by which building construction is regulated in the United States to assure the health and safety of the general public. Inspectors make an initial inspection during the first phase of construction, and follow-up inspections throughout the construction project to monitor compliance with regulations. However, no inspection is ever exactly the same. In areas where certain types of severe weather or natural disasters are more common, inspectors monitor compliance with additional safety regulations designed to protect structures and occupants during these events.

Building inspectors inspect the structural quality and general safety of buildings. Some specialize in such areas as structural steel or reinforced concrete structures. Before construction begins, *plan examiners* determine whether the plans for the building or other structure comply with building code regulations and if they are suited to the engineering and environmental demands of the building site. Inspectors visit the work site before the foundation is poured to inspect the soil condition and positioning and depth of the footings. Later, they return to the site to inspect the foundation after it has been completed. The size and type of structure, as well as the rate of completion, determine the number of other site visits they must make. Upon completion of the project, they make a final comprehensive inspection.

In addition to structural characteristics, a primary concern of building inspectors is fire safety. They inspect structures' fire sprinklers, alarms, and smoke control systems, as well as fire exits. Inspectors assess the type of construction, building contents, adequacy of fire protection equipment, and risks posed by adjoining buildings.

In the past, most localities based their building codes on regional model codes established by the Building Officials and Code Administration (BOCA), the International Conference of Building Officials (ICBO), or the Southern Building Code Congress International (SBCCI). Therefore, building inspectors in one region who were experts in one code found it difficult to move to an area of the country using another code. To eliminate differences among the three sets of codes, these organizations jointly created the International Code Council (ICC), which released the nation's first set of uniform building code regulations. This makes it much easier for construction and building inspectors to move to different regions within the United States.

There are many types of inspectors. *Electrical inspectors* examine the installation of electrical systems and equipment to ensure that they function properly and comply with electrical codes and standards. They visit work sites to inspect new and existing sound and security systems, wiring, lighting, motors, and generating equipment. They also inspect the installation of the electrical wiring for heating and air-conditioning systems, appliances, and other components.

Elevator inspectors examine lifting and conveying devices such as elevators, escalators, moving sidewalks, lifts and hoists, inclined railways, ski lifts, and amusement rides.

Mechanical inspectors inspect the installation of the mechanical components of commercial kitchen appliances, heating and air-conditioning equipment, gasoline and butane tanks, gas and oil piping, and gas-fired and oil-fired appliances. Some specialize in boilers or ventilating equipment as well.

Plumbing inspectors examine plumbing systems, including private disposal systems, water supply and distribution systems, plumbing fixtures and traps, and drain, waste, and vent lines.

Public works inspectors ensure that federal, state, and local government construction of water and sewer systems, highways, streets, bridges, and dams conforms to detailed contract specifications. They inspect excavation and fill operations, the placement of forms for concrete, concrete mixing and pouring, asphalt paving, and grading operations. They record the work and materials used so that contract payments can be calculated. Public works inspectors may specialize in highways, structural steel, reinforced concrete, or ditches. Others specialize in dredging operations required for bridges and dams or for harbors.

Home inspectors generally conduct inspections of newly built or previously owned homes. Increasingly, prospective home buyers hire home inspectors to inspect and report the condition of a home's systems, components, and structure. They typically are hired either immediately prior to a purchase offer on a home, or as a contingency to a sales contract. In addition to structural quality, home inspectors must be able to inspect all home systems and features, from plumbing, electrical, and heating or cooling systems to roofing.

The owner of a building or structure under construction employs *specification inspectors* to ensure that work is done according to design specifications. They represent the owner's interests, not those of the general public. Insurance companies and financial institutions also may use specification inspectors.

Details concerning construction projects, building and occupancy permits, and other documentation generally are stored on computers so that they can easily be retrieved, kept accurate, and updated. For example, inspectors may use laptop computers to record their findings while inspecting a site. Most inspectors use computers to help them monitor the status of construction inspection activities and keep track of issued permits.

Although inspections are primarily visual, inspectors may use tape measures, survey instruments, metering devices, and test equipment such as concrete strength measurers. They keep a log of their work, take photographs, file reports, and, if necessary, act on their findings. For example, construction inspectors notify the construction contractor, superintendent, or supervisor when they discover a code or ordinance violation or something that does not comply with the contract specifications or approved plans. If the problem is not corrected within a reasonable or specified period, government inspectors have authority to issue a "stop-work" order.

Many inspectors also investigate construction or alterations being done without proper permits. Inspectors who are employees of municipalities enforce laws pertaining to the proper design, construction, and use of buildings. They direct violators of permit laws to obtain permits and submit to inspection.

Working Conditions

Construction and building inspectors usually work alone. However, several may be assigned to large, complex projects, particularly because inspectors tend to specialize in different areas of construction. Although they spend considerable time inspecting construction work sites, in-

spectors also spend time in a field office reviewing blueprints, answering letters or telephone calls, writing reports, and scheduling inspections.

Inspection sites are dirty and may be cluttered with tools, materials, or debris. Inspectors may have to climb ladders or many flights of stairs, or crawl around in tight spaces. Although their work generally is not considered hazardous, inspectors, like other construction workers, wear hard hats and adhere to other safety requirements while at a construction site.

Inspectors normally work regular hours. However, they may work additional hours during periods when a lot of construction is taking place. Also, if an accident occurs at a construction site, inspectors must respond immediately and may work additional hours to complete their report.

Employment

Construction and building inspectors held about 75,000 jobs in 2000. Local governments, primarily municipal or county building departments, employed 49 percent. Employment of local government inspectors is concentrated in cities and in suburban areas undergoing rapid growth. Local governments employ large inspection staffs, including many plan examiners or inspectors who specialize in structural steel, reinforced concrete, boiler, electrical, and elevator inspection.

Another 17 percent of construction and building inspectors worked for engineering and architectural services firms, conducting inspections for a fee or on a contract basis. Many of these are home inspectors working on the behalf of potential real estate purchasers. Most of the remaining inspectors were employed in other services industries or by state governments.

Training, Other Qualifications, and Advancement

Although requirements vary considerably depending upon where one is employed, individuals who want to become construction and building inspectors should have a thorough knowledge of construction materials and practices in either a general area, such as structural or heavy construction, or in a specialized area, such as electrical or plumbing systems, reinforced concrete, or structural steel. Applicants for construction or building inspection jobs need several years of experience as a construction manager, supervisor, or craftworker. Many inspectors previously worked as carpenters, electricians, plumbers, or pipefitters.

Because inspectors must possess the right mix of technical knowledge, experience, and education, employers prefer applicants who have formal training as well as experience. Most employers require at least a high school diploma or equivalent, even for workers with considerable experience. More often, employers look for persons who have studied engineering or architecture, or who have a degree from a community or junior college, with courses in building inspection, home inspection, construction technology, drafting, and mathematics. Many community colleges offer certificate or associate degree programs in building inspection technology. Courses in algebra, geometry, English, and blueprint reading also are useful.

Construction and building inspectors must be in good physical condition in order to walk and climb about construction sites. They must also have a driver's license. In addition, federal, state, and many local governments may require that inspectors pass a civil service exam.

Construction and building inspectors usually receive much of their training on the job, although they must learn building codes and standards on their own. Working with an experienced inspector, they learn about inspection techniques; codes, ordinances, and regulations; contract specifications; and record keeping and reporting duties. They may begin by inspecting less complex types of construction, such as residential buildings, and then progress to more difficult assignments. An engineering or architectural degree is often required for advancement to supervisory positions.

Because they advise builders and the general public on building codes, construction practices, and technical developments, construction and building inspectors must keep abreast of changes in these areas. Continuing education is imperative in this field. Many employers provide formal training programs to broaden inspectors' knowledge of construction materials, practices, and techniques. Inspectors who work for small agencies or firms that do not conduct training programs can expand their knowledge and upgrade their skills by attending state-sponsored training programs, by taking college or correspondence courses, or by attending seminars sponsored by various related organizations, such as model code organizations.

Most states and cities require some type of certification for employment; even if not required, certification can enhance an inspector's opportunities for employment and advancement to more responsible positions. To become certified, inspectors with substantial experience and education must pass stringent examinations on code requirements, construction techniques, and materials. The three major model code organizations offer voluntary certification, as do other professional membership associations. In most cases, there are no education or experience prerequisites, and certification consists of passing an examination in a designated field. Many categories of certification are awarded for inspectors and plan examiners in a variety of disciplines, including the designation "CBO," Certified Building Official, offered by the International Code Council.

Job Outlook

Employment of construction and building inspectors is expected to grow as fast as the average for all occupations through 2010. Growing concern for public safety and improvements in the quality of construction should continue to stimulate demand for construction and building inspectors. In addition to the expected employment growth, some job openings will arise from the need to replace inspectors who transfer to other occupations or leave the labor force. Well-trained workers will have especially favorable opportunities.

Opportunities should be best for highly experienced supervisors and craftworkers who have some college education, engineering or architectural training, or certification as inspectors or plan examiners. Thorough knowledge of construction practices and skills in areas such as reading and evaluating blueprints and plans are essential.

Inspectors are involved in all phases of construction, including maintenance and repair work, and are therefore less likely to lose jobs when new construction slows during recessions. As the population grows and the volume of real estate transactions increases, greater emphasis on home inspections should result in rapid growth in employment of home inspectors. In addition, there should be good opportunities in engineer-ing, architectural, and management services firms due to the tendency of governments—particularly federal and state—to contract out inspection work, and due to expected growth in private inspection services.

Earnings

Median annual earnings of construction and building inspectors were $38,750 in 2000. The middle 50 percent earned between $30,640 and $47,860. The lowest 10 percent earned less than $24,370, and the highest 10 percent earned more than $56,570. Median annual earnings in the industries employing the largest numbers of construction and building inspectors in 2000 were:

Local government	$39,410
State government	38,370
Engineering and architectural services	37,810

Generally, building inspectors, including plan examiners, earn the highest salaries. Salaries in large metropolitan areas are substantially higher than those in small local jurisdictions.

Related Occupations

Construction and building inspectors combine knowledge of construction principles and law with an ability to coordinate data, diagnose problems, and communicate with people. Workers in other occupations using a similar combination of skills include architects, except landscape and naval; construction managers; civil engineers; cost estimators; drafters; engineering technicians; and surveyors, cartographers, photogrammetrists, and surveying technicians.

Sources of Additional Information

Information about certification and a career as a construction or building inspector is available from the following model code organizations:

- International Conference of Building Officials, 5360 Workman Mill Rd., Whittier, CA 90601-2298. Internet: http://www.icbo.org

- Building Officials and Code Administrators International, Inc., 4051 West Flossmoor Rd., Country Club Hills, IL 60478. Internet: http://www.bocai.org

- Southern Building Code Congress International, Inc., 900 Montclair Rd., Birmingham, AL 35213. Internet: http://sbcci.org

Information about training for construction inspectors is available from:

- Association of Construction Inspectors, 1224 North Nokomis NE., Alexandria, MN 56308. Internet: http://www.iami.org

General information about electrical inspection is available from:

- International Association of Electrical Inspectors, 901 Waterfall Way, Suite 602, Richardson, TX 75080

Information about a career as a home inspector is available from:

- American Society of Home Inspectors, Inc., 932 Lee St., Suite 101, Des Plaines, IL 60016

For information about a career as a state or local government construction or building inspector, contact your state or local employment service.

Construction Equipment Operators

O*NET 47-2071.00, 47-2072.00, 47-2073.01, 47-2073.02

Significant Points

- Most construction equipment operators acquire their skills on the job, but formal apprenticeship programs provide more comprehensive training.

- Job opportunities are expected to be good, despite slower-than-average employment growth.

- Hourly pay is relatively high but, because construction equipment operators cannot work in inclement weather, total earnings may be reduced.

Nature of the Work

Construction equipment operators use machinery to move construction materials, earth, and other heavy materials and to apply asphalt and concrete to roads and other structures. Operators control equipment by moving levers or foot pedals, operating switches, or turning dials. The operation of much of this equipment is becoming more complex as a result of computerized controls. Construction equipment operators may also set up and inspect equipment, make adjustments, and perform minor repairs.

Construction equipment operators include operating engineers and other construction equipment operators; paving, surfacing, and tamping equipment operators; and pile driver operators. *Operating engineers and other construction equipment operators* operate one or several types of power construction equipment. They may operate excavation and loading machines equipped with scoops, shovels, or buckets that dig sand, gravel, earth, or similar materials and load it into trucks or onto conveyors. In addition to the familiar bulldozers, they operate trench excavators, road graders, and similar equipment. Sometimes, they may drive and control industrial trucks or tractors equipped with a forklift or boom for lifting materials, or hitches for pulling trailers. They also may operate and maintain air compressors, pumps, and other power equipment at construction sites. Construction equipment operators who are classified as operating engineers have the capability of operating several different types of construction equipment.

Paving and surfacing equipment operators use levers and other controls to operate machines that spread and level asphalt or spread and smooth concrete for roadways or other structures. *Asphalt paving machine operators* turn valves to regulate the temperature and flow of asphalt onto the roadbed. They must take care that the machine distributes the paving material evenly and without voids, and make sure that there is a constant flow of asphalt going into the hopper. *Concrete paving machine operators* move levers and turn handwheels to lower an attachment that spreads, vibrates, and levels wet concrete within forms. They must observe the surface of concrete to identify low spots into which workers must add concrete. They use other attachments to the machine to smooth the surface of the concrete, spray on a curing compound, and cut ex-

pansion joints. *Tamping equipment operators* operate tamping machines that compact earth and other fill materials for roadbeds. They also may operate machines with interchangeable hammers to cut or break up old pavement and drive guardrail posts into the earth.

Pile driver operators operate pile drivers—large machines mounted on skids, barges, or cranes, which hammer piles into the ground. Piles are long heavy beams of wood or steel that are driven into the ground to support retaining walls, bulkheads, bridges, piers, or building foundations. Some pile driver operators work on offshore oil rigs. Pile driver operators move hand and foot levers and turn valves to activate, position, and control the pile-driving equipment.

Working Conditions

Many construction equipment operators work outdoors, in nearly every type of climate and weather condition. Some machines, including bulldozers, scrapers, and especially tampers and pile drivers, are noisy and shake or jolt the operator. Operating heavy construction equipment can be dangerous. As with most machinery, accidents generally can be avoided by observing proper operating procedures and safety practices. Construction equipment operators can expect to be cold in the winter and hot in the summer, and often get dirty, greasy, muddy, or dusty.

Operators may have irregular hours because work on some construction projects continues around the clock. Some operators work in remote locations on large construction projects, such as highways and dams, or in factory or mining operations.

Employment

Construction equipment operators held about 416,000 jobs in 2000. Jobs were found in every section of the country and were distributed among various types of operators as follows:

Operating engineers and other construction equipment operators	357,000
Paving, surfacing, and tamping equipment operators	55,000
Pile-driver operators	4,400

About 3 out of every 5 construction equipment operators worked in the construction industry. Many equipment operators worked in heavy construction, building highways, bridges, or railroads. About 81,000 of all construction equipment operators worked in state and local government. Others—mostly grader, bulldozer, and scraper operators—worked in mining. Some also worked in manufacturing and for utility companies. About 1 in 20 construction equipment operators was self-employed.

Training, Other Qualifications, and Advancement

Construction equipment operators usually learn their skills on the job. However, it is generally accepted that formal training provides more comprehensive skills. Some construction equipment operators train in formal 3-year operating engineer apprenticeship programs administered by union-management committees of the International Union of Operating Engineers and the Associated General Contractors of America. Because apprentices learn to operate a wider variety of machines than do other beginners, they usually have better job opportunities. Apprenticeship programs consist of at least 3 years, or 6,000 hours, of on-the-job training and 144 hours a year of related classroom instruction.

Employers of construction equipment operators generally prefer to hire high school graduates, although some employers may train persons having less education to operate some types of equipment. The more technologically advanced construction equipment has computerized controls and improved hydraulics and electronics, requiring more skill to operate than previously was necessary. Operators of such equipment may need more training and some understanding of electronics. Mechanical aptitude and high school training in automobile mechanics are helpful because workers may perform some maintenance on their machines. Also, high school courses in science and mechanical drawing are useful. Experience operating related mobile equipment, such as farm tractors or heavy equipment, in the armed forces or elsewhere is an asset.

Private vocational schools offer instruction in the operation of certain types of construction equipment. Completion of such a program may help a person get a job as a trainee or apprentice. However, persons considering such training should check the reputation of the school among employers in the area.

Beginning construction equipment operators handle light equipment under the guidance of an experienced operator. Later, they may operate heavier equipment such as bulldozers and cranes. Operators need to be in good physical condition and have a good sense of balance, the ability to judge distance, and eye-hand-foot coordination. Some operator positions require the ability to work at heights.

Job Outlook

Job opportunities for construction equipment operators are expected to be good through 2010. This is due in part to the shortage of adequate training programs. In addition, many potential workers may prefer work that is less strenuous and has more comfortable working conditions. Well-trained workers will have especially favorable opportunities.

Employment of construction equipment operators is expected to increase more slowly than the average for all occupations through the year 2010 because equipment improvements are expected to continue to raise worker productivity and to moderate demand for skilled construction equipment operators. Employment is expected to increase as population and business growth create a need for new houses, industrial facilities, schools, hospitals, offices, and other structures. Also stimulating demand is the expected growth in highway, bridge, and street construction. Bridge construction is expected to grow the fastest, due to the need to repair or replace structures before they become unsafe. Poor highway conditions also will spur demand for highway maintenance and repair. In the last several years, Congress has passed substantial public works bills designed to provide money for such construction projects, including mass transit systems. In addition to employment growth in this occupation, many job openings will arise because of the need to replace experienced workers who transfer to other occupations or leave the labor force.

Employment of construction equipment operators is sensitive to fluctuations in the economy. Workers may experience periods of unemployment when the level of construction activity falls.

Earnings

Earnings for construction equipment operators vary. In 2000, median hourly earnings of operating engineers and other construction equipment operators were $15.99. The middle 50 percent earned between $12.21 and $21.68. The lowest 10 percent earned less than $10.00, and the highest 10 percent earned more than $27.29. Median hourly earnings in the industries employing the largest numbers of operating engineers in 2000 were:

Highway and street construction	$18.68
Miscellaneous special trade contractors	16.68
Heavy construction, except highway	16.63
Local government	13.95
State government	12.83

Median hourly earnings of paving, surfacing, and tamping equipment operators were $12.88 in 2000. The middle 50 percent earned between $10.04 and $17.57. The lowest 10 percent earned less than $8.51, and the highest 10 percent earned more than $23.57. Median hourly earnings in the industries employing the largest numbers of paving, surfacing, and tamping equipment operators in 2000 were:

Highway and street construction	$13.45
Concrete work	12.91
Local government	12.57

In 2000, median hourly earnings of pile driver operators were $19.85. The middle 50 percent earned between $13.36 and $26.03. The lowest 10 percent earned less than $10.99, and the highest 10 percent earned more than $31.04.

Pay scales generally are higher in metropolitan areas. Annual earnings of some workers may be lower than hourly rates would indicate because worktime may be limited by bad weather.

Related Occupations

Other workers who operate heavy mechanical equipment include bus drivers; truck drivers and driver/sales workers; farmers, ranchers, and agricultural managers; agricultural workers; and forest, conservation, and logging workers.

Sources of Additional Information

For further information about apprenticeships or work opportunities for construction equipment operators, contact a local of the International Union of Operating Engineers, a local apprenticeship committee, or the nearest office of the state apprenticeship agency or employment service. For general information about the work of construction equipment operators, contact:

- Associated General Contractors of America, 333 John Carlyle St., Suite 200, Alexandria, VA 22314. Internet: http://www.agc.org

- International Union of Operating Engineers, 1125 17th St. NW., Washington, DC 20036. Internet: http://www.iuoe.org

Construction Laborers

O*NET 47-2061.00

Significant Points

- Job opportunities should be good.

- The work can be physically demanding and sometimes dangerous.

- Most construction laborers learn through informal on-the-job training; some complete formal apprenticeship programs.

Nature of the Work

Construction laborers perform a wide range of physically demanding tasks involving building and highway construction, tunnel and shaft excavation, hazardous waste removal, and demolition. Although the term "laborer" implies work that requires relatively low skill or training, many tasks that these workers perform require a fairly high level of training and experience. Construction laborers clean and prepare construction sites to eliminate possible hazards, dig trenches, mix and place concrete, and set braces to support the sides of excavations. They load, unload, identify, and distribute building materials to the appropriate location according to project plans and specifications on building construction projects. They also tend machines; for example, they may mix concrete using a portable mixer or tend a machine that pumps concrete, grout, cement, sand, plaster, or stucco through a spray gun for application to ceilings and walls. Construction laborers may sometimes help other craft workers including carpenters, plasterers, and masons.

At heavy and highway construction sites, construction laborers clear and prepare highway work zones and rights of way; install traffic barricades, cones, and markers; and control traffic passing near, in, and around work zones. They also install sewer, water, and storm drain pipes, build manholes, and lay cement and asphalt on roads.

At hazardous waste removal sites, construction laborers prepare the site and safely remove asbestos, lead, radioactive waste, and other hazardous materials. They operate, read, and maintain air monitoring and other sampling devices in confined and/or hazardous environments. They also safely sample, identify, handle, pack, and transport hazardous and/or radioactive materials and clean and decontaminate equipment, buildings, and enclosed structures. Other highly specialized tasks include operating laser guidance equipment to place pipes, operating air and pneumatic drills, and transporting and setting explosives for tunnel, shaft, and road construction.

Construction laborers operate a variety of equipment including pavement breakers; jackhammers; earth tampers; concrete, mortar, and plaster mixers; electric and hydraulic boring machines; torches; small mechanical hoists; laser beam equipment; and surveying and measuring equipment. They operate pipe-laying machinery and use computers and other high-tech input devices to control robotic pipe cutters and cleaners. To perform their jobs effectively, construction laborers must be familiar with the duties of other craft workers and with the materials, tools, and machinery they use.

Construction laborers often work as part of a team with other skilled craft workers, jointly carrying out assigned construction tasks. At other times, construction laborers may work alone, reading and interpreting instructions, plans, and specifications with little or no supervision.

While most construction laborers tend to specialize in a type of construction such as highway or tunnel construction, they are skilled generalists who perform many different tasks during all stages of construction. However, construction laborers who work in underground construction (such as in tunnels) or in demolition are more likely to specialize in only those areas.

Working Conditions

Most laborers do physically demanding work. They may lift and carry heavy objects, and stoop, kneel, crouch, or crawl in awkward positions. Some work at great heights, or outdoors in all weather conditions. Some jobs expose workers to harmful materials or chemicals, fumes, odors, loud noise, or dangerous machinery. To avoid injury, workers in these jobs wear safety clothing, such as gloves, hard hats, protective chemical suits, and devices to protect their eyes, respiratory system, or hearing. While working in underground construction, construction laborers must be especially alert to safely follow procedures and must deal with a variety of hazards.

Construction laborers generally work 8-hour shifts, although longer shifts also are common. They may work only during certain seasons, when the weather permits construction activity.

Employment

Construction laborers held about 791,000 jobs in 2000. They worked throughout the country but, like the general population, are concentrated in metropolitan areas. Almost all construction laborers work in the construction industry and almost 38 percent work for special trade contractors. Only about 8 percent worked part-time in 2000.

Training, Other Qualifications, and Advancement

For some construction laborer jobs, employers hire people without experience or specific training in the occupation. However, the work requires more strength and stamina than most occupations, as well as a basic education. Basic literacy is a must if a worker is to read and comprehend warning signs and labels and understand instructions and specifications.

Most construction laborers learn their skills informally, observing and learning from experienced workers. Individuals who learn the trade on the job usually start as helpers. These workers perform routine tasks, such as cleaning and preparing the work site and unloading materials. When the opportunity arises, they learn how to do more difficult tasks, such as operating tools and equipment, from experienced craft workers. Becoming a fully skilled construction laborer by training on the job normally takes longer than the 2 to 4 years required to complete an apprenticeship program.

Formal apprenticeship programs provide more thorough preparation for jobs as construction laborers than does on-the-job training. Local apprenticeship programs are operated under guidelines established by the Laborers–Associated General Contractors of America Education and Training Fund. These programs typically require at least 4,000 hours of supervised on-the-job training and approximately 400 hours of classroom training. Depending on the availability of work and on local training schedules, it can take an individual from 2 to 4 years to complete the apprenticeship. A core curriculum consisting of basic construction skills such as blueprint reading, the correct use of tools and equipment, and knowledge of safety procedures comprises the first 200 hours. The remainder of the curriculum consists of specialized skills training in three of the largest segments of the construction industry: building construction, heavy/highway construction, and environmental remediation (cleaning up debris, landscaping, and restoring the environment to its original state). Workers who use dangerous equipment or handle toxic chemicals usually receive specialized training in safety awareness and procedures. Apprentices must complete at least 144 hours of classroom work each year.

Most apprenticeship programs require workers to be at least 18 years old (17 years of age or older in the case of some school-to-work and career preparation programs) and physically able to perform the work. Many apprenticeship programs require a high school diploma or equivalent. High school and junior college courses in science, physics, chemistry, and mathematics are helpful. Vocational classes in welding, construction, and other general building skills can give anyone wishing to become a construction laborer a significant head start.

Experience is helpful but usually is not necessary to obtain a job. Relevant work experience that provides construction-related job skills can often reduce or eliminate a wide range of training and apprenticeship requirements. Finally, most apprenticeship programs, local unions, and employers look very favorably on military service and/or service in the Job Corps, as veterans and Job Corps graduates have already demonstrated a high level of responsibility and reliability and may have gained many valuable job skills.

Construction laborers need good manual dexterity, hand-eye coordination, and balance. They also need the ability to read and comprehend all warning signs and labels on a construction site and the reading skills sufficient to understand and interpret plans, drawings, and written instructions and specifications. They should be capable of working as a member of a team and have basic problem-solving and math skills. Employers want workers who are hard-working, reliable, and diligent about being on time. Additionally, construction laborers who wish to work in environmental remediation must pass a physical test that measures the ability to wear a respirator. Computer skills also are important as construction becomes increasingly mechanized and computerized.

Experience in many construction laborer jobs may allow some workers to advance to positions such as supervisor or construction superintendent. A few become independent contractors.

Job Outlook

Job opportunities for construction laborers are expected to be good due to the numerous openings arising each year from laborers who leave the occupation. In addition, many potential workers may prefer work that is less strenuous and has more comfortable working conditions. Employment of construction laborers is expected to grow about as fast as the average for all occupations through the year 2010. Opportunities will be best for well-trained workers who are willing to relocate to different work sites.

Growth of construction laborer employment will be spurred by continuing emphasis on environmental remediation and on rebuilding infrastructure—roads, airports, bridges, tunnels, and communications facilities, for example. However, employment growth will be adversely affected by automation as new machines and equipment that improve productivity and quality replace some jobs.

Employment of construction laborers, like that of many other construction workers, can be variable or intermittent due to the limited duration of construction projects and the cyclical nature of the construction industry. During economic downturns, job openings for construction laborers decrease as the level of construction activity declines.

Earnings

Median hourly earnings of construction laborers in 2000 were $11.15. The middle 50 percent earned between $8.79 and $16.23. The lowest 10 percent earned less than $7.22 and the highest 10 percent earned more than $21.88. Median hourly earnings in the largest industries employing construction laborers in 2000 were as follows:

Nonresidential building construction $11.85
Miscellaneous special trade contractors 11.71
Concrete work 11.27
Heavy construction, except highway 10.90
Residential building construction 10.62

Earnings for construction laborers can be reduced by poor weather or by downturns in construction activity, which sometimes result in layoffs.

Apprentices or helpers usually start at about 50 percent of the wage rate paid to experienced workers. Pay increases as apprentices gain experience and learn new skills.

Almost 1 in 5 construction laborers is a member of a union. Many belong to the Laborers' International Union of North America.

Related Occupations

The work of construction laborers is closely related to other construction occupations. Other workers who perform similar physical work include persons in material moving occupations; forest, conservation, and logging workers; and grounds maintenance workers.

Sources of Additional Information

For information about jobs as construction laborers, contact local building or construction contractors, local joint labor-management apprenticeship committees, apprenticeship agencies, or the local office of your state employment service.

For general information about the work of construction laborers, contact:

● Laborers' International Union of North America, 905 16th St. NW., Washington, DC 20006. Internet: http://www.liuna.org

Construction Managers

O*NET 11-9021.00

Significant Points

● Construction managers must be available—often 24 hours a day—to deal with delays, bad weather, or emergencies at the job site.

- Employers prefer individuals who combine construction industry work experience with a bachelor's degree in construction science, construction management, or civil engineering.

- Excellent opportunities are expected for qualified managers.

- Employment can be sensitive to the short-term nature of many construction projects and cyclical fluctuations in construction activity.

Nature of the Work

Construction managers plan and direct construction projects. They may have job titles such as constructor, construction superintendent, general superintendent, project engineer, project manager, general construction manager, or executive construction manager. Construction managers may be owners or salaried employees of a construction management or contracting firm, or may work under contract or as a salaried employee of the owner, developer, contractor, or management firm overseeing the construction project. The term construction manager describes salaried or self-employed managers who oversee construction supervisors and workers.

A construction manager is defined more narrowly within the construction industry to denote a management firm, or an individual employed by such a firm, involved in managerial oversight of a construction project. Under this definition, construction managers usually represent the owner or developer with other participants throughout the project. Although they usually play no direct role in the actual construction of a structure, they typically schedule and coordinate all design and construction processes, including the selection, hiring, and oversight of specialty trade contractors.

Managers who work in the construction industry, such as general managers, project engineers, and others, increasingly are called constructors. Through education and past work experience, this broad group of managers manages, coordinates, and supervises the construction process from the conceptual development stage through final construction on a timely and economical basis. Given designs for buildings, roads, bridges, or other projects, constructors oversee the organization, scheduling, and implementation of the project to execute those designs. They are responsible for coordinating and managing people, materials, and equipment; budgets, schedules, and contracts; and safety of employees and the general public.

On large projects, construction managers may work for a general contractor, the firm with overall responsibility for all activities. There, they oversee the completion of all construction in accordance with the engineer's and architect's drawings and specifications and prevailing building codes. They arrange for trade contractors to perform specialized craftwork or other specified construction work. On small projects, such as remodeling a home, a self-employed construction manager or skilled trades worker who directs and oversees employees often is referred to as the construction "contractor."

Large construction projects, such as an office building or industrial complex, are too complicated for one person to manage. These projects are divided into many segments: site preparation, including land clearing and earth moving; sewage systems; landscaping and road construction; building construction, including excavation and laying foundations, erection of structural framework, floors, walls, and roofs; and building systems, including fire-protection, electrical, plumbing, air-conditioning, and heating. Construction managers may be in charge of one or more of these activities. Construction managers often team with workers in other occupations, such as engineers and architects.

Construction managers evaluate various construction methods and determine the most cost-effective plan and schedule. They determine the appropriate construction methods and schedule all required construction site activities into logical, specific steps, budgeting the time required to meet established deadlines. This may require sophisticated estimating and scheduling techniques and use of computers with specialized software. This also involves the selection and coordination of trade contractors hired to complete specific pieces of the project, which could include everything from structural metalworking and plumbing to painting and carpet installation. Construction managers determine the labor requirements and, in some cases, supervise or monitor the hiring and dismissal of workers. They oversee the performance of all trade contractors and are responsible for ensuring that all work is completed on schedule.

Construction managers direct and monitor the progress of construction activities, at times through other construction supervisors. They oversee the delivery and use of materials, tools, and equipment; and the quality of construction, worker productivity, and safety. They are responsible for obtaining all necessary permits and licenses and, depending upon the contractual arrangements, direct or monitor compliance with building and safety codes and other regulations. They may have several subordinates, such as assistant managers or superintendents, field engineers, or crew supervisors, reporting to them.

Construction managers regularly review engineering and architectural drawings and specifications to monitor progress and ensure compliance with plans and schedules. They track and control construction costs against the project budget to avoid cost overruns. Based upon direct observation and reports by subordinate supervisors, managers may prepare daily reports of progress and requirements for labor, material, machinery, and equipment at the construction site. They meet regularly with owners, trade contractors, architects, and others to monitor and coordinate all phases of the construction project.

Working Conditions

Construction managers work out of a main office from which the overall construction project is monitored, or out of a field office at the construction site. Management decisions regarding daily construction activities generally are made at the job site. Managers usually travel when the construction site is in another state or when they are responsible for activities at two or more sites. Management of overseas construction projects usually entails temporary residence in another country.

Construction managers may be "on call"—often 24 hours a day—to deal with delays, bad weather, or emergencies at the site. Most work more than a standard 40-hour week because construction may proceed around the clock. They may have to work this type of schedule for days, even weeks, to meet special project deadlines, especially if there are delays.

Although the work usually is not considered inherently dangerous, construction managers must be careful while touring construction sites. Managers must establish priorities and assign duties. They need to observe job conditions and be alert to changes and potential problems, particularly those involving safety on the job site and adherence to regulations.

Employment

Construction managers held about 308,000 jobs in 2000. Around 75,000 were self-employed. About 59 percent of construction managers were employed in the construction industry, about 24 percent by specialty trade contractors—for example, plumbing, heating and air-conditioning, and electrical contractors—and about 28 percent by general building contractors. Engineering, architectural, and construction management services firms, as well as local governments, educational institutions, and real estate developers employed others.

Training, Other Qualifications, and Advancement

Persons interested in becoming a construction manager need a solid background in building science, business, and management, as well as related work experience within the construction industry. They need to understand contracts, plans, and specifications, and to be knowledgeable about construction methods, materials, and regulations. Familiarity with computers and software programs for job costing, scheduling, and estimating also is important.

Traditionally, persons advance to construction management positions after having substantial experience as construction craftworkers—carpenters, masons, plumbers, or electricians, for example—or after having worked as construction supervisors or as owners of independent specialty contracting firms overseeing workers in one or more construction trades. However, employers—particularly large construction firms—increasingly prefer individuals who combine industry work experience with a bachelor's degree in construction science, construction management, or civil engineering. Practical industry experience also is very important, whether it is acquired through internships, cooperative education programs, or work experience in the industry.

Construction managers should be flexible and work effectively in a fast-paced environment. They should be decisive and work well under pressure, particularly when faced with unexpected occurrences or delays. The ability to coordinate several major activities at once, while analyzing and resolving specific problems, is essential, as is an understanding of engineering, architectural, and other construction drawings. Good oral and written communication skills also are important, as are leadership skills. Managers must be able to establish a good working relationship with many different people, including owners, other managers, designers, supervisors, and craftworkers.

Advancement opportunities for construction managers vary depending upon an individual's performance and the size and type of company for which they work. Within large firms, managers may eventually become top-level managers or executives. Highly experienced individuals may become independent consultants; some serve as expert witnesses in court or as arbitrators in disputes. Those with the required capital may establish their own construction management services, specialty contracting, or general contracting firm.

In 2000, more than 100 colleges and universities offered 4-year degree programs in construction management or construction science. These programs include courses in project control and development, site planning, design, construction methods, construction materials, value analysis, cost estimating, scheduling, contract administration, accounting, business and financial management, building codes and standards, inspection procedures, engineering and architectural sciences, mathematics, statistics, and information technology. Graduates from 4-year degree programs usually are hired as assistants to project managers, field engineers, schedulers, or cost estimators. An increasing number of graduates in related fields—engineering or architecture, for example—also enter construction management, often after having had substantial experience on construction projects or after completing graduate studies in construction management or building science.

Around 20 colleges and universities offer a master's degree program in construction management or construction science. Master's degree recipients, especially those with work experience in construction, typically become construction managers in very large construction or construction management companies. Often, individuals who hold a bachelor's degree in an unrelated field seek a master's degree in order to work in the construction industry. Some construction managers obtain a master's degree in business administration or finance to further their career prospects. Doctoral degree recipients usually become college professors or conduct research.

Many individuals also attend training and educational programs sponsored by industry associations, often in collaboration with postsecondary institutions. A number of 2-year colleges throughout the country offer construction management or construction technology programs.

Both the American Institute of Constructors (AIC) and the Construction Management Association of America (CMAA) have established voluntary certification programs for construction managers. Requirements combine written examinations with verification of professional experience. AIC awards the Associate Constructor (AC) and Certified Professional Constructor (CPC) designations to candidates who meet the requirements and pass appropriate construction examinations. CMAA awards the Certified Construction Manager (CCM) designation to practitioners who meet the requirements in a construction management firm and pass a technical examination. Applicants for the CMAA certification also must complete a self-study course that covers a broad range of topics central to construction management, including the professional role of a construction manager, legal issues, and allocation of risk. Although certification is not required to work in the construction industry, voluntary certification can be valuable because it provides evidence of competence and experience.

Job Outlook

Excellent employment opportunities for construction managers are expected through 2010 because the number of job openings arising from job growth and replacement needs is expected to exceed the number of qualified managers seeking to enter the occupation. Because the construction industry often is seen as having dirty, strenuous, and hazardous working conditions, even for managers, many potential managers chose other types of careers.

Employment of construction managers is expected to increase about as fast as the average for all occupations through 2010, as the level and complexity of construction activity continues to grow. Prospects in construction management, engineering and architectural services, and construction contracting firms should be best for persons who have a bachelor's or higher degree in construction science, construction management, or construction engineering, as well as practical experience working in construction. Employers prefer applicants with previous construction work experience who can combine a strong background in building technology with proven supervisory or managerial skills. In addition to job growth, many openings should result annually from the need to replace workers who transfer to other occupations or leave the labor force.

The increasing complexity of construction projects should boost demand for management-level personnel within the construction industry, as sophisticated technology and the proliferation of laws setting standards for buildings and construction materials, worker safety, energy efficiency, and environmental protection have further complicated the construction process. Advances in building materials and construction methods; the need to replace much of the nation's infrastructure; and the growing number of multipurpose buildings, electronically operated "smart" buildings, and energy-efficient structures will further add to the demand for more construction managers. However, employment of construction managers can be sensitive to the short-term nature of many projects and to cyclical fluctuations in construction activity.

Earnings

Earnings of salaried construction managers and self-employed independent construction contractors vary depending upon the size and nature of the construction project, its geographic location, and economic conditions. In addition to typical benefits, many salaried construction managers receive benefits such as bonuses and use of company motor vehicles.

Median annual earnings of construction managers in 2000 were $58,250. The middle 50 percent earned between $44,710 and $76,510. The lowest 10 percent earned less than $34,820, and the highest 10 percent earned more than $102,860. Median annual earnings in the industries employing the largest numbers of managers in 2000 are shown in the following table:

Electrical work	$60,300
Nonresidential building construction	59,470
Plumbing, heating, and air-conditioning	58,500
Heavy construction, except highway	57,280
Residential building construction	53,510

According to a 2001 salary survey by the National Association of Colleges and Employers, candidates with a bachelor's degree in construction science/management received job offers averaging $40,740 a year.

Related Occupations

Construction managers participate in the conceptual development of a construction project and oversee its organization, scheduling, and implementation. Occupations in which similar functions are performed include architects, except landscape and naval; civil engineers; cost estimators; landscape architects; and engineering and natural sciences managers.

Sources of Additional Information

For information about constructor certification, contact:

● American Institute of Constructors, 466 94th Ave. North, St. Petersburg, FL 33702. Internet: http://www.aicnet.org

For information about construction management and construction manager certification, contact:

● Construction Management Association of America, 7918 Jones Branch Dr., Suite 540, McLean, VA 22102-3307. Internet: http://www.cmaanet.org

Information on accredited construction science and management programs and accreditation requirements is available from:

● American Council for Construction Education, 1300 Hudson Lane, Suite 3, Monroe, LA 71201. Internet: http://www.acce-hq.org

Correctional Officers

O*NET 33-1011.00, 33-3011.00, 33-3012.00

Significant Points

● The work can be stressful and hazardous.

● Job opportunities are expected to be excellent, due to fast growth and high replacement needs.

● Most jobs are in prisons in rural areas or in large regional jails.

Nature of the Work

Correctional officers are responsible for overseeing individuals who have been arrested and are awaiting trial or who have been convicted of a crime and sentenced to serve time in a jail, reformatory, or penitentiary. They maintain security and inmate accountability to prevent disturbances, assaults, or escapes. Officers have no law enforcement responsibilities outside the institution where they work.

Police and sheriffs' departments in county and municipal jails or precinct station houses employ many correctional officers, also known as *detention officers*. Most of the approximately 3,300 jails in the United States are operated by county governments, with about three-quarters of all jails under the jurisdiction of an elected sheriff. Individuals in the jail population change constantly as some are released, some are convicted and transferred to prison, and new offenders are arrested and enter the system. Correctional officers in the American jail system admit and process more than 11 million people a year, with about half a million offenders in jail at any given time. When individuals are first arrested, the jail staff may not know their true identity or criminal record, and violent detainees may be placed in the general population. This is the most dangerous phase of the incarceration process for correctional officers.

Most correctional officers are employed in large jails or state and federal prisons, watching over the approximately one million offenders who are incarcerated in federal and state prisons at any given time. In addition to jails and prisons, a relatively small number of correctional officers oversee individuals being held by the U.S. Immigration and Naturalization Service before they are released or deported, or they work for correctional institutions that are run by private for-profit organizations. While both jails and prisons can be dangerous places to work, prison populations are more stable than jail populations, and correctional officers in prisons know the security and custodial requirements of the prisoners with whom they are dealing.

Regardless of the setting, correctional officers maintain order within the institution, and enforce rules and regulations. To help ensure that inmates are orderly and obey rules, correctional officers monitor the activities and supervise the work assignments of inmates. Sometimes, it is necessary for officers to search inmates and their living quarters for contraband like weapons or drugs, settle disputes between inmates, and enforce discipline. Correctional officers periodically inspect the facilities, checking cells and other areas of the institution for unsanitary conditions, contraband, fire hazards, and any evidence of infractions of rules. In addition, they routinely inspect locks, window bars, grilles, doors, and gates for signs of tampering. Finally, officers inspect mail and visitors for prohibited items.

Correctional officers report orally and in writing on inmate conduct and on the quality and quantity of work done by inmates. Officers also report security breaches, disturbances, violations of rules, and any unusual occurrences. They usually keep a daily log or record of their activities. Correctional officers cannot show favoritism and must report any inmate who violates the rules. Should the situation arise, they help the responsible law enforcement authorities investigate crimes committed within their institution or search for escaped inmates.

In jail and prison facilities with direct supervision cellblocks, officers work unarmed. They are equipped with communications devices so that they can summon help if necessary. These officers often work in a cellblock alone, or with another officer, among the 50 to 100 inmates who reside there. The officers enforce regulations primarily through their interpersonal communications skills and the use of progressive sanctions, such as loss of some privileges.

In the highest security facilities where the most dangerous inmates are housed, correctional officers often monitor the activities of prisoners from a centralized control center with the aid of closed-circuit television cameras and a computer tracking system. In such an environment, the inmates may not see anyone but officers for days or weeks at a time and only leave their cells for showers, solitary exercise time, or visitors. Depending on the offender's security classification within the institution, correctional officers may have to restrain inmates in handcuffs and leg irons to safely escort them to and from cells and other areas to see authorized visitors. Officers also escort prisoners between the institution and courtrooms, medical facilities, and other destinations outside the institution.

Working Conditions

Working in a correctional institution can be stressful and hazardous. Every year, a number of correctional officers are injured in confrontations with inmates. Correctional officers may work indoors or outdoors. Some correctional institutions are well lit, temperature controlled, and ventilated; others are old, overcrowded, hot, and noisy. Correctional officers usually work an 8-hour day, 5 days a week, on rotating shifts. Prison and jail security must be provided around the clock, which often means that officers work all hours of the day and night, weekends, and holidays. In addition, officers may be required to work paid overtime.

Employment

Correctional officers held about 457,000 jobs in 2000. Almost 6 of every 10 jobs were in state correctional institutions such as prisons, prison camps, and youth correctional facilities. Most of the remaining jobs were in city and county jails or other institutions run by local governments. About 15,000 jobs for correctional officers were in federal correctional institutions, and about 19,000 jobs were in privately owned and managed prisons.

There are 118 jail systems in the United States that house over 1,000 inmates, all of which are located in urban areas. However, most correc-

tional officers work in institutions located in rural areas with smaller inmate populations. A significant number work in jails and other facilities located in law enforcement agencies throughout the country.

Training, Other Qualifications, and Advancement

Most institutions require correctional officers to be at least 18 to 21 years of age and a U.S. citizen; have a high school education or its equivalent; demonstrate job stability, usually by accumulating two years of work experience; and have no felony convictions. Promotion prospects may be enhanced through obtaining a postsecondary education.

Correctional officers must be in good health. Candidates for employment are generally required to meet formal standards of physical fitness, eyesight, and hearing. In addition, many jurisdictions use standard tests to determine applicant suitability to work in a correctional environment. Good judgment and the ability to think and act quickly are indispensable. Applicants are typically screened for drug abuse, subject to background checks, and required to pass a written examination.

Federal, state, and some local departments of corrections provide training for correctional officers based on guidelines established by the American Correctional Association and the American Jail Association. Some states have regional training academies which are available to local agencies. All states and local correctional agencies provide on-the-job training at the conclusion of formal instruction, including legal restrictions and interpersonal relations. Many systems require firearms proficiency and self-defense skills. Officer trainees typically receive several weeks or months of training in an actual job setting under the supervision of an experienced officer. However, specific entry requirements and on-the-job training vary widely from agency to agency.

Academy trainees generally receive instruction on a number of subjects, including institutional policies, regulations, and operations, as well as custody and security procedures. As a condition of employment, new federal correctional officers must undergo 200 hours of formal training within the first year of employment. They also must complete 120 hours of specialized training at the U.S. Federal Bureau of Prisons residential training center at Glynco, Ga., within the first 60 days after appointment. Experienced officers receive annual in-service training to keep abreast of new developments and procedures.

Some correctional officers are members of prison tactical response teams, which are trained to respond to disturbances, riots, hostage situations, forced cell moves, and other potentially dangerous confrontations. Team members receive training and practice with weapons, chemical agents, forced entry methods, crisis management, and other tactics.

With education, experience, and training, qualified officers may advance to correctional sergeant. Correctional sergeants supervise correctional officers and usually are responsible for maintaining security and directing the activities of other officers during an assigned shift or in an assigned area. Ambitious and qualified correctional officers can be promoted to supervisory or administrative positions all the way up to warden. Officers sometimes transfer to related areas, such as probation officer, parole officer, or correctional treatment specialist.

Job Outlook

Job opportunities for correctional officers are expected to be excellent through 2010. The need to replace correctional officers who transfer to other occupations, retire, or leave the labor force, coupled with rising employment demand, will generate thousands of job openings each year. In the past, some local and state corrections agencies have experienced difficulty in attracting and keeping qualified applicants, largely due to relatively low salaries and the concentration of jobs in rural locations. This situation is expected to continue.

Employment of correctional officers is expected to increase faster than the average for all occupations through 2010, as additional officers are hired to supervise and control a growing inmate population. The adoption of mandatory sentencing guidelines calling for longer sentences and reduced parole for inmates will continue to spur demand for correctional officers. Moreover, expansion and new construction of corrections facilities also are expected to create many new jobs for correctional officers, although state and local government budgetary constraints could affect the rate at which new facilities are built and staffed. Some employment opportunities also will arise in the private sector as public authorities contract with private companies to provide and staff corrections facilities.

Layoffs of correctional officers are rare because of increasing offender populations. While officers are allowed to join bargaining units, they are not allowed to strike.

Earnings

Median annual earnings of correctional officers were $31,170 in 2000. The middle 50 percent earned between $24,650 and $40,100. The lowest 10 percent earned less than $20,010, and the highest 10 percent earned more than $49,310. Median annual earnings the public sector were $37,430 in the federal government, $31,860 in state government, and $29,240 in local government. In the management and public relations industry, where officers employed by privately operated prisons are classified, median annual earnings were $21,600. According to the Federal Bureau of Prisons, the starting salary for federal correctional officers was about $27,000 a year in 2001. Starting federal salaries were slightly higher in selected areas where prevailing local pay levels were higher.

Median annual earnings of first-line supervisors/managers of correctional officers were $41,880 in 2000. The middle 50 percent earned between $32,460 and $55,540. The lowest 10 percent earned less than $28,280, and the highest 10 percent earned more than $67,280. Median annual earnings were $40,560 in state government and $49,680 in local government.

In addition to typical benefits, correctional officers employed in the public sector usually are provided with uniforms or a clothing allowance to purchase their own uniforms. Civil service systems or merit boards cover officers employed by the federal government and most state governments. Their retirement coverage entitles them to retire at age 50 after 20 years of service or at any age with 25 years of service.

Related Occupations

A number of options are available to those interested in careers in protective services and security. Security guards and gaming surveillance officers protect people and property against theft, vandalism, illegal entry, and fire. Police and detectives maintain law and order, prevent crime, and arrest offenders. Probation officers and correctional treatment specialists monitor and counsel offenders in the community and evaluate their progress in becoming productive members of society.

Sources of Additional Information

Information about correctional jobs in a jail setting is available from:

- The American Jail Association, 2053 Day Rd., Suite 100, Hagerstown, MD 21740

Information on entrance requirements, training, and career opportunities for correctional officers at the federal level may be obtained by calling:

- The Federal Bureau of Prisons at (800) 347-7744. Internet: http://www.bop.gov

Information on obtaining a position as a correctional officer with the federal government is available from the Office of Personnel Management (OPM) through a telephone-based system. Consult your telephone directory under U.S. Government for a local number or call (912) 757-3000; Federal Relay Service: (800) 877-8339. The first number is not toll free, and charges may result. Information also is available from:

- OPM Internet site: http://www.usajobs.opm.gov

Cost Estimators

O*NET 13-1051.00

Significant Points

- Fifty percent work in the construction industry, and another 20 percent are found in manufacturing industries.

- Growth of the construction industry will be the driving force behind the demand for cost estimators; employment of cost estimators in manufacturing should remain relatively stable.

- In construction and manufacturing, job prospects should be best for those with industry work experience and a degree in a related field.

Nature of the Work

Accurately forecasting the cost of future projects is vital to the survival of any business. Cost estimators develop the cost information that business owners or managers need to make a bid for a contract or to determine if a proposed new product will be profitable. They also determine which endeavors are making a profit.

Regardless of the industry in which they work, estimators compile and analyze data on all the factors that can influence costs—such as materials, labor, location, and special machinery requirements, including computer hardware and software. Job duties vary widely depending on the type and size of the project.

The methods of and motivations for estimating costs can vary greatly, depending on the industry. On a construction project, for example, the estimating process begins with the decision to submit a bid. After reviewing various preliminary drawings and specifications, the estimator visits the site of the proposed project. The estimator needs to gather information on access to the site and availability of electricity, water, and other services, as well as on surface topography and drainage. The information developed during the site visit usually is recorded in a signed report that is included in the final project estimate.

After the site visit is completed, the estimator determines the quantity of materials and labor the firm will need to furnish. This process, called the quantity survey or "takeoff," involves completing standard estimating forms, filling in dimensions, number of units, and other information. A cost estimator working for a general contractor, for example, will estimate the costs of all items the contractor must provide. Although subcontractors will estimate their costs as part of their own bidding process, the general contractor's cost estimator often analyzes bids made by subcontractors as well. Also during the takeoff process, the estimator must make decisions concerning equipment needs, sequence of operations, and crew size. Allowances for the waste of materials, inclement weather, shipping delays, and other factors that may increase costs also must be incorporated in the estimate.

On completion of the quantity surveys, the estimator prepares a total project-cost summary, including the costs of labor, equipment, materials, subcontracts, overhead, taxes, insurance, markup, and any other costs that may affect the project. The chief estimator then prepares the bid proposal for submission to the owner.

Construction cost estimators also may be employed by the project's architect or owner to estimate costs or track actual costs relative to bid specifications as the project develops. In large construction companies employing more than one estimator, it is common practice for estimators to specialize. For example, one may estimate only electrical work and another may concentrate on excavation, concrete, and forms.

In manufacturing and other firms, cost estimators usually are assigned to the engineering, cost, or pricing departments. The estimators' goal in manufacturing is to accurately estimate the costs associated with making products. The job may begin when management requests an estimate of the costs associated with a major redesign of an existing product or the development of a new product or production process. When estimating the cost of developing a new product, for example, the estimator works with Engineers, first reviewing blueprints or conceptual drawings to determine the machining operations, tools, gauges, and materials that would be required for the job. The estimator then prepares a parts list and determines whether it is more efficient to produce or to purchase the parts. To do this, the estimator must initiate inquiries for price information from potential suppliers. The next step is to determine the cost of manufacturing each component of the product. Some high technology products require a tremendous amount of computer programming during the design phase. The cost of software development is one of the fastest growing and most difficult activities to estimate. Some cost estimators now specialize in estimating only computer software development and related costs.

The cost estimator then prepares time-phase charts and learning curves. Time-phase charts indicate the time required for tool design and fabrication, tool "debugging"—finding and correcting all problems—manufacturing of parts, assembly, and testing. Learning curves graphically represent the rate at which performance improves with practice. These curves are commonly called "cost reduction" curves because many problems—such as engineering changes, rework, parts shortages, and lack of operator skills—diminish as the number of parts produced increases, resulting in lower unit costs.

Using all of this information, the estimator then calculates the standard labor hours necessary to produce a predetermined number of units. Standard labor hours are then converted to dollar values, to which are added factors for waste, overhead, and profit to yield the unit cost in dollars. The estimator then compares the cost of purchasing parts with the firm's cost of manufacturing them to determine which is cheaper.

Computers play an integral role in cost estimation because estimating often involves complex mathematical calculations and requires advanced mathematical techniques. For example, to undertake a parametric analysis (a process used to estimate project costs on a per unit basis, subject to the specific requirements of a project), cost estimators use a computer database containing information on costs and conditions of many other similar projects. Although computers cannot be used for the entire estimating process, they can relieve estimators of much of the drudgery associated with routine, repetitive, and time-consuming calculations. Computers also are used to produce all of the necessary documentation with the help of word-processing and spreadsheet software, leaving estimators more time to study and analyze projects.

Operations research, production control, cost, and price analysts who work for government agencies also may do significant amounts of cost estimating in the course of their regular duties. In addition, the duties of Construction Managers also may include estimating costs.

Working Conditions

Although estimators spend most of their time in an office, construction estimators must make visits to project work sites that can be dusty, dirty, and occasionally hazardous. Likewise, estimators in manufacturing must spend time on the factory floor where it also can be noisy and dirty. In some industries, frequent travel between a firm's headquarters and its subsidiaries or subcontractors also may be required.

Although estimators normally work a 40-hour week, overtime is common. Cost estimators often work under pressure and stress, especially when facing bid deadlines. Inaccurate estimating can cause a firm to lose out on a bid or lose money on a job that was not accurately estimated.

Employment

Cost estimators held about 211,000 jobs in 2000, about 50 percent of which were in the construction industry. Another 20 percent of cost estimators were employed in manufacturing industries. The remainder worked for engineering and architectural services firms and business services firms, and throughout a wide range of other industries.

Cost estimators work throughout the country, usually in or near major industrial, commercial, and government centers, and in cities and suburban areas undergoing rapid change or development.

Training, Other Qualifications, and Advancement

Entry requirements for cost estimators vary by industry. In the construction industry, employers increasingly prefer individuals with a degree in building construction, construction management, construction science, engineering, or architecture. However, most construction estimators also have considerable construction experience, gained through work in the industry, internships, or cooperative education programs. Applicants with a thorough knowledge of construction materials, costs, and procedures in areas ranging from heavy construction to electrical work, plumbing systems, or masonry work have a competitive edge.

In manufacturing industries, employers prefer to hire individuals with a degree in engineering, physical science, operations research, mathematics, or statistics; or in accounting, finance, business, economics, or a related subject. In most industries, great emphasis is placed on experience involving quantitative techniques.

Cost estimators should have an aptitude for mathematics, be able to quickly analyze, compare, and interpret detailed and sometimes poorly defined information, and be able to make sound and accurate judgments based on this knowledge. Assertiveness and self-confidence in presenting and supporting their conclusions are important, as are strong communications and interpersonal skills, because estimators may work as part of a project team alongside managers, owners, engineers, and design professionals. Cost estimators also need knowledge of computers, including word-processing and spreadsheet packages. In some instances, familiarity with special estimation software or programming skills also may be required.

Regardless of their background, estimators receive much training on the job because every company has its own way of handling estimates. Working with an experienced estimator, they become familiar with each step in the process. Those with no experience reading construction specifications or blueprints first learn that aspect of the work. They then may accompany an experienced estimator to the construction site or shop floor, where they observe the work being done, take measurements, or perform other routine tasks. As they become more knowledgeable, estimators learn how to tabulate quantities and dimensions from drawings and how to select the appropriate material prices.

For most estimators, advancement takes the form of higher pay and prestige. Some move into management positions, such as project manager for a construction firm or manager of the industrial engineering department for a manufacturer. Others may go into business for themselves as consultants, providing estimating services for a fee to government, construction, or manufacturing firms.

Many colleges and universities include cost estimating as part of bachelor's and associate degree curriculums in civil engineering, industrial engineering, and construction management or construction engineering technology. In addition, cost estimating is a significant part of many master's degree programs in construction science or construction management. Organizations representing cost estimators, such as the Association for the Advancement of Cost Engineers (AACE) International and the Society of Cost Estimating and Analysis (SCEA), also sponsor educational and professional development programs. These programs help students, estimators-in-training, and experienced estimators stay abreast of changes affecting the profession. Many technical schools, community colleges, and universities also offer specialized courses and programs in cost-estimating techniques and procedures.

Voluntary certification can be valuable to cost estimators because it provides professional recognition of the estimator's competence and experience. In some instances, individual employers may even require professional certification for employment. Both AACE International and SCEA administer certification programs. To become certified, estimators usually must have between 3 and 7 years of estimating experience and must pass an examination. In addition, certification requirements may include publication of at least one article or paper in the field.

Job Outlook

Overall employment of cost estimators is expected to grow about as fast as the average for all occupations through the year 2010. In addition to openings created by growth, some job openings also will arise from the need to replace workers who transfer to other occupations or leave the labor force.

Growth of the construction industry, in which half of all cost estimators are employed, will be the driving force behind the demand for these workers. Construction and repair of highways and streets, bridges, and construction of more subway systems, airports, water and sewage systems, and electric power plants and transmission lines will stimulate demand for many more cost estimators. The increasing population and its changing demographics that will increase the demand for residential construction and remodeling also will spur demand for cost estimators. As the population ages, the demand for nursing and extended care facilities will increase. School construction and repair also will add to the demand for cost estimators. Job prospects in construction should be best for cost estimators with a degree in construction management or construction science, engineering, or architecture who have practical experience in various phases of construction or in a specialty craft area.

Employment of cost estimators in manufacturing should remain relatively stable as firms continue to use their services to identify and control their operating costs. Experienced estimators with degrees in engineering, science, mathematics, business administration, or economics should have the best job prospects in manufacturing.

Earnings

Salaries of cost estimators vary widely by experience, education, size of firm, and industry. Median annual earnings of cost estimators in 2000 were $45,800. The middle 50 percent earned between $35,040 and $59,410. The lowest 10 percent earned less than $27,710, and the highest 10 percent earned more than $75,460. Median annual earnings in the industries employing the largest numbers of cost estimators in 2000 were as follows:

Nonresidential building construction	$50,930
Electrical work	49,630
Plumbing, heating, and air-conditioning	47,680
Residential building construction	46,360
Miscellaneous special trade contractors	45,740

College graduates with degrees in fields that provide a strong background in cost estimating, such as engineering or construction management, could start at a higher level. According to a 2001 salary survey by the National Association of Colleges and Employers, bachelor's degree candidates with degrees in construction science/management received job offers averaging about $40,740 a year.

Related Occupations

Other workers who quantitatively analyze information include accountants and auditors; budget analysts; claims adjusters, appraisers, examiners, and investigators; economists and market and survey researchers; financial analysts and personal financial advisors; insurance underwriters; loan counselors and officers; and operations research analysts. In addition, the duties of industrial production managers and construction managers also may involve analyzing costs.

Sources of Additional Information

Information about career opportunities, certification, educational programs, and cost-estimating techniques may be obtained from:

- Association for the Advancement of Cost Engineering International, 209 Prairie Ave., Suite 100, Morgantown, WV 26501. Internet: http://www.aacei.org

- Society of Cost Estimating and Analysis, 101 S. Whiting St., Suite 201, Alexandria, VA 22304. Internet: http://www.erols.com/scea

Counter and Rental Clerks

O*NET 41-2021.00

Significant Points

- Jobs primarily are entry-level and require little or no experience and minimal formal education.

- Average employment growth is expected as businesses strive to improve customer service.

- Part-time employment opportunities should be plentiful.

Nature of the Work

Whether renting videotapes, moving trucks, or air compressors, dropping off clothes to be dry cleaned or appliances to be serviced, we rely on counter and rental clerks to handle these transactions efficiently. Although specific duties vary by establishment, counter and rental clerks answer questions involving product availability, cost, and rental provisions. Counter and rental clerks also take orders, calculate fees, receive payments, and accept returns.

Regardless of where they work, counter and rental clerks must be knowledgeable about the company's services, policies, and procedures. Depending on the type of establishment, counter and rental clerks use their special knowledge to give advice on a wide variety of products and services, which may range from hydraulic tools to shoe repair. For example, in the car rental industry, they inform customers about the features of different types of automobiles, as well as daily and weekly rental costs. They also ensure that customers meet age and other requirements for rental cars, and indicate when and in what condition cars must be returned. Those in the equipment rental industry have similar duties, but must also know how to operate and care for the machinery rented. In dry-cleaning establishments, counter clerks inform customers when items will be ready and what the effects of the chemicals used on garments are, if any. In video rental stores, they advise customers about the use of video and game players and the length of rental, scan returned movies and games, restock the shelves, handle money, and log daily reports.

When taking orders, counter and rental clerks use various types of equipment. In some establishments, they write out tickets and order forms, although most use computers or bar code scanners. Most of these computer systems are user-friendly, require very little data entry, and are customized for the firm. Scanners read the product code and display a description of the item on a computer screen. However, clerks must ensure that the data on the screen accurately matches the product.

Working Conditions

Firms employing counter and rental clerks usually operate nights and weekends for the convenience of their customers. However, many employers offer flexible schedules. Some counter and rental clerks work 40-hour weeks, but about half are on part-time schedules—usually during rush periods, such as weekends, evenings, and holidays.

Working conditions usually are pleasant; most stores and service establishments are clean, well-lighted, and temperature-controlled. However, clerks are on their feet much of the time and may be confined behind a small counter area or be exposed to harmful chemicals. This job requires constant interaction with the public and can be stressful, especially during busy periods.

Employment

Counter and rental clerks held 423,000 jobs in 2000. About 1 of every 6 clerks worked in a videotape rental store. Other large employers included dry-cleaners, automobile rental firms, equipment rental firms, and miscellaneous amusement and recreation establishments.

Counter and rental clerks are employed throughout the country but are concentrated in metropolitan areas, where personal services and renting and leasing services are in greater demand.

Training, Other Qualifications, and Advancement

Counter and rental clerk jobs primarily are entry-level and require little or no experience and minimal formal education. However, many employers prefer workers with at least a high school diploma.

In most companies, counter and rental clerks are trained on the job, sometimes through the use of videotapes, brochures, and pamphlets. Clerks usually learn how to operate the equipment and become familiar with the establishment's policies and procedures under the observation of a more experienced worker. However, some employers have formal classroom training programs lasting from a few hours to a few weeks. Topics covered in this training include a description of the industry, the company and its policies and procedures, equipment operation, sales techniques, and customer service. Counter and rental clerks also must become familiar with the different products and services rented or provided by their company in order to give customers the best possible service.

Counter and rental clerks should enjoy working with people and have the ability to deal tactfully with difficult customers. They should be able to handle several tasks at once, while continuing to provide friendly service. In addition, good oral and written communication skills are essential.

Advancement opportunities depend on the size and type of company. Many establishments that employ counter or rental clerks tend to be small businesses, making advancement difficult. But in larger establishments with a corporate structure, jobs as counter and rental clerks offer good opportunities for workers to learn about their company's products and business practices. These jobs can lead to more responsible positions. It is common in many establishments to promote counter and rental clerks to event planner, assistant manager, or sales positions. Workers may choose to pursue related positions, such as mechanic, or even establish their own business.

In certain industries, such as equipment repair, counter and rental jobs may be an additional or alternate source of income for workers who are unemployed or entering semiretirement. For example, retired mechanics could prove invaluable at tool rental centers because of their relevant knowledge.

Job Outlook

Employment of counter and rental clerks is expected to increase about as fast as the average for all occupations through the year 2010, as all types of businesses strive to improve customer service. In addition, some industries employing counter and rental clerks are expected to grow rapidly, including equipment rental and leasing and amusement and recreation services. Nevertheless, most job openings will arise from the need to replace experienced workers who transfer to other occupations or leave the labor force. Part-time employment opportunities are expected to be plentiful.

Earnings

Counter and rental clerks typically start at the minimum wage, which, in establishments covered by federal law, was $5.15 an hour in 2001. In some states, the law sets the minimum wage higher and establishments must pay at least that amount. Wages also tend to be higher in areas where there is intense competition for workers. In addition to wages, some counter and rental clerks receive commissions, based on the number of contracts they complete or services they sell.

Median hourly earnings of counter and rental clerks in 2000 were $7.87. The middle 50 percent earned between $6.51 and $10.22 an hour. The lowest 10 percent earned less than $5.80 an hour, and the highest 10 percent earned more than $13.75 an hour. Median hourly earnings in the industries employing the largest number of counter and rental clerks in 2000 were as follows:

New and used car dealers	$14.90
Miscellaneous equipment rental and leasing	9.54
Automotive rentals, no drivers	9.16
Grocery stores	7.66
Video tape rental	6.60

Full-time workers typically receive health and life insurance, paid vacation, and sick leave. Benefits for counter and rental clerks who work part-time or for independent stores tend to be significantly less than for those who work full time. Many companies offer discounts to both full- and part-time employees on the services they provide.

Related Occupations

Counter and rental clerks take orders and receive payment for services rendered. Other workers with similar duties include tellers, cashiers, food and beverage serving and related workers, gaming cage workers, postal service workers, and retail salespersons.

Sources of Additional Information

For general information on employment in the equipment rental industry, contact:

- American Rental Association, 1900 19th St., Moline, IL 61265. Internet: http://www.ararental.org

For more information about the work of counter clerks in dry-cleaning and laundry establishments, contact:

- International Fabricare Institute, 12251 Tech Rd., Silver Spring, MD 20904. Internet: http://www.ifi.org

Couriers and Messengers

O*NET 43-5021.00

Significant Points

- Many courier and messenger jobs are entry level and do not require more than a high school diploma.

- Workers develop the necessary skills through on-the-job training lasting from several days to a few months.

- Employment of couriers and messengers is expected to decline through 2010 due to the more widespread use of electronic information-handling technology.

Nature of the Work

Couriers and messengers move and distribute information, documents, and small packages for businesses, institutions, and government agencies. They pick up and deliver letters, important business documents, or packages that need to be sent or received quickly within a local area. Trucks and vans are used for larger deliveries, such as legal caseloads and conference materials. By sending an item by courier or messenger, the sender ensures that it reaches its destination the same day or even within the hour. Couriers and messengers also deliver items that the sender is unwilling to entrust to other means of delivery, such as important legal or financial documents, passports, airline tickets, or medical samples to be tested.

Couriers and messengers receive their instructions either by reporting to their office in person, by telephone, by two-way radio, or wireless data service. They then pick up the item and carry it to its destination. After each pickup or delivery, they check in with dispatch to receive instructions. Sometimes dispatch will contact them while they are between stops; they may be routed to go past a stop that has very recently called in a delivery. Since most couriers and messengers work on commission, they are carrying more than one package at any given time of the day. Consequently, most couriers and messengers spend much of their time outdoors or in their vehicle. They usually maintain records of deliveries and often obtain signatures from the persons receiving the items.

Most couriers and messengers deliver items within a limited geographic area, such as a city or metropolitan area. Items that need to go longer distances usually are sent by mail or by an overnight delivery service. Some couriers and messengers carry items only for their employer, which typically might be a law firm, bank, or financial institution. Others may act as part of an organization's internal mail system and mainly carry items among an organization's buildings or entirely within one building. Many couriers and messengers work for messenger or courier services; for a fee, they pick up items from anyone and deliver them to specified destinations within a local area. Most are paid on a commission basis.

Couriers and messengers reach their destination by several methods. Many drive vans or cars or ride motorcycles. A few travel by foot, especially in urban areas or when making deliveries nearby. In congested urban areas, messengers often use bicycles to make deliveries. Bicycle messengers usually are employed by messenger or courier services. Although e-mail and fax machines can deliver information faster than couriers and messengers can and a great deal of information is available over the Internet, an electronic copy cannot substitute for the original document for many types of business transactions.

Working Conditions

Couriers and messengers spend most of their time alone making deliveries and usually are not closely supervised. Those who deliver by bicycle must be physically fit and are exposed to all weather conditions, as well as to the many hazards associated with heavy traffic. Car, van, and truck couriers must sometimes carry heavy loads, either manually or with the aid of a handtruck. They also have to deal with difficult parking situations as well as traffic jams and road construction. The pressure of making as many deliveries as possible to increase earnings can be stressful and may lead to unsafe driving or bicycling practices.

The typical workweek is Monday through Friday.

Employment

Couriers and messengers together held about 141,000 jobs in 2000. About 9 percent of couriers and messengers worked for law firms, another 10 percent worked for hospitals and medical and dental laboratories, and 29 percent were employed by local and long-distance trucking establishments. Financial institutions, such as commercial banks, savings institutions, and credit unions, employed 10 percent. The rest were employed in a variety of other industries. Technically, many messengers are self-employed independent contractors because they provide their vehicles and, to a certain extent, set their own schedules but, in many respects, they are like employees because they usually work for one company.

Training, Other Qualifications, and Advancement

Many courier and messenger jobs are entry level and do not require more than a high school diploma. Employers, however, prefer to hire those who are familiar with computers and other electronic office and business equipment. Those who have taken business courses or have previous business, dispatching, or specific job-related experience may be preferred. Because communication with other people is an integral part of these jobs, good oral and written communications skills are essential.

Couriers and messengers usually learn on the job, training with a veteran for a short time. Those who work as independent contractors for a messenger or delivery service may be required to have a valid driver's license, a registered and inspected vehicle, a good driving record, and insurance coverage. Many couriers and messengers who are employees, rather than independent contractors, also are required to provide and maintain their own vehicle. Although some companies have spare bicycles or mopeds that their riders may rent for a short period, almost all

two-wheeled couriers own their own bicycle, moped, or motorcycle. A good knowledge of the geographic area in which they travel, as well as a good sense of direction, also are important.

Couriers and messengers, especially those who work for messenger or courier services, have limited advancement opportunities; a small fraction move into the office to learn dispatching or to take service requests by phone.

Job Outlook

Employment of couriers and messengers is expected to decline through 2010 despite an increasing volume of parcels, business documents, promotional materials, and other written information that must be handled and delivered as the economy expands. Employment of couriers and messengers will continue to be adversely impacted by the more widespread use of electronic information-handling technology. For example, fax machines that allow copies of documents to be immediately sent across town or around the world have become standard office equipment. The transmission of information using e-mail also has become commonplace and will continue to reduce the demand for messengers. Many documents, forms, and application that people used to have delivered by hand are now downloaded from the Internet. However, couriers and messengers still will be needed to transport materials that cannot be sent electronically—such as legal documents, blueprints and other oversized materials, large multipage documents, securities, passports, financial statements, and airline tickets. Also, they still will be required by medical and dental laboratories to pick up and deliver medical samples, specimens, and other materials.

Earnings

Median hourly earnings in 2000 for couriers and messengers were $8.96.

Couriers and messengers agents usually receive the same benefits as most other workers. If uniforms are required, employers usually provide either the uniforms or an allowance to purchase them.

Related Occupations

Messengers and couriers deliver letters, parcels, and other items. They also keep accurate records of their work. Others who do similar work are postal service workers; truckdrivers and driver/sales workers; shipping, receiving, and traffic clerks; and cargo and freight agents.

Sources of Additional Information

Information about job opportunities may be obtained from local employers and local offices of the state employment service. Persons interested in courier and messenger jobs also may contact messenger and courier services, mail-order firms, banks, printing and publishing firms, utility companies, retail stores, or other large firms.

Court Reporters

O*NET 23-2091.00

Significant Points

● Court reporters usually need a 2- or 4-year postsecondary school degree.

● Demand for realtime and broadcast captioning and translating will result in employment growth of court reporters.

● Job opportunities should be best for those with certification from the National Court Reporters Association.

Nature of the Work

Court reporters typically take verbatim reports of speeches, conversations, legal proceedings, meetings, and other events when written accounts of spoken words are necessary for correspondence, records, or legal proof. Court reporters not only play a critical role in judicial proceedings, but every meeting where the spoken word must be preserved as a written transcript. They are responsible for ensuring a complete, accurate, and secure legal record. In addition to preparing and protecting the legal record, many court reporters assist judges and trial attorneys in a variety of ways, such as organizing and searching for information in the official record or making suggestions to judges and attorneys regarding courtroom administration and procedure. Increasingly, court reporters are providing closed-captioning and realtime translating services to the deaf and hard-of-hearing community.

Court reporters document all statements made in official proceedings using a stenotype machine, which allows them to press multiple keys at a time to record combinations of letters representing sounds, words, or phrases. These symbols are then recorded on computer disks or CD-ROM, which are then translated and displayed as text in a process called computer-aided transcription (CAT). In all cases, accuracy is crucial because there is only one person creating an official transcript. In a judicial setting, for example, appeals often depend on the court reporter's transcript.

Stenotype machines used for realtime captioning are linked directly to the computer. As the reporter keys in the symbols, they instantly appear as text on the screen. This process, called Communications Access Realtime Translation (CART), is used in courts, classrooms, meetings, and for closed captioning for the hearing-impaired on television.

Court reporters are responsible for a number of duties both before and after transcribing events. First, they must create and maintain the computer dictionary that they use to translate stenographic strokes into written text. They may customize the dictionary with word parts, words, or terminology specific to the proceeding, program, or event—such as a religious service—they plan to transcribe. After documenting proceedings, court reporters must edit their CART translation for correct grammar, accurate identification of proper names and places, and to ensure the record or testimony is distinguishable. They usually prepare written transcripts, make copies, and provide transcript information to court, counsel, parties, and the public upon request. They also develop procedures for easy storage and retrieval of all stenographic notes and files in paper or digital format.

Although many court reporters record official proceedings in the courtroom, the majority of them work outside the courtroom. Freelance reporters, for example, take depositions for attorneys in offices and document proceedings of meetings, conventions, and other private activities. Others capture the proceedings in government agencies of all levels, from the U.S. Congress to state and local governing bodies. Court reporters who specialize in captioning live television programming for people with hearing loss are commonly known as *stenocaptioners*. They work for television networks or cable stations captioning news, emergency broadcasts, sporting events, and other programming. With CART and broadcast captioning, the level of understanding gained by a person with hearing loss depends entirely on the skill of the stenocaptioner. In an emergency situation, such as a tornado or hurricane, peoples' safety may depend entirely on the information provided in the form of captioning.

Medical transcriptionists have similar duties, but with a different focus. They translate and edit recorded dictation by physicians and other healthcare providers regarding patient assessment and treatment.

Working Conditions

The majority of court reporters work in comfortable settings, such as in offices of attorneys, courtrooms, legislatures, and conventions. An increasing number of court reporters work from home-based offices as independent contractors.

Work in this occupation presents few hazards, although sitting in the same position for long periods can be tiring, and workers can suffer wrist, back, neck, or eye problems due to strain and risk repetitive motion injuries such as carpal tunnel syndrome. Also, the pressure to be accurate and fast also can be stressful.

Many official court reporters work a standard 40-hour week. Self-employed court reporters usually work flexible hours—including part-time, evenings, weekends, or on an on-call basis.

Employment

Court reporters held about 18,000 jobs in 2000. Of those who worked for a wage or salary, about 11,000 worked for state and local governments, a reflection of the large number of court reporters working in courts, legislatures, and various agencies. Most of the rest worked as independent contractors or employees of court reporting agencies. About 13 percent were self-employed.

Training, Other Qualifications, and Advancement

Court reporters usually complete a 2- or 4-year training program, offered by about 160 postsecondary vocational and technical schools and colleges. Currently, the National Court Reporters Association (NCRA) has approved about 86 programs, all of which offer courses in computer-aided transcription and real-time reporting. NCRA-approved programs require students to capture a minimum of 225 words per minute. Court reporters in the federal government must capture at least 225 words a minute.

Some states require court reporters to be Notary Publics, or to be a Certified Court Reporter (CCR); reporters must pass a state certification test administered by a board of examiners to earn this designation. The National Court Reporters Association confers the entry-level designation, Registered Professional Reporter (RPR), upon those who pass a four-part examination and participate in mandatory continuing education programs. Although voluntary, the RPR designation is recognized as a mark of distinction in this field. A reporter may obtain additional certifica-

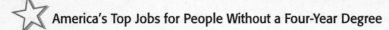

tions that demonstrate higher levels of competency. The NCRA also offers a designation called Certified Realtime Reporter (CRR). This designation promotes and recognizes competence in the specialized skill of converting the spoken word into the written word instantaneously. Reporters, working as stenocaptioners or CART providers, use realtime skills to produce captions for the deaf and hard-of-hearing viewers.

Court reporters must have excellent listening skills, as well as good English grammar and punctuation skills. They must also be aware of business practices and current events, especially the correct spelling of names of people, places, and events that may be mentioned in a broadcast or in court proceedings. For those who work in courtrooms, an expert knowledge of legal terminology and criminal and appellate procedure is essential. Because stenographic capturing of proceedings requires a computerized stenography machine, court reporters must be knowledgeable about computer hardware and software applications.

With experience and education, court reporters can advance to administrative and management positions, consulting, or teaching.

Job Outlook

Employment of court reporters is projected to grow about as fast as the average for all occupations through 2010. Demand for court reporter services will be spurred by the continuing need for accurate transcription of proceedings in courts and in pretrial depositions, and by the growing need to create captions of live or prerecorded television and provide other realtime translating services for the deaf and hard-of-hearing community.

Federal legislation mandates that a by 2006, all new television programming must be captioned for the deaf and hard-of-hearing. Additionally, the American with Disabilities Act gives deaf and hard-of-hearing students in colleges and universities the right to request access to realtime translation in their classes. Both of these factors are expected to increase demand for trained stenographic court reporters to provide realtime captioning and Communications Access Realtime Translation (CART) services. Although these services are transcript-free and differ from traditional court reporting, which uses computer-aided transcription to turn spoken words into permanent text, they require the same skills that court reporters learn in their training.

Despite increasing numbers of civil and criminal cases, budget constraints are expected to limit the ability of federal, state, and local courts to expand, also limiting the demand for traditional court reporting services in courtrooms and other legal venues. Also, in efforts to keep costs down, many courtrooms have installed tape recorders to maintain records of proceedings. Despite the use of audiotape and videotape technology, court reporters can quickly turn spoken words into readable, searchable, permanent text so they will continue to be needed to produce written legal transcripts and proceedings for publication.

The Internet is expected to affect how reporting services are provided as online video technology improves and more meetings, college classes, and even depositions take place on the Internet. Court reporters will be in demand online to provide instantaneous text of those meetings in a searchable, easy-to-access medium.

Job opportunities should be best for those with certification from the National Court Reporters Association.

Earnings

Court reporters had median annual earnings of $39,660 in 2000. The middle 50 percent earned between $28,630 and $51,740. The lowest paid 10 percent earned less than $18,750, and the highest paid 10 percent earned over $69,060. Median annual earnings in 2000 were $37,640 for court reporters working in local government.

Compensation methods for court reporters vary, depending on the type of reporting jobs, the experience of the individual reporter, the level of certification achieved and the region. Official court reporters earn a salary and a per-page fee for transcripts. Many salaried court reporters supplement their income by doing additional freelance work. Freelance court reporters are paid per job and receive a per-page fee for transcripts. Communication access realtime translation providers are paid hourly. Stenocaptioners are paid a salary and benefits if they work as employees of a captioning company; stenocaptioners working as independent contractors are paid hourly.

According to a National Court Reporters Association survey of its members, average annual earnings for court reporters were $61,830 in 1999.

Related Occupations

A number of other workers type, record information, and process paperwork. Among these are secretaries and administrative assistants, medical transcriptionists, receptionists and information clerks, and human resources assistants, except payroll and timekeeping. Other workers who provide legal support include paralegals and legal assistants.

Sources of Additional Information

State employment service offices can provide information about job openings for court reporters. For information about careers, training, and certification in court reporting, contact:

- National Court Reporters Association, 8224 Old Courthouse Rd., Vienna, VA 22182. Internet: http://www.ncraonline.org and http://www.bestfuture.com

- United States Court Reporters Association, 1904 Marvel Lane, Liberty, MO 64068. Internet: http://www.uscra.org

Credit Authorizers, Checkers, and Clerks

O*NET 43-4041.01, 43-4041.02

Significant Points

- Slower-than-average employment growth for credit authorizers, checkers, and clerks is expected through 2010, as technological advancements continue to automate many of their job duties. Some job openings should arise due to the need to replace workers who leave these occupations.

- A high school diploma or its equivalent is the most common educational requirement.

● Because many credit authorizers, checkers, and clerks deal directly with the public by telephone, a professional attitude and pleasant personality are imperative.

Nature of the Work

Credit authorizers, checkers, and clerks review credit history and obtain the information needed to determine the creditworthiness of individuals or businesses applying for credit. They spend much of their day on the telephone obtaining information from credit bureaus, employers, banks, credit institutions, and other sources to determine applicants' credit history and ability to pay back the charge.

Credit authorizers, checkers, and clerks process and authorize applications for credit, including credit cards. Although the distinctions among the three job titles are becoming less, some general differences remain. *Credit clerks* typically handle the processing of credit applications by verifying the information on the application, calling applicants if additional data are needed, contacting credit bureaus for a credit rating, and obtaining any other information necessary to determine applicants' creditworthiness. If the clerk works in a department store or other establishment that offers instant credit, he or she enters applicant information into a computer at the point-of-sale. A credit rating will then be transmitted from a central office within seconds to indicate whether the application should be rejected or approved.

Some organizations have *credit checkers*, who investigate a person's or business's credit history and current credit standing prior to the issuance of a loan or line of credit. Credit checkers also may telephone or write to credit departments of businesses and service companies to obtain information about an applicant's credit standing. Credit reporting agencies and bureaus hire a number of checkers to secure, update, and verify information for credit reports. These workers often are called credit investigators or reporters.

Credit authorizers approve charges against customers' existing accounts. Most charges are approved automatically by computer. When accounts are past due, overextended, or invalid, or show a change of address, however, sales persons refer transactions to credit authorizers located in a central office. These authorizers evaluate the customers' computerized credit records and payment histories to quickly decide whether or not to approve new charges.

Working Conditions

Most credit authorizers, checkers, and clerks work in areas that are clean, well lit, and relatively quiet. Because a number of clerks may share the same workspace, it may be crowded and noisy.

Most credit authorizers, checkers, and clerks work a standard 40-hour week. Some jobs may require working evenings, late night shifts, weekends, and holidays. In general, employees with the least seniority tend to be assigned the less desirable shifts.

The work performed by credit authorizers, checkers, and clerks may be repetitious and stressful. Stress is caused by technology that enables management to electronically monitor use of computer systems, tape record telephone calls, or limit the time spent on each call.

In addition, prolonged exposure to a video display terminal may lead to eyestrain for the many information clerks who work with computers.

Employment

Credit authorizers, checkers, and clerks held about 86,000 jobs in 2000. About 4 out of 10 were employed by commercial and savings banks, credit unions, mortgage banks, and personal and business credit institutions. Credit reporting and collection agencies and establishments in wholesale and retail trade also employ these clerks.

Training, Other Qualifications, and Advancement

Although hiring requirements for credit authorizers, checkers, and clerks vary from industry to industry, a high school diploma or its equivalent is the most common educational requirement. Increasingly, familiarity or experience with computers and good interpersonal skills is equally important to employers.

Many credit authorizers, checkers, and clerks deal with the public, so a pleasant personality is important. A clear speaking voice and fluency in the English language also are essential because these employees frequently use the telephone. Good spelling and computer literacy often are needed, particularly because most work involves considerable computer use.

Orientation and training for credit authorizers, checkers, and clerks usually takes place on the job. Under the guidance of a supervisor or other senior workers, new employees learn company procedures. Some formal classroom training also may be necessary, such as training in specific computer software. Most credit authorizers, checkers, and clerks continue to receive instruction on new procedures and company policies after their initial training ends.

Advancement for credit authorizers, checkers, and clerks usually comes by transfer to a position with more responsibilities or by promotion to a supervisory position. Most companies fill office and administrative support supervisory and managerial positions by promoting individuals within their organization, so clerks who acquire additional skills, experience, and training improve their advancement opportunities.

Job Outlook

Slower-than-average employment growth for credit authorizers, checkers, and clerks is expected through 2010. Despite a projected increase in the number of credit applications, automation will allow fewer workers to process, check, and authorize applications than in the past.

Credit scoring is a major development that has improved the productivity of these workers, thus limiting employment growth. Companies and credit bureaus now can purchase software that quickly analyzes an applicant's creditworthiness and summarizes it into a "score." Credit issuers then can easily decide whether to accept or reject the application depending on the score, speeding up the authorization of loans or credit. Obtaining credit ratings also is much easier for credit checkers and authorizers, as businesses now have computer systems that are directly linked to credit bureaus that provide immediate access to a person's credit history.

The job outlook for credit authorizers, checkers, and clerks is sensitive to overall economic activity. A downturn in the economy or a rise in interest rates usually lead to a decline in demand for credit. Even in slow economic times, however, job openings will arise from the need to replace workers who leave the occupation for various reasons.

Earnings

In 2000, the median annual earnings for credit authorizers, checkers, and clerks were $24,570.

In addition to their hourly wage, full-time credit authorizers, checkers, and clerks who work evenings, nights, weekends, or holidays may receive shift differential pay.

Related Occupations

A number of other workers deal with the public, receive and provide information, or direct people to others who can assist them. Among these are dispatchers, security guards and gaming surveillance workers, tellers, and counter and rental clerks.

Sources of Additional Information

State employment service offices can provide information about employment opportunities.

Customer Service Representatives

O*NET 43-4051.00, 43-4051.01, 43-4051.02

Significant Points

- Numerous job openings should arise for customer service representatives due to employment growth and the need to replace workers who leave these occupations.

- A high school diploma or its equivalent is the most common educational requirement.

- Because many customer service representatives deal directly with the public, a professional appearance and pleasant personality are imperative.

Nature of the Work

Customer service representatives interact with customers to provide information in response to inquires about products and services. They also handle and resolve customer's complaints. Some customer service representatives assist individuals interested in opening accounts for various utilities such as electricity and gas, or for communication services such as cable television and telephone. In many cases, they gather information by phone or in person. They receive orders for services to be installed, turned on, turned off, or changed. They may look into and resolve complaints about billings and service provided by phone, cable television, and utility companies. Customer service representatives also may explain how to use equipment and solve any equipment problems. Others explain to users how to navigate an Internet site.

Many customer service representatives use multiline telephones, fax machines, and personal computers. Because banks are highly automated,

their customer service call centers route each call to the first available representative as quickly as possible. Insurance agencies, on the other hand, often use time-consuming searches for files and related paperwork in providing customer service.

Self-service Web sites and e-mail are providing more efficient and targeted customer service. Many companies are starting to transform conventional call centers, and e-mail has become a principal method through which to serve customers. The challenge of providing customer service via e-mail is having enough representatives to deal with the large volume of mail.

Working Conditions

Most customer service representatives work in areas that are clean, well lit, and relatively quiet. This is especially true for clerks who greet customers and visitors; they usually work in highly visible areas that are furnished to make a good impression. Because a number of customer service representatives may share the same workspace, it may be crowded and noisy.

Most customer service representatives work a standard 40-hour week. Some high school and college students work part-time as information clerks, after school or during vacations. Some jobs may require working evenings, late night shifts, weekends, and holidays. This is the case for a growing number of customer service representatives who work for large banks with call centers that are staffed around the clock. In general, employees with the least seniority tend to be assigned the less desirable shifts.

The work performed by customer service representatives may be repetitious and stressful. Stress is caused by technology that enables management to electronically monitor use of computer systems, tape record telephone calls, or limit the time spent on each call.

The work of customer service representatives also can be stressful when trying to serve the needs of difficult or angry customers. In addition, prolonged exposure to a video display terminal may lead to eyestrain for the many customer service representatives who work with computers.

Employment

Customer service representatives held about 1.9 million jobs in 2000. Although they were found in all industries, about 1 in 4 customer service representatives worked in finance, insurance, and real estate. Telephone communications and cable television services also employed a large number of customer service representatives.

Training, Other Qualifications, and Advancement

Although hiring requirements for customer service representatives vary from industry to industry, a high school diploma or its equivalent is the most common educational requirement. For customer service representatives, some college education may be preferred.

Increasingly, familiarity or experience with computers and good interpersonal skills is equally important to employers.

Customer service representatives deal with the public, so a pleasant personality is important. A clear speaking voice and fluency in the English language also are essential because these employees frequently use the telephone or public address systems. Good spelling and computer literacy often are needed, particularly because most work involves considerable computer use.

Some entry-level customer service representatives are college graduates with degrees in business, finance, or liberal arts. Although a degree rarely is required, many graduates accept entry-level clerical positions to get into a particular company or to enter a particular field. Workers with college degrees are likely to start at higher salaries and advance more easily than those without degrees do.

Customer service representatives also receive on-the-job training, which includes instructions on how to operate telephone and computer systems. These workers must possess strong communication skills since they are constantly interacting with customers. During this period, supervisors may monitor telephone conversations to improve the quality of customer service. Agents are expected to provide good service while limiting the time spent on each call without being discourteous to customers.

Some formal classroom training also may be necessary, such as training in specific computer software. Most customer service representatives continue to receive instruction on new procedures and company policies after their initial training ends.

Advancement for customer service representatives usually comes by transfer to a position with more responsibilities or by promotion to a supervisory position. Most companies fill office and administrative support supervisory and managerial positions by promoting individuals within their organization, so customer service representatives who acquire additional skills, experience, and training improve their advancement opportunities.

Job Outlook

Overall employment of customer service representatives is expected to increase faster than the average for all occupations through the year 2010. In addition to many new openings occurring as businesses and organizations expand, numerous job openings will result from the need to replace experienced customer service representatives who transfer to other occupations or leave the labor force. Replacement needs are expected to be significant in this large occupation as many young people work as customer service representatives for a few years before switching to other, higher paying jobs. This occupation is well-suited to flexible work schedules, and many opportunities for part-time work will continue to be available, particularly as organizations attempt to cut labor costs by hiring more temporary workers.

Customer service is critical to the success of any organization that deals with customers. Strong customer service can build sales and visibility as companies try to distinguish themselves from competitors. Advances in technology, especially the increased use of the Internet and the expected growth in electronic commerce, should result in rapid employment growth among customer service representatives. Web sites, e-mail, and more recently, wireless communications, are proving more efficient because they provide targeted customer service. As more business is conducted over the Internet, more customer service representatives will be needed over the next decade to answer questions, provide assistance in navigating Web sites, make product recommendations, and quickly and efficiently respond to the growing volume of e-mail.

Earnings

In 2000, the median annual earnings for customer service representatives were $24,600.

In early 2001, the federal government typically paid salaries ranging from $18,667 to $22,734 a year to beginning receptionists with a high school diploma or 6 months of experience. The average annual salary for all receptionists employed by the federal government was about $24,477 in 2001.

In addition to their hourly wage, full-time customer service representatives who work evenings, nights, weekends, or holidays may receive shift differential pay. Some employers offer educational assistance to their employees.

Related Occupations

A number of other workers deal with the public, receive and provide information, or direct people to others who can assist them. Among these are dispatchers, security guards and gaming surveillance workers, tellers, and counter and rental clerks.

Sources of Additional Information

State employment service offices can provide information about employment opportunities.

Dancers and Choreographers

O*NET 27-2031.00, 27-2032.00

Significant Points

- Many dancers stop performing by their late thirties; however, some remain in the field as choreographers, dance teachers, or artistic directors.

- Most dancers begin formal training at an early age (between 5 and 15) and many have their first professional audition by age 17 or 18.

- Dancers and choreographers face intense competition (only the most talented find regular work).

Nature of the Work

From ancient times to the present, dancers have expressed ideas, stories, rhythm, and sound with their bodies. They use a variety of dance forms that allow free movement and self-expression, including classical ballet, modern dance, and culturally specific dance styles. Many dancers combine performance work with teaching or choreography.

Dancers perform in a variety of settings, such as musical productions, and may present folk, ethnic, tap, jazz, and other popular kinds of dance. They also perform in opera, musical theater, television, movies, music videos, and commercials, in which they may sing and act. Dancers most often perform as part of a group, although a few top artists perform solo.

Many dancers work with choreographers, who create original dances and develop new interpretations of existing dances. Because few dance routines are written down, choreographers instruct performers at rehearsals to achieve the desired effect. In addition, choreographers often are involved in auditioning performers.

Working Conditions

Dance is strenuous. Many dancers stop performing by their late thirties because of the physical demands on the body. However, some continue to work in the field as choreographers, dance teachers and coaches, or artistic directors. Others move into administrative positions, such as company manager. Some celebrated dancers, however, continue performing beyond the age of 50.

Daily rehearsals require very long hours. Many dance companies tour for part of the year to supplement a limited performance schedule at home. Dancers who perform in musical productions and other family entertainment spend much of their time on the road; others work in nightclubs or on cruise ships. Most dance performances are in the evening, while rehearsals and practice take place during the day. As a result, dancers often work very long and late hours. Generally, dancers and choreographers work in modern and temperature-controlled facilities; however, some studios may be older and less comfortable.

Employment

Professional dancers and choreographers held about 26,000 jobs at any one time in 2000. Many others were between engagements, so that the total number of people available for work as dancers over the course of the year was greater. Dancers and choreographers worked in a variety of settings, including eating and drinking establishments, theatrical and television productions, dance studios and schools, dance companies and bands, concert halls, and theme parks. Dancers who give lessons worked in secondary schools, colleges and universities, and private studios.

New York City is home to many major dance companies; however, full-time professional dance companies operate in most major cities.

Training, Other Qualifications, and Advancement

Training varies depending upon the type of dance and is a continuous part of all dancers' careers. Many dancers and dance instructors believe dancers should start with a good foundation in classical dance before selecting a particular dance style. Ballet training for women usually begins at 5 to 8 years of age with a private teacher or through an independent ballet school. Serious training traditionally begins between the ages of 10 and 12. Men often begin their ballet training between the ages of 10 and 15. Students who demonstrate potential in their early teens receive more intensive and advanced professional training. At about this time, students should begin to focus their training on a particular style and decide whether to pursue additional training through a dance company's school or a college dance program. Leading dance school companies often have summer training programs from which they select candidates for admission to their regular full-time training program. Formal training for modern and culturally specific dancers often begins

later than training in ballet; however, many folk dance forms are taught to very young children.

Many dancers have their first professional auditions by age 17 or 18. Training is an important component of professional dancers' careers. Dancers normally spend 8 hours a day in class and rehearsal, keeping their bodies in shape and preparing for performances. Their daily training period includes time to warm up and cool down before and after classes and rehearsals.

Because of the strenuous and time-consuming dance training required, some dancers view formal education as secondary. However, a broad, general education including music, literature, history, and the visual arts is helpful in the interpretation of dramatic episodes, ideas, and feelings. Dancers sometimes conduct research to learn more about the part they are playing.

Many colleges and universities confer bachelor's or master's degrees in dance, typically through departments of music, theater, or fine arts. Many programs concentrate on modern dance, but some also offer courses in jazz, culturally specific, ballet, or classical techniques; dance composition, history, and criticism; and movement analysis.

A college education is not essential to obtain employment as a professional dancer; however, many dancers obtain degrees in unrelated fields to prepare themselves for careers after dance. Completion of a college program in dance and education is essential in order to qualify to teach dance in college, high school, or elementary school. Colleges and conservatories sometimes require graduate degrees, but may accept performance experience. A college background is not necessary, however, for teaching dance or choreography in local recreational programs. Studio schools usually require teachers to have experience as performers.

Because of the rigorous practice schedules of most dancers, self-discipline, patience, perseverance, and a devotion to dance are essential for success in the field. Dancers also must possess good problem-solving skills and an ability to work with people. Good health and physical stamina also are necessary attributes. Above all, dancers must have flexibility, agility, coordination, grace, a sense of rhythm, a feeling for music, and a creative ability to express themselves through movement.

Dancers seldom perform unaccompanied, so they must be able to function as part of a team. They should also be highly motivated and prepared to face the anxiety of intermittent employment and rejections when auditioning for work. For dancers, advancement takes the form of a growing reputation, more frequent work, bigger and better roles, and higher pay.

Choreographers typically are older dancers with years of experience in the theater. Through their performance as dancers, they develop reputations as skilled artists that often lead to opportunities to choreograph productions.

Job Outlook

Dancers and choreographers face intense competition for jobs. Only the most talented find regular employment.

Employment of dancers and choreographers is expected to increase about as fast as the average for all occupations through 2010, reflecting the public's continued interest in this form of artistic expression. However, funding from public and private organizations is not expected to keep pace with rising production costs, resulting in slower employment growth. Although job openings will arise each year because dancers and choreographers retire or leave the occupation for other reasons, the number of applicants will continue to vastly exceed the number of job openings.

National dance companies should continue to provide most jobs in this field. Opera companies and dance groups affiliated with colleges and universities and with television and motion pictures also will offer some opportunities. Moreover, the growing popularity of dance in recent years has resulted in increased opportunities to teach dance. Additionally, music video channels will provide some opportunities for both dancers and choreographers.

Earnings

Median annual earnings of dancers were $22,470 in 2000. The middle 50 percent earned between $14,260 and $34,600. The lowest 10 percent earned less than $12,520, and the highest 10 percent earned more than $55,220. Median annual earnings were $29,980 in the producers, orchestras, and entertainers industry and $16,290 in eating and drinking places.

Median annual earnings of choreographers were $27,010 in 2000. The middle 50 percent earned between $17,970 and $42,080. The lowest 10 percent earned less than $13,370, and the highest 10 percent earned more than $55,800. Median annual earnings were $25,860 in dance studios, schools, and halls.

Dancers on tour received an additional allowance for room and board, and extra compensation for overtime. Earnings from dancing are usually low because employment is part year and irregular. Dancers often supplement their income by working as guest artists with other dance companies, teaching dance, or taking jobs unrelated to the field.

Earnings of many professional dancers are governed by union contracts. Dancers in the major opera ballet, classical ballet, and modern dance corps belong to the American Guild of Musical Artists, Inc., AFL-CIO; those who appear on live or videotaped television programs belong to the American Federation of Television and Radio Artists; those who perform in films and on television belong to the Screen Actors Guild; and those in musical theater are members of Actors' Equity Association. The unions and producers sign basic agreements specifying minimum salary rates, hours of work, benefits, and other conditions of employment. However, the contract each dancer signs with the producer of the show may be more favorable than the basic agreement.

Dancers and choreographers covered by union contracts are entitled to some paid sick leave, paid vacations, and various health and pension benefits, including extended sick pay and family leave provisions provided by their unions. Employers contribute toward these benefits. Those not covered by union contracts usually do not enjoy such benefits.

Related Occupations

People who work in other performing arts occupations include actors, producers, and directors; and musicians, singers, and related workers. Those directly involved in the production of dance programs include set and exhibit designers; fashion designers; sound engineering technicians; and hairdressers, hairstylists, and cosmetologists. Like dancers, athletes, coaches, umpires, and related workers in most sports need strength, flexibility, and agility.

Sources of Additional Information

For general information about dance and a list of accredited college-level programs, contact:

- National Association of Schools of Dance, 11250 Roger Bacon Dr., Suite 21, Reston, VA 20190. Internet: http://www.arts-accredit.org/nasd/default.htm

- Dance/USA, 1156 15th St. NW., Suite 820, Washington, DC 20005. Internet: http://www.danceusa.org

Data Entry and Information Processing Workers

O*NET 43-9021.00, 43-9022.00

Significant Points

- Workers can acquire their skills through high schools, community colleges, business schools, or self-teaching aids such as books, tapes, or Internet tutorial applications.

- Overall employment is projected to decline due to the proliferation of personal computers and other technologies; however, the need to replace workers who leave this large occupation each year should produce many job openings.

- Those with expertise in appropriate computer software applications should have the best job prospects.

Nature of the Work

Organizations need to process a rapidly growing amount of information. Data entry and information processing workers help ensure this work is handled smoothly and efficiently. By typing texts, entering data into a computer, operating a variety of office machines, and performing other clerical duties, these workers help organizations keep up with the rapid changes of the "Information Age."

Word processors and *typists* usually set up and prepare reports, letters, mailing labels, and other text material. *Typists* make neat, typed copies of materials written by other clerical, professional, or managerial workers. They may begin as entry-level workers by typing headings on form letters, addressing envelopes, or preparing standard forms on typewriters or computers. As they gain experience, they often are assigned tasks requiring a higher degree of accuracy and independent judgment. Senior typists may work with highly technical material, plan and type complicated statistical tables, combine and rearrange materials from different sources, or prepare master copies.

Most keyboarding is now done on word processing equipment—usually a personal computer or part of a larger computer system—which normally includes a keyboard, video display terminal, and printer, and may have "add-on" capabilities such as optical character recognition readers. *Word processors* use this equipment to record, edit, store, and revise letters, memos, reports, statistical tables, forms, and other printed materials. Although it is becoming less common, some word processing workers are employed in centralized word processing teams that handle the transcription and typing for several departments.

In addition to the duties mentioned above, word processors and typists often perform other office tasks, such as answering telephones, filing, and operating copiers or other office machines. Job titles of these workers often vary to reflect these duties. Clerk typists, for example, combine typing with filing, sorting mail, answering telephones, and other general office work. Note readers transcribe stenotyped notes of court proceedings into standard formats.

Data entry keyers usually input lists of items, numbers, or other data into computers or complete forms that appear on a computer screen. They may also manipulate existing data, edit current information, or proofread new entries to a database for accuracy. Some examples of data sources include customers' personal information, medical records, and membership lists. Usually this information is used internally by a company and may be reformatted before use by other departments or by customers.

Keyers use various types of equipment to enter data. Many keyers use a machine that converts the information they type to magnetic impulses on tapes or disks for entry into a computer system. Others prepare materials for printing or publication by using data entry composing machines. Some keyers operate online terminals or personal computers. Data entry keyers increasingly also work with non-keyboard forms of data entry such as scanners and electronically transmitted files. When using these new character recognition systems, data entry keyers often enter only those data that cannot be recognized by machines. In some offices, keyers also operate computer peripheral equipment such as printers and tape readers, act as tape librarians, and perform other clerical duties.

Working Conditions

Data entry and information processing workers usually work a standard 40-hour week in clean offices. They sit for long periods and sometimes must contend with high noise levels caused by various office machines. These workers are susceptible to repetitive strain injuries, such as carpal tunnel syndrome and neck, back, and eyestrain. To help prevent these from occurring, many offices have scheduled exercise breaks, ergonomically designed keyboards, and work stations that allow workers to stand or sit as they wish.

Employment

Data entry and information processing workers held about 806,000 jobs in 2000 and were employed in every sector of the economy; 509,000 were data entry keyers, and 297,000 were word processors and typists. Some workers telecommute by working from their homes on personal computers linked by telephone lines to those in the main office. This enables them to type material at home while still being able to produce printed copy in their offices.

About 1 out of 3 data entry and information processing workers held jobs in firms providing business services, including temporary help, word processing, and computer and data processing. Nearly 1 out of 5 worked in federal, state, and local government agencies.

Training, Other Qualifications, and Advancement

Employers generally hire high school graduates who meet their requirements for keyboarding speed. Increasingly, employers also expect applicants to have word processing or data entry training or experience. Spelling, punctuation, and grammar skills are important, as is familiarity with standard office equipment and procedures.

Students acquire skills in keyboarding and in the use of word processing, spreadsheet, and database management computer software packages through high schools, community colleges, business schools, temporary help agencies, or self-teaching aids such as books, tapes, or Internet tutorials applications.

For many people, a job as a data entry and information-processing worker is their first job after graduating from high school or after a period of full-time family responsibilities. This work frequently serves as a steppingstone to higher paying jobs with increased responsibilities. Large companies and government agencies usually have training programs to help administrative employees upgrade their skills and advance to other positions. It is common for data entry and information processing workers to transfer to other administrative jobs, such as secretary, administrative assistant, statistical clerk, or to be promoted to a supervisory job in a word processing or data entry center.

Job Outlook

Overall employment of data entry and information processing workers is projected to decline through 2010. Nevertheless, the need to replace those who transfer to other occupations or leave this large occupation for other reasons will produce numerous job openings each year. Job prospects will be most favorable for those with the best technical skills—in particular, expertise in appropriate computer software applications. Data entry and information processing workers must be willing to continuously upgrade their skills to remain marketable.

Although data entry and information processing workers are all affected by productivity gains stemming from organizational restructuring and the implementation of new technologies, projected growth differs among these workers. Employment of word processors and typists is expected to decline due to the proliferation of personal computers which allows other workers to perform duties formerly assigned to word processors and typists. Most professionals and managers, for example, now use desktop personal computers to do their own word processing. Because technologies affecting data entry keyers tend to be costlier to implement, however, these workers will be less affected by technology and should experience slower-than-average growth.

Employment growth of data entry keyers will still be dampened by productivity gains, as various data capturing technologies, such as bar code scanners, voice recognition technologies, and sophisticated character recognition readers, become more prevalent. These technologies can be applied to a variety of business transactions, such as inventory tracking, invoicing, and order placement. Moreover, as telecommunications technology improves, many organizations will increasingly take advantage of computer networks that allow data to be transmitted electronically, thereby avoiding the reentry of data. These technologies will allow more data to be entered automatically into computers, reducing the demand for data entry keyers.

In addition to technology, employment of data entry and information processing workers will be adversely affected as businesses increasingly contract out their work. Many organizations have reduced or even eliminated permanent in-house staff, for example, in favor of temporary-help and staffing services firms. Some large data entry and information processing firms increasingly employ workers in nations with low wages to enter data. As international trade barriers continue to fall and telecommunications technology improves, this transfer will mean reduced demand for data entry keyers in the United States.

Earnings

Median annual earnings of word processors and typists in 2000 were $24,710. The middle 50 percent earned between $20,070 and $29,500. The lowest 10 percent earned less than $16,410, while the highest 10 percent earned more than $35,410. The salaries of these workers vary by industry and by region. In 2000, median annual earnings in the industries employing the largest numbers of word processors and typists were:

Local government	$25,710
State government	24,850
Federal government	23,890
Elementary and secondary schools	23,300
Personnel supply services	22,720

Median annual earnings of data entry keyers in 2000 were $21,300. The middle 50 percent earned between $17,850 and $25,820. The lowest 10 percent earned less than $15,140, and the highest 10 percent earned more than $30,910. In 2000, median annual earnings in the industries employing the largest numbers of data entry keyers were:

Federal government	$27,260
Accounting, auditing, and bookkeeping	22,310
Computer and data processing services	20,480
Commercial banks	20,410
Personnel supply services	20,070

In the federal government, clerk-typists and data entry keyers without work experience started at $16,015 a year in 2001. Beginning salaries were slightly higher in selected areas where the prevailing local pay level was higher. The average annual salary for all clerk-typists in the federal government was $24,934 in 2001.

Related Occupations

Data entry and information processing workers must transcribe information quickly. Other workers who deliver information in a timely manner are dispatchers and communications equipment operators. Data entry and information processing workers also must be comfortable working with office automation, and in this regard they are similar to court reporters, medical records and health information technicians, secretaries and administrative assistants, and computer operators.

Sources of Additional Information

For information about job opportunities for data entry and information processing workers, contact the nearest office of the state employment service.

Demonstrators, Product Promoters, and Models

O*NET 41-9011.00, 41-9012.00

Significant Points

● Job openings should be plentiful for demonstrators and product promoters, but keen competition is expected for modeling jobs.

● Most jobs are part-time or have variable work schedules.

● Many jobs require frequent travel.

Nature of the Work

Demonstrators, product promoters, and models create public interest in buying products such as clothing, cosmetics, food items, and housewares. The information they provide helps consumers make educated choices among the wide variety of products and services available.

Demonstrators and product promoters create public interest in buying a product by demonstrating it to prospective customers and answering their questions. They may sell the demonstrated merchandise, or gather names of prospects to contact at a later date or to pass on to a sales staff. *Demonstrators* promote sales of a product to consumers, while *product promoters* try to induce retail stores to sell particular products and market them effectively. Product demonstration is an effective technique used by both to introduce new products or promote sales of old products. It allows face-to-face interaction with potential customers.

Demonstrators and product promoters build current and future sales of both sophisticated and simple products, ranging from computer software to mops. They attract an audience by offering samples, administering contests, distributing prizes, and using direct-mail advertising. They must greet and catch the attention of possible customers and quickly identify those who are interested and qualified. They inform and educate customers about the features of products and demonstrate their use with apparent ease to inspire confidence in the product and its manufacturer. They also distribute information, such as brochures and applications. Some demonstrations are intended to generate immediate sales through impulse buying, while others are considered an investment to generate future sales and increase brand awareness.

Demonstrations and product promotions are conducted in retail and grocery stores, shopping malls, trade shows, and outdoor fairs. Locations are selected based on both the nature of the product and the type of audience. Demonstrations at large events may require teams of demonstrators to efficiently handle large crowds. Some demonstrators promote products on videotape or on television programs, such as "infomercials" or home shopping programs.

Demonstrators and product promoters may prepare the content of a presentation and alter it to target a specific audience or to keep it current. They may participate in the design of an exhibit or customize exhibits for particular audiences. Results obtained by demonstrators and product promoters are analyzed, and presentations are adjusted to make them more effective. Demonstrators and product promoters also may be involved in transporting, assembling, and disassembling materials used in demonstrations.

A demonstrator's presentation may include visuals, models, case studies, testimonials, test results, and surveys. The equipment used for a demonstration varies with the product being demonstrated. A food product demonstration might require the use of cooking utensils, while a software demonstration could require the use of a multimedia computer. Demonstrators must be familiar with the product to be able to relate detailed information to customers and to answer any questions that arise before, during, or after a demonstration. Therefore, they may research the product to be presented, the products of competitors, and the interests and concerns of the target audience before conducting a demonstration. Demonstrations of complex products can require practice.

Models pose for photos or as subjects for paintings or sculptures. They display clothing, such as dresses, coats, underclothing, swimwear, and suits, for a variety of audiences and in various types of media. They model accessories, such as handbags, shoes, and jewelry, and promote beauty products, including fragrances and cosmetics. The most successful models, called supermodels, hold celebrity status and often use their image to sell products such as books, calendars, and fitness videos. In addition to modeling, they may appear in movies and television shows.

Models' clients use printed publications, live modeling, and television to advertise and promote products and services. There are different categories of modeling jobs within these media, and the nature of a model's work may vary with each. Most modeling jobs are for printed publications, and models usually do a combination of editorial, commercial, and catalog work. Editorial print modeling uses still photographs of models for fashion magazine covers and to accompany feature articles, but does not include modeling for advertisements. Commercial print modeling includes work for advertisements in magazines and newspapers, and for outdoor advertisements such as billboards. Catalog models appear in department store and mail order catalogs.

During a photo shoot, a model poses to demonstrate the features of clothing and products. Models make small changes in posture and facial expression to capture the look desired by the client. As they shoot film, photographers instruct models to pose in certain positions and to interact with their physical surroundings. Models work closely with photographers, hair and clothing stylists, makeup artists, and clients to produce the desired look and to finish the photo shoot on schedule. Stylists and makeup artists prepare the model for the photo shoot, provide touchups, and change the look of models throughout the day. If stylists are not provided, models must apply their own makeup and bring their own clothing. Because the client spends time and money planning for and preparing an advertising campaign, the client usually is present to ensure that the work is satisfactory. The client also may offer suggestions.

Editorial printwork generally pays less than other types of modeling, but provides exposure for a model and can lead to commercial modeling opportunities. Often, beginning fashion models work in foreign countries, where fashion magazines are more plentiful.

Live modeling is done in a variety of locations. Live models stand, turn, and walk to demonstrate clothing to a variety of audiences. At fashion shows and in showrooms, garment buyers are the primary audience. Runway models display clothes that either are intended for direct sale to consumers or are the artistic expressions of the designer. High fashion, or haute couture, runway models confidently walk a narrow run-

way before an audience of photographers, journalists, designers, and garment buyers. Live modeling also is done in apparel marts, department stores, and fitting rooms of clothing designers. In retail establishments, models display clothing directly for shoppers and may be required to describe the features and price of the clothing. Other models pose for sketching artists, painters, and sculptors.

Models may compete with actors and actresses for work in television and may even receive speaking parts. Television work includes commercials, cable television programs, and even game shows. However, competition for television work is intense because of the potential for high earnings and extensive exposure.

Because advertisers need to target very specific segments of the population, models may specialize in a certain area. Petite and plus-size fashions are modeled by women whose dress sizes are smaller or larger than the typical model. Models who are disabled may be used to model fashions or products for disabled consumers. "Parts" models have a body part, such as a hand or foot, that is particularly well-suited to model products such as fingernail polish or shoes.

Almost all models work through agents. Agents provide a link between models and clients. Clients pay models, while the agency receives a portion of the model's earnings for its services. Agents scout for new faces, advise and train new models, and promote them to clients. A typical modeling job lasts only 1 day, so modeling agencies differ from other employment agencies in that they maintain an ongoing relationship with the model. Agents find and nurture relationships with clients, arrange auditions called "go-sees," and book shoots if a model is hired. They also provide bookkeeping and billing services to models and may offer them financial planning services. Relatively short careers and high incomes make financial planning an important issue for successful models.

With the help of agents, models spend a considerable amount of time promoting and developing themselves. Models assemble and maintain portfolios, print composite cards, and travel to go-sees. A portfolio is a collection of model's previous work that is carried to all go-sees and bookings. A composite card, or comp card, contains the best photographs from a model's portfolio, along with his or her measurements.

Models must gather information before a job. From an agent, they learn the pay, date, time, and length of the shoot. Also, models must ask agents if hair, makeup, and clothing stylists will be provided. It is helpful to know what product is being promoted and what image they should project. Some models research the client and the product being modeled to prepare for a shoot. Models use a document called a voucher to record the rate of pay and the actual duration of the job. The voucher is used for billing purposes after both the client and model sign it. Once a job is completed, models must check in with their agency and plan for the next appointment.

Working Conditions

Over half of all demonstrators, product promoters, and models work part-time and almost a quarter have variable work schedules. Many positions last 6 months or less.

Demonstrators and product promoters may work long hours while standing or walking, with little opportunity to rest. Some of them travel frequently, and night and weekend work often is required. The atmosphere of a crowded trade show or state fair often is hectic, and demonstrators and product promoters may feel pressure to influence the greatest number of consumers possible in a very limited amount of time. However, many enjoy the opportunity to interact with a variety of people.

The work of models is both glamorous and difficult, and they may work under a variety of conditions. The coming season's fashions may be modeled in a comfortable, climate-controlled studio or in a cold, damp outdoor location. Schedules can be demanding, and models must keep in constant touch with an agent so that they do not miss an opportunity for work. Being away from friends and family, and needing to focus on the photographer's instructions despite constant interruption for touchups, clothing, and set changes can be stressful. Yet, successful models interact with a variety of people and enjoy frequent travel. They may meet potential clients at several go-sees in one day and often travel to work in distant cities, foreign countries, and exotic locations.

Employment

Demonstrators, product promoters, and models held about 121,000 jobs in 2000. Models alone held only about 3,700 jobs in 2000. About 14 percent of all salaried jobs were in miscellaneous business services (which includes trade shows and demonstration services), and about 13 percent were in personnel-supply services (which includes modeling agencies). Others worked in advertising, department stores, drug stores, grocery and related products wholesalers, grocery stores, management and public relations, and computer and data processing services.

Demonstrator and product promoter jobs may be found in communities throughout the nation, but modeling jobs are concentrated in New York, Miami, and Los Angeles.

Training, Other Qualifications, and Advancement

Formal training and education requirements are limited for demonstrators, product promoters, and models. Training usually is short-term, occurring over a period of days or weeks. Postsecondary education, while helpful, usually is not required. About 55 percent of these workers have no more than a high school diploma.

Demonstrators and product promoters usually receive on-the-job training. Training is primarily product-oriented because a demonstrator must be familiar with the product to demonstrate it properly. The length of training varies with the complexity of the product. Experience with the product or familiarity with similar products may be required for demonstration of complex products, such as computers. During the training process, demonstrators may be introduced to the manufacturer's corporate philosophy and preferred methods for dealing with customers.

Employers look for demonstrators and product promoters with good communication skills and a pleasant appearance and personality. Demonstrators and product promoters must be comfortable with public speaking. They should be able to entertain an audience and use humor, spontaneity, and personal interest in the product as promotional tools. Foreign language skills are helpful.

While no formal training is required to begin a modeling career, models should be photogenic and have a basic knowledge of hair styling, makeup, and clothing. Some local governments require models under the age of 18 to hold a work permit. An attractive physical appearance is necessary to become a successful model. A model should have flawless skin, healthy hair, and attractive facial features. Models must be within certain ranges for height, weight, and dress or coat size in order to meet the practical needs of fashion designers, photographers, and advertisers. Requirements may change slightly from time to time as our society's perceptions about physical beauty change; however, most fashion designers feel their clothing looks its best on tall, thin models. Although physical requirements may be relaxed for some types of modeling jobs, opportunities are limited for those who do not meet these basic requirements.

Because a model's career depends on preservation of his or her physical characteristics, models must control their diet, exercise regularly, and get enough sleep in order to stay healthy. Haircuts, pedicures, and manicures are necessary work-related expenses for models.

In addition to being attractive, models must be photogenic. The ability to relate to the camera in order to capture the desired look on film is essential and agents test prospective models using snapshots or professional photographs. For photographic and runway work, models must be able to move gracefully and confidently. Training in acting, voice, and dance is useful and allows a model to be considered for television work. Foreign language skills are useful because successful models travel frequently to foreign countries.

Because models must interact with a large number of people, personality plays an important role in success. Models must be professional, polite, and prompt; every contact could lead to future employment. Organizational skills are necessary to manage personal lives, financial matters, and busy work and travel schedules. Because competition for jobs is stiff and clients' needs are very specific, patience and persistence are essential.

Modeling schools provide training in posing, walking, makeup application, and other basic tasks, but attending such schools does not necessarily lead to job opportunities. In fact, many agents prefer beginning models with little or no previous experience and discourage models from attending modeling schools and purchasing professional photographs. A model's selection of an agency is an important factor for advancement in the occupation. The better the reputation and skill of the agency, the more assignments a model is likely to get. Because clients prefer to work with agents, it is very difficult for a model to pursue a freelance career.

Agents continually scout for new faces, and many of the top models are discovered in this way. Most agencies review snapshots or have open calls, during which models are seen in person; this service usually is provided free of charge. Some agencies sponsor modeling contests and searches. Very few people who send in snapshots or attend open calls are offered contracts.

Agencies advise models on how to dress, wear makeup, and conduct themselves properly during go-sees and bookings. Because models' advancement depends on their previous work, development of a good portfolio is key to getting assignments. Models accumulate and display current tear sheets—examples of a model's editorial print work—and photographs in the portfolio. The higher the quality and currency of the photos in the portfolio, the more likely it is that the model will find work.

Demonstrators and product promoters who perform well and show leadership ability may advance to other marketing and sales occupations or open their own businesses. Because modeling careers are relatively short, most models eventually transfer to other occupations.

Job Outlook

Employment of demonstrators, product promoters, and models is expected to grow faster than the average for all occupations through 2010. Job growth should be driven by increases in the number and size of trade shows and greater use of demonstrators and product promoters in department stores and various retail shops for in-store promotions. Additional job openings will arise from the need to replace demonstrators, product promoters, and models who transfer to other occupations, retire, or stop working for other reasons.

Job openings should be plentiful for demonstrators and product promoters. Employers may have difficulty finding qualified demonstrators who are willing to fill part-time, short-term positions. In addition, product demonstration is considered a very effective marketing tool. New jobs should arise as firms devote a greater percentage of marketing budgets to product demonstration.

On the other hand, modeling is considered a glamorous occupation, with limited formal entry requirements. Consequently, those who wish to pursue a modeling career can expect keen competition for jobs. The modeling profession typically attracts many more job seekers than there are job openings available. Only models who closely meet the unique requirements of the occupation will achieve regular employment. The increasing diversification of the general population should increase demand for models more representative of diverse racial and ethnic groups. Work for male models should increase as society becomes more receptive to the marketing of men's fashions. Because fashions change frequently, demand for a model's look may fluctuate; most models experience periods of unemployment.

Employment of demonstrators, product promoters, and models is affected by downturns in the business cycle. Many firms tend to reduce advertising budgets during recessions.

Earnings

Demonstrators and product promoters had median hourly earnings of $9.51 in 2000. The middle 50 percent earned between $7.71 and $13.51. The lowest 10 percent earned less than $6.82, and the highest 10 percent earned more than $19.76. Median hourly earnings in the largest industries that employed demonstrators and product promoters in 2000 were as follows:

Personnel supply services	$10.47
Advertising	8.90
Miscellaneous business services	8.29
Department stores	8.28

Employers of demonstrators, product promoters, and models generally pay for job-related travel expenses.

Median hourly earnings of models were $9.17 in 2000. The middle 50 percent earned between $7.00 and $13.70. The lowest 10 percent earned less than $6.11, and the highest 10 percent earned more than $16.94. Earnings vary for different types of modeling, and depend on the experience and reputation of the model. Female models typically earn more than male models for similar work. Hourly earnings can be relatively high, particularly for supermodels and others in high demand, but models may not have work every day, and jobs may last only a few hours. Models occasionally receive clothing or clothing discounts instead of, or in addition to, regular earnings. Almost all models work with agents, and pay 15 to 20 percent of their earnings in return for an agent's services. Models who do not find immediate work may receive payments, called advances, from agents to cover promotional and living expenses. Models must provide their own health and retirement benefits.

Related Occupations

Demonstrators, product promoters, and models create public interest in buying clothing and products. Others who create interest in a product or service include actors, producers, and directors; insurance sales agents; real estate brokers and sales agents; retail salespersons; sales representatives, wholesale and manufacturing; and travel agents.

Sources of Additional Information

For information about careers in modeling, contact:

- Models Guild, Office and Professional Employees International Union, 265 W. 14th St., Suite 203, New York, NY 10011. Internet: http://www.opeiu.org/models/index.asp

For information about modeling schools and agencies in your area, contact a local consumer affairs organization such as the Better Business Bureau.

Dental Assistants

O*NET 31-9091.00

Significant Points

- Rapid employment growth and substantial replacement needs should result in good job opportunities.

- Dentists are expected to hire more assistants to perform routine tasks so that they may devote their own time to more profitable procedures.

- Infection control is a crucial responsibility of dental assistants. Proper infection control protects patients and members of the dental health team.

Nature of the Work

Dental assistants perform a variety of patient care, office, and laboratory duties. They work chairside as dentists examine and treat patients. They make patients as comfortable as possible in the dental chair, prepare them for treatment, and obtain dental records. Assistants hand instruments and materials to dentists, and keep patients' mouths dry and clear by using suction or other devices. Assistants also sterilize and disinfect instruments and equipment, prepare tray setups for dental procedures, and instruct patients on postoperative and general oral healthcare.

Some dental assistants prepare materials for making impressions and restorations, expose radiographs, and process dental X-ray film as directed by a dentist. They also may remove sutures, apply anesthetics to gums or cavity-preventive agents to teeth, remove excess cement used in the filling process, and place rubber dams on the teeth to isolate them for individual treatment.

Those with laboratory duties make casts of the teeth and mouth from impressions taken by dentists, clean and polish removable appliances, and make temporary crowns. Dental assistants with office duties schedule and confirm appointments, receive patients, keep treatment records, send bills, receive payments, and order dental supplies and materials.

Dental assistants should not be confused with dental hygienists, who are licensed to perform different clinical tasks.

Working Conditions

Dental assistants work in a well-lighted, clean environment. Their work area usually is near the dental chair so that they can arrange instruments, materials, and medication and hand them to the dentist when needed. Dental assistants wear gloves, masks, eyewear, and protective clothing to protect themselves and their patients from infectious diseases. Following safety procedures also minimizes the risks associated with the use of radiographic equipment.

Almost half of dental assistants have a 35- to 40-hour work week, which may include work on Saturdays or evenings.

Employment

Dental assistants held about 247,000 jobs in 2000. Almost 2 out of 5 worked part-time, sometimes in more than one dental office.

Virtually all dental assistants work in a private dental office. A small number work in dental schools, private and government hospitals, state and local public health departments, or clinics.

Training, Other Qualifications, and Advancement

Most assistants learn their skills on the job, although some are trained in dental assisting programs offered by community and junior colleges, trade schools, technical institutes, or the armed forces. Assistants must be a dentist's "third hand"; therefore, dentists look for people who are reliable, can work well with others, and have good manual dexterity. High school students interested in a career as a dental assistant should take courses in biology, chemistry, health, and office practices.

The American Dental Association's Commission on Dental Accreditation approved 248 dental assisting training programs in 2000. Programs include classroom, laboratory, and preclinical instruction in dental assisting skills and related theory. In addition, students gain practical experience in dental schools, clinics, or dental offices. Most programs take 1 year or less to complete and lead to a certificate or diploma. Two-year programs offered in community and junior colleges lead to an associate degree. All programs require a high school diploma or its equivalent, and some require a typing or science course for admission. Some private vocational schools offer 4- to 6-month courses in dental assisting, but the Commission on Dental Accreditation does not accredit these.

Some states regulate the duties dental assistants may complete through licensure or registration. Licensure or registration may require passing a written or practical examination. States offering licensure or registration have a variety of schools offering courses—approximately 10 to 12 months in length—that meet their state's requirements. Some states require continuing education to maintain licensure or registration. A few states allow dental assistants to perform any function delegated to them by the dentist.

Individual states have adopted different standards for dental assistants who perform certain medical duties, such as radiological procedures. Completion of the Radiation Health and Safety examination offered by the Dental Assisting National Board, Inc. (DANB) meets those standards in 31 states. Some states require the completion of a state-approved course in radiology as well.

Certification is available through DANB and is recognized or required in 20 states. Other organizations offer registration, most often at the state level. Certification is an acknowledgment of an assistant's qualifications and professional competence, and may be an asset when seeking employment. Candidates may qualify to take the DANB certification examination by graduating from an accredited training program or by having 2 years of full-time, or 4 years of part-time, experience as a dental assistant. In addition, applicants must have current certification in cardiopulmonary resuscitation. Recertification is offered annually for applicants who have earned continuing education credits.

Without further education, advancement opportunities are limited. Some dental assistants become office managers, dental assisting instructors, or dental product sales representatives. Others go back to school to become dental hygienists. For many, this entry-level occupation provides basic training and experience and serves as a steppingstone to more highly skilled and higher paying jobs.

Job Outlook

Job prospects for dental assistants should be good. Employment is expected to grow much faster than the average for all occupations through the year 2010. In addition, numerous job openings will occur due to the need to replace assistants who transfer to other occupations, retire, or leave the labor force for other reasons. Many opportunities are for entry-level positions offering on-the-job training.

Population growth and greater retention of natural teeth by middle-aged and older people will fuel demand for dental services. Older dentists, who are less likely to employ assistants, will leave and be replaced by recent graduates, who are more likely to use one, or even two. In addition, as dentists' work loads increase, they are expected to hire more assistants to perform routine tasks, so that they may devote their own time to more profitable procedures.

Earnings

Median hourly earnings of dental assistants were $12.49 in 2000. The middle 50 percent earned between $9.99 and $15.51 an hour. The lowest 10 percent earned less than $8.26, and the highest 10 percent earned more than $18.57 an hour.

Benefits vary substantially by practice setting and may be contingent upon full-time employment. According to the American Dental Association's 1999 Workforce Needs Assessment Survey, almost all full-time dental assistants employed by private practitioners received paid vacation. The survey also found that 9 out of 10 full- and part-time dental assistants received dental coverage.

Related Occupations

Workers in other occupations supporting health practitioners include medical assistants, occupational therapist assistants and aides, pharmacy aides, pharmacy technicians, physical therapist assistants and aides, and veterinary technologists, technicians, and assistants.

Sources of Additional Information

Information about career opportunities and accredited dental assistant programs is available from:

- Commission on Dental Accreditation, American Dental Association, 211 E. Chicago Ave., Suite 1814, Chicago, IL 60611. Internet: http://www.ada.org

For information on becoming a Certified Dental Assistant and a list of state boards of dentistry, contact:

- Dental Assisting National Board, Inc., 676 North Saint Clair, Suite 1880, Chicago, IL 60611. Internet: http://www.danb.org

For general information about continuing education for dental assistants, contact:

- American Dental Assistants Association, 203 North LaSalle St., Suite 1320, Chicago, IL 60601. Internet: http://www.dentalassistant.org

Dental Hygienists

O*NET 29-2021.00

Significant Points

- Dental hygienists are projected to be one of the 30 fastest growing occupations.

- Population growth and greater retention of natural teeth will stimulate demand for dental hygienists.

- Opportunities for part-time work and flexible schedules are common.

Nature of the Work

Dental hygienists remove soft and hard deposits from teeth, teach patients how to practice good oral hygiene, and provide other preventive dental care. Hygienists examine patients' teeth and gums, recording the presence of diseases or abnormalities. They remove calculus, stains, and plaque from teeth; take and develop dental X rays; and apply cavity-preventive agents such as fluorides and pit and fissure sealants. In some states, hygienists administer anesthetics; place and carve filling materials, temporary fillings, and periodontal dressings; remove sutures; perform root-planing as a periodontal therapy; and smooth and polish metal restorations. Although hygienists may not diagnose diseases, they can prepare clinical and laboratory diagnostic tests for the dentist to interpret. Hygienists sometimes work chairside with the dentist during treatment.

Dental hygienists also help patients develop and maintain good oral health. For example, they may explain the relationship between diet and oral health, or even the link between oral health and such serious conditions as heart disease and stroke. They also inform patients how to select toothbrushes and show them how to brush and floss their teeth.

Dental hygienists use hand and rotary instruments and ultrasonics to clean and polish teeth, X-ray machines to take dental pictures, syringes with needles to administer local anesthetics, and models of teeth to explain oral hygiene.

Working Conditions

Flexible scheduling is a distinctive feature of this job. Full-time, part-time, evening, and weekend schedules are widely available. Dentists frequently hire hygienists to work only 2 or 3 days a week, so hygienists may hold jobs in more than one dental office.

Dental hygienists work in clean, well-lighted offices. Important health safeguards include strict adherence to proper radiological procedures, and use of appropriate protective devices when administering anesthetic gas. Dental hygienists also wear safety glasses, surgical masks, and gloves to protect themselves from infectious diseases.

Employment

Dental hygienists held about 147,000 jobs in 2000. Because multiple jobholding is common in this field, the number of jobs exceeds the number of hygienists. More than half of all dental hygienists worked part-time—less than 35 hours a week.

Almost all dental hygienists work in private dental offices. Some work in public health agencies, hospitals, and clinics.

Training, Other Qualifications, and Advancement

Dental hygienists must be licensed by the state in which they practice. To qualify for licensure, a candidate must graduate from an accredited dental hygiene school and pass both a written and clinical examination. The American Dental Association Joint Commission on National Dental Examinations administers the written examination accepted by all states and the District of Columbia. State or regional testing agencies administer the clinical examination. In addition, most states require an examination on legal aspects of dental hygiene practice. Alabama allows candidates to take its examinations if they have been trained through a state-regulated on-the-job program in a dentist's office.

In 2000, the Commission on Dental Accreditation accredited about 256 programs in dental hygiene. Although some programs lead to a bachelor's degree, most grant an associate degree. A dozen universities offer master's degree programs in dental hygiene or a related area.

An associate degree is sufficient for practice in a private dental office. A bachelor's or master's degree usually is required for research, teaching, or clinical practice in public or school health programs.

About half of the dental hygiene programs prefer applicants who have completed at least 1 year of college. However, requirements vary from one school to another. Schools offer laboratory, clinical, and classroom instruction in subjects such as anatomy, physiology, chemistry, microbiology, pharmacology, nutrition, radiography, histology (the study of tissue structure), periodontology (the study of gum diseases), pathology, dental materials, clinical dental hygiene, and social and behavioral sciences.

Dental hygienists should work well with others and must have good manual dexterity because they use dental instruments within a patient's mouth, with little room for error. High school students interested in becoming a dental hygienist should take courses in biology, chemistry, and mathematics.

Job Outlook

Employment of dental hygienists is expected to grow much faster than the average for all occupations through 2010, in response to increasing demand for dental care and the greater substitution of the services of hygienists for those previously performed by dentists. Job prospects are expected to remain very good unless the number of dental hygienist program graduates grows much faster than during the last decade, and results in a much larger pool of qualified applicants.

Population growth and greater retention of natural teeth will stimulate demand for dental hygienists. Older dentists, who are less likely to employ dental hygienists, will leave and be replaced by recent graduates, who are more likely to do so. In addition, as dentists' work loads increase, they are expected to hire more hygienists to perform preventive dental care such as cleaning, so that they may devote their own time to more profitable procedures.

Earnings

Median hourly earnings of dental hygienists were $24.68 in 2000. The middle 50 percent earned between $20.46 and $29.72 an hour. The lowest 10 percent earned less than $15.53, and the highest 10 percent earned more than $35.39 an hour.

Earnings vary by geographic location, employment setting, and years of experience. Dental hygienists who work in private dental offices may be paid on an hourly, daily, salary, or commission basis.

Benefits vary substantially by practice setting, and may be contingent upon full-time employment. According to the American Dental Association's 1999 Workforce Needs Assessment Survey, almost all full-time dental hygienists employed by private practitioners received paid vacation. The survey also found that 9 out of 10 full- and part-time dental hygienists received dental coverage. Dental hygienists who work for school systems, public health agencies, the federal government, or state agencies usually have substantial benefits.

Related Occupations

Workers in other occupations supporting health practitioners in an office setting include dental assistants, medical assistants, occupational therapist assistants and aides, physical therapist assistants and aides, physician assistants, and registered nurses.

Sources of Additional Information

For information on a career in dental hygiene and the educational requirements to enter this occupation, contact:

● Division of Professional Development, American Dental Hygienists' Association, 444 N. Michigan Ave., Suite 3400, Chicago, IL 60611. Internet: http://www.adha.org

For information about accredited programs and educational requirements, contact:

● Commission on Dental Accreditation, American Dental Association, 211 E. Chicago Ave., Suite 1814, Chicago, IL 60611. Internet: http://www.ada.org

The State Board of Dental Examiners in each state can supply information on licensing requirements.

Dental Laboratory Technicians

O*NET 51-9081.00

Significant Points

● Employment should increase slowly, as the public's improving dental health requires fewer dentures but more bridges and crowns.

● Dental laboratory technicians need artistic aptitude for detailed and precise work, a high degree of manual dexterity, and good vision.

Nature of the Work

Dental laboratory technicians fill prescriptions from dentists for crowns, bridges, dentures, and other dental prosthetics. First, dentists send a specification of the item to be fabricated, along with an impression (mold) of the patient's mouth or teeth. Then, dental laboratory technicians, also called dental technicians, create a model of the patient's mouth by pouring plaster into the impression and allowing it to set. Next, they place the model on an apparatus that mimics the bite and movement of the patient's jaw. The model serves as the basis of the prosthetic device. Technicians examine the model, noting the size and shape of the adjacent teeth, as well as gaps within the gumline. Based upon these observations and the dentist's specifications, technicians build and shape a wax tooth or teeth model, using small hand instruments called wax spatulas and wax carvers. They use this wax model to cast the metal framework for the prosthetic device.

After the wax tooth has been formed, dental technicians pour the cast and form the metal and, using small hand-held tools, prepare the surface to allow the metal and porcelain to bond. They then apply porcelain in layers, to arrive at the precise shape and color of a tooth. Technicians place the tooth in a porcelain furnace to bake the porcelain onto the metal framework, and then adjust the shape and color, with subsequent grinding and addition of porcelain to achieve a sealed finish. The final product is nearly an exact replica of the lost tooth or teeth.

In some laboratories, technicians perform all stages of the work, whereas in other labs, each technician does only a few. Dental laboratory technicians can specialize in one of five areas: Orthodontic appliances, crowns and bridges, complete dentures, partial dentures, or ceramics. Job titles can reflect specialization in these areas. For example, technicians who make porcelain and acrylic restorations are called *dental ceramists*.

Working Conditions

Dental laboratory technicians generally work in clean, well-lighted, and well-ventilated areas. Technicians usually have their own workbenches, which can be equipped with Bunsen burners, grinding and polishing equipment, and hand instruments, such as wax spatulas and wax carvers.

The work is extremely delicate and time consuming. Salaried technicians usually work 40 hours a week, but self-employed technicians frequently work longer hours.

Employment

Dental laboratory technicians held about 43,000 jobs in 2000. Most jobs were in commercial dental laboratories, which usually are small, privately owned businesses with fewer than five employees. However, some laboratories are large; a few employ more than 50 technicians.

Some dental laboratory technicians work in dentists' offices. Others work for hospitals providing dental services, including U.S. Department of Veterans Affairs' hospitals. Some technicians work in dental laboratories in their homes, in addition to their regular job.

Training, Other Qualifications, and Advancement

Most dental laboratory technicians learn their craft on the job. They begin with simple tasks, such as pouring plaster into an impression, and progress to more complex procedures, such as making porcelain crowns and bridges. Becoming a fully trained technician requires an average of 3 to 4 years, depending upon the individual's aptitude and ambition, but it may take a few years more to become an accomplished technician.

Training in dental laboratory technology also is available through community and junior colleges, vocational-technical institutes, and the armed forces. Formal training programs vary greatly both in length and in the level of skill they impart.

In 2000, 30 programs in dental laboratory technology were accredited by the Commission on Dental Accreditation in conjunction with the American Dental Association (ADA). These programs provide classroom instruction in dental materials science, oral anatomy, fabrication procedures, ethics, and related subjects. In addition, each student is given supervised practical experience in a school or an associated dental laboratory. Accredited programs normally take 2 years to complete and lead to an associate degree.

Graduates of 2-year training programs need additional hands-on experience to become fully qualified. Each dental laboratory owner operates in a different way, and classroom instruction does not necessarily expose students to techniques and procedures favored by individual laboratory owners. Students who have taken enough courses to learn the basics of the craft usually are considered good candidates for training, regardless of whether they have completed a formal program. Many employers will train someone without any classroom experience.

The National Board for Certification, an independent board established by the National Association of Dental Laboratories, offers certification in dental laboratory technology. Certification, which is voluntary, can be obtained in five specialty areas: crowns and bridges, ceramics, partial dentures, complete dentures, and orthodontic appliances.

In large dental laboratories, technicians may become supervisors or managers. Experienced technicians may teach or may take jobs with dental suppliers in such areas as product development, marketing, and sales. Still, for most technicians, opening one's own laboratory is the way toward advancement and higher earnings.

A high degree of manual dexterity, good vision, and the ability to recognize very fine color shadings and variations in shape are necessary. An artistic aptitude for detailed and precise work also is important. High school students interested in becoming dental laboratory technicians should take courses in art, metal and wood shop, drafting, and sciences. Courses in management and business may help those wishing to operate their own laboratories.

Job Outlook

Job opportunities for dental laboratory technicians should be favorable, despite very slow growth in the occupation. Employers have difficulty filling trainee positions, probably because entry-level salaries are relatively low and because the public is not familiar with the occupation.

Although job opportunities are favorable, slower-than-average growth in the employment of dental laboratory technicians is expected through the year 2010, due to changes in dental care. The overall dental health of the population has improved because of fluoridation of drinking water, which has reduced the incidence of dental cavities, and greater emphasis on preventive dental care since the early 1960s. As a result, full dentures will be less common, as most people will need only a bridge or crown. However, during the last few years, demand has arisen from an aging public that is growing increasingly interested in cosmetic prostheses. For example, many dental laboratories are filling orders for composite fillings that are the same shade of white as natural teeth to replace older, less attractive fillings.

Earnings

Median hourly earnings of dental laboratory technicians were $12.94 in 2000. The middle 50 percent earned between $9.83 and $16.82 an hour. The lowest 10 percent earned less than $7.78, and the highest 10 percent earned more than $21.47 an hour. Median hourly earnings of dental laboratory technicians in 2000 were $12.88 in offices and clinics of dentists and $12.87 in medical and dental laboratories.

Technicians in large laboratories tend to specialize in a few procedures, and, therefore, tend to be paid a lower wage than those employed in small laboratories that perform a variety of tasks.

Related Occupations

Dental laboratory technicians fabricate artificial teeth, crowns and bridges, and orthodontic appliances, following specifications and instructions provided by dentists. Other workers who make and repair medical devices include dispensing opticians, ophthalmic laboratory technicians, orthotists and prosthetists, and precision instrument and equipment repairers.

Sources of Additional Information

For a list of accredited programs in dental laboratory technology, contact:

- Commission on Dental Accreditation, American Dental Association, 211 E. Chicago Ave., Chicago, IL 60611. Internet: http://www.ada.org

For information on requirements for certification, contact:

- National Board for Certification in Dental Technology, 1530 Metropolitan Blvd., Tallahassee, FL 32308. Internet: http://www.nadl.org/html/certification.html

For information on career opportunities in commercial laboratories, contact:

- National Association of Dental Laboratories, 1530 Metropolitan Blvd., Tallahassee, FL 32308. Internet: http://www.nadl.org

General information on grants and scholarships is available from dental technology schools.

Desktop Publishers

O*NET 43-9031.00

Significant Points

- Desktop publishers rank among the 10 fastest growing occupations.
- Most jobs are in firms that handle commercial or business printing, and in newspaper plants.
- Although formal training is not always required, those with certification or degrees will have the best job opportunities.

Nature of the Work

Using computer software, desktop publishers format and combine text, numerical data, photographs, charts, and other visual graphic elements to produce publication-ready material. Depending on the nature of a particular project, desktop publishers may write and edit text, create graphics to accompany text, convert photographs and drawings into digital images and then manipulate those images. They also design page layouts, create proposals, develop presentations and advertising campaigns, typeset and do color separation, and translate electronic information onto film or other traditional forms. Materials produced by desktop publishers include books, business cards, calendars, magazines, newsletters and newspapers, packaging, slides, and tickets. As companies have brought the production of marketing, promotional, and other kinds of materials in-house, they increasingly have employed people who can produce such materials.

Desktop publishers use a keyboard to enter and select formatting specifics such as size and style of type, column width, and spacing, and store them in the computer. The computer then displays and arranges columns of type on a video display terminal or computer monitor. An entire newspaper, catalog, or book page, complete with artwork and graphics, can be created on the screen exactly as it will appear in print. Operators transmit the pages for production either into film and then into printing plates, or directly into plates.

Desktop publishing is a rapidly changing field that encompasses a number of different kinds of jobs. Personal computers enable desktop publishers to perform publishing tasks that would otherwise require complicated equipment and human effort. Advances in computer software and printing technology continue to change and enhance desktop publishing work. Instead of receiving simple typed text from customers, desktop publishers get the material on a computer disk. Other innovations in desktop publishing work include digital color page makeup systems, electronic page layout systems, and off-press color proofing systems.

And because most materials today often are published on the Internet, desktop publishers may need to know electronic publishing technologies, such as Hypertext Markup Language (HTML), and may be responsible for converting text and graphics to an Internet-ready format.

Typesetting and page layout have been affected by the technological changes shaping desktop publishing. Increasingly, desktop publishers use computers to do much of the typesetting and page layout work formerly done by prepress workers, posing new challenges for the printing industry. The old "hot type" method of text composition—which used molten lead to create individual letters, paragraphs, and full pages of text—is nearly extinct. Today, composition work is primarily done with computers. Improvements in desktop publishing software also allow customers to do much more of their own typesetting.

Desktop publishers use scanners to capture photographs, images or art as digital data that can be incorporated directly into electronic page layouts or further manipulated using computer software. The desktop publisher then can correct for mistakes or compensate for deficiencies in the original color print or transparency. Digital files are used to produce printing plates. Like photographers and multimedia artists and animators, desktop publishers also can create special effects or other visual images using film, video, computers, or other electronic media.

Depending on the establishment employing these workers, desktop publishers also may be referred to as publications specialists, electronic publishers, DTP operators, desktop publishing editors, electronic prepress technicians, electronic publishing specialists, image designers, typographers, compositors, layout artists, and Web publications designers.

Working Conditions

Desktop publishers usually work in clean, air-conditioned office areas with little noise. Desktop publishers usually work an 8-hour day, 5 days a week. Some workers—particularly those self-employed—work night shifts, weekends, and holidays.

Desktop publishers often are subject to stress and the pressures of short deadlines and tight work schedules. Like other workers who spend long hours working in front of a computer monitor, they may be susceptible to eyestrain, back discomfort, and hand and wrist problems.

Employment

Desktop publishers held about 38,000 jobs in 2000. Nearly all worked in the printing and publishing industries. About 1,000 desktop publishers were self-employed.

Most desktop publishing jobs were found in firms that handle commercial or corporate printing, and in newspaper plants. Commercial printing firms print a wide range of products (newspaper inserts, catalogs, pamphlets, and advertisements); business form establishments print material such as sales receipts. A large number of desktop publishers also were found in printing trade services firms. Establishments in printing trade services typically perform custom compositing, platemaking, and related prepress services. Others work printing or publishing materials "in-house" or "in-plant" for business services firms, government agencies, hospitals, or universities, typically in a reproduction or publications department that operates within the organization.

The printing and publishing industry is one of the most geographically dispersed in the United States, and desktop publishing jobs are found throughout the country. However, job prospects may be best in large metropolitan cities.

Training, Other Qualifications, and Advancement

Most workers qualify for jobs as desktop publishers by taking classes or completing certificate programs at vocational schools, universities and colleges, or via the Internet. Programs range in length, but the average nondegree certification training program takes approximately 1 year. However, some desktop publishers train on the job to develop the necessary skills. The length of training on the job varies by company. An internship or part-time desktop publishing assignment is another way to gain experience as a desktop publisher.

Students interested in pursuing a career in desktop publishing also may obtain an associate degree in applied science or a bachelor's degree in graphic arts, graphic communications or graphic design. Graphic arts programs are a good way to learn about desktop publishing software used to format pages, assign type characteristics, and import text and graphics into electronic page layouts to produce printed materials such as advertisements, brochures, newsletters, and forms. Applying this knowledge of graphic arts techniques and computerized typesetting usually are intended for students who may eventually move into management positions, while 2-year associate degree programs are designed to train skilled workers. Students also develop finely tuned skills in typography, print mediums, packaging, branding and identity, Web design and motion graphics. These programs teach print and graphic design fundamentals and provide an extensive background in imaging, prepress, print reproduction, and emerging media. Courses in other aspects of printing also are available at vocational-technical institutes, industry-sponsored update and retraining programs, and private trade and technical schools.

Although formal training is not always required, those with certification or degrees will have the best job opportunities. Most employers prefer to hire people who have at least a high school diploma, possess good communication skills, basic computer skills, and a strong work ethic. Desktop publishers should be able to deal courteously with people because in small shops they may have to take customer orders. They also may add, subtract, multiply, divide, and compute ratios to estimate job costs. Persons interested in working for firms using advanced printing technology need to know the basics of electronics and computers.

Desktop publishers need good manual dexterity, and they must be able to pay attention to detail and work independently. Good eyesight, including visual acuity, depth perception, field of view, color vision, and the ability to focus quickly, also are assets. Artistic ability often is a plus. Employers also seek persons who are even-tempered and adaptable (important qualities for workers who often must meet deadlines and learn how to operate new equipment).

Workers with limited training and experience may start as helpers. They begin with instruction from an experienced desktop publisher and advance based on their demonstrated mastery of skills at each level. All workers should expect to be retrained from time to time to handle new, improved software and equipment. As workers gain experience, they advance to positions with greater responsibility. Some move into supervisory or management positions. Other desktop publishers may start their own company or work as an independent consultant, while those with more artistic talent and further education may find opportunities in graphic design or commercial art.

Job Outlook

Employment of desktop publishers is expected to grow much faster than the average for all occupations through 2010, as more page layout and design work is performed in-house using computers and sophisticated publishing software. Desktop publishing is replacing much of the prepress work done by compositors and typesetters, enabling organizations to reduce costs while increasing production speeds. Many new jobs for desktop publishers are expected to emerge in commercial printing and publishing establishments. However, more companies also are turning to in-house desktop publishers, as computers with elaborate text and graphics capabilities have become common, and desktop publishing software has become cheaper and easier to use. In addition to employment growth, many job openings for desktop publishers also will result from the need to replace workers who move into managerial positions, transfer to other occupations, or who leave the labor force.

Printing and publishing costs represent a significant portion of a corporation's expenses, no matter the industry, and corporations are finding it more profitable to print their own newsletters and other reports than to send them out to trade shops. Desktop publishing reduces the time needed to complete a printing job, and allows commercial printers to make inroads into new markets that require fast turnaround.

Most employers prefer to hire experienced desktop publishers. As more people gain desktop publishing experience, however, competition for jobs may increase. Among persons without experience, opportunities should be best for those with computer backgrounds who are certified or who have completed postsecondary programs in desktop publishing or graphic design. Many employers prefer graduates of these programs because the comprehensive training they receive helps them learn the page layout process and adapt more rapidly to new software and techniques.

Earnings

Earnings for desktop publishers vary according to level of experience, training, location, and size of firm. Median annual earnings of desktop publishers were $30,600 in 2000. The middle 50 percent earned between $22,890 and $40,210. The lowest 10 percent earned less than $17,800, and the highest 10 percent earned more than $50,920 a year. Median annual earnings in the industries employing the largest numbers of these workers in 2000 are shown in the following:

Commercial printing $30,940
Newspapers 24,520

Related Occupations

Desktop publishers use artistic and editorial skills in their work. These skills also are essential for artists and related workers; designers; news analysts, reporters, and correspondents; public relations specialists; writers and editors; and prepress technicians and workers.

Sources of Additional Information

Details about apprenticeship and other training programs may be obtained from local employers such as newspapers and printing shops, or from local offices of the state employment service.

For information on careers and training in printing, desktop publishing, and graphic arts, write to:

- Graphic Communications Council, 1899 Preston White Dr., Reston, VA 20191. Internet: http://www.npes.org

- Graphic Arts Technical Foundation, 200 Deer Run Rd., Sewickley, PA 15143. Internet: http://www.gatf.org

For information on benefits and compensation in desktop publishing, write to:

- Printing Industries of America, Inc., 100 Daingerfield Rd., Alexandria, VA 22314. Internet: http://www.gain.org

Diagnostic Medical Sonographers

O*NET 29-2032.00

Significant Points

- Sonographers should experience favorable job opportunities as ultrasound becomes an increasingly attractive alternative to radiologic procedures.

- More than half of all sonographers are employed by hospitals, and most of the remainder work in physicians' offices and clinics, including diagnostic imaging centers.

- Beginning in 2005, an associate or higher degree from an accredited program will be required for registration.

Nature of the Work

Diagnostic imaging embraces several procedures that aid in diagnosing ailments, the most familiar being the X ray. Another increasingly common diagnostic imaging method, called magnetic resonance imaging (MRI), uses giant magnets and radio waves rather than radiation to create an image. Not all imaging technologies use ionizing radiation or radio waves, however. Sonography, or ultrasonography, is the use of sound waves to generate an image used for assessment and diagnosis of various medical conditions. Many people associate sonography with obstetrics and the viewing of the fetus in the womb. But this technology has many other applications in the diagnosis and treatment of medical conditions.

Diagnostic medical sonographers, also known as *ultrasonographers*, use special equipment to direct nonionizing, high frequency sound waves into areas of the patient's body. Sonographers operate the equipment, which collects reflected echoes and forms an image that may be videotaped, transmitted, or photographed for interpretation and diagnosis by a physician.

Sonographers begin by explaining the procedure to the patient and recording any additional medical history that may be relevant to the condition being viewed. They then select appropriate equipment settings and direct the patient to move into positions that will provide the best view. To perform the exam, sonographers use a transducer, which transmits sound waves in a cone- or rectangle-shaped beam. Although techniques vary based on the area being examined, sonographers usually spread a special gel on the skin to aid the transmission of sound waves.

Viewing the screen during the scan, sonographers look for subtle visual cues that contrast healthy areas from unhealthy ones. They decide whether the images are satisfactory for diagnostic purposes and select which ones to show to the physician.

Diagnostic medical sonographers may specialize in obstetric and gynecologic sonography (the female reproductive system), abdominal sonography (the liver, kidneys, gallbladder, spleen, and pancreas), neurosonography (the brain), or ophthalmologic sonography (the eyes). In addition, sonographers also may specialize in vascular technology or echocardiography.

Obstetric and gynecologic sonographers specialize in the study of the female reproductive system. This includes one of the more well known uses of sonography: examining the fetus of a pregnant woman to track its growth and health.

Abdominal sonographers inspect a patient's abdominal cavity to help diagnose and treat conditions involving primarily the gallbladder, bile ducts, kidneys, liver, pancreas, and spleen. Abdominal sonographers also are able to scan parts of the heart, although diagnosis of the heart using ultrasound usually is done by echocardiographers.

Neurosonographers use ultrasound technology to focus on the nervous system, including the brain. In neonatal care, neurosonographers study and diagnose neurological and nervous system disorders in premature infants. They also may scan blood vessels to check for abnormalities indicating a stroke in infants diagnosed with sickle cell anemia. Like other sonographers, neurosonographers operate transducers to perform the ultrasound, but use different frequencies and beam shapes than obstetric and abdominal sonographers.

Ophthalmologic sonographers use ultrasound to study the eyes. Ultrasound aids in the insertion of prosthetic lenses by allowing accurate measurement of the eyes. Ophthalmologic ultrasound also helps diagnose and track tumors, blood supply conditions, separated retinas, and other ailments of the eye and the surrounding tissue. Ophthalmologic sonographers use high frequency transducers made exclusively to study the eyes, which are much smaller than those used in other specialties.

In addition to working directly with patients, diagnostic medical sonographers keep patient records and adjust and maintain equipment. They also may prepare work schedules, evaluate equipment purchases, or manage a sonography or diagnostic imaging department.

Working Conditions

Most full-time sonographers work about 40 hours a week; they may have evening weekend hours and times when they are on call and must be ready to report to work on short notice.

Sonographers typically work in healthcare facilities that are clean and well lit. Some travel to patients in large vans equipped with sophisticated diagnostic equipment. Sonographers are on their feet for long periods and may have to lift or turn disabled patients. They work at diagnostic imaging machines but may also do some procedures at patients' bedsides.

Employment

Diagnostic medical sonographers held about 33,000 jobs in 2000. More than half of all sonographer jobs are in hospitals. Most of the rest are in physicians' offices and clinics, primarily in offices specializing in obstetrics and in diagnostic imaging centers. According to the 2000 Sonography Benchmark Survey conducted by the Society of Diagnostic Medical Sonographers (SDMS), about three out of four sonographers worked in urban areas.

Training, Other Qualifications, and Advancement

There are several avenues for entry into the field of diagnostic medical sonography. Sonographers may train in hospitals, vocational-technical institutions, colleges and universities, and the armed forces. Some training programs prefer applicants with a background in science or experience in other health professions, but also will consider high school graduates with courses in math and science, as well as applicants with liberal arts backgrounds.

Colleges and universities offer formal training in both 2- and 4-year programs, culminating in an associate or bachelor's degree. Two-year programs are most prevalent. Course work includes classes in anatomy, physiology, instrumentation, basic physics, patient care, and medical ethics. The Joint Review Committee on Education for Diagnostic Medical Sonography accredits most formal training programs (76 programs in 1999).

Some health workers, such as obstetric nurses and radiologic technologists, seek to increase their marketability by cross-training in fields such as sonography. Many take 1-year programs resulting in a certificate. Additionally, sonographers specializing in one discipline often seek competency in others; for example, obstetric sonographers might seek training in and exposure to abdominal sonography to broaden their opportunities.

While no state requires licensure in diagnostic medical sonography, the American Registry of Diagnostic Medical Sonographers (ARDMS) certifies the competency of sonographers through registration. Because registration provides an independent, objective measure of an individual's professional standing, many employers prefer to hire registered sonographers. Registration with ARDMS requires passing a general physics and instrumentation examination, in addition to passing an exam in a specialty such as obstetrics/gynecology, abdominal, or neurosonography.

While formal education is not necessary to take the exams, an associate or bachelor's degree from an accredited program is preferred. Beginning in 2005, ARDMS will consider for registration only those holding an associate or higher degree. To keep their registration current, sonographers must complete 30 hours of continuing education every 3 years to stay abreast of advances in the occupation and in technology.

Sonographers need good communication and interpersonal skills because they must be able to explain technical procedures and results to their patients, some of whom may be nervous about the exam or the problems it may reveal. They also should have some background in math and science, especially when they must perform mathematical and scientific calculations in analyses for diagnosis.

Job Outlook

Employment of diagnostic medical sonographers is expected to grow faster than the average for all occupations through 2010 as the population grows and ages, increasing the demand for diagnostic imaging and therapeutic technology. Some job openings also will arise from the need to replace sonographers who leave the occupation.

Ultrasound is becoming an increasingly attractive alternative to radiologic procedures as patients seek safer treatment methods. Because ultrasound—unlike most diagnostic imaging methods—does not involve radiation, harmful side effects and complications from repeated use are rarer for both the patient and the sonographer. Sonographic technology is expected to evolve rapidly and to spawn many new ultrasound procedures, such as 3D-ultrasonography for use in obstetric and ophthalmologic diagnosis. However, high costs may limit the rate at which some promising new technologies are adopted.

Hospitals will remain the principal employer of diagnostic medical sonographers. However, employment is expected to grow more rapidly in offices and clinics of physicians, including diagnostic imaging centers. Health facilities such as these are expected to grow very rapidly through 2010 due to the strong shift toward outpatient care, encouraged by third-party payers and made possible by technological advances that permit more procedures to be performed outside the hospital.

Earnings

Median annual earnings of diagnostic medical sonographers were $44,820 in 2000. The middle 50 percent earned between $38,390 and $52,750 a year. The lowest 10 percent earned less than $32,470, and the highest 10 percent earned more than $59,310. Median annual earnings of diagnostic medical sonographers in 2000 were $43,950 in hospitals and $46,190 in offices and clinics of medical doctors.

Related Occupations

Diagnostic medical sonographers operate sophisticated equipment to help physicians and other health practitioners diagnose and treat patients. Workers in related occupations include cardiovascular technologists and technicians, clinical laboratory technologists and technicians, nuclear medicine technologists, radiologic technologists and technicians, and respiratory therapists.

Sources of Additional Information

For more information on a career as a diagnostic medical sonographer, contact:

- Society of Diagnostic Medical Sonographers, 12770 Coit Rd., Suite 708, Dallas, TX 75251. Internet: http://www.sdms.org

- The American Registry of Diagnostic Medical Sonographers, 600 Jefferson Plaza, Suite 360, Rockville, MD 20852-1150. Internet: http://www.ardms.org

For a current list of accredited education programs in diagnostic medical sonography, write to:

- The Joint Review Committee on Education in Diagnostic Medical Sonography, 1248 Harwood Rd., Bedford, TX 76021-4244. Internet: http://www.caahep.org

Diesel Service Technicians and Mechanics

O*NET 49-3031.00

Significant Points

● A career as a diesel service technician or mechanic offers relatively high wages and the challenge of skilled repair work.

● Opportunities are expected to be good for persons who complete formal training programs.

● National certification is the recognized standard of achievement for diesel service technicians and mechanics.

Nature of the Work

The diesel engine is the workhorse powering the nation's trucks and buses, because it delivers more power and is more durable than its gasoline-burning counterpart. Diesel-powered engines also are becoming more prevalent in light vehicles, including pickups and other work trucks.

Diesel service technicians and mechanics, also known as *bus and truck mechanics and diesel engine specialists*, repair and maintain the diesel engines that power transportation equipment such as heavy trucks, buses, and locomotives. Some diesel technicians and mechanics also work on heavy vehicles and mobile equipment such as bulldozers, cranes, road graders, farm tractors, and combines. A small number of technicians repair diesel-powered passenger automobiles, light trucks, or boats.

Technicians who work for organizations that maintain their own vehicles spend most of their time doing preventive maintenance, to ensure that equipment will operate safely. These workers also eliminate unnecessary wear on and damage to parts that could result in costly breakdowns. During a routine maintenance check on a vehicle, technicians follow a checklist that includes inspection of brake systems, steering mechanisms, wheel bearings, and other important parts. Following inspection, technicians repair or adjust parts that do not work properly or remove and replace parts that cannot be fixed.

Increasingly, technicians must be flexible, in order to adapt to customer needs and new technologies. It is common for technicians to handle all kinds of repairs, from working on a vehicle's electrical system one day, to doing major engine repairs the next. Diesel maintenance is becoming increasingly complex, as more electronic components are used to control engine operation. For example, microprocessors regulate and manage fuel timing, increasing engine efficiency. In modern shops, diesel service technicians use hand-held computers to diagnose problems and adjust engine functions. Technicians must continually learn about new techniques and advanced materials.

Diesel service technicians use a variety of tools in their work, including power tools, such as pneumatic wrenches, to remove bolts quickly; machine tools, such as lathes and grinding machines, to rebuild brakes; welding and flame-cutting equipment to remove and repair exhaust systems; and jacks and hoists to lift and move large parts. Common handtools—screwdrivers, pliers, and wrenches—are used to work on small parts and get at hard-to-reach places. Diesel service technicians and mechanics also use a variety of computerized testing equipment to pinpoint and analyze malfunctions in electrical systems and engines.

In large shops, technicians generally receive their assignments from shop supervisors or service managers. Most supervisors and managers are experienced technicians who also assist in diagnosing problems and maintaining quality standards. Technicians may work as a team or be assisted by an apprentice or helper when doing heavy work, such as removing engines and transmissions.

Working Conditions

Diesel technicians usually work indoors, although they occasionally make repairs to vehicles on the road. Diesel technicians may lift heavy parts and tools, handle greasy and dirty parts, and stand or lie in awkward positions to repair vehicles and equipment. Minor cuts, burns, and bruises are common, although serious accidents can usually be avoided if the shop is kept clean and orderly and safety procedures are followed. Technicians normally work in well-lighted, heated, and ventilated areas; however, some shops are drafty and noisy. Many employers provide lockers and shower facilities.

Employment

Diesel service technicians and mechanics held about 285,000 jobs in 2000. About 25 percent serviced buses, trucks, and other diesel-powered equipment for customers of vehicle and equipment dealers, automotive rental and leasing agencies, or independent automotive repair shops. About 20 percent worked for local and long-distance trucking companies, and another 19 percent maintained the buses, trucks, and other equipment of buslines, public transit companies, school systems, or federal, state, and local governments. The remaining technicians maintained vehicles and other equipment for manufacturing, construction, or other companies. A relatively small number were self-employed. Nearly every section of the country employs diesel service technicians and mechanics, although most work in towns and cities where trucking companies, buslines, and other fleet owners have large operations.

Training, Other Qualifications, and Advancement

Although many persons qualify for diesel service technician and mechanic jobs through years of on-the-job training, authorities recommend completion of a formal diesel engine training program. Employers prefer to hire graduates of formal training programs because these workers often have a head start in training and are able to quickly advance to the journey level.

Many community colleges and trade and vocational schools offer programs in diesel repair. These programs, lasting 6 months to 2 years, lead to a certificate of completion or an associate degree. Programs vary in the degree of hands-on training they provide on equipment. Some offer about 30 hours per week on equipment, whereas others offer more lab or classroom instruction. Training provides a foundation in the latest diesel technology and instruction in the service and repair of the vehicles and equipment that technicians will encounter on the job. Training programs also improve the skills needed to interpret technical manuals and to communicate with coworkers and customers. In addition to the hands-on aspects of the training, many institutions teach communication skills, customer service, basic understanding of physics, and logical thought. Increasingly, employers work closely with representatives of training programs, providing instructors with the latest equipment, techniques, and tools and offering jobs to graduates.

Whereas most employers prefer to hire persons who have completed formal training programs, some technicians and mechanics continue to learn their skills on the job. Unskilled beginners usually are assigned tasks such as cleaning parts, fueling and lubricating vehicles, and driving vehicles into and out of the shop. Beginners usually are promoted to trainee positions, as they gain experience and as vacancies become available. In some shops, beginners with experience in automobile service start as trainee technicians.

Most trainees perform routine service tasks and make minor repairs after a few months' experience. These workers advance to increasingly difficult jobs as they prove their ability and competence. After technicians master the repair and service of diesel engines, they learn to work on related components, such as brakes, transmissions, and electrical systems. Generally, technicians with at least 3 to 4 years of on-the-job experience will qualify as journey-level diesel technicians. Completion of a formal training program speeds advancement to the journey level.

For unskilled entry-level jobs, employers usually look for applicants who have mechanical aptitude and strong problem-solving skills, and who are at least 18 years of age and in good physical condition. Nearly all employers require completion of high school. Courses in automotive repair, electronics, English, mathematics, and physics provide a strong educational background for a career as a diesel service technician or mechanic. Technicians need a state commercial driver's license to test-drive trucks or buses on public roads. Practical experience in automobile repair at a gasoline service station, in the armed forces, or as a hobby is also valuable.

Employers often send experienced technicians and mechanics to special training classes conducted by manufacturers and vendors, in which workers learn the latest technology and repair techniques. Technicians constantly receive updated technical manuals and service procedures outlining changes in techniques and standards for repair. It is essential for technicians to read, interpret, and comprehend service manuals, in order to keep abreast of engineering changes.

Voluntary certification by the National Institute for Automotive Service Excellence (ASE) is recognized as the standard of achievement for diesel service technicians and mechanics. Technicians may be certified as Master Heavy-Duty Truck Technicians or in specific areas of heavy-duty truck repair, such as gasoline engines, drive trains, brakes, suspension and steering, electrical and electronic systems, or preventive maintenance and inspection.

For certification in each area, a technician must pass one or more of the ASE-administered exams and present proof of 2 years of relevant hands-on work experience. Two years of relevant formal training from a high school, vocational or trade school, or community or junior college program may be substituted for up to 1 year of the work experience requirement. To remain certified, technicians must retest every 5 years. This ensures that service technicians and mechanics keep up with changing technology.

Diesel service technicians and mechanics may opt for ASE certification as schoolbus technicians. The certification identifies and recognizes technicians with the knowledge and skills required to diagnose, service, and repair different subsystems of schoolbuses. The ASE School Bus Techni-

cian Test Series includes seven certification exams: Body Systems and Special Equipment (S1), Diesel Engines (S2), Drive Train (S3), Brakes (S4), Suspension and Steering (S5), Electrical/Electronic Systems (S6), and Air Conditioning Systems and Controls (S7). Whereas several of these tests parallel existing ASE truck tests, each one is designed to test knowledge of systems specific to schoolbuses. In order to become ASE-certified in schoolbus repair, technicians must pass one or more of the exams and present proof of 2 years of relevant hands-on work experience. Technicians who pass tests S1 through S6 become ASE-Certified Master School Bus Technicians.

The most important work possessions of technicians and mechanics are their handtools. Technicians and mechanics usually provide their own tools, and many experienced workers have thousands of dollars invested in them. Employers typically furnish expensive power tools, computerized engine analyzers, and other diagnostic equipment; but individual workers ordinarily accumulate handtools with experience.

Experienced technicians and mechanics with leadership ability may advance to shop supervisor or service manager. Technicians and mechanics with sales ability sometimes become sales representatives. Some open their own repair shops.

Job Outlook

Employment of diesel service technicians and mechanics is expected to increase about as fast as the average for all occupations through the year 2010. Besides openings resulting from employment growth, opportunities will be created by the need to replace workers who retire or transfer to other occupations.

Employment of diesel service technicians and mechanics is expected to grow as freight transportation by truck increases. Additional trucks will be needed to keep pace with the increasing volume of freight shipped nationwide. Trucks also serve as intermediaries for other forms of transportation, such as rail and air. Due to the greater durability and economy of the diesel engine relative to the gasoline engine, buses and trucks of all sizes are expected to be increasingly powered by diesels. In addition, diesel service technicians will be needed to maintain and repair the growing number of schoolbuses in operation.

Careers as diesel service technicians attract many because of relatively high wages and the challenge of skilled repair work. Opportunities should be good for persons who complete formal training in diesel mechanics at community and junior colleges and vocational and technical schools. Applicants without formal training may face stiffer competition for entry-level jobs.

Most persons entering this occupation can expect steady work, because changes in economic conditions have little effect on the diesel repair business. During a financial downturn, however, some employers may be reluctant to hire new workers.

Earnings

Median hourly earnings of bus and truck mechanics and diesel engine specialists, including incentive pay, were $15.55 in 2000. The middle 50 percent earned between $12.33 and $19.30 an hour. The lowest 10 percent earned less than $9.88, and the highest 10 percent earned more than $22.63 an hour. Median hourly earnings in the industries employing the largest numbers of bus and truck mechanics and diesel engine specialists in 2000 were as follows:

Local government	$17.93
Motor vehicles, parts, and supplies	15.48
Automotive repair shops	14.74
Trucking and courier services, except air	14.65
Elementary and secondary schools	14.63

Because many experienced technicians employed by truck fleet dealers and independent repair shops receive a commission related to the labor cost charged to the customer, weekly earnings depend on the amount of work completed. Beginners usually earn from 50 to 75 percent of the rate of skilled workers and receive increases, as they become more skilled, until they reach the rates of skilled service technicians.

The majority of service technicians work a standard 40-hour week, although some work longer hours, particularly if they are self-employed. A growing number of shops have expanded their hours to better perform repairs and routine service when needed, or as a convenience to customers. Those employed by truck and bus firms providing service around the clock may work evenings, nights, and weekends. These technicians usually receive a higher rate of pay for working non-traditional hours.

Many diesel service technicians and mechanics are members of labor unions, including the International Association of Machinists and Aerospace Workers; the Amalgamated Transit Union; the International Union, United Automobile, Aerospace and Agricultural Implement Workers of America; the Transport Workers Union of America; the Sheet Metal Workers' International Association; and the International Brotherhood of Teamsters.

Related Occupations

Diesel service technicians and mechanics repair trucks, buses, and other diesel-powered equipment. Related technician and mechanic occupations include aircraft and avionics equipment mechanics and service technicians, automotive service technicians and mechanics, heavy vehicle and mobile equipment service technicians and mechanics, and small engine mechanics.

Sources of Additional Information

More details about work opportunities for diesel service technicians and mechanics may be obtained from local employers such as trucking companies, truck dealers, or bus lines; locals of the unions previously mentioned; and local offices of your state employment service. Local state employment service offices also may have information about training programs. State boards of postsecondary career schools also have information on licensed schools with training programs for diesel service technicians and mechanics.

For general information about a career as a diesel service technician or mechanic, write:

- Detroit Diesel, Personnel Director, MS B39, 13400 West Outer Dr., Detroit, MI 48239

Information on how to become a certified medium/heavy-duty diesel technician or bus technician is available from:

- ASE, 101 Blue Seal Dr. S.E., Suite 101, Leesburg, VA 20175. Internet: http://www.asecert.org

For a directory of accredited private trade and technical schools with training programs for diesel service technicians and mechanics, contact:

- Accrediting Commission of Career Schools and Colleges of Technology, 2101 Wilson Blvd., Suite 302, Arlington, VA 22201. Internet: http://www.accsct.org

- National Automotive Technicians Education Foundation, 101 Blue Seal Dr. S.E., Suite 101, Leesburg, VA 20175. Internet: http://www.natef.org

For a directory of public training programs for diesel service technicians and mechanics, contact:

- SkillsUSA-VICA, P.O. Box 3000, 14001 James Monroe Hwy., Leesburg, VA 22075. Internet: http://www.skillsusa.org

Dispatchers

O*NET 43-5031.00, 43-5032.00

Significant Points

- Many dispatcher jobs are entry level and do not require more than a high school diploma.

- Dispatchers develop necessary skills through extensive on-the-job training lasting up to a few months.

- Numerous job openings will arise each year from the need to replace workers who leave this very large occupational group.

Nature of the Work

Dispatchers schedule and dispatch workers, equipment, or service vehicles for conveyance of materials or passengers. They keep records, logs, and schedules of the calls they receive, the transportation vehicles they monitor and control, and the actions they take. They maintain information on each call, and then prepare a detailed report on all activities occurring during the shift. Many dispatchers employ computer-aided dispatch systems to accomplish these tasks. The work of dispatchers varies greatly, depending on the industry in which they work.

Regardless of where they work, all dispatchers are assigned a specific territory and have responsibility for all communications within this area. Many work in teams, especially in large communications centers or companies. One person usually handles all dispatching calls to the response units or company drivers, while the other members of the team usually receive the incoming calls and deal with the public.

Police, fire, and ambulance dispatchers, also called public safety dispatchers, monitor the location of emergency services personnel from any one or all of the jurisdiction's emergency services departments. They dispatch the appropriate type and number of units in response to calls for assistance. Dispatchers, or call takers, often are the first people the public contacts when they call for emergency assistance. If certified for emergency medical services, the dispatcher may provide medical instruction to those on the scene of the emergency until the medical staff arrives.

Police, fire, and ambulance dispatchers work in a variety of settings; they may work in a police station, a fire station, a hospital, or, increasingly, in a centralized communications center. In many areas, the police department serves as the communications center. In these situations, all 911 emergency calls go to the police department, where a dispatcher handles the police calls and screens the others before transferring them to the appropriate service.

When handling calls, dispatchers carefully question each caller to determine the type, seriousness, and location of the emergency. This information is posted either electronically by computer or, with decreasing frequency, by hand. It is communicated immediately to uniformed or supervisory personnel, who quickly decide on the priority of the incident, the kind and number of units needed, and the location of the closest and most suitable units available. Usually, dispatchers constitute the communications workforce on a shift. Typically, there is a team of call takers who answer calls and relay the information to be dispatched. Responsibility then shifts to the dispatchers who send response units to the scene and monitor the activity of the public safety personnel answering the dispatch. During the course of the shift, dispatchers may rotate these functions.

When appropriate, dispatchers stay in close contact with other service providers—for example, a police dispatcher would monitor the response of the fire department when there is a major fire. In a medical emergency, dispatchers keep in close touch not only with the dispatched units, but also with the caller. They may give extensive pre-arrival first-aid instructions while the caller is waiting for the ambulance. They continuously give updates on the patient's condition to the ambulance personnel, and often serve as a link between the medical staff in a hospital and the emergency medical technicians in the ambulance.

Other dispatchers coordinate deliveries, service calls, and related activities for a variety of firms. *Truck dispatchers,* who work for local and long-distance trucking companies, coordinate the movement of trucks and freight between cities. They direct the pickup and delivery activities of drivers. They receive customers' requests for pickup and delivery of freight; consolidate freight orders into truckloads for specific destinations; assign drivers and trucks; and draw up routes and pickup and delivery schedules. *Bus dispatchers* make sure that local and long-distance buses stay on schedule. They handle all problems that may disrupt service, and dispatch other buses or arrange for repairs in order to restore service and schedules. *Train dispatchers* ensure the timely and efficient movement of trains according to train orders and schedules. They must be aware of track switch positions, track maintenance areas, and the location of other trains running on the track. *Taxicab dispatchers,* or starters, dispatch taxis in response to requests for service and keep logs on all road service calls. *Tow truck dispatchers* take calls for emergency road service. They relay the nature of the problem to a nearby service station or a tow truck service and see to it that the emergency road service is completed. *Gas and water service dispatchers* monitor gaslines and water mains and send out service trucks and crews to take care of emergencies.

Working Conditions

The work of dispatchers can be very hectic when many calls come in at the same time. The job of public safety dispatcher is particularly stressful because slow or improper response to a call can result in serious injury or further harm. Also, callers who are anxious or afraid may become excited and be unable to provide needed information; some may even become abusive. Despite provocations, dispatchers must remain calm, objective, and in control of the situation.

Dispatchers sit for long periods, using telephones, computers, and two-way radios. Much of their time is spent at video display terminals, viewing monitors and observing traffic patterns. As a result of working for long stretches with computers and other electronic equipment, dispatchers can experience significant eyestrain and back discomfort. Generally, dispatchers work a 40-hour week; however, rotating shifts and compressed work schedules are common. Alternative work schedules are necessary to accommodate evening, weekend, and holiday work, as well as 24-hour-per-day, 7-day-per-week operations.

The typical work week is Monday through Friday; however, evening and weekend hours are common for some jobs, and may be required in other jobs when large shipments are involved.

Employment

Dispatchers held 254,000 jobs in 2000. About one-third were police, fire, and ambulance dispatchers, almost all of whom worked for state and local governments—primarily for local police and fire departments. Most of the remaining dispatchers worked for local and long-distance trucking companies and buslines; air carriers; wholesale establishments; railroads; taxicab companies; and companies providing business services.

Although dispatching jobs are found throughout the country, most dispatchers work in urban areas, where large communications centers and businesses are located.

Training, Other Qualifications, and Advancement

Many dispatcher jobs are entry level and do not require more than a high school diploma. Employers, however, prefer to hire those who are familiar with computers and other electronic office and business equipment. Those who have taken business courses or have previous business, dispatching, or specific job-related experience may be preferred. Because communication with other people is an integral part of these jobs, good oral and written communications skills are essential. Typing, filing, recordkeeping, and other clerical skills also are important.

State or local government civil service regulations usually govern police, fire, emergency medical, and ambulance dispatching jobs. Candidates for these positions may have to pass written, oral, and performance tests. Also, they may be asked to attend training classes and attain the proper certification in order to qualify for advancement.

Trainees usually develop the necessary skills on the job. This informal training lasts from several days to a few months, depending on the complexity of the job. Dispatchers usually require the most extensive training. Working with an experienced dispatcher, they monitor calls and learn how to operate a variety of communications equipment, including telephones, radios, and various wireless devices. As trainees gain confidence, they begin to handle calls themselves. In smaller operations, dispatchers sometimes act as customer service representatives, processing orders themselves. Many public safety dispatchers also participate in structured training programs sponsored by their employer. Some employers offer a course designed by the Association of Public Safety Communications Officials. This course covers topics such as interpersonal communications; overview of the police, fire, and rescue functions; modern public safety telecommunications systems; basic radio broadcasting; local, state, and national crime information computer systems; and telephone complaint/report processing procedures. Other employers develop in-house programs based on their own needs. Emergency medical dispatchers often receive special training or have special skills. Increasingly, public safety dispatchers receive training in stress and crisis management, as well as family counseling. Employers are recognizing the toll this work has on daily living and the potential impact that stress has on the job, on the work environment, and in the home.

Communications skills and the ability to work under pressure are important personal qualities for dispatchers. Residency in the city or county of employment frequently is required for public safety dispatchers. Dispatchers in transportation industries must be able to deal with sudden influxes of shipments and disruptions of shipping schedules caused by bad weather, road construction, or accidents.

Although there are no mandatory licensing or certification requirements, some states require that public safety dispatchers possess a certificate to work on a state network, such as the Police Information Network. The Association of Public Safety Communications Officials, the National Academy of Emergency Medical Dispatch, and the International Municipal Signal Association all offer certification programs. Many dispatchers participate in these programs in order to improve their prospects for career advancement.

Dispatchers who work for private firms, which usually are small, will find few opportunities for advancement. Public safety dispatchers, on the other hand, may become a shift or divisional supervisor or chief of communications, or move to higher paying administrative jobs. Some become police officers or firefighters.

Job Outlook

Employment of dispatchers is expected to grow as fast as the average for all occupations through 2010. In addition to those resulting from job growth, openings will arise from the need to replace workers who transfer to other occupations or leave the labor force.

Projected employment growth of police, fire, and ambulance dispatchers, or public safety dispatchers, stems from increased demand for emergency services. Many districts are consolidating their communications centers into a shared, areawide facility. Individuals with computer skills and experience will have a greater opportunity for employment as public safety dispatchers.

Population growth and economic expansion are expected to spur employment growth for other types of dispatchers. Employment of some dispatchers is more adversely affected by economic downturns than that of other dispatchers. When economic activity falls, demand for transportation services declines. As a result, taxicab, train, and truck dispatchers may experience layoffs or a shortened work week, and job seekers may have some difficulty finding entry-level jobs. Employment of tow truck dispatchers, on the other hand, is seldom affected by general economic conditions because of the emergency nature of their business.

Earnings

Median hourly earnings in 2000 for dispatchers were $13.66.

Dispatchers usually receive the same benefits as most other workers. If uniforms are required, employers usually provide either the uniforms or an allowance to purchase them.

Related Occupations

Other occupations that involve directing and controlling the movement of vehicles, freight, and personnel, as well as distributing information and messages, include air traffic controllers, communications equipment operators, customer service representatives, and reservation and transportation ticket agents and travel clerks.

Sources of Additional Information

For further information on training and certification for police, fire, and emergency dispatchers, contact:

- National Academy of Emergency Medical Dispatch, 139 East South Temple, Suite 530, Salt Lake City, UT 84111. Internet: http://www.emergencydispatch.org

- Association of Public Safety Communications Officials, 2040 S. Ridgewood, South Daytona, FL 32119-2257. Internet: http://www.apcointl.org

- International Municipal Signal Association, 165 East Union St., P.O. Box 539, Newark, NY 14513-0539. Internet: http://www.imsasafety.org

For information on train dispatchers, contact:

- American Train Dispatchers Association, 1370 Ontario St., Cleveland, OH 44113

Information on job opportunities for police, fire, and emergency dispatchers is available from personnel offices of state and local governments or police departments. Information about work opportunities for other types of dispatchers is available from local employers and state employment service offices.

Drafters

O*NET 17-3011.01, 17-3011.02, 17-3012.01, 17-3012.02, 17-3013.00

Significant Points

- The type and quality of postsecondary drafting programs vary considerably; prospective students should be careful in selecting a program.

- Opportunities should be best for individuals who have at least 2 years of postsecondary training in drafting and considerable skill and experience using computer-aided drafting (CAD) systems.

- Demand for particular drafting specializations varies geographically, depending on the needs of local industry.

Nature of the Work

Drafters prepare technical drawings and plans used by production and construction workers to build everything from manufactured products, such as toys, toasters, industrial machinery, or spacecraft, to structures, such as houses, office buildings, or oil and gas pipelines. Their drawings provide visual guidelines, showing the technical details of the products and structures and specifying dimensions, materials to be used, and procedures and processes to be followed. Drafters fill in technical details, using drawings, rough sketches, specifications, codes, and calculations previously made by engineers, surveyors, architects, or scientists. For example, they use their knowledge of standardized building techniques to draw in the details of a structure. Some drafters use their knowledge of engineering and manufacturing theory and standards to draw the parts of a machine in order to determine design elements, such as the number and kind of fasteners needed to assemble it. They use technical handbooks, tables, calculators, and computers to do this.

Traditionally, drafters sat at drawing boards and used pencils, pens, compasses, protractors, triangles, and other drafting devices to prepare a drawing manually. Most drafters now use computer-aided drafting (CAD) systems to prepare drawings. Consequently, some drafters are referred to as CAD operators. CAD systems employ computer work stations to create a drawing on a video screen. The drawings are stored electronically so that revisions or duplications can be made easily. These systems also permit drafters to easily and quickly prepare variations of a design. Although drafters use CAD extensively, it is only a tool. Persons who produce technical drawings using CAD still function as drafters, and need the knowledge of traditional drafters—relating to drafting skills and standards—in addition to CAD skills. Despite the near-universal use of CAD systems, manual drafting still is used in certain applications.

Drafting work has many specialties, and titles may denote a particular discipline of design or drafting. *Aeronautical drafters* prepare engineering drawings detailing plans and specifications used for the manufacture of aircraft, missiles, and related parts.

Architectural drafters draw architectural and structural features of buildings and other structures. They may specialize by the type of structure, such as residential or commercial, or by the kind of material used, such as reinforced concrete, masonry, steel, or timber.

Civil drafters prepare drawings and topographical and relief maps used in major construction or civil engineering projects, such as highways, bridges, pipelines, flood control projects, and water and sewage systems.

Electrical drafters prepare wiring and layout diagrams used by workers who erect, install, and repair electrical equipment and wiring in communication centers, powerplants, electrical distribution systems, and buildings.

Electronic drafters draw wiring diagrams, circuitboard assembly diagrams, schematics, and layout drawings used in the manufacture, installation, and repair of electronic devices and components.

Mechanical drafters prepare detail and assembly drawings of a wide variety of machinery and mechanical devices, indicating dimensions, fastening methods, and other requirements.

Process piping or *pipeline drafters* prepare drawings used for layout, construction, and operation of oil and gas fields, refineries, chemical plants, and process piping systems.

Working Conditions

Drafters usually work in comfortable offices furnished to accommodate their tasks. They may sit at adjustable drawing boards or drafting tables when doing manual drawings, although most drafters work at computer terminals much of the time. Because they spend long periods in front of computer terminals doing detailed work, drafters may be susceptible to eyestrain, back discomfort, and hand and wrist problems.

Employment

Drafters held about 213,000 jobs in 2000. More than 40 percent of drafters worked in engineering and architectural services firms that design construction projects or do other engineering work on a contract basis for organizations in other industries. Another 29 percent worked in durable goods manufacturing industries, such as machinery, electrical equipment, and fabricated metals. The remainder were mostly employed in the construction; government; transportation, communications, and utilities; and personnel-supply services industries. About 10,000 were self-employed in 2000.

Training, Other Qualifications, and Advancement

Employers prefer applicants who have completed postsecondary school training in drafting, which is offered by technical institutes, community colleges, and some 4-year colleges and universities. Employers are most interested in applicants who have well-developed drafting and mechanical drawing skills; a knowledge of drafting standards, mathematics, science, and engineering technology; and a solid background in computer-aided drafting and design techniques. In addition, communication and problem-solving skills are important.

Individuals planning careers in drafting should take courses in math, science, computer technology, design or computer graphics, and any high school drafting courses available. Mechanical ability and visual aptitude also are important. Prospective drafters should be able to draw three-dimensional objects as well as draw freehand. They also should do detailed work accurately and neatly. Artistic ability is helpful in some specialized fields, as is knowledge of manufacturing and construction methods. In addition, prospective drafters should have good interpersonal skills because they work closely with engineers, surveyors, architects, other professionals, and sometimes customers.

Training and coursework differ somewhat within the drafting specialties. The initial training for each specialty is similar. All incorporate math and communication skills, for example, but coursework relating to the specialty varies. In an electronics drafting program, for example, students learn the ways that electronic components and circuits are depicted in drawings.

Entry-level or junior drafters usually do routine work under close supervision. After gaining experience, intermediate-level drafters progress to more difficult work with less supervision. They may be required to exercise more judgment and perform calculations when preparing and modifying drawings. Drafters may eventually advance to senior drafter, designer, or supervisor. Many employers pay for continuing education and, with appropriate college degrees, drafters may go on to become engineering technicians, engineers, or architects.

Many types of publicly and privately operated schools provide some form of drafting training. The kind and quality of programs vary considerably. Therefore, prospective students should be careful in selecting a program. They should contact prospective employers regarding their preferences and ask schools to provide information about the kinds of jobs obtained by graduates, type and condition of instructional facilities and equipment, and faculty qualifications.

Technical institutes offer intensive technical training but less general education than junior and community colleges. Certificates or diplomas based on completion of a certain number of course hours may be rewarded. Many technical institutes offer 2-year associate degree programs, which are similar to, or part of, the programs offered by community colleges or state university systems. Other technical institutes are run by private, often for-profit, organizations, sometimes called proprietary schools. Their programs vary considerably in both length and type of courses offered.

Community colleges offer curriculums similar to those in technical institutes but include more courses on theory and liberal arts. Often, there is little or no difference between technical institute and community college programs. However, courses taken at community colleges are more likely to be accepted for credit at 4-year colleges than are those at technical institutes. After completing a 2-year associate degree program, graduates may obtain jobs as drafters or continue their education in a related field at 4-year colleges. Four-year colleges usually do not offer drafting training, but college courses in engineering, architecture, and mathematics are useful for obtaining a job as a drafter.

Area vocational-technical schools are postsecondary public institutions that serve local students and emphasize training needed by local employers. Many offer introductory drafting instruction. Most require a high school diploma, or its equivalent, for admission.

Technical training obtained in the armed forces also can be applied in civilian drafting jobs. Some additional training may be necessary, depending on the technical area or military specialty.

The American Design Drafting Association (ADDA) has established a certification program for drafters. Although drafters usually are not required to be certified by employers, certification demonstrates that the understanding of nationally recognized practices and knowledge standards have been met. Individuals who wish to become certified must pass the Drafter Certification Test, which is administered periodically at ADDA-authorized test sites. Applicants are tested on their knowledge and understanding of basic drafting concepts such as geometric construction, working drawings, and architectural terms and standards.

Job Outlook

Employment of drafters is expected to grow about as fast as the average for all occupations through 2010. Industrial growth and increasingly complex design problems associated with new products and manufacturing processes will increase the demand for drafting services. Further, drafters are beginning to break out of the traditional drafting role and increasingly do work traditionally performed by engineers and architects, thus increasing the need for drafters. However, the greater use of CAD equipment by drafters, as well as by architects and engineers, should limit demand for lesser-skilled drafters. In addition to those created by employment growth, many job openings are expected to arise as drafters move to other occupations or leave the labor force.

Opportunities should be best for individuals who have at least 2 years of postsecondary training in a drafting program that provides strong technical skills, and who have considerable skill and experience using CAD systems. CAD has increased the complexity of drafting applications while enhancing the productivity of drafters. It also has enhanced the nature of drafting by creating more possibilities for design and drafting. As technology continues to advance, employers will look for drafters with a strong background in fundamental drafting principles, a higher level of technical sophistication, and an ability to apply this knowledge to a broader range of responsibilities.

Demand for particular drafting specialties varies throughout the country because employment usually is contingent upon the needs of local industry. Employment of drafters remains highly concentrated in industries that are sensitive to cyclical changes in the economy, such as engineering and architectural services and durable-goods manufacturing. During recessions, drafters may be laid off. However, a growing number of drafters should continue to be employed on a temporary or contract basis, as more companies turn to the personnel-supply services industry to meet their changing needs.

Earnings

Earnings for drafters vary by specialty and level of responsibility. Median hourly earnings of architectural and civil drafters were $16.93 in 2000. The middle 50 percent earned between $13.79 and $20.86. The lowest 10 percent earned less than $11.18, and the highest 10 percent earned more than $26.13. Median hourly earnings of architectural and civil drafters in engineering and architectural services in 2000 were $16.75.

Median hourly earnings of electrical and electronics drafters were $18.37 in 2000. The middle 50 percent earned between $14.19 and $23.76. The lowest 10 percent earned less than $11.30, and the highest 10 percent earned more than $29.46. In engineering and architectural services, the average hourly earnings for electrical and electronics drafters were $17.30.

Median hourly earnings of mechanical drafters were $18.19 in 2000. The middle 50 percent earned between $14.43 and $23.20. The lowest 10 percent earned less than $11.70, and the highest 10 percent earned more than $28.69. The average hourly earnings for mechanical drafters in engineering and architectural services were $16.98.

Related Occupations

Other workers who prepare or analyze detailed drawings and make precise calculations and measurements include architects, except landscape and naval; landscape architects; designers; engineers; engineering technicians; science technicians; and surveyors, cartographers, photogrammetrists, and surveying technicians.

Sources of Additional Information

Information on schools offering programs in drafting and related fields is available from:

- Accrediting Commission of Career Schools and Colleges of Technology, 2101 Wilson Blvd., Suite 302, Arlington, VA 22201. Internet: http://www.accsct.org

Information about certification is available from:

- American Design Drafting Association, P.O. Box 11937, Columbia, SC 29211. Internet: http://www.adda.org

Drywall Installers, Ceiling Tile Installers, and Tapers

O*NET 47-2081.01, 47-2081.02, 47-2082.00

Significant Points

- Most workers learn the trade on the job, either by working as helpers or through a formal apprenticeship.

- Job prospects are expected to be excellent.

- Inclement weather seldom interrupts work, but workers may be idled when downturns in the economy slow new construction activity.

Nature of the Work

Drywall consists of a thin layer of gypsum between two layers of heavy paper. It is used for walls and ceilings in most buildings today because it is both faster and cheaper to install than plaster.

There are two kinds of drywall workers—installers and tapers—although many workers do both types of work. Installers, also called *applicators*, fasten drywall panels to the inside framework of residential houses and other buildings. *Tapers*, or *finishers*, prepare these panels for painting by taping and finishing joints and imperfections.

Because drywall panels are manufactured in standard sizes—usually 4 feet by 8 or 12 feet—drywall installers must measure, cut, and fit some pieces around doors and windows. They also saw or cut holes in panels for electrical outlets, air-conditioning units, and plumbing. After making these alterations, installers may glue, nail, or screw the wallboard panels to the wood or metal framework. Because drywall is heavy and cumbersome, a helper generally assists the installer in positioning and securing the panel. A lift often is used when placing ceiling panels.

After the drywall is installed, tapers fill joints between panels with a joint compound. Using the wide, flat tip of a special trowel, they spread the compound into and along each side of the joint with brush-like strokes. They immediately use the trowel to press a paper tape—used to reinforce the drywall and to hide imperfections—into the wet compound and to smooth away excess material. Nail and screw depressions also are covered with this compound, as are imperfections caused by the installation of air-conditioning vents and other fixtures. On large commercial projects, finishers may use automatic taping tools that apply the joint compound and tape in one step. Tapers apply second and third coats of the compound, sanding the treated areas after each coat to make them as smooth as the rest of the wall surface. This results in a very smooth and almost perfect surface. Some tapers apply textured surfaces to walls and ceilings with trowels, brushes, or spray guns.

Ceiling tile installers, or *acoustical carpenters*, apply or mount acoustical tiles or blocks, strips, or sheets of shock-absorbing materials to ceilings and walls of buildings to reduce reflection of sound or to decorate rooms. First, they measure and mark the surface according to blueprints and drawings. Then, they nail or screw moldings to the wall to support and seal the joint between the ceiling tile and the wall. Finally, they mount the tile, either by applying a cement adhesive to the back of the tile and then pressing the tile into place or by nailing, screwing, stapling, or wire-tying the lath directly to the structural framework.

Also included in this occupation are *lathers*. Lathers fasten metal or rockboard lath to walls, ceilings, and partitions of buildings. Lath forms the support base for plaster, fireproofing, or acoustical materials. At one time, lath was made of wooden strips. Now, lathers work mostly with wire, metal mesh, or rockboard lath. Metal lath is used where the plaster application will be exposed to weather or water or for curved or irregular surfaces for which drywall is not a practical material. Using hand tools and portable power tools, lathers nail, screw, staple, or wire-tie the lath directly to the structural framework.

Working Conditions

As in many other construction trades, this work sometimes is strenuous. Drywall installers, ceiling tile installers, and tapers spend most of the day on their feet, either standing, bending, or kneeling. Some tapers use stilts to tape and finish ceiling and angle joints. Installers have to lift and maneuver heavy panels. Hazards include falls from ladders and scaffolds and injuries from power tools and from working with sharp materials. Because sanding a joint compound to a smooth finish creates a great deal of dust, some finishers wear masks for protection.

Employment

Drywall installers, ceiling tile installers, and tapers held about 188,000 jobs in 2000. Most worked for contractors specializing in drywall and ceiling tile installation; others worked for contractors doing many kinds of construction. About 38,000 were self-employed independent contractors.

Most installers and tapers are employed in populous areas. In other areas, where there may not be enough work to keep a drywall or a ceiling tile installer employed full time, carpenters and painters usually do the work.

Training, Other Qualifications, and Advancement

Most drywall installers, ceiling tile installers, and tapers start as helpers and learn their skills on the job. Installer helpers start by carrying materials, lifting and holding panels, and cleaning up debris. Within a few weeks, they learn to measure, cut, and install materials. Eventually, they become fully experienced workers. Taper apprentices begin by taping joints and touching up nail holes, scrapes, and other imperfections. They soon learn to install corner guards and to conceal openings around pipes. At the end of their training, drywall installers, ceiling tile installers, and tapers learn to estimate the cost of installing and finishing drywall.

Some drywall installers, ceiling tile installers, and tapers learn their trade in an apprenticeship program. The United Brotherhood of Carpenters and Joiners of America, in cooperation with local contractors, administers an apprenticeship program in both drywall installation and finishing and acoustical carpentry. Apprenticeship programs consist of at least 3 years, or 6,000 hours, of on-the-job training and 144 hours a year of related classroom instruction. In addition, local affiliates of the Associated Builders and Contractors and the National Association of Home Builders conduct training programs for nonunion workers. The International Brotherhood of Painters and Allied Trades conducts an apprenticeship program in drywall finishing that lasts 2 to 3 years.

Employers prefer high school graduates who are in good physical condition, but they frequently hire applicants with less education. High school or vocational school courses in carpentry provide a helpful background for drywall work. Regardless of educational background, installers must be good at simple arithmetic. Other useful high school courses include English, wood shop, metal shop, blueprint reading, and mechanical drawing.

Drywall installers, ceiling tile installers, and tapers with a few years' experience and with leadership ability may become supervisors. Some workers start their own contracting businesses.

Job Outlook

Job opportunities for drywall installers, ceiling tile installers, and tapers are expected to be excellent through 2010, partly due to a shortage of adequate training programs. In addition, many potential workers may prefer work that is less strenuous and has mor e comfortable working conditions. Well-trained workers will have especially favorable opportunities.

Employment is expected to grow more slowly than the average for all occupations over the 2000–2010 period, reflecting increases in new construction and remodeling. In addition to traditional interior work, the growing acceptance of insulated exterior wall systems will provide additional jobs for drywall workers.

In addition to those resulting from job growth, many jobs will open up each year because of the need to replace workers who transfer to other occupations or leave the labor force. Because of their relatively weak attachment to the occupation, many drywall installers, ceiling tile installers, and tapers with limited skills leave the occupation when they find that they dislike the work or fail to find steady employment.

Despite the growing use of exterior panels, most drywall installation and finishing is done indoors. Therefore, drywall workers lose less work time because of inclement weather than do some other construction workers. Nevertheless, they may be unemployed between construction projects and during downturns in construction activity.

Earnings

In 2000, the median hourly earnings of drywall and ceiling tile installers were $15.80. The middle 50 percent earned between $12.27 and $20.81. The lowest 10 percent earned less than $9.68, and the highest 10 percent earned more than $26.86. The median hourly earnings in the largest industries employing drywall and ceiling tile installers in 2000 were:

Nonresidential building construction $16.18
Residential building construction 15.96
Masonry, stonework, and plastering 15.93

In 2000, the median hourly earnings of tapers were $17.81. The middle 50 percent earned between $13.99 and $23.34. The lowest 10 percent earned less than $11.06, and the highest 10 percent earned more than $27.62. The median hourly earnings of tapers in 2000 in masonry, stonework, and plastering were $17.67.

Trainees usually started at about half the rate paid to experienced workers, and received wage increases as they became more highly skilled.

Some contractors pay these workers according to the number of panels they install or finish per day; others pay an hourly rate. A 40-hour week is standard, but the work week may sometimes be longer. Workers who are paid hourly rates receive premium pay for overtime.

Related Occupations

Drywall installers, ceiling tile installers, and tapers combine strength and dexterity with precision and accuracy to make materials fit according to a plan. Other occupations that require similar abilities include carpenters; carpet, floor, and tile installers and finishers; insulation workers; and plasterers and stucco masons.

Sources of Additional Information

For information about work opportunities in drywall application and finishing and ceiling tile installation, contact local drywall installation and ceiling tile installation contractors, union locals, or a local joint union-management apprenticeship committee. Information is also available from the state or local chapter of the Associated Builders and Contractors and the nearest office of the state employment service or apprenticeship agency.

For details about job qualifications and training programs in drywall application and finishing and ceiling tile installation, write to:

- Associated Builders and Contractors, Inc., 1300 N. 17th St., Arlington, VA 22209. Internet: http://www.abc.org

- National Association of Home Builders, 1201 15th St. NW., Washington, DC 20005. International Brotherhood of Painters and Allied Trades, 1750 New York Ave. NW., Washington, DC 20006. Internet: http://www.ibpat.org

- United Brotherhood of Carpenters and Joiners of America, 101 Constitution Ave. NW., Washington, DC 20001

Electrical and Electronics Installers and Repairers

O*NET 49-2092.01, 49-2092.02, 49.2092.03, 49-2092.04, 49-2092.05, 49-2092.06, 49-2093.00, 49-2094.00, 49-2095.00, 49-2096.00

Significant Points

- Knowledge of electrical equipment and electronics is necessary for employment; many applicants complete 1 to 2 years at vocational schools and community colleges, although some less skilled repairers may have only a high school diploma.

- Projected employment growth will be slower than average, but varies by occupational specialty.

- Job opportunities will be best for applicants with a thorough knowledge of electrical and electronic equipment, as well as repair experience.

Nature of the Work

Businesses and other organizations depend on complex electronic equipment for a variety of functions. Industrial controls automatically monitor and direct production processes on the factory floor. Transmitters and antennae provide communications links for many organizations. Electric power companies use electronic equipment to operate and control generating plants, substations, and monitoring equipment. The federal government uses radar and missile control systems to provide for the national defense and to direct commercial air traffic. These complex pieces of electronic equipment are installed, maintained, and repaired by electrical and electronics installers and repairers.

Electrical equipment and electronics equipment are two distinct types of industrial equipment, although much equipment contains both electrical and electronic components. In general, electrical portions of equipment provide the power for the equipment while electronic components control the device, although many types of equipment still are controlled with electrical devices. Electronic sensors monitor the equipment and the manufacturing process, providing feedback to the programmable logic control (PLC) that controls the equipment. The PLC processes the information provided by the sensors and makes adjustments to optimize output. To adjust the output the PLC sends signals to the electrical, hydraulic, and pneumatic devices that power the machine—changing feed rates, pressures, and other variables in the manufacturing process. Many installers and repairers, known as *field technicians*, travel to factories or other locations to repair equipment. These workers often have assigned areas where they perform preventive maintenance on a regular basis. When equipment breaks down, field technicians go to a customer's site to repair the equipment. *Bench technicians* work in repair shops located in factories and service centers. They work on components that cannot be repaired on the factory floor.

Some industrial electronic equipment is self-monitoring and alerts repairers to malfunctions. When equipment breaks down, repairers first check for common causes of trouble, such as loose connections or obviously defective components. If routine checks do not locate the trouble, repairers may refer to schematics and manufacturers' specifications that show connections and provide instructions on how to locate problems. Automated electronic control systems are increasing in complexity, making diagnosing problems more challenging. Repairers use software programs and testing equipment to diagnose malfunctions. They use multimeters, which measure voltage, current, and resistance; advanced multimeters also measure capacitance, inductance, and current gain of transistors. They also use signal generators that provide test signals, and oscilloscopes that graphically display signals. Repairers use handtools such as pliers, screwdrivers, soldering irons, and wrenches to replace faulty parts and to adjust equipment.

Because component repair is complex and factories cannot allow production equipment to stand idle, repairers on the factory floor usually remove and replace defective units, such as circuit boards, instead of fixing them. Defective units are discarded or returned to the manufacturer or to a specialized shop for repair. Bench technicians at these locations have the training, tools, and parts to thoroughly diagnose and repair circuit boards or other complex components. These workers also locate and repair circuit defects, such as poorly soldered joints, blown fuses, or malfunctioning transistors.

Electrical and electronics installers often fit older manufacturing equipment with new automated control devices. Older manufacturing machines are frequently in good working order, but are limited by inefficient control systems that lack replacement parts. Installers replace old electronic control units with new PLCs. Setting up and installing a new PLC involves connecting it to different sensors and electrically powered devices (electric motors, switches, pumps) and writing a computer program to operate the PLC. Electronics installers coordinate their efforts with other workers installing and maintaining equipment.

Electronic equipment installers and repairers, motor vehicles have a significantly different job. They install, diagnose, and repair communications, sound, security, and navigation equipment in motor vehicles. Most installation work involves either new alarm or sound systems. New sound systems vary significantly in cost and complexity of installation. Replacing a head unit (radio) with a new computer disc (CD) player is quite simple, requiring removing a few screws and connecting a few wires. Installing a new sound system with a subwoofer, amplifier, and fuses is far more complicated. The installer builds a box, of fiberglass or wood, designed to hold the subwoofer and to fit in the unique dimensions of the automobile. Installing sound-deadening material, which often is necessary with more powerful speakers, requires an installer to remove many parts of a car (seats, carpeting, interiors of doors), add sound-absorbing material in empty spaces, and reinstall the interior parts. They also run new speaker and electrical cables. Additional electrical power may require additional fuses; a new electrical line to be run from the battery, through a newly drilled hole in the fire wall into the interior of the vehicle; or an additional or more powerful alternator and/or battery.

Repairing automotive electronic equipment is similar to other electronic installation and repair work. Multimeters are used to diagnose the source of the problem. Many parts often are removed and replaced, rather than repaired. Many repairs are quite simple, only requiring a fuse to be replaced. Motor vehicle installers and repairs work with an increasingly complex range of electronic equipment, including DVD players, VCRs, satellite navigation equipment, passive security tracking systems, and active security systems.

Working Conditions

Many electrical and electronics installers and repairers work on factory floors where they are subject to noise, dirt, vibration, and heat. Bench technicians work primarily in repair shops where the surroundings are relatively quiet, comfortable, and well-lighted. Field technicians spend much time on the road, traveling to different customer locations.

Because electronic equipment is critical to industries and other organizations, repairers work around the clock. Their schedules may include evening, weekend, and holiday shifts; shifts may be assigned on the basis of seniority.

Installers and repairers may have to do heavy lifting and work in a variety of positions. They must follow safety guidelines and often wear protective goggles and hardhats. When working on ladders or on elevated equipment, repairers must wear harnesses to prevent falls. Before repairing a piece of machinery, these workers must follow procedures to insure that others cannot start the equipment during the repair process. They also must take precautions against electric shock by locking off power to the unit under repair.

Electronic equipment installers and repairers, motor vehicles normally work indoors in well-ventilated and well-lighted repair shops. Minor cuts and bruises are common, but serious accidents usually are avoided when safety practices are observed.

Employment

Electrical and electronics installers and repairers held about 171,000 jobs in 2000. The following table breaks down employment by occupational specialty:

Electrical and electronics repairers, commercial and
   industrial equipment 90,000
Electric motor, power tools, and related repairers 37,000

Electrical and electronics repairers, powerhouse, substation, and relay	18,000
Electrical and electronics installers and repairers, transportation equipment	14,000
Electronic equipment installers and repairers, motor vehicles	13,000

Many repairers worked for wholesale trade companies, general electrical work companies, the federal government, electrical repair shops, and manufacturers of electronic components and accessories and communications equipment.

Training, Other Qualifications, and Advancement

Knowledge of electrical equipment and electronics is necessary for employment. Many applicants gain this training through programs lasting 1 to 2 years at vocational schools and community colleges, although some less skilled repairers may have only a high school diploma. Entry-level repairers may work closely with more experienced technicians who provide technical guidance.

Installers and repairers should have good eyesight and color perception in order to work with the intricate components used in electronic equipment. Field technicians work closely with customers and should have good communications skills and a neat appearance. Employers also may require that field technicians have a driver's license.

The International Society of Certified Electronics Technicians (ISCET) and the Electronics Technicians Association (ETA) administer certification programs for electronics installation and repair technicians. Repairers may specialize—in industrial electronics, for example. To receive certification, repairers must pass qualifying exams corresponding to their level of training and experience. Both programs offer associate certifications to entry-level repairers.

Experienced repairers with advanced training may become specialists or troubleshooters who help other repairers diagnose difficult problems. Workers with leadership ability may become supervisors of other repairers. Some experienced workers open their own repair shops.

Job Outlook

Job opportunities should be best for applicants with a thorough knowledge of electrical equipment and electronics, as well as repair experience. Overall employment of electrical and electronics installers and repairers is expected to grow more slowly than the average for all occupations over the 2000–2010 period, but varies by occupational specialty. In addition to employment growth, many job openings should result from the need to replace workers who transfer to other occupations or leave the labor force.

Average employment growth is projected for electrical and electronics installers and repairers of transportation equipment. Commercial and industrial electronic equipment will become more sophisticated and used more frequently, as businesses strive to lower costs by increasing and improving automation. Companies will install electronic controls, robots, sensors, and other equipment to automate processes such as assembly and testing. As prices decline, applications will be found across a number of industries, including services, utilities, and construction, as well as manufacturing. Improved equipment reliability should not constrain employment growth, however; companies increasingly will rely on repairers, because any malfunction that idles commercial and industrial equipment is costly.

Employment of electronics installers and repairers of motor vehicles also is expected to grow about as fast as average. Motor vehicle manufacturers will install more and better sound, security, entertainment, and navigation systems in new vehicles, limiting employment growth for after-market electronic equipment installers. However, repairing the new electronic systems should help drive employment growth.

On the other hand, employment of electric motor, power tool, and related repairers is expected to grow more slowly than average. Improvements in electrical and electronic equipment design should limit job growth by simplifying repair tasks. More parts are being designed to be easily disposable, further reducing employment growth.

Employment of electrical and electronics installers and repairers, powerhouse, substation, and relay is expected to decline slightly. Consolidation and privatization in utilities industries should improve productivity, reducing employment. Newer equipment will be more reliable and easier to repair, further limiting employment.

Earnings

Median hourly earnings of electrical and electronics repairers, commercial and industrial equipment were $17.75 in 2000. The middle 50 percent earned between $13.92 and $21.32. The lowest 10 percent earned less than $10.90, and the highest 10 percent earned more than $25.78.

Median hourly earnings of electric motor, power tool, and related repairers were $15.80 in 2000. The middle 50 percent earned between $11.91 and $20.04. The lowest 10 percent earned less than $9.13, and the highest 10 percent earned more than $25.17.

Median hourly earnings of electrical and electronics repairers, powerhouse, substation, and relay were $23.34 in 2000. The middle 50 percent earned between $19.07 and $26.21. The lowest 10 percent earned less than $14.79, and the highest 10 percent earned more than $29.00.

Median hourly earnings of electrical and electronics repairers, transportation equipment were $16.93 in 2000. The middle 50 percent earned between $12.25 and $21.54. The lowest 10 percent earned less than $9.60, and the highest 10 percent earned more than $25.76.

Median hourly earnings of electronics installers and repairers, motor vehicles were $12.06 in 2000. The middle 50 percent earned between $9.60 and $15.25. The lowest 10 percent earned less than $7.98, and the highest 10 percent earned more than $18.69.

Related Occupations

Workers in other occupations who install and repair electronic equipment include broadcast and sound engineering technicians and radio operators; computer, automated teller, and office machine repairers; electronic home entertainment equipment installers and repairers; and radio and telecommunications equipment installers and repairers. Industrial machinery installation, repair, and maintenance workers also install, maintain, and repair industrial machinery.

Sources of Additional Information

For information on careers and certification, contact:

- International Society of Certified Electronics Technicians, 3608 Pershing Ave., Fort Worth, TX 76107-4527. Internet: http://www.iscet.org

- Electronics Technicians Association, 502 North Jackson, Greencastle, IN 46135

Electricians

O*NET 47-2111.00

Significant Points

- Job opportunities are expected to be excellent for qualified electricians.

- Most electricians acquire their skills by completing a formal 4- or 5-year apprenticeship program.

- About one-third of all electricians work in industries other than construction.

Nature of the Work

Electricity is essential for light, power, air conditioning, and refrigeration. Electricians install, connect, test, and maintain electrical systems for a variety of purposes, including climate control, security, and communications. They also may install and maintain the electronic controls for machines in business and industry. Although most electricians specialize in either construction or maintenance, a growing number do both.

Electricians work with blueprints when they install electrical systems in factories, office buildings, homes, and other structures. Blueprints indicate the locations of circuits, outlets, load centers, panel boards, and other equipment. Electricians must follow the National Electric Code and comply with state and local building codes when they install these systems. In factories and offices, they first place conduit (pipe or tubing) inside designated partitions, walls, or other concealed areas. They also fasten to the wall small metal or plastic boxes that will house electrical switches and outlets. They then pull insulated wires or cables through the conduit to complete circuits between these boxes. In lighter construction, such as residential, plastic-covered wire usually is used instead of conduit.

Regardless of the type of wire used, electricians connect it to circuit breakers, transformers, or other components. They join the wires in boxes with various specially designed connectors. After they finish the wiring, they use testing equipment, such as ohmmeters, voltmeters, and oscilloscopes, to check the circuits for proper connections, ensuring electrical compatibility and safety of components.

In addition to wiring a building's electrical system, electricians may install coaxial or fiber optic cable for computers and other telecommunications equipment. A growing number of electricians install telephone

systems, computer wiring and equipment, street lights, intercom systems, and fire alarm and security systems. They also may connect motors to electrical power and install electronic controls for industrial equipment.

Maintenance work varies greatly, depending on where the electrician is employed. Electricians who specialize in residential work may rewire a home and replace an old fuse box with a new circuit breaker to accommodate additional appliances. Those who work in large factories may repair motors, transformers, generators, and electronic controllers on machine tools and industrial robots. Those in office buildings and small plants may repair all types of electrical equipment.

Maintenance electricians spend much of their time in preventive maintenance. They periodically inspect equipment, and locate and correct problems before breakdowns occur. Electricians may also advise management on whether continued operation of equipment could be hazardous. When needed, they install new electrical equipment. When breakdowns occur, they must make the necessary repairs as quickly as possible in order to minimize inconvenience. Electricians may replace items such as circuit breakers, fuses, switches, electrical and electronic components, or wire. When working with complex electronic devices, they may work with engineers, engineering technicians, or industrial machinery installation, repair, and maintenance workers.

Electricians use handtools such as screwdrivers, pliers, knives, and hacksaws. They also use power tools and testing equipment such as oscilloscopes, ammeters, and test lamps.

Working Conditions

Electricians' work is sometimes strenuous. They may stand for long periods and frequently work on ladders and scaffolds. Their working environment varies, depending on the type of job. Some may work in dusty, dirty, hot, or wet conditions, or in confined areas, ditches, or other uncomfortable places. Electricians risk injury from electrical shock, falls, and cuts; to avoid injuries, they must follow strict safety procedures. Some electricians may have to travel to job sites, which may be up to 100 miles away.

Most electricians work a standard 40-hour week, although overtime may be required. Those in maintenance work may work nights or weekends, and be on call. Companies that operate 24 hours a day may employ three shifts of electricians.

Employment

Electricians held about 698,000 jobs in 2000. About two-thirds were employed in the construction industry. About one-third worked as maintenance electricians and were employed outside the construction industry. In addition, about 8 percent of electricians were self-employed.

Because of the widespread need for electrical services, jobs for electricians are found in all parts of the country.

Training, Other Qualifications, and Advancement

Most people learn the electrical trade by completing a 4- or 5-year apprenticeship program. Apprenticeship gives trainees a thorough knowledge of all aspects of the trade and generally improves their ability to find a job. Although more electricians are trained through apprenticeship than are workers in other construction trades, some still learn their skills informally, on the job.

Apprenticeship programs may be sponsored by joint training committees made up of local unions of the International Brotherhood of Electrical Workers and local chapters of the National Electrical Contractors Association; company management committees of individual electrical contracting companies; or local chapters of the Associated Builders and Contractors and the Independent Electrical Contractors Association. Training also may be provided by company management committees of individual electrical contracting companies and by local chapters of the Associated Builders and Contractors and the Independent Electrical Contractors. Because of the comprehensive training received, those who complete apprenticeship programs qualify to do both maintenance and construction work.

The typical large apprenticeship program provides at least 144 hours of classroom instruction each year, and 8,000 hours of on-the-job training over the course of the apprenticeship. In the classroom, apprentices learn blueprint reading, electrical theory, electronics, mathematics, electrical code requirements, and safety and first aid practices. They also may receive specialized training in welding, communications, fire alarm systems, and cranes and elevators. On the job, under the supervision of experienced electricians, apprentices must demonstrate mastery of the electrician's work. At first, they drill holes, set anchors, and set up conduit. Later, they measure, fabricate, and install conduit, as well as install, connect, and test wiring, outlets, and switches. They also learn to set up and draw diagrams for entire electrical systems.

Those who do not enter a formal apprenticeship program can begin to learn the trade informally by working as helpers for experienced electricians. While learning to install conduit, connect wires, and test circuits, helpers also learn safety practices. Many helpers supplement this training with trade school or correspondence courses.

Regardless of how one learns the trade, previous training is very helpful. High school courses in mathematics, electricity, electronics, mechanical drawing, science, and shop provide a good background. Special training offered in the armed forces and by postsecondary technical schools also is beneficial. All applicants should be in good health and have at least average physical strength. Agility and dexterity also are important. Good color vision is needed because workers must frequently identify electrical wires by color.

Most apprenticeship sponsors require applicants for apprentice positions to be at least 18 years old and have a high school diploma or its equivalent. For those interested in becoming maintenance electricians, a background in electronics is increasingly important because of the growing use of complex electronic controls on manufacturing equipment.

Most localities require electricians to be licensed. Although licensing requirements vary from area to area, electricians usually must pass an examination that tests their knowledge of electrical theory, the National Electrical Code, and local electric and building codes.

Electricians periodically take courses offered by their employer or union to keep abreast of changes in the National Electrical Code, materials, or methods of installation.

Experienced electricians can become supervisors and then superintendents. Those with sufficient capital and management skills may start their own contracting business, although this may require an electrical contractor's license.

Job Outlook

Job opportunities for skilled electricians are expected to be excellent, largely due to the numerous openings arising each year from experienced electricians who leave the occupation. In addition, many potential workers may prefer work that is less strenuous and has more comfortable working conditions. Well-trained workers will have especially favorable opportunities.

Employment of electricians is expected to increase about as fast as the average for all occupations through the year 2010. As the population and economy grow, more electricians will be needed to install and maintain electrical devices and wiring in homes, factories, offices, and other structures. New technologies also are expected to continue to stimulate the demand for these workers. Increasingly, buildings will be prewired during construction to accommodate use of computers and telecommunications equipment. More factories will be using robots and automated manufacturing systems. Installation of this equipment, which is expected to increase, should also stimulate demand for electricians. Additional jobs will be created by rehabilitation and retrofitting of existing structures.

In addition to jobs created by increased demand for electrical work, many openings will occur each year as electricians transfer to other occupations, retire, or leave the labor force for other reasons. Because of their lengthy training and relatively high earnings, a smaller proportion of electricians than of other craftworkers leave their occupation each year. The number of retirements is expected to rise, however, as more electricians reach retirement age.

Employment of construction electricians, like that of many other construction workers, is sensitive to changes in the economy. This results from the limited duration of construction projects and the cyclical nature of the construction industry. During economic downturns, job openings for electricians are reduced as the level of construction activity declines. Apprenticeship opportunities also are less plentiful during these periods.

Although employment of maintenance electricians is steadier than that of construction electricians, those working in the automotive and other manufacturing industries that are sensitive to cyclical swings in the economy may be laid off during recessions. Also, efforts to reduce operating costs and increase productivity, through the increased use of contracting out for electrical services, may limit opportunities for maintenance electricians in many industries. However, this should be partially offset by increased demand by electrical contracting firms.

Job opportunities for electricians also vary by area. Employment opportunities follow the movement of people and businesses among states and local areas, and reflect differences in local economic conditions. The number of job opportunities in a given year may fluctuate widely from area to area.

Earnings

In 2000, median hourly earnings of electricians were $19.29. The middle 50 percent earned between $14.49 and $25.41. The lowest 10 percent earned less than $11.31, and the highest 10 percent earned more than $31.71. Median hourly earnings in the industries employing the largest numbers of electricians in 2000 are shown in the following table:

Motor vehicles and equipment $26.71
Local government 19.88
Electrical work 19.22
Heavy construction, except highway 17.92
Plumbing, heating, and air-conditioning 17.26

Depending on experience, apprentices usually start at between 30 and 50 percent of the rate paid to experienced electricians. As they become more skilled, they receive periodic increases throughout the course of the apprenticeship program. Many employers also provide training opportunities for experienced electricians to improve their skills.

Many construction electricians are members of the International Brotherhood of Electrical Workers. Among unions organizing maintenance electricians are the International Brotherhood of Electrical Workers; the International Union of Electronic, Electrical, Salaried, Machine, and Furniture Workers; the International Association of Machinists and Aerospace Workers; the International Union, United Automobile, Aircraft and Agricultural Implement Workers of America; and the United Steelworkers of America.

Related Occupations

To install and maintain electrical systems, electricians combine manual skill and knowledge of electrical materials and concepts. Workers in other occupations involving similar skills include heating, air-conditioning, and refrigeration mechanics and installers; line installers and repairers; electrical and electronics installers and repairers; electronic home entertainment equipment installers and repairers; and elevator installers and repairers.

Sources of Additional Information

For details about apprenticeships or other work opportunities in this trade, contact the offices of the state employment service, the state apprenticeship agency, local electrical contractors or firms that employ maintenance electricians, or local union-management electrician apprenticeship committees. This information may also be available from local chapters of the Independent Electrical Contractors, Inc.; the National Electrical Contractors Association; the Home Builders Institute; the Associated Builders and Contractors; and the International Brotherhood of Electrical Workers.

For general information about the work of electricians, contact:

- Independent Electrical Contractors, Inc., 2010-A Eisenhower Ave., Alexandria, VA 22314. Internet: http://www.ieci.org

- National Electrical Contractors Association (NECA), 3 Metro Center, Suite 1100, Bethesda, MD 20814. Internet: http://www.necanet.org

- International Brotherhood of Electrical Workers (IBEW), 1125 15th St. NW., Washington, DC 20005. Internet: http://www.ibew.org

- Associated Builders and Contractors, 1300 N. 17th St., Arlington, VA 22209. Internet: http://www.abc.org

- National Association of Home Builders, 1201 15th St. NW., Washington, DC 20005. Internet: http://www.nahb.org

Electronic Home Entertainment Equipment Installers and Repairers

O*NET 49-2097.00

Significant Points

- Employment is expected to decline because it often is cheaper to replace than to repair equipment.

- Job opportunities will be best for applicants with knowledge of electronics and related hands-on experience.

Nature of the Work

Electronic home entertainment equipment installers and repairers, also called *service technicians*, repair a variety of equipment, including televisions and radios, stereo components, video and audio disc players, video cameras, and videocassette recorders. They also repair home security systems, intercom equipment, and home theater equipment, which consist of large-screen televisions and sophisticated, surround-sound systems.

Customers usually bring small, portable equipment to repair shops for servicing. Repairers at these locations, known as *bench technicians*, are equipped with a full array of electronic tools and parts. When larger, less mobile equipment breaks down, customers may pay repairers to come to their homes. These repairers, known as *field technicians*, travel with a limited set of tools and parts, and attempt to complete the repair at the customer's location. If the repair is complex, technicians may bring defective components back to the repair shop for a thorough diagnosis and repair.

When equipment breaks down, repairers check for common causes of trouble, such as dirty or defective components. Many repairs consist of simply cleaning and lubricating equipment. For example, cleaning the tape heads on a videocassette recorder will prevent tapes from sticking to the equipment. If routine checks do not locate the trouble, repairers may refer to schematics and manufacturers' specifications that provide instructions on how to locate problems. Repairers use a variety of test equipment to diagnose and identify malfunctions. They use multimeters to detect short circuits, failed capacitors, and blown fuses by measuring the voltage, current, and resistance. They use color bar and dot generators to provide onscreen test patterns, signal generators to test signals, and oscilloscopes and digital storage scopes to measure complex waveforms produced by electronic equipment. Repairs may involve removing and replacing a failed capacitor, transistor, or fuse. Repairers use handtools such as pliers, screwdrivers, soldering irons, and wrenches to replace faulty parts. They also make adjustments to equipment, such as focusing and converging the picture of a television set or balancing the audio on a surround-sound system.

Improvements in technology have miniaturized and digitized many audio and video recording devices. Miniaturization has made repairwork significantly more difficult, as both the components and acceptable tolerances are smaller. For example, an analog video camera operates at 1800 revolutions per minute (rpm), while a digital video camera may operate at 9000 rpm. Components now are mounted on the surface of circuit boards, instead of plugged into slots, requiring more precise soldering when a new part is installed. Improved technologies also have lowered the price of electronic home entertainment equipment. As a result, customers often replace broken equipment instead of repairing it.

Working Conditions

Most repairers work in well-lighted electrical repair shops. Field technicians, however, spend much time traveling in service vehicles and working in customers' residences.

Repairers may have to work in a variety of positions and carry heavy equipment. Although the work of repairers is comparatively safe, they must take precautions against minor burns and electric shock. Because television monitors carry high voltage even when turned off, repairers need to discharge the voltage before servicing such equipment.

Employment

Electronic home entertainment equipment installers and repairers held about 37,000 jobs in 2000. Most repairers work in stores that sell and service electronic home entertainment products, or in electrical repair shops and service centers. About 1 in 6 electronic home entertainment equipment installers and repairers is self-employed.

Training, Other Qualifications, and Advancement

Employers prefer applicants who have basic knowledge and skills in electronics. Applicants should be familiar with schematics and have some hands-on experience repairing electronic equipment. Many applicants gain these skills at vocational training programs and community colleges. Training programs should include both a hands-on and theoretical education in digital consumer electronics. Entry-level repairers may work closely with more experienced technicians, who provide technical guidance.

Field technicians work closely with customers and must have good communications skills and a neat appearance. Employers also may require that field technicians have a driver's license.

The International Society of Certified Electronics Technicians (ISCET) and the Electronics Technicians Association (ETA) administer certification programs for electronics technicians. Repairers may specialize in a variety of skill areas, including consumer electronics. To receive certification, repairers must pass qualifying exams corresponding to their level of training and experience. Both programs offer associate certifications to entry-level repairers.

Experienced repairers with advanced training may become specialists or troubleshooters, who help other repairers diagnose difficult problems. Workers with leadership ability may become supervisors of other repairers. Some experienced workers open their own repair shops.

Job Outlook

Employment of electronic home entertainment equipment installers and repairers is expected to decline through 2010, due to decreased demand

for repair work. Some job openings will occur, however, as repairers retire or gain higher paying jobs in other occupations requiring electronics experience. Opportunities will be best for applicants with hands-on experience and knowledge of electronics.

The need for repairers is declining because home entertainment equipment is less expensive than in the past. As technological developments have lowered equipment prices and improved reliability, the demand for repair services has decreased. When malfunctions do occur, it often is cheaper for consumers to replace equipment rather than to pay for repairs.

Employment of repairers will continue to decline despite the introduction of sophisticated digital equipment, such as DVDs, digital televisions, and digital camcorders. So long as the price of such equipment remains high, purchasers will be willing to hire repairers when malfunctions occur. However, the need for repairers to maintain this costly equipment will not be great enough to offset the overall decline in demand for their services.

Earnings

Median hourly earnings of electronic home entertainment equipment installers and repairers were $12.72 in 2000. The middle 50 percent earned between $9.90 and $16.63. The lowest 10 percent earned less than $7.84, and the highest 10 percent earned more than $20.72. Median hourly earnings in the industries employing the largest numbers of electronic home entertainment equipment repairers in 2000 are shown in the following table:

Electrical repair shops $12.30
Radio, television, and computer stores 11.67

Related Occupations

Other workers who repair and maintain electronic equipment include broadcast and sound engineering technicians and radio operators; computer, automated teller, and office machine repairers; electrical and electronics installers and repairers; and radio and telecommunications equipment installers and repairers.

Sources of Additional Information

For information on careers and certification, contact:

- The International Society of Certified Electronics Technicians, 3608 Pershing Ave., Fort Worth, TX 76107. Internet: http://www.iscet.org

- Electronics Technicians Association, 502 North Jackson, Greencastle, IN 46135

Elevator Installers and Repairers

O*NET 47-4021.00

Significant Points

- Workers learn the trade through 4 to 5 years of on-the-job training and classroom instruction.

- Elevator installers and repairers have one of the highest rates of union membership.

- Job opportunities are expected to be limited in this small occupation; prospects should be best for those with postsecondary education in electronics.

Nature of the Work

Elevator installers and repairers—also called *elevator constructors* or *elevator mechanics*—assemble, install, and replace elevators, escalators, dumbwaiters, moving walkways, and similar equipment in new and old buildings. Once the equipment is in service, they maintain and repair it as well. They also are responsible for modernizing older equipment.

To install, repair, and maintain modern elevators, which are almost all electronically controlled, elevator installers and repairers must have a thorough knowledge of electronics, electricity, and hydraulics. Many elevators are controlled with microprocessors, which are programmed to analyze traffic conditions in order to dispatch elevators in the most efficient manner. With these computer controls, it is possible to get the greatest amount of service with the least number of cars.

When installing a new elevator, installers and repairers begin by studying blueprints to determine the equipment needed to install rails, machinery, car enclosures, motors, pumps, cylinders, and plunger foundations. Once this has been done, they begin equipment installation. Working on scaffolding or platforms, installers bolt or weld steel rails to the walls of the shaft to guide the elevator.

Elevator installers put in electrical wires and controls by running tubing, called conduit, along a shaft's walls from floor to floor. Once it is in place, mechanics pull plastic-covered electrical wires through the conduit. They then install electrical components and related devices required at each floor and at the main control panel in the machine room.

Installers bolt or weld together the steel frame of an elevator car at the bottom of the shaft; install the car's platform, walls, and doors; and attach guide shoes and rollers to minimize the lateral motion of the car as it travels through the shaft. They also install the outer doors and door frames at the elevator entrances on each floor.

For cabled elevators, these workers install geared or gearless machines with a traction-drive wheel that guides and moves heavy steel cables connected to the elevator car and counterweight. The counterweight moves in the opposite direction from the car and balances most of the weight of the car to reduce the weight that the elevator's motor must lift. Elevator installers also install elevators in which a car sits on a hydraulic plunger that is driven by a pump. The plunger pushes the elevator car up from underneath, similar to a lift in an auto service station.

Installers and repairers also install escalators. They put in place the steel framework, the electrically powered stairs, and the tracks and install associated motors and electrical wiring. In addition to elevators and escalators, they also may install devices such as dumbwaiters and material lifts—which are similar to elevators in design—as well as moving walkways, stair lifts, and wheelchair lifts.

The most highly skilled elevator installers and repairers, called "adjusters," specialize in fine-tuning all the equipment after installation. Adjusters make sure that an elevator is working according to specifications, such as stopping correctly at each floor within a specified time. Once an elevator is operating properly, it must be maintained and serviced regularly to keep it in safe working condition. Elevator installers and repairers generally do preventive maintenance—such as oiling and greasing moving parts, replacing worn parts, testing equipment with meters and gauges, and adjusting equipment for optimal performance. They also troubleshoot and may be called in to do emergency repairs.

A service crew usually handles major repairs—for example, replacing cables, elevator doors, or machine bearings. This may require the use of cutting torches or rigging equipment—tools an elevator repairer normally would not carry. Service crews also do major modernization and alteration work, such as moving and replacing electrical motors, hydraulic pumps, and control panels.

Elevator installers and repairers usually specialize in installation, maintenance, or repair work. Maintenance and repair workers generally need more knowledge of electricity and electronics than installers do, because a large part of maintenance and repair work is troubleshooting. Similarly, adjusters need a thorough knowledge of electricity, electronics, and computers to ensure that newly installed elevators operate properly.

Working Conditions

Most elevator installers and repairers work a 40-hour week. However, overtime is required when essential elevator equipment must be repaired, and some workers are on 24-hour call. Unlike most elevator installers, workers who specialize in elevator maintenance are on their own most of the day and typically service the same elevators periodically.

Elevator installers lift and carry heavy equipment and parts, and may work in cramped spaces or awkward positions. Potential hazards include falls, electrical shock, muscle strains, and other injuries related to handling heavy equipment. Because most of their work is performed indoors in buildings under construction or in existing buildings, elevator installers and repairers lose less work time due to inclement weather than do other construction trades workers.

Employment

Elevator installers and repairers held about 23,000 jobs in 2000. Special trade contractors employed most. Others were employed by field offices of elevator manufacturers, wholesale distributors, small-elevator maintenance and repair contractors, government agencies, or businesses that do their own elevator maintenance and repair.

Training, Other Qualifications, and Advancement

Most elevator installers and repairers apply for their jobs through a local of the International Union of Elevator Constructors. Applicants for trainee positions must be at least 18 years old, have a high school diploma or equivalent, and pass an aptitude test. Good physical condition and mechanical aptitude also are important.

Elevator installers and repairers learn their trade in a program administered by local joint educational committees representing the employers and the union. These programs, through which the trainee learns everything from installation to repair, combine on-the-job training with classroom instruction in blueprint reading, electrical and electronic theory, mathematics, applications of physics, and safety. In nonunion shops, workers may complete training programs sponsored by independent contractors.

Generally, trainees or helpers must complete a 6-month probationary period. After successful completion, they work toward becoming fully qualified within 4 to 5 years. To be classified as a fully qualified elevator installer or repairer, union trainees must pass a standard examination administered by the National Elevator Industry Educational Program. Most states and cities also require elevator installers and repairers to pass a licensing examination.

Most trainees or helpers assist experienced elevator installers and repairers. Beginners carry materials and tools, bolt rails to walls, and assemble elevator cars. Eventually, trainees learn more difficult tasks such as wiring, which requires knowledge of local and national electrical codes.

High school courses in electricity, mathematics, and physics provide a useful background. As elevators become increasingly sophisticated, workers may find it necessary to acquire more advanced formal education—for example, in postsecondary technical school or junior college—with an emphasis on electronics. Workers with more formal education usually advance more quickly than their counterparts.

Many elevator installers and repairers also receive training from their employers or through manufacturers to become familiar with a company's particular equipment. Retraining is very important to keep abreast of technological developments in elevator repair. In fact, union elevator installers and repairers typically receive continual training throughout their careers, through correspondence courses, seminars, or formal classes. Although voluntary, this training greatly improves one's chances for promotion.

Some installers may receive further training in specialized areas and advance to mechanic-in-charge, adjuster, supervisor, or elevator inspector. Adjusters, for example, may be picked for their position because they possess particular skills or are electronically inclined. Other workers may move into management, sales, or product design jobs.

Job Outlook

Job opportunities are expected to be somewhat limited in this small occupation. A large proportion of elevator installer and repairer jobs are unionized and involve a significant investment in training. As a result, workers tend to stay in this occupation for a long time. This investment in training, as well as good benefits and relatively high wages, results in fewer openings due to turnover, thus reducing job opportunities. Job prospects should be best for those with postsecondary education in electronics.

Employment of elevator installers and repairers is expected to increase about as fast as the average for all occupations through the year 2010. Job growth is related to the growth of nonresidential construction, such as commercial office buildings and stores that have elevators and escalators, which is expected to increase about as fast as the average over the 2000–2010 period. The need to continually update and modernize old equipment, including improvements in appearance and the installation of increasingly sophisticated equipment and computerized controls, also should add to the demand for elevator installers and repairers.

Because it is desirable that equipment always be kept in good working condition, economic downturns will have less of an effect on employment of elevator installers and repairers than on other construction trades.

Earnings

Median hourly earnings of elevator installers and repairers were $22.78 in 2000. The middle 50 percent earned between $16.38 and $27.38. The lowest 10 percent earned less than $11.19, and the top 10 percent earned more than $33.23. In 2000, median hourly earnings in the miscellaneous special trade contractors industry were $23.29.

In addition to free continuing education, elevator installers and repairers receive basic benefits enjoyed by most other workers.

Elevator installers and repairers have one of the highest rates of union membership, about 9 out of 10. Most elevator installers and repairers belong to the International Union of Elevator Constructors.

Related Occupations

Elevator installers and repairers combine electrical and mechanical skills with construction skills, such as welding, rigging, measuring, and blueprint reading. Other occupations that require many of these skills are boilermakers; electricians; electrical and electronics installers and repairers; industrial machinery installation, repair, and maintenance workers; sheet metal workers; and structural and reinforcing iron and metal workers.

Sources of Additional Information

For further details about opportunities as an elevator installer and repairer, contact elevator manufacturers, elevator repair and maintenance contractors, a local of the International Union of Elevator Constructors, or the nearest local public employment service office.

Emergency Medical Technicians and Paramedics

O*NET 29-2041.00

Significant Points

- Job stress is common due to irregular hours and treating patients in life-or-death situations.

- Formal training and certification are required but state requirements vary.

- Employment is projected to grow faster than average as paid emergency medical technician positions replace unpaid volunteers.

Nature of the Work

People's lives often depend on the quick reaction and competent care of emergency medical technicians (EMTs) and paramedics, EMTs with additional advanced training to perform more difficult pre-hospital medical procedures. Incidents as varied as automobile accidents, heart attacks, drownings, childbirth, and gunshot wounds all require immediate medical attention. EMTs and paramedics provide this vital attention as they care for and transport the sick or injured to a medical facility.

Depending on the nature of the emergency, EMTs and paramedics typically are dispatched to the scene by a 911 operator and often work with police and fire department personnel. Once they arrive, they determine the nature and extent of the patient's condition while trying to ascertain whether the patient has pre-existing medical problems. Following strict rules and guidelines, they give appropriate emergency care and, when necessary, transport the patient. Some paramedics are trained to treat patients with minor injuries on the scene of an accident or at their home without transporting them to a medical facility. Emergency treatments for more complicated problems are carried out under the direction of medical doctors by radio preceding or during transport.

EMTs and paramedics may use special equipment such as backboards to immobilize patients before placing them on stretchers and securing them in the ambulance for transport to a medical facility. Usually, one EMT or paramedic drives while the other monitors the patient's vital signs and gives additional care as needed. Some EMTs work as part of the flight crew of helicopters that transport critically ill or injured patients to hospital trauma centers.

At the medical facility, EMTs and paramedics help transfer patients to the emergency department, report their observations and actions to staff, and may provide additional emergency treatment. After each run, EMTs and paramedics replace used supplies and check equipment. If a transported patient had a contagious disease, EMTs and paramedics decontaminate the interior of the ambulance and report cases to the proper authorities.

Beyond these general duties, the specific responsibilities of EMTs and paramedics depend on their level of qualification and training. To determine this, the National Registry of Emergency Medical Technicians (NREMT) registers emergency medical service (EMS) providers at four levels: First Responder, EMT-Basic, EMT-Intermediate, and EMT-Paramedic. Some states, however, do their own certification and use numeric ratings from 1 to 4 to distinguish levels of proficiency.

The lowest level workers—First Responders—are trained to provide basic emergency medical care because they tend to be the first persons to arrive at the scene of an incident. Many firefighters, police officers, and other emergency workers have this level of training. The EMT-Basic, also known as EMT-1, represents the first component of the emergency medical technician system. An EMT-1 is trained to care for patients on accident scenes and on transport by ambulance to the hospital under medical direction. The EMT-1 has the emergency skills to assess a patient's condition and manage respiratory, cardiac, and trauma emergencies.

The EMT-Intermediate (EMT-2 and EMT-3) has more advanced training that allows administration of intravenous fluids, use of manual defibrillators to give lifesaving shocks to a stopped heart, and use of advanced airway techniques and equipment to assist patients experiencing respiratory emergencies. EMT-Paramedics (EMT-4) provide the most extensive pre-hospital care. In addition to the procedures already described, paramedics may administer drugs orally and intravenously, interpret electrocardiograms (EKGs), perform endotracheal intubations, and use monitors and other complex equipment.

Working Conditions

EMTs and paramedics work both indoors and outdoors, in all types of weather. They are required to do considerable kneeling, bending, and heavy lifting. These workers risk noise-induced hearing loss from sirens and back injuries from lifting patients. In addition, EMTs and paramedics may be exposed to diseases such as Hepatitis-B and AIDS, as well as violence from drug overdose victims or mentally unstable patients. The work is not only physically strenuous, but also stressful, involving life-or-death situations and suffering patients. Nonetheless, many people find the work exciting and challenging and enjoy the opportunity to help others.

EMTs and paramedics employed by fire departments work about 50 hours a week. Those employed by hospitals frequently work between 45 and 60 hours a week, and those in private ambulance services, between 45 and 50 hours. Some of these workers, especially those in police and fire departments, are on call for extended periods. Because emergency services function 24 hours a day, EMTs and paramedics have irregular working hours that add to job stress.

Employment

EMTs and paramedics held about 172,000 jobs in 2000. Most career EMTs and paramedics work in metropolitan areas. There are many more volunteer EMTs and paramedics, especially in smaller cities, towns, and rural areas. They volunteer for fire departments, emergency medical services (EMS), or hospitals and may respond to only a few calls for service per month, or may answer the majority of calls, especially in smaller communities. EMTs and paramedics work closely with firefighters, who often are certified as EMTs as well and act as first responders.

Full- and part-time paid EMTs and paramedics were employed in a number of industries. About 4 out of 10 worked in local and suburban transportation, as employees of private ambulance services. About 3 out of 10 worked in local government for fire departments, public ambulance services and EMS. Another 2 out 10 were found in hospitals, where they worked full time within the medical facility or responded to calls in ambulances or helicopters to transport critically ill or injured patients. The remainder worked in various industries providing emergency services.

Training, Other Qualifications, and Advancement

Formal training and certification is needed to become an EMT or paramedic. All 50 states possess a certification procedure. In 38 states and the District of Columbia, registration with the National Registry of Emergency Medical Technicians (NREMT) is required at some or all levels of certification. Other states administer their own certification examination or provide the option of taking the NREMT examination. To maintain certification, EMTs and paramedics must reregister, usually every 2 years. In order to re-register, an individual must be working as an EMT or paramedic and meet a continuing education requirement.

Training is offered at progressive levels: EMT-Basic, also known as EMT-1; EMT-Intermediate, or EMT-2 and EMT-3; and EMT-paramedic, or EMT-4. The EMT-Basic represents the first level of skills required to work in the emergency medical system. Coursework typically emphasizes emergency skills such as managing respiratory, trauma, and cardiac emergencies and patient assessment. Formal courses are often combined with time in an emergency room or ambulance. The program also provides instruction and practice in dealing with bleeding, fractures, airway obstruction, cardiac arrest, and emergency childbirth. Students learn to use and maintain common emergency equipment, such as backboards, suction devices, splints, oxygen delivery systems, and stretchers. Graduates of approved EMT basic training programs who pass a written and practical examination administered by the state certifying agency or the NREMT earn the title of Registered EMT-Basic. The course also is a prerequisite for EMT-Intermediate and EMT-Paramedic training.

EMT-Intermediate training requirements vary from state to state. Applicants can opt to receive training in EMT-Shock Trauma, where the caregiver learns to start intravenous fluids and give certain medications, or in EMT-Cardiac, which includes learning heart rhythms and administering advanced medications. Training commonly includes 35 to 55 hours of additional instruction beyond EMT-Basic coursework and covers patient assessment, as well as the use of advanced airway devices and intravenous fluids. Prerequisites for taking the EMT-Intermediate examination include registration as an EMT-Basic, required classroom work, and a specified amount of clinical experience.

The most advanced level of training for this occupation is EMT-Paramedic. At this level, the caregiver receives additional training in body function and more advanced skills. The Paramedic Technology program usually lasts up to 2 years and results in an associate degree in applied science. Such education prepares the graduate to take the NREMT examination and become certified as an EMT-Paramedic. Extensive related coursework and clinical and field experience is required. Due to the longer training requirement, almost all EMT-Paramedics are in paid positions. Refresher courses and continuing education are available for EMTs and paramedics at all levels.

EMTs and paramedics should be emotionally stable, have good dexterity, agility, and physical coordination, and be able to lift and carry heavy loads. They also need good eyesight (corrective lenses may be used) with accurate color vision.

Advancement beyond the EMT-Paramedic level usually means leaving fieldwork. An EMT-Paramedic can become a supervisor, operations manager, administrative director, or executive director of emergency services. Some EMTs and paramedics become instructors, dispatchers, or physician assistants, while others move into sales or marketing of emergency medical equipment. A number of people become EMTs and paramedics to assess their interest in healthcare and then decide to return to school and become registered nurses, physicians, or other health workers.

Job Outlook

Employment of emergency medical technicians and paramedics is expected to grow faster than the average for all occupations through 2010. Population growth and urbanization will increase the demand for full-time paid EMTs and paramedics rather than for volunteers. In addition, a large segment of the population—the aging baby boomers—will further spur demand for EMT services, as they become more likely to have medical emergencies. There will still be demand for part-time, volunteer EMTs and paramedics in rural areas and smaller metropolitan areas. In addition to job growth, openings will occur because of replacement needs; some workers leave because of stressful working conditions, lim-

ited advancement potential, and the modest pay and benefits in the private sector.

Most opportunities for EMTs and paramedics are expected to arise in hospitals and private ambulance services. Competition will be greater for jobs in local government, including fire, police, and independent third service rescue squad departments, where salaries and benefits tend to be slightly better. Opportunities will be best for those who have advanced certifications, such as EMT-Intermediate and EMT-Paramedic, as clients and patients demand higher levels of care before arriving at the hospital.

Earnings

Earnings of EMTs and paramedics depend on the employment setting and geographic location as well as the individual's training and experience. Median annual earnings of EMTs and paramedics were $22,460 in 2000. The middle 50 percent earned between $17,930 and $29,270. The lowest 10 percent earned less than $14,660, and the highest 10 percent earned more than $37,760. Median annual earnings in the industries employing the largest numbers of EMTs and paramedics in 2000 were:

Local government	$24,800
Hospitals	23,590
Local and suburban transportation	20,950

Those in emergency medical services who are part of fire or police departments receive the same benefits as firefighters or police officers. For example, many are covered by pension plans that provide retirement at half pay after 20 or 25 years of service or if disabled in the line of duty.

Related Occupations

Other workers in occupations that require quick and level-headed reactions to life-or-death situations are air traffic controllers, firefighting occupations, physician assistants, police and detectives, and registered nurses.

Sources of Additional Information

General information about emergency medical technicians and paramedics is available from:

- National Association of Emergency Medical Technicians, 408 Monroe St., Clinton, MS 39056. Internet: http://www.naemt.org

- National Registry of Emergency Medical Technicians, P.O. Box 29233, Columbus, OH 43229. Internet: http://www.nremt.org

- National Highway Transportation Safety Administration, EMS Division, 400 7th St. SW., NTS-14, Washington, DC. Internet: http://www.nhtsa.dot.gov/people/injury/ems

Engineering Technicians

O*NET 17-3021.00, 17-3022.00, 17-3023.01, 17-3023.02, 17-3023.03, 17-3024.00, 17-3025.00, 17-3026.00, 17-3027.00

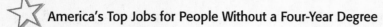

Significant Points

- Electrical and electronic engineering technicians make up about 45 percent of all engineering technicians.

- Because the type and quality of training programs vary considerably, prospective students should carefully investigate training programs before enrolling.

- Opportunities will be best for individuals with an associate degree or extensive job training in engineering technology.

Nature of the Work

Engineering technicians use the principles and theories of science, engineering, and mathematics to solve technical problems in research and development, manufacturing, sales, construction, inspection, and maintenance. Their work is more limited in scope and more practically oriented than that of scientists and engineers. Many engineering technicians assist engineers and scientists, especially in research and development. Others work in quality control—inspecting products and processes, conducting tests, or collecting data. In manufacturing, they may assist in product design, development, or production. Many workers who repair or maintain various types of electrical, electronic, or mechanical equipment often are called technicians.

Engineering technicians who work in research and development build or set up equipment, prepare and conduct experiments, collect data, calculate or record the results, and help Engineers or scientists in other ways, such as making prototype versions of newly designed equipment. They also assist in design work, often using computer-aided design equipment.

Most engineering technicians specialize in certain areas, learning skills and working in the same disciplines as engineers. Occupational titles, therefore, tend to follow the same structure as those of engineers.

Aerospace engineering and operations technicians install, construct, maintain, and test systems used to test, launch, or track aircraft and space vehicles. They may calibrate test equipment and determine the cause of equipment malfunctions. Using computer and communications systems, aerospace engineering and operations technicians often record and interpret test data.

Chemical engineering technicians usually are employed in industries producing pharmaceuticals, chemicals, and petroleum products, among others. They work in laboratories as well as processing plants. They help develop new chemical products and processes, test processing equipment and instrumentation, gather data, and monitor quality.

Civil engineering technicians help civil engineers plan and build highways, buildings, bridges, dams, wastewater treatment systems, and other structures, and perform related surveys and studies. Some estimate construction costs and specify materials to be used, and some may even prepare drawings or perform land-surveying duties. Others may set up and monitor instruments used to study traffic conditions.

Electrical and electronics engineering technicians help design, develop, test, and manufacture electrical and electronic equipment such as communication equipment, radar, industrial and medical measuring or control devices, navigational equipment, and computers. They may work in product evaluation and testing, using measuring and diagnostic devices to adjust, test, and repair equipment.

Electrical and electronic engineering technology is also applied to a wide variety of systems such as communications and process controls. *Electromechanical engineering technicians* combine fundamental principles of mechanical engineering technology with knowledge of electrical and electronic circuits to design, develop, test, and manufacture electrical and computer-controlled mechanical systems.

Environmental engineering technicians work closely with environmental engineers and scientists in developing methods and devices used in the prevention, control, or correction of environmental hazards. They inspect and maintain equipment affecting air pollution and recycling. Some inspect water and wastewater treatment systems to ensure that pollution control requirements are met.

Industrial engineering technicians study the efficient use of personnel, materials, and machines in factories, stores, repair shops, and offices. They prepare layouts of machinery and equipment, plan the flow of work, make statistical studies, and analyze production costs.

Mechanical engineering technicians help engineers design, develop, test, and manufacture industrial machinery, consumer products, and other equipment. They may assist in product tests—by setting up instrumentation for auto crash tests, for example. They may make sketches and rough layouts, record data, make computations, analyze results, and write reports. When planning production, mechanical engineering technicians prepare layouts and drawings of the assembly process and of parts to be manufactured. They estimate labor costs, equipment life, and plant space. Some test and inspect machines and equipment in manufacturing departments or work with engineers to eliminate production problems.

Working Conditions

Most engineering technicians work at least 40 hours a week in laboratories, offices, or manufacturing or industrial plants, or on construction sites. Some may be exposed to hazards from equipment, chemicals, or toxic materials.

Employment

Engineering technicians held about 519,000 jobs in 2000. About 233,000 of these were electrical and electronics engineering technicians. About 35 percent of all engineering technicians worked in durable goods manufacturing, mainly in the electrical and electronic equipment, industrial machinery and equipment, instruments and related products, and transportation equipment industries. Another 26 percent worked in service industries, mostly in engineering or business services companies that do engineering work on contract for government, manufacturing firms, or other organizations.

In 2000, the federal government employed about 23,000 engineering technicians. The major employer was the Department of Defense, followed by the Departments of Transportation, Agriculture, and Interior, the Tennessee Valley Authority, and the National Aeronautics and Space Administration. State governments employed about 22,000, and local governments, about 21,000.

Training, Other Qualifications, and Advancement

Although it may be possible to qualify for a few engineering technician jobs without formal training, most employers prefer to hire someone with at least a 2-year associate degree in engineering technology. Training is available at technical institutes, community colleges, extension divisions of colleges and universities, public and private vocational-technical schools, and the armed forces. Persons with college courses in science, engineering, and mathematics may qualify for some positions but may need additional specialized training and experience. Although employers usually do not require engineering technicians to be certified, such certification may provide job seekers a competitive advantage.

Prospective engineering technicians should take as many high school science and math courses as possible to prepare for postsecondary programs in engineering technology. Most 2-year associate degree programs accredited by the Technology Accreditation Commission of the Accreditation Board for Engineering and Technology (TAC/ABET) require, at a minimum, college algebra and trigonometry, and one or two basic science courses. Depending on the specialty, more math or science may be required.

The type of technical courses required also depends on the specialty. For example, prospective mechanical engineering technicians may take courses in fluid mechanics, thermodynamics, and mechanical design; electrical engineering technicians may take classes in electric circuits, microprocessors, and digital electronics; and those preparing to work in environmental engineering technology need courses in environmental regulations and safe handling of hazardous materials.

Because many engineering technicians may assist in design work, creativity is desirable. Good communication skills and the ability to work well with others also is important because these workers often are part of a team of Engineers and other technicians.

Engineering technicians usually begin by performing routine duties under the close supervision of an experienced technician, technologist, engineer, or scientist. As they gain experience, they are given more difficult assignments with only general supervision. Some engineering technicians eventually become supervisors.

Many publicly and privately operated schools provide technical training; the type and quality of programs vary considerably. Therefore, prospective students should be careful in selecting a program. They should contact prospective employers regarding their preferences and ask schools to provide information about the kinds of jobs obtained by graduates, instructional facilities and equipment, and faculty qualifications. Graduates of ABET-accredited programs usually are recognized to have achieved an acceptable level of competence in the mathematics, science, and technical courses required for this occupation.

Technical institutes offer intensive technical training through application and practice, but less theory and general education than community colleges. Many offer 2-year associate degree programs, and are similar to or part of a community college or state university system. Other technical institutes are run by private, often for-profit, organizations, sometimes called proprietary schools. Their programs vary considerably in length and types of courses offered, although some are 2-year associate degree programs.

Community colleges offer curriculums that are similar to those in technical institutes, but that may include more theory and liberal arts. Often there may be little or no difference between technical institute and community college programs, as both offer associate degrees. After completing the 2-year program, some graduates get jobs as engineering technicians, while others continue their education at 4-year colleges.

However, there is a difference between an associate degree in pre-engineering and one in engineering technology. Students who enroll in a 2-year pre-engineering program may find it very difficult to find work as an engineering technician should they decide not to enter a 4-year engineering program, because pre-engineering programs usually focus less on hands-on applications and more on academic preparatory work. Conversely, graduates of 2-year engineering technology programs may not receive credit for many of the courses they have taken if they choose to transfer to a 4-year engineering program. Colleges with these 4-year programs usually do not offer engineering technician training, but college courses in science, engineering, and mathematics are useful for obtaining a job as an engineering technician. Many 4-year colleges offer bachelor's degrees in engineering technology, but graduates of these programs often are hired to work as technologists or applied engineers, not technicians.

Area vocational-technical schools, another source of technical training, include postsecondary public institutions that serve local students and emphasize training needed by local employers. Most require a high school diploma or its equivalent for admission.

Other training in technical areas may be obtained in the armed forces. Many military technical training programs are highly regarded by employers. However, skills acquired in military programs are often narrowly focused, so they may not be useful in civilian industry, which often requires broader training. Therefore, some additional training may be needed, depending on the acquired skills and the kind of job.

The National Institute for Certification in Engineering Technologies (NICET) has established a voluntary certification program for engineering technicians. Certification is available at various levels, each level combining a written examination in 1 of more than 30 specialties with a certain amount of job-related experience, a supervisory evaluation, and a recommendation.

Job Outlook

Opportunities will be best for individuals with an associate degree or extensive job training in engineering technology. As technology becomes more sophisticated, employers continue to look for technicians who are skilled in new technology and require a minimum of additional job training. An increase in the number of jobs affecting public health and safety should create job opportunities for certified engineering technicians.

Overall employment of engineering technicians is expected to increase about as fast as the average for all occupations through 2010. As production of technical products continues to grow, competitive pressures will force companies to improve and update manufacturing facilities and product designs more rapidly than in the past. However, the growing availability and use of advanced technologies, such as computer-aided design and drafting and computer simulation, will continue to increase productivity and limit job growth. In addition to growth, many job openings will stem from the need to replace technicians who retire or leave the labor force.

Like engineers, employment of engineering technicians is influenced by local and national economic conditions. As a result, the employment outlook varies with industry and specialization. Some types of engineering technicians, such as civil engineering and aerospace engineering and operations technicians, experience greater cyclical fluctuations in employment than do others. Increasing demand for more sophisticated electrical and electronic products, as well as the expansion of these products and systems into all areas of industry and manufacturing processes, will contribute to average growth in the largest specialty—electrical and electronics engineering technicians. At the same time, new specializations will contribute to growth among all other engineering technicians; fire protection engineering, water quality control, and environmental technology are some of many new specialties for which demand is increasing.

Earnings

Median annual earnings of electrical and electronics engineering technicians were $40,020 in 2000. The middle 50 percent earned between $31,570 and $49,680. The lowest 10 percent earned less than $25,210, and the highest 10 percent earned more than $58,320. Median annual earnings in the industries employing the largest numbers of electrical and electronics engineering technicians in 2000 are shown below.

Federal government	$50,000
Telephone communication	45,640
Engineering and architectural services	40,690
Electrical goods	38,120
Electronic components and accessories	35,500

Median annual earnings of civil engineering technicians were $35,990 in 2000. The middle 50 percent earned between $27,810 and $44,740. The lowest 10 percent earned less than $21,830, and the highest 10 percent earned more than $54,770. Median annual earnings in the industries employing the largest numbers of civil engineering technicians in 2000 are shown below.

Local government	$39,080
Engineering and architectural services	36,670
State government	32,160

In 2000, the average annual salary for aerospace engineering and operations technicians in the aircraft and parts industry was $53,340, and the average annual salary for environmental engineering technicians in engineering and architectural services was $29,960. The average annual salary for industrial engineering technicians in computer and data processing services and electric components and accessories was $73,320 and $36,300, respectively. In engineering and architectural services, the average annual salary for mechanical engineering technicians was $40,580.

Related Occupations

Engineering technicians apply scientific and engineering principles usually acquired in postsecondary programs below the baccalaureate level. Similar occupations include science technicians; drafters; surveyors, cartographers, photogrammetrists, and surveying technicians; and broadcast and sound engineering technicians and radio operators.

Sources of Additional Information

For $3.50, a full package of guidance materials and information (product number SP-01) on a variety of engineering technician and technology careers is available from:

● Junior Engineering Technical Society (JETS), 1420 King St., Suite 405, Alexandria, VA 22314-2794. Internet: http://www.jets.org

Information on ABET-accredited engineering technology programs is available from:

● Accreditation Board for Engineering and Technology, Inc., 111 Market Place, Suite 1050, Baltimore, MD 21202. Internet: http://www.abet.org

Information on certification of engineering technicians is available from:

● National Institute for Certification in Engineering Technologies (NICET), 1420 King St., Alexandria, VA 22314-2794. Internet: http://www.nicet.org

Farmers, Ranchers, and Agricultural Managers

O*NET 11-9011.01, 11-9011.02, 11-9011.03, 11-9012.00

Significant Points

● Modern farming requires college training in agriculture and work experience acquired through growing up on a farm or through a small number of internships now available.

● Overall employment is projected to decline because of increasing productivity and consolidation of farms.

● Aquaculture should provide some new employment opportunities; in addition, developments in value-added marketing and organic farming are making small-scale farming economically viable again.

● Self-employed farmers' and ranchers' incomes vary greatly from year to year.

Nature of the Work

American farmers, ranchers, and agricultural managers direct the activities of one of the world's largest and most productive agricultural sectors. They produce enough food and fiber to meet the needs of the United States and produce a surplus for export.

Farmers and ranchers may be owners or tenants who rent the use of land. The type of farm they operate determines their specific tasks. On crop farms—farms growing grain, cotton, and other fibers, fruit, and vegetables—farmers are responsible for planning, tilling, planting, fertilizing, cultivating, spraying, and harvesting. After the harvest, they make sure the crops are properly packaged, stored, or marketed. Livestock, dairy, and poultry farmers must feed, plan, and care for the animals and keep barns, pens, coops, and other farm buildings clean and in good condition. They also oversee breeding and marketing activities. Horticultural specialty farmers oversee the production of ornamental plants, nursery products—such as flowers, bulbs, shrubbery, and sod—and fruits and vegetables grown in greenhouses. Aquaculture farmers raise fish and shellfish in marine, brackish, or fresh water, usually in ponds, floating net pens, raceways, or recirculating systems. They stock, feed, protect, and otherwise manage aquatic life sold for consumption or used for recreational fishing.

Farmers and ranchers make many managerial decisions. Their farm output is strongly influenced by the weather, disease, fluctuations in prices of domestic and foreign farm products, and federal farm programs. In a crop operation, farmers usually determine the best time to plant seed, apply fertilizer and chemicals, harvest, and market. They use different strategies to protect themselves from unpredictable changes in the markets for agricultural products. Many farmers carefully plan the combination of crops they grow so that if the price of one crop drops, they will have sufficient income from another to make up for the loss. Others, particularly operators of smaller farms, may choose to sell their goods directly through farmers' markets, or use cooperatives to reduce their financial risk and to gain a larger share of consumers' expenditures on food. For example, in Community Supported Agriculture (CSA), cooperatives sell to consumers shares of a harvest prior to the planting season, thus freeing the farmer from having to bear all the financial risks and ensuring the farmer a market for the produce of the coming season.

Farmers and ranchers who plan ahead may be able to store their crops or keep their livestock to take advantage of better prices later in the year. Those who participate in the risky futures market—in which contracts and options on futures contracts on commodities are traded through stockbrokers—try to anticipate or track changes in the supply of and demand for agricultural commodities, and thus changes in the prices of farm products. By buying or selling futures contracts, or by pricing their products in advance of future sales, they attempt to either limit their risk or reap greater profits than would normally be realized. They may have to secure loans from credit agencies to finance the purchase of machinery, fertilizer, livestock, and feed. Like other businesses, farming operations have become more complex in recent years, so many farmers use computers to keep financial and inventory records. They also use computer databases and spreadsheets to manage breeding, dairy, and other farm operations.

Responsibilities of farmers and ranchers range from caring for livestock, to operating machinery, to maintaining equipment and facilities. The size of the farm or ranch often determines which of these tasks farmers and ranchers will handle themselves. Operators of small farms usually perform all tasks, physical and administrative. They keep records for tax purposes, service machinery, maintain buildings, and grow vegetables and raise animals. Operators of large farms, on the other hand, have employees who help with the physical work that small-farm operators do themselves. Although employment on most farms is limited to the farmer and one or two family workers or hired employees, some large farms have 100 or more full-time and seasonal workers. Some of these employees are in nonfarm occupations, working as truck drivers, sales representatives, bookkeepers, and computer specialists.

Agricultural managers guide and assist farmers and ranchers in maximizing the financial returns to their land by managing the day-to-day activities. Their duties and responsibilities vary widely. For example, the owner of a very large livestock farm may employ a manager to oversee a single activity, such as feeding the livestock. On the other hand, when managing a small crop farm for an absentee owner, a manager may assume responsibility for all functions, from selecting the crops to participating in planting and harvesting. Farm management firms and corporations involved in agriculture employ highly trained professional farm managers who may manage farm operations or oversee tenant operators of several farms. In these cases, managers may establish output goals; determine financial constraints; monitor production and marketing; hire, assign, and supervise workers; determine crop transportation and storage requirements; and oversee maintenance of the property and equipment.

There are several types of agricultural managers. Nursery and greenhouse managers make decisions about the type and quality of horticultural plants—trees, shrubs, flowers, or mushrooms, for example—to be grown. They also select and purchase seed, fertilizers, and chemicals used for disease control. Crop farm managers and fish hatchery managers direct farm workers involved in crop and fish hatchery production.

Working Conditions

The work of farmers, ranchers, and agricultural managers is often strenuous; work hours are frequently long; and they rarely have days off during the planting, growing, and harvesting seasons. Nevertheless, for those who enter farming or ranching, these disadvantages are outweighed by the quality of life in a rural area, working outdoors, being self-employed, and making a living working the land. Farmers and farm managers on crop farms usually work from sunrise to sunset during the planting and harvesting seasons. During the rest of the year they plan next season's crops, market their output, and repair machinery; some may earn additional income by working a second job off the farm.

On livestock producing farms and ranches, work goes on throughout the year. Animals, unless they are grazing, must be fed and watered every day, and dairy cows must be milked two or three times a day. Many livestock and dairy farmers monitor and attend to the health of their herds, which may include assisting in the birthing of animals. Such farmers rarely get the chance to get away unless they hire an assistant or arrange for a temporary substitute.

Farmers who grow produce and perishables have different demands on their time. For example, organic farmers must maintain cover crops during the cold months, which keeps them occupied with farming beyond the typical growing season.

Farm work also can be hazardous. Tractors and other farm machinery can cause serious injury, and workers must be constantly alert on the job. The proper operation of equipment and handling of chemicals is necessary to avoid accidents and protect the environment.

On very large farms, farmers spend substantial time meeting with farm managers or farm supervisors in charge of various activities. Professional farm managers overseeing several farms may divide their time between traveling to meet farmers or landowners and planning the farm operations in their offices. As farming practices and agricultural technology become more sophisticated, farmers and farm managers are spending more time in offices and at computers, where they electronically manage many aspects of their businesses. Some farmers also spend time at conferences, particularly during the winter months, exchanging information.

Employment

Farmers, ranchers, and agricultural managers held nearly 1.5 million jobs in 2000. About 86 percent were self-employed farmers and ranchers. Most farmers, ranchers, and agricultural managers oversee crop production activities, while others manage livestock and dairy production. A smaller number are involved in agricultural services, such as contract harvesting and farm labor contracting.

The soil, topography of the land, and the climate of an area generally determine the type of farming and ranching done. For example, California, Wisconsin, New York, and Pennsylvania lead the country in milk production, while Ohio, California, Pennsylvania, and Indiana lead in egg production. Texas, California, Georgia, and Mississippi are the biggest cotton producers, and Kansas, North Dakota, Montana, and Washington are the biggest wheat producers.

Training, Other Qualifications, and Advancement

Growing up on a family farm and participating in agricultural programs for young people (sponsored by the National FFA Organization, formerly known as the Future Farmers of America, or the 4-H youth educational programs) are important sources of training for those interested in pursuing agriculture as a career. However, modern farming requires increasingly complex scientific, business, and financial decisions. Therefore, even people who were raised on farms must acquire the appropriate education.

Not all agricultural managers grew up on farms or ranches. For these people, a bachelor's degree in business with a concentration in agriculture is important. In addition to formal education, they need several years of work experience in the different aspects of farm and ranch operations in order to qualify for an agricultural manager position.

Students should select the college most appropriate to their specific interests and location. In the United States, all state university systems have one land-grant university with a school of agriculture. Common programs of study include agronomy, dairy science, agricultural economics and business, horticulture, crop and fruit science, and animal science. For students interested in aquaculture, formal programs are available, and include coursework in fisheries biology, fish culture, hatchery management and maintenance, and hydrology. Whatever one's interest, the college curriculum should include courses in agricultural production, marketing, and economics.

Professional status can be enhanced through voluntary certification as an Accredited Farm Manager (AFM) by the American Society of Farm Managers and Rural Appraisers. Certification requires several years of farm management experience, the appropriate academic background—a bachelor's degree or, preferably, a master's degree in a field of agricultural science—and the passing of courses and examinations relating to business, financial, and legal aspects of farm and ranch management.

Farmers, ranchers, and agricultural managers need to keep abreast of continuing advances in agricultural methods both in the United States and abroad, as well as changes in governmental regulations that may impact methods or markets for particular crops. Besides print journals that inform the agricultural community, the spread of the Internet allows quick access to the latest developments in areas such as agricultural marketing, legal arrangements, or growing crops, vegetables, and livestock. Electronic mail, on-line journals, and newsletters from agricultural organizations also speed the exchange of information directly between farming associations and individual farmers.

Farmers, ranchers, and agricultural managers also must have enough technical knowledge of crops, growing conditions, and plant diseases to make decisions ensuring the successful operation of their farms. A rudimentary knowledge of veterinary science, as well as animal husbandry, is important for livestock and dairy farmers. Knowledge of the relationship between farm operations—for example, the use of pesticides—and environmental conditions is essential. Mechanical aptitude and the ability to work with tools of all kinds are also valuable skills for the operator of a small farm, who often maintains and repairs machinery or farm structures.

Farmers, ranchers, and agricultural managers need the managerial skills necessary to organize and operate a business. A basic knowledge of accounting and bookkeeping is essential in keeping financial records, while a knowledge of credit sources is vital for buying seed, fertilizer, and other inputs necessary for planting. It is also necessary to be familiar with complex safety regulations and requirements of governmental agricultural support programs. Computer skills are increasingly important, especially on large farms, where computers are widely used for recordkeeping and business analysis. For example, some farmers, ranchers, and agricultural managers use personal computers to access the Internet to get the latest information on prices of farm products and other agricultural news.

High school training should include courses in mathematics and in biology and other life sciences. Completion of a 2-year degree, and preferably a 4-year bachelor's degree program in a college of agriculture, is becoming increasingly important. But even after obtaining formal education, novices may need to spend time working under an experienced farmer to learn how to put into practice the skills learned through academic training. A small number of farms offer, on a formal basis, apprenticeships to help young people acquire such practical skills.

Job Outlook

Demand for food and fiber will increase due to growth in world population and in demand for U.S. agricultural exports as developing nations improve their economies and personal incomes. However, increasing productivity in the U.S. agricultural production industry is expected to meet domestic consumption needs and export requirements with fewer workers. Employment of farmers and ranchers, is expected to continue to decline through 2010, while employment for farm, ranch, and agricultural managers is expected to grow slower than average. The overwhelming majority of job openings for self-employed farmers and ranchers will result from the need to replace farmers who retire or leave the occupation for economic or other reasons.

Market pressures will continue the long-term trend toward consolidation into fewer and larger farms over the 2000–2010 period, further reducing the number of jobs for farmers and ranchers, but increasing employment of agricultural managers. Some farmers acquire farms by inheritance; however, purchasing a farm or additional land is expensive and requires substantial capital. In addition, sufficient funds are required to withstand the adverse effects of climate and price fluctuations upon farm output and income and to cover operating costs—livestock, feed, seed, and fuel. Also, the complexity of modern farming and keen competition among farmers leaves little room for the marginally successful farmer.

Despite the expected continued consolidation of farm land and the projected decline in overall employment of farmers, ranchers, and agricultural managers, an increasing number of small-scale farmers have developed successful market niches that involve personalized, direct contact with their customers. Many are finding opportunities in organic food production, as more consumers demand food grown without pesticides or chemicals. Others use farmers' markets that cater directly to urban and suburban consumers, allowing the farmers to capture a greater share of consumers' food dollars. Some small-scale farmers, such as some dairy farmers, belong to collectively owned marketing cooperatives that process and sell their product. Other farmers participate in community-supported agriculture cooperatives that allow consumers to directly buy a share of the farmer's harvest.

Aquaculture also should continue to provide some new employment opportunities over the 2000–2010 period. Overfishing has resulted in declining ocean catches, and the growing demand for certain seafood items—such as shrimp, salmon, and catfish—has spurred the growth of aquaculture farms. Aquaculture output increased strongly between the early 1980s and mid-1990s, and continued growth is expected.

Earnings

Incomes of farmers and ranchers vary greatly from year to year because prices of farm products fluctuate depending upon weather conditions and other factors that influence the quantity and quality of farm output and the demand for those products. A farm that shows a large profit in one year may show a loss in the following year. Under the 1996 Farm Act, federal government subsidy payments, which have traditionally shielded some grain producers from the ups and downs of the market, were set at fixed levels regardless of yields or prices. Consequently, these farmers may experience more income variability from year to year than in the past. The Farm Act also phases out price supports for dairy farmers, and may result in lower incomes for dairy producers. Many farmers—primarily operators of small farms—have income from off-farm business activities, often greater than that of their farm income.

Full-time, salaried farm managers, with the exception of horticultural managers, had median weekly earnings of $542 in 2000. The middle half earned between $221 and $655. The highest-paid 10 percent earned more than $756, and the lowest-paid 10 percent earned less than $187. Horticultural specialty farm managers generally earn considerably more.

Farmers and self-employed farm managers make their own provisions for benefits. As members of farm organizations, they may derive benefits such as group discounts on health and life insurance premiums.

Related Occupations

Farmers, ranchers, and agricultural managers strive to improve the quality of agricultural products and the efficiency of farms. Others whose work is related to agricultural products include agricultural engineers, agricultural and food scientists, agricultural workers, and purchasing agents and buyers of farm products.

Sources of Additional Information

For general information about farming and agricultural occupations, contact:

- Center for Rural Affairs, P.O. Box 406, Walthill, NE 68067. Internet: http://www.cfra.org

For information about certification as an accredited farm manager, contact:

- American Society of Farm Managers and Rural Appraisers, 950 Cherry St., Suite 508, Denver, CO 80222. Internet: http://www.asfmra.org

- Small Farm Program, U.S. Department of Agriculture, Cooperative State, Research, Education, and Extension Service, Stop 2220, Washington, DC 20250-2220. Internet: http://www.reeusda.gov/agsys/smallfarm

For information on aquaculture, education, training, or Community Supported Agriculture, contact:

- Alternative Farming System Information Center (AFSIC), National Agricultural Library USDA, 10301 Baltimore Ave., Room 132, Beltsville, MD 20705-2351. Internet: http://www.nal.usda.gov/afsic

- Appropriate Technology Transfer for Rural Areas, P.O. Box 3657, Fayetteville, AR 72702. Internet: http://www.attra.org

File Clerks

O*NET 43-4071.00

Significant Points

- Numerous job openings should arise for most types of file clerks due to employment growth and the need to replace workers who leave these occupations.

- A high school diploma or its equivalent is the most common educational requirement.

Nature of the Work

The amount of information generated by organizations continues to grow rapidly. File clerks classify, store, retrieve, and update this information. In many small offices, they often have additional responsibilities, such as data entry, word processing, sorting mail, and operating copying or fax machines. They are employed across the nation by organizations of all types.

File clerks, also called records, information, or record center clerks, examine incoming material and code it numerically, alphabetically, or by subject matter. They then store forms, letters, receipts, or reports in paper form or enter necessary information into other storage devices. Some clerks operate mechanized files that rotate to bring the needed records to them; others convert documents to films that are then stored on microforms, such as microfilm or microfiche. A growing number of file clerks use imaging systems that scan paper files or film and store the material on optical disks.

In order for records to be useful they must be up-to-date and accurate. File clerks ensure that new information is added to the files in a timely manner and may get rid of outdated file materials or transfer them to inactive storage. They also check files at regular intervals to make sure that all items are correctly sequenced and placed. Whenever records cannot be found, the file clerk attempts to locate the missing material. As an organization's needs for information change, file clerks also implement changes to the filing system established by supervisory personnel.

When records are requested, file clerks locate them and give them to the borrower. The record may be a sheet of paper stored in a file cabinet or an image on microform. In the first example, the clerk manually retrieves the document and hands or forwards it to the borrower. In the latter example, the clerk retrieves the microform and displays it on a microform reader. If necessary, file clerks make copies of records and distribute them. In addition, they keep track of materials removed from the files to ensure that borrowed files are returned.

Increasingly, file clerks use computerized filing and retrieval systems. These systems use a variety of storage devices, such as a mainframe computer, CD-ROM, or floppy disk. To retrieve a document in these systems, the clerk enters the document's identification code, obtains the location, and pulls the document. Accessing files in a computer database is much quicker than locating and physically retrieving paper files. Even when files are stored electronically, however, backup paper or electronic copies usually are also kept.

Working Conditions

Most file clerks work in areas that are clean, well lit, and relatively quiet. Because a number of file clerks may share the same workspace, it may be crowded and noisy.

Most file clerks work a standard 40-hour week.

The work performed by file clerks may be repetitive and stressful. Stress is caused by technology that enables management to electronically monitor use of computer systems, tape record telephone calls, or limit the time spent on each call. In addition, prolonged exposure to a video display terminal may lead to eyestrain for the many file clerks who work with computers.

Employment

File clerks held about 288,000 jobs in 2000. Although file clerk jobs are found in nearly every sector of the economy, about 85 percent of these workers are employed in services, government, finance, insurance, and real estate. More than 1 out of every 7 are employed in temporary services firms, and about 1 out of 3 worked part-time in 2000.

Training, Other Qualifications, and Advancement

Although hiring requirements for file clerks vary from industry to industry, a high school diploma or its equivalent is the most common educational requirement. Increasingly, familiarity or experience with computers and good interpersonal skills is equally important to employers.

Good spelling and computer literacy often are needed, particularly because most work involves considerable computer use.

File clerks often learn the skills they need in high schools, business schools, and community colleges. Business education programs offered by these institutions typically include courses in typing, word processing, shorthand, business communications, records management, and office systems and procedures.

Some entry-level clerks are college graduates with degrees in business, finance, or liberal arts. Although a degree rarely is required, many graduates accept entry-level clerical positions to get into a particular company or to enter a particular field. Workers with college degrees are likely to start at higher salaries and advance more easily than those without degrees do.

Orientation and training for file usually takes place on the job. New employees usually receive on-the-job training. Under the guidance of a supervisor or other senior workers, new employees learn company procedures. Some formal classroom training also may be necessary, such as training in specific computer software. Most file clerks continue to receive instruction on new procedures and company policies after their initial training ends.

Job Outlook

Employment of file clerks is expected to grow more slowly than the average for all occupations through 2010. Projected job growth stems from rising demand for file clerks to record and retrieve information in organizations across the economy. This growth will be slowed, however, by productivity gains stemming from office automation and the consolidation of clerical jobs. Nonetheless, job opportunities for file clerks should be plentiful because a large number of workers will be needed to replace workers who leave the occupation each year. Job turnover among file clerks reflects the lack of formal training requirements, limited advancement potential, and relatively low pay.

Job seekers who have typing and other secretarial skills and are familiar with a wide range of office machines, especially personal computers, should have the best job opportunities. File clerks should find many opportunities for temporary or part-time work, especially during peak business periods.

Earnings

In 2000, median annual earnings for file clerks were $18,700.

Related Occupations

A number of other workers deal with the public, receive and provide information, or direct people to others who can assist them. Among these are dispatchers, security guards and gaming surveillance workers, tellers, and counter and rental clerks.

Sources of Additional Information

State employment service offices can provide information about employment opportunities.

Financial Analysts and Personal Financial Advisors

O*NET 13-2051.00, 13-2052.00

Significant Points

- A college degree and good interpersonal skills are among the most important qualifications for these workers.

- Although both occupations will benefit from an increase in investing by individuals, personal financial advisors will benefit more.

- Financial analysts may face keen competition for jobs, especially at top securities firms, where pay can be lucrative.

Nature of the Work

Financial analysts and personal financial advisors provide investment analysis and guidance to businesses and individuals to help them with their investment decisions. They gather financial information, analyze it, and make recommendations. However, their job duties differ because of the type of investment information they provide and the clients they work for. Financial analysts assess the economic performance of companies and industries for firms and institutions with money to invest. Personal financial advisors generally assess the financial needs of individuals, providing them a wide range of options.

Financial analysts, also called security analysts and investment analysts, work for banks, insurance companies, mutual and pension funds, securities firms, and other businesses helping the company or their clients make investment decisions. They read company financial statements and analyze commodity prices, sales, costs, expenses, and tax rates in order to determine a company's value and project future earnings. They often meet with company officials to get better insight into a company and determine managerial effectiveness. Usually financial analysts study an entire industry, assessing current trends in business practices, products, and industry competition. They must keep abreast of new regulations or policies that may affect the industry, as well as monitor the economy to determine its effect on earnings.

Financial analysts use spreadsheet and statistical software packages to analyze financial data, spot trends, and develop forecasts. Based on their results, they write reports and make presentations, usually making recommendations to buy or sell a particular investment or security. Senior analysts may actually make the decision to buy or sell for the company or client if they are the ones responsible for managing the assets. Other analysts use the data to measure the financial risks associated with making a particular investment decision.

Financial analysts in investment banking departments of securities or banking firms often work in teams analyzing the future prospects of companies that want to sell shares to the public for the first time. They also ensure that the forms and written materials necessary for compliance with Securities and Exchange Commission regulations are accurate and complete. They may make presentations to prospective investors about the merits of investing in the new company. Financial analysts also work in mergers and acquisitions departments, preparing analyses on the costs and benefits of a proposed merger or takeover.

Some financial analysts, called ratings analysts, evaluate the ability of companies or governments issuing bonds to repay their debt. Based on their evaluation, a management team assigns a rating to a company's or government's bonds. Other financial analysts perform budget, cost, and credit analysis as part of their responsibilities.

Personal financial advisors, also called financial planners or financial consultants, use their knowledge of investments, tax laws, insurance, and real estate to recommend financial options to individuals based on their short-term and long-term goals. Some of the issues they address are retirement planning, estate planning, tax issues, funding for college, and general investment options. While most planners offer advice on a wide range of topics, some specialize in areas such as estate planning or risk management.

An advisor's work begins with a consultation with the client, where the advisor obtains information on the client's finances and financial goals. The advisor then develops a comprehensive financial plan that identifies problem areas, makes recommendations for improvement, and selects appropriate investments based on their goals, attitude toward risk, and expectations or needs for a return on the investment. Often, this plan is written, but it can be in the form of verbal advice. Financial advisors usually meet with established clients at least once a year to update

them on potential investments and determine if there have been any life changes—such as marriage, disability, or retirement—that might affect the clients' financial goals. Financial advisors also answer questions from clients regarding changes in benefit plans or consequences of a job change. Some advisors buy and sell financial products, such as mutual funds or insurance, or refer clients to other companies for products and services such as preparation of taxes or wills. A number of advisors take on the responsibility of managing the client's investments for them.

Finding clients and building a customer base is one of the most important parts of a financial advisor's job. Many advisors contact potential clients by giving seminars or lectures or meeting clients through business and social contacts.

Working Conditions

Financial analysts and personal financial advisors usually work indoors in safe, comfortable offices or their own homes. Many of these workers enjoy the challenge of helping firms or people make financial decisions. However, financial analysts may face long hours, frequent travel to visit companies and talk to potential investors, and deadline pressure. Much of their research must be done after office hours, because their day is filled with phone calls and meetings. Personal financial advisors usually work standard business hours, but they also schedule meetings with clients in the evenings or on weekends. Many teach evening classes or put on seminars in order to bring in more clients.

Employment

Financial analysts and personal financial advisors held 239,000 jobs in 2000; financial analysts accounted for about 6 in 10 of the total. Many financial analysts work at the headquarters of large financial companies, several of which are based in New York. One-fourth of financial analysts work for security and commodity brokers, exchanges, and investment services firms; and one-fifth work for depository and nondepository institutions, including banks, credit institutions, and mortgage bankers and brokers. The remainder primarily work for insurance carriers, computer and data processing services, and management and public relations firms.

Approximately one fourth of personal financial advisors are self-employed, operating small investment advisory firms, usually located in urban areas. The majority of salaried advisors—nearly 6 in 10—work for security and commodity brokers, exchanges, and investment services firms. About 1 in 7 personal financial advisors works for commercial banks, saving institutions, and credit unions. A small number work for insurance carriers and insurance agents, brokers, and services.

Training, Other Qualifications, and Advancement

A college education is required for financial analysts and strongly preferred for personal financial advisors. Most companies require financial analysts to have at least a bachelor's degree in business administration, accounting, statistics, or finance. Coursework in statistics, economics, and business is required, and knowledge of accounting policies and procedures, corporate budgeting, and financial analysis methods is recommended. A master of business administration is desirable. Advanced courses in options pricing or bond valuation and knowledge of risk management are also suggested.

Employers usually do not require a specific field of study for personal financial advisors, but a bachelor's degree in accounting, finance, economics, business, mathematics, or law provides good preparation for the occupation. Courses in investments, taxes, estate planning, and risk management also are helpful. Programs in financial planning are becoming more widely available in colleges and universities. However, many financial planners enter the field after working in a related occupation, such as securities and financial services sales representative, insurance agent, accountant, or lawyer.

Mathematical, computer, analytical, and problem-solving skills are all essential qualifications for financial analysts and personal financial advisors. Good communication skills also are necessary because these workers must present complex financial concepts and strategies in easy-to-understand language to clients and other professionals. Self-confidence, maturity, and the ability to work independently are important as well.

Financial analysts must be detail-oriented, motivated to seek out obscure information, and familiar with the workings of the economy, tax laws, and money markets. For financial advisors, strong interpersonal skills and sales ability are crucial to success.

Certification, although not required for financial analysts or personal financial advisors to practice, can enhance professional standing and is strongly recommended by many financial companies. Financial analysts may receive the title Chartered Financial Analyst (CFA), sponsored by the Association of Investment Management and Research. To qualify for CFA designation, applicants must have a bachelor's degree, 3 years of work experience in a related field, and pass a series of three examinations. The essay exams, administered once a year for 3 years, cover subjects such as accounting, economics, securities analysis, asset valuation, and portfolio management.

Personal financial advisors may obtain a Certified Financial Planner (CFP) or Chartered Financial Consultant (ChFC) designation. Both designations demonstrate to potential customers that a planner has extensive training and competency in the area of financial planning. The CFP designation, issued by the CFP Board of Standards, requires relevant experience, completion of education requirements, passage of a comprehensive examination, and adherence to an enforceable code of ethics. The ChFC designation, issued by the American College in Bryn Mawr, PA, requires experience and completion of an eight-course study program. Both programs have a continuing education requirement.

A license is not required to work as a personal financial advisor, but advisors who sell stocks, bonds, mutual funds, insurance, or real estate, may need licenses to perform these additional services. Also, if legal advice is provided, a license to practice law may be required. Financial advisors that do not provide these additional services often refer clients to those qualified to provide them.

Financial analysts may advance by becoming portfolio managers or financial managers, directing the investment policies of their companies or those of clients. Personal financial advisors who work in firms also may move into managerial positions, but most advisors advance by accumulating clients and managing more assets.

Job Outlook

Increased investment by businesses and individuals is expected to result in faster-than-average employment growth of financial analysts and personal financial advisors through 2010. Both occupations will benefit as baby boomers save for retirement and a generally better educated and wealthier population requires investment advice. In addition, people are living longer and must plan to finance more years of retirement. The rapid expansion of self-directed retirement plans, such as the 401(k) plans, is expected to continue. Most of the money in these plans is invested in mutual funds. As the number of mutual funds and the amount of assets invested in the funds increases, mutual fund companies will need increase numbers of financial analysts to recommend which financial products the funds should buy or sell. Growth in retirement plans will also increase demand for personal financial advisors to provide advice on how to invest this money.

Deregulation of the financial services industry is also expected to spur demand for financial analysts and personal financial advisors. Since 1999, banks, insurance companies, and brokerage firms have been allowed to broaden their financial services. Many firms are adding investment advice to their list of services and are expected to increase their hiring of personal financial advisors. Many banks are now entering the securities brokerage and investment banking fields and will increasingly need the skills of financial analysts in these areas.

The globalization of the securities markets as well as the increased complexity of many financial products also will increase the need for analysts and advisors to help investors make financial choices. In addition, business mergers and acquisitions seem likely to continue, requiring the services of financial analysts. However, in the field of investment banking, the demand for financial analysts may fluctuate because investment banking is sensitive to changes in the stock market. And further consolidation in the financial services industry may eliminate some financial analyst positions, somewhat dampening overall employment growth. Competition is expected to be keen for these highly lucrative positions, with many more applicants than jobs.

Earnings

Median annual earnings of financial analysts were $52,420 in 2000. The middle half earned between $40,210 and $70,840. The lowest 10 percent earned less than $31,880, and the top 10 percent earned more than $101,760.

Median annual earnings of personal financial advisors were $55,320 in 2000. The middle half earned between $34,420 and $96,360. The lowest 10 percent earned less than $25,110, and the top 10 percent earned more than $145,600.

Many financial analysts receive a bonus in addition to their salary, which can add substantially to their earnings. The bonus is usually based on how well their predictions compare to the actual performance of a benchmark investment. Personal financial advisors who work for financial services firms are generally paid a salary plus bonus. Advisors who work for financial planning firms or who are self-employed either charge hourly fees for their services or charge one set fee for a comprehensive plan based on its complexity. Advisors who manage a client's assets usually charge a percentage of the assets under management. A majority of advisors receive commissions for financial products they sell in addition to a fee.

Related Occupations

Other jobs requiring expertise in finance and investments or sales of financial products include accountants, financial managers, insurance sales agents, real estate agents, and securities, commodities and financial services sales representatives.

Sources of Additional Information

For information on a career in financial planning, contact:

- The Financial Planning Association, 1700 Broadway, Suite 708, Denver, CO 80290. Internet: http://www.fpanet.org

For information about the Certified Financial Planner certification, contact:

- The Certified Financial Planner Board of Standards, 1700 Broadway, Suite 2100, Denver, CO 80290-2101. Internet: http://www.cfp-board.org

For information about the Chartered Financial Consultant designation, contact:

- The American College, 270 South Bryn Mawr Ave., Bryn Mawr, PA 19010. Internet: http://www.amercoll.edu

For information on about the Chartered Financial Analyst designation, contact:

- Association of Investment Management and Research, P.O. Box 3668, 560 Ray C. Hunt Drive, Charlottesville, VA 22903. Internet: http://www.aimr.org

Financial Clerks

O*NET 43-3011.00, 43-3021.01, 43-3021.02, 43-3021-03, 43-3031.00, 43-3041.00, 43-3051.00, 43-3061.00, 43-3071.00

Significant Points

- Most jobs require only a high school diploma.

- Numerous job opportunities should arise due to high turnover.

- Slower-than-average growth is expected in overall employment, reflecting the spread of computers and other office automation as well as organizational restructuring.

Nature of the Work

Financial clerks keep track of money. They record all amounts coming into or leaving an organization. Their records are vital to an organization's need to keep track of all revenues and expenses. While most financial clerks work in offices maintaining and processing various accounting records, some deal directly with customers, taking in and paying out money. When bills are not paid on time, financial clerks must contact customers to find out why and attempt to resolve the problem. Other clerks keep track of a store's inventory and order replacement stock when supplies are low.

Depending on their specific titles, these workers perform a wide variety of financial record keeping duties. *Bill and account collectors* notify customers with delinquent accounts in order to solicit payment. *Billing and posting clerks and machine operators* prepare bills and invoices. *Bookkeeping, accounting, and auditing clerks* maintain financial data in computer and paper files. *Payroll and timekeeping clerks* compute wages for payroll records and review employee timecards. *Procurement clerks* prepare purchase orders and monitor purchase requests. *Tellers* receive and pay out money for financial institutions, while *gaming cage workers* perform many of the same services for casinos.

The duties of financial clerks vary with the size of the firm. In a small business, a bookkeeper may handle all financial records and transactions, as well as payroll and billing duties. A large firm, on the other hand, may employ specialized accounting, payroll, and billing clerks. In general, however, clerical staffs in firms of all sizes increasingly perform a broader variety of tasks than in the past.

Another change in these occupations is the growing use of financial software to enter and manipulate data. Computer programs automatically perform calculations on data that were previously calculated manually. Computers also enable clerks to access data within files more quickly and even generate statements automatically. Nevertheless, most workers still keep backup paper records for research, auditing, and reference purposes, although a paperless office is increasingly the goal for many organizations.

Despite the growing use of automation, interaction with the public and coworkers remains a basic part of the job for many financial clerks. Payroll clerks, for example, answer questions concerning employee benefits; tellers and gaming cage workers help customers with their financial needs, and procurement clerks often have to deal with an organization's suppliers.

Working Conditions

With the exception of gaming cage workers, financial clerks typically are employed in an office environment. Bill collectors who work for third-party collection agencies may spend most of their days on the phone in a call center environment. However, a growing number of financial clerks, particularly medical billets, work at home and many work part-time.

Because the majority of financial clerks use computers on a daily basis, these workers may experience eye and muscle strain, backaches, headaches, and repetitive motion injuries. Also, clerks who review detailed data may have to sit for extended periods of time.

Most financial clerks work regular business hours. However, since most casinos are open 24 hours a day, gaming cage workers often work in shifts, including nights and weekends. Tellers can work some evenings and Saturday mornings, while bill collectors often have to work evenings and weekends when it is easier to reach people. Accounting clerks may work longer hours to meet deadlines at the end of the fiscal year, during tax time, or when monthly and yearly accounting audits are performed. Billing, bookkeeping, and accounting clerks in hotels, restaurants, and stores may work overtime during peak holiday and vacation seasons.

Employment

Financial clerks held more than 3.7 million jobs in 2000. The following table shows employment in individual clerical occupations:

Bookkeeping, accounting, and auditing clerks	1,991,000
Billing and posting clerks and machine operators	506,000
Tellers	499,000
Bill and account collectors	400,000

Payroll and timekeeping clerks 201,000
Procurement clerks 76,000
Gaming cage workers 22,000

These workers are employed in virtually every industry, including manufacturing, business and health services, and government. However, it is becoming more common for these clerks to work for companies that specialize in performing specific accounting services, such as bill collection, medical billing, and payroll services as companies seek to cut costs and outsource many administrative functions. Also, more financial clerks are finding jobs with personnel-supply agencies, as companies increasingly hire temporary workers for peak periods.

All financial clerk occupations have some part-time workers, but tellers and bookkeeping, accounting, and auditing clerks have the most with more than one-fourth working part-time.

Training, Other Qualifications, and Advancement

Most financial clerks are required to have at least a high school diploma. However, having some college is becoming increasingly important, particularly for those occupations requiring knowledge of accounting. For occupations such as bookkeepers, accounting clerks, and procurement clerks, an associate degree in business or accounting often is required. Some financial clerks have bachelor's degrees in business, accounting, or liberal arts. Although a degree is rarely required, many graduates accept entry-level clerical positions to get into a particular company or to enter the finance or accounting field with the hope of being promoted to professional or managerial positions. Some companies have a set plan of advancement that tracks college graduates from entry-level clerical jobs into managerial positions. Workers with bachelor's degrees are likely to start at higher salaries and advance more easily than those without degrees do.

Experience in a related job also is recommended for a number of these positions. For example, cash-handling experience is important for gaming cage workers and tellers. Telemarketing experience is useful for bill and account collectors. For other financial clerks, experience working in an office environment or in customer service is always beneficial. Regardless of the type of work, most employers prefer workers with good communication skills who are computer-literate; knowledge of word processing and spreadsheet software is especially valuable.

Gaming cage workers have additional requirements. They must be at least 21 years old and they are required to obtain a license by the state gaming commission or other regulatory body. In addition to a fee, applicants must provide a photograph and proof of age and residence. A background check is conducted to make sure that applicants do not have a criminal history.

Once hired, financial clerks usually receive on-the-job training. Under the guidance of a supervisor or other senior worker, new employees learn company procedures. Some formal classroom training also may be necessary, such as training in specific computer software. Bill and account collectors generally receive training in telephone techniques, negotiation skills, and the laws governing the collection of debt. Financial clerks must be careful, orderly, and detail-oriented in order to avoid making errors and recognize errors made by others. These workers also should be discreet and trustworthy, because they frequently come in contact with confidential material. Additionally, all financial clerks should have a strong aptitude for numbers.

Bookkeepers, particularly those who handle all the recordkeeping for companies, may find it beneficial to become certified. The Certified Bookkeeper designation, awarded by the American Institute of Professional Bookkeepers, assures employers that individuals have the skills and knowledge required to carry out all the bookkeeping and accounting functions up through the adjusted trial balance, including payroll functions. For certification, candidates must have at least 2 years bookkeeping experience, pass three tests, and adhere to a code of ethics. Collection agencies may require their collectors to become certified by the American Collectors Association (ACA). ACA seminars concentrate on current state and federal compliance laws. Since most states recognize these credentials, ACA-certified collectors have greater career mobility. Tellers can prepare for better jobs by taking courses offered or accredited by the American Institute of Banking (an educational affiliate of the American Bankers Association) or the Institute of Financial Education (an affiliate of the Bank Administration Institute). These organizations have several hundred chapters in cities across the country and numerous study groups in small communities.

Financial clerks usually advance by taking on more duties in the same occupation for higher pay or by transferring to a closely related occupation. For example, procurement clerks with the appropriate experience often become buyers. Most companies fill office and administrative support supervisory and managerial positions by promoting individuals from within their organization, so financial clerks who acquire additional skills, experience, and training improve their advancement opportunities. With appropriate experience and education, some clerks may become accountants, human resource specialists, or buyers.

Job Outlook

Overall employment of financial clerks is expected to grow more slowly than the average for all occupations through 2010. Despite continued growth in the volume of business transactions, rising productivity stemming from the spread of office automation, as well as organizational restructuring, will adversely affect demand for financial clerks. Turnover in this large occupation, however, will provide the most job openings. As a result, opportunities should be plentiful for full-time and part-time employment as financial clerks transfer to other occupations or leave the labor force.

Many basic data entry accounting and clerical jobs already have become heavily automated. Productivity has increased significantly, as workers increasingly use personal computers instead of manual entry and time-consuming equipment such as typewriters, adding machines, and calculators. The growing use of bar code readers, point-of-sale terminals, automated teller machines, and optical scanners that record transactions reduces much of the data entry handled by financial clerks. In addition, the use of local area networks also is facilitating electronic data interchange—the sending of data from computer to computer—abolishing the need for clerks to reenter the data. To further eliminate duplicate functions, many large companies are consolidating their clerical operations in a central office where accounting, billing, personnel, and payroll functions are performed for all offices—main and satellite—within the organization. In addition, as more companies merge or are acquired, accounting departments also are usually merged, reducing the number of financial clerks. More companies also are outsourcing their accounting functions to specialized companies that can do the job more efficiently.

Despite the expected slow growth, some financial clerks will fare better than others. The number of gaming cage workers should grow over time as more Indian tribes become involved in gaming. Also, the number of bill collectors is expected to increase as consumer debt continues to rise. The healthcare services industry is expected to hire more financial clerks, particularly billing clerks, to match the explosive growth of this sector and to process the large amounts of paperwork required to process patient claims.

Earnings

Salaries of financial clerks vary considerably. The region of the country, size of city, and type and size of establishment all influence salary levels. Also, the level of expertise required and the complexity and uniqueness of a clerk's responsibilities also may affect earnings. Median hourly earnings of full-time financial clerks in 2000 were as follows:

Procurement clerks	$13.33
Payroll and timekeeping clerks	13.07
Bookkeeping, accounting, and auditing clerks	12.34
Bill and account collectors	12.17
Billing and posting clerks and machine operators	11.81
Gaming cage workers	9.99
Tellers	9.21

In addition to their salary, some bill and account collectors receive commissions or bonuses based on the number of cases they close.

Related Occupations

Financial clerks enter data into a computer, handle cash, and keep track of business and other financial transactions. Higher level financial clerks can generate reports and perform analysis of the financial data. Other occupations that perform these duties include brokerage clerks; cashiers; credit authorizers, checkers, and clerks; loan interviewers and clerks; new accounts clerks; order clerks; and secretaries and administrative assistants.

Sources of Additional Information

Information on employment opportunities for financial clerks is available from local offices of the state employment service.

Career information on bill and account collectors is available from:

- American Collectors Association, Inc., P.O. Box 39106, Minneapolis, MN 55439-0106

For information on the Certified Bookkeeper designation, contact:

- The American Institute of Professional Bookkeepers, 6001 Montrose Rd., Rockville, MD 20852. Internet: http://www.aipb.org

Firefighting Occupations

O*NET 33-1021.01, 33-1021.02, 33-2011.01, 33-2011.02, 33-2021.01, 33-2021.02, 33-2022.00

Significant Points

- Firefighting involves hazardous conditions and long, irregular hours.

- Keen competition for jobs is expected; many people are attracted to the occupation because it provides considerable job security and the opportunity to perform an essential public service.

Nature of the Work

Every year, fires and other emergencies take thousands of lives and destroy property worth billions of dollars. Firefighters help protect the public against these dangers by rapidly responding to a variety of emergencies. They are frequently the first emergency personnel at the scene of a traffic accident or medical emergency and may be called upon to put out a fire, treat injuries, or perform other vital functions.

During duty hours, firefighters must be prepared to respond immediately to a fire or any other emergency that arises. Because fighting fires is dangerous and complex, it requires organization and teamwork. At every emergency scene, firefighters perform specific duties assigned by a superior officer. At fires, they connect hose lines to hydrants, operate a pump to send water to high pressure hoses, and position ladders to enable them to deliver water to the fire. They also rescue victims and provide emergency medical attention as needed, ventilate smoke-filled areas, and attempt to salvage the contents of buildings. Their duties may change several times while the company is in action. Sometimes they remain at the site of a disaster for days at a time, rescuing trapped survivors and assisting with medical treatment.

Firefighters have assumed a range of responsibilities, including emergency medical services. In fact, most calls to which firefighters respond involve medical emergencies, and about half of all fire departments provide ambulance service for victims. Firefighters receive training in emergency medical procedures, and many fire departments require them to be certified as emergency medical technicians.

Firefighters work in a variety of settings, including urban and suburban areas, airports, chemical plants, other industrial sites, and rural areas like grasslands and forests. In addition, some firefighters work in hazardous materials units that are trained for the control, prevention, and cleanup of oil spills and other hazardous materials incidents. Workers in urban and suburban areas, airports, and industrial sites typically use conventional firefighting equipment and tactics, while forest fires and major hazardous materials spills call for different methods.

In national forests and parks, *forest fire inspectors and prevention specialists* spot fires from watchtowers and report their findings to headquarters by telephone or radio. Forest rangers patrol to ensure travelers and campers comply with fire regulations. When fires break out, crews of firefighters are brought in to suppress the blaze using heavy equipment, handtools, and water hoses. Forest firefighting, like urban firefighting, can be rigorous work. One of the most effective means of battling the blaze is by creating fire lines through cutting down trees and digging out grass and all other combustible vegetation, creating bare land in the path of the fire that deprives it of fuel. Elite firefighters, called smoke jumpers, parachute from airplanes to reach otherwise inaccessible areas. This can be extremely hazardous because the crews have no way to escape if the wind shifts and causes the fire to burn toward them.

Between alarms, firefighters clean and maintain equipment, conduct practice drills and fire inspections, and participate in physical fitness activities. They also prepare written reports on fire incidents and review fire science literature to keep abreast of technological developments and changing administrative practices and policies.

Most fire departments have a fire prevention division, usually headed by a fire marshal and staffed by *fire inspectors*. Workers in this division conduct inspections of structures to prevent fires and ensure fire code compliance. These firefighters also work with developers and planners to check and approve plans for new buildings. Fire prevention personnel often speak on these subjects in schools and before public assemblies and civic organizations.

Some firefighters become *fire investigators*, who determine the origin and causes of fires. They collect evidence, interview witnesses, and prepare reports on fires in cases where the cause may be arson or criminal negligence. They often are called upon to testify in court.

Working Conditions

Firefighters spend much of their time at fire stations, which usually have features common to a residential facility like a dormitory. When an alarm sounds, firefighters respond rapidly, regardless of the weather or hour. Firefighting involves risk of death or injury from sudden cave-ins of floors, toppling walls, traffic accidents when responding to calls, and exposure to flames and smoke. Firefighters may also come in contact with poisonous, flammable, or explosive gases and chemicals, as well as radioactive or other hazardous materials that may have immediate or long-term effects on their health. For these reasons, they must wear protective gear that can be very heavy and hot.

Work hours of firefighters are longer and vary more widely than hours of most other workers. Many work more than 50 hours a week, and sometimes they may work even longer. In some agencies, they are on duty for 24 hours, then off for 48 hours, and receive an extra day off at intervals. In others, they work a day shift of 10 hours for 3 or 4 days, a night shift of 14 hours for 3 or 4 nights, have 3 or 4 days off, and then repeat the cycle. In addition, firefighters often work extra hours at fires and other emergencies and are regularly assigned to work on holidays. Fire lieutenants and fire captains often work the same hours as the firefighters they supervise. Duty hours include time when firefighters study, train, and perform fire prevention duties.

Employment

Employment figures in this statement include only paid career firefighters; they do not cover volunteer firefighters, who perform the same duties and may comprise the majority of firefighters in a residential area. Paid career firefighters held about 258,000 jobs in 2000. First-line supervisors/managers of firefighting and prevention workers held about 62,000 jobs; and fire inspectors held about 13,000. More than 9 out of 10 worked in municipal or county fire departments. Some large cities have thousands of career firefighters, while many small towns have only a few. Most of the remainder worked in fire departments on federal and state installations, including airports. Private firefighting companies employ a small number of firefighters and usually operate on a subscription basis.

In response to the expanding role of firefighters, some municipalities have combined fire prevention, public fire education, safety, and emergency medical services into a single organization commonly referred to as a public safety organization. Some local and regional fire departments are being consolidated into countywide establishments in order to reduce administrative staffs and cut costs, and to establish consistent training standards and work procedures.

Training, Other Qualifications, and Advancement

Applicants for municipal firefighting jobs generally must pass a written exam; tests of strength, physical stamina, coordination, and agility; and a medical examination that includes drug screening. Workers may be monitored on a random basis for drug use after accepting employment. Examinations are generally open to persons who are at least 18 years of age and have a high school education or the equivalent. Those who receive the highest scores in all phases of testing have the best chances for appointment. The completion of community college courses in fire science may improve an applicant's chances for appointment. In recent years, an increasing proportion of entrants to this occupation has had some postsecondary education.

As a rule, entry-level workers in large fire departments are trained for several weeks at the department's training center or academy. Through classroom instruction and practical training, the recruits study firefighting techniques, fire prevention, hazardous materials control, local building codes, and emergency medical procedures, including first aid and cardiopulmonary resuscitation. They also learn how to use axes, chain saws, fire extinguishers, ladders, and other firefighting and rescue equipment. After successfully completing this training, they are assigned to a fire company, where they undergo a period of probation.

A number of fire departments have accredited apprenticeship programs lasting up to 5 years. These programs combine formal, technical instruction with on-the-job training under the supervision of experienced firefighters. Technical instruction covers subjects such as firefighting techniques and equipment, chemical hazards associated with various combustible building materials, emergency medical procedures, and fire prevention and safety. Fire departments frequently conduct training programs, and some firefighters attend training sessions sponsored by the U.S. National Fire Academy. These training sessions cover topics including executive development, anti-arson techniques, disaster preparedness, hazardous materials control, and public fire safety and education. Some states also have extensive firefighter training and certification programs. In addition, a number of colleges and universities offer courses leading to 2- or 4-year degrees in fire engineering or fire science. Many fire departments offer firefighters incentives such as tuition reimbursement or higher pay for completing advanced training.

Among the personal qualities firefighters need are mental alertness, self-discipline, courage, mechanical aptitude, endurance, strength, and a sense of public service. Initiative and good judgment are also extremely important because firefighters make quick decisions in emergencies. Because members of a crew live and work closely together under conditions of stress and danger for extended periods, they must be dependable and able to get along well with others. Leadership qualities are necessary for officers, who must establish and maintain discipline and efficiency, as well as direct the activities of firefighters in their companies.

Most experienced firefighters continue studying to improve their job performance and prepare for promotion examinations. To progress to higher level positions, they acquire expertise in advanced firefighting equipment and techniques, building construction, emergency medical technology, writing, public speaking, management and budgeting procedures, and public relations.

Opportunities for promotion depend upon written examination results, job performance, interviews, and seniority. Increasingly, fire departments use assessment centers, which simulate a variety of actual job performance tasks, to screen for the best candidates for promotion. The line of promotion usually is to engineer, lieutenant, captain, battalion chief, assistant chief, deputy chief, and finally to chief. Many fire departments now require a bachelor's degree, preferably in fire science, public administration, or a related field, for promotion to positions higher than battalion chief. A master's degree is required for executive fire officer certification from the National Fire Academy and for state chief officer certification.

Job Outlook

Prospective firefighters are expected to face keen competition for available job openings. Many people are attracted to firefighting because it is challenging and provides the opportunity to perform an essential public service, a high school education is usually sufficient for entry, and a pension is guaranteed upon retirement after 20 years. Consequently, the number of qualified applicants in most areas exceeds the number of job openings, even though the written examination and physical requirements eliminate many applicants. This situation is expected to persist in coming years.

Employment of firefighters is expected to increase more slowly than the average for all occupations through 2010 as fire departments continue to compete with other public safety providers for funding. Most job growth will occur as volunteer firefighting positions are converted to paid positions. In addition to job growth, openings are expected to result from the need to replace firefighters who retire, stop working for other reasons, or transfer to other occupations.

Layoffs of firefighters are uncommon. Fire protection is an essential service, and citizens are likely to exert considerable pressure on local officials to expand or at least preserve the level of fire protection. Even when budget cuts do occur, local fire departments usually cut expenses by postponing equipment purchases or not hiring new firefighters, rather than by laying off staff.

Earnings

Median hourly earnings of firefighters were $16.43 in 2000. The middle 50 percent earned between $11.82 and $21.75. The lowest 10 percent earned less than $8.03, and the highest 10 percent earned more than $26.58. Median hourly earnings were $16.71 in local government and $15.00 in federal government.

Median annual earnings of first-line supervisors/managers of firefighting and prevention workers were $51,990 in 2000. The middle 50 percent earned between $40,920 and $64,760. The lowest 10 percent earned less than $31,820, and the highest 10 percent earned more than $77,700. First-line supervisors/managers of firefighting and prevention workers employed in local government earned about $52,390 a year in 2000.

Median annual earnings of fire inspectors and investigators were $41,630 in 2000. The middle 50 percent earned between $31,630 and $53,130 a year. The lowest 10 percent earned less than $24,790, and the highest 10 percent earned more than $65,030. Fire inspectors and investigators employed in local government earned about $44,030 a year in 2000.

Median annual earnings of forest fire inspectors and prevention specialists were $32,140 in 2000. The middle 50 percent earned between $22,930 and $41,150 a year. The lowest 10 percent earned less than $17,060, and the highest 10 percent earned more than $50,680.

The International City-County Management Association's annual Police and Fire Personnel, Salaries, and Expenditures Survey revealed that 89 percent of the municipalities surveyed provided fire protection services in 2000. The following 2000 salaries pertain to sworn full-time positions.

	Minimum annual average base salary	Maximum annual average base salary
Fire chief	$58,156	$74,749
Deputy chief	52,174	65,112
Battalion chief	50,164	62,309
Assistant fire chief	48,391	60,179
Fire captain	41,816	50,848
Fire lieutenant	38,875	46,327
Fire prevention/code inspector	37,142	46,798
Engineer	35,090	44,310
Firefighter	29,316	39,477

Firefighters who average more than a certain number of hours a week are required to be paid overtime. The hours threshold is determined by the department during the firefighter's work period, which ranges from 7 to 28 days. Firefighters often earn overtime for working extra shifts to maintain minimum staffing levels or for special emergencies.

Firefighters receive benefits usually including medical and liability insurance, vacation and sick leave, and some paid holidays. Almost all fire departments provide protective clothing (helmets, boots, and coats) and breathing apparatus, and many also provide dress uniforms. Firefighters are generally covered by pension plans, often providing retirement at half pay after 25 years of service or if disabled in the line of duty.

Related Occupations

Like firefighters, emergency medical technicians and paramedics and police and detectives respond to emergencies and save lives.

Sources of Additional Information

Information about a career as a firefighter may be obtained from local fire departments and from:

- International Association of Firefighters, 1750 New York Ave. NW., Washington, DC 20006. Internet: http://www.iaff.org/iaff/index.html

- U.S. Fire Administration, 16825 South Seton Ave., Emmitsburg, MD 21727

Information about firefighter professional qualifications and a list of colleges and universities offering 2- or 4-year degree programs in fire science or fire prevention may be obtained from:

- National Fire Academy, Degrees at a Distance Program, 16825 South Seton Ave., Emmitsburg, MD 21727. Internet: http://www.usfa.fema.gov/nfa/index.htm

Fishers and Fishing Vessel Operators

O*NET 45-3011.00

Significant Points

- Over 60 percent of the workers are self-employed, among the highest proportion in the workforce.

- Many jobs require strenuous work and long hours, and provide only seasonal employment.

- Employment is projected to decline, due to depletion of fish stocks and new federal and state laws restricting both commercial and recreational fishing.

Nature of the Work

Fishers and fishing vessel operators catch and trap various types of marine life for human consumption, animal feed, bait, and other uses.

Fishing hundreds of miles from shore with commercial fishing vessels—large boats capable of hauling a catch of tens of thousands of pounds of fish—requires a crew including a captain, or skipper, a first mate and sometimes a second mate, boatswain (called a deckboss on some smaller boats), and deckhands with specialized skills.

The *fishing boat captain* plans and oversees the fishing operation—the fish to be sought, the location of the best fishing grounds, the method of capture, the duration of the trip, and the sale of the catch.

The captain ensures the fishing vessel is seaworthy; oversees the purchase of supplies, gear, and equipment such as fuel, netting, and cables; obtains the required fishing permits and licenses; and hires qualified crew members and assigns their duties. The captain plots the vessel's course, using navigation instruments and aids such as compasses, sextants, and charts, in addition to electronic navigational equipment such as autopilots, loran systems, and satellite navigation systems. Ships also use radar to avoid obstacles and depth sounders to indicate the water depth and the existence of marine life between the vessel and sea bottom. Sophisticated tracking technology allows captains to better locate and analyze schools of fish. The captain directs the fishing operation through the officers, and records daily activities in the ship's log. Upon returning to port, the captain arranges for the sale of the catch—directly to buyers or through a fish auction—and ensures that each crew member receives the prearranged portion of adjusted net proceeds from the sale of the catch. Some captains have begun buying and selling fish via the Internet; and as electronic commerce grows as a method to find buyers for fresh catch, more captains may use computers.

The *first mate*—the captain's assistant, who must be familiar with navigation requirements and the operation of all electronic equipment—assumes control of the vessel when the captain is off duty. Duty shifts, called watches, usually last 6 hours. The mate's regular duty, with the help of the boatswain and under the captain's oversight, is to direct the fishing operations and sailing responsibilities of the deckhands. These include the operation, maintenance, and repair of the vessel, and the gathering, preservation, stowing, and unloading of the catch.

The *boatswain*, a highly experienced deckhand with supervisory responsibilities, directs the *deckhands* as they carry out the sailing and fishing operations. Before departure, the boatswain directs the deckhands to load equipment and supplies, either by hand or with hoisting equipment, and to untie lines from other boats and the dock. When necessary, boatswains repair fishing gear, equipment, nets, and accessories. They operate the fishing gear, letting out and pulling in nets and lines. They extract the catch such as pollock, flounder, menhaden, and tuna, from the nets or lines' hooks. Deckhands use dip nets to prevent the escape of small fish and gaffs to facilitate the landing of large fish. They then wash, salt, ice, and stow away the catch. Deckhands also must ensure that decks are clear and clean at all times and the vessel's engines and equipment are kept in good working order. Upon return to port, they secure the vessel's lines to and from the docks and other vessels. Unless "lumpers" (laborers or longshore workers) are hired, the deckhands unload the catch.

Large fishing vessels that operate in deep water generally have technologically advanced equipment, and some may have facilities on board where the fish are processed and prepared for sale. Such vessels are equipped for long stays at sea and can perform the work of several smaller boats.

Some full-time and many part-time fishers work on small boats in relatively shallow waters, often in sight of land. Navigation and communication needs are vital and constant for almost all types of boats. Crews are small; usually only one or two people collaborate on all aspects of the fishing operation. This may include placing gill nets across the mouths of rivers or inlets, entrapment nets in bays and lakes, or pots and traps for fish or shellfish such as lobsters and crabs. Dredges and scrapes are sometimes used to gather shellfish such as oysters and scallops. A very small proportion of commercial fishing is conducted as diving operations. Depending upon the water's depth, divers—wearing regulation diving suits with an umbilical (air line) or a scuba outfit and equipment—use spears to catch fish and use nets and other equipment to gather shellfish, coral, sea urchins, abalone, and sponges. In very shallow waters, fish are caught from small boats having an outboard motor, from rowboats, or by wading or seining from shore. Fishers use a wide variety of hand-operated equipment—for example, nets, tongs, rakes, hoes, hooks, and shovels—to gather fish and shellfish; catch amphibians and reptiles such as frogs and turtles; and harvest marine vegetation, such as Irish moss and kelp.

Although historically most fishers were involved with the traditional commercial fishery, some captains and deckhands are primarily employed in support of the sport or recreational fishery. Typically, a group of people charter a fishing vessel, for periods ranging from several hours to a number of days. for sport fishing, socializing, and relaxation and employ a captain and possibly several deckhands. This industry had experienced significant growth in the 1970s and 1980s, but declined in the 1990s because of the limited availability of fish.

Working Conditions

Fishing operations are conducted under various environmental conditions, depending on the region of the country and the kind of species sought. Storms, fog, and wind may hamper fishing vessels. Divers are affected by murky water and unexpected shifts in underwater currents. In relatively busy fisheries, smaller boats have to take care not to be hit by larger vessels.

Fishers and fishing vessel operators work under hazardous conditions, and often help is not readily available. Malfunctioning navigation or communication equipment may lead to collisions or shipwrecks. Malfunctioning fishing gear poses the danger of injury to the crew, who also must guard against entanglement in fishing nets and gear, slippery decks resulting from fish processing operations, ice formation in the winter, or being swept overboard—a fearsome situation. Also, treatment for any serious injuries may have to await transfer to a hospital. Divers must guard against entanglement of air lines, malfunction of scuba equipment, decompression problems, and attacks by predatory fish.

Fishers and fishing vessel operators face strenuous outdoor work and long hours. Commercial fishing trips may require a stay of several weeks, or even months—hundreds of miles away from home port. The pace of work may vary, but even during travel between home port and the fishing grounds, deckhands on smaller boats try to finish their cleaning duties so that there are no chores remaining to be done at port. However, lookout watches are a regular responsibility, and crew members must be prepared to stand watch at prearranged times of the day or night. Although fishing gear has improved, and operations have become more mechanized, netting and processing fish are strenuous activities. Whereas newer vessels have improved living quarters and amenities, such as television and shower stalls, crews still experience the aggravations of confined conditions, continuous close personal contact, and the absence of family.

Employment

Fishers and fishing vessel operators held an estimated 53,000 jobs in 2000. More than 6 out of 10 were self-employed. Besides fishing conducted primarily to harvest food, some jobs involved sport fishing activities.

Training, Other Qualifications, and Advancement

Fishers usually acquire occupational skills on the job, many as members of families involved in fishing activities. No formal academic requirements exist. Operators of large commercial fishing vessels are required to complete a Coast Guard-approved training course. Students can expedite their entrance into these occupations by enrolling in 2-year vocational-technical programs offered by secondary schools. In addition, some community colleges and universities offer fishery technology and related programs that include courses in seamanship, vessel operations, marine safety, navigation, vessel repair and maintenance, health emergencies, and fishing gear technology. Courses include hands-on experience. Secondary and postsecondary programs are normally offered in or near coastal areas.

Experienced fishers may find short-term workshops offered through various postsecondary institutions especially useful. These programs provide a good working knowledge of electronic equipment used in navigation and communication, and the latest improvements in fishing gear.

Captains and mates on large fishing vessels of at least 200 gross tons must be licensed. Captains of sport fishing boats used for charter, regardless of size, must also be licensed. Crew members on certain fish processing vessels may need a merchant mariner's document. The U.S. Coast Guard issues these documents and licenses to individuals who meet the stipulated health, physical, and academic requirements.

Fishers must be in good health and possess physical strength. Good coordination, mechanical aptitude, and the ability to work under difficult or dangerous conditions are necessary to operate, maintain, and repair equipment and fishing gear. Fishers need stamina to work long hours at sea, often under difficult conditions. On large vessels, they must be able to work as members of a team. Fishers must be patient, yet always alert, to overcome the boredom of long watches, when not engaged in fishing operations. The ability to assume any deckhand's functions, on short notice, is important. As supervisors, mates must be able to assume all duties, including the captain's, when necessary. The captain must be highly experienced, mature, decisive, and possess the business skills needed to run business operations.

On fishing vessels, most fishers begin as deckhands. Deckhands who acquire experience and whose interests are in ship engineering—maintenance and repair of ship engines and equipment—can eventually become licensed chief engineers on large commercial vessels, after meeting the Coast Guard's experience, physical, and academic requirements. Experienced, reliable deckhands who display supervisory qualities may become boatswains. Boatswains may, in turn, become second mates, first mates, and finally captains. Almost all captains become self-employed, and the overwhelming majority eventually own, or have an interest in, one or more fishing ships. Some may choose to run a sport or recreational fishing operation. When their seagoing days are over, experienced individuals may work in or, with the necessary capital, own stores selling fishing and marine equipment and supplies. Some captains may assume advisory or administrative positions in industry trade associations or government offices, such as harbor development commissions or in teaching positions in industry-sponsored workshops or educational institutions. Divers in fishing operations can enter commercial diving activity—for example, repairing ships or maintaining piers and marinas—usually after completion of a certified training program sponsored by an educational institution or industry association.

Job Outlook

Employment of fishers and fishing vessel operators is expected to decline through the year 2010. These occupations depend on the natural ability of fish stocks to replenish themselves through growth and reproduction, as well as on governmental regulation of fisheries. Many operations are currently at or beyond maximum sustainable yield, partially because of habitat destruction, and the number of workers who can earn an adequate income from fishing is expected to decline. Job openings will arise from the need to replace workers who retire or leave the occupation. Some fishers and fishing vessel operators leave the occupation because of the strenuous and hazardous nature of the job and the lack of steady, year-round income.

In many areas, particularly the North Atlantic and Pacific Northwest, damage to spawning grounds and excessive fishing have adversely affected the stock of fish and, consequently, the employment opportunities for fishers. In some areas, states have greatly reduced permits to fishers, to allow stocks of fish and shellfish to replenish, idling many fishers. Other factors contributing to the projected decline in employment of fishers include the use of sophisticated electronic equipment for navigation, communication, and fish location; improvements in fishing gear, which have greatly increased the efficiency of fishing operations; and the use of highly automated floating processors, where the catch is processed aboard the vessel. Sport fishing boats will continue to provide some job opportunities.

Earnings

The majority of fishers earn between $300 and $750 per week. Earnings of fishers and fishing vessel operators normally are highest in the summer and fall—when demand for services peaks and environmental conditions are favorable—and lowest during the winter. Many full-time and most part-time workers supplement their income by working in other activities during the off-season. For example, fishers may work in seafood processing plants, establishments selling fishing and marine equipment, or in construction, or in a number of non-related, seasonal occupations.

Earnings of fishers vary widely, depending upon their position, ownership percentage of the vessel, size of ship, and the amount and value of the catch. The costs of the fishing operation—the physical aspects of operating the ship such as the fuel costs, repair and maintenance of gear and equipment, and the crew's supplies—are deducted from the sale of the catch. Net proceeds are distributed among the crew members in accordance with a prearranged percentage. Generally, the ship's owner—usually its captain—receives half of the net proceeds. From this, the owner pays for depreciation, maintenance and repair, replacement and insurance costs of the ship and equipment; the money remaining is the owner's profit.

Related Occupations

Other occupations that involve outdoor work with fish and watercraft include water transportation occupations and fish and game wardens.

Sources of Additional Information

Names of postsecondary schools offering fishing and related marine educational programs are available from:

● Marine Technology Society, 1828 L St. NW., Suite 906, Washington, DC 20036-5104. Internet: http://www.mtsociety.org

Information on licensing of fishing vessel captains and mates, and requirements for merchant mariner documentation, is available from the U.S. Coast Guard Marine Inspection Office or Marine Safety Office in your state, or from:

● Office of Compliance, Commandant (G-MOC-3) 2100 Second St. SW., Washington, DC 20593. Licensing and Evaluation Branch, National Maritime Center, 4200 Wilson Blvd., Suite 630, Arlington, VA 22203-1804

Flight Attendants

O*NET 39-6031.00

Significant Points

● Job duties are learned through intensive formal training after workers are hired.

● The opportunity for travel attracts many to this career, but the job requires working nights, weekends, and holidays and frequently being away from home.

Nature of the Work

Major airlines are required by law to provide flight attendants for the safety of the traveling public. Although the primary job of the flight attendants is to ensure that safety regulations are followed, they also try to make flights comfortable and enjoyable for passengers.

At least 1 hour before each flight, flight attendants are briefed by the captain, the pilot in command, on such things as emergency evacuation procedures, crew coordination, length of flight, expected weather conditions, and special passenger issues. Flight attendants make sure that first aid kits and other emergency equipment are aboard and in working order and that the passenger cabin is in order, with adequate supplies of food, beverages, and blankets. As passengers board the plane, flight attendants greet them, check their tickets, and tell them where to store coats and carry-on items.

Before the plane takes off, flight attendants instruct all passengers in the use of emergency equipment and check to see that seat belts are fastened, seat backs are in upright positions, and all carry-on items are properly stowed. In the air, helping passengers in the event of an emergency is the most important responsibility of a flight attendant. Safety-related actions may range from reassuring passengers during occasional encounters with strong turbulence to directing passengers who must evacuate a plane following an emergency landing. Flight attendants also answer questions about the flight; distribute reading material, pillows, and blankets; and help small children, elderly or disabled persons, and any others needing assistance. They may administer first aid to passengers who become ill. Flight attendants generally serve beverages and other refreshments and, on many flights, heat and distribute precooked meals or snacks. Prior to landing, flight attendants take inventory of headsets, alcoholic beverages, and moneys collected. They also report any medical problems passengers may have had, and the condition of cabin equipment. In addition to performing flight duties, flight attendants sometimes make public relations appearances for the airlines during "career days" at high schools and at fundraising campaigns, sales meetings, conventions, and other goodwill occasions.

Lead, or first, flight attendants, sometimes known as pursers, oversee the work of the other attendants aboard the aircraft, while performing most of the same duties.

Working Conditions

Because airlines operate around-the-clock and year-round, flight attendants may work nights, holidays, and weekends. In most cases, agreements between the airline and the employees' union determine the total monthly working time. Attendants usually fly 75 to 85 hours a month and, in addition, generally spend about 75 to 85 hours a month on the ground preparing planes for flights, writing reports following completed flights, and waiting for planes to arrive. Because of variations in scheduling and limitations on flying time, many flight attendants have 11 or more days off each month. They may be away from their home base at least one-third of the time. During this period, the airlines provide hotel accommodations and an allowance for meal expenses.

The combination of free time and discount air fares provides flight attendants the opportunity to travel and see new places. However, the work can be strenuous and trying. Short flights require speedy service if meals are served, and turbulent flights can make serving drinks and meals difficult. Flight attendants stand during much of the flight and must remain pleasant and efficient, regardless of how tired they are or how demanding passengers may be. Occasionally, flight attendants must deal with disruptive passengers.

Flight attendants are susceptible to injuries because of the job demands in a moving aircraft. Back injuries and mishaps opening overhead compartments are common. In addition, medical problems can occur from irregular sleeping and eating patterns, dealing with stressful passengers, working in a pressurized environment, and breathing recycled air.

Employment

Flight attendants held about 124,000 jobs in 2000. Commercial airlines employed the vast majority of all flight attendants, most of whom live in their employer's home base city. A small number of flight attendants worked for large companies that operated company aircraft for business purposes.

Training, Other Qualifications, and Advancement

Airlines prefer to hire poised, tactful, and resourceful people who can interact comfortably with strangers and remain calm under duress. Applicants usually must be at least 18 to 21 years old. Flight attendants must have excellent health and the ability to speak clearly. In addition, there generally are height requirements, and most airlines want candidates with weight proportionate to height.

Prospective flight attendants usually must be willing to relocate, although many flight attendants are able to commute to and from their home base. Applicants must be high school graduates. Those having several years of college or experience in dealing with the public are preferred. More and more flight attendants being hired are college graduates. Highly desirable areas of concentration include such people-oriented disciplines as psychology and education. Flight attendants for international airlines generally must speak a foreign language fluently. Some of the major airlines prefer candidates who can speak two major foreign languages for their international flights.

Once hired, candidates must undergo a period of formal training. The length of training, ranging from 4 to 7 weeks, depends on the size and type of carrier and takes place in the airline's flight training center. Airlines that do not operate training centers generally send new employees to the center of another airline. Airlines may provide transportation to the training centers and an allowance for board, room, and school supplies. However, new trainees are not considered employees of the airline until they successfully complete the training program. Some airlines may actually charge individuals for training. Trainees learn emergency procedures such as evacuating an airplane, operating emergency systems and equipment, administering first aid, and water survival tactics. In addition, trainees are taught how to deal with disruptive passengers and hijacking and terrorist situations. New hires learn flight regulations and duties, company operations and policies, and receive instruction on personal grooming and weight control. Trainees for the international routes get additional instruction in passport and customs regulations. Towards the end of their training, students go on practice flights. Additionally, flight attendants must receive 12 to 14 hours of annual training in emergency procedures and passenger relations.

After completing initial training, flight attendants are assigned to one of their airline's bases. New flight attendants are placed on "reserve sta-

tus" and are called on either to staff extra flights or to fill in for crewmembers who are sick or on vacation or rerouted. When not on duty, reserve flight attendants must be available to report for flights on short notice. They usually remain on reserve for at least 1 year but, in some cities, it may take 5 to 10 years or longer to advance from reserve status. Flight attendants who no longer are on reserve bid monthly for regular assignments. Because assignments are based on seniority, usually only the most experienced attendants get their choice of assignments. Advancement takes longer today than in the past because experienced flight attendants are remaining in this career longer than they used to.

Some flight attendants become supervisors, or take on additional duties such as recruiting and instructing. Their experience also may qualify them for numerous airline-related jobs involving contact with the public, such as reservation ticket agents or public relations specialists.

Job Outlook

Opportunities should be favorable for persons seeking flight attendant jobs because the number of applicants is expected to be roughly the same as the number of job openings. Those with at least 2 years of college and experience in dealing with the public should have the best chance of being hired. The majority of job openings through the year 2010 should be due to the need to replace flight attendants who transfer to other occupations or who leave the labor force. Many flight attendants are attracted to the occupation by the glamour of the airline industry and the opportunity to travel, but some eventually leave in search of jobs that offer higher earnings and require fewer nights away from their families.

Employment of flight attendants is expected to grow about as fast as the average for all occupations through the year 2010. Growth in population and income is expected to boost the number of airline passengers. Airlines enlarge their capacity by increasing the number and size of planes in operation. Because FAA safety rules require one attendant for every 50 seats, more flight attendants will be needed.

Employment of flight attendants is sensitive to cyclical swings in the economy. During recessions, when the demand for air travel declines, many flight attendants are put on part-time status or laid off. Until demand increases, few new flight attendants are hired.

Earnings

Median annual earnings of flight attendants were $38,820 in 2000. The middle 50 percent earned between $28,200 and $56,610. The lowest 10 percent earned less than $18,090, and the highest 10 percent earned more than $83,630.

According to data from the Association of Flight Attendants, beginning flight attendants had median earnings of about $14,847 a year in 2000. However, beginning pay scales for flight attendants vary by carrier. New hires usually begin at the same pay scale regardless of experience, and all flight attendants receive the same future pay increases. Flight attendants receive extra compensation for night and international flights and for increased hours. In addition, some airlines offer incentive pay for working holidays or taking positions that require additional responsibility or paperwork. Most airlines guarantee a minimum of 65 to 75 flight hours per month, with the option to work additional hours. Flight attendants also receive a "per diem" allowance for meal expenses while on duty away from home. In addition, flight attendants and their immediate families are entitled to free fares on their own airline and reduced fares on most other airlines.

Flight attendants are required to purchase uniforms and wear them while on duty. The airlines usually pay for uniform replacement items, and may provide a small allowance to cover cleaning and upkeep of the uniforms.

The majority of flight attendants hold union membership, primarily with the Association of Flight Attendants. Others may be members of the Transport Workers Union of America, the International Brotherhood of Teamsters, or other unions.

Related Occupations

Other jobs that involve helping people as a safety professional, while requiring the ability to be calm even under trying circumstances, include emergency medical technicians and paramedics and firefighting occupations.

Sources of Additional Information

Information about job opportunities and qualifications required for work at a particular airline may be obtained by writing to the airline's personnel office.

Food and Beverage Serving and Related Workers

O*NET 35-3011.00, 35-3021.00, 35-3022.00, 35-3031.00, 35-3041.00, 35-9011.00, 35-9021.00, 35-9031.00

Significant Points

- Most jobs are part-time and many opportunities exist for young people. Nearly 2 out of 3 food counter and fountain workers are 16 to 19 years old.

- Job openings are expected to be abundant through 2010, reflecting substantial turnover.

- Tips comprise a major portion of earnings; consequently, keen competition is expected for bartender, waiter and waitress, and other jobs in popular restaurants and fine dining establishments where potential earnings from tips are greatest.

Nature of the Work

Whether they work in small, informal diners or large, elegant restaurants, all food and beverage serving and related workers aim to help customers have a positive dining experience in their establishments. These workers greet customers, take food and drink orders, serve food, clean up after patrons, and prepare tables and dining areas.

The largest group of these workers, *waiters and waitresses,* take customers' orders, serve food and beverages, prepare itemized checks, and sometimes accept payments. Their specific duties vary considerably, depending on the establishment where they work. In coffee shops, they are expected to provide fast and efficient, yet courteous service. In fine restaurants, where gourmet meals are accompanied by attentive formal service, waiters and waitresses serve meals at a more leisurely pace and offer more personal service to patrons. For example, servers may recommend a certain wine as a complement to a particular entree, explain how various items on the menu are prepared, or complete preparations on a salad or other special dishes at tableside. Additionally, waiters and waitresses may check the identification of patrons to ensure they meet the minimum age requirement for the purchase of alcohol and tobacco products.

Depending on the type of restaurant, waiters and waitresses may perform additional duties usually associated with other food and beverage service occupations. These tasks may include escorting guests to tables, serving customers seated at counters, setting up and clearing tables, or operating a cash register. However, formal restaurants frequently hire other staff to perform these duties, allowing their waiters and waitresses to concentrate on customer service.

Bartenders fill drink orders that waiters and waitresses take from customers. They prepare standard mixed drinks and, occasionally, are asked to mix drinks to suit a customer's taste. Most bartenders know dozens of drink recipes and are able to mix drinks accurately, quickly, and without waste, even during the busiest periods. Besides mixing and serving drinks, bartenders collect payment, operate the cash register, clean up after customers leave, and often serve food to customers seated at the bar. Bartenders also check identification of customers seated at the bar, to ensure they meet the minimum age requirement for the purchase of alcohol and tobacco products. Bartenders usually are responsible for ordering and maintaining an inventory of liquor, mixes, and other bar supplies. They often form attractive displays out of bottles and glassware and wash the glassware and utensils after each use.

The majority of bartenders who work in eating and drinking establishments directly serve and interact with patrons. Because customers typically frequent drinking establishments for the friendly atmosphere, most bartenders must be friendly and helpful with customers. Bartenders at service bars, on the other hand, have little contact with customers because they work in small bars in restaurants, hotels, and clubs where only waiters and waitresses serve drinks. Some establishments, especially larger ones, use automatic equipment to mix drinks of varying complexity at the push of a button. Even in these establishments, however, bartenders still must be efficient and knowledgeable in case the device malfunctions or a customer requests a drink not handled by the equipment.

Hosts and hostesses try to create a good impression of a restaurant by warmly welcoming guests. Because hosts and hostesses are restaurants' personal representatives, they try to insure that service is prompt and courteous and that the meal meets expectations. They may courteously direct patrons to where coats and other personal items may be left and indicate where patrons can wait until their table is ready. Hosts and hostesses assign guests to tables suitable for the size of their group, escort patrons to their seats, and provide menus. They also schedule dining reservations, arrange parties, and organize any special services that are required. In some restaurants, they also act as cashiers.

Dining room and cafeteria attendants and bartender helpers assist waiters, waitresses, and bartenders by cleaning tables, removing dirty dishes, and keeping serving areas stocked with supplies. They replenish the supply of clean linens, dishes, silverware, and glasses in the dining room and keep the bar stocked with glasses, liquor, ice, and drink garnishes. Bartender helpers also keep bar equipment clean and wash glasses. Dining room attendants set tables with clean tablecloths, napkins, silverware, glasses, and dishes and serve ice water, rolls, and butter. At the conclusion of meals, they remove dirty dishes and soiled linens from tables. Cafeteria attendants stock serving tables with food, trays, dishes, and silverware and may carry trays to dining tables for patrons. *Dishwashers* clean dishes, kitchen and food preparation equipment, and utensils.

Counter attendants take orders and serve food at counters. In cafeterias, they serve food displayed on counters and steam tables, carve meat, dish out vegetables, ladle sauces and soups, and fill beverage glasses. In lunchrooms and coffee shops, counter attendants take orders from customers seated at the counter, transmit orders to the kitchen, and pick up and serve food. They also fill cups with coffee, soda, and other beverages and prepare fountain specialties, such as milkshakes and ice cream sundaes. Counter attendants prepare some short-order items, such as sandwiches and salads, and wrap or place orders in containers for carry out. They also clean counters, write itemized checks, and sometimes accept payment.

Some food and beverage serving workers take orders from customers at counters or drive-through windows at fast-food restaurants. They pick up the ordered beverage and food items, serve them to a customer, and accept payment. Many of these are *combined food preparation and serving workers* who also cook and package food, make coffee, and fill beverage cups using drink-dispensing machines.

Other workers serve food to patrons outside of a restaurant environment, such as in hotels, hospital rooms, or cars.

Working Conditions

Food and beverage service workers are on their feet most of the time and often carry heavy trays of food, dishes, and glassware. During busy dining periods, they are under pressure to serve customers quickly and efficiently. The work is relatively safe, but care must be taken to avoid slips, falls, and burns.

Part-time work is more common among food and beverage serving and related workers than among workers in almost any other occupation. Those on part-time schedules include nearly half of all waiters and waitresses, and about 6 out of 10 food counter attendants, as compared to almost 1 out of 7 workers throughout the economy. While about half of all bartenders work full time, 36 percent work part-time and the remainder work a variable schedule.

The wide range in dining hours creates work opportunities attractive to homemakers, students, and others seeking supplemental income. In fact, nearly 2 out of 3 food counter attendants are between 16 and 19 years old. Many food and beverage serving and related workers work evenings, weekends, and holidays. Some work split shifts. They work for several hours during the middle of the day, take a few hours off in the afternoon, and then return to their jobs for evening hours.

Employment

Food and beverage serving and related workers held 6.5 million jobs in 2000. Combined food preparation and serving workers held about 2.2 million of these jobs; waiters and waitresses, about 2 million; dishwashers, 525,000; dining room and cafeteria attendants and bartender helpers, 431,000; counter attendants, 421,000; bartenders, 387,000; hosts and hostesses, 343,000; and nonrestaurant food servers, 205,000.

Restaurants, coffee shops, bars, and other retail eating and drinking places employed the overwhelming majority of food and beverage service workers. Others worked in hotels and other lodging places, bowling alleys, casinos, country clubs, and other membership organizations.

Jobs are located throughout the country but are typically plentiful in large cities and tourist areas. Vacation resorts offer seasonal employment, and some workers alternate between summer and winter resorts, instead of remaining in one area the entire year.

Training, Other Qualifications, and Advancement

There are no specific educational requirements for food and beverage service jobs. Although many employers prefer to hire high school graduates for waiter and waitress, bartender, and host and hostess positions, completion of high school usually is not required for fast-food workers, counter attendants, and dining room attendants and bartender helpers. For many people, a job as a food and beverage service worker serves as a source of immediate income, rather than a career. Many entrants to these jobs are in their late teens or early twenties and have a high school education or less. Usually, they have little or no work experience. Many are full-time students or homemakers. Food and beverage service jobs are a major source of part-time employment for high school and college students.

Because maintaining a restaurant's image is important to its success, employers emphasize personal qualities. Food and beverage serving and related workers are in close contact with the public, so these workers should be well spoken and have a neat, clean appearance. They should enjoy dealing with all kinds of people and possess a pleasant disposition.

Waiters and waitresses need a good memory to avoid confusing customers' orders and to recall faces, names, and preferences of frequent patrons. These workers should also be good at arithmetic so they can total bills without the assistance of a calculator or cash register if necessary. In restaurants specializing in foreign foods, knowledge of a foreign language is helpful. Prior experience waiting on tables is preferred by restaurants and hotels that have rigid table service standards. Jobs at these establishments often have higher earnings, but they may also have higher educational requirements than less demanding establishments.

Usually, bartenders must be at least 21 years of age, but employers prefer to hire people who are 25 or older. Bartenders should be familiar with state and local laws concerning the sale of alcoholic beverages.

Most food and beverage serving and related workers pick up their skills on the job by observing and working with more experienced workers. Some employers, particularly those in fast-food restaurants, use self-instruction programs with audiovisual presentations and instructional booklets to teach new employees food preparation and service skills. Some public and private vocational schools, restaurant associations, and large restaurant chains provide classroom training in a generalized food service curriculum.

Some bartenders acquire their skills by attending a bartending or vocational and technical school. These programs often include instruction on state and local laws and regulations, cocktail recipes, attire and conduct, and stocking a bar. Some of these schools help their graduates find jobs. Although few employers require any level of educational attainment, some specialized training is usually needed including food handling training and legal issues including serving alcoholic beverages and tobacco. Employers are more likely to hire and promote based on people skills and personal qualities rather than education. Food and beverage service workers are in close contact with the public, so they should present themselves well and have a neat and clean appearance.

Due to the relatively small size of most food-serving establishments, opportunities for promotion are limited. After gaining some experience, some dining room and cafeteria attendants and bartender helpers are able to advance to waiter, waitress, or bartender jobs. For waiters, waitresses, and bartenders, advancement usually is limited to finding a job in a more expensive restaurant or bar where prospects for tip earnings are better. A few bartenders open their own businesses. Some hosts and hostesses and waiters and waitresses advance to supervisory jobs, such as maitre d'hotel, dining room supervisor, or restaurant manager. In larger restaurant chains, food and beverage service workers who excel at their work often are invited to enter the company's formal management training program.

Job Outlook

Job openings are expected to be abundant for food and beverage serving and related workers. Overall employment of these workers is expected to grow about as fast as the average for all occupations over the 2000–2010 period, stemming from increases in population, personal incomes, and leisure time. While employment growth will produce many new jobs, the overwhelming majority of openings will arise from the need to replace the high proportion of workers who leave this occupation each year. There is substantial movement into and out of the occupation because education and training requirements are minimal, and the predominance of part-time jobs is attractive to people seeking a short-term source of income rather than a career. However, keen competition is expected for bartender, waiter and waitress, and other food and beverage service jobs in popular restaurants and fine dining establishments, where potential earnings from tips are greatest.

Projected employment growth between 2000 and 2010 varies by type of job. Employment of combined food preparation and serving workers, which includes fast-food workers, is expected to increase faster than average in response to the continuing fast-paced lifestyle of many Americans and the addition of healthier foods at many fast-food restaurants. Increases in the number of families and the more affluent, 55-and-older population will result in more restaurants that offer table service and more varied menus—leading to fast as average growth for waiters and waitresses and hosts and hostesses. Average employment growth is projected for bartenders as drinking of alcoholic beverages outside the home—particularly cocktails—continues among after-work "happy hour" groups and weekend patrons. A decline is expected in the employment of dining room attendants, as waiters and waitresses increasingly assume their duties.

Earnings

Food and beverage serving and related workers derive their earnings from a combination of hourly wages and customer tips. Earnings vary greatly, depending on the type of job and establishment. For example, fast-food workers and hosts and hostesses usually do not receive tips, so their wage rates may be higher than those of waiters and waitresses and bartenders, who may earn more from tips than from wages. In some restaurants, these workers contribute a portion of their tips to a tip pool,

which is distributed among the establishment's other food and beverage serving and related workers and kitchen staff. Tip pools allow workers who normally do not receive tips, such as dining room attendants and dishwashers, to share in the rewards of a well-served meal.

In 2000, median hourly earnings (not including tips) of waiters and waitresses were $6.42. The middle 50 percent earned between $5.88 and $7.26. The lowest 10 percent earned less than $5.49, and the highest 10 percent earned more than $10.15 per hour. For most waiters and waitresses, higher earnings are primarily the result of receiving more in tips rather than higher hourly wages. Tips usually average between 10 and 20 percent of guests' checks, so waiters and waitresses working in busy, expensive restaurants earn the most.

Bartenders had median hourly earnings (not including tips) of $6.86 in 2000. The middle 50 percent earned between $6.10 and $8.44. The lowest 10 percent earned less than $5.59, and the highest 10 percent earned more than $11.14 an hour. Like waiters and waitresses, bartenders employed in public bars may receive more than half of their earnings as tips. Service bartenders often are paid higher hourly wages to offset their lower tip earnings.

Median hourly earnings (not including tips) of dining room and cafeteria attendants and bartender helpers were $6.53 in 2000. The middle 50 percent earned between $5.97 and $7.62. The lowest 10 percent earned less than $5.54, and the highest 10 percent earned more than $9.26 an hour. Most received over half of their earnings as wages; the rest of their income was a share of the proceeds from tip pools.

Median hourly earnings of hosts and hostesses were $6.95 in 2000. The middle 50 percent earned between $6.18 and $8.11. The lowest 10 percent earned less than $5.65, and the highest 10 percent earned more than $9.59 an hour. The majority of their earnings are received from wages. In some cases, wages were supplemented by a share of the proceeds from tip pools.

Median hourly earnings of counter attendants in cafeterias, food concessions, and coffee shops (not including tips) were $6.72 in 2000. The middle 50 percent earned between $6.07 and $8.05 an hour. The lowest 10 percent earned less than $5.59, and the highest 10 percent earned more than $9.92 and hour.

Median hourly earnings of combined food preparation and serving workers, including fast food, were $6.52 in 2000. The middle 50 percent earned between $5.92 and $7.52. The lowest 10 percent earned less than $5.51, and the highest 10 percent earned more than $8.64 an hour. Although some counter attendants receive part of their earnings as tips, fast-food workers usually do not.

Median hourly earnings of dishwashers were $6.69 in 2000. The middle 50 percent earned between $6.05 and $7.86. The lowest 10 percent earned less than $5.58, and the highest 10 percent earned more than $8.81 an hour. Generally these are part-time positions receiving very low wages due to the nature of the work and automation.

Median hourly earnings of nonrestaurant food servers were $7.07 in 2000.

In establishments covered by federal law, most workers beginning at the minimum wage earned $5.15 an hour in 2000. However, various minimum wage exceptions apply under specific circumstances to disabled workers, full-time students, youth under age 20 in their first 90 days of employment, tipped employees, and student-learners. Tipped employees are those who customarily and regularly receive more than $30 a month in tips. The employer may consider tips as part of wages, but the employer must pay at least $2.13 an hour in direct wages. Employers also are permitted to deduct from wages the cost, or fair value, of any meals or lodging provided. However, many employers provide free meals and furnish uniforms. Food and beverage service workers who work full time often receive typical benefits, while part-time workers usually do not.

In some large restaurants and hotels, food and beverage serving and related workers belong to unions—principally the Hotel Employees and Restaurant Employees International Union and the Service Employees International Union.

Related Occupations

Other workers whose jobs involve serving customers and helping them enjoy themselves include flight attendants, tour and travel guides, and gaming services workers.

Sources of Additional Information

Information about job opportunities may be obtained from local employers and local offices of the state employment service.

A guide to careers in restaurants, a list of 2- and 4-year colleges that have food service programs, and information on scholarships to those programs is available from:

- National Restaurant Association, 1200 17th St. NW., Washington, DC 20036-3097. Internet: http://www.restaurant.org

For general information on hospitality careers, contact:

- International Council on Hotel, Restaurant, and Institutional Education, 3205 Skipwith Rd., Richmond, VA 23294-4442. Internet: http://www.chrie.org

Food Processing Occupations

O*NET 51-3011.01, 51-3011.02, 51-3021.00, 51-3022.00, 51-3023.00, 51-3091.00, 51-3092.00, 51-3093.00

Significant Points

- Workers in meatpacking plants have among the highest incidences of injury and illness of all workers.

- Most employees in manual food processing jobs require little or no training prior to being hired.

- Job growth will be concentrated among lower skilled workers.

Nature of the Work

Food processing occupations include many different types of workers involved in processing raw food products into finished goods ready for sale by grocers or wholesalers, restaurants, or institutional food services.

These workers perform a variety of tasks and are responsible for producing many of the food products found in every household.

Butchers and meat, poultry, and fish cutters and trimmers are employed at different stages in the process by which animal carcasses are converted into manageable pieces of meat suitable for sale to wholesales or consumers. Meat, poultry, and fish cutters and trimmers commonly work in meatpacking or fish and poultry processing plants, while butchers and meatcutters usually are employed at the retail level. As a result of this distinction, the nature of these jobs varies significantly.

In meatpacking plants, *slaughterers and meatpackers* slaughter cattle, hogs, goats, and sheep and cut the carcasses into large wholesale cuts, such as rounds, loins, ribs, and chucks, to facilitate the handling, distribution, and marketing of meat. In some of these plants, slaughterers and meatpackers also further process these primal parts into cuts that are ready for retail use. These workers also produce hamburger meat and meat trimmings, which are used to prepare sausages, luncheon meats, and other fabricated meat products. Slaughterers and meatpackers usually work on assembly lines, with each individual responsible for only a few of the many cuts needed to process a carcass. Depending on the type of cut, they use knives, cleavers, meat saws, bandsaws, or other, often dangerous, equipment.

In grocery stores, wholesale establishments that supply meat to restaurants, and institutional food service facilities, *butchers and meatcutters* separate wholesale cuts of meat into retail cuts or individual size servings. They cut meat into steaks and chops, shape and tie roasts, and grind beef for sale as chopped meat. Boneless cuts are prepared using knives, slicers, or power cutters, while bandsaws are required to carve bone-in pieces. Butchers and meatcutters in retail food stores may also weigh, wrap, and label the cuts of meat, arrange them in refrigerated cases for display, and prepare special cuts of meat to fill unique orders.

Poultry cutters and trimmers slaughter and cut up chickens, turkeys, and other types of poultry. Although the poultry processing industry is becoming increasingly automated, many jobs such as trimming, packing, and deboning are still done manually. As in the meatpacking industry, most poultry cutters and trimmers perform routine cuts on poultry as it moves along production lines.

Unlike some of the occupations listed above, *fish cutters and trimmers*, also called *fish cleaners*, are likely to be employed in both manufacturing and retail establishments. These workers primarily cut, scale, and dress fish by removing the head, scales, and other inedible portions and cutting the fish into steaks or boneless fillets. In retail markets, they may also wait on customers and clean fish to order.

Meat, poultry, and fish cutters and trimmers also prepare ready-to-heat foods. This often entails filleting meat or fish or cutting it into bite-sized pieces, preparing and adding vegetables, or applying sauces or breading.

Bakers mix and bake ingredients in accordance with recipes to produce varying quantities of breads, pastries, and other baked goods for consumption. Bakers commonly are employed in grocery stores and specialty shops and produce small quantities of breads, pastries, and other baked goods for consumption on premises or for sale as specialty baked goods. In manufacturing, bakers produce goods in large quantities, using high-volume mixing machines, ovens, and other equipment. Goods produced in large quantities usually are for sale through establishments such as grocery stores.

Other food processing occupations include *food batchmakers,* who set up and operate equipment that mixes, blends, or cooks ingredients used in the manufacturing of food products, according to formulas or recipes; *food cooking machine operators and tenders,* who operate or tend cooking equipment, such as steam cooking vats, deep-fry cookers, pressure cookers, kettles, and boilers, to prepare food products, such as meats, sugar, cheese, and grain; and *food and tobacco roasting, baking, and drying machine operators,* who utilize equipment to reduce moisture content of food or tobacco products or to process food in preparation for canning. Some of the machines used include hearth ovens, kiln driers, roasters, char kilns, steam ovens, and vacuum drying equipment.

Working Conditions

Working conditions vary by type and size of establishment. In meatpacking plants and large retail food establishments, butchers and meat cutters work in large meatcutting rooms equipped with power machines and conveyors. In small retail markets, the butcher or fish cleaner may work in a space behind the meat counter. To prevent viral and bacterial infections, work areas must be kept clean and sanitary.

Butchers and meatcutters, poultry and fish cutters and trimmers, and slaughterer and meatpackers often work in cold, damp rooms, which are refrigerated to prevent meat from spoiling and are damp because meatcutting generates large amounts of blood, condensation, and fat. Cool damp floors increase the likelihood of slips and falls. In addition, the low temperature, combined with the need to stand for long periods and perform physical tasks, makes the work tiring. As a result, butchers and meat, poultry, and fish cutters are more susceptible to injury than are most other workers. In fact, meatpacking plants had the highest incidence of work-related injury and illness of any industry in 1999. More than 1 in 4 employees experienced a work-related injury or illness during that year.

Injuries include cuts, and even amputations, that occur when knives, cleavers, and power tools are used improperly. Also, repetitive slicing and lifting often lead to cumulative trauma injuries, such as carpal tunnel syndrome. To reduce the incidence of cumulative trauma disorders, some employers have reduced workloads, redesigned jobs and tools, and increased awareness of early warning signs. Nevertheless, workers in this occupation still face the serious threat of disabling injuries.

Most traditional bakers work in bakeries, cakeshops, hot breadshops, hotels, restaurants, cafeterias, and factories. They also may work in the bakery department of supermarkets and on cruise ships. Conditions for bakers may be hot and noisy. Stress is another potential factor in the bakery world, as bakers often work to strict deadlines. Bakers usually work in shifts, and may work early mornings, evenings, weekends, and holidays. While many bakers often work as part of a team, they also may work alone when baking particular items. They may supervise assistants and teach apprentices and trainees. Bakers also may be required to serve customers.

Other food processing workers such as food batchmakers, food and tobacco roasting, baking, and drying machine operators, and food cooking machine operators and tenders typically work in production areas that are specially designed for food preservation or processing. Food batchmakers in particular work in kitchen-type, assembly-line production facilities. Because this work involves food, work areas must be sanitary and governmental regulations must be met. The ovens, as well as the motors of other equipment, often make work areas very warm. There are some hazards, such as burns, created by the equipment that these

workers use. Food batchmakers, food and tobacco roasting, baking, and drying machine operators, and food cooking machine operators and tenders workers spend a great deal of time on their feet and generally work a regular 40-hour week that may include evening and night shifts.

Employment

Food processing workers held 760,000 jobs in 2000. Employment among the various types of food processing occupations was distributed as follows:

Bakers	160,000
Meat, poultry, and fish cutters and trimmers	148,000
Butchers and meatcutters	141,000
Slaughterers and meatpackers	122,000
Food batchmakers	66,000
Food cooking machine operators and tenders	37,000
Food and tobacco roasting, baking, and drying machine operators and tenders	18,000
All other food processing workers	69,000

About 33 percent of all food processing workers were employed in meatpacking or poultry and fish processing plants. Many others in this occupation were employed at the retail level in grocery stores, meat and fish markets, restaurants, or hotels. Highly skilled butchers and meatcutters, and slaughterers and meatpackers, are employed in almost every city and town in the nation, while lower skilled meat, poultry, and fish cutter and trimmer jobs are concentrated in communities with food processing plants. Bakers and food machine operators are more commonly employed in retail establishments.

Training, Other Qualifications, and Advancement

Training varies widely among food processing occupations. However, most manual food processing workers require little or no training prior to being hired.

Most butchers, poultry, and fish cutters and trimmers acquire their skills on the job through formal and informal training programs. The length of training varies significantly. Simple cutting operations requiring a few days to learn, while more complex tasks, like eviscerating, generally require about a month to learn. On the other hand, the training period for a highly skilled butcher at the retail level may be 1 or 2 years.

Generally, on-the-job trainees begin by doing less difficult jobs, such as simple cuts or removing bones. Under the guidance of experienced workers, trainees learn the proper use of tools and equipment and how to prepare various cuts of meat. After demonstrating skill with various meatcutting tools, they learn to divide carcasses into wholesale cuts and wholesale cuts into retail and individual portions. Trainees also may learn to roll and tie roasts, prepare sausage, and cure meat. Those employed in retail food establishments often are taught operations such as inventory control, meat buying, and recordkeeping. In addition, growing concern about the safety of meats has led employers to offer extensive training in food safety to employees.

Skills important to meat, poultry, and fish cutters and trimmers include manual dexterity, good depth perception, color discrimination, and good hand-eye coordination. Physical strength often is needed to lift and move heavy pieces of meat. Butchers and fish cleaners who wait on customers should have a pleasant personality, a neat appearance, and the ability to communicate clearly. In some states, a health certificate is required for employment.

Bakers often start off as apprentices or trainees. Apprentice bakers usually start in craft bakeries, while in store bakeries such as supermarkets often employ trainees. Bakers need to be skilled in baking, icing, cake decorating and making calculations. They also need to be able to follow instructions, organize others, have an eye for detail, and communicate well with others. Knowledge of bakery products and ingredients, as well as mechanical mixing and baking equipment, is important. Many apprentice bakers participate in correspondence study and may work towards a certificate in baking. Working as a baker's assistant or at other activities involving handling food also is a useful tool for training. The complexity of the skills required for baker certification often is underestimated. Creating and marketing bakery products requires knowledge of applied chemistry, ingredients and nutrition, government regulations, business concepts, and production processes, including the operation and maintenance of machinery. Modern food plants utilize high-speed, automated machinery that often is operated by computers.

Food machine operators and tenders usually are trained on the job. They learn to run the different types of equipment by watching and helping other workers. Training can last anywhere from 1 month to a year, depending on the complexity of the tasks and the number of products involved. A degree in the appropriate area—dairy processing for those working in diary product operations, for example—is helpful for advancement to a lead worker or supervisory role. Most food batchmakers participate in on-the-job training. The training period usually is moderate in length, ranging from about a month to a year. Some food batchmakers learn their trade through an approved apprenticeship program.

Food processing workers in retail or wholesale establishments may progress to supervisory jobs, such as department managers in supermarkets. A few of these workers may become buyers for wholesalers or supermarket chains. Some open their own markets or bakeries. In processing plants, workers may advance to supervisory positions or become team leaders.

Job Outlook

Overall employment of the food processing occupations is expected to grow more slowly than the average for all occupations through 2010. Job growth will be concentrated among lower skilled workers, as more meat cutting and processing shifts from retail stores to food processing plants. Nevertheless, job opportunities should be available at all levels of the occupation due to the need to replace experienced workers who transfer to other occupations or leave the labor force.

As the nation's population grows, the demand for meat, poultry, and seafood should continue to increase. Successful marketing by the poultry industry is likely to increase demand for rotisserie chicken and ready-to-heat products. Similarly, the development of lower fat and ready-to-heat products promises to stimulate the consumption of red meat. Although per capita consumption of fish and other seafood has been constant over the last decade, population growth is expected to push consumption to record levels in coming years.

Employment growth of lower skilled meat, poultry, and fish cutters—who work primarily in meatpacking, poultry, and fish processing plants—is expected to increase about as fast as the average for all occupations in coming years. Although the growing popularity of labor-intensive, ready-to-heat goods promises to spur demand for poultry workers, much of the production of poultry and fabricated poultry products is performed by machines. Meat and fish cutters also will be in demand, as the task of preparing ready-to-heat meat and fish goods slowly shifts from retail stores to processing plants. Also, advances in fish farming, or "aquaculture," should help meet the growing demand for fish and produce ample opportunities for fish cutters.

Employment of more highly skilled butchers and meatcutters, who work primarily in retail stores, is expected to gradually decline. New automation and the consolidation of the meatpacking and poultry processing industries are enabling employers to transfer employment from higher paid butchers to lower wage slaughterers and meatpackers in meatpacking plants. At present, most red meat arrives at grocery stores partially cut up, but a growing share of meat is being delivered prepackaged, with additional fat removed, to wholesalers and retailers. This trend is resulting in less work and, thus, fewer jobs for retail butchers.

While high-volume production equipment limits the demand for bakers in manufacturing, overall employment of bakers is expected to increase due to growing numbers of large wholesale bakers, in store and specialty shops, and traditional bakeries. In addition to those of cookie, muffin, and cinnamon roll bakeries, the numbers of specialty bread and bagel shops also have been growing, spurring demand for bread and pastry bakers.

Employment of food batchmakers, food and tobacco cooking and roasting machine operators and tenders, and all other food processing workers is expected to show little or no change or decline. Although more of this work is being done at the manufacturing level rather than at the retail level, increasingly automated cooking and roasting equipment appears to be leading to reductions in employment levels.

Earnings

Earnings vary by industry, skill, geographic region, and educational level. Median annual earnings of butchers and meatcutters were $24,120 in 2000. The middle 50 percent earned between $18,170 and $32,440. The highest paid 10 percent earned more than $40,240 annually, while the lowest 10 percent earned less than $14,340. Butchers and meatcutters employed at the retail level typically earn more than do those in manufacturing. Median annual earnings in the industries employing the largest numbers of butchers and meatcutters in 2000 were as follows:

Grocery stores	$25,680
Groceries and related products	22,090
Meat and fish markets	20,820
Meat products	17,980

Meat, poultry, and fish cutters and trimmers typically earn less than butchers and meatcutters. In 2000, median annual earnings for these lower skilled workers were $16,760. The middle 50 percent earned between $14,920 and $19,900. The highest 10 percent earned more than $23,490, while the lowest 10 percent earned less than $13,310. Median annual earnings in the industries employing the largest numbers of meat, poultry, and fish cutters and trimmers in 2000 are shown in the following table:

Grocery stores	$18,540
Groceries and related products	18,060
Meat products	16,750
Miscellaneous food and kindred products	14,370

Median annual earnings of bakers were $19,710 in 2000. The middle 50 percent earned between $15,630 and $25,570. The highest 10 percent earned more than $31,720, and the lowest 10 percent earned less than $13,170. Median annual earnings in the industries employing the largest numbers of bakers in 2000 are shown in the following table:

Bakery products	$23,010
Department stores	21,320
Grocery stores	19,220
Eating and drinking places	18,710
Retail bakeries	18,060

Median annual earnings of food batchmakers were $20,990 in 2000. The middle 50 percent earned between $15,980 and $27,600. The highest 10 percent earned more than $33,660, and the lowest 10 percent earned less than $13,250. Median annual earnings in the industries employing the largest numbers of food batchmakers in 2000 are shown in the following table:

Bakery products	$24,660
Preserved fruits and vegetables	21,070
Sugar and confectionery products	20,510
Meat products	20,100
Miscellaneous food and kindred products	19,170

In 2000, median annual earnings for slaughterers and meatpackers were $19,410. The middle 50 percent earned between $16,620 and $21,790. The highest 10 percent earned more than $24,690, and the lowest 10 percent earned less than $14,690. Median annual earnings in meat products, the industry employing the largest number of slaughters and meatpackers, were $19,460 in 2000.

Median annual earnings for food cooking machine operators and tenders were $20,630 in 2000. The middle 50 percent earned between $16,000 and $26,750. The highest 10 percent earned more than $32,780 and the lowest 10 percent earned less than $13,420. Median annual earnings in preserved fruits and vegetables, the industry employing the largest number of food cooking machine operators and tenders, were $21,700 in 2000.

In 2000, median annual earnings for food and tobacco roasting, baking, and drying machine operators and tenders were $22,690, and for all other food processing workers, $18,170.

Food processing workers generally received typical benefits, including pension plans for union members or those employed by grocery stores. However, poultry workers rarely earned substantial benefits. In 2000, more than a third of all butchers and meatcutters were union members or covered by a union contract. Fifteen percent of all bakers and 19 percent of all food batchmakers also were union members or were covered by a union contract. Many food processing workers are members of the United Food and Commercial Workers International Union.

Related Occupations

Food processing workers must be skilled at both hand work and machinework and must have some knowledge of processes and techniques involved in handling and preparing food. Other occupations that require similar skills and knowledge include chefs, cooks, and food preparation workers.

Sources of Additional Information

Information about work opportunities can be obtained from local employers or local offices of the state employment service. For information on training and other aspects of this trade, contact:

● United Food and Commercial Workers International Union, 1775 K St. NW., Washington, DC 20006

Food Service Managers

O*NET 11-9051.00

Significant Points

● Although many experienced food and beverage preparation and service workers are promoted to fill managerial jobs, applicants with a bachelor's or associate degree in restaurant and institutional food service management should have the best job opportunities.

● Most new jobs will arise in eating and drinking places as the number of establishments increases along with the population, personal incomes, and leisure time.

● As more restaurant managers are employed by larger companies to run establishments, job opportunities should be better for salaried managers than for self-employed managers.

Nature of the Work

The daily responsibilities of many food service managers can often be as complicated as some of the meals prepared by a fine chef. In addition to the traditional duties of selecting and pricing menu items, using food and other supplies efficiently, and achieving quality in food preparation and service, managers now are responsible for a growing number of administrative and human resource tasks. For example, managers must carefully find and evaluate new ways of recruiting employees in a tight job market. Once hired, managers also must find creative ways to retain experienced workers.

In most restaurants and institutional food service facilities, the manager is assisted in these duties by one or more assistant managers, depending on the size and operating hours of the establishment. In most large establishments, as well as in many smaller ones, the management team consists of a general manager, one or more assistant managers, and an executive chef. The executive chef is responsible for the operation of the kitchen, while the assistant managers oversee service in the dining room and other areas. In smaller restaurants, the executive chef also may be the general manager, and sometimes an owner. In fast-food restaurants and other food service facilities open for long hours—often 7 days a week—several assistant managers, each of whom supervises a shift of workers, aid the manager.

One of the most important tasks of food service managers is selecting successful menu items. This task varies by establishment because, although many restaurants rarely change their menu, others make frequent alterations. Managers or executive chefs select menu items, taking into account the likely number of customers and the past popularity of dishes. Other issues taken into consideration when planning a menu include unserved food left over from prior meals that should not be wasted, the need for variety, and the seasonal availability of foods. Managers or executive chefs analyze the recipes of the dishes to determine food, labor, and overhead costs, and to assign prices to various dishes. Menus must be developed far enough in advance that supplies can be ordered and received in time.

On a daily basis, managers estimate food consumption, place orders with suppliers, and schedule the delivery of fresh food and beverages. They receive and check the content of deliveries, evaluating the quality of meats, poultry, fish, fruits, vegetables, and baked goods. To ensure good service, managers meet with sales representatives from restaurant suppliers to place orders replenishing stocks of tableware, linens, paper, cleaning supplies, cooking utensils, and furniture and fixtures. They also arrange for equipment maintenance and repairs, and coordinate a variety of services such as waste removal and pest control.

The quality of food dishes and services in restaurants depends largely on a manager's ability to interview, hire, and, when necessary, fire employees. This is especially true in tight labor markets, when many managers report difficulty in hiring experienced food and beverage preparation and service workers. Managers may attend career fairs or arrange for newspaper advertising to expand their pool of applicants. Once a new employee is hired, managers explain the establishment's policies and practices and oversee any necessary training. Managers also schedule the work hours of employees, making sure there are enough workers present to cover peak dining periods. If employees are unable to work, managers may have to fill in for them. Some managers regularly help with cooking, clearing of tables, or other tasks.

Another fundamental responsibility of food service managers is supervising the kitchen and dining room. For example, managers often oversee all food preparation and cooking, examining the quality and portion sizes to ensure that dishes are prepared and garnished correctly and in a timely manner. They also investigate and resolve customers' complaints about food quality or service. To maintain company and government sanitation standards, they direct the cleaning of the kitchen and dining areas and washing of tableware, kitchen utensils, and equipment. Managers also monitor the actions of their employees and patrons on a continual basis to ensure that health and safety standards and local liquor regulations are obeyed.

In addition to their regular duties, food service managers have a variety of administrative responsibilities. Managers in most smaller establishments, such as fast-food restaurants, must keep records of the hours and wages of employees, prepare the payroll, and fill out paperwork in compliance with licensing laws and reporting requirements of tax, wage and hour, unemployment compensation, and Social Security laws. (In a larger establishment, much of this work may be delegated to a bookkeeper.) Managers also maintain records of supply and equipment purchases and ensure that accounts with suppliers are paid on a regular basis. In addition, managers in full-service restaurants record the number, type, and cost of items sold to evaluate and discontinue dishes that may be unpopular or less profitable.

Many managers are able to ease the burden of recordkeeping and paperwork through the use of computers. Point-of-service (POS) systems are used in many restaurants to increase employee productivity and allow managers to track the sales of specific menu items. Using a POS system, a server keys in the customer's order, and the computer immediately sends the order to the kitchen so that preparation can begin. The same

system totals checks, acts as a cash register and credit card authorizer, and tracks daily sales. To minimize food costs and spoilage, many managers use inventory-tracking software to compare the record of daily sales from the POS with a record of present inventory. In some establishments, when supplies needed for the preparation of popular menu items run low, additional inventory can be ordered directly from the supplier using the computer. Computers also allow restaurant and food service managers to more efficiently keep track of employee schedules and pay.

Technology also impacts the job of food service managers in many other ways, helping to enhance efficiency and productivity. According to the 2000 National Restaurant Association's Tableservice Operator Survey, for example, Internet uses by food service managers included tracking industry news, finding recipes, conducting market research, purchasing supplies or equipment, recruiting employees, and training staff. Internet access also makes service to customers more efficient. Many restaurants maintain Web sites that include menus and online promotions and provide information about the restaurant's location and the option to make a reservation.

Managers are among the first to arrive in the morning and the last to leave. At the conclusion of each day, or sometimes each shift, managers tally the cash and charge receipts received and balance them against the record of sales. In most cases, they are responsible for depositing the day's receipts at the bank or securing them in a safe place. Finally, managers are responsible for locking up, checking that ovens, grills, and lights are off, and switching on alarm systems.

Working Conditions

Evenings and weekends are popular dining periods, making night and weekend work common among managers. Many managers of institutional food service facilities work more conventional hours because factory and office cafeterias usually are open only on weekdays for breakfast and lunch. However, hours for many managers are unpredictable, as managers may have to fill in for absent workers on short notice. It is common for food service managers to work 50 or more hours per week, 7 days a week, and 12 to 15 hours per day.

Managers often experience the pressure of simultaneously coordinating a wide range of activities. When problems occur, it is the responsibility of the manager to resolve them with minimal disruption to customers. The job can be hectic during peak dining hours, and dealing with irate customers or uncooperative employees can be stressful.

Employment

Food service managers held about 465,000 jobs in 2000. Most managers are salaried, but about 1 in 3 was self-employed. Most work in restaurants or for contract institutional food service companies, while a smaller number are employed by educational institutions, hospitals, nursing and personal care facilities, and civic, social, and fraternal organizations. Jobs are located throughout the country, with large cities and tourist areas providing more opportunities for full-service dining positions.

Training, Other Qualifications, and Advancement

Most food service management companies and national or regional restaurant chains recruit management trainees from 2- and 4-year college hospitality management programs. Food service and restaurant chains prefer to hire people with degrees in restaurant and institutional food service management, but they often hire graduates with degrees in other fields who have demonstrated interest and aptitude. Some restaurant and food service manager positions, particularly self-service and fast food, are filled by promoting experienced food and beverage preparation and service workers. Waiters, waitresses, chefs, and fast-food workers demonstrating potential for handling increased responsibility sometimes advance to assistant manager or management trainee jobs. Executive chefs need extensive experience working as chefs, and general managers need experience as assistant managers.

A bachelor's degree in restaurant and food service management provides a particularly strong preparation for a career in this occupation. A number of colleges and universities offer 4-year programs in restaurant and hotel management or institutional foodservice management. For those not interested in pursuing a 4-year degree, community and junior colleges, technical institutes, and other institutions offer programs in these fields leading to an associate degree or other formal certification. Both 2- and 4-year programs provide instruction in subjects such as nutrition and food planning and preparation, as well as accounting, business law and management, and computer science. Some programs combine classroom and laboratory study with internships that provide on-the-job experience. In addition, many educational institutions offer culinary programs that provide food preparation training. This training can lead to a career as a cook or chef and provide a foundation for advancement to an executive chef position.

Most restaurant chains and food service management companies have rigorous training programs for management positions. Through a combination of classroom and on-the-job training, trainees receive instruction and gain work experience in all aspects of the operations of a restaurant or institutional food service facility. Topics include food preparation, nutrition, sanitation, security, company policies and procedures, personnel management, recordkeeping, and preparation of reports. Training on use of the restaurant's computer system is increasingly important as well. Usually after 6 months or a year, trainees receive their first permanent assignment as an assistant manager.

Most employers emphasize personal qualities when hiring managers. For example, self-discipline, initiative, and leadership ability are essential. Managers must be able to solve problems and concentrate on details. They need good communication skills to deal with customers and suppliers, as well as to motivate and direct their staff. A neat and clean appearance is a must because they often are in close personal contact with the public. Food service management can be demanding, so good health and stamina also are important.

The certified Foodservice Management Professional (FMP) designation is a measure of professional achievement for food service managers. Although not a requirement for employment or advancement in the occupation, voluntary certification provides recognition of professional competence, particularly for managers who acquired their skills largely on the job. The Educational Foundation of the National Restaurant Association awards the FMP designation to managers who achieve a qualifying score on a written examination, complete a series of courses that cover a range of food service management topics, and meet standards of work experience in the field.

Willingness to relocate often is essential for advancement to positions with greater responsibility. Managers typically advance to larger establishments or regional management positions within restaurant chains.

Some eventually open their own eating and drinking establishments. Others transfer to hotel management positions because their restaurant management experience provides a good background for food and beverage manager jobs in hotels and resorts.

Job Outlook

Employment of food service managers is expected to increase about as fast as the average for all occupations through 2010. In addition to employment growth, the need to replace managers who transfer to other occupations or stop working will create many job openings. Applicants with a bachelor's or associate degree in restaurant and institutional food service management should have the best job opportunities.

Projected employment growth varies by industry. Most new jobs will arise in eating and drinking places as the number of establishments increases along with the population, personal incomes, and leisure time. In addition, manager jobs will increase in eating and drinking places as schools, hospitals, and other businesses contract out more of their food services to institutional food service companies within the eating and drinking industry. Food service manager jobs still are expected to increase in many of the latter industries, but growth will be slowed as contracting out becomes more common. Growth in the elderly population should result in more food service manager jobs in nursing homes and other healthcare institutions, and in residential-care and assisted-living facilities.

Job opportunities should be better for salaried managers than for self-employed managers. New restaurants are increasingly affiliated with national chains rather than being independently owned and operated. As this trend continues, fewer owners will manage restaurants themselves, and more restaurant managers will be employed by larger companies to run establishments.

Earnings

Median annual earnings of food service managers were $31,720 in 2000. The middle 50 percent earned between $24,500 and $41,000. The lowest 10 percent earned less than $19,200, and the highest 10 percent earned more than $53,090. Median annual earnings in the industries employing the largest numbers of food service managers in 2000 follow.

Miscellaneous amusement and recreation services	$37,000
Hotels and motels	36,460
Nursing and personal care facilities	31,400
Eating and drinking places	31,380
Elementary and secondary schools	28,310

In addition to typical benefits, most salaried restaurant and food service managers receive free meals and the opportunity for additional training, depending on their length of service.

Related Occupations

Food service managers direct the activities of businesses, which provide a service to customers. Other managers and supervisors in service-oriented businesses include lodging managers, medical and health services managers, sales worker supervisors, financial managers, social and community service managers, and first line supervisors/managers of food preparation and serving workers.

Sources of Additional Information

Information about a career as a food service manager, 2- and 4-year college programs in restaurant and food service management, and certification as a Foodservice Management Professional is available from:

- National Restaurant Association Educational Foundation, Suite 1400, 250 South Wacker Dr., Chicago, IL 60606

General information on hospitality careers may be obtained from:

- The International Council on Hotel, Restaurant, and Institutional Education, 3205 Skipwith Rd., Richmond, VA 23294. Internet: http://www.chrie.org

Additional information about job opportunities in food service management may be obtained from local employers and from local offices of the state employment service.

Forest, Conservation, and Logging Workers

O*NET 45-4011.00, 45-4021.00, 45-4022.01, 45-4023.00

Significant Points

- Workers spend all their time outdoors, sometimes in poor weather and often in isolated areas.

- Most jobs are physically demanding and can be hazardous.

- A small decline is expected in overall employment.

Nature of the Work

The nation's forests are a rich natural resource, providing beauty and tranquillity, varied recreational areas, and wood for commercial use. Managing forests and woodlands requires many different kinds of workers. Forest and conservation workers help develop, maintain, and protect these forests by growing and planting new tree seedlings, fighting insects and diseases that attack trees, and helping to control soil erosion. Timber cutting and logging workers harvest thousands of acres of forests each year for the timber that provides the raw material for countless consumer and industrial products.

Forest and conservation workers perform a variety of tasks to reforest and conserve timberlands and maintain forest facilities, such as roads and campsites. Some forest workers, called tree planters, use digging and planting tools called "dibble bars" and "hoedads" to plant tree seedlings to reforest timberland areas. Forest workers also remove diseased or undesirable trees with a powersaw or handsaw and spray trees with insecticides to kill insects and to protect against disease and herbicides to reduce competing vegetation. Forest workers in private industry usually work for professional foresters and paint boundary lines, assist with prescribed burning, and aid in tree marking and measuring by keeping a tally of the trees examined and counted. Those who work for state and local governments or under contract to the federal government also clear away brush and debris from jurisdictional camp trails, roadsides, and camping areas. Some clean kitchens and restrooms at recreational facilities and campgrounds.

Other forest and conservation workers work in forest nurseries, sorting out tree seedlings and discarding those that do not meet prescribed standards of root formation, stem development, and foliage condition.

Some forest workers are employed on tree farms, where they plant, cultivate, and harvest many different kinds of trees. Duties vary depending on the type of tree farm. Those who work on specialty farms, such as those growing Christmas or ornamental trees for nurseries, are responsible for shearing tree tops and limbs to control growth, increase limb density, and improve tree shape. In addition, duties include planting, spraying to control surrounding weed growth and insects, and harvesting.

Other forest workers gather, by hand or using hand tools, products from the woodlands such as decorative greens, tree cones and barks, moss, and other wild plant life. Still others tap trees for sap to make syrup or to produce chemicals.

The timber cutting and logging process is carried out by a variety of workers who make up a logging crew. *Fallers* cut down trees with hand-held power chain saws or occasionally axes. Usually using gas-powered chain saws, *buckers* trim off the tops and branches and buck (cut) the resulting logs into specified lengths.

Choke setters fasten chokers (steel cables or chains) around logs to be skidded (dragged) by tractors or forwarded by the cable yarding system to the landing or deck area where logs are separated by species and product type, such as pulpwood, sawlogs, or veneer logs, and loaded onto trucks. *Rigging slingers* and *chasers* set up and dismantle the cables and guy wires of the cable yarding system. *Log sorters*, *markers*, *movers*, and *debarkers* sort, mark, and move logs, based on species, size, and ownership, and tend machines that debarks logs.

Logging equipment operators on a logging crew perform a number of duties. They drive crawler or wheeled tractors called skidders, or forwarders, which drag or transport logs from the felling site in the woods to the log landing area for loading. They operate grapple loaders, which lift and load logs into trucks, and tree fellers or shears, which cut the trees. They use tree harvesters to shear the tops off of trees, cut and limb the trees, and then cut the logs into desired lengths. Some logging equipment operators use tracked or wheeled equipment similar to a forklift to unload logs and pulpwood off trucks or gondola railroad cars, usually in a sawmill or pulpmill woodyard.

Log graders and *scalers* inspect logs for defects, measure logs to determine their volume, and estimate the marketable content or value of logs or pulpwood. These workers often use hand-held data collection terminals to enter data about individual trees, which can later be downloaded or sent, via modem, from the scaling area to a central computer.

Other timber cutting and logging workers have a variety of responsibilities. Some workers hike through forests to assess logging conditions. Laborers clear areas of brush and other growth to prepare for logging activities or to promote growth of desirable species of trees.

The timber cutting and logging industry is characterized by a large number of small crews of four to eight workers. A typical crew might consist of one or two fallers or one feller machine operator, one bucker, two logging tractor operators to drag cut trees to the loading deck, and one equipment operator to load the logs onto trucks. Most crews work for self-employed logging contractors who possess substantial logging experience, the capital to purchase equipment, and skills needed to run a small business successfully. Most contractors work alongside their crews as working supervisors and often operate one of the logging machines, such as the grapple loader or the tree harvester. Many manage more than one crew and function as owner-supervisors.

Although timber cutting and logging equipment has greatly improved and operations are becoming increasingly mechanized, many logging jobs are still labor intensive. These jobs require various levels of skill, ranging from the unskilled task of manually moving logs, branches, and equipment to skillfully using chain saws, peavies (hooked poles), and log jacks to cut and position logs for further processing or loading. To keep costs down, some timber cutting and logging workers maintain and repair the equipment they use. A skillful, experienced logger is expected to handle a variety of logging operations.

Working Conditions

Forestry and logging jobs are physically demanding. These workers spend all their time outdoors, sometimes in poor weather and often in isolated areas. The increased use of enclosed machines has decreased some of the discomforts caused by inclement weather. A few lumber camps in Alaska house workers in bunkhouses or company towns. Workers in sparsely populated western states commute long distances between their homes and logging sites. In the more densely populated eastern and southern states, commuting distances are much shorter.

Most logging occupations involve lifting, climbing, and other strenuous activities, although machinery has eliminated some of the heavy labor. Loggers work under unusually hazardous conditions. Falling trees and branches are a constant menace, as are the dangers associated with log handling operations and use of sawing equipment, especially delimbing devices. Special care must be taken during strong winds, which can even halt operations. Slippery or muddy ground and hidden roots or vines not only reduce efficiency but also present a constant danger, especially in the presence of moving vehicles and machinery. Poisonous plants, brambles, insects, snakes, and heat and humidity are minor annoyances. If safety precautions are not taken, the high noise level of sawing and skidding operations over long periods of time may impair hearing. Experience, exercise of caution, and use of proper safety measures and equipment—such as hardhats, eye and ear protection, and safety clothing and boots—are extremely important to avoid injury.

The jobs of forest and conservation workers generally are much less hazardous. It may be necessary for some forestry aides or forest workers to walk long distances through densely wooded areas to do their work.

Employment

Forest, conservation, and logging workers held about 90,000 jobs in 2000, distributed among the following occupations:

Logging equipment operators	47,000
Forest and conservation workers	21,000
Fallers	13,000
Log graders and scalers	8,000

Additional employment of choke setters, buckers, rigging slingers, and other logging workers is not included in the employment above.

Most wage and salary fallers and logging equipment operators are employed in the logging camps and logging contractors industry, although some work in sawmills and planing mills. Employment of log graders and scalers is largely concentrated in sawmills and planing mills. Although logging operations are found in most states, the southeast employs the most, about 37 percent of all logging workers, followed by the northwest, which employs 30 percent.

About 2 in 5 wage and salary forest and conservation workers are employed by companies that operate timber tracts, tree farms, or forest nurseries, or for establishments that supply forestry services. Some of those employed in forestry services work on a contract basis for the U.S. Department of Agriculture's Forest Service. Most of the remainder of forest and conservation workers are employed by state or local governments; about 4,300 work for state governments, and 1,900 work for local governments. A small number work in sawmills and planing mills. Although forest and conservation workers are located in every state, employment is concentrated in the west and southeast where many national and private forests and parks are located.

Self-employed forestry, conservation, and logging workers account for about 1 of every 5 logging workers—a much higher proportion of self-employment than for most occupations.

Seasonal demand for forest, conservation, and logging workers varies by region. For example, in the northern states, winter work is common because the frozen ground facilitates logging. In the southeast, logging and related activities occur year round.

Training, Other Qualifications, and Advancement

Most forest, conservation, and logging workers develop skills through on-the-job training with instruction coming primarily from experienced workers. Logging workers must familiarize themselves with the character and potential dangers of the forest environment and the operation of logging machinery and equipment. However, large logging companies and trade associations, such as the Northeastern Loggers Association and the Forest Resources Association, Inc., offer special programs, particularly for workers training to operate large, expensive machinery and equipment. Often, a representative of the manufacturer or company spends several days in the field explaining and overseeing the operation of newly purchased machinery. Safety training is a vital part of instruction for all logging workers.

Many state forestry or logging associations provide training sessions for fallers, whose job duties require more skill and experience than other positions on the logging team. Sessions may take place in the field, where trainees, under the supervision of an experienced logger, have the opportunity to practice various felling techniques. Fallers learn how to manually cut down extremely large or expensive trees safely and with minimal damage to the felled or surrounding trees.

Training programs for loggers are becoming common in many states, in response to a collaborative effort by the American Forest and Paper Association and others in the forestry industry. Such programs are designed to encourage the health and productivity of the nation's forests through the Sustainable Forest Initiative (SFI) program. Logger training programs vary by state, but generally include some type of classroom or field training in a number of areas—best management practices, safety, endangered species, reforestation, and business management. Some programs lead to logger certification.

Experience in other occupations can expedite entry into some logging occupations. For example, equipment operators, such as truck drivers and bulldozer and crane operators, can assume skidding and yarding functions. Some loggers have worked in sawmills or on family farms with extensive wooded areas. Some logging contractors were formerly crew members of family-owned businesses operated over several generations.

Generally, little formal education is required for most forest, conservation, and logging occupations. Many secondary schools, including vocational and technical schools, and some community colleges offer courses or a 2-year degree in general forestry, wildlife, conservation, and forest harvesting, which could be helpful in obtaining a job. A curriculum that includes field trips to observe or participate in forestry or logging activities provides a particularly good background. There are no educational requirements for forest worker jobs. Many of these workers are high school or college students who are hired on a part-time or seasonal basis to perform short-term, labor-intensive tasks, such as planting tree seedlings.

Forest, conservation, and logging workers must be in good health and able to work outdoors every day. They also must be able to work as part of a team. Many logging occupations require physical strength and stamina. Maturity and good judgment are important in making quick, intelligent decisions in dealing with hazards as they arise. Mechanical aptitude and coordination are necessary qualities for operators of machinery and equipment, who often are responsible for repair and maintenance as well. Initiative and managerial and business skills are necessary for success as a self-employed logging contractor.

Experience working at a nursery or as a laborer can be useful in obtaining a job as a forest or conservation worker. Logging workers generally advance from occupations involving primarily manual labor to those involving the operation of expensive, sometimes complicated, machinery and other equipment. Inexperienced entrants usually begin as laborers, who carry tools and equipment, clear brush, and load and unload logs and brush. For some, familiarization with logging operations may lead to jobs such as log handling equipment operator. Further experience may lead to jobs involving the operation of more complicated machinery and yarding towers to transport, load, and unload logs. Those who have the motor skills required for the efficient use of power saws and other equipment may become fallers and buckers.

Job Outlook

Overall employment of forest, conservation, and logging workers is expected to decline slightly through the year 2010. Most job openings will result from replacement needs. Many logging workers are older and will retire, or transfer to other jobs that are less physically demanding and dangerous. In addition, some forestry workers are young workers who are not committed to the occupation on a long-term basis. Some take jobs to earn money for school; others only work in this occupation until they find a better paying job.

Slower-than-average employment growth is expected for forest and conservation workers. Environmental concerns may spur limited demand for these workers, especially at the state and local government levels. If more land is set aside to protect natural resources or wildlife habitats, more forest and conservation workers will be needed to maintain these lands.

Despite steady demand for lumber and other wood products, employment of timber cutting and logging occupations is expected to decline.

Forest conservation efforts may restrict the volume of public timber available for harvesting, particularly in federal forests in the west and northwest, dampening demand for timber cutting and logging workers. The best job opportunities will be with privately owned forests and tree farms, which are not subject to the same restrictions in timber harvesting as forests on federal land. Domestic timber producers also face increasing competition from foreign producers who can harvest the same amount of timber at lower cost. As competition increases, the logging industry is expected to continue to consolidate in order to reduce costs, eliminating some jobs.

Increased mechanization of logging operations and improvements in logging equipment will also continue to depress demand for many timber cutting and logging workers. Employment of fallers, buckers, choke setters, and other workers—whose jobs are labor intensive—should decline, as safer, laborsaving machinery and other equipment are increasingly used. Employment of machinery and equipment operators, such as logging tractor and log handling equipment operators, should be less adversely affected.

Weather can force curtailment of logging operations during the muddy spring season and cold winter months, depending on the geographic region. Changes in the level of construction, particularly residential construction, also affect logging activities in the short term. In addition, logging operations must be relocated when timber harvesting in a particular area has been completed. During prolonged periods of inactivity, some workers may stay on the job to maintain or repair logging machinery and equipment; others are forced to find jobs in other occupations or be without work.

Earnings

Earnings vary depending on the particular forestry or logging occupation and experience, ranging from the minimum wage in some beginning forestry and conservation positions to about $27.00 an hour for some experienced fallers. Median hourly earnings in 2000 for forest, conservation, and logging occupations were as follows:

Log graders and scalers	$13.07
Fallers	12.33
Logging equipment operators	12.07
Forest and conservation workers	8.97

Earnings of logging workers vary by size of establishment and by geographic area. Workers in the largest establishments earn more than those in the smallest establishments earn. Workers in Alaska and the northwest earn more than those in the south, where the cost of living is generally lower.

Forest and conservation workers who work for state and local governments and large private firms generally enjoy more generous benefits than workers in smaller firms do. Small logging contractors generally offer timber cutting and logging workers few benefits. However, some employers offer full-time workers basic benefits, such as medical coverage, and provide safety apparel and equipment.

Related Occupations

Other occupations concerned with the care of trees and their environment include conservation scientists and foresters, forest and conservation technicians, and grounds maintenance workers. Logging equipment operators have skills similar to material moving equipment operators, such as industrial truck and tractor operators and crane and tower operators.

Sources of Additional Information

For information about timber cutting and logging careers and secondary and postsecondary programs offering training for logging occupations, contact:

- Northeastern Loggers Association, P.O. Box 69, Old Forge, NY 13420. Forest Resources Association, Inc., 600 Jefferson Plaza, Suite 350, Rockville, MD 20852. Internet: http://www.forestresources.org

For information on the Sustainable Forestry Initiative (SFI) training programs, contact:

- American Forest and Paper Association, 1111 19th St. NW., Suite 800, Washington, DC 20036. Internet: http://www.afandpa.org

Schools of forestry at states' land-grant colleges or universities also should be able to provide useful information.

A list of state forestry associations and other forestry-related state associations is available at most public libraries.

Funeral Directors

O*NET 11-9061.00, 39-4011.00

Significant Points

- Funeral directors must be licensed by their state.

- Job opportunities should be good, but mortuary science graduates may have to relocate to find jobs as funeral directors.

- Job outlook should be best for those who also embalm.

Nature of the Work

Funeral practices and rites vary greatly among various cultures and religions. Among the many diverse groups in the United States, funeral practices usually share some common elements: removal of the deceased to a mortuary, preparation of the remains, performance of a ceremony that honors the deceased and addresses the spiritual needs of the family, and the burial or destruction of the remains. Funeral directors arrange and direct these tasks for grieving families.

Funeral directors also are called morticians or undertakers. This career may not appeal to everyone, but those who work as funeral directors take great pride in their ability to provide efficient and appropriate services. They also comfort the family and friends of the deceased.

Funeral directors arrange the details and handle the logistics of funerals. They interview the family to learn what they desire with regard to the nature of the funeral, the clergy members or other persons who will officiate, and the final disposition of the remains. Sometimes the deceased leaves detailed instructions for their own funerals. Together with the family, funeral directors establish the location, dates, and times of

wakes, memorial services, and burials. They arrange for a hearse to carry the body to the funeral home or mortuary.

Funeral directors also prepare obituary notices and have them placed in newspapers, arrange for pallbearers and clergy, schedule the opening and closing of a grave with the cemetery, decorate and prepare the sites of all services, and provide transportation for the remains, mourners, and flowers between sites. They also direct preparation and shipment of remains for out-of-state burial.

Most funeral directors also are trained, licensed, and practicing embalmers. Embalming is a sanitary, cosmetic, and preservative process through which the body is prepared for interment. If more than 24 hours elapses between death and interment, state laws usually require that the remains be refrigerated or embalmed.

The embalmer washes the body with germicidal soap and replaces the blood with embalming fluid to preserve the body. Embalmers may reshape and reconstruct disfigured or maimed bodies using materials, such as clay, cotton, plaster of Paris, and wax. They also may apply cosmetics to provide a natural appearance, and then dress the body and place it in a casket. Embalmers maintain records such as embalming reports, and itemized lists of clothing or valuables delivered with the body. In large funeral homes, an embalming staff of two or more embalmers, plus several apprentices, may be employed.

Funeral services may take place in a home, house of worship, funeral home or at the gravesite or crematory. Services may be nonreligious, but often they reflect the religion of the family, so funeral directors must be familiar with the funeral and burial customs of many faiths, ethnic groups, and fraternal organizations. For example, members of some religions seldom have the bodies of the deceased embalmed or cremated.

Burial in a casket is the most common method of disposing of remains in this country, although entombment also occurs. Cremation, which is the burning of the body in a special furnace, is increasingly selected because it can be more convenient and less costly. Cremations are appealing because the remains can be easily shipped, kept at home, buried, or scattered. Memorial services can be held anywhere, and at any time, sometimes months later when all relatives and friends can get together. Even when the remains are cremated, many people still want a funeral service.

A funeral service followed by cremation need not be any different from a funeral service followed by a burial. Usually cremated remains are placed in some type of permanent receptacle, or urn, before being committed to a final resting place. The urn may be buried, placed in an indoor or outdoor mausoleum or columbarium, or interred in a special urn garden that many cemeteries provide for cremated remains.

Funeral directors handle the paperwork involved with the person's death, such as submitting papers to state authorities so that a formal certificate of death may be issued and copies distributed to the heirs. They may help family members apply for veterans' burial benefits, and notify the Social Security Administration of the death. Also, funeral directors may apply for the transfer of any pensions, insurance policies, or annuities on behalf of survivors.

Funeral directors also prearrange funerals. Increasingly, they arrange funerals in advance of need to provide peace of mind by ensuring that the client's wishes will be taken care of in a way that is satisfying to the person and to those who will survive.

Most funeral homes are small, family-run businesses, and the funeral directors either are owner-operators or employees of the operation. Funeral directors, therefore, are responsible for the success and the profitability of their businesses. Directors keep records of expenses, purchases, and services rendered; prepare and send invoices for services; prepare and submit reports for unemployment insurance; prepare federal, state, and local tax forms; and prepare itemized bills for customers. Funeral directors increasingly are using computers for billing, bookkeeping and marketing. Some are beginning to use the Internet to communicate with clients who are preplanning their funerals, or to assist clients by developing electronic obituaries and guest books. Directors strive to foster a cooperative spirit and friendly attitude among employees and a compassionate demeanor towards the families. A growing number of funeral directors also are involved in helping individuals adapt to changes in their lives following a death through postdeath support group activities.

Most funeral homes have a chapel, one or more viewing rooms, a casket-selection room, and a preparation room. An increasing number also have a crematory on the premises. Equipment may include a hearse, a flower car, limousines, and sometimes an ambulance. They usually stock a selection of caskets and urns for families to purchase or rent.

Working Conditions

Funeral directors often work long, irregular hours, and the occupation can be considered a very high-stress job. Many work on an on-call basis, because they may be needed to remove remains in the middle of the night. Shift work sometimes is necessary because funeral home hours include evenings and weekends. In smaller funeral homes, working hours vary, but in larger homes employees usually work 8 hours a day, 5 or 6 days a week.

Funeral directors occasionally come into contact with the remains of persons who had contagious diseases, but the possibility of infection is remote if strict health regulations are followed.

To show proper respect and consideration for the families and the dead, funeral directors must dress appropriately. The profession usually requires short, neat haircuts and trim beards, if any, for men. Suits, ties, and dresses are customary for a conservative look.

Employment

Funeral directors held about 32,000 jobs in 2000. Almost 1 in 5 was self-employed. Nearly all worked in the funeral service and crematory industry. Embalmers held about 7,200 jobs in 2000. Most funeral directors also are trained, licensed, and practicing embalmers.

Training, Other Qualifications, and Advancement

Funeral directors must be licensed in all but one state, Colorado. Licensing laws vary from state to state, but most require applicants to be 21 years old, have 2 years of formal education that includes studies in mortuary science, serve a 1-year apprenticeship, and pass a qualifying examination. After becoming licensed, new funeral directors may join the staff of a funeral home. Embalmers must be licensed in all states, and some states issue a single license for both funeral directors and embalmers. In states that have separate licensing requirements for the two positions, most people in the field obtain both licenses. Persons interested

in a career as a funeral director should contact their state licensing board for specific requirements.

College programs in mortuary science usually last from 2 to 4 years; the American Board of Funeral Service Education accredits 49 mortuary science programs. Two-year programs are offered by a small number of community and junior colleges, and a few colleges and universities offer both 2- and 4-year programs. Mortuary science programs include courses in anatomy, physiology, pathology, embalming techniques, restorative art, business management, accounting and use of computers in funeral home management, and client services. They also include courses in the social sciences and legal, ethical, and regulatory subjects, such as psychology, grief counseling, oral and written communication, funeral service law, business law, and ethics.

The Funeral Service Educational Foundation and many state associations offer continuing education programs designed for licensed funeral directors. These programs address issues in communications, counseling, and management. Thirty-two states have requirements that funeral directors receive continuing education credits in order to maintain their licenses.

Apprenticeships must be completed under an experienced and licensed funeral director or embalmer. Depending on state regulations, apprenticeships last from 1 to 3 years and may be served before, during, or after mortuary school. Apprenticeships provide practical experience in all facets of the funeral service from embalming to transporting remains.

State board licensing examinations vary, but they usually consist of written and oral parts and include a demonstration of practical skills. Persons who want to work in another state may have to pass the examination for that state; however, some states have reciprocity arrangements and will grant licenses to funeral directors from another state without further examination.

High school students can start preparing for a career as a funeral director by taking courses in biology and chemistry and participating in public speaking or debate clubs. Part-time or summer jobs in funeral homes consist mostly of maintenance and cleanup tasks, such as washing and polishing limousines and hearses, but these tasks can help students become familiar with the operation of funeral homes.

Important personal traits for funeral directors are composure, tact, and the ability to communicate easily with the public. They also should have the desire and ability to comfort people in their time of sorrow.

Advancement opportunities are best in larger funeral homes; funeral directors may earn promotions to higher paying positions such as branch manager or general manager. Some directors eventually acquire enough money and experience to establish their own funeral home businesses.

Job Outlook

Little or no change is expected in overall employment through 2010. Employment of funeral directors is projected to increase more slowly than the average for all occupations as the number of deaths increase, spurring demand for funeral services. Employment of embalmers, however, is expected to decline slightly since most funeral directors also are trained, licensed, and practicing embalmers.

The need to replace funeral directors who retire or leave the occupation for other reasons will account for more job openings than employment growth. Typically, a number of mortuary science graduates leave the profession shortly after becoming licensed funeral directors to pursue other career interests, and this trend is expected to continue. Also, more funeral directors are 55 years old and over as compared with workers in other occupations, and will be retiring in greater numbers between 2000 and 2010. Although employment opportunities for funeral directors are expected to be good, mortuary science graduates may have to relocate to find jobs in funeral services.

Earnings

Median annual earnings for funeral directors were $41,110 in 2000. The middle 50 percent earned between $30,680 and $57,290. The lowest 10 percent earned less than $22,140, and the top 10 percent more than $85,780.

Salaries of funeral directors depend on the number of years of experience in funeral service, the number of services performed, the number of facilities operated, the area of the country, the size of the community, and the level of formal education. Funeral directors in large cities earned more than their counterparts in small towns and rural areas.

Median annual earnings for embalmers were $32,870 in 2000. The middle 50 percent earned between $25,840 and $41,760. The lowest 10 percent earned less than $18,840, and the top 10 percent more than $52,130.

Related Occupations

The job of a funeral director requires tact, discretion, and compassion when dealing with grieving people. Others who need these qualities include members of the clergy, social workers, psychologists, physicians and surgeons, and other health diagnosing and treating practitioners.

Sources of Additional Information

For a list of accredited mortuary science programs and information on the funeral service profession, write to:

- The National Funeral Directors Association, 13625 Bishop's Dr., Brookfield, WI 53005. Internet: http://www.nfda.org

For information about college programs in mortuary science, scholarships, and funeral service as a career, contact:

- The American Board of Funeral Service Education, 38 Florida Ave., Portland, ME 04103. Internet: http://www.abfse.org/index.html

For information on continuing education programs in funeral service, contact:

- The Funeral Service Educational Foundation, 13625 Bishop's Dr., Brookfield, WI 53005. Internet: http://www.fsef.org

Gaming Cage Workers

O*NET 43-3041.00

Significant Points

- Most jobs require only a high school diploma.
- Numerous job opportunities should arise due to high turnover.

- Slower-than-average growth is expected in overall employment, reflecting the spread of computers and other office automation as well as organizational restructuring.

Nature of the Work

Gaming cage workers, more commonly called *cage cashiers*, work in casinos and other gaming establishments. The "cage," where these workers can be found, is the central depository for money, gaming chips, and paperwork necessary to support casino play. Cage workers perform a wide range of financial transactions and handle any paperwork that may be required. They perform credit checks and verify credit references for people who want to open a house credit account. They cash checks according to rules established by the casino. Cage workers sell gambling chips, tokens, or tickets to patrons or to other workers for resale to patrons and exchange chips and tokens for cash. They may use cash registers, adding machines, or computers to calculate and record transactions. At the end of their shift, cage cashiers must reconcile the books and make sure they balance.

Cage workers must follow a number of rules and regulations related to their handling of money as this industry is highly scrutinized. Large cash transactions, for example, must be reported to the Internal Revenue Service. Also, when determining when to extend credit or cash a check, very detailed procedures must be followed.

Working Conditions

Gaming cage workers work in casinos and other gaming establishments. These workers may use computers on a daily basis, and subsequently may experience eye and muscle strain, backaches, headaches, and repetitive motion injuries. Also, clerks who review detailed data may have to sit for extended periods of time.

Because most casinos are open 24 hours a day, gaming cage workers often work in shifts, including nights and weekends.

Employment

Gaming cage workers held about 22,000 jobs in 2000. All of them work in the gaming industry, which is heavily concentrated in Nevada and Atlantic City, New Jersey. However, a growing number of states and Indian reservations have legalized gambling and gaming establishments can now be found in many parts of the country.

Training, Other Qualifications, and Advancement

Most gaming cage workers are required to have at least a high school diploma. Although a degree is rarely required, many graduates accept entry-level positions to get into a particular company or with the hope of being promoted to professional or managerial positions. Some companies have a set plan of advancement that tracks college graduates from entry-level clerical jobs into managerial positions. Workers with bachelor's degrees are likely to start at higher salaries and advance more easily than those without degrees do.

Experience in a related job also is recommended. For example, cash-handling experience is important for gaming cage workers. Regardless of the type of work, most employers prefer workers with good communication skills who are computer-literate; knowledge of word processing and spreadsheet software is especially valuable.

Gaming cage workers have additional requirements. They must be at least 21 years old, and they are required to obtain a license by the state gaming commission or other regulatory body. In addition to a fee, applicants must provide a photograph and proof of age and residence. A background check is conducted to make sure that applicants do not have a criminal history.

Once hired, gaming cage workers usually receive on-the-job training. Under the guidance of a supervisor or other senior worker, new employees learn company procedures. Some formal classroom training also may be necessary, such as training in specific computer software. Gaming cage workers must be careful, orderly, and detail-oriented in order to avoid making errors and recognize errors made by others. These workers also should be discreet and trustworthy because they frequently come in contact with confidential material. Additionally, all gaming cage workers should have a strong aptitude for numbers.

Gaming cage workers usually advance by taking on more duties in the same occupation for higher pay or by transferring to a closely related occupation.

Job Outlook

Employment of gaming cage workers is expected to increase faster than the average for all occupations through 2010. In addition, even more job openings should result from high turnover in this occupation due to the high level of scrutiny workers in this occupation receive and the need to be very accurate. Opportunities for gaming cage workers depend on the health of the gaming industry. The industry as a whole is strong and demand will remain high as gambling becomes a more popular and acceptable leisure pursuit. However, as a result of a boom in casino building in the 1990s, slower growth in casino building in established markets is expected. New casinos will be built on Indian reservations, especially in California, where the legislature recently passed a law allowing casinos on tribal lands in that state. Persons with good math skills, some background in accounting or bookkeeping, and good customer service skills should have the best opportunities.

Earnings

Salaries of gaming cage workers vary considerably. The region of the country, size of city, and type and size of establishment all influence salary levels. Also, the level of expertise required and the complexity and uniqueness of a worker's responsibilities also may affect earnings. Median hourly earnings of full-time gaming cage workers in 2000 were $9.99.

Related Occupations

Gaming cage workers enter data into a computer, handle cash, and keep track of business and other financial transactions. Higher level clerks can generate reports and perform analysis of the financial data.

Sources of Additional Information

Information on employment opportunities for gaming cage workers is available from local offices of the state employment service.

Gaming Services Occupations

O*NET 39-1011.00, 39-1012.00, 39-3011.00, 39-3012.00, 39-3019.99, 39-3099.99

Significant Points

- Usually there are no minimum educational requirements; each casino establishes its own requirements for education, training, and experience.

- Workers need a license issued by a regulatory agency, such as a casino control board or commission; licensure requires proof of residency in the state in which gaming workers are employed.

- Job prospects are best for those with a degree or certification in gaming or a hospitality-related field, previous casino gaming training or experience, and strong interpersonal and customer service skills.

Nature of the Work

Legalized gambling in the United States today includes casino gaming, state lotteries, parimutuel wagering on contests such as horseracing, and charitable gaming. Gaming, the playing of games of chance, is a multibillion-dollar industry that is responsible for the creation of a number of unique service occupations.

The majority of all gaming services workers are employed in casinos. Their duties and titles may vary from one establishment to another. Despite differences in job title and task, however, workers perform many of the same basic functions in all casinos. Some positions are associated with oversight and direction—supervision, surveillance, and investigation—while others involve working with the games or patrons themselves, performing such activities as tending slot machines, handling money, writing and running tickets, and dealing cards.

Like nearly every business establishment, casinos have workers who direct and oversee day-to-day operations. *Gaming supervisors* oversee the gaming operations and personnel in an assigned area. They circulate among the tables and observe the operations to ensure that all of the stations and games are covered for each shift. It also is not uncommon for gaming supervisors to explain and interpret the operating rules of the house to the patrons who may have difficulty understanding the rules. Gaming supervisors also may plan and organize activities to create a friendly atmosphere for the guests staying in their hotels or casino hotels; and, periodically, they address and adjust service complaints.

Some gaming occupations demand specially acquired skills—dealing blackjack, for example—that are unique to casino work. Others require skills common to most businesses, such as the ability to conduct financial transactions. In both capacities, the workers in these jobs interact directly with patrons in attending to slot machines, making change, cashing or selling tokens and coins, writing and running for other games, and dealing cards at table games. Part of their responsibility is to make those interactions enjoyable.

Slot key persons, also called slot attendants, slot technicians or slot key persons, coordinate and supervise the slot department and its workers. Their duties include verifying and handling payoff winnings to patrons, resetting slot machines after completing the payoff, and refilling machines with money. Slot key persons must be familiar with a variety of slot machines and be able to make minor repairs and adjustments to the machines as needed. If major repairs are required, slot key persons determine whether the slot machine should be removed from the floor. Working the floor as front-line personnel, they enforce safety rules and report hazards.

Gaming and sportsbook writers and runners assist in the operations of games such as bingo and keno. They scan tickets presented by patrons and calculate and distribute winnings. Some writers and runners operate the equipment that randomly selects the numbers. Others may announce numbers selected, pick up tickets from patrons, collect bets, or receive, verify, and record patrons' cash wagers.

Gaming dealers operate table games such as craps, blackjack, and roulette. Standing or sitting behind the table, dealers provide dice, dispense cards to players, or run the equipment. Some dealers also monitor the patrons for infractions of casino rules. Gaming dealers must be skilled in customer service and in executing their game. Dealers determine winners, calculate and pay winning bets, and collect losing bets. Because of the fast-paced work environment, most gaming dealers are competent in at least two games—usually blackjack and craps.

Working Conditions

The atmosphere in casinos is generally fun-filled and often considered glamorous. However, casino work can also be physically demanding. Most occupations require that workers stand for long periods; some require the lifting of heavy items. The "glamorous" atmosphere exposes casino workers to certain hazards, such as cigarette, cigar, and pipe smoke. Noise from slot machines, gaming tables, and talking workers and patrons may be distracting to some workers, although workers wear protective headgear in areas where loud machinery is used to count money.

Most casinos are open 24 hours a day and offer three staggered shifts.

Employment

Gaming services' occupations held 167,000 jobs in 2000. Employment by occupational specialty was distributed as follows:

Gaming dealers	88,000
Gaming supervisors	31,000
Slot key persons	14,000
Gaming and sports book writers and runners	12,000
All other gaming service workers	21,000

The majority are found in the hotel and amusement and recreation services industries. Gaming services workers are employed in land-based or riverboat casinos in 11 states—Colorado, Illinois, Indiana, Iowa, Louisiana, Michigan, Mississippi, Missouri, Nevada, New Jersey, and South Dakota. The largest number works in land-based casinos in Nevada, and the second-largest group works in similar establishments in New Jersey. Mississippi, which boasts the greatest number of riverboat casinos in operation, employs the most workers in that venue. In addition, there are 27 states with Indian casinos. Legal lotteries are held in 37 states and the District of Columbia, and parimutuel wagering is legal in 40 states.

Forty-six states and the District of Columbia also allow charitable gaming.

For most workers, gaming licensure requires proof of residency in the state in which gaming workers are employed. But some gaming services workers do not limit themselves to one state, or even one country. Some workers find jobs on the small number of casinos located on luxury cruise liners, traveling the world while living and working aboard.

Training, Other Qualifications, and Advancement

Usually, there are no minimum educational requirements for entry-level gaming workers, although most employers prefer a high school diploma or GED. However, entry-level gaming services workers are required to have a license issued by a regulatory agency, such as a casino control board or commission. Applicants for a license must provide photo identification, proof of residency in the state in which they anticipate working, and pay a fee. Age requirements vary by state. The licensing application process also includes a background investigation.

In addition to a license, gaming services workers need superior customer service skills. Casino gaming workers provide entertainment and hospitality to patrons, and the quality of their service contributes to an establishment's success or failure. Therefore, gaming workers need good communication skills, an outgoing personality, and the ability to maintain their composure even when dealing with angry or demanding patrons. Personal integrity also is important because workers handle large amounts of money.

Each casino establishes its own requirements for education, training, and experience. Almost all casinos provide some in-house training in addition to requiring certification. The type and quantity of classes needed may vary.

Many institutions of higher learning offer training classes toward certification in gaming, as well as offering an associate, bachelor's, or master's degree in a hospitality-related field such as hospitality management, hospitality administration, or hotel management. One example is the Atlantic Cape Community College's Casino Career Institute in Atlantic City, New Jersey. Using a combination of a large mock casino and classroom instruction, the institute offers training in games, supervisory programs, slot attendant and slot repair technician work, slot department management, and surveillance and security.

Gaming services workers who manage money should have some experience handling cash or using calculators or adding machines. For such positions, most casinos administer a math test to assess an applicant's level of competency.

Most casino supervisory staff have an associate or bachelor's degree. Supervisors who do not have a degree usually substitute hands-on experience for formal education. Regardless of their educational background, however, most supervisors gain experience in other gaming occupations before moving into supervisory positions because knowledge of games and casino operations is essential for these workers. Gaming supervisors must have leadership qualities and good communication skills to supervise employees effectively and to deal with patrons in a way that encourages return visits.

Slot key persons do not need to meet formal educational requirements to enter the occupation, but completion of slot attendant or slot technician training is helpful. As with most other gaming workers, slot key persons receive on-the-job training during the first several weeks of employment. Most slot key positions are entry level, so a desire to learn is important. Slot key persons need good communication skills and an ability to remain calm, even when dealing with angry or demanding patrons. Personal integrity also is important because these workers handle large sums of money.

Gaming and sportsbook writers and runners must have at least a high school diploma or GED. Most of these workers receive on-the-job training. Because gaming and sportsbook writers and runners work closely with patrons, they need excellent customer service skills.

Nearly all gaming dealers are certified. Certification is available through 2- or 4-year programs in gaming or a hospitality-related field. Experienced dealers, who often are able to attract new or return business, have the best job prospects. Dealers with more experience are placed at the "high roller" tables.

Advancement opportunities in casino gaming depend less on workers' previous casino duties and titles than on their ability and eagerness to learn new jobs. For example, an entry-level gaming worker eventually might advance to become a dealer or card room manager or to assume some other supervisory position.

Job Outlook

Employment in gaming services occupations is projected to grow faster than the average for all occupations through 2010. As a direct result of increasing demand for additional table games in gaming establishments, the most rapid growth is expected among gaming dealers. Job prospects in gaming services occupations are best for those with a degree or certification in gaming or a hospitality-related field, previous casino gaming training or experience, and strong interpersonal and customer service skills. In addition to job openings arising from employment growth, opportunities will result from the need to replace workers transferring to other occupations or leaving the labor force.

Gaming has increased, reflecting growth in the population and in disposable income. More domestic and international competition for gaming patrons, and higher expectations among gaming patrons for customer service, should result in more jobs for gaming services workers. Job growth is expected in established gaming areas such as Las Vegas, Nevada, and Atlantic City, New Jersey, and in other states and areas that may legalize gaming in the coming years, including the development of more gaming establishments on Indian tribal lands.

Earnings

Wage earnings for gaming services workers vary according to occupation, level of experience, training, location, and size of the gaming establishment. The following table shows the range of median earnings for various gaming services occupations in 2000:

Gaming supervisors	$37,900
Slot key persons	21,620
Gaming and sports book writers and runners	17,100
Gaming dealers	13,330

Related Occupations

Many other occupations provide hospitality and customer service. Some examples of related occupations are security guards and gaming surveillance officers, recreation and fitness workers, sales worker supervisors, cashiers, gaming change persons and booth cashiers, retail salespersons, gaming cage workers, and tellers.

Sources of Additional Information

For additional information on careers in gaming, visit your public library and your state gaming regulatory agency or casino control commission.

Information on careers in gaming also is available from:

- American Gaming Association, 555 13th St. NW., Suite 1010 East, Washington, DC 20004. Internet: http://www.americangaming.org

Glaziers

O*NET 47-2121.00

Significant Points

- Glaziers may be injured by broken glass or cutting tools, falls from scaffolds, or from improperly lifting heavy glass panels.

- Many glaziers learn the trade by working as helpers to experienced glaziers; however, employers recommend a 3- to 4-year apprenticeship program.

- Job opportunities are expected to be excellent.

Nature of the Work

Glass serves many uses in modern buildings. Insulated and specially treated glass keeps in warmed or cooled air and provides good condensation and sound control qualities; tempered and laminated glass makes doors and windows more secure. In large commercial buildings, glass panels give office buildings a distinctive look while reducing the need for artificial lighting. The creative use of large windows, glass doors, skylights, and sun-room additions makes homes bright, airy, and inviting.

Glaziers are responsible for selecting, cutting, installing, replacing, and removing all types of glass. They generally work on one of several types of projects. Residential glazing involves work such as replacing glass in home windows; installing glass mirrors, shower doors, and bathtub enclosures; and fitting glass for table tops and display cases. On commercial interior projects, glaziers install items such as heavy, often etched, decorative room dividers or security windows. Glazing projects also may involve replacement of storefront windows for establishments such as supermarkets, auto dealerships, or banks. In the construction of large commercial buildings, glaziers build metal framework extrusions and install glass panels or curtain walls.

Besides working with glass, glaziers also may work with plastics, granite, marble, and similar materials used as glass substitutes. They may mount steel and aluminum sashes or frames and attach locks and hinges to glass doors. For most jobs, the glass is precut and mounted in frames at a factory or a contractor's shop. It arrives at the job site ready for glaziers to position and secure it in place. They may use a crane or hoist with suction cups to lift large, heavy pieces of glass. They then gently guide the glass into position by hand.

Once glaziers have the glass in place, they secure it with mastic, putty, or other pastelike cement, or with bolts, rubber gaskets, glazing compound, metal clips, or metal or wood moldings. When they secure glass using a rubber gasket—a thick, molded rubber half-tube with a split running its length—they first secure the gasket around the perimeter within the opening, then set the glass into the split side of the gasket, causing it to clamp to the edges and hold the glass firmly in place.

When they use metal clips and wood moldings, glaziers first secure the molding to the opening, place the glass in the molding, and then force springlike metal clips between the glass and the molding. The clips exert pressure and keep the glass firmly in place.

When a glazing compound is used, glaziers first spread it neatly against and around the edges of the molding on the inside of the opening. Next, they install the glass. Pressing it against the compound on the inside molding, workers screw or nail outside molding that loosely holds the glass in place. To hold it firmly, they pack the space between the molding and the glass with glazing compound and then trim any excess material with a glazing knife.

For some jobs, the glazier must cut the glass manually at the job site. To prepare the glass for cutting, glaziers rest it either on edge on a rack, or "A-frame," or flat against a cutting table. They then measure and mark the glass for the cut.

Glaziers cut glass with a special tool that has a small, very hard metal wheel. Using a straightedge as a guide, the glazier presses the cutter's wheel firmly on the glass, guiding and rolling it carefully to make a score just below the surface. To help the cutting tool move smoothly across the glass, workers brush a thin layer of oil along the line of the intended cut or dip the cutting tool in oil. Immediately after cutting, the glazier presses on the shorter end of the glass to break it cleanly along the cut.

Glaziers also replace or repair broken or pitted windshields and window glass on automobiles and other vehicles. They first remove the broken glass, which may involve cutting it free from the adhesive holding it down. They then install the glass in the vehicle, often using a special adhesive. They also may weatherproof the window or windshield and prevent it from rattling by installing rubber strips around the sides of the glass.

In addition to handtools such as glass cutters, suction cups, and glazing knives, glaziers use power tools such as saws, drills, cutters, and grinders. An increasing number of glaziers use computers in the shop or at the job site to improve their layout work and reduce the amount of glass that is wasted.

Working Conditions

Glaziers often work outdoors, sometimes in inclement weather. At times, they work on scaffolds at great heights. They do a considerable amount of bending, kneeling, lifting, and standing. Glaziers may be injured by broken glass or cutting tools, by falls from scaffolds, or by improperly lifting heavy glass panels.

Employment

Glaziers held about 49,000 jobs in 2000. About 3 out of every 5 glaziers worked for glazing contractors engaged in new construction, alteration, and repair. About 1 out of 5 worked in retail glass shops that install or replace glass and for wholesale distributors of products containing glass. Others worked in automotive repair shops.

Training, Other Qualifications, and Advancement

Many glaziers learn the trade informally on the job. They usually start as helpers, carrying glass and cleaning up debris in glass shops. They often practice cutting on discarded glass. After a while, they are given an opportunity to cut glass for a job. Eventually, helpers assist experienced workers on simple installation jobs. By working with experienced glaziers, they eventually acquire the skills of a fully qualified glazier.

Employers recommend that glaziers learn the trade through a formal apprenticeship program that lasts 3 to 4 years. Apprenticeship programs, which are administered by the National Glass Association and local union-management committees or local contractors' associations, consist of on-the-job training, as well as 144 hours of classroom instruction or home study each year. On the job, apprentices learn to use the tools and equipment of the trade; handle, measure, cut, and install glass and metal framing; cut and fit moldings; and install and balance glass doors. In the classroom, they are taught basic mathematics, blueprint reading and sketching, general construction techniques, safety practices, and first aid. Learning the trade through an apprenticeship program usually takes less time and provides more complete training than acquiring skills informally on the job, but opportunities for apprenticeships are declining.

Local apprenticeship administrators determine the physical, age, and educational requirements needed by applicants for apprenticeships and for helper positions. In general, applicants must be in good physical condition and be at least 17 years old. High school or vocational school graduates are preferred. In some areas, applicants must take mechanical-aptitude tests. Courses in general mathematics, blueprint reading or mechanical drawing, general construction, and shop provide a good background.

Standards for acceptance into apprenticeship programs are rising to reflect changing requirements associated with new products and equipment. In addition, the growing use of computers in glass layout requires that glaziers be familiar with personal computers.

Because many glaziers do not learn the trade through a formal apprenticeship program, the National Glass Association (NGA) offers a series of written examinations that certify an individual's competency to perform glazier work at three progressively more difficult levels of proficiency. These levels include Level I, Glazier; Level II, Commercial Interior/Residential Glazier or Storefront/Curtainwall Glazier; and Level III, Master Glazier. Recently, the NGA has added a new certification program for auto-glass repair.

Advancement generally consists of increases in pay for most glaziers; some advance to supervisory jobs or become contractors or estimators.

Job Outlook

Job opportunities are expected to be excellent for glaziers, largely due to the numerous openings arising each year as experienced glaziers leave the occupation. In addition, many potential workers may prefer work that is less strenuous and has more comfortable working conditions. Well-trained worksers will have especially favorable opportunities.

Employment of glaziers is expected to increase about as fast as the average for all occupations through the year 2010, as a result of growth in residential and nonresidential construction. Demand for glaziers will be spurred by the continuing need to modernize and repair existing structures and the popularity of glass in bathroom and kitchen design. Improved glass performance in the areas of insulation, privacy, safety, condensation control, and noise reduction also are expected to contribute to the demand for glaziers in both residential and nonresidential remodeling. A continuing emphasis on energy management, which encourages people to replace their old windows and doors with high-efficiency products, also will spur the demand for glaziers.

Similar to other construction-trades workers, construction glaziers should expect to experience periods of unemployment resulting from the limited duration of construction projects and the cyclical nature of the construction industry. During bad economic times, job openings for glaziers are reduced as the level of construction declines. Because construction activity varies from area to area, job openings, as well as apprenticeship opportunities, fluctuate with local economic conditions. Employment and apprenticeship opportunities should be greatest in metropolitan areas, where most glazing contractors and glass shops are located.

Earnings

In 2000, median hourly earnings of glaziers were $14.32. The middle 50 percent earned between $10.88 and $19.35. The lowest 10 percent earned less than $8.50, and the highest 10 percent earned more than $25.78. Median hourly earnings in the industries employing the largest numbers of glaziers in 2000 are shown in the following table:

Miscellaneous special trade contractors $15.39
Paint, glass, and wallpaper stores 12.60

Glaziers covered by union contracts generally earn more than their non-union counterparts. Apprentice wage rates usually start at 50 to 60 percent of the rate paid to experienced glaziers and increase every 6 months. Because glaziers can lose time due to weather conditions and fluctuations in construction activity, their overall earnings may be lower than their hourly wages suggest.

Many glaziers employed in construction are members of the International Brotherhood of Painters and Allied Trades.

Related Occupations

Glaziers use their knowledge of construction materials and techniques to install glass. Other construction workers whose jobs also involve skilled, custom work are brickmasons, blockmasons, and stonemasons; carpenters; carpet, floor, and tile installers and finishers; cement masons, concrete finishers, segmental pavers, and terrazzo workers; and painters and paperhangers.

Sources of Additional Information

For more information about glazier apprenticeships or work opportunities, contact local glazing or general contractors, a local of the International Brotherhood of Painters and Allied Trades, a local joint union-management apprenticeship agency, or the nearest office of the state employment service or state apprenticeship agency.

For general information about the work of glaziers, contact:

● International Brotherhood of Painters and Allied Trades, 1750 New York Ave. NW., Washington, DC 20006

For information concerning training for glaziers, contact:

● National Glass Association, Education and Training Department, 8200 Greensboro Dr., Suite 302, McLean, VA 22102-3881. Internet: http://www.glass.org

Grounds Maintenance Workers

O*NET 37-1012.01, 37-1012.02, 37-3011.00, 37-3012.00, 37-3013.00

Significant Points

● Opportunities, especially for seasonal or part-time work, should be excellent due to significant job turnover.

● Many beginning jobs have low earnings and are physically demanding.

● Most workers learn through short-term on-the-job training.

Nature of the Work

Attractively designed, healthy, and well-maintained lawns, gardens, and grounds create a positive first impression, establish a peaceful mood, and increase property values. Grounds maintenance workers perform the variety of tasks necessary to achieve a pleasant and functional outdoor environment. They also care for indoor gardens and plantings in commercial and public facilities, such as malls, hotels, and botanical gardens.

The duties of *landscaping workers* and *groundskeeping workers* are similar, and often overlap. Landscaping workers physically install and maintain landscaped areas. They grade property, install lighting or sprinkler systems, and build walkways, terraces, patios, decks, and fountains. In addition to initially transporting and planting new vegetation, they also transplant, mulch, fertilize, and water flowering plants, trees, and shrubs, and mow and water lawns. A growing number of residential and commercial clients, such as managers of office buildings, shopping malls, multiunit residential buildings, and hotels and motels, favor full-service landscape maintenance. Landscaping workers perform a range of duties for such clients on a regular basis during the growing season, including mowing, edging, trimming, fertilizing, dethatching, and mulching.

Groundskeeping workers, also called *groundskeepers*, maintain a variety of facilities, including athletic fields, golf courses, cemeteries, university campuses, and parks. In addition to caring for sod, plants, and trees, they also rake and mulch leaves, clear snow from walkways and parking lots, and use irrigation methods to adjust the amount of water consumption and prevent waste. They see to the proper upkeep and repair of sidewalks, parking lots, groundskeeping equipment, pools, fountains, fences, planters, and benches.

Groundskeeping workers who care for athletic fields keep natural and artificial turf fields in top condition and mark out boundaries and paint turf with team logos and names before events. They must make sure that the underlying soil on natural turf fields has the required composition to allow proper drainage and to support the appropriate grasses used on the field. They regularly mow, water, fertilize, and aerate the fields. Groundskeeping workers also vacuum and disinfect synthetic turf after use in order to prevent growth of harmful bacteria, and periodically remove the turf and replace the cushioning pad.

Workers who maintain golf courses are called *greenskeepers*. Greenskeepers do many of the same things that other groundskeepers do. In addition, greenskeepers periodically relocate the holes on putting greens to eliminate uneven wear of the turf and to add interest and challenge to the game. Greenskeepers also keep canopies, benches, ball washers, and tee markers repaired and freshly painted.

Some groundskeeping workers specialize in caring for cemeteries and memorial gardens. They dig graves to specified depths, generally using a backhoe. They may place concrete slabs on the bottom and around the sides of the grave to line it for greater support. When preparing a site for the burial ceremony, they position the casket-lowering device over the grave, cover the immediate area with an artificial grass carpet, erect a canopy, and arrange folding chairs to accommodate mourners. They regularly mow grass, apply fertilizers and other chemicals, prune shrubs and trees, plant flowers, and remove debris from graves. They also must periodically build the ground up around new gravesites to compensate for settling.

Groundskeeping workers in parks and recreation facilities care for lawns, trees, and shrubs, maintain athletic fields and playgrounds, clean buildings, and keep parking lots, picnic areas, and other public spaces free of litter. They also may remove snow and ice from roads and walkways, erect and dismantle snow fences, and maintain swimming pools. These workers inspect buildings and equipment, make needed repairs, and keep everything freshly painted.

Landscaping and groundskeeping workers use handtools such as shovels, rakes, pruning and regular saws, hedge and brush trimmers, and axes, as well as power lawnmowers, chain saws, snowblowers, and electric clippers. Some use equipment such as tractors and twin-axle vehicles. Landscaping and groundskeeping workers at parks, schools, cemeteries, and golf courses may use sod cutters to harvest sod that will be replanted elsewhere.

Pesticide handlers, sprayers, and applicators, vegetation, mix or apply pesticides, herbicides, fungicides, or insecticides through sprays, dusts, vapors, soil incorporation, or chemical application on trees, shrubs, lawns, or botanical crops. Those working for chemical lawn service firms are more specialized. They inspect lawns for problems and apply fertilizers, herbicides, pesticides, and other chemicals to stimulate growth and prevent or control weed, disease, or insect infestation, as well as practice integrated pest management techniques.

Tree trimmers and pruners cut away dead or excess branches from trees or shrubs to maintain rights-of-way for roads, sidewalks, or utilities, or to improve the appearance, health, and value of trees. Tree trimmers also may fill cavities in trees to promote healing and prevent deterioration. Workers who specialize in pruning trim and shape ornamental trees and shrubs for private residences, golf courses, or other institutional grounds. Tree trimmers and pruners use handsaws, pruning hooks, shears, and clippers. When trimming near powerlines, they usually use truck-mounted lifts and power pruners.

Working Conditions

Many of the jobs for grounds maintenance workers are seasonal, meaning that they are in demand mainly in the spring, summer, and fall when most planting, mowing and trimming, and cleanup is necessary. The work, most of which is performed outdoors in all kinds of weather, can be physically demanding and repetitive, involving much bending, lifting, and shoveling. Workers in landscaping and groundskeeping may be under pressure to get the job completed, especially when preparing for scheduled events such as athletic competitions or burials.

Those who work with pesticides, fertilizers, and other chemicals, as well as potentially dangerous equipment and tools such as power lawnmowers, chain saws, and power clippers, must exercise safety precautions. Workers who use motorized equipment must take care to protect themselves against hearing damage.

Employment

Grounds maintenance workers held about 1.1 million jobs in 2000. Employment was distributed as follows:

Landscaping and groundskeeping workers	894,000
First-line supervisors/managers of landscaping, lawn service, and groundskeeping workers	159,000
Tree trimmers and pruners	52,000
Pesticide handlers, sprayers, and applicators, vegetation	27,000

About 42 percent of wage and salary workers in grounds maintenance were employed in companies providing landscape and horticultural services. Others worked for firms operating and building real estate, amusement and recreation facilities such as golf courses and racetracks, and retail nurseries and garden stores. Some were employed by local governments, installing and maintaining landscaping for parks, schools, hospitals, and other public facilities.

More than 1 out of every 6 grounds maintenance workers were self-employed, providing landscape maintenance directly to customers on a contract basis. About 1 of every 7 worked part-time; many of these were of school age.

Training, Other Qualifications, and Advancement

There usually are no minimum educational requirements for entry-level positions in grounds maintenance. In 2000, most workers had a high school education or less, although a diploma is necessary for some jobs. Short-term on-the-job training usually is sufficient to teach new hires how to operate equipment such as mowers, trimmers, leafblowers, and small tractors, and to follow correct safety procedures. Entry-level workers must be able to follow directions and learn proper planting procedures. If driving is an essential part of a job, employers look for applicants with a good driving record and some experience driving a truck. Workers who deal directly with customers must get along well with people. Employers also look for responsible, self-motivated individuals, because grounds maintenance workers often work with little supervision.

Laborers who demonstrate a willingness to work hard and quickly, have good communication skills, and take an interest in the business may advance to crew leader or other supervisory positions. Advancement or entry into positions such as grounds manager or landscape contractor usually requires some formal education beyond high school, and several years of progressively more responsible experience.

Most states require certification for workers who apply pesticides. Certification requirements vary, but usually include passing a test on the proper and safe use and disposal of insecticides, herbicides, and fungicides. Some states require that landscape contractors be licensed.

The Professional Grounds Management Society (PGMS) offers certification to grounds managers who have a combination of 8 years of experience and formal education beyond high school, and pass an examination covering subjects such as equipment management, personnel management, environmental issues, turf care, ornamentals, and circulatory systems. The PGMS also offers certification to groundskeepers who have a high school diploma or equivalent, plus 2 years of experience in the grounds maintenance field.

The Associated Landscape Contractors of America (ALCA) offers the designations Certified Landscape Professional or Certified Landscape Technician to those who meet established education and experience standards and pass an ALCA examination. The hands-on test for technicians covers areas such as maintenance equipment operation and the installation of plants by reading a plan. A written safety test also is administered.

Some workers with groundskeeping backgrounds may start their own businesses after several years of experience.

Job Outlook

Those interested in grounds maintenance occupations should find plentiful job opportunities in the future. Because of high turnover, a large number of job openings is expected to result from the need to replace workers who transfer to other occupations or leave the labor force. These occupations attract many part-time workers. Some take grounds maintenance jobs to earn money for school or simply to secure an income until they find a better-paying job. Because wages for beginners are low and the work is physically demanding, many employers have difficulty attracting enough workers to fill all openings.

Employment of grounds maintenance workers is expected to grow faster than the average for all occupations through the year 2010, in response to increasing demand for groundskeeping and related services. Expected growth in the construction of commercial and industrial buildings, shopping malls, homes, highways, and recreational facilities should contribute to demand for these workers.

The upkeep and renovation of existing landscaping and grounds are continuing sources of demand for grounds maintenance workers. Owners of many existing buildings and facilities, including colleges and universities, recognize the importance of "curb appeal" and are expected to use grounds maintenance services more extensively to maintain and upgrade their properties. Homeowners also are expected to continue using landscaping services to maintain the beauty and value of their property. As the "echo" boom generation (children of baby boomers) comes of age, the demand for parks, athletic fields, and recreational facilities also can be expected to sustain the demand for grounds maintenance workers.

Job opportunities for nonseasonal work are more numerous in regions with temperate climates, where landscaping and lawn services are required all year. However, opportunities may vary depending on local economic conditions.

Earnings

Median hourly earnings in 2000 of grounds maintenance workers were as follows:

First-line supervisors/managers of landscaping, lawn
service, and groundskeeping workers $14.70
Tree trimmers and pruners 11.41
Pesticide handlers, sprayers, and applicators, vegetation 11.11
Landscaping and groundskeeping workers 8.80

Median hourly earnings in the industries employing the largest numbers of landscaping and groundskeeping workers in 2000 were as follows:

Local government $11.41
Real estate agents and managers 9.05
Subdividers and developers 8.71
Landscape and horticultural services 8.63
Miscellaneous amusement and recreation services 8.34
Real estate operators and lessors 8.18

Related Occupations

Grounds maintenance workers perform most of their work outdoors and have some knowledge of plants and soils. Others whose jobs may require that they work outdoors and are otherwise related are agricultural workers; farmers, ranchers, and agricultural managers; forest, conservation, and logging workers; landscape architects; and biological scientists.

Sources of Additional Information

For career and certification information on tree trimmers and pruners, contact:

● National Arborist Association, 3 Perimeter Rd., Unit I, Manchester, NH 03103

For information on work as a landscaping and groundskeeping worker, contact:

● Professional Lawn Care Association of America, 1000 Johnson Ferry Rd. NE., Suite C-135, Marietta, GA 30068-2112. Internet: http://www.plcaa.org

● Associated Landscape Contractors of America, 150 Elden St., Suite 270, Herndon, VA 20170

For information on becoming a licensed pesticide sprayer, contact your state's department of agriculture.

Hazardous Materials Removal Workers

O*NET 47-4041.00

Significant Points

- Working conditions can be difficult, and the use of protective clothing is often required.

- Formal education beyond high school is not required, but a training program leading to a federal license is mandatory.

- Excellent job opportunities are expected.

Nature of the Work

Increased public awareness and federal and state regulations are resulting in the removal of hazardous materials from buildings, facilities, and the environment to prevent further contamination of natural resources and to promote public health and safety. Hazardous-materials removal workers identify, remove, package, transport, and dispose of various hazardous materials, including asbestos, lead, and radioactive and nuclear materials. The removal of hazardous materials, or "hazmats," from public places and the environment also is called abatement, remediation, and decontamination.

Hazardous-materials removal workers use a variety of tools and equipment, depending on the work at hand. Equipment ranges from brooms to personal protective suits that completely isolate workers from the hazardous material. Depending on the threat of contamination, equipment required can include disposable or reusable coveralls, gloves, hard hats, shoe covers, safety glasses or goggles, chemical-resistant clothing, face shields, and hearing protection. Most workers also are required to wear respirators while working to protect them from airborne particles. These respirators range from simple versions that cover only the mouth and nose to self-contained suits with their own air supply.

Asbestos is a material used in the past for fireproofing roofing and flooring, for heat insulation, and for a variety of other uses. While materials containing asbestos rarely are used in buildings anymore, there still are structures containing the material. When embedded in materials, asbestos is fairly harmless; when airborne, however, asbestos can cause several lung diseases, including lung cancer and asbestosis.

Lead was a common building component found in paint and plumbing fixtures and pipes until the late 1970s. Because lead is easily absorbed into the bloodstream, it can travel to vital organs and build up there. The health risks associated with lead poisoning include fatigue, loss of appetite, miscarriage, and learning disabilities and decreased IQ in children. Due to these risks, it has become necessary to remove lead-based products and asbestos from buildings and structures.

Asbestos-abatement and *lead-abatement workers* remove these and other materials from buildings scheduled to be renovated or demolished. They use a variety of hand and power tools, such as vacuums and scrapers, to remove asbestos and lead from surfaces. The vacuums used by asbestos-abatement workers have special, highly efficient filters designed to trap the asbestos, which is later disposed of or stored. During the abatement, special monitors for asbestos and lead content sample the air to protect the workers; lead-abatement workers also wear a personal air monitor that indicates how much lead the worker has been exposed to. Workers also use monitoring devices to identify the asbestos, lead, and other materials that need to be removed from the surfaces of walls and structures.

A typical residential lead-abatement project involves using a chemical to strip the lead-based paint from the walls of the home. Lead-abate-

ment workers apply the compound with a putty knife and allow it to dry. Then, they scrape the hazardous material into an impregnable container for transport and storage. They also use sandblasters and high-pressure water sprayers to remove lead from large structures.

Radioactive materials are classified as either high- or low-level wastes. High-level wastes primarily are nuclear-reactor fuels used to produce electricity. Low-level wastes include any radioactively contaminated protective clothing, tools, filters, medical equipment, and other items. *Decontamination technicians* perform duties similar to janitors and cleaners. They use brooms, mops, and other tools to clean exposed areas and remove exposed items for decontamination or disposal. With experience, these workers can advance to *radiation-protection technician* jobs and use radiation survey meters to locate and evaluate materials, operate high-pressure cleaning equipment for decontamination, and package radioactive materials for transportation or disposal.

Decommissioning and decontamination (D&D) workers remove and treat radioactive materials generated by nuclear facilities and power plants. They use a variety of handtools to break down contaminated items such as "gloveboxes," which are used to process radioactive materials. At decommissioning sites, the workers clean and decontaminate the facility, as well as remove any radioactive or contaminated materials.

Treatment, storage, and disposal (TSD) workers transport and prepare materials for treatment or disposal. To ensure proper treatment of materials, laws require workers in this field to be able to verify shipping manifests. At incinerator facilities, these workers transport materials from the customer or service center to the incinerator. At landfills, they follow a strict procedure for the processing and storage of hazardous materials. They organize and track the location of items in the fill and may help change the state of a material from liquid to solid in preparation for its storage. These workers typically operate heavy machinery such as forklifts, earthmoving machinery, and large trucks and rigs.

Hazardous-materials removal workers also may be required to construct scaffolding or erect containment areas prior to the abatement or decontamination. Government regulation, in most cases, dictates that hazardous-materials removal workers are closely supervised on the work site. The standard usually is 1 supervisor to every 10 workers. The work is very structured, planned out sometimes years in advance, and team-oriented. There is a great deal of cooperation among supervisors and coworkers. Due to the nature of the materials being removed, work areas are restricted to licensed hazardous-materials removal workers, thus minimizing exposure to the public.

Working Conditions

Hazardous-materials removal workers face different working conditions depending on their area of expertise. Although many work a standard 40-hour week, overtime and shiftwork is not uncommon, especially in asbestos and lead abatement. Asbestos- and lead-abatement workers tend to work primarily in buildings and other structures, such as office buildings and schools. Because they are under pressure to complete their work within certain deadlines, workers may experience fatigue. Completing projects frequently requires night and weekend work, because hazardous-materials removal workers often work around the schedules of others. Treatment, storage, and disposal workers are employed primarily at facilities such as landfills, incinerators, boilers, and industrial furnaces. These facilities often are located in remote areas due to the kinds of work being done. As a result, workers employed by treatment, storage, or disposal facilities may commute long distances to work.

Decommissioning and decontamination workers, decontamination technicians, and radiation protection technicians work at nuclear facilities and electrical power plants. These sites, like treatment, storage, and disposal facilities, often are far from urban areas. Workers, who often perform jobs in cramped conditions, may need to use sharp tools to dismantle contaminated objects. A hazardous-materials removal worker must have great self-control and a level head to cope with the daily stress associated with working with hazardous materials.

Hazardous-materials removal employees work in a highly structured environment to minimize danger. Each phase of an operation is planned in advance, and workers are trained to deal with safety breaches and hazardous situations. Crews and supervisors take every precaution to ensure that the work site is safe. Hazardous-materials removal workers, whether working in asbestos and lead abatement or in radioactive decontamination, must stand, stoop, and kneel for long periods. Some hazardous-materials removal workers must wear fully enclosed personal protective suits for several hours at a time; these suits may be hot and uncomfortable and cause some individuals to experience claustrophobia.

Hazardous-materials removal workers may be required to travel outside their normal working area in order to respond to emergency situations. These emergency cleanups sometimes take several days or weeks to complete, and workers usually are away from home for the duration of the project.

Employment

Hazardous-materials removal workers held about 37,000 jobs in 2000. Nearly half were employed by special trade contractors, primarily in asbestos and lead abatement. Almost a quarter worked in water supply and sanitary services. A small number worked in electric services at nuclear and electric plants as decommissioning and decontamination workers and radiation safety and decontamination technicians.

Training, Other Qualifications, and Advancement

Formal education beyond a high school diploma is not required to become a hazardous materials removal worker. However, workers must be able to perform basic mathematical conversions and calculations, manipulating readings for consideration during the abatement. To perform the job duties, workers also should have good physical strength and manual dexterity.

Because of the nature of the work to be done and the time constraints sometimes involved, employers prefer people who are dependable, prompt, and detail-oriented. Because much of the work is done in buildings, a background in construction is helpful.

Federal regulations require a license to work as a hazardous-materials removal worker. Most employers provide technical training on the job, but a formal 32- to 40-hour training program must be completed to be licensed to work as an asbestos- and lead-abatement worker or a treatment, storage, and disposal worker. The program covers health hazards, personal protective equipment and clothing, site safety, hazard recognition and identification, and decontamination. In some cases, workers will discover one hazardous material while abating another. If the workers are not licensed to work with the newly discovered material, they cannot continue to work. Many experienced workers opt to take courses

in additional disciplines to avoid this situation. Some employers prefer to hire workers licensed in multiple disciplines.

For decommissioning and decontamination workers employed at nuclear facilities, training is more extensive. In addition to the standard 40-hour training course in asbestos, lead, and hazardous waste, workers must take courses on regulations governing nuclear materials and radiation safety. These courses add up to approximately 3 months of training, although most are not taken consecutively. Many agencies, organizations, and companies throughout the country provide training programs that are approved by the U.S. Environmental Protection Agency, the U.S. Department of Energy, and other regulatory bodies. Workers in all fields are required to take refresher courses every year to maintain their license.

Job Outlook

Job opportunities are expected to be excellent for hazardous-materials removal workers, largely due to the numerous openings arising each year as experienced workers leave the occupation. In addition, many potential workers may prefer work that is less strenuous and has more comfortable working conditions. Well-trained workers will have especially favorable opportunities.

The overall employment in this occupation is expected to grow faster than average for all occupations through the year 2010. Employment of the largest group of workers, asbestos- and lead-abatement workers, is expected to grow as fast as other occupations in special trade contractors, but opportunities will be best in lead abatement. Compared with other construction trades occupations, employment of lead-abatement workers is much less affected by slowdowns in the economy.

Employment of decontamination technicians, radiation safety technicians, and decommissioning and decontamination workers is expected to grow in response to increased pressure for safer and cleaner nuclear and electric generator facilities. In addition, the number of closed facilities that need decommissioning may continue to grow due to federal legislation. These workers also are less affected by fluctuations in the economy because the facilities they work in must operate regardless of the state of the economy.

Opportunities will be best in the private sector as more state and local governments contract out hazardous-materials removal work to private companies.

Earnings

Median hourly earnings of hazardous materials removal workers were $13.71 in 2000. The middle 50 percent earned between $11.34 and $18.56 per hour. The lowest 10 percent earned less than $9.33 per hour, and the highest 10 percent earned more than $24.01 per hour. The median hourly earnings in the largest industries employing hazardous materials removal workers in 2000 are shown in the following table.

Miscellaneous special trade contractors	$13.78
Sanitary services	13.30

According to the limited data available, treatment, storage, and disposal workers usually earn slightly more than asbestos- and lead-abatement workers or decontamination technicians. Decontamination and decommissioning workers and radiation protection technicians, although constituting the smallest group, tend to earn the highest wages.

Related Occupations

Asbestos- and lead-abatement workers share skills with other construction trades workers, including brickmasons, blockmasons, and stonemasons; cement masons, concrete finishers, segmental pavers, and terrazzo workers; insulation workers; and sheet metal workers. Treatment, storage, and disposal workers, decommissioning and decontamination workers, and decontamination and radiation safety technicians work closely with plant and system operators, such as power plant operators, distributors, and dispatchers and water and wastewater treatment plant operators.

Sources of Additional Information

For more information on hazardous-materials removal workers, including training information, contact:

- Laborers-AGC Education and Training Fund, 37 Deerfield Rd., P.O. Box 37, Promfret, CT 06259

Heating, Air-Conditioning, and Refrigeration Mechanics and Installers

O*NET 49-9021.01, 49-9021.02

Significant Points

- Opportunities should be very good for mechanics and installers with technical school or formal apprenticeship training.

- Mechanics and installers need a basic understanding of microelectronics because they increasingly install and service equipment with electronic controls.

Nature of the Work

What would people living in Chicago do without heating, people in Miami do without air-conditioning, or blood banks all over the country do without refrigeration? Heating and air-conditioning systems control the temperature, humidity, and the total air quality in residential, commercial, industrial, and other buildings. Refrigeration systems make it possible to store and transport food, medicine, and other perishable items. *Heating, air-conditioning, and refrigeration mechanics and installers*—also called *technicians*—install, maintain, and repair such systems.

Heating, air-conditioning, and refrigeration systems consist of many mechanical, electrical, and electronic components such as motors, compressors, pumps, fans, ducts, pipes, thermostats, and switches. In central heating systems, for example, a furnace heats air that is distributed throughout the building via a system of metal or fiberglass ducts. Technicians must be able to maintain, diagnose, and correct problems throughout the entire system. To do this, they adjust system controls to recommended settings and test the performance of the entire system using special tools and test equipment.

Although they are trained to do both, technicians often specialize in either installation or maintenance and repair. Some specialize in one type of equipment—for example, oil burners, solar panels, or commercial refrigerators. Technicians may work for large or small contracting companies or directly for a manufacturer or wholesaler. Those working for smaller operations tend to do both installation and servicing, and work with heating, cooling, and refrigeration equipment.

Heating and air-conditioning mechanics install, service, and repair heating and air-conditioning systems in both residences and commercial establishments. *Furnace installers*, also called *heating equipment technicians*, follow blueprints or other specifications to install oil, gas, electric, solid-fuel, and multiple-fuel heating systems. *Air-conditioning mechanics* install and service central air-conditioning systems. After putting the equipment in place, they install fuel and water supply lines, air ducts and vents, pumps, and other components. They may connect electrical wiring and controls and check the unit for proper operation. To ensure the proper functioning of the system, furnace installers often use combustion test equipment such as carbon dioxide and oxygen testers.

After a furnace has been installed, heating equipment technicians often perform routine maintenance and repairwork to keep the system operating efficiently. During the fall and winter, for example, when the system is used most, they service and adjust burners and blowers. If the system is not operating properly, they check the thermostat, burner nozzles, controls, or other parts to diagnose and then correct the problem.

During the summer, when the heating system is not being used, heating equipment technicians do maintenance work, such as replacing filters, ducts, and other parts of the system that may accumulate dust and impurities during the operating season. During the winter, air-conditioning mechanics inspect the systems and do required maintenance, such as overhauling compressors.

Refrigeration mechanics install, service, and repair industrial and commercial refrigerating systems and a variety of refrigeration equipment. They follow blueprints, design specifications, and manufacturers' instructions to install motors, compressors, condensing units, evaporators, piping, and other components. They connect this equipment to the ductwork, refrigerant lines, and electrical power source. After making the connections, they charge the system with refrigerant, check it for proper operation, and program control systems.

When heating, air-conditioning, and refrigeration mechanics service equipment, they must use care to conserve, recover, and recycle chlorofluorocarbon (CFC) and hydrochlorofluorocarbon (HCFC) refrigerants used in air-conditioning and refrigeration systems. The release of CFCs and HCFCs contributes to the depletion of the stratospheric ozone layer, which protects plant and animal life from ultraviolet radiation. Technicians conserve the refrigerant by making sure that there are no leaks in the system; they recover it by venting the refrigerant into proper cylinders; and they recycle it for reuse with special filter-dryers.

Heating, air-conditioning, and refrigeration mechanics and installers are adept at using a variety of tools, including hammers, wrenches, metal snips, electric drills, pipe cutters and benders, measurement gauges, and acetylene torches, to work with refrigerant lines and air ducts. They use voltmeters, thermometers, pressure gauges, manometers, and other testing devices to check air flow, refrigerant pressure, electrical circuits, burners, and other components.

New technology, in the form of cellular "Web" phones that allow technicians to tap into the Internet, may soon affect the way technicians diagnose problems. Computer hardware and software have been developed that allows heating, venting, and refrigeration units to automatically contact the maintenance establishment when problems arise. The maintenance establishment can then notify the mechanic in the field via cellular phone. The mechanic can then access the Internet to "talk" with the unit needing maintenance. While this technology is cutting-edge and not yet widespread, its potential for cost-savings may spur its acceptance.

Other craft workers sometimes install or repair cooling and heating systems. For example, on a large air-conditioning installation job, especially where workers are covered by union contracts, ductwork might be done by sheet metal workers and duct installers; electrical work by electricians; and installation of piping, condensers, and other components by pipelayers, plumbers, pipefitters, and steamfitters. Home appliance repairers usually service room air conditioners and household refrigerators.

Working Conditions

Heating, air-conditioning, and refrigeration mechanics and installers work in homes, stores of all kinds, hospitals, office buildings, and factories—anywhere there is climate-control equipment. They may be assigned to specific job sites at the beginning of each day, or if they are making service calls, they may be dispatched to jobs by radio, telephone, or pagers. Increasingly, employers are using cell phones to coordinate technicians' schedules.

Technicians may work outside in cold or hot weather or in buildings that are uncomfortable because the air-conditioning or heating equipment is broken. In addition, technicians might have to work in awkward or cramped positions and sometimes are required to work in high places. Hazards include electrical shock, burns, muscle strains, and other injuries from handling heavy equipment. Appropriate safety equipment is necessary when handling refrigerants because contact can cause skin damage, frostbite, or blindness. Inhalation of refrigerants when working in confined spaces is also a possible hazard.

The majority of mechanics and installers work more than a 40-hour week, particularly during peak seasons when they often work overtime or irregular hours. Maintenance workers, including those who provide maintenance services under contract, often work evening or weekend shifts, and are on call. Most employers try to provide a full workweek the year round by scheduling both installation and maintenance work, and many manufacturers and contractors now provide or even require service contracts. In most shops that service both heating and air-conditioning equipment, employment is very stable throughout the year.

Employment

Heating, air-conditioning, and refrigeration mechanics and installers held about 243,000 jobs in 2000; approximately one third of these worked for cooling and heating contractors. The remainder were employed in a variety of industries throughout the country, reflecting a widespread dependence on climate-control systems. Some worked for fuel oil dealers, refrigeration and air-conditioning service and repair shops, schools, and department stores that sell heating and air-conditioning systems. Local governments, the federal government, hospitals, office buildings, and other organizations that operate large air-conditioning, refrigeration, or heating systems employed others. Approximately 1 of every 5 mechanics and installers was self-employed.

Training, Other Qualifications, and Advancement

Because of the increasing sophistication of heating, air-conditioning, and refrigeration systems, employers prefer to hire those with technical school or apprenticeship training. A sizable number of mechanics and installers, however, still learn the trade informally on the job.

Many secondary and postsecondary technical and trade schools, junior and community colleges, and the armed forces offer 6-month to 2-year programs in heating, air-conditioning, and refrigeration. Students study theory, design, and equipment construction, as well as electronics. They also learn the basics of installation, maintenance, and repair.

Apprenticeship programs are frequently run by joint committees representing local chapters of the Air-Conditioning Contractors of America, the Mechanical Contractors Association of America, the National Association of Plumbing-Heating-Cooling Contractors, and locals of the Sheet Metal Workers' International Association or the United Association of Journeymen and Apprentices of the Plumbing and Pipefitting Industry of the United States and Canada. Other apprenticeship programs are sponsored by local chapters of the Associated Builders and Contractors and the National Association of Home Builders. Formal apprenticeship programs normally last 3 to 5 years and combine on-the-job training with classroom instruction. Classes include subjects such as the use and care of tools, safety practices, blueprint reading, and the theory and design of heating, ventilation, air-conditioning, and refrigeration systems. Applicants for these programs must have a high school diploma or equivalent.

Those who acquire their skills on the job usually begin by assisting experienced technicians. They may begin performing simple tasks such as carrying materials, insulating refrigerant lines, or cleaning furnaces. In time, they move on to more difficult tasks, such as cutting and soldering pipes and sheet metal and checking electrical and electronic circuits.

Courses in shop math, mechanical drawing, applied physics and chemistry, electronics, blueprint reading, and computer applications provide a good background for those interested in entering this occupation. Some knowledge of plumbing or electrical work is also helpful. A basic understanding of microelectronics is becoming more important because of the increasing use of this technology in solid-state equipment controls. Because technicians frequently deal directly with the public, they should be courteous and tactful, especially when dealing with an aggravated customer. They also should be in good physical condition because they sometimes have to lift and move heavy equipment.

All technicians who purchase or work with refrigerants must be certified in their proper handling. To become certified to purchase and handle refrigerants, technicians must pass a written examination specific to the type of work in which they specialize. The three possible areas of certification are: Type I—small appliances, Type II—high pressure refrigerants, and Type III—low pressure refrigerants. Exams are administered by organizations approved by the U.S. Environmental Protection Agency, such as trade schools, unions, contractor associations, or building groups.

Several organizations have begun to offer basic self-study, classroom, and Internet courses for individuals with limited experience. In addition to understanding how systems work, technicians must be knowledgeable about refrigerant products, and legislation and regulation that govern their use. The industry recently announced the adoption of one standard for certification of experienced technicians—the Air-Conditioning Excellence program, which is offered through North American Technician Excellence, Inc. (NATE).

Advancement usually takes the form of higher wages. Some technicians, however, may advance to positions as supervisor or service manager. Others may move into areas such as sales and marketing. Still others may become building superintendents, cost estimators, or, with the necessary certification, teachers. Those with sufficient money and managerial skill can open their own contracting business.

Job Outlook

Job prospects for highly skilled heating, air-conditioning, and refrigeration mechanics and installers are expected to be very good, particularly for those with technical school or formal apprenticeship training to install, remodel, and service new and existing systems. In addition to job openings created by employment growth, thousands of openings will result from the need to replace workers who transfer to other occupations or leave the labor force.

Employment of heating, air-conditioning, and refrigeration mechanics and installers is expected to increase faster than the average for all occupations through the year 2010. As the population and economy grow, so does the demand for new residential, commercial, and industrial climate-control systems. Technicians who specialize in installation work may experience periods of unemployment when the level of new construction activity declines, but maintenance and repair work usually remains relatively stable. People and businesses depend on their climate control systems and must keep them in good working order, regardless of economic conditions.

Renewed concern for energy conservation should continue to prompt the development of new energy-saving heating and air-conditioning systems. An emphasis on better energy management should lead to the replacement of older systems and the installation of newer, more efficient systems in existing homes and buildings. Also, demand for maintenance and service work should increase as businesses and home owners strive to keep systems operating at peak efficiency. Regulations prohibiting the discharge of CFC and HCFC refrigerants took effect in 1993, and regulations banning CFC production became effective in 2000. Consequently, these regulations should continue to result in demand for technicians to replace many existing systems, or modify them to use new environmentally safe refrigerants. In addition, the continuing focus on improving indoor air quality should contribute to the growth of jobs for heating, air-conditioning, and refrigeration technicians. Also, growth of business establishments that use refrigerated equipment—such as supermarkets and convenience stores—will contribute to a growing need for technicians.

Earnings

Median hourly earnings of heating, air-conditioning, and refrigeration mechanics and installers were $15.76 in 2000. The middle 50 percent earned between $12.25 and $19.92 an hour. The lowest 10 percent earned less than $9.71, and the top 10 percent earned more than $24.58. Median hourly earnings in the industries employing the largest numbers of heating, air-conditioning, and refrigeration mechanics and installers in 2000 were as follows:

Hardware, plumbing, and heating equipment $16.83
Elementary and secondary schools 16.45
Fuel dealers 16.40
Colleges and universities 16.12
Electrical repair shops 15.16
Plumbing, heating, and air-conditioning 15.08

Apprentices usually begin at about 50 percent of the wage rate paid to experienced workers. As they gain experience and improve their skills, they receive periodic increases until they reach the wage rate of experienced workers.

Heating, air-conditioning, and refrigeration mechanics and installers enjoy a variety of employer-sponsored benefits. In addition to typical benefits like health insurance and pension plans, some employers pay for work-related training and provide uniforms, company vans, and tools.

More than 1 out of every 5 heating, air-conditioning, and refrigeration mechanics and installers is a member of a union. The unions to which the greatest numbers of mechanics and installers belong are the Sheet Metal Workers' International Association and the United Association of Journeymen and Apprentices of the Plumbing and Pipefitting Industry of the United States and Canada.

Related Occupations

Heating, air-conditioning, and refrigeration mechanics and installers work with sheet metal and piping, and repair machinery, such as electrical motors, compressors, and burners. Other workers who have similar skills are boilermakers; home appliance repairers; electricians; sheet metal workers; and pipelayers, plumbers, pipefitters, and steamfitters.

Sources of Additional Information

For more information about opportunities for training, certification, and employment in this trade, contact local vocational and technical schools; local heating, air-conditioning, and refrigeration contractors; a local of the unions previously mentioned; a local joint union-management apprenticeship committee; a local chapter of the Associated Builders and Contractors; or the nearest office of the state employment service or apprenticeship agency.

For information on career opportunities, training, and technician certification, contact:

- Air-Conditioning Contractors of America (ACCA), Suite 300, 2800 Shirlington Rd., Arlington, VA 22206. Internet: http://www.acca.org

- Refrigeration Service Engineers Society (RSES), 1666 Rand Rd., Des Plaines, IL 60016-3552

- National Association of Plumbing-Heating-Cooling Contractors (PHCC), 180 S. Washington St., P.O. Box 6808, Falls Church, VA 22046. Internet: http://www.naphcc.org

- Northamerican Heating, Refrigeration, and Air-conditioning Wholesalers Association (NHRAW),1389 Dublin Road, PO Box 16790, Columbus, OH 43216-6790. Internet: http://www.nhraw.org

For information on technician testing and certification, contact:

- North American Technician Excellence (NATE), Suite 300, 8201 Greensboro Dr., McLean, VA 22102. Internet: http://www.natex.org

For information on career opportunities and training, write to:

- Associated Builders and Contractors, Suite 800, 1300 North 17th St., Rosslyn, VA 22209. Internet: http://www.abc.org

- Home Builders Institute, National Association of Home Builders, 1201 15th St. NW., 6th Floor, Washington, DC 20005. Internet: http://www.hbi.org

- Mechanical Contractors Association of America, 1385 Piccard Dr., Rockville, MD 20850-4329. Internet: http://www.mcca.org

- Air-Conditioning and Refrigeration Institute, 4301 North Fairfax Dr., Suite 425, Arlington, VA 22203. Internet: http://www.coolcareers.org

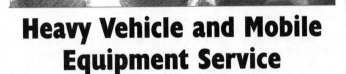

Heavy Vehicle and Mobile Equipment Service Technicians and Mechanics

O*NET 49-3041.00, 49-3042.00, 49-3043.00

Significant Points

- Opportunities should be good for persons with formal postsecondary training in diesel or heavy equipment mechanics, especially if they also have training in basic electronics and hydraulics.

- This occupation offers relatively high wages and the challenge of skilled repair work.

- Skill in using computerized diagnostic equipment is becoming more important.

Nature of the Work

Heavy vehicles and mobile equipment are indispensable to many industrial activities, from construction to railroads. Various types of equipment move materials, till land, lift beams, and dig earth to pave the way for development and production. *Heavy vehicle and mobile equipment service technicians and mechanics* repair and maintain engines and hydraulic, transmission, and electrical systems powering farm equipment, cranes, bulldozers, and railcars.

Service technicians perform routine maintenance checks on diesel engines and fuel, brake, and transmission systems to ensure peak performance, safety, and longevity of the equipment. Maintenance checks and comments from equipment operators usually alert technicians to problems. With many types of modern heavy and mobile equipment, technicians can plug hand-held diagnostic computers into onboard computers to diagnose any component needing adjustment or repair. After locating the problem, these technicians rely on their training and experience to use the best possible technique to solve the problem. If necessary, they may partially dismantle the component to examine parts for damage or excessive wear. Then, using hand-held tools, they repair, replace, clean, and lubricate parts, as necessary. In some cases, technicians calibrate systems by typing codes into the onboard computer. After reassembling the component and testing it for safety, they put it back into the equipment and return the equipment to the field.

Many types of heavy and mobile equipment use hydraulics to raise and lower movable parts, such as scoops, shovels, log forks, and scraper blades.

When hydraulic components malfunction, technicians examine them for hydraulic fluid leaks, ruptured hoses, or worn gaskets on fluid reservoirs. Occasionally, the equipment requires extensive repairs, such as replacing a defective hydraulic pump.

In addition to routine maintenance checks, service technicians perform a variety of other repairs. They diagnose electrical problems and adjust or replace defective components. They also disassemble and repair undercarriages and track assemblies. Occasionally, technicians weld broken equipment frames and structural parts, using electric or gas welders.

It is common for technicians in large shops to specialize in one or two types of repair. For example, a shop may have individual specialists in major engine repair, transmission work, electrical systems, and suspension or brake systems. The technology used in heavy equipment is becoming more sophisticated with the increased use of electronic and computer-controlled components. Training in electronics is essential for these technicians to make engine adjustments and diagnose problems. Training in the use of hand-held computers also is necessary, because computers help technicians diagnose problems and adjust component functions.

Service technicians use a variety of tools in their work. They use power tools, such as pneumatic wrenches to remove bolts quickly, machine tools like lathes and grinding machines to rebuild brakes, welding and flame-cutting equipment to remove and repair exhaust systems, and jacks and hoists to lift and move large parts. They also use common handtools—screwdrivers, pliers, and wrenches—to work on small parts and to get at hard-to-reach places. Service technicians may use a variety of computerized testing equipment to pinpoint and analyze malfunctions in electrical systems and other essential systems. For example, they use tachometers and dynamometers to locate engine malfunctions. Service technicians also use ohmmeters, ammeters, and voltmeters when working on electrical systems.

Mobile heavy equipment mechanics and service technicians keep construction and surface mining equipment such bulldozer, cranes, crawlers, draglines, graders, excavators, and other equipment in working order. They typically work for equipment wholesale distribution and leasing firms, large construction and mining companies, local and federal governments, or other organizations operating and maintaining heavy machinery and equipment fleets. Service technicians employed by the federal government may work on tanks and other armored equipment.

Farm equipment mechanics service, maintain, and repair farm equipment as well as smaller lawn and garden tractors sold to suburban homeowners. What typically was a general repairer's job around the farm has evolved into a specialized technical career. Farmers have increasingly turned to farm equipment dealers to service and repair their equipment because the machinery has grown in complexity. Modern equipment uses more electronics and hydraulics making it difficult to perform repairs without some specialized training.

Farm equipment mechanics work mostly on equipment brought into the shop for repair and adjustment. During planting and harvesting seasons, they may travel to farms to make emergency repairs to minimize delays in farm operations.

Railcar repairers specialize in servicing railroad locomotives and other rolling stock, streetcars and subway cars, or mine cars. Most work for railroads, public and private transit companies, and underground mine operators.

Working Conditions

Service technicians usually work indoors, although many make repairs at the work site. Technicians often lift heavy parts and tools, handle greasy and dirty parts, and stand or lie in awkward positions, to repair vehicles and equipment. Minor cuts, burns, and bruises are common; but serious accidents are normally avoided when the shop is kept clean and orderly and safety practices are observed. Technicians usually work in well-lighted, heated, and ventilated areas. However, some shops are drafty and noisy. Many employers provide uniforms, locker rooms, and shower facilities.

When heavy and mobile equipment breaks down at a construction site, it may be too difficult or expensive to bring it into a repair shop, so the shop often sends a field service technician to the job site to make repairs. Field service technicians work outdoors and spend much of their time away from the shop. Generally, more experienced service technicians specialize in field service. They usually drive trucks specially equipped with replacement parts and tools. On occasion, they must travel many miles to reach disabled machinery. Field technicians normally earn a higher wage than their counterparts, because they are required to make on-the-spot decisions necessary to serve their customers.

The hours of work for farm equipment mechanics vary according to the season of the year. During the busy planting and harvesting seasons, mechanics often work 6 or 7 days a week, 10 to 12 hours daily. In slow winter months, however, mechanics may work fewer than 40 hours a week.

Employment

Heavy vehicle and mobile equipment service technicians and mechanics held about 185,000 jobs in 2000. About 130,000 were mobile heavy equipment mechanics; 41,000 were farm equipment mechanics; and 14,000 were railcar repairers. Heavy and mobile equipment dealers and distributors employed more than 40 percent. About 11 percent were employed by federal, state, and local governments; and nearly 9 percent worked for construction contractors. Other service technicians worked for agricultural production and services, mine operators, public utilities, or heavy equipment rental and leasing companies. Still others repaired equipment for machinery manufacturers, airlines, railroads, steel mills, or oil and gas field companies. Less than 4 percent of service technicians were self-employed.

Nearly every section of the country employs heavy and mobile equipment service technicians and mechanics, although most work in towns and cities where equipment dealers, equipment rental and leasing companies, and construction companies have repair facilities.

Training, Other Qualifications, and Advancement

Although many persons qualify for service technician jobs through years of on-the-job training, most employers prefer that applicants complete a formal diesel or heavy equipment mechanic training program after graduating from high school. They seek persons with mechanical aptitude who are knowledgeable about the fundamentals of diesel engines, transmissions, electrical systems, and hydraulics. Additionally, the constant change in equipment technology makes it necessary for technicians to be flexible and have the capacity to learn new skills quickly.

Many community colleges and vocational schools offer programs in diesel technology. Some tailor programs to heavy equipment mechanics. These programs educate the student in the basics of analysis and diagnostic techniques, electronics, and hydraulics. The increased use of electronics and computers makes training in the fundamentals of electronics essential for new heavy and mobile equipment mechanics. Some 1- to 2-year programs lead to a certificate of completion, whereas others lead to an associate degree in diesel or heavy equipment mechanics. These programs provide a foundation in the components of diesel and heavy equipment technology. These programs also enable trainee technicians to advance more rapidly to the journey, or experienced worker, level.

A combination of formal and on-the-job training prepares trainee technicians with the knowledge to efficiently service and repair equipment handled by a shop. Most beginners perform routine service tasks and make minor repairs, after a few months' experience. They advance to harder jobs, as they prove their ability and competence. After trainees master the repair and service of diesel engines, they learn to work on related components, such as brakes, transmissions, and electrical systems. Generally, a service technician with at least 3 to 4 years of on-the-job experience is accepted as fully qualified.

Many employers send trainee technicians to training sessions conducted by heavy equipment manufacturers. These sessions, which typically last up to 1 week, provide intensive instruction in the repair of a manufacturer's equipment. Some sessions focus on particular components found in the manufacturer's equipment, such as diesel engines, transmissions, axles, and electrical systems. Other sessions focus on particular types of equipment, such as crawler-loaders and crawler-dozers. As they progress, trainees may periodically attend additional training sessions. When appropriate, experienced technicians attend training sessions to gain familiarity with new technology or equipment.

High school courses in automobile repair, physics, chemistry, and mathematics provide a strong foundation for a career as a service technician or mechanic. It is also essential for technicians to be able to read and interpret service manuals to keep abreast of engineering changes. Experience working on diesel engines and heavy equipment acquired in the armed forces also is valuable.

Voluntary certification by the National Institute for Automotive Service Excellence (ASE) is recognized as the standard of achievement for heavy and mobile equipment diesel service technicians. Technicians may be certified as a Master Heavy-Duty Diesel Technician or in 1 or more of 6 different areas of heavy-duty equipment repair: brakes, gasoline engines, diesel engines, drive trains, electrical systems, and suspension and steering. For certification in each area, technicians must pass a written examination and have at least 2 years' experience. High school, vocational or trade school, or community or junior college training in gasoline or diesel engine repair may substitute for up to 1 year's experience. To remain certified, technicians must retest every 5 years. This ensures that service technicians keep up with changing technology. However, there are currently no certification programs for other heavy vehicle and mobile equipment repair specialties.

The most important work possessions of technicians are their handtools. Service technicians typically buy their own handtools, and many experienced technicians have thousands of dollars invested in them. Employers typically furnish expensive power tools, computerized engine analyzers, and other diagnostic equipment; but handtools are normally accumulated with experience.

Experienced technicians may advance to field service jobs, where they have a greater opportunity to tackle problems independently and earn additional pay. Technicians with leadership ability may become shop supervisors or service managers. Some technicians open their own repair shops or invest in a franchise.

Job Outlook

Opportunities for heavy vehicle and mobile equipment service technicians and mechanics should be good for persons who have completed formal training programs in diesel or heavy equipment mechanics. Persons without formal training are expected to encounter growing difficulty entering these jobs.

Employment of heavy vehicle and mobile equipment service technicians and mechanics is expected to grow slower than the average for all occupations through the year 2010. Most job openings will arise from the need to replace experienced repairers who retire. Employers report difficulty finding candidates with formal postsecondary training to fill available service technician positions because many young people with mechanic training prefer to take jobs as automotive service technicians, diesel service technicians, or industrial machinery repairers—jobs that offer relatively higher earnings and a wider variety of locations in which to work.

Increasing numbers of service technicians will be required to support growth in the construction industry, equipment dealers, and rental and leasing companies. Because of the nature of construction activity, demand for service technicians follows the nation's economic cycle. As the economy expands, construction activity increases, resulting in the use of more mobile heavy equipment. More equipment is needed to grade construction sites, excavate basements, and lay water and sewer lines, increasing the need for periodic service and repair. In addition, the construction and repair of highways and bridges also requires more technicians to service equipment. Also, as equipment becomes more complex, repairs increasingly must be made by specially trained technicians. Job openings for farm equipment mechanics and railcar repairers are mostly expected to arise due to replacement needs.

Construction and mining are particularly sensitive to changes in the level of economic activity; therefore, heavy and mobile equipment may be idled during downturns. In addition, winter is traditionally the slow season for construction and farming activity, particularly in cold regions. Few technicians may be needed during periods when equipment is used less; however, employers usually try to retain experienced workers. Employers may be reluctant to hire inexperienced workers during slow periods though.

Earnings

Median hourly earnings of mobile heavy equipment mechanics were $16.32 in 2000. The middle 50 percent earned between $13.32 and $19.86. The lowest 10 percent earned less than $10.93, and the highest 10 percent earned more than $23.29. Median hourly earnings in the industries employing the largest numbers of mobile heavy equipment mechanics in 2000 were as follows:

Federal government	$18.67
Local government	17.09
Machinery, equipment, and supplies	16.05
Miscellaneous equipment rental and leasing	15.95
Heavy construction, except highway	15.54

Median hourly earnings of farm equipment mechanics were $12.38 in 2000. The middle 50 percent earned between $9.99 and $15.29. The lowest 10 percent earned less than $8.15, and the highest 10 percent earned more than $18.23.

Median hourly earnings of railcar repairers were $16.19 in 2000. The middle 50 percent earned between $12.31 and $19.34. The lowest 10 percent earned less than $9.78, and the highest 10 percent earned more than $21.19.

About one-fourth of all service technicians and mechanics are members of unions including the International Association of Machinists and Aerospace Workers, the International Union of Operating Engineers, and the International Brotherhood of Teamsters.

Related Occupations

Workers in related repair occupations include aircraft and avionics equipment mechanics and service technicians; automotive service technicians and mechanics; diesel service technicians and mechanics; heating, air-conditioning, and refrigeration mechanics and installers; and small engine mechanics.

Sources of Additional Information

More details about job openings for heavy vehicle and mobile equipment service technicians and mechanics may be obtained from local heavy and mobile equipment dealers and distributors, construction contractors, and government agencies. Local offices of the state employment service also may have information on job openings and training programs.

For general information about a career as a heavy vehicle and mobile equipment service technician or mechanic, contact:

- The Equipment Maintenance Counsel, P.O. Box 1368, Glenwood Springs, CO 81602. Internet: http://www.equipment.org

- Specialized Carriers and Rigging Association, 2750 Prosperity Ave., Suite 620, Fairfax, VA 22031-4312

- The AED Foundation (Associated Equipment Dealers affiliate), 615 W. 22nd St., Oak Brook, IL 60523. Internet: http://www.aednet.org/aed_foundation

For a directory of public training programs in heavy and mobile equipment mechanics, contact:

- SkillsUSA-VICA, P.O. Box 3000, 1401 James Monroe Hwy., Leesburg, VA 22075. Internet: http://www.skillsusa.org

A list of certified diesel service technician training programs can be obtained from:

- National Automotive Technician Education Foundation (NATEF), 101 Blue Seal Dr. S.E., Suite 101, Leesburg, VA 20175. Internet: http://www.natef.org

Information on certification as a heavy-duty diesel service technician is available from:

- ASE, 101 Blue Seal Dr. S.E., Suite 101, Leesburg, VA 20175. Internet: http://www.asecert.org

Home Appliance Repairers

O*NET 49-9031.00, 49-9031.01, 49-9031.02

Significant Points

- Although employment of home appliance repairers is expected to grow slowly, opportunities should be good for skilled repairers.

- Many repairers are high school graduates who are trained on the job.

- Knowledge of basic electronics is becoming increasingly important.

Nature of the Work

Anyone whose washer, dryer, or refrigerator has ever broken knows the importance of a dependable repair person. Home appliance repairers, often called service technicians, keep home appliances working and help prevent unwanted breakdowns. Some repairers work specifically on small appliances such as microwaves and vacuum cleaners; others specialize in major appliances such as refrigerators, dishwashers, washers, and dryers.

Home appliance repairers visually inspect appliances and check for unusual noises, excessive vibration, fluid leaks, or loose parts to determine why they fail to operate properly. They use service manuals, troubleshooting guides, and experience to diagnose particularly difficult problems. They disassemble the appliance to examine its internal parts for signs of wear or corrosion. Repairers follow wiring diagrams and use testing devices such as ammeters, voltmeters, and wattmeters to check electrical systems for shorts and faulty connections.

After identifying problems, they replace or repair defective belts, motors, heating elements, switches, gears, or other items. They tighten, align, clean, and lubricate parts as necessary. Repairers use common hand tools, including screwdrivers, wrenches, files, and pliers, as well as soldering guns and special tools designed for particular appliances. When repairing appliances with electronic parts, they may replace circuit boards or other electronic components.

Many manufacturers incorporate "fuzzy logic" technology into their newer and more expensive appliances. Fuzzy logic technology involves sensors, or inputs, strategically placed inside an appliance to transmit information to an on-board computer. The computer processes this information and adjusts variables such as water and electricity, to optimize appliance performance and reduce wasted resources. Fuzzy logic uses 1 input; "neurofuzzy logic" uses up to 5 inputs; and "chaos logic" uses up to 10 inputs. Dishwashers, washers, and dryers commonly use neurofuzzy logic in their components.

When repairing refrigerators and window air-conditioners, repairers must use care to conserve, recover, and recycle chlorofluorocarbon (CFC) and hydrochlorofluorocarbon (HCFC) refrigerants used in their cooling systems as required by law. Repairers conserve the refrigerant by making sure there are no leaks in the system; they recover the refrigerant by venting it into proper cylinders; and they recycle the refrigerant for re-

use with special filter-dryers. Federal regulations also require that home appliance repairers document the capture and disposal of refrigerants.

Home appliance installers generally install "white goods" such as refrigerators, washing machines and stoves. They may have to install pipes in a customer's home to connect the appliances to the gas line. They measure, lay out, cut, and thread pipe and connect it to a feeder line and to the appliance. They may have to saw holes in walls or floors and hang steel supports from beams or joists to hold gas pipes in place. Once the gas line is in place, they turn on the gas and check for leaks. *Gas appliance repairers* check the heating unit and replace tubing, thermocouples, thermostats, valves, and indicator spindles. They also answer emergency calls for gas leaks.

Repairers also answer customers' questions about the care and use of appliances. For example, they demonstrate how to load automatic washing machines, arrange dishes in dishwashers, or sharpen chain saws to maximize performance.

Repairers write up estimates of the cost of repairs for customers, keep records of parts used and hours worked, prepare bills, and collect payments. Self-employed repairers also deal with the original appliance manufacturers to recoup monetary claims for work performed on appliances still under warranty.

Working Conditions

Home appliance repairers who handle portable appliances usually work in repair shops that are generally quiet, well lighted, and adequately ventilated. Those who repair major appliances usually make service calls to customers' homes. They carry their tools and a number of commonly used parts with them in a truck or van for use on their service calls. A repairer may spend several hours a day driving to and from appointments and emergency calls. They may work in clean comfortable rooms such as kitchens, or in damp, dirty, or dusty areas of a home. Repairers sometimes work in cramped and uncomfortable positions when they're replacing parts in hard-to-reach areas of appliances.

Repairer jobs generally are not hazardous, but they must exercise care and follow safety precautions to avoid electrical shocks and injuries when lifting and moving large appliances. When repairing gas appliances and microwave ovens, they must be aware of the dangers of gas and radiation leaks.

Many home appliance repairers work a standard 40-hour week. Some repairers work early morning, evening, and weekend shifts. Many repairers remain on-call in case of emergency. Many repairers work overtime and weekend hours in the summer months, when they are in high demand to fix air-conditioners and refrigerators.

Home appliance repairers usually work with little or no direct supervision, a feature of the job that appeals to many people.

Employment

Home appliance repairers held nearly 43,000 jobs in 2000. More than 20 percent of repairers are self-employed. About 40 percent of salaried repairers worked in retail establishments such as department stores, household appliance stores, and fuel dealers. Others worked for gas and electric utility companies, electrical repair shops, and wholesalers.

Almost every community in the country employs appliance repairers; a high concentration of jobs are found in more populated areas.

Training, Other Qualifications, and Advancement

Employers generally require a high school diploma for home appliance repairer jobs. Repairers of small appliances commonly learn the trade on the job; repairers of large household appliances often receive their training in a formal trade school, community college, or directly from the appliance manufacturer. Mechanical aptitude is desirable, and those who work in customers' homes must be courteous and tactful.

Employers prefer to hire people with formal training in appliance repair and electronics. Many repairers complete 1- or 2-year formal training programs in appliance repair and related subjects in high schools, private vocational schools, and community colleges. Courses in basic electricity and electronics are becoming increasingly necessary as more manufacturers install circuit boards and other electronic control systems in home appliances.

Whether their basic skills are developed through formal training or on the job, trainees usually receive additional training from their employer and manufacturers. In shops that fix portable appliances, they work on a single type of appliance, such as a vacuum cleaner, until they master its repair. Then they move on to others, until they can repair all those handled by the shop. In companies that repair major appliances, beginners assist experienced repairers on service visits. They may also study on their own. They learn to read schematic drawings, analyze problems, determine whether to repair or replace parts, and follow proper safety procedures. Up to 3 years of on-the-job training may be needed for a technician to become skilled in all aspects of repair.

Some appliance manufacturers and department store chains have formal training programs that include home study and shop classes, in which trainees work with demonstration appliances and other training equipment. Many repairers receive supplemental instruction through 2- or 3-week seminars conducted by appliance manufacturers. Experienced repairers also often attend training classes and study service manuals. Repairers authorized for warranty work by manufacturers are required to attend periodic training sessions.

The U.S. Environmental Protection Agency (EPA) has mandated that all repairers who buy or work with refrigerants must be certified in their proper handling; a technician must pass a written examination to become certified to buy and handle refrigerants. Exams are administered by organizations approved by the EPA, such as trade schools, unions, and employer associations. There are even EPA-approved take-home certification exams. Although no formal training is required for certification, many of these organizations offer training programs designed to prepare workers for the certification examination.

To protect consumers and recognize highly skilled home appliance repairers, the Association of Home Appliance Manufacturers has instituted the National Appliance Service Technician Certification Program (NASTeC). Together, manufacturers, schools, and field experts write questions that measure the skills of their trade. To become certified, technicians must pass a comprehensive examination testing their competence in the diagnosis, repair, and maintenance of major home appliances. The examination is given on demand at locations throughout the country. While there has not previously been standardized certification, growing numbers of employers now encourage repairers to become certified.

The Professional Service Association (PSA) has a certification program with similar goals to the NASTeC program—to recognize skilled repairers. To become certified, technicians must pass an examination. The PSA certification is valid for 4 years. If certified technicians complete at least 15 credit hours of instruction every year during the 4 years, then the technicians need not sit for the examination for recertification. Otherwise, they must retake the examination.

Repairers in large shops or service centers may be promoted to supervisor, assistant service manager, or service manager. A few repairers advance to managerial positions such as regional service manager or parts manager for appliance or tool manufacturers. Preference is given to those who demonstrate technical competence and show an ability to get along with coworkers and customers. Experienced repairers who have sufficient funds and knowledge of small business management may open their own repair shop.

Job Outlook

Employment of home appliance repairers is expected to increase more slowly than the average for all occupations through the year 2010. Prospects should continue to be good for well-trained repairers, particularly those with a strong background in electronics. The number of home appliances in use is expected to increase with growth in the number of households and businesses. In the past, employment growth of home appliance repairers has been limited because of the need for less frequent repairs due to solid-state circuitry, microprocessors, and sensing devices in appliances. Also, many consumers tended to purchase new appliances when existing warranties expired rather than invest in repairs on old appliances, further reducing the need for home appliance repairers. These employment limitations could be somewhat offset over the next decade as more consumers purchase higher priced appliances designed to have much longer lives, making consumers more likely to use repair service than to purchase new appliances. Moreover, as home appliance repairers retire or transfer to other occupations, additional job openings will arise.

The availability of manufacturer-sponsored training programs could limit employment growth. Manufacturers often make these programs available only to large equipment dealers, thereby discouraging repairers from becoming self-employed or working for small shops. Many self-employed repairers are forced to join larger shops so that they can stay abreast of developments in the industry. Jobs are expected to be increasingly concentrated in larger companies as the number of smaller shops and family-owned businesses declines. However, those repairers that maintain strong industry relationships may still go into business for themselves.

Employment is relatively steady because the demand for appliance repair services continues even during economic downturns. However, during economic slowdowns some repair shops may lay off repairers.

Earnings

Median annual earnings, including commission, of home appliance repairers were $28,860 in 2000. The middle 50 percent earned between $21,840 and $38,040 a year. The lowest 10 percent earned less than $17,300, and the highest 10 percent earned more than $45,750 a year. Median annual earnings in the two industries employing the largest numbers of home appliance repairers in 2000 were $27,560 in electrical repair shops and $24,860 in household appliance stores.

Earnings of home appliance repairers vary according to the skill level required to fix equipment, geographic location, and the type of equipment repaired. Because many repairers receive commission along with their salary, earnings increase along with the number of jobs a repairer can complete in a day.

Many larger dealers, manufacturers and service stores offer benefits such as health insurance coverage, sick leave, and retirement and pension programs. Some home appliance repairers belong to the International Brotherhood of Electrical Workers.

Related Occupations

Other workers who repair electrical and electronic equipment include heating, air-conditioning, and refrigeration mechanics and installers; small engine mechanics; office machine and cash register servicers; electronic home entertainment equipment installers and repairers; and coin, vending, and amusement machine servicers and repairers.

Sources of Additional Information

For information about jobs in the home appliance repair field, contact local appliance repair shops, manufacturers, vocational trade schools, appliance dealers, and utility companies, or the local office of the state employment service.

For general information about the work of home appliance repairers, contact:

- Appliance Service News, P.O. Box 809, St. Charles, IL 60174

- North American Retail Dealers Association, 10 E. 22nd St., Suite 310, Lombard, IL 60148-4915

- National Appliance Service Association, 9247 N. Meridian, Suite 105, Indianapolis, IN 46260

For information on technician certification, as well as general information about the work of home appliance repairers, contact:

- National Appliance Service Technician Certification Program (NASTeC), 10 E. 22nd St., Suite 310, Lombard, IL 60148. Internet: http://www.nastecnet.org

- Professional Service Association, 71 Columbia St., Cohoes, NY 12047

Hotel, Motel, and Resort Desk Clerks

O*NET 43-4081.00

Significant Points

- Numerous job openings should arise for hotel, motel, and resort desk clerks due to employment growth and the need to replace workers who leave these occupations.

- A high school diploma or its equivalent is the most common educational requirement.

- Because many information and record clerks deal directly with the public, a professional appearance and pleasant personality are imperative.

Nature of the Work

Hotel, motel, and resort desk clerks perform a variety of services for guests of hotels, motels, and other lodging establishments. Regardless of the type of accommodation, most desk clerks have similar responsibilities. Primarily, they register arriving guests, assign rooms, and check out guests at the end of their stay. They also keep records of room assignments and other registration information on computers. When guests check out, they prepare and explain the charges, as well as process payments.

Front desk clerks always are in the public eye and, through their attitude and behavior, greatly influence the public's impressions of the establishment. When answering questions about services, checkout times, the local community, or other matters of public interest, clerks must be courteous and helpful. Should guests report problems with their rooms, clerks contact members of the housekeeping or maintenance staff to correct them.

In some smaller hotels and motels, clerks may have a variety of additional responsibilities usually performed by specialized employees in larger establishments. In these places, the desk clerk often is responsible for all front office operations, information, and services. These clerks, for example, may perform the work of a bookkeeper, advance reservation agent, cashier, laundry attendant, and telephone switchboard operator.

Working Conditions

Working conditions vary for different types of hotel, motel, and resort desk clerks, but work in areas that are clean, well lit, and relatively quiet. This is especially true for clerks who greet customers and visitors; they usually work in highly visible areas that are furnished to make a good impression. Because a number of clerks may share the same workspace, it may be crowded and noisy.

Although some information and record clerks work a standard 40-hour week, about 3 in 10 hotel clerks works part-time. Because hotels and motels need to be staffed 24 hours a day, evening, holiday, and weekend work is common. In general, employees with the least seniority tend to be assigned the less desirable shifts.

Some high school and college students work part-time as information clerks, after school or during vacations.

The work performed by hotel, motel, and resort desk clerks may be repetitious and stressful, especially when trying to serve the needs of difficult or angry customers. When flights are canceled, reservations mishandled, or guests are dissatisfied, these clerks must bear the brunt of the customers' anger. Hotel desk clerks may be on their feet most of the time.

In addition, prolonged exposure to a video display terminal may lead to eyestrain for the many clerks who work with computers.

Employment

Hotel, motel, and resort desk clerks held about 177,000 jobs in 2000. This occupation is well suited to flexible work schedules, as about 3 in 10 hotel clerks works part-time. Because hotels and motels need to be staffed 24 hours a day, evening and weekend work is common.

Training, Other Qualifications, and Advancement

Although hiring requirements for hotel, motel, and resort desk clerks vary from industry to industry, a high school diploma or its equivalent is the most common educational requirement. Increasingly, familiarity or experience with computers and good interpersonal skills is equally important to employers.

Many hotel, motel, and resort desk clerks deal with the public, so a pleasant personality is important. A clear speaking voice and fluency in the English language also are essential because these employees frequently use the telephone or public address systems. Good spelling and computer literacy often are needed, particularly because most work involves considerable computer use.

Orientation and training for hotel, motel, and resort desk usually takes place on the job. It usually includes an explanation of the job duties and information about the establishment, such as room locations and available services. New employees learn job tasks through on-the-job training under the guidance of a supervisor or an experienced clerk. They often need additional training in how to use the computerized reservation, room assignment, and billing systems and equipment. Desk clerks usually receive training in procedures for greeting visitors, operating telephone and computer systems, and distributing mail, fax, and parcel deliveries.

Most hotel, motel, and resort desk continue to receive instruction on new procedures and company policies after their initial training ends.

Advancement for hotel, motel, and resort desk clerks usually comes by transfer to a position with more responsibilities or by promotion to a supervisory position. Clerks can improve their chances for advancement by taking home or group study courses in lodging management, such as those sponsored by the Educational Institute of the American Hotel and Motel Association.

Job Outlook

Employment of hotel, motel, and resort desk clerks is expected to grow faster than the average for all occupations through 2010, as more hotels, motels, and other lodging establishments are built and occupancy rates rise. Job opportunities for hotel and motel desk clerks also will result from a need to replace workers, as thousands of workers transfer to other occupations that offer better pay and advancement opportunities or simply leave the work force altogether. Opportunities for part-time work should continue to be plentiful, as front desks often are staffed 24 hours a day, 7 days a week.

Employment of hotel and motel desk clerks should be favorably affected by an increase in business and leisure travel. Shifts in travel preference away from long vacations and toward long weekends and other, more frequent, shorter trips also should increase demand as this trend increases the total number of nights spent in hotels. The expansion of budget and extended-stay hotels relative to larger, luxury establishments reflects a change in the composition of the hotel and motel industry. As employment shifts from luxury hotels to these extended-stay establishments offering larger rooms with kitchenettes and laundry services, the proportion of hotel desk clerks should increase in relation to staff such as waiters and waitresses and recreation workers. Desk clerks are able to handle more of the guest's needs in these establishments, answering the main switchboard, providing business services, and coordinating services like dry cleaning or grocery shopping.

New technologies automating check-in and check-out procedures now allow some guests to bypass the front desk in many larger establishments, reducing staffing needs. As some of the more traditional duties are automated, however, many desk clerks are assuming a wider range of responsibilities.

Employment of desk clerks is sensitive to cyclical swings in the economy. During recessions, vacation and business travel declines, and hotels and motels need fewer clerks. Similarly, desk clerk employment is affected by seasonal fluctuations in travel during high and low tourist seasons.

Earnings

In 2000, annual earnings were less than $12,370 for the lowest paid 10 percent of hotel clerks. The median annual earnings for hotel, motel, and resort desk clerks were $16,380.

Earnings of hotel and motel desk clerks also vary considerably depending on the location, size, and type of establishment in which they work. For example, large luxury hotels and those located in metropolitan and resort areas generally pay clerks more than less exclusive or "budget" establishments and those located in less populated areas.

In addition to their hourly wage, full-time hotel, motel and resort desk clerks who work evenings, nights, weekends, or holidays may receive shift differential pay. Some employers offer educational assistance to their employees.

Related Occupations

A number of other workers deal with the public, receive and provide information, or direct people to others who can assist them. Among these are dispatchers, security guards and gaming surveillance workers, tellers, and counter and rental clerks.

Sources of Additional Information

State employment service offices can provide information about employment opportunities.

Information on careers in the lodging industry, as well as information about professional development and training programs, may be obtained from:

- Educational Institute of the American Hotel and Lodging Association, 800 N. Magnolia Ave., Suite 1800, Orlando, FL 32803. Internet: http://www.ei-ahma.org

Human Resources Assistants, Except Payroll and Timekeeping

O*NET 43-4161.00

America's Top Jobs for People Without a Four-Year Degree

Significant Points

- Numerous job openings should arise for human resources assistants due to employment growth and the need to replace workers who leave these occupations.

- A high school diploma or its equivalent is the most common educational requirement.

- Because many human resources assistants may deal directly with employees and job applicants, a professional appearance and pleasant personality are imperative.

Nature of the Work

Human resources assistants maintain the personnel records of an organization's employees. These records include information such as name, address, job title, and earnings, benefits such as health and life insurance, and tax withholding. On a daily basis, these assistants record and answer questions about employee absences and supervisory reports on job performance. When an employee receives a promotion or switches health insurance plans, the human resources assistant updates the appropriate form. Human resources assistants also may prepare reports for managers elsewhere within the organization. For example, they might compile a list of employees eligible for an award.

In smaller organizations, some human resources assistants perform a variety of other clerical duties. They answer telephone or letter inquiries from the public, send out announcements of job openings or job examinations, and issue application forms. When credit bureaus and finance companies request confirmation of a person's employment, the human resources assistant provides authorized information from the employee's personnel records. Payroll departments and insurance companies also may be contacted to verify changes to records.

Some human resources assistants also are involved in hiring. They screen job applicants to obtain information such as education and work experience; administer aptitude, personality, and interest tests; explain the organization's employment policies and refer qualified applicants to the employing official; and request references from present or past employers. Also, human resources assistants inform job applicants, by telephone or letter, of their acceptance or rejection for employment.

In some job settings, human resources assistants have specific job titles. For example, *assignment clerks* notify a firm's existing employees of position vacancies and identify and assign qualified applicants. They keep track of vacancies throughout the organization and complete and distribute vacancy advertisement forms. These clerks review applications in response to advertisements and verify information, using personnel records. After a selection is made, they notify all the applicants of their acceptance or rejection.

For another example, *identification clerks* are responsible for security matters at defense installations. They compile and record personal data about vendors, contractors, and civilian and military personnel and their dependents. Job duties include interviewing applicants; corresponding with law enforcement authorities; and preparing badges, passes, and identification cards.

Working Conditions

Most human resources assistants work in areas that are clean, well lit, and relatively quiet.

Most information and record clerks work a standard 40-hour week.

The work performed by information clerks may be repetitious and stressful. Prolonged exposure to a video display terminal may lead to eyestrain for the many human resources assistants who work with computers.

Employment

Human resources assistants held about 177,000 jobs in 2000. Although these workers are found in most industries, about 1 in every 6 works for a government agency. Colleges and universities, hospitals, department stores, and banks also employ large numbers of human resources assistants.

Training, Other Qualifications, and Advancement

Although hiring requirements for human resources assistants vary from industry to industry, a high school diploma or its equivalent is the most common educational requirement. Increasingly, familiarity or experience with computers and good interpersonal skills is equally important to employers.

Many human resources assistants deal with the public, so a professional appearance and pleasant personality is important. A clear speaking voice and fluency in the English language also are essential because these employees frequently use the telephone. Good spelling and computer literacy often are needed, particularly because most work involves considerable computer use.

Human resources assistants often learn the skills they need in high schools, business schools, and community colleges. Business education programs offered by these institutions typically include courses in typing, word processing, shorthand, business communications, records management, and office systems and procedures.

Some entry-level human resources assistants are college graduates who accept entry-level clerical positions to get into a particular company or to enter a particular field. Workers with college degrees are likely to start at higher salaries and advance more easily than those without degrees do.

Orientation and training for human resources assistants usually takes place on the job. New employees usually receive on-the-job training. Under the guidance of a supervisor or other senior workers, new employees learn company procedures. Some formal classroom training also may be necessary, such as training in specific computer software. Most human resources assistants continue to receive instruction on new procedures and company policies after their initial training ends.

Advancement usually comes by transfer to a position with more responsibilities or by promotion to a supervisory position. Most companies fill office and administrative support supervisory and managerial positions by promoting individuals within their organization, so human resources assistants who acquire additional skills, experience, and training improve their advancement opportunities.

Job Outlook

Employment of human resources assistants is expected to grow about as fast as the average for all occupations through the year 2010, as assistants continue to take on more responsibilities. For example, workers conduct Internet research to locate resumes, must be able to scan resumes of job candidates quickly and efficiently, and must be increasingly sensitive to confidential information such as salaries and social security numbers. In a favorable job market, more emphasis is placed on human resources departments, thus increasing the demand for human resources assistants. However, even in economic downturns, there will be continuing demand for human resources assistants as human resources departments in all industries try to make their organizations more efficient by determining what type of employees to hire and strategically filling job openings. Human resources assistants may play an instrumental role in their organization's human resources policies. For example, they may talk to staffing firms and consulting firms and conduct other research, and then offer their ideas on issues such as whether to hire temporary contract workers or full-time staff.

Similar to other office and administrative support occupations, the growing use of computers in human resources departments means that a lot of data entry done by human resources assistants can be eliminated, as employees themselves enter the data and send it to the human resources office. This is most feasible in large organizations with multiple human resources offices and, to some extent, could limit job growth among human resources assistants.

In addition to job growth, replacement needs will account for many job openings for human resources assistants as they advance within the human resources department, take jobs unrelated to human resources administration, or leave the labor force.

Earnings

In 2000, median annual earnings for human resources assistants, except for those in payroll and timekeeping, were $28,340.

Related Occupations

A number of other workers deal with the public, receive and provide information, or direct people to others who can assist them. Among these are dispatchers, security guards and gaming surveillance workers, tellers, and counter and rental clerks.

Sources of Additional Information

State employment service offices can provide information about employment opportunities.

Industrial Machinery Installation, Repair, and Maintenance Workers

O*NET 49-9041.00, 49-9042.00, 49-9043.00, 49-9044.00

Significant Points

● Workers learn their trade through a 4-year apprenticeship program, or through informal on-the-job training supplemented by classroom instruction.

● Despite slower-than-average employment growth resulting from technological advancements in machinery, applicants with broad skills in machine repair should have favorable job prospects.

Nature of the Work

When production workers encounter problems with the machines they operate, they call industrial machinery installation, repair, and maintenance workers. These workers include industrial machinery mechanics, millwrights, and general maintenance and repair and machinery maintenance workers. Their work is important not only because an idle machine will delay production, but also because a machine that is not properly repaired and maintained may damage the final product or injure the operator.

Industrial machinery mechanics repair, install, adjust, or maintain industrial production and processing machinery or refinery and pipeline distribution systems. *Millwrights* install, dismantle, or move machinery and heavy equipment according to layout plans, blueprints, or other drawings. *General maintenance and repair workers* perform work involving the skills of two or more maintenance or craft occupations to keep machines, mechanical equipment, or the structure of an establishment in repair. *Machinery maintenance workers* lubricate machinery, change parts, or perform other routine machinery maintenance.

Much of the work begins when machinery arrives at the job site. New equipment must be unloaded, inspected, and moved into position. To lift and move light machinery, industrial machinery installation, repair, and maintenance workers use rigging and hoisting devices, such as pulleys and cables. In other cases, they require the assistance of hydraulic lift-truck or crane operators to position the machinery. Because industrial machinery installation, repair, and maintenance workers often decide which device to use for moving machinery, they must know the load-bearing properties of ropes, cables, hoists, and cranes.

Industrial machinery installation, repair, and maintenance workers consult with production managers and others to determine the optimal placement of machines in a plant. In some instances, this placement requires building a new foundation. Industrial machinery installation, repair, and maintenance workers either prepare the foundation themselves or supervise its construction, so they must know how to read blueprints and work with building materials, such as concrete, wood, and steel.

When assembling machinery, industrial machinery installation, repair, and maintenance workers fit bearings, align gears and wheels, attach motors, and connect belts, according to the manufacturer's blueprints and drawings. Precision leveling and alignment are important in the assembly process; industrial machinery installation, repair, and maintenance workers must have good mathematical skills, so that they can measure angles, material thickness, and small distances with tools such as squares, calipers, and micrometers. When a high level of precision is required, devices such as lasers and ultrasonic measuring tools may be used. Industrial machinery installation, repair, and maintenance workers also work with hand and power tools, such as cutting torches, welding machines, and soldering guns. Some of these workers use metalworking equipment, such as lathes or grinders, to modify parts to specifications.

Maintenance mechanics must be able to detect and diagnose minor problems and correct them before they become major ones. For example, after hearing a vibration from a machine, the mechanic must decide whether it is due to worn belts, weak motor bearings, or some other problem. Computerized maintenance, vibration analysis techniques, and self-diagnostic systems are making this task easier. Self-diagnostic features on new industrial machinery can determine the cause of a malfunction and, in some cases, alert the mechanic to potential trouble spots before symptoms develop.

After diagnosing the problem, the mechanic disassembles the equipment and repairs or replaces the necessary parts. Once the machine is reassembled, the final step is to test it to ensure that it is running smoothly. When repairing electronically controlled machinery, maintenance mechanics may work closely with electronic repairers or electricians who maintain the machine's electronic parts. However, industrial machinery installation, repair, and maintenance workers increasingly need electronic and computer skills to repair sophisticated equipment on their own.

Although repairing machines is the most important job of industrial machinery installation, repair, and maintenance workers, they also perform preventive maintenance. This includes keeping machines and their parts well oiled, greased, and cleaned. Repairers regularly inspect machinery and check performance. For example, they adjust and calibrate automated manufacturing equipment such as industrial robots, and rebuild components of other industrial machinery. By keeping complete and up-to-date records, mechanics try to anticipate trouble and service equipment before factory production is interrupted.

A wide range of tools may be used when performing repairs or preventive maintenance. Repairers may use a screwdriver and wrench to adjust a motor, or a hoist to lift a printing press off the ground. When replacements for broken or defective parts are not readily available, or when a machine must be quickly returned to production, repairers may sketch a part that can be fabricated by the plant's machine shop. Repairers use catalogs to order replacement parts and often follow blueprints and engineering specifications to maintain and fix equipment.

Installation of new machinery is another responsibility of industrial machinery installation, repair, and maintenance workers. As plants retool and invest in new equipment, they increasingly rely on these workers to properly situate and install the machinery. As employers increasingly seek workers who have a variety of skills, industrial machinery installation, repair, and maintenance workers are taking on new responsibilities.

Working Conditions

Working conditions for repairers who work in manufacturing are similar to those of production workers. These workers are subject to common shop injuries such as cuts and bruises, and use protective equipment such as hardhats, protective glasses, and safety belts. Industrial machinery installation, repair, and maintenance workers also may face additional hazards because they often work on top of a ladder or underneath or above large machinery in cramped conditions. Industrial machinery installation, repair, and maintenance workers may work independently or as part of a team. They must work quickly and precisely, because disabled machinery costs a company time and money.

Because factories and other facilities cannot afford breakdowns of industrial machinery, repairers may be called to the plant at night or on weekends for emergency repairs. Overtime is common among industrial machinery installation, repair, and maintenance workers—more than a third work over 40 hours a week. During power outages, industrial machinery installation, repair, and maintenance workers may be assigned overtime and be required to work in shifts to deal with the emergency.

Employment

Industrial machinery installation, repair, and maintenance workers held about 1.6 million jobs in 2000. Employment was distributed among the following occupations:

Maintenance and repair workers, general 1,251,000
Industrial machinery mechanics 198,000
Maintenance workers, machinery 114,000
Millwrights 72,000

About 1 of every 3 worked in manufacturing industries, primarily food processing, textile mill products, chemicals, fabricated metal products, and primary metals. Others worked for government agencies, public utilities, mining companies, and other establishments in which industrial machinery is used.

Industrial machinery installation, repair, and maintenance workers are found in a wide variety of plants and in every part of the country. However, employment is concentrated in heavily industrialized areas.

Training, Other Qualifications, and Advancement

Most industrial machinery installation, repair, and maintenance workers, including millwrights, learn their trade through a 4-year apprenticeship program combining classroom instruction with on-the-job training. These programs usually are sponsored by a local trade union. Other machinery maintenance workers start as helpers and pick up the skills of the trade informally and by taking courses offered by machinery manufacturers and community colleges.

Trainee repairers learn from experienced repairers how to operate, disassemble, repair, and assemble machinery. Trainees also may work with concrete and receive instruction in related skills, such as carpentry, welding, and sheet metal work. Classroom instruction focuses on subjects such as shop mathematics, blueprint reading, welding, electronics, and computer training.

Most employers prefer to hire those who have completed high school or its equivalency, and who have some vocational training or experience. High school courses in mechanical drawing, mathematics, blueprint reading, physics, computers, and electronics are especially useful.

Mechanical aptitude and manual dexterity are important characteristics for workers in this trade. Good physical conditioning and agility also are necessary because repairers sometimes have to lift heavy objects or climb to reach equipment located high above the floor.

Opportunities for advancement are limited. Industrial machinery installation, repair, and maintenance workers advance either by working with more complicated equipment or by becoming supervisors. The most highly skilled repairers can be promoted to master mechanic or can become machinists or tool and die makers.

Job Outlook

Overall employment of industrial machinery installation, repair, and maintenance workers is projected to grow more slowly than the average for all occupations through 2010. Nevertheless, applicants with broad skills in machine repair should have favorable job prospects. As more firms introduce automated production equipment, industrial machinery installation, repair, and maintenance workers will be needed to ensure that these machines are properly maintained and consistently in operation. However, many new machines are capable of self-diagnosis, increasing their reliability and, thus, reducing the need for repairers. As a result, the majority of job openings will stem from the need to replace repairers who transfer to other occupations or leave the labor force.

As automation of machinery becomes more widespread, there is a greater need for repair work than for the installation of new machinery. Industrial machinery installation, repair, and maintenance workers are becoming more productive through the use of technologies such as hydraulic torque wrenches, ultrasonic measuring tools, and laser shaft alignment, as these technologies allow fewer workers to perform more work. In addition, the demand for industrial machinery installation, repair, and maintenance workers will be adversely affected as lower-paid workers, such as electronics technicians, increasingly assume some installation and maintenance duties.

Unlike many other occupations concentrated in manufacturing industries, industrial machinery installation, repair, and maintenance workers usually are not affected by seasonal changes in production. During slack periods, when some plant workers are laid off, repairers often are retained to do major overhaul jobs. Although these workers may face layoff or a reduced workweek when economic conditions are particularly severe, they usually are less affected than are other workers because machines have to be maintained regardless of production level.

Earnings

Earnings of industrial machinery installation, repair, and maintenance workers vary by industry and geographic region. Median hourly earnings of industrial machinery mechanics were $17.30 in 2000. The middle 50 percent earned between $13.73 and $21.93. The lowest 10 percent earned less than $11.31, and the highest 10 percent earned more than $26.26. Median hourly earnings in the industries employing the largest numbers of industrial machinery mechanics in 2000 are shown in the following table:

Motor vehicles and equipment	$24.28
Electric services	24.12
Plastics materials and synthetics	20.14
Machinery, equipment, and supplies	15.01
Meat products	13.06

Median hourly earnings of general maintenance and repair workers were $13.39 in 2000. The middle 50 percent earned between $10.05 and $17.47. The lowest 10 percent earned less than $7.84, and the highest 10 percent earned more than $21.43. Median hourly earnings in the industries employing the largest numbers of general maintenance and repair workers in 2000 are shown in the following table:

Local government	$13.99
Elementary and secondary schools	13.17
Real estate agents and managers	10.85
Real estate operators and lessors	10.71
Hotels and motels	10.07

Median hourly earnings of millwrights were $19.33 in 2000. The middle 50 percent earned between $15.19 and $23.98. The lowest 10 percent earned less than $12.02, and the highest 10 percent earned more than $27.07. Median hourly earnings in the industries employing the largest numbers of millwrights in 2000 are shown in the following table:

Motor vehicles and equipment	$25.73
Miscellaneous special trade contractors	19.64
Blast furnace and basic steel products	18.85

Median hourly earnings of machinery maintenance workers were $14.89 in 2000. The middle 50 percent earned between $11.54 and $18.79. The lowest 10 percent earned less than $9.20, and the highest 10 percent earned more than $22.74. Median hourly earnings in miscellaneous plastics products, the industry employing the largest numbers of machinery maintenance workers, were $15.28 in 2000.

More than 25 percent of industrial machinery mechanics are union members. More than 67 percent of millwrights belong to labor unions, one of the highest rates of unionization in the economy. Labor unions that represent industrial machinery installation, repair, and maintenance workers include the United Steelworkers of America; the United Automobile, Aerospace and Agricultural Implement Workers of America; the International Association of Machinists and Aerospace Workers; and the International Union of Electronic, Electrical, Salaried, Machine, and Furniture Workers.

Related Occupations

Other occupations that involve repairing machinery include aircraft and avionics equipment mechanics and service technicians; electrical and electronics installers and repairers; coin, vending, and amusement machine servicers and repairers; automotive body and related repairers; automotive service technicians and mechanics; electronic home entertainment equipment installers and repairers; heating, air-conditioning, and refrigeration mechanics and installers; and radio and telecommunications equipment installers and repairers.

Sources of Additional Information

Information about employment and apprenticeship opportunities for industrial machinery installation, repair, and maintenance workers may be obtained from local offices of the state employment service or from:

- United Brotherhood of Carpenters and Joiners of America, 101 Constitution Ave. NW., Washington, DC 20001

- The National Tooling and Machining Association, 9300 Livingston Rd., Fort Washington, MD 20744. Internet: http://www.ntma.org

- Precision Machined Products Association, 6700 West Snowville Rd., Brecksville, OH 44141. Internet: http://www.pmpa.org

- Associated General Contractors of America, 1957 E St. NW., Washington, DC 20006. Internet: http://www.agc.org

Information and Record Clerks

O*NET 43-4011.00, 43-4021.00, 43-4031.01, 43-4031.02, 43-4031.03, 43-4041.01, 43-4041.02, 43-4051.01, 43-4051.02, 43-4061.01, 43-4061.02, 43-4071.00, 43-4081.00, 43-4111.00, 43-4121.00, 43-4131.00, 43-4141.00, 43-4151.00, 43-4161.00, 43-4171.00, 43-4171.00, 43-4181.01, 43-4181.02

Significant Points

- Numerous job openings should arise for most types of information and record clerks due to employment growth and the need to replace workers who leave these occupations.

- A high school diploma or its equivalent is the most common educational requirement.

- Because many information and record clerks deal directly with the public, a professional appearance and pleasant personality are imperative.

Nature of the Work

Information and record clerks are found in nearly every industry in the nation, gathering data and providing information to the public. The specific duties of these clerks vary as widely as the job titles they hold.

Although their day-to-day duties vary widely, most information clerks greet customers, guests, or other visitors. Many also answer telephones and either obtain information from or provide information to the public. Most information clerks use multiline telephones, fax machines, and personal computers. *Hotel, motel, and resort desk clerks*, for example, are a guest's first contact for check-in, check-out, and other services within hotels, motels, and resorts. *Interviewers, except eligibility and loan*, found most often in medical facilities, research firms, and financial institutions, assist the public in completing forms, applications, or questionnaires. *Eligibility interviewers, government programs* determine eligibility of individuals applying to receive assistance. *Receptionists and information clerks* often are a visitor's or caller's first contact within an organization, providing information and routing calls. *Reservation and transportation ticket agents and travel clerks* assist the public in making travel plans, reservations, and purchasing tickets for a variety of transportation services.

Court, municipal, and license clerks perform administrative duties in courts of law, municipalities, and governmental licensing agencies and bureaus. Court clerks prepare the docket of cases to be called, secure information for judges, and contact witnesses, attorneys, and litigants to obtain information for the court. Municipal clerks prepare draft agendas or by-laws for town or city councils, answer official correspondence, and keep fiscal records and accounts. License clerks issue licenses or permits, record data, administer tests, and collect fees.

New account clerks interview individuals desiring to open bank accounts. Their principal tasks include handling customer inquiries, explaining the institution's products and services to people, and referring customers to the appropriate sales personnel. If a customer wants to open a checking or savings account, or an IRA, the new account clerk will interview the customer and enter the required information into a computer for processing.

Customer service representatives interact with customers to provide information in response to inquires about products and services and to handle and resolve complaints.

Record clerks, on the other hand, maintain, update, and process a variety of records, ranging from payrolls to information on the shipment of goods or bank statements. They ensure that other workers get paid on time, customers' questions are answered, and records are kept of all transactions.

Depending on their specific titles, these workers perform a wide variety of record keeping duties. *Brokerage clerks* prepare and maintain the records generated when stocks, bonds, and other types of investments are traded. *File clerks* store and retrieve various kinds of office information for use by staff members. *Human resources assistants, except payroll and timekeeping* maintain employee records. *Library assistants, clerical* assist library patrons. *Order clerks* process incoming orders for goods and services. *Correspondence clerks* reply to customers regarding damage claims, delinquent accounts, incorrect billings, complaints of unsatisfactory service, and requests for merchandise exchanges or returns. *Loan interviewers and clerks* and *credit authorizers, checkers, and clerks* review credit history and obtain the information needed to determine the creditworthiness of loan and credit card applications.

The duties of record clerks vary with the size of the firm. In a small business, a bookkeeping clerk may handle all financial records and transactions, as well as payroll and personnel duties. A large firm, on the other hand, may employ specialized accounting, payroll, and human resources clerks. In general, however, clerical staffs in firms of all sizes increasingly perform a broader variety of tasks than in the past. This is especially true for clerical occupations involving accounting work. As the growing use of computers enables bookkeeping, accounting, and auditing clerks to become more productive, these workers may assume billing, payroll, and timekeeping duties.

Another change in these occupations is the growing use of financial software to enter and manipulate data. Computer programs automatically perform calculations on data that were previously calculated manually. Computers also enable clerks to access data within files more quickly than the former method of reviewing stacks of paper. Nevertheless, most workers still keep backup paper records for research, auditing, and reference purposes. Despite the growing use of automation, interaction with the public and coworkers remains a basic part of the job for many records processing clerks.

Working Conditions

Working conditions vary for different types of information and record clerks, but most clerks work in areas that are clean, well lit, and relatively quiet. This is especially true for information clerks who greet customers and visitors and usually work in highly visible areas that are furnished to make a good impression. Reservation agents and interviewing clerks who spend much of their day talking on the telephone, however, commonly work away from the public, often in large centralized reservation or phone centers. Because a number of agents or clerks may share the same workspace, it may be crowded and noisy. Interviewing clerks may conduct surveys on the street, in shopping malls, or go door to door.

Although most information and record clerks work a standard 40-hour week, about 1 out of 5 works part-time. Some high school and college students work part-time as information clerks, after school or during vacations. Some jobs—such as those in the transportation industry, hospitals, and hotels, in particular—may require working evenings, late night shifts, weekends, and holidays. This also is the case for a growing number of customer service representatives who work for large banks with call centers that are staffed around the clock. Interviewing clerks conducting surveys or other research may mainly work evenings or weekends. In general, employees with the least seniority tend to be assigned the less desirable shifts.

The work performed by information clerks may be repetitious and stressful. For example, many receptionists spend all day answering telephones while performing additional clerical or secretarial tasks. Reservation agents and travel clerks work under stringent time constraints or have quotas on the number of calls answered or reservations made. Additional stress is caused by technology that enables management to electronically monitor use of computer systems, tape record telephone calls, or limit the time spent on each call.

The work of hotel, motel, and resort desk clerks and transportation ticket agents also can be stressful when trying to serve the needs of difficult or angry customers. When flights are canceled, reservations mishandled, or guests are dissatisfied, these clerks must bear the brunt of the customers' anger. Hotel desk clerks and ticket agents may be on their feet most of the time, and ticket agents may have to lift heavy baggage. In addition, prolonged exposure to a video display terminal may lead to eyestrain for the many information clerks who work with computers.

Employment

Information and record clerks held 5.1 million jobs in 2000. The following table shows employment for the individual occupations.

Customer service representatives	1,900,000
Receptionists and information clerks	1,100,000
Order clerks	348,000
File clerks	288,000
Reservation and transportation ticket agents and travel clerks	191,000
Human resources assistants, except payroll and timekeeping	177,000
Hotel, motel, and resort desk clerks	177,000
Interviewers, except eligibility and loan	154,000
Loan interviewers and clerks	139,000
Eligibility interviewers, government programs	117,000
Court, municipal, and license clerks	105,000
Library assistants, clerical	98,000
New accounts clerks	87,000
Credit authorizers, checkers, and clerks	86,000
Brokerage clerks	70,000
Correspondence clerks	38,000

Although information and record clerks are found in a variety of industries, employment is concentrated in health services; finance, insurance, and real estate; transportation, communications, and utilities; and business services.

Training, Other Qualifications, and Advancement

Although hiring requirements for information and record clerk jobs vary from industry to industry, a high school diploma or its equivalent is the most common educational requirement. Increasingly, familiarity or experience with computers and good interpersonal skills is equally important to employers. Although many employers prefer to hire information and record clerks with a higher level of education, it is only required in a few of these clerical occupations. For example, brokerage firms usually seek college graduates for brokerage clerk jobs, and order clerks in high-technology firms often need to understand scientific and mechanical processes, which may require some college education. For customer service representatives, new account clerks, and airline reservation and ticket agent jobs, some college education may be preferred.

Many information clerks deal directly with the public, so a professional appearance and pleasant personality are important. A clear speaking voice and fluency in the English language also are essential because these employees frequently use the telephone or public address systems. Good spelling and computer literacy often are needed, particularly because most work involves considerable computer use. It also is increasingly helpful for those wishing to enter the lodging or travel industries to speak a foreign language fluently.

With the exception of airline reservation and transportation ticket agents, orientation and training for information clerks usually takes place on the job. For example, orientation for hotel and motel desk clerks usually includes an explanation of the job duties and information about the establishment, such as room locations and available services. New employees learn job tasks through on-the-job training under the guidance of a supervisor or an experienced clerk. They often need additional training in how to use the computerized reservation, room assignment, and billing systems and equipment. Most clerks continue to receive instruction on new procedures and company policies after their initial training ends.

Receptionists usually receive on-the-job training, which may include procedures for greeting visitors, operating telephone and computer systems, and distributing mail, fax, and parcel deliveries. Some employers look for applicants who already possess certain skills, such as prior computer and word processing experience, or previous formal education. Customer service representatives also receive on-the-job training, which includes instructions on how to operate telephone and computer systems. These workers must possess strong communication skills since they are constantly interacting with customers.

Most airline reservation and ticket agents learn their skills through formal company training programs. In a classroom setting, they learn company and industry policies, computer systems, and ticketing procedures. They also learn to use the airline's computer system to obtain information on schedules, seat availability, and fares; to reserve space for passengers; and to plan passenger itineraries. They also must become familiar with airport and airline code designations, regulations, and safety procedures, and may be tested on this knowledge. After completing classroom instruction, new agents work on the job with supervisors or experienced agents for a period. During this period, supervisors may monitor telephone conversations to improve the quality of customer service. Agents are expected to provide good service while limiting the time spent on each call without being discourteous to customers. In contrast to the airlines, automobile clubs, bus lines, and railroads tend to train their ticket agents or travel clerks on the job through short in-house classes that last several days.

Most banks prefer to hire college graduates for new account clerk positions. Nevertheless, many new account clerks without college degrees start out as bank tellers and are promoted by demonstrating excellent communication skills and motivation to learn new skills. If a new account clerk has not been a teller before, he or she often will receive such training and work for several months as a teller. In both cases, new account clerks undergo formal training regarding the bank's procedures, products, and services.

Record clerks often learn the skills they need in high schools, business schools, and community colleges. Business education programs offered by these institutions typically include courses in typing, word processing, shorthand, business communications, records management, and office systems and procedures. Specialized order clerks in technical positions obtain their training from technical institutes and 2- and 4-year colleges.

Some entry-level record clerks are college graduates with degrees in business, finance, or liberal arts. Although a degree rarely is required, many graduates accept entry-level clerical positions to get into a particular company or to enter a particular field. Some companies, such as brokerage and accounting firms, have a set plan of advancement that tracks college graduates from entry-level clerical jobs into managerial positions. Workers with college degrees are likely to start at higher salaries and advance more easily than those without degrees do.

Once hired, record clerks usually receive on-the-job training. Under the guidance of a supervisor or other senior workers, new employees learn company procedures. Some formal classroom training also may be necessary, such as training in specific computer software.

Advancement for information and record clerks usually comes by transfer to a position with more responsibilities or by promotion to a supervisory position. Most companies fill office and administrative support supervisory and managerial positions by promoting individuals within their organization, so information clerks who acquire additional skills, experience, and training improve their advancement opportunities. Receptionists, interviewers, and new account clerks with word processing or other clerical skills may advance to a better paying job as a secretary or administrative assistant. Within the airline industry, a ticket agent may advance to lead worker on the shift.

Additional training is helpful in preparing information clerks for promotion. In the lodging industry, clerks can improve their chances for advancement by taking home or group study courses in lodging management, such as those sponsored by the Educational Institute of the American Hotel and Motel Association. In some industries—such as lodging, banking, insurance, or the airlines—workers commonly are promoted through the ranks. Information and record clerk positions offer good opportunities for qualified workers to get started in the business. In a number of industries, a college degree may be required for advancement to management ranks.

Job Outlook

Overall employment of information and record clerks is expected grow about as fast as the average for all occupations through 2010. In addition to many openings occurring as businesses and organizations expand, numerous job openings for information and record clerks will result from the need to replace experienced workers who transfer to other occupations or leave the labor force. Replacement needs are expected to be significant in this large occupational group, as many young people work as clerks for a few years before switching to other, higher paying jobs. The occupation is well suited to flexible work schedules, and many opportunities for part-time work will continue to be available, particularly as organizations attempt to cut labor costs by hiring more part-time or temporary workers.

The outlook for different types of information and record clerks is expected to vary in the coming decade. Customer service representatives are expected to grow faster than the average for all occupations, as they increasingly take over the duties of a variety of other workers. Economic growth and general business expansion are expected to stimulate faster-than-average growth among receptionists and information clerks. Hotel, motel, and resort desk clerks are expected to grow faster than the average, as the occupational composition of the lodging industry changes and services provided by these workers expand. Employment of interviewers, except eligibility and loan also is expected to grow faster than average, as these workers will benefit from rapid growth in the health services industry.

Library assistants and human resources assistants are expected to grow about as fast as average as these workers take on more responsibilities. Average employment growth also is projected for court, municipal, and license clerks as the number of court cases and demand for citizen services continues to increase. Reservation and transportation ticket agents and travel clerks also are expected to grow about as fast as average due to rising demand for travel services. Employment of correspondence clerks; credit authorizers, checkers, and clerks; file clerks; and new account clerks, on the other hand, is expected to grow more slowly than the average for all occupations due to automation and the consolidation of record keeping functions across all industries.

The remainder of the information and record clerks are expected to decline. Employment of eligibility interviewers will decline as government programs, such as welfare, continue to be reformed, reducing the need for these types of workers. Both brokerage clerks and loan interviewers are expected to decline as online trading and other technological innovations continue to automate more of this type of work. And, employment of order clerks is expected to decline as advances in electronic commerce continue to increase the efficiency of transactions among businesses, consumers, and government.

Earnings

Earnings vary widely by occupation and experience. Annual earnings ranged from less than $12,370 for the lowest paid 10 percent of hotel clerks to over $51,410 for the top 10 percent of brokerage clerks in 2000. Salaries of reservation and transportation ticket agents and travel clerks tend to be significantly higher than for other information and record clerks, while hotel, motel, and resort desk clerks tend to earn quite a bit less, as the following table of median annual earnings shows.

Brokerage clerks $31,060
Eligibility interviewers, government programs 28,380
Human resources assistants, except payroll and
    timekeeping 28,340
Loan interviewers and clerks 26,410
Court, municipal, and license clerks 26,150
Customer service representatives 24,600
Credit authorizers, checkers, and clerks 24,570
Correspondence clerks 24,150

Earnings of hotel and motel desk clerks also vary considerably depending on the location, size, and type of establishment in which they work. For example, clerks at large luxury hotels and those located in metropolitan and resort areas generally pay clerks more than less exclusive or "budget" establishments and those located in less populated areas.

In early 2001, the federal government typically paid salaries ranging from $18,667 to $22,734 a year to beginning receptionists with a high school diploma or 6 months of experience. The average annual salary for all receptionists employed by the federal government was about $24,477 in 2001.

In addition to their hourly wage, full-time information and record clerks who work evenings, nights, weekends, or holidays may receive shift differential pay. Some employers offer educational assistance to their employees. Reservation and transportation ticket agents and travel clerks receive free or reduced rate travel on their company's carriers for themselves and their immediate family and, in some companies, for friends.

Related Occupations

A number of other workers deal with the public, receive and provide information, or direct people to others who can assist them. Among these are dispatchers, security guards and gaming surveillance workers, tellers, and counter and rental clerks.

Sources of Additional Information

State employment service offices can provide information about employment opportunities.

For specific information on a career as a loan processor or loan closer, contact:

- Mortgage Bankers Association of America, 1125 15th St. NW., Washington, DC 20005. Internet: http://www.mbaa.org

Information on careers in the lodging industry, as well as information about professional development and training programs, may be obtained from:

- Educational Institute of the American Hotel and Lodging Association, 800 N. Magnolia Ave., Suite 1800, Orlando, FL 32803. Internet: http://www.ei-ahma.org

Information about a career as a library assistant can be obtained from:

- Council on Library/Media Technology, P.O. Box 951, Oxon Hill, MD 20750. Internet: http://library.ucr.edu/COLT

- American Library Association, 50 East Huron St., Chicago, IL 60611. Internet: http://www.ala.org/hrdr

Public libraries and libraries in academic institutions can provide information about job openings for library assistants.

For information about job opportunities as reservation and transportation ticket agents and travel clerks, write the personnel manager of individual transportation companies. Addresses of airlines are available from:

- Air Transport Association of America, 1301 Pennsylvania Ave. NW., Suite 1100, Washington, DC 20004-1707

Inspectors, Testers, Sorters, Samplers, and Weighers

O*NET 51-9061.01, 51-9061.02, 51-9061.03, 51-9061.04, 51-9061.05

Significant Points

- For workers who perform relatively simple tests of products, a high school diploma is sufficient; experienced production workers fill more complex inspecting positions.

- Employment is expected to decline, reflecting the growth of automated inspection and the redistribution of quality-control responsibilities from inspectors to other production workers.

Nature of the Work

Inspectors, testers, sorters, samplers, and weighers ensure that your food will not make you sick, your car will run properly, and your pants will not split the first time you wear them. These workers monitor or audit quality standards for virtually all manufactured products, including foods, textiles, clothing, glassware, motor vehicles, electronic components, computers, and structural steel. As quality becomes increasingly important to the success of many production firms, daily duties of inspectors have changed. In some cases, their titles also have changed to *quality-control inspector* or a similar name, reflecting the growing importance of quality.

Regardless of title, all inspectors, testers, sorters, samplers, and weighers work to guarantee the quality of the goods their firms produce. Job duties, even within one company, vary by the type of products produced or the stage of production. Specific job duties also vary across the wide range of industries in which these workers are found. For example, inspectors may check products by sight, sound, feel, smell, or even taste to locate imperfections such as cuts, scratches, bubbles, missing pieces, misweaves, or crooked seams. These workers also may verify dimensions, color, weight, texture, strength, or other physical characteristics of objects. Machinery testers generally verify that parts fit, move correctly, and are properly lubricated; check the pressure of gases and the level of liquids; test the flow of electricity; and do a test run to check for proper operation. Some jobs involve only a quick visual inspection; others require a longer, detailed one. Sorters may separate goods according to length, size, fabric type, or color, while samplers test or inspect a sample taken from a batch or production run for malfunctions or defects. Weighers weigh quantities of materials for use in production.

Inspectors, testers, sorters, samplers, and weighers are involved at every stage of the production process. Some inspectors examine materials received from a supplier before sending them to the production line. Others inspect components, subassemblies, and assemblies or perform a final check on the finished product. Depending on the skill level of the inspectors, they also may set up and test equipment, calibrate precision instruments, repair defective products, or record data.

Inspectors, testers, sorters, samplers, and weighers rely on a number of tools to perform their jobs. Many use micrometers, calipers, alignment gauges, and other instruments to check and compare the dimensions of parts against the parts' specifications. They also may operate electronic equipment, such as measuring machines, which use sensitive probes to measure a part's dimensional accuracy. Inspectors testing electrical devices may use voltmeters, ammeters, and oscilloscopes to test insulation, current flow, and resistance.

Inspectors mark, tag, or note problems. They may reject defective items outright, send them for repair or correction, or fix minor problems themselves. If the product is acceptable, inspectors may screw on a nameplate, tag it, stamp it with a serial number, or certify it in some other way. Inspectors, testers, sorters, samplers, and weighers record the results of their inspections, compute the percentage of defects and other statistical measures, and prepare inspection and test reports. Some electronic inspection equipment automatically provides test reports containing these inspection results. When defects are found, inspectors notify supervisors and help analyze and correct the production problems.

Increased emphasis on quality control in manufacturing means that inspection is more fully integrated into the production process than in the past. For example, some companies have set up teams of inspection and production workers to jointly review and improve product quality. In addition, many companies now use self-monitoring production machines to ensure that the output is produced within quality standards. Self-monitoring machines can alert inspectors to production problems and automatically repair defects in some cases. Many firms have completely automated inspection with the help of advanced vision systems, using machinery installed at one or several points in the production process. Inspectors in these firms calibrate and monitor the equipment, review output, and perform random product checks.

Working Conditions

Working conditions vary by industry and establishment size. As a result, some inspectors examine similar products for an entire shift, whereas others examine a variety of items. In manufacturing, it is common for most inspectors to remain at one workstation; in transportation, some travel from place to place to do inspections. Inspectors in some industries may be on their feet all day and may have to lift heavy objects, whereas, in other industries, they sit during most of their shift and do little strenuous work. Workers in heavy manufacturing plants may be exposed to the noise and grime of machinery; in other plants, inspectors work in clean, air-conditioned environments suitable for carrying out controlled tests.

Some inspectors work evenings, nights, or weekends. Shift assignments generally are made on the basis of seniority. Overtime may be required to meet production goals.

Employment

Inspectors, testers, sorters, samplers, and weighers held about 602,000 jobs in 2000. About 7 out of 10 worked in manufacturing establishments that produced such products as industrial machinery and equip-

ment, motor vehicles and equipment, aircraft and parts, primary and fabricated metals, electronic components and accessories, food, textiles, and apparel. Inspectors, testers, sorters, samplers, and weighers also were found in personnel supply services, transportation, wholesale trade, engineering and management services, and government agencies.

Training, Other Qualifications, and Advancement

Training requirements vary, based on the responsibilities of the inspector, tester, sorter, sampler, or weigher. For workers who perform simple "pass/fail" tests of products, a high school diploma is preferred and may be required for some jobs. Simple jobs may be filled by beginners provided with in-house training. Training for new inspectors may cover the use of special meters, gauges, computers, or other instruments; quality-control techniques; blueprint reading; safety; and reporting requirements. There are some postsecondary training programs in testing, but many employers prefer to train inspectors on the job.

Complex precision-inspecting positions are filled by experienced assemblers, machine operators, or mechanics who already have a thorough knowledge of the products and production processes. To advance to these positions, experienced workers may need training in statistical process control, new automation, or the company's quality assurance policies. As automated inspection equipment becomes more common, computer skills are increasingly important.

In general, inspectors, testers, sorters, samplers, and weighers need mechanical aptitude, math and communication skills, and good hand-eye coordination and vision. Advancement for these workers frequently takes the form of higher pay. They also may advance to inspector of more complex products, supervisor, or related positions, such as purchaser of materials and equipment.

Job Outlook

Like many other occupations concentrated in manufacturing industries, employment of inspectors, testers, sorters, samplers, and weighers is expected to decline through the year 2010. The projected decline stems primarily from the growing use of automated inspection and the redistribution of quality-control responsibilities from inspectors to production workers. In spite of declining employment, numerous job openings will arise due to turnover in this large occupation. Many of these jobs, however, will be open only to experienced production workers with advanced skills.

Employment of inspectors, testers, sorters, samplers, and weighers will be significantly affected by the increased focus on quality in American industry. The emphasis on quality has led manufacturers to invest in automated inspection equipment and to take a more systematic approach to quality inspection. Continued improvements in technologies, such as spectrophotometers and computer-assisted visual inspection systems, allow firms to effectively automate simple inspection tasks, increasing worker productivity and reducing the demand for inspectors. As the price of these technologies continues to decrease, they will become more cost effective and will be more widely implemented in a broad range of industries.

Apart from automation, firms are improving quality by building it into the production process. Many inspection duties are being redistributed from inspectors, testers, sorters, samplers, and weighers to other production workers who monitor quality at every stage of the process. In addition, the growing implementation of statistical process control is resulting in smarter inspection. Using this system, firms survey the sources and incidence of defects so that they can better focus their efforts and reduce production of defective products.

In many industries, however, automation is not being aggressively pursued as an alternative to manual inspection. Where key inspection elements are oriented toward size, such as length, width, or thickness, automation may play some role in the future. But where taste, smell, texture, appearance, fabric complexity, or product performance is important, inspection will probably continue to be done by humans. Employment of inspectors, testers, sorters, samplers, and weighers is expected to increase in the rapidly growing personnel supply services industry, as more manufacturers and industrial firms hire temporary inspectors to increase the flexibility of their staffing strategies, and in wholesale trade.

Earnings

Median hourly earnings of inspectors, testers, sorters, samplers, and weighers were $12.22 in 2000. The middle 50 percent earned between $9.26 and $16.55 an hour. The lowest 10 percent earned less than $7.33 an hour; the highest 10 percent earned more than $22.21 an hour. Median hourly earnings in the industries employing the largest number of inspectors, testers, sorters, samplers, and weighers in 2000 were as follows:

Motor vehicles and equipment	$21.50
Aircraft and parts	17.00
Electronic components and accessories	11.55
Miscellaneous plastics products, not elsewhere classified	11.24
Personnel supply services	8.25

Related Occupations

Other inspectors include construction and building inspectors, who examine buildings and other structures to ensure compliance with building codes, zoning regulations, and contract specifications.

Sources of Additional Information

For general information about inspectors, testers, sorters, samplers, and weighers, contact:

- The American Society for Quality, 600 North Plankinton Ave., Milwaukee, WI 53203. Internet: http://www.asq.org

Insulation Workers

O*NET 47-2131.00, 47-2132.00

Significant Points

- Workers must follow strict safety guidelines to protect themselves from the dangers of insulating irritants.

- Most insulation workers learn informally on the job; others complete formal apprenticeship programs.

- Excellent employment opportunities are expected, resulting largely from job turnover.

Nature of the Work

Properly insulated buildings reduce energy consumption by keeping heat in during the winter and out in the summer. Refrigerated storage rooms, vats, tanks, vessels, boilers, and steam and hot water pipes also are insulated to prevent the wasteful transfer of heat. Insulation workers install the materials used to insulate buildings and equipment.

Insulation workers cement, staple, wire, tape, or spray insulation. When covering a steam pipe, for example, insulation workers measure and cut sections of insulation to the proper length, stretch it open along a cut that runs the length of the material, and slip it over the pipe. They fasten the insulation with adhesive, staples, tape, or wire bands. Sometimes, they wrap a cover of aluminum, plastic, or canvas over it and cement or band the cover in place. Insulation workers may screw on sheet metal around insulated pipes to protect the insulation from weather conditions or physical abuse.

When covering a wall or other flat surface, workers may use a hose to spray foam insulation onto a wire mesh. The wire mesh provides a rough surface to which the foam can cling and adds strength to the finished surface. Workers may then install drywall or apply a final coat of plaster for a finished appearance.

In attics or exterior walls of uninsulated buildings, workers blow in loose-fill insulation. A helper feeds a machine with fiberglass, cellulose, or rock wool insulation while another worker blows the insulation with a compressor hose into the space being filled.

In new construction or major renovations, insulation workers staple fiberglass or rockwool batts to exterior walls and ceilings before drywall, paneling, or plaster walls are put in place. In making major renovations to old buildings or when putting new insulation around pipes and industrial machinery, insulation workers often must first remove the old insulation. In the past, asbestos—now known to cause cancer in humans—was used extensively in walls and ceilings and for covering pipes, boilers, and various industrial equipment. Because of this danger, U.S. Environmental Protection Agency regulations require that asbestos be removed before a building undergoes major renovations or is demolished. When asbestos is present, specially trained workers must remove the asbestos before insulation workers can install the new insulating materials.

Insulation workers use common handtools—trowels, brushes, knives, scissors, saws, pliers, and stapling guns. They use power saws to cut insulating materials, welding machines to join sheet metal or secure clamps, and compressors to blow or spray insulation.

Working Conditions

Insulation workers generally work indoors. They spend most of the workday on their feet, either standing, bending, or kneeling. Sometimes, they work from ladders or in tight spaces. The work requires more coordination than strength. Insulation work often is dusty and dirty, and the summer heat can make the insulation worker very uncomfortable.

Minute particles from insulation materials, especially when blown, can irritate the eyes, skin, and respiratory system. Workers must follow strict safety guidelines to protect themselves from the dangers of insulating irritants. They keep work areas well-ventilated; wear protective suits, masks, and respirators; and take decontamination showers when necessary.

Employment

Insulation workers held about 53,000 jobs in 2000. The construction industry employed 9 out of 10 of these workers; most worked for insulation or other construction trades contractors. Small numbers of insulation workers held jobs in the federal government, in wholesale trade, and in shipbuilding and other manufacturing industries that have extensive installations for power, heating, and cooling. Most worked in urban areas. In less populated areas, carpenters, heating and air-conditioning installers, or drywall installers may do insulation work.

Training, Other Qualifications, and Advancement

Most insulation workers learn their trade informally on the job, although some workers complete formal apprenticeship programs. For entry jobs, insulation contractors prefer high school graduates who are in good physical condition and licensed to drive. High school courses in blueprint reading, shop math, science, sheet-metal layout, woodworking, and general construction provide a helpful background. Applicants seeking apprenticeship positions must have a high school diploma or its equivalent, and be at least 18 years old.

Trainees who learn on the job receive instruction and supervision from experienced insulation workers. Trainees begin with simple tasks, such as carrying insulation or holding material while it is fastened in place. On-the-job training can take up to 2 years, depending on the nature of the work. Learning to install insulation in homes generally requires less training than does insulation application in commercial and industrial settings. As they gain experience, trainees receive less supervision, more responsibility, and higher pay.

In contrast, trainees in formal apprenticeship programs receive in-depth instruction in all phases of insulation. Apprenticeship programs may be provided by a joint committee of local insulation contractors and the local union of the International Association of Heat and Frost Insulators and Asbestos Workers, to which many insulation workers belong. Programs normally consist of 4 years of on-the-job training coupled with classroom instruction, and trainees must pass practical and written tests to demonstrate knowledge of the trade.

Skilled insulation workers may advance to supervisor, shop superintendent, or insulation contract estimator, or they may set up their own insulation business.

Job Outlook

Job opportunities are expected to be excellent for insulation workers, largely due to the numerous openings arising each year as experienced insulation workers move to other occupations. Because there are no strict training requirements for entry, many people with limited skills work as insulation workers for a short time and then move on to other types of work, creating many job openings. Other opportunities will arise from the need to replace workers who leave the labor force. In addition, many potential workers may prefer work that is less strenuous and has more comfortable working conditions. Well-trained workers will have especially favorable opportunities.

In addition to replacement needs, new jobs will arise as employment of insulation workers increases about as fast as the average for all occupations through the year 2010 as a result of growth in residential and nonresidential construction. Demand for insulation workers will be spurred by the continuing concerns about the efficient use of energy to heat and cool buildings, resulting in increased demand for insulation workers in the construction of new residential, industrial, and commercial buildings. In addition, renovation and efforts to improve insulation in existing structures also will increase demand.

Insulation workers in the construction industry may experience periods of unemployment because of the short duration of many construction projects and the cyclical nature of construction activity. Workers employed in industrial plants generally have more stable employment because maintenance and repair must be done on a continuing basis. Most insulation is applied after buildings are enclosed, so weather conditions have less effect on the employment of insulation workers than on that of some other construction occupations.

Earnings

In 2000, median hourly earnings of insulation workers were $13.05. The middle 50 percent earned between $9.99 and $17.00. The lowest 10 percent earned less than $7.96, and the highest 10 percent earned more than $24.75. Median hourly earnings in the industries employing the largest numbers of insulation workers in 2000 are shown in the following table:

Miscellaneous special trade contractors $13.91
Masonry, stonework, and plastering 12.24

Union workers tend to earn more than nonunion workers. Apprentices start at about one-half of the journeyworker's wage. Insulation workers doing commercial and industrial work earn substantially more than those working in residential construction, which does not require as much skill.

Related Occupations

Insulation workers combine their knowledge of insulation materials with the skills of cutting, fitting, and installing materials. Workers in occupations involving similar skills include carpenters; carpet, floor, and tile installers and finishers; drywall installers, ceiling tile installers, and tapers; roofers; and sheet metal workers.

Sources of Additional Information

For information about training programs or other work opportunities in this trade, contact a local insulation contractor, a local chapter of the International Association of Heat and Frost Insulators and Asbestos Workers, the nearest office of the state employment service or apprenticeship agency, or:

- International Association of Heat and Frost Insulators and Asbestos Workers, 1776 Massachusetts Ave. NW., Suite 301, Washington, DC 20036. Internet: http://www.insulators.org

- National Insulation and Abatement Contractors Association, 99 Canal Center Plaza, Suite 222, Alexandria, VA 22314

- Insulation Contractors Association of America, 1321 Duke St., Suite 303, Alexandria, VA 22314

Insurance Sales Agents

O*NET 41-3021.00

Significant Points

- Despite slower-than-average growth, job opportunities should be good for people with the right skills.

- Employers prefer to hire college graduates and persons with proven sales ability or success in other occupations.

- In addition to insurance policies, agents are beginning to sell more financial products such as mutual funds, retirement funds, and securities.

Nature of the Work

Most people have their first contact with an insurance company through an insurance sales agent. These workers help individuals, families, and businesses select insurance policies that provide the best protection for their lives, health, and property. Insurance sales agents who work exclusively for one insurance company are referred to as captive agents. Independent insurance agents, or brokers, represent several companies and place insurance policies for their clients with the company that offers the best rate and coverage. In either case, agents prepare reports, maintain records, seek out new clients, and, in the event of a loss, help policyholders settle insurance claims. Increasingly, some may also offer their clients financial analysis or advice on ways they can minimize risk.

Insurance sales agents sell one or more types of insurance, such as property and casualty, life, health, disability, and long-term care. Property and casualty insurance agents sell policies that protect individuals and businesses from financial loss resulting from automobile accidents, fire, theft, storms, and other events that can damage property. For businesses, property and casualty insurance can also cover injured workers' compensation, product liability claims, or medical malpractice claims.

Life insurance agents specialize in selling policies that pay beneficiaries when a policyholder dies. Depending on the policyholder's circumstances, a cash-value policy can be designed to provide retirement income, funds for the education of children, or other benefits. Life insurance agents also sell annuities that promise a retirement income. Health insurance agents sell health insurance policies that cover the costs of medical care and loss of income due to illness or injury. They may also sell dental insurance and short- and long-term disability insurance policies.

An increasing number of insurance sales agents offer comprehensive financial planning services to their clients, such as retirement planning, estate planning, or assistance in setting up pension plans for businesses. As a result, many insurance agents are involved in "cross-selling" or "total account development." Besides insurance, these agents may become licensed to sell mutual funds, variable annuities, and other securi-

ties. This is most common for life insurance agents who already sell annuities; however, property and casualty agents also sell financial products.

Technology has greatly impacted the insurance agency, making it much more efficient and giving the agent the ability to take on more clients. Agents' computers are now linked directly to the insurance companies via the Internet, making the tasks of obtaining price quotes and processing applications and service requests, faster and easier. Computers also allow agents to be better informed about new products that the insurance carriers may be offering.

The growth of the Internet in the insurance industry is gradually changing the relationship between the agent and client. In the past, agents devoted much of their time to marketing and selling products to new clients; however, this is changing. Increasingly, clients obtain insurance quotes from a company's Web site, then contact the company directly to purchase policies. This gives the client a more active role in selecting a policy at the best price, while reducing the amount of time agents spend actively seeking new clients. Because insurance sales agents also obtain many new accounts through referrals, it is important that agents maintain regular contact with their clients to ensure that their financial needs are being met. Developing a satisfied clientele who will recommend an agent's services to other potential customers is a key to success in this field.

Increasing competition in the insurance industry means that carriers and agents must find new ways to keep their clients satisfied. One solution is the increasing use of call centers, which usually are accessible to clients 24 hours a day, 7 days a week. Insurance carriers and sales agents are hiring customer service representatives to handle the routine tasks such as answering questions, making policy changes, processing claims, and selling more products to clients. This opportunity to cross-sell new products to clients will help agents' business grow. The use of call centers also allows agents to concentrate their efforts on seeking out new clients and maintaining relationships with old ones.

Working Conditions

Most insurance sales agents are based in small offices, from which they contact clients and provide insurance policy information. However, much of their time may be spent outside their offices, traveling locally to meet with clients, close sales, or investigate claims. Agents usually determine their own hours of work and often schedule evening and weekend appointments for the convenience of clients. Although most agents work a 40-hour week, some work 60 hours a week or longer. Commercial sales agents, in particular, may meet with clients during business hours and then spend evenings doing paperwork and preparing presentations to prospective clients.

Employment

Insurance sales agents held about 378,000 jobs in 2000. The following table shows the percent distribution of wage and salary jobs by industry:

Insurance agents, brokers, and services	34
Life insurance carriers	16
Property and casualty insurance carriers	8
Medical service and health insurance carriers	3
Pension funds and miscellaneous insurance carriers	2
Other industries	37

Most insurance sales agents employed in wage and salary positions work for insurance agencies. A decreasing number work directly for insurance carriers. Most of these are employed by life insurance companies, and a smaller number work for property, casualty, and medical and health insurance companies. Although most insurance agents specialize in life and health or property and casualty insurance, a growing number of "multiline" agents sell all lines of insurance. Approximately 1 out of 3 insurance sales agents is self-employed.

Many agents also work for banking institutions, nondepository institutions, or security and commodity brokers. As more of these types of institutions begin to sell insurance policies, an increasing number of agents should be employed here, rather than in insurance agencies.

Insurance sales agents are employed throughout the country, but most work in or near large urban centers. Some are employed in the headquarters of insurance companies, but the majority work out of local offices or independent agencies.

Training, Other Qualifications, and Advancement

For insurance agency jobs, most companies and independent agencies prefer to hire college graduates—particularly those who have majored in business or economics. A few hire high school graduates with proven sales ability or who have been successful in other types of work. In fact, many entrants to insurance sales agent jobs transfer from other occupations. In selling commercial insurance, technical experience in a field can be very beneficial in helping to sell policies to those in the same profession. As a result, new agents tend to be older than entrants in many other occupations.

College training may help agents grasp the technical aspects of insurance policies and the fundamentals and procedures of selling insurance. Many colleges and universities offer courses in insurance, and a few schools offer a bachelor's degree in insurance. College courses in finance, mathematics, accounting, economics, business law, marketing, and business administration enable insurance sales agents to understand how social and economic conditions relate to the insurance industry. Courses in psychology, sociology, and public speaking can prove useful in improving sales techniques. In addition, familiarity with computers and popular software packages has become very important, as computers provide instantaneous information on a wide variety of financial products and greatly improve agents' efficiency.

Insurance sales agents must obtain a license in the states where they plan to sell insurance. Separate licenses are required for agents to sell life and health insurance and property and casualty insurance. In most states, licenses are issued only to applicants who complete specified prelicensing courses and pass state examinations covering insurance fundamentals and state insurance laws.

A number of organizations offer professional designation programs, which certify expertise in specialties such as life, health, property, and casualty insurance, or financial consulting. Although these are voluntary, such programs assure clients and employers that an agent has a thorough understanding of the relevant specialty. Many professional societies now require agents to commit to continuing education in order to retain their designations.

Indeed, as the diversity of financial products sold by insurance agents increases, employers are placing greater emphasis on continuing professional education. It is important for insurance agents to keep up to date with issues concerning clients. Changes in tax laws, government benefits programs, and other state and federal regulations can affect the insurance needs of clients and the way in which agents conduct business. Agents can enhance their selling skills and broaden their knowledge of insurance and other financial services by taking courses at colleges and universities and by attending institutes, conferences, and seminars sponsored by insurance organizations. Most states have mandatory continuing education requirements focusing on insurance laws, consumer protection, and the technical details of various insurance policies.

As the role of financial planners increases, many insurance agents are choosing to gain the proper licensing and certification to sell securities and other financial products. This includes passing an additional examination. Before agents can qualify as securities representatives, they must pass the General Securities Registered Representative Examination (Series 7 exam), administered by the National Association of Securities Dealers (NASD). To further demonstrate competency in the area of financial planning, many agents also find it worthwhile to obtain a Certified Financial Planner (CFP) or Chartered Financial Consultant (ChFC) designation.

Insurance sales agents should be flexible, enthusiastic, confident, disciplined, hardworking, willing to solve problems, and able to communicate effectively. They should be able to inspire customer confidence. Because they usually work without supervision, sales agents must be able to plan their time well and have the initiative to locate new clients.

An insurance sales agent who shows ability and leadership may become a sales manager in a local office. A few advance to agency superintendent or executive positions. However, many who have built up a good clientele prefer to remain in sales work. Some, particularly in the property/casualty field, establish their own independent agencies or brokerage firms.

Job Outlook

Although slower-than-average employment growth is expected among insurance agents through 2010, opportunities for agents will be favorable for persons with the right qualifications and skills. This includes flexible and ambitious people who enjoy competitive sales work, have excellent interpersonal skills, and have developed expertise in a wide range of insurance and financial services. Multilingual agents also should be in high demand because they can serve a wider range of customers. Insurance language tends to be very technical, so it is important for insurance sales agents to have a firm understanding of relevant technical and legal terms. Because many beginners find it difficult to establish a sufficiently large clientele in this commission-based occupation, some eventually leave for other jobs. Most job openings are likely to result from the need to replace agents who leave the occupation and the large number of agent retirements expected in coming years.

Future demand for insurance sales agents depends largely on the volume of sales of insurance and other financial products. While sales of life insurance are down, rising incomes and a concern for financial security during retirement are lifting sales of annuities, mutual funds, and other financial products sold by insurance agents. Sales of health and long-term care insurance also are expected to rise sharply as the population ages and as the law provides more people access to health insurance. In addition, a growing population will increase the demand for insurance for automobiles, homes, and high-priced valuables and equipment. As new businesses emerge and existing firms expand coverage, sales of commercial insurance also should increase, including coverage such as product liability, workers' compensation, employee benefits, and pollution liability insurance.

Employment of agents will not keep up with the rising level of insurance sales, however. Many insurance companies are trying to contain costs. As a result, many are shedding their captive agents—those agents working directly for insurance carriers—and are relying more on independent agents or direct marketing through the mail, by phone, or on the Internet.

Agents who incorporate new technology into their existing business will remain competitive. More clients are turning to the Internet first as a source of information. Those agents who use the Internet to market their products will reach a broader client base, and expand their business. But because most clients value their relationship with their agent, the Internet should not be a much of a threat to jobs. Many individuals prefer discussing their policies directly with their agents, rather than through a computer.

Agents will face increased competition from traditional securities brokers and bankers as they begin to sell insurance policies. Because of increasing consolidation among insurance companies, banks, and brokerage firms and increasing demands from clients for more comprehensive financial planning, insurance sales agents will need to expand the products and services they offer.

Agents who offer better customer service also will remain competitive. Call centers are the primary way companies and agents are offering better service because customers are demanding greater access to their policies.

Insurance and investments are becoming more complex, and many people and businesses lack the time and expertise to buy insurance without the advice of an agent. Insurance agents who are knowledgeable about their products and sell multiple lines of insurance and other financial products will remain in demand. Additionally, agents who take advantage of direct mail and Internet resources to advertise and promote their products can reduce the time it takes to develop sales leads, allowing them to concentrate on following up on potential clients. Most individuals and businesses consider insurance a necessity, regardless of economic conditions. Therefore, agents are not likely to face unemployment because of a recession.

Earnings

The median annual earnings of wage and salary insurance sales agents were $38,750 in 2000. The middle 50 percent earned between $26,920 and $59,370. The lowest 10 percent had earnings of $20,070 or less, while the highest 10 percent earned more than $91,530. Median annual earnings in the industries employing the largest number of insurance sales agents in 2000 were:

Fire, marine, and casualty insurance	$46,320
Medical service and health insurance	38,900
Insurance agents, brokers, and service	38,470
Life insurance	35,920

Many independent agents are paid by commission only, whereas sales workers who are employees of an agency or an insurance carrier may be paid in one of three ways—salary only, salary plus commission, or salary plus bonus. In general, commissions are the most common form of compensation, especially for experienced agents. The amount of commission depends on the type and amount of insurance sold, and whether the transaction is a new policy or a renewal. Bonuses usually are awarded when agents meet their sales goals or when an agency's profit goals are met. Some agents involved with financial planning receive a fee for their services, rather than a commission.

Company-paid benefits to insurance sales agents usually include continuing education, paid licensing training, group insurance plans, and office space and clerical support services. Some may pay for automobile and transportation expenses, attendance at conventions and meetings, promotion and marketing expenses, and retirement plans. Independent agents working for insurance agencies receive fewer benefits, but their commissions may be higher to help them pay for marketing and other expenses.

Related Occupations

Other workers who sell financial products or services include real estate agents and brokers; securities, commodities, and financial services sales representatives; financial analysts and personal financial advisors; and financial managers. Other occupations in the insurance industry include insurance underwriters; claims adjusters, examiners, and investigators; and insurance appraisers.

Sources of Additional Information

Occupational information about insurance sales agents is available from the home office of many life and casualty insurance companies. Information on state licensing requirements may be obtained from the department of insurance at any state capital.

For information about insurance sales careers and training, contact:

- Independent Insurance Agents of America, 127 S. Peyton St., Alexandria, VA 22314. Internet: http://www.iiaa.org

- Insurance Vocational Education Student Training (InVEST), 127 S. Peyton St., Alexandria, VA 22314

- National Association of Professional Insurance Agents, 400 N. Washington St., Alexandria, VA 22314

For information about health insurance sales careers, contact:

- National Association of Health Underwriters, 2000 N. 14th St., Suite 450, Arlington, VA 22201. Internet: http://www.nahu.org

- Health Insurance Association of America, 555 13th St. NW., Suite 600 East, Washington, DC, 20004. Internet: http://www.hiaa.org

For information on the property and casualty field, contact:

- Insurance Information Institute, 110 William St., New York, NY 10038. Internet: http://www.iii.org

For information regarding training for life insurance sales careers, contact:

- LIMRA International, P.O. Box 203, Hartford, CT, 06141

For information about professional designation programs, contact:

- The American College, 270 Bryn Mawr Ave., Bryn Mawr, PA 19010-2195. Internet: http://www.amercoll.edu

- The National Alliance for Insurance Education and Research, P.O. Box 27027, Austin, TX 78755

Interviewers

O*NET 43-4061.01, 43-4061.02, 43-4111.00, 43-4131.00

Significant Points

- Most interviewer job openings should arise from the need to replace those who leave the occupation each year. Applicants with a broad range of job skills, such as good customer service, math, and telephone skills, have the best prospects for filling these openings.

- A high school diploma or its equivalent is the most common educational requirement.

- Because many interviewers deal directly with the public, a professional appearance and pleasant personality are imperative.

Nature of the Work

Interviewers obtain information from individuals and business representatives who are opening bank accounts, trying to obtain loans, seeking admission to medical facilities, participating in consumer surveys, applying to receive aid from government programs, and providing data for various other purposes. By mail, telephone, or in person, these workers solicit and verify information, create files, and perform a number of other related tasks.

The specific duties and job titles of *interviewers*, except those of *eligibility and loan interviewers*, depend upon the type of employer. In doctors' offices and other healthcare facilities, for example, *interviewing clerks* also are known as *admitting interviewers* or *patient representatives*. These workers obtain all preliminary information required for a patient's record or for his or her admission to a hospital, such as the patient's name, address, age, medical history, present medications, previous hospitalizations, religion, persons to notify in case of emergency, attending physician, and the party responsible for payment. In some cases, interviewing clerks may be required to verify that an individual is eligible for health benefits or to work out financing options for those who might need them.

Other duties of interviewers in healthcare include assigning patients to rooms and summoning escorts to take patients to their rooms; sometimes, interviewers may escort patients themselves. Using the facility's computer system, they schedule laboratory work, X rays, and surgeries, and prepare admitting and discharge records and route them to appropriate departments. They also may bill patients, receive payments, and answer the telephone. In an outpatient or office setting, they schedule appointments, keep track of cancellations, and provide general information about care. In addition, the role of the admissions staff, particularly in hospitals, is expanding to include a wide range of patient services, from assisting patients with financial and medical questions to helping family members find hotel rooms.

Interviewing clerks who conduct market research surveys and polls for research firms have somewhat different responsibilities. These interviewers ask a series of prepared questions, record the responses, and forward the results to management. They may ask individuals questions about their occupation and earnings, political preferences, buying habits, customer satisfaction, or other aspects of their lives. Although most interviews are conducted over the telephone, some are conducted in focus groups or by randomly polling people in a public place. More recently, the Internet is being used to elicit people's opinions. Almost all interviewers use computers or similar devices to enter the responses to questions.

Eligibility interviewers, government programs determine the eligibility of individuals applying to receive assistance from government programs such as welfare, unemployment benefits, social security, and public housing. They gather the relevant personal and financial information on an applicant and, based on the rules and regulations of the particular government program, they grant, modify, deny, or terminate individuals' eligibility for the program in question. These interviewers also are involved in the detection of fraud committed by persons who try to obtain benefits although they are not eligible to receive them.

Loan interviewers and clerks review credit history and obtain the information needed to determine the creditworthiness of loan and credit card applicants. They spend much of their day on the phone obtaining credit information from credit bureaus, employers, banks, credit institutions, and other sources to determine applicants' credit history and ability to pay back the loan or charge.

Loan clerks, also called *loan processing clerks*, *loan closers*, or *loan service clerks*, assemble loan documents, process the paperwork associated with the loan, and ensure that all information is complete and verified. Mortgage loans are the primary type of loan handled by loan clerks, who also may have to order appraisals on the property, set up escrow accounts, and secure any additional information required to transfer the property.

The specific duties of loan clerks vary by specialty. Loan closers, for example, complete the loan process by gathering the proper documents for signature at the closing, including deeds of trust, property insurance papers, and title commitments. They set the time and place for the closing, make sure that all parties are present, and ensure that all conditions for settlement have been met. After settlement, the loan closer records all documents and submits the final loan package to the owner of the loan. Loan service clerks maintain the payment records once the loan is issued. These clerical workers process the paperwork for payment of fees to insurance companies and tax authorities, and also may record changes to client addresses and loan ownership. When necessary, they answer calls from customers with routine inquiries.

Loan interviewers have duties that are similar to those of loan clerks. They interview potential borrowers and help them fill out loan applications. Interviewers may then investigate the applicant's background and references, verify information on the application, and forward any findings, reports, or documents to the appraisal department. Finally, interviewers inform the applicant whether the loan has been accepted or denied.

Working Conditions

Most interviewers work in areas that are clean, well lit, and relatively quiet. This is especially true for interviewers who greet customers and visitors and usually work in highly visible areas that are furnished to make a good impression. Interviewing clerks who spend much of their work time talking on the telephone, however, commonly work away from the public, often in large centralized reservation or phone centers. Because a number of interviewers may share the same workspace, it may be crowded and noisy. Interviewing clerks may conduct surveys on the street, in shopping malls, or go door to door.

Although most interviewers work a standard 40-hour week, about 3 out of 10 works part-time. Some interviewing jobs—such as those in marketing or healthcare—may require working evenings, late night shifts, weekends, and holidays. Interviewing clerks conducting surveys or other research may mainly work evenings or weekends. In general, employees with the least seniority tend to be assigned the less desirable shifts.

The work performed by interviewers may be repetitive and stressful, especially when trying to serve the needs of difficult or angry clients.

Additional stress is caused by technology that enables management to electronically monitor use of computer systems, tape record telephone calls, or limit the time spent on each call. Prolonged exposure to a video display terminal may lead to eyestrain for the many information clerks who work with computers.

Employment

Interviewers held about 410,000 jobs in 2000. About 154,000 were interviewers, except eligibility and loan; 139,000 were loan interviewers and clerks; and 117,000 were eligibility interviewers, government programs. Almost 1 out of every 5 interviewers worked in health services, while most loan interviewers and clerks worked in financial institutions. Almost 3 out of every 10 interviewers worked part-time.

Training, Other Qualifications, and Advancement

Although hiring requirements for interviewers vary from industry to industry, a high school diploma or its equivalent is the most common educational requirement. Increasingly, familiarity or experience with computers and good interpersonal skills is equally important to employers.

Many interviewers deal with the public, so a professional appearance and pleasant personality is important. A clear speaking voice and fluency in the English language also are essential because these employees frequently use the telephone or public address systems. Good spelling and computer literacy often are needed, particularly because most work involves considerable computer use.

Some interviewers are college graduates with degrees in business, finance, or liberal arts. Although a degree rarely is required, many graduates accept entry-level clerical positions to get into a particular company or to enter a particular field.

Orientation and training for interviewers usually takes place on the job. Under the guidance of a supervisor or other senior workers, new employees learn company procedures. Some formal classroom training also may be necessary, such as training in specific computer software. Most interviewers continue to receive instruction on new procedures and company policies after their initial training ends.

Job Outlook

Little or no change is expected in overall employment of interviewers through 2010. However, the projected change in employment varies by specialty. Most job openings should arise from the need to replace the numerous interviewers who leave the occupation or the labor force each year. Prospects for filling these openings will be best for applicants with a broad range of job skills, such as good customer service, math, and telephone skills. In addition to full-time jobs, opportunities also should be available for part-time and temporary jobs.

The number of interviewers, except eligibility and loan, is projected to grow faster than average, reflecting growth in the health services industry. This industry will hire more admissions interviewers as healthcare facilities consolidate staff and expand the role of the admissions staff, and as an aging and growing population requires more visits to healthcare practitioners. In addition, increasing use of market research will create more jobs requiring interviewers to collect data. In the future, though, more market research is expected to be conducted over the Internet, thus reducing the need for telephone interviewers to make individual calls.

The number of loan interviewers and clerks is projected to decline, due to advances in technology that are making these workers more productive. Despite a projected increase in the number of loan applications, automation will allow fewer workers to process, check, and authorize applications than in the past. The effects of automation on employment will be moderated, however, by the many interpersonal aspects of the job. Mortgage loans, for example, require loan processors to personally verify financial data on the application, and loan closers are needed to assemble documents and prepare them for settlement. Employment also will be adversely affected by changes in the financial services industry. For example, significant consolidation has occurred among mortgage loan servicing companies. As a result, fewer mortgage banking companies are involved in loan servicing, making the function more efficient and reducing the need for loan servicing clerks.

The job outlook for loan interviewers and clerks is sensitive to overall economic activity. A downturn in the economy or a rise in the interest rates usually leads to a decline in the demand for loans, particularly mortgage loans, and can result in layoffs. Even in slow economic times, however, job openings will arise from the need to replace workers who leave the occupation for various reasons.

Like loan interviewers and clerks, employment of eligibility interviewers for government programs also is projected to decline, due to technology advances and the transformation of government aid programs that have taken place over the last decade. Automation should have a significant effect on these workers because, as with credit and loan ratings, eligibility for government aid programs can be determined instantaneously by entering information into a computer. The job outlook for eligibility interviewers, however, also is sensitive to overall economic activity; a severe slowdown in the economy will cause more people to apply for government aid programs, increasing demand for eligibility interviewers.

Earnings

In 2000, median annual earnings for the three basic types of interviewers were as follows:

Eligibility interviewers, government programs $28,380
Loan interviewers and clerks 26,410
Interviewers, except eligibility and loan 20,840

Related Occupations

A number of other workers deal with the public, receive and provide information, or direct people to others who can assist them. Among these are dispatchers, security guards and gaming surveillance workers, tellers, and counter and rental clerks.

Sources of Additional Information

State employment service offices can provide information about employment opportunities.

For specific information on a career as a loan processor or loan closer, contact:

● Mortgage Bankers Association of America, 1125 15th St. NW., Washington, DC 20005. Internet: http://www.mbaa.org

Jewelers and Precious Stone and Metal Workers

O*NET 51-9071.01, 51-9071.02, 51-9071.03, 51-9071.04, 51-9071.05, 51-9071.06

Significant Points

● About 30 percent of all jewelers are self-employed.

● Jewelers usually learn their trade in vocational or technical schools, through correspondence courses, or on the job.

● Although employment is expected to experience little or no change, prospects should be excellent; as more jewelers retire, many employers have difficulty finding and retaining workers with the right skills.

Nature of the Work

Jewelers use a variety of common and specialized handtools to design and manufacture new pieces of jewelry; cut, set, and polish stones; and repair or adjust rings, necklaces, bracelets, earrings, and other jewelry. Jewelers usually specialize in one or more of these areas, and may work for large jewelry manufacturing firms or small retail jewelry shops, or may open their own business. Regardless of the type of work done or the work setting, jewelers require a high degree of skill, precision, and attention to detail.

Some jewelers design or make their own jewelry. Following their own designs, or those created by designers or customers, they begin by shaping the metal or by carving wax to make a model for casting the metal. The individual parts then are soldered together, and the jeweler may mount a diamond or other gem, or engrave a design into the metal. Others do finishing work, such as setting stones, polishing, or engraving. Typical repairwork includes enlarging or reducing ring sizes, resetting stones, and replacing broken clasps and mountings. In manufacturing, jewelers usually specialize in a single operation. *Mold and model makers* create models or tools for the jewelry that is to be pro-

duced. *Assemblers* connect by soldering or fusing the metal and may set stones. *Engravers* may etch designs into the metal, and *polishers* polish the metal and stones to perfect the piece. In small retail stores or repairshops, jewelers may be involved in all aspects of the work. Jewelers who own or manage stores or shops also hire and train employees; order, market, and sell merchandise; and perform other managerial duties.

Jewelers typically do the handiwork required in producing a piece of jewelry, while *gemologists* study the quality, characteristics, and value of gemstones. Gemologists usually sell jewelry and provide appraisal services. A few gemologists are employed by insurance companies that offer their own appraisal services for those customers who wish to insure certain pieces of jewelry. Many jewelers also study gemology in order to become familiar with the physical properties of the gemstones with which they work, so that they do not unknowingly damage stones while setting and polishing them.

Although the quality of a piece of jewelry is the direct reflection of a particular jeweler's skills, and many procedures have been performed the same way for hundreds of years, new technology is helping to produce higher quality pieces of jewelry at a reduced cost and in a shorter amount of time. A growing number of jewelers use lasers for cutting and improving the quality of stones, intricate engraving or design work, and identification (ID) inscription. Jewelers also use lasers to weld metals together in milliseconds with no seams or blemishes, improving the quality and appearance of the jewelry. Some manufacturing firms use computer-aided design and manufacturing (CAD/CAM) to facilitate product design and automate some steps in the mold- and model-making process. CAD allows a jeweler to create a virtual reality model of a piece of jewelry, modify the design, and find mistakes, all on the computer screen. Once a jeweler is satisfied with the model, CAM produces the model in a wax-like material. Once the model is made, it is easier for manufacturing firms to produce numerous pieces of the jewelry, which are distributed to different retail establishments across the country.

Working Conditions

A jeweler's work involves a great deal of concentration and attention to detail. Working on precious stones and metals while trying to satisfy customers' and employers' demands for speed and quality can cause fatigue or stress. However, the use of more ergonomically correct jewelers' benches has eliminated the strain and discomfort formerly caused by spending long periods bending over a workbench in one position. In larger manufacturing plants and some smaller repairshops, chemicals, sharp or pointed tools, and jewelers' torches pose potential safety threats and may cause injury if proper care is not taken; however, most dangerous chemicals have been replaced with synthetic, less toxic products to meet safety requirements.

In repairshops, jewelers usually work alone with little supervision. In retail stores, on the other hand, they may talk with customers about repairs, perform custom design work, and even do some sales work. Because many of their materials are very valuable, jewelers must observe strict security procedures. These include locked doors that are opened only by a buzzer, barred windows, burglar alarms, and, for large jewelry establishments, the presence of armed guards.

Employment

Jewelers and precious stone and metal workers held about 43,000 jobs in 2000. About one-third of all these workers were self-employed; many operated their own store or repairshop, and some specialized in designing and creating custom jewelry.

Over 40 percent of all salaried jewelers worked in retail establishments, while another 40 percent were employed in manufacturing plants. Although jewelry stores and repairshops can be found in every city and in many small towns, most job opportunities are in larger metropolitan areas. Many jewelers employed in manufacturing work in Rhode Island, New York, and California.

Training, Other Qualifications, and Advancement

Jewelers usually learn their trade in vocational or technical schools, through correspondence courses, or on the job. Colleges and art and design schools also offer programs that can lead to a bachelor's or master's degree of fine arts in jewelry design. Formal training in the basic skills of the trade enhances one's employment and advancement opportunities. Many employers prefer jewelers with design, repair, and sales skills.

For those interested in working in a jewelry store or repairshop, vocational and technical training or courses offered by public and private colleges and schools are the best sources of training. In these programs, which can vary in length from 6 months to 1 year, students learn the use and care of jewelers' tools and machines and basic jewelry-making and jewelry-repairing skills, such as design, casting, stone setting, and polishing. Technical school courses also cover topics including blueprint reading, math, and shop theory. To enter some technical school and most college programs, a high school diploma or its equivalent is required. However, some schools specializing in jewelry training do not require a high school diploma. Because computer-aided design is used increasingly in the jewelry field, it is recommended that students—especially those interested in design and manufacturing—obtain training in CAD.

The Gemological Institute of America (GIA) offers programs lasting about 6 months and self-paced correspondence courses that may last longer. The GIA offers the graduate gemologist (G.G.) and graduate jeweler (G.J.) diplomas, along with a variety of courses in gemology and jewelry manufacturing and design. Advanced programs cover a wide range of topics, including the identification and grading of diamonds and gemstones.

Most employers feel that vocational and technical school graduates need several more years of supervised, on-the-job training, or apprenticeship, to refine their repair skills and learn more about the operation of the store or shop. In addition, some employers encourage workers to improve their skills by enrolling in short-term technical school courses such as samplemaking, wax carving, or gemology. Many employers pay all or part of the cost of this additional training.

In jewelry manufacturing plants, workers traditionally develop their skills through informal apprenticeships and on-the-job training. This training lasts 3 to 4 years, depending on the difficulty of the specialty. Training usually focuses on casting, stonesetting, modelmaking, or engraving. In recent years, a growing number of technical schools and colleges have begun to offer training designed for jewelers working in manufacturing. Like employers in retail trade, though, those in manufacturing now prefer graduates of these programs because they are familiar with the production process, requiring less on-the-job training.

The precise and delicate nature of jewelry work requires finger and hand dexterity, good hand-eye coordination, patience, and concentration.

Artistic ability and fashion consciousness are major assets because jewelry must be stylish and attractive. Those who work in jewelry stores have frequent contact with customers and should be neat, personable, and knowledgeable about the merchandise. In addition, employers require workers of good character because jewelers work with very valuable materials.

Advancement opportunities are limited and depend greatly on an individual's skill and initiative. In manufacturing, some jewelers advance to supervisory jobs, such as master jeweler or head jeweler but, for most, advancement takes the form of higher pay for doing the same job. Jewelers who work in jewelry stores or repairshops may become managers; some open their own businesses.

Those interested in starting their own business should first establish themselves and build a reputation for their work within the jewelry trade. Then, they can obtain sufficient credit from jewelry suppliers and wholesalers to acquire the necessary inventory. Also, because the jewelry business is highly competitive, jewelers who plan to open their own store should have experience in selling, as well as knowledge of marketing and business management. Courses in these areas often are available from technical schools and community colleges.

Job Outlook

Employment of jewelers and precious stone and metal workers is expected to experience little or no change through 2010. Employment opportunities, however, should be excellent, because while jewelers are retiring, jewelry sales are increasing at rates that exceed the number of new jewelers entering the profession. When master jewelers retire, they take with them years of experience that require substantial time and financial resources to replace, in the form of training new jewelers. As a result, many employers have difficulty finding and retaining jewelers with the right skills. Those who devote the time and effort to mastering their trade should have excellent job prospects. Even though some technological advances have made jewelry making more efficient, many of the skills require excellent handiwork and cannot be fully automated.

The demand for jewelry depends largely on the amount of disposable income people have. Therefore, the increasing numbers of affluent individuals, working women, double-income households, and fashion-conscious men are expected to keep jewelry sales strong. The population aged 45 and older, which accounts for a major portion of jewelry sales, also is on the rise.

Recently, nontraditional jewelry marketers, such as discount stores, mail-order catalogue companies, television shopping networks, and Internet retailers have limited the growth of sales by traditional jewelers. Because these establishments require fewer sales and marketing staff, employment opportunities for jewelers and precious stone and metal workers who work mainly in sales will be limited. As these marketers enjoy increases in sales, however, they will need highly skilled jewelers to make the jewelry.

Opportunities in jewelry stores and repairshops will be best for graduates from a jeweler or gemologist training program. Despite an increase in sales by nontraditional jewelry marketers, traditional jewelers should not be greatly affected. Traditional jewelers have the advantage of being able to build client relationships based on trust. Many clients prefer to work directly with a jeweler to ensure that the product is of the highest quality and meets their specifications. Many traditional jewelers expand their business as clients recommend their services to friends and relatives.

The jewelry industry can be cyclical. During economic downturns, demand for jewelry products, and jewelers, tends to decrease. However, demand for repair workers should remain strong, even during economic slowdowns, because maintaining and repairing jewelry is an ongoing process. In fact, demand for jewelry repair may increase during recessions, as people repair or restore existing pieces rather than purchase new ones. Also, many nontraditional vendors typically do not offer repair services.

Within manufacturing, increasing automation will adversely affect employment of low-skilled occupations, such as assembler and polisher. Automation will have a lesser impact on more creative, highly skilled positions, such as mold- and modelmaker. Furthermore, small manufacturers, which typify the industry, will have an increasingly difficult time competing with the larger manufacturers when it comes to supplying large retailers. Because of recent international trade agreements, exports are increasing modestly as manufacturers become more competitive in foreign markets. However, imports from foreign manufacturers are increasing more rapidly than exports due to these same agreements.

Earnings

Median annual earnings for jewelers and precious stone and metal workers were $26,330 in 2000. The middle 50 percent earned between $19,140 and $35,150. The lowest 10 percent earned less than $14,550, and the highest 10 percent earned more than $44,120. In 2000, median annual earnings in the industries employing the largest numbers of jewelers and precious stone and metal workers were as follows:

Miscellaneous shopping goods stores	$32,290
Jewelry, silverware, and plated ware	22,920

Most jewelers start out with a base salary but, once they become more proficient, they might begin charging by the number of pieces completed. Jewelers who work in retail stores may earn a commission for each piece of jewelry sold, in addition to their base salary. Many jewelers also enjoy a variety of benefits, including reimbursement from their employers for work-related courses and discounts on jewelry purchases.

Related Occupations

Jewelers and precious stone and metal workers do precision handwork. Other skilled workers who do similar jobs include precision instrument and equipment repairers; welding, soldering, and brazing workers; and woodworkers. Some jewelers and precious stone and metal workers create their own jewelry designs. Other visually artistic occupations include artists and related workers, and designers. And, some jewelers and precious stone and metal workers are involved in the buying and selling of stones and metals or of the finished piece of jewelry. Similar occupations include retail salespersons and sales representatives in wholesale trade.

Sources of Additional Information

Information on job opportunities and training programs for jewelers is available from:

- Gemological Institute of America, 5345 Armada Dr., Carlsbad, CA 92008. Internet: http://www.gia.org

- California Institute of Jewelry Training, 5800 Winding Way, Carmichael, CA 95608

General career information is available from:

- Manufacturing Jewelers and Suppliers of America, 45 Royal Little Dr., Providence, RI 02904. Internet: http://mjsa.polygon.net

To receive a list of technical schools which have programs in jewelry design, accredited by the Accrediting Commission of Career Schools and Colleges of Technology, contact:

- Accrediting Commission of Career Schools and Colleges of Technology, 2101 Wilson Blvd., Suite 302, Arlington, VA 22201. Internet: http://www.accsct.org

Job Opportunities in the Armed Forces

O*NET 55-1011.00, 55-1012.00, 55-1013.00, 55-1014.00, 55-1015.00, 55-1016.00, 55-1017.00, 55-1019.99, 55-2011.00, 55-2012.00, 55-2013.00, 55-3011.00, 55-3012.00, 55-3013.00, 55-3014.00, 55-3015.00, 55-3016.00, 55-3017.00, 55-3018.00, 55-3019.99

Significant Points

- Opportunities should be good in all branches of the armed forces for applicants who meet designated standards.

- Most enlisted personnel need at least a high school diploma, while officers need a bachelor's or advanced degree.

- Hours and working conditions can be arduous and vary substantially.

- Some training and duty assignments are hazardous, even in peacetime.

Nature of the Work

Maintaining a strong national defense encompasses such diverse activities as running a hospital, commanding a tank, programming computers, operating a nuclear reactor, or repairing and maintaining a helicopter. The military provides training and work experience in these fields and many others for more than 1.5 million people who serve in the active Army, Navy, Marine Corps, Air Force, and Coast Guard, their Reserve components, and the Air and Army National Guard.

The military distinguishes between enlisted and officer careers. Enlisted personnel, who make up about 85 percent of the armed forces, carry out the fundamental operations of the military in areas such as combat, administration, construction, engineering, healthcare, and human services. Officers, who make up the remaining 15 percent of the armed forces, are the leaders of the military. They supervise and manage activities in every occupational specialty in the military.

The following sections discuss the major occupational groups for enlisted personnel and officers.

Enlisted occupational groups:

Administrative careers include a wide variety of positions. The military must keep accurate information for planning and managing its operations. Paper and electronic records are kept on personnel and on equipment, funds, supplies, and other property of the military. Enlisted administrative personnel record information, type reports, maintain files, and review information to assist military offices. Personnel may work in a specialized area such as finance, accounting, legal, maintenance, supply, or transportation. Some examples of administrative specialists are recruiting specialists, who recruit and place qualified personnel and provide information about military careers to young people, parents, schools, and local communities; training specialists and instructors, who provide the training programs necessary to help people perform their jobs effectively; and personnel specialists, who collect and store information about individuals in the military, including training, job assignment, promotion, and health information.

Combat specialty occupations refer to enlisted specialties, such as infantry, artillery, and special forces, whose members operate weapons or execute special missions during combat situations. Persons in these occupations normally specialize by the type of weapon system or combat operation. These personnel maneuver against enemy forces, and position and fire artillery, guns, and missiles to destroy enemy positions. They also may operate tanks and amphibious assault vehicles in combat or scouting missions. When the military has difficult and dangerous missions to perform, they call upon special operations teams. These elite combat forces stay in a constant state of readiness to strike anywhere in the world on a moment's notice. Special operations forces team members conduct offensive raids, demolitions, intelligence, search and rescue, and other missions from aboard aircraft, helicopters, ships, or submarines.

Construction occupations in the military include personnel who build or repair buildings, airfields, bridges, foundations, dams, bunkers, and the electrical and plumbing components of these structures. Enlisted personnel in construction occupations operate bulldozers, cranes, graders, and other heavy equipment. Construction specialists also may work with engineers and other building specialists as part of military construction teams. Some personnel specialize in areas such as plumbing or electrical wiring. Plumbers and pipefitters install and repair the plumbing and pipe systems needed in buildings and on aircraft and ships. Building electricians install and repair electrical wiring systems in offices, airplane hangars, and other buildings on military bases.

Electronic and electrical equipment repair personnel repair and maintain electronic and electrical equipment used in the military. Repairers normally specialize by type of equipment, such as avionics, computer, optical, communications, or weapons systems. For example, electronic instrument repairers install, test, maintain, and repair a wide variety of electronic systems, including navigational controls and biomedical instruments. Weapons maintenance technicians maintain and repair weapons used by combat forces, most of which have electronic components and systems that assist in locating targets and in aiming and firing weapons.

The military has many *engineering, science, and technical occupations,* whose members require specific knowledge to operate technical equipment, solve complex problems, or provide and interpret information. Enlisted personnel normally specialize in one area, such as space operations, emergency management, environmental health and safety, or intelligence. Space operations specialists use and repair spacecraft ground control command equipment, including electronic systems that track spacecraft location and operation. Emergency management specialists prepare emergency procedures for all types of disasters, such as floods, tornadoes, and earthquakes. Environmental health and safety specialists inspect military facilities and food supplies for the presence of disease, germs, or other conditions hazardous to health and the environment. Intelligence specialists gather and study information using aerial photographs and various types of radar and surveillance systems.

Healthcare personnel assist medical professionals in treating and providing services for men and women in the military. They may work as part of a patient service team in close contact with doctors, dentists, nurses, and physical therapists to provide the necessary support functions within a hospital or clinic. Healthcare specialists normally specialize in a particular area. They may provide emergency medical treatment, operate diagnostic equipment such as X-ray and ultrasound equipment, conduct laboratory tests on tissue and blood samples, maintain pharmacy supplies, or maintain patient records.

Human services specialists help military personnel and their families with social or personal problems, or assist chaplains. For example, caseworkers and counselors work with personnel who may be experiencing social problems, such as drug or alcohol dependence or depression. Religious program specialists assist chaplains with religious services, religious education programs, and administrative duties.

Machine operator and production occupations operate industrial equipment, machinery, and tools to fabricate and repair parts for a variety of items and structures. They may operate engines, turbines, nuclear reactors, and water pumps. Personnel often specialize by type of work performed. Welders and metal workers, for instance, work with various types of metals to repair or form the structural parts of ships, submarines, buildings, or other equipment. Survival equipment specialists inspect, maintain, and repair survival equipment such as parachutes and aircraft life support equipment. Dental and optical laboratory technicians construct and repair dental equipment and eyeglasses for military personnel.

Media and public affairs occupations are involved in the public presentation and interpretation of military information and events. Enlisted media and public affairs personnel take and develop photographs; film, record, and edit audio and video programs; present news and music programs; and produce graphic artwork, drawings, and other visual displays. Other public affairs specialists act as interpreters and translators to convert written or spoken foreign languages into English or other languages.

Service personnel include those who enforce military laws and regulations, provide emergency response to natural and manmade disasters, and maintain food standards. Personnel normally specialize by function. Military police control traffic, prevent crime, and respond to emergencies. Other law enforcement and security specialists investigate crimes committed on military property and guard inmates in military correctional facilities. Firefighters put out, control, and help prevent fires in buildings, on aircraft, and aboard ships. Food service specialists prepare all types of food in dining halls, hospitals, and ships.

Transportation and material handling specialists ensure the safe transport of people and cargo. Most personnel within this occupational group are classified according to mode of transportation, such as aircraft, motor vehicle, or ship. Aircrew members operate equipment on board aircraft during operations. Vehicle drivers operate all types of heavy military vehicles including fuel or water tank trucks, semi-tractor trailers, heavy troop transports, and passenger buses. Quartermasters and boat operators navigate and pilot many types of small watercraft, including tugboats, gunboats, and barges. Cargo specialists load and unload military supplies and material using equipment such as forklifts and cranes.

Vehicle and machinery mechanics conduct preventive and corrective maintenance on aircraft, ships, automotive and heavy equipment, heating and cooling systems, marine engines, and powerhouse station equipment. They typically specialize by the type of equipment that they maintain. For example, aircraft mechanics inspect, service, and repair helicopters and airplanes. Automotive and heavy equipment mechanics maintain and repair vehicles such as jeeps, cars, trucks, tanks, self-propelled missile launchers, and other combat vehicles. They also repair bulldozers, power shovels, and other construction equipment. Heating and cooling mechanics install and repair air-conditioning, refrigeration, and heating equipment. Marine engine mechanics repair and maintain gasoline and diesel engines on ships, boats, and other watercraft. They also repair shipboard mechanical and electrical equipment. Powerhouse mechanics install, maintain, and repair electrical and mechanical equipment in power-generating stations.

Officer occupational groups:

Combat specialty officers plan and direct military operations, oversee combat activities, and serve as combat leaders. This category includes officers in charge of tanks and other armored assault vehicles, artillery systems, special operations forces, and infantry. They normally specialize by type of unit that they lead. Within the unit, they may specialize by the type of weapon system. Artillery and missile system officers, for example, direct personnel as they target, launch, test, and maintain various types of missiles and artillery. Special-operations officers lead their units in offensive raids, demolitions, intelligence gathering, and search and rescue missions.

Engineering, science, and technical officers have a wide range of responsibilities based on their area of expertise. They lead or perform activities in areas such as space operations, environmental health and safety, and engineering. These officers may direct the operations of communications centers or the development of complex computer systems. Environmental health and safety officers study the air, ground, and water to identify and analyze sources of pollution and its effects. They also direct programs to control safety and health hazards in the workplace. Other personnel work as aerospace engineers to design and direct the development of military aircraft, missiles, and spacecraft.

Executive, administrative, and managerial officers oversee and direct military activities in key functional areas such as finance, accounting, health administration, international relations, and supply. Health services administrators, for instance, are responsible for the overall quality of care provided at the hospitals and clinics they operate. They must ensure that each department works together to provide the highest quality of care. Purchasing and contracting managers are another example: they negotiate and monitor contracts for the purchase of the billions of dollars worth of equipment, supplies, and services that the military buys from private industry each year.

Healthcare officers provide health services at military facilities, based on their area of specialization. Officers who assist in examining, diagnosing, and treating patients with illness, injury, or disease include physician assistants and registered nurses. Other healthcare officers provide therapy, rehabilitative treatment, and other services for patients. Physical and occupational therapists plan and administer therapy to help patients adjust to disabilities, regain independence, and return to work. Speech therapists evaluate and treat patients with hearing and speech problems. Dietitians manage food service facilities, and plan meals for hospital patients and for outpatients who need special diets. Pharmacists manage the purchasing, storing, and dispensing of drugs and medicines.

Health diagnosing and treating practitioner officers examine, diagnose, and provide treatment for illnesses, injuries, and disorders. For example, physicians and surgeons in this occupational group provide the majority of medical services to the military and their families. Dentists treat diseases and disorders of the mouth. Optometrists treat vision problems by prescribing eyeglasses or contact lenses. Psychologists provide mental healthcare, and also conduct research on behavior and emotions.

Human services officers perform services in support of the morale and well-being of military personnel and their families. Social workers focus on improving conditions that cause social problems, such as drug and alcohol abuse, racism, and sexism. Chaplains conduct worship services for military personnel and perform other spiritual duties covering beliefs and practices of all religious faiths.

Media and public affairs officers oversee the development, production, and presentation of information or events for the public. These officers may produce and direct motion pictures, videotapes, and television and radio broadcasts that are used for training, news, and entertainment. Some plan, develop, and direct the activities of military bands. Public information officers respond to inquiries about military activities and prepare news releases and reports to keep the public informed.

Officers in *transportation occupations* manage and perform activities related to the safe transport of military personnel and material by air and water. Officers normally specialize by mode of transportation or area of expertise because, in many cases, they must meet licensing and certification requirements. Pilots in the military fly various types of specialized airplanes and helicopters to carry troops and equipment and execute combat missions. Navigators use radar, radio, and other navigation equipment to determine their position and plan their route of travel. Officers on ships and submarines work as a team to manage the various departments aboard their vessels. Ship engineers direct engineering departments aboard ships and submarines, including engine operations, maintenance, repair, heating, and power generation.

Employment

In 2000, more than 1.5 million individuals were on active duty in the armed forces—about 530,500 in the Army, 400,000 in the Navy, 385,000 in the Air Force, 174,000 in the Marine Corps, and 37,000 in the Coast Guard. Table 1 shows the occupational composition of enlisted personnel in 2001, while Table 2 presents similar information for officers.

TABLE 1

Military Enlisted Personnel by Broad Occupational Category and Branch of Military Service, April 2001

Occupational Group—Enlisted	Army	Air Force	Coast Guard	Marine Corps	Navy	Total, All Services
Administrative occupations	19,862	23,124	2,211	11,560	16,760	73,517
Combat specialty occupations	102,844	1,092	—	33,127	4,242	141,305
Construction occupations	15,815	6,130	881	5,503	5,897	34,226
Electronic and electrical repair occupations	29,628	47,485	1,725	15,828	62,269	156,935
Engineering, science, and technical occupations	43,368	42,018	2,153	25,098	44,979	157,616
Healthcare occupations	26,443	19,140	664	—	24,559	70,806
Human resource development occupations	13,287	12,514	654	5,097	4,557	36,109
Machine operator and precision work occupations	2,881	9,729	4,410	2,275	6,870	26,165
Media and public affairs occupations	7,740	6,683	114	1,974	3,578	20,089
Protective service occupations	21,731	31,123	1,913	5,801	14,780	75,348
Support services occupations	12,651	7,029	1,173	3,062	9,254	33,169
Transportation and material handling occupations	54,555	36,534	10,355	25,911	65,825	193,180
Vehicle machinery mechanic occupations	45,921	37,477	1,626	17,536	48,174	150,734

SOURCE: U.S. Department of Defense, Defense Manpower Data Center East

TABLE 2

Military Officer Personnel by Broad Occupational Category and Branch of Military Service, April 2001

Occupational Group—Officer	Army	Air Force	Coast Guard	Marine Corps	Navy	Total, All Services
Combat specialty occupations	18,714	5,260	38	4,741	4,068	32,821
Engineering, science, and technical occupations	16,095	17,257	1,315	3,027	10,431	48,125
Executive, administrative, and managerial occupations	10,619	8,613	578	2,220	7,163	29,193
Healthcare occupations	10,829	10,383	16	—	8,327	29,555
Human resource development occupations	1,828	2,471	275	659	3,658	8,891
Media and public affairs occupations	601	468	20	152	370	1,611
Protective service occupations	2,063	1,207	981	350	917	5,518
Support services occupations	1,578	1,214	—	44	1,164	4,000
Transportation occupations	12,749	20,846	3,645	6,916	16,774	60,930
Total, by service	75,076	67,719	6,868	18,109	52,872	220,644

SOURCE: U.S. Department of Defense, Defense Manpower Data Center East

Military personnel are stationed throughout the United States and in many countries around the world. More than half of all military jobs are located in California, Texas, North Carolina, Virginia, Florida, and Georgia. About 258,000 individuals were stationed outside the United States in 2000, including those assigned to ships at sea. More than 117,000 of these were stationed in Europe, mainly in Germany, and another 101,000 were assigned to East Asia and the Pacific area, mostly in Japan and the Republic of Korea.

Training, Other Qualifications, and Advancement

Enlisted personnel. In order to join the services, enlisted personnel must sign a legal agreement called an enlistment contract, which usually involves a commitment to 8 years of service. Depending on the terms of the contract, 2 to 6 years are spent on active duty and the balance is spent in the reserves. The enlistment contract obligates the service to provide the agreed-upon job, rating, pay, cash bonuses for enlistment in certain occupations, medical and other benefits, occupational training, and continuing education. In return, enlisted personnel must serve satisfactorily for the period specified.

Requirements for each service vary, but certain qualifications for enlistment are common to all branches. In order to enlist, one must be between 17 and 35 years old, be a U.S. citizen or immigrant alien holding permanent resident status, not have a felony record, and possess a birth certificate. Applicants who are aged 17 must have the consent of a parent or legal guardian before entering the service. Coast Guard enlisted personnel must enter active duty before their 28th birthday, while Marine Corps enlisted personnel must not be over the age of 29. Applicants must both pass a written examination—the Armed Services Vocational Aptitude Battery—and meet certain minimum physical standards such as height, weight, vision, and overall health. All branches of the armed forces require high school graduation or its equivalent for certain enlistment options. In 2000, more than 9 out of 10 recruits were high school graduates.

People thinking about enlisting in the military should learn as much as they can about military life before making a decision. This is especially important if you are thinking about making the military a career. Speaking to friends and relatives with military experience is a good idea. Determine what the military can offer you and what it will expect in return. Then, talk to a recruiter, who can determine if you qualify for enlistment, explain the various enlistment options, and tell you which military occupational specialties currently have openings. Bear in mind that the recruiter's job is to recruit promising applicants into his or her branch of military service, so the information that the recruiter gives you is likely to stress the positive aspects of military life in the branch in which he or she serves.

Ask the recruiter for the branch you have chosen to assess your chances of being accepted for training in the occupation of your choice, or, better still, take the aptitude exam to see how well you score. The military uses the aptitude exam as a placement exam, and test scores largely determine an individual's chances of being accepted into a particular training program. Selection for a particular type of training depends on the needs of the service, your general and technical aptitudes, and your personal preference. Because all prospective recruits are required to take the exam, those who do so before committing themselves to enlist have the advantage of knowing in advance whether they stand a good chance of being accepted for training in a particular specialty. The recruiter can schedule you for the Armed Services Vocational Aptitude Battery without any obligation. Many high schools offer the exam as an easy way for students to explore the possibility of a military career, and the test also provides insight into career areas in which the student has demonstrated aptitudes and interests.

If you decide to join the military, the next step is to pass the physical examination and sign an enlistment contract. Negotiating the contract involves choosing, qualifying, and agreeing on a number of enlistment options such as length of active duty time, which may vary according to the enlistment option. Most active duty programs have first-term enlistments of 4 years, although there are some 2-, 3-, and 6-year programs. The contract also will state the date of enlistment and other options, such as bonuses and types of training to be received. If the service is unable to fulfill its part of the contract, such as providing a certain kind of training, the contract may become null and void.

All services offer a "delayed entry program" by which an individual can delay entry into active duty for up to 1 year after enlisting. High school students can enlist during their senior year and enter a service after graduation. Others choose this program because the job training they desire is not currently available but will be within the coming year, or because they need time to arrange personal affairs.

Women are eligible to enter most military specialties—for example, mechanics, missile maintenance technicians, heavy equipment operators, and fighter pilots, as well as medical care, administrative support, and intelligence specialties. Generally, only occupations involving direct exposure to combat are excluded.

People planning to apply the skills gained through military training to a civilian career should first determine how good the prospects are for civilian employment in jobs related to the military specialty that interests them. Second, they should know the prerequisites for the related civilian job. Because many civilian occupations require a license, certification, or minimum level of education, it is important to determine whether military training is sufficient to enter the civilian equivalent or, if not, what additional training will be required. Additional information often can be obtained from school counselors.

Following enlistment, new members of the armed forces undergo recruit training, which is better known as "basic" training. Recruit training provides a 6-to-12–week introduction to military life with courses in military skills and protocol. Days and nights are carefully structured, and include rigorous physical exercise designed to improve strength and endurance and build unit cohesion.

Following basic training, most recruits take additional training at technical schools that prepare them for a particular military occupational specialty. The formal training period generally lasts from 10 to 20 weeks, although training for certain occupations—nuclear power plant operator, for example—may take as long as a year. Recruits not assigned to classroom instruction receive on-the-job training at their first duty assignment.

Many service people get college credit for the technical training they receive on duty, which, combined with off-duty courses, can lead to an associate degree through community college programs such as the Community College of the Air Force. In addition to on-duty training, military personnel may choose from a variety of educational programs. Most military installations have tuition assistance programs for people wishing to take courses during off-duty hours. These may be correspondence courses or degree programs offered by local colleges or universities. Tuition assistance pays up to 75 percent of college costs. Also available are courses designed to help service personnel earn high school equivalency diplomas. Each service branch provides opportunities for full-time study to a limited number of exceptional applicants. Military personnel accepted into these highly competitive programs—in law or medicine, for example—receive full pay, allowances, tuition, and related fees. In return, they must agree to serve an additional amount of time in the service. Other very selective programs enable enlisted personnel to qualify as commissioned officers through additional military training.

Warrant officers. Warrant officers are technical and tactical leaders who specialize in a specific technical area; for example, Army aviators make up one group of warrant officers. The Army Warrant Officer Corps constitutes less than 5 percent of the total Army. Although the Corps is small in size, its level of responsibility is high. Its members receive extended career opportunities, worldwide leadership assignments, and increased pay and retirement benefits. Selection to attend the Warrant Officer Candidate School is highly competitive and restricted to those with the rank of E5 or higher. (See Table 3.)

Officers. Officer training in the armed forces is provided through the federal service academies (Military, Naval, Air Force, and Coast Guard); the Reserve Officers Training Corps (ROTC) program offered at many colleges and universities; Officer Candidate School (OCS) or Officer Training School (OTS); the National Guard (State Officer Candidate School programs); the Uniformed Services University of Health Sciences; and other programs. All are very selective and are good options for those wishing to make the military a career. Persons interested in obtaining training through the federal service academies must be single to enter and graduate, while those seeking training through OCS, OTS, or ROTC need not be single. Single parents with one or more minor dependents are not eligible for officer commissioning.

Federal service academies provide a 4-year college program leading to a Bachelor of Science degree. Midshipmen or cadets are provided free room and board, tuition, medical and dental care, and a monthly allowance. Graduates receive regular or reserve commissions and have a 5-year active duty obligation, or more if they are entering flight training.

To become a candidate for appointment as a cadet or midshipman in one of the service academies, applicants are required to obtain a nomination from an authorized source, usually a member of Congress. Candidates do not need to know a member of Congress personally to request a nomination. Nominees must have an academic record of the requisite quality, college aptitude test scores above an established minimum, and recommendations from teachers or school officials; they also must pass a medical examination. Appointments are made from the list of eligible nominees. Appointments to the Coast Guard Academy, however, are based strictly on merit and do not require a nomination.

ROTC programs train students in about 950 Army, 67 Navy and Marine Corps, and 1,000 Air Force units at participating colleges and universities. Trainees take 2 to 5 hours of military instruction a week, in addition to regular college courses. After graduation, they may serve as officers on active duty for a stipulated period. Some may serve their obligation in the Reserves or National Guard. In the last 2 years of a ROTC program, students receive a monthly allowance while attending school, and additional pay for summer training. ROTC scholarships for 2, 3, and 4 years are available on a competitive basis. All scholarships pay for tuition and have allowances for subsistence, textbooks, supplies, and other costs.

College graduates can earn a commission in the armed forces through OCS or OTS programs in the Army, Navy, Air Force, Marine Corps, Coast Guard, and National Guard. These officers generally must serve their obligation on active duty. Those with training in certain health professions may qualify for direct appointment as officers. In the case of persons studying for the health professions, financial assistance and internship opportunities are available from the military in return for specified periods of military service. Prospective medical students can apply to the Uniformed Services University of Health Sciences, which offers free tuition in a program leading to a Doctor of Medicine (M.D.) degree. In return, graduates must serve for 7 years in either the military or the U.S. Public Health Service. Direct appointments also are available for those qualified to serve in other specialty areas, such as the judge advocate general (legal) or chaplain corps. Flight training is available to commissioned officers in each branch of the armed forces. In addition, the Army has a direct enlistment option to become a warrant officer aviator.

Each service has different criteria for promoting personnel. Generally, the first few promotions for both enlisted and officer personnel come easily; subsequent promotions are much more competitive. Criteria for promotion may include time in service and grade, job performance, a fitness report (supervisor's recommendation), and written examinations. People who are passed over for promotion several times generally must leave the military. Table 3 shows the officer, warrant officer, and enlisted ranks by service.

TABLE 3

Military Rank and Employment for Active Duty Personnel, April 2001

Grade   Rank and Title

Grade	Army	Navy and Coast Guard	Air Force	Marine Corps	Total DOD Employment
Commissioned Officers:					
O-10	General	Admiral	General	General	34
O-9	Lieutenant General	Vice Admiral	Lieutenant General	Lieutenant General	118
O-8	Major General	Rear Admiral Upper	Major General	Major General	282
O-7	Brigadier General	Rear Admiral Lower	Brigadier General	Brigadier General	441
O-6	Colonel	Captain	Colonel	Colonel	11,302
O-5	Lieutenant Colonel	Commander	Lieutenant Colonel	Lieutenant Colonel	27,543
O-4	Major	Lieutenant Commander	Major	Major	43,151
O-3	Captain	Lieutenant	Captain	Captain	65,917
O-2	1st Lieutenant	Lieutenant (JG)	1st Lieutenant	1st Lieutenant	24,759
O-1	2nd Lieutenant	Ensign	2nd Lieutenant	2nd Lieutenant	25,303
Warrant Officers:					
W-5	Chief Warrant Officer	Chief Warrant Officer	—	Chief Warrant Officer	476
W-4	Chief Warrant Officer	Chief Warrant Officer	—	Chief Warrant Officer	1,958
W-3	Chief Warrant Officer	Chief Warrant Officer	—	Chief Warrant Officer	3,837
W-2	Chief Warrant Officer	Chief Warrant Officer	—	Chief Warrant Officer	6,350
W-1	Warrant Officer	Warrant Officer	—	Warrant Officer	2,302
Enlisted Personnel:					
E-9	Sergeant Major	Master Chief Petty Officer	Chief Master Sergeant	Sergeant Major	10,197
E-8	1st Sergeant/Master Sergeant	Sr. Chief Petty Officer	Senior Master Sergeant	Master Sergeant/1st Sergeant	25,399
E-7	Sergeant First Class	Chief Petty Officer	Master Sergeant	Gunnery Sergeant	97,052
E-6	Staff Sergeant	Petty Officer 1st Class	Technical Sergeant	Staff Sergeant	165,130
E-5	Sergeant	Petty Officer 2nd Class	Staff Sergeant	Sergeant	231,750
E-4	Corporal/Specialist	Petty Officer 3rd Class	Senior Airman	Corporal	247,691
E-3	Private First Class	Seaman	Airman 1st Class	Lance Corporal	207,432
E-2	Private	Seaman Apprentice	Airman	Private 1st Class	96,420
E-1	Private	Seaman Recruit	Airman Basic	Private	60,228

Source: U.S. Department of Defense

Job Outlook

Opportunities should be good for qualified individuals in all branches of the armed forces through 2010. Many military personnel retire with a pension after 20 years of service, while they still are young enough to start a new career. More than 365,000 enlisted personnel and officers must be recruited each year to replace those who complete their commitment or retire. Since the end of the draft in 1973, the military has met its personnel requirements with volunteers. When the economy is good, it is more difficult for all the services to meet their recruitment quotas, while it is much easier to do so during a recession.

America's strategic position is stronger than it has been in decades. Despite reductions in personnel due to the decreasing threat from Eastern Europe and Russia, the number of active duty personnel is expected to remain roughly constant through 2010. The U.S. Armed Forces' current goal is to maintain a sufficient force to fight and win two major regional conflicts occurring at the same time. Political events, however, could cause these plans to change.

Educational requirements will continue to rise as military jobs become more technical and complex. High school graduates and applicants with a college background will be sought to fill the ranks of enlisted personnel, while virtually all officers will need at least a bachelor's degree and, in some cases, an advanced degree as well.

Earnings

The earnings structure for military personnel is shown in Table 4. Most enlisted personnel started as recruits at Grade E-1 in 2000; however, those with special skills or above-average education started as high as Grade E-4. Most warrant officers started at Grade W-1 or W-2, depending upon their occupational and academic qualifications and the branch of service, but warrant officer is not an entry-level occupation and, consequently, these individuals all had previous military service. Most commissioned officers started at Grade O-1, while some with advanced education started as Grade O-2 and some highly trained officers—for example, physicians and dentists—started as high as Grade O-3. Pay varies by total years of service as well as rank. Because it usually takes many years to reach the higher ranks, most personnel in higher ranks receive the higher pay rates awarded to those with many years of service.

TABLE 4

Military Basic Monthly Pay by Grade for Active Duty Personnel, July 1, 2001

Grade	Years of Service					
	Less than 2	Over 4	Over 8	Over 12	Over 16	Over 20
O-10	$8,518.80	—	$9,156.90	$9,664.20	$10,356.00	$11,049.30
O-9	7,550.10	—	8,114.10	8,451.60	9,156.90	9,664.20
O-8	6,838.20	$7,252.20	7,747.80	8,114.10	8,451.60	9,156.90
O-7	5,682.30	6,112.50	6,514.50	6,915.90	7,747.80	—
O-6	4,211.40	—	5,160.90	—	6,005.40	6,617.40
O-5	3,368.70	4,280.40	—	4,831.80	5,481.60	5,790.30
O-4	2,839.20	3,739.50	4,127.70	4,629.30	4,935.00	—
O-3	2,638.20	3,489.30	3,839.70	4,189.80	—	—
O-2	2,301.00	3,120.30	—	—	—	—
O-1	1,997.70	—	—	—	—	—
W-5	—	—	—	—	—	4,640.70
W-4	2,688.00	3,056.70	3,336.30	3,614.10	3,892.50	4,168.20
W-3	2,443.20	2,684.10	2,919.00	3,184.80	3,420.30	3,669.90
W-2	2,139.60	2,391.00	2,649.90	2,851.50	3,058.20	3,280.80
W-1	1,782.60	2,214.60	2,419.20	2,626.80	2,835.90	3,018.60
E-9	—	—	—	3,197.40	3,392.40	3,601.80
E-8	—	—	2,622.00	2,768.40	2,945.10	3,138.00
E-7	1,831.20	2,149.80	2,362.20	2,512.80	2,666.10	2,817.90
E-6	1,575.00	1,891.80	2,097.30	2,248.80	2,379.60	—
E-5	1,381.80	1,701.00	1,888.50	1,811.10	2,040.30	—
E-4	1,288.80	1,576.20	—	—	—	—
E-3	1,214.70	1,385.40	—	—	—	—
E-2	1,169.10	—	—	—	—	—
E-1 4mos+	1,042.80	—	—	—	—	—
E-1 <4mos	964.80	—	—	—	—	—

SOURCE: U.S. Department of Defense—Defense Finance and Accounting Service

In addition to basic pay, military personnel receive free room and board (or a tax-free housing and subsistence allowance), medical and dental care, a military clothing allowance, military supermarket and department store shopping privileges, 30 days of paid vacation a year (referred to as leave), and travel opportunities. In many duty stations, military personnel may receive a housing allowance that can be used for off-base housing. This allowance can be substantial, but varies greatly by rank and duty station. For example, in July 2001, the housing allowance for an E-4 with dependents was $462.90 per month; for a comparable individual without dependents, it was $323.40. The allowance for an O-4 with dependents was $881.70 per month; for a person without dependents, it was $766.50. Other allowances are paid for foreign duty, hazardous duty, submarine and flight duty, and employment as a medical officer. Athletic and other facilities—such as gymnasiums, tennis courts, golf courses, bowling centers, libraries, and movie theaters—are available on many military installations. Military personnel are eligible for retirement benefits after 20 years of service.

The Veterans Administration (VA) provides numerous benefits to those who have served at least 2 years in the armed forces. Veterans are eligible for free care in VA hospitals for all service-related disabilities, regardless of time served; those with other medical problems are eligible for free VA care if they are unable to pay the cost of hospitalization elsewhere. Admission to a VA medical center depends on the availability of beds, however. Veterans also are eligible for certain loans, including home loans. Veterans, regardless of health, can convert a military life insurance policy to an individual policy with any participating company in the veteran's state of residence. In addition, job counseling, testing, and placement services are available.

Veterans who participate in the New Montgomery GI Bill Program receive educational benefits. Under this program, armed forces personnel may elect to deduct up to $100 a month from their pay during the first 12 months of active duty, putting this money toward their future education. Veterans who serve on active duty for more than 2 years, or 2 years active duty plus 4 years in the Selected Reserve, will receive $528 a month in basic benefits for 36 months. Those who enlist and serve for 2 years will receive $429 a month for 36 months. In addition, each service provides its own additional contributions for future education. This sum becomes the service member's educational fund. Upon separation from active duty, the fund can be used to finance educational costs at any VA-approved institution. VA-approved schools include many vocational, correspondence, certification, business, technical, and flight training schools; community and junior colleges; and colleges and universities.

Sources of Additional Information

Each of the military services publishes handbooks, fact sheets, and pamphlets describing entrance requirements, training and advancement opportunities, and other aspects of military careers. These publications are widely available at all recruiting stations, at most state employment service offices, and in high schools, colleges, and public libraries. Information on educational and other veterans' benefits is available from VA offices located throughout the country.

In addition, the Defense Manpower Data Center, an agency of the U.S. Department of Defense, publishes *Military Career Guide Online*, a compendium of military occupational, training, and career information designed for use by students and job seekers.

Library Assistants, Clerical

O*NET 43-4121.00

Significant Points

● Numerous job openings should arise for most types of information and record clerks due to employment growth and the need to replace workers who leave these occupations.

● A high school diploma or its equivalent is the most common educational requirement.

● Because many clerical library assistants deal directly with the public, a professional appearance and pleasant personality are imperative.

Nature of the Work

Library assistants organize library resources and make them available to users. They assist librarians and, in some cases, library technicians.

Clerical library assistants—sometimes referred to as library media assistants, library aides, or circulation assistants—register patrons so they can borrow materials from the library. They record the borrower's name and address from an application and then issue a library card. Most library assistants enter and update patrons' records using computer databases.

At the circulation desk, assistants lend and collect books, periodicals, videotapes, and other materials. When an item is borrowed, assistants stamp the due date on the material and record the patron's identification from his or her library card. They inspect returned materials for damage, check due dates, and compute fines for overdue material. Library assistants review records to compile a list of overdue materials and send out notices. They also answer patrons' questions and refer those they cannot answer to a librarian.

Throughout the library, assistants sort returned books, periodicals, and other items and return them to their designated shelves, files, or storage areas. They locate materials to be loaned, either for a patron or another library. Many card catalogues are computerized, so library assistants must be familiar with the computer system. If any materials have been damaged, these workers try to repair them. For example, they use tape or paste to repair torn pages or book covers and other specialized processes to repair more valuable materials.

Some library assistants specialize in helping patrons who have vision problems. Sometimes referred to as library clerks, talking-books clerks, or Braille-and-talking-books clerks, they review the borrower's list of desired reading material. They locate those materials or closely related substitutes from the library collection of large type or Braille volumes, tape cassettes, and open-reel talking books. They complete the paperwork and give or mail them to the borrower.

Working Conditions

Most library assistants work in areas that are clean, well lit, and relatively quiet.

Opportunities for flexible schedules are abundant; more than half of all library assistants work part-time. Some high school and college students work part-time as library assistants, after school or during vacations. Some jobs may require working evenings or weekends. In general, employees with the least seniority tend to be assigned the less desirable shifts.

The work performed by library assistants may be repetitive. In addition, prolonged exposure to a video display terminal may lead to eyestrain for the many library assistants who work with computers.

Employment

Library assistants held about 98,000 jobs in 2000. More than one-half of these workers were employed by local government in public libraries; most of the remaining worked in school libraries. Opportunities for flexible schedules are abundant; more than one-half of these workers were on part-time schedules.

Training, Other Qualifications, and Advancement

Although hiring requirements for library assistants vary, a high school diploma or its equivalent is the most common educational requirement. Increasingly, familiarity or experience with computers and good interpersonal skills is equally important to employers.

Many library assistants deal with the public, so a professional appearance and pleasant personality is important. A clear speaking voice and fluency in the English language also are essential because these employees frequently use the telephone or public address systems. Good spelling and computer literacy often are needed, particularly because most work involves considerable computer use.

Orientation and training for library assistants usually takes place on the job. Under the guidance of a supervisor or other senior workers, new employees learn company procedures. Some formal classroom training also may be necessary, such as training in specific computer software. Most library assistants continue to receive instruction on new procedures and company policies after their initial training ends.

Additional training in library science or library-related computer software is helpful in preparing library assistants for promotion.

Job Outlook

Opportunities should be good for persons interested in jobs as library assistants through 2010. Turnover of these workers is quite high, reflecting the limited investment in training and subsequent weak attachment to this occupation. This work is attractive to retirees, students, and others who want a part-time schedule, and there is a lot of movement into and out of the occupation. Many openings will become available each year to replace workers who transfer to another occupation or leave the labor force. Some positions become available as library assistants move within the organization. Library assistants can be promoted to library technicians, and eventually supervisory positions in public service or technical service areas. Advancement opportunities are greater in larger libraries and may be more limited in smaller ones.

Employment is expected to grow about as fast as the average for all occupations through 2010. The vast majority of library assistants work in public or school libraries. Efforts to contain costs in local governments and academic institutions of all types may result in more hiring of library support staff than librarians. Also, due to changing roles within libraries, library assistants are taking on more responsibility. Because most are employed by public institutions, library assistants are not directly affected by the ups and downs of the business cycle. Some of these workers may lose their jobs, however, if there are cuts in government budgets.

Earnings

In 2000, median annual earnings for clerical library assistants were $17,980. In addition to their hourly wage, full-time library assistants who work evenings, nights, and weekends may receive shift differential pay. Some employers offer educational assistance to their employees.

Related Occupations

A number of other workers deal with the public, receive and provide information, or direct people to others who can assist them. Among these are dispatchers, security guards and gaming surveillance workers, tellers, and counter and rental clerks.

Sources of Additional Information

Information about a career as a library assistant can be obtained from:

- Council on Library/Media Technology, P.O. Box 951, Oxon Hill, MD 20750. Internet: http://library.ucr.edu/COLT

- American Library Association, 50 East Huron St., Chicago, IL 60611. Internet: http://www.ala.org/hrdr

Public libraries and libraries in academic institutions can provide information about job openings for library assistants.

Library Technicians

O*NET 25-4031.00

Significant Points

- Training requirements range from a high school diploma to an associate or bachelor's degree, but computer skills are needed for many jobs.

- Increasing use of computerized circulation and information systems should spur job growth, but budget constraints of many libraries should moderate growth.

- Employment should grow rapidly in special libraries as growing numbers of professionals and other workers use those libraries.

Nature of the Work

Library technicians help Librarians acquire, prepare, and organize material, and assist users in finding information. Library technicians usually work under the supervision of a librarian, although they work independently in certain situations. Technicians in small libraries handle a range of duties; those in large libraries usually specialize. As libraries increasingly use new technologies—such as CD-ROM, the Internet, virtual libraries, and automated databases—the duties of library technicians will expand and evolve accordingly. Library technicians are assuming greater responsibilities, in some cases taking on tasks previously performed by librarians.

Depending on the employer, library technicians can have other titles, such as library technical assistant or media aide. Library technicians direct library users to standard references, organize and maintain periodicals, prepare volumes for binding, handle interlibrary loan requests, prepare invoices, perform routine cataloguing and coding of library materials, retrieve information from computer databases, and supervise support staff.

The widespread use of computerized information storage and retrieval systems has resulted in technicians handling more technical and user services—such as entering catalogue information into the library's computer—that were once performed by librarians. Technicians assist with customizing databases. In addition, technicians instruct patrons how to use computer systems to access data. The increased automation of recordkeeping has reduced the amount of clerical work performed by library technicians. Many libraries now offer self-service registration and circulations with computers, decreasing the time library technicians spend manually recording and inputting records.

Some library technicians operate and maintain audiovisual equipment, such as projectors, tape recorders, and videocassette recorders, and assist users with microfilm or microfiche readers. They also design posters, bulletin boards, or displays.

Library technicians in school libraries encourage and teach students to use the library and media center. They also help teachers obtain instructional materials and assist students with special assignments. Some work in special libraries maintained by government agencies, corporations, law firms, advertising agencies, museums, professional societies, medical centers, and research laboratories, where they conduct literature searches, compile bibliographies, and prepare abstracts, usually on subjects of particular interest to the organization.

To extend library services to more patrons, many libraries operate bookmobiles. Bookmobile drivers take trucks stocked with books to designated sites on a regular schedule. Bookmobiles serve community organizations such as shopping centers, apartment complexes, schools, and nursing homes. They also may be used to extend library service to patrons living in remote areas. Depending on local conditions, drivers may operate a bookmobile alone or may be accompanied by another library employee.

When working alone, the drivers answer patrons' questions, receive and check out books, collect fines, maintain the book collection, shelve materials, and occasionally operate audiovisual equipment to show slides or films. They participate and may assist in planning programs sponsored by the library such as reader advisory programs, used book sales, or outreach programs. Bookmobile drivers keep track of their mileage, the materials lent out, and the amount of fines collected. In some areas, they are responsible for maintenance of the vehicle and any photocopiers or other equipment in it. They record statistics on circulation and the number of people visiting the bookmobile. Drivers also may record requests for special items from the main library and arrange for the

materials to be mailed or delivered to a patron during the next scheduled visit. Many bookmobiles are equipped with personal computers and CD-ROM systems linked to the main library system; this allows bookmobile drivers to reserve or locate books immediately. Some bookmobiles now offer Internet access to users.

Working Conditions

Technicians answer questions and provide assistance to library users. Those who prepare library materials sit at desks or computer terminals for long periods and can develop headaches or eyestrain from working with video display terminals. Some duties, like calculating circulation statistics, can be repetitive and boring. Others, such as performing computer searches using local and regional library networks and cooperatives, can be interesting and challenging. Library technicians may lift and carry books, and climb ladders to reach high stacks.

Library technicians in school libraries work regular school hours. Those in public libraries and college and university (academic) libraries also work weekends, evenings and some holidays. Library technicians in special libraries usually work normal business hours, although they often work overtime as well.

The schedules of bookmobile drivers depend on the size of the area being served. Some of these workers go out on their routes every day, while others go only on certain days. On these other days, they work at the library. Some also work evenings and weekends to give patrons as much access to the library as possible. Because bookmobile drivers may be the only link some people have to the library, much of their work is helping the public. They may assist handicapped or elderly patrons to the bookmobile, or shovel snow to assure their safety. They may enter hospitals or nursing homes to deliver books to patrons who are bedridden.

Employment

Library technicians held about 109,000 jobs in 2000. Most worked in school, academic, or public libraries. Some worked in hospitals and religious organizations. The federal government, primarily the U.S. Department of Defense and the U.S. Library of Congress, and state and local governments also employed library technicians.

Training, Other Qualifications, and Advancement

Training requirements for library technicians vary widely, ranging from a high school diploma to specialized postsecondary training. Some employers hire individuals with work experience or other training; others train inexperienced workers on the job. Other employers require that technicians have an associate or bachelor's degree. Given the rapid spread of automation in libraries, computer skills are needed for many jobs. Knowledge of databases, library automation systems, online library systems, online public access systems, and circulation systems is valuable.

Some 2-year colleges offer an associate of arts degree in library technology. Programs include both liberal arts and library-related study. Students learn about library and media organization and operation, and how to order, process, catalogue, locate, and circulate library materials and work with library automation. Libraries and associations offer continuing education courses to keep technicians abreast of new developments in the field.

Library technicians usually advance by assuming added responsibilities. For example, technicians often start at the circulation desk, checking books in and out. After gaining experience, they may become responsible for storing and verifying information. As they advance, they may become involved in budget and personnel matters in their department. Some library technicians advance to supervisory positions and are in charge of the day-to-day operation of their department.

Many bookmobile drivers are required to have a commercial driver's license.

Job Outlook

Employment of library technicians is expected to grow about as fast as the average for all occupations through 2010. In addition to employment growth, some job openings will result from the need to replace library technicians who transfer to other fields or leave the labor force.

The increasing use of library automation is expected to spur job growth among library technicians. Computerized information systems have simplified certain tasks, such as descriptive cataloguing, which can now be handled by technicians instead of Librarians. For example, technicians can now easily retrieve information from a central database and store it in the library's computer. Although efforts to contain costs could dampen employment growth of library technicians in school, public, and college and university libraries, cost containment efforts could also result in more hiring of library technicians than Librarians. Growth in the number of professionals and other workers who use special libraries should result in good job opportunities for library technicians in those settings.

Earnings

Median annual earnings of library technicians in 2000 were $23,170. The middle 50 percent earned between $17,820 and $29,840. The lowest 10 percent earned less than $13,810, and the highest 10 percent earned more than $35,660. Median annual earnings in the industries employing the largest numbers of library technicians in 2000 were as follows:

Colleges and universities	$25,320
Local government	22,910
Elementary and secondary schools	21,120

Salaries of library technicians in the federal government averaged $33,224 in 2001.

Related Occupations

Library technicians perform organizational and administrative duties. Workers in other occupations with similar duties include library assistants, clerical; information and record clerks; and medical records and health information technicians.

Sources of Additional Information

For information on training programs for library/media technical assistants, write to:

- American Library Association, Office for Human Resource Development and Recruitment, 50 East Huron St., Chicago, IL 60611. Internet: http://www.ala.org

Information on acquiring a job as a library technician with the federal government may be obtained from the Office of Personnel Management through a telephone-based system. Consult your telephone directory under U.S. Government for a local number, or call (912) 757-3000; Federal Relay Service (800) 877-8339. The first number is not toll free and charges may result. Information also is available on the Internet: http://www.usajobs.opm.gov

Information concerning requirements and application procedures for positions in the Library of Congress can be obtained directly from:

- Human Resources Office, Library of Congress, 101 Independence Ave. SE, Washington, DC 20540-2231

State library agencies can furnish information on requirements for technicians, and general information about career prospects in the state. Several of these agencies maintain job hotlines reporting openings for library technicians.

State departments of education can furnish information on requirements and job opportunities for school library technicians.

Licensed Practical and Licensed Vocational Nurses

O*NET 29-2061.00

Significant Points

- Training lasting about 1 year is available in about 1,100 state-approved programs, mostly in vocational or technical schools.

- Nursing homes will offer the most new jobs.

- Job seekers in hospitals may face competition as the number of hospital jobs for LPNs declines.

Nature of the Work

Licensed practical nurses (LPNs), or licensed vocational nurses (LVNs) as they are called in Texas and California, care for the sick, injured, convalescent, and disabled under the direction of physicians and registered nurses.

Most LPNs provide basic bedside care. They take vital signs such as temperature, blood pressure, pulse, and respiration. They also treat bedsores, prepare and give injections and enemas, apply dressings, give alcohol rubs and massages, apply ice packs and hot water bottles, and monitor catheters. LPNs observe patients and report adverse reactions to medications or treatments. They collect samples for testing, perform routine laboratory tests, feed patients, and record food and fluid intake and output. They help patients with bathing, dressing, and personal hygiene, keep them comfortable, and care for their emotional needs. In states where the law allows, they may administer prescribed medicines or start intravenous fluids. Some LPNs help deliver, care for, and feed infants. Experienced LPNs may supervise nursing assistants and aides.

LPNs in nursing homes provide routine bedside care, help evaluate residents' needs, develop care plans, and supervise the care provided by nursing aides. In doctors' offices and clinics, they also may make appointments, keep records, and perform other clerical duties. LPNs who work in private homes also may prepare meals and teach family members simple nursing tasks.

Working Conditions

Most licensed practical nurses in hospitals and nursing homes work a 40-hour week, but because patients need around-the-clock care, some work nights, weekends, and holidays. They often stand for long periods and help patients move in bed, stand, or walk.

LPNs may face hazards from caustic chemicals, radiation, and infectious diseases such as hepatitis. They are subject to back injuries when moving patients and shock from electrical equipment. They often must deal with the stress of heavy workloads. In addition, the patients they care for may be confused, irrational, agitated, or uncooperative.

Employment

Licensed practical nurses held about 700,000 jobs in 2000. Twenty-nine percent of LPNs worked in nursing homes, 28 percent worked in hospitals, and 14 percent in physicians' offices and clinics. Others worked for home healthcare services, residential care facilities, schools, temporary help agencies, or government agencies; about 1 in 5 worked part-time.

Training, Other Qualifications, and Advancement

All states and the District of Columbia require LPNs to pass a licensing examination after completing a state-approved practical nursing program. A high school diploma, or equivalent, usually is required for entry, although some programs accept candidates without a diploma or are designed as part of a high school curriculum.

In 2000, approximately 1,100 state-approved programs provided practical nursing training. Almost 6 out of 10 students were enrolled in technical or vocational schools, while 3 out of 10 were in community and junior colleges. Others were in high schools, hospitals, and colleges and universities.

Most practical nursing programs last about 1 year and include both classroom study and supervised clinical practice (patient care). Classroom study covers basic nursing concepts and patient-care related subjects, including anatomy, physiology, medical-surgical nursing, pediatrics, obstetrics, psychiatric nursing, administration of drugs, nutrition, and first aid. Clinical practice usually is in a hospital, but sometimes includes other settings.

LPNs should have a caring, sympathetic nature. They should be emotionally stable because work with the sick and injured can be stressful. They also should have keen observational, decision making, and communication skills. As part of a healthcare team, they must be able to follow orders and work under close supervision.

Job Outlook

Employment of LPNs is expected to grow about as fast as the average for all occupations through 2010 in response to the long-term care needs of a rapidly growing elderly population and the general growth of healthcare. Replacement needs will be a major source of job openings, as many workers leave the occupation permanently.

Employment of LPNs in nursing homes is expected to grow faster than the average. Nursing homes will offer the most new jobs for LPNs as the number of aged and disabled persons in need of long-term care rises. In addition to caring for the aged and disabled, nursing homes will be called on to care for the increasing number of patients who have been discharged from the hospital but who have not recovered enough to return home.

LPNs seeking positions in hospitals may face competition, as the number of hospital jobs for LPNs declines. An increasing proportion of sophisticated procedures, which once were performed only in hospitals, are being performed in physicians' offices and clinics, including ambulatory surgicenters and emergency medical centers, due largely to advances in technology. As a result, employment of LPNs is projected to grow much faster than average in these places as healthcare expands outside the traditional hospital setting.

Employment of LPNs is expected to grow much faster than average in home healthcare services. This is in response to a growing number of older persons with functional disabilities, consumer preference for care in the home, and technological advances, which make it possible to bring increasingly complex treatments into the home.

Earnings

Median annual earnings of licensed practical nurses were $29,440 in 2000. The middle 50 percent earned between $24,920 and $34,800. The lowest 10 percent earned less than $21,520, and the highest 10 percent earned more than $41,800. Median annual earnings in the industries employing the largest numbers of licensed practical nurses in 2000 were as follows:

Personnel supply services	$35,750
Home healthcare services	31,220
Nursing and personal care facilities	29,980
Hospitals	28,450
Offices and clinics of medical doctors	27,520

Related Occupations

LPNs work closely with people while helping them. So do emergency medical technicians and paramedics, social and human service assistants, surgical technologists, and teacher assistants.

Sources of Additional Information

For information about practical nursing, contact:

- National League for Nursing, 61 Broadway, New York, NY 10006. Internet: http://www.nln.org

- National Association for Practical Nurse Education and Service, Inc., 1400 Spring St., Suite 330, Silver Spring, MD 20910

- National Federation of Licensed Practical Nurses, Inc., 893 US Highway 70 West, Suite 202, Garner, NC 27529-2597

Line Installers and Repairers

O*NET 49-9051.00, 49-9052.00

Significant Points

- Projected employment growth reflects the expansion of telecommunications and cable networks.

- Line installers and repairers work outdoors; the work can be hazardous.

- Earnings are relatively high.

Nature of the Work

Vast networks of wires and cables provide customers with electrical power and communications services. Networks of electrical power lines deliver electricity from generating plants to customers. Communications networks of telephone and cable television lines provide voice, video, and other communications services. These networks are constructed and maintained by line installers and repairers.

Line installers, or line erectors, install new lines by constructing utility poles, towers, and underground trenches to carry the wires and cables. Line erectors use a variety of construction equipment including digger derricks, trenchers, cable plows, and borers. Digger derricks are trucks equipped with augers and cranes; augers dig holes in the ground, and cranes set utility poles in place. Trenchers, cable plows, and borers cut openings in the earth for laying underground cables.

When construction is complete, line installers string cable along the poles, towers, tunnels, and trenches. While working on poles and towers, installers first use truck-mounted buckets to reach the top of the structure or, less often, climb the pole or tower. Next, they pull up cable by hand from large reels mounted on trucks. The line is then set in place and pulled so that it has the correct amount of tension. Finally, line installers attach the cable to the structure using hand and hydraulic tools. When working with electrical powerlines, installers bolt or clamp insulators onto the poles before attaching the cable. Underground cable is laid directly in the trench, pulled through a tunnel, or strung through a conduit running through the trench.

Other installation duties include setting up service for customers and installing network equipment. To set up service, line installers string cable between the customers' premises and the lines running on poles or towers or in trenches. They place wiring in houses and check that transmission signals are strong. Line installers may also install a variety of equipment. Workers on telephone and cable television lines install amplifiers and repeaters that maintain the strength of communications transmissions. Workers on electrical powerlines install and replace transformers, circuit breakers, switches, fuses, and other equipment to control and direct the electrical current.

In addition to installation, line installers and repairers also are responsible for maintenance of electrical, telephone, and cable television lines.

Workers periodically travel in trucks, helicopters, and airplanes to visually inspect the wires and cables. Sensitive monitoring equipment can automatically detect malfunctions on the network, such as loss of current flow. When line repairers identify a problem, they travel to the location of the malfunction and repair or replace defective cables or equipment. Bad weather or natural disasters can cause extensive damage to networks. Line installers and repairers must respond quickly to these emergencies to restore critical utility and communications services. This can often involve working outdoors in adverse weather conditions.

Installation and repair work may require splicing, or joining together, separate pieces of cable. Each cable contains numerous individual wires; splicing the cables together requires that each wire in one piece of cable be joined to another wire in the matching piece. Line installers splice cables using small hand tools, epoxy, or mechanical equipment. At each splice, they place insulation over the conductor and seal the splice with moisture-proof covering.

Many communications networks now use fiber optic cables instead of conventional wire or metal cables. Fiber optic cables are made of hair-thin strands of glass, which convey pulses of light. These cables can carry much more information at higher speeds than conventional cables. The higher transmission capacity of fiber optic cable has allowed communication networks to offer upgraded services, such as high speed Internet access. Splicing fiber optic cable requires specialized equipment that carefully slices, matches, and aligns individual glass fibers. The fibers are joined by either electrical fusion (welding) or a mechanical fixture and gel (glue).

Working Conditions

Line installers and repairers must climb and maintain their balance while working on poles and towers. They lift equipment and work in a variety of positions, such as stooping or kneeling. Their work often requires that they drive utility vehicles, travel long distances, and work outdoors under a variety of weather conditions. Many line installers and repairers work a 40-hour week; however, emergencies may require overtime work. For example, when severe weather damages electrical and communications lines, line installers and repairers may work long and irregular hours to restore service.

Line installers and repairers encounter serious hazards on their jobs and must follow safety procedures to minimize potential danger. They wear safety equipment when entering utility holes and test for the presence of gas before going underground. Electric powerline workers have the most hazardous jobs. High voltage powerlines can cause electrocution, and line installers and repairers must consequently use electrically insulated protective devices and tools when working with live cables. Powerlines are typically higher than telephone and cable television lines, increasing the risk of severe injury due to falls. To prevent these injuries, line installers and repairers must use fall-protection equipment when working on poles or towers.

Employment

Line installers and repairers held about 263,000 jobs in 2000. Approximately 164,000 were telecommunications line installers and repairers; the remainder were electrical power-line installers and repairers. Nearly all line installers and repairers worked for telephone, cable television, electric power, or construction companies.

Training, Other Qualifications, and Advancement

Line installers and repairers are trained on the job, and most employers generally require at least a high school diploma. However, employers prefer a technical knowledge of electricity and electronics obtained through vocational programs, community colleges, or experience in the armed forces. Prospective employees should possess a basic knowledge of algebra and trigonometry, and mechanical ability. Customer service and interpersonal skills also are important. Because the work entails lifting heavy objects (many employers require applicants to be able to lift at least 60 pounds), climbing, and other physical activity, applicants should have stamina, strength, and coordination, and must be unafraid of heights. The ability to distinguish colors is necessary because wires and cables may be color-coded.

Line installers and repairers working for electric power companies generally complete formal apprenticeship or employer training programs. These are sometimes administered jointly by the employer and the union representing the workers. The unions include the International Brotherhood of Electrical Workers, the Communications Workers of America, and the Utility Workers Union of America. Apprenticeship programs last up to 5 years and combine formal instruction with on-the-job training.

Line installers and repairers in telephone and cable television companies receive several years of on-the-job training. They may also attend training or take online courses provided by equipment manufacturers, schools, unions, or industry training organizations. The Society of Cable Television Engineers (SCTE) provides certification programs for line installers and repairers. Applicants for certification must be employed in the cable television industry, and attend training sessions at local SCTE chapters.

Entry-level line installers may be hired as ground workers, helpers, or tree trimmers, who clear branches from telephone and power lines. These workers may advance to positions stringing cable and performing service installations. With experience, they may advance to more sophisticated maintenance and repair positions responsible for increasingly larger portions of the network. Promotion to supervisory or training positions also is possible, but more advanced supervisory positions often require a college diploma.

Job Outlook

Overall employment of line installers and repairers is expected to grow faster than the average for all occupations through 2010. Much of this increase will result from growth in the telecommunications industry. The introduction of new technologies, especially fiber optic cable, has increased the transmission capacity of telephone and cable television networks. This higher capacity has allowed the creation of new and extremely popular services, such as high-speed Internet access. At the same time, deregulation of the telecommunications industry has reduced barriers to competition. As a result, numerous companies are installing high-capacity networks in order to compete for the increasing demand for telecommunications services. Competition for local phone service and demand for high-speed Internet access is forcing former local telephone companies to update and modernize their networks. In some regions, underground telephone lines may be 50 years old, and are incapable of providing advanced services. Strong job growth is expected due to the expansion, maintenance, and modernization of telecommunications networks. Besides employment growth, many job openings will result from the need to replace the large number of older workers reaching retirement age.

Employment of telecommunications line installers and repairers is expected to grow faster than average. Telephone and cable television companies will create new networks and improve existing ones to provide customers with high-speed access to data, video, and graphics. Line installers and repairers will be needed not only to construct and install networks, but also to maintain the ever-growing systems of wires and cables. Businesses will install extensive private networks as they increasingly use telecommunications lines for access to suppliers and customers. The average residential customer already has more than two telephone lines. Increased demand for high-speed Internet access, fax lines, and multiple phone lines will require the improvement and expansion of local phone line networks.

Employment of electrical powerline installers and repairers, on the other hand, should grow more slowly than the average for all occupations through 2010. The demand for electricity has been consistently rising, driving the expansion of powerline networks, which tends to increase employment. However, industry deregulation is pushing companies to cut costs and maintenance, which tends to reduce employment. Also, many power companies are using their existing networks of towers and rights-of-way to expand into the telecommunications industry. Because electrical power companies have reduced hiring and training in recent years, opportunities should be best for workers who possess experience and training.

Earnings

Earnings for line installers and repairers are higher than in most other occupations that do not require postsecondary education. Median hourly earnings for electrical powerline installers and repairers were $22.01 in 2000. The middle 50 percent earned between $16.99 and $26.09. The lowest 10 percent earned less than $12.36, and the highest 10 percent earned more than $30.35. Median hourly earnings in the industries employing the largest numbers of electrical powerline installers and repairers in 2000 are shown in the following table:

Combination utility services	$25.86
Telephone communication	22.80
Electric services	22.70
Heavy construction, except highway	16.86
Electrical work	16.84

Median hourly earnings for telecommunications line installers and repairers were $18.32 in 2000. The middle 50 percent earned between $12.82 and $23.82. The lowest 10 percent earned less than $9.79, and the highest 10 percent earned more than $26.68. Median hourly earnings in the industries employing the largest numbers of telephone and cable television line installers and repairers in 2000 are shown in the following table:

Telephone communication	$22.88
Electrical work	14.88
Cable and other pay TV services	14.86
Heavy construction, except highway	12.26

Most line installers and repairers belong to unions, principally the Communications Workers of America, the International Brotherhood of Electrical Workers, and the Utility Workers Union of America. For these workers, union contracts set wage rates, wage increases, and the time needed to advance from one job level to the next.

Related Occupations

Other workers who install and repair electronic equipment include broadcast and sound engineering technicians and radio operators, electricians, and radio and telecommunications equipment installers and repairers.

Sources of Additional Information

For more details about employment opportunities, contact the telephone, cable television, or electrical power companies in your community. For general information on line installer and repairer jobs, write to:

- Communications Workers of America, 501 3rd St. NW., Washington, DC 20001. Internet: http://www.cwa-union.org

- International Brotherhood of Electrical Workers, Utility Department, 1125 15th St. NW., Washington, DC 20005

For information on training and certification programs in the cable industry, contact:

- Society of Cable Telecommunications Engineers, Certification Department, 140 Phillips Rd., Exton, PA 19341. Internet: http://www.scte.org

Lodging Managers

O*NET 11-9081.00

Significant Points

- Employment is projected to grow more slowly than average.

- College graduates with degrees in hotel or restaurant management should have the best job opportunities.

Nature of the Work

A comfortable room, good food, and a helpful staff can make being away from home an enjoyable experience for both vacationing families and business travelers. While most lodging managers work in traditional hotels and motels, some work in other lodging establishments, such as camps, inns, boardinghouses, dude ranches, and recreational resorts. In full-service hotels, lodging managers help their guests have a pleasant stay by providing many of the comforts of home, including cable television, fitness equipment, and voice mail, as well as specialized services such as health spas. For business travelers, lodging managers often schedule available meeting rooms and electronic equipment, including slide projectors and fax machines.

Lodging managers are responsible for keeping their establishments efficient and profitable. In a small establishment with a limited staff, the manager may oversee all aspects of operations. However, large hotels may employ hundreds of workers, and the general manager usually is aided by a number of assistant managers assigned to the various departments of the operation. In hotels of every size, managerial duties vary significantly by job title.

The general manager, for example, has overall responsibility for the operation of the hotel. Within guidelines established by the owners of the hotel or executives of the hotel chain, the general manager sets room rates, allocates funds to departments, approves expenditures, and establishes expected standards for guest service, decor, housekeeping, food quality, and banquet operations. Managers who work for chains also may organize and staff a newly built hotel, refurbish an older hotel, or reorganize a hotel or motel that is not operating successfully. In order to fill low-paying service and clerical jobs in hotels, some managers attend career fairs.

Resident managers live in hotels and are on call 24 hours a day to resolve problems or emergencies. In general, though, they typically work an 8-hour day and oversee the day-to-day operations of the hotel. In many hotels, the general manager also is the resident manager.

Executive housekeepers ensure that guest rooms, meeting and banquet rooms, and public areas are clean, orderly, and well maintained. They also train, schedule, and supervise the work of housekeepers; inspect rooms; and order cleaning supplies.

Front office managers coordinate reservations and room assignments, as well as train and direct the hotel's front desk staff. They ensure that guests are treated courteously, complaints and problems are resolved, and requests for special services are carried out. Front office managers often have authorization to adjust charges posted on a customer's bill.

Convention services managers coordinate the activities of large hotels' various departments for meetings, conventions, and special events. They meet with representatives of groups or organizations to plan the number of rooms to reserve, the desired configuration of hotel meeting space, and the banquet services. During the meeting or event, they resolve unexpected problems and monitor activities to ensure that hotel operations conform to the expectations of the group.

Assistant managers help run the day-to-day operations of the hotel. In large hotels, they may be responsible for activities such as personnel, accounting, office administration, marketing and sales, purchasing, security, maintenance, and pool, spa, or recreational facilities. In smaller hotels, these duties may be combined into one position. Some hotels allow an assistant manager to make decisions regarding hotel guest charges when a manager is unavailable.

Computers are used extensively by lodging managers and their assistants to keep track of the guest's bill, reservations, room assignments, meetings, and special events. In addition, computers are used to order food, beverages, and supplies, as well as to prepare reports for hotel owners and top-level managers. Managers work with computer specialists to ensure that the hotel's computer system functions properly. Should the hotel's computer system fail, managers must continue to meet guests' needs.

Working Conditions

Because hotels are open around the clock, night and weekend work is common. Many lodging managers work more than 40 hours per week. Managers who live in the hotel usually have regular work schedules, but they may be called to work at any time. Some employees of resort hotels are managers during the busy season and have other duties during the rest of the year.

Lodging managers sometimes experience the pressures of coordinating a wide range of functions. Conventions and large groups of tourists may present unusual problems. Moreover, dealing with irate guests can be stressful. The job can be particularly hectic for front office managers during check-in and check-out time. Computer failures can further complicate an already busy time.

Employment

Lodging managers held about 68, 000 jobs in 2000. Self-employed managers—primarily owners of small hotels and motels—held about half of these jobs. Companies that manage hotels and motels under contract employed some managers.

Training, Other Qualifications, and Advancement

Hotels increasingly emphasize specialized training. Postsecondary training in hotel or restaurant management is preferred for most hotel management positions, although a college liberal arts degree may be sufficient when coupled with related hotel experience. Internships or part-time or summer work are an asset to students seeking a career in hotel management. The experience gained and the contacts made with employers can greatly benefit students after graduation. Most bachelor's degree programs include work-study opportunities.

In the past, many managers were promoted from the ranks of front desk clerks, housekeepers, waiters, chefs, and hotel sales workers. Although some employees still advance to hotel management positions without education beyond high school, postsecondary education is preferred. Restaurant management training or experience also is a good background for entering hotel management because the success of a hotel's food service and beverage operations often is of great importance to the profitability of the entire establishment.

Community colleges, junior colleges and some universities offer associate, bachelor's, and graduate degree programs in hotel or restaurant management. When combined with technical institutes, vocational and trade schools, and other academic institutions, over 800 educational facilities have programs leading to formal recognition in hotel or restaurant management. Hotel management programs include instruction in hotel administration, accounting, economics, marketing, housekeeping, food service management and catering, and hotel maintenance engineering. Computer training also is an integral part of hotel management training due to the widespread use of computers in reservations, billing, and housekeeping management.

Lodging managers must be able to get along with many different people, even in stressful situations. They must be able to solve problems and concentrate on details. Initiative, self-discipline, effective communication skills, and the ability to organize and direct the work of others also are essential for managers at all levels.

Most hotels promote employees who have proven their ability and completed formal education in hotel management. Graduates of hotel or restaurant management programs usually start as trainee assistant managers. Some large hotels sponsor specialized on-the-job management training programs allowing trainees to rotate among various departments and gain a thorough knowledge of the hotel's operation. Other hotels may help finance formal training in hotel management for outstanding employees. Newly built hotels, particularly those without well-established, on-the-job training programs, often prefer experienced personnel for managerial positions.

Large hotel and motel chains may offer better opportunities for advancement than small, independently owned establishments, but relocation every several years often is necessary for advancement. The large chains have more extensive career ladder programs and offer managers the opportunity to transfer to another hotel or motel in the chain or to the central office. Career advancement can be accelerated by completion of certification programs offered by the associations listed in the following "Sources of Additional Information" section. These programs usually require a combination of coursework, examinations, and experience. Outstanding lodging managers may advance to higher-level manager positions.

Job Outlook

Employment of lodging managers is expected to grow more slowly than the average for all occupations through 2010. Additional job openings are expected to occur as experienced managers transfer to other occupations or leave the labor force, in part because of the long hours and stressful working conditions. Job opportunities in hotel management are expected to be best for persons with college degrees in hotel or restaurant management.

Increasing business travel and domestic and foreign tourism will drive employment growth of lodging managers. Managerial jobs are not expected to grow as rapidly as the hotel industry overall, however. As the industry consolidates, many chains and franchises will acquire independently owned establishments and increase the numbers of economy-class rooms to accommodate bargain-conscious guests. Economy hotels offer clean, comfortable rooms and front desk services without costly extras like restaurants and room service. Because there are not as many departments in these hotels, fewer managers will be needed. Similarly, the increasing number of extended-stay hotels will temper demand for managers because in these establishments, management is not required to be available 24 hours a day. In addition, front desk clerks increasingly are assuming some responsibilities previously reserved for managers, further limiting the growth of managers and their assistants.

Additional demand for managers, however, is expected in suite hotels as some guests, especially business customers, are willing to pay higher prices for rooms with kitchens and suites that provide the space needed to conduct meetings. In addition, large full-service hotels—offering restaurants, fitness centers, large meeting rooms, and play areas for children, among other amenities—will continue to offer many trainee and managerial opportunities.

Earnings

Median annual earnings of lodging managers were $30,770 in 2000. The middle 50 percent earned between $23,670 and $41,830. The lowest 10 percent earned less than $19,080, and the highest 10 percent earned more than $55,050.

Salaries of lodging managers vary greatly according to their responsibilities and the segment of the hotel industry in which they are employed. Managers may earn bonuses of up to 25 percent of their basic salary in some hotels and also may be furnished with lodging, meals, parking, laundry, and other services. In addition to typical benefits, some hotels offer profit-sharing plans and educational assistance to their employees.

Related Occupations

Other occupations concerned with organizing and directing a business where customer service is the cornerstone of their success include food service managers, gaming managers, sales worker supervisors, and property, real estate, and community association managers.

Sources of Additional Information

For information on careers and scholarships in hotel management, contact:

- American Hotel and Lodging Association, 1201 New York Ave. NW., #600, Washington, DC 20005-3931. Internet: http://www.ahlaonline.org

Information on careers in the lodging industry and professional development and training programs may be obtained from:

- Educational Institute of the American Hotel and Lodging Association, 800 N. Magnolia Ave., Suite 1800, Orlando, FL 32853-1126. Internet: http://www.ei-ahma.org

For information on educational programs, including correspondence courses, in hotel and restaurant management, write to:

- International Council on Hotel, Restaurant, and Institutional Education, 3205 Skipwith Rd., Richmond, VA 23294-4442. Internet: http://www.chrie.org

Information on careers in housekeeping management may be obtained from:

- International Executive Housekeepers Association, Inc., 1001 Eastwind Dr., Suite 301, Westerville, OH 43081. Internet: http://www.ieha.org

Machine Setters, Operators, and Tenders— Metal and Plastic

O*NET 51-4021.00, 51-4022.00, 51-4023.00, 51-4031.01, 51-4031.02, 51-4031.03, 51-4031.04, 51-4032.00, 51-4033.01, 51-4033.02, 51-4034.00, 51-4035.00, 51-4051.00, 51-4052.00, 51-4061.00, 51-4062.00, 51-4071.00, 51-4072.01, 51-4072.02, 51-4072.03, 51-4072.04, 51-4072.05, 51-4081.01, 51-4081.02, 51-4191.01, 51-4191.02, 51-4191.03, 51-4192.00, 51-4193.01, 51-4193.02, 51-4193.03, 51-4193.04, 51-4194.00, 51-4199.99

Significant Points

- A few weeks of on-the-job training is sufficient for most workers to learn basic machine operations, but several years are required to become a skilled operator.

- Employment of most operators is expected to decline, while employment of multiple machine tool operators is projected to grow.

Nature of the Work

Consider the parts of a toaster, such as the metal or plastic housing or the lever that lowers the toast. These parts, and many other metal and plastic products, are produced by metalworking and plastics-working machine operators. In fact, machine tool operators in the metalworking and plastics industries play a major part in producing most of the consumer products on which we rely daily.

In general, these workers can be separated into two groups—those who set up machines for operation and those who tend the machines during production. Setup workers prepare the machines prior to production and may adjust the machinery during operation. Operators and tenders, on the other hand, primarily monitor the machinery during operation, sometimes loading or unloading the machine or making minor adjustments to the controls. Many workers both set up and operate equipment. Because the setup process requires an understanding of the entire production process, setters usually have more training and are more highly skilled than those who simply operate or tend machinery. As new automation simplifies the setup process, however, less skilled workers also are increasingly able to set up machines for operation.

Setters, operators, tenders, and setup operators usually are identified by the type of machine with which they work. Some examples of specific titles are drilling and boring machine toolsetters, milling and planing machine tenders, and lathe and turning-machine tool operators. Job duties usually vary based on the size of the firm and on the type of machine being operated. Although some workers specialize in one or two types of machinery, many are trained to set up or operate a variety of machines. Newer production techniques require machine operators to rotate between, and be proficient with, different machines. The rotating of assignments allows workers more varied work, but also requires them to have a wider range of skills.

Metalworking-machine setters and operators set up and tend machines that cut and form all types of metal parts. Traditionally, setup workers plan and set up the sequence of operations according to blueprints, layouts, or other instructions. They adjust speed, feed, and other controls; choose the proper coolants and lubricants; and select the instruments or tools for each operation. Using micrometers, gauges, and other precision measuring instruments, they also may compare the completed work with the tolerance limits stated in the specifications.

Although there are many different types of metalworking machine tools that require specific knowledge and skills, most operators perform similar tasks. Whether tending grinding machines that remove excess material from the surface of machined products or presses that extrude metal through a die to form wire, operators usually perform simple, repetitive operations that can be learned quickly. Typically, these workers place metal stock in a machine on which the operating specifications have already been set. They may watch one or more machines and make minor adjustments according to their instructions. Regardless of the type of machine they operate, machine tenders usually depend on skilled setup workers for major adjustments when the machines are not functioning properly.

Plastics-working machine operators set up and tend machines that transform plastic compounds—chemical-based products that can be produced in powder, pellet, or syrup form—into a wide variety of consumer goods such as toys, tubing, and auto parts. These products are manufactured using various methods, of which injection molding is the most common. The injection-molding machine heats and liquefies a plastic compound and forces it into a mold. After the part has cooled and hardened, the mold opens and the part is released. Many common kitchen products are produced using this method. To produce long parts such as pipes or window frames, an extruding machine usually is employed. These machines force a plastic compound through a die that contains an opening of the desired shape of the final product. Blow molding is another common plastics-working technique. Blow-molding machines force hot air into a mold that contains a plastic tube. As the air moves into the mold, the plastic tube is inflated to the shape of the mold, and a plastic container is formed. The familiar 2-liter soft drink bottles are produced using this method.

Workers in three different specialized occupations operate injection-molding machines: tenders, operators, and setters. Most other types of plastic machines function in a similar manner. Tenders remove the cooled plastic from the mold, loading the product into boxes. Operators monitor the many gauges on injection-molding machines, adjusting different inputs, pressures, and speeds to maintain quality. A typical injection-molding machine may have 25 different controls that can be adjusted. Setters or technicians set up the machines prior to operations. They are responsible for repairing any major problem.

Working Conditions

Most machine setters, operators, and tenders—metal and plastic work in areas that are clean, well lit, and well ventilated. Nevertheless, many operators require stamina because they are on their feet much of the day and may do moderately heavy lifting. Also, these workers operate powerful, high-speed machines that can be dangerous if strict safety rules are not observed. Most operators wear protective equipment, such as safety glasses and earplugs, to protect against flying particles of metal or plastic and against noise from the machines. However, many modern machines are totally enclosed, minimizing the exposure of workers to noise, dust, and lubricants used during machining. Other required safety equipment varies by work setting and machine. For example, workers in the plastics industry who work near materials that emit dangerous fumes or dust must wear face masks or self-contained breathing apparatus.

Most metalworking and plastics-working machine operators work a 40-hour week, but overtime is common during periods of increased production. Because many metalworking and plastics-working shops operate more than one shift daily, some operators work nights and weekends.

Employment

Machine setters, operators, and tenders—metal and plastic held about 1.6 million jobs in 2000. About 3 out of every 4 metalworking and plastics-working machine operators are found in 5 manufacturing industries—fabricated metal products, industrial machinery and equipment, rubber and miscellaneous plastics products, transportation equipment, and primary metals. The following table shows the distribution of employment of metalworking and plastics-working machine operators by detailed occupation.

Cutting, punching, and press machine setters, operators, and tenders, metal and plastic	372,000
Molders and molding machine setters, operators, and tenders, metal and plastic	235,000
All other metal workers and plastic workers	150,000
Grinding, lapping, polishing, and buffing machine tool setters, operators, and tenders, metal and plastic	145,000
Extruding and drawing machine setters, operators, and tenders, metal and plastic	126,000
Multiple machine tool setters, operators, and tenders, metal and plastic	105,000
Lathe and turning machine tool setters, operators, and tenders, metal and plastic	84,000
Drilling and boring machine tool setters, operators, and tenders, metal and plastic	71,000
Plating and coating machine setters, operators, and tenders, metal and plastic	65,000
Forging machine setters, operators, and tenders, metal and plastic	54,000
Rolling machine setters, operators, and tenders, metal and plastic	49,000
Heat treating equipment setters, operators, and tenders, metal and plastic	43,000
Metal-refining furnace operators and tenders	40,000
Milling and planing machine setters, operators, and tenders, metal and plastic	34,000
Tool grinders, filers, and sharpeners	29,000
Model makers and patternmakers, metal and plastic	19,000
Lay-out workers, metal and plastic	18,000

Training, Other Qualifications, and Advancement

Machine setters, operators, and tenders—metal and plastic learn their skills on the job. Trainees begin by observing and assisting experienced workers, sometimes in formal training programs. Under supervision, they may start as tenders, supplying materials, starting and stopping the machine, or removing finished products from it. They then advance to the more difficult tasks performed by operators, such as adjusting feed speeds, changing cutting tools, or inspecting a finished product for defects. Eventually they become responsible for their own machines.

The complexity of the equipment largely determines the time required to become an operator. Most operators learn the basic machine operations and functions in a few weeks, but they may need several years to become skilled operators or to advance to the more highly skilled job of setter.

Setters or technicians normally need a thorough knowledge of the machinery and of the products being manufactured because they often plan the sequence of work, make the first production run, and determine which adjustments need to be made. Strong analytical abilities are particularly important to perform this job. Some companies have formal training programs for operators and setters, which combine classroom instruction with on-the-job training.

Although no special education is required for most operating jobs, employers prefer to hire applicants with good basic skills. Many require employees to have a high school education and to read, write, and speak English. Because machinery is becoming more complex and shop-floor organization is changing, employers increasingly look for persons with good communication and interpersonal skills. Mechanical aptitude, manual dexterity, and experience working with machinery also are helpful. Those interested in becoming machine setters, operators, and tenders can improve their employment opportunities by completing high school courses in shop and blueprint reading and by gaining a working knowledge of the properties of metals and plastics. A solid math background including courses in algebra, geometry, trigonometry, and basic statistics also is useful.

Job opportunities and advancement also can be enhanced by becoming certified in a particular machining skill. The National Institute for Metalworking Skills has developed standards for metalworking-machine operators. After taking a course approved by the organization and passing a written exam and performance requirement, the worker is issued a credential that formally recognizes him or her as competent in a specific machining operation. The Society of Plastics Industry, Inc., the national trade association representing plastics manufacturers, also certifies workers in the plastics industry. To achieve machine-operator certification, 2 years of experience operating a plastics-processing machine is recommended, and one must pass a computer-based exam.

Advancement for operators usually takes the form of higher pay, although there are some limited opportunities for operators to advance to new positions as well. For example, they can become multiple machine operators, setup operators, or trainees for the more highly skilled positions of machinist, tool and die maker, or computer control programmers or operators. Some setup workers may advance to supervisory positions.

Job Outlook

Employment trends for among the various machine setters, operators, and tenders—metal and plastic are expected to diverge over the 2000–2010 period. In general, employment of these workers will be affected by the rate of technological implementation, the demand for the goods they produce, the effects of trade, and the reorganization of production processes. These trends are expected to spur employment growth among multiple machine tool operators; plastics-molding, core-making, and casting machine operators; and a number of miscellaneous operating positions. On the other hand, a decline in employment is projected for many machine tool operators, including cutting, punching, and press machine setters, operators, and tenders; and lathe and turning-machine tool workers. Despite differing rates of employment change, a large number of machine setter, operator, and tender jobs will become available due to an expected surge in retirements as the first of the baby boomers become eligible for retirement by the end of this decade.

One of the most important factors influencing employment change in this occupation is the implementation of laborsaving machinery. In order to remain competitive by improving quality and lowering production costs, many firms are adopting new technologies, such as computer-controlled machine tools and robots. Computer-controlled equipment allows operators to simultaneously tend a greater number of machines and often makes setup easier, thereby reducing the amount of time setup workers spend on each machine. Robots are being used to load and unload parts from machines. The lower-skilled manual machine tool operators and tenders are more likely to be eliminated by these new technologies because the functions they perform are more easily automated.

The demand for metalworking and plastics-working machine operators largely mirrors the demand for the parts that they produce. Recent growth in the domestic economy, for example, has led to increased employment in a number of machine-operating occupations. In addition, the consumption of plastic products has grown as they have been substituted for metal goods in many consumer and manufactured products in recent years. This process is likely to continue and should result in stronger demand for machine operators in plastics than in metalworking.

Both the plastics and metal industries, however, face stiff foreign competition that is limiting the demand for domestically produced parts. One way in which larger U.S. producers have responded to this competition is by moving production operations to other countries where labor costs are lower. These moves are likely to continue, and will further reduce employment opportunities for many machine operators, setters, and tenders—metal and plastic in the United States.

Workers with a thorough background in machine operations, exposure to a variety of machines, and a good working knowledge of the properties of metals and plastics will be best able to adjust to this changing environment. In addition, new shop-floor arrangements will reward workers with good basic mathematics and reading skills, good communication skills, and the ability and willingness to learn new tasks. As workers are called upon to adapt to new production methods and to operate more machines, the number of multiple machine tool operators, setters, and tenders—metal and plastic will continue to rise.

Earnings

Earnings for machine operators can vary by size of the company, union/nonunion status, industry, and skill level and experience of the operator. Also, temporary employees, who are being hired in greater numbers, usually get paid less than company-employed workers get. The median hourly earnings in 2000 for a variety of machine setters, operators, and tenders—metal and plastic were as follows:

Model makers and patternmakers, metal and plastic $16.07
Lay-out workers, metal and plastic 14.27
Lathe and turning machine tool setters, operators,
   and tenders, metal and plastic 13.77
Metal-refining furnace operators and tenders 13.47
Milling and planing machine setters, operators,
   and tenders, metal and plastic 13.25
Tool grinders, filers, and sharpeners 13.22
Multiple machine tool setters, operators, and tenders,
   metal and plastic 12.96
Rolling machine setters, operators, and tenders,
   metal and plastic 12.85
Heat treating equipment setters, operators, and tenders,
   metal and plastic 12.64
Drilling and boring machine tool setters, operators,
   and tenders, metal and plastic 12.25
Forging machine setters, operators, and tenders,
   metal and plastic 12.11
Grinding, lapping, polishing, and buffing machine
   tool setters, operators, and tenders, metal and plastic 11.71
Extruding and drawing machine setters, operators,
   and tenders, metal and plastic 11.66
Plating and coating machine setters, operators,
   and tenders, metal and plastic 11.23
Cutting, punching, and press machine setters,
   operators, and tenders, metal and plastic 11.03
Molders and molding machine setters, operators,
   and tenders, metal and plastic 10.40
All other metal workers and plastic workers 13.26

Approximately one-third of these workers are union members, about double the rate for other workers in the economy. Metalworking industries have a higher rate of unionization than does the plastics industry.

Related Occupations

Workers in occupations closely related to machine setters, operators, and tenders—metal and plastic include machinists, tool and die makers, assemblers and fabricators, computer control programmers and operators, and woodworkers.

Sources of Additional Information

For general information about machine setters, operators, and tenders—metal and plastic, contact:

- National Tooling and Metalworking Association, 9300 Livingston Rd., Fort Washington, MD 20744. Internet: http://www.ntma.org

- Precision Machining Association Educational Foundation, 6363 Oak Tree Blvd., Independence, OH 44131. Internet: http://www.pmaef.org

- Precision Machine Products Association, 6700 West Snowville Rd., Brecksville, OH 44141-3292. Internet: http://www.pmpa.org

- Society of Plastics Industry, 1801 K St. NW., Suite 600K, Washington, DC 20006-1301. Internet: http://www.socplas.org and http://www.certifyme.org

Machinists

O*NET 51-4041.00

Significant Points

- Machinists learn in apprenticeship programs, informally on the job, and in high schools, vocational schools, or community or technical colleges.

- Many entrants previously have worked as machine setters, operators, or tenders.

- Job opportunities are expected to be excellent.

Nature of the Work

Machinists use machine tools, such as lathes, milling machines, and spindles, to produce precision metal parts. Although they may produce large quantities of one part, precision machinists often produce small batches or one-of-a-kind items. They use their knowledge of the working properties of metals and their skill with machine tools to plan and carry out the operations needed to make machined products that meet precise specifications.

Before they machine a part, machinists must carefully plan and prepare the operation. These workers first review blueprints or written specifications for a job. Next, they calculate where to cut or bore into the workpiece (the piece of metal that is being shaped), how fast to feed the metal into the machine, and how much metal to remove. They then select tools and materials for the job, plan the sequence of cutting and finishing operations, and mark the metal stock to show where cuts should be made.

After this layout work is completed, machinists perform the necessary machining operations. They position the metal stock on the machine tool—spindle, drill press, lathe, milling machine, or other—set the controls, and make the cuts. During the machining process, they must constantly monitor the feed and speed of the machine. Machinists also ensure that the workpiece is being properly lubricated and cooled, because the machining of metal products generates a significant amount of heat. The temperature of the workpiece is a key concern because most metals expand when heated; machinists must adjust the size of their cuts relative to the temperature. Some rarer, but increasingly popular, metals, such as titanium, are machined at extremely high temperatures. Machinists also adjust cutting speeds to compensate for harmonic vibrations, which can decrease the accuracy of cuts, particularly on newer high-speed spindles and lathes.

Some machinists, often called production machinists, may produce large quantities of one part, especially parts requiring the use of complex operations and great precision. Production machinists work with complex computer numerically controlled (CNC) cutting machines. Frequently, machinists work with computer-control programmers to determine how the automated equipment will cut a part. The programmer determines the path of the cut, and the machinist determines the type of cutting tool, the speed of the cutting tool, and the feed rate. After the production process is designed, relatively simple and repetitive operations normally are performed by machine setters, operators, and tenders. Other machinists do maintenance work, repairing or making new parts for existing machinery. To repair a broken part, maintenance machinists may refer to blueprints and perform the same machining operations that were needed to create the original part.

Working Conditions

Most machine shops of today are relatively clean, well lit, and ventilated. Many computer-controlled machines are totally enclosed, minimizing the exposure of workers to noise, dust, and the lubricants used to cool workpieces during machining. Nevertheless, working around machine tools presents certain dangers, and workers must follow safety precautions. Machinists wear protective equipment such as safety glasses to shield against bits of flying metal and earplugs to dampen machinery noise. They also must exercise caution when handling hazardous coolants and lubricants. The job requires stamina, because machinists stand most of the day and, at times, may need to lift moderately heavy workpieces.

Most machinists work a 40-hour week. Evening and weekend shifts are becoming more common as companies justify investments in more expensive machinery by extending hours of operation. Overtime is common during peak production periods.

Employment

Machinists held about 430,000 jobs in 2000. Most machinists work in small machining shops or in manufacturing firms that produce durable goods, such as metalworking and industrial machinery, aircraft, or motor vehicles. Maintenance machinists work in most industries that use production machinery. Although machinists work in all parts of the country, jobs are most plentiful in the northeast, midwest, and west, where manufacturing is concentrated.

Training, Other Qualifications, and Advancement

Machinists train in apprenticeship programs, informally on the job, and in high schools, vocational schools, or community or technical colleges. Experience with machine tools is helpful. In fact, many entrants previously have worked as machine setters, operators, or tenders. Persons interested in becoming machinists should be mechanically inclined, able to work independently, and able to do highly accurate work that requires concentration and physical effort.

High school or vocational school courses in mathematics, blueprint reading, metalworking, and drafting are highly recommended. Apprenticeship programs consist of shop training and related classroom instruction. In shop training, apprentices work almost full time, and are supervised by an experienced machinist while learning to operate various machine tools. Classroom instruction includes math, physics, blueprint reading, mechanical drawing, and quality and safety practices. In addition, as machine shops have increased their use of computer-controlled equipment, training in the operation and programming of CNC machine tools has become essential. Apprenticeship classes are taught in cooperation with local community or vocational colleges. A growing number of machinists learn the trade through 2-year associate degree programs at community or technical colleges. Graduates of these programs still need significant on-the-job experience before they are fully qualified.

To boost the skill level of machinists and to create a more uniform standard of competency, a number of training facilities and colleges have recently begun implementing curriculums incorporating national skills standards developed by the National Institute of Metalworking Skills (NIMS). After completing such a curriculum and passing a performance requirement and written exam, a NIMS credential is granted to trainees, providing formal recognition of competency in a metalworking field. Completing a recognized certification program provides a machinist with better career opportunities.

As new automation is introduced, machinists normally receive additional training to update their skills. This training usually is provided by a representative of the equipment manufacturer or a local technical school. Some employers offer tuition reimbursement for job-related courses.

Machinists can advance in several ways. Experienced machinists may become computer-control programmers and operators, and some are promoted to supervisory or administrative positions in their firms. A few open their own shops.

Job Outlook

Despite projected slower-than-average employment growth, job opportunities for machinists should continue to be excellent. Many young people with the necessary educational and personal qualifications needed to obtain machining skills may prefer to attend college or may not wish to enter production-related occupations. Therefore, the number of workers obtaining the skills and knowledge necessary to fill machinist jobs is expected to be less than the number of job openings arising each year from employment growth and from the need to replace experienced machinists who transfer to other occupations or retire.

Employment of machinists is expected to grow more slowly than the average for all occupations over the 2000–2010 period because of rising productivity among machinists. Productivity gains are resulting from the expanded use of computer-controlled machine tools and new technologies, such as high-speed machining, which reduce the time required for machining operations. This allows fewer machinists to accomplish the same amount of work previously performed by more workers. Technology is not expected to affect the employment of machinists as significantly as that of most other production occupations, however, because many of the unique operations performed by machinists cannot be efficiently automated. Due to modern production techniques, employers prefer workers, such as machinists, who have a wide range of skills and are capable of performing almost any task in a machine shop. In addition, firms are likely to retain their most skilled workers to operate and maintain expensive new machinery.

Employment levels in this occupation are influenced by economic cycles—as the demand for machined goods falls, machinists involved in production may be laid off or forced to work fewer hours. Employment of machinists involved in plant maintenance, however, often is more stable because proper maintenance and repair of costly equipment remain vital concerns, even when production levels fall.

Earnings

Median hourly earnings of machinists were $14.78 in 2000. The middle 50 percent earned between $11.43 and $18.39. The lowest 10 percent earned less than $9.01, while the top 10 percent earned more than $21.84. Median hourly earnings in the manufacturing industries employing the largest number of machinists in 2000 were as follows:

Aircraft and parts	$16.86
Metalworking machinery	15.89
Industrial machinery, not elsewhere classified	14.66
Motor vehicles and equipment	14.24
Personnel supply services	8.80

Related Occupations

Occupations most closely related to that of machinist are other machining occupations. These include tool and die makers; machine setters, operators, and tenders—metal and plastic; and computer-control programmers and operators. Another occupation that requires precision and skill in working with metal is welding, soldering, and brazing workers.

Sources of Additional Information

For general information about machinists, contact:

- Precision Machine Products Association, 6700 West Snowville Rd., Brecksville, OH 44141-3292. Internet: http://www.pmpa.org

For a list of training centers and apprenticeship programs, contact:

- National Tooling and Metalworking Association, 9300 Livingston Rd., Fort Washington, MD 20744. Internet: http://www.ntma.org

For general occupational information and a list of training programs, contact:

- PMA Educational Foundation, 6363 Oak Tree Blvd., Independence, OH 44131-2500. Internet: http://www.pmaef.org

Material Moving Occupations

O*NET 53-1021.00, 53-7011.00, 53-7021.00, 53-7031.00, 53-7032.01, 53-7032.02, 53-7033.00, 53-7041.00, 53-7051.00, 53-7061.00, 53-7062.01, 53-7062.02, 53-7062.03, 53-7063.00, 53-7064.00, 53-7071.01, 53-7071.02, 53-7072.00, 53-7073.00, 53-7081.00, 53-7111.00, 53-7121.00, 53-7199.99

Significant Points

● Job openings should be numerous because the occupation is very large.

● Most jobs require little work experience or specific training, but earnings are low.

● Pay is highest in jobs that require the most experience or that have the greatest responsibilities, but seasonal work may reduce earnings.

Nature of the Work

Material moving workers are categorized into two groups: operators and laborers. Operators use machinery to move construction materials, earth, petroleum products, and other heavy materials. Generally, they move materials over short distances—around a construction site, factory, or warehouse. Some move materials on or off trucks and ships. Operators control equipment by moving levers or foot pedals, operating switches, or turning dials. They may also set up and inspect equipment, make adjustments, and perform minor repairs when needed. Laborers and hand material movers manually handle freight, stock, or other materials; clean vehicles, machinery, and other equipment; feed materials into or remove materials from machines or equipment; and pack or package products and materials.

Material moving occupations are classified by the type of equipment they operate or goods they handle. Each piece of equipment requires different skills to move different types of loads.

Industrial truck and tractor operators drive and control industrial trucks or tractors equipped to move materials around a warehouse, storage yard, factory, or construction site. A typical industrial truck, often called a forklift or lift truck, has a hydraulic lifting mechanism and forks. They also may operate tractors that pull trailers loaded with materials, goods, or equipment within factories and warehouses, or around outdoor storage area.

Excavating and loading machine and dragline operators operate or tend machinery equipped with scoops, shovels, or buckets, to dig and load sand, gravel, earth, or similar materials into trucks or onto conveyors. Construction and mining industries employ the majority of excavation and loading machine and dragline operators.

Crane and tower operators operate mechanical boom and cable or tower and cable equipment to lift and move materials, machinery, or other heavy objects. They extend or retract a horizontally mounted boom to lower or raise a hook attached to the loadline. Most operators coordi-

nate their maneuvers in response to hand signals and radioed instructions. Operators position the loads from the on-board console or from a remote console at the site. While crane and tower operators are noticeable at office building and other construction sites, the biggest group works in primary metal, metal fabrication, and transportation equipment manufacturing industries that use heavy, bulky materials.

Hoist and winch operators control movement of cables, cages, and platforms to move workers and materials for manufacturing, logging, and other industrial operations. They work in such positions as derrick operators and hydraulic boom operators. One half of all jobs for hoist and winch operators were found in manufacturing or construction industries.

Pump operators and their helpers tend, control, or operate power-driven pumps and manifold systems that transfer gases, oil, or other materials to vessels or equipment. They maintain the equipment to regulate the flow of materials according to a schedule set up by petroleum engineers and production supervisors.

Gas compressor and gas pumping station operators operate steam, gas, electric motor, or internal combustion engine driven compressors. They transmit, compress, or recover gases, such as butane, nitrogen, hydrogen, and natural gas. *Wellhead pumpers* operate power pumps and auxiliary equipment to produce flow of oil or gas from wells in oil fields.

Tank, car, truck and ship loaders operate ship loading and unloading equipment, conveyors, hoists, and other specialized material handling equipment such as railroad tank car unloading equipment. They may gauge or sample shipping tanks and test them for leaks. *Conveyor operators and tenders* control or tend conveyor systems that move materials to or from stockpiles, processing stations, departments, or vehicles.

Laborers and hand freight, stock, and material movers manually move materials or perform other unskilled general labor. These workers move freight, stock, and other materials to and from storage and production areas, loading docks, delivery vehicles, ships, and containers. Their specific duties vary by industry and work setting. Specialized workers within this group include baggage and cargo handlers, who work in transportation industries; and truck loaders and unloaders. In factories, they may move raw materials, components, and finished goods between loading docks, storage areas, and work areas. They receive and sort materials and supplies and prepare them according to work orders for delivery to work or storage areas.

Hand packers and *packagers* manually pack, package, or wrap a variety of materials. They may inspect items for defects, label cartons, stamp information on products, keep records of items packed, and stack packages on loading docks. This group also includes order fillers, who pack materials for shipment, as well as grocery store courtesy clerks. In grocery stores, they may bag groceries, carry packages to customers' cars, and return shopping carts to designated areas.

Machine feeders and *offbearers* feed materials into or remove materials from automatic equipment or machines tended by other workers. *Cleaners of vehicle and equipment* clean machinery, vehicles, storage tanks, pipelines, and similar equipment using water and other cleaning agents, vacuums, hoses, brushes, cloths, and other cleaning equipment. *Refuse and recyclable material collectors* gather trash, garbage, and recyclables from homes and businesses along a regularly scheduled route, and deposit the refuse in their truck for transport to a dump, landfill, or recycling center. They lift and empty garbage cans or recycling bins by hand, or operate a hydraulic lift truck that picks up and empties dumpsters.

Working Conditions

Many material moving workers work outdoors in every type of climate and weather condition. The work tends to be repetitive and physically demanding. They may lift and carry heavy objects, and stoop, kneel, crouch, or crawl in awkward positions. Some work at great heights, or outdoors in all weather conditions. Some jobs expose workers to harmful materials or chemicals, fumes, odors, loud noise, or dangerous machinery. To avoid injury, these workers wear safety clothing, such as gloves and hard hats, and devices to protect their eyes, mouth, or hearing. These jobs have become much safer as safety equipment such as overhead guards on forklift trucks has become common. As with most machinery, most accidents can be avoided by observing proper operating procedures and safety practices.

Material movers generally work 8-hour shifts, although longer shifts are also common. In many industries that work around the clock, material movers work evening or "graveyard" shifts. Some may work at night because the establishment may not want to disturb customers during normal business hours. Refuse and recyclable material collectors often work shifts starting at 5:00 or 6:00 a.m. Some material movers only work during certain seasons, such as when the weather permits construction activity.

Employment

Material movers held about 5 million jobs in 2000. They were distributed among the detailed occupations as follows:

Laborers and freight, stock, and material movers, hand	2,084,000
Hand packers and packagers	1,091,000
Industrial truck and tractor operators	635,000
Cleaners of vehicles and equipment	322,000
Machine feeders and offbearers	182,000
First-line supervisors/managers of helpers, laborers, and material movers, hand	153,000
Refuse and recyclable materials collectors	124,000
Excavating and loading machine and dragline operators	76,000
Conveyer operators and tenders	63,000
Crane and tower operators	55,000
Tank, car, truck, and ship loaders	19,000
Pump operators, except wellhead pumpers	14,000
Wellhead pumpers	12,000
Hoist and winch operators	9,000
Gas compressor and gas pumping station operators	7,000
All other material moving workers	142,000

More than 44 percent of all material movers worked in transportation, public utilities, wholesale trade, or retail trade industries. Another 26 percent worked in manufacturing. Significant numbers of material movers also worked in construction, mining, and service industries. A small proportion of material movers were self-employed. A growing number are employed on a temporary or contract basis, many through firms providing personnel supply services. For example, companies that only need workers for a few days to move materials or clean up a site may contract with temporary help agencies specializing in providing this type of worker on a short-term basis.

Material movers work in every part of the country. Some work in remote locations on large construction projects, such as highways and dams, or in factory or mining operations.

Training, Other Qualifications, and Advancement

Most material moving jobs require no work experience or specific training. Some employers prefer applicants with a high school diploma, but most simply require workers to be at least 18 years old and physically able to perform the work. For those jobs requiring physical exertion, employers may require that applicants pass a physical exam. Some employers also require drug testing or background checks before employment. These workers often are younger than workers in other occupations are, reflecting the limited training but significant physical requirements of many of these jobs.

Material movers generally learn skills informally, on the job from more experienced workers or supervisors. However, workers who use dangerous equipment or handle toxic chemicals usually receive specialized training in safety awareness and procedures. Many of the training requirements are standardized through the U.S. Occupational Safety and Health Administration (OSHA).

Material moving equipment operators need a good sense of balance, distance judgment, and eye-hand-foot coordination. For those jobs that involve dealing with the public, such as grocery store courtesy clerks, workers should be pleasant and courteous. Most jobs require reading and basic mathematics skills to read procedures manuals, billing, and other documents. Mechanical aptitude and high school training in automobile or diesel mechanics are helpful because workers may perform some maintenance on their equipment. Experience operating mobile equipment, such as farm tractors or heavy equipment in the armed forces, is an asset.

Experience in many of these jobs may allow workers to qualify or become trainees for other skilled positions such as construction trades workers; assemblers or other production workers; motor vehicle operators; or vehicle and mobile equipment mechanics, installers, and repairers. In fact, many employers prefer to promote qualified material movers as openings arise. Some may eventually advance to become supervisors.

Job Outlook

Employment in material moving occupations will increase about as fast as average for all occupations through 2010. Employment growth will stem from an expanding economy and increased spending on the nation's infrastructure of highways, bridges, and dams. However, equipment improvements, including the growing automation of material handling in factories and warehouses, will continue to raise productivity and moderate the demand for material movers.

Job growth for material movers largely depends on growth in the industries employing them and the type of equipment the workers operate or the materials they handle. For example, employment of operators in manufacturing will decline slightly due to increased automation and efficiency in the production process. On the other hand, employment will grow rapidly in temporary help organizations as firms contract out material moving services.

Job openings should be numerous because the occupation is very large and turnover is relatively high—characteristic of occupations requiring little formal training. Many openings will arise from the need to replace workers who retire, transfer to other occupations, or leave the labor force for other reasons.

Both construction and manufacturing are very sensitive to changes in economic conditions, so the number of job openings in these industries may fluctuate from year to year.

Earnings

Median hourly earnings of material moving workers in 2000 were as follows:

Gas compressor and gas pumping station operators $20.32
Pump operators, except wellhead pumpers 17.16
First-line supervisors/managers of helpers, laborers,
    and material movers, hand 16.73
Wellhead pumpers 16.35
Crane and tower operators 15.89
Excavating and loading machine and dragline operators 14.94
Hoist and winch operators 14.40
Tank, car, truck, and ship loaders 13.78
Refuse and recyclable materials collectors 11.83
Industrial truck and tractor operators 11.74
Conveyer operators and tenders 10.70
Machine feeders and offbearers 9.69
Laborers and freight, stock, and material movers, hand 9.04
Cleaners of vehicles and equipment 7.55
Hand packers and packagers 7.53

Pay rates vary according to experience and job responsibilities. Pay usually is higher in metropolitan areas. Seasonal work may reduce earnings.

Related Occupations

Other workers who operate mechanical equipment include busdrivers; construction equipment operators; machine setters, operators, and tenders—metal and plastic; rail transportation workers; and truckdrivers and driver/sales workers. Other entry-level workers who perform mostly physical work are agricultural workers; building cleaning workers; construction laborers; forest, conservation, and logging workers; and grounds maintenance workers.

Sources of Additional Information

For information about job opportunities and training programs, contact local state employment service offices, building or construction contractors, manufacturers, and wholesale and retail establishments.

Information on safety and training requirements is available from:

- U.S. Department of Labor, Occupational Safety and Health Administration (OSHA), 200 Constitution Ave. NW., Washington, D.C. 20210. Internet: http://www.osha.gov

Information on industrial truck and tractor operators is available from:

- Industrial Truck Association, 1750 K St. NW., Suite 460, Washington, DC 20006. Specialized Carriers and Rigging Association, 2750 Prosperity Ave., Suite 620, Fairfax, VA 22301

Material Recording, Scheduling, Dispatching, and Distributing Occupations, Except Postal Workers

O*NET 43-5011.00, 43-5021.00, 43-5031.00, 43-5032.00, 43-5041.00, 43-5061.00, 43-5071.00, 43-5081.01, 43-5081.02, 43-5081.03, 43-5081.04, 43-5111.00

Significant Points

- Many of these occupations are entry level and do not require more than a high school diploma.

- Workers develop the necessary skills through on-the-job training lasting from several days to a few months; dispatchers usually require the most extensive training.

- Numerous job openings will arise each year from the need to replace workers who leave this very large occupational group.

Nature of the Work

Workers in this group are responsible for a variety of communications, record keeping, and scheduling operations. Typically, they coordinate, expedite, and track orders for personnel, materials, and equipment. *Cargo and freight agents* route and track cargo and freight shipments, whether from airline, train, or truck terminals, or shipping docks. They keep records of any missing or damaged items and any excess supplies. The agents sort cargo according to its destination and separate any items that cannot be packed together. They also coordinate payment schedules with customers and arrange for the pick-up or delivery of freight.

Couriers and messengers deliver letters, important business documents, or packages within a firm, to other businesses, or to customers. They usually keep records of deliveries and sometimes obtain the recipient's signature. Couriers and messengers travel by car, van, bicycle, or even by foot when making nearby deliveries.

Dispatchers receive requests for service and initiate action to provide that service. Duties vary, depending on the needs of the employer. Police, fire, and ambulance dispatchers, also called public safety dispatchers, handle calls from people reporting crimes, fires, and medical emergencies. Truck, bus, and train dispatchers schedule and coordinate the movement of these vehicles to ensure that they arrive on schedule. Taxicab dispatchers relay requests for cabs to individual drivers, tow truck dispatchers take calls for emergency road service, and utility company dispatchers handle calls related to utility and telephone service. Courier and messenger service dispatchers route drivers, riders, and walkers around a usually urban area. They distribute work by radio, email, or phone, making sure that service deadlines are met.

Meter readers read meters and record consumption of electricity, gas, water, or steam. They serve a variety of consumers and travel along designated routes to track consumption. Although many meters still are read at the house or building, many newer meters can be read remotely from a central point. Meter readers also look for evidence of unauthorized utility usage.

Production, planning, and expediting clerks coordinate and expedite the flow of information, work, and materials, usually according to a production or work schedule. They gather information for reports on work progress and production problems. They also may schedule workers or parts shipments, estimate costs, and keep inventories of materials.

Shipping, receiving, and traffic clerks track all incoming and outgoing shipments of goods transferred between businesses, suppliers, and customers. These clerks may be required to lift cartons of various sizes. Shipping clerks assemble, address, stamp, and ship merchandise or materials. Receiving clerks unpack, verify, and record incoming merchandise. Traffic clerks record the destination, weight, and cost of all incoming and outgoing shipments. In a small company, one clerk may perform all of these tasks.

Stock clerks and order fillers receive, unpack, and store materials and equipment, and maintain and distribute inventories. Inventories may include merchandise in wholesale and retail establishments, or equipment, supplies, or materials in other kinds of organizations. In small firms, stock clerks and order fillers may perform all of the above tasks, as well as those usually handled by shipping and receiving clerks. In large establishments, they may be responsible for only one task.

Weighers, measurers, checkers, and samplers check and record the weight and measurement of various materials and equipment. They use scales, measuring and counting devices, and calculators to compare the weight, measurements, or other specifications against bills or invoices. They also prepare reports on inventory levels.

Working Conditions

Working conditions vary considerably by occupation and employment setting. Couriers and messengers spend most of their time alone making deliveries and usually are not closely supervised. Those who deliver by bicycle must be physically fit and are exposed to all weather conditions, as well as to the many hazards associated with heavy traffic. Car, van, and truck couriers must sometimes carry heavy loads, either manually or with the aid of a handtruck. They also have to deal with difficult parking situations as well as traffic jams and road construction. The pressure of making as many deliveries as possible to increase earnings can be stressful and may lead to unsafe driving or bicycling practices.

Meter readers, usually working 40 hours a week, work outdoors in all types of weather as they travel through communities and neighborhoods taking readings.

The work of dispatchers can be very hectic when many calls come in at the same time. The job of public safety dispatcher is particularly stressful because slow or improper response to a call can result in serious injury or further harm. Also, callers who are anxious or afraid may become excited and be unable to provide needed information; some may even become abusive. Despite provocations, dispatchers must remain calm, objective, and in control of the situation.

Dispatchers sit for long periods, using telephones, computers, and two-way radios. Much of their time is spent at video display terminals, viewing monitors and observing traffic patterns. As a result of working for long stretches with computers and other electronic equipment, dispatchers can experience significant eyestrain and back discomfort. Generally, dispatchers work a 40-hour week; however, rotating shifts and compressed work schedules are common. Alternative work schedules are necessary to accommodate evening, weekend, and holiday work, as well as 24-hour-per-day, 7-day-per-week operations.

Other workers in this group—cargo and freight agents; shipping, receiving, and traffic clerks; stock clerks and order fillers; production, planning, and expediting clerks; and weighers, measurers, checkers, and samplers—work in a wide variety of businesses, institutions, and industries. Some work in warehouses, stockrooms, or shipping and receiving rooms that may not be temperature controlled. Others may spend time in cold storage rooms or outside on loading platforms, where they are exposed to the weather.

Production, planning, and expediting clerks work closely with supervisors who must approve production and work schedules. Most jobs for shipping, receiving, and traffic clerks, stock clerks and order fillers, and cargo and freight agents involve frequent standing, bending, walking, and stretching. Some lifting and carrying of smaller items also may be involved. Although automation devices have lessened the physical demands of this occupation, their use remains somewhat limited. Work still can be strenuous, even though mechanical material handling equipment is employed to move heavy items.

The typical work week is Monday through Friday; however, evening and weekend hours are common for some jobs, such as stock clerks and order fillers in retail trade and couriers and messengers, and may be required in other jobs when large shipments are involved or when inventory is taken.

Employment

In 2000, material recording, scheduling, dispatching, and distributing workers held about 3.5 million jobs. Employment was distributed among the detailed occupations as follows:

Stock clerks and order fillers	1,679,000
Shipping, receiving, and traffic clerks	890,000
Production, planning, and expediting clerks	332,000
Dispatchers	254,000
Couriers and messengers	141,000
Weighers, measurers, checkers, and samplers, recordkeeping	83,000
Cargo and freight agents	60,000
Meter readers, utilities	49,000
All other material recording, scheduling, dispatching, and distributing workers	63,000

About two-thirds of material recording, scheduling, dispatching, and distributing jobs were in services or wholesale and retail trade. Although these workers are found throughout the country, most work near population centers where retail stores, warehouses, factories, and large communications centers are concentrated.

Training, Other Qualifications, and Advancement

Many material recording, scheduling, dispatching, and distributing occupations are entry level and do not require more than a high school diploma. Employers, however, prefer to hire those who are familiar with computers and other electronic office and business equipment. Those who have taken business courses or have previous business, dispatching, or specific job-related experience may be preferred. Because communication with other people is an integral part of these jobs, good oral and written communications skills are essential. Typing, filing, recordkeeping, and other clerical skills also are important.

State or local government civil service regulations usually govern police, fire, emergency medical, and ambulance dispatching jobs. Candidates for these positions may have to pass written, oral, and performance tests. Also, they may be asked to attend training classes and attain the proper certification in order to qualify for advancement.

Trainees usually develop the necessary skills on the job. This informal training lasts from several days to a few months, depending on the complexity of the job. Dispatchers usually require the most extensive training. Working with an experienced dispatcher, they monitor calls and learn how to operate a variety of communications equipment, including telephones, radios, and various wireless devices. As trainees gain confidence, they begin to handle calls themselves. In smaller operations, dispatchers sometimes act as customer service representatives, processing orders themselves. Many public safety dispatchers also participate in structured training programs sponsored by their employer. Some employers offer a course designed by the Association of Public Safety Communications Officials. This course covers topics such as interpersonal communications; overview of the police, fire, and rescue functions; modern public safety telecommunications systems; basic radio broadcasting; local, state, and national crime information computer systems; and telephone complaint/report processing procedures. Other employers develop in-house programs based on their own needs. Emergency medical dispatchers often receive special training or have special skills. Increasingly, public safety dispatchers receive training in stress and crisis management, as well as family counseling. Employers are recognizing the toll this work has on daily living and the potential impact that stress has on the job, on the work environment, and in the home.

Communications skills and the ability to work under pressure are important personal qualities for dispatchers. Residency in the city or county of employment frequently is required for public safety dispatchers. Dispatchers in transportation industries must be able to deal with sudden influxes of shipments and disruptions of shipping schedules caused by bad weather, road construction, or accidents.

Although there are no mandatory licensing or certification requirements, some states require that public safety dispatchers possess a certificate to work on a state network, such as the Police Information Network. The Association of Public Safety Communications Officials, the National Academy of Emergency Medical Dispatch, and the International Municipal Signal Association all offer certification programs. Many dispatchers participate in these programs in order to improve their prospects for career advancement.

Couriers and messengers usually learn on the job, training with a veteran for a short time. Those who work as independent contractors for a messenger or delivery service may be required to have a valid driver's license, a registered and inspected vehicle, a good driving record, and insurance coverage. Many couriers and messengers who are employees, rather than independent contractors, also are required to provide and maintain their own vehicle. Although some companies have spare bicycles or mopeds that their riders may rent for a short period, almost all two-wheeled couriers own their own bicycle, moped, or motorcycle. A good knowledge of the geographic area in which they travel, as well as a good sense of direction, also are important.

Utility meter readers usually shadow a more experienced meter reader until they feel comfortable doing the job on their own. They learn how to read the meters and determine the consumption rate. They also must learn the route that they need to travel in order to read all their customers' meters.

Production, planning, and expediting clerks; weighers, measurers, checkers, and samplers; stock clerks and order fillers; and shipping, receiving, and traffic clerks usually learn the job by doing routine tasks under close supervision. They learn how to count and mark stock, and then start keeping records and taking inventory. Strength, stamina, good eyesight, and an ability to work at repetitive tasks, sometimes under pressure, are important characteristics. Production, planning, and expediting clerks must learn how their company operates along with its priorities before they can begin to efficiently write production and work schedules. Stock clerks, whose sole responsibility is to bring merchandise to the sales floor to stock shelves and racks, need little training. Shipping, receiving, and traffic clerks and stock clerks and order fillers who handle jewelry, liquor, or drugs may be bonded.

Shipping, receiving, and traffic clerks, as well as cargo and freight agents, start out by checking items to be shipped and then attaching labels and making sure the addresses are correct. Training in the use of automated equipment usually is done informally, on the job. As these occupations become more automated, however, workers in these jobs may need longer training in order to master the use of the equipment.

Advancement opportunities for material recording, scheduling, dispatching, and distributing workers vary with the place of employment. Dispatchers who work for private firms, which usually are small, will find few opportunities for advancement. Public safety dispatchers, on the other hand, may become a shift or divisional supervisor or chief of communications, or move to higher paying administrative jobs. Some become police officers or firefighters. Couriers and messengers, especially those who work for messenger or courier services, have limited advancement opportunities; a small fraction move into the office to learn dispatching or to take service requests by phone. In large firms, stock clerks can advance to invoice clerk, stock control clerk, or procurement clerk. Shipping, receiving, and traffic clerks are promoted to head clerk, and those with a broad understanding of shipping and receiving may enter a related field such as industrial traffic management. With additional training, some stock clerks and order fillers and shipping, receiving, and traffic clerks advance to jobs as warehouse manager or purchasing agent.

Job Outlook

Overall employment of material recording, scheduling, dispatching, and distributing workers is expected to grow about as fast as the average for all occupations through 2010. In addition, numerous job openings will arise each year from the need to replace workers who leave this very large occupational group.

Projected employment growth varies by detailed occupation. Meter readers will experience a decline in employment due to automated meter reading systems that greatly increase productivity. The use of e-mail and fax will contribute to a decline for couriers and messengers as well. New technologies will enable stock clerks and order fillers to handle more stock, resulting in slower-than-average employment growth. Employment of shipping, receiving, and traffic clerks and of cargo and freight agents also will grow more slowly than average due to the increasing use of automation that enables these workers to handle materials and shipments more efficiently and more accurately.

Employment of dispatchers; production, planning, and expediting clerks; and weighers, measurers, checkers, and samplers is projected to grow about as fast as the average for all occupations through 2010. Population growth, in addition to the expanded role of dispatchers stemming from advances in telecommunications, should boost employment levels. Employment of production, planning, and expediting clerks should benefit from more emphasis on efficiency in the production process, while the growing need for accurate inventory records spurs employment of weighers, measurers, checkers, and samplers.

Earnings

Earnings of material recording, scheduling, dispatching, and distributing occupations vary somewhat by occupation and industry. The range of median hourly earnings in 2000 are shown in the following table:

Production, planning, and expediting clerks $14.71
Cargo and freight agents 13.73
Dispatchers 13.66
Meter readers, utilities 13.32
Weighers, measurers, checkers, and samplers,
    recordkeeping 11.36
Shipping, receiving, and traffic clerks 10.52
Couriers and messengers 8.96
Stock clerks and order fillers 8.75
All other material recording, scheduling, dispatching,
    and distributing workers 11.66

Workers in material recording, scheduling, dispatching, and distributing occupations usually receive the same benefits as most other workers. If uniforms are required, employers usually provide either the uniforms or an allowance to purchase them.

Related Occupations

Material recording, scheduling, dispatching, and distributing workers who determine and document characteristics of materials or equipment include cargo and freight agents; production, planning, and expediting clerks; shipping, receiving, and traffic clerks; stock clerks and order fillers; and procurement clerks.

Workers who also handle, move, organize, store, and keep records of materials include shipping, receiving, and traffic clerks; production, planning, and expediting clerks; cargo and freight agents; and procurement clerks.

Shipping, receiving, and traffic clerks record, check, and often store materials that a company receives. They also process and pack goods for shipment. Other workers who perform similar duties are stock clerks

and order fillers; production, planning, and expediting clerks; and cargo and freight agents.

Workers who coordinate the flow of information to assist the production process include cargo and freight agents; shipping, receiving, and traffic clerks; stock clerks and order fillers; and weighers, measurers, checkers, and samplers, recordkeeping. Other workers responsible for the distribution and control of utilities include powerplant operators, distributors, and dispatchers.

Occupations that involve directing and controlling the movement of vehicles, freight, and personnel, as well as distributing information and messages, include air traffic controllers, communications equipment operators, customer service representatives, and reservation and transportation ticket agents and travel clerks.

Messengers and couriers deliver letters, parcels, and other items. They also keep accurate records of their work. Others who do similar work are postal service workers; truckdrivers and driver/sales workers; shipping, receiving, and traffic clerks; and cargo and freight agents.

Cargo and freight agents plan and coordinate cargo shipments using airlines, trains, and trucks. They also arrange freight pickup with customers. Others who do similar work are couriers and messengers; shipping, receiving, and traffic clerks; weighers, measurers, checkers, and samplers; truckdrivers and driver/sales workers; and postal service workers.

Sources of Additional Information

Information about job opportunities may be obtained from local employers and local offices of the state employment service.

Information on employment as a meter reader, and on automatic meter reading technology, can be obtained from:

- Automatic Meter Reading Association. Internet: http://www.amra-intl.org

General information about stock clerks and order fillers in retail trade can be obtained from:

- National Retail Federation, 325 Seventh St. NW., Suite 1000, Washington, DC 20004

For further information on training and certification for police, fire, and emergency dispatchers, contact:

- National Academy of Emergency Medical Dispatch, 139 East South Temple, Suite 530, Salt Lake City, UT 84111. Internet: http://www.emergencydispatch.org

- Association of Public Safety Communications Officials, 2040 S. Ridgewood, South Daytona, FL 32119-2257. Internet: http://www.apcointl.org

- International Municipal Signal Association, 165 East Union St., P.O. Box 539, Newark, NY 14513-0539. Internet: http://www.imsasafety.org

For information on train dispatchers, contact:

- American Train Dispatchers Association, 1370 Ontario St., Cleveland, OH 44113

Information on job opportunities for police, fire, and emergency dispatchers is available from personnel offices of state and local governments or police departments.

Persons interested in courier and messenger jobs also may contact messenger and courier services, mail-order firms, banks, printing and publishing firms, utility companies, retail stores, or other large firms.

Medical Assistants

O*NET 31-9092.00

Significant Points

● The job of medical assistant is expected to be one of the fastest growing occupations through the year 2010.

● Job prospects should be best for medical assistants with formal training or experience.

Nature of the Work

Medical assistants perform routine administrative and clinical tasks to keep the offices and clinics of physicians, podiatrists, chiropractors, and optometrists running smoothly. They should not be confused with physician assistants who examine, diagnose, and treat patients under the direct supervision of a physician.

The duties of medical assistants vary from office to office, depending on office location, size, and specialty. In small practices, medical assistants usually are "generalists," handling both administrative and clinical duties and reporting directly to an office manager, physician, or other health practitioner. Those in large practices tend to specialize in a particular area under the supervision of department administrators.

Medical assistants perform many administrative duties. They answer telephones, greet patients, update and file patient medical records, fill out insurance forms, handle correspondence, schedule appointments, arrange for hospital admission and laboratory services, and handle billing and bookkeeping.

Clinical duties vary according to state law and include taking medical histories and recording vital signs, explaining treatment procedures to patients, preparing patients for examination, and assisting the physician during the examination. Medical assistants collect and prepare laboratory specimens or perform basic laboratory tests on the premises, dispose of contaminated supplies, and sterilize medical instruments. They instruct patients about medication and special diets, prepare and administer medications as directed by a physician, authorize drug refills as directed, telephone prescriptions to a pharmacy, draw blood, prepare patients for X rays, take electrocardiograms, remove sutures, and change dressings.

Medical assistants also may arrange examining room instruments and equipment, purchase and maintain supplies and equipment, and keep waiting and examining rooms neat and clean.

Assistants who specialize have additional duties. *Podiatric medical assistants* make castings of feet, expose and develop X rays, and assist podiatrists in surgery. *Ophthalmic medical assistants* help ophthalmologists provide medical eye care. They conduct diagnostic tests, measure and record vision, and test eye muscle function. They also show patients how to insert, remove, and care for contact lenses; and they apply eye dressings. Under the direction of the physician, they may administer eye medications. They also maintain optical and surgical instruments and may assist the ophthalmologist in surgery.

Working Conditions

Medical assistants work in well-lighted, clean environments. They constantly interact with other people, and may have to handle several responsibilities at once.

Most full-time medical assistants work a regular 40-hour week. Some work part-time, evenings, or weekends.

Employment

Medical assistants held about 329,000 jobs in 2000. Sixty percent were in physicians' offices, and about 15 percent were in hospitals, including inpatient and outpatient facilities. The rest were in nursing homes, offices of other health practitioners, and other healthcare facilities.

Training, Other Qualifications, and Advancement

Most employers prefer graduates of formal programs in medical assisting. Such programs are offered in vocational-technical high schools, postsecondary vocational schools, community and junior colleges, and in colleges and universities. Postsecondary programs usually last either 1 year, resulting in a certificate or diploma, or 2 years, resulting in an associate degree. Courses cover anatomy, physiology, and medical terminology as well as typing, transcription, recordkeeping, accounting, and insurance processing. Students learn laboratory techniques, clinical and diagnostic procedures, pharmaceutical principles, medication administration, and first aid. They study office practices, patient relations, medical law, and ethics. Accredited programs include an internship that provides practical experience in physicians' offices, hospitals, or other healthcare facilities.

Two agencies recognized by the U.S. Department of Education accredit programs in medical assisting: the Commission on Accreditation of Allied Health Education Programs (CAAHEP) and the Accrediting Bureau of Health Education Schools (ABHES). In 2001, there were about 500 medical assisting programs accredited by CAAHEP and about 170 accredited by ABHES. The Committee on Accreditation for Ophthalmic Medical Personnel approved 14 programs in ophthalmic medical assisting.

Formal training in medical assisting, while generally preferred, is not always required. Some medical assistants are trained on the job, although this is less common than in the past. Applicants usually need a high school diploma or the equivalent. Recommended high school courses include mathematics, health, biology, typing, bookkeeping, computers, and office skills. Volunteer experience in the healthcare field also is helpful.

Although there is no licensing for medical assistants, some states require them to take a test or a course before they can perform certain tasks, such as taking X rays. Employers prefer to hire experienced workers or certified applicants who have passed a national examination, indicating that the medical assistant meets certain standards of competence. The American Association of Medical Assistants awards the

Certified Medical Assistant credential. The American Medical Technologists awards the Registered Medical Assistant credential. The American Society of Podiatric Medical Assistants awards the Podiatric Medical Assistant Certified credential, and the Joint Commission on Allied Health Personnel in Ophthalmology awards credentials at three levels—Certified Ophthalmic Assistant, Certified Ophthalmic Technician, and Certified Ophthalmic Medical Technologist.

Medical assistants may be able to advance to office manager. They may qualify for a variety of administrative support occupations, or may teach medical assisting. Some, with additional education, enter other health occupations such as nursing and medical technology.

Medical assistants deal with the public; therefore, they must be neat and well-groomed and have a courteous, pleasant manner. Medical assistants must be able to put patients at ease and explain physicians' instructions. They must respect the confidential nature of medical information. Clinical duties require a reasonable level of manual dexterity and visual acuity.

Job Outlook

Employment of medical assistants is expected to grow much faster than the average for all occupations through the year 2010 as the health services industry expands because of technological advances in medicine, and a growing and aging population. It is one of the fastest growing occupations.

Employment growth will be driven by the increase in the number of group practices, clinics, and other healthcare facilities that need a high proportion of support personnel, particularly the flexible medical assistant who can handle both administrative and clinical duties. Medical assistants primarily work in outpatient settings, where much faster-than-average growth is expected.

In view of the preference of many healthcare employers for trained personnel, job prospects should be best for medical assistants with formal training or experience, particularly those with certification.

Earnings

The earnings of medical assistants vary, depending on experience, skill level, and location. Median annual earnings of medical assistants were $23,000 in 2000. The middle 50 percent earned between $19,460 and $27,460 a year. The lowest 10 percent earned less than $16,700, and the highest 10 percent earned more than $32,850 a year. Median annual earnings in the industries employing the largest number of medical assistants in 2000 were as follows:

Offices and clinics of medical doctors	$23,610
Hospitals	22,950
Health and allied services, not elsewhere classified	22,860
Offices of osteopathic physicians	21,420
Offices of other health practitioners	20,860

Related Occupations

Workers in other medical support occupations include dental assistants, medical records and health information technicians, medical secretaries, occupational therapist assistants and aides, pharmacy aides, and physical therapist assistants and aides.

Sources of Additional Information

Information about career opportunities, CAAHEP-accredited educational programs in medical assisting, and the Certified Medical Assistant exam is available from:

- The American Association of Medical Assistants, 20 North Wacker Dr., Suite 1575, Chicago, IL 60606. Internet: http://www.aama-ntl.org

Information about career opportunities and the Registered Medical Assistant certification exam is available from:

- Registered Medical Assistants of American Medical Technologists, 710 Higgins Rd., Park Ridge, IL 60068-5765

For a list of ABHES-accredited educational programs in medical assisting, contact:

- Accrediting Bureau of Health Education Schools, 803 West Broad St., Suite 730, Falls Church, VA 22046. Internet: http://www.abhes.org

Information about career opportunities, training programs, and the Certified Ophthalmic Assistant exam is available from:

- Joint Commission on Allied Health Personnel in Ophthalmology, 2025 Woodlane Dr., St. Paul, MN 55125-2995. Internet: http://www.jcahpo.org

Information about careers for podiatric assistants is available from:

- American Society of Podiatric Medical Assistants, 2124 S. Austin Blvd., Cicero, IL 60650

Medical Records and Health Information Technicians

O*NET 29-2071.00

Significant Points

- Medical records and health information technicians are projected to be one of the fastest growing occupations.

- High school students can improve chances of acceptance into a medical record and health information education program by taking anatomy, physiology, medical terminology, and computer courses.

- Most technicians will be employed by hospitals, but job growth will be faster in offices and clinics of physicians, nursing homes, and home health agencies.

Nature of the Work

Every time healthcare personnel treat a patient, they record what they observed, and how the patient was treated medically. This record includes information the patient provides concerning their symptoms and medical history, the results of examinations, reports of X rays and laboratory tests, diagnoses, and treatment plans. Medical records and health information technicians organize and evaluate these records for completeness and accuracy.

Medical records and health information technicians begin to assemble patients' health information by first making sure their initial medical charts are complete. They ensure all forms are completed and properly identified and signed, and all necessary information is in the computer. Sometimes, they communicate with physicians or others to clarify diagnoses or get additional information.

Technicians assign a code to each diagnosis and procedure. They consult classification manuals and rely, also, on their knowledge of disease processes. Technicians then use a software program to assign the patient to one of several hundred "diagnosis-related groups," or DRGs. The DRG determines the amount the hospital will be reimbursed if the patient is covered by Medicare or other insurance programs using the DRG system. Technicians who specialize in coding are called health information coders, medical record coders, coder/abstractors, or coding specialists. In addition to the DRG system, coders use other coding systems, such as those geared towards ambulatory settings.

Technicians also use computer programs to tabulate and analyze data to help improve patient care, control costs, for use in legal actions, in response to surveys, or for use in research studies. *Tumor registrars* compile and maintain records of patients who have cancer to provide information to physicians and for research studies.

Medical records and health information technicians' duties vary with the size of the facility. In large to medium facilities, technicians may specialize in one aspect of health information, or supervise health information clerks and transcriptionists while a *medical records and health information administrator* manages the department. In small facilities, a credentialed medical records and health information technician sometimes manages the department.

Working Conditions

Medical records and health information technicians usually work a 40-hour week. Some overtime may be required. In hospitals (where health information departments often are open 24 hours a day, 7 days a week) technicians may work day, evening, and night shifts.

Medical records and health information technicians work in pleasant and comfortable offices. This is one of the few health occupations in which there is little or no physical contact with patients. Because accuracy is essential, technicians must pay close attention to detail. Technicians who work at computer monitors for prolonged periods must guard against eyestrain and muscle pain.

Employment

Medical records and health information technicians held about 136,000 jobs in 2000. About 4 out of 10 jobs were in hospitals. The rest were mostly in nursing homes, medical group practices, clinics, and home health agencies. Insurance firms that deal in health matters employ a small number of health information technicians to tabulate and analyze health information. Public health departments also hire technicians to supervise data collection from healthcare institutions and to assist in research.

Training, Other Qualifications, and Advancement

Medical records and health information technicians entering the field usually have an associate degree from a community or junior college. In addition to general education, coursework includes medical terminology, anatomy and physiology, legal aspects of health information, coding and abstraction of data, statistics, database management, quality improvement methods, and computer training. Applicants can improve their chances of admission into a program by taking biology, chemistry, health, and computer courses in high school.

Hospitals sometimes advance promising health information clerks to jobs as medical records and health information technicians, although this practice may be less common in the future. Advancement usually requires 2 to 4 years of job experience and completion of a hospital's in-house training program.

Most employers prefer to hire Registered Health Information Technicians (RHIT), who must pass a written examination offered by AHIMA. To take the examination, a person must graduate from a 2-year associate degree program accredited by the Commission on Accreditation of Allied Health Education Programs (CAAHEP) of the American Medical Association. Technicians trained in non-CAAHEP accredited programs, or on the job, are not eligible to take the examination. In 2001, CAAHEP accredited 177 programs for health information technicians. Technicians who specialize in coding may also obtain voluntary certification.

Experienced medical records and health information technicians usually advance in one of two ways—by specializing or managing. Many senior technicians specialize in coding, particularly Medicare coding, or in tumor registry.

In large medical records and health information departments, experienced technicians may advance to section supervisor, overseeing the work of the coding, correspondence, or discharge sections, for example. Senior technicians with RHIT credentials may become director or assistant director of a medical records and health information department in a small facility. However, in larger institutions, the director is usually an administrator, with a bachelor's degree in medical records and health information administration.

Job Outlook

Job prospects for formally trained technicians should be very good. Employment of medical records and health information technicians is expected to grow much faster than the average for all occupations through 2010, due to rapid growth in the number of medical tests, treatments, and procedures which will be increasingly scrutinized by third-party payers, regulators, courts, and consumers.

Hospitals will continue to employ a large percentage of health information technicians, but growth will not be as fast as in other areas. Increasing demand for detailed records in offices and clinics of physicians should result in fast employment growth, especially in large group practices. Rapid growth is also expected in nursing homes and home health agencies.

Earnings

Median annual earnings of medical records and health information technicians were $22,750 in 2000. The middle 50 percent earned between

$18,700 and $28,590. The lowest 10 percent earned less than $15,710, and the highest 10 percent earned more than $35,170. Median annual earnings in the industries employing the largest numbers of medical records and health information technicians in 2000 were as follows:

Nursing and personal care facilities $23,760
Hospitals 23,540
Offices and clinics of medical doctors 21,090

Related Occupations

Medical records and health information technicians need a strong clinical background to analyze the contents of medical records. Workers in other occupations requiring knowledge of medical terminology, anatomy, and physiology without physical contact with the patient are medical secretaries and medical transcriptionists.

Sources of Additional Information

Information on careers in medical records and health information technology, including a list of CAAHEP-accredited programs, is available from:

● American Health Information Management Association, 233 N. Michigan Ave., Suite 2150, Chicago, IL 60601-5800. Internet: http://www.ahima.org

Medical Transcriptionists

O*NET 31-9094.00

Significant Points

● Employers prefer medical transcriptionists who have completed a vocational school or community college program.

● Employment is projected to grow faster than average due to increasing demand for medical transcription services.

● Some medical transcriptionists enjoy the flexibility of working at home, especially those with previous experience in a hospital or clinic setting.

Nature of the Work

Medical transcriptionists, also called *medical transcribers* and *medical stenographers*, listen to dictated recordings made by physicians and other healthcare professionals and transcribe them into medical reports, correspondence, and other administrative material. They generally listen to recordings on a special headset, using a foot pedal to pause the recording when necessary, and key the text into a personal computer or word processor, editing as necessary for grammar and clarity. The documents they produce include discharge summaries, history and physical examination reports, operating room reports, consultation reports, autopsy reports, diagnostic imaging studies, and referral letters. Medical transcriptionists return transcribed documents to the dictator for review and signature, or correction. These documents eventually become part of patients' permanent files.

To understand and accurately transcribe dictated reports into a format that is clear and comprehensible for the reader, medical transcriptionists must understand medical terminology, anatomy and physiology, diagnostic procedures, and treatment. They also must be able to translate medical jargon and abbreviations into their expanded forms. To help identify terms appropriately, transcriptionists refer to standard medical reference materials—both printed and electronic. Some of these are available over the Internet. Medical transcriptionists must comply with specific standards that apply to the style of medical records, in addition to the legal and ethical requirements involved with keeping patient records confidential.

Experienced transcriptionists spot mistakes or inconsistencies in a medical report and check back with the dictator to correct the information. Their ability to understand and correctly transcribe patient assessments and treatments reduces the chance of patients receiving ineffective or even harmful treatments and ensures high quality patient care.

Currently, most healthcare providers transmit dictation to medical transcriptionists using either digital or analog dictating equipment. With the emergence of the Internet, some transcriptionists receive dictation over the Internet and are able to quickly return transcribed documents to clients for approval. As confidentiality concerns are resolved, this practice will become more prevalent. Another emerging trend is the implementation of speech recognition technology, which electronically translates sound into text and creates drafts of reports. Reports are then formatted; edited for mistakes in translation, punctuation, or grammar; and checked for consistency and possible medical errors. Transcriptionists working in specialized areas with more standard terminology, such as radiology or pathology, are more likely to encounter speech recognition technology. However, use of speech recognition technology will become more widespread as the technology becomes more sophisticated.

Medical transcriptionists who work in physicians' offices and clinics may have other office duties, such as receiving patients, scheduling appointments, answering the telephone, and handling incoming and outgoing mail. Medical secretaries may also transcribe as part of their jobs. Court reporters have similar duties, but with a different focus. They take verbatim reports of speeches, conversations, legal proceedings, meetings, and other events when written accounts of spoken words are necessary for correspondence, records, or legal proof.

Working Conditions

The majority of these workers are employed in comfortable settings, such as hospitals, physicians' offices, clinics, laboratories, medical libraries, government medical facilities, or at home. An increasing number of medical transcriptionists telecommute from home-based offices as employees or subcontractors for hospitals and transcription services or as self-employed independent contractors.

Work in this occupation presents few hazards, although sitting in the same position for long periods can be tiring, and workers can suffer wrist, back, neck, or eye problems due to strain and risk repetitive motion injuries such as carpal tunnel syndrome. The pressure to be accurate and fast also can be stressful.

Many medical transcriptionists work a standard 40-hour week. Self-employed medical transcriptionists are more likely to work irregular hours—including part-time, evenings, weekends, or on an on-call basis.

Employment

Medical transcriptionists held about 102,000 jobs in 2000. About 2 out of 5 worked in hospitals and about another 2 out of 5 in physicians' offices and clinics. Others worked for laboratories, colleges and universities, transcription services, and temporary help agencies.

Training, Other Qualifications, and Advancement

Employers prefer to hire transcriptionists who have completed postsecondary training in medical transcription, offered by many vocational schools, community colleges, and distance-learning programs. Completion of a 2-year associate degree or 1-year certificate program—including coursework in anatomy, medical terminology, medicolegal issues, and English grammar and punctuation—is highly recommended, but not always required. Many of these programs include supervised on-the-job experience. Some transcriptionists, especially those already familiar with medical terminology due to previous experience as a nurse or medical secretary, become proficient through on-the-job training.

The American Association for Medical Transcription (AAMT) awards the voluntary designation, Certified Medical Transcriptionist (CMT), to those who earn passing scores on written and practical examinations. As in many other fields, certification is recognized as a sign of competence. Because medical terminology is constantly evolving, medical transcriptionists are encouraged to regularly update their skills. Every 3 years, CMTs must earn continuing education credits to be recertified.

In addition to understanding medical terminology, transcriptionists must have good English grammar and punctuation skills, as well as familiarity with personal computers and word processing software. Normal hearing acuity and good listening skills also are necessary. Employers often require applicants to take pre-employment tests.

With experience, medical transcriptionists can advance to supervisory positions, home-based work, consulting, or teaching. With additional education or training, some become medical records and health information technicians, medical coders, or medical records and health information administrators.

Job Outlook

Employment of medical transcriptionists is projected to grow faster than the average for all occupations through 2010. Demand for medical transcription services will be spurred by a growing and aging population. Older age groups receive proportionately greater numbers of medical tests, treatments, and procedures that require documentation. A high level of demand for transcription services also will be sustained by the continued need for electronic documentation that can be easily shared among providers, third-party payers, regulators, and consumers. Growing numbers of medical transcriptionists will be needed to amend patients' records, edit for grammar, and discover discrepancies in medical records.

Advancements in speech recognition technology are not projected to significantly reduce the need for medical transcriptionists because these workers will continue to be needed to review and edit drafts for accuracy. In spite of the advances in this technology, it has been difficult for the software to grasp and analyze the human voice and the English language with all its diversity. There will continue to be a need for skilled medical transcriptionists to identify and appropriately edit the inevitable errors created by speech recognition systems, and create a final document.

Hospitals will continue to employ a large percentage of medical transcriptionists, but job growth will not be as fast as in other areas. Increasing demand for standardized records in offices and clinics of physicians should result in rapid employment growth, especially in large group practices. Job opportunities should be the best for those who earn an associate degree or certification from the American Association for Medical Transcription.

Earnings

Medical transcriptionists had median hourly earnings of $12.15 in 2000. The middle 50 percent earned between $10.07 and $14.41. The lowest 10 percent earned less than $8.66, and the highest 10 percent earned more than $16.70. Median hourly earnings in the industries employing the largest numbers of medical transcriptionists in 2000 were as follows:

Offices and clinics of medical doctors	$12.25
Hospitals	12.14
Mailing, reproduction, and stenographic services	11.47

Compensation methods for medical transcriptionists vary. Some are paid based on the number of hours they work or on the number of lines they transcribe. Others receive a base pay per hour with incentives for extra production. Large hospitals and healthcare organizations usually prefer to pay for the time an employee works. Independent contractors and employees of transcription services almost always receive production-based pay.

According to a 1999 study conducted by Hay Management Consultants for the American Association for Medical Transcription, entry-level medical transcriptionists had median hourly earnings of $10.32 and the most experienced transcriptionists had median hourly earnings of $13.00. Earnings were highest in organizations employing 1,000 or more workers. Transcriptionists receiving production-based pay earned about 7 to 8.5 cents per standardized line (based on a 65-character line, counting all keystrokes). However, independent contractors—who have higher expenses than their corporate counterparts, receive no benefits, and face higher risk of termination than employed transcriptionists—typically charge about 12 to 13 cents per standardized line.

Related Occupations

A number of other workers type, record information, and process paperwork. Among these are court reporter, secretaries and administrative assistants, receptionists and information clerks, and human resources assistants, except payroll and timekeeping. Other workers who provide medical support include medical assistants and medical records and health information technicians.

Sources of Additional Information

For information on a career as a medical transcriptionist, send a self-addressed, stamped envelope to:

● American Association for Medical Transcription, 3460 Oakdale Rd., Suite M, Modesto, CA 95355-9690. Internet: http://www.aamt.org

State employment service offices can provide information about job openings for medical transcriptionists.

Meter Readers, Utilities

O*NET 43-5041.00

Significant Points

- Many utilities meter reader jobs are entry level and do not require more than a high school diploma.

- Workers develop the necessary skills through on-the-job training lasting from several days to a few months.

- Employment of meter readers is expected to decline through 2010 due to the use of automated meter reading (AMR) systems. However, because it will be many years before AMR systems can be implemented in all locations, there still will be some openings for meter readers, mainly to replace workers who leave the occupation.

Nature of the Work

Meter readers read electric, gas, water, or steam consumption meters and record the volume used. They serve both residential and commercial consumers, either walking or driving along the designated route. Their duties include inspecting the meters and their connections for any defects or damage, supplying meter repair and maintenance workers with the necessary information to fix damaged meters, and keeping track of the average usage and record reasons for any extreme fluctuations in volume.

Meter readers are constantly aware of any abnormal behavior or consumption that might indicate an unauthorized connection. They may turn off service for questionable behavior or nonpayment of charges, and also are responsible for turning on service for new occupants. They usually keep a record of receipt and completion of meter service.

Working Conditions

Meter readers usually work 40 hours a week, Monday through Friday. They work outdoors in all types of weather as they travel through communities and neighborhoods taking readings.

Employment

Meter readers held about 49,000 jobs in 2000. About half were employed by electric, gas, and water utilities. Most of the rest were employed in local government, reading water meters or meters for other government-owned utilities.

Training, Other Qualifications, and Advancement

Many meter reader jobs are entry level and do not require more than a high school diploma. Employers, however, prefer to hire those who are familiar with computers and other electronic office and business equipment. Those who have taken business courses or have previous business, dispatching, or specific job-related experience may be preferred. Because communication with other people is an integral part of these jobs, good oral and written communications skills are essential.

State or local government civil service regulations usually govern police, fire, emergency medical, and ambulance dispatching jobs. Candidates for these positions may have to pass written, oral, and performance tests. Also, they may be asked to attend training classes and attain the proper certification in order to qualify for advancement.

Trainees usually develop the necessary skills on the job. This informal training lasts from several days to a few months, depending on the complexity of the job.

Utility meter readers usually shadow a more experienced meter reader until they feel comfortable doing the job on their own. They learn how to read the meters and determine the consumption rate. They also must learn the route that they need to travel in order to read all their customers' meters.

Job Outlook

Employment of meter readers is expected to decline through 2010. New automated meter reading (AMR) systems allow meters to be monitored and billed from a central point, reducing the need for meter readers. However, because it will be many years before AMR systems can be implemented in all locations, there still will be some openings for meter readers, mainly to replace workers who leave the occupation.

Earnings

Median hourly earnings in 2000 for meter readers were $13.32.

Meter readers usually receive the same benefits as most other workers. If uniforms are required, employers usually provide either the uniforms or an allowance to purchase them.

Related Occupations

Other workers responsible for the distribution and control of utilities include powerplant operators, distributors, and dispatchers.

Sources of Additional Information

Information on employment as a meter reader, and on automatic meter reading technology, can be obtained from:

- Automatic Meter Reading Association, 60 Revere Dr., Suite 500, Northbrook, IL 60062. Internet: http://www.amra-intl.org

Musicians, Singers, and Related Workers

O*NET 27-2041.01, 27-2041.02, 27-2041.03, 27-2042.01, 27-2042.02

Significant Points

- Part-time schedules and intermittent unemployment are common; many musicians supplement their income with earnings from other sources.

- Aspiring musicians begin studying an instrument or training their voices at an early age.

- Competition for jobs is keen; those who can play several instruments and types of music should enjoy the best job prospects.

Nature of the Work

Musicians, singers, and related workers play musical instruments, sing, compose, arrange, or conduct groups in instrumental or vocal performances. They may perform solo or as part of a group. Musicians, singers, and related workers entertain live audiences in nightclubs, concert halls, and theaters featuring opera, musical theater, or dance. Although most of these entertainers play for live audiences, some perform exclusively for recording or production studios. Regardless of the setting, musicians, singers, and related workers spend considerable time practicing, alone and with their band, orchestra, or other musical ensemble.

Musicians often gain their reputation or professional standing in a particular kind of music or performance. However, those who learn several related instruments, such as the flute and clarinet, and can perform equally well in a several musical styles, have better employment opportunities. Instrumental musicians, for example, may play in a symphony orchestra, rock group, or jazz combo one night, appear in another ensemble the next, and in a studio band the following day. Some play a variety of string, brass, woodwind, or percussion instruments or electronic synthesizers.

Singers interpret music using their knowledge of voice production, melody, and harmony. They sing character parts or perform in their own individual style. Singers are often classified according to their voice range—soprano, contralto, tenor, baritone, or bass—or by the type of music they sing, such as opera, rock, popular, folk, rap, or country and western.

Music directors conduct, direct, plan, and lead instrumental or vocal performances by musical groups, such as orchestras, choirs, and glee clubs. *Conductors* lead instrumental music groups, such as symphony orchestras, dance bands, show bands, and various popular ensembles. These leaders audition and select musicians, choose the music most appropriate for their talents and abilities, and direct rehearsals and performances. Choral directors lead choirs and glee clubs, sometimes working with a band or orchestra conductor. Directors audition and select singers and lead them at rehearsals and performances to achieve harmony, rhythm, tempo, shading, and other desired musical effects.

Composers create original music such as symphonies, operas, sonatas, radio and television jingles, film scores, or popular songs. They transcribe ideas into musical notation using harmony, rhythm, melody, and tonal structure. Although most composers and songwriters practice their craft on instruments and transcribe the notes with pen and paper, some use computer software to compose and edit their music.

Arrangers transcribe and adapt musical composition to a particular style for orchestras, bands, choral groups, or individuals. Components of music—including tempo, volume, and the mix of instruments needed—are arranged to express the composer's message. While some arrangers write directly into a musical composition, others use computer software to make changes.

Working Conditions

Musicians typically perform at night and on weekends. They spend much of their remaining time practicing or in rehearsal. Full-time musicians with long-term employment contracts, such as those with symphony orchestras and television and film production companies, enjoy steady work and less travel. Nightclub, solo, or recital musicians frequently travel to perform in a variety of local settings and may tour nationally or internationally. Because many musicians find only part-time or intermittent work, experiencing unemployment between engagements, they often supplement their income with other types of jobs. The stress of constantly looking for work leads many musicians to accept permanent, full-time jobs in other occupations, while working only part-time as musicians.

Most instrumental musicians work closely with a variety of other people, including their colleagues, agents, employers, sponsors, and audiences. Although they usually work indoors, some perform outdoors for parades, concerts, and dances. In some nightclubs and restaurants, smoke and odors may be present, and lighting and ventilation may be inadequate.

Employment

Musicians, singers, and related workers held about 240,000 jobs in 2000. More than 40 percent worked part-time, and more than 40 percent were self-employed. Many jobs were found in cities in which entertainment and recording activities are concentrated, such as New York, Los Angeles, and Nashville.

Musicians, singers, and related workers are employed in a variety of settings. More than half of those who earn a wage or salary are employed by religious organizations. Classical musicians may perform with professional orchestras or in small chamber music groups like trios or quartets. Musicians may work in opera, musical theater, and ballet productions. They also perform in nightclubs and restaurants, and for weddings and other events. Well-known musicians and groups may perform in concert, appear on radio and television broadcasts, and make recordings and music videos. The armed forces also offer careers in their bands and smaller musical groups.

Training, Other Qualifications, and Advancement

Aspiring musicians begin studying an instrument at an early age. They may gain valuable experience playing in a school or community band or orchestra or with a group of friends. Singers usually start training when their voices mature. Participation in school musicals or choirs often provides good early training and experience.

Musicians need extensive and prolonged training to acquire the necessary skills, knowledge, and ability to interpret music. Like other artists, musicians and singers continually strive to stretch themselves, musically, and explore different music forms. Formal training may be obtained through private study with an accomplished musician, in a college or university music program, or in a music conservatory. For university or conservatory study, an audition generally is necessary. Courses typically include musical theory, music interpretation, composition, conducting, and performance in their particular instrument or voice. Music directors, composers, conductors, and arrangers need considerable related work experience or advanced training in these subjects.

Many colleges, universities, and music conservatories grant bachelor's degrees or higher degrees in music. A master's or doctoral degree is usually required to teach advanced music courses in colleges and universities; a bachelor's degree may be sufficient to teach basic courses. A degree in music education qualifies graduates for a state certificate to teach music in public elementary or secondary schools. Musicians who do not meet public school music education requirements may teach in private schools and recreation associations, or instruct individual students in private sessions.

Musicians must be knowledgeable about the broad range of music styles, but keenly aware of the form that interests them most. This broader range of interest, knowledge, and training can help expand employment opportunities and musical abilities. Voice training and private instrumental lessons, especially when young, also help develop technique and enhance performance.

Young persons considering careers in music should have musical talent, versatility, creativity, poise, and a good stage presence. Because quality performance requires constant study and practice, self-discipline is vital. Moreover, musicians who play concert and nightclub engagements and who tour must have physical stamina to endure frequent travel and an irregular performance schedule. Musicians and singers always must make their performances look effortless; therefore, preparations and practice are important. They also must be prepared to face the anxiety of intermittent employment and rejections when auditioning for work.

Advancement for musicians usually means becoming better known and performing for higher earnings. Successful musicians often rely on agents or managers to find them performing engagements, negotiate contracts, and develop their careers.

Job Outlook

Competition for musician, singer, and related worker jobs is expected to be keen. The vast number of persons with the desire to perform will exceed the number of openings. Talent alone is no guarantee of success. Many people start out to become musicians or singers, but leave the profession because they find the work difficult, the discipline demanding, and the long periods of intermittent unemployment unendurable.

Overall employment of musicians, singers, and related workers is expected to grow about as fast as the average for all occupations through 2010. Most new wage and salary jobs for musicians will arise in religious organizations, where the majority of these workers are employed. Average growth also is expected for self-employed musicians, who generally perform in nightclubs, concert tours, and other venues. Although growth in demand for musicians will generate a number of job opportunities, many openings also will arise from the need to replace those who leave the field each year because they are unable to make a living solely as musicians or for other reasons.

Earnings

Median annual earnings of salaried musicians and singers were $36,740 in 2000. The middle 50 percent earned between $19,590 and $59,330.

The lowest 10 percent earned less than $13,250, and the highest 10 percent earned more than $88,640. Median annual earnings were $41,520 in the producers, orchestras, and entertainers industry and $16,570 in religious organizations.

Median annual earnings of salaried music directors and composers were $31,510 in 2000. The middle 50 percent earned between $21,080 and $45,000. The lowest 10 percent earned less than $13,530, and the highest 10 percent earned more than $66,140.

Earnings often depend on the number of hours and weeks worked, a performer's professional reputation, and setting. The most successful musicians earn performance or recording fees that far exceed the median earnings indicated above.

According to the American Federation of Musicians, minimum salaries in major orchestras ranged from $24,720 to $100,196 per year during the 2000–2001 performing season. Each orchestra works out a separate contract with its local union. Top orchestras have a season ranging from 24 to 52 weeks, with 18 orchestras reporting 52 week contracts. In regional orchestras, minimum salaries are often less because fewer performances are scheduled. Community orchestras often have more limited levels of funding and offer salaries that are much lower for seasons of shorter duration. Regional orchestra musicians often are paid per service without guarantees.

Although musicians employed by some symphony orchestras work under master wage agreements, which guarantee a season's work up to 52 weeks, many other musicians face relatively long periods of unemployment between jobs. Even when employed, many musicians and singers work part-time in unrelated occupations. Thus, their earnings usually are lower than earnings in many other occupations. Moreover, because they may not work steadily for one employer, some performers cannot qualify for unemployment compensation, and few have typical benefits such as sick leave or paid vacations. For these reasons, many musicians give private lessons or take jobs unrelated to music to supplement their earnings as performers.

Many musicians belong to a local of the American Federation of Musicians. Professional singers usually belong to a branch of the American Guild of Musical Artists.

Related Occupations

Musical instrument repairers and tuners (part of precision instrument and equipment repairers) require technical knowledge of musical instruments. Others whose work involves music include actors, producers, and directors; announcers; broadcast and sound engineering technicians and radio operators; and dancers and choreographers.

Sources of Additional Information

For general information about music and music teacher education and a list of accredited college-level programs, contact:

● National Association of Schools of Music, 11250 Roger Bacon Dr., Suite 21, Reston, VA 22091. Internet: http://www.arts-accredit.org/nasm/nasm.htm

Nuclear Medicine Technologists

O*NET 29-2033.00

Significant Points

- Faster-than-average growth will arise from an increase in the number of middle-aged and elderly persons, who are the primary users of diagnostic procedures.

- Technologists with cross training in radiologic technology or other modalities will have the best prospects.

Nature of the Work

In nuclear medicine, radionuclides—unstable atoms that emit radiation spontaneously—are used to diagnose and treat disease. Radionuclides are purified and compounded like other drugs to form radiopharmaceuticals. Nuclear medicine technologists administer these radiopharmaceuticals to patients, then monitor the characteristics and functions of tissues or organs in which they localize. Abnormal areas show higher or lower concentrations of radioactivity than normal.

Nuclear medicine technologists operate cameras that detect and map the radioactive drug in the patient's body to create an image on photographic film or a computer monitor. Radiologic technologists and technicians also operate diagnostic imaging equipment, but their equipment creates an image by projecting an X ray through the patient.

Nuclear medicine technologists explain test procedures to patients. They prepare a dosage of the radiopharmaceutical and administer it by mouth, injection, or other means. When preparing radiopharmaceuticals, technologists adhere to safety standards that keep the radiation dose to workers and patients as low as possible.

Technologists position patients and start a gamma scintillation camera, or "scanner," which creates images of the distribution of a radiopharmaceutical as it localizes in and emits signals from the patient's body. Technologists produce the images on a computer screen or on film for a physician to interpret. Some nuclear medicine studies, such as cardiac function studies, are processed with the aid of a computer.

Nuclear medicine technologists also perform radioimmunoassay studies that assess the behavior of a radioactive substance inside the body. For example, technologists may add radioactive substances to blood or serum to determine levels of hormones or therapeutic drug content.

Technologists keep patient records and record the amount and type of radionuclides received, used, and disposed of.

Working Conditions

Nuclear medicine technologists generally work a 40-hour week. This may include evening or weekend hours in departments that operate on an extended schedule. Opportunities for part-time and shift work are also available. In addition, technologists in hospitals may have on-call duty on a rotational basis.

Because technologists are on their feet much of the day, and may lift or turn disabled patients, physical stamina is important.

Although there is potential for radiation exposure in this field, it is kept to a minimum by the use of shielded syringes, gloves, and other protective devices and adherence to strict radiation safety guidelines. Technologists also wear badges that measure radiation levels. Because of safety programs, however, badge measurements rarely exceed established safety levels.

Employment

Nuclear medicine technologists held about 18,000 jobs in 2000. About two-thirds of all jobs were in hospitals. The rest were in physicians' offices and clinics, including diagnostic imaging centers.

Training, Other Qualifications, and Advancement

Nuclear medicine technology programs range in length from 1 to 4 years and lead to a certificate, associate degree, or bachelor's degree. Generally, certificate programs are offered in hospitals, associate programs in community colleges, and bachelor's programs in 4-year colleges and in universities. Courses cover physical sciences, the biological effects of radiation exposure, radiation protection and procedures, the use of radiopharmaceuticals, imaging techniques, and computer applications.

One-year certificate programs are for health professionals, especially radiologic technologists and diagnostic medical sonographers, who wish to specialize in nuclear medicine. They also attract medical technologists, registered nurses, and others who wish to change fields or specialize. Others interested in the nuclear medicine technology field have three options: A 2-year certificate program, a 2-year associate program, or a 4-year bachelor's program.

The Joint Review Committee on Education Programs in Nuclear Medicine Technology accredits most formal training programs in nuclear medicine technology. In 2000, there were 95 accredited programs in the continental United States and Puerto Rico.

All nuclear medicine technologists must meet the minimum federal standards on the administration of radioactive drugs and the operation of radiation detection equipment. In addition, about half of all states require technologists to be licensed. Technologists also may obtain voluntary professional certification or registration. Registration or certification is available from the American Registry of Radiologic Technologists and from the Nuclear Medicine Technology Certification Board. Most employers prefer to hire certified or registered technologists.

Nuclear medicine technologists should be sensitive to patients' physical and psychological needs. They must pay attention to detail, follow instructions, and work as part of a team. In addition, operating complicated equipment requires mechanical ability and manual dexterity.

Technologists may advance to supervisor, then to chief technologist, and to department administrator or director. Some technologists specialize in a clinical area such as nuclear cardiology or computer analysis or leave patient care to take positions in research laboratories. Some become instructors or directors in nuclear medicine technology programs, a step that usually requires a bachelor's degree or a master's in nuclear medicine technology. Others leave the occupation to work as sales or training representatives for medical equipment and radiopharmaceutical manufacturing firms, or as radiation safety officers in regulatory agencies or hospitals.

Job Outlook

Employment of nuclear medicine technologists is expected to grow faster than the average for all occupations through the year 2010. The number of openings each year will be very low because the occupation is small. Growth will arise from an increase in the number of middle-aged and older persons who are the primary users of diagnostic procedures, including nuclear medicine tests.

Technological innovations may increase the diagnostic uses of nuclear medicine. One example is the use of radiopharmaceuticals in combination with monoclonal antibodies to detect cancer at far earlier stages than is customary today, and without resorting to surgery. Another is the use of radionuclides to examine the heart's ability to pump blood. Wider use of nuclear medical imaging to observe metabolic and biochemical changes for neurology, cardiology, and oncology procedures, also will spur some demand for nuclear medicine technologists.

On the other hand, cost considerations will affect the speed with which new applications of nuclear medicine grow. Some promising nuclear medicine procedures, such as positron emission tomography (PET), are extremely costly, and hospitals contemplating them will have to consider equipment costs, reimbursement policies, and the number of potential users.

Earnings

Median annual earnings of nuclear medicine technologists were $44,130 in 2000. The middle 50 percent earned between $38,150 and $52,190. The lowest 10 percent earned less than $31,910, and the highest 10 percent earned more than $58,500. Median annual earnings of nuclear medicine technologists in 2000 were $44,000 in hospitals.

Related Occupations

Nuclear medical technologists operate sophisticated equipment to help physicians and other health practitioners diagnose and treat patients. Cardiovascular technologists and technicians, clinical laboratory technologists and technicians, diagnostic medical sonographers, radiation therapists, radiologic technologists and technicians, and respiratory therapists also perform similar functions.

Sources of Additional Information

Additional information on a career as a nuclear medicine technologist is available from:

- The Society of Nuclear Medicine–Technologist Section, 1850 Samuel Morse Dr., Reston, VA 22090. Internet: http://www.snm.org

For career information, send a stamped, self-addressed business size envelope with your request to:

- American Society of Radiologic Technologists, Customer Service Department, 15000 Central Ave. SE., Albuquerque, NM 87123-3917, or call (800) 444-2778. Internet: http://www.asrt.org/asrt.htm

For a list of accredited programs in nuclear medicine technology, write to:

- Joint Review Committee on Educational Programs in Nuclear Medicine Technology, PMB 418, 1 2nd Avenue East, Suite C, Polson, MT 59860-2107. Internet: http://www.jrcnmt.org

Information on certification is available from:

- American Registry of Radiologic Technologists, 1255 Northland Dr., St. Paul, MN 55120-1155. Internet: http://www.arrt.org

- Nuclear Medicine Technology Certification Board, 2970 Clairmont Rd., Suite 610, Atlanta, GA 30329. Internet: http://www.nmtcb.org

Nursing, Psychiatric, and Home Health Aides

O*NET 31-1011.00, 31-1012.00, 31-1013.00

Significant Points

- Job prospects for nursing and home health aides will be very good because of fast growth and high replacement needs in these large occupations.

- Minimum education or training is generally required for entry-level jobs, but earnings are low.

Nature of the Work

Nursing and psychiatric aides help care for physically or mentally ill, injured, disabled, or infirm individuals confined to hospitals, nursing and personal care facilities, and mental health settings. Home health aides duties are similar, but they work in patients' homes or residential care facilities.

Nursing aides, also known as nursing assistants, geriatric aides, unlicensed assistive personnel, or hospital attendants, perform routine tasks under the supervision of nursing and medical staff. They answer patients' call bells, deliver messages, serve meals, make beds, and help patients eat, dress, and bathe. Aides also may provide skin care to patients; take temperatures, pulse, respiration, and blood pressure; and help patients get in and out of bed and walk. They also may escort patients to operating and examining rooms, keep patients' rooms neat, set up equipment, store and move supplies, or assist with some procedures. Aides observe patients' physical, mental, and emotional conditions and report any change to the nursing or medical staff.

Nursing aides employed in nursing homes often are the principal caregivers, having far more contact with residents than other members of the staff. Because some residents may stay in a nursing home for months or even years, aides develop ongoing relationships with them and interact with them in a positive, caring way.

Psychiatric aides, also known as mental health assistants or psychiatric nursing assistants, care for mentally impaired or emotionally disturbed individuals. They work under a team that may include psychiatrists, psychologists, psychiatric nurses, social workers, and therapists. In addition to helping patients dress, bathe, groom, and eat, psychiatric aides socialize with them and lead them in educational and recreational activities. Psychiatric aides may play games such as cards with the patients, watch television with them, or participate in group activities such as sports or field trips. They observe patients and report any physical or behavioral signs that might be important for the professional staff to know. They accompany patients to and from examinations and treatments. Because they have such close contact with patients, psychiatric aides can have a great deal of influence on their outlook and treatment.

Home health aides help elderly, convalescent, or disabled persons live in their own homes instead of in a health facility. Under the direction of nursing or medical staff, they provide health-related services, such as administering oral medications. Like nursing aides, home health aides may check pulse, temperature, and respiration; help with simple prescribed exercises; keep patients' rooms neat; and help patients move from bed, bathe, dress, and groom. Occasionally, they change nonsterile dressings, give massages and alcohol rubs, or assist with braces and artificial limbs. Experienced home health aides also may assist with medical equipment such as ventilators, which help patients breathe.

Most home health aides work with elderly or disabled persons who need more extensive care than family or friends can provide. Some help discharged hospital patients who have relatively short-term needs.

In home healthcare agencies, a registered nurse, physical therapist, or social worker usually assigns specific duties and supervises home health aides. Aides keep records of services performed and patients' condition and progress. They report changes in patients' conditions to the supervisor or case manager.

Working Conditions

Most full-time aides work about 40 hours a week, but because patients need care 24 hours a day, some aides work evenings, nights, weekends, and holidays. Many work part-time. Aides spend many hours standing and walking, and they often face heavy workloads. Because they may have to move patients in and out of bed or help them stand or walk, aides must guard against back injury. Aides also may face hazards from minor infections and major diseases, such as hepatitis, but can avoid infections by following proper procedures.

Aides often have unpleasant duties, such as emptying bedpans and changing soiled bed linens. The patients they care for may be disoriented, irritable, or uncooperative. Psychiatric aides must be prepared to care for patients whose illness may cause violent behavior. While their work can be emotionally demanding, many aides gain satisfaction from assisting those in need.

Home health aides may go to the same patient's home for months or even years. However, most aides work with a number of different patients, each job lasting a few hours, days, or weeks. Home health aides often visit multiple patients on the same day.

Home health aides generally work alone, with periodic visits by their supervisor. They receive detailed instructions explaining when to visit patients and what services to perform. Aides are individually responsible for getting to patients' homes, and they may spend a good portion of the working day traveling from one patient to another. Because mechanical lifting devices available in institutional settings are seldom available in patients' homes, home health aides are particularly susceptible to injuries resulting from overexertion when assisting patients.

Employment

Nursing, psychiatric, and home health aides held about 2.1 million jobs in 2000. Nursing aides held about 1.4 million jobs, home health aides held roughly 615,000 jobs, and psychiatric aides held about 65,000 jobs. About one-half of nursing aides worked in nursing homes, and about one-fourth worked in hospitals. Most home health aides were employed by home health agencies, visiting nurse associations, social services agencies, residential care facilities, and temporary-help firms. Others worked for home health departments of hospitals and nursing facilities, public health agencies, and community volunteer agencies. Most psychiatric aides worked in psychiatric units of general hospitals, psychiatric hospitals, state and county mental institutions, homes for mentally retarded and psychiatric patients, and community mental health centers.

Training, Other Qualifications, and Advancement

In many cases, neither a high school diploma nor previous work experience is necessary for a job as a nursing, psychiatric, or home health aide. A few employers, however, require some training or experience. Hospitals may require experience as a nursing aide or home health aide. Nursing homes often hire inexperienced workers who must complete a minimum of 75 hours of mandatory training and pass a competency evaluation program within 4 months of employment. Aides who complete the program are certified and placed on the state registry of nursing aides. Some states require psychiatric aides to complete a formal training program.

The federal government has enacted guidelines for home health aides whose employers receive reimbursement from Medicare. Federal law requires home health aides to pass a competency test covering 12 areas: communication skills; documentation of patient status and care provided; reading and recording vital signs; basic infection control procedures; basic body functions; maintenance of a healthy environment; emergency procedures; physical, emotional, and developmental characteristics of patients; personal hygiene and grooming; safe transfer techniques; normal range of motion and positioning; and basic nutrition.

A home health aide may take training before taking the competency test. Federal law suggests at least 75 hours of classroom and practical training supervised by a registered nurse. Training and testing programs may be offered by the employing agency, but must meet the standards of the Healthcare Financing Administration. Training programs vary depending upon state regulations.

The National Association for Home Care offers national certification for home health aides. The certification is a voluntary demonstration that the individual has met industry standards.

Nursing aide training is offered in high schools, vocational-technical centers, some nursing homes, and some community colleges. Courses cover body mechanics, nutrition, anatomy and physiology, infection control, communication skills, and resident rights. Personal care skills such as how to help patients bathe, eat, and groom also are taught.

Some facilities, other than nursing homes, provide classroom instruction for newly hired aides, while others rely exclusively on informal on-the-job instruction from a licensed nurse or an experienced aide. Such training may last several days to a few months. From time to time, aides may also attend lectures, workshops, and in-service training.

These occupations can offer individuals an entry into the world of work. The flexibility of night and weekend hours also provides high school and college students a chance to work during the school year.

Applicants should be tactful, patient, understanding, healthy, emotionally stable, dependable, and have a desire to help people. They should also be able to work as part of a team, have good communication skills, and be willing to perform repetitive, routine tasks. Home health aides should be honest, and discreet because they work in private homes.

Aides must be in good health. A physical examination, including state regulated tests such as those for tuberculosis, may be required.

Opportunities for advancement within these occupations are limited. To enter other health occupations, aides generally need additional formal training. Some employers and unions provide opportunities by simplifying the educational paths to advancement. Experience as an aide can also help individuals decide whether to pursue a career in the healthcare field.

Job Outlook

Overall employment of nursing, psychiatric, and home health aides is projected to grow faster than the average through the year 2010, although individual occupational growth rates vary. *Home health aides* are expected to grow the fastest, as a result of growing demand for home healthcare from an aging population and efforts to contain healthcare costs by moving patients out of hospitals and nursing facilities as quickly as possible. Consumer preference for care in the home and improvements in medical technologies for in-home treatment also will contribute to much faster-than-average employment growth for home health aides.

Nursing aide employment will not grow as fast as home health aide employment, largely because nursing aides are concentrated in the relatively slower-growing nursing home sector. Nevertheless, employment of nursing aides is expected to grow faster than the average for all occupations in response to increasing emphasis on rehabilitation and the long-term care needs of a rapidly growing elderly population. Financial pressure on hospitals to discharge patients as soon as possible should produce more nursing home admissions. Modern medical technology will also increase the employment of nursing aides. This technology, while saving and extending more lives, increases the need for long-term care provided by aides.

Employment of *psychiatric aides*—the smallest of the three occupation—is expected to grow as fast as the average. The number of jobs for psychiatric aides in hospitals, where one-half of psychiatric aides work, will decline due to attempts to contain costs by limiting inpatient psychiatric treatment. Employment in other sectors will rise in response to growth in the number of older persons. Many elderly will require mental health services, increasing public acceptance of formal treatment for drug abuse and alcoholism, and a lessening of the stigma attached to those receiving mental healthcare.

Numerous openings for nursing and home health aides will arise from a combination of fast growth and high replacement needs for these large occupations. Turnover is high, a reflection of modest entry requirements, low pay, high physical and emotional demands, and lack of advancement opportunities. For these same reasons, many people are unwilling to perform this kind of work. Therefore, persons who are interested in this work and suited for it should have excellent job opportunities.

Earnings

Median hourly earnings of nursing aides, orderlies, and attendants were $8.89 in 2000. The middle 50 percent earned between $7.51 and $10.59 an hour. The lowest 10 percent earned less than $6.48, and the highest 10 percent earned more than $12.69 an hour. Median hourly earnings in the industries employing the largest numbers of nursing aides, orderlies, and attendants in 2000 were as follows:

Personnel supply services	$9.82
Local government	9.66
Hospitals	9.42
Nursing and personal care facilities	8.61
Residential care	7.96

Median hourly earnings of psychiatric aides were $10.45 in 2000. The middle 50 percent earned between $8.38 and $13.02 an hour. The lowest 10 percent earned less than $7.10, and the highest 10 percent earned more than $15.50 an hour. Median hourly earnings of psychiatric aides in 2000 were $12.61 in state government and $10.50 in hospitals.

Nursing and psychiatric aides in hospitals generally receive at least one week's paid vacation after 1 year of service. Paid holidays and sick leave, hospital and medical benefits, extra pay for late-shift work, and pension plans also are available to many hospital and some nursing home employees.

Median hourly earnings of home health aides were $8.23 in 2000. The middle 50 percent earned between $7.13 and $9.88 an hour. The lowest 10 percent earned less than $6.14, and the highest 10 percent earned more than $11.93 an hour. Median hourly earnings in the industries employing the largest numbers of home health aides in 2000 were as follows:

Nursing and personal care facilities	$8.65
Personnel supply services	8.60
Residential care	8.16
Home healthcare services	7.91
Individual and family services	7.89

Home health aides receive slight pay increases with experience and added responsibility. They usually are paid only for the time worked in the home; they normally are not paid for travel time between jobs. Most employers hire only on-call hourly workers and provide no benefits.

Related Occupations

Nursing, psychiatric, and home health aides help people who need routine care or treatment. So do childcare workers, medical assistants, occupational therapist assistants and aides, personal and home care aides, and physical therapist assistants and aides.

Sources of Additional Information

Information about employment opportunities may be obtained from local hospitals, nursing homes, home healthcare agencies, psychiatric facilities, state boards of nursing, and local offices of the state employment service.

General information about training and referrals to state and local agencies about opportunities for home health aides, a list of relevant publications, and information on certification are available from:

National Association for Home Care, 228 7th St. SE., Washington, DC 20003. Internet: http://www.nahc.org

Occupational Health and Safety Specialists and Technicians

O*NET 29-9011.00, 29-9012.00

Significant Points

● Almost half of occupational health and safety specialists and technicians work in federal, state, and local government agencies that enforce rules on health and safety.

● For positions as specialists, many employers, including the federal government, require 4-year college degrees in safety or a related field.

Nature of the Work

Occupational health and safety specialists and technicians, also known as *occupational health and safety inspectors* and *industrial hygienists*, help keep workplaces safe and workers unscathed. They promote occupational health and safety within organizations by developing safer, healthier, and more efficient ways of working. *Occupational health and safety specialists* analyze work environments and design programs to control, eliminate, and prevent disease or injury caused by chemical, physical, and biological agents or ergonomic factors. They may conduct inspections and enforce adherence to laws, regulations, or employer policies governing worker health and safety. *Occupational health and safety technicians* collect data on work environments for analysis by occupational health and safety specialists. Usually working under the supervision of specialists, they help implement and evaluate programs designed to limit risks to workers.

Occupational health and safety specialists and technicians identify hazardous conditions and practices. Sometimes, they develop methods to predict hazards from experience, historical data, and other information sources. Then they identify potential hazards in existing or future systems, equipment, products, facilities, or processes. After reviewing the causes or effects of hazards, they evaluate the probability and severity of accidents that may result. For example, they might uncover patterns in injury data that implicate a specific cause such as system failure, human error, incomplete or faulty decision making, or a weakness in existing policies or practices. Then they develop and help enforce a plan to eliminate hazards, conducting training sessions for management, supervisors, and workers on health and safety practices and regulations, as necessary. Lastly, they may check on the progress of the safety plan after its implementation. If improvements are not satisfactory, a new plan might be designed and put into practice.

Many occupational health and safety specialists inspect and test machinery and equipment, such as lifting devices, machine shields, or scaffolding, to ensure they meet appropriate safety regulations. They may check that personal protective equipment, such as masks, respirators, safety glasses, or safety helmets, is being used in workplaces according to regulations. They also check that dangerous materials are stored correctly. They test and identify work areas for potential accident and health hazards, such as toxic fumes and explosive gas-air mixtures, and may implement appropriate control measures, such as adjustments to ventilation systems. Their investigations might involve talking with workers and observing their work, as well as inspecting elements in their work environment, such as lighting, tools, and equipment.

To measure and control hazardous substances, such as the noise or radiation levels, occupational health and safety specialists and technicians prepare and calibrate scientific equipment. Samples of dust, gases, vapors, and other potentially toxic materials must be collected and handled properly to ensure safety and accurate test results.

If an accident occurs, occupational health and safety specialists help investigate unsafe working conditions, study possible causes, and recommend remedial action. Some occupational health and safety specialists and technicians assist with the rehabilitation of workers after accidents and injuries, and make sure they return to work successfully.

Frequent communication with management may be necessary to report on the status of occupational health and safety programs. Consultation with engineers or physicians also may be required.

Occupational health and safety specialists prepare reports including observations, analysis of contaminants, and recommendation for control and correction of hazards. Those who develop expertise in certain areas may develop occupational health and safety systems, including policies, procedures, and manuals.

Working Conditions

Occupational health and safety specialists and technicians work with many different people in a variety of environments. Their jobs often involve considerable fieldwork, and some travel frequently. Many occupational health and safety specialists and technicians work long and often irregular hours.

Occupational health and safety specialists and technicians may experience unpleasant, stressful, and dangerous working conditions. For example, health and safety inspectors are exposed to many of the same physically strenuous conditions and hazards as industrial employees, and the work may be performed in unpleasant, stressful, and dangerous working conditions. Health and safety inspectors may find themselves in adversarial roles when the organization or individual being inspected objects to the process or its consequences.

Employment

Occupational health and safety specialists and technicians held about 35,000 jobs in 2000. The federal government—chiefly the Department of Labor—employed 8 percent, state governments employed 17 percent, and local governments employed 19 percent. The remainder were employed throughout the private sector in schools, hospitals, management consulting firms, public utilities, and manufacturing firms.

Within the federal government, most jobs are as Occupational Health and Safety Administration (OSHA) inspectors, who enforce U.S. Department of Labor regulations that ensure adequate safety principles, practices, and techniques are applied in workplaces. Employers may be fined for violation of OSHA standards. Within the U.S. Department of Health and Human Services, occupational health and safety specialists working for the National Institute of Occupational Safety and Health (NIOSH) provide private companies with an avenue to evaluate the health and safety of their employees without the risk of being fined. Most large government agencies also employ occupational health and safety specialists and technicians who work to protect agency employees.

Most private companies either employ their own safety personnel or contract safety professionals to ensure OSHA compliance, as needed.

Training, Other Qualifications, and Advancement

Requirements include a combination of education, experience, and passing scores on written examinations. Many employers, including the federal government, require a 4-year college degree in safety or a related field for some positions. Experience as a safety professional is also a prerequisite for many positions.

All occupational health and safety specialists and technicians are trained in the applicable laws or inspection procedures through some combination of classroom and on-the-job training. In general, people who want to enter this occupation should be responsible and like detailed work. Occupational health and safety specialists and technicians should be able to communicate well. Recommended high school courses include English, chemistry, biology, and physics.

Certification is available through the Board of Certified Safety Professionals (BCSP) and the American Board of Industrial Hygiene (ABIH). The BCSP offers the Certified Safety Professional (CSP) credential, while the ABIH proffers the Certified Industrial Hygienist (CIH) credential. Also, the Council on Certification of Health, Environmental, and Safety Technologists, a joint effort between the BCSP and ABIH, awards the Occupational Health and Safety Technologist (OHST) credential. Requirements for the OHST credential are less stringent than those for the CSP or CIH credentials. Once education and experience requirements have been met, certification may be obtained through an examination. Continuing education is required for recertification. Although voluntary, many employers encourage certification.

Federal government occupational health and safety specialists and technicians whose job performance is satisfactory advance through their career ladder to a specified full-performance level. For positions above this level, usually supervisory positions, advancement is competitive and based on agency needs and individual merit. Advancement opportunities in state and local governments and the private sector are often similar to those in the federal government.

With additional experience or education, promotion to a managerial position is possible. Research or related teaching positions at the college level require advanced education.

Job Outlook

Employment of occupational health and safety specialists and technicians is expected to grow about as fast as the average for all occupations through 2010, reflecting a balance of continuing public demand for a safe and healthy work environment against the desire for smaller government and fewer regulations. Additional job openings will arise from the need to replace those who transfer to other occupations, retire, or leave the labor force for other reasons. In private industry, employment growth will reflect industry growth and the continuing self-enforcement of government and company regulations and policies.

Employment of occupational health and safety specialists and technicians is seldom affected by general economic fluctuations. Federal, state, and local governments—which employ almost half of all specialists and technicians—provide considerable job security.

Earnings

Median annual earnings of occupational health and safety specialists and technicians were $42,750 in 2000. The middle 50 percent earned between $32,060 and $54,880. The lowest 10 percent earned less than $23,780, while the highest 10 percent earned over $67,760. Median annual earnings of occupational health and safety specialists and technicians in 2000 were $41,330 in local government and $41,110 in state government.

Most occupational health and safety specialists and technicians work for federal, state, and local governments or in large private firms. The latter generally offer more generous benefits than smaller firms offer.

Related Occupations

Occupational health and safety specialists and technicians ensure that laws and regulations are obeyed. Others who enforce laws and regulations include agricultural inspectors, construction and building inspectors, correctional officers, financial examiners, fire inspectors, police and detectives, and transportation inspectors.

Sources of Additional Information

Information about jobs in federal, state, and local government as well as in private industry is available from the states' employment service offices.

For information on a career as an industrial hygienist and a list of colleges and universities offering programs in industrial hygiene, contact:

- American Industrial Hygiene Association, 2700 Prosperity Ave., Suite 250, Fairfax, VA 22031. Internet: http://www.aiha.org

For a list of colleges and universities offering safety and related degrees, including correspondence courses, contact:

- American Society of Safety Engineers, 1800 E Oakton St., Des Plaines, IL 60018. Internet: http://www.asse.org

For information on the Certified Safety Professional credential, contact:

- Board of Certified Safety Professionals, 208 Burwash Ave., Savoy, IL 61874. Internet: http://www.bcsp.org

For information on the Certified Industrial Hygiene credential, contact:

- American Board of Industrial Hygiene, 6015 West St. Joseph, Suite 102, Lansing, MI 48917. Internet: http://www.abih.org

For information on the Occupational Health and Safety Technologist credential, contact:

- Council on Certification of Health, Environmental, and Safety Technologists, 208 Burwash Ave., Savoy, IL 61874. Internet: http://www.cchest.org

For additional career information, contact:

- U.S. Department of Health and Human Services, Center for Disease Control and Prevention, National Institute of Occupational Safety and Health, Hubert H. Humphrey Bldg., 200 Independence Ave. SW, Room 715H, Washington, DC 20201. Internet: http://www.cdc.gov/niosh/homepage.html

- U.S. Department of Labor, Occupational Safety and Health Administration, 200 Constitution Ave. NW, Washington, DC 20210. Internet: http://www.osha.gov

Information on obtaining positions as occupational health and safety specialists and technicians with the federal government is available from the Office of Personnel Management through a telephone-based system. Consult your telephone directory under U.S. Government for a local number or call (912) 757-3000; Federal Relay Service: (800) 877-8339. The first number is not toll free, and charges may result. Information also is available from the Internet site: http://www.usajobs.opm.gov

Occupational Therapist Assistants and Aides

O*NET 31-2011.00, 31-2012.00

Significant Points

- Certified occupational therapist assistants must complete an associate degree or certificate program. In contrast, occupational therapist aides usually receive most of their training on the job.

- Aides are not licensed, so by law they are not allowed to perform as wide a range of tasks as occupational therapist assistants do.

- Employment is projected to increase much faster than the average, as rapid growth in the number of middle-aged and elderly individuals increases the demand for therapeutic services.

Nature of the Work

Occupational therapist assistants and aides work under the direction of occupational therapists to provide rehabilitative services to persons with mental, physical, emotional, or developmental impairments. The ultimate goal is to improve clients' quality of life by helping them compensate for limitations. For example, occupational therapist assistants help injured workers reenter the labor force by helping them improve their motor skills or help persons with learning disabilities increase their independence, by teaching them to prepare meals or use public transportation.

Occupational therapist assistants help clients with rehabilitative activities and exercises outlined in a treatment plan developed in collaboration with an occupational therapist. Activities range from teaching the proper method of moving from a bed into a wheelchair, to the best way to stretch and limber the muscles of the hand. Assistants monitor an individual's activities to make sure they are performed correctly and to provide encouragement. They also record their client's progress for use by the occupational therapist. If the treatment is not having the in-

tended effect, or the client is not improving as expected, the therapist may alter the treatment program in hopes of obtaining better results. In addition, occupational therapist assistants document billing of the client's health insurance provider.

Occupational therapist aides typically prepare materials and assemble equipment used during treatment and are responsible for a range of clerical tasks. Duties can include scheduling appointments, answering the telephone, restocking or ordering depleted supplies, and filling out insurance forms or other paperwork. Aides are not licensed, so by law they are not allowed to perform as wide a range of tasks as occupational therapist assistants.

Working Conditions

The hours and days that occupational therapist assistants and aides work vary, depending on the facility and whether they are full or part-time employees. Many outpatient therapy offices and clinics have evening and weekend hours, to help coincide with patients' personal schedules.

Occupational therapist assistants and aides need to have a moderate degree of strength, due to the physical exertion required in assisting patients with their treatment. For example, in some cases, assistants and aides need to help lift patients. Additionally, constant kneeling, stooping, and standing for long periods all are part of the job.

Employment

Occupational therapist assistants and aides held 25,000 jobs in 2000. Occupational therapist assistants held about 17,000 jobs, and occupational therapist aides held about 8,500. About 30 percent of assistants and aides worked in hospitals, 25 percent worked in offices of occupational therapists, and 20 percent worked in nursing and personal care facilities. The remainder primarily worked in offices and clinics of physicians, social services agencies, outpatient rehabilitation centers, and home health agencies.

Training, Other Qualifications, and Advancement

Persons must complete an associate degree or certificate program from an accredited community college or technical school to qualify for occupational therapist assistant jobs. In contrast, occupational therapist aides usually receive most of their training on the job.

There were 185 accredited occupational therapist assistant programs in the United States in 2000. The first year of study typically involves an introduction to healthcare, basic medical terminology, anatomy, and physiology. In the second year, courses are more rigorous and usually include occupational therapist courses in areas such as mental health, gerontology, and pediatrics. Students also must complete supervised fieldwork in a clinic or community setting. Applicants to occupational therapist assistant programs can improve their chances of admission by taking high school courses in biology and health and by performing volunteer work in nursing homes, occupational or physical therapist's offices, or elsewhere in the healthcare field.

Occupational therapist assistants are regulated in most states, and must pass a national certification examination after they graduate. Those who pass the test are awarded the title of certified occupational therapist assistant.

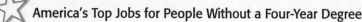

Occupational therapist aides usually receive most of their training on the job. Qualified applicants must have a high school diploma, strong interpersonal skills, and a desire to help people in need. Applicants may increase their chances of getting a job by volunteering their services, thus displaying initiative and aptitude to the employer.

Assistants and aides must be responsible, patient, and willing to take directions and work as part of a team. Furthermore, they should be caring and want to help people who are not able to help themselves.

Job Outlook

Employment of occupational therapist assistants and aides is expected to grow much faster than the average for all occupations through 2010. Federal legislation imposing limits on reimbursement for therapy services may adversely affect the job market for occupational therapist assistants and aides in the near term. However, over the long run, demand for occupational therapist assistants and aides will continue to rise, with growth in the number of individuals with disabilities or limited function. Growth will result from an increasing population in older age groups, including the baby-boom generation, which increasingly needs occupational therapy services as they become older. Demand also will result from advances in medicine that allow more people with critical problems to survive and then need rehabilitative therapy. Third-party payers, concerned with rising healthcare costs may begin to encourage occupational therapists to delegate more of the hands-on therapy work to occupational therapist assistants and aides. By having assistants and aides work more closely with clients under the guidance of a therapist, the cost of therapy should be more modest than otherwise.

Earnings

Median annual earnings of occupational therapist assistants were $34,340 in 2000. The middle 50 percent earned between $29,280 and $40,690. The lowest 10 percent earned less than $23,970, and the highest 10 percent earned more than $45,370. Median annual earnings of occupational therapist assistants in 2000 were $33,390 in hospitals.

Median annual earnings of occupational therapist aides were $20,710 in 2000. The middle 50 percent earned between $16,510 and $28,470. The lowest 10 percent earned less than $14,370, and the highest 10 percent earned more than $35,900.

Related Occupations

Occupational therapist assistants and aides work under the direction of occupational therapists. Other occupations in the healthcare field that work under the supervision of professionals include dental assistants, medical assistants, pharmacy technicians, and physical therapist assistants and aides.

Sources of Additional Information

For information on a career as an occupational therapist assistant and a list of accredited programs, contact:

● The American Occupational Therapy Association, 4720 Montgomery Ln., P.O. Box 31220, Bethesda, MD 20824-1220. Internet: http://www.aota.org

Office and Administrative Support Worker Supervisors and Managers

O*NET 43-1011.01, 43-1011.02

Significant Points

● Most jobs are filled by promoting individuals from within the organization, very often from the ranks of clerks whom they will subsequently supervise.

● Office automation will cause employment in some office and administrative support occupations to slow or even decline, but supervisors are more likely to retain their jobs because of their relatively higher skills and longer tenure.

● Applicants for office and administrative support supervisor or manager jobs are likely to encounter keen competition because their number should greatly exceed the number of job openings.

Nature of the Work

All organizations need timely and effective office and administrative support to operate efficiently. *Office and administrative support supervisors and managers* coordinate this support. These workers are employed in virtually every sector of the economy, working in positions as varied as *customer services manager, teller supervisor,* and *shipping-and-receiving supervisor.*

Although specific functions of office and administrative support supervisors and managers vary considerably, they share many common duties. For example, supervisors perform administrative tasks to ensure that their staffs can work efficiently. Equipment and machinery used in their departments must be in good working order. If the computer system goes down or a facsimile machine malfunctions, they must try to correct the problem or alert repair personnel. They also request new equipment or supplies for their department when necessary.

Planning the work of their staff and supervising them are key functions of this job. To do these effectively, the supervisor must know the strengths and weaknesses of each member of the staff, as well as the required level of quality and time allotted to each job. They must make allowances for unexpected absences and other disruptions by adjusting assignments or performing the work themselves if the situation requires it.

After allocating work assignments and issuing deadlines, office and administrative support supervisors and managers oversee the work to ensure that it is proceeding on schedule and meets established quality standards. This may involve reviewing each person's work on a computer—as in the case of accounting clerks—or listening to how they deal with customers—as in the case of customer services representatives. When supervising long-term projects, the supervisor may meet regularly with staff members to discuss their progress.

Office and administrative support supervisors and managers also evaluate each worker's performance. If a worker has done a good job, the supervisor records it in the employee's personnel file and may recommend a promotion or other award. Alternatively, if a worker is performing poorly, the supervisor discusses the problem with the employee to determine the cause and helps the worker improve his or her performance. This might require sending the employee to a training course or arranging personal counseling. If the situation does not improve, the supervisor may recommend a transfer, demotion, or dismissal.

Office and administrative support supervisors and managers usually interview and evaluate prospective clerical employees. When new workers arrive on the job, supervisors greet them and provide orientation to acquaint them with the organization and its operating routines. Some supervisors may be actively involved in recruiting new workers, for example, by making presentations at high schools and business colleges. They may also serve as the primary liaisons between their offices and the general public through direct contact and by preparing promotional information.

Supervisors also help train new employees in organization and office procedures. They may teach new employees how to use the telephone system and operate office equipment. Because much clerical work is computerized, they must also teach new employees to use the organization's computer system. When new office equipment or updated computer software is introduced, supervisors retrain experienced employees in using it efficiently. If this is not possible, they may arrange for special outside training for their employees.

Office and administrative support supervisors and managers often act as liaisons between the clerical staff and the professional, technical, and managerial staff. This may involve implementing new company policies or restructuring the workflow in their departments. They must also keep their superiors informed of their progress and abreast of any potential problems. Often this communication takes the form of research projects and progress reports. Because they have access to information such as their department's performance records, they may compile and present these data for use in planning or designing new policies.

Office and administrative support supervisors and managers also may have to resolve interpersonal conflicts among the staff. In organizations covered by union contracts, supervisors must know the provisions of labor-management agreements and run their departments accordingly. They may meet with union representatives to discuss work problems or grievances.

Working Conditions

Office and administrative support supervisors and managers are employed in a wide variety of work settings, but most work in clean, well-lit, offices that usually are comfortable.

Most work a standard 40-hour week. Because some organizations operate around the clock, office and administrative support supervisors and managers may have to work nights, weekends, and holidays. Sometimes supervisors rotate among the three shifts; in other cases, shifts are assigned on the basis of seniority.

Employment

Office and administrative support supervisors and managers held almost 1.4 million jobs in 2000. Although jobs for office and administrative support supervisors and managers are found in practically every industry, the largest number are found in organizations with a large clerical workforce such as banks, wholesalers, government agencies, retail establishments, business service firms, healthcare facilities, schools, and insurance companies. Because of most organizations' need for continuity of supervision, few office and administrative support supervisors and managers work on a temporary or part-time basis.

Training, Other Qualifications, and Advancement

Most firms fill office and administrative support supervisory and managerial positions by promoting clerical or administrative support workers from within their organizations. To become eligible for promotion to a supervisory position, clerical or administrative support workers must prove they are capable of handling additional responsibilities. When evaluating candidates, superiors look for strong teamwork, problem-solving, leadership, and communication skills, as well as determination, loyalty, poise, and confidence. They also look for more specific supervisory attributes, such as the ability to organize and coordinate work efficiently, to set priorities, and to motivate others. Increasingly, supervisors need a broad base of office skills coupled with personal flexibility to adapt to changes in organizational structure and move among departments when necessary.

In addition, supervisors must pay close attention to detail in order to identify and correct errors made by the staff they oversee. Good working knowledge of the organization's computer system is also an advantage. Many employers require postsecondary training—in some cases, an associate or even a bachelor's degree.

A clerk with potential supervisory abilities may be given occasional supervisory assignments. To prepare for full-time supervisory duties, he or she may attend in-house training or take courses in time management or interpersonal relations.

Some office and administrative support supervisor positions are filled with people from outside the organization. These positions may serve as entry-level training for potential higher level managers. New college graduates may rotate through departments of an organization at this level to learn the work of the organization.

Job Outlook

Like other supervisory occupations, applicants for jobs as office and administrative support supervisors or managers are likely to encounter keen competition because the number of applicants should greatly exceed the number of job openings. Employment is expected to grow more slowly than the average for all occupations through 2010. In addition to the job openings arising from growth, a larger number of openings will stem from the need to replace workers who transfer to other occupations or leave this large occupation for other reasons.

Employment of office and administrative support supervisors and managers is largely affected by the demand for administrative support workers. The continuing increase in office automation due to new technology should increase support workers' productivity and allow a wider variety of tasks to be performed by more people in professional positions, requiring fewer office and administrative support workers. The result will be to cause employment growth in some clerical occupations to slow or even decline. Supervisors will direct smaller permanent staffs—supplemented by increased use of temporary clerical staff—and perform more professional tasks. Office and administrative support managers will coordinate the increasing amount of administrative work and make sure the technology is applied and running properly. However, organizational restructuring should continue to reduce some manager positions, distributing more responsibility to office and administrative support supervisors.

Earnings

Median annual earnings of office and administrative support supervisors and managers were $36,420 in 2000; the middle 50 percent earned between $28,090 and $47,350. The lowest paid 10 percent earned less than $22,070, while the highest paid 10 percent earned more than $60,600. In 2000, median annual earnings in the industries employing the largest numbers of office and administrative support supervisors and managers were:

Federal government	$48,870
State government	40,050
Local government	38,450
Offices and clinics of medical doctors	35,140
Commercial banks	34,240
Department stores	20,370

In addition to typical benefits, some office and administrative support supervisors and managers in the private sector may receive additional compensation in the form of bonuses and stock options.

Related Occupations

Office and administrative support supervisors and managers must understand and sometimes perform the work of those whom they oversee, including bookkeeping, accounting, and auditing clerks; cashiers; communications equipment operators; customer service representatives; data entry and information processing workers; general office clerks; receptionists and information clerks; stock clerks and order fillers; and tellers. Their supervisory and administrative duties are similar to those of other supervisors and managers.

Sources of Additional Information

For a wide variety of information related to management occupations, including educational programs, contact:

- American Management Association, 1601 Broadway, New York, NY 10019-7420. Internet: http://www.amanet.org

- National Management Association, 2210 Arbor Blvd., Dayton, OH 45439. Internet: http://www.nma1.org

- Association of Records Managers and Administrators, 4200 Somerset Dr., Suite 215, Prairie Village, KS 66208-0540. Internet: http://www.arma.org

- International Association of Administrative Professionals, 10502 NW Ambassador Dr., P.O. Box 20404, Kansas City, MO 64195-0404. Internet: http://www.iaap-hq.org

Office Clerks, General

O*NET 43-9061.00

Significant Points

- Although most jobs are entry level, applicants with previous office experience, computer skills, and sound communication abilities may have an advantage.

- Plentiful job opportunities will stem from employment growth, the large size of the occupation, and high replacement needs.

Nature of the Work

Rather than performing a single specialized task, the daily responsibilities of general office clerks change with the needs of the specific job and the employer. Whereas some clerks spend their days filing or typing, others enter data at a computer terminal. They can also be called upon to operate photocopiers, fax machines, and other office equipment; prepare mailings; proofread copies; and answer telephones and deliver messages.

The specific duties assigned to a clerk vary significantly, depending upon the type of office in which a clerk works. An office clerk in a doctor's office, for example, would not perform the same tasks as a clerk in a large financial institution or in the office of an auto-parts wholesaler. Although they may sort checks, keep payroll records, take inventory, and access information, clerks also perform duties unique to their employer, such as organizing medications, making transparencies for a presentation, or filling orders received by fax machine.

The specific duties assigned to a clerk also vary by level of experience. Whereas inexperienced employees make photocopies, stuff envelopes, or record inquiries, experienced clerks usually are given additional responsibilities. For example, they may maintain financial or other records, set up spreadsheets, verify statistical reports for accuracy and completeness, handle and adjust customer complaints, work with vendors, make travel arrangements, take inventory of equipment and supplies, answer questions on departmental services and functions, or help prepare invoices or budgetary requests. Senior office clerks may be expected to monitor and direct the work of lower level clerks.

Working Conditions

For the most part, general office clerks work in comfortable office settings. Those on full-time schedules usually work a standard 40-hour week; however, some work shifts or overtime during busy periods. About 1 in 4 clerks works part-time, and about 1 in 10 works on a temporary basis.

Employment

General office clerks held about 2.7 million jobs in 2000. Most are employed in relatively small businesses. Although they work in every sector of the economy, more than 60 percent worked in the services and wholesale and retail trade industries.

Training, Other Qualifications, and Advancement

Although most office clerk jobs are entry-level administrative support positions, some previous office or business experience may be needed. Employers usually require a high school diploma, and some require typing, basic computer skills, and other general office skills. Familiarity with computer word-processing software and applications is becoming increasingly important.

Training for this occupation is available through business education programs offered in high schools, community and junior colleges, and postsecondary vocational schools. Courses in word processing, other computer applications, and office practices are particularly helpful.

Because general office clerks usually work with other office staff, they should be cooperative and able to work as part of a team. Employers prefer individuals who are able to perform a variety of tasks and satisfy the needs of the many departments within a company. In addition, applicants should have good communication skills, be detail-oriented, and adaptable.

General office clerks who exhibit strong communication, interpersonal, and analytical skills may be promoted to supervisory positions. Others may move into different, more senior clerical or administrative jobs, such as receptionist, secretary, or administrative assistant. After gaining some work experience or specialized skills, many workers transfer to jobs with higher pay or greater advancement potential. Advancement to professional occupations within an establishment normally requires additional formal education, such as a college degree.

Job Outlook

Employment of general office clerks is expected to grow about as fast as the average for all occupations through the year 2010. Employment growth, the large size of the occupation, and high replacement needs should result in plentiful job opportunities for general office clerks in many industries. Furthermore, growth in part-time and temporary clerical positions will lead to a large number of job openings. Prospects should be brightest for those who have knowledge of basic computer applications and office machinery, such as fax machines and copiers. Job opportunities will also be most favorable for those with good writing and communication skills. As general clerical duties continue to be consolidated and the ability to perform multiple tasks becomes increasingly necessary, employers will seek well-rounded individuals with highly developed communication skills.

The employment outlook for general office clerks will be affected by the increasing use of computers, expanding office automation, and the consolidation of clerical tasks. Automation has led to productivity gains, allowing a wide variety of duties to be performed by few office workers. However, automation also has led to a consolidation of clerical staffs and a diversification of job responsibilities. This consolidation increases the demand for general office clerks, because they perform a variety of clerical tasks. It will become increasingly common within small businesses to find a single general office clerk in charge of all clerical work.

Job opportunities may vary from year to year, because the strength of the economy affects demand for general office clerks. Companies tend to hire more when the economy is strong. Industries least likely to be affected by economic fluctuation tend to be the most stable places for employment.

Earnings

Median annual earnings of general office clerks were $21,130 in 2000; the middle 50 percent earned between $16,710 and $26,670 annually. Ten percent earned less than $13,650, and 10 percent more than $33,050.

Median annual salaries in the industries employing the largest numbers of general office clerks in 2000 are shown in the following:

State government	$24,830
Local government	24,100
Commercial banks	22,320
Hospitals	22,310
Elementary and secondary schools	21,560
Offices and clinics of medical doctors	20,440
Colleges and universities	20,220
Personnel supply services	19,510

Related Occupations

The duties of general office clerks can include a combination of bookkeeping, typing, office machine operation, and filing. Other office and administrative support workers who perform similar duties include information and record clerks, and secretaries and administrative assistants. Nonclerical entry-level workers include cashiers, medical assistants, and food and beverage serving and related workers.

Sources of Additional Information

State employment service offices and agencies can provide information about job openings for general office clerks.

Ophthalmic Laboratory Technicians

O*NET 51-9083.01, 51-9083.02

Significant Points

● Nearly all ophthalmic laboratory technicians learn their skills on the job.

● Increasing use of automated equipment will result in relatively slow job growth.

● Only a small number of job openings will be created each year because the occupation is small and slower-than-average growth is expected.

Nature of the Work

Ophthalmic laboratory technicians—also known as *manufacturing opticians*, *optical mechanics* or *optical goods workers*—make prescription eyeglass or contact lenses. Prescription lenses are curved in such a way that light is correctly focused onto the retina of the patient's eye, improving vision. Some ophthalmic laboratory technicians manufacture lenses for other optical instruments, such as telescopes and binoculars. Ophthalmic laboratory technicians cut, grind, edge, and finish lenses according to specifications provided by dispensing opticians, optometrists, or ophthalmologists. They also may insert lenses into frames to produce finished glasses. Although some lenses still are produced by hand, technicians increasingly use automated equipment to make lenses.

Ophthalmic laboratory technicians should not be confused with workers in other vision care occupations. Ophthalmologists and optometrists are "eye doctors" who examine eyes, diagnose and treat vision problems, and prescribe corrective lenses. Ophthalmologists are physicians who perform eye surgery. Dispensing opticians, who also may do work described here, help patients select frames and lenses, and adjust finished eyeglasses.

Ophthalmic laboratory technicians read prescription specifications, then select standard glass or plastic lens blanks and mark them to indicate where the curves specified on the prescription should be ground. They place the lens in the lens grinder, set the dials for the prescribed curvature, and start the machine. After a minute or so, the lens is ready to be "finished" by a machine that rotates it against a fine abrasive to grind it and smooth out rough edges. The lens is then placed in a polishing machine with an even finer abrasive, to polish it to a smooth, bright finish.

Next, the technician examines the lens through a lensometer, an instrument similar in shape to a microscope, to make sure the degree and placement of the curve is correct. The technician then cuts the lenses and bevels the edges to fit the frame, dips each lens into dye if the prescription calls for tinted or coated lenses, polishes the edges, and assembles the lenses and frame parts into a finished pair of glasses.

In small laboratories, technicians usually handle every phase of the operation. In large ones, technicians may be responsible for operating computerized equipment where virtually every phase of the operation is automated. Technicians also inspect the final product for quality and accuracy.

Working Conditions

Ophthalmic laboratory technicians work in relatively clean and well-lighted laboratories and have limited contact with the public. Surroundings are relatively quiet despite the humming of machines. At times, technicians wear goggles to protect their eyes, and may spend a great deal of time standing.

Most ophthalmic laboratory technicians work a 5-day, 40-hour week, which may include weekends, evenings, or occasionally some overtime. Some work part-time.

Ophthalmic laboratory technicians need to take precautions against the hazards associated with cutting glass, handling chemicals, and working near machinery.

Employment

Ophthalmic laboratory technicians held about 32,000 jobs in 2000. Thirty-one percent were in retail optical stores that manufacture and sell prescription glasses and contact lenses, and 23 percent were in optical laboratories. These laboratories manufacture eyewear and contact lenses for sale by retail stores, as well as by ophthalmologists and optometrists. Most of the rest were in wholesalers or in optical laboratories that manufacture lenses for other optical instruments, such as telescopes and binoculars.

Training, Other Qualifications, and Advancement

Nearly all ophthalmic laboratory technicians learn their skills on the job. Employers filling trainee jobs prefer applicants who are high school graduates. Courses in science, mathematics, and computers are valuable; manual dexterity and the ability to do precision work are essential.

Technician trainees producing lenses by hand start on simple tasks such as marking or blocking lenses for grinding, then progress to lens grinding, lens cutting, edging, beveling, and eyeglass assembly. Depending on individual aptitude, it may take up to 6 months to become proficient in all phases of the work.

Technicians using automated systems will find computer skills valuable. Training is completed on the job and varies in duration depending on the type of machinery and individual aptitude.

A very small number of ophthalmic laboratory technicians learn their trade in the armed forces or in the few programs in optical technology offered by vocational-technical institutes or trade schools. These programs have classes in optical theory, surfacing and lens finishing, and the reading and applying of prescriptions. Programs vary in length from 6 months to 1 year and award certificates or diplomas.

Ophthalmic laboratory technicians can become supervisors and managers. Some technicians become dispensing opticians, although further education or training generally is required.

Job Outlook

Overall employment of ophthalmic laboratory technicians is expected to grow more slowly than the average for all occupations through the year 2010. Employment is expected to increase slowly in manufacturing as firms invest in automated machinery.

Demographic trends make it likely that many more Americans will need vision care in the years ahead. Not only will the population grow, but also the proportion of middle-aged and older adults is projected to increase rapidly. Middle age is a time when many people use corrective lenses for the first time, and elderly persons usually require more vision care than others.

Fashion, too, influences demand. Frames come in a variety of styles and colors, which encourages people to buy more than one pair. Demand also is expected to grow in response to the availability of new technologies that improve the quality and look of corrective lenses, such as antireflective coatings and bifocal lenses without the line visible in traditional bifocals.

Most job openings will arise from the need to replace technicians who transfer to other occupations or leave the labor force. However, only a small number of job openings will be created each year because the occupation is small.

Earnings

Median hourly earnings of ophthalmic laboratory technicians were $9.88 in 2000. The middle 50 percent earned between $8.25 and $12.07 an hour. The lowest 10 percent earned less than $7.19, and the highest 10 percent earned more than $14.71 an hour. In 2000, median hourly earnings of ophthalmic laboratory technicians were $10.25 in ophthalmic goods manufacturing and $9.79 in retail stores, not elsewhere classified, including optical goods stores.

Related Occupations

Workers in other precision production occupations include dental laboratory technicians, orthotists and prosthetists, and precision instrument and equipment repairers.

Sources of Additional Information

For a list of accredited programs in ophthalmic laboratory technology, contact:

- Commission on Opticianry Accreditation, 7023 Little River Turnpike, Suite 207, Annandale, VA 22003

State employment service offices can provide information about job openings for ophthalmic laboratory technicians.

Opticians, Dispensing

O*NET 29-2081.00

Significant Points

- Most dispensing opticians receive training on-the-job or through apprenticeships lasting 2 or more years; 22 states require a license.

- Projected employment growth reflects steadfast demand for corrective lenses and trends in fashion.

- The number of job openings will be relatively small because the occupation is small.

Nature of the Work

Dispensing opticians fit eyeglasses and contact lenses, following prescriptions written by ophthalmologists or Optometrists.

Dispensing opticians examine written prescriptions to determine lens specifications. They recommend eyeglass frames, lenses, and lens coatings after considering the prescription and the customer's occupation, habits, and facial features. Dispensing opticians measure clients' eyes, including the distance between the centers of the pupils and the distance between the eye surface and the lens. For customers without prescriptions, dispensing opticians may use a lensometer to record the present eyeglass prescription. They also may obtain a customer's previous record, or verify a prescription with the examining optometrist or ophthalmologist.

Dispensing opticians prepare work orders that give ophthalmic laboratory technicians information needed to grind and insert lenses into a frame. The work order includes lens prescriptions and information on lens size, material, color, and style. Some dispensing opticians grind and insert lenses themselves. After the glasses are made, dispensing opticians verify that the lenses have been ground to specifications. Then they may reshape or bend the frame, by hand or using pliers, so that the

eyeglasses fit the customer properly and comfortably. Some also fix, adjust, and refit broken frames. They instruct clients about adapting to, wearing, or caring for eyeglasses.

Some dispensing opticians specialize in fitting contacts, artificial eyes, or cosmetic shells to cover blemished eyes. To fit contact lenses, dispensing opticians measure eye shape and size, select the type of contact lens material, and prepare work orders specifying the prescription and lens size. Fitting contact lenses requires considerable skill, care, and patience. Dispensing opticians observe customers' eyes, corneas, lids, and contact lenses with special instruments and microscopes. During several visits, opticians show customers how to insert, remove, and care for their contacts, and ensure the fit is correct.

Dispensing opticians keep records on customer prescriptions, work orders, and payments; track inventory and sales; and perform other administrative duties.

Working Conditions

Dispensing opticians work indoors in attractive, well-lighted, and well-ventilated surroundings. They may work in medical offices or small stores where customers are served one at a time, or in large stores where several dispensing opticians serve a number of customers at once. Opticians spend a lot of time on their feet. If they prepare lenses, they need to take precautions against the hazards associated with glass cutting, chemicals, and machinery.

Most dispensing opticians work a 40-hour week, although some work longer hours. Those in retail stores may work evenings and weekends. Some work part-time.

Employment

Dispensing opticians held about 68,000 jobs in 2000. Almost half worked for ophthalmologists or Optometrists who sell glasses directly to patients. Many also work in retail optical stores that offer one-stop shopping. Customers may have their eyes examined, choose frames, and have glasses made on the spot. Some work in optical departments of drug and department stores.

Training, Other Qualifications, and Advancement

Employers usually hire individuals with no background in opticianry or those who have worked as Ophthalmic Laboratory Technicians and then provide the required training. Most dispensing opticians receive training on-the-job or through apprenticeships lasting 2 or more years. Some employers, however, seek people with postsecondary training in opticianry.

Knowledge of physics, basic anatomy, algebra, geometry, and mechanical drawing is particularly valuable because training usually includes instruction in optical mathematics, optical physics, and the use of precision measuring instruments and other machinery and tools. Dispensing opticians deal directly with the public, so they should be tactful, pleasant, and communicate well. Manual dexterity and the ability to do precision work are essential.

Large employers usually offer structured apprenticeship programs, and small employers provide more informal on-the-job training. In the 22 states that require dispensing opticians to be licensed, individuals without postsecondary training work from 2 to 4 years as apprentices. Apprenticeship or formal training is offered in most states as well.

Apprentices receive technical training and learn office management and sales. Under the supervision of an experienced optician, optometrist, or ophthalmologist, apprentices work directly with patients, fitting eyeglasses and contact lenses. In the 21 states requiring licensure, information about apprenticeships and licensing procedures is available from the state board of occupational licensing.

Formal opticianry training is offered in community colleges and a few colleges and universities. In 2000, the Commission on Opticianry Accreditation accredited 25 programs that awarded 2-year associate degrees in opticianry. There also are shorter programs of 1 year or less. Some states that offer a license to dispensing opticians allow graduates to take the licensure exam immediately upon graduation; others require a few months to a year of experience.

Dispensing opticians may apply to the American Board of Opticianry (ABO) and the National Contact Lens Examiners (NCLE) for certification of their skills. Certification must be renewed every 3 years through continuing education. Those licensed in states where licensing renewal requirements include continuing education credits may use proof of their renewed state license to meet the recertification requirements of the ABO. Likewise, the NCLE will accept proof of license renewal from any state that has contact lens requirements.

Many experienced dispensing opticians open their own optical stores. Others become managers of optical stores or sales representatives for wholesalers or manufacturers of eyeglasses or lenses.

Job Outlook

Employment of dispensing opticians is expected to increase about as fast as the average for all occupations through 2010 as demand grows for corrective lenses. The number of middle-aged and elderly persons is projected to increase rapidly. Middle age is a time when many individuals use corrective lenses for the first time, and elderly persons generally require more vision care than others.

Fashion, too, influences demand. Frames come in a growing variety of styles and colors, which encourages people to buy more than one pair. Demand also is expected to grow in response to the availability of new technologies that improve the quality and look of corrective lenses, such as anti-reflective coatings and bifocal lenses without the line visible in old-style bifocals. Improvements in bifocal, extended wear, and disposable contact lenses also will spur demand.

The need to replace those who leave the occupation will result in additional job openings. Nevertheless, the total number of job openings will be relatively small because the occupation is small. This occupation is vulnerable to changes in the business cycle because eyewear purchases often can be deferred for a time. Employment of opticians can fall somewhat during economic downturns.

Earnings

Median annual earnings of dispensing opticians were $24,430 in 2000. The middle 50 percent earned between $19,200 and $31,770. The lowest 10 percent earned less than $15,900, and the highest 10 percent earned more than $39,660.

Related Occupations

Other workers who deal with customers and perform delicate work include camera and photographic equipment repairers, dental laboratory technicians, jewelers and precious stone and metal workers, locksmiths and safe repairers, ophthalmic laboratory technicians, orthotists and prosthetists, and watch repairers.

Sources of Additional Information

For general information about a career as a dispensing optician and about continuing education, as well as a list of state licensing boards for opticianry, contact:

- Opticians Association of America, 7023 Little River Turnpike, Suite 207, Annandale, VA 22003. Internet: http://www.opticians.org

For general information about a career as a dispensing optician and a list of accredited training programs, contact:

- Commission on Opticianry Accreditation, 7023 Little River Turnpike, Suite 207, Annandale, VA 22003

For general information on opticianry and a list of home-study programs, seminars, and review materials, contact:

- National Academy of Opticianry, 8401 Corporate Dr., Suite 605, Landover, MD 20785. Internet: http://www.nao.org

To learn about voluntary certification for opticians who fit spectacles, as well as state licensing boards of opticianry, contact:

- American Board of Opticianry, 6506 Loisdale Rd., Suite 209, Springfield, VA 22150. Internet: http://www.abo.org

For information on voluntary certification for dispensing opticians who fit contact lenses, contact:

- National Contact Lens Examiners, 6506 Loisdale Rd., Suite 209, Springfield, VA 22150. Internet: http://www.abo.org

Order Clerks

O*NET 43-4151.00

Significant Points

- While overall employment of order clerks is expected to decline through the year 2010, numerous openings will become available each year to replace order clerks who transfer to other occupations or leave the labor force.

- Many openings will be for seasonal work, especially for catalogue companies or online retailers.

- A high school diploma or its equivalent is the most common educational requirement.

- Because many order clerks deal directly with the public, a professional appearance and pleasant personality are imperative.

Nature of the Work

Order clerks receive and process incoming orders for a wide variety of goods or services, such as spare parts for machines, consumer appliances, gas and electric power connections, film rentals, and articles of clothing. They sometimes are called order-entry clerks, sales representatives, order processors, or order takers.

Orders for materials, merchandise, or services can come from inside or from outside of an organization. In large companies with many work sites, such as automobile manufacturers, clerks order parts and equipment from the company's warehouses. Inside order clerks receive orders from other workers employed by the same company or from salespersons in the field.

Many other order clerks, however, receive orders from outside companies or individuals. Order clerks in wholesale businesses, for instance, receive orders from retail establishments for merchandise that the retailer, in turn, sells to the public. An increasing number of order clerks work for catalogue companies and online retailers, receiving orders from individual customers by telephone, fax, regular mail, or e-mail. Order clerks dealing primarily with the public sometimes are referred to as outside order clerks.

Computers provide order clerks with ready access to information such as stock numbers, prices, and inventory. The successful filling of an order frequently depends on having the right products in stock and being able to determine which products are most appropriate for the customer's needs. Some order clerks, especially those in industrial settings, must be able to give price estimates for entire jobs, not just single parts. Others must be able to take special orders, give expected arrival dates, prepare contracts, and handle complaints.

Many order clerks receive orders directly by telephone, entering the required information as the customer places the order. However, a rapidly increasing number of orders now are received through computer systems, the Internet, faxes, and e-mail. In some cases, these orders are sent directly from the customer's terminal to the order clerk's terminal. Orders received by regular mail are sometimes scanned into a database that is instantly accessible to clerks.

Clerks review orders for completeness and clarity. They may complete missing information or contact the customer for the information. Similarly, clerks contact customers if the customers need additional information, such as prices or shipping dates, or if delays in filling the order are anticipated. For orders received by regular mail, clerks extract checks or money orders, sort them, and send them for processing.

After an order has been verified and entered, the customer's final cost is calculated. The clerk then routes the order to the proper department, such as the warehouse, that actually sends out or delivers the item in question.

In organizations with sophisticated computer systems, inventory records are adjusted automatically, as sales are made. In less automated organizations, order clerks may adjust inventory records. Clerks also may notify other departments when inventories are low or when filling certain orders would deplete supplies.

Some order clerks must establish priorities in filling orders. For example, an order clerk in a blood bank may receive a request from a hospital for a certain type of blood. The clerk must first find out if the request is routine or an emergency, and then take appropriate action.

Working Conditions

Most order clerks work in areas that are clean, well lit, and relatively quiet. Because a number of clerks may share the same workspace, it may be crowded and noisy.

Although most order clerks work a standard 40-hour week, some jobs may require working evenings, late night shifts, and weekends.

The work performed by order clerks may be repetitious and stressful. Stress is caused by technology that enables management to electronically monitor use of computer systems, tape record telephone calls, or limit the time spent on each call. In addition, prolonged exposure to a video display terminal may lead to eyestrain for the many order clerks who work with computers.

Employment

Order clerks held about 348,000 jobs in 2000. About one-half were in wholesale and retail establishments and about one-fifth were in manufacturing firms. Most of the remaining jobs for order clerks were in business services.

Training, Other Qualifications, and Advancement

Although hiring requirements for order clerks vary from industry to industry, a high school diploma or its equivalent is the most common educational requirement. Specialized order clerks in technical positions obtain their training from technical institutes and 2- and 4-year colleges. Increasingly, familiarity or experience with computers and good interpersonal skills is important to employers.

Many order clerks deal with the public, so a pleasant personality is important. A clear speaking voice and fluency in the English language also are essential because these employees frequently use the telephone or public address systems. Good spelling and computer literacy often are needed, particularly because most work involves considerable computer use.

Orientation and training for order clerks usually take place on the job. Under the guidance of a supervisor or other senior workers, new employees learn company procedures. Some formal classroom training also may be necessary, such as training in specific computer software. Most order clerks continue to receive instruction on new procedures and company policies after their initial training ends.

Order clerks positions can offer good opportunities for qualified workers to get started in the business. Advancement usually comes by transfer to a position with more responsibilities or by promotion to a supervisory position. Most companies fill office and administrative support supervisory and managerial positions by promoting individuals within their organization, so clerks who acquire additional skills, experience, and training improve their advancement opportunities.

Job Outlook

Job openings for order clerks should be limited, as improvements in technology and office automation continue to increase worker productivity. While overall employment of order clerks is expected to decline through the year 2010, numerous openings will become available each year to replace order clerks who transfer to other occupations or leave the labor force completely. Many of these openings will be for seasonal work, especially in catalogue companies or online retailers catering to holiday gift buyers.

The growth in online retailing, business-to-business electronic commerce, and the use of automated systems that make placing orders easy and convenient will decrease demand for order clerks. The spread of electronic data interchange, a system enabling computers to communicate directly with each other, allows orders within establishments to be placed with little human intervention. Besides electronic data interchange, extranets and other internal systems allowing a firm's employees to place orders directly are increasingly common. Outside orders placed over the Internet often are entered directly into the computer by the customer; thus, the order clerk is not involved at all in placing the order. Some companies also use automated phone menus accessible with a touch-tone phone to receive orders, and others use answering machines. Developments in voice recognition technology may further reduce the demand for order clerks.

Furthermore, increased automation will allow current order clerks to be more productive, as each clerk is able to handle an increasingly higher volume of orders. Sophisticated inventory control and automatic billing systems permit companies to track inventory and accounts with much less help from order clerks than in the past.

Earnings

In 2000, median annual earnings for order clerks were $23,620.

In addition to their hourly wage, full-time order clerks who work evenings, nights, weekends, or holidays may receive shift differential pay.

Related Occupations

A number of other workers deal with the public, receive and provide information, or direct people to others who can assist them. Among these are dispatchers, security guards and gaming surveillance workers, tellers, and counter and rental clerks.

Sources of Additional Information

State employment service offices can provide information about employment opportunities.

Painters and Paperhangers

O*NET 47-2141.00, 47-2142.00

Significant Points

- Working conditions can be hazardous.

- Most workers learn informally on the job as helpers; however, training authorities recommend completion of an apprenticeship program.

- Due to worker turnover, employment prospects should be good.

Nature of the Work

Paint and wall coverings make surfaces clean, attractive, and bright. In addition, paints and other sealers protect outside walls from wear caused by exposure to the weather. Although some people do both painting and paperhanging, each requires different skills.

Painters apply paint, stain, varnish, and other finishes to buildings and other structures. They choose the right paint or finish for the surface to be covered, taking into account durability, ease of handling, method of application, and customers' wishes. Painters first prepare the surfaces to be covered, so that the paint will adhere properly. This may require removing the old coat of paint by stripping, sanding, wire brushing, burning, or water and abrasive blasting. Painters also wash walls and trim to remove dirt and grease, fill nail holes and cracks, sandpaper rough spots, and brush off dust. On new surfaces, they apply a primer or sealer to prepare the surface for the finish coat. Painters also mix paints and match colors, relying on knowledge of paint composition and color harmony. In large paint shops or hardware stores, these functions are automated.

There are several ways to apply paint and similar coverings. Painters must be able to choose the right paint applicator for each job, depending on the surface to be covered, the characteristics of the finish, and other factors. Some jobs need only a good bristle brush with a soft, tapered edge; others require a dip or fountain pressure roller; still others can best be done using a paint sprayer. Many jobs need several types of applicators. The right tools for each job not only expedite the painter's work but also produce the most attractive surface.

When working on tall buildings, painters erect scaffolding, including "swing stages," scaffolds suspended by ropes, or cables attached to roof hooks. When painting steeples and other conical structures, they use a bosun's chair, a swing-like device.

Paperhangers cover walls and ceilings with decorative wall coverings made of paper, vinyl, or fabric. They first prepare the surface to be covered by applying "sizing," which seals the surface and makes the covering stick better. When redecorating, they may first remove the old covering by soaking, steaming, or applying solvents. When necessary, they patch holes and take care of other imperfections before hanging the new wall covering.

After the surface has been prepared, paperhangers must prepare the paste or other adhesive. Then, they measure the area to be covered, check the covering for flaws, cut the covering into strips of the proper size, and closely examine the pattern to match it when the strips are hung.

The next step is to brush or roll the adhesive onto the back of the covering and to then place the strips on the wall or ceiling, making sure the pattern is matched, the strips are hung straight, and the edges are butted together to make tight, closed seams. Finally, paperhangers smooth the strips to remove bubbles and wrinkles, trim the top and bottom with a razor knife, and wipe off any excess adhesive.

Working Conditions

Most painters and paperhangers work 40 hours a week or less; about 1 out of 10 works part-time. Painters and paperhangers must stand for long periods. Their jobs also require a considerable amount of climbing and bending. These workers must have stamina, because much of the work is done with their arms raised overhead. Painters often work outdoors but seldom in wet, cold, or inclement weather.

Painters and paperhangers risk injury from slips or falls off ladders and scaffolds. They sometimes may work with materials that can be hazardous if masks are not worn or if ventilation is poor. Some painting jobs can leave a worker covered with paint.

Employment

Painters and paperhangers held about 518,000 jobs in 2000; most were painters. More than 1 out of every 3 painters and paperhangers works for contractors engaged in new construction, repair, restoration, or remodeling work. In addition, organizations that own or manage large buildings—such as apartment complexes—employ maintenance painters, as do some schools, hospitals, factories, and government agencies.

Self-employed independent painting contractors accounted for 47 percent of all painters and paperhangers. This is significantly greater than the corresponding proportion of building trades workers in general.

Training, Other Qualifications, and Advancement

Painting and paperhanging are learned through apprenticeship or informal, on-the-job instruction. Although training authorities recommend completion of an apprenticeship program as the best way to become a painter or paperhanger, most painters learn the trade informally on the job as a helper to an experienced painter. Few opportunities for informal training exist for paperhangers because few paperhangers have a need for helpers.

The apprenticeship for painters and paperhangers consists of 3 to 4 years of on-the-job training, in addition to 144 hours of related classroom instruction each year. Apprentices receive instruction in color harmony, use and care of tools and equipment, surface preparation, application techniques, paint mixing and matching, characteristics of different finishes, blueprint reading, wood finishing, and safety.

Whether a painter learns the trade through a formal apprenticeship or informally as a helper, on-the-job instruction covers similar skill areas. Under the direction of experienced workers, trainees carry supplies, erect scaffolds, and do simple painting and surface preparation tasks while they learn about paint and painting equipment. As they gain experience, trainees learn to prepare surfaces for painting and paperhanging, to mix paints, and to apply paint and wall coverings efficiently and neatly. Near the end of their training, they may learn decorating concepts, color coordination, and cost-estimating techniques. In addition to learning craft skills, painters must become familiar with safety and health regulations so that their work is in compliance with the law.

Apprentices or helpers generally must be at least 16 years old and in good physical condition. A high school education or its equivalent, with courses in mathematics, usually is required to enter an apprenticeship program. Applicants should have good manual dexterity and color sense.

Painters and paperhangers may advance to supervisory or estimating jobs with painting and decorating contractors. Many establish their own painting and decorating businesses.

Job Outlook

Job prospects should be good, as thousands of painters and paperhangers transfer to other occupations or leave the labor force each year. Because there are no strict training requirements for entry, many people with limited skills work as painters or paperhangers for a short time and then move on to other types of work. Many fewer openings will occur for paperhangers because the number of these jobs is comparatively small.

In addition to the need to replace experienced workers, new jobs will be created. Employment of painters and paperhangers is expected to grow about as fast as the average for all occupations through the year 2010, reflecting increases in the level of new construction and in the stock of buildings and other structures that require maintenance and renovation. Painting is very labor-intensive and not suitable to the kinds of technological changes that might make workers more productive and thus restrict employment growth.

Job seekers considering these occupations should expect some periods of unemployment, especially until they become fully skilled. Many construction projects are of short duration, and construction activity is cyclical and seasonal in nature. Remodeling, restoration, and maintenance projects, however, often provide many jobs for painters and paperhangers even when new construction activity declines. The most versatile painters and skilled paperhangers generally are best able to keep working steadily during downturns in the economy.

Earnings

In 2000, median hourly earnings of painters, construction and maintenance, were $13.10. The middle 50 percent earned between $10.36 and $16.81. The lowest 10 percent earned less than $8.56, and the highest 10 percent earned more than $22.39. Median hourly earnings in the industries employing the largest numbers of painters in 2000 are shown in the following table:

Painting and paper hanging	$13.03
Residential building construction	12.79
Real estate operators and lessors	10.95
Real estate agents and managers	10.77
Personnel supply services	10.63

In 2000, median earnings for paperhangers were $15.33. The middle 50 percent earned between $10.89 and $19.91. The lowest 10 percent earned less than $8.04, and the highest 10 percent earned more than $24.16. Earnings for painters may be reduced on occasion because of bad weather and the short-term nature of many construction jobs. Hourly wage rates for apprentices usually start at 40 to 50 percent of the rate for experienced workers and increase periodically.

Some painters and paperhangers are members of the International Brotherhood of Painters and Allied Trades. Some maintenance painters are members of other unions.

Related Occupations

Painters and paperhangers apply various coverings to decorate and protect wood, drywall, metal, and other surfaces. Other construction occupations in which workers do finishing work include carpenters; carpet, floor, and tile installers and finishers; drywall installers, ceiling tile installers, and tapers; and plasterers and stucco masons.

Sources of Additional Information

For details about painting and paperhanging apprenticeships or work opportunities, contact local painting and decorating contractors, a local of the International Brotherhood of Painters and Allied Trades, a local joint union-management apprenticeship committee, or an office of the state apprenticeship agency or employment service.

For general information about the work of painters and paperhangers, contact:

- International Brotherhood of Painters and Allied Trades, 1750 New York Ave. NW., Washington, DC 20006

For information on training programs, contact:

- Associated Builders and Contractors, 1300 N. 17th St., Arlington, VA 22209. Internet: http://www.abc.org

- Painting and Decorating Contractors of America, 3913 Old Lee Highway, Suite 33B, Fairfax, VA, 22030

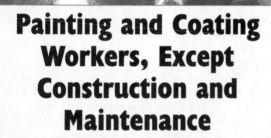

Painting and Coating Workers, Except Construction and Maintenance

O*NET 51-9121.01, 51-9121.02, 51-9122.00, 51-9123.00

Significant Points

- Most workers acquire their skills on the job; for most operators, training lasts from a few days to several months, but becoming skilled in all aspects of automotive painting usually requires 1 to 2 years.

- Employment growth for highly skilled transportation painters and automotive refinishers is projected to be slightly faster than for lesser skilled painting, coating, and spraying machine operators.

Nature of the Work

Millions of items ranging from cars to candy are covered by paint, plastic, varnish, chocolate, or some other type of coating solution. Often the protection provided by the paint or coating is essential to the product, as with the coating of insulating material covering wires and other electrical and electronic components. Many paints and coatings have dual purposes, such as the paint finish on an automobile, which heightens the visual appearance of the vehicle while providing protection from corrosion.

Painting, coating, and spraying machine setters, operators, and tenders control the machinery that applies these paints and coatings to a wide range of manufactured products. Perhaps the most straightforward technique is simply dipping an item in a large vat of paint or other coating. This is the technique used by *dippers*, who immerse racks or baskets of articles in vats of paint, liquid plastic, or other solutions using a power hoist. Similarly, *tumbling barrel painters* deposit articles made of porous materials in a barrel of paint, varnish, or other coating, which is then rotated to insure thorough coverage.

Another familiar technique is spraying products with a solution of paint or other coating. *Spray-machine operators* use spray guns to coat metal, wood, ceramic, fabric, paper, and food products with paint and other coating solutions. Following a formula, operators fill the equipment's tanks with a mixture of paints or chemicals, adding prescribed amounts of solution. They adjust nozzles on the spray guns to obtain the proper dispersion of the spray and hold or position the guns to direct the spray onto the article. Operators also check the flow and viscosity of the paint or solution and visually inspect the quality of the coating. When products are drying, these workers often must regulate the temperature and air circulation in drying ovens. Individuals who paint, coat, or decorate articles such as furniture, glass, pottery, toys, and books are known as *painting, coating, and decorating workers*.

Painting workers use various types of machines to coat a range of products. Often, their job title reflects the specialized nature of the machine or the coating being applied. For example, *enrobing machine operators* coat, or "enrobe," confectionery, bakery, and other food products with melted chocolate, cheese, oils, sugar, or other substances. *Paper coating machine operators* spray "size" on rolls of paper to give it its gloss or finish. And *silvering applicators* spray silver, tin, and copper solutions on glass in the manufacture of mirrors.

In response to concerns about air pollution and worker safety, manufacturers increasingly use new types of paints and coatings on their products instead of high-solvent paints. Water-based paints and powder coatings are two of the most common. These compounds do not emit as many volatile organic compounds into the air and can be applied to a variety of products. Powder coatings are sprayed much like liquid paints and then heated to melt and cure the coating.

The adoption of new types of paints often is accompanied by a conversion to more automated painting equipment that the operator sets and monitors. When using these machines, operators position the automatic spray guns, set the nozzles, and synchronize the action of the guns with the speed of the conveyor carrying articles through the machine and drying ovens. The operator also may add solvents or water to the paint vessel that prepares the paint for application. During operation, these workers tend painting machines, observe gauges on the control panel, and randomly check articles for evidence of any variation from specifications. The operator then uses a spray gun to "touch up" spots where necessary.

Although the majority of workers are employed in manufacturing, the best known group of these workers refinish old and damaged cars, trucks, and buses in automotive body repair and paintshops. *Transportation equipment* or *automotive painters* are among the most highly skilled manual spray operators because they perform intricate, detailed work and mix paints to match the original color, a task that is especially difficult if the color has faded.

To prepare a vehicle for painting, painters or their helpers use power sanders and sandpaper to remove the original paint or rust, and then fill small dents and scratches with body filler. They also remove or mask parts they do not want to paint, such as chrome trim, headlights, windows, and mirrors. Automotive painters use a spray gun to apply several coats of paint. They apply lacquer, enamel, or water-based primers to vehicles with metal bodies, and flexible primers to newer vehicles with plastic body parts. Controlling the spray gun by hand, they apply successive coats until the finish of the repaired sections of the vehicle matches that of the original undamaged portions. To speed drying between coats, they may place the freshly painted vehicle under heat lamps or in a special infrared oven. After each coat of primer dries, they sand the surface to remove any irregularities and to improve the adhesion of the next coat. Final sanding of the primers may be done by hand with a fine grade of sandpaper. A sealer then is applied and allowed to dry, followed by the final topcoat. When lacquer is used, painters or their helpers usually polish the finished surface after the final coat has dried.

Working Conditions

Painting and coating workers typically work indoors and may be exposed to dangerous fumes from paint and coating solutions. Although painting usually is done in special ventilated booths, many operators wear masks or respirators that cover their noses and mouths. In addition, the Clean Air Act of 1990 has led to a decrease in workers' exposure to hazardous chemicals by regulating emissions of volatile organic compounds from paints and other chemicals. This legislation also has led to increasing use of more sophisticated paint booths and fresh air systems which provide a safer work environment.

Operators have to stand for long periods of time and, when using a spray gun, they may have to bend, stoop, or crouch in uncomfortable positions to reach different parts of the article. Most operators work a normal 40-hour week, but self-employed automotive painters sometimes work more than 50 hours a week, depending on the number of vehicles customers want repainted.

Employment

Painting and coating workers held about 195,000 jobs in 2000. Lesser skilled coating, painting, and spraying machine setters, operators, and tenders accounted for about 108,000 jobs, while more skilled transportation equipment painters accounted for about 49,000. About 38,000 workers were painting, coating, and decorating workers.

Seventy-one percent of jobs for salaried workers were found in manufacturing establishments, where they applied coatings to items such as fabricated metal products, motor vehicles and related equipment, industrial machines, household and office furniture, and plastics, wood, and paper products. Other workers included automotive painters employed by independent automotive repair shops and body repair and paintshops operated by retail motor vehicle dealers. About 7 percent of painting and coating machine operators were self-employed; most of these were transportation equipment painters.

Training, Other Qualifications, and Advancement

Most painting and coating workers acquire their skills on the job, usually by watching and helping other experienced workers. For most setters, operators and tenders, as well as painting, coating, and decorating workers, training lasts from a few days to several months. Coating, painting, and spraying machine setters, operators, and tenders who modify the operation of computer-controlled equipment during operation may require additional training in computer operations and minor programming.

Similarly, most transportation equipment painters start as helpers and gain their skills informally on the job. Becoming skilled in all aspects of automotive painting usually requires 1 to 2 years of on-the-job training. Beginning helpers usually remove trim, clean and sand surfaces to be painted, mask surfaces that they do not want painted, and polish finished work. As helpers gain experience, they progress to more complicated tasks, such as mixing paint to achieve a good match and using spray guns to apply primer coats or final coats to small areas.

Painters should have keen eyesight and a good sense of color. Completion of high school generally is not required but is advantageous. Additional instruction is offered at many community colleges and vocational or technical schools. Such programs enhance one's employment prospects and can speed promotion to the next level.

Some employers sponsor training programs to help their workers become more productive. This training is available from manufacturers of chemicals, paints, or equipment or from other private sources. It may include safety and quality tips and knowledge of products, equipment, and general business practices. Some automotive painters are sent to technical schools to learn the intricacies of mixing and applying different types of paint.

Voluntary certification by the National Institute for Automotive Service Excellence (ASE) is recognized as the standard of achievement for automotive painters. For certification, painters must pass a written examination and have at least 2 years of experience in the field. High school, trade or vocational school, or community or junior college training in automotive painting and refinishing may substitute for up to 1 year of experience. To retain certification, painters must retake the examination at least every 5 years.

Experienced painting and coating workers with leadership ability may become team leaders or supervisors. Those who acquire practical experience or college or other formal training may become sales or technical representatives for chemical or paint companies. Eventually, some automotive painters open their own shops.

Job Outlook

Overall employment of painting and coating workers is expected to grow about as fast as the average for all occupations through the year 2010. Employment growth for highly skilled transportation painters and automotive refinishers is projected to be slightly faster than for lesser skilled painting, coating, and spraying machine operators. In addition to job growth, some jobs will become available each year as employers replace experienced operators who transfer to other occupations or leave the labor force.

An increasing population demanding more manufactured goods will spur employment growth among coating, painting, and spraying machine operators. Similarly, increasing demand for hand-painted tiles and related specialty products will lead to growth among painting, coating, and decorating workers. Employment growth will be limited, however, by improvements in the automation of paint and coating applications that will raise worker productivity. For example, operators will be able to coat goods more rapidly as they use sophisticated industrial robots that move and aim spray guns increasingly more like humans; as the cost of robots continues to fall, they will be more widely used. The Clean Air Act of 1990, which sets limits on the emissions of ozone-forming volatile organic compounds, also is expected to impede the employment growth of operators in manufacturing because firms tend to introduce more efficient automation as they switch to water-based and powder coatings to comply with the law.

Because the detailed work of refinishing automobiles in collision repair shops and motor vehicle dealerships does not lend itself to automation, painters employed in these establishments are projected to experience slightly faster growth. As the demand for refinishing continues to grow, slower productivity growth among these workers will lead to employment increases more in line with the growing demand for their services.

The number of job openings for painting and coating workers may fluctuate from year to year due to cyclical changes in economic conditions. When demand for manufactured goods lessens, production may be suspended or reduced, and workers may be laid off or face a shortened workweek. Automotive painters, on the other hand, can expect relatively steady work because automobiles damaged in accidents require repair and refinishing regardless of the state of the economy.

Earnings

Median hourly earnings of coating, painting, and spraying machine setters, operators, and tenders, were $11.37 in 2000. The middle 50 percent earned between $9.11 and $14.11 an hour. The lowest 10 percent earned less than $7.54, and the highest 10 percent earned more than $17.65 an hour.

Median hourly earnings of transportation equipment painters were $14.64 in 2000. The middle 50 percent earned between $11.43 and $19.45 an hour. The lowest 10 percent earned less than $9.12, and the highest 10 percent earned more than $24.79 an hour. Median hourly earnings of transportation equipment painters were $14.45 in automotive repair shops and $18.77 in motor vehicle and equipment manufacturing.

Median hourly earnings of painting, coating, and decorating workers were $9.55 in 2000. The middle 50 percent earned between $7.56 and $12.48 an hour. The lowest 10 percent earned less than $6.45, and the highest 10 percent earned more than $16.07 an hour.

Many automotive painters employed by motor vehicle dealers and independent automotive repair shops receive a commission based on the labor cost charged to the customer. Under this method, earnings depend largely on the amount of work a painter does and how fast it is completed. Employers frequently guarantee commissioned painters a minimum weekly salary. Helpers and trainees usually receive an hourly rate until they become sufficiently skilled to work on commission. Trucking companies, bus lines, and other organizations that repair and refinish their own vehicles usually pay by the hour.

Many painting and coating machine operators belong to unions. Most union operators work for manufacturers and the larger motor vehicle dealers.

Related Occupations

Other occupations in which workers apply paints and coatings include painters and paperhangers, woodworker, and machine setters, operators, and tenders—metal and plastic.

Sources of Additional Information

For more details about work opportunities, contact local manufacturers, automotive body repair shops, motor vehicle dealers, and vocational schools; locals of unions representing these workers; or the local office of the state employment service. The state employment service also may be a source of information about training programs.

Information on how to become a certified automotive painter is available from:

● National Institute for Automotive Service Excellence (ASE), 101 Blue Seal Dr. S.E., Leesburg, VA 20175. Internet: http://www.asecert.org

Paralegals and Legal Assistants

O*NET 23-2011.00

Significant Points

● While some paralegals train on the job, employers increasingly prefer graduates of postsecondary paralegal education programs, especially graduates of 4-year paralegal programs or college graduates who have completed paralegal certificate programs.

● Paralegals are projected to rank among the fastest growing occupations in the economy, as they increasingly perform many legal tasks formerly carried out by lawyers.

● Stiff competition is expected, as the number of graduates of paralegal training programs and others seeking to enter the profession outpaces job growth.

Nature of the Work

While lawyers assume ultimate responsibility for legal work, they often delegate many of their tasks to paralegals. In fact, paralegals—also called legal assistants—continue to assume a growing range of tasks in the nation's legal offices and perform many of the same tasks as lawyers. Nevertheless, they are still explicitly prohibited from carrying out duties that are considered to be the practice of law, such as setting legal fees, giving legal advice, and presenting cases in court.

One of a paralegal's most important tasks is helping Lawyers prepare for closings, hearings, trials, and corporate meetings. Paralegals investigate the facts of cases and ensure that all relevant information is considered. They also identify appropriate laws, judicial decisions, legal articles, and other materials that are relevant to assigned cases. After they analyze and organize the information, paralegals may prepare written reports that attorneys use in determining how cases should be handled. Should attorneys decide to file lawsuits on behalf of clients, paralegals may help prepare the legal arguments, draft pleadings and motions to be filed with the court, obtain affidavits, and assist attorneys during trials. Paralegals also organize and track files of important case documents and make them available and easily accessible to attorneys.

In addition to this preparatory work, paralegals also perform a number of other vital functions. For example, they help draft contracts, mortgages, separation agreements, and trust instruments. They also may assist in preparing tax returns and planning estates. Some paralegals coordinate the activities of other law office employees and maintain financial office records. Various additional tasks may differ, depending on the employer.

Paralegals are found in all types of organizations, but most are employed by law firms, corporate legal departments, and various government offices. In these organizations, they may work in all areas of the law, including litigation, personal injury, corporate law, criminal law, employee benefits, intellectual property, labor law, bankruptcy, immigration, family law, and real estate. Within specialties, functions often are broken down further so that paralegals may deal with a specific area. For example, paralegals specializing in labor law may deal exclusively with employee benefits.

The duties of paralegals also differ widely based on the type of organization in which they are employed. Paralegals who work for corporations often assist attorneys with employee contracts, shareholder agreements, stock-option plans, and employee benefit plans. They also may help prepare and file annual financial reports, maintain corporate minute books and resolutions, and secure loans for the corporation. Paralegals often monitor and review government regulations to ensure that the corporation operates within the law.

The duties of paralegals who work in the public sector usually vary within each agency. In general, they analyze legal material for internal use, maintain reference files, conduct research for attorneys, and collect and analyze evidence for agency hearings. They may then prepare informative or explanatory material on laws, agency regulations, and agency policy for general use by the agency and the public. Paralegals employed in community legal-service projects help the poor, the aged, and others in need of legal assistance. They file forms, conduct research, prepare documents, and when authorized by law, may represent clients at administrative hearings.

Paralegals in small and medium-sized law firms usually perform a variety of duties that require a general knowledge of the law. For example, they may research judicial decisions on improper police arrests or help prepare a mortgage contract. Paralegals employed by large law firms, government agencies, and corporations, however, are more likely to specialize in one aspect of the law.

Computer use and technical knowledge has become essential to paralegal work. Computer software packages and the Internet are increasingly used to search legal literature stored in computer databases and on CD-ROM. In litigation involving many supporting documents, paralegals may use computer databases to retrieve, organize, and index various materials. Imaging software allows paralegals to scan documents directly into a database, while billing programs help them to track hours billed to clients. Computer software packages also may be used to perform tax computations and explore the consequences of possible tax strategies for clients.

Working Conditions

Paralegals employed by corporations and government usually work a standard 40-hour week. Although most paralegals work year round, some are temporarily employed during busy times of the year, then released when the workload diminishes. Paralegals who work for law firms sometimes work very long hours when they are under pressure to meet deadlines. Some law firms reward such loyalty with bonuses and additional time off.

These workers handle many routine assignments, particularly when they are inexperienced. As they gain experience, paralegals usually assume more varied tasks with additional responsibility. Paralegals do most of their work at desks in offices and law libraries. Occasionally, they travel to gather information and perform other duties.

Employment

Paralegals and legal assistants held about 188,000 jobs in 2000. Private law firms employed the vast majority; most of the remainder worked for corporate legal departments and various levels of government. Within the federal government, the U.S. Department of Justice is the largest employer, followed by the U.S. Departments of Treasury and Defense, and the Federal Deposit Insurance Corporation. Other employers include state and local governments, publicly funded legal-service centers, banks, real estate development companies, and insurance companies. A small number of paralegals own their own businesses and work as freelance legal assistants, contracting their services to attorneys or corporate legal departments.

Training, Other Qualifications, and Advancement

There are several ways to become a paralegal. Employers usually require formal paralegal training obtained through associate or bachelor's degree programs or through a certification program. Increasingly, employers prefer graduates of 4-year paralegal programs or college graduates who have completed paralegal certificate programs. Some employers prefer to train paralegals on the job, hiring college graduates with no legal experience or promoting experienced legal secretaries. Other entrants have experience in a technical field that is useful to law firms, such as a background in tax preparation for tax and estate practice, or nursing or health administration for personal injury practice.

More than 800 formal paralegal training programs are offered by 4-year colleges and universities, law schools, community and junior colleges, business schools, and proprietary schools. There are currently 247 programs approved by the American Bar Association (ABA). Although this approval is neither required nor sought by many programs, graduation from an ABA-approved program can enhance one's employment opportunities. The requirements for admission to these programs vary. Some require certain college courses or a bachelor's degree; others accept high school graduates or those with legal experience; and a few schools require standardized tests and personal interviews.

Paralegal programs include 2-year associate degree programs, 4-year bachelor's degree programs, and certificate programs that take only a few months to complete. Many certificate programs only require a high school diploma or GED for admission, but they usually are designed for students who already hold an associate or baccalaureate degree. Programs typically include courses on law and legal research techniques, in addition to courses covering specialized areas of law, such as real estate, estate planning and probate, litigation, family law, contracts, and criminal law. Many employers prefer applicants with specialized training.

The quality of paralegal training programs varies; the better programs usually include job placement. Programs increasingly include courses introducing students to the legal applications of computers. Many paralegal training programs include an internship in which students gain practical experience by working for several months in a private law firm, office of a public defender or attorney general, bank, corporate legal department, legal-aid organization, or government agency. Experience gained in internships is an asset when seeking a job after graduation. Prospective students should examine the experiences of recent graduates before enrolling in those programs.

Although most employers do not require certification, earning a voluntary certificate from a professional society may offer advantages in the labor market. The National Association of Legal Assistants, for example, has established standards for certification requiring various combinations of education and experience. Paralegals who meet these standards are eligible to take a 2-day examination, given three times each year at several regional testing centers. Those who pass this examination may use the designation Certified Legal Assistant (CLA). In addition, the Paralegal Advanced Competency Exam, established in 1996 and administered through the National Federation of Paralegal Associations, offers professional recognition to paralegals with a bachelor's degree and at least 2 years of experience. Those who pass this examination may use the designation Registered Paralegal (RP).

Paralegals must be able to document and present their findings and opinions to their supervising attorney. They need to understand legal terminology and have good research and investigative skills. Familiarity with the operation and applications of computers in legal research and litigation support also is increasingly important. Paralegals should stay informed of new developments in the laws that affect their area of practice. Participation in continuing legal education seminars allows paralegals to maintain and expand their legal knowledge.

Because paralegals frequently deal with the public, they should be courteous and uphold the ethical standards of the legal profession. The National Association of Legal Assistants, the National Federation of Paralegal Associations, and a few states have established ethical guidelines for paralegals to follow.

Paralegals usually are given more responsibilities and less supervision as they gain work experience. Experienced paralegals who work in large law firms, corporate legal departments, and government agencies may supervise and delegate assignments to other paralegals and clerical staff. Advancement opportunities also include promotion to managerial and other law-related positions within the firm or corporate legal department. However, some paralegals find it easier to move to another law firm when seeking increased responsibility or advancement.

Job Outlook

Paralegals and legal assistants are projected to rank among the fastest growing occupations in the economy through 2010. Employment growth stems from law firms and other employers with legal staffs increasingly hiring paralegals to lower the cost and increase the availability and efficiency of legal services. The majority of job openings for paralegals in the future will be new jobs created by rapid employment growth, but additional job openings will arise as people leave the occupation. Despite projections of fast employment growth, stiff competition for jobs should continue as the number of graduates of paralegal training programs and others seeking to enter the profession outpaces job growth.

Private law firms will continue to be the largest employers of paralegals, but a growing array of other organizations, such as corporate legal departments, insurance companies, real estate and title insurance firms, and banks will also continue to hire paralegals. Demand for paralegals is expected to grow as an increasing population requires additional legal services, especially in areas such as intellectual property, healthcare, international, elder, sexual harassment, and environmental law. The growth of prepaid legal plans also should contribute to the demand for legal services. Paralegal employment is expected to increase as organizations presently employing paralegals assign them a growing range of tasks, and as paralegals are increasingly employed in small and medium-sized

establishments. A growing number of experienced paralegals are expected to establish their own businesses.

Job opportunities for paralegals will expand in the public sector as well. Community legal-service programs, which provide assistance to the poor, aged, minorities, and middle-income families, will employ additional paralegals to minimize expenses and serve the most people. Federal, state, and local government agencies, consumer organizations, and the courts also should continue to hire paralegals in increasing numbers.

To a limited extent, paralegal jobs are affected by the business cycle. During recessions, demand declines for some discretionary legal services, such as planning estates, drafting wills, and handling real estate transactions. Corporations are less inclined to initiate litigation when falling sales and profits lead to fiscal belt tightening. As a result, full-time paralegals employed in offices adversely affected by a recession may be laid off or have their work hours reduced. On the other hand, during recessions, corporations and individuals are more likely to face other problems that require legal assistance, such as bankruptcies, foreclosures, and divorces. Paralegals, who provide many of the same legal services as Lawyers at a lower cost, tend to fare relatively better in difficult economic conditions.

Earnings

Earnings of paralegals and legal assistants vary greatly. Salaries depend on education, training, experience, type and size of employer, and geographic location of the job. In general, paralegals who work for large law firms or in large metropolitan areas earn more than those who work for smaller firms or in less populated regions. In 2000, full-time, wage and salary paralegals and legal assistants had median annual earnings of $35,360. The middle 50 percent earned between $28,700 and $45,010. The top 10 percent earned more than $56,060, while the bottom 10 percent earned less than $23,350. Median annual earnings in the industries employing the largest numbers of paralegals in 2000 were as follows:

Federal government	$48,560
Legal services	34,230
Local government	34,120
State government	32,680

According to the National Association of Legal Assistants, paralegals had an average salary of $38,000 in 2000. In addition to a salary, many paralegals received a bonus, which averaged about $2,400. According to the National Federation of Paralegal Associations, starting salaries of paralegals with 1 year or less experience averaged $38,100 in 1999.

Related Occupations

Several other occupations call for a specialized understanding of the law and the legal system, but do not require the extensive training of a lawyer. These include law clerks; title examiners, abstractors, and searchers; claims adjusters, appraisers, examiners, and investigators; and occupational health and safety specialists and technicians.

Sources of Additional Information

General information on a career as a paralegal can be obtained from:

- Standing Committee on Legal Assistants, American Bar Association, 541 North Fairbanks Court, Chicago, IL 60611. Internet: http://www.abanet.org

For information on the Certified Legal Assistant exam, schools that offer training programs in a specific state, and standards and guidelines for paralegals, contact:

- National Association of Legal Assistants, Inc., 1516 South Boston St., Suite 200, Tulsa, OK 74119. Internet: http://www.nala.org

Information on a career as a paralegal, schools that offer training programs, job postings for paralegals, the Paralegal Advanced Competency Exam, and local paralegal associations can be obtained from:

- National Federation of Paralegal Associations, P.O. Box 33108, Kansas City, MO 64114. Internet: http://www.paralegals.org

Information on paralegal training programs, including the pamphlet "How to Choose a Paralegal Education Program," may be obtained from:

- American Association for Paralegal Education, 2965 Flowers Road South, Atlanta, GA 30341. Internet: http://www.aafpe.org

Information on obtaining a position as a paralegal specialist with the federal government is available from the Office of Personnel Management (OPM) through a telephone-based system. Consult your telephone directory under U.S. Government for a local number or call (912) 757-3000; Federal Relay Service: (800) 877-8339. The first number is not toll free, and charges may result. Information also is available from the OPM Internet site: http://www.usajobs.opm.gov

Payroll and Timekeeping Clerks

O*NET 43-3051.00

Significant Points

- Most jobs require only a high school diploma.

- Numerous job opportunities should arise due to high turnover.

- Slower-than-average growth is expected in overall employment, reflecting the spread of computers and other office automation as well as organizational restructuring.

Nature of the Work

Payroll and timekeeping clerks perform a vital function, ensuring that employees are paid on time and that their paychecks are accurate. If inaccuracies arise, such as monetary errors or incorrect amounts of vacation time, these workers research and correct the records. In addition, they may also perform various other clerical tasks. Automated timekeeping systems that allow employees to directly enter their hours worked into a computer have eliminated much of the data entry and review by timekeepers and has elevated the job of payroll clerk. But in offices that have not automated this function, payroll and timekeeping clerks still perform many of the following functions.

The fundamental task of *timekeeping clerks* is distributing and collecting timecards each pay period. They review employee workcharts, timesheets, and timecards to ensure that information is properly recorded and that

records have the signatures of authorizing officials. In companies that bill for the time spent by staff, such as law or accounting firms, timekeeping clerks make sure the hours recorded are charged to the correct job, so clients can be properly billed. These clerks also review computer reports listing timecards that cannot be processed because of errors, and they contact the employee or the employee's supervisor to resolve the problem. In addition, timekeeping clerks are responsible for informing managers and other employees of procedural changes in payroll policies.

Payroll clerks, also called payroll technicians, screen timecards for calculating, coding, or other errors. They compute pay by subtracting allotments, including federal and state taxes, retirement, insurance, and savings, from gross earnings. Increasingly, computers perform these calculations and alert payroll clerks to problems or errors in the data. In small organizations, or for new employees whose records are not yet entered into a computer system, clerks may perform the necessary calculations manually. In some small offices, clerks or other employees in the accounting department process payroll.

Payroll clerks record changes in employee addresses; close out files when workers retire, resign, or transfer; and advise employees on income tax withholding and other mandatory deductions. They also issue and record adjustments to pay because of previous errors or retroactive increases. Payroll clerks need to follow changes in tax and deduction laws, so they are aware of the most recent revisions. Finally, they prepare and mail earnings and tax withholding statements for employees' use in preparing income tax returns.

In small offices, payroll and timekeeping duties are likely to be included in the duties of a general office clerk, secretary, or accounting clerk. However, large organizations employ specialized payroll and timekeeping clerks to perform these functions. In offices that have automated timekeeping systems, payroll clerks perform more analysis of the data, look at trends, and work with computer systems. They also spend more time answering employee questions and processing unique data.

Working Conditions

Payroll and timekeeping clerks typically are employed in an office environment.

Because the majority of payroll and timekeeping clerks use computers on a daily basis, these workers may experience eye and muscle strain, backaches, headaches, and repetitive motion injuries. Also, clerks who review detailed data may have to sit for extended periods of time.

Most payroll and timekeeping clerks work regular business hours.

Employment

Payroll and timekeeping clerks held about 201,000 jobs in 2000. They can be found in every industry, but a growing number work for personnel-supply companies and for accounting firms, which are taking on payroll duties as an additional service. About 13 percent of all payroll and timekeeping clerks worked part-time in 2000.

Training, Other Qualifications, and Advancement

Most payroll and timekeeping clerks are required to have at least a high school diploma. However, having some college is becoming increasingly important, particularly for those occupations requiring knowledge of accounting. Some payroll and timekeeping clerks have bachelor's degrees in business, accounting, or liberal arts. Although a degree is rarely required, many graduates accept entry-level clerical positions to get into a particular company or to enter the finance or accounting field with the hope of being promoted to professional or managerial positions. Some companies have a set plan of advancement that tracks college graduates from entry-level clerical jobs into managerial positions. Workers with bachelor's degrees are likely to start at higher salaries and advance more easily than those without degrees do.

Experience in a related job also is recommended. Experience working in an office environment or in customer service is always beneficial. Regardless of the type of work, most employers prefer workers with good communication skills who are computer-literate; knowledge of word processing and spreadsheet software is especially valuable.

Once hired, payroll and timekeeping clerks usually receive on-the-job training. Under the guidance of a supervisor or other senior worker, new employees learn company procedures. Some formal classroom training also may be necessary, such as training in specific computer software. Payroll and timekeeping clerks must be careful, orderly, and detail-oriented in order to avoid making errors and recognize errors made by others. These workers also should be discreet and trustworthy, because they frequently come in contact with confidential material. Additionally, all payroll and timekeeping clerks should have a strong aptitude for numbers.

Payroll and timekeeping clerks usually advance by taking on more duties in the same occupation for higher pay or by transferring to a closely related occupation. Most companies fill office and administrative support supervisory and managerial positions by promoting individuals from within their organization, so payroll and timekeeping clerks who acquire additional skills, experience, and training improve their advancement opportunities. With appropriate experience and education, some clerks may become accountants, human resource specialists, or buyers.

Job Outlook

Little or no change is expected in the employment of payroll and timekeeping clerks through 2010, due to the continuing automation of payroll and timekeeping functions and the consolidation of clerical jobs. A growing number of mergers and acquisitions also will adversely affect payroll departments as administrative offices are usually the first to be downsized. Nevertheless, a number of job openings should arise in coming years as payroll and timekeeping clerks leave the labor force or transfer to other occupations. Many payroll clerks use this position as a steppingstone to higher level accounting jobs.

As in many other clerical occupations, new technology will continue to allow many of the tasks formerly handled by payroll and timekeeping clerks to be partially or completely automated. For example, automated timeclocks, which calculate employee hours, allow large organizations to centralize their timekeeping duties in one location. At individual sites, employee hours are increasingly tracked by computer and verified by managers. This information is then compiled and sent to a central office to be processed by payroll clerks, eliminating the need to have payroll clerks at every site. In addition, the growing use of direct deposit eliminates the need to draft paychecks, because these funds are automatically transferred each pay period. Also, a growing number of organizations are allowing employees to automatically update their payroll records. Furthermore, payroll and timekeeping duties are increasingly

being distributed to secretaries, general office clerks, or accounting clerks or are being contracted out to organizations that specialize in these services.

Earnings

Salaries of payroll and timekeeping clerks vary considerably. The region of the country, size of city, and type and size of establishment all influence salary levels. Also, the level of expertise required and the complexity and uniqueness of a clerk's responsibilities also may affect earnings. Median hourly earnings of full-time payroll and timekeeping clerks in 2000 were $13.07.

Related Occupations

Payroll and timekeeping clerks enter data into a computer and keep track of business and other financial transactions. Higher level clerks can generate reports and perform analysis of the financial data. Other occupations that perform these duties include brokerage clerks; cashiers; credit authorizers, checkers, and clerks; loan interviewers and clerks; new accounts clerks; order clerks; and secretaries and administrative assistants.

Sources of Additional Information

Information on employment opportunities for payroll and timekeeping clerks is available from local offices of the state employment service.

Personal and Home Care Aides

O*NET 39-9021.00

Significant Points

- Numerous job openings will result from very fast employment growth and high replacement needs.

- Education required for entry-level jobs is generally minimal, but earnings are low.

Nature of the Work

Personal and home care aides help elderly, disabled, and ill persons live in their own homes or in residential care facilities instead of in a health facility. Most work with elderly or disabled clients who need more extensive care than family or friends can provide. Some aides work with families in which a parent is incapacitated and small children need care. Others help discharged hospital patients who have relatively short-term needs.

Personal and home care aides (also called homemakers, caregivers, companions, and personal attendants) provide housekeeping and routine personal care services. They clean clients' houses, do laundry, and change bed linens. Aides may plan meals (including special diets), shop for food, and cook. Aides also may help clients move from bed, bathe, dress, and groom. Some accompany clients outside the home, serving as a guide and companion.

Personal and home care aides also provide instruction and psychological support. They may advise families and patients on such things as nutrition, cleanliness, and household tasks. Aides also may assist in toilet training a severely mentally handicapped child, or just listen to clients talk about their problems.

In home care agencies, it usually is a registered nurse, a physical therapist, or a social worker who assigns specific duties and supervises personal and home care aides. Aides keep records of services performed and of clients' condition and progress. They report changes in the client's condition to the supervisor or case manager. Aides work in cooperation with other healthcare professionals, including registered nurses, therapists, and other medical staff.

Working Conditions

The personal and home care aide's daily routine may vary. Aides may go to the same home every day for months or even years. However, most aides work with a number of different clients, each job lasting a few hours, days, or weeks. Aides often visit four or five clients on the same day.

Surroundings differ from case to case. Some homes are neat and pleasant, while others are untidy or depressing. Some clients are pleasant and cooperative; others are angry, abusive, depressed, or otherwise difficult.

Personal and home care aides generally work on their own, with periodic visits by their supervisor. They receive detailed instructions explaining when to visit clients and what services to perform. Many aides work part-time, and weekend hours are common.

Aides are individually responsible for getting to the client's home. They may spend a good portion of the working day traveling from one client to another. They are particularly susceptible to falls inside and outside clients' homes and injuries resulting from all types of overexertion when assisting patients. Mechanical lifting devices that are available in institutional settings are seldom available in patients' homes.

Employment

Personal and home care aides held about 414,000 jobs in 2000. Most aides are employed by social services agencies, home health agencies, or residential care facilities. Self-employed aides have no agency affiliation or supervision, and accept clients, set fees, and arrange work schedules on their own.

Training, Other Qualifications, and Advancement

In some states, this occupation is open to individuals with no formal training. On-the-job training is generally provided. Other states may require formal training, depending on state law. The National Association for Home Care offers national certification for personal and home care aides. Certification is a voluntary demonstration that the individual has met industry standards.

Successful personal and home care aides like to help people and do not mind hard work. They should be responsible, compassionate, emotionally stable, and cheerful. In addition, aides should be tactful, honest, and discreet because they work in private homes. Aides also must be in good health. A physical examination including state-mandated tests, such as those for tuberculosis, may be required.

Advancement for personal and home care aides is limited. In some agencies, workers start out performing homemaker duties, such as cleaning. With experience and training, they may take on personal care duties.

Job Outlook

A large number of job openings are expected for personal and home care aides because of much faster-than-average employment growth and high replacement needs. Personal and home care aides is expected to be one of the fastest growing occupations through the year 2010.

The number of elderly people is projected to rise substantially. This age group is characterized by mounting health problems requiring some assistance. In addition to the elderly, there will be an increasing reliance on home care for patients of all ages. This trend reflects several developments: efforts to contain costs by moving patients out of hospitals and nursing facilities as quickly as possible; the realization that treatment can be more effective in familiar surroundings rather than clinical surroundings; and the development and improvement of medical technologies for in-home treatment.

In addition to job openings created by the increase in demand for these workers, replacement needs are expected to produce numerous openings. Turnover is high, a reflection of the relatively low skill requirements, low pay, and high emotional demands of the work. For these same reasons, many people are reluctant to seek these jobs. Therefore, persons who are interested in this work and suited for it should have excellent job opportunities, particularly those with experience or training as personal care, home health, or nursing aides.

Earnings

Median hourly earnings of personal and home care aides were $7.50 in 2000. The middle 50 percent earned between $6.43 and $8.53 an hour. The lowest 10 percent earned less than $5.74, and the highest 10 percent earned more than $10.13 an hour. Median hourly earnings in the industries employing the largest numbers of personal and home care aides in 2000 are shown in the following table:

Residential care	$7.97
Job training and related services	7.85
Nursing and personal care facilities	7.82
Individual and family services	7.75
Home healthcare services	6.49

Most employers give slight pay increases with experience and added responsibility. Aides usually are paid only for the time worked in the home. They normally are not paid for travel time between jobs. Employers often hire on-call hourly workers and provide no benefits.

Related Occupations

Personal and home care aide is a service occupation combining duties of caregivers and social service workers. Workers in related occupations that involve personal contact to help others include childcare workers; nursing, psychiatric, and home health aides; occupational therapist assistants and aides; and physical therapist assistants and aides.

Sources of Additional Information

General information about training and referrals to state and local agencies about opportunities for personal and home care aides, a list of relevant publications, and information on certification are available from:

- National Association for Home Care, 228 7th St. SE., Washington, DC 20003. Internet: http://www.nahc.org

Pest Control Workers

O*NET 37-2021.00

Significant Points

- Pesticides used by pest control workers can pose health risks.

- Federal and state laws require licensure through training and examination.

- Job prospects should be favorable for qualified applicants because many people do not find pest control work appealing.

Nature of the Work

Roaches, rats, mice, spiders, termites, fleas, ants, and bees—few people welcome them into their homes or offices. Unwanted creatures that infest households, buildings, or surrounding areas are pests that can pose serious risks to human health and safety. It is a pest control worker's job to eliminate them.

Pest control workers locate, identify, destroy, and repel pests. They use their knowledge of pests' lifestyles and habits, along with an arsenal of pest management techniques—applying chemicals, setting traps, operating equipment, and even modifying structures—to alleviate pest problems.

The best known method of pest control is pesticide application. Pest control workers use two different types of pesticides—general use and restricted use. General use pesticides are the most widely used and are readily available; in diluted concentrations, they are available to the public. Restricted use pesticides are available only to certified professionals for controlling the most severe infestations. Their registration, labeling, and application are regulated by federal law, interpreted by the U.S. Environmental Protection Agency (EPA), because of their potential harm to pest control workers, customers, and the environment.

Pesticides are not pest control workers' only tool, however. Pest control workers increasingly use a combination of pest management techniques, known as integrated pest management. One method involves using proper sanitation and creating physical barriers, for pests cannot survive without food and will not infest a building if they cannot enter it. Another method involves using baits, some of which destroy the pests, and others that prevent them from reproducing. Yet another method involves using mechanical devices, such as traps, that do not allow pests to reenter the environment.

Integrated pest management is becoming popular for several reasons. First, pesticides can pose environmental and health risks. Second, some pests are becoming more resistant to pesticides in certain situations. Finally, an integrated pest management plan is more effective in the long term than use of a pesticide alone.

Most pest control workers work in one of three positions—pest control technician, applicator, or supervisor. Position titles vary by state, but the hierarchy—based on training and responsibility required—remains consistent.

Pest control technicians identify problem areas and operate and maintain traps. They assist applicators by carrying supplies, organizing materials, and preparing equipment. In addition, they may make sales presentations on pest control products or services. Technicians are licensed to apply pesticides only under an applicator's supervision.

Certified pest control applicators, sometimes called exterminators, perform the same tasks technicians do. But they also are certified to apply all pesticides, both general use and restricted use, without supervision and are licensed to supervise and train technicians in pesticide use. Within this group of workers are several subspecialties, including termite exterminators and fumigators.

Termite exterminators are applicators who specialize in controlling termites. They use chemicals and modify structures to eliminate termites and prevent reinfestation. To treat infested areas, termite exterminators drill holes and cut openings into buildings to access infestations. To prevent further infestation, they modify foundations and dig holes and trenches around buildings. Some termite exterminators even repair structural damage caused by termites.

Fumigators are applicators who control pests using poisonous gases called fumigants. Fumigators pretreat infested buildings by examining, measuring, and sealing the buildings. Then, using cylinders, hoses, and valves, they fill structures with the proper amount and concentration of fumigant. They also monitor the premises during treatment for leaking gas. To prevent accidental fumigant exposure, fumigators padlock doors and post warning signs.

Pest control supervisors, also known as operators, direct service technicians and certified applicators. Supervisors are licensed to apply pesticides, but they usually are more involved in running the business. Supervisors are responsible for ensuring employee adherence to rules and must resolve problems with regulatory officials. Most states require each pest control establishment to have a supervisor; self-employed business owners usually are supervisors.

Working Conditions

Pest control workers must kneel, bend, reach, and crawl to inspect, modify, and treat structures. They work both indoors and out, in all weather conditions. During warm weather, applicators may be uncomfortable wearing the heavy protective gear—such as respirators, gloves, and goggles—required for working with pesticides.

Almost half of all pest control workers work a 40-hour week, but about a quarter work more hours. Pest control workers often work evenings and weekends, but many work consistent shifts.

There are health risks associated with pesticide use. Various pest control chemicals are toxic and could pose health risks if not used properly. Extensive training required for certification and the use of recommended protective equipment minimizes these health risks, resulting in fewer reported cases of lost work. Because pest control workers travel to visit clients, the potential risk of motor vehicle accidents is another occupational hazard.

Employment

Pest control workers held about 58,000 jobs in 2000; 79 percent of workers were employed in the services to buildings industry. They are concentrated in states with warmer climates. About 14 percent were self-employed.

Training, Other Qualifications, and Advancement

A high school diploma or equivalent is the minimum qualification for most pest control jobs. Although a college degree is not required, almost half of all pest control workers have either attended college or earned a degree.

Pest control workers must have basic skills in math, chemistry, and writing. Because of the extensive interaction that pest control workers have with their customers, employers prefer to hire people who have good communication and interpersonal skills. In addition, most pest control companies require their employees to have a good driving record. Pest control workers must be in good health because of the physical demands of the job, and they also must be able to withstand extreme conditions—such as the heat of climbing into an attic in the summertime or the chill of sliding into a crawlspace during winter.

Both federal and state laws regulate pest control workers. These laws require them to be certified through training and examination, for which most pest control firms help their employees prepare. Workers may receive both formal classroom and on-the-job training, but they also must study on their own. Because the pest control industry is constantly changing, workers must attend continuing education classes to maintain their certification.

Requirements for pest control workers vary by state. Pest control workers usually begin their careers as apprentice technicians. Before performing any pest control services, apprentices must attend general training in pesticide safety and use. In addition, they must train in each pest control category in which they wish to practice. Categories may include general pest control, rodent control, termite control, fumigation, and ornamental and turf control.

Training usually involves spending 10 hours in the classroom and 60 hours on the job for each category. After completing the required training, apprentices can provide supervised pest control services. Apprentices have up to 1 year to prepare for and pass the written examinations. Upon successful completion of the exams, the apprentice becomes licensed as a technician.

To be eligible to become applicators, technicians need 1 year of experience, 6 months of which must be as a licensed technician. This requirement is sometimes waived for individuals who have either a college degree in biological sciences or extensive related work experience. To become certified as applicators, technicians must pass an additional set of category exams. Depending on the state, applicators must attend additional classes every 1 to 6 years to be recertified.

Applicators with several years of experience often become supervisors. To qualify as a pest control supervisor, applicators must pass state-administered exams and have experience in the industry, usually a minimum of 2 years. Many supervisors are self-employed, reflecting the relative ease of entry into the field and the growing need for pest control. Therefore, the pest control industry provides a good opportunity for people interested in operating their own business.

Job Outlook

Job prospects should be favorable for qualified applicants because many people do not find pest control work appealing. Employment of pest control workers is expected to grow faster than the average for all occupations through 2010. In addition to job openings arising from employment growth, opportunities will result from workers transferring to other occupations or leaving the labor force.

Demand for pest control workers is projected to increase for a number of reasons. An expanding client base will develop as environmental and health concerns, greater numbers of dual-income households, and improvements in the standard of living convince more people to hire professionals rather than attempt pest control work themselves. In addition, tougher regulations limiting pesticide use will demand more complex integrated pest management strategies. Greater concerns about the effects of pesticide use in schools has increasingly prompted more school districts to investigate alternative means of pest control, such as integrated pest management. Furthermore, use of some newer materials for insulation around foundations has made many homes more susceptible to pest infestation. Finally, continuing population shifts to the more pest-prone sunbelt state laws should increase the number of households in need of pest control.

Earnings

The hierarchy of pest control positions also applies to earnings. Pest control supervisors usually earn the most and technicians the least, with earnings of certified applicators falling somewhere in between. Earnings data do not distinguish among job titles, however.

Median hourly earnings of full-time wage and salary pest control workers were $10.65 in 2000. The middle 50 percent earned between $8.73 and $13.58. The lowest 10 percent earned less than $7.09, and the top 10 percent earned over $16.95.

Many pest control workers are employed under a wage plus commission system, which rewards workers who do their job well. Some firms offer bonuses to workers who exceed their performance goals.

Related Occupations

Pest control workers visit homes and places of business to provide building services. Other workers who provide services to buildings include building cleaning workers; various construction trades workers, including carpenters and electricians; and heating, air-conditioning, and refrigeration mechanics and installers.

Sources of Additional Information

Private employment agencies and state employment services offices have information about available job opportunities for pest control workers.

For information about the training and certification required in your state, contact your local office of the U.S. Department of Agriculture or your state's Environmental Protection Agency.

Pharmacy Aides

O*NET 31-9095.00

Significant Points

- Many pharmacy aides work evenings, weekends, and some holidays.

- Eight out of 10 jobs are in retail pharmacies.

- Job opportunities are expected to be good, especially for those with related work experience.

Nature of the Work

Pharmacy aides help licensed pharmacists with administrative duties in running a pharmacy. Aides often are clerks or cashiers who primarily answer telephones, handle money, stock shelves, and perform other clerical duties. They work closely with pharmacy technicians. *Pharmacy technicians* usually perform more complex tasks than do assistants, although, in some states, their duties and job titles overlap. Aides refer any questions regarding prescriptions, drug information, or health matters to a pharmacist.

Aides have several important duties that help the pharmacy to function smoothly. They may establish and maintain patient profiles, prepare insurance claim forms, and stock and take inventory of prescription and over-the-counter medications. Accurate recordkeeping is necessary to help avert a potentially dangerous drug interaction. Because many people have medical insurance to help pay for the prescription, it is essential that pharmacy aides efficiently and correctly correspond with the third-party insurance providers to obtain payment. They also maintain the inventory and inform the supervisor of stock needs so that the pharmacy has the vital medications for those who need them. Some also clean pharmacy equipment, help with the maintenance of equipment and supplies, and manage the cash register.

Working Conditions

Pharmacy aides work in clean, organized, well-lighted, and well-ventilated areas. Most of their workday is spent on their feet. They may be required to lift heavy boxes or to use stepladders to retrieve supplies from high shelves.

Aides work the same hours as pharmacists. This includes evenings, nights, weekends, and some holidays. Because some hospital and retail pharmacies are open 24 hours a day, aides may work varying shifts. There are many opportunities for part-time work in both retail and hospital settings.

Employment

Pharmacy aides held about 57,000 jobs in 2000. Over 80 percent were in retail pharmacies, either independently owned or part of a drug store chain, grocery store, department store, or mass retailer. The vast majority of these are in drug stores. Thirteen percent were in hospitals, and the rest were in mail-order pharmacies, clinics, pharmaceutical wholesalers, and the federal government.

Training, Other Qualifications, and Advancement

Most pharmacy aides receive informal on-the-job training, but employers favor those with at least a high school diploma. Prospective pharmacy aides with experience working as a cashier may have an advantage. Employers also prefer applicants with strong customer service and communication skills and experience managing inventories and using a computer. Aides entering the field need strong spelling, reading, and mathematics skills.

Successful pharmacy aides are organized, dedicated, friendly, and responsible. They should be willing and able to take directions. Candidates interested in becoming pharmacy aides cannot have prior records of drug or substance abuse. Strong interpersonal and communication skills are needed because there is a lot of interaction with patients, coworkers, and healthcare professionals. Teamwork is very important because aides are often required to work with technicians and pharmacists.

Pharmacy aides almost always are trained on the job. They may begin by observing a more experienced worker. After they become familiar with the store's equipment, policies, and procedures, they begin to work on their own. Once they become experienced workers, they are not likely to receive additional training, except when new equipment is introduced or when policies or procedures change.

To become a pharmacy aide, one should be able to perform repetitious work accurately. Aides need good basic mathematics skills and good manual dexterity. Because they deal constantly with the public, pharmacy aides should be neat in appearance and able to deal pleasantly and tactfully with customers. Some employers may prefer people with experience typing, handling money, or operating specialized equipment, including computers.

Advancement usually is limited, although some aides may decide to become a pharmacy technician or to enroll in pharmacy school to become a pharmacist.

Job Outlook

Job opportunities for full- and part-time work are expected to be good, especially for aides with related work experience. Job openings will be created by employment growth and by the need to replace workers who transfer to other occupations or leave the labor force.

Employment of pharmacy aides is expected to grow about as fast as the average for all occupations through 2010 due to the increased pharmaceutical needs of a larger and older population and to the greater use of medication. The increased number of middle-aged and elderly people—

who, on average, use more prescription drugs than do younger people—will spur demand for aides in all practice settings.

Cost-conscious insurers, pharmacies, and health systems will continue to emphasize the role of aides. As a result, pharmacy aides will assume responsibility for more routine tasks previously performed by pharmacists and pharmacy technicians, thereby giving pharmacists more time to interact with patients and affording technicians more time to prepare medications.

Earnings

Median hourly earnings of pharmacy aides were $8.52 in 2000. The middle 50 percent earned between $7.16 and $10.58; the lowest 10 percent earned less than $6.12, and the highest 10 percent earned more than $13.14. Median hourly earnings of pharmacy aides were $8.02 in drug stores and proprietary stores, $11.17 in hospitals, and $8.47 in grocery stores in 2000.

Related Occupations

The work of pharmacy aides is closely related to that of pharmacy technicians. Workers in other medical support occupations include dental assistants, licensed practical and licensed vocational nurses, medical transcriptionists, medical records and health information technicians, occupational therapist assistants and aides, physical therapist assistants and aides, and surgical technologists.

Sources of Additional Information

For information on employment opportunities, contact local employers or local offices of the state employment service.

Pharmacy Technicians

O*NET 29-2052.00

Significant Points

- Job opportunities are expected to be good, especially for those with certification or previous work experience.

- Many technicians work evenings, weekends, and some holidays.

- Two-thirds of all jobs are in retail pharmacies.

Nature of the Work

Pharmacy technicians help licensed pharmacists provide medication and other healthcare products to patients. Technicians usually perform routine tasks to help prepare prescribed medication for patients, such as counting tablets and labeling bottles. Technicians refer any questions regarding prescriptions, drug information, or health matters to a pharmacist.

Pharmacy aides work closely with pharmacy technicians. They are often clerks or Cashiers who primarily answer telephones, handle money,

stock shelves, and perform other clerical duties. Pharmacy technicians usually perform more complex tasks than do pharmacy aides, although, in some states, their duties and job titles overlap.

Pharmacy technicians who work in retail pharmacies have varying responsibilities, depending on state rules and regulations. Technicians receive written prescriptions or requests for prescription refills from patients. They also may receive prescriptions sent electronically from the doctor's office. They must verify that the information on the prescription is complete and accurate. To prepare the prescription, technicians must retrieve, count, pour, weigh, measure, and sometimes mix the medication. Then, they prepare the prescription labels, select the type of prescription container, and affix the prescription and auxiliary labels to the container. Once the prescription is filled, technicians price and file the prescription, which must be checked by a pharmacist before it is given to a patient. Technicians may establish and maintain patient profiles, prepare insurance claim forms, and stock and take inventory of prescription and over-the-counter medications.

In hospitals, technicians have added responsibilities. They read patient charts and prepare and deliver the medicine to patients. The pharmacist must check the order before it is delivered to the patient. The technician then copies the information about the prescribed medication onto the patient's profile. Technicians also may assemble a 24-hour supply of medicine for every patient. They package and label each dose separately. The package is then placed in the medicine cabinet of each patient until the supervising pharmacist checks it for accuracy. It is then given to the patient.

Working Conditions

Pharmacy technicians work in clean, organized, well-lighted, and well-ventilated areas. Most of their workday is spent on their feet. They may be required to lift heavy boxes or to use stepladders to retrieve supplies from high shelves.

Technicians work the same hours as pharmacists. This may include evenings, nights, weekends, and holidays. Because some hospital and retail pharmacies are open 24 hours a day, technicians may work varying shifts. As their seniority increases, technicians often have increased control over the hours they work. There are many opportunities for part-time work in both retail and hospital settings.

Employment

Pharmacy technicians held about 190,000 jobs in 2000. Two-thirds of all jobs were in retail pharmacies, either independently owned or part of a drug store chain, grocery store, department store, or mass retailer. More than 2 out of 10 jobs were in hospitals and a small number were in mail-order and Internet pharmacies, clinics, pharmaceutical wholesalers, and the federal government.

Training, Other Qualifications, and Advancement

Although most pharmacy technicians receive informal on-the-job training, employers favor those who have completed formal training and certification. However, there are currently few state and no federal requirements for formal training or certification of pharmacy technicians. Employers who can neither afford, nor have the time to give, on-the-job training often seek formally educated pharmacy technicians. Formal education programs and certification emphasize the technicians' interest in and dedication to the work to potential employers. In addition to the military, some hospitals, proprietary schools, vocational or technical colleges, and community colleges offer formal education programs.

Formal pharmacy-technician education programs require classroom and laboratory work in a variety of areas, including medical and pharmaceutical terminology, pharmaceutical calculations, pharmacy recordkeeping, pharmaceutical techniques, and pharmacy law and ethics. Technicians also are required to learn medication names, actions, uses, and doses. Many training programs include internships, in which students gain hands-on experience in actual pharmacies. Students receive a diploma, certificate, or an associate degree, depending on the program.

Prospective pharmacy technicians with experience working as an aide in a community pharmacy or volunteering in a hospital may have an advantage. Employers also prefer applicants with strong customer service and communication skills and with experience managing inventories, counting, measuring, and using computers. Technicians entering the field need strong mathematics, spelling, and reading skills. A background in chemistry, English, and health education also may be beneficial. Some technicians are hired without formal training, but under the condition that they obtain certification within a specified period to retain employment.

The Pharmacy Technician Certification Board administers the National Pharmacy Technician Certification Examination. This exam is voluntary and displays the competency of the individual to act as a pharmacy technician. Eligible candidates must have a high school diploma or GED, and those who pass the exam earn the title of Certified Pharmacy Technician (CPhT). The exam is offered several times per year at various locations nationally. Employers, often pharmacists, know that individuals who pass the exam have a standardized body of knowledge and skills.

Certified technicians must be recertified every 2 years. Technicians must complete 20 contact hours of pharmacy-related topics within the 2-year certification period to become eligible for recertification. Contact hours are awarded for on-the-job training, attending lectures, and college coursework. At least 1 contact hour must be in pharmacy law. Contact hours can be earned from several different sources, including pharmacy associations, pharmacy colleges, and pharmacy technician training programs. Up to 10 contact hours can be earned when the technician is employed under the direct supervision and instruction of a pharmacist.

Successful pharmacy technicians are alert, observant, organized, dedicated, and responsible. They should be willing and able to take directions. They must enjoy precise work: details are sometimes a matter of life and death. Although a pharmacist must check and approve all their work, they should be able to work on their own without constant instruction from the pharmacist. Candidates interested in becoming pharmacy technicians cannot have prior records of drug or substance abuse.

Strong interpersonal and communication skills are needed because there is a lot of interaction with patients, coworkers, and healthcare professionals. Teamwork is very important because technicians are often required to work with pharmacists, aides, and other technicians.

Job Outlook

Good job opportunities are expected for full-time and part-time work, especially for technicians with formal training or previous experience. Job openings for pharmacy technicians will result from the expansion of retail pharmacies and other employment settings, and from the need to replace workers who transfer to other occupations or leave the labor force.

Employment of pharmacy technicians is expected to grow much faster than the average for all occupations through 2010 due to the increased pharmaceutical needs of a larger and older population, and to the greater use of medication. The increased number of middle-aged and elderly people—who, on average, use more prescription drugs than do younger people—will spur demand for technicians in all practice settings. With advances in science, more medications are becoming available to treat more conditions.

Cost-conscious insurers, pharmacies, and health systems will continue to emphasize the role of technicians. As a result, pharmacy technicians will assume responsibility for more routine tasks previously performed by pharmacists. Pharmacy technicians also will need to learn and master new pharmacy technology as it surfaces. For example, robotic machines are used to dispense medicine into containers; technicians must oversee the machines, stock the bins, and label the containers. Thus, while automation is increasingly incorporated into the job, it will not necessarily reduce the need for technicians.

Almost all states have legislated the maximum number of technicians who can safely work under a pharmacist at a time. In some states, increased demand for technicians has encouraged an expanded ratio of technicians to pharmacists. Changes in these laws could directly affect employment.

Earnings

Median hourly earnings of pharmacy technicians in 2000 were $9.93. The middle 50 percent earned between $8.12 and $12.26; the lowest 10 percent earned less than $7.00, and the highest 10 percent earned more than $14.56. Median hourly earnings in the industries employing the largest numbers of pharmacy technicians in 2000 were as follows:

Hospitals	$11.44
Grocery stores	10.57
Drugs, proprietaries, and sundries	10.09
Drug stores and proprietary stores	9.00
Department stores	8.75

Certified technicians may earn more. Shift differentials for working evenings or weekends also can increase earnings. Some technicians belong to unions representing hospital or grocery store workers.

Related Occupations

This occupation is most closely related to pharmacists and pharmacy aides. Workers in other medical support occupations include dental assistants, licensed practical and licensed vocational nurses, medical transcriptionists, medical records and health information technicians, occupational therapist assistants and aides, physical therapist assistants and aides, secretaries and administrative assistants, and surgical technologists.

Sources of Additional Information

For information on certification and a National Pharmacy Technician Certification Examination Candidate Handbook, contact:

● Pharmacy Technician Certification Board, 2215 Constitution Ave. NW, Washington, DC 20037. Internet: http://www.ptcb.org

Photographers

O*NET 27-4021.01, 27-4021.02

Significant Points

● Technical expertise, a "good eye," imagination, and creativity are essential.

● Only the most skilled and talented who have good business sense maintain long-term careers.

● More than half of all photographers are self-employed, a much higher proportion than the average for all occupations.

Nature of the Work

Photographers produce and preserve images that paint a picture, tell a story, or record an event. To create commercial quality photographs, photographers need both technical expertise and creativity. Producing a successful picture requires choosing and presenting a subject to achieve a particular effect and selecting the appropriate equipment. For example, photographers may enhance the subject's appearance with lighting or draw attention to a particular aspect of the subject by blurring the background.

Today, many cameras adjust settings like shutter speed and aperture automatically. They also let the photographer adjust these settings manually, allowing greater creative and technical control over the picture-taking process. In addition to automatic and manual cameras, photographers use an array of film, lenses, and equipment—from filters, tripods, and flash attachments to specially constructed lighting equipment.

Photographers use either a traditional camera or a newer digital camera that electronically records images. A traditional camera records images on silver halide film that is developed into prints. Some photographers send their film to laboratories for processing. Color film requires expensive equipment and exacting conditions for correct processing and printing. Other photographers, especially those who use black-and-white film or require special effects, prefer to develop and print their own photographs. Photographers who do their own film developing must have the technical skill to operate a fully equipped darkroom or the appropriate computer software to process prints digitally.

Recent advances in electronic technology now make it possible for the professional photographer to develop and scan standard 35mm or other types of film, and use flatbed scanners and photofinishing laboratories to produce computer-readable, digital images from film. After converting the film to a digital image, photographers can edit and electronically transmit images, making it easier and faster to shoot, develop, and transmit pictures from remote locations.

Using computers and specialized software, photographers also can manipulate and enhance the scanned or digital image to create a desired effect. Images can be stored on compact disc (CD) the same way as music. Digital technology also allows the production of larger, more colorful, and more accurate prints or images for use in advertising, photographic art, and scientific research. Some photographers use this technology to create electronic portfolios, as well. Because much photography now involves the use of computer technology, photographers must have hands-on knowledge of computer editing software.

Some photographers specialize in areas such as portrait, commercial and industrial, scientific, news, or fine arts photography. *Portrait photographers* take pictures of individuals or groups of people and often work in their own studios. Some specialize in weddings or school photographs and may work on location. Portrait photographers who are business owners arrange for advertising, schedule appointments, set and adjust equipment, develop and retouch negatives, and mount and frame pictures. They also purchase supplies, keep records, bill customers, and may hire and train employees.

Commercial and industrial photographers take pictures of various subjects, such as buildings, models, merchandise, artifacts, and landscapes. These photographs are used in a variety of media, including books, reports, advertisements, and catalogs. Industrial photographers often take pictures of equipment, machinery, products, workers, and company officials. The pictures then are used for analyzing engineering projects, publicity, or as records of equipment development or deployment, such as placement of an offshore rig. This photography frequently is done on location.

Scientific photographers photograph a variety of subjects to illustrate or record scientific or medical data or phenomena, using knowledge of scientific procedures. They typically possess additional knowledge in areas such as engineering, medicine, biology, or chemistry.

News photographers, also called *photojournalists*, photograph newsworthy people, places, sports, political activities, and community events for newspapers, journals, magazines, or television. Some news photographers are salaried staff; others are self-employed and are known as freelance photographers.

Fine arts photographers sell their photographs as fine artwork. In addition to technical proficiency, fine arts photographers need artistic talent and creativity.

Self-employed, or freelance, photographers may license the use of their photographs through stock photo agencies or contract with clients or agencies to provide photographs as necessary. Stock agencies grant magazines and other customers the right to purchase the use of photographs, and, in turn, pay the photographer on a commission basis. Stock photo agencies require an application from the photographer and a sizable portfolio. Once accepted, a large number of new submissions usually are required from the photographer each year.

Working Conditions

Working conditions for photographers vary considerably. Photographers employed in government and advertising agencies usually work a 5-day, 40-hour week. On the other hand, news photographers often work long, irregular hours and must be available to work on short notice. Many photographers work part-time or variable schedules.

Portrait photographers usually work in their own studios but also may travel to take photographs at the client's location, such as a school, a company office, or a private home. News and commercial photographers frequently travel locally, stay overnight on assignments, or travel to distant places for long periods.

Some photographers work in uncomfortable, or even dangerous surroundings, especially news photographers covering accidents, natural disasters, civil unrest, or military conflicts. Many photographers must wait long hours in all kinds of weather for an event to take place and stand or walk for long periods while carrying heavy equipment. News photographers often work under strict deadlines.

Self-employment allows for greater autonomy, freedom of expression, and flexible scheduling. However, income can be uncertain and the continuous, time-consuming search for new clients can be stressful. Some self-employed photographers hire assistants who help seek out new business.

Employment

Photographers held about 131,000 jobs in 2000. More than half were self-employed, a much higher proportion than the average for all occupations. Some self-employed photographers contracted with advertising agencies, magazines, or others to do individual projects at a predetermined fee, while others operated portrait studios or provided photographs to stock photo agencies.

Most salaried photographers worked in portrait or commercial photography studios. Newspapers, magazines, television broadcasters, advertising agencies, and government agencies employed most of the others. Most photographers worked in metropolitan areas.

Training, Other Qualifications, and Advancement

Employers usually seek applicants with a "good eye," imagination, and creativity, as well as a good technical understanding of photography. Entry-level positions in photojournalism, industrial, or scientific photography generally require a college degree in journalism or photography. Freelance and portrait photographers need technical proficiency, whether gained through a degree program, vocational training, or extensive work experience.

Many universities, community and junior colleges, vocational-technical institutes, and private trade and technical schools offer photography courses. Basic courses in photography cover equipment, processes, and techniques. Bachelor's degree programs, especially those including business courses, provide a well-rounded education. Art schools offer useful training in design and composition.

Individuals interested in photography should subscribe to photographic newsletters and magazines, join camera clubs, and seek summer or part-time employment in camera stores, newspapers, or photo studios.

Photographers may start out as assistants to experienced photographers. Assistants learn to mix chemicals, develop film, print photographs, and the other skills necessary to run a portrait or commercial photography business. Freelance photographers also should develop an individual style of photography in order to differentiate themselves from the competition. Some photographers enter the field by submitting unsolicited photographs to magazines and art directors at advertising agencies. For freelance photographers, a good portfolio of their work is critical.

Photographers need good eyesight, artistic ability, and hand-eye coordination. They should be patient, accurate, and detail-oriented. Photographers should be able to work well with others, as they frequently deal with clients, graphic designers, or advertising and publishing specialists. Increasingly, photographers need to know computer software programs and applications that allow them to prepare and edit images.

Portrait photographers need the ability to help people relax in front of the camera. Commercial and fine arts photographers must be imaginative and original. News photographers not only must be good with a camera, but also must understand the story behind an event so their pictures match the story. They must be decisive in recognizing a potentially good photograph and act quickly to capture it.

Photographers who operate their own businesses, or freelance, need business skills as well as talent. These individuals must know how to prepare a business plan; submit bids; write contracts; hire models, if needed; get permission to shoot on locations that normally are not open to the public; obtain releases to use photographs of people; license and price photographs; secure copyright protection for their work; and keep financial records.

After several years of experience, magazine and news photographers may advance to photography or picture editor positions. Some photographers teach at technical schools, film schools, or universities.

Job Outlook

Photographers can expect keen competition for job openings because the work is attractive to many people. The number of individuals interested in positions as commercial and news photographers usually is much greater than the number of openings. Those who succeed in landing a salaried job or attracting enough work to earn a living by freelancing are likely to be the most creative, able to adapt to rapidly changing technologies, and adept at operating a business. Related work experience, job-related training, or some unique skill or talent—such as a background in computers or electronics—also are beneficial to prospective photographers.

Employment of photographers is expected to increase about as fast as the average for all occupations through 2010. Demand for portrait photographers should increase as the population grows. And, as the number of electronic versions of magazines, journals, and newspapers grows on the Internet, photographers will be needed to provide digital images.

Employment growth of photographers will be constrained somewhat by the widespread use of digital photography. Besides increasing photographers' productivity, improvements in digital technology will allow individual consumers and businesses to produce, store, and access photographic images on their own. Declines in the newspaper industry will reduce demand for photographers to provide still images for print.

Earnings

Median annual earnings of salaried photographers were $22,300 in 2000. The middle 50 percent earned between $16,790 and $33,020. The lowest 10 percent earned less than $13,760, and the highest 10 percent earned more than $46,890.

© 2003 • JIST Works • Indianapolis, IN

Salaried photographers (more of whom work full time) tend to earn more than those who are self-employed. Because most freelance and portrait photographers purchase their own equipment, they incur considerable expense acquiring and maintaining cameras and accessories. Unlike news and commercial photographers, few fine arts photographers are successful enough to support themselves solely through their art.

Related Occupations

Other occupations requiring artistic talent include architects, except landscape and naval; artists and related workers; designers; and television, video, and motion picture camera operators and editors.

Sources of Additional Information

Career information on photography is available from:

- Professional Photographers of America, Inc., 229 Peachtree St. NE., Suite 2200, Atlanta, GA 30303

- National Press Photographers Association, Inc., 3200 Croasdaile Dr., Suite 306, Durham, NC 27705. Internet: http://www.nppa.org/default.cfm

Photographic Process Workers and Processing Machine Operators

O*NET 51-9131.01, 51-9131.02, 51-9131.03, 51-9131.04, 51-9132.00

Significant Points

- Employment is expected to show little or no change as digital photography becomes commonplace.

- Most receive on-the-job training from their companies, manufacturers' representatives, and experienced workers.

Nature of the Work

Both amateur and professional photographers rely heavily on photographic process workers and processing machine operators to develop film, make prints or slides, and do related tasks, such as enlarging or retouching photographs. *Photographic processing machine operators* operate various machines, such as mounting presses and motion picture film printing, photographic printing, and film developing machines. *Photographic process workers* perform more delicate tasks, such as retouching photographic negatives and prints to emphasize or correct specific features.

Photographic processing machine operators often have specialized jobs. *Film process technicians* operate machines that develop exposed photographic film or sensitized paper in a series of chemical and water baths to produce negative or positive images. First, technicians mix developing and fixing solutions, following a formula. They then load the film

in the machine, which immerses the exposed film in a developer solution. This brings out the latent image. The next steps include immersing the negative in a stop-bath to halt the developer action, transferring it to a hyposolution to fix the image, and then immersing it in water to remove the chemicals. The technician then dries the film. In some cases, these steps are performed by hand.

Color printer operators control equipment that produces color prints from negatives. These workers read customer instructions to determine processing requirements. They load film into color printing equipment, examine negatives to determine equipment control settings, set controls, and produce a specified number of prints. Finally, they inspect the finished prints for defects, remove any that are found, and insert the processed negatives and prints into an envelope for return to the customer.

Photographic process workers, sometimes known as *digital imaging technicians*, use computer images of conventional negatives and specialized computer software to vary the contrast of images, remove unwanted background, or combine features from different photographs. Although computers and digital technology are replacing much manual work, some photographic process workers, especially those who work in portrait studios, still perform many specialized tasks by hand directly on the photo or negative. *Airbrush artists* restore damaged and faded photographs, and may color or shade drawings to create photographic likenesses using an airbrush. *Photographic retouchers* alter photographic negatives, prints, or images to accentuate the subject. *Colorists* apply oil colors to portrait photographs to create natural, lifelike appearances. *Photographic spotters* remove imperfections on photographic prints and images.

Working Conditions

Photographic process workers and processing machine operators generally spend their work hours in clean, appropriately lighted, well-ventilated and air-conditioned offices, photofinishing laboratories, or 1-hour minilabs. In recent years, more commercial photographic processing has been done on computers than in darkrooms; and this trend is expected to continue.

Some photographic process workers and processing machine operators are exposed to the chemicals and fumes associated with developing and printing. These workers must wear rubber gloves and aprons and take precautions against these hazards. Those who use computers for extended periods may experience back pain, eye strain, or fatigue.

Photographic processing machine operators must do repetitive work at a rapid pace without any loss of accuracy. Photographic process workers do detailed tasks, such as airbrushing and spotting, which can contribute to eye fatigue.

Many photo laboratory employees work a 40-hour week, including evenings and weekends, and may work overtime during peak seasons.

Employment

Photographic process workers held about 26,000 jobs in 2000. Nearly one-third of photographic process workers were employed in photofinishing laboratories and 1-hour minilabs. About one-fourth worked for portrait studios or commercial laboratories that specialize in processing the work of professional photographers for advertising and other industries.

Photographic processing machine operators held about 50,000 jobs in 2000. One-half worked in retail establishments, such as department stores and drug stores. About one-quarter worked in photofinishing laboratories and 1-hour minilabs. A small number were self-employed.

Employment fluctuates somewhat over the course of the year. Typically, employment peaks during school graduation and summer vacation periods, and again during the winter holiday season.

Training, Other Qualifications, and Advancement

Most photographic process workers and processing machine operators receive on-the-job training from their companies, manufacturers' representatives, and experienced workers. New employees gradually learn to use the machines and chemicals that develop and print film.

Employers prefer applicants who are high school graduates or those who have some experience in the field. Familiarity with computers is essential for photographic processing machine operators. The ability to perform simple mathematical calculations also is helpful. Photography courses that include instruction in film processing are valuable preparation. Such courses are available through high schools, vocational-technical institutes, private trade schools, and colleges and universities.

On-the-job training in photographic processing occupations can range from just a few hours for print machine operators to several months for photographic processing workers like airbrush artists and colorists. Some workers attend periodic training seminars to maintain a high level of skill. Manual dexterity, good hand-eye coordination, and good vision, including normal color perception, are important qualifications for photographic process workers.

Photographic process machine workers can sometimes advance from jobs as machine operators to supervisory positions in laboratories or to management positions within retail stores.

Job Outlook

Overall employment of photographic process workers and processing machine operators is expected to show little or no change through the year 2010. Employment of processing machine operators will grow slower than average, while employment of photographic process workers will decline. Most openings will result from replacement needs, which are higher for machine operators than for photographic process workers.

In recent years, the use of digital cameras, which use electronic memory rather than film to record images, has grown rapidly among professional photographers and advanced amateurs. As the cost of digital photography drops, the use of such cameras will become more widespread among amateur photographers, reducing the demand for traditional photographic processing machine operators. However, conventional cameras, which use film to record images, are expected to continue to be the camera of choice among most casual photographers. Population growth and the popularity of amateur and family photography will contribute to an ongoing need for photographic processing machine operators to process the film used in conventional cameras, including increasingly sophisticated disposable cameras. This need will prevent what otherwise would be even slower growth in the numbers of these workers.

Employment of photographic process workers is expected to decline, as digital cameras and imaging become more commonplace. Using digital cameras and technology, consumers who have a personal computer and the proper software will be able to download and view pictures on their computer, as well as manipulate, correct, and retouch their own photographs. No matter what improvements occur in camera technology though, there will be some photographic processing tasks that require skillful manual treatment.

Earnings

Earnings of photographic process workers vary greatly depending on skill level, experience, and geographic location. Median hourly earnings for photographic process workers were $9.44 in 2000. The middle 50 percent earned between $7.56 and $12.54. The lowest 10 percent earned less than $6.44, and the highest 10 percent earned more than $16.61. Median hourly earnings were $9.55 in miscellaneous business services, including photofinishing laboratories.

Median hourly earning for photographic processing machine operators were $8.39 in 2000. The middle 50 percent earned between $7.06 and $10.56. The lowest 10 percent earned less than $6.06, and the highest 10 percent earned more than $14.48. Median hourly earnings in the industries employing the largest numbers of photographic processing machine operators were as follows:

Miscellaneous business services $9.03
Department stores 7.97
Drug stores and proprietary stores 6.89

Related Occupations

Photographic process workers and processing machine operators need specialized knowledge of the photodeveloping process. Other workers who apply specialized technical knowledge include clinical laboratory technologists and technicians, computer operators, jewelers and precious stone and metal workers, prepress technicians and workers; printing machine operators; and science technicians.

Sources of Additional Information

For information about employment opportunities in photographic laboratories and schools that offer degrees in photographic technology, contact:

● Photo Marketing Association International, 3000 Picture Place, Jackson, MI 49201

Physical Therapist Assistants and Aides

O*NET 31-2021.00, 31-2022.00

Significant Points

● Employment is projected to increase much faster than the average, as rapid growth in the number of middle-aged and elderly individuals increases the demand for therapeutic services.

- Licensed physical therapist assistants have an associate degree, but physical therapist aides usually learn skills on the job.

- More than two-thirds of jobs for physical therapist assistants and aides were in hospitals or offices of physical therapists.

Nature of the Work

Physical therapist assistants and aides perform components of physical therapy procedures and related tasks selected by a supervising physical therapist. These workers assist physical therapists in providing services that help improve mobility, relieve pain, and prevent or limit permanent physical disabilities of patients suffering from injuries or disease. Patients include accident victims and individuals with disabling conditions, such as low back pain, arthritis, heart disease, fractures, head injuries, and cerebral palsy.

Physical therapist assistants perform a variety of tasks. Components of treatment procedures performed by these workers, under the direction and supervision of physical therapists, involve exercises, massages, electrical stimulation, paraffin baths, hot and cold packs, traction, and ultrasound. Physical therapist assistants record the patient's responses to treatment and report to the physical therapist the outcome of each treatment.

Physical therapist aides help make therapy sessions productive, under the direct supervision of a physical therapist or physical therapist assistant. They usually are responsible for keeping the treatment area clean and organized and preparing for each patient's therapy. When patients need assistance moving to or from a treatment area, aides push them in a wheelchair, or provide them with a shoulder to lean on. Because they are not licensed, aides do not perform the clinical tasks of a physical therapist assistant.

The duties of aides include some clerical tasks, such as ordering depleted supplies, answering the phone, and filling out insurance forms and other paperwork. The extent to which an aide or an assistant performs clerical tasks depends on the size and location of the facility.

Working Conditions

The hours and days that physical therapist assistants and aides work vary, depending on the facility and on whether they are full or part-time employees. Many outpatient physical therapy offices and clinics have evening and weekend hours, to help coincide with patients' personal schedules.

Physical therapist assistants and aides need to have a moderate degree of strength, due to the physical exertion required in assisting patients with their treatment. For example, in some cases, assistants and aides need to help lift patients. Additionally, constant kneeling, stooping, and standing for long periods are all part of the job.

Employment

Physical therapist assistants and aides held 80,000 jobs in 2000. Physical therapist assistants held about 44,000 jobs; and physical therapist aides held about 36,000. They work alongside physical therapists in a variety of settings. More than two-thirds of jobs for assistants and aides were in hospitals or offices of physical therapists. Others work in nursing and personal care facilities, outpatient rehabilitation centers, offices and clinics of physicians, and home health agencies.

Training, Other Qualifications, and Advancement

Physical therapist aides are trained on the job, but physical therapist assistants typically earn an associate degree from an accredited physical therapist assistant program. Licensure or registration is not required in all states for the physical therapist assistant to practice. The states that require licensure stipulate specific educational and examination criteria. Complete information on practice acts and regulations can be obtained from the state licensing boards. Additional requirements may include certification in CPR and other first aid and a minimum number of hours of clinical experience.

According to the American Physical Therapy Association, there were 268 accredited physical therapist assistant programs in the United States as of 2001. Accredited physical therapist assistant programs are designed to last 2 years, or 4 semesters, and culminate in an associate degree. Programs are divided into academic study and hands on clinical experience. Academic coursework includes algebra, anatomy and physiology, biology, chemistry, and psychology. Before students begin their clinical field experience, many programs require that they complete a semester of anatomy and physiology and have certifications in CPR and other first aid. Both educators and prospective employers view clinical experience as an integral part of ensuring that students understand the responsibilities of a physical therapist assistant.

Employers typically require physical therapist aides to have a high school diploma, strong interpersonal skills, and a desire to assist people in need. Most employers provide clinical on-the-job training.

Job Outlook

Employment of physical therapist assistants and aides is expected to grow much faster than the average through the year 2010. Federal legislation imposing limits on reimbursement for therapy services may adversely affect the job market for physical therapist assistants and aides in the near term. However, over the long run, demand for physical therapist assistants and aides will continue to rise, with growth in the number of individuals with disabilities or limited function. The rapidly growing elderly population is particularly vulnerable to chronic and debilitating conditions that require therapeutic services. These patients often need additional assistance in their treatment, making the roles of assistants and aides vital. The large baby-boom generation is entering the prime age for heart attacks and strokes, further increasing the demand for cardiac and physical rehabilitation. Additionally, future medical developments should permit an increased percentage of trauma victims to survive, creating added demand for therapy services.

Licensed physical therapist assistants can enhance the cost-effective provision of physical therapy services. Once a patient is evaluated, and a treatment plan is designed by the physical therapist, the physical therapist assistant can provide many aspects of treatment, as prescribed by the therapist.

Earnings

Median annual earnings of physical therapist assistants were $33,870 in 2000. The middle 50 percent earned between $28,830 and $40,440. The lowest 10 percent earned less than $23,150, and the highest 10 percent earned more than $45,610. Median annual earnings of physical therapist assistants in 2000 were $33,660 in offices of other healthcare practitioners and $33,820 in hospitals.

Median annual earnings of physical therapist aides were $19,670 in 2000. The middle 50 percent earned between $16,460 and $23,390. The lowest 10 percent earned less than $14,590, and the highest 10 percent earned more than $28,800. Median annual earnings of physical therapist aides in 2000 were $18,320 in offices of other healthcare practitioners and $19,840 in hospitals.

Related Occupations

Physical therapist assistants and aides work under the supervision of physical therapists. Other occupations in the healthcare field that work under the supervision of professionals include dental assistants, medical assistants, occupational therapist assistants and aides, and pharmacy technicians.

Sources of Additional Information

Information on a career as a physical therapist assistant and a list of schools offering accredited programs can be obtained from:

- The American Physical Therapy Association, 1111 North Fairfax St., Alexandria, VA 22314-1488. Internet: http://www.apta.org

Pipelayers, Plumbers, Pipefitters, and Steamfitters

O*NET 47-2151.00, 47-2152.01, 47-2152.02, 47-2152.03

Significant Points

- Job opportunities should be excellent because not enough people are seeking training.

- Most workers learn the trade through 4 or 5 years of formal apprenticeship training.

- Pipelayers, plumbers, pipefitters, and steamfitters make up one of the largest and highest paid construction occupations.

Nature of the Work

Most people are familiar with plumbers, who come to their home to unclog a drain or install an appliance. In addition to these activities, however, pipelayers, plumbers, pipefitters, and steamfitters install, maintain, and repair many different types of pipe systems. For example, some systems move water to a municipal water treatment plant and then to residential, commercial, and public buildings. Other systems dispose of waste, provide gas to stoves and furnaces, or supply air-conditioning. Pipe systems in powerplants carry the steam that powers huge turbines. Pipes also are used in manufacturing plants to move material through the production process.

Although pipelaying, plumbing, pipefitting, and steamfitting sometimes are considered a single trade, workers generally specialize in one of the four areas. *Pipelayers* lay clay, concrete, plastic, or cast-iron pipe for drains, sewers, water mains, and oil or gas lines. Before laying the pipe, pipelayers prepare and grade the trenches either manually or with machines. *Plumbers* install and repair the water, waste disposal, drainage, and gas systems in homes and commercial and industrial buildings. Plumbers also install plumbing fixtures—bathtubs, showers, sinks, and toilets—and appliances such as dishwashers and water heaters. *Pipefitters* install and repair both high- and low-pressure pipe systems used in manufacturing, in the generation of electricity, and in heating and cooling buildings. They also install automatic controls that are increasingly being used to regulate these systems. Some pipefitters specialize in only one type of system. *Steamfitters*, for example, install pipe systems that move liquids or gases under high pressure. *Sprinklerfitters* install automatic fire sprinkler systems in buildings.

Pipelayers, plumbers, pipefitters, and steamfitters use many different materials and construction techniques, depending on the type of project. Residential water systems, for example, incorporate copper, steel, and plastic pipe that can be handled and installed by one or two workers. Municipal sewerage systems, on the other hand, are made of large cast-iron pipes; installation normally requires crews of pipefitters. Despite these differences, all pipelayers, plumbers, pipefitters, and steamfitters must be able to follow building plans or blueprints and instructions from supervisors, lay out the job, and work efficiently with the materials and tools of the trade. Computers often are used to create blueprints and plan layouts.

When construction plumbers install piping in a house, for example, they work from blueprints or drawings that show the planned location of pipes, plumbing fixtures, and appliances. They first lay out the job to fit the piping into the structure of the house with the least waste of material and within the confines of the structure. They then measure and mark areas where pipes will be installed and connected. Construction plumbers also check for obstructions such as electrical wiring and, if necessary, plan the pipe installation around the problem.

Sometimes, plumbers have to cut holes in walls, ceilings, and floors of a house. For some systems, they may hang steel supports from ceiling joists to hold the pipe in place. To assemble a system, plumbers—using saws, pipe cutters, and pipe-bending machines—cut and bend lengths of pipe. They connect lengths of pipe with fittings, using methods that depend on the type of pipe used. For plastic pipe, plumbers connect the sections and fittings with adhesives. For copper pipe, they slide a fitting over the end of the pipe and solder it in place with a torch.

After the piping is in place in the house, plumbers install the fixtures and appliances and connect the system to the outside water or sewer lines. Finally, using pressure gauges, they check the system to ensure that the plumbing works properly.

Working Conditions

Because pipelayers, plumbers, pipefitters, and steamfitters frequently must lift heavy pipes, stand for long periods, and sometimes work in uncomfortable or cramped positions, they need physical strength as well as stamina. They also may have to work outdoors in inclement weather. In addition, they are subject to possible falls from ladders, cuts from sharp tools, and burns from hot pipes or soldering equipment.

Pipelayers, plumbers, pipefitters, and steamfitters engaged in construction generally work a standard 40-hour week; those involved in maintaining pipe systems, including those who provide maintenance services under contract, may have to work evening or weekend shifts, as well as be on call. These maintenance workers may spend quite a bit of time traveling to and from work sites.

Employment

Pipelayers, plumbers, pipefitters, and steamfitters constitute one of the largest construction occupations, holding about 568,000 jobs in 2000. About 52 percent worked for plumbing, heating, and air conditioning contractors engaged in new construction, repair, modernization, or maintenance work. Others did maintenance work for a variety of industrial, commercial, and government employers. For example, pipefitters were employed as maintenance personnel in the petroleum and chemical industries, where manufacturing operations require the moving of liquids and gases through pipes. About 1 of every 7 pipelayers, plumbers, pipefitters, and steamfitters was self-employed.

Jobs for pipelayers, plumbers, pipefitters, and steamfitters are distributed across the country in about the same proportion as the general population.

Training, Other Qualifications, and Advancement

Virtually all pipelayers, plumbers, pipefitters, and steamfitters undergo some type of apprenticeship training. Many programs are administered by local union-management committees made up of members of the United Association of Journeymen and Apprentices of the Plumbing and Pipefitting Industry of the United States and Canada. Local employers might also sponsors program, particularly those who are members of the Mechanical Contractors Association of America, the National Association of Plumbing-Heating-Cooling Contractors, or the National Fire Sprinkler Association.

Nonunion training and apprenticeship programs are administered by local chapters of the Associated Builders and Contractors, the National Association of Plumbing-Heating-Cooling Contractors, the American Fire Sprinkler Association, or the Home Builders Institute of the National Association of Home Builders.

Apprenticeships—both union and nonunion—consist of 4 or 5 years of on-the-job training, in addition to at least 144 hours per year of related classroom instruction. Classroom subjects include drafting and blueprint reading, mathematics, applied physics and chemistry, safety, and local plumbing codes and regulations. On the job, apprentices first learn basic skills, such as identifying grades and types of pipe, using the tools of the trade, and safely unloading materials. As apprentices gain experience, they learn how to work with various types of pipe and how to install different piping systems and plumbing fixtures. Apprenticeship gives trainees a thorough knowledge of all aspects of the trade. Although most pipelayers, plumbers, pipefitters, and steamfitters are trained through apprenticeship, some still learn their skills informally on the job.

Applicants for union or nonunion apprentice jobs must be at least 18 years old and in good physical condition. Apprenticeship committees may require applicants to have a high school diploma or its equivalent. Armed forces training in pipelaying, plumbing, and pipefitting is considered very good preparation. In fact, persons with this background may be given credit for previous experience when entering a civilian apprenticeship program. Secondary or postsecondary courses in shop, plumbing, general mathematics, drafting, blueprint reading, computers, and physics also are good preparation.

Although there are no uniform national licensing requirements, most communities require plumbers to be licensed. Licensing requirements vary from area to area, but most localities require workers to pass an examination that tests their knowledge of the trade and of local plumbing codes.

Some pipelayers, plumbers, pipefitters, and steamfitters may become supervisors for mechanical and plumbing contractors; others go into business for themselves.

Job Outlook

Job opportunities are expected to be excellent, as increased demand for skilled pipelayers, plumbers, pipefitters, and steamfitters is expected to outpace the supply of workers trained in this craft. Employment of pipelayers, plumbers, pipefitters, and steamfitters is expected to grow about as fast as the average for all occupations through the year 2010. In addition, many potential workers may prefer work that is less strenuous and has more comfortable working conditions. Well-trained workers will have especially favorable opportunities.

Demand for plumbers will stem from building renovation, including the increasing installation of sprinkler systems; repair and maintenance of existing residential systems; and maintenance activities for places having extensive systems of pipes, such as power plants, water and wastewater treatment plants, pipelines, office buildings, and factories. However, the growing use of plastic pipe and fittings, which are much easier to install and repair than other types; increasingly efficient sprinkler systems; and other new technologies will restrict the number of new jobs. In addition to those resulting from employment growth, many positions will become available each year from the need to replace experienced workers who retire or leave the occupation for other reasons.

Traditionally, many organizations with extensive pipe systems have employed their own plumbers or pipefitters to maintain equipment and keep systems running smoothly. But, to reduce labor costs, many of these firms no longer employ a full-time, in-house plumber or pipefitter. Instead, when they need a plumber, they rely on workers provided under service contracts by plumbing and pipefitting contractors.

Construction projects provide only temporary employment. So, when a project ends, pipelayers, plumbers, pipefitters, and steamfitters working on the project may experience bouts of unemployment. Because construction activity varies from area to area, job openings, as well as apprenticeship opportunities, fluctuate with local economic conditions. However, employment of pipelayers, plumbers, pipefitters, and steamfitters generally is less sensitive to changes in economic conditions than is that of some other construction trades. Even when construction activity declines, maintenance, rehabilitation, and replacement of existing piping systems, as well as the increasing installation of fire sprinkler systems, provide many jobs for pipelayers, plumbers, pipefitters, and steamfitters.

Earnings

Pipelayers, plumbers, pipefitters, and steamfitters are among the highest paid construction occupations; in 2000, median hourly earnings of plumbers, pipefitters, and steamfitters were $18.19. The middle 50 percent earned between $14.00 and $24.24. The lowest 10 percent earned less than $10.71, and the highest 10 percent earned more than $30.06. Median hourly earnings in the industries employing the largest numbers of plumbers, pipefitters, and steamfitters in 2000 are shown in the following table.

Plumbing, heating, and air-conditioning	$18.20
Nonresidential building construction	17.80
Heavy construction, except highway	17.26
Local government	17.12
Miscellaneous special trade contractors	16.92

In 2000, median hourly earnings of pipelayers were $13.20. The middle 50 percent earned between $10.17 and $17.71. The lowest 10 percent earned less than $8.61, and the highest 10 percent earned more than $23.16.

Apprentices usually begin at about 50 percent of the wage rate paid to experienced pipelayers, plumbers, pipefitters, and steamfitters. Wages increase periodically as skills improve. After an initial waiting period, apprentices receive the same benefits as experienced pipelayers, plumbers, pipefitters, and steamfitters do.

Many pipelayers, plumbers, pipefitters, and steamfitters are members of the United Association of Journeymen and Apprentices of the Plumbing and Pipefitting Industry of the United States and Canada.

Related Occupations

Other occupations in which workers install and repair mechanical systems in buildings are boilermakers; electricians; elevator installers and repairers; heating, air-conditioning, and refrigeration mechanics and installers; industrial machinery installation, repair, and maintenance workers; sheet metal workers; and stationary engineers and boiler operators.

Sources of Additional Information

For information about apprenticeships or work opportunities in pipelaying, plumbing, pipefitting, and steamfitting, contact local plumbing, heating, and air-conditioning contractors; a local or state chapter of the National Association of Plumbing, Heating, and Cooling Contractors; a local chapter of the Mechanical Contractors Association; or a local chapter of the United Association of Journeymen and Apprentices of the Plumbing and Pipefitting Industry of the United States and Canada. You can also check with the nearest office of your state employment service or apprenticeship agency.

For information about apprenticeship opportunities for pipelayers, plumbers, pipefitters, and steamfitters, contact:

- United Association of Journeymen and Apprentices of the Plumbing and Pipefitting Industry, 901 Massachusetts Ave. NW., Washington, DC 20001

For more information about training programs for pipelayers, plumbers, pipefitters, and steamfitters, contact:

- Associated Builders and Contractors, 1300 N. 17th St., Arlington, VA 22209. Internet: http://www.abc.org

- National Association of Home Builders, 15th and M St. NW., Washington, DC 20005. Internet: http://www.hbi.org

For general information about the work of pipelayers, plumbers, and pipefitters, contact:

- Mechanical Contractors Association of America, 1385 Piccard Dr., Rockville, MD 20850. Internet: http://www.mcaa.org

- National Association of Plumbing-Heating-Cooling Contractors, 180 S. Washington St., P.O. Box 6808, Falls Church, VA 22040

For general information about the work of sprinklerfitters, contact:

- American Fire Sprinkler Association, Inc., 12959 Jupiter Rd., Suite 142, Dallas, TX 75238-3200. Internet: http://www.firesprinkler.org

- National Fire Sprinkler Association, Robin Hill Corporate Park, Rt. 22, Box 1000, Patterson, NY 12563. Internet: http://www.nfsa.org

Plasterers and Stucco Masons

O*NET 47-2161.00

Significant Points

- Plastering is physically demanding.

- Plastering is learned on the job, either through a formal apprenticeship program or by working as a helper.

- Job opportunities are expected to be good, particularly in the south and southwest.

Nature of the Work

Plastering—one of the oldest crafts in the building trades—is enjoying resurgence in popularity because of the introduction of newer, less costly materials and techniques. *Plasterers* apply plaster to interior walls and ceilings to form fire-resistant and relatively soundproof surfaces. They also apply plaster veneer over drywall to create smooth or textured abrasion-resistant finishes. In addition, plasterers install prefabricated exterior insulation systems over existing walls—for good insulation and interesting architectural effects—and cast ornamental designs in plaster. Stucco masons apply durable plasters, such as polymer-based acrylic finishes and stucco, to exterior surfaces. Drywall installers, ceiling tile installers, and tapers use drywall instead of plaster when erecting interior walls and ceilings.

When plasterers work with interior surfaces such as concrete block and concrete, they first apply a brown coat of gypsum plaster that provides a base, followed by a second, or finish, coat—also called "white coat"—which is a lime-based plaster. When plastering metal lath (supportive wire mesh) foundations, they apply a preparatory, or "scratch," coat with a trowel. They spread this rich plaster mixture into and over the metal lath. Before the plaster sets, plasterers scratch its surface with a rake-like tool to produce ridges, so that the subsequent brown coat will bond tightly.

Laborers prepare a thick, smooth plaster for the brown coat. Plasterers spray or trowel this mixture onto the surface, then finish by smoothing it to an even, level surface.

For the finish coat, plasterers prepare a mixture of lime, plaster of Paris, and water. They quickly apply this to the brown coat using a "hawk"—a light, metal plate with a handle—trowel, brush, and water. This mixture, which sets very quickly, produces a very smooth, durable finish.

Plasterers also work with a plaster material that can be finished in a single coat. This "thin-coat" or gypsum veneer plaster is made of lime and plaster of Paris and is mixed with water at the job site. This plaster provides a smooth, durable, abrasion-resistant finish on interior masonry surfaces, special gypsum baseboard, or drywall prepared with a bonding agent.

Plasterers create decorative interior surfaces as well. They do this by pressing a brush or trowel firmly against a wet plaster surface and using a circular hand motion to create decorative swirls.

For exterior work, stucco masons usually apply stucco—a mixture of Portland cement, lime, and sand—over cement, concrete, masonry, or lath. Stucco may also be applied directly to a wire lath with a scratch coat, followed by a brown coat and then a finish coat. Stucco masons may also embed marble or gravel chips into the finish coat to achieve a pebblelike, decorative finish.

Increasingly, plasterers apply insulation to the exteriors of new and old buildings. They cover the outer wall with rigid foam insulation board and reinforcing mesh, and then trowel on a polymer-based or polymer-modified base coat. They may apply an additional coat of this material with a decorative finish.

Plasterers sometimes do complex decorative and ornamental work that requires special skill and creativity. For example, they may mold intricate wall and ceiling designs. Following an architect's blueprint, plasterers pour or spray a special plaster into a mold and allow it to set. Workers then remove the molded plaster and put it in place, according to the plan.

Working Conditions

Most plastering jobs are indoors; however, plasterers and stucco masons work outside when applying stucco or exterior wall insulation and decorative finish systems. Sometimes, plasterers work on scaffolds high above the ground.

Plastering is physically demanding, requiring considerable standing, bending, lifting, and reaching overhead. The work can be dusty and dirty, soiling shoes and clothing, and can irritate the skin and eyes.

Employment

Plasterers and stucco masons held about 54,000 jobs in 2000. Most plasterers and stucco masons work on new construction sites, particularly where special architectural and lighting effects are part of the work. Some repair and renovate older buildings. Many plasterers and stucco masons are employed in Florida, California, and the southwest, where exterior plasters with decorative finishes are very popular.

Most plasterers and stucco masons work for independent contractors. About 1 out of every 6 plasterers and stucco masons is self-employed.

Training, Other Qualifications, and Advancement

Although most employers recommend apprenticeship as the best way to learn plastering, many people learn the trade by working as helpers to experienced plasterers and stucco masons. Those who learn the trade informally as helpers usually start by carrying materials, setting up scaffolds, and mixing plaster. Later, they learn to apply the scratch, brown, and finish coats.

Apprenticeship programs, sponsored by local joint committees of contractors and unions, generally consist of 2 or 3 years of on-the-job training, in addition to at least 144 hours annually of classroom instruction in drafting, blueprint reading, and mathematics for layout work.

In the classroom, apprentices start with a history of the trade and the industry. They also learn about the uses of plaster, estimating materials and costs, and casting ornamental plaster designs. On the job, they learn about lath bases, plaster mixes, methods of plastering, blueprint reading, and safety. They also learn how to use various tools, such as hand and powered trowels, floats, brushes, straightedges, power tools, plaster-mixing machines, and piston-type pumps. Some apprenticeship programs allow individuals to obtain training in related occupations, such as cement masonry and bricklaying.

Applicants for apprentice or helper jobs normally must be at least 17 years old, in good physical condition, and have good manual dexterity. Applicants who have a high school education are preferred. Courses in general mathematics, mechanical drawing, and shop provide a useful background.

Plasterers and stucco masons may advance to supervisors, superintendents, or estimators for plastering contractors or may become self-employed contractors.

Job Outlook

Job opportunities for plasterers and stucco masons are expected to be good through 2010 because many potential workers may prefer work that is less strenuous and has more comfortable working conditions. Well-trained workers will have especially favorable opportunities.

Employment of plasterers and stucco masons is expected to increase about as fast as the average for all occupations through the year 2010. In addition to job openings due to rising demand for plastering and stucco work, jobs will become available as plasterers and stucco masons transfer to other occupations or leave the labor force.

In past years, employment of plasterers declined as more builders switched to drywall construction. This decline has halted, however, and employment of plasterers is expected to continue growing as a result of the appreciation for the durability and attractiveness that troweled finishes provide. Thin-coat plastering—or veneering—in particular is gaining wide acceptance as more builders recognize its ease of application, durability, quality of finish, and fire-retarding qualities. Prefabricated wall systems and new polymer-based or polymer-modified acrylic exterior insulating finishes also are gaining popularity, particularly in the south and southwest regions of the country. This is not only because of their durability, attractiveness, and insulating properties but also because of their relatively low cost. In addition, plasterers will be needed to renovate plasterwork in old structures and to create special architectural effects, such as curved surfaces, which are not practical with drywall materials.

Most plasterers and stucco masons work in construction, where prospects fluctuate from year to year due to changing economic conditions. Bad weather affects plastering less than other construction trades because most work is indoors. On exterior surfacing jobs, however, plasterers and stucco masons may lose time because materials cannot be applied under wet or freezing conditions. Best employment opportunities should continue to be in Florida, California, and the southwest, where exterior plaster and decorative finishes are expected to remain popular.

Earnings

In 2000, median hourly earnings of plasterers and stucco masons were $16.00. The middle 50 percent earned between $12.41 and $20.83. The lowest 10 percent earned less than $9.72, and the top 10 percent earned more than $26.08.

The median hourly earnings in the largest industries employing plasterers and stucco masons in 2000 were $16.03 in masonry, stonework, and plastering and $14.51 in concrete work.

Apprentice wage rates start at about half the rate paid to experienced plasterers and stucco masons. Annual earnings for plasterers and stucco masons and apprentices can be less than the hourly rate would indicate, because poor weather and periodic declines in construction activity can limit worktime.

Many plasterers and stucco masons are members of unions. They are represented by the Operative Plasterers' and Cement Masons' International Association of the United States and Canada, or by the International Union of Bricklayers and Allied Craftsmen.

Related Occupations

Other construction workers who use a trowel as their primary tool include brickmasons, blockmasons, and stonemasons; cement masons, concrete finishers, segmental pavers, and terrazzo workers; and drywall installers, ceiling tile installers, and tapers.

Sources of Additional Information

For information about apprenticeships or other work opportunities, contact local plastering contractors, locals of the unions previously mentioned, a local joint union-management apprenticeship committee, or the nearest office of your state apprenticeship agency or employment service.

For general information about the work of plasterers and stucco masons, contact:

- International Union of Bricklayers and Allied Craftsmen, 815 15th St. NW., Washington, DC 20005. Internet: http://www.bacweb.org

- Operative Plasterers' and Cement Masons' International Association of the United States and Canada, 14405 Laurel Place, Suite 300, Laurel, MD 20707

Police and Detectives

O*NET 33-1012.00, 33-3021.01, 33-3021.02, 33-3021.03, 33-3021.04, 33-3021.05, 33-3031.00, 33-3051.01, 33-3051.02, 33-3051.03, 33-3052.00

Significant Points

- Police work can be dangerous and stressful.

- The number of qualified candidates exceeds the number of job openings in federal and state law enforcement agencies but is inadequate to meet growth and replacement needs in many local and special police departments.

- The largest number of employment opportunities will arise in urban communities with relatively low salaries and high crime rates.

Nature of the Work

People depend on police officers and detectives to protect their lives and property. Law enforcement officers, some of whom are state or federal special agents or inspectors, perform these duties in a variety of ways, depending on the size and type of their organization. In most jurisdictions, they are expected to exercise authority when necessary, whether on or off duty. According to the U.S. Bureau of Justice Statistics, about 65 percent of state and local law enforcement officers are uniformed personnel.

Uniformed police officers who work in municipal police departments of various sizes, small communities, and rural areas have general law enforcement duties including maintaining regular patrols and responding to calls for service. They may direct traffic at the scene of a fire, investigate a burglary, or give first aid to an accident victim. In large police departments, officers usually are assigned to a specific type of duty. Many urban police agencies are becoming more involved in community policing—a practice in which an officer builds relationships with the citizens of local neighborhoods and mobilizes the public to help fight crime.

Police agencies are usually organized into geographic districts, with uniformed officers assigned to patrol a specific area, such as part of the business district or outlying residential neighborhoods. Officers may work alone, but in large agencies they often patrol with a partner. While on patrol, officers attempt to become thoroughly familiar with their patrol area and remain alert for anything unusual. Suspicious circumstances and hazards to public safety are investigated or noted, and officers are dispatched to individual calls for assistance within their district. During their shift, they may identify, pursue, and arrest suspected criminals, resolve problems within the community, and enforce traffic laws.

Public college and university police forces, public school district police, and agencies serving transportation systems and facilities are examples of special police agencies. There are more than 1,300 of these agencies with special geographic jurisdictions or enforcement responsibilities in the United States. More than 75 percent of the sworn personnel in special agencies are uniformed officers, and about 15 percent are investigators.

Some police officers specialize in such diverse fields as chemical and microscopic analysis, training and firearms instruction, or handwriting and fingerprint identification. Others work with special units such as horseback, bicycle, motorcycle or harbor patrol, canine corps, or special weapons and tactics (SWAT) or emergency response teams. About 10 percent of local and special law enforcement officers perform jail-related duties, and around 4 percent work in courts. Regardless of job duties or location, police officers and detectives at all levels must write reports and maintain meticulous records that will be needed if they testify in court.

Sheriffs and deputy sheriffs enforce the law on the county level. Sheriffs are usually elected to their posts and perform duties similar to those of a local or county police chief. Sheriffs' departments tend to be relatively small, most having fewer than 25 sworn officers. A deputy sheriff in a large agency will have law enforcement duties similar to those of officers in urban police departments. Nationwide, about 40 percent of full-time sworn deputies are uniformed officers assigned to patrol and respond to calls, 12 percent are investigators, 30 percent are assigned to jail-related duties, and 11 percent perform court-related duties, with the balance in administration. Police and sheriffs' deputies who provide security in city and county courts are sometimes called bailiffs.

State police officers (sometimes called *state troopers* or *highway patrol officers*) arrest criminals statewide and patrol highways to enforce motor vehicle laws and regulations. Uniformed officers are best known for issuing traffic citations to motorists who violate the law. At the scene of accidents, they may direct traffic, give first aid, and call for emergency equipment. They also write reports used to determine the cause of the accident. State police officers are frequently called upon to render assistance to other law enforcement agencies, especially those in rural areas or small towns.

State law enforcement agencies operate in every state except Hawaii. Seventy percent of the full-time sworn personnel in the 49 state police agencies are uniformed officers who regularly patrol and respond to calls for service. Fifteen percent are investigators; 2 percent are assigned to court-related duties; and the remaining 13 percent work in administrative or other assignments.

Detectives are plainclothes investigators who gather facts and collect evidence for criminal cases. Some are assigned to interagency task forces to combat specific types of crime. They conduct interviews, examine records, observe the activities of suspects, and participate in raids or arrests. Detectives and state and federal agents and inspectors usually specialize in one of a wide variety of violations such as homicide or fraud. They are assigned cases on a rotating basis and work on them until an arrest and conviction occurs or the case is dropped.

The federal government maintains a high profile in many areas of law enforcement. The U.S. Department of Justice is the largest employer of sworn federal officers. *Federal Bureau of Investigation (FBI) agents* are the Government's principal investigators, responsible for investigating violations of more than 260 statutes and conducting sensitive national security investigations. Agents may conduct surveillance, monitor court-authorized wiretaps, examine business records, investigate white-collar crime, track the interstate movement of stolen property, collect evidence of espionage activities, or participate in sensitive undercover assignments. The FBI investigates organized crime, public corruption, financial crime, fraud against the government, bribery, copyright infringement, civil rights violations, bank robbery, extortion, kidnapping,

air piracy, terrorism, espionage, interstate criminal activity, drug trafficking, and other violations of federal statutes.

U.S. Drug Enforcement Administration (DEA) agents enforce laws and regulations relating to illegal drugs. Not only is the DEA the lead agency for domestic enforcement of federal drug laws, it also has sole responsibility for coordinating and pursuing U.S. drug investigations abroad. Agents may conduct complex criminal investigations, carry out surveillance of criminals, and infiltrate illicit drug organizations using undercover techniques.

U.S. marshals and deputy marshals protect the federal courts and ensure the effective operation of the judicial system. They provide protection for the federal judiciary, transport federal prisoners, protect federal witnesses, and manage assets seized from criminal enterprises. They enjoy the widest jurisdiction of any federal law enforcement agency and are involved to some degree in nearly all federal law enforcement efforts. In addition, U.S. marshals pursue and arrest federal fugitives.

U.S. Immigration and Naturalization Service (INS) agents and inspectors facilitate the entry of legal visitors and immigrants to the United States and detain and deport those arriving illegally. They consist of border patrol agents, immigration inspectors, criminal investigators and immigration agents, and detention and deportation officers. Nearly half of sworn INS officers are border patrol agents. *U.S. Border Patrol agents* protect more than 8,000 miles of international land and water boundaries. Their missions are to detect and prevent the smuggling and unlawful entry of undocumented foreign nationals into the United States, apprehend those persons found in violation of the immigration laws, and interdict contraband, such as narcotics. *Immigration inspectors* interview and examine people seeking entrance to the United States and its territories. They inspect passports to determine whether people are legally eligible to enter the United States. Immigration inspectors also prepare reports, maintain records, and process applications and petitions for immigration or temporary residence in the United States.

Special agents and inspectors employed by the U.S. Department of the Treasury work for the Bureau of Alcohol, Tobacco, and Firearms; the Customs Service; and the Secret Service. *Bureau of Alcohol, Tobacco, and Firearms (ATF) agents* regulate and investigate violations of federal firearms and explosives laws, as well as federal alcohol and tobacco tax regulations. *Customs agents* investigate violations of narcotics smuggling, money laundering, child pornography, customs fraud, and enforcement of the Arms Export Control Act. Domestic and foreign investigations involve the development and use of informants, physical and electronic surveillance, and examination of records from importers/exporters, banks, couriers, and manufacturers. They conduct interviews, serve on joint task forces with other agencies, and get and execute search warrants.

Customs inspectors inspect cargo, baggage, and articles worn or carried by people and carriers including vessels, vehicles, trains and aircraft entering or leaving the United States to enforce laws governing imports and exports. These inspectors examine, count, weigh, gauge, measure, and sample commercial and noncommercial cargoes entering and leaving the United States. Customs inspectors seize prohibited or smuggled articles, intercept contraband, and apprehend, search, detain, and arrest violators of U.S. laws. *U.S. Secret Service special agents* protect the president, vice president, and their immediate families, presidential candidates, former presidents, and foreign dignitaries visiting the United States. Secret Service agents also investigate counterfeiting, forgery of Government checks or bonds, and fraudulent use of credit cards.

The U.S. Department of State *Bureau of Diplomatic Security special agents* are engaged in the battle against terrorism. Overseas, they advise ambassadors on all security matters and manage a complex range of security programs designed to protect personnel, facilities, and information. In the United States, they investigate passport and visa fraud, conduct personnel security investigations, issue security clearances, and protect the Secretary of state and a number of foreign dignitaries. They also train foreign civilian police and administer a counter-terrorism reward program.

Other federal agencies employ police and special agents with sworn arrest powers and the authority to carry firearms. These agencies include the U.S. Postal Service, the Bureau of Indian Affairs Office of Law Enforcement under the U.S. Department of the Interior, the U.S. Forest Service under the U.S. Department of Agriculture, the National Park Service under the U.S. Department of the Interior, and Federal Air Marshals under the U.S. Department of Transportation. Other police agencies have evolved from the need for security for the agency's property and personnel. The largest such agency is the General Services Administration's Federal Protective Service, which provides security for federal workers, buildings, and property.

Working Conditions

Police work can be very dangerous and stressful. In addition to the obvious dangers of confrontations with criminals, officers need to be constantly alert and ready to deal appropriately with a number of other threatening situations. Many law enforcement officers witness death and suffering resulting from accidents and criminal behavior. A career in law enforcement may take a toll on officers' private lives.

Uniformed officers, detectives, agents, and inspectors are usually scheduled to work 40-hour weeks, but paid overtime is common. Shiftwork is necessary because protection must be provided around the clock. Junior officers frequently work weekends, holidays, and nights. Police officers and detectives are required to work at any time their services are needed and may work long hours during investigations. In most jurisdictions, whether on or off duty, officers are expected to be armed and to exercise their arrest authority whenever necessary.

The jobs of some federal agents such as U.S. Secret Service and DEA special agents require extensive travel, often on very short notice. They may relocate a number of times over the course of their careers. Some special agents in agencies such as the U.S. Border Patrol work outdoors in rugged terrain for long periods and in all kinds of weather.

Employment

Police and detectives held about 834,000 jobs in 2000. About 80 percent were employed by local governments. State police agencies employed about 13 percent and various federal agencies employed about 6 percent. A small proportion worked for schools, railroads, transit agencies, or private detective, guard, and armored car services.

According to the U.S. Bureau of Justice Statistics, police and detectives employed by local governments primarily worked in cities with more than 25,000 inhabitants. Some cities have very large police forces, while thousands of small communities employ fewer than 25 officers each. Forty-six local, special, and state agencies employed 1,000 or more full-time sworn officers, while approximately 7,000 departments employed fewer than 10 each.

Training, Other Qualifications, and Advancement

Civil service regulations govern the appointment of police and detectives in practically all states, large municipalities, and special police agencies, as well as in many smaller ones. Candidates must be U.S. citizens, usually at least 20 years of age, and must meet rigorous physical and personal qualifications. In the federal government, candidates must be at least 21 years of age but less than 37 years of age at the time of appointment. Physical examinations for entrance into law enforcement often include tests of vision, hearing, strength, and agility. Eligibility for appointment usually depends on performance in competitive written examinations and previous education and experience. In larger departments, where the majority of law enforcement jobs are found, applicants usually must have at least a high school education. Federal and state agencies typically require a college degree. Candidates should enjoy working with people and meeting the public.

Because personal characteristics such as honesty, sound judgement, integrity, and a sense of responsibility are especially important in law enforcement, candidates are interviewed by senior officers, and their character traits and backgrounds are investigated. In some agencies, candidates are interviewed by a psychiatrist or a psychologist, or given a personality test. Most applicants are subjected to lie detector examinations or drug testing. Some agencies subject sworn personnel to random drug testing as a condition of continuing employment.

Before their first assignments, officers usually go through a period of training. In state and large local departments, recruits get training in their agency's police academy, often for 12 to 14 weeks. In small agencies, recruits often attend a regional or state academy. Training includes classroom instruction in constitutional law and civil rights, state laws and local ordinances, and accident investigation. Recruits also receive training and supervised experience in patrol, traffic control, use of firearms, self-defense, first aid, and emergency response. Police departments in some large cities hire high school graduates who are still in their teens as police cadets or trainees. They do clerical work and attend classes, usually for 1 to 2 years, at which point they reach the minimum age requirement and may be appointed to the regular force.

Police officers usually become eligible for promotion after a probationary period ranging from 6 months to 3 years. In a large department, promotion may enable an officer to become a detective or specialize in one type of police work, such as working with juveniles. Promotions to corporal, sergeant, lieutenant, and captain usually are made according to a candidate's position on a promotion list, as determined by scores on a written examination and on-the-job performance.

The FBI has the largest number of special agents. To be considered for appointment as an FBI agent, an applicant either must be a graduate of an accredited law school or a college graduate with a major in accounting, fluency in a foreign language, or 3 years of related full-time work experience. All new agents undergo 16 weeks of training at the FBI academy on the U.S. Marine Corps base in Quantico, Virginia.

Applicants for special agent jobs with the U.S. Department of Treasury's Secret Service and the Bureau of Alcohol, Tobacco, and Firearms must have a bachelor's degree or a minimum of 3 years' related work experience. Prospective special agents undergo 10 weeks of initial criminal investigation training at the Federal Law Enforcement Training Center in Glynco, Georgia, and another 17 weeks of specialized training with their particular agencies.

Applicants for special agent jobs with the U.S. Drug Enforcement Administration (DEA) must have a college degree and either 1 year of experience conducting criminal investigations, 1 year of graduate school, or have achieved at least a 2.95 grade point average while in college. DEA special agents undergo 14 weeks of specialized training at the FBI Academy in Quantico, Va.

U.S. Border Patrol agents must be U.S. citizens, younger than 37 years of age at the time of appointment, possess a valid driver's license, and pass a three-part examination on reasoning and language skills. A bachelor's degree or previous work experience that demonstrates the ability to handle stressful situations, make decisions, and take charge is required for a position as a Border Patrol agent. Applicants may qualify through a combination of education and work experience.

Postal inspectors must have a bachelor's degree and 1 year of related work experience. It is desirable that they have one of several professional certifications, such as that of certified public accountant. They also must pass a background suitability investigation, meet certain health requirements, undergo a drug screening test, possess a valid state driver's license, and be a U.S. citizen between 21 and 36 years of age when hired.

Law enforcement agencies are encouraging applicants to take postsecondary school training in law enforcement-related subjects. Many entry-level applicants for police jobs have completed some formal postsecondary education and a significant number are college graduates. Many junior colleges, colleges, and universities offer programs in law enforcement or administration of justice. Other courses helpful in preparing for a career in law enforcement include accounting, finance, electrical engineering, computer science, and foreign languages. Physical education and sports are helpful in developing the competitiveness, stamina, and agility needed for many law enforcement positions. Knowledge of a foreign language is an asset in many federal agencies and urban departments.

Continuing training helps police officers, detectives, and special agents improve their job performance. Through police department academies, regional centers for public safety employees established by the states, and federal agency training centers, instructors provide annual training in self-defense tactics, firearms, use-of-force policies, sensitivity and communications skills, crowd-control techniques, relevant legal developments, and advances in law enforcement equipment. Many agencies pay all or part of the tuition for officers to work toward degrees in criminal justice, police science, administration of justice, or public administration, and pay higher salaries to those who earn such a degree.

Job Outlook

The opportunity for public service through law enforcement work is attractive to many because the job is challenging and involves much personal responsibility. Furthermore, law enforcement officers in many agencies may retire with a pension after 20 or 25 years of service, allowing them to pursue a second career while still in their 40s. Because of relatively attractive salaries and benefits, the number of qualified candidates exceeds the number of job openings in federal law enforcement agencies and in most state police departments—resulting in increased hiring standards and selectivity by employers. Competition is expected to remain keen for the higher paying jobs with state and federal agencies and police departments in more affluent areas. Opportunities will be better in local and special police departments, especially in departments that offer relatively low salaries or urban communities where the crime rate is relatively high. Applicants with college training in police

science, military police experience, or both should have the best opportunities.

Employment of police and detectives is expected to increase faster than the average for all occupations through 2010. A more security-conscious society and concern about drug-related crimes should contribute to the increasing demand for police services. At the local and state levels, growth is likely to continue as long as crime remains a serious concern. However, employment growth at the federal level will be tempered by continuing budgetary constraints faced by law enforcement agencies.

The level of government spending determines the level of employment for police officers, detectives, and special agents. The number of job opportunities, therefore, can vary from year to year and from place to place. Layoffs, on the other hand, are rare because retirements enable most staffing cuts to be handled through attrition. Trained law enforcement officers who lose their jobs because of budget cuts usually have little difficulty finding jobs with other agencies. The need to replace workers who retire, transfer to other occupations, or stop working for other reasons will be the source of many job openings.

Earnings

Police and sheriff's patrol officers had median annual earnings of $39,790 in 2000. The middle 50 percent earned between $30,460 and $50,230. The lowest 10 percent earned less than $23,790, and the highest 10 percent earned more than $58,900. Median annual earnings were $44,400 in state government, $39,710 in local government, and $37,760 in federal government.

In 2000, median annual earnings of police and detective supervisors were $57,210. The middle 50 percent earned between $43,630 and $70,680. The lowest 10 percent earned less than $34,660, and the highest 10 percent earned more than $86,060. Median annual earnings were $74,070 in federal government, $57,030 in local government, and $53,960 in state government.

In 2000, median annual earnings of detectives and criminal investigators were $48,870. The middle 50 percent earned between $37,240 and $61,750. The lowest 10 percent earned less than $29,600, and the highest 10 percent earned more than $72,160. Median annual earnings were $61,180 in federal government, $46,340 in local government, and $43,050 in state government.

Federal law provides special salary rates to federal employees who serve in law enforcement. Additionally, federal special agents and inspectors receive law enforcement availability pay (LEAP)—equal to 25 percent of the agent's grade and step—awarded because of the large amount of overtime that these agents are expected to work. For example, in 2001 FBI agents enter federal service as GS-10 employees on the pay scale at a base salary of $36,621, yet earned about $45,776 a year with availability pay. They can advance to the GS-13 grade level in field non-supervisory assignments at a base salary of $57,345 which is worth almost $71,681 with availability pay. FBI supervisory, management, and executive positions in grades GS-14 and GS-15 pay a base salary of about $67,765 or $79,710 a year, respectively, and equaled $84,706 or $99,637 per year including availability pay. Salaries were slightly higher in selected areas where the prevailing local pay level was higher. Because federal agents may be eligible for a special law enforcement benefits package, applicants should ask their recruiter for more information.

The International City-County Management Association's annual Police and Fire Personnel, Salaries, and Expenditures Survey revealed that

84 percent of the municipalities surveyed provided police services in 2000. The following table shows minimum and maximum annual base salaries for sworn full-time positions in 2000.

	Minimum	Maximum
Police chief	$62,640	$78,580
Deputy chief	53,740	67,370
Police captain	51,680	64,230
Police lieutenant	47,750	57,740
Police sergeant	42,570	50,670
Police corporal	35,370	43,830
Police officer	31,410	43,450

Total earnings for local, state, and special police and detectives frequently exceed the stated salary because of payments for overtime, which can be significant. In addition to the common benefits—paid vacation, sick leave, and medical and life insurance—most police and sheriffs' departments provide officers with special allowances for uniforms. Because police officers usually are covered by liberal pension plans, many retire at half-pay after 20 or 25 years of service.

Related Occupations

Police and detectives maintain law and order, collect evidence and information, and conduct investigations and surveillance. Workers in related occupations include correctional officers, private detectives and investigators, and security guards and gaming surveillance officers.

Sources of Additional Information

Information about entrance requirements may be obtained from federal, state, and local law enforcement agencies.

Further information about qualifications for employment as a FBI Special Agent is available from the nearest state FBI office. The address and phone number are listed in the local telephone directory.

● Internet: http://www.fbi.gov

Information about qualifications for employment as a DEA Special Agent is available from the nearest DEA office, or call:

● (800) DEA-4288. Internet: http://www.usdoj.gov/dea

Information about career opportunities, qualifications, and training to become a deputy marshal is available from:

● United States Marshals Service, Employment and Compensation Division, Field Staffing Branch, 600 Army Navy Dr., Arlington, VA 22202. Internet: http://www.usdoj.gov/marshals

Career opportunities, qualifications, and training for U.S. Secret Service Special Agents is available from:

● U.S. Secret Service, Personnel Division, Suite 7400, 950 H St. NW., Washington, DC 20223. Internet: http://www.treas.gov/usss

For information on career opportunities and U.S. Bureau of Alcohol, Tobacco and Firearms operations, contact:

● U.S. Bureau of Alcohol, Tobacco and Firearms, Personnel Division, 650 Massachusetts Avenue NW., Room 4100, Washington, DC 20226. Internet: http://www.atf.treas.gov

Information about careers in the United States Border Patrol is available from:

● U.S. Border Patrol, Chester A. Arthur Building, 425 I St. NW., Washington DC 20536. Internet: http://www.ins.usdoj.gov/graphics/workfor/careers/bpcareer/index.htm

Postal Service Workers

O*NET 43-5051.00, 43-5052.00, 43-5053.00

Significant Points

● Qualification is based on an examination.

● Employment is expected to decline slightly.

● Keen competition is expected because the number of qualified applicants should continue to exceed the number of job openings.

Nature of the Work

Each week, the U.S. Postal Service delivers billions of pieces of mail, including letters, bills, advertisements, and packages. To do this in an efficient and timely manner, the postal service employs about 860,000 individuals. Most postal service workers are postal clerks or mail carriers. Postal clerks include a wide variety of workers such as window clerks, distribution clerks, and mail processors. Window clerks wait on customers at post offices, whereas distribution clerks and mail processors sort mail. Mail carriers deliver mail to urban and rural residences and businesses throughout the United States.

Postal clerks, who typically are classified by job duties, perform a variety of functions in the nation's post offices. Those who work as window or counter clerks, for example, sell stamps, money orders, postal stationary, and mailing envelopes and boxes. They also weigh packages to determine postage and check that packages are in satisfactory condition for mailing. These clerks register, certify, and insure mail and answer questions about postage rates, post office boxes, mailing restrictions, and other postal matters. Window and counter clerks also help customers file claims for damaged packages.

Distribution clerks sort local mail for delivery to individual customers. Other clerks, known as mail processors, operate optical character readers (OCRs) and barcode sorters to arrange mail according to destination. OCRs "read" the ZIP code and spray a barcode onto the mail. Barcode sorters then scan the code and sort the mail. Because this is significantly faster than older sorting methods, it is becoming the standard sorting technology in mail processing centers.

Nevertheless, in some locations, mail still is sorted using electronic letter-sorting machines. Workers who operate these machines push keys corresponding to the ZIP code of the local post office to which each letter will be delivered. The machine then drops the letter into the proper slot. Odd-sized letters, magazines, and newspapers still are sorted by hand. In small post offices, some workers perform all of the functions listed above.

Once the mail has been processed and sorted, it is ready to be delivered by mail carriers. Although carriers are classified by their type of route—either city or rural—duties of city and rural carriers are similar. Most travel established routes, delivering and collecting mail. Mail carriers start work at the post office early in the morning, when they arrange the mail in delivery sequence. Recently, automated equipment has reduced the time that carriers need to sort the mail, allowing them to spend more time delivering mail.

Mail carriers cover their routes on foot, by vehicle, or a combination of both. On foot, they carry a heavy load of mail in a satchel or push it on a cart. In most urban and rural areas, they use a car or small truck. Although the postal service provides vehicles to city carriers, most rural carriers must use their own automobiles. Deliveries are made house-to-house, to roadside mailboxes, and to large buildings such as offices or apartments, which generally have all the mailboxes at one location.

Besides delivering and collecting mail, carriers collect money for postage-due and COD (cash-on-delivery) fees and obtain signed receipts for registered, certified, and insured mail. If a customer is not home, the carrier leaves a notice that tells where special mail is being held. After completing their routes, carriers return to the post office with mail gathered from street collection boxes, homes, and businesses and turn in the mail, receipts, and money collected during the day.

The duties of some city carriers can be specialized, with some delivering only parcel post, whereas others pick up mail from mail collection boxes. In contrast to city carriers, rural carriers provide a wider range of postal services, in addition to delivering and picking up mail. For example, rural carriers may sell stamps and money orders and register, certify, and insure parcels and letters. All carriers, however, must be able to answer customers' questions about postal regulations and services and provide change-of-address cards and other postal forms when requested.

Working Conditions

Window clerks usually work in the public portion of clean, well-ventilated, and well lit buildings. They have a variety of duties and frequent contact with the public, but they rarely work at night. However, they may have to deal with upset customers, stand for long periods, and be held accountable for an assigned stock of stamps and funds. Depending on the size of the post office in which they work, they also may be required to sort mail.

The working conditions of other postal clerks can vary. In small post offices, workers may sort mail by hand. In large post offices and mail processing centers, chutes and conveyors move the mail, and machines do much of the sorting. Despite the use of automated equipment, the work of postal clerks can be physically demanding. These workers usually are on their feet, reaching for sacks and trays of mail or placing packages and bundles into sacks and trays.

Mail distribution clerks and mail processors can become tired and bored with the endless routine of moving and sorting mail. Many work at night or on weekends, because most large post offices process mail around the clock, and the largest volume of mail is sorted during the evening and night shifts. Workers can experience stress, as they process ever-larger quantities of mail under tight production deadlines and quotas.

Most carriers begin work early in the morning. Those with routes in a business district can start as early as 4 a.m. Overtime hours are frequently required for urban carriers during peak delivery times, such as before the winter holidays. A carrier's schedule has its advantages, however. Carriers who begin work early in the morning are through by early afternoon and spend most of the day on their own, relatively free from direct supervision. Carriers spend most of their time outdoors, delivering mail in all kinds of weather. Even those who drive often must walk periodically when making deliveries and must lift heavy sacks of parcel post items when loading their vehicles. In addition, carriers must be cautious of potential hazards on their routes. Wet and icy roads and sidewalks can be treacherous, and each year dogs attack numerous carriers.

Employment

The U.S. Postal Service employed 74,000 clerks; 324,000 mail carriers; and 289,000 mail sorters, processors, and processing-machine operators in 2000. Most of them worked full time. While some postal clerks provided window service, most processed mail. Many distribution clerks and mail processors sorted mail at major metropolitan post offices; others worked at mail-processing centers. The majority of mail carriers worked in cities and suburbs, while the rest worked in rural areas.

Postal service workers are classified as casual, part-time flexible, part-time regular, or full time. Casuals are hired for 90 days at a time to help process and deliver mail during peak mailing or vacation periods. Part-time flexible workers do not have a regular work schedule or weekly guarantee of hours but are called in as the need arises. Part-time regulars have a set work schedule of fewer than 40 hours per week, often replacing regular full-time workers on their scheduled day off. Full-time postal employees work a 40-hour week over a 5-day period.

Training, Other Qualifications, and Advancement

Postal service workers must be at least 18 years old and U.S. citizens or have been granted permanent resident-alien status in the United States. Qualification is based on a written examination that measures speed and accuracy at checking names and numbers and the ability to memorize mail distribution procedures. Applicants must pass a physical examination and drug test, and may be asked to show that they can lift and handle mail sacks weighing 70 pounds. Applicants for mail carrier positions must have a driver's license and a good driving record, and receive a passing grade on a road test.

Job seekers should contact the post office or mail processing center where they wish to work to determine when an exam will be given. Applicants' names are listed in order of their examination scores. Five points are added to the score of an honorably discharged veteran and 10 points to the score of a veteran who was wounded in combat or is disabled. When a vacancy occurs, the appointing officer chooses one of the top three applicants; the rest of the names remain on the list to be considered for future openings until their eligibility expires—usually 2 years after the examination date.

Relatively few people become postal clerks or mail carriers as their first job, because of keen competition and the customary waiting period of 1 to 2 years or more after passing the examination. It is not surprising, therefore, that most entrants transfer from other occupations.

New postal service workers are trained on the job by experienced workers. Many post offices offer classroom instruction on safety and defensive driving. Workers receive additional instruction when new equipment or procedures are introduced. In these cases, workers usually are trained by another postal employee or a training specialist.

Postal clerks and mail carriers should be courteous and tactful when dealing with the public, especially when answering questions or receiving complaints. A good memory and the ability to read rapidly and accurately are important. Good interpersonal skills also are vital, because mail distribution clerks work closely with other postal workers, frequently under the tension and strain of meeting dispatch or transportation deadlines and quotas.

Postal service workers often begin on a part-time, flexible basis and become regular or full time, in order of seniority as vacancies occur. Full-time workers may bid for preferred assignments, such as the day shift or a high-level nonsupervisory position. Carriers can look forward to obtaining preferred routes as their seniority increases, or to high-level jobs, such as carrier technician. Postal service workers can advance to supervisory positions on a competitive basis.

Job Outlook

Employment of postal service workers is expected to decline slightly through 2010. However, many jobs still will become available because of the need to replace those who retire or leave the occupation. Those seeking jobs as postal service workers can expect to encounter keen competition, because the number of applicants will continue to exceed the number of openings.

Although efforts by the U.S. Postal Service to provide better service will increase the number of window clerks, the demand for such clerks will be offset by the use of electronic communications technologies and private delivery companies. Employment of distribution clerks and mail processors is expected to decline because of the increasing use of automated materials handling equipment and optical character readers, barcode sorters, and other automated sorting equipment. The expected decline in mail volume also may have a negative impact on the employment of distribution clerks and mail processors.

Several factors are expected to influence demand for mail carriers. The competition from alternative delivery systems and new forms of electronic communication could drastically affect the total volume of mail handled. The postal service expects mail volume to increase through 2002, and then decrease through 2010. Most of the decrease is expected to come from first-class and standard mail. The postal service expects an increase in package deliveries due to the rising number of purchases made through the Internet by businesses and consumers and to partnerships the postal service has made with its competitors. Although total mail volume is projected to decrease, perhaps significantly, the number of addresses to which mail must be delivered will continue to increase. However, increased use of the "delivery point sequencing" system, which allows machines to sort mail directly by the order of delivery, should reduce the amount of time carriers spend sorting their mail, allowing them more time to handle these longer routes. In addition, the postal service is moving toward more centralized mail delivery, such as the increased use of cluster boxes, to cut down on the number of door-to-door deliveries. These trends are expected to increase carrier productivity, causing slow employment growth.

Currently the role of the postal service as a government-approved monopoly is a topic of debate. Any legislative changes that would privatize or deregulate the U.S. Postal Service may affect employment of all its workers. Employment and schedules in the postal service fluctuate with the demand for its services. When mail volume is high, full-time workers work overtime, part-time workers work additional hours, and casual workers may be hired. When mail volume is low, overtime is curtailed, part-timers work fewer hours, and casual workers are discharged.

Earnings

Median annual earnings of postal mail carriers were $38,420 in 2000. The middle 50 percent earned between $33,620 and $41,930. The lowest 10 percent had earnings of less than $26,140, while the top 10 percent earned over $44,040. Rural mail carriers are reimbursed for mileage put on their own vehicles while delivering mail.

Median annual earnings of postal service clerks were $39,010 in 2000. The middle 50 percent earned between $36,140 and $41,870. The lowest 10 percent had earnings of less than $31,980, while the top 10 percent earned more than $43,590.

Median annual earnings of mail sorters, processors, and processing-machine operators were $32,080 in 2000. The middle 50 percent earned between $22,560 and $39,300. The lowest 10 percent had earnings of less than $18,940, while the top 10 percent earned more than $42,570.

Postal service workers enjoy a variety of employer-provided benefits similar to those enjoyed by federal government workers. The American Postal Workers Union or the National Association of Letter Carriers, both of which are affiliated with the AFL-CIO, represent most of these workers.

Related Occupations

Other occupations with duties similar to those of postal clerks include cashiers; counter and rental clerks; file clerks; and shipping, receiving, and traffic clerks. Others with duties related to those of mail carriers include couriers and messengers and truckdrivers and driver/sales workers. Occupations whose duties are related to those of mail sorters, processors, and processing-machine operators include inspectors, testers, sorters, samplers, and weighers, and material moving occupations.

Sources of Additional Information

Local post offices and state employment service offices can supply details about entrance examinations and specific employment opportunities for postal service workers.

Power Plant Operators, Distributors, and Dispatchers

O*NET 51-8011.00, 51-8012.00, 51-8013.01, 51-8013.02

Significant Points

● Overall employment of operators, distributors, and dispatchers is expected to change little due to increasing industry competition.

- Opportunities will be best for operators with training in automated systems.

- Little or no change in employment and low turnover will result in few job opportunities.

Nature of the Work

Electricity is vital for most everyday activities. From the moment you flip the first switch each morning, you are connecting to a huge network of people, electric lines, and generating equipment. Power plant operators control the machinery that generates electricity. Power distributors and dispatchers control the flow of electricity from the power plant over a network of transmission lines, to industrial plants and substations, and, finally, over distribution lines to residential users.

Power plant operators control and monitor boilers, turbines, generators, and auxiliary equipment in power generating plants. Operators distribute power demands among generators, combine the current from several generators, and monitor instruments to maintain voltage and regulate electricity flows from the plant. When power requirements change, these workers start or stop generators and connect or disconnect them from circuits. They often use computers to keep records of switching operations and loads on generators, lines, and transformers. Operators also may use computers to prepare reports of unusual incidents, malfunctioning equipment, or maintenance performed during their shift.

Operators in plants with automated control systems work mainly in a central control room and usually are called *control room operators* and *control room operator trainees* or *assistants*. In older plants, the controls for the equipment are not centralized, and *switchboard operators* control the flow of electricity from a central point, whereas *auxiliary equipment operators* work throughout the plant, operating and monitoring valves, switches, and gauges.

The Nuclear Regulatory Commission (NRC) licenses operators of nuclear power plants. *Reactor operators* are authorized to control equipment that affects the power of the reactor in a nuclear power plant. In addition, an NRC-licensed *senior reactor operator* must be on duty during each shift to act as the plant supervisor and supervise the operation of all controls in the control room.

Power distributors and dispatchers, also called *load dispatchers* or *systems operators*, control the flow of electricity through transmission lines to industrial plants and substations that supply residential electric needs. They operate current converters, voltage transformers, and circuit breakers. Dispatchers monitor equipment and record readings at a pilot board, which is a map of the transmission grid system showing the status of transmission circuits and connections with substations and industrial plants.

Dispatchers also anticipate power needs, such as those caused by changes in the weather. They call control room operators to start or stop boilers and generators, to bring production into balance with needs. They handle emergencies such as transformer or transmission line failures and route current around affected areas. They also operate and monitor equipment in substations, which step up or step down voltage, and operate switchboard levers to control the flow of electricity in and out of substations.

Working Conditions

Because electricity is provided around the clock, operators, distributors, and dispatchers usually work one of three daily 8-hour shifts or one of two 12-hour shifts on a rotating basis. Shift assignments may change periodically, so that all operators can share duty on less desirable shifts. Work on rotating shifts can be stressful and fatiguing, because of the constant change in living and sleeping patterns. Operators, distributors, and dispatchers who work in control rooms generally sit or stand at a control station. This work is not physically strenuous but requires constant attention. Operators who work outside the control room may be exposed to danger from electric shock, falls, and burns.

Nuclear power plant operators are subject to random drug and alcohol tests, as are most workers at nuclear power plants.

Employment

Power plant operators, distributors, and dispatchers held about 55,000 jobs in 2000. Jobs are located throughout the country. About 8 in 10 worked for utility companies and government agencies that produced electricity. Others worked for manufacturing establishments that produced electricity for their own use.

Training, Other Qualifications, and Advancement

Employers seek high school graduates for entry-level operator, distributor, and dispatcher positions. Candidates with strong math and science skills are preferred. College-level courses or prior experience in a mechanical or technical job may be helpful. Employers increasingly require computer proficiency, as computers are used to keep records, generate reports, and track maintenance. Most entry-level positions are helper or laborer jobs, such as in powerline construction. Depending on the results of aptitude tests, worker preferences, and availability of openings, workers may be assigned to train for one of many utility positions.

Workers selected for training as a fossil-fueled power plant operator or distributor undergo extensive on-the-job and classroom training. Several years of training and experience are required to become a fully qualified control room operator or power distributor. With further training and experience, workers may advance to shift supervisor. Utilities generally promote from within; therefore, opportunities to advance by moving to another employer are limited.

Extensive training and experience are necessary to pass the Nuclear Regulatory Commission (NRC) examinations for reactor operators and senior reactor operators. To maintain their license, licensed reactor operators must pass an annual practical plant operation exam and a biennial written exam administered by their employer. Training may include simulator and on-the-job training, classroom instruction, and individual study. Entrants to nuclear power plant operator trainee jobs must have strong math and science skills. Experience in other power plants or with Navy nuclear propulsion plants also is helpful. With further training and experience, reactor operators may advance to senior reactor operator positions.

In addition to preliminary training as a power plant operator, distributor, or dispatcher, most workers are given periodic refresher training. Nuclear power plant operators are given frequent refresher training. This training is usually taken on plant simulators designed specifically to replicate procedures and situations that might be encountered working at the trainee's plant.

Job Outlook

Little or no change in employment of power plant operators, distributors, and dispatchers is expected through the year 2010, as the industry continues to restructure in response to deregulation and increasing competition. The Energy Policy Act of 1992 has had a tremendous impact on the organization of the utilities industry. This legislation has increased competition in power generating utilities by allowing independent power producers to sell power directly to industrial and other wholesale customers. Utilities, which historically operated as regulated local monopolies, are restructuring operations to reduce costs and compete effectively and, as a result, the number of jobs is decreasing.

People who want to become power plant operators, distributors, and dispatchers are expected to encounter keen competition for these high-paying jobs. Little or no change in employment and low turnover in this occupation will result in few job opportunities. The slow pace of new plant construction also will limit opportunities for power plant operators, distributors, and dispatchers. Increasing use of automatic controls and more efficient equipment should increase productivity and decrease the demand for operators. Individuals with training in computers and automated equipment will have the best job prospects.

Earnings

Median annual earnings of power plant operators were $46,090 in 2000. The middle 50 percent earned between $37,320 and $54,200 a year. The lowest 10 percent earned less than $28,700, and the highest 10 percent earned more than $62,020 a year. Median annual earnings of power plant operators in 2000 were $48,350 in electric services and $40,160 in local government.

Median annual earnings of nuclear power reactor operators were $57,220 in 2000. The middle 50 percent earned between $50,720 and $67,320 a year. The lowest 10 percent earned less than $46,890, and the highest 10 percent earned more than $74,370 a year.

Median annual earnings of power distributors and dispatchers were $48,570 in 2000. The middle 50 percent earned between $39,880 and $58,290 a year. The lowest 10 percent earned less than $31,760, and the highest 10 percent earned more than $69,260 a year. Median annual earnings in electric services, the industry employing the largest numbers of power distributors and dispatchers, were $49,070.

Related Occupations

Other workers who monitor and operate plant and systems equipment include chemical plant and system operators; petroleum pump system operators, refinery operators, and gaugers; stationary engineers and boiler operators; and water and wastewater treatment plant and system operators.

Sources of Additional Information

For information about employment opportunities, contact local electric utility companies, locals of unions mentioned below, and state employment service offices.

For general information about power plant operators, nuclear power reactor operators, and power distributors and dispatchers, contact:

- International Brotherhood of Electrical Workers, 1125 15th St. NW., Washington, DC 20005.

- Utility Workers Union of America, 815 16th St. NW., Suite 605, Washington, DC 20006

Precision Instrument and Equipment Repairers

O*NET 49-9061.00, 49-9062.00, 49-9063.01, 49-9063.02, 49-9063.03, 49-9063.04, 49-9064.00, 49-9069.99

Significant Points

- Training requirements include a high school diploma and, in some cases, postsecondary education, coupled with significant on-the-job training.

- Good opportunities are expected for most types of jobs.

- Overall employment is expected to grow about as fast as average, but projected growth varies by detailed occupation.

- About 1 out of 4 is self-employed.

Nature of the Work

Repairing and maintaining watches, cameras, musical instruments, medical equipment, and other precision instruments requires a high level of skill and attention to detail. For example, some devices contain tiny gears that must be manufactured to within one one-hundredth of a millimeter of design specifications, and other devices contain sophisticated electronic controls.

Camera and photographic equipment repairers work through a series of steps in fixing a camera. The first step is determining whether a repair would be profitable. Many inexpensive cameras cost more to repair than to replace. The most complicated or expensive problems are referred back to the manufacturer. If the repairers decide to proceed, they diagnose the problem, often by disassembling numerous small parts in order to reach the source. They then make needed adjustments or replace a defective part. Many problems are caused by the electronic circuits used in many cameras, which require an understanding of electronics. Camera repairers also maintain cameras by removing and replacing broken or worn parts and cleaning and lubricating gears and springs. Many of the components and parts involved are extremely small, requiring a great deal of manual dexterity. Frequently, older camera parts are no longer available, requiring repairers to build replacement parts or strip junked cameras. When machining new parts, workers often use a small lathe, a grinding wheel, and other metalworking tools.

Camera repairers also repair the increasingly popular digital cameras. Repairs on such cameras are similar to those for most modern cameras, but, because digital cameras have no film to wind, they employ fewer moving parts.

Watch and clock repairers work almost exclusively on expensive timepieces, as moderately priced timepieces are cheaper to replace than to repair. Electrically powered quartz watches and clocks function with almost no moving parts, limiting necessary maintenance to replacing the battery. Many expensive timepieces still employ old-style mechanical movements and a manual winding mechanism or spring. This type of timepiece requires regular adjustment and maintenance. Any repair or maintenance work on a mechanical timepiece requires the disassembly of many fine gears and components. Each part is inspected for signs of significant wear. Some gears or springs may need to be replaced or machined. All of the parts are cleaned and oiled.

As for older cameras, replacement parts are frequently unavailable for antique watches or clocks. In such cases, watch repairers must machine their own parts. They employ small lathes and other machines in creating tiny parts.

Musical instrument repairers and tuners combine their love of music with a highly skilled craft. Musical instrument repairers and tuners, often referred to as technicians, work in four specialties: band instruments, pianos and organs, violins, and guitars.

Band instrument repairers, brass and wind instrument repairers, and percussion instrument repairers focus on woodwind, brass, reed, and percussion instruments damaged through deterioration or by accident. They move mechanical parts or play scales to find problems. They may unscrew and remove rod pins, keys, worn cork pads, and pistons and remove soldered parts using gas torches. They repair dents in metal and wood using filling techniques or a mallet. Drums often need new drumheads, which are cut from animal skin. These repairers use gas torches, grinding wheels, shears, mallets, and small hand tools.

Piano repairers use similar techniques, skills, and tools. Repairers often earn additional income by tuning pianos, which involves tightening and loosening different strings to achieve the proper tone or pitch. Pipe-organ repairers do work similar to that of piano repairers on a larger scale. Additionally, they assemble new organs. Because pipe organs are too large to transport, they must be assembled on site. Even with repairers working in teams or with assistants, the organ assembly process can take several weeks or even months, depending upon the size of the organ.

Violin repairers and guitar repairers adjust and repair string instruments. Initially, repairers play and inspect the instrument to find any defects. They replace or repair cracked or broken sections and damaged parts. They also restring the instruments and repair damage to their finish.

The work of *medical equipment repairers* differs significantly from other precision instrument and equipment repair work. Although medical equipment repairers work on fine mechanical systems, the larger scale of their tasks requires less precision. The machines that they repair include electric wheelchairs, mechanical lifts, hospital beds, and customized vehicles.

Medical equipment repairers use various tools, including ammeters, voltmeters, and other measuring devices to diagnose problems. They use handtools and machining equipment, such as small lathes and other metalworking equipment, to make repairs.

Other precision instrument and equipment repairers service, repair, and replace a wide range of equipment associated with automated or instrument-controlled manufacturing processes. A precision instrument repairer working at an electric power plant, for example, would repair and maintain instruments that monitor the operation of the plant, such as pressure and temperature gauges. These workers use many of the same tools that medical equipment repairers use. Malfunctioning parts are often replaced, but sometimes repair is necessary. Replacement parts are not always available, so repairers sometimes machine or fabricate a new part. Preventive maintenance involves regular lubrication, cleaning, and adjustment of many measuring devices.

Working Conditions

Camera, watch, and musical instrument repairers work under fairly similar solitary, low-stress conditions with minimal supervision. A quiet, well-lighted workshop or repair shop is typical, while a few of these repairers travel to the instrument being repaired, such as a piano, organ, or grandfather clock.

Medical equipment and precision instrument and equipment repairers normally work daytime hours. But, like other hospital and factory employees, some repairers work irregular hours. Precision instrument repairers work under a wide array of conditions, from hot, dirty, noisy factories to air-conditioned workshops to outdoor fieldwork. Attention to safety is essential, as the work sometimes involves dangerous machinery or toxic chemicals. Due to the individual nature of the work, supervision is fairly minimal.

Employment

Precision instrument and equipment repairers held 63,000 jobs in 2000. The overwhelming majority of medical equipment repairers and other precision instrument and equipment repairers were wage and salary workers. Medical equipment repairers often work for hospitals or wholesale equipment suppliers, while most precision instrument repairers work in manufacturing. On the other hand, about 1 out of 4 watch, camera and photographic equipment, and musical instrument repairers was self-employed. The following table presents employment by occupation:

Medical equipment repairers	28,000
All other precision instrument and equipment repairers	15,000
Camera and photographic equipment repairers	7,200
Musical instrument repairers and tuners	7,100
Watch repairers	5,200

Training, Other Qualifications, and Advancement

Most employers require at least a high school diploma for beginning precision instrument and equipment repairers. Many employers prefer applicants with some postsecondary education. Much training takes place on the job. The ability to read and understand technical manuals is important. Necessary physical qualities include good fine motor skills and vision. Also, precision equipment repairers must be able to pay close attention to details, enjoy problem solving, and have the desire to disassemble machines to see how they work. Most precision equipment repairers must be able to work alone with minimal supervision.

The educational background required for camera and photographic equipment repairers varies, but some background in electronics is necessary. Some workers complete postsecondary training, such as an associate degree, in this field. The job requires the ability to read an electronic schematic diagram and comprehend other technical information, in addition to good manual dexterity. New employees are trained on the job in two stages over about a year. First, they assist a senior repairer for about 6 months. Then, they refine their skills by performing repairs on their own for an additional 6 months. Finally, repairers continually hone and improve their skills by attending manufacturer-sponsored seminars on the specifics of particular models.

Medical equipment repairers are trained in a similar manner. A background in electronics is helpful, but not required. Like camera repairers, they often specialize in a model or brand. Medical equipment repair requires less training than other precision equipment repair specialties. There are no schools to train these repairers; instead, they learn through hands-on experience and observation. New repairers begin by observing and assisting an experienced worker over a period of 3 to 6 months. Gradually, they begin working independently, while still under close supervision.

Training also varies for watch and clock repairers. Several associations, including the American Watchmakers-Clockmakers Institute (AWI) and the National Association of Watch and Clock Collectors, offer certifications. Some certifications can be completed in a few months; some require simply passing an examination; and the most demanding certifications require 3,000 hours, over 2 years, of classroom time in technical institutes or colleges. (Clock repairers generally require less training than watch repairers because watches have smaller components and require greater precision.) Some repairers opt to learn through assisting a master watch repairer. Nevertheless, developing proficiency in watch or clock repair requires several years of education and experience.

For musical instrument repairers and tuners, employers prefer people with post-high school training in music repair technology. According to a 1997 Piano Technicians Guild membership survey, more than 85 percent of respondents had completed at least some college work; at least 50 percent had a bachelor's or higher degree, although not always in music repair technology. A few technical schools and colleges offer courses in instrument repair. Graduates of these programs normally receive additional training on the job, working with an experienced repairer. A few musical instrument repairers and tuners begin learning their trade on the job as assistants, but employers strongly prefer those with technical school training. Trainees perform a variety of tasks around the shop. Full qualification usually requires 2 to 5 years of training and practice.

Educational requirements for other precision instrument and equipment repair jobs also vary, but include a high school diploma, with a focus on mathematics and science courses. Most employers require postsecondary courses, as repairers need to understand blueprints, electrical schematic diagrams, and electrical, hydraulic, and electromechanical systems. In addition to formal education, a year or two of on-the-job training is required before a repairer is considered fully qualified. Some advancement opportunities exist, but many supervisory positions require more formal education.

Job Outlook

Good opportunities are expected for most types of precision instrument and equipment repairer jobs. Overall employment is projected to grow about as fast as the average for all occupations over the 2000–2010 period. However, projected growth varies by detailed occupation.

Job growth among medical equipment repairers should grow about as fast as the average for all occupations over the projected period. The expanding elderly population should spark strong demand for medical equipment and, in turn, create good employment opportunities in this occupation.

On the other hand, employment of musical instrument repairers is expected to increase more slowly than average. Replacement needs will provide the most job opportunities as many repairers and tuners near retirement. While the expected increase in the number of school-age children involved with music should spur demand for repairers, music must compete with other extracurricular activities and interests. Without new musicians, there will be a slump in instrument rentals, purchases, and repairs. Because training in the repair of musical instruments is difficult to obtain—there are only a few schools that offer training programs, and few experienced workers are willing to take on apprentices—opportunities should be good for those who receive training.

Employment of camera and photographic equipment repairers is expected to decline. The camera repair business is fairly immune to downturns in the business cycle, as consumers are more likely to repair an expensive camera than to buy a new one. However, the popularity of inexpensive cameras adversely affects employment in this occupation, as most point-and-shoot cameras are cheaper to replace than repair.

Employment of watch repairers is expected to grow more slowly than average. However, applicants should have very good opportunities because a large proportion of watch and clock repairers are approaching retirement age and because of trends in watch fashions. Over the past few decades, changes in technology, including the invention of digital and quartz watches that need few repairs, caused a significant decline in the demand for watch repairers. In recent years, there has been a rapidly growing demand for antique and expensive mechanical watches, resulting in increased need for watch repairers.

The projected slower-than-average employment growth of other precision instrument and equipment repairers reflects the expected lack of employment growth in manufacturing and other industries in which they are employed. Nevertheless, good employment opportunities are expected for other precision instrument and equipment repairers due to the relatively small number of people entering the occupation and the need to replace repairers who retire.

Earnings

The following table shows median hourly earnings for various precision instrument and equipment repairers in 2000. Earnings ranged from less than $6.48 for the lowest 10 percent of watch repairers, to more than $31.47 for the highest 10 percent of musical instrument repairers and tuners.

Medical equipment repairers	$16.99
Musical instrument repairers and tuners	15.10
Camera and photographic equipment repairers	13.94
Watch repairers	12.08
All other precision instrument and equipment repairers	19.87

Earnings within the different occupations vary significantly, depending upon skill levels. For example, a watch and clock repairer may simply change batteries and replace worn wrist straps, while highly skilled watch and clock repairers, with years of training and experience, may rebuild and replace worn parts. According to a survey by the American Watchmakers-Clockmakers Institute, the median annual earnings of highly skilled watch and clock repairers were about $40,000 in 2000.

Related Occupations

Many precision instrument and equipment repairers work with precision mechanical and electronic equipment. Other workers who repair precision mechanical and electronic equipment include computer, automated teller, and office machine repairers and coin, vending, and amusement machine servicers and repairers. Other workers who make precision items include dental laboratory technicians and ophthalmic laboratory technicians. Some precision instrument and equipment repairers work with a wide array of industrial equipment. Their work environment and responsibilities are similar to those of industrial machinery installation, maintenance, and repair workers. Much of the work of watch repairers is similar to that of jewelers and precious stone and metal workers. Camera repairers' work is similar to that of electronic home entertainment equipment installers and repairers. Both occupations work with consumer electronics that are based around a circuit board, but that also involve numerous moving mechanical parts.

Sources of Additional Information

For more information about camera repair careers, contact:

- The National Association of Photo Equipment Technicians (NAPET), 3000 Picture Pl., Jackson, MI 49201

For additional information on medical equipment repair, contact your local medical equipment repair shop or hospital.

For information on musical instrument repair, including schools offering training, contact:

- National Association of Professional Band Instrument Repair Technicians (NAPBIRT), P.O. Box 51, Normal, IL 61761. Internet: http://www.napbirt.org

For additional information on piano repair work, contact:

- Piano Technicians Guild, 3930 Washington St., Kansas City, MO 64111-2963. Internet: http://www.ptg.org

For information about training, mentoring programs, and schools with programs in precision instrument repair, contact:

- ISA-The Instrumentation, Systems, and Automation Society, 67 Alexander Dr., P.O. Box 12277, Research Triangle Park, NC 27709. Internet: http://www.isa.org

For information about watch and clock repair and a list of schools with related programs of study, contact:

- American Watchmakers-Clockmakers Institute (AWI), 701 Enterprise Dr., Harrison, OH 45030-1696. Internet: http://www.awi-net.org

Prepress Technicians and Workers

O*NET 51-5021.00, 51-5022.01, 51-5022.02, 51-5022.03, 51-5022.04, 51-5022.05, 51-5022.06, 51-5022.07, 51-5022.08, 51-5022.09, 51-5022.10, 51-5022.11, 51-5022.12, 51-5022.13

Significant Points

- Most workers train on-the-job; some complete formal graphics arts programs or other postsecondary programs in printing technology. Most employers prefer to hire experienced prepress technicians and workers.

- Employment is projected to decline as the increased use of computers in typesetting and page layout eliminates many prepress jobs.

Nature of the Work

The printing process has three stages—prepress, press, and binding or postpress. Prepress technicians and workers prepare material for printing presses. They perform a variety of tasks involved with transforming text and pictures into finished pages and making printing plates of the pages.

Advances in computer software and printing technology continue to change prepress work. Customers, as well as prepress technicians and workers, use their computers to produce material that looks like the desired finished product. Customers, using their own computers, increasingly do much of the typesetting and page layout work formerly done by prepress technicians and workers. This process, called "desktop publishing," poses new challenges for the printing industry. Instead of receiving simple typed text from customers, prepress technicians and workers get the material on a computer disk. Because of this, customers are increasingly likely to have already settled on a format on their own, rather than relying on suggestions from prepress technicians and workers. Furthermore, the printing industry is rapidly moving toward complete "digital imaging," by which customers' material received on computer disks is converted directly into printing plates. Other innovations in prepress work are digital color page makeup systems, electronic page layout systems, and off-press color proofing systems.

Typesetting and page layouts also have been affected by technological changes. The old "hot type" method of text composition—which used molten lead to create individual letters, paragraphs, and full pages of text—is nearly extinct. Today, composition work is done with computers and "cold type" technology. Cold type, which is any of a variety of methods creating type without molten lead, has traditionally used "photo typesetting" to ready text and pictures for printing. Although this method has many variations, all use photography to create images on paper. The images are assembled into page format and re-photographed to create film negatives from which the actual printing plates are made. However, newer cold type methods are becoming more common. These automate the photography or make printing plates directly from electronic files.

In one common form of phototypesetting, text is entered into a computer programmed to hyphenate, space, and create columns of text. Typesetters or data entry clerks may do keyboarding of text at the printing establishment. Increasingly, however, authors do this work before the job is sent out for composition. The coded text then is transferred to a typesetting machine, which uses photography, a cathode-ray tube, or a laser to create an image on typesetting paper or film. Once it has been developed the paper or film is sent to a lithographer who makes the actual printing plate.

New technologies have had a significant impact on the role of other composition workers. Sophisticated publishing software allows an entire newspaper, catalog, or book page, complete with artwork and graphics, to be made up on the computer screen exactly as it will appear in print. Although generally this is the work of desktop publishers, improvements in packaged software allow customers to do more of their own typesetting and layout work. Operators, however, still transmit the pages for production into film and then into plates or directly into plates. "Imagesetters" read text from computer memory and then "beam" it directly onto film, paper, or plates, bypassing the slower photographic process traditionally used. In small shops, *job printers* may be responsible for composition and page layout, reading proofs for errors and clarity, correcting mistakes, and printing.

With traditional photographic processes, the material is arranged and typeset, and then passed on to workers who further prepare it for the presses. *Camera operators* usually are classified as line camera operators, halftone operators, or color separation photographers. Line camera operators start the process of making a lithographic plate by photographing and developing film negatives or positives of the material to be printed. They adjust light and expose film for a specified length of time, and then develop film in a series of chemical baths. They may load exposed film in machines that automatically develop and fix the image. The use of film in printing will decline, as electronic imaging becomes more prevalent. With decreased costs and improved quality, electronic imaging has become the method of choice in the industry.

The lithographic printing process requires that images be made up of tiny dots coming together to form a picture. Photographs cannot be printed without them. When normal "continuous-tone" photographs need to be reproduced, halftone camera operators separate the photograph into pictures containing the dots. Color separation photography is more complex. In this process, camera operators produce four-color separation negatives from a continuous-tone color print or transparency.

Most of this separation work is done electronically on scanners. *Scanner operators* use computerized equipment to capture photographs or art as digital data, or to create film negatives or positives of photographs or art. The computer controls the color separation of the scanning process, and with the help of the operator, corrects for mistakes, or compensates for deficiencies in the original color print or transparency. Each scan produces a dotted image, or halftone, of the original in one of four primary printing colors—yellow, magenta, cyan, and black. The images are used to produce printing plates that print each of these colors, with transparent colored inks, one at a time. These produce "secondary" color combinations of red, green, blue, and black, which can be combined to produce the colors and hues of the original photograph.

Scanners that can perform color correction during the color separation procedure are rapidly replacing *lithographic dot etchers*, who retouch film negatives or positives by sharpening or reshaping images. They work by hand, using chemicals, dyes, and special tools. Dot etchers must know the characteristics of all types of paper and must produce fine shades of color. Like camera operators, they are usually assigned to only one phase of the work, and may have job titles such as dot etcher, retoucher, or letterer.

New technology also is lessening the need for *film strippers*, who cut the film to the required size and arrange and tape the negatives onto "flats"— or layout sheets used by platemakers to make press plates. When completed, flats resemble large film negatives of the text in its final form. In large printing establishments such as newspapers, arrangement is done automatically.

Platemakers use a photographic process to make printing plates. The film assembly or flat is placed on top of a thin metal plate coated with a light-sensitive resin. Exposure to ultraviolet light activates the chemical in parts not protected by the film's dark areas. The plate then is developed in a solution that removes the unexposed non-image area, exposing bare metal. The chemical on areas of the plate exposed to the light hardens and becomes water repellent. The hardened parts of the plate form the text.

A growing number of printing plants use lasers to directly convert electronic data to plates without any use of film. Entering, storing, and retrieving information from computer-aided equipment require technical skills. In addition to operating and maintaining the equipment, lithographic platemakers must make sure that plates meet quality standards.

During the printing process, the plate is first covered with a thin coat of water. The water adheres only to the bare metal non-image areas, and is repelled by the hardened areas that were exposed to light. Next, the plate comes in contact with a rubber roller covered with oil-based ink. Because oil and water do not mix, the ink is repelled by the water-coated area and sticks to the hardened areas. The ink covering the hardened text is transferred to paper.

Although computers perform a wider variety of tasks, printing still involves text composition, page layout, and plate making, so printing still will require prepress technicians and workers. As computer skills become increasingly important, these workers will need to demonstrate a desire and an ability to benefit from the frequent retraining required by rapidly changing technology.

Working Conditions

Prepress technicians and workers usually work in clean, air-conditioned areas with little noise. Some workers, such as typesetters and compositors, may develop eyestrain from working in front of a video display terminal, or musculoskeletal problems such as backaches. Lithographic artists and film strippers may find working with fine detail tiring to the eyes. Platemakers, who work with toxic chemicals, face the hazard of skin irritations. Workers often are subject to stress and the pressures of short deadlines and tight work schedules.

Prepress employees usually work an 8-hour day. Some workers—particularly those employed by newspapers—work night shifts, weekends, and holidays.

Employment

Prepress technicians and workers held about 162,000 jobs in 2000. Of these, almost 56,000 were job printers.

Most prepress jobs were found in firms that handle commercial or business printing, and in newspaper plants. Commercial printing firms print newspaper inserts, catalogs, pamphlets, and advertisements, while business form establishments print material such as sales receipts. A large number of jobs also are found in printing trade services firms and "in-plant" operations. Establishments in printing trade services typically perform custom compositing, platemaking, and related prepress services.

The printing and publishing industry is one of the most geographically dispersed in the United States, and prepress jobs are found throughout the country. However, job prospects may be best in large metropolitan cities such as New York, Chicago, Los Angeles, Philadelphia, Dallas, and Washington, DC.

Training, Other Qualifications, and Advancement

Most prepress technicians and workers train on the job; the length of training varies by occupation. Some skills, such as typesetting, can be learned in a few months, but they are the most likely to be automated in the future. Other skills, such as stripping (image assembly), require years of experience to master. However, these workers also should expect to receive intensive retraining.

Workers often start as helpers who are selected for on-the-job training programs after demonstrating their reliability and interest in the occupation. They begin with instruction from an experienced craft worker and advance based on their demonstrated mastery of skills at each level. All workers should expect to be retrained from time to time to handle new, improved equipment. As workers gain experience, they advance to positions with greater responsibility. Some move into supervisory positions.

Apprenticeship is another way to become a skilled prepress worker, although few apprenticeships have been offered in recent years. Apprenticeship programs emphasize a specific craft—such as camera operator, film stripper, lithographic etcher, scanner operator, or platemaker—but apprentices are introduced to all phases of printing.

Usually, most employers prefer to hire high school graduates who possess good communication skills, both oral and written. Prepress technicians and workers should be able to deal courteously with people, because in small shops they may take customer orders. They also may perform computations to estimate job costs. Persons interested in working for firms using advanced printing technology need to know the basics of electronics and computers. Mathematical skills also are essential for operating many of the software packages used to run modern, computerized prepress equipment.

Prepress technicians and workers need good manual dexterity, and they must be able to pay attention to detail and work independently. Good eyesight, including visual acuity, depth perception, field of view, color vision, and the ability to focus quickly, also are assets. Artistic ability is often a plus. Employers also seek persons who are even-tempered and adaptable, important qualities for workers who often must meet deadlines and learn how to operate new equipment.

Formal graphic arts programs, offered by community and junior colleges and some 4-year colleges, are a good way to learn about the industry. These programs provide job-related training, which will help when seeking full-time employment. Bachelor's degree programs in graphic arts usually are intended for students who may eventually move into management positions, and 2-year associate degree programs are designed to train skilled workers.

Courses in various aspects of printing also are available at vocational-technical institutes, industry-sponsored update and retraining programs, and private trade and technical schools.

As workers gain experience, they may advance to positions with greater responsibility. Some move into supervisory positions.

Job Outlook

Overall employment of prepress technicians and workers is expected to decline through 2010. Demand for printed material should continue to grow, spurred by rising levels of personal income, increasing school enrollments, higher levels of educational attainment, and expanding markets. However, increased use of computers in desktop publishing should eliminate many prepress jobs.

Technological advances will have a varying effect on employment among the prepress occupations. This reflects the increasing proportion of page layout and design that will be performed using computers. Most prepress technicians and workers such as paste-up, composition and typesetting, photoengraving, platemaking, film stripping, and camera operator occupations are expected to experience declines as handwork becomes automated. Computerized equipment allowing reporters and editors to specify type and style, and to format pages at a desktop computer terminal, already has eliminated many typesetting and composition jobs; more may disappear in the years ahead. In contrast, employment of job printers is expected to grow slightly because at certain times, it is more advantageous for a company to contract out this same service to a small shop. Contracting out is likely to benefit job printers because they usually are found in small shops.

Job prospects also will vary by industry. Changes in technology have shifted many employment opportunities away from the traditional printing plants into advertising agencies, public relations firms, and large corporations. Many companies are turning to in-house typesetting or desktop publishing, as personal computers with elaborate graphic capabilities have become common. Corporations are finding it more profitable to print their own newsletters and other reports than to send them out to trade shops.

Some new jobs for prepress technicians and workers are expected to emerge in commercial printing establishments. New equipment should reduce the time needed to complete a printing job, and allow commercial printers to make inroads into new markets that require fast turnaround. Because small establishments predominate, commercial printing should provide the best opportunities for inexperienced workers who want to gain a good background in all facets of printing.

Most employers prefer to hire experienced prepress technicians and workers. Among persons without experience, however, opportunities should be best for those with computer backgrounds who have completed postsecondary programs in printing technology. Many employers prefer graduates of these programs because the comprehensive training they receive helps them learn the printing process and adapt more rapidly to new processes and techniques.

Earnings

Median hourly earnings of prepress technicians and workers were $14.57 in 2000. The middle 50 percent earned between $10.70 and $19.12 an hour. The lowest 10 percent earned less than $8.20, and the highest 10 percent earned more than $23.57 an hour. Median hourly earnings in commercial printing, the industry employing the largest number of prepress technicians and workers, were $15.26 in 2000.

Median hourly earnings of job printers were $13.61 in 2000. The middle 50 percent earned between $10.00 and $17.67 an hour. The lowest 10 percent earned less than $7.81, and the highest 10 percent earned more than $21.88 an hour. Median hourly earnings in commercial printing, the industry employing the largest number of job printers, were $14.68 in 2000.

Wage rates for prepress technicians and workers vary according to occupation, level of experience, training, location, and size of the firm, and whether they are union members.

Related Occupations

Prepress technicians and workers use artistic skills in their work. These skills also are essential for artists and related workers, etchers and engravers, designers, and desktop publishers. In addition to typesetters, other workers who operate machines equipped with keyboards include data entry and information processing workers.

Sources of Additional Information

Details about apprenticeship and other training programs may be obtained from local employers such as newspapers and printing shops, or from local offices of the state employment service.

For information on careers and training in printing and the graphic arts, write to:

- Printing Industries of America, 100 Daingerfield Rd., Alexandria, VA 22314. Internet: http://www.gain.org/servlet/gateway/PIA_GATF/non_index.html

- Graphic Communications Council, 1899 Preston White Dr., Reston, VA 20191. Internet: http://www.npes.org/edcouncil/index.html

- Graphic Communications International Union, 1900 L St. NW., Washington, DC 20036. Internet: http://www.gciu.org

- Graphic Arts Technical Foundation, 200 Deer Run Rd., Sewickley, PA 15143. Internet: http://www.gatf.org

Printing Machine Operators

O*NET 51-5023.01, 51-5023.02, 51-5023.03, 51-5023.04, 51-5023.05, 51-5023.06, 51-5023.07, 51-5023.08, 51-5023.09

Significant Points

- Most are trained informally on the job.

- Employment growth will be slowed by the increasing use of new, more efficient computerized printing presses.

- Job seekers are likely to face keen competition; opportunities should be best for persons who qualify for formal apprenticeship training or who complete postsecondary training programs.

Nature of the Work

Printing machine operators prepare, operate, and maintain the printing presses in a pressroom. Duties of printing machine operators vary according to the type of press they operate—offset lithography, gravure,

flexography, screen printing, or letterpress. Offset lithography, which transfers an inked impression from a rubber-covered cylinder to paper or other material, is the dominant printing process. With gravure, the recesses on an etched plate or cylinder are inked and pressed to paper. Flexography is a form of rotary printing in which ink is applied to the surface by a flexible rubber printing plate with a raised image area. Gravure and flexography should increase in use, but letterpress, in which an inked, raised surface is pressed against paper, will be phased out. In addition to the major printing processes, plateless or nonimpact processes are coming into general use. Plateless processes—including electronic, electrostatic, and ink-jet printing—are used for copying, duplicating, and document and specialty printing, usually by quick and in-house printing shops.

To prepare presses for printing, machine operators install and adjust the printing plate, adjust pressure, ink the presses, load paper, and adjust the press to the paper size. Press operators ensure that paper and ink meet specifications, and adjust margins and the flow of ink to the inking rollers accordingly. They then feed paper through the press cylinders and adjust feed and tension controls.

While printing presses are running, press operators monitor their operation and keep the paper feeders well stocked. They make adjustments to correct uneven ink distribution, speed, and temperatures in the drying chamber, if the press has one. If paper jams or tears and the press stops, which can happen with some offset presses, operators quickly correct the problem to minimize downtime. Similarly, operators working with other high-speed presses constantly look for problems, making quick corrections to avoid expensive losses of paper and ink. Throughout the run, operators occasionally pull sheets to check for any printing imperfections.

In most shops, press operators also perform preventive maintenance. They oil and clean the presses and make minor repairs.

Machine operators' jobs differ from one shop to another because of differences in the kinds and sizes of presses. Small commercial shops are operated by one person and tend to have relatively small presses, which print only one or two colors at a time. Operators who work with large presses have assistants and helpers. Large newspaper, magazine, and book printers use giant "in-line web" presses that require a crew of several press operators and press assistants. These presses are fed paper in big rolls, called "webs," up to 50 inches or more in width. Presses print the paper on both sides; trim, assemble, score, and fold the pages; and count the finished sections as they come off the press.

Most plants have or will soon have installed printing presses with computers and sophisticated instruments to control press operations, making it possible to set up for jobs in less time. Computers allow press operators to perform many of their tasks electronically. With this equipment, press operators monitor the printing process on a control panel or computer monitor, which allows them to adjust the press electronically.

Working Conditions

Operating a press can be physically and mentally demanding, and sometimes tedious. Printing machine operators are on their feet most of the time. Often, operators work under pressure to meet deadlines. Most printing presses are capable of high printing speeds, and adjustments must be made quickly to avoid waste. Pressrooms are noisy, and workers in certain areas wear ear protectors. Working with press machinery can be hazardous, but accidents can be avoided when safe work practices are observed. The threat of accidents is less with newer computerized presses because operators make most adjustments from a control panel. Many press operators work evening, night, and overtime shifts.

Employment

Printing machine operators held about 222,000 jobs in 2000. Most press operator jobs were in newspaper plants or in firms handling commercial or business printing. Commercial printing firms print newspaper inserts, catalogs, pamphlets, and the advertisements found in mailboxes, and business form establishments print items such as business cards, sales receipts, and paper used in computers. Additional jobs were in the "in-plant" section of organizations and businesses that do their own printing—such as banks, insurance companies, and government agencies.

The printing and publishing industry is one of the most geographically dispersed in the United States, and press operators can find jobs throughout the country. However, jobs are concentrated in large printing centers such as New York, Los Angeles, Chicago, Philadelphia, Dallas, and Washington, DC.

Training, Other Qualifications, and Advancement

Although completion of a formal apprenticeship or a postsecondary program in printing equipment operation continue to be the best ways to learn the trade, most printing machine operators are trained informally on the job while working as assistants or helpers to experienced operators. Beginning press operators load, unload, and clean presses. With time, they move up to operating one-color sheet-fed presses and eventually advance to multicolor presses. Operators are likely to gain experience on many kinds of printing presses during the course of their career.

Apprenticeships for press operators in commercial shops take 4 years. In addition to on-the-job instruction, apprenticeships include related classroom or correspondence school courses. Once the dominant method for preparing for this occupation, apprenticeships are becoming less prevalent.

In contrast, formal postsecondary programs in printing equipment operation offered by technical and trade schools and community colleges are growing in importance. Some postsecondary school programs require 2 years of study and award an associate degree, but most programs can be completed in 1 year or less. Postsecondary courses in printing are increasingly important because they provide the theoretical knowledge needed to operate advanced equipment.

Persons who wish to become printing machine operators need mechanical aptitude to make press adjustments and repairs. Oral and writing skills also are required. Operators should possess the mathematical skills necessary to compute percentages, weights, and measures, and to calculate the amount of ink and paper needed to do a job. Because of technical developments in the printing industry, courses in chemistry, electronics, color theory, and physics are helpful.

Technological changes have had a tremendous effect on the skills needed by printing machine operators. New presses now require operators to possess basic computer skills. Even experienced operators periodically receive retraining and skill updating. For example, printing plants that change from sheet-fed offset presses to Web offset presses have to retrain the entire press crew because skill requirements for the two types of presses are different. Web offset presses, with their faster operating speeds, require faster decisions, monitoring of more variables, and greater physical effort. In the future, workers are expected to need to retrain several times during their career.

Printing machine operators may advance in pay and responsibility by working on a more complex printing press. Through experience and demonstrated ability, for example, a one-color sheet-fed press operator may become a four-color sheet-fed press operator. Others may advance to pressroom supervisor and become responsible for an entire press crew.

Job Outlook

Persons seeking jobs as printing machine operators are likely to face keen competition from experienced operators and prepress workers who have been displaced by new technology, particularly those who have completed retraining programs. Opportunities to become printing machine operators are likely to be best for persons who qualify for formal apprenticeship training or who complete postsecondary training programs.

Employment of printing machine operators is expected to grow more slowly than the average for all occupations through 2010. Although demand for printed materials will grow, employment growth will be slowed by the increased use of new, more efficient computerized printing presses. Most job openings will result from the need to replace operators who retire or leave the occupation.

Most new jobs will result from expansion of the printing industry as demand for printed material increases in response to demographic trends, U.S. expansion into foreign markets, and growing use of direct mail by advertisers. Demand for books and magazines will increase as school enrollments rise, and as substantial growth in the middle-aged and older population spurs adult education and leisure reading. Additional growth should stem from increased foreign demand for domestic trade publications, professional and scientific works, and mass-market books such as paperbacks.

Continued employment in commercial printing will be spurred by increased expenditures for print advertising materials to be mailed directly to prospective customers. New market research techniques are leading advertisers to increase spending on messages targeted to specific audiences, and should continue to require the printing of a wide variety of newspaper inserts, catalogs, direct mail enclosures, and other kinds of print advertising.

Other printing, such as newspapers, books, and greeting cards, also will provide jobs. Experienced press operators will fill most of these jobs because many employers are under severe pressure to meet deadlines and have limited time to train new employees.

Earnings

Median hourly earnings of printing machine operators were $13.57 in 2000. The middle 50 percent earned between $10.38 and $17.80 an hour. The lowest 10 percent earned less than $8.09, and the highest 10 percent earned more than $21.92 an hour. Median hourly earnings in the industries employing the largest numbers of printing machine operators in 2000, were as follows:

Commercial printing	$14.91
Newspapers	14.71
Paperboard containers and boxes	14.44
Miscellaneous converted paper products	13.78
Mailing, reproduction, and stenographic services	10.92

The basic wage rate for a printing machine operator depends on the type of press being run and the geographic area in which the work is located. Workers covered by union contracts usually had higher earnings.

Related Occupations

Other workers who set up and operate production machinery include machine setters, operators, and tenders—metal and plastic, bookbinders and bindery workers, and various precision machine operators.

Sources of Additional Information

Details about apprenticeships and other training opportunities may be obtained from local employers such as newspapers and printing shops, local offices of the Graphic Communications International Union, local affiliates of Printing Industries of America, or local offices of the state employment service.

For general information about press operators, write to:

- Graphic Communications International Union, 1900 L St. NW., Washington, DC 20036. Internet: http://www.gciu.org

For information on careers and training in printing and the graphic arts, write to:

- Printing Industries of America, 100 Daingerfield Rd., Alexandria, VA 22314. Internet: http://www.gain.org/servlet/gateway/PIA_GATF/non_index.html

- Graphic Communications Council, 1899 Preston White Dr., Reston, VA 20191. Internet: http://www.npes.org/edcouncil/index.html

- Graphic Arts Technical Foundation, 200 Deer Run Rd., Sewickley, PA 15143. Internet: http://www.gatf.org

Private Detectives and Investigators

O*NET 33-9021.00

Significant Points

- Work hours often are irregular for beginning detectives and investigators, many of whom work part-time.

- Most applicants have related experience in areas such as law enforcement, insurance, or the military.

- Stiff competition is expected for better paying jobs because of the large number of qualified people who are attracted to this occupation.

Nature of the Work

Private detectives and investigators use many means to determine the facts in a variety of matters. To carry out investigations, they may use various types of surveillance or searches. To verify facts, such as an individual's place of employment or income, they may make phone calls or visit a subject's workplace. In other cases, especially those involving missing persons and background checks, investigators often interview people to gather as much information as possible about an individual. In all cases, private detectives and investigators assist attorneys, businesses, and the public with a variety of legal, financial, and personal problems.

Private detectives and investigators offer many services, including executive, corporate, and celebrity protection; pre-employment verification; and individual background profiles. They also provide assistance in civil liability and personal injury cases, insurance claims and fraud, child custody and protection cases, and premarital screening. Increasingly, they are hired to investigate individuals to prove or disprove infidelity.

Most detectives and investigators are trained to perform physical surveillance, often for long periods, in a car or van. They may observe a site, such as the home of a subject, from an inconspicuous location. The surveillance continues using still and video cameras, binoculars, and a cell phone, until the desired evidence is obtained. They also may perform computer database searches, or work with someone who does. Computers allow detectives and investigators to quickly obtain massive amounts of information on individuals' prior arrests, convictions, and civil legal judgments; telephone numbers; motor vehicle registrations; association and club memberships; and other matters.

The duties of private detectives and investigators depend on the needs of their client. In cases for employers involving workers' fraudulent compensation claims, for example, investigators may carry out long-term covert observation of subjects. If an investigator observes a subject performing an activity that contradicts injuries stated in a workers' compensation claim, the investigator would take video or still photographs to document the activity and report it to the client.

Private detectives and investigators often specialize. Those who focus on intellectual property theft, for example, investigate and document acts of piracy, help clients stop the illegal activity, and provide intelligence for prosecution and civil action. Other investigators specialize in developing financial profiles and asset searches. Their reports reflect information gathered through interviews, investigation and surveillance, and research, including review of public documents.

Legal investigators specialize in cases involving the courts and are normally employed by law firms or lawyers. They frequently assist in preparing criminal defenses, locating witnesses, serving legal documents, interviewing police and prospective witnesses, and gathering and reviewing evidence. Legal investigators also may collect information on the parties to the litigation, take photographs, testify in court, and assemble evidence and reports for trials.

Corporate investigators conduct internal and external investigations for corporations other than investigative firms. In internal investigations, they may investigate drug use in the workplace, ensure that expense accounts are not abused, or determine if employees are stealing merchandise or information. External investigations typically prevent criminal schemes originating outside the corporation, such as theft of company assets through fraudulent billing of products by suppliers.

Financial investigators may be hired to develop confidential financial profiles of individuals or companies who are prospective parties to large financial transactions. They often are Certified Public Accountants (CPAs) and work closely with investment bankers and accountants. They search for assets in order to recover damages awarded by a court in fraud or theft cases.

Detectives who work for retail stores or hotels are responsible for loss control and asset protection. *Store detectives*, also known as *loss prevention agents*, safeguard the assets of retail stores by apprehending anyone attempting to steal merchandise or destroy store property. They prevent theft by shoplifters, vendor representatives, delivery personnel, and even store employees. Store detectives also conduct periodic inspections of stock areas, dressing rooms, and restrooms, and sometimes assist in opening and closing the store. They may prepare loss prevention and security reports for management and testify in court against persons they apprehend. *Hotel detectives* protect guests of the establishment from theft of their belongings and preserve order in hotel restaurants and bars. They also may keep undesirable individuals, such as known thieves, off the premises.

Working Conditions

Private detectives and investigators often work irregular hours because of the need to conduct surveillance and contact people who are not available during normal working hours. Early morning, evening, weekend, and holiday work is common.

Many detectives and investigators spend time away from their offices conducting interviews or doing surveillance, but some work in their office most of the day conducting computer searches and making phone calls. Those who have their own agencies and employ other investigators may work primarily in an office and have normal business hours.

When working on a case away from the office, the environment might range from plush boardrooms to seedy bars. Store and hotel detectives work in the businesses that they protect. Investigators generally work alone, but they sometimes work with others during surveillance or when following a subject in order to avoid detection by the subject.

Some of the work involves confrontation, so the job can be stressful and dangerous. Some situations call for the investigator to be armed, such as certain bodyguard assignments for corporate or celebrity clients. Detectives and investigators who carry handguns must be licensed by the appropriate authority. In most cases, however, a weapon is not necessary because the purpose of their work is gathering information and not law enforcement or criminal apprehension. Owners of investigative agencies have the added stress of having to deal with demanding and sometimes distraught clients.

Employment

Private detectives and investigators held about 39,000 jobs in 2000. About 2 out of 5 were self-employed. Approximately a third of salaried private detectives and investigators worked for detective agencies, while another third were employed as store detectives in department or clothing and accessories stores. The remainder worked for hotels and other lodging places, legal services firms, and in other industries.

Training, Other Qualifications, and Advancement

There are no formal education requirements for most private detective and investigator jobs, although many private detectives have college degrees. Almost all private detectives and investigators have previous experience in other occupations. Some work initially for insurance or collections companies or in the private security industry. Many investigators enter the field after serving in law enforcement, the military, government auditing and investigative positions, or federal intelligence jobs.

Former law enforcement officers, military investigators, and government agents often become private detectives or investigators as a second career because they are frequently able to retire after 20 years of service. Others enter from such diverse fields as finance, accounting, commercial credit, investigative reporting, insurance, and law. These individuals often can apply their prior work experience in a related investigative specialty. A few enter the occupation directly after graduation from college, generally with associate or bachelor of criminal justice or police science degrees.

The majority of the states and the District of Colombia require private detectives and investigators to be licensed. Licensing requirements vary widely, but convicted felons cannot receive a license in most states and a growing number of states are enacting mandatory training programs for private detectives and investigators. Some states have few requirements, and 6 states—Alabama, Alaska, Colorado, Idaho, Mississippi, and South Dakota—have no statewide licensing requirements while others have stringent regulations. For example, the Bureau of Security and Investigative Services of the California Department of Consumer Affairs requires private investigators to be 18 years of age or older and have a combination of education in police science, criminal law, or justice. They also must have experience equaling 3 years (6,000 hours) of investigative experience; pass an evaluation by the Federal Department of Justice and a criminal history background check; and receive a qualifying score on a 2-hour written examination covering laws and regulations. There are additional requirements for a firearms permit.

For private detective and investigator jobs, most employers look for individuals with ingenuity, persistence and assertiveness. A candidate must not be afraid of confrontation, should communicate well, and should be able to think on his or her feet. Good interviewing and interrogation skills also are important and usually are acquired in earlier careers in law enforcement or other fields. Because the courts often are the ultimate judge of a properly conducted investigation, the investigator must be able to present the facts in a manner a jury will believe.

Training in subjects such as criminal justice is helpful to aspiring private detectives and investigators. Most corporate investigators must have a bachelor's degree, preferably in a business-related field. Some corporate investigators have master's degrees in business administration or law, while others are certified public accountants. Corporate investigators hired by large companies may receive formal training from their employers on business practices, management structure, and various finance-related topics. The screening process for potential employees typically includes a background check of candidates' criminal history.

Some investigators receive certification from a professional organization to demonstrate competency in a field. For example, the National Association of Legal Investigators (NALI) confers the designation Certified Legal Investigator to licensed investigators who devote a majority of their practice to negligence or criminal defense investigations. To receive the designation, applicants must satisfy experience, educational, and continuing training requirements, and must pass written and oral exams administered by the NALI.

Most private detective agencies are small, with little room for advancement. Usually there are no defined ranks or steps, so advancement takes the form of increases in salary and assignment status. Many detectives and investigators work for detective agencies at the beginning of their careers and after a few years start their own firms. Corporate and legal investigators may rise to supervisor or manager of the security or investigations department.

Job Outlook

Keen competition is expected because private detective and investigator careers attract many qualified people, including relatively young retirees from law enforcement and military careers. Opportunities will be best for entry-level jobs with detective agencies or as store detectives on a part-time basis. Those seeking store detective jobs have the best prospects with large chains and discount stores.

Employment of private detectives and investigators is expected to grow faster than the average for all occupations through 2010. In addition to growth, replacement of those who retire or leave the occupation for other reasons should create many additional job openings. Increased demand for private detectives and investigators will result from fear of crime, increased litigation, and the need to protect confidential information and property of all kinds. More private investigators also will be needed to assist attorneys working on criminal defense and civil litigation. Growing financial activity worldwide will increase the demand for investigators to control internal and external financial losses, and to monitor competitors and prevent industrial spying.

Earnings

Median annual earnings of salaried private detectives and investigators were $26,750 in 2000. The middle 50 percent earned between $20,040 and $38,240. The lowest 10 percent earned less than $16,210, and the highest 10 percent earned more than $52,200. Median annual earnings were $21,180 in department stores, the industry employing the largest numbers of private detectives and investigators.

Earnings of private detectives and investigators vary greatly depending on their employer, specialty, and the geographic area in which they work. According to a study by Abbott, Langer & Associates, security/loss prevention directors and vice presidents had a median income of $77,500 per year in 2000; investigators, $39,800; and store detectives, $25,000. In addition to typical benefits, most corporate investigators received profit-sharing plans.

Related Occupations

Private detectives and investigators often collect information and protect the property and other assets of companies. Others with related duties include bill and account collectors; claims adjusters, appraisers, examiners, and investigators; police and detectives; and security guards and gaming surveillance officers. Investigators who specialize in conducting financial profiles and asset searches perform work closely related to that of accountants and auditors and financial analysts and personal finance advisors.

Sources of Additional Information

For information on local licensing requirements, contact your state Department of Public Safety, state Division of Licensing, or your local or state police headquarters.

For information on a career as a legal investigator, contact:

- The National Association of Legal Investigators, P.O. Box 905, Grand Blanc, MI 48439

Probation Officers and Correctional Treatment Specialists

O*NET 21-1092.00

Significant Points

- Probation officers and correctional treatment specialists work with criminal offenders, some of whom may be dangerous.

- A bachelor's degree in social work, criminal justice, or a related field usually is required.

- Good employment opportunities are expected.

Nature of the Work

Many people who are convicted of crimes are placed on probation instead of being sent to prison. During probation, offenders must stay out of trouble and meet various other requirements. Probation officers, who also may be referred to as community supervision officers in some states, supervise people who have been placed on probation. Parole officers perform many of the same duties that probation officers perform. However, parole officers supervise offenders who have been released from prison on parole to ensure that they comply with the conditions of their parole. In some states, the job of parole and probation officer is combined.

Probation and parole officers supervise offenders on probation or parole through personal contact with the offender and his or her family. Some offenders are required to wear an electronic device so that probation officers can monitor their activities. Officers may arrange for offenders to get substance abuse rehabilitation or job training. They also attend court hearings to update the court on the offender's compliance with the terms of his or her sentence and on the offender's efforts at rehabilitation.

Probation officers also spend much of their time working for the courts. They investigate the background of offenders brought before the court, write presentence reports, and make sentencing recommendations for each offender. Officers review sentencing recommendations with offenders and their families before submitting them to the court. Officers may be required to testify in court as to their findings and recommendations.

Probation officers usually work with either adults or juveniles exclusively. Only in small, usually rural jurisdictions do probation officers counsel both adults and juveniles. Occasionally, in the federal courts system, probation officers may undertake the job of a pretrial services officer. Pretrial services officers conduct pretrial investigations and make bond recommendations for defendants.

Correctional treatment specialists work in correctional institutions (jails and prisons) or in parole or probation agencies. In jails and prisons, they evaluate the progress of inmates. They also work with inmates, probation officers, and other agencies to develop parole and release plans. Their case reports are provided to the appropriate parole board when their clients are eligible to be released. In addition, they plan educational and training programs to provide offenders with job skills, and counsel offenders either individually or in groups regarding their coping skills, anger management skills, and drug or sexual abuse. They usually write treatment plans and summaries for each client. Correctional treatment specialists working in parole and probation agencies perform many of the same duties as their counterparts who work in correctional institutions. Correctional treatment specialists may also be known as case managers or drug treatment specialists.

The number of cases a probation officer or correctional treatment specialist handles at one time depends on the counseling needs of offenders and the risks they pose. Higher-risk offenders and those who need a greater amount of counseling usually command more of the officer's time and resources. Caseload size also varies by jurisdiction of the agency. Consequently, officers may handle from 20 to more than 300 active cases at a time.

The nature of the work of many probation officers and correctional treatment specialists has been affected by recent changes in the parole and probation system brought about by public debate on the proper role of prisons, probation, and parole. This has resulted in more community involvement on the part of probation and parole officers in many jurisdictions. Instead of requiring offenders to meet officers in their offices, many officers are going into the community to meet the offenders in their homes and at their places of employment or therapy. Probation and parole agencies also are employing the assistance of community organizations, such as religious institutions, neighborhood groups, and local residents, to monitor the behavior of many offenders. The ability to do this additional fieldwork is facilitated by telecommuting methods, such as the use of computers, phones, and faxes. Probation officers also may telecommute from their own homes. Other technological advancements, such as electronic monitoring devices and drug screening, also have assisted probation officers and correctional treatment specialists in supervising and counseling offenders.

A debate also has emerged about privatizing the probation and parole systems. Many services, such as emotional counseling, job training, drug rehabilitation, and urine testing, already are contracted out to private firms. Some states, including Georgia and Tennessee, have already completely privatized some of their probation agencies. Another recent trend in corrections has involved abolishing parole, either altogether or for certain crimes. In some cases, states have placed many restrictions on the types of offenders who can be paroled and on how much of their sentence must be completed before being paroled. In states where parole has been abolished, another form of supervised release has been established.

Working Conditions

Probation officers and correctional treatment specialists work with criminal offenders, some of whom may be dangerous. In the course of supervising offenders, they usually interact with many other individuals, such as family members and friends of their clients, who may be angry, upset, or difficult to work with. Workers may be assigned to fieldwork in high crime areas or in institutions where there is a risk of violence or communicable diseases. Probation officers and correctional treatment specialists are required to meet many deadlines, most of which are imposed by courts, which contributes to their heavy workloads. All of these factors contribute to a stressful work environment. Although the high stress levels can make these jobs very difficult at times, they also can be very rewarding. Many workers obtain personal satisfaction from counseling members of their community and helping them become productive citizens.

In addition, extensive travel and fieldwork may be required to meet with offenders who are on probation or parole. Workers may be required to carry a firearm or other weapon for protection. Workers generally work a 40-hour workweek, but some may work longer. They may be on call 24 hours a day to supervise and assist offenders at any time. They also may be required to collect and transport urine samples of offenders for drug testing.

Employment

About 84,000 people were employed as probation officers and correctional treatment specialists in 2000. Most of these workers work for state or local governments. The government level that employs these workers varies by state. In some states, the state government employs all probation officers and correctional treatment specialists, while in other states, local governments are the only employers. In still other states, both levels of government employ these workers. Currently, California and Texas have the highest probation and parole populations. Together these two states account for about one-fourth of the country's correctional supervision population. Jobs also are more plentiful in urban areas.

Training, Other Qualifications, and Advancement

Background qualifications for probation officers and correctional treatment specialists vary by state, but a bachelor's degree in social work, criminal justice, or a related field from a 4-year college or university is usually required. Some states also require 1 year of work experience in a related field or 1 year of graduate study in criminal justice, social work, or psychology to become a probation officer. Some employers may require previous experience or a master's degree in criminal justice, social work, or psychology, of applicants wishing to become correctional treatment specialists.

Applicants usually are administered written, oral, psychological, and physical examinations. Most probation officers and some correctional treatment specialists are required to complete a training program sponsored by their state government or the federal government. A certification test also may be required in some states during or after the completion of training.

Prospective probation officers or correctional treatment specialists should be in good physical and emotional condition. Most agencies require applicants to be at least 21 years old and, for federal employment, not older than 37. Those convicted of felonies may not be eligible for employment in this occupation. Familiarity with the use of computers often is required due to the increasing use of computer technology in probation and parole work. Candidates also should be knowledgeable about laws and regulations pertaining to corrections. Probation officers and correctional treatment specialists should possess strong writing skills due to the large numbers of reports they are required to prepare.

Most probation officers and correctional treatment specialists work as trainees for about 6 months. After successfully completing the training period, workers obtain a permanent position. A typical agency has several levels of probation and parole officers and correctional treatment specialists, as well as supervisors. A graduate degree, such as a master's degree in criminal justice, social work, or psychology, may be helpful for advancement.

Job Outlook

This occupation is not attractive to some potential entrants due to relatively low earnings, heavy workloads, and high stress levels. Therefore, the number of entrants to the occupation may not be enough to fill all expected openings, resulting in good employment opportunities over the projection period.

Employment of probation officers and correctional treatment specialists is projected to grow faster than the average for all occupations through 2010. Despite recent decreases in the crime rate, vigorous law enforcement is expected to result in a continuing increase in the prison population. Overcrowding in prisons also has increased the probation population, as judges and prosecutors search for alternate forms of punishments, such as electronic monitoring and day reporting centers. The number of offenders released on parole is expected to increase to create room for other offenders in prison. The increasing prison, parole, and probation populations should spur more demand for probation and parole officers and correctional treatment specialists.

In addition to openings due to growth, many openings will be created by replacement needs, especially openings due to the large number of these workers who are expected to retire over the projection period.

The job outlook depends on the amount of government funding that is allocated to corrections, and especially to probation systems. Although community supervision is far less expensive than keeping offenders in prison, a change in political trends toward more imprisonment and away from community supervision could result in reduced employment opportunities.

Earnings

Median annual earnings of probation officers and correctional treatment specialists in 2000 were $38,150. The middle 50 percent earned between $30,270 and $49,030. The lowest 10 percent earned less than $25,010, and the highest 10 percent earned more than $59,010. In 2000, median annual earnings for probation officers and correctional treatment specialists employed in state government were $36,980; those employed in local government earned $40,820. Higher wages tend to be found in urban areas.

Related Occupations

Probation officers and correctional treatment specialists counsel criminal offenders as they re-enter society. Other occupations that involve similar responsibilities include social workers, social and human service assistants, and counselors.

Probation officers and correctional treatment also play a major role in maintaining public safety. Other occupations related to corrections and law enforcement include police and detectives, correctional officers, and firefighting occupations.

Sources of Additional Information

For information about criminal justice job opportunities in your area, contact your state's department of corrections, criminal justice, or probation.

Further information about probation officers and correctional treatment specialists is available from:

- The American Probation and Parole Association, P.O. Box 11910, Lexington, KY 40578-1910. Internet: http://www.appa-net.org

Procurement Clerks

O*NET 43-3061.00

Significant Points

- Most jobs require only a high school diploma.
- Numerous job opportunities should arise due to high turnover.
- Slower-than-average growth is expected in overall employment, reflecting the spread of computers and other office automation as well as organizational restructuring.

Nature of the Work

Procurement clerks compile requests for materials, prepare purchase orders, keep track of purchases and supplies, and handle inquiries about orders. Usually called *purchasing clerks*, or *purchasing technicians*, they perform a variety of tasks related to the ordering of goods and supplies for an organization and make sure that what was purchased arrives when scheduled and meets the purchaser's specifications.

Automation is having a profound effect on the occupation. Orders for goods can now be placed electronically when supplies are low. For example, computers integrated with cash registers at stores record purchases and automatically reorder goods when supplies reach a certain target level. However, automation is still years away for many firms and the role of the procurement clerk is unchanged in many organizations.

There is a wide range of tasks performed by procurement clerks and a wide range of responsibilities. Some clerks may act more like buyers, particularly at small to medium-sized companies, while others perform strictly clerical functions. In general, procurement clerks process requests for purchases. They first determine if there is any product left in inventory and may go through catalogs or to the Internet to find suppliers. They may prepare invitation-to-bid forms and mail them to suppliers or distribute them for public posting. Once suppliers are found, they may interview the suppliers to check on prices and specifications and put together spreadsheets with price comparisons and other facts about each supplier. Upon approval of a supplier, purchase orders are prepared, mailed, and recorded into computers. Procurement clerks keep track of orders and determine the causes of any delays. If the supplier has questions, clerks try to answer them and resolve any problems. When the shipment arrives, procurement clerks may reconcile the purchase order with the shipment, making sure they match, notify the vendors when invoices not received, and make sure the bills concur with the purchase orders.

Some purchasing departments, particularly in small companies, are responsible for overseeing the organization's inventory control system. At these organizations, procurement clerks monitor in-house inventory movement and complete inventory transfer forms for bookkeeping purposes. They may keep inventory spreadsheets and place orders when materials on hand are insufficient.

Working Conditions

Procurement clerks typically are employed in an office environment.

Because the majority of procurement clerks use computers on a daily basis, these workers may experience eye and muscle strain, backaches, headaches, and repetitive motion injuries. Also, clerks who review detailed data may have to sit for extended periods of time.

Most procurement clerks work regular business hours.

Employment

In 2000, procurement clerks held about 76,000 jobs. Procurement clerks are found in every industry, including manufacturing, retail and wholesale trade, healthcare, and government.

Training, Other Qualifications, and Advancement

Most procurement clerks are required to have at least a high school diploma. However, having some college is becoming increasingly important, and, an associate degree in business or accounting often is required for procurement clerks. Some clerks have bachelor's degrees in business, accounting, or liberal arts. Many graduates accept entry-level clerical positions to get into a particular company or to enter the finance or accounting field with the hope of being promoted to professional or managerial positions. Some companies have a set plan of advancement that tracks college graduates from entry-level clerical jobs into managerial positions. Workers with bachelor's degrees are likely to start at higher salaries and advance more easily than those without degrees do.

Experience in a related job also is recommended. Experience working in an office environment or in customer service is always beneficial. Regardless of the type of work, most employers prefer workers with good communication skills who are computer-literate; knowledge of word processing and spreadsheet software is especially valuable.

Once hired, procurement clerks usually receive on-the-job training. Under the guidance of a supervisor or other senior worker, new employees learn company procedures. Some formal classroom training also may be necessary, such as training in specific computer software. Procurement clerks must be careful, orderly, and detail-oriented in order to avoid making errors and recognize errors made by others. These workers also should be discreet and trustworthy, because they frequently come in contact with confidential material. Additionally, all procurement clerks should have a strong aptitude for numbers.

Procurement clerks usually advance by taking on more duties in the same occupation for higher pay or by transferring to a closely related occupation. For example, procurement clerks with the appropriate experience often become buyers. Most companies fill office and administrative support supervisory and managerial positions by promoting individuals from within their organization, so clerks who acquire additional skills, experience, and training improve their advancement opportunities.

Job Outlook

Employment of procurement clerks is expected to decline through 2010 as a result of increasing automation. The need for procurement clerks will be reduced as the use of computers to place orders directly with suppliers—called electronic data interchange—and as ordering over the Internet—known as "e-procurement"—become more commonplace. In addition, procurement responsibilities are gradually being decentralized within organizations and are increasingly being performed in the originating departments by managers or by a designated employee. These departments may be issued procurement cards, which are similar to credit cards, that enable a department to charge purchases up to a specified amount.

Although employment in the occupation is expected to decline, job openings will occur for qualified individuals as workers transfer to other occupations or leave the labor force. Persons with good writing and communication skills, along with computer skills, will have the best opportunities for employment.

Earnings

Salaries of procurement clerks vary considerably. The region of the country, size of city, and type and size of establishment all influence salary levels. Also, the level of expertise required and the complexity and uniqueness of a clerk's responsibilities also may affect earnings. Median hourly earnings of full-time procurement clerks in 2000 were $13.33.

Related Occupations

Procurement clerks enter data into a computer and keep track of business and other financial transactions. Higher level clerks can generate reports and perform analysis of the financial data. Other occupations that perform these duties include brokerage clerks; cashiers; credit authorizers, checkers, and clerks; loan interviewers and clerks; new accounts clerks; order clerks; and secretaries and administrative assistants.

Sources of Additional Information

Information on employment opportunities for procurement clerks is available from local offices of the state employment service.

Production, Planning, and Expediting Clerks

O*NET 43-5061.00

Significant Points

- Many production, planning, and expediting clerk jobs are entry level and do not require more than a high school diploma.

- Workers develop the necessary skills through on-the-job training lasting from several days to a few months.

- Numerous job openings will arise each year from the need to replace workers who leave this very large occupational group.

Nature of the Work

Production, planning, and expediting clerks coordinate and expedite the flow of information, work, and materials within or among offices. Most of their work is done according to production, work, or shipment schedules. The schedules are reviewed and distributed after being considered by supervisors who determine work progress and completion dates. Production, planning, and expediting clerks compile reports on progress of work and production problems. They also may schedule workers, estimate costs, schedule shipment of parts, keep inventory of materials, inspect and assemble materials, and write special orders for services and merchandise. In addition, they may route and deliver parts to ensure that production quotas are met and that merchandise is delivered on the date promised.

Production and planning clerks compile records and reports on various aspects of production, such as materials and parts used, products produced, machine and instrument readings, and frequency of defects. They prepare and distribute work tickets or other production guides to workers. They coordinate, schedule, monitor, and chart production and its progress, either manually or using electronic equipment. Production and planning clerks also gather information from customer orders or other specifications to prepare a detailed production sheet that serves as a guide in assembly or manufacture of the product.

Expediting clerks contact vendors and shippers to ensure that merchandise, supplies, and equipment are forwarded on the specified shipping dates. They communicate with transportation companies to prevent delays in transit, and they may arrange for distribution of materials upon arrival. They may even visit work areas of vendors and shippers to check the status of orders. Expediting clerks locate and distribute materials to specified production areas. They may inspect products for quality and quantity to ensure adherence to specifications. They also keep a chronological list of due dates and may move work not meeting the production schedule to the front.

Working Conditions

Production, planning, and expediting clerks work in a wide variety of businesses, institutions, and industries. Some work in warehouses, stock-rooms, or shipping and receiving rooms that may not be temperature controlled. Others may spend time in cold storage rooms or outside on loading platforms, where they are exposed to the weather.

Production, planning, and expediting clerks work closely with supervisors who must approve production and work schedules.

The typical workweek is Monday through Friday; however, evening and weekend hours are common for some jobs, and may be required in other jobs when large shipments are involved or when inventory is taken.

Employment

In 2000, production, planning, and expediting clerks held 332,000 jobs. Jobs in manufacturing made up 44 percent and jobs in wholesale trade and groceries and related products comprised about 6 percent. About 8 percent worked in the personnel supply services industry.

Training, Other Qualifications, and Advancement

Many jobs for production, planning, and expediting clerks are entry level and do not require more than a high school diploma. Employers, however, prefer to hire those who are familiar with computers and other electronic office and business equipment. Those who have taken business courses or have previous business, dispatching, or specific job-related experience may be preferred. Because communication with other people is an integral part of these jobs, good oral and written communications skills are essential. Typing, filing, recordkeeping, and other clerical skills also are important.

Production, planning, and expediting clerks usually learn the job by doing routine tasks under close supervision. They learn how to count and mark stock, and then start keeping records and taking inventory. Strength, stamina, good eyesight, and an ability to work at repetitive tasks, sometimes under pressure, are important characteristics. Production, planning, and expediting clerks must learn how their company operates along with its priorities before they can begin to efficiently write production and work schedules.

Advancement opportunities for production, planning, and expediting clerks vary with the place of employment.

Job Outlook

Employment of production, planning, and expediting clerks is expected to grow about as fast as the average for all occupations through 2010. As increasing pressure is put on companies to get things produced and delivered more quickly and efficiently, the need for production, planning, and expediting clerks will grow. The work of production, planning, and expediting clerks is less likely to be automated than is that of many other administrative support occupations. In addition to openings due to employment growth, many additional job openings will arise from the need to replace production, planning, and expediting clerks who leave the labor force or transfer to other occupations.

Earnings

Median hourly earnings in 2000 for production, planning, and expediting clerks were $14.71.

Production, planning, and expediting clerks usually receive the same benefits as most other workers. If uniforms are required, employers usually provide either the uniforms or an allowance to purchase them.

Related Occupations

Other workers who coordinate the flow of information to assist the production process include cargo and freight agents; shipping, receiving, and traffic clerks; stock clerks and order fillers; and weighers, measurers, checkers, and samplers, recordkeeping.

Sources of Additional Information

Information about job opportunities may be obtained from local employers and local offices of the state employment service.

Property, Real Estate, and Community Association Managers

O*NET 11-9141.00

Significant Points

- Many enter the occupation as onsite managers of apartment buildings, office complexes, or community associations, or as employees of property management firms or community association management companies.

- Almost half of all property and real estate managers were self-employed, as compared with only 8 percent of all workers combined.

- Opportunities should be best for those with college degrees in business administration or related fields, as well as professional designations.

Nature of the Work

Buildings can be homes, stores, or offices to those who use them. To businesses and investors, properly managed real estate is a potential source of income and profits, and to homeowners, it is a way to preserve and enhance resale values. Property, real estate, and community association managers maintain and increase the value of real estate investments. Property and real estate managers oversee the performance of income-producing commercial or residential properties, and ensure that real estate investments achieve their expected revenues. Community association managers manage the common property and services of condominiums, cooperatives, and planned communities through their homeowners' or community associations.

When owners of apartments, office buildings, or retail or industrial properties lack the time or expertise needed for day-to-day management of their real estate investments or homeowners' associations, they often hire a property or real estate manager, or community association man-

ager. The manager is employed either directly by the owner or indirectly through a contract with a property management firm.

Generally, property and real estate managers handle the financial operations of the property, ensuring that mortgages, taxes, insurance premiums, payroll, and maintenance bills are paid on time. In community associations, however, homeowners pay their own real estate taxes and mortgages. Some property managers, called asset property managers, supervise the preparation of financial statements and periodically report to the owners on the status of the property, occupancy rates, dates of lease expirations, and other matters.

Often, property managers negotiate contracts for janitorial, security, groundskeeping, trash removal, and other services. When contracts are awarded competitively, managers solicit bids from several contractors and recommend to the owners who bid to accept. They monitor the performance of contractors and investigate and resolve complaints from residents and tenants when services are not properly provided. Managers also purchase supplies and equipment for the property and make arrangements with specialists for repairs that cannot be handled by regular property maintenance staff.

In addition to these duties, property managers must understand and comply with provisions of legislation, such as the Americans with Disabilities Act and the Federal Fair Housing Amendment Act, as well as local fair housing laws. They must ensure that their renting and advertising practices are not discriminatory and that the property itself complies with all of the local, state, and federal regulations and building codes.

Onsite property managers are responsible for day-to-day operations for one piece of property, such as an office building, shopping center, community association, or apartment complex. To ensure that the property is safe and properly maintained, onsite managers routinely inspect the grounds, facilities, and equipment to determine if repairs or maintenance are needed. They meet not only with current residents when handling requests for repairs or trying to resolve complaints, but also with prospective residents or tenants to show vacant apartments or office space. Onsite managers also are responsible for enforcing the terms of rental or lease agreements, such as rent collection, parking and pet restrictions, and termination-of-lease procedures. Other important duties of onsite managers include keeping accurate, up-to-date records of income and expenditures from property operations and submitting regular expense reports to the asset property manager or owners.

Property managers who do not work onsite act as a liaison between the onsite manager and the owner. They also market vacant space to prospective tenants through the use of a leasing agent, advertising, or by other means, and establish rental rates in accordance with prevailing local economic conditions.

Some property and real estate managers, often called real estate asset managers, act as the property owners' agent and adviser for the property. They plan and direct the purchase, development, and disposition of real estate on behalf of the business and investors. These managers focus on long-term strategic financial planning rather than on day-to-day operations of the property.

When deciding to acquire property, real estate asset managers take several factors into consideration, such as property values, taxes, zoning, population growth, transportation, and traffic volume and patterns. Once a site is selected, they negotiate contracts for the purchase or lease of the property, securing the most beneficial terms. Real estate asset managers periodically review their company's real estate holdings and identify properties that are no longer financially profitable. They then negotiate the sale or termination of the lease of such properties.

Property and real estate managers who work for homebuilders, real estate developers, and land development companies acquire land and plan construction of shopping centers, houses, apartments, office buildings, or industrial parks. They negotiate with representatives of local governments, other businesses, community and public interest groups, and public utilities to eliminate obstacles to the development of land and to gain support for a planned project. It sometimes takes years to win approval for a project and, in the process, managers may have to modify plans for the project many times. Once cleared to proceed with a project, managers may help to negotiate short-term loans to finance the construction of the project, and later negotiate long-term permanent mortgage loans. They then help choose, assist, and advise the architectural firms that draw up detailed plans and the construction companies that build the project.

In many respects, the work of community association managers parallels that of property managers. They collect monthly assessments, prepare financial statements and budgets, negotiate with contractors, and help resolve complaints. In other respects, however, the work of community association managers differs from that of other residential property and real estate managers. They interact on a daily basis with homeowners and other residents, rather than with renters. Hired by the volunteer board of directors of the association, community association managers administer the daily affairs, and oversee the maintenance of property and facilities that the homeowners own and use jointly through the association. They also assist the board and owners in complying with association and government rules and regulations.

Some associations encompass thousands of homes and employ their own onsite staff and managers. In addition to administering the associations' financial records and budget, managers may be responsible for the operation of community pools, golf courses, and community centers, and for the maintenance of landscaping and parking areas. Community association managers also may meet with the elected boards of directors to discuss and resolve legal issues or disputes between neighbors, as well as to review any proposed changes or improvements by homeowners to their properties, to make sure they fit within community guidelines.

Working Conditions

Offices of most property, real estate, and community association managers are clean, modern, and well lighted. However, many managers spend a major portion of their time away from their desks. Onsite managers, in particular, may spend a large portion of their workday away from their office, visiting the building engineer, showing apartments, checking on the janitorial and maintenance staff, or investigating problems reported by tenants. Property and real estate managers frequently visit the properties they oversee, sometimes on a daily basis when contractors are doing major repair or renovation work. Real estate asset managers may spend time away from home while traveling to company real estate holdings or searching for properties to acquire.

Property, real estate, and community association managers often must attend meetings in the evening with residents, property owners, community association boards of directors, or civic groups. Not surprisingly, many managers put in long workweeks, especially before financial and tax reports are due. Some apartment managers are required to live in apartment complexes where they work so that they are available to handle any emergency that occurs, even when they are off duty. They usually receive compensatory time off for working nights or weekends. Many apartment managers receive time off during the week so that they are available on weekends to show apartments to prospective residents.

Employment

Property, real estate, and community association managers held about 270,000 jobs in 2000. Two of every 5 worked for real estate agents and managers, real estate operators and lessors, or property management firms. Others worked for real estate development companies, government agencies that manage public buildings, and corporations with extensive holdings of commercial properties. Forty-eight percent of property and real estate managers were self-employed, as compared with only 8 percent for all workers combined.

Training, Other Qualifications, and Advancement

Most employers prefer to hire college graduates for property management positions. Entrants with degrees in business administration, accounting, finance, real estate, public administration, or related fields are preferred, but those with degrees in the liberal arts also may qualify. Good speaking, writing, computer, and financial skills, as well as an ability to tactfully deal with people, are essential in all areas of property management.

Many people enter property management as onsite managers of apartment buildings, office complexes, or community associations, or as employees of property management firms or community association management companies. As they acquire experience working under the direction of a property manager, they may advance to positions with greater responsibility at larger properties. Those who excel as onsite managers often transfer to assistant property manager positions in which they can acquire experience handling a broad range of property management responsibilities.

Previous employment as a real estate sales agent may be an asset to onsite managers because it provides experience useful in showing apartments or office space. In the past, those with backgrounds in building maintenance have advanced to onsite manager positions on the strength of their knowledge of building mechanical systems, but this is becoming less common as employers place greater emphasis on administrative, financial, and communication abilities for managerial jobs.

Although many people entering jobs such as assistant property manager do so by having previously gained onsite management experience, employers increasingly hire inexperienced college graduates with bachelor's or master's degrees in business administration, accounting, finance, or real estate for these positions. Assistants work closely with a property manager and learn how to prepare budgets, analyze insurance coverage and risk options, market property to prospective tenants, and collect overdue rent payments. In time, many assistants advance to property manager positions.

The responsibilities and compensation of property, real estate, and community association managers increase as they manage more and larger properties. Most property managers are responsible for several properties at a time. As their careers advance, they gradually are entrusted with larger properties whose management is more complex. Many specialize in the management of one type of property, such as apartments, office buildings, condominiums, cooperatives, homeowner associations, or retail properties. Managers who excel at marketing properties to tenants may specialize in managing new properties, while those who are particularly knowledgeable about buildings and their mechanical systems might specialize in the management of older properties requiring renovation or more frequent repairs. Some experienced managers open their own property management firms.

Persons most commonly enter real estate asset manager jobs by transferring from positions as property managers or real estate brokers. Real estate asset managers must be good negotiators, adept at persuading and handling people, and good at analyzing data in order to assess the fair market value of property or its development potential. Resourcefulness and creativity in arranging financing are essential for managers who specialize in land development.

Many employers encourage attendance at short-term formal training programs conducted by various professional and trade associations active in the real estate field. Employers send managers to these programs to improve their management skills and expand their knowledge of specialized subjects, such as the operation and maintenance of building mechanical systems, enhancement of property values, insurance and risk management, personnel management, business and real estate law, community association risks and liabilities, tenant relations, communications, and accounting and financial concepts. Managers also participate in these programs to prepare themselves for positions of greater responsibility in property management. Completion of these programs, related job experience, and a satisfactory score on a written examination lead to certification, or the formal award of a professional designation, by the sponsoring association. (Some organizations offering such programs are listed at the end of this statement.) In addition to these qualifications, some associations require their members to adhere to a specific code of ethics. In some states, community association managers must be licensed.

Managers of public housing subsidized by the federal government are required to be certified. Many property, real estate, and community association managers, who work with all types of property, choose to earn a professional designation voluntarily because it represents formal industry recognition of their achievements and status in the occupation. Real estate asset managers who buy or sell property are required to be licensed by the state in which they practice.

Job Outlook

Employment of property, real estate, and community association managers is projected to increase faster than the average for all occupations through the year 2010. Many job openings are expected to occur as managers transfer to other occupations or leave the labor force. Opportunities should be best for those with a college degree in business administration, real estate, or a related field, and for those who attain a professional designation.

Job growth among onsite property managers in commercial real estate is expected to accompany the projected expansion in several industry groups: wholesale and retail trade; finance, insurance, and real estate; and services. Additional employment growth will stem from expansion of existing buildings.

An increase in the nation's stock of apartments, houses, and offices also should require more property managers. Developments of new homes increasingly are being organized with community or homeowner associations that provide community services and oversee jointly owned common areas, requiring professional management. To help properties become more profitable or to enhance the resale values of homes, more commercial and residential property owners are expected to place their investments in the hands of professional managers.

The changing demographic composition of the population also should create more jobs for property, real estate, and community association managers. The number of older people will grow during the 2000–2010 projection period, increasing the need for various types of suitable housing, such as assisted-living facilities and retirement communities. Accordingly, there will be demand for property and real estate managers to operate these facilities, and especially for those who have a background in the operation and administrative aspects of running a health unit.

Earnings

Median annual earnings of salaried property, real estate, and community association managers were $36,020 in 2000. The middle 50 percent earned between $24,100 and $53,780 a year. The lowest 10 percent earned less than $16,720, and the highest 10 percent earned more than $80,360 a year. Median annual earnings of salaried property, real estate, and community association managers in 2000 were as follows:

Local government	$50,410
Real estate agents and managers	36,070
Real estate operators and lessors	30,150

Many resident apartment managers and onsite association managers receive the use of an apartment as part of their compensation package. Managers often are reimbursed for the use of their personal vehicles, and managers employed in land development often receive a small percentage of ownership in the projects they develop.

According to a survey conducted by the Community Association Institute, the median annual salary for community managers was $42,000 in 2000, with the middle 50 percent earning between $34,000 and $55,000 a year. For assistant community managers, the median annual salary was $30,000, with the middle 50 percent earning between $25,000 and $38,000 a year.

Related Occupations

Property, real estate, and community association managers plan, organize, staff, and manage the real estate operations of businesses. Workers who perform similar functions in other fields include administrative services managers, education administrators, food service managers, lodging managers, medical and health services managers, real estate brokers and sales agents, and urban and regional planners.

Sources of Additional Information

General information about education and careers in property management is available from:

● Institute of Real Estate Management, 430 N. Michigan Ave., Chicago, IL 60611. Internet: http://www.irem.org

For information on careers and certification programs in commercial property management, contact:

- Building Owners and Managers Institute, 1521 Ritchie Hwy., Arnold, MD 21012. Internet: http://www.bomi-edu.org

For information on careers and professional designation and certification programs in residential property and community association management, contact:

- Community Associations Institute, 225 Reinekers Ln., Suite 300, Alexandria, VA 22314. Internet: http://www.caionline.org

- National Board of Certification for Community Association Managers, P.O. Box 25037, Alexandria, VA 22313. Internet: http://www.nbccam.org

Purchasing Managers, Buyers, and Purchasing Agents

O*NET 11-3061.00, 13-1021.00, 13-1022.00, 13-1023.00

Significant Points

- More than half were employed in wholesale trade or manufacturing establishments.

- Some firms promote qualified employees to these positions, while other employers recruit college graduates; regardless of academic preparation, new employees must learn the specifics of their employers' business.

- Overall employment is expected to experience little or no change due to productivity improvements brought about by the increasing use of computers and the Internet; however, employment will vary by occupational specialty.

Nature of the Work

Purchasing managers, buyers, and purchasing agents seek to obtain the highest quality merchandise at the lowest possible purchase cost for their employers. In general, purchasers buy goods and services for their company or organization, whereas buyers typically buy items for resale. Purchasers and buyers determine which commodities or services are best, choose the suppliers of the product or service, negotiate the lowest price, and award contracts that ensure that the correct amount of the product or service is received at the appropriate time. In order to accomplish these tasks successfully, purchasing managers, buyers, and purchasing agents study sales records and inventory levels of current stock, identify foreign and domestic suppliers, and keep abreast of changes affecting both the supply of and demand for needed products and materials.

Purchasing managers, buyers, and purchasing agents evaluate suppliers based upon price, quality, service support, availability, reliability, and selection. To assist them in their search, they review catalogs, industry and company publications, directories, and trade journals. Much of this information is now available on the Internet. They research the reputation and history of the suppliers and may advertise anticipated purchase actions in order to solicit bids. At meetings, trade shows, conferences, and suppliers' plants and distribution centers, they examine products and services, assess a supplier's production and distribution capabilities, and discuss other technical and business considerations that influence the purchasing decision. Once all the necessary information on suppliers is gathered, orders are placed and contracts are awarded to those suppliers who meet the purchasers' needs. Contracts often are for several years and may stipulate the price or a narrow range of prices, allowing purchasers to reorder as necessary. Other specific job duties and responsibilities vary by employer and by the type of commodities or services to be purchased.

Purchasing specialists employed by government agencies or manufacturing firms usually are called purchasing directors, managers, or agents; buyers or industrial buyers; or contract specialists. These workers acquire materials, parts, machines, supplies, services, and other materials used in the production of a final product. Some purchasing managers specialize in negotiating and supervising supply contracts and are called contract or supply managers. Purchasing agents and managers obtain items ranging from raw materials, fabricated parts, machinery, and office supplies to construction services and airline tickets. The flow of work—or even the entire production process—can be slowed or halted if the right materials, supplies, or equipment are not on hand when needed. To be effective, purchasing specialists must have a working technical knowledge of the goods or services to be purchased.

In large industrial organizations, a distinction often is drawn between the work of a buyer or purchasing agent and that of a purchasing manager. Purchasing agents and buyers commonly focus on routine purchasing tasks, often specializing in a commodity or group of related commodities, such as steel, lumber, cotton, grains, fabricated metal products, or petroleum products. Purchasing agents usually track market conditions, price trends, or futures markets. Purchasing managers usually handle the more complex or critical purchases and may supervise a group of purchasing agents handling other goods and services. Whether a person is titled purchasing manager, buyer, or purchasing agent depends more on specific industry and employer practices than on specific job duties.

Changing business practices have altered the traditional roles of purchasing or supply management specialists in many industries. For example, manufacturing companies increasingly involve purchasing workers at most stages of product development because of their ability to forecast a part's or material's cost, availability, and suitability for its intended purpose. Furthermore, potential problems with the supply of materials may be avoided by consulting the purchasing department in the early stages of product design.

Businesses also might enter into integrated supply contracts. These contracts increase the importance of supplier selection because agreements are larger in scope and longer in duration. Integrated supply incorporates all members of the supply chain including the supplier, transportation companies, and the retailer. A major responsibility of most purchasers is to work out problems that may occur with a supplier because the success of the relationship affects the buying firm's performance.

Purchasing specialists often work closely with other employees in their organizations when deciding on purchases, an arrangement sometimes called team buying. For example, they may discuss the design of custom-made products with company design engineers, quality problems in purchased goods with quality assurance engineers and production supervisors, or shipment problems with managers in the receiving department before submitting an order.

Contract specialists and managers in various levels of government award contracts for an array of items, including office and building supplies, services for the public, and construction projects. For example, they may oversee the contract for cleaning services of a government office building to verify that the work is being done on schedule and on budget, even though the cleaners are not government employees. They may use sealed bids to award contracts, but usually establish negotiated agreements for complex items. Often, purchasing specialists in government place solicitations for services and accept bids and offers through the Internet. Government purchasing agents and managers must follow strict laws and regulations in their work to avoid any appearance of impropriety. These legal requirements are occasionally changed, so agents and contract specialists must stay informed about the latest regulations.

Other purchasing specialists, who buy finished goods for resale, are employed by wholesale and retail establishments where they commonly are known as buyers or merchandise managers. Wholesale and retail buyers are an integral part of a complex system of distribution and merchandising that caters to the vast array of consumer needs and desires. Wholesale buyers purchase goods directly from manufacturers or from other wholesale firms for resale to retail firms, commercial establishments, institutions, and other organizations. In retail firms, buyers purchase goods from wholesale firms or directly from manufacturers for resale to the public. Buyers largely determine which products their establishment will sell. Therefore, it is essential that they have the ability to accurately predict what will appeal to consumers. They must constantly stay informed of the latest trends because failure to do so could jeopardize profits and the reputation of their company. Buyers also follow ads in newspapers and other media to check competitors' sales activities and watch general economic conditions to anticipate consumer-buying patterns. Buyers working for large and medium-sized firms usually specialize in acquiring one or two lines of merchandise, whereas buyers working for small stores may purchase their complete inventory.

The use of private-label merchandise and the consolidation of buying departments have increased the responsibilities of retail buyers. Private-label merchandise, produced for a particular retailer, requires buyers to work closely with vendors to develop and obtain the desired product. The downsizing and consolidation of buying departments increases the demands placed on buyers because, although the amount of work remains unchanged, there are fewer people to accomplish it. The result is an increase in the workloads and levels of responsibility.

Many merchandise managers assist in the planning and implementation of sales promotion programs. Working with merchandise executives, they determine the nature of the sale and purchase accordingly. They may work with advertising personnel to create an ad campaign. For example, they may determine in which media the advertisement will be placed—newspapers, direct mail, television, or some combination of these. In addition, merchandise managers often visit the selling floor to ensure that the goods are properly displayed. Often, assistant buyers are responsible for placing orders and checking shipments.

Computers continue to have a major effect on the jobs of purchasing managers, buyers, and purchasing agents. In manufacturing and service industries, computers handle most of the routine tasks, enabling pur-

chasing workers to concentrate mainly on the analytical and qualitative aspects of the job. Computers are used to obtain instant and accurate product and price listings, to track inventory levels, to process orders, and to help determine when to make purchases. Computers also maintain lists of bids and offers, record the history of supplier performance, and issue purchase orders.

Computerized systems have dramatically simplified many of the acquisition functions and improved the efficiency of determining which products are selling. For example, cash registers connected to computers, known as point-of-sale terminals, allow organizations to maintain instant access to current sales and inventory records. This information can be used to produce sales reports that reflect customer-buying habits. The ability to quickly know which products or combination of products are selling well provides powerful data that buyers and supply managers can use to increase sales and reduce costs. Buyers can gain instant access to the specifications for thousands of commodities, inventory records, and their customers' purchase records to avoid overpaying for goods and to avoid shortages of popular goods or surpluses of goods that do not sell as well. Firms are linked with manufacturers and wholesalers by electronic purchasing systems, the Internet, or extranets. These systems improve the speed for selection, customization, and ordering, and they provide information on availability and shipment, allowing buyers to better concentrate on the selection of goods and suppliers.

Working Conditions

Most purchasing managers, buyers, and purchasing agents work in comfortable, well-lighted offices. They frequently work more than the standard 40-hour week because of special sales, conferences, or production deadlines. Evening and weekend work also is common. For those working in retail trade, this is especially true prior to holiday and back-to-school seasons. Consequently, many retail firms discourage the use of vacation time during peak periods.

Buyers and merchandise managers often work under great pressure. Because wholesale and retail stores are so competitive, buyers need physical stamina to keep up with the fast-paced nature of their work.

Many purchasing managers, buyers, and purchasing agents travel at least several days a month. Purchasers for worldwide manufacturing companies and large retailers, and buyers of high fashion, may travel outside the United States.

Employment

Purchasing managers, buyers, and purchasing agents held about 536,000 jobs in 2000. More than one-half worked in wholesale trade or manufacturing establishments such as distribution centers or factories, and another one-sixth worked in retail trade establishments such as grocery or department stores. The remainder worked mostly in service establishments or different levels of government. A small number were self-employed.

The following table shows the distribution of employment by occupational specialty:

Purchasing agents, except wholesale, retail, and farm products	237,000
Wholesale and retail buyers, except farm products	148,000
Purchasing managers	132,000
Purchasing agents and buyers, farm products	20,000

Training, Other Qualifications, and Advancement

Qualified persons may begin as trainees, purchasing clerks, expediters, junior buyers, or assistant buyers. Retail and wholesale firms prefer to hire applicants who have a college degree, and who are familiar with the merchandise they sell and with wholesaling and retailing practices. Some retail firms promote qualified employees to assistant buyer positions; others recruit and train college graduates as assistant buyers. Most employers use a combination of methods.

Educational requirements tend to vary with the size of the organization. Large stores and distributors, especially those in wholesale and retail trade, prefer applicants who have completed a bachelor's degree program with a business emphasis. Many manufacturing firms put a greater emphasis on formal training. They prefer applicants with a bachelor's or master's degree in engineering, business, economics, or one of the applied sciences.

Regardless of academic preparation, new employees must learn the specifics of their employers' business. Training periods vary in length, with most lasting 1 to 5 years. In wholesale and retail establishments, most trainees begin by selling merchandise, supervising sales workers, checking invoices on material received, and keeping track of stock. As they progress, retail trainees are given increased buying-related responsibilities.

In manufacturing, new purchasing employees often are enrolled in company training programs and spend a considerable amount of time learning about company operations and purchasing practices. They work with experienced purchasers to learn about commodities, prices, suppliers, and markets. In addition, they may be assigned to the production planning department to learn about the material requirements system and the inventory system the company uses to keep production and replenishment functions working smoothly.

Purchasing managers, buyers, and purchasing agents must know how to use word processing as well as spreadsheet software and the Internet. Other important qualities include the ability to analyze technical data in suppliers' proposals; good communication, negotiation, and mathematical skills; knowledge of supply-chain management; and the ability to perform financial analyses.

Persons who wish to become wholesale or retail buyers should be good at planning and decision making and have an interest in merchandising. Anticipating consumer preferences and ensuring that goods are in stock when they are needed require resourcefulness, good judgment, and self-confidence. Buyers must be able to quickly make decisions and to take risks. Marketing skills and the ability to identify products that will sell also are very important. Employers often look for leadership ability because buyers spend a large portion of their time supervising assistant buyers and dealing with manufacturers' representatives and store executives.

Experienced buyers may advance by moving to a department that manages a larger volume or by becoming a merchandise manager. Others may go to work in sales for a manufacturer or wholesaler.

An experienced purchasing agent or buyer may become an assistant purchasing manager in charge of a group of purchasing professionals before advancing to purchasing manager, supply manager, or director of materials management. At the top levels, duties may overlap with other management functions such as production, planning, logistics, and marketing.

Regardless of industry, continuing education is essential for advancement. Many purchasers participate in seminars offered by professional societies and take college courses in supply management. Professional certification is increasingly important.

In private industry, recognized marks of experience and professional competence are the Accredited Purchasing Practitioner (APP) and Certified Purchasing Manager (CPM) designations, conferred by the Institute for Supply Management, and the Certified Purchasing Professional (CPP) designation and the Certified Professional Purchasing Manager (CPPM), conferred by the American Purchasing Society. In federal, state, and local government, the indications of professional competence are Certified Professional Public Buyer (CPPB) and Certified Public Purchasing Officer (CPPO), conferred by the National Institute of Governmental Purchasing. Most of these certifications are awarded only after work-related experience and education requirements are met, and written or oral exams are successfully completed.

Job Outlook

Overall employment of purchasing managers, buyers, and purchasing agents is expected to experience little or no change through the year 2010. Demand for these workers will not keep up with the rising level of economic activity. The increasing use of computers has allowed the paperwork involved in ordering and procuring supplies to be eliminated, reducing the demand for lower-level buyers who perform these duties and for the managers who supervise them. In addition, the increased use of credit cards by some employees to purchase supplies without using the services of the procurement or purchasing office, combined with the growing number of buys being made electronically, will restrict demand for purchasing agents. Despite little or no change in employment, some job openings will result from the need to replace workers who transfer to other occupations or leave the labor force.

Projected employment varies by occupational specialty. Employment of purchasing managers is expected to decline through 2010. The use of the Internet to conduct electronic commerce has made information easier to obtain, thus increasing the productivity of purchasing managers. The Internet also allows both large and small companies to bid on contracts. Exclusive supply contracts and long-term contracting have allowed companies to negotiate with fewer suppliers less frequently, further reducing demand for purchasing managers.

Employment of wholesale and retail buyers, except farm products, also is projected to decline. In retail trade, mergers and acquisitions have forced the consolidation of buying departments, hence eliminating jobs. In addition, larger retail stores are removing their buying departments from geographic markets and centralizing them at their headquarters, thus eliminating more jobs.

Employment of purchasing agents, except wholesale, retail, and farm products, is expected to increase about as fast as the average for all occupations through 2010. Despite the greater use of electronic transactions, purchases of complex equipment is more difficult to automate, or transact electronically. Employment of purchasing agents and buyers, farm products, also is projected to increase about as fast as the average for all occupations, as the more technical nature of farm products limits the ease of making purchases electronically.

Persons who have a bachelor's degree in business should have the best chance of obtaining a buyer job in wholesale or retail trade or within government. A bachelor's degree, combined with industry experience and knowledge of a technical field, will be an advantage for those interested in working for a manufacturing or industrial company. Government agencies and larger companies usually require a master's degree in business or public administration for top-level purchasing positions.

Earnings

Median annual earnings of purchasing managers were $53,030 in 2000. The middle 50 percent earned between $38,770 and $71,480 a year. The lowest 10 percent earned less than $29,100, and the highest 10 percent earned more than $93,040 a year.

Median annual earnings for purchasing agents and buyers, farm products were $37,560 in 2000. The middle 50 percent earned between $29,150 and $52,600 a year. The lowest 10 percent earned less than $21,550, and the highest 10 percent earned more than $80,320 a year.

Median annual earnings for wholesale and retail buyers, except farm products were $37,200 in 2000. The middle 50 percent earned between $27,480 and $51,560 a year. The lowest 10 percent earned less than $21,570, and the highest 10 percent earned more than $70,750 a year. Median annual earnings in the industries employing the largest numbers of wholesale and retail buyers, except farm products in 2000 were as follows:

Groceries and related products	$41,020
Electrical goods	38,220
Machinery, equipment, and supplies	35,170
Miscellaneous shopping goods stores	33,730
Grocery stores	29,650

Median annual earnings for purchasing agents, except wholesale, retail, and farm products were $41,370 in 2000. The middle 50 percent earned between $32,050 and $53,830 a year. The lowest 10 percent earned less than $25,650, and the highest 10 percent earned more than $67,980 a year. Median annual earnings in the industries employing the largest numbers of purchasing agents, except wholesale, retail, and farm products in 2000 were as follows:

Federal government	$53,010
Aircraft and parts	49,430
Electronic components and accessories	40,880
Local government	40,330
Hospitals	32,800

Purchasing managers, buyers, and purchasing agents receive the same benefits package as other workers, including vacations, sick leave, life and health insurance, and pension plans. In addition to standard benefits, retail buyers often earn cash bonuses based on their performance and may receive discounts on merchandise bought from their employer.

Related Occupations

Workers in other occupations who need a knowledge of marketing and the ability to assess consumer demand include advertising, marketing, promotions, public relations, and sales managers; insurance sales agents; material recording, scheduling, dispatching, and distributing occupa-

tions, expect postal workers; sales engineers; and sales representatives, wholesale and manufacturing.

Sources of Additional Information

Further information about education, training, employment, and certification for purchasing careers is available from:

- American Purchasing Society, North Island Center, Suite 203, 8 East Galena Blvd., Aurora, IL 60506. Internet: http://www.american-purchasing.com

- Institute for Supply Management, P.O. Box 22160, Tempe, AZ 85285-2160. Internet: http://www.napm.org

- National Institute of Governmental Purchasing, Inc., 151 Spring St., Suite 300, Herndon, VA 20170-5223. Internet: http://www.nigp.org

Radio and Telecommunications Equipment Installers and Repairers

O*NET 49-2021.00, 49-2022.01, 49-2022.02, 49-2022.03, 49-2022.04, 49-2022.05

Significant Points

- Employment is projected to decline.

- Applicants with electronics training and computer skills should have the best opportunities.

- Weekend and holiday hours are common; repairers may be on call around the clock in case of emergencies.

Nature of the Work

Telephones and radios depend on a variety of equipment to transmit communications signals. Electronic switches route telephone signals to their destinations. Switchboards direct telephone calls within a single location or organization. Radio transmitters and receivers relay signals from wireless phones and radios to their destinations. Newer telecommunications equipment is computerized and can communicate a variety of information, including data, graphics, and video. The workers who set up and maintain this sophisticated equipment are radio and telecommunications equipment installers and repairers.

Central office installers set up switches, cables, and other equipment in central offices. These locations are the hubs of a telecommunications network—they contain the switches and routers that direct packets of information to their destinations. *PBX installers and repairers* set up private branch exchange (PBX) switchboards, which relay incoming, outgoing, and interoffice calls within a single location or organization. To install switches and switchboards, installers first connect the equipment to power lines and communications cables and install frames and supports. They test the connections to ensure that adequate power is available and that the communication links function. They also install equipment such as power systems, alarms, and telephone sets. New switches and switchboards are computerized; workers install software or may program the equipment to provide specific features. For example, as a cost-cutting feature, an installer may program a PBX switchboard to route calls over different lines at different times of the day. However, other workers, such as computer support specialists, rather than installers, generally handle complex programming. Finally, the installer performs tests to verify that the newly installed equipment functions properly.

The increasing reliability of telephone switches and routers has simplified maintenance. New telephone switches are self-monitoring and alert repairers to malfunctions. Some switches allow repairers to diagnose and correct problems from remote locations. When faced with a malfunction, the repairer may refer to manufacturers' manuals that provide maintenance instructions. PBX repairers determine if the problem is located within the PBX system, or if it originates in the telephone lines maintained by the local phone company.

When problems with telecommunications equipment arise, telecommunications equipment repairers diagnose the source of the problem by testing each of the different parts of the equipment, which requires an understanding of how the software and hardware interact. Repairers often use spectrum and/or network analyzers to locate the problem. A network analyzer sends a signal through the equipment to detect any distortion in the signal. The nature of the signal distortion often directs the repairer to the source of the problem. To fix the equipment, repairers may use small hand tools, including pliers and screwdrivers, to remove and replace defective components such as circuit boards or wiring. Newer equipment is easier to repair, since whole boards and parts are designed to be quickly removed and replaced. Repairers also may install updated software or programs that maintain existing software.

Station installers and repairers, telephone—commonly known as *telephone installers and repairers*—install and repair telephone wiring and equipment on customers' premises. They install telephone service by connecting customers' telephone wires to outside service lines. These lines run on telephone poles or in underground conduits. The installer may climb poles or ladders to make the connections. Once the telephone is connected, the line is tested to insure that it receives a dial tone. When a maintenance problem occurs, repairers test the customers' lines to determine if the problem is located in the customers' premises or in the outside service lines. When onsite procedures fail to resolve installation or maintenance problems, repairers may request support from their technical service center. Line installers and repairers install the wires and cables that connect customers with central offices.

Radio mechanics install and maintain radio transmitting and receiving equipment. This includes stationary equipment mounted on transmission towers and mobile equipment, such as radio communications systems in service and emergency vehicles. Their work does not include cellular communications towers and equipment. Newer radio equipment is self-monitoring and may alert mechanics to potential malfunctions. When malfunctions occur, these mechanics examine equipment for damaged components and loose or broken wires. They use electrical measuring instruments to monitor signal strength, transmission capacity, interference, and signal delay, as well as hand tools to replace defective components and parts and to adjust equipment so it performs within required specifications.

Working Conditions

Radio and telecommunications equipment installers and repairers generally work in clean, well-lighted, air-conditioned surroundings, such as a telephone company's central office, a customer's PBX location, or an electronic repair shop or service center. Telephone installers and repairers work on rooftops, ladders, and telephone poles. Radio mechanics may maintain equipment located on the tops of transmissions towers. While working outdoors, these workers are subject to a variety of weather conditions.

Nearly all radio and telecommunications equipment installers and repairers work full time. Many work regular business hours to meet the demand for repair services during the workday. Schedules are more irregular at companies that need repair services 24 hours a day or where installation and maintenance must take place after business hours. At these locations, mechanics work a variety of shifts, including weekend and holiday hours. Repairers may be on call around the clock, in case of emergencies, and may have to work overtime.

The work of most repairers involves lifting, reaching, stooping, crouching, and crawling. Adherence to safety precautions is important to guard against work hazards. These hazards include falls, minor burns, electrical shock, and contact with hazardous materials.

Employment

Radio and telecommunications equipment installers and repairers held about 196,000 jobs in 2000. About 189,000 were telecommunications equipment installers and repairers, except line installers, and the rest were radio mechanics. Most worked for telephone communications companies but many radio mechanics worked in electrical repair shops.

Training, Other Qualifications, and Advancement

Most employers seek applicants with postsecondary training in electronics and a familiarity with computers. Training sources include 2- and 4-year college programs in electronics or communications, trade schools, and equipment and software manufacturers. Military experience with communications equipment is highly valued by many employers.

Newly hired repairers usually receive some training from their employers. This may include formal classroom training in electronics, communications systems, or software and informal, hands-on training with communications equipment. Large companies may send repairers to outside training sessions to keep these employees informed of new equipment and service procedures. As networks have become more sophisticated—often including equipment from a variety of companies—the knowledge needed for installation and maintenance also has increased.

Repairers must be able to distinguish colors, because wires are color-coded, and they must be able to hear distinctions in the various tones on a telephone system. For positions that require climbing poles and towers, workers must be in good physical shape. Repairers who handle assignments alone at a customer's site must be able to work without close supervision. For workers who frequently contact customers, a pleasant personality, neat appearance, and good communications skills also are important.

Experienced repairers with advanced training may become specialists or troubleshooters who help other repairers diagnose difficult problems, or may work with engineers in designing equipment and developing maintenance procedures. Because of their familiarity with equipment, repairers are particularly well qualified to become manufacturers' sales workers. Workers with leadership ability also may become maintenance supervisors or service managers. Some experienced workers open their own repair services or shops or become wholesalers or retailers of electronic equipment.

Job Outlook

Employment of radio and telecommunications equipment installers and repairers is expected to decline through 2010. Although the need for installation work will grow as companies seek to upgrade their telecommunications networks, there will be a declining need for maintenance work—performed by telecommunications equipment installers and repairers, except line installers—because of increasingly reliable self-monitoring and self-diagnosing equipment. The replacement of two-way radio systems by wireless systems, especially in service vehicles, has eliminated the need in many companies for onsite radio mechanics. The increased reliability of wireless equipment and the use of self-monitoring systems also will continue to lessen the need for radio mechanics. Applicants with electronics training and computer skills should have the best opportunities for radio and telecommunications equipment installer and repairer jobs.

Job opportunities will vary by specialty. For example, opportunities should be available for central office and PBX installers and repairers as the growing popularity of the Internet, expanded multimedia offerings such as video on demand, and other telecommunications services continue to place additional demand on telecommunications networks. These new services require high data transfer rates, which can only be achieved by installing new optical switching and routing equipment. Extending high speed communications from central offices to customers also will require the installation of more advanced switching and routing equipment. Whereas increased reliability and automation of switching equipment will limit opportunities, these effects will be offset by the strong demand for installation and upgrading of switching equipment.

Station installers and repairers, on the other hand, can expect keen competition. Pre-wired buildings and the increasing reliability of telephone equipment will reduce the need for installation and maintenance of customers' telephones. The number of pay phones is declining as cellular telephones have increased in popularity, which also will adversely affect employment in this specialty as pay phone installation and maintenance is one of their major functions.

Earnings

In 2000, median hourly earnings of telecommunications equipment installers and repairers, except line installers were $21.17. The middle 50 percent earned between $16.55 and $24.99. The bottom 10 percent earned less than $12.04, whereas the top 10 percent earned more than $27.23. Median hourly earnings in the telephone communications industry were $22.88 in 2000.

Median hourly earnings of radio mechanics in 2000 were $15.86. The middle 50 percent earned between $12.57 and $20.60. The bottom 10 percent earned less than $9.39, whereas the top 10 percent earned more than $25.62.

Related Occupations

Related occupations that work with electronic equipment include broadcast and sound engineering technicians and radio operators; computer, automated teller, and office machine repairers; electronic home entertainment equipment installers and repairers; and electrical and electronics installers and repairers. Engineering technicians also may repair electronic equipment as part of their duties.

Sources of Additional Information

For information on career opportunities, contact:

- International Brotherhood of Electrical Workers, Telecommunications Department, 1125 15th St. NW., Room 807, Washington, DC 20005

- Communications Workers of America, 501 3rd St. NW., Washington, DC 20001. Internet: http://www.cwa-union.org

For information on careers and schools, contact:

- Electronics Technicians Association International, 502 North Jackson, Greencastle, IN 46135

- National Association of Radio and Telecommunications engineers, P.O. Box 678, Medway, MA 02053. Internet: http://www.narte.org

Radiologic Technologists and Technicians

O*NET 29-2034.01, 29-2034.02

Significant Points

- Faster-than-average growth will arise from an increase in the number of middle-aged and older persons, who are the primary users of diagnostic procedures.

- Although hospitals will remain the primary employer of radiologic technologists and technicians, a greater number of new jobs will be found in offices and clinics of physicians, including diagnostic imaging centers.

- Radiologic technologists and technicians with cross training in nuclear medicine technology or other modalities will have the best prospects.

Nature of the Work

Radiologic technologists and technicians take X rays and administer nonradioactive materials into patients' blood streams for diagnostic purposes. Some specialize in diagnostic imaging technologies such as computed tomography (CT) and magnetic resonance imaging (MRI).

In addition to radiologic technologists and technicians, others who assist in diagnostic imaging procedures include Cardiovascular Technologists and Technicians, Diagnostic Medical Sonographers, and Nuclear Medicine Technologists.

Radiologic technologists and technicians, also referred to as *radiographers*, produce X-ray films (radiographs) of parts of the human body for use in diagnosing medical problems. They prepare patients for radiologic examinations by explaining the procedure, removing articles such as jewelry, through which X rays cannot pass, and positioning patients so that the parts of the body can be appropriately radiographed. To prevent unnecessary radiation exposure, they surround the exposed area with radiation protection devices, such as lead shields, or limit the size of the X-ray beam. Radiographers position radiographic equipment at the correct angle and height over the appropriate area of a patient's body. Using instruments similar to a measuring tape, they may measure the thickness of the section to be radiographed and set controls on the X-ray machine to produce radiographs of the appropriate density, detail, and contrast. They place the X-ray film under the part of the patient's body to be examined and make the exposure. They then remove the film and develop it.

Experienced radiographers may perform more complex imaging procedures. For fluoroscopies, radiographers prepare a solution of contrast medium for the patient to drink, allowing the radiologist, a physician who interprets radiographs, to see soft tissues in the body. Some radiographers, called *CT technologists,* operate computerized tomography scanners to produce cross sectional images of patients. Others operate machines using strong magnets and radio waves rather than radiation to create an image and are called *magnetic resonance imaging (MRI) technologists.*

Radiologic technologists and technicians must follow physicians' orders precisely and conform to regulations concerning use of radiation to protect themselves, their patients, and coworkers from unnecessary exposure.

In addition to preparing patients and operating equipment, radiologic technologists and technicians keep patient records and adjust and maintain equipment. They also may prepare work schedules, evaluate equipment purchases, or manage a radiology department.

Working Conditions

Most full-time radiologic technologists and technicians work about 40 hours a week; they may have evening, weekend, or on-call hours. Opportunities for part-time and shift work are also available.

Because technologists and technicians are on their feet for long periods and may lift or turn disabled patients, physical stamina is important. Technologists and technicians work at diagnostic machines but may also do some procedures at patients' bedsides. Some travel to patients in large vans equipped with sophisticated diagnostic equipment.

Although potential radiation hazards exist in this occupation, they are minimized by the use of lead aprons, gloves, and other shielding devices, as well as by instruments monitoring radiation exposure. Technologists and technicians wear badges measuring radiation levels in the radiation area, and detailed records are kept on their cumulative lifetime dose.

Employment

Radiologic technologists and technicians held about 167,000 jobs in 2000. About 1 in 5 worked part-time. More than half of all jobs are in hospitals. Most of the rest are in physicians' offices and clinics, including diagnostic imaging centers.

Training, Other Qualifications, and Advancement

Preparation for this profession is offered in hospitals, colleges and universities, vocational-technical institutes, and the U.S. Armed Forces. Hospitals, which employ most radiologic technologists and technicians, prefer to hire those with formal training.

Formal training programs in radiography range in length from 1 to 4 years and lead to a certificate, associate degree, or bachelor's degree. Two-year associate degree programs are most prevalent.

Some 1-year certificate programs are available for experienced radiographers or individuals from other health occupations, such as medical technologists and registered nurses, who want to change fields or specialize in computerized tomography or magnetic resonance imaging. A bachelor's or master's degree in one of the radiologic technologies is desirable for supervisory, administrative, or teaching positions.

The Joint Review Committee on Education in Radiologic Technology accredits most formal training programs for this field. They accredited 584 radiography programs in 2000. Radiography programs require, at a minimum, a high school diploma or the equivalent. High school courses in mathematics, physics, chemistry, and biology are helpful. The programs provide both classroom and clinical instruction in anatomy and physiology, patient care procedures, radiation physics, radiation protection, principles of imaging, medical terminology, positioning of patients, medical ethics, radiobiology, and pathology.

In 1981, Congress passed the Consumer-Patient Radiation Health and Safety Act, which aims to protect the public from the hazards of unnecessary exposure to medical and dental radiation by ensuring operators of radiologic equipment are properly trained. Under the act, the federal government sets voluntary standards that the states, in turn, may use for accrediting training programs and certifying individuals who engage in medical or dental radiography.

In 1999, 35 states and Puerto Rico licensed radiologic technologists and technicians. The American Registry of Radiologic Technologists (ARRT) offers voluntary registration in radiography. To be eligible for registration, technologists generally must graduate from an accredited program and pass an examination. Many employers prefer to hire registered radiographers. To be recertified, radiographers must complete 24 hours of continuing education every other year.

Radiologic technologists and technicians should be sensitive to patients' physical and psychological needs. They must pay attention to detail, follow instructions, and work as part of a team. In addition, operating complicated equipment requires mechanical ability and manual dexterity.

With experience and additional training, staff technologists may become specialists, performing CT scanning, angiography, and magnetic resonance imaging. Experienced technologists may also be promoted to supervisor, chief radiologic technologist, and ultimately department administrator or director. Depending on the institution, courses or a master's degree in business or health administration may be necessary for the director's position. Some technologists progress by becoming instructors or directors in radiologic technology programs; others take jobs as sales representatives or instructors with equipment manufacturers.

Job Outlook

Employment of radiologic technologists and technicians is expected to grow faster than the average for all occupations through 2010, as the population grows and ages, increasing the demand for diagnostic imaging. Opportunities are expected to be favorable. Some employers report shortages of radiologic technologists and technicians. Imbalances between the supply of qualified workers and demand should spur efforts to attract and retain qualified radiologic technologists and technicians. For example, employers may provide more flexible training programs, or improve compensation and working conditions.

Although physicians are enthusiastic about the clinical benefits of new technologies, the extent to which they are adopted depends largely on cost and reimbursement considerations. For example, digital imaging technology can improve quality and efficiency, but remains expensive. Some promising new technologies may not come into widespread use because they are too expensive and third-party payers may not be willing to pay for their use.

Radiologic technologists who are educated and credentialed in more than one type of diagnostic imaging technology, such as radiography and sonography or nuclear medicine, will have better employment opportunities as employers look for new ways to control costs. In hospitals, multi-skilled employees will be the most sought after, as hospitals respond to cost pressures by continuing to merge departments.

Hospitals will remain the principal employer of radiologic technologists and technicians. However, a greater number of new jobs will be found in offices and clinics of physicians, including diagnostic imaging centers. Health facilities such as these are expected to grow very rapidly through 2010 due to the strong shift toward outpatient care, encouraged by third-party payers and made possible by technological advances that permit more procedures to be performed outside the hospital. Some job openings will also arise from the need to replace technologists and technicians who leave the occupation.

Earnings

Median annual earnings of radiologic technologists and technicians were $36,000 in 2000. The middle 50 percent earned between $30,220 and $43,380. The lowest 10 percent earned less than $25,310, and the highest 10 percent earned more than $52,050. Median annual earnings in the industries employing the largest numbers of radiologic technologists and technicians in 2000 were:

Medical and dental laboratories	$39,400
Hospitals	36,280
Offices and clinics of medical doctors	34,870

Related Occupations

Radiologic technologists and technicians operate sophisticated equipment to help physicians, dentists, and other health practitioners diagnose and treat patients. Workers in related occupations include cardiovascular technologists and technicians, clinical laboratory technologists and technicians, diagnostic medical sonographers, nuclear medicine technologists, radiation therapists, and respiratory therapists.

Sources of Additional Information

For career information, send a stamped, self-addressed business size envelope with your request to:

- American Society of Radiologic Technologists, 15000 Central Ave. SE, Albuquerque, NM 87123-3917. Internet: http://www.asrt.org/asrt.htm

For the current list of accredited education programs in radiography, write to:

- Joint Review Committee on Education in Radiologic Technology, 20 N. Wacker Dr., Suite 600, Chicago, IL 60606-2901. Internet: http://www.jrcert.org

For information on certification, contact:

- American Registry of Radiologic Technologists, 1255 Northland Dr., St. Paul, MN 55120-1155. Internet: http://www.arrt.org

Rail Transportation Occupations

O*NET 53-4011.00, 53-4012.00, 53-4013.00, 53-4021.01, 53-4021.02, 53-4031.00, 53-4041.00, 53-4099.99

Significant Points

- Overall employment in the railroad transportation industry is expected to decline due to productivity gains.

- Employment of locomotive engineers is projected to grow slowly, but all other rail transportation occupations are projected to decline.

- Nearly 8 out of 10 rail transportation workers are members of unions and many have relatively high earnings.

Nature of the Work

More than a century ago, freight and passenger railroads were the ties binding the nation together and the engine driving the economy. Today, rail transportation remains a vital link in our nation's transportation network and economy. Railroads deliver billions of tons of freight and thousands of travelers to destinations throughout the nation, while subways and streetcars transport millions of passengers within metropolitan areas.

Locomotive engineers are among the most experienced and skilled workers on the railroad. Locomotive engineers operate large trains carrying cargo and passengers between stations. Most engineers run diesel locomotives, while a few operate electrically powered locomotives.

Before and after each run, engineers check the mechanical condition of their locomotive, and make minor adjustments on the spot. Engineers receive starting instructions from conductors and move controls such as throttles and air brakes to drive the locomotive. They monitor gauges and meters that measure speed, amperage, battery charge, and air pressure both in the brakelines and in the main reservoir.

On the open rail and in the yard, engineers confer with conductors and traffic control center personnel via two-way radio or mobile telephone to issue or receive information concerning stops, delays, and train locations. They interpret and comply with train orders, train signals, speed limits, and railroad rules and regulations. They must have a thorough knowledge of the signaling systems, yards, and terminals on routes over which they operate. Engineers must be constantly aware of the condition and makeup of their train. This is extremely important because trains react differently to acceleration, braking, and curves, depending on the grade and condition of the rail, number of cars, ratio of empty to loaded cars, and amount of slack in the train.

Locomotive firers, or *assistant engineers*, monitor instruments during runs and watch for dragging equipment, track obstructions, and train signals. In rail yards, they watch for and relay traffic signals from yard workers to yard engineers. *Rail yard engineers, dinkey operators, and hostlers* drive switching or small "dinkey" engines within railroad yards, industrial plants, mines and quarries, or construction projects.

Railroad conductors coordinate the activities of freight and passenger train crews. Railroad conductors assigned to freight trains review schedules, switching orders, way bills, and shipping records to obtain cargo loading and unloading information. Conductors assigned to passenger trains ensure passenger safety and comfort. They collect tickets and fares, and coordinate crew activities to provide boarding, porter, maid, and meal services.

Before a train leaves the terminal, the conductor and engineer discuss instructions received from the dispatcher concerning the train's route, timetable, and cargo. During the run, conductors use two-way radios and mobile telephones to communicate with dispatchers, engineers, and conductors of other trains. Conductors receive information from dispatch or electronic monitoring devices that relay any equipment problems on the train or the rail. They may arrange for the removal of defective cars from the train for repairs at the nearest station or stop. Additionally, conductors may discuss alternative routes if there is a defect or obstruction on the rail.

Yardmasters coordinate activities of workers engaged in railroad traffic operations. These activities include the makeup or breakup of trains and switching inbound or outbound traffic to a specific section of the line. Some cars are sent to unload their cargo on special tracks, while other cars are moved to other tracks to await assemblage into new trains destined for different cities. Yardmasters inform engineers where to move the cars to fit the planned train configuration. Computerized switches divert the locomotive or cars to the proper track for coupling and uncoupling.

Other *railroad brake, signal, and switch operators* perform a variety of activities such as operating track switches to route cars to different sections of the yard. They may signal engineers and set warning signals, help couple and uncouple rolling stock to make up or break up trains, or inspect couplings, air-hoses, and hand brakes.

Traditionally, freight train crews included either one or two brake operators—one in the locomotive with the engineer and the firer and another who rode with the conductor in the rear car. Brake operators worked under the direction of conductors and did the physical work involved in adding and removing cars at railroad stations and assembling and disassembling trains in railroad yards. In an effort to reduce costs and take advantage of new technology, most railroads have phased out locomotive firers and brake operators. Many modern freight trains only use an engineer and a conductor, stationed with the engineer, because new visual instrumentation and monitoring devices have eliminated the need for crewmembers located at the rear of the train.

In contrast to other rail transportation workers, subway and streetcar operators generally work for public transit authorities instead of railroads. *Subway operators* control trains that transport passengers throughout a city and its suburbs. The trains run on rail-guided tracks in underground tunnels, on the surface, or on elevated platforms above streets. Operators must stay alert to observe signals along the track that indicate when they must start, slow, or stop their train. They also make announcements to riders, may open and close the doors, and ensure that passengers get on and off the subway safely.

To meet predetermined schedules, operators must control the train's speed and the amount of time spent at each station. Increasingly, however, these functions are controlled by computers and not by the operator. When breakdowns or emergencies occur, operators contact their dispatcher or supervisor and may have to evacuate cars.

Streetcar operators drive electric-powered streetcars or trolleys that transport passengers in metropolitan areas. Some tracks may be recessed in city streets or have grade crossings, so operators must observe traffic signals and cope with car and truck traffic. Operators start, slow, and stop their cars so passengers may get on or off with ease. They may collect fares, and issue change and transfers. They also answer questions from passengers concerning fares, schedules, and routes.

Working Conditions

Many rail transportation employees work nights, weekends, and holidays because trains operate 24 hours a day, 7 days a week. Nearly 40 percent work more than a 40-hour workweek. Seniority usually dictates who receives the more desirable shifts.

Most freight trains are unscheduled, and few workers on these trains have scheduled assignments. Instead, workers place their names on a list and wait their turn to work. Jobs are usually handed out on short notice and often at odd hours. Those who work on trains operating between stations that are hundreds of miles apart may spend several nights at a time away from home.

Workers on passenger trains ordinarily have more regular and reliable shifts. The appearance, temperature, and accommodations of the passenger trains are also more comfortable than freight trains.

Rail yard workers spend most of their time outdoors in varying weather. The work of conductors and engineers on local runs, where trains frequently stop at stations to pick up and deliver cars, is physically demanding. Climbing up and down and getting off moving cars is strenuous and can be dangerous.

Employment

Rail transportation workers held 115,000 jobs in 2000—including 37,000 locomotive engineers and firers; 3,800 rail yard engineers, dinkey operators, and hostlers; 45,000 railroad conductors and yardmasters; and 22,000 railroad brake, signal, and switch operators. Railroads employ more than 92 percent of all rail transportation workers. The rest primarily work for local governments as subway and streetcar operators, and for mining and manufacturing establishments operating their own locomotives and dinkey engines that move rail cars containing ore, coal, and other bulk materials.

Training, Other Qualifications, and Advancement

Most railroad transportation workers begin as yard laborers, and later may have the opportunity to train for engineer or conductor jobs. Railroads require that applicants have a minimum of a high school diploma or equivalent. Applicants must have good hearing, eyesight, and color vision, as well as good hand-eye coordination, manual dexterity, and mechanical aptitude. Physical stamina is required for these entry-level jobs. Employers require railroad transportation job applicants to pass a physical examination and drug and alcohol screening. Under federal law, all train crewmembers are subject to random drug and alcohol testing while on duty.

Applicants for locomotive engineer jobs must be at least 21 years old. Frequently, employers fill engineer positions with workers who have experience in other railroad operating occupations. Federal regulations require beginning engineers to complete a formal engineer training program, including classroom, simulator, and hands-on instruction in locomotive operation. The instruction is usually administered by the rail company in programs approved by the Federal Railroad Administration. At the end of the training period, they must pass a hearing and visual acuity test, a safety conduct background check, a railroad operation knowledge test, and a skills performance test. The company issues the engineer a license after the applicant successfully passes the examinations. Other conditions and rules may apply to entry-level engineers, and these rules usually vary by employer.

To maintain certification, railroad companies must monitor their engineers. Additionally, engineers must periodically pass an operational rules efficiency test. The test is an unannounced event requiring engineers to take active or responsive action in certain situations such as maintaining a certain speed through a turn or yard.

Engineers undergo periodic physical examinations and drug and alcohol testing to determine their fitness to operate locomotives. In some cases, engineers who fail to meet these physical and conduct standards are restricted to yard service; in other instances, they may be disciplined, trained to perform other work, or discharged.

Conductor jobs are generally filled from the ranks of experienced rail transportation workers who have passed tests covering signals, timetables, operating rules, and related subjects. Seniority usually is the main factor in determining promotion to conductor. On some railroads, conductors start in the yards, then move to freight or passenger service.

Newly trained engineers and conductors are placed on the "extra board" until permanent positions become available. Extra board workers only receive assignments when the railroad needs substitutes for regular workers who are absent because of vacation, illness, or other personal reasons. Seniority rules may also allow workers with greater seniority to select their type of assignment. For example, an engineer may move from an initial regular assignment in yard service to road service.

For subway and streetcar operator jobs, subway transit systems prefer applicants with a high school education. Applicants also must be in good health, have good communication skills, and be able to make quick, responsible judgments.

New operators generally complete training programs that last from a few weeks to 6 months. At the end of the period of classroom and on-the-job training, operators usually must pass qualifying examinations covering the operating system, troubleshooting, and evacuation and emergency procedures. Some operators with sufficient seniority can advance to station managers or other supervisory positions.

Job Outlook

Competition for available opportunities is expected to be keen. Many persons qualify for rail transportation occupations because education beyond high school is generally not required. Many more desire employment than can be hired because the pay is good and the work steady.

Employment for a majority of railroad transportation occupations is expected to decline through the year 2010, with only locomotive engineers expected to grow. The need to replace workers who transfer to other occupations or retire will be the main source of job openings. Employment in most rail occupations, other than locomotive engineers, will continue to decline due to consolidation of railroads and job duties. To remain competitive with other modes of transportation, railroads will strive to control labor costs.

Demand for railroad freight service will grow as the economy and the intermodal transportation of goods expand. Intermodal systems use trucks to pick-up and deliver the shippers' sealed trailers or containers, and trains to transport them long distance. This saves customers time and money by efficiently carrying goods across the country. For railroads, the benefit has been the increased efficiency of equipment use, allowing increases in the number of runs each train makes in a year. In order to compete with other modes of transportation such as trucks, ships, and aircraft, railroads are improving delivery times and on-time service while reducing shipping rates. As a result, businesses are expected to increasingly use railroads to carry their goods.

However, growth in the number of railroad transportation workers will be adversely affected by innovations such as larger, faster, more fuel-efficient trains and computerized classification yards that make it possible to move freight more economically. Computers help keep track of freight cars, match empty cars with the closest loads, and dispatch trains. Computer-assisted devices alert engineers to train malfunctions and new work rules have become widespread allowing trains to operate with two- or three-person crews instead of the traditional five-person crews.

Earnings

Median hourly earnings of locomotive engineers were $21.26 in 2000. The middle 50 percent earned between $15.77 and $25.30 an hour. The lowest 10 percent earned less than $12.84, and the highest 10 percent earned more than $29.67 an hour.

Median hourly earnings of railroad conductors and yardmasters were $18.86 in 2000. The middle 50 percent earned between $15.47 and $22.08 an hour. The lowest 10 percent earned less than $12.92, and the highest 10 percent earned more than $31.03 an hour.

Median hourly earnings of railroad brake, signal, and switch operators were $18.82 in 2000. The middle 50 percent earned between $14.60 and $25.26 an hour. The lowest 10 percent earned less than $11.87, and the highest 10 percent earned more than $31.83 an hour.

Median hourly earnings of rail yard engineers, dinkey operators, and hostlers were $17.69 in 2000. The middle 50 percent earned between $14.43 and $20.38 an hour. The lowest 10 percent earned less than $11.70, and the highest 10 percent earned more than $24.66 an hour.

Most railroad workers in road service are paid according to miles traveled or hours worked; whichever leads to higher earnings. Full-time employees have steadier work, more regular hours, increased opportunities for overtime work, and higher earnings than do those assigned to the extra board.

According to the National Railroad Labor Conference (NRLC) in 1999, the average annual earnings for Class I railroad engineers ranged from $61,400 for yard-freight engineers, to $81,000 for passenger engineers. For conductors, earnings ranged from $53,500 for yard-freight conductors, up to $68,300 for passenger conductors. The NRLC reported that brake operators averaged from $40,800 for yard-freight operators, up to $58,700 for local-freight operators.

According to data from the American Public Transportation Association, in early 2001 the top-rate full-time hourly earnings of operators for commuter rail ranged from $17.50 to $30.10; operators for heavy rail from $16.20 to $27.70; and operators for light rail from $14.40 to $23.90. Transit workers in the northeastern United States typically had the highest wages.

Nearly 80 percent of railroad transportation workers are members of unions. Many different railroad unions represent various crafts on the railroads. Most railroad engineers are members of the Brotherhood of Locomotive engineers, while most other railroad transportation workers are members of the United Transportation Union. Many subway operators are members of the Amalgamated Transit Union, while others belong to the Transport Workers Union of North America.

Related Occupations

Other related transportation workers include aircraft pilots and flight engineers, busdrivers, truckdrivers and driver/sales workers, and water transportation occupations.

Sources of Additional Information

To obtain information on employment opportunities, contact the employment offices of the various railroads and rail transit systems, or state employment service offices.

For general information about the rail transportation industry, contact:

- Association of American Railroads, 50 F St. NW., Washington, DC 20001. Internet: http://www.aar.org

- Federal Railroad Administration, 400 7th St. SW., Washington, DC 20590. Internet: http://www.fra.dot.gov

For general information about career opportunities in passenger transportation, contact:

- American Public Transportation Association, 1666 K St. NW., Suite 1100, Washington, DC 20006

General information on rail transportation occupations and career opportunities as a locomotive engineer is available from:

- Brotherhood of Locomotive engineers, 1370 Ontario Ave., Cleveland, OH 44113-1702. Internet: http://www.ble.org

Real Estate Brokers and Sales Agents

O*NET 41-9021.00, 41-9022.00

Significant Points

- Real estate brokers and sales agents often work evenings and weekends, and are always on call to suit the needs of clients.

- A license is required in every state and the District of Columbia.

- Not everyone is successful in this highly competitive field; well-trained, ambitious people who enjoy selling should have the best chance for success.

Nature of the Work

One of the most complex and important financial events in peoples' lives is the purchase or sale of a home or investment property. As a result, people usually seek the help of real estate brokers and sales agents when buying or selling real estate.

Real estate brokers and sales agents have a thorough knowledge of the real estate market in their community. They know which neighborhoods will best fit clients' needs and budgets. They are familiar with local zoning and tax laws and know where to obtain financing. Agents and brokers also act as an intermediary in price negotiations between buyers and sellers.

Real estate agents usually are independent sales workers who provide their services to a licensed real estate broker on a contract basis. In return, the broker pays the agent a portion of the commission earned from the agent's sale of the property. Brokers are independent business people who sell real estate owned by others; they also may rent and manage properties for a fee. When selling real estate, brokers arrange for title searches and for meetings between buyers and sellers where details of the transactions are agreed upon and the new owners take possession. A broker may help to arrange favorable financing from a lender for the prospective buyer that often makes the difference between success and failure in closing a sale. In some cases, brokers and agents assume primary responsibility for closing sales; in others, lawyers or lenders do this. Brokers supervise agents who may have many of the same job duties. Brokers also manage their own offices, advertise properties, and handle other business matters. Some combine other types of work, such as selling insurance or practicing law, with their real estate business.

There is more to an agent or broker's job than making sales. They must have properties to sell. Consequently, they spend a significant amount of time obtaining listings—owner agreements to place properties for sale with the firm. When listing a property for sale, agents and brokers compare the listed property with similar properties that have recently sold to determine its competitive market price. Once the property is sold, the agent who sold the property and the agent who obtained the listing both receive a portion of the commission. Thus, agents who sell a property they also listed can increase their commission.

Most real estate brokers and sales agents sell residential property. A small number, usually employed in large or specialized firms, sell commercial, industrial, agricultural, or other types of real estate. Every specialty requires knowledge of that particular type of property and clientele. Selling or leasing business property requires an understanding of leasing practices, business trends, and location needs. Agents who sell or lease industrial properties must know about the region's transportation, utilities, and labor supply. Whatever the type of property, the agent or broker must know how to meet the client's particular requirements.

Before showing residential properties to potential buyers, agents meet with buyers to get a feeling for the type of home the buyers would like. In this prequalifying phase, the agent determines how much buyers can afford to spend. In addition, they usually sign a loyalty contract which states the agent will be the only one to show them houses. An agent or broker uses a computer to generate lists of properties for sale, their location and description, and available sources of financing. In some cases, agents and brokers use computers to give buyers a virtual tour of properties in which they are interested. Buyers can view interior and exterior images or floor plans without leaving the real estate office.

Agents may meet several times with prospective buyers to discuss and visit available properties. Agents identify and emphasize the most pertinent selling points. To a young family looking for a house, they may emphasize the convenient floor plan, the area's low crime rate, and the proximity to schools and shopping centers. To a potential investor, they may point out the tax advantages of owning a rental property and the ease of finding a renter. If bargaining over price becomes necessary, agents must carefully follow their client's instructions and may have to present counter-offers in order to get the best possible price.

Once both parties have signed the contract, the real estate broker or agent must see to it that all special terms of the contract are met before the closing date. For example, the agent must make sure the mandated and agreed-to inspections, including the home, termite, and radon inspections, take place. Also, if the seller agrees to any repairs, the broker or agent must see they are made. Increasingly, brokers and agents handle environmental problems by making sure the properties they sell meet environmental regulations. For example, they may be responsible for dealing with lead paint on the walls. While loan officers, attorneys, or other persons handle many details, the agent must ensure that they are completed.

Working Conditions

Advances in telecommunications and the ability to retrieve data on properties over the Internet allows many real estate brokers and sales agents to work out of their homes, instead of real estate offices. Even with this convenience, much of their time is spent away from their desk—showing properties to customers, analyzing properties for sale, meeting with prospective clients, or researching the state of the market.

Agents and brokers often work more than a standard 40-hour week; nearly 1 out of every 4 full-time workers worked 50 hours or more a week in 2000. They often work evenings and weekends, and are always on call to suit the needs of clients. Business usually is slower during the winter season. Although the hours are long and often irregular, most agents and brokers also have the freedom to determine their own schedule. Consequently, they can arrange their work so they can have time off when they want it.

Employment

In 2000, real estate brokers held about 93,000 jobs; real estate sales agents held 339,000 jobs. Many worked part-time, combining their real estate activities with other careers. More than two-thirds of real estate agents and brokers were self-employed. Real estate is sold in all areas, but employment is concentrated in large urban areas and in smaller, but rapidly growing communities.

Most real estate firms are relatively small; indeed, some are a one-person business. Some large real estate firms have several hundred agents operating out of many branch offices. Many brokers have franchise agreements with national or regional real estate organizations. Under this type of arrangement, the broker pays a fee in exchange for the privilege of using the more widely known name of the parent organization. Although franchised brokers often receive help training sales staff and running their offices, they bear the ultimate responsibility for the success or failure of their firm.

Real estate brokers and sales agents are older, on average, than most other workers. Historically, many homemakers and retired persons were attracted to real estate sales by the flexible and part-time work schedules characteristic of this field. They could enter, leave, and later re-enter the occupation, depending on the strength of the real estate market, family responsibilities, or other personal circumstances. Recently, however, the attractiveness of part-time work has declined as increasingly complex legal and technological requirements raise start-up costs associated with becoming an agent.

Training, Other Qualifications, and Advancement

In every state and the District of Columbia, real estate brokers and sales agents must be licensed. Prospective agents must be a high school graduate, at least 18 years old, and pass a written test. The examination—more comprehensive for brokers than for agents—includes questions on basic real estate transactions and laws affecting the sale of property. Most states require candidates for the general sales license to complete between 30 and 90 hours of classroom instruction. Those seeking a broker's license need between 60 and 90 hours of formal training and a specific amount of experience selling real estate, usually 1 to 3 years. Some states waive the experience requirements for the broker's license for applicants who have a bachelor's degree in real estate.

State licenses typically must be renewed every 1 or 2 years, usually without examination. However, many states require continuing education for license renewal. Prospective agents and brokers should contact the real estate licensing commission of the state in which they wish to work to verify exact licensing requirements.

As real estate transactions have become more legally complex, many firms have turned to college graduates to fill positions. A large number of agents and brokers have some college training. College courses in real estate, finance, business administration, statistics, economics, law, and English are helpful. For those who intend to start their own company, business courses such as marketing and accounting are as important as those in real estate or finance.

Personality traits are equally as important as academic background. Brokers look for applicants who possess a pleasant personality, honesty, and a neat appearance. Maturity, tact, trustworthiness, and enthusiasm for the job are required in order to motivate prospective customers in this highly competitive field. Agents should be well organized, detail oriented, and have a good memory for names, faces, and business details.

Those interested in jobs as real estate agents often begin in their own communities. Their knowledge of local neighborhoods is a clear advantage. Under the direction of an experienced agent, beginners learn the practical aspects of the job, including the use of computers to locate or list available properties and identify sources of financing.

Many firms offer formal training programs for both beginners and experienced agents. Larger firms usually offer more extensive programs than smaller firms. More than 1,000 universities, colleges, and junior colleges offer courses in real estate. At some, a student can earn an associate or bachelor's degree with a major in real estate; several offer advanced degrees. Many local real estate associations that are members of the National Association of Realtors sponsor courses covering the fundamentals and legal aspects of the field. Advanced courses in mortgage financing, property development and management, and other subjects also are available through various affiliates of the National Association of Realtors.

Advancement opportunities for agents may take the form of higher commission rates. As agents gain knowledge and expertise, they become more efficient in closing a greater number of transactions and increase their earnings. Experienced agents can advance in many large firms to sales or general manager. Persons who have received their broker's license may open their own offices. Others with experience and training in estimating property value may become real estate appraisers, and people familiar with operating and maintaining rental properties may become property managers. Experienced agents and brokers with a thorough knowledge of business conditions and property values in their localities may enter mortgage financing or real estate investment counseling.

Job Outlook

Employment of real estate brokers and sales agents is expected to grow more slowly than the average for all occupations through the year 2010. However, a large number of job openings will arise each year from the need to replace workers who transfer to other occupations or leave the labor force. Not everyone is successful in this highly competitive field; many beginners become discouraged by their inability to get listings and to close a sufficient number of sales. Well-trained, ambitious people who enjoy selling should have the best chance for success.

Increasing use of electronic information technology will continue to increase the productivity of agents and brokers, thus limiting job growth. Real estate companies use computer-generated images to show houses to customers without leaving the office. Internet sites contain information on vast numbers of homes for sale with maps and directions to find them, available to anyone. In addition, wireless products such as cellular phones and pagers that can send and receive large amounts of data allow agents and brokers to become more efficient and to serve a greater number of customers. Use of this technology may eliminate some marginal agents such as those practicing real estate part-time or between jobs. These workers will not be able to compete as easily with full-time agents who have invested in this technology. Changing legal requirements, like disclosure laws, may dissuade some who are not serious about practicing full time from continuing to work part-time.

Another factor expected to adversely impact the need for agents and brokers is the ability of prospective customers to conduct their own searches for properties that meet their criteria by accessing real estate information on the Internet. While they are not able to conduct the entire real estate transaction online, it does allow the prospective buyer the convenience of making a more informed choice of properties to visit, as well as the ability to find out about financing, inspections, and appraisals.

Employment growth in this field will stem primarily from increased demand for home purchases and rental units. Shifts in the age distribution of the population over the next decade will result in a growing number of retirements and persons moving to smaller accommodations, often in quieter, smaller cities and towns or retirement communities. At the same time, younger families are expected to move out of apartments or smaller houses to larger accommodations.

Employment of real estate brokers and sales agents is very sensitive to swings in the economy. During periods of declining economic activity and tight credit, the volume of sales and the resulting demand for sales workers falls. During these periods, the earnings of agents and brokers decline, and many work fewer hours or leave the occupation altogether.

Earnings

The median annual earnings of salaried real estate agents, including commission, were $27,640 in 2000. The middle 50 percent earned between $19,530 and $45,740 a year. The lowest 10 percent earned less than $14,460, and the highest 10 percent earned more than $78,540. Median annual earnings in the industries employing the largest number of salaried real estate agents in 2000 were as follows:

Residential building construction	$44,940
Subdividers and developers	32,030
Real estate agents and managers	27,770
Real estate operators and lessors	20,770

Median annual earnings of salaried real estate brokers, including commission, were $47,690 in 2000. The middle 50 percent earned between $30,630 and $80,250 a year. The lowest 10 percent earned less than $18,080, and the highest 10 percent earned more than $143,560 a year.

Commissions on sales are the main source of earnings of real estate agents and brokers. The rate of commission varies according to agent and broker agreement, the type of property, and its value. The percentage paid on the sale of farm and commercial properties or unimproved land usually is higher than the percentage paid for selling a home.

Commissions may be divided among several agents and brokers. The broker and the agent in the firm who obtained the listing usually share their commission when the property is sold; the broker and the agent in the firm who made the sale also usually share their part of the commission. Although an agent's share varies greatly from one firm to another, often it is about half of the total amount received by the firm. Agents who both list and sell a property maximize their commission.

Income usually increases as an agent gains experience, but individual ability, economic conditions, and the type and location of the property also affect earnings. Sales workers who are active in community organizations and local real estate associations can broaden their contacts and increase their earnings. A beginner's earnings often are irregular because a few weeks or even months may go by without a sale. Although some brokers allow an agent a drawing account against future earnings, this practice is not usual with new employees. The beginner, therefore, should have enough money to live on for about 6 months or until commissions increase.

Related Occupations

Selling expensive items such as homes requires maturity, tact, and a sense of responsibility. Other sales workers who find these character traits important in their work include insurance sales agents; retail salespersons; sales representatives, wholesale and manufacturing; and securities, commodities, and financial services sales agents.

Sources of Additional Information

Information on license requirements for real estate brokers and sales agents is available from most local real estate organizations or from the state real estate commission or board.

For more information about opportunities in real estate, contact:

● National Association of Realtors, 700 11th St. NW., Washington, DC 20001

Receptionists and Information Clerks

O*NET 43-4171.00

Significant Points

● Numerous job openings should arise for receptionists and information clerks due to employment growth and the need to replace workers who leave these occupations.

● A high school diploma or its equivalent is the most common educational requirement.

● Because receptionists and information clerks deal directly with the public, a professional appearance and pleasant personality are imperative.

Nature of the Work

Receptionists and information clerks are charged with a responsibility that may have a lasting impact on the success of an organization—making a good first impression. These workers often are the first representatives of an organization a visitor encounters, so they need to be courteous, professional, and helpful. Receptionists answer telephones, route calls, greet visitors, respond to inquiries from the public and provide information about the organization. In addition, receptionists contribute to the security of an organization by helping to monitor the access of visitors.

Whereas some tasks are common to most receptionists and information clerks, the specific responsibilities of receptionists vary depending upon the type of establishment in which they work. For example, reception-

ists in hospitals and doctors' offices may gather personal and financial information and direct patients to the proper waiting rooms. In beauty or hair salons, however, they arrange appointments, direct customers to the hairstylist, and may serve as cashier. In factories, large corporations, and government offices, they may provide identification cards and arrange for escorts to take visitors to the proper office. Those working for bus and train companies respond to inquiries about departures, arrivals, stops, and other related matters.

Increasingly, receptionists use multiline telephone systems, personal computers, and fax machines. Despite the widespread use of automated answering systems or voice mail, many receptionists still take messages and inform other employees of visitors' arrivals or cancellation of an appointment. When they are not busy with callers, most receptionists are expected to perform a variety of office duties including opening and sorting mail, collecting and distributing parcels, making fax transmittals and deliveries, updating appointment calendars, preparing travel vouchers, and performing basic bookkeeping, word processing, and filing.

Working Conditions

Most receptionists and information clerks work in areas that are clean, well lit, and relatively quiet. This is especially true for receptionists who greet customers and visitors; they usually work in highly visible areas that are furnished to make a good impression.

Most receptionists and information clerks work a standard 40-hour week, although about 3 of every 10 receptionists and information clerks work part-time.

The work performed by information clerks may be repetitious and stressful. For example, many receptionists spend all day answering telephones while performing additional clerical or secretarial tasks. Additional stress is caused by technology that enables management to electronically monitor use of computer systems, tape record telephone calls, or limit the time spent on each call. Prolonged exposure to a video display terminal may lead to eyestrain for the many information clerks who work with computers.

Employment

Receptionists and information clerks held about 1.1 million jobs in 2000. Almost two-thirds worked in services industries, and a little less than half of these were employed in the health services industry in doctors' and dentists' offices, hospitals, nursing homes, urgent care centers, surgical centers, and clinics. Manufacturing, wholesale and retail trade, government, and real estate industries also employed large numbers of receptionists and information clerks. About 3 of every 10 receptionists and information clerks worked part-time.

Training, Other Qualifications, and Advancement

Although hiring requirements for receptionists and information clerks vary, a high school diploma or its equivalent is the most common educational requirement. Increasingly, familiarity or experience with computers and good interpersonal skills is equally important to employers.

Many receptionists and information clerks deal with the public, so a pleasant personality is important. A clear speaking voice and fluency in the English language also are essential because these employees frequently use the telephone or public address systems. Good spelling and computer literacy often are needed, particularly because most work involves considerable computer use.

Receptionists and information clerks often learn the skills they need in high schools, business schools, and community colleges. Business education programs offered by these institutions typically include courses in typing, word processing, shorthand, business communications, records management, and office systems and procedures.

Receptionists usually receive on-the-job training, which may include procedures for greeting visitors, operating telephone and computer systems, and distributing mail, fax, and parcel deliveries. Some employers look for applicants who already possess certain skills, such as prior computer and word processing experience, or previous formal education.

Receptionists with word processing or other clerical skills may advance to a better paying job as a secretary or administrative assistant.

Job Outlook

Employment of receptionists and information clerks is expected to grow faster than the average for all occupations through 2010. This increase will result from rapid growth in services industries—including physician's offices, law firms, temporary help agencies, and consulting firms—where most are employed. In addition, turnover in this large occupation will create numerous openings as receptionists and information clerks transfer to other occupations or leave the labor force altogether. Opportunities should be best for experienced persons with a wide range of clerical and technical skills.

Technology should have conflicting effects on the demand for receptionists and information clerks. The increasing use of voice mail and other telephone automation reduces the need for receptionists by allowing one receptionist to perform work that formerly required several receptionists. However, increasing use of technology also has caused a consolidation of clerical responsibilities and growing demand for workers with diverse clerical and technical skills. Because receptionists and information clerks may perform a wide variety of clerical tasks, they should continue to be in demand. Further, they perform many tasks that are of an interpersonal nature and are not easily automated, ensuring continued demand for their services in a variety of establishments.

Earnings

In 2000, median annual earnings for all receptionists and information clerks were $20,040.

In early 2001, the federal government typically paid salaries ranging from $18,667 to $22,734 a year to beginning receptionists with a high school diploma or 6 months of experience. The average annual salary for all receptionists employed by the federal government was about $24,477 in 2001.

Related Occupations

A number of other workers deal with the public, receive and provide information, or direct people to others who can assist them. Among these are dispatchers, security guards and gaming surveillance workers, tellers, and counter and rental clerks.

Sources of Additional Information

State employment offices can provide information on job openings for receptionists.

Recreation and Fitness Workers

O*NET 39-9031.00, 39-9032.00

Significant Points

- Educational requirements for recreation workers range from a high school diploma to a graduate degree, whereas fitness workers usually need certification.

- Competition will remain keen for full-time career positions in recreation; however, job prospects for fitness workers will be more favorable.

Nature of the Work

People spend much of their leisure time participating in a wide variety of organized recreational activities, such as aerobics, arts and crafts, the performing arts, camping, and sports. Recreation and fitness workers plan, organize, and direct these activities in local playgrounds and recreation areas, parks, community centers, health clubs, fitness centers, religious organizations, camps, theme parks, and tourist attractions. Increasingly, recreational and fitness workers also are found in workplaces, where they organize and direct leisure activities and athletic programs for employees of all ages.

Recreation workers hold a variety of positions at different levels of responsibility. Recreation leaders, who are responsible for a recreation program's daily operation, primarily organize and direct participants. They may lead and give instruction in dance, drama, crafts, games, and sports; schedule use of facilities; keep records of equipment use; and ensure that recreation facilities and equipment are used properly. Workers who provide instruction and coach groups in specialties such as art, music, drama, swimming, or tennis may be called activity specialists. Recreation supervisors oversee recreation leaders and plan, organize, and manage recreational activities to meet the needs of a variety of populations. These workers often serve as liaisons between the director of the park or recreation center and the recreation leaders. Recreation supervisors with more-specialized responsibilities also may direct special activities or events or oversee a major activity, such as aquatics, gymnastics, or performing arts.

Directors of recreation and parks develop and manage comprehensive recreation programs in parks, playgrounds, and other settings. Directors usually serve as technical advisors to state and local recreation and park commissions and may be responsible for recreation and park budgets.

Camp counselors lead and instruct children and teenagers in outdoor-oriented forms of recreation, such as swimming, hiking, horseback riding, and camping. In addition, counselors provide campers with specialized instruction in activities such as archery, boating, music, drama, gymnastics, tennis, and computers. In resident camps, counselors also provide guidance and supervise daily living and general socialization.

Fitness workers instruct or coach groups or individuals in various exercise activities. Because gyms and health clubs offer a variety of exercise activities such as weightlifting, yoga, aerobics, and karate, fitness workers typically specialize in only a few areas. Fitness trainers help clients assess their level of physical fitness and help them set and reach fitness goals. They also demonstrate various exercise activities and help clients improve their techniques. They may keep records of their clients' exercise sessions to analyze their progress towards physical fitness. Personal trainers work with clients on a one-on-one basis in either a gym or the client's home. Aerobics instructors conduct group exercise sessions that involve aerobic exercise, stretching, and muscle conditioning. Some fitness workers may perform the duties of both aerobics instructors and fitness trainers. Fitness directors oversee the operations of a health club or fitness center. Their work involves creating and maintaining programs that meet the needs of the club's members.

Working Conditions

Recreation and fitness workers may work in a variety of settings—for example, a health club, cruise ship, woodland recreational park, or a playground in the center of a large urban community. Regardless of setting, most recreation workers spend much of their time outdoors and may work in a variety of weather conditions, whereas most fitness workers spend their time indoors at fitness centers and health clubs. Recreation and fitness directors and supervisors, however, typically spend most of their time in an office, planning programs and special events. Directors and supervisors generally engage in less physical activity than do lower-level recreation and fitness workers. Nevertheless, recreation and fitness workers at all levels risk suffering injuries during physical activities.

Most recreation and fitness workers work about 40 hours a week. People entering this field, especially camp counselors, should expect some night and weekend work and irregular hours. About 3 out of 10 work part time, and many recreation jobs are seasonal.

Employment

Recreation and fitness workers held about 427,000 jobs in 2000, and many additional workers held summer jobs in this occupation. About 63 percent were recreation workers; the rest were fitness trainers and aerobics instructors. Of those with year-round jobs as recreation workers, more than one-third worked in park and recreation departments of municipal and county governments. Nearly 1 in 5 recreation workers worked in membership organizations, such as the Boy or Girl Scouts or Red Cross, or worked for programs run by social service organizations, including senior centers, adult daycare programs, or residential care facilities like halfway houses, group homes, and institutions for delinquent youths. Another 1 out of 10 recreation workers worked for nursing and other personal care facilities.

Almost all fitness trainers and aerobics instructors were employed in physical fitness facilities, health clubs, and fitness centers, mainly within the amusement and recreation services industry or membership organizations. Other employers of recreation and fitness workers included commercial recreation establishments, amusement parks, sports and entertainment centers, wilderness and survival enterprises, tourist attractions, vacation excursion companies, hotels and resorts, summer camps, and apartment complexes. About 26,000 recreation and fitness workers were self-employed; many of these were personal trainers.

The recreation field has an unusually large number of part-time, seasonal, and volunteer jobs. These jobs include summer camp counselors, lifeguards, craft specialists, and after-school and weekend recreation program leaders. In addition, many teachers and college students accept jobs as recreation and fitness workers when school is not in session. The vast majority of volunteers serve as activity leaders at local day-camp programs, or in youth organizations, camps, nursing homes, hospitals, senior centers, and other settings. Some volunteers serve on local park and recreation boards and commissions. Volunteer experience, part-time work during school, or a summer job can lead to a full-time career as a recreation worker.

Training, Other Qualifications, and Advancement

Educational requirements for recreation workers range from a high school diploma—or sometimes less for many summer jobs—to graduate degrees for some administrative positions in large public recreation systems. Full-time career professional positions usually require a college degree with a major in parks and recreation or leisure studies, but a bachelor's degree in any liberal arts field may be sufficient for some jobs in the private sector. In industrial recreation, or "employee services" as it is more commonly called, companies prefer to hire those with a bachelor's degree in recreation or leisure studies and a background in business administration.

Specialized training or experience in a particular field, such as art, music, drama, or athletics, is an asset for many jobs. Some jobs also require certification. For example, a lifesaving certificate is a prerequisite for teaching or coaching water-related activities. Graduates of associate degree programs in parks and recreation, social work, and other human services disciplines also enter some career recreation positions. High school graduates occasionally enter career positions, but this is not common. Some college students work part time as recreation workers while earning degrees.

A bachelor's degree and experience are preferred for most recreation supervisor jobs and required for most higher level administrator jobs. However, increasing numbers of recreation workers who aspire to administrator positions obtain master's degrees in parks and recreation or related disciplines. Certification in the recreation field also may be helpful for advancement. Also, many persons in other disciplines, including social work, forestry, and resource management, pursue graduate degrees in recreation.

Programs leading to an associate or bachelor's degree in parks and recreation, leisure studies, or related fields are offered at several hundred colleges and universities. Many also offer master's or doctoral degrees in this field. In 2000, 100 bachelor's degree programs in parks and recreation were accredited by the National Recreation and Park Association (NRPA). Accredited programs provide broad exposure to the history, theory, and practice of park and recreation management. Courses offered include community organization; supervision and administration; recreational needs of special populations, such as the elderly or disabled; and supervised fieldwork. Students may specialize in areas such as therapeutic recreation, park management, outdoor recreation, industrial or commercial recreation, or camp management.

Certification in the recreation field is offered by the NRPA National Certification Board. The NRPA, along with its state chapters, offers certification as a Certified Park and Recreation Professional (CPRP) for those with a college degree in recreation, and as a Certified Park and Recreation Associate (CPRA) for those with less than 4 years of college. Other NRPA certifications include Certified Playground Safety Inspector (CPSI) and Aquatic Facility Operator (AFO) Certification. Continuing education is necessary to remain certified.

Generally, fitness trainers and aerobics instructors must obtain a certification in the fitness field to obtain employment. Certification may be offered in various areas of exercise such as personal training, weight training, and aerobics. There are many organizations that offer certification testing in the fitness field, including the American College of Sports Medicine, American Council on Exercise, and National Strength and Conditioning Association. Certification generally is good for two years, after which workers must become recertified. Recertification is accomplished by attending continuing education classes. Most fitness workers are required to maintain a cardiopulmonary resuscitation (CPR) certification. Some employers also require workers to be certified in first aid.

An increasing number of employers require fitness workers to have a bachelor's degree in fields related to health or fitness, such as exercise science or physical education. Some employers allow workers to substitute a college degree for certification, while others require both a degree and certification. A bachelor's degree (and, in some cases, a master's degree in exercise science, physical education, or a related area), along with experience, usually is required to advance to management positions in a health club or fitness center. Many fitness workers become personal trainers, in addition to their main job in a fitness center or as a full-time job. Some workers go into business for themselves and open up their own fitness centers.

Persons planning recreation and fitness careers should be outgoing, good at motivating people, and sensitive to the needs of others. Excellent health and physical fitness are required due to the physical nature of the job. As in many fields, managerial skills are needed to advance to supervisory or managerial positions. College courses in management, business administration, accounting, and personnel management are helpful for advancement to supervisory or managerial positions.

Job Outlook

Competition will be keen for career positions for recreation workers because this field attracts many applicants and because the number of career positions is limited compared with the numerous lower level seasonal jobs. Opportunities for staff positions should be best for persons with formal training and experience gained in part-time or seasonal recreation jobs. Those with graduate degrees should have the best opportunities for supervisory or administrative positions. Opportunities are expected to be better for fitness trainers and aerobics instructors because of relatively rapid growth in employment. Job openings for both recreation and fitness workers also will stem from the need to replace the large numbers of workers who leave these occupations each year.

The recreation field provides a large number of temporary, seasonal jobs. These positions, which typically are filled by high school or college students, generally do not have formal education requirements and are open to anyone with the desired personal qualities. Employers compete for a share of the vacationing student labor force and, although salaries in recreation often are lower than those in other fields, the nature of the

work and the opportunity to work outdoors are attractive to many. Seasonal employment prospects as program directors should be best for applicants with specialized training and certification in certain activities, such as swimming.

Overall employment of recreation and fitness workers is expected to grow faster than the average for all occupations through 2010, as increasing numbers of people spend more time and money on leisure and fitness services. Average employment growth is projected for recreation workers—reflecting growth in local government and civic and social associations, industries that employ about half of all recreation workers. Employment of fitness workers—who are concentrated in the rapidly growing amusement and recreation services industry—is expected to increase much faster than average due to rising interest in personal training, aerobics instruction, and other fitness activities.

Projected job growth stems, in part, from rising demand for recreational and fitness activities for older adults in senior centers, retirement communities, and other settings. In order to prevent many illnesses, such as heart disease, strokes, and arthritis, the general population has increasingly sought the benefits of exercise and its effects on overall health and well-being. In addition, more workers will be needed to develop and lead activity programs in halfway houses, children's homes, and daycare programs for people with special needs. Recreation and fitness jobs also will continue to increase as more businesses recognize the benefits of recreation and fitness programs and other services such as wellness programs. Job growth also will occur in amusement parks, athletic clubs, camps, sports clinics, and swimming pools.

Earnings

Median hourly earnings of recreation workers who worked full time in 2000 were $8.24. The middle 50 percent earned between about $6.75 and $10.65, while the top 10 percent earned $14.61 or more. However, earnings of recreation directors and others in supervisory or managerial positions can be substantially higher. Most public and private recreation agencies provide full-time recreation workers with typical benefits; part-time workers receive few, if any, benefits. Hourly earnings in the industries employing the largest number of recreation workers in 2000 were:

Nursing and personal care facilities	$8.70
Local government, except education and hospitals	8.40
Individual and family services	8.27
Civic and social associations	7.62
Miscellaneous amusement and recreation services	7.46

Median hourly earnings of fitness trainers and aerobics instructors in 2000 were $10.96. The middle 50 percent earned between $7.65 and $17.84, while the top 10 percent earned $25.98 or more. In 2000, earnings of these workers in the miscellaneous amusement and recreation services industry, which includes commercial fitness clubs, were $12.22 an hour; fitness trainers and aerobics instructors in civic and social associations earned $9.03. Earnings for successful self-employed personal trainers can be much higher.

Related Occupations

Recreation workers must exhibit leadership and sensitivity when dealing with people. Other occupations that require similar personal qualities include counselors, probation officers and correctional treatment specialists, psychologists, recreational therapists, and social workers. Occupations that focus on physical fitness, as do fitness workers, include athletes, coaches, umpires, and related workers.

Sources of Additional Information

For information on jobs in recreation, contact employers such as local government departments of parks and recreation, nursing and personal care facilities, local YMCAs, or the Boy or Girl Scouts.

Ordering information for materials describing careers and academic programs in recreation is available from:

- National Recreation and Park Association, Division of Professional Services, 22377 Belmont Ridge Rd., Ashburn, VA 20148. Internet: http://www.activeparks.org

For information on careers and certification in the fitness field, contact:

- American Council on Exercise, 5820 Oberlin Dr., Suite 102, San Diego, CA 92121-3787. Internet: http://www.acefitness.org

- American College of Sports Medicine, P.O. Box 1440, Indianapolis, IN 46206-1440. Internet: http://www.acsm.org

- National Strength and Conditioning Association, 1955 North Union Blvd., Colorado Springs, CO 80909. Internet: http://www.nsca-lift.org

Reservation and Transportation Ticket Agents and Travel Clerks

O*NET 43-4181.01, 43-4181.02

Significant Points

- Applicants for reservation and transportation ticket agent and travel clerk jobs are likely to encounter considerable competition.

- Job openings should arise due to employment growth and the need to replace workers who leave these occupations.

- A high school diploma or its equivalent is the most common educational requirement.

- Because reservation and transportation ticket agents and travel clerks deal directly with the public, a professional appearance and pleasant personality are imperative.

Nature of the Work

Each year, millions of Americans travel by plane, train, ship, bus, and automobile. Many of these travelers rely on the services of reservation and transportation ticket agents and travel clerks. These ticket agents and clerks perform functions as varied as selling tickets, confirming reservations, checking baggage, and providing tourists with useful travel information.

Most *reservation agents* work for large hotel chains or airlines, helping people plan trips and make reservations. They usually work in large reservation centers answering telephone or e-mail inquiries and offering suggestions on travel arrangements, such as routes, time schedules, rates, and types of accommodation. Reservation agents quote fares and room rates, provide travel information, and make and confirm transportation and hotel reservations. Most agents use proprietary networks to quickly obtain information needed to make, change, or cancel reservations for customers.

Transportation ticket agents are sometimes known as passenger service agents, passenger-booking clerks, reservation clerks, airport service agents, ticket clerks, or ticket sellers. They work in airports, train, and bus stations selling tickets, assigning seats to passengers, and checking baggage. In addition, they may answer inquiries and give directions, examine passports and visas, or check in pets. Other ticket agents, more commonly known as *gate* or *station agents*, work in airport terminals assisting passengers boarding airplanes. These workers direct passengers to the correct boarding area, check tickets and seat assignments, make boarding announcements, and provide special assistance to young, elderly, or disabled passengers when they board or disembark.

Most *travel clerks* are employed by membership organizations, such as automobile clubs. These workers, sometimes called *member services counselors* or *travel counselors*, plan trips, calculate mileage, and offer travel suggestions, such as the best route from the point of origin to the destination, for club members. Travel clerks also may prepare an itinerary indicating points of interest, restaurants, overnight accommodations, and availability of emergency services during the trip. In some cases, they make rental car, hotel, and restaurant reservations for club members.

Passenger rate clerks generally work for bus companies. They sell tickets for regular bus routes and arrange nonscheduled or chartered trips. They plan travel routes, compute rates, and keep customers informed of appropriate details. They also may arrange travel accommodations.

Working Conditions

Most transportation ticket agents and travel clerks work in areas that are clean, well lit, and relatively quiet. Reservation agents who spend much of their day talking on the telephone, however, commonly work away from the public, often in large centralized reservation or phone centers. Because a number of agents or clerks may share the same workspace, it may be crowded and noisy.

Most reservation and transportation ticket agents and travel clerks work a standard 40-hour week. Some jobs—such as those in the transportation industry and hotels—may require working evenings, late night shifts, weekends, and holidays. In general, employees with the least seniority tend to be assigned the less desirable shifts.

The work performed by reservation and transportation ticket agents and travel clerks may be repetitious and stressful. Reservation agents and travel clerks work under stringent time constraints or have quotas on the number of calls answered or reservations made. Additional stress is caused by technology that enables management to electronically monitor use of computer systems, tape record telephone calls, or limit the time spent on each call.

The work of transportation ticket agents also can be stressful when trying to serve the needs of difficult or angry customers. When flights are canceled or reservations mishandled, these clerks must bear the brunt of the customers' anger. Ticket agents may be on their feet most of the time, and may have to lift heavy baggage. In addition, prolonged exposure to a video display terminal may lead to eyestrain for the many clerks or agents who work with computers.

Employment

Reservation and transportation ticket agents and travel clerks held about 191,000 jobs in 2000. More than 6 of every 10 are employed by airlines. Others work for membership organizations, such as automobile clubs; hotels and other lodging places; railroad companies; bus lines; and other companies that provide transportation services.

Although agents and clerks are found throughout the country, most work in large metropolitan airports, downtown ticket offices, large reservation centers, and train or bus stations. The remainder work in small communities served only by intercity bus or railroad lines.

Training, Other Qualifications, and Advancement

Although hiring requirements for reservation and transportation ticket agents and travel clerks vary from industry to industry, a high school diploma or its equivalent is the most common educational requirement. For airline reservation and ticket agent jobs, some college education may be preferred.

Increasingly, familiarity or experience with computers and good interpersonal skills is equally important to employers.

Many reservation and transportation ticket agents and travel clerks deal with the public, so a pleasant personality is important. A clear speaking voice and fluency in the English language also are essential because these employees frequently use the telephone or public address systems. Good spelling and computer literacy often are needed, particularly because most work involves considerable computer use. It also is increasingly helpful for those wishing to enter the lodging or travel industries to speak a foreign language fluently.

Most airline reservation and ticket agents learn their skills through formal company training programs. In a classroom setting, they learn company and industry policies, computer systems, and ticketing procedures. They also learn to use the airline's computer system to obtain information on schedules, seat availability, and fares; to reserve space for passengers; and to plan passenger itineraries. They also must become familiar with airport and airline code designations, regulations, and safety procedures, and may be tested on this knowledge. After completing classroom instruction, new agents work on the job with supervisors or experienced agents for a period. During this period, supervisors may monitor telephone conversations to improve the quality of customer service. Agents are expected to provide good service while limiting the time spent on each call without being discourteous to customers.

In contrast to the airlines, automobile clubs, bus lines, and railroads tend to train their ticket agents or travel clerks on the job through short in-house classes that last several days.

Advancement for reservation and transportation ticket agents and travel clerks usually comes by transfer to a position with more responsibilities or by promotion to a supervisory position. Within the airline industry, a ticket agent may advance to lead worker on the shift. In the lodging industry, clerks can improve their chances for advancement by taking home or group study courses in lodging management, such as those sponsored by the Educational Institute of the American Hotel and Motel Association.

Job Outlook

Applicants for reservation and transportation ticket agent jobs are likely to encounter considerable competition, because the supply of qualified applicants exceeds the expected number of job openings. Entry requirements for these jobs are minimal, and many people seeking to get into the airline industry or travel business often start out in these types of positions. These jobs provide excellent travel benefits, and many people view airline and other travel-related jobs as glamorous.

Employment of reservation and transportation ticket agents and travel clerks is expected to grow about as fast as the average for all occupations through 2010. Although a growing population will demand additional travel services, employment of these workers will grow more slowly than this demand, because of the significant impact of technology on productivity. Automated reservations and ticketing, as well as "ticketless" travel, for example, are reducing the need for some workers. Most train stations and airports now have satellite ticket printer locations, or "kiosks," that enable passengers to make reservations and purchase tickets themselves. Many passengers also are able to check flight times and fares, make reservations, and purchase tickets on the Internet. Nevertheless, all travel-related passenger services can never be fully automated, primarily for safety and security reasons. As a result, job openings will continue to become available as the occupation grows and as workers transfer to other occupations, retire, or leave the labor force altogether.

Employment of reservation and transportation ticket agents and travel clerks is sensitive to cyclical swings in the economy. During recessions, discretionary passenger travel declines, and transportation service companies are less likely to hire new workers and even may resort to layoffs.

Earnings

Salaries of reservation and transportation ticket agents and travel clerks tend to be significantly higher than for other types of information and record clerks. In 2000, median annual earnings for reservation and transportation ticket agents and travel clerks were $22,620.

In addition to their hourly wage, full-time reservation and transportation ticket agents and travel clerks who work evenings, nights, weekends, or holidays may receive shift differential pay. Some employers offer educational assistance to their employees. Reservation and transportation ticket agents and travel clerks receive free or reduced rate travel on their company's carriers for themselves and their immediate family and, in some companies, for friends.

Related Occupations

A number of other workers deal with the public, receive and provide information, or direct people to others who can assist them. Among these are dispatchers, security guards and gaming surveillance workers, tellers, and counter and rental clerks.

Sources of Additional Information

For information about job opportunities as reservation and transportation ticket agents and travel clerks, write the personnel manager of individual transportation companies. Addresses of airlines are available from:

● Air Transport Association of America, 1301 Pennsylvania Ave. NW., Suite 1100, Washington, DC 20004-1707

Respiratory Therapists

O*NET 29-1126.00, 29-2054.00

Significant Points

● Hospitals will continue to employ more than 8 out of 10 respiratory therapists, but a growing number of therapists will work in respiratory therapy clinics, nursing homes, home health agencies, and firms that supply respiratory equipment for home use.

● Job opportunities will be best for therapists with cardiopulmonary care skills or experience working with newborns and infants.

Nature of the Work

Respiratory therapists and respiratory therapy technicians (also known as *respiratory care practitioners*) evaluate, treat, and care for patients with breathing disorders. *Respiratory therapists* assume primary responsibility for all respiratory care treatments, including the supervision of respiratory therapy technicians. *Respiratory therapy technicians* provide specific, well-defined respiratory care procedures under the direction of respiratory therapists and physicians. In clinical practice, many of the daily duties of therapists and technicians overlap, although therapists generally have more experience than technicians. In this statement, the term *respiratory therapists* includes both respiratory therapists and respiratory therapy technicians.

To evaluate patients, respiratory therapists test the capacity of the lungs and analyze oxygen and carbon dioxide concentration. They also measure the patient's potential of hydrogen (pH), which indicates the acidity or alkalinity level of the blood. To measure lung capacity, patients breathe into an instrument that measures the volume and flow of oxygen during inhalation and exhalation. By comparing the reading with the norm for the patient's age, height, weight, and sex, respiratory therapists can determine whether lung deficiencies exist. To analyze oxygen, carbon dioxide, and pH levels, therapists draw an arterial blood sample, place it in a blood gas analyzer, and relay the results to a physician.

Respiratory therapists treat all types of patients, ranging from premature infants whose lungs are not fully developed, to elderly people whose lungs are diseased. These workers provide temporary relief to patients with chronic asthma or emphysema, as well as emergency care to patients who are victims of a heart attack, stroke, drowning, or shock.

To treat patients, respiratory therapists use oxygen or oxygen mixtures, chest physiotherapy, and aerosol medications. To increase a patient's concentration of oxygen, therapists place an oxygen mask or nasal cannula on a patient and set the oxygen flow at the level prescribed by a physician. Therapists also connect patients who cannot breathe on their own to ventilators that deliver pressurized oxygen into the lungs. They insert a tube into a patient's trachea, or windpipe; connect the tube to the ventilator; and set the rate, volume, and oxygen concentration of the oxygen mixture entering the patient's lungs.

Therapists regularly check on patients and equipment. If the patient appears to be having difficulty, or if the oxygen, carbon dioxide, or pH level of the blood is abnormal, they change the ventilator setting according to the doctor's order or check equipment for mechanical problems. In homecare, therapists teach patients and their families to use ventilators and other life support systems. Additionally, they visit several times a month to inspect and clean equipment and ensure its proper use and make emergency visits, if equipment problems arise.

Respiratory therapists perform chest physiotherapy on patients to remove mucus from their lungs and make it easier for them to breathe. For example, during surgery, anesthesia depresses respiration, so this treatment may be prescribed to help get the patient's lungs back to normal and to prevent congestion. Chest physiotherapy also helps patients suffering from lung diseases, such as cystic fibrosis, that cause mucus to collect in the lungs. In this procedure, therapists place patients in positions to help drain mucus, thump and vibrate patients' rib cages, and instruct them to cough.

Respiratory therapists also administer aerosols—liquid medications suspended in a gas that forms a mist which is inhaled—and teach patients how to inhale the aerosol properly to assure its effectiveness.

In some hospitals, therapists perform tasks that fall outside their traditional role. Tasks are expanding into cardiopulmonary procedures like electrocardiograms and stress testing, as well as other tasks like drawing blood samples from patients. Therapists also keep records of materials used and charges to patients.

Working Conditions

Respiratory therapists generally work between 35 and 40 hours a week. Because hospitals operate around the clock, therapists may work evenings, nights, or weekends. They spend long periods standing and walking between patients' rooms. In an emergency, therapists work under a great deal of stress.

Because gases used by respiratory therapists are stored under pressure, they are potentially hazardous. However, adherence to safety precautions and regular maintenance and testing of equipment minimize the risk of injury. As in many other health occupations, respiratory therapists run a risk of catching infectious diseases, but carefully following proper procedures minimizes this risk.

Employment

Respiratory therapists held about 110,000 jobs in 2000. More than 4 out of 5 jobs were in hospital departments of respiratory care, anesthesiology, or pulmonary medicine. Respiratory therapy clinics, offices of physicians, nursing homes, and firms that supply respiratory equipment for home use accounted for most of the remaining jobs.

Training, Other Qualifications, and Advancement

Formal training is necessary for entry to this field. Training is offered at the postsecondary level by medical schools, colleges and universities, trade schools, vocational-technical institutes, and the armed forces. Formal training programs vary in length and in the credential or degree awarded. Some programs award associate or bachelor's degrees and prepare graduates for jobs as registered respiratory therapists (RRTs). Other, shorter programs award certificates and lead to jobs as entry-level certified respiratory therapists (CRTs). According to the Committee on Accreditation for Respiratory Care (CoARC), there were 334 accredited RRT programs and 102 accredited CRT programs in the United States in 2000.

Areas of study for respiratory therapy programs include human anatomy and physiology, chemistry, physics, microbiology, and mathematics. Technical courses deal with procedures, equipment, and clinical tests.

More than 40 states license respiratory care personnel. Aspiring respiratory care practitioners should check on licensure requirements with the board of respiratory care examiners for the state in which they plan to work.

The National Board for Respiratory Care (NBRC) offers voluntary certification and registration to graduates of CoARC-accredited programs. Two credentials are awarded to respiratory therapists who satisfy the requirements: Registered Respiratory Therapist (RRT) and Certified Respiratory Therapist (CRT). Graduates from 2- and 4-year programs in respiratory therapy may take the CRT examination. CRTs who meet education and experience requirements can take two separate examinations, leading to the award of the RRT. Either the CRT or RRT examination is the standard in the states requiring licensure.

Most employers require applicants for entry-level or generalist positions to hold the CRT or be eligible to take the certification examination. Supervisory positions and those in intensive care specialties usually require the RRT (or RRT eligibility).

Therapists should be sensitive to patients' physical and psychological needs. Respiratory care practitioners must pay attention to detail, follow instructions, and work as part of a team. In addition, operating complicated equipment requires mechanical ability and manual dexterity.

High school students interested in a career in respiratory care should take courses in health, biology, mathematics, chemistry, and physics. Respiratory care involves basic mathematical problem solving and an understanding of chemical and physical principles. For example, respiratory care workers must be able to compute medication dosages and calculate gas concentrations.

Respiratory therapists advance in clinical practice by moving from care of general to critical patients who have significant problems in other organ systems, such as the heart or kidneys. Respiratory therapists, especially those with 4-year degrees, may also advance to supervisory or managerial positions in a respiratory therapy department. Respiratory therapists in home care and equipment rental firms may become branch managers. Some respiratory therapists advance by moving into teaching positions.

Job Outlook

Job opportunities are expected to remain good. Employment of respiratory therapists is expected to increase faster than the average for all occupations through the year 2010, because of substantial growth of the middle-aged and elderly population—a development that will heighten the incidence of cardiopulmonary disease.

Older Americans suffer most from respiratory ailments and cardiopulmonary diseases such as pneumonia, chronic bronchitis, emphysema, and heart disease. As their numbers increase, the need for respiratory therapists will increase, as well. In addition, advances in treating victims of heart attacks, accident victims, and premature infants (many of

whom are dependent on a ventilator during part of their treatment) will increase the demand for the services of respiratory care practitioners.

Opportunities are expected to be favorable for respiratory therapists with cardiopulmonary care skills and experience working with infants.

Although hospitals will continue to employ the vast majority of therapists, a growing number of therapists can expect to work outside of hospitals in respiratory therapy clinics, offices of physicians, nursing homes, or homecare.

Earnings

Median annual earnings of respiratory therapists were $37,680 in 2000. The middle 50 percent earned between $32,140 and $43,430. The lowest 10 percent earned less than $28,620, and the highest 10 percent earned more than $50,660. In hospitals, median annual earnings of respiratory therapists were $38,040 in 2000.

Median annual earnings of respiratory therapy technicians were $32,860 in 2000. The middle 50 percent earned between $27,280 and $39,740. The lowest 10 percent earned less than $22,830, and the highest 10 percent earned more than $46,800. Median annual earnings of respiratory therapy technicians employed in hospitals were $32,830 in 2000.

Related Occupations

Respiratory therapists, under the supervision of a physician, administer respiratory care and life support to patients with heart and lung difficulties. Other workers who care for, treat, or train people to improve their physical condition include registered nurses, occupational therapists, physical therapists, and radiation therapists.

Sources of Additional Information

Information concerning a career in respiratory care is available from:

● American Association for Respiratory Care, 11030 Ables Ln., Dallas, TX 75229-4593. Internet: http://www.aarc.org

For the current list of CoARC-accredited educational programs for respiratory care practitioners, write to:

● Committee on Accreditation for Respiratory Care, 1248 Harwood Rd., Bedford, TX 76021-4244

Information on gaining credentials in respiratory care and a list of state licensing agencies can be obtained from:

● The National Board for Respiratory Care, Inc., 8310 Nieman Rd., Lenexa, KS 66214-1579. Internet: http://www.nbrc.org

Retail Salespersons

O*NET 41-2031.00

Significant Points

● Good employment opportunities are expected due to the need to replace the large number of workers who leave the occupation each year.

- Many salespersons work evenings, weekends, and long hours from Thanksgiving through the beginning of January, during sales, and in other peak retail periods.

- Opportunities for part-time work are plentiful, attracting people looking to supplement their income. However, most of those selling high-priced items work full time and have substantial experience.

Nature of the Work

Whether selling shoes, computer equipment, or automobiles, retail salespersons assist customers in finding what they are looking for and try to interest them in buying the merchandise. They describe a product's features, demonstrate its use, or show various models and colors. For some sales jobs, particularly those involving expensive and complex items, retail salespersons need special knowledge or skills. For example, salespersons who sell automobiles must be able to explain to customers the features of various models, warranty information, the meaning of manufacturers' specifications, and the types of options and financing available.

Consumers spend millions of dollars every day on merchandise and often form their impressions of a store by evaluating its sales force. Therefore, retailers stress the importance of providing courteous and efficient service in order to remain competitive. When a customer wants an item that is not on the sales floor, for example, the salesperson may check the stockroom, place a special order, or call another store to locate the item.

In addition to selling, most retail salespersons, especially those who work in department and apparel stores, make out sales checks; receive cash, check, and charge payments; bag or package purchases; and give out change and receipts. Depending on the hours they work, retail salespersons may have to open or close cash registers. This may include counting the money; separating charge slips, coupons, and exchange vouchers; and making deposits at the cash office. Salespersons often are held responsible for the contents of their registers, and repeated shortages are cause for dismissal in many organizations.

Salespersons also may handle returns and exchanges of merchandise, wrap gifts, and keep their work areas neat. In addition, they may help stock shelves or racks, arrange for mailing or delivery of purchases, mark price tags, take inventory, and prepare displays.

Frequently, salespersons must be aware of special sales and promotions. They must also recognize possible security risks and thefts and know how to handle or prevent such situations.

Working Conditions

Most salespersons in retail trade work in clean, comfortable, well-lighted stores. However, they often stand for long periods and may need supervisory approval to leave the sales floor.

The Monday-through-Friday, 9-to-5 work week is the exception rather than the rule in retail trade. Most salespersons work evenings and weekends, particularly during sales and other peak retail periods. Because the holiday season is the busiest time for most retailers, many employers restrict the use of vacation time from Thanksgiving through the beginning of January.

This job can be rewarding for those who enjoy working with people. Patience and courtesy are required, especially when the work is repetitious and the customers are demanding.

Employment

Retail salespersons held about 4.1 million jobs in 2000. They worked in stores ranging from small specialty shops employing a few workers, to giant department stores with hundreds of salespersons. In addition, some were self-employed representatives of direct sales companies and mail-order houses. The largest employers of retail salespersons are department stores, clothing and accessories stores, furniture and home furnishing stores, and motor vehicle dealers.

This occupation offers many opportunities for part-time work and is especially appealing to students, retirees, and others looking to supplement their income. However, most of those selling "big-ticket" items, such as cars, jewelry, furniture, and electronic equipment, work full time and have substantial experience.

Because retail stores are found in every city and town, employment is distributed geographically in much the same way as the population.

Training, Other Qualifications, and Advancement

There usually are no formal education requirements for this type of work, although a high school diploma or equivalent is preferred. Employers look for people who enjoy working with others and have the tact and patience to deal with difficult customers. Among other desirable characteristics are an interest in sales work, a neat appearance, and the ability to communicate clearly and effectively. The ability to speak more than one language may be helpful for employment in communities where people from various cultures tend to live and shop. Before hiring a salesperson, some employers may conduct a background check, especially for a job selling high-priced items.

In most small stores, an experienced employee, or the proprietor, instructs newly hired sales personnel in making out sales checks and operating cash registers. In large stores, training programs are more formal and usually conducted over several days. Topics usually discussed are customer service, security, the store's policies and procedures, and how to work a cash register. Depending on the type of product they are selling, they may be given additional specialized training by manufacturers' representatives. For example, those working in cosmetics receive instruction on the types of products available and for whom the cosmetics would be most beneficial. Likewise, salespersons employed by motor vehicle dealers may be required to participate in training programs designed to provide information on the technical details of standard and optional equipment available on new models. Because providing the best service to customers is a high priority for many employers, employees often are given periodic training to update and refine their skills.

As salespersons gain experience and seniority, they usually move to positions of greater responsibility and may be given their choice of departments. This often means moving to areas with potentially higher earnings and commissions. The highest earnings potential usually is found in selling big-ticket items. This type of position often requires the most knowledge of the product and the greatest talent for persuasion.

Opportunities for advancement vary in small stores. In some establishments, advancement is limited, because one person, often the owner, does most of the managerial work. In others, however, some salespersons are promoted to assistant managers.

Traditionally, capable salespersons without college degrees could advance to management positions. Today, however, large retail businesses usually prefer to hire college graduates as management trainees, making a college education increasingly important. Despite this trend, motivated and capable employees without college degrees still may advance to administrative or supervisory positions in large establishments.

Retail selling experience may be an asset when applying for sales positions with larger retailers or in other industries, such as financial services, wholesale trade, or manufacturing.

Job Outlook

As in the past, employment opportunities for retail salespersons are expected to be good because of the need to replace the large number of workers who transfer to other occupations or leave the labor force each year. In addition, many new jobs will be created for retail salespersons. Employment is expected to grow about as fast as the average for all occupations through the year 2010, reflecting rising retail sales stemming from a growing population. Opportunities for part-time work should be abundant, and demand will be strong for temporary workers during peak selling periods, such as the end-of-the-year holiday season.

During economic downturns, sales volumes and the resulting demand for sales workers usually decline. Purchases of costly items, such as cars, appliances, and furniture, tend to be postponed during difficult economic times. In areas of high unemployment, sales of many types of goods decline. However, because turnover of sales workers usually is very high, employers often can adjust employment levels by simply not replacing all those who leave.

Earnings

The starting wage for many retail sales positions is the federal minimum wage, which was $5.15 an hour in 2001. In areas where employers have difficulty attracting and retaining workers, wages tend to be higher than the legislated minimum.

Median hourly earnings of retail salespersons, including commission, were $8.02 in 2000. The middle 50 percent earned between $6.63 and $10.54 an hour. The lowest 10 percent earned less than $5.86, and the highest 10 percent earned more than $15.86 an hour. Median hourly earnings in the industries employing the largest numbers of retail salespersons in 2000 were as follows:

New and used car dealers	$17.81
Lumber and other building materials	10.38
Department stores	7.63
Miscellaneous shopping goods stores	7.50
Family clothing stores	7.39

Compensation systems vary by type of establishment and merchandise sold. Salespersons receive hourly wages, commissions, or a combination of wages and commissions. Under a commission system, salespersons receive a percentage of the sales that they make. This system offers sales workers the opportunity to significantly increase their earnings,

but they may find that their earnings strongly depend on their ability to sell their product and on the ups and downs of the economy. Employers may use incentive programs such as awards, banquets, bonuses, and profit-sharing plans to promote teamwork among the sales staff.

Benefits may be limited in smaller stores, but benefits in large establishments usually are comparable to those offered by other employers. In addition, nearly all salespersons are able to buy their store's merchandise at a discount, with the savings depending upon the type of merchandise.

Related Occupations

Salespersons use sales techniques, coupled with their knowledge of merchandise, to assist customers and encourage purchases. Workers in a number of other occupations use these same skills, including sales representatives, wholesale and manufacturing; securities, commodities, and financial services sales agents; counter and rental clerks; real estate brokers and sales agents; purchasing managers, buyers, and purchasing agents; insurance sales agents; sales engineers; and cashiers.

Sources of Additional Information

Information on careers in retail sales may be obtained from the personnel offices of local stores or from state merchants' associations.

General information about retailing is available from:

- National Retail Federation, 325 7th St. NW., Suite 1100, Washington, DC 20004

Information about retail sales employment opportunities is available from:

- Retail, Wholesale, and Department Store Union, 30 East 29th St., 4th Floor, New York, NY 10016

Information about training for a career in automobile sales is available from:

- National Automobile Dealers Association, Public Relations Department, 8400 Westpark Dr., McLean, VA 22102-3591. Internet: http://www.nada.org

Roofers

O*NET 47-2181.00

Significant Points

- Most roofers acquire their skills informally on the job; some roofers train through 3-year apprenticeship programs.

- Jobs for roofers should be plentiful because the work is hot, strenuous, and dirty, resulting in high job turnover.

- Demand for roofers is less susceptible to downturns in the economy than that for other construction trades because most roofing work consists of repair and reroofing.

Nature of the Work

A leaky roof can damage ceilings, walls, and furnishings. To protect buildings and their contents from water damage, roofers repair and install roofs made of tar or asphalt and gravel; rubber or thermoplastic; metal; or shingles made of asphalt, slate, fiberglass, wood, tile, or other material. Repair and reroofing—replacing old roofs on existing buildings—provide many job opportunities for these workers. Roofers also may waterproof foundation walls and floors.

There are two types of roofs—flat and pitched (sloped). Most commercial, industrial, and apartment buildings have flat or slightly sloping roofs. Most houses have pitched roofs. Some roofers work on both types; others specialize.

Most flat roofs are covered with several layers of materials. Roofers first put a layer of insulation on the roof deck. Over the insulation, they then spread a coat of molten bitumen, a tar-like substance. Next, they install partially overlapping layers of roofing felt—a fabric saturated in bitumen—over the surface. Roofers use a mop to spread hot bitumen over the surface and under the next layer. This seals the seams and makes the surface watertight. Roofers repeat these steps to build up the desired number of layers, called "plies." The top layer either is glazed to make a smooth finish or has gravel embedded in the hot bitumen to create a rough surface.

An increasing number of flat roofs are covered with a single-ply membrane of waterproof rubber or thermoplastic compounds. Roofers roll these sheets over the roof's insulation and seal the seams. Adhesive, mechanical fasteners, or stone ballasts hold the sheets in place. The building must be of sufficient strength to hold the ballast.

Most residential roofs are covered with shingles. To apply shingles, roofers first lay, cut, and tack 3-foot strips of roofing felt lengthwise over the entire roof. Then, starting from the bottom edge, they staple or nail overlapping rows of shingles to the roof. Workers measure and cut the felt and shingles to fit intersecting roof surfaces and to fit around vent pipes and chimneys. Wherever two roof surfaces intersect, or shingles reach a vent pipe or chimney, roofers cement or nail flashing-strips of metal or shingle over the joints to make them watertight. Finally, roofers cover exposed nailheads with roofing cement or caulking to prevent water leakage.

Some roofers also waterproof and dampproof masonry and concrete walls and floors. To prepare surfaces for waterproofing, they hammer and chisel away rough spots, or remove them with a rubbing brick, before applying a coat of liquid waterproofing compound. They also may paint or spray surfaces with a waterproofing material, or attach waterproofing membrane to surfaces. When dampproofing, they usually spray a bitumen-based coating on interior or exterior surfaces.

Working Conditions

Roofing work is strenuous. It involves heavy lifting, as well as climbing, bending, and kneeling. Roofers work outdoors in all types of weather, particularly when making repairs. These workers risk slips or falls from scaffolds, ladders, or roofs, or burns from hot bitumen. In addition, roofs become extremely hot during the summer.

Employment

Roofers held about 158,000 jobs in 2000. Almost all wage and salary roofers worked for roofing contractors. About 1 out of every 4 roofers was self-employed. Many self-employed roofers specialized in residential work.

Training, Other Qualifications, and Advancement

Most roofers acquire their skills informally by working as helpers for experienced roofers. They start by carrying equipment and material, and erecting scaffolds and hoists. Within 2 or 3 months, trainees are taught to measure, cut, and fit roofing materials and, later, to lay asphalt or fiberglass shingles. Because some roofing materials are used infrequently, it can take several years to get experience working on all the various types of roofing applications.

Some roofers train through 3-year apprenticeship programs administered by local union-management committees representing roofing contractors and locals of the United Union of Roofers, Waterproofers, and Allied Workers. The apprenticeship program generally consists of a minimum of 2,000 hours of on-the-job training annually, plus 144 hours of classroom instruction a year in subjects such as tools and their use, arithmetic, and safety. On-the-job training for apprentices is similar to that for helpers, except that the apprenticeship program is more structured. Apprentices also learn to dampproof and waterproof walls.

Good physical condition and good balance are essential for roofers. A high school education, or its equivalent, is helpful, as are courses in mechanical drawing and basic mathematics. Most apprentices are at least 18 years old.

Roofers may advance to supervisor or estimator for a roofing contractor, or become contractors themselves.

Job Outlook

Jobs for roofers should be plentiful through the year 2010, primarily because of the need to replace workers who transfer to other occupations or leave the labor force. Turnover is high; roofing work is hot, strenuous, and dirty, and a significant number of workers treat roofing as a temporary job until something better comes along. Some roofers leave the occupation to go into other construction trades.

Employment of roofers is expected to grow about as fast as the average for all occupations through the year 2010. Roofs deteriorate faster than most other parts of buildings and periodically need to be repaired or replaced. About three-fourths of roofing work is repair and replacement, a higher proportion than in most other construction work. As a result, demand for roofers is less susceptible to downturns in the economy than that for other construction trades. In addition to repair and reroofing work on the growing stock of buildings, new construction of industrial, commercial, and residential buildings will add to the demand for roofers. Jobs should be easiest to find during spring and summer, when most roofing is done.

Earnings

In 2000, median hourly earnings of roofers were $13.95. The middle 50 percent earned between $10.72 and $18.86. The lowest 10 percent earned less than $8.68, and the highest 10 percent earned more than $24.47. The median hourly earnings in 2000 of roofers in the roofing, siding, and sheet metal work industry were $14.00.

Some roofers are members of the United Union of Roofers, Waterproofers, and Allied Workers.

Apprentices usually start at about 40 percent of the rate paid to experienced roofers and receive periodic raises as they acquire the skills of the trade. Earnings for roofers are reduced on occasion because poor weather often limits the time they can work.

Related Occupations

Roofers use shingles, bitumen and gravel, single-ply plastic or rubber sheets, or other materials to waterproof building surfaces. Workers in other occupations who cover surfaces with special materials for protection and decoration include carpenters; carpet, floor, and tile installers and finishers; cement masons, concrete finishers, segmental pavers, and terrazzo workers; drywall installers, ceiling tile installers, and tapers; and plasterers and stucco masons.

Sources of Additional Information

For information about apprenticeships or job opportunities in roofing, contact local roofing contractors, a local chapter of the roofers union, a local joint union-management apprenticeship committee, or the nearest office of your state employment service or apprenticeship agency.

For information about the work of roofers, contact:

- National Roofing Contractors Association, 10255 W. Higgins Rd., Rosemont, IL 60018-5607. Internet: http://www.nrca.net

- United Union of Roofers, Waterproofers, and Allied Workers, 1660 L St. NW., Suite 800, Washington, DC 20036

Sales Representatives, Wholesale and Manufacturing

O*NET 41-4011.01, 41-4011.02, 41-4011.03, 41-4011.04, 41-4011.05, 41-4011.06, 41-4012.00

Significant Points

- Many are self-employed manufacturers' agents who work for a commission.

- A bachelor's degree increasingly is required; nevertheless, some individuals with previous sales experience enter the occupation without a college degree.

- Prospects will be best for those with the appropriate knowledge or technical expertise, as well as the personal traits necessary for successful selling.

Nature of the Work

Sales representatives are an important part of manufacturers' and wholesalers' success. Regardless of the type of product they sell, their primary duties are to interest wholesale and retail buyers and purchasing agents in their merchandise, and to address any of the client's questions or concerns. Sales representatives represent one or several manufacturers or wholesale distributors by selling one product or a complimentary line of products. Sales representatives also advise clients on methods to reduce costs, use their products, and increase sales. They market their company's products to manufacturers, wholesale and retail establishments, construction contractors, government agencies, and other institutions. Retail salespersons sell directly to consumers, and sales engineers specialize in sales of technical products and services.

Depending on where they work, sales representatives have different job titles. Those employed directly by a manufacturer or wholesaler often are called *sales representatives*. *Manufacturers' agents* or *manufacturers' representatives* are self-employed sales workers who contract their services to all types of manufacturing companies. However, many of these titles are used interchangeably.

Sales representatives spend much of their time traveling to and visiting with prospective buyers and current clients. During a sales call, they discuss the client's needs and suggest how their merchandise or services can meet those needs. They may show samples or catalogs that describe items their company stocks and inform customers about prices, availability, and ways in which their products can save money and improve productivity. Because a vast number of manufacturers and wholesalers sell similar products, sales representatives must emphasize any unique qualities of their products and services. As independent agents, they might sell several complimentary products made by different manufacturers and, thus, take a broad approach to their customers' business. Sales representatives may help install new equipment and train employees. They also take orders and resolve any problems with or complaints about the merchandise.

Obtaining new accounts is an important part of the job. Sales representatives follow leads from other clients, track advertisements in trade journals, participate in trade shows and conferences, and may visit potential clients unannounced. In addition, they may spend time meeting with and entertaining prospective clients during evenings and weekends.

In a process that may take several months, sales representatives present their product and negotiate the sale. Aided by a laptop computer connected to the Internet, they often can answer technical and nontechnical questions immediately.

Frequently, sales representatives who lack technical expertise work as a team with a technical expert. In this arrangement, the technical expert—sometimes a sales engineer—will attend the sales presentation to explain the product and answer questions or concerns. The sales representative makes the preliminary contact with customers, introduces the company's product, and closes the sale. The representative is then able to spend more time maintaining and soliciting accounts and less time acquiring technical knowledge. After the sale, representatives may make follow-up visits to ensure that the equipment is functioning properly and may even help train customers' employees to operate and maintain new equipment. Those selling consumer goods often suggest how and where merchandise should be displayed. Working with retailers, they may help arrange promotional programs, store displays, and advertising.

Sales representatives have several duties beyond selling products. They also analyze sales statistics; prepare reports; and handle administrative duties, such as filing their expense account reports, scheduling appointments, and making travel plans. They study literature about new and existing products and monitor the sales, prices, and products of their competitors.

Manufacturers' agents who operate a sales agency must also manage their business. This requires organizational skills as well as knowledge of accounting, marketing, and administration.

Working Conditions

Some sales representatives have large territories and travel considerably. A sales region may cover several states, so they may be away from home for several days or weeks at a time. Others work near their "home base" and travel mostly by automobile. Due to the nature of the work and the amount of travel, sales representatives typically work more than 40 hours per week.

Although the hours are long and often irregular, most sales representatives have the freedom to determine their own schedule. Consequently, they can arrange their appointments so they can have time off when they want it. Sales representatives are often on their feet for long periods and may carry heavy sample products, which necessitates some physical stamina.

Dealing with different types of people can be stimulating but demanding. Sales representatives often face competition from representatives of other companies. Companies usually set goals or quotas that representatives are expected to meet. Because their earnings depend on commissions, manufacturers' agents are also under the added pressure to maintain and expand their clientele.

Employment

Manufacturers' and wholesale sales representatives held about 1.8 million jobs in 2000. Nearly three of every 5 salaried representatives worked in wholesale trade—mostly for distributors of machinery and equipment, groceries and related products, and motor vehicles and parts. Others were employed in manufacturing and mining. Due to the diversity of products and services sold, employment opportunities are available in every part of the country in a wide range of industries.

In addition to those working directly for a firm, many sales representatives are self-employed manufacturers' agents. They often form small sales firms and work for a straight commission based on the value of their own sales. However, manufacturers' agents usually gain experience and recognition with a manufacturer or wholesaler before becoming self-employed.

Training, Other Qualifications, and Advancement

The background needed for sales jobs varies by product line and market. Most firms require a strong educational background and increasingly prefer or require a bachelor's degree as the job requirements have become more technical and analytical. Nevertheless, many employers still hire individuals with previous sales experience who do not have a college degree. For some consumer products, factors such as sales ability, personality, and familiarity with brands are as important as a degree. On the other hand, firms selling complex, technical products may require a technical degree in addition to some sales experience. Many sales representatives attend seminars in sales techniques or take courses in marketing, economics, communication, or even a foreign language

to provide the extra edge needed to make sales. In general, companies are looking for the best and brightest individuals who have the personality and desire to sell.

Many companies have formal training programs for beginning sales representatives lasting up to 2 years. However, most businesses are accelerating these programs to reduce costs and expedite the returns from training. In some programs, trainees rotate among jobs in plants and offices to learn all phases of production, installation, and distribution of the product. In others, trainees take formal classroom instruction at the plant, followed by on-the-job training under the supervision of a field sales manager. Some sales representatives complete certification courses to become Certified Professional Manufacturers' Representatives (CPMRs).

New workers may get training by accompanying experienced workers on their sales calls. As they gain familiarity with the firm's products and clients, these workers are given increasing responsibility until they are eventually assigned their own territory. As businesses experience greater competition, increased pressure is placed upon sales representatives to produce sales.

Sales representatives stay abreast of new products and the changing needs of their customers in a variety of ways. They attend trade shows where new products and technologies are showcased. They also attend conferences and conventions to meet other sales representatives and clients and discuss new product developments. In addition, the entire sales force may participate in company-sponsored meetings to review sales performance, product development, sales goals, and profitability.

Those who want to become sales representatives should be goal-oriented and persuasive, and work well both independently and as part of a team. A pleasant personality and appearance, the ability to communicate well with people, and problem-solving skills are highly valued. Furthermore, completing a sale can take several months and thus requires patience and perseverance.

Frequently, promotion takes the form of an assignment to a larger account or territory where commissions are likely to be greater. Experienced sales representatives may move into jobs as sales trainers, who instruct new employees on selling techniques and company policies and procedures. Those who have good sales records and leadership ability may advance to sales supervisor or district manager.

In addition to advancement opportunities within a firm, some manufacturers' agents go into business for themselves. Others find opportunities in purchasing, advertising, or marketing research.

Job Outlook

Employment of sales representatives, wholesale and manufacturing, is expected to grow more slowly than the average for all occupations through the year 2010. Continued growth due to the increasing variety and number of goods to be sold will be tempered by the increased effectiveness and efficiency of sales workers. Many job openings will result from the need to replace workers who transfer to other occupations or leave the labor force.

Prospective customers will still require sales workers to demonstrate or illustrate the particulars about the good or service. However, computer technology makes them more effective and productive, for example, by allowing them to provide accurate and current information to customers during sales presentations. In addition, electronic commerce provides sales representatives another way to advertise and sell, thus requiring fewer sales representatives to do the same amount of work.

Manufacturers are expected to continue outsourcing sales duties to independent agents rather than using in-house or direct selling personnel. To their advantage, these agents are more likely to work in a sales area or territory longer than representatives, creating a better working relationship and understanding of how customers operate their businesses. Agents are paid only if they sell, which reduces the overhead cost to their clients. Also, by using an agent who usually lends his or her services to more than one company, companies can share costs with the other companies involved with that agent.

Those interested in this occupation should keep in mind that direct selling opportunities in manufacturing are likely to be best for products with strong demand. Furthermore, jobs will be most plentiful in small wholesale and manufacturing firms because a growing number of these companies will rely on agents to market their products as a way to control their costs and expand their customer base.

Employment opportunities and earnings may fluctuate from year to year because sales are affected by changing economic conditions, legislative issues, and consumer preferences. Prospects will be best for those with the appropriate knowledge or technical expertise as well as the personal traits necessary for successful selling.

Earnings

Compensation methods vary significantly by the type of firm and product sold. Most employers use a combination of salary and commission or salary plus bonus. Commissions usually are based on the amount of sales, whereas bonuses may depend on individual performance, on the performance of all sales workers in the group or district, or on the company's performance.

Median annual earnings of sales representatives, wholesale and manufacturing, technical and scientific products, were $52,620, including commission, in 2000. The middle 50 percent earned between $37,420 and $74,470 a year. The lowest 10 percent earned less than $27,450, and the highest 10 percent earned more than $102,000 a year. Median annual earnings in the industries employing the largest number of sales representatives, technical and scientific products, in 2000 were as follows:

Computer and data processing services	$62,310
Professional and commercial equipment	56,840
Drugs, proprietaries, and sundries	56,660
Machinery, equipment, and supplies	52,820
Electrical goods	51,650

Median annual earnings of sales representatives, wholesale and manufacturing, except technical and scientific products, were $40,340, including commission, in 2000. The middle 50 percent earned between $28,850 and $57,280 a year. The lowest 10 percent earned less than $21,450, and the highest 10 percent earned more than $82,830 a year. Median annual earnings in the industries employing the largest number of sales representatives, except technical and scientific products, in 2000 were as follows:

Machinery, equipment, and supplies	$43,190
Professional and commercial equipment	41,880
Electrical goods	41,390
Groceries and related products	37,220
Miscellaneous nondurable goods	33,630

In addition to their earnings, sales representatives are usually reimbursed for expenses such as transportation costs, meals, hotels, and entertaining customers. They often receive benefits such as health and life insurance, pension plan, vacation and sick leave, personal use of a company car, and frequent flyer mileage. Some companies offer incentives such as free vacation trips or gifts for outstanding sales workers.

Unlike those working directly for a manufacturer or wholesaler, manufacturers' agents are paid strictly on commission and are usually not reimbursed for expenses. Depending on the type of product or products they are selling, their experience in the field, and the number of clients, their earnings can be significantly higher or lower than those working in direct sales.

Related Occupations

Sales representatives, wholesale and manufacturing, must have sales ability and knowledge of the products they sell. Other occupations that require similar skills include advertising, marketing, promotions, and public relations, and sales managers; insurance sales agents; purchasing managers, buyers, and purchasing agents; real estate brokers and sales agents; retail salespersons; sales engineers; and securities, commodities, and financial services sales agents.

Sources of Additional Information

Career information on manufacturers' agents is available from:

- Manufacturers' Agents National Association, P.O. Box 3467, Laguna Hills, CA 92654-3467. Internet: http://www.manaonline.org

Career and certification information is available from:

- Manufacturers' Representatives Educational Research Foundation, P.O. Box 247, Geneva, IL 60134. Internet: http://www.mrerf.org

Sales Worker Supervisors

O*NET 41-1011.00, 41-1012.00

Significant Points

- Applicants with experience as a retail salesperson, cashier, or customer service representative should have the best job opportunities.

- The number of self-employed sales worker supervisors in retail trade is expected to decline as independent retailers face increasing competition from national chains.

- Work schedules may be irregular and often include evenings and weekends.

- A postsecondary degree is increasingly needed for advancement into management.

Nature of the Work

Sales worker supervisors oversee the work of sales and related workers such as retail salespersons, cashiers, customer service representatives, stock clerks and order fillers, sales engineers, and wholesale and manufacturing sales representatives. They are responsible for interviewing, hiring, and training employees, as well as preparing work schedules and assigning workers to specific duties. Many of these workers hold job titles such as *sales manager* or *department manager*. They might also be called *supervisors* rather than *managers,* even though many of these workers often perform many managerial functions. Sales worker supervisors oversee retail salespersons, cashiers, customer service representatives, stock clerks and order fillers, sales engineers, and sales representatives, wholesale and manufacturing.

In retail establishments, sales worker supervisors ensure that customers receive satisfactory service and quality goods. They also answer customers' inquiries and deal with complaints, and may handle purchasing, budgeting, and accounting. Their responsibilities vary, depending on the size and type of establishment. As the size of retail stores and the types of goods and services increase, these workers tend to specialize in one department or one aspect of merchandising.

Sales worker supervisors in large retail establishments, often referred to as department managers, provide day-to-day oversight of individual departments, such as shoes, cosmetics, or housewares in large department stores; produce and meat in grocery stores; and sales in automotive dealerships. These workers establish and implement policies, goals, objectives, and procedures for their specific departments; coordinate activities with other department heads; and strive for smooth operations within their departments. They supervise employees who price and ticket goods and place them on display; clean and organize shelves, displays, and inventory in stockrooms; and inspect merchandise to ensure that nothing is outdated. Sales worker supervisors also review inventory and sales records, develop merchandising techniques, coordinate sales promotions, and may greet and assist customers and promote sales and good public relations.

Sale workers supervisors in nonretail establishments supervise and coordinate the activities of sales workers who sell industrial products, automobiles, or services such as advertising or Internet services. They may prepare budgets, make personnel decisions, devise sales-incentive programs, assign sales territories, or approve sales contracts.

In small or independent companies and retail stores, sales worker supervisors not only directly supervise sales associates, but are also responsible for the operation of the entire company or store. Some are also self-employed business or store owners.

Working Conditions

Most sales worker supervisors have offices. In retail trade, their offices are within the stores, usually close to the area they oversee. Although some time is spent in the office completing merchandise orders or arranging work schedules, a large portion of their workday is spent on the sales floor, supervising employees or selling.

Work hours of supervisors vary greatly among establishments, because work schedules usually depend on customers' needs. Most supervisors work 40 hours or more a week; long hours are common. This is particularly true during sales, holidays, busy shopping hours, and times during which inventory is taken. They are expected to work evenings and weekends, but usually are compensated with a day off during the week. Hours can change weekly, and managers sometimes must report to work on short notice, especially when employees are absent. Independent owners can often set their own schedules, but hours must be convenient to customers.

Employment

Sales worker supervisors held about 2.5 million jobs in 2000. About one-third were self-employed; most of these were store owners. Most are found in grocery and department stores, motor vehicle dealerships, and clothing and accessory stores, and in services such as advertising or other business services.

Training, Other Qualifications, and Advancement

Sales worker supervisors usually acquire knowledge of management principles and practices—an essential requirement for a supervisory or managerial position in retail trade—through work experience. Many supervisors begin their careers on the sales floor as salespersons, cashiers, or customer service representatives. In these positions, they learn merchandising, customer service, and the basic policies and procedures of the company.

The educational background of sales worker supervisors varies widely. Regardless of the education received, recommended courses include accounting, marketing, management, and sales, as well as psychology, sociology, and communication. Supervisors must be computer literate because almost all cash registers, inventory control systems, and sales quotes and contracts are computerized.

Most supervisors who have postsecondary education hold associate or bachelor's degrees in liberal arts, social sciences, business, or management. To gain experience, many college students participate in internship programs that usually are developed jointly by individual schools and firms.

Once supervisors are on the job, the type and amount of training available to them varies from company to company. Many national retail chains and companies have formal training programs for management trainees that include both classroom and onsite training. Training time may be as brief as 1 week but may also last up to 1 year or more, because many organizations require that trainees gain experience during all sales seasons.

Ordinarily, classroom training includes such topics as interviewing and customer service skills, employee and inventory management, and scheduling. Management trainees may work in one specific department while training on the job, or they may rotate through several departments to gain a well-rounded knowledge of the company's operation. Training programs for retail franchises are generally extensive, covering all functions of the company's operation, including budgeting, marketing, management, finance, purchasing, product preparation, human resource management, and compensation. College graduates usually can enter management training programs directly.

Sales worker supervisors must get along with all types of people. They need initiative, self-discipline, good judgment, and decisiveness. Patience and a mild temperament are necessary when dealing with demanding customers. Sales worker supervisors must also be able to motivate, organize, and direct the work of subordinates and communicate clearly and persuasively with customers and other supervisors.

Individuals who display leadership and team-building skills, self-confidence, motivation, and decisiveness become candidates for promotion to assistant manager or manager. A postsecondary degree may speed advancement, because it is viewed by employers as a sign of motivation and maturity—qualities deemed important for promotion to more responsible positions. In many retail establishments, managers are promoted from within the company. In small retail establishments, where the number of positions is limited, advancement to a higher management position may come slowly. Large establishments often have extensive career ladder programs, and may offer supervisors the opportunity to transfer to another store in the chain or to the central office if an opening occurs. Although promotions may occur more quickly in large establishments, some managers may need to relocate every several years to advance. Supervisors also can become advertising, marketing, promotions, public relations, and sales managers—workers who coordinate marketing plans, monitor sales, and propose advertisements and promotions; or purchasing managers, buyers, or purchasing agents—workers who purchase goods and supplies for their organization or for resale.

Some supervisors who have worked in their industry for a long time open their own stores or sales firms. However, retail trade and sales are highly competitive and, although many independent owners succeed, some fail to cover expenses and eventually go out of business. To prosper, owners usually need good business sense and strong customer service and public relations skills.

Job Outlook

Candidates who have retail experience will have the best job opportunities. As in other fields, competition is expected for sales worker supervisor jobs with the most attractive earnings and working conditions.

Employment of sales worker supervisors is expected to grow more slowly than the average for all occupations through the year 2010. Growth in this occupation will be restrained somewhat as retail companies hire more sales staff, but increase the responsibilities of sales worker supervisors. However, many job openings are expected to occur as experienced supervisors and managers move into higher levels of management, transfer to other occupations, or leave the labor force.

The Internet and electronic commerce are creating new opportunities to reach and communicate with potential customers. Some firms are hiring Internet sales managers, who are in charge of maintaining an Internet site and answering inquiries relating to the product, price, and delivery terms—a trend that will increase demand for these supervisors. Overall, however, Internet sales and electronic commerce will reduce somewhat the number of additional sales workers needed, thus reducing the number of additional supervisors needed.

Projected employment growth of sales worker supervisors will mirror, in part, the patterns of employment growth in the industries in which they work. For example, faster-than-average employment growth is expected in rapidly growing services industries. The number of self-employed retail sales worker supervisors is expected to decline, as independent retailers face increasing competition from national chains.

Unlike middle- and upper-level management positions, store-level retail supervisors generally will not be affected by the restructuring and consolidation taking place at the corporate and headquarters levels of many retail chains.

Earnings

Salaries of sales worker supervisors vary substantially, depending upon the level of responsibility; length of service; and type, size, and location of the firm.

In 2000, median annual earnings of salaried sales worker supervisors of retail sales workers, including commission, were $27,510. The middle 50 percent earned between $21,050 and $37,200 a year. The lowest 10 percent earned less than $16,910, and the highest 10 percent earned more than $52,590 a year. Median annual earnings in the industries employing the largest numbers of salaried sales worker supervisors of retail sales workers in 2000 were as follows:

Grocery stores	$27,380
Drug stores and proprietary stores	27,250
Miscellaneous shopping goods stores	25,750
Gasoline service stations	23,630
Department stores	23,530

In 2000, median annual earnings of salaried sales worker supervisors of non-retail sales workers, including commission, were $48,960. The middle 50 percent earned between $33,270 and $72,770 a year. The lowest 10 percent earned less than $23,850, and the highest 10 percent earned more than $107,520 a year. Median annual earnings in the industries employing the largest numbers of salaried sales worker supervisors of non-retail sales workers in 2000 were as follows:

Professional and commercial equipment	$66,610
Machinery, equipment, and supplies	56,380
Groceries and related products	47,920
Telephone communication	47,540
Miscellaneous business services	31,600

Compensation systems vary by type of establishment and merchandise sold. Many supervisors receive a commission, or a combination of salary and commission. Under a commission system, supervisors receive a percentage of department or store sales. Under these systems, supervisors have the opportunity to significantly increase their earnings, but they may find that their earnings depend on their ability to sell their product and the condition of the economy. Those who sell large amounts of merchandise or exceed sales goals often receive bonuses or other awards.

Related Occupations

Sales worker supervisors serve customers, supervise workers, and direct and coordinate the operations of an establishment. Others with similar responsibilities include financial managers, food service managers, lodging managers, and medical and health services managers.

Sources of Additional Information

Information on employment opportunities for retail sales worker supervisors may be obtained from the employment offices of various retail establishments or state employment service offices.

General information on management careers in retail establishments is available from:

● National Retail Federation, 325 7th St. NW., Suite 1100, Washington, DC 20004

Information on management careers in grocery stores, and on schools offering related programs, is available from:

● Food Distributors International, 201 Park Washington Ct., Falls Church, VA 22046-4521. Internet: http://fdi.org

Information about management careers and training programs in the motor vehicle dealers industry is available from:

● National Automobile Dealers Association, Public Relations Dept., 8400 Westpark Dr., McLean, VA 22102-3591. Internet: http://www.nada.org

Information about management careers in convenience stores is available from:

● National Association of Convenience Stores, 1605 King St., Alexandria, VA 22314-2792

Science Technicians

O*NET 19-4011.01, 19-4011.02, 19-4021.00, 19-4031.00, 19-4041.01, 19-4041.02, 19-4051.01, 19-4051.02, 19-4091.00, 19-4092.00, 19-4093.00

Significant Points

● Science technicians in production jobs often work in 8-hour shifts around the clock.

● Job opportunities are expected to be best for qualified graduates of science technician training programs or applied science technology programs.

Nature of the Work

Science technicians use the principles and theories of science and mathematics to solve problems in research and development and to help invent and improve products and processes. However, their jobs are more practically oriented than those of scientists. Technicians set up, operate, and maintain laboratory instruments, monitor experiments, make observations, calculate and record results, and often develop conclusions. They must keep detailed logs of all their work-related activities. Those who work in production monitor manufacturing processes and may be involved in ensuring quality by testing products for proper proportions of ingredients, purity, or for strength and durability.

As laboratory instrumentation and procedures have become more complex in recent years, the role of science technicians in research and development has expanded. In addition to performing routine tasks, many technicians also develop and adapt laboratory procedures to achieve the best results, interpret data, and devise solutions to problems, under the direction of scientists. Moreover, technicians must master the laboratory equipment so that they can adjust settings when necessary and recognize when equipment is malfunctioning.

The increasing use of robotics to perform many routine tasks has freed technicians to operate more sophisticated laboratory equipment. Science technicians make extensive use of computers, computer-interfaced equipment, robotics, and high-technology industrial applications, such as biological engineering.

Most science technicians specialize, learning skills and working in the same disciplines as scientists. Occupational titles, therefore, tend to follow the same structure as scientists. *Agricultural technicians* work with agricultural scientists in food, fiber, and animal research, production, and processing. Some conduct tests and experiments to improve the yield and quality of crops or to increase the resistance of plants and animals to disease, insects, or other hazards. Other agricultural technicians do animal breeding and nutrition work. *Food science technicians* assist food scientists and technologists in research and development, production technology, and quality control. For example, food science technicians may conduct tests on food additives and preservatives to ensure FDA compliance on factors such as color, texture, and nutrients. They analyze, record, and compile test results; order supplies to maintain laboratory inventory; and clean and sterilize laboratory equipment.

Biological technicians work with biologists studying living organisms. Many assist scientists who conduct medical research—helping to find a cure for cancer or AIDS, for example. Those who work in pharmaceutical companies help develop and manufacture medicinal and pharmaceutical preparations. Those working in the field of microbiology generally work as lab assistants, studying living organisms and infectious agents. Biological technicians also analyze organic substances, such as blood, food, and drugs, and some examine evidence in criminal investigations. Biological technicians working in biotechnology labs use the knowledge and techniques gained from basic research by scientists, including gene splicing and recombinant DNA, and apply these techniques in product development.

Chemical technicians work with chemists and chemical engineers, developing and using chemicals and related products and equipment. Most do research and development, testing, or other laboratory work. For example, they might test packaging for design, integrity of materials, and environmental acceptability; assemble and operate new equipment to develop new products; monitor product quality; or develop new production techniques. Some chemical technicians collect and analyze samples of air and water to monitor pollution levels. Those who focus on basic research might produce compounds through complex organic synthesis. Chemical technicians within chemical plants are also referred to as *process technicians*. They may operate equipment, monitor plant processes and analyze plant materials.

Environmental science and protection technicians perform laboratory and field tests to monitor environmental resources and determine the contaminants and sources of pollution. They may collect samples for testing or be involved in abating, controlling, or remediating sources of environmental pollutants. Some are responsible for waste management operations, control and management of hazardous materials inventory, or general activities involving regulatory compliance. There is a growing emphasis on pollution prevention activities.

Forensic science technicians investigate crimes by collecting and analyzing physical evidence. Often, they specialize in areas such as DNA analysis or firearm examination, performing tests on weapons or substances, such as fiber, hair, tissue, or body fluids to determine significance to the investigation. They also prepare reports to document their findings and the laboratory techniques used. When criminal cases come to trial, forensic science technicians often provide testimony, as expert witnesses, on specific laboratory findings by identifying and classifying substances, materials, and other evidence collected at the crime scene.

Forest and conservation technicians compile data on the size, content, and condition of forest land tracts. These workers travel through sections of forest to gather basic information, such as species and population of trees, disease and insect damage, tree seedling mortality, and conditions that may cause fire danger. Forest and conservation technicians also train and lead forest and conservation workers in seasonal activities, such as planting tree seedlings, putting out forest fires, and maintaining recreational facilities.

Geological and petroleum technicians measure and record physical and geologic conditions in oil or gas wells, using instruments lowered into wells or by analysis of the mud from wells. In oil and gas exploration, these technicians collect and examine geological data or test geological samples to determine petroleum and mineral content. Some petroleum technicians, called *scouts*, collect information about oil and gas well drilling operations, geological and geophysical prospecting, and land or lease contracts.

Nuclear technicians operate nuclear test and research equipment, monitor radiation, and assist nuclear engineers and physicists in research. Some also operate remote control equipment to manipulate radioactive materials or materials to be exposed to radioactivity.

Other science technicians collect weather information or assist oceanographers.

Working Conditions

Science technicians work under a wide variety of conditions. Most work indoors, usually in laboratories, and have regular hours. Some occasionally work irregular hours to monitor experiments that can not be completed during regular working hours. Production technicians often work in 8-hour shifts around the clock. Others, such as agricultural, forest and conservation, geological and petroleum, and environmental science and protection technicians, perform much of their work outdoors, sometimes in remote locations.

Some science technicians may be exposed to hazards from equipment, chemicals, or toxic materials. Chemical technicians sometimes work with toxic chemicals or radioactive isotopes, nuclear technicians may be exposed to radiation, and biological technicians sometimes work with disease-causing organisms or radioactive agents. Forensic science technicians often are exposed to human body fluids and firearms. However, these working conditions pose little risk, if proper safety procedures are followed. For forensic science technicians, collecting evidence from crime scenes can be distressing and unpleasant.

Employment

Science technicians held a total of about 198,000 jobs in 2000. Employment was distributed as follows:

Chemical technicians	73,000
Biological technicians	41,000
Environmental science and protection technicians, including health	27,000
Forest and conservation technicians	18,000
Agricultural and food science technicians	18,000
Geological and petroleum technicians	10,000
Forensic science technicians	6,400
Nuclear technicians	3,300

Chemical technicians held jobs in a wide range of manufacturing and service industries, but were concentrated in chemical manufacturing, where they held over 30,000 jobs. A significant number, 12,000, worked in research and testing firms. About 45 percent of biological technicians also worked in research and testing firms. Most of the rest of biological technicians worked in drug manufacturing or for federal, state, or local governments. Significant numbers of environmental science and protection technicians also worked for state and local governments and

research and testing services. Others worked for engineering and architectural services and management and public relations firms. Nearly 68 percent of forest and conservation technicians held jobs in federal government; another 22 percent worked for state governments. More than 30 percent of agricultural and food science technicians worked for food processing companies; the rest worked for research and testing firms, state governments, and non-veterinary animal services. More than 47 percent of geological and petroleum technicians worked for oil and gas extraction companies, and forensic science technicians worked primarily for state and local governments.

Training, Other Qualifications, and Advancement

There are several ways to qualify for a job as a science technician. Many employers prefer applicants who have at least 2 years of specialized training or an associate degree in applied science or science-related technology. Because employers' preferences vary, however, some science technicians have a bachelor's degree in chemistry, biology, or forensic science, or have taken several science and math courses at 4-year colleges.

Many technical and community colleges offer associate degrees in a specific technology or a more general education in science and mathematics. A number of 2-year associate degree programs are designed to provide easy transfer to a 4-year college or university, if desired. Technical institutes usually offer technician training, but provide less theory and general education than technical or community colleges. The length of programs at technical institutes varies, although 1-year certificate programs and 2-year associate degree programs are common.

About 20 colleges or universities offer bachelor's degree programs in forensic technology, often with an emphasis in a specialty area, such as criminalistics, pathology, jurisprudence, odontology, or toxicology. In contrast to some other science technician positions that require only a 2-year degree, a 4-year degree in forensics science is usually necessary to work in the field. Forestry and conservation technicians can choose from 23 associate degree programs accredited by the Society of American Foresters.

Some schools offer cooperative-education or internship programs, allowing students the opportunity to work at a local company or other workplace, while attending classes in alternate terms. Participation in such programs can significantly enhance a student's employment prospects.

Persons interested in careers as science technicians should take as many high school science and math courses as possible. Science courses taken beyond high school, in an associate or bachelor's program, should be laboratory oriented, with an emphasis on bench skills. Because computers and computer-interfaced equipment often are used in research and development laboratories, technicians should have strong computer skills. Communication skills are also important; technicians often are required to report their findings both through speaking and in writing. Additionally, technicians should be able to work well with others, because teamwork is common. Organizational ability, an eye for detail, and skill in interpreting scientific results are also important.

Prospective science technicians can acquire good career preparation through 2-year formal training programs that combine the teaching of scientific principles and theory with practical hands-on application in a laboratory setting with up-to-date equipment. Graduates of 4-year bachelor's degree programs in science who have considerable experience in laboratory-based courses, have completed internships, or held summer jobs in laboratories, are also well-qualified for science technician positions and are preferred by some employers. However, those with a bachelor's degree who accept technician jobs generally cannot find employment that uses their advanced academic education.

Technicians usually begin work as trainees in routine positions, under the direct supervision of a scientist or a more experienced technician. Job candidates whose training or educational background encompasses extensive hands-on experience with a variety of laboratory equipment, including computers and related equipment, usually require a short period of on-the-job training. As they gain experience, technicians take on more responsibility and carry out assignments under only general supervision, and some eventually become supervisors. However, technicians employed at universities often have their fortunes tied to particular professors; when professors retire or leave, these technicians face uncertain employment prospects.

Job Outlook

Overall employment of science technicians is expected to increase about as fast as the average for all occupations through the year 2010. Continued growth of scientific and medical research, as well as the development and production of technical products, should stimulate demand for science technicians in many industries. In particular, the growing number of agricultural and medicinal products developed from using biotechnology techniques will increase the need for biological technicians. Also, stronger competition among drug companies and an aging population are expected to contribute to the need for innovative and improved drugs, further spurring demand for biological technicians. Fastest employment growth of biological technicians should occur in the drug manufacturing industry and research and testing service firms.

The chemical and drug industry, the major employers of chemical technicians, should face stable demand for new and better pharmaceuticals and personal care products. To meet these demands, chemical and drug manufacturing firms are expected to continue to devote money to research and development, either through in-house teams or outside contractors, spurring employment growth of chemical technicians. An increasing focus on quality assurance will further stimulate demand for these workers. However, growth will be moderated somewhat by an expected slowdown in overall employment in the chemical industry.

Overall employment growth of science technicians will also be fueled by demand for environmental technicians to help regulate waste products; to collect air, water, and soil samples for measuring levels of pollutants; to monitor compliance with environmental regulations; and to clean up contaminated sites.

Demand for forest and conservation technicians at the federal and state government levels will result from a continuing emphasis on sustainability issues, such as environmental protection and responsible land management. However, employment growth may be moderated by downsizing in the federal government and continuing reductions in timber harvesting on federal lands.

Agricultural and food science technicians will be needed to assist agricultural scientists in biotechnology research as it becomes increasingly important to balance greater agricultural output with protection and preservation of soil, water, and the ecosystem. Jobs for forensic science technicians are expected to grow slowly. Crime scene technicians who work for state public safety departments may experience favorable employment prospects if the number of qualified applicants remains low.

Job opportunities are expected to be best for qualified graduates of science technician training programs or applied science technology programs who are well-trained on equipment used in industrial and government laboratories and production facilities. As the instrumentation and techniques used in industrial research, development, and production become increasingly more complex, employers are seeking well-trained individuals with highly developed technical and communication skills.

Along with opportunities created by growth, many job openings should arise from the need to replace technicians who retire or leave the labor force for other reasons. During periods of economic recession, layoffs of science technicians may occur.

Earnings

Median hourly earnings of science technicians in 2000 were as follows:

Nuclear technicians	$28.44
Forensic science technicians	18.04
Geological and petroleum technicians	17.55
Chemical technicians	17.05
Environmental science and protection technicians, including health	16.26
Biological technicians	15.16
Forest and conservation technicians	14.22
Agricultural and food science technicians	13.02

In the federal government in 2001, science technicians started at $17,483, $19,453, or $22,251, depending on education and experience. Beginning salaries were slightly higher in selected areas of the country where the prevailing local pay level was higher. The average annual salary for biological science technicians in nonsupervisory, supervisory, and managerial positions employed by the federal government in 2001 was $32,753; for physical science technicians, $42,657; for geodetic technicians, $53,143; for hydrologic technicians, $39,518; and for meteorologic technicians, $48,630.

Related Occupations

Other technicians who apply scientific principles at a level usually taught in 2-year associate degree programs include engineering technicians, broadcast technicians and sound engineering technicians and radio operators, drafters, and various health technologists and technicians, including clinical laboratory technologists and technicians, diagnostic medical sonographers, and radiologic technologists and technicians.

Sources of Additional Information

For information about a career as a chemical technician, contact:

- American Chemical Society, Education Division, Career Publications, 1155 16th St. NW., Washington, DC 20036. Internet: http://www.acs.org

For career information and a list of undergraduate, graduate, and doctoral programs in forensics sciences, contact:

- American Academy of Forensic Sciences, P.O. BOX 669, Colorado Springs, CO, 80901. Internet: http://www.aafs.org

For information on forestry technicians and lists of schools offering education in forestry, send a self-addressed, stamped business envelope to:

- Society of American Foresters, 5400 Grosvenor Ln., Bethesda, MD 20814. Internet: http://www.safnet.org

Secretaries and Administrative Assistants

O*NET 43-6011.00, 43-6012.00, 43-6013.00, 43-6014.00

Significant Points

- Increasing office automation and organizational restructuring will lead to slow growth in overall employment of secretaries and administrative assistants.

- Job openings will stem primarily from the need to replace workers who transfer to other occupations or leave this very large occupation for other reasons each year. Opportunities should be best for skilled and experienced secretaries.

Nature of the Work

As technology continues to expand in offices across the nation, the role of the office professional has greatly evolved. Office automation and organizational restructuring have led secretaries and administrative assistants to assume a wider range of new responsibilities once reserved for managerial and professional staff. Many secretaries and administrative assistants now provide training and orientation for new staff, conduct research on the Internet, and operate and troubleshoot new office technologies. In the midst of these changes, however, their core responsibilities have remained much the same, although changed from manual to electronic—performing and coordinating an office's administrative activities, storing retrieving, and integrating information for dissemination to staff and clients.

Secretaries and administrative assistants are responsible for a variety of administrative and clerical duties necessary to run an organization efficiently. They serve as an information manager for an office, schedule meetings and appointments, organize and maintain paper and electronic files, manage projects, conduct research, and provide information via the telephone, postal mail, and e-mail. They also may prepare correspondence and handle travel arrangements.

Secretaries and administrative assistants are aided in these tasks by a variety of office equipment, such as facsimile machines, photocopiers, and telephone systems. In addition, secretaries and administrative assistants increasingly use personal computers to create spreadsheets, compose correspondence, manage databases, and create reports and documents via desktop publishing, and using digital graphics—all tasks previously handled by managers and other professionals. At the same time, these other office workers have assumed many tasks traditionally assigned to secretaries and administrative assistants, such as word processing and answering the telephone. Because secretaries and administrative assistants are often relieved from dictation and typing, they can support more members of the executive staff. In a number of organizations, secretaries and administrative assistants work in teams in order to work flexibly and share their expertise.

Specific job duties vary with experience and titles. *Executive secretaries and administrative assistants*, for example, perform fewer clerical tasks than other secretaries. In addition to arranging conference calls, and scheduling meetings, they may handle more complex responsibilities such as conducting research, preparing statistical reports, training employees, and supervising other clerical staff.

Some secretaries and administrative assistants, such as legal and medical secretaries, perform highly specialized work requiring knowledge of technical terminology and procedures. For instance, *legal secretaries* prepare correspondence and legal papers such as summonses, complaints, motions, responses, and subpoenas under the supervision of an attorney or paralegal. They also may review legal journals and assist in other ways with legal research, such as verifying quotes and citations in legal briefs. *Medical secretaries* transcribe dictation, prepare correspondence, and assist physicians or medical scientists with reports, speeches, articles, and conference proceedings. They also record simple medical histories, arrange for patients to be hospitalized, and order supplies. Most medical secretaries need to be familiar with insurance rules, billing practices, and hospital or laboratory procedures. Other technical secretaries who assist engineers or scientists may prepare correspondence, maintain the technical library, and gather and edit materials for scientific papers.

Working Conditions

Secretaries and administrative assistants usually work in offices with other professionals in schools, hospitals, corporate settings, or in legal and medical offices. Their jobs often involve sitting for long periods. If they spend a lot of time typing, particularly at a video display terminal, they may encounter problems of eyestrain, stress, and repetitive motion, such as carpal tunnel syndrome.

Office work can lend itself to alternative or flexible working arrangements, such as part-time work or telecommuting, especially if their jobs require extensive computer use. More than 1 secretary in 7 works part-time and many others work in temporary positions. A few participate in job sharing arrangements in which two people divide responsibility for a single job. The majority of secretaries, however, are full-time employees who work a standard 40-hour week.

Employment

Secretaries and administrative assistants held about 3.9 million jobs in 2000, ranking among the largest occupations in the U.S. economy. The following table shows the distribution of employment by secretarial specialty:

Secretaries, except legal, medical, and executive 1,864,000
Executive secretaries and administrative assistants 1,445,000
Medical secretaries 314,000
Legal secretaries 279,000

Secretaries and administrative assistants are employed in organizations of every type. Almost 3 out of 5 secretaries and administrative assistants are employed in firms providing services, ranging from education and health to legal and business services. Others work for firms engaged in manufacturing, construction, wholesale and retail trade, transportation, and communications. Banks, insurance companies, investment firms, and real estate firms are also important employers, as are federal, state, and local government agencies.

Training, Other Qualifications, and Advancement

High school graduates who have basic office skills may qualify for entry-level secretarial positions. However, employers increasingly require extensive knowledge of software applications, such as word processing, spreadsheets, and database management. Secretaries and administrative assistants should be proficient in keyboarding and good at spelling, punctuation, grammar, and oral communication. Because secretaries and administrative assistants must be tactful in their dealings with people, employers also look for good interpersonal skills. Discretion, good judgment, organizational or management ability, initiative, and the ability to work independently are especially important for higher-level administrative positions.

As office automation continues to evolve, retraining and continuing education will remain an integral part of secretarial jobs. Changes in the office environment have increased the demand for secretaries and administrative assistants who are adaptable and versatile. Secretaries and administrative assistants may have to attend classes to learn how to operate new office technologies, such as information storage systems, scanners, the Internet, or new updated software packages, or utilize online education.

Secretaries and administrative assistants acquire skills in various ways. Training ranges from high school vocational education programs that teach office skills and keyboarding to 1- and 2-year programs in office administration offered by business schools, vocational-technical institutes, and community colleges. Many temporary placement agencies also provide formal training in computer and office skills. Many skills are often acquired, however, through on-the-job instruction by other employees or by equipment and software vendors. Specialized training programs are available for students planning to become medical or legal secretaries or administrative technology specialists. Bachelor's degrees and professional certifications are becoming increasingly important as business continues to become more global.

Testing and certification for entry-level office skills is available through the International Association of Administrative Professionals and NALS, the association for legal professionals. As secretaries and administrative assistants gain experience, they can earn the Certified Professional Secretary (CPS) designation or the Certified Administrative Professional (CAP) designation by meeting certain experience and/or educational requirements and passing an examination. Similarly, those with one year's experience in the legal field or who have concluded an approved training course and who want to be certified as a legal support professional can acquire the basic designation of Accredited Legal Secretary (ALS) by a testing process administered by NALS. NALS also offers an examination to confer the designation of Professional Legal Secretary (PLS), an advanced certification for legal support professionals. Legal Secretaries International confers the Certified Legal Secretary Specialist

(CLSS) designation in specialized areas such as civil trial, real estate, probate, and business law, to those who have 5 years of law-related experience and pass an examination. In some instances, waivers of certain requirements may be available.

Secretaries generally advance by being promoted to other administrative positions with more responsibilities. Qualified secretaries who broaden their knowledge of a company's operations and enhance their skills may be promoted to other positions such as senior or executive secretary, clerical supervisor, or office manager. Secretaries with word processing or data entry experience can advance to jobs as word processing or data entry trainers, supervisors, or managers within their own firms or in a secretarial, word processing or data entry service bureau. Secretarial experience can also lead to jobs such as instructor or sales representative with manufacturers of software or computer equipment. With additional training, many legal secretaries become paralegals.

Job Outlook

Overall, employment of secretaries and administrative assistants is expected to grow more slowly than the average for all occupations over the 2000–2010 period. In addition to openings due to growth, numerous job openings will result from the need to replace workers who transfer to other occupations or leave this very large occupation for other reasons each year. Opportunities should be best for well-qualified and experienced secretaries.

Projected employment of secretaries will vary by occupational specialty. Employment growth in the health and legal services industries should lead to average growth for medical and legal secretaries. Employment of executive secretaries and administrative assistants also is projected to grow about as fast as the average for all occupations. Fast growing industries—such as personnel supply, computer and data processing services, health and legal services education, and engineering and management—will continue to generate most new job opportunities. A decline in employment is expected for all other secretaries except legal, medical, or executive. They account for almost half of all secretaries and administrative assistants.

Growing levels of office automation and organizational restructuring will continue to make secretaries and administrative assistants more productive in coming years. Personal computers, electronic mail, scanners, and voice message systems will allow secretaries to accomplish more in the same amount of time. The use of automated equipment is also changing the distribution of work in many offices. In some cases, such traditional secretarial duties as keyboarding, filing, photocopying, and bookkeeping are being assigned to workers in other units or departments. Professionals and managers increasingly do their own word processing and data entry; and handle much of their own correspondence rather than submit the work to secretaries and other support staff. Also, in some law offices and physicians' offices, paralegals and medical assistants are assuming some tasks formerly done by secretaries. As other workers assume more of these duties, there is a trend in many offices for professionals and managers to "share" secretaries and administrative assistants. The traditional arrangement of one secretary per manager is becoming less prevalent; instead, secretaries and administrative assistants increasingly support systems, departments, or units. This approach often means secretaries and administrative assistants assume added responsibilities and are seen as valuable members of a team, but it also contributes to the decline in employment projected for overall numbers of secretaries and administrative assistants.

Developments in office technology are certain to continue, and they will bring about further changes in the secretary's and administrative assistant's work environment. However, many secretarial and administrative duties are of a personal, interactive nature and, therefore, not easily automated. Responsibilities such as planning conferences, working with clients, and transmitting staff instructions require tact and communication skills. Because technology cannot substitute for these personal skills, secretaries and administrative assistants will continue to play a key role in most organizations.

Earnings

Median annual earnings of executive secretaries and administrative assistants were $31,090 in 2000. The middle 50 percent earned between $24,970 and $38,370 in 2000. The lowest 10 percent earned less than $20,350, and the highest 10 percent earned more than $46,250. Median annual earnings in the industries employing the largest numbers of executive secretaries and administrative assistants in 2000, were:

Computer and data processing services $33,720
Local government 32,100
Elementary and secondary schools 30,470
Colleges and universities 29,710
Personnel supply services 28,020

Median annual earnings of legal secretaries, were $34,740 in 2000. The middle 50 percent earned between $27,650 and $42,510. The lowest 10 percent earned less than $22,440, and the highest 10 percent earned more than $50,970. Medical secretaries earned a median annual salary of $23,430 in 2000. The middle 50 percent earned between $19,530 and $28,120. The lowest 10 percent earned less than $16,510, and the highest 10 percent earned more than $34,510. Median annual earnings of all other secretaries, excluding legal, medical, and executive secretaries, were about $23,870 in 2000.

Salaries vary a great deal, however, reflecting differences in skill, experience, and level of responsibility. Salaries also vary in different parts of the country; earnings are usually lowest in southern cities, and highest in northern and western cities. In addition, salaries vary by industry; salaries of secretaries tend to be highest in transportation, legal services, and public utilities, and lowest in retail trade and finance, insurance, and real estate. Certification in this field usually is rewarded by a higher salary.

The starting salary for inexperienced secretaries in the federal government was $17,474 a year in 2001. Beginning salaries were slightly higher in selected areas where the prevailing local pay level was higher. All secretaries employed by the federal government averaged about $33,354 a year in early 2001.

Related Occupations

A number of other workers type, record information, and process paperwork. Among them are bookkeeping, accounting, and auditing clerks; receptionists and information clerks; court reporters; human resources assistants, except payroll and timekeeping; computer operators; data entry and information processing workers; paralegals and legal assistants; medical assistants; and medical records and health information technicians. A growing number of secretaries share in managerial and human resource responsibilities. Occupations requiring these skills include office and administrative support supervisors and managers, com-

puter and information systems managers, administrative services managers, and human resources, training, and labor relations managers and specialists.

Sources of Additional Information

State employment offices provide information about job openings for secretaries. For information on the Certified Professional Secretary designation or the Certified Administrative Professional designation, contact:

● International Association of Administrative Professionals, 10502 NW Ambassador Dr., P.O. Box 20404, Kansas City, MO 64195-0404. Internet: http://www.iaap-hq.org

Information on the Certified Legal Secretary Specialist designation can be obtained from:

● Legal Secretaries International Inc., 8902 Sunnywood Dr., Houston, TX 77088-3729. Internet: http://www.legalsecretaries.org

Information on the Accredited Legal Secretary (ALS) and the Professional Legal Secretary (PLS) certifications is available from:

● NALS, Inc., 314 East 3rd St., Suite 210, Tulsa, OK 74120. Internet: http://www.nals.org

Securities, Commodities, and Financial Services Sales Agents

O*NET 41-3031.01, 41-3031.02

Significant Points

● Employment is expected to grow faster than average, but competition for entry-level jobs is expected to be keen because sales agents who succeed often have high earnings.

● A college degree, sales ability, good interpersonal and communication skills, and a strong desire to succeed are important qualifications for this profession.

● Beginning securities and commodities sales agents must pass a licensing exam to sell securities and commodities. Many eventually leave the occupation because they are unable to establish a sufficient clientele.

Nature of the Work

Most investors, whether they are individuals with a few hundred dollars to invest or large institutions with millions, use *securities, commodities, and financial services sales agents* when buying or selling stocks, bonds, shares in mutual funds, insurance annuities, or other financial products. In addition, many clients seek out these agents for advice on investments, estate planning, and other financial matters.

Securities and commodities sales agents, also called brokers, stockbrokers, registered representatives, account executives, or financial consultants, perform a variety of tasks depending on their specific job duties. When an investor wishes to buy or sell a security, for example, sales agents may relay the order through their firm's computers to the floor of a securities exchange, such as the New York Stock Exchange. There, securities and commodities sales agents known as *floor brokers* negotiate the price with other floor brokers, make the sale, and forward the purchase price to the sales agents. If a security is not traded on an exchange, as in the case of bonds and over-the-counter stocks, the broker sends the order to the firm's trading department. Here, other securities sales agents, known as *dealers,* buy and sell securities directly from other dealers using their own funds or those of the firm, with the intention of reselling the security to customers at a profit. After the transaction has been completed, the broker notifies the customer of the final price.

Securities and commodities sales agents also provide many related services for their customers. They may explain stock market terms and trading practices, offer financial counseling or advice on the purchase or sale of particular securities, and devise an individual client's financial portfolio, which could include securities, life insurance, corporate and municipal bonds, mutual funds, certificates of deposit, annuities, and other investments.

Not all customers have the same investment goals. Some individuals prefer long-term investments for capital growth or to provide income over a number of years; others might want to invest in speculative securities that they hope will quickly rise in price. Securities and commodities sales agents furnish information about advantages and disadvantages of an investment based on each customer's objectives. They also supply the latest price quotes on any security, as well as information on the activities and financial positions of the corporations issuing these securities.

Most securities and commodities sales agents serve individual investors, but others specialize in institutional investors, such as banks and pension funds. In institutional investing, sales agents usually concentrate on a specific financial product, such as stocks, bonds, options, annuities, or commodity futures. At other times, they may also handle the sale of new issues, such as corporate securities issued to finance plant expansion.

The most important part of a sales representative's job is finding clients and building a customer base. Thus, beginning securities and commodities sales agents spend much of their time searching for customers—relying heavily on telephone solicitation. They also may meet clients through business and social contacts. Many sales agents find it useful to contact potential clients by teaching adult education investment courses, or by giving lectures at libraries or social clubs. Brokerage firms may give sales agents lists of people with whom the firm has done business in the past. Some agents inherit the clients of agents who have retired.

Financial services sales agents sell a wide variety of banking and related services. They contact potential customers to explain their services and to ascertain customers' banking and other financial needs. In doing so, they discuss services such as loans, deposit accounts, lines of credit, sales or inventory financing, certificates of deposit, cash management, or investment services. They also may solicit businesses to participate in consumer credit card programs. Financial services sales agents who serve all the financial needs of a single affluent individual or a business often are called private bankers or relationship managers.

As deregulation of the financial services industry is implemented, the distinctions among these sales agents become less clear as securities firms, banks and insurance companies begin to offer each other's products and services. The agents' jobs are also becoming more important as competition between the firms intensifies.

Working Conditions

Most securities and commodities sales agents work in offices under fairly stressful conditions. They have access to "quote boards" or computer terminals that continually provide information on the prices of securities. When sales activity increases, due perhaps to unanticipated changes in the economy, the pace can become very hectic.

Established securities and commodities sales agents usually work a standard 40 hour week. Beginners who are seeking customers may work longer hours. New brokers spend a great deal of time learning the firm's products and services and studying for exams in order to qualify to sell other products, such as insurance and commodities. Most securities and commodities sales agents accommodate customers by meeting with them in the evenings or on weekends.

A growing number of securities sales agents, employed mostly by discount or online brokerage firms, work in call center environments. In these centers, hundreds of agents spend much of the day on the telephone taking orders from clients or offering advice and information on different securities. Often, these call centers operate 24 hours a day, requiring agents to work in shifts.

Financial services sales agents normally work 40 hours a week in a comfortable, less stressful office environment. They may spend considerable time outside the office meeting with current and prospective clients, attending civic functions, and participating in trade association meetings. Some financial services sales agents work exclusively inside banks, providing service to "walk-in" customers.

Employment

Securities, commodities, and financial services sales agents held 367,000 jobs in 2000, including 90,000 who were self-employed. Of the wage and salary workers, 7 out of 10 worked for securities and commodities brokers, exchanges, and investment services companies. One in seven worked for commercial banks, savings institutions and credit unions. Although securities and commodities sales agents are employed by firms in all parts of the country, many sales agents work for a small number of large securities and investment banking firms headquartered in New York City.

Training, Other Qualifications, and Advancement

Because securities and commodities sales agents must be knowledgeable about economic conditions and trends, a college education is important, especially in larger securities firms. In fact, the overwhelming majority of workers in this occupation are college graduates. Although employers seldom require specialized academic training, courses in business administration, economics, and finance are helpful.

Many employers consider personal qualities and skills more important than academic training. Employers seek applicants who have considerable sales ability, good interpersonal and communication skills, and a strong desire to succeed. Some employers also make sure that applicants have a good credit history and a clean record. Self-confidence and an ability to handle frequent rejections also are important ingredients for success.

Because maturity and the ability to work independently are important, many employers prefer to hire those who have achieved success in other jobs. Some firms prefer candidates with sales experience, particularly those who have worked on commission in areas such as real estate or insurance. Therefore, most entrants to this occupation transfer from other jobs. Some begin working as securities and commodities sales agents following retirement from other fields.

Securities and commodities sales agents must meet state licensing requirements, which usually include passing an examination and, in some cases, furnishing a personal bond. In addition, sales agents must register as representatives of their firm with the National Association of Securities Dealers, Inc. (NASD). Before beginners can qualify as registered representatives, they must pass the General Securities Registered Representative Examination (Series 7 exam), administered by the NASD, and be an employee of a registered firm for at least 4 months. Most states require a second examination—the Uniform Securities Agents State Law Examination. These tests measure the prospective representative's knowledge of the securities business in general, customer protection requirements, and record keeping procedures. Many take correspondence courses in preparation for the securities examinations. Within 2 years, brokers are encouraged to take additional licensing exams in order to sell mutual funds, insurance, and commodities.

Most employers provide on-the-job training to help securities and commodities sales agents meet the registration requirements for certification. In most firms, this training period takes about 4 months. Trainees in large firms may receive classroom instruction in securities analysis, effective speaking, and the finer points of selling; take courses offered by business schools and associations; and undergo a period of on-the-job training lasting up to 2 years. Many firms like to rotate their trainees among various departments to give them a broad perspective of the securities business. In small firms, sales agents often receive training in outside institutions and on the job.

Securities and commodities sales agents must understand the basic characteristics of the wide variety of financial products offered by brokerage firms. Brokers periodically take training through their firms or outside institutions to keep abreast of new financial products and improve their sales techniques. Computer training also is important, as the securities sales business is highly automated. Since 1995, it also has become mandatory for all registered securities and commodities sales agents to attend periodic continuing-education classes to maintain their licenses. Courses consist of computer-based training in regulatory matters and company training on new products and services.

The principal form of advancement for securities and commodities sales agents is an increase in the number and size of the accounts they handle. Although beginners usually service the accounts of individual investors, they may eventually handle very large institutional accounts, such as those of banks and pension funds. After taking a series of tests, some brokers become portfolio managers and have greater authority to make investment decisions regarding an account. Some experienced sales agents become branch office managers and supervise other sales agents while continuing to provide services for their own customers. A few agents advance to top management positions or become partners in their firms.

Banks and other credit institutions prefer to hire college graduates for financial services sales jobs. A business administration degree with a specialization in finance or a liberal arts degree including courses in accounting, economics, and marketing serves as excellent preparation for this job. Often, financial services sales agents learn their jobs through on-the-job training under the supervision of bank officers. However, those who wish to sell mutual funds and insurance products may need to undergo formal training and pass some of the same exams required of securities sales agents.

Job Outlook

Barring a significant decline in the stock market, the number of securities, commodities, and financial services sales agents should grow faster than the average for all occupations through 2010. As people's incomes continue to climb and they seek better returns on their investments, they will increasingly need the advice and services of securities, commodities, and financial services sales agents to realize their financial goals. Growth in the volume of trade in stocks over the Internet will reduce the need for brokers for many transactions. Nevertheless, the rapid overall increase in investment is expected to spur employment growth among these workers, as a majority of transactions will still require the advice and services of securities, commodities, and financial services sales agents.

Baby boomers in their peak savings years will fuel much of the investment boom. Saving for retirement is being made much easier by the government, which continues to offer a number of tax-favorable pension plans, such as the 401(k) and the Roth IRA. The participation of more women in the workforce also means higher household incomes and more women qualifying for pensions. And many of these pensions are self-directed—meaning that the recipient has the responsibility for investing the money. With such large amounts of money to invest, sales agents, in their role as financial advisors, will be in great demand.

Other factors that will impact the demand for brokers are the increasing number and complexity of investment products, as well as the effects of globalization. As the public and businesses become more sophisticated about investing, they are venturing into the options and futures markets. Brokers are needed to buy or sell these products, which are not traded online. Also, markets for investment are expanding with the increase in global trading of stocks and bonds. Furthermore, the New York Stock Exchange has announced its intention to extend its trading hours to accommodate trading in foreign stocks and compete with foreign exchanges. If this takes place, it will vastly increase the demand for brokers, both on the floor of the exchange and in brokerage firms, to handle the larger volume of trades.

Employment of brokers, however, will be adversely affected if the stock market or the economy suddenly declines. Even in good times, turnover is relatively high for beginning brokers who are unable to establish a sizable clientele. Once established, securities and commodities sales agents have a very strong attachment to their occupation because of their high earnings and the considerable investment in training. Competition usually is intense, especially in larger companies with more applicants than jobs. Opportunities for beginning brokers should be better in smaller firms.

The number of financial services sales agents in banks will increase faster than average as banks expand their product offerings in order to compete directly with other investment firms.

Earnings

Median annual earnings of securities, commodities, and financial services sales agents were $56,080 in 2000. The middle half earned between $33,630 and $107,800. The lowest 10 percent earned less than $24,770; more than 10 percent earned $145,600 or more.

Median annual earnings in the industries employing the largest numbers of securities and financial services sales agents in 2000 were:

Security and commodity services	$71,260
Security brokers and dealers	69,550
Mortgage bankers and brokers	39,740
Personal credit institutions	37,690
Mortgage bankers and brokers	36,590

Stockbrokers, who provide personalized service and more guidance with respect to a client's investments, usually are paid a commission based on the amount of stocks, bonds, mutual funds, insurance, and other products they sell. Commission earnings are likely to be high when there is much buying and selling, and low when there is a slump in market activity. Most firms provide sales agents with a steady income by paying a "draw against commission"—a minimum salary based on commissions they can be expected to earn. Securities and commodities sales agents who can provide their clients with the most complete financial services should enjoy the greatest income stability. Trainee brokers usually are paid a salary until they develop a client base. The salary gradually decreases in favor of commissions as the broker gains clients. A small but increasing number of full-service brokers are paid a percentage of the assets they oversee. This fee often covers a certain number of trades done for free.

Brokers who work for discount brokerage firms that promote the use of telephone and online trading services usually are paid a salary. Sometimes this salary is boosted by bonuses that reflect the profitability of the office. Financial services sales agents usually are paid a salary; however, bonuses or commissions from sales are starting to account for a larger share of their income.

Related Occupations

Other jobs requiring knowledge of finance and an ability to sell include insurance sales agents, real estate agents, and personal financial advisors.

Sources of Additional Information

For general information on the securities industry, contact:

● The Securities Industry Association, 120 Broadway, New York, NY 10271

For information about job opportunities for financial services sales agents in various states, contact state bankers' associations or write directly to a particular bank.

Security Guards and Gaming Surveillance Officers

O*NET 33-9031.00, 33-9032.00

Significant Points

● Favorable opportunities are expected for lower paying jobs, but stiff competition is likely for higher paying positions at facilities requiring a high level of security, such as nuclear plants and government installations.

● Some positions, such as those of armored car guards, are hazardous.

● Because of limited formal training requirements and flexible hours, this occupation attracts many individuals seeking a second or part-time job.

Nature of the Work

Guards, who are also called *security officers*, patrol and inspect property to protect against fire, theft, vandalism, and illegal activity. These workers protect their employer's investment, enforce laws on the property, and deter criminal activity or other problems. They use radio and telephone communications to call for assistance from an ambulance, wrecker, or the police or fire departments as the situation dictates. Security guards write comprehensive reports outlining their observations and activities during their assigned shift. They may also interview witnesses or victims, prepare case reports, and testify in court.

Although all security guards perform many of the same duties, specific duties vary based on whether the guard works in a "static" security position or on a mobile patrol. Guards assigned to static security positions usually serve the client at one location for a specific length of time. These guards must become closely acquainted with the property and people associated with it, complete all tasks assigned them, and often monitor alarms and closed-circuit TV cameras. In contrast, guards assigned to mobile patrol duty drive or walk from location to location and conduct security checks within an assigned geographical zone. They may detain or arrest criminal violators, answer service calls concerning criminal activity or problems, and issue traffic violation warnings.

Specific job responsibilities also vary with the size, type, and location of the employer. In department stores, guards protect people, records, merchandise, money, and equipment. They often work with undercover store detectives to prevent theft by customers or store employees and help in the apprehension of shoplifting suspects prior to arrival by police. Some shopping centers and theaters have officers mounted on horses or bicycles who patrol their parking lots to deter car theft and robberies. In office buildings, banks, and hospitals, guards maintain order and protect the institutions' property, staff, and customers. At air, sea, and rail terminals and other transportation facilities, guards protect people, freight, property, and equipment. They may screen passengers and visitors for weapons and explosives using metal detectors and high-tech equipment, ensure nothing is stolen while being loaded or unloaded, and watch for fires and criminals.

Guards who work in public buildings such as museums or art galleries protect paintings and exhibits by inspecting people and packages entering and leaving the building. In factories, laboratories, government buildings, data processing centers, and military bases, security officers protect information, products, computer codes, and defense secrets and check the credentials of people and vehicles entering and leaving the premises. Guards working at universities, parks, and sports stadiums perform crowd control, supervise parking and seating, and direct traffic. Security guards stationed at the entrance to bars and places of adult entertainment, such as nightclubs, prevent access by minors, collect cover charges at the door, maintain order among customers, and protect property and patrons.

Armored car guards protect money and valuables during transit. In addition, they protect individuals responsible for making commercial bank deposits from theft or bodily injury. When the armored car arrives at the door of a business, an armed guard enters, signs for the money, and returns to the truck with the valuables in hand. Carrying money between the truck and the business can be extremely hazardous for guards, and a number of them have been robbed and shot in recent years, so armored car guards usually wear bullet-proof vests.

All security officers must show good judgment and common sense, follow directions and directives from supervisors, accurately testify in court, and follow company policy and guidelines. Guards should have a professional appearance and attitude and be able to interact with the public. They also must be able to take charge and direct others in emergencies or other dangerous incidents. In a large organization, the security manager is often in charge of a trained guard force divided into shifts; whereas in a small organization, a single worker may be responsible for all security.

Gaming surveillance officers and gaming investigators act as security agents for casino managers and patrons. They observe casino operations for irregular activities, such as cheating or theft, by either employees or patrons. To do this, surveillance officers and investigators monitor activities from a catwalk over one-way mirrors located above the casino floor. Many casinos use audio and video equipment, allowing surveillance officers and investigators to observe these same areas via monitors. Recordings are kept as a record and are sometimes used as evidence against alleged criminals in police investigations.

Working Conditions

Most security guards and gaming surveillance officers spend considerable time on their feet, either assigned to a specific post or patrolling buildings and grounds. Guards may be stationed at a guard desk inside a building to monitor electronic security and surveillance devices or to check the credentials of persons entering or leaving the premises. They also may be stationed at a guardhouse outside the entrance to a gated facility or communities and use a portable radio or telephone that allows them to be in constant contact with a central station. Guard work usually is routine, but guards must be constantly alert for threats to themselves and the property they are protecting. Guards who work during the day may have a great deal of contact with other employees and members of the public. Gaming surveillance often takes place behind a bank of monitors controlling several cameras in a casino, which can cause eyestrain.

Guards usually work at least 8-hour shifts for 40 hours per week and often are on call in case an emergency arises. Some employers have three shifts, and guards rotate to equally divide daytime, weekend, and holiday work. Guards usually eat on the job instead of taking a regular break away from the site.

Employment

Security guards and gaming surveillance officers held more than 1.1 million jobs in 2000. Industrial security firms and guard agencies employed 60 percent of all wage and salary guards. These organizations provide security services on a contract basis, assigning their guards to buildings and other sites as needed. Most other security officers were employed by the organization they are responsible for guarding, such as banks, building management companies, hotels, hospitals, retail stores, restaurants, bars, schools, and governments. Guard jobs are found throughout the country, most commonly in metropolitan areas. More than 1 in 7 guards worked part-time, and many individuals held a second job as a guard to supplement their primary earnings. Gaming surveillance officers work exclusively in casinos and other gaming facilities and are employed only in those states and Indian reservations where gambling has been legalized.

A significant number of law-enforcement officers work as security guards when off-duty to supplement their incomes. Often working in uniform and with the official cars assigned to them, they add a high profile security presence to the establishment with which they have contracted. At construction sites and apartment complexes, for example, their presence often prevents trouble before it starts.

Training, Other Qualifications, and Advancement

Most states require that guards be licensed. To be licensed as a guard, individuals must usually be at least 18 years old, pass a background check, and complete classroom training in such subjects as property rights, emergency procedures, and detention of suspected criminals. Drug testing often is required, and may be random and ongoing.

Many employers of unarmed guards do not have any specific educational requirements. For armed guards, employers usually prefer individuals who are high school graduates or hold an equivalent certification. Many jobs require a driver's license. For positions as armed guards, employers often seek people who have had responsible experience in other occupations.

Guards who carry weapons must be licensed by the appropriate government authority, and some receive further certification as special police officers, which allows them to make limited types of arrests while on duty. Armed guard positions have more stringent background checks and entry requirements than those of unarmed guards because of greater insurance liability risks. Compared to unarmed security guards, armed guards and special police typically enjoy higher earnings and benefits, greater job security, more advancement potential, and usually are given more training and responsibility.

Rigorous hiring and screening programs consisting of background, criminal record, and fingerprint checks are becoming the norm in the occupation. Applicants are expected to have good character references, no serious police record, and good health. They should be mentally alert, emotionally stable, and physically fit in order to cope with emergencies. Guards who have frequent contact with the public should communicate well.

Candidates for guard jobs in the federal government must have some experience in the occupation and pass a written examination to be certified by the U.S. General Services Administration. Armed forces experience is an asset. For federal guard positions, applicants also must qualify in the use of firearms and pass a first aid test.

The amount of training guards receive varies. Training requirements are higher for armed guards because their employers are legally responsible for any use of force. Armed guards receive formal training in areas such as weapons retention and laws covering the use of force.

Many employers give newly hired guards instruction before they start the job and also provide on-the-job training. An increasing number of states are making ongoing training a legal requirement for retention of certification. Guards may receive training in protection, public relations, report writing, crisis deterrence, and first aid, as well as specialized training relevant to their particular assignment.

Guards employed at establishments placing a heavy emphasis on security usually receive extensive formal training. For example, guards at nuclear power plants undergo several months of training before being placed on duty under close supervision. They are taught to use firearms, administer first aid, operate alarm systems and electronic security equipment, and spot and deal with security problems. Guards authorized to carry firearms may be periodically tested in their use.

Although guards in small companies may receive periodic salary increases, advancement opportunities are limited. Most large organizations use a military type of ranking that offers the possibility of advancement in position and salary. Some guards may advance to supervisor or security manager positions. Guards with management skills may open their own contract security guard agencies.

In addition to the keen observation skills required to perform their jobs, gaming surveillance officers and gaming investigators must have excellent verbal and writing abilities to document violations or suspicious behavior. They also need to be physically fit and have quick reflexes because they sometimes must detain individuals until local law enforcement officials arrive.

Surveillance officers and investigators usually do not need a bachelor's degree, but some training beyond high school is required; previous security experience is a plus. Several educational institutes offer certification programs. Training classes usually are conducted in a casino-like atmosphere using surveillance camera equipment.

Job Outlook

Opportunities for most jobs as security guards and gaming surveillance officers should be very favorable through the year 2010. Numerous job openings will stem from employment growth attributable to the desire for increased security, and from the need to replace those who leave this large occupation each year. Many opportunities are expected for persons seeking full-time employment, as well as for those seeking part-time or second jobs. However, competition is expected for higher paying positions that require longer periods of training; these positions usually are found at facilities that require a high level of security, such as nuclear power plants or weapons installations.

Employment of security guards and gaming surveillance officers is expected to grow faster than the average for all occupations through 2010

as concern about crime, vandalism, and terrorism continue to increase the need for security. Demand for guards also will grow as private security firms increasingly perform duties—such as monitoring crowds at airports and providing security in courts—which were formerly handled by government police officers and marshals. Because enlisting the services of a security guard firm is easier and less costly than assuming direct responsibility for hiring, training, and managing a security guard force, job growth is expected to be concentrated among contract security guard agencies. Casinos will continue to hire more surveillance officers as more states legalize gambling and as the number of casinos increases in states where gambling is already legal. Additionally, casino security forces will employ more technically trained personnel as technology becomes increasingly important in thwarting casino cheating and theft.

Earnings

Median annual earnings of security guards were $17,570 in 2000. The middle 50 percent earned between $14,930 and $21,950. The lowest 10 percent earned less than $12,860, and the highest 10 percent earned more than $28,660. Median annual earnings in the industries employing the largest numbers of security guards in 2000 were as follows:

Hospitals	$22,260
Elementary and secondary schools	22,240
Hotels and motels	20,230
Miscellaneous business services	16,830
Eating and drinking places	15,870

Depending on their experience, newly hired guards in the federal government earned $21,950 to $27,190 a year in 2001. Beginning salaries were slightly higher in selected areas where the prevailing local pay level was higher. Guards employed by the federal government averaged $28,960 a year in 2001. These workers usually receive overtime pay as well as a wage differential for the second and third shifts.

Gaming surveillance officers and gaming investigators had median annual earnings of $21,220 in 2000. The middle 50 percent earned between $18,080 and $25,950. The lowest 10 percent earned less than $14,520, and the highest 10 percent earned more than $32,890. Median annual earnings in 2000 in miscellaneous amusement and recreation services, the industry employing the largest numbers of gaming surveillance officers and gaming investigators, were $20,650.

Related Occupations

Guards protect property, maintain security, and enforce regulations and standards of conduct in the establishments at which they work. Related security and protective service occupations include correctional officers, police and detectives, and private detectives and investigators.

Sources of Additional Information

Further information about work opportunities for guards is available from local security and guard firms and state employment service offices. Information about licensing requirements for guards may be obtained from the state licensing commission or the state police department. In states where local jurisdictions establish licensing requirements, contact a local government authority such as the sheriff, county executive, or city manager.

Semiconductor Processors

O*NET 51-9141.00

Significant Points

- Semiconductor processors is the only production occupation whose employment expected to grow much is expected to grow faster than the average for all occupations.

- An associate degree in a relevant curriculum is increasingly required.

Nature of the Work

Electronic semiconductors—also known as computer chips, microchips, or integrated chips—are the miniature but powerful brains of high technology equipment. They are comprised of a myriad of tiny aluminum wires and electric switches, which manipulate the flow of electrical current. Semiconductor processors are responsible for many of the steps necessary to manufacture each semiconductor that goes into a personal computer, missile guidance system, and a host of other electronic equipment.

Semiconductor processors manufacture semiconductors in disks about the size of dinner plates. These disks, called wafers, are thin slices of silicon on which the circuitry of the microchips is layered. Each wafer is eventually cut into dozens of individual chips.

Semiconductor processors make wafers using photolithography, a printing process for creating plates from photographic images. Operating automated equipment, workers imprint precise microscopic patterns of the circuitry on the wafers, etch out the patterns with acids, and replace the patterns with metals that conduct electricity. Then the wafers receive a chemical bath to make them smooth, and the imprint process begins again on a new layer with the next pattern. Wafers usually have from 8 to 20 such layers of microscopic, three-dimensional circuitry.

Semiconductors are produced in semiconductor fabricating plants, or "fabs." Within fabs, the manufacture and cutting of wafers to create semiconductors takes place in "clean rooms." Clean rooms are production areas that must be kept free of any airborne matter, because the least bit of dust can damage a semiconductor. All semiconductor processors working in clean rooms—both operators and technicians—must wear special lightweight outer garments known as "bunny suits." Bunny suits fit over clothing to prevent lint and other particles from contaminating semiconductor processing work sites.

Operators, who make up the majority of the workers in clean rooms, start and monitor the sophisticated equipment that performs the various tasks during the many steps of the semiconductor production sequence. They spend a great deal of time at computer terminals, monitoring the operation of the equipment to ensure that each of the tasks in the production of the wafer is performed correctly. They also may transfer wafer carriers from one development station to the next; in newer fabs, the lifting of heavy wafer carriers and the constant monitoring for quality control are increasingly being automated, however.

Once begun, production of semiconductor wafers is continuous. Operators work to the pace of the machinery that has largely automated the production process. Operators are responsible for keeping the automated machinery within proper operating parameters.

Technicians account for a smaller percentage of the workers in clean rooms, but they troubleshoot production problems and make equipment adjustments and repairs. They also take the lead in assuring quality control and in maintaining equipment. In order to prevent the need for repairs, technicians perform diagnostic analyses and run computations. For example, technicians may determine if a flaw in a chip is due to contamination and peculiar to that wafer, or if the flaw is inherent in the manufacturing process.

Working Conditions

The work pace in cleanrooms is deliberately slow. Limited movement keeps the air in cleanrooms as free as possible of dust and other particles, which can destroy semiconductors during production. Because the machinery sets operators' rate of work in the largely automated production process, workers keep an easy-going pace. Although workers spend some time alone monitoring equipment, operators and technicians spend much of their time working in teams.

Technicians are on their feet most of the day, walking through the clean room to oversee production activities. Operators spend a great deal of time sitting or standing at workstations, monitoring computer readouts and gauges. Sometimes, they must retrieve wafers from one station and take them to another.

The temperature in the cleanrooms must be kept within narrow ranges, usually a comfortable 72 degrees Fahrenheit. Although bunny suits cover virtually the entire body, except perhaps the eyes, their light-weight fabric keeps the temperature inside fairly comfortable as well. However, entry and exit of workers in bunny suits from the clean room is controlled to minimize contamination, and workers must be reclothed in a clean suit and decontaminated each time they return to the clean room.

The work environment of semiconductor fabricating plants is one of the safest in any industry. Measures taken to avoid contamination of the wafers lead to more than just antiseptically clean rooms—they result in a work environment nearly free of conditions that cause occupational illnesses and accidents.

Semiconductor fabricating plants operate around the clock. For this reason, night and weekend work is common. In some plants, workers maintain standard 8-hour shifts, 5 days a week. In other plants, employees are on duty for 12-hour shifts to minimize the disruption of clean room operations brought about by shift changes. Managers in some plants allow workers to alternate schedules for equitable distribution of the "graveyard" shift.

Employment

Electronic semiconductor processors held 52,000 jobs in 2000. Nearly all of them were employed in facilities that manufacture electronic components and accessories, although a small percentage worked in plants that primarily manufacture computers and office equipment.

Training, Other Qualifications, and Advancement

People interested in becoming semiconductor processors—either operators or technicians—need a solid background in mathematics and physical sciences. In addition to their application to the complex manufacturing processes performed in fabs, math and science knowledge are essentials for pursuing higher education in semiconductor technology—and knowledge of both subjects is one of the best ways to advance in the semiconductor fabricating field.

Semiconductor processor workers must also be able to think analytically and critically to anticipate problems and avoid costly mistakes. Communication skills also are vital, as workers must be able to convey their thoughts and ideas both orally and in writing.

Employers prefer to hire persons who have completed associate degree programs for semiconductor processor jobs. A high school diploma or equivalent is the minimum requirement for entry-level operator jobs in semiconductor fabrication plants. Although completion of a 1-year certificate program in semiconductor technology offered by some community colleges is an asset, technicians must have at least an associate degree in electronics technology or a related field.

Degree or certificate candidates who get hands-on training while attending school look even more attractive to prospective employers. Semiconductor technology programs in a growing number of community colleges include an internship at a semiconductor fabricating plant; many students in these programs already hold full- or part-time jobs in the industry and work toward degrees in semiconductor technology in their spare time to update their skills or qualify for promotion to technician jobs. In addition, to ensure that operators and technicians keep their skills current, most employers provide 40 hours of formal training annually. Some employers also provide financial assistance to employees who want to earn associate and bachelor's degrees.

Summer and part-time employment provide another option for getting started in the field for those who live near a semiconductor processing plant. Students often are hired to work during the summer, and some students are allowed to continue working part-time during the school year. Students in summer and part-time semiconductor processor jobs learn what education they need to prosper in the field. They also gain valuable experience that may lead to full-time employment after graduation.

Some semiconductor processing technicians transfer to sales engineer jobs with suppliers of the machines that manufacture the semiconductors or become field support personnel.

Job Outlook

Between 2000 and 2010, employment of semiconductor processors is projected to increase faster than the average for all occupations. Besides the creation of new jobs, additional openings will result from the need to replace workers who leave the occupation. Growing demand for semiconductors and semiconductor processors will stem from the many existing and future applications for semiconductors in computers, appliances, machinery, vehicles, cell phones and other telecommunications devices, and other equipment. Job prospects should be best for people with postsecondary education in electronics or semiconductor technology.

The electronic components and accessories industry is projected to be one of the most rapidly growing manufacturing industries. Moreover, industry development of semiconductors made from better materials means that semiconductors will become even smaller, more powerful, and more durable. For example, the industry has begun producing a new generation of microchips, made with copper rather than aluminum wires, which will better conduct electricity. Also, technology to develop chips based on plastic, rather than on silicon, will make computers durable enough to be used in a variety of applications in which they could not easily have been used previously. These technological developments and new applications will lead to employment growth in the industry and more semiconductor processor jobs.

Earnings

Median hourly earnings of electronic semiconductor processors were $12.23 in 2000. The middle 50 percent earned between $10.02 and $15.36 an hour. The lowest 10 percent earned less than $8.85, and the top 10 percent earned more than $19.10 an hour.

Technicians with an associate degree in electronics or semiconductor technology generally started at higher salaries than those with less education. Almost one fourth of all electronic semiconductor processors belong to a union, considerably higher than the rate for all occupations.

Related Occupations

Electronic semiconductor processors do production work that resembles the work of precision assemblers and fabricators of electrical and electronic equipment. Also, many electronic semiconductor processors have academic training in semiconductor technology, which emphasizes scientific and engineering principles. Other occupations that require some college or postsecondary vocational training emphasizing such principles are engineering technicians, electrical and electronics engineers, and science technicians.

Sources of Additional Information

For more information on semiconductor processor careers, contact:

- Semiconductor Industry Association, 181 Metro Dr., Suite 450, San Jose, CA 95110. Internet: http://www.semichips.org

- SEMATECH, 2706 Montopolis Dr., Austin, TX 78741. Maricopa Advanced Technology Education Center (MATEC), 2323 West 14th St., Suite 540, Tempe, AZ 85281. Internet: http://matec.org

Sheet Metal Workers

O*NET 47-2211.00

Significant Points

- Two out of 3 jobs are found in the construction industry; about 1 out of 3 is in manufacturing.

- Apprenticeship programs lasting 4 or 5 years are considered the best training.

- Job opportunities should be excellent in construction.

Nature of the Work

Sheet metal workers make, install, and maintain air-conditioning, heating, ventilation, and pollution control duct systems; roofs; siding; rain gutters; downspouts; skylights; restaurant equipment; outdoor signs; and many other products made from metal sheets. They also may work with fiberglass and plastic materials. Although some workers specialize in fabrication, installation, or maintenance, most do all three jobs. In addition to construction-related sheet metal work, some sheet metal workers are employed in the mass production of sheet metal products in manufacturing.

Sheet metal workers first study plans and specifications to determine the kind and quantity of materials they will need. They then measure, cut, bend, shape, and fasten pieces of sheet metal to make ductwork, counter tops, and other custom products. In an increasing number of shops, sheet metal workers use computerized metalworking equipment. This enables them to experiment with different layouts and to select the one that results in the least waste of material. They cut or form parts with computer-controlled saws, lasers, shears, and presses.

In shops without computerized equipment, and for products that cannot be made on such equipment, sheet metal workers use hand calculators to make the required calculations and use tapes, rulers, and other measuring devices for layout work. They then cut or stamp the parts on machine tools.

Before assembling pieces, sheet metal workers check each part for accuracy using measuring instruments such as calipers and micrometers and, if necessary, finish it by using hand, rotary, or squaring shears and hacksaws. After the parts have been inspected, workers fasten seams and joints together with welds, bolts, cement, rivets, solder, specially formed sheet metal drive clips, or other connecting devices. They then take the parts to the construction site where they further assemble the pieces as they install them. These workers install ducts, pipes, and tubes by joining them end to end and hanging them with metal hangers secured to a ceiling or a wall. They also use shears, hammers, punches, and drills to make parts at the work site or to alter parts made in the shop.

Some jobs are done completely at the job site. When installing a metal roof, for example, sheet metal workers measure and cut the roofing panels that are needed to complete the job. They secure the first panel in place and interlock and fasten the grooved edge of the next panel into the grooved edge of the first. Then, they nail or weld the free edge of the panel to the structure. This two-step process is repeated for each additional panel. Finally, the workers fasten machine-made molding at joints, along corners, and around windows and doors for a neat, finished effect.

In addition to installation, some sheet metal workers specialize in testing, balancing, adjusting, and servicing existing air-conditioning and ventilation systems to make sure they are functioning properly and to improve their energy efficiency.

Sheet metal workers in manufacturing plants make sheet metal parts for products such as aircraft or industrial equipment. Although some of the fabrication techniques used in large-scale manufacturing are similar to those used in smaller shops, the work may be highly automated and repetitive.

Working Conditions

Sheet metal workers usually work a 40-hour week. Those who fabricate sheet metal products work in shops that are well-lighted and well-ventilated. However, they stand for long periods and lift heavy materials and finished pieces. Sheet metal workers must follow safety practices because working around high-speed machines can be dangerous. They also are subject to cuts from sharp metal, burns from soldering and welding, and falls from ladders and scaffolds. They usually wear safety glasses but must not wear jewelry or loose-fitting clothing that could easily be caught in a machine.

Those performing installation work do considerable bending, lifting, standing, climbing, and squatting, sometimes in close quarters or in awkward positions. Although duct systems and kitchen equipment are installed indoors, the installation of siding, roofs, and gutters involves much outdoor work, requiring sheet metal workers to work in various kinds of weather.

Employment

Sheet metal workers held about 224,000 jobs in 2000. Two-thirds of all sheet metal workers were found in the construction industry. Of those employed in construction, three-fourths worked for plumbing, heating, and air-conditioning contractors; most of the rest worked for roofing and sheet metal contractors. Some worked for other special trade contractors and for general contractors engaged in residential and commercial building. Most of the sheet metal workers outside of construction are found in manufacturing industries, such as the fabricated structural metal products, industrial machinery equipment, and aircraft and parts industries. Some work for the federal government.

Compared with workers in most construction craft occupations, relatively few sheet metal workers are self-employed.

Training, Other Qualifications, and Advancement

Apprenticeship generally is considered to be the best way to learn this trade. The apprenticeship program consists of 4 or 5 years of on-the-job training and a minimum of 144 hours per year of classroom instruction. Apprenticeship programs provide comprehensive instruction in both sheet metal fabrication and installation. They are administered by local joint committees composed of the Sheet Metal Workers' International Association and local chapters of the Sheet Metal and Air Conditioning Contractors National Association.

On the job, apprentices learn the basics of pattern layout and how to cut, bend, fabricate, and install sheet metal. They begin with basic ductwork and gradually advance to more difficult jobs, such as making more complex ducts, fittings, and decorative pieces. They also use materials such as fiberglass, plastics, and other nonmetallic materials.

In the classroom, apprentices learn drafting, plan and specification reading, trigonometry and geometry applicable to layout work, the use of computerized equipment, welding, and the principles of heating, air-conditioning, and ventilating systems. Safety is stressed throughout the program. In addition, apprentices learn the relationship between sheet metal work and other construction work.

Some persons pick up the trade informally, usually by working as helpers to experienced sheet metal workers. Most begin by carrying metal and cleaning up debris in a metal shop while they learn about materials and tools and their uses. Later, they learn to operate machines that bend or cut metal. In time, helpers go out on the job site to learn installation. Those who acquire their skills this way often take vocational school courses in mathematics or sheet metal fabrication to supplement their work experience. To be promoted to the journey level, helpers usually must pass the same written examination as apprentices. Most sheet metal workers in large-scale manufacturing receive on-the-job training.

Applicants for jobs as apprentices or helpers should be in good physical condition and have mechanical and mathematical aptitude. Good eye-hand coordination, spatial and form perception, and manual dexterity also are important. Local apprenticeship committees require a high school education or its equivalent. Courses in algebra, trigonometry, geometry, mechanical drawing, and shop provide a helpful background for learning the trade, as does related work experience obtained in the Armed Services.

It is important for experienced sheet metal workers to keep abreast of new technological developments, such as the growing use of computerized layout and laser cutting machines. Workers often take additional training provided by the union or by their employer, to improve existing skills or to acquire new ones.

Sheet metal workers may advance to supervisory jobs. Some of these workers take additional training in welding and do work that is more specialized. Others go into the contracting business for themselves. Because a sheet metal contractor must have a shop with equipment to fabricate products, this type of contracting business is more expensive to start than other types of construction contracting.

Job Outlook

Job opportunities are expected to be excellent for sheet metal workers in the construction industry and in construction-related sheet metal fabrication, reflecting both rapid employment growth and openings arising each year as experienced sheet metal workers leave the occupation. In addition, many potential workers may prefer work that is less strenuous and that has more comfortable working conditions, thus limiting the number of applicants for sheet metal jobs. Opportunities should be particularly good for individuals who acquire apprenticeship training. Prospects are expected to be better for sheet metal workers in the construction industry than for those in manufacturing because construction is expected to grow faster than the manufacturing industries that employ sheet metal workers.

Employment of sheet metal workers in construction is expected to increase faster than the average for all occupations through 2010, reflecting growth in the demand for sheet metal installations as more industrial, commercial, and residential structures are built. The need to install energy-efficient air-conditioning, heating, and ventilation systems in the increasing stock of old buildings and to perform other types of renovation and maintenance work also should boost employment. In addition, the popularity of decorative sheet metal products and increased architectural restoration are expected to add to the demand for sheet metal workers. On the other hand, average job growth is projected for sheet metal workers in manufacturing.

Sheet metal workers in construction may experience periods of unemployment, particularly when construction projects end and economic conditions dampen construction activity. Nevertheless, employment of sheet metal workers is less sensitive to declines in new construction than is the employment of some other construction workers, such as carpenters. Maintenance of existing equipment—which is less affected by economic fluctuations than is new construction—makes up a large part of the work done by sheet metal workers. Installation of new air-conditioning and heating systems in existing buildings continues during construction slumps, as individuals and businesses adopt more energy-efficient equipment to cut utility bills. In addition, a large proportion of sheet metal installation and maintenance is done indoors, so sheet metal workers usually lose less worktime due to bad weather than other construction workers do.

Earnings

In 2000, median hourly earnings of sheet metal workers employed in all industries were $15.31. The lowest 10 percent of all sheet metal workers earned less than $8.90, and the highest 10 percent earned more than $27.54.

The median hourly earnings of the largest industries employing sheet metal workers in 2000 are shown in the following table:

Federal government	$18.85
Plumbing, heating, and air-conditioning	16.06
Roofing, siding, and sheet metal work	15.37
Fabricated structural metal products	14.11
Aircraft and parts	13.47

Apprentices normally start at about 40 percent of the rate paid to experienced workers. As apprentices acquire more skills throughout the course of their training, they receive periodic increases until their pay approaches that of experienced workers. In addition, union workers in some areas receive supplemental wages from the union when they are on layoff or shortened workweeks. Many sheet metal workers are members of the Sheet Metal Workers' International Association.

Related Occupations

To fabricate and install sheet metal products, sheet metal workers combine metalworking skills and knowledge of construction materials and techniques. Other occupations in which workers lay out and fabricate metal products include assemblers and fabricators; machinists; machine setters, operators, and tenders—metal and plastic; and tool and die makers. Construction occupations requiring similar skills and knowledge include glaziers and heating, air-conditioning, and refrigeration mechanics and installers.

Sources of Additional Information

For more information about apprenticeships or other work opportunities, contact local sheet metal contractors or heating, refrigeration, and air-conditioning contractors; a local of the Sheet Metal Workers; a local of the Sheet Metal and Air-Conditioning Contractors National Association; a local joint union-management apprenticeship committee; or the nearest office of your state employment service or apprenticeship agency.

For general information about sheet metal workers, contact:

- International Training Institute for the Sheet Metal and Air-Conditioning Industry, 601 N. Fairfax St., Suite 240, Alexandria, VA 22314

- Sheet Metal and Air-Conditioning Contractors National Association, 4201 Lafayette Center Dr., Chantilly, VA 20151-1209. Internet: http://www.smacna.org

- Sheet Metal Workers International Association, 1750 New York Ave. NW., Washington, DC 20006. Internet: http://www.smwia.org

Shipping, Receiving, and Traffic Clerks

O*NET 43-5071.00

Significant Points

- Many shipping, receiving, and traffic clerk jobs are entry level and do not require more than a high school diploma.

- Workers develop the necessary skills through on-the-job training lasting from several days to a few months.

- Employment of shipping, receiving, and traffic clerks is expected to grow more slowly than the average for all occupations through 2010 due to the effects of automation.

Nature of the Work

Shipping, receiving, and traffic clerks keep records of all goods shipped and received. Their duties depend on the size of the establishment and the level of automation used. Larger companies typically are better able to finance the purchase of computers and other equipment to handle some or all of a clerk's responsibilities. In smaller companies, a clerk maintains records, prepares shipments, and accepts deliveries. In both environments, shipping, receiving, and traffic clerks may lift cartons of various sizes.

Shipping clerks keep records of all outgoing shipments. They prepare shipping documents and mailing labels, and make sure orders have been filled correctly. Also, they record items taken from inventory and note when orders were filled. Sometimes they fill the order themselves, obtaining merchandise from the stockroom, noting when inventories run low, and wrapping or packing the goods in shipping containers. They also address and label packages, look up and compute freight or postal rates, and record the weight and cost of each shipment. Shipping clerks also may prepare invoices and furnish information about shipments to other parts of the company, such as the accounting department. Once a shipment is checked and ready to go, shipping clerks may move the goods from the plant—sometimes by forklift truck—to the shipping dock and direct its loading.

Receiving clerks perform tasks similar to those of shipping clerks. They determine whether orders have been filled correctly by verifying incoming shipments against the original order and the accompanying bill of lading or invoice. They make a record of the shipment and the condition of its contents. In many firms, receiving clerks use hand-held scan-

ners to record barcodes on incoming products or enter the information into a computer. These data then can be transferred to the appropriate departments. The shipment is checked for any discrepancies in quantity, price, and discounts. Receiving clerks may route or move shipments to the proper department, warehouse section, or stockroom. They also may arrange for adjustments with shippers whenever merchandise is lost or damaged. Receiving clerks in small businesses also may perform duties similar to those of stock clerks. In larger establishments, receiving clerks may control all receiving-platform operations, such as truck scheduling, recording of shipments, and handling of damaged goods.

Traffic clerks maintain records on the destination, weight, and charges on all incoming and outgoing freight. They verify rate charges by comparing the classification of materials with rate charts. In many companies, this work may be automated. Information either is scanned or is hand-entered into a computer for use by accounting or other departments within the company. Also, they keep a file of claims for overcharges and for damage to goods in transit.

Working Conditions

Shipping, receiving, and traffic clerks work in a wide variety of businesses, institutions, and industries. Some work in warehouses, stockrooms, or shipping and receiving rooms that may not be temperature controlled. Others may spend time in cold storage rooms or outside on loading platforms, where they are exposed to the weather.

Most jobs for shipping, receiving, and traffic clerks, involve frequent standing, bending, walking, and stretching. Some lifting and carrying of smaller items also may be involved. Although automation devices have lessened the physical demands of this occupation, their use remains somewhat limited. Work still can be strenuous, even though mechanical material handling equipment is employed to move heavy items.

The typical workweek is Monday through Friday; however, evening and weekend hours are common for some jobs, and may be required when large shipments are involved or when inventory is taken.

Employment

Shipping, receiving, and traffic clerks held about 890,000 jobs in 2000. Nearly 4 out of 5 were employed in manufacturing or by wholesale and retail establishments. Although jobs for shipping, receiving, and traffic clerks are found throughout the country, most clerks work in urban areas, where shipping depots in factories and wholesale establishments usually are located.

Training, Other Qualifications, and Advancement

Many shipping, receiving, and traffic clerk jobs are entry level and do not require more than a high school diploma. Employers, however, prefer to hire those who are familiar with computers and other electronic office and business equipment. Those who have taken business courses or have previous business, dispatching, or specific job-related experience may be preferred. Because communication with other people is an integral part of these jobs, good oral and written communications skills are essential. Typing, filing, recordkeeping, and other clerical skills also are important.

Shipping, receiving, and traffic clerks usually learn the job by doing routine tasks under close supervision. They learn how to count and mark stock, and then start keeping records and taking inventory. Strength, stamina, good eyesight, and an ability to work at repetitive tasks, sometimes under pressure, are important characteristics. Shipping, receiving, and traffic clerks and stock clerks and order fillers who handle jewelry, liquor, or drugs may be bonded.

Such clerks start out by checking items to be shipped and then attaching labels and making sure the addresses are correct. Training in the use of automated equipment usually is done informally, on the job. As these occupations become more automated, however, workers in these jobs may need longer training in order to master the use of the equipment.

Shipping, receiving, and traffic clerks are often promoted to head clerk, and those with a broad understanding of shipping and receiving may enter a related field such as industrial traffic management. With additional training, some clerks advance to jobs as warehouse manager or purchasing agent.

Job Outlook

Employment of shipping, receiving, and traffic clerks is expected to grow more slowly than the average for all occupations through 2010. Employment growth will continue to be affected by automation, as all but the smallest firms move to reduce labor costs by using computers to store and retrieve shipping and receiving records.

Methods of material handling have changed significantly in recent years. Large warehouses are increasingly automated, using equipment such as computerized conveyor systems, robots, computer-directed trucks, and automatic data storage and retrieval systems. Automation, coupled with the growing use of hand-held scanners and personal computers in shipping and receiving departments, has increased the productivity of these workers.

Despite technology, job openings will continue to arise due to increasing economic and trade activity, and because certain tasks cannot be automated. For example, someone needs to check shipments before they go out and when they arrive to ensure that everything is in order. In addition to those arising from job growth, openings will occur because of the need to replace shipping, receiving, and traffic clerks who leave the occupation. Because this is an entry-level occupation, many vacancies are created by normal career progression.

Earnings

Median hourly earnings in 2000 for shipping, receiving, and traffic clerks were $10.52.

Shipping, receiving, and traffic clerks usually receive the same benefits as most other workers. If uniforms are required, employers usually provide either the uniforms or an allowance to purchase them.

Related Occupations

Shipping, receiving, and traffic clerks record, check, and often store materials that a company receives. They also process and pack goods for shipment. Other workers who perform similar duties are stock clerks and order fillers; production, planning, and expediting clerks; and cargo and freight agents.

Sources of Additional Information

Information about job opportunities may be obtained from local employers and local offices of the state employment service.

Small Engine Mechanics

O*NET 49-3051.00, 49-3052.00, 49-3053.00

Significant Points

- Employment is expected to grow slowly, but persons with formal mechanic training should enjoy good job prospects.

- Because the use of motorcycles, motorboats, and outdoor power equipment is seasonal in many areas, mechanics may service other types of equipment or work reduced hours in the winter.

Nature of the Work

Although smaller, engines powering motorcycles, motorboats, and outdoor power equipment share many characteristics with their larger counterparts, including breakdowns. Small engine mechanics repair and service power equipment ranging from racing motorcycles to chain saws.

Small engines, like large engines, require periodic service to minimize the chance of breakdowns and to keep them operating at peak performance. During routine equipment maintenance, mechanics follow a checklist including the inspection and cleaning of brakes, electrical systems, fuel injection systems, plugs, carburetors, and other parts. Following inspection, mechanics usually repair or adjust parts that do not work properly, or replace unfixable parts. Routine maintenance is normally a major part of the mechanic's work.

When equipment breakdowns occur, mechanics use various techniques to diagnose the source and extent of the problem. The mark of a skilled mechanic is the ability to diagnose mechanical, fuel, and electrical problems, and to make repairs in a minimal amount of time. Quick and accurate diagnosis requires problem-solving ability and a thorough knowledge of the equipment's operation.

In larger repair shops, mechanics may use special computerized diagnostic testing equipment as a preliminary tool in analyzing equipment. These computers provide a systematic performance report of various components to compare them to normal ratings. After pinpointing the problem, the mechanic makes the needed adjustments, repairs, or replacements. Some jobs require minor adjustments or the replacement of a single item, such as a carburetor or fuel pump. In contrast, a complete engine overhaul requires a number of hours to disassemble the engine and replace worn valves, pistons, bearings, and other internal parts. Some highly skilled mechanics use highly specialized components and the latest computerized equipment to customize and tune motorcycles and motorboats for racing.

Small engine mechanics use common handtools such as wrenches, pliers, and screwdrivers. They also use power tools, such as drills and grinders when customized repairs warrant. Computerized engine analyzers, compression gauges, ammeters and voltmeters, and other testing devices help mechanics locate faulty parts and tune engines. Hoists may be used to lift heavy equipment such as motorcycles, snowmobiles, or motorboats. Mechanics often refer to service manuals for detailed directions and specifications while performing repairs.

Motorcycle mechanics repair and overhaul motorcycles, motor scooters, mopeds, dirt bikes, and all-terrain vehicles. Besides engines, they may work on transmissions, brakes, and ignition systems, and make minor body repairs. Mechanics usually specialize in the service and repair of one type of equipment, although they may work on closely related products. Mechanics may only service a few makes and models of motorcycles because usually the dealers only service the products they sell.

Motorboat mechanics, or *marine equipment mechanics,* repair and adjust the electrical and mechanical equipment of inboard and outboard boat engines. Most small boats have portable outboard engines that are removed and brought into the repair shop. Larger craft, such as cabin cruisers and commercial fishing boats, are powered by diesel or gasoline inboard or inboard-outboard engines, which are only removed for major overhauls. Most of these repairs are performed at the docks or marinas. Motorboat mechanics may also work on propellers, steering mechanisms, marine plumbing, and other boat equipment.

Outdoor power equipment and other small engine mechanics service and repair outdoor power equipment such as lawnmowers, garden tractors, edge trimmers, and chain saws. They may also occasionally work on portable generators and go-carts. In addition, small engine mechanics in northern parts of the country may work on snowblowers and snowmobiles, but demand for this type of repair is seasonal.

Working Conditions

Small engine mechanics usually work in repair shops that are well-lighted and ventilated, but are sometimes noisy when testing engines. Motorboat mechanics may work outdoors at docks or marinas, as well as in all weather conditions when making repairs aboard boats. They may work in cramped or awkward positions to reach a boat's engine.

During the winter months in the northern United States, mechanics may work fewer than 40 hours a week because the amount of repair and service work declines when lawnmowers, motorboats, and motorcycles are not in use. Many mechanics only work during the busy spring and summer seasons. However, many mechanics schedule time-consuming engine overhauls and work on snowmobiles and snowblowers during winter downtime. Mechanics may work considerably more than 40 hours a week when demand is strong.

Employment

Small-engine mechanics held about 73,000 jobs in 2000. Motorcycle mechanics held about 14,000 jobs; motorboat mechanics held about 25,000; and outdoor power equipment and other small engine mechanics held about 33,000. About one-third worked for retail hardware and garden stores, or retail dealers of motorboats, motorcycles, and miscellaneous vehicles. Most of the remainder were employed by independent repair shops, marinas and boat yards, equipment rental companies, wholesale distributors, and landscaping services. About 1 in 4 was self-employed.

Training, Other Qualifications, and Advancement

Due to the increasing complexity of motorcycles and motorboats, most employers prefer to hire mechanics who graduate from formal training programs for small engine mechanics. Because the number of these specialized postsecondary programs is limited, most mechanics learn their skills on the job or while working in related occupations. For trainee jobs, employers hire persons with mechanical aptitude who are knowledgeable about the fundamentals of small 2- and 4-stroke engines. Many trainees develop an interest in mechanics and acquire some basic skills through working on automobiles, motorcycles, motorboats, or outdoor power equipment as a hobby. Others may be introduced to mechanics through vocational automotive training in high school, or one of many postsecondary institutions.

Trainees learn routine service tasks under the guidance of experienced mechanics by replacing ignition points and spark plugs or by taking apart, assembling, and testing new equipment. As trainees gain experience and proficiency, they progress to more difficult tasks such as advanced computerized diagnosis and engine overhauls. Up to 3 years of on-the-job training may be necessary before a novice worker becomes competent in all aspects of the repair of motorcycle and motorboat engines.

Employers often send mechanics and trainees to special training courses conducted by motorcycle, motorboat, and outdoor power equipment manufacturers or distributors. These courses, which can last as long as 2 weeks, upgrade the worker's skills and provide information on repairing new models. They are usually a prerequisite for any mechanic who performs warranty work for manufacturers or insurance companies.

Most employers prefer to hire high school graduates for trainee mechanic positions, but will accept applicants with less education if they possess adequate reading, writing, and arithmetic skills. Many equipment dealers employ students part-time and during the summer to help assemble new equipment and perform minor repairs. Helpful high school courses include small engine repair, automobile mechanics, science, and business arithmetic.

Knowledge of basic electronics is essential for small engine mechanics. Electronic components control engine performance, instrument displays, and a variety of other functions of motorcycles, motorboats, and outdoor power equipment. To recognize and fix potential problems, mechanics should be familiar with the basic principles of electronics.

The most important work possessions of mechanics are their hand tools. Mechanics usually provide their own tools and many experienced mechanics have invested thousands of dollars in them. Employers typically furnish expensive powertools, computerized engine analyzers, and other diagnostic equipment, but mechanics accumulate hand tools with experience.

The skills used as a small engine mechanic generally transfer to other occupations such as automobile, diesel, or heavy vehicle and mobile equipment mechanics. Experienced mechanics with leadership ability may advance to shop supervisor or service manager jobs. Mechanics with sales ability sometimes become sales representatives or open their own repair shops.

Job Outlook

Employment of small engine mechanics is expected to grow slower than the average for all occupations through the year 2010. The majority of job openings are expected to be replacement jobs because many experienced small engine mechanics leave each year to transfer to other occupations, retire, or stop working for other reasons. Job prospects should be especially favorable for persons who complete mechanic training programs.

Growth of personal disposable income over the 2000–2010 period should provide consumers with more discretionary dollars to buy motorboats, lawn and garden power equipment, and motorcycles. This will require more mechanics to keep the growing amount of equipment in operation. In addition, routine service will always be a significant source of work for mechanics. While advancements in technology will lengthen the interval between checkups, the need for qualified mechanics to perform this service will increase.

Employment of motorcycle mechanics should increase slowly as the popularity of motorcycles rebounds. Motorcycle usage should continue to be popular with persons between the ages of 18 and 24, an age group which historically has had the greatest proportion of motorcycle enthusiasts. Motorcycles also are increasingly popular with persons over the age of 40. Traditionally, this group has disposable income to spend on recreational equipment such as motorcycles and motorboats.

Over the next decade, more people will be entering the 40 and over age group; this group is responsible for the largest segment of marine craft purchases. These potential buyers will help expand the market for motorboats, while helping to maintain the demand for qualified mechanics. Construction of new single-family houses will result in an increase in the lawn and garden equipment in operation, increasing the need for mechanics. However, equipment growth will be slowed by trends toward smaller lawns and contracting out their maintenance to lawn service firms. Growth also will be tempered by the tendency of many consumers to dispose of and replace relatively inexpensive items rather than have them repaired.

Earnings

Median annual earnings of motorcycle mechanics were $25,100 in 2000. The middle 50 percent earned between $19,660 and $32,490. The lowest 10 percent earned less than $15,980, and the highest 10 percent earned more than $41,180. Median annual earnings in 2000 in motorcycle dealers, the industry employing the largest numbers of motorcycle mechanics, were $25,650.

Median annual earnings of motorboat mechanics were $26,660 in 2000. The middle 50 percent earned between $20,760 and $33,680. The lowest 10 percent earned less than $17,320, and the highest 10 percent earned more than $41,490. Median annual earnings in 2000 in boat dealers, the industry employing the largest numbers of motorboat mechanics, were $26,350.

Median annual earnings of outdoor power equipment and other small engine mechanics were $23,780 in 2000. The middle 50 percent earned between $18,930 and $29,370. The lowest 10 percent earned less than $14,830, and the highest 10 percent earned more than $35,250.

Small engine mechanics tend to receive few benefits in small shops, but those employed in larger shops often receive paid vacations, sick leave, and health insurance. Some employers also pay for work-related training and provide uniforms.

Related Occupations

Mechanics and repairers who work on other types of mobile equipment include automotive service technicians and mechanics, diesel service technicians and mechanics, and heavy vehicle and mobile equipment service technicians and mechanics.

Sources of Additional Information

For more details about work opportunities, contact local motorcycle, motorboat, and lawn and garden equipment dealers, boat yards, and marinas. Local offices of the state employment service may also have information about employment and training opportunities.

General information about motorcycle mechanic careers may be obtained from:

- American Motorcycle Institute, 3042 West International Speedway Blvd., Daytona Beach, FL 32124. Telephone (toll free): 800-874-0645. Internet: http://www.amiwrench.org

- Motorcycle Mechanics Institute, 2844 West Deer Valley Rd., Phoenix, AZ 85027. Telephone (toll free): 800-582-7995

General information about motorboat mechanic careers is available from:

- American Marine Institute, 3042 West International Speedway Blvd., Daytona Beach, FL 32124. Telephone (toll free): 800-874-0645. Internet: http://www.amiwrench.org

- American Watercraft Institute, 3042 West International Speedway Blvd., Daytona Beach, FL 32124. Telephone (toll free): 800-342-9253. Internet: http://www.amiwrench.org

- Marine Mechanics Institute, 9751 Delegates Dr., Orlando, FL 32827. Telephone (toll free): 800-342-9253

Social and Human Service Assistants

O*NET 21-1093.00

Significant Points

- While a bachelor's degree usually is not required, employers increasingly seek individuals with relevant work experience or education beyond high school.

- Social and human service assistants are projected to be among the fastest growing occupations.

- Job opportunities should be excellent, particularly for applicants with appropriate postsecondary education, but pay is low.

Nature of the Work

Social and human service assistant is a generic term for people with various job titles, including human service worker, case management aide, social work assistant, community support worker, mental health aide, community outreach worker, life skill counselor, or gerontology aide. They usually work under the direction of professionals from a variety of fields, such as nursing, psychiatry, psychology, rehabilitative or physical therapy, or social work. The amount of responsibility and supervision they are given varies a great deal. Some have little direct supervision; others work under close direction.

Social and human service assistants provide direct and indirect client services. They assess clients' needs, establish their eligibility for benefits and services, and help clients obtain them. They examine financial documents such as rent receipts and tax returns to determine whether the client is eligible for Food Stamps, Medicaid, welfare, and other human service programs. They also arrange for transportation and escorts, if necessary, and provide emotional support. Social and human service assistants monitor and keep case records on clients and report progress to supervisors and case managers. They also may transport or accompany clients to group meal sites, adult daycare centers, or doctors' offices; telephone or visit clients' homes to make sure services are being received; or help resolve disagreements, such as those between tenants and landlords. They also may help some clients complete insurance or medical forms, as well as applications for financial assistance, and may assist others with daily living needs.

Social and human service assistants play a variety of roles in a community. They may organize and lead group activities, assist clients in need of counseling or crisis intervention, or administer a food bank or emergency fuel program. In halfway houses, group homes, and government-supported housing programs, they assist adults who need supervision with personal hygiene and daily living skills. They review clients' records, ensure that they take correct doses of medication, talk with family members, and confer with medical personnel and other caregivers to gain better insight into clients' backgrounds and needs. Social and human service assistants also provide emotional support and help clients become involved in their own well-being, in community recreation programs, and in other activities.

In psychiatric hospitals, rehabilitation programs, and outpatient clinics, social and human service assistants work with professional care providers, such as psychiatrists, psychologists, and social workers, to help clients master everyday living skills, to teach them how to communicate more effectively, and to get along better with others. They support the client's participation in a treatment plan, such as individual or group counseling or occupational therapy.

Working Conditions

Working conditions of social and human service assistants vary. Some work in offices, clinics, and hospitals, while others work in group homes, shelters, sheltered workshops, and day programs. Many spend their time in the field visiting clients. Most work a 40-hour week, although some work in the evening and on weekends.

The work, while satisfying, can be emotionally draining. Understaffing and relatively low pay may add to the pressure. Turnover is reported to be high, especially among workers without academic preparation for this field.

Employment

Social and human service assistants held about 271,000 jobs in 2000. Approximately half worked in private social or human services agencies, offering a variety of services, including adult daycare, group meals, crisis intervention, counseling, and job training. Many social and human service assistants supervised residents of group homes and halfway houses. About one-quarter were employed by state and local governments, primarily in public welfare agencies and facilities for mentally disabled and developmentally challenged individuals. Social and human service assistants also held jobs in clinics, detoxification facilities, community mental health centers, psychiatric hospitals, day-treatment programs, and sheltered workshops.

Training, Other Qualifications, and Advancement

While a bachelor's degree usually is not required for entry into this occupation, employers increasingly seek individuals with relevant work experience or education beyond high school. Certificates or associate degrees in subjects such as social work, human services, gerontology, or one of the social or behavioral sciences meet most employers' requirements.

Human services programs have a core curriculum that trains students to observe patients and record information, conduct patient interviews, implement treatment plans, employ problem-solving techniques, handle crisis intervention matters, and use proper case management and referral procedures. General education courses in liberal arts, sciences, and the humanities also are part of the curriculum. Many degree programs require completion of a supervised internship.

Educational attainment often influences the kind of work employees may be assigned and the degree of responsibility that may be entrusted to them. For example, workers with no more than a high school education are likely to receive extensive on-the-job training to work in direct-care services, while employees with a college degree might be assigned to do supportive counseling, coordinate program activities, or manage a group home. Social and human service assistants with proven leadership ability, either from previous experience or as a volunteer in the field, often have greater autonomy in their work. Regardless of the academic or work background of employees, most employers provide some form of in-service training, such as seminars and workshops, to their employees.

Hiring requirements in group homes tend to be more stringent than those in other settings. For example, employers may require employees to have a valid driver's license or to submit to a criminal background investigation.

Employers try to select applicants who have effective communication skills, a strong sense of responsibility, and the ability to manage time effectively. Many human services jobs involve direct contact with people who are vulnerable to exploitation or mistreatment; therefore, patience, understanding, and a strong desire to help others are highly valued characteristics.

Formal education almost always is necessary for advancement. In general, advancement requires a bachelor's or master's degree in counseling, rehabilitation, social work, human services, psychology, or a related field.

Job Outlook

Job opportunities for social and human service assistants are expected to be excellent, particularly for applicants with appropriate postsecondary education. The number of social and human service assistants is projected to grow much faster than the average for all occupations between 2000 and 2010—ranking among the most rapidly growing occupations. The need to replace workers who move into new positions due to advancement or retirement or for other reasons will create many additional job opportunities. This occupation, however, is not attractive to everyone. It can be draining emotionally, and the pay is relatively low. There will be more competition for jobs in urban areas than in rural areas, but qualified applicants should have little difficulty finding employment.

Faced with rapid growth in the demand for social and human services, employers are developing new strategies for delivering and funding services. Many employers increasingly rely on social and human service assistants to undertake greater responsibility in delivering services to clients.

Opportunities are expected to be best in job-training programs, residential care facilities, and private social service agencies, which include such services as adult daycare and meal delivery programs. Demand for these services will expand with the growing elderly population, who are more likely to need services. In addition, social and human service assistants will continue to be needed to provide services to pregnant teenagers, the homeless, the mentally disabled and developmentally challenged, and those with substance-abuse problems.

Job-training programs also are expected to require additional social and human service assistants. As social welfare policies shift focus from benefit-based programs to work-based initiatives, there will be more demand for people to teach job skills to the people who are new to, or returning to, the workforce. Additionally, streamlined and downsized businesses create demand for persons with job-retraining expertise. Social and human service assistants will help companies to cope with new modes of conducting business and employees to master new job skills.

Residential care establishments should face increased pressures to respond to the needs of the chronically and mentally ill. Many of these patients have been deinstitutionalized and lack the knowledge or the ability to care for themselves. Also, more community-based programs, supported independent-living sites, and group residences are expected to be established to house and assist the homeless and the chronically and mentally ill. Because more substance abusers are being sent to treatment programs instead of to prison, employment of social and human service assistants in substance abuse programs will also grow.

The number of jobs for social and human service assistants will grow more rapidly than overall employment in state and local governments. State and local governments employ many of their social and human service assistants in corrections and public-assistance departments. Although employment in corrections departments is growing, employment of social and human service assistants is not expected to grow as rapidly as employment in other corrections jobs, such as correctional officers. Public-assistance programs have been employing more social and human service assistants in an attempt to employ fewer social workers, who are more educated, and thus more highly paid.

Earnings

Median annual earnings of social and human service assistants were $22,330 in 2000. The middle 50 percent earned between $17,820 and $27,930. The top 10 percent earned more than $35,220, while the lowest 10 percent earned less than $14,660.

Median annual earnings in the industries employing the largest numbers of social and human service assistants in 2000 were:

State government, except education and hospitals	$27,130
Local government, except education and hospitals	25,320
Social services, not elsewhere classified	21,820
Individual and family services	21,350
Residential care	19,880

Related Occupations

Workers in other occupations that require skills similar to those of social and human service assistants include social workers; clergy; counselors; childcare workers; occupational-therapist assistants and aides; physical-therapist assistants and aides; and nursing, psychiatric, and home-health aides.

Sources of Additional Information

Information on academic programs in human services may be found in most directories of 2- and 4-year colleges, available at libraries or career counseling centers.

For information on programs and careers in human services, contact:

- National Organization for Human Service Education, University of Rhode Island, Quinn 107-URI, Kingston, RI 02881

- Council for Standards in Human Services Education, Northern Essex Community College, 100 Elliot Way, Haverhill, MA 01830

Information on job openings may be available from state employment service offices or directly from city, county, or state departments of health, mental health and mental retardation, and human resources.

Stationary Engineers and Boiler Operators

O*NET 51-8021.01, 51-8021.02

Significant Points

- Job opportunities will be best for workers with computer skills.

- Stationary engineers and boiler operators usually acquire their skills through a formal apprenticeship program or informal on-the-job training supplemented by courses at a trade or technical school.

- A license to operate boilers, ventilation, air conditioning, and other equipment is required in most states and cities.

Nature of the Work

Heating, air-conditioning, and ventilation systems keep large buildings comfortable all year long. Industrial plants often have facilities to provide electrical power, steam, or other services. Stationary engineers and boiler operators control and maintain these systems, which include boilers, air-conditioning and refrigeration equipment, diesel engines, turbines, generators, pumps, condensers, and compressors. The equipment that stationary engineers and boiler operators control is similar to equipment operated by locomotive or marine engineers, except that it is not on a moving vehicle.

Stationary engineers and boiler operators start up, regulate, and shut down equipment. They ensure that it operates safely, economically, and within established limits by monitoring meters, gauges, and computerized controls. They manually control equipment and, if necessary, make adjustments. They use hand and power tools to perform repairs and maintenance ranging from a complete overhaul to replacing defective valves, gaskets, or bearings. They also record relevant events and facts concerning operation and maintenance in an equipment log. On steam boilers, for example, they observe, control, and record steam pressure, temperature, water level and chemistry, power output, fuel consumption, and emissions. They watch and listen to machinery and routinely check safety devices, identifying and correcting any trouble that develops.

Stationary engineers and boiler operators may use computers to operate the mechanical systems of new buildings and plants. Engineers and operators monitor, adjust, and diagnose these systems from a central location using a computer linked into the buildings' communications network.

Routine maintenance, such as lubricating moving parts, replacing filters, and removing soot and corrosion that can reduce operating efficiency, is a regular part of the work of stationary engineers and boiler operators. They test boiler water and add chemicals to prevent corrosion and harmful deposits. They also may check the air quality of the ventilation system and make adjustments to keep within mandated guidelines.

In a large building or industrial plant, a stationary engineer may be in charge of all mechanical systems in the building. Engineers may supervise the work of assistant stationary engineers, turbine operators, boiler tenders, and air-conditioning and refrigeration operators and mechanics. Some perform other maintenance duties, such as carpentry, plumbing, and electrical repairs. In a small building or industrial plant, there may be only one stationary engineer.

Working Conditions

Stationary engineers and boiler operators generally have steady, year-round employment. The average workweek is 40 hours. In facilities that operate around the clock, engineers and operators usually work one of three daily 8-hour shifts on a rotating basis. Weekend and holiday work often is required.

Engine rooms, power plants, and boiler rooms usually are clean and well lighted. Even under the most favorable conditions, however, some stationary engineers and boiler operators are exposed to high temperatures, dust, dirt, and high noise levels from the equipment. General maintenance duties also may require contact with oil, grease, or smoke. Workers spend much of the time on their feet. They may also have to crawl inside boilers and work in crouching or kneeling positions to inspect, clean, or repair equipment.

Stationary engineers and boiler operators work around potentially hazardous machinery such as boilers and electrical equipment. They must follow procedures to guard against burns, electric shock, and exposure to hazardous materials such as asbestos or certain chemicals.

Employment

Stationary engineers and boiler operators held about 57,000 jobs in 2000. They worked in a variety of places, including factories, hospitals, hotels, office and apartment buildings, schools, and shopping malls. Some are employed as contractors to a building or plant.

Stationary engineers and boiler operators work throughout the country, generally in the more heavily populated areas in which large industrial and commercial establishments are located.

Training, Other Qualifications, and Advancement

Stationary engineers and boiler operators usually acquire their skills through a formal apprenticeship program or informal on-the-job training supplemented by courses at a trade or technical school. In addition, valuable experience can be obtained in the Navy or the Merchant Marine because marine-engineering plants are similar to many stationary power and heating plants. Most employers prefer to hire persons with at least a high school diploma, or equivalent, due to the increasing complexity of the equipment with which engineers and operators work. Many stationary engineers and boiler operators have some college education. Mechanical aptitude, manual dexterity, and good physical condition also are important.

The International Union of Operating Engineers sponsors apprenticeship programs and is the principal union for stationary engineers and boiler operators. In selecting apprentices, most local labor-management apprenticeship committees prefer applicants with education or training in mathematics, computers, mechanical drawing, machine-shop practice, physics, and chemistry. An apprenticeship usually lasts 4 years and includes 8,000 hours of on-the-job training. In addition, apprentices receive 600 hours of classroom instruction in subjects such as boiler design and operation, elementary physics, pneumatics, refrigeration, air conditioning, electricity, and electronics.

Those who acquire their skills on the job usually start as boiler tenders or helpers to experienced stationary engineers and boiler operators. This practical experience may be supplemented by postsecondary vocational training in computerized controls and instrumentation. However, becoming an engineer or operator without completing a formal apprenticeship program usually requires many years of work experience.

Most large and some small employers encourage and pay for skill-improvement training for their employees. Training almost always is provided when new equipment is introduced or when regulations concerning some aspect of the workers' duties change.

Most states and cities have licensing requirements for stationary engineers and boiler operators. Applicants usually must be at least 18 years of age, reside for a specified period in the state or locality, meet experience requirements, and pass a written examination. A stationary engineer or boiler operator who moves from one state or city to another may have to pass an examination for a new license due to regional differences in licensing requirements.

There are several classes of stationary engineer licenses. Each class specifies the type and size of equipment the engineer can operate without supervision. A licensed first-class stationary engineer is qualified to run a large facility, supervise others, and operate equipment of all types and capacities. An applicant for this license may be required to have a high school education, apprenticeship or on-the-job training, and several years of experience. Licenses below first class limit the types or capacities of equipment the engineer may operate without supervision.

Stationary engineers and boiler operators advance by being placed in charge of larger, more powerful, or more varied equipment. Generally, engineers advance to these jobs as they obtain higher class licenses. Some stationary engineers and boiler operators advance to boiler inspectors, chief plant engineers, building and plant superintendents, or building managers. A few obtain jobs as examining engineers or technical instructors.

Job Outlook

Persons wishing to become stationary engineers and boiler operators may face competition for job openings. Employment opportunities will be best for those with apprenticeship training or vocational school courses covering systems operation using computerized controls and instrumentation.

Employment of stationary engineers and boiler operators is expected to decline through the year 2010. Continuing commercial and industrial development will increase the amount of equipment to be operated and maintained. However, automated systems and computerized controls are making newly installed equipment more efficient, thus reducing the number of jobs needed for its operation. Some job openings will arise from the need to replace experienced workers who transfer to other occupations or leave the labor force. However, turnover in this occupation is low, partly due to its high wages. Consequently, relatively few replacement openings are expected.

Earnings

Median annual earnings of stationary engineers and boiler operators were $40,420 in 2000. The middle 50 percent earned between $31,490 and $51,090 a year. The lowest 10 percent earned less than $24,470, and the highest 10 percent earned more than $61,530 a year. Median annual earnings of stationary engineers and boiler operators in 2000 were $46,600 in local government and $37,680 in hospitals.

Related Occupations

Other workers who monitor and operate stationary machinery include chemical plant and system operators; gas plant operators; petroleum pump system operators, refinery operators, and gaugers; power plant operators, distributors, and dispatchers; and water and wastewater treatment plant and system operators. Other workers who maintain the equipment and machinery in a building or plant are industrial machinery repairers and millwrights.

Sources of Additional Information

Information about apprenticeships, vocational training, and work opportunities is available from state employment service offices, locals of the International Union of Operating Engineers, vocational schools, and state and local licensing agencies.

Specific questions about this occupation should be addressed to:

● International Union of Operating Engineers, 1125 17th St. NW., Washington, DC 20036. Internet: http://www.iuoe.org

● National Association of Power Engineers, Inc., 1 Springfield St., Chicopee, MA 01013

● Building Owners and Managers Institute International, 1521 Ritchie Hwy., Arnold, MD 21012. Internet: http://www.bomi-edu.org

Stock Clerks and Order Fillers

O*NET 43-5081.01, 43-5081.02, 43-5081.03, 43-5081.04

Significant Points

● Many stock clerk and order filler jobs are entry level and do not require more than a high school diploma.

● Workers develop the necessary skills through on-the-job training lasting from several days to a few months.

● Numerous job openings will arise each year from the need to replace workers who leave this very large occupational group.

Nature of the Work

Stock clerks and order fillers receive, unpack, check, store, and track merchandise or materials. They keep records of items entering or leaving the stockroom and inspect damaged or spoiled goods. They sort, organize, and mark items with identifying codes, such as prices or stock or inventory control codes, so that inventories can be located quickly and easily. They also may be required to lift cartons of various sizes. In larger establishments, where they may be responsible for only one task, they may be called *stock-control clerk*, *merchandise distributor*, or *property custodian*. In smaller firms, they also may perform tasks usually handled by shipping and receiving clerks.

In many firms, stock clerks and order fillers use hand-held scanners connected to computers to keep inventories up to date. In retail stores, stock clerks bring merchandise to the sales floor and stock shelves and racks. In stockrooms and warehouses, stock clerks store materials in bins, on floors, or on shelves. Instead of putting the merchandise on the sales floor or on shelves, order fillers take customer orders and either hold the merchandise until the customer can pick it up or send it to them.

Working Conditions

Stock clerks and order fillers work in a wide variety of businesses, institutions, and industries. Some work in warehouses, stockrooms, or shipping and receiving rooms that may not be temperature controlled. Others may spend time in cold storage rooms or outside on loading platforms, where they are exposed to the weather.

Most jobs for stock clerks and order fillers involve frequent standing, bending, walking, and stretching. Some lifting and carrying of smaller items also may be involved. Although automation devices have lessened the physical demands of this occupation, their use remains somewhat limited. Work still can be strenuous, even though mechanical material handling equipment is employed to move heavy items.

The typical workweek is Monday through Friday; however, evening and weekend hours are common for some jobs, such as stock clerks and order fillers in retail trade, and may be required in other jobs when large shipments are involved or when inventory is taken.

Employment

Stock clerks and order fillers held about 1.7 million jobs in 2000; they were, by far, the largest material recording, scheduling, dispatching, and distributing occupation. About 76 percent work in wholesale and retail trade. The greatest numbers are found in grocery stores, followed by department stores. Jobs for stock clerks are found in all parts of the country, but most work in large urban areas that have many large suburban shopping centers, warehouses, and factories.

Training, Other Qualifications, and Advancement

Many stock clerks and order filler jobs are entry level and do not require more than a high school diploma. Employers, however, prefer to hire those who are familiar with computers and other electronic office and business equipment. Those who have taken business courses or have previous business, dispatching, or specific job-related experience may be preferred. Because communication with other people is an integral part of these jobs, good oral and written communications skills are essential. Typing, filing, recordkeeping, and other clerical skills also are important.

Stock clerks and order fillers usually learn the job by doing routine tasks under close supervision. They learn how to count and mark stock, and then start keeping records and taking inventory. Strength, stamina, good eyesight, and an ability to work at repetitive tasks, sometimes under pressure, are important characteristics. Stock clerks, whose sole responsibility is to bring merchandise to the sales floor to stock shelves and racks, need little training. Stock clerks and order fillers who handle jewelry, liquor, or drugs may be bonded.

In large firms, stock clerks can advance to invoice clerk, stock control clerk, or procurement clerk. With additional training, some stock clerks and order fillers advance to jobs as warehouse manager or purchasing agent.

Job Outlook

Employment of stock clerks and order fillers is projected to grow more slowly than the average for all occupations through 2010, due to the use of automation in factories and stores. Because this occupation is very large and many jobs are entry level, however, numerous job openings will occur each year to replace those who transfer to other jobs or leave the labor force.

The growing use of computers for inventory control and the installation of new, automated equipment are expected to slow growth in demand for stock clerks and order fillers. This is especially true in

manufacturing and wholesale trade industries whose operations are most easily automated. In addition to computerized inventory control systems, firms in these industries rely more on sophisticated conveyor belts and automatic high stackers to store and retrieve goods. Also, expanded use of battery-powered, driverless, automatically guided vehicles can be expected.

Employment of stock clerks and order fillers who work in grocery, general merchandise, department, apparel, and accessories stores is expected to be somewhat less affected by automation because much of their work is done manually and is difficult to automate. In addition, the increasing role of large retail outlets and warehouses, as well as catalogue, mail, telephone, and Internet shopping services, should bolster employment of stock clerks and order fillers in these sectors of retail trade.

Earnings

Median hourly earnings in 2000 for stock clerks and order fillers were $8.75.

Stock clerks and order fillers usually receive the same benefits as most other workers. If uniforms are required, employers usually provide either the uniforms or an allowance to purchase them.

Related Occupations

Workers who also handle, move, organize, store, and keep records of materials include shipping, receiving, and traffic clerks; production, planning, and expediting clerks; cargo and freight agents; and procurement clerks.

Sources of Additional Information

State employment service offices can provide information about job openings for stock clerks and order fillers.

General information about stock clerks and order fillers in retail trade can be obtained from:

- National Retail Federation, 325 Seventh St. NW., Suite 1000, Washington, DC 20004

Structural and Reinforcing Iron and Metal Workers

O*NET 47-2171.00, 47-2221.00

Significant Points

- Most employers recommend a 3- or 4-year apprenticeship.

- During economic downturns, workers can experience high rates of unemployment.

- The danger of injuries due to falls is great; therefore, those who work at great heights do not work during wet, icy, or extremely windy conditions.

Nature of the Work

Builders use materials made from iron, steel, aluminum, fiberglass, or precast concrete to construct highways, bridges, office and other large buildings, and power transmission towers. These structures have frames made of steel columns, beams, and girders. In addition, reinforced concrete—concrete containing steel bars or wire fabric—is an important material in buildings, bridges, and other structures, as the steel gives the concrete additional strength. Moreover, metal stairways, catwalks, floor gratings, ladders, window frames, lampposts, railings, fences, and decorative ironwork increase the functionality and attractiveness of these structures. Structural and reinforcing iron and metal workers fabricate, assemble, and install these products. They also repair, renovate, and maintain older buildings and structures, such as manufacturing plants, highways, and bridges.

Even though the primary metal involved in this work is steel, workers often are known as *ironworkers*. Before construction can begin, ironworkers must erect steel frames and assemble the cranes and derricks that move structural steel, reinforcing bars, buckets of concrete, lumber, and other materials and equipment around the construction site. The structural metal arrives at the construction site in sections. There, it is lifted into position by a crane. Ironworkers then connect the sections and set the cables to do the hoisting.

Once this job has been completed, workers begin to connect steel columns, beams, and girders according to blueprints and instructions from supervisors and superintendents. Structural steel, reinforcing rods, and ornamental iron generally come to the construction site ready for erection—cut to the proper size, with holes drilled for bolts and numbered for assembly.

Ironworkers at the construction site unload and stack the prefabricated steel so that it can be hoisted easily when needed. To hoist the steel, metal workers attach cables from a crane or derrick. One worker directs the hoist operator with hand signals. Another worker holds a rope (tag line) attached to the steel to prevent it from swinging. The crane or derrick hoists steel into place in the framework, where several workers, using spud wrenches, position the steel with connecting bars and jacks. Workers using drift pins or the handle of a spud wrench—a long wrench with a pointed handle—align the holes in the steel with the holes in the framework. Then, they temporarily bolt the piece in place; check vertical and horizontal alignment with plumb bobs, laser equipment, transits, or levels; and bolt or weld the piece permanently in place.

Reinforcing iron and rebar workers set the bars in the forms that hold concrete, following blueprints showing the location, size, and number of reinforcing bars (rebar). They then fasten the bars together by tying wire around them with pliers. When reinforcing floors, workers place blocks under the rebar to hold the bars off the deck. Although these materials usually arrive ready to use, ironworkers occasionally must cut bars with metal shears or acetylene torches, bend them by hand or machine, or weld them with arc-welding equipment. Some concrete is reinforced with welded wire fabric. Using hooked rods, workers cut and fit the fabric and, while a concrete crew places the concrete, metal workers properly position the fabric in the concrete. Post-tensioning is another technique used in reinforcing concrete; workers substitute cables for reinforcing bars. When the concrete is poured, the ends of the cables are left exposed. After the concrete dries, ironworkers tighten the cable. Post-tensioning allows designers to create larger open areas in a building because supports can be placed further apart. This technique is commonly employed in parking garages and arenas.

Ornamental ironworkers install elevator shafts, stairs, curtain walls (the nonstructural walls and window frames of many large buildings), and other ornamentation pieces after the structure of the building has been completed. As they hoist pieces into position, ornamental ironworkers check that the pieces are properly fitted and aligned before bolting, brazing, or welding them for a secure fit.

Working Conditions

Structural and reinforcing iron and metal workers usually work outside in all kinds of weather. However, those who work at great heights do not work during wet, icy, or extremely windy conditions. Because the danger of injuries due to falls is great, ironworkers use safety devices such as safety belts, scaffolding, and nets to reduce risk.

Some ironworkers fabricate structural metal in fabricating shops, which usually are located away from the construction site.

Employment

Structural and reinforcing iron and metal workers held about 111,000 jobs in 2000. About half worked for structural steel erection contractors. Most of the remainder worked for contractors specializing in the construction of homes; factories; commercial buildings; churches; schools; bridges and tunnels; and water, sewer, communications, and power lines.

Structural and reinforcing iron and metal workers are employed in all parts of the country, but most work in metropolitan areas, where most commercial and industrial construction takes place.

Training, Other Qualifications, and Advancement

Most employers recommend a 3- or 4-year apprenticeship, consisting of on-the-job training and evening classroom instruction, as the best way to learn this trade. Apprenticeship programs usually are administered by committees made up of representatives of local unions of the International Association of Bridge, Structural, Ornamental and Reinforcing Iron Workers or the local chapters of contractors' associations.

Ironworkers must be at least 18 years old. A high school diploma may be preferred by employers and may be required by some local apprenticeship committees. High school courses in general mathematics, mechanical drawing, and shop are helpful. Because materials used in iron working are heavy and bulky, metal workers must be in good physical condition. They also need good agility, balance, eyesight, and depth perception to safely work at great heights on narrow beams and girders. Ironworkers should not be afraid of heights or suffer from dizziness.

In the classroom, apprentices study blueprint reading; mathematics for layout work; the basics of structural erecting, rigging, reinforcing, welding, and burning; ornamental erection; and assembling. Apprentices also study the care and safe use of tools and materials. On the job, apprentices work in all aspects of the trade, such as unloading and storing materials at the job site, rigging materials for movement by crane or derrick, connecting structural steel, and welding.

Some ironworkers learn the trade informally on the job without completing an apprenticeship. These workers generally do not receive classroom training, although some large contractors have extensive training programs. On-the-job trainees usually begin by assisting experienced ironworkers by doing simple jobs, such as carrying various materials.

With experience, trainees perform more difficult tasks like cutting and fitting different parts; however, learning through work experience alone may not provide training as complete as an apprenticeship program and usually takes longer.

Some experienced workers are promoted to supervisor. Others may go into the contracting business for themselves.

Job Outlook

Employment of structural and reinforcing iron and metal workers is expected to rise about as fast as the average for all occupations through the year 2010, largely based on the continued growth in industrial and commercial construction. The rehabilitation, maintenance, and replacement of a growing number of older buildings, factories, power plants, and highways and bridges is expected to create employment opportunities. While some new jobs will arise, most openings will result from the need to replace experienced ironworkers who transfer to other occupations or leave the labor force.

The number of job openings fluctuates from year to year as economic conditions and the level of construction activity change. During economic downturns, ironworkers can experience high rates of unemployment. Similarly, job opportunities for ironworkers may vary widely by geographic area. Job openings for ironworkers usually are more abundant during the spring and summer months, when the level of construction activity increases.

Earnings

In 2000, median hourly earnings of structural iron and steel workers in all industries were $17.92. The middle 50 percent earned between $13.34 and $24.16. The lowest 10 percent earned less than $10.05, and the highest 10 percent earned more than $29.62. In 2000, median hourly earnings of reinforcing iron and rebar workers in all industries were $16.78. The middle 50 percent earned between $12.57 and $23.64. The lowest 10 percent earned less than $9.90, and the highest 10 percent earned more than $27.86. Median hourly earnings in the industries employing the largest number of structural iron and steel workers in 2000 were:

Miscellaneous special trade contractors	$19.59
Heavy construction, except highway	17.55
Nonresidential building construction	15.86
Fabricated structural metal products	13.71

Many workers in this trade are members of the International Association of Bridge, Structural, Ornamental, and Reinforcing Iron Workers. According to the union, average hourly earnings, including benefits, for structural and reinforcing metal workers who belonged to a union and worked full time ranged between $18 and $50 in 2000. Structural and reinforcing iron and metal workers in New York, Boston, San Francisco, Chicago, Los Angeles, Philadelphia, and other large cities received the highest wages.

Apprentices generally start at about 50 to 60 percent of the rate paid to experienced journey workers. They receive periodic increases throughout the course of the apprenticeship program, as they acquire the skills of the trade, until their pay approaches that of experienced workers.

Earnings for ironworkers may be reduced on occasion because work can be limited by bad weather, the short-term nature of construction jobs, and economic downturns.

Related Occupations

Structural and reinforcing iron and metal workers play an essential role in erecting buildings, bridges, highways, powerlines, and other structures. Others who also work on these construction jobs include assemblers and fabricators; boilermakers; civil engineers; cement masons, concrete finishers, segmental pavers, and terrazzo workers; construction managers; and welding, soldering, and brazing workers.

Sources of Additional Information

For more information on apprenticeships or other work opportunities, contact local general contractors; a local of the International Association of Bridge, Structural, Ornamental, and Reinforcing Iron Workers Union; a local ironworkers' joint union-management apprenticeship committee; a local or state chapter of the Associated Builders and Contractors; or the nearest office of your state employment service or apprenticeship agency.

For apprenticeship information, contact:

- International Association of Bridge, Structural, Ornamental, and Reinforcing Iron Workers, Apprenticeship Department, 1750 New York Ave. NW., Suite 400, Washington, DC 20006

For general information about ironworkers, contact:

- The Associated General Contractors of America, 333 John Carlyle St., Suite 200, Alexandria, VA 22314

Surgical Technologists

O*NET 29-2055.00

Significant Points

- Most educational programs for surgical technologists last approximately 1 year and result in a certificate.

- Employment of surgical technologists is expected to grow faster than average as the number of surgical procedures grows.

Nature of the Work

Surgical technologists, also called *scrubs* and *surgical or operating room technicians*, assist in surgical operations under the supervision of surgeons, registered nurses, or other surgical personnel. Surgical technologists are members of operating room teams, which most commonly include surgeons, anesthesiologists, and circulating nurses. Before an operation, surgical technologists help prepare the operating room by setting up surgical instruments and equipment, sterile drapes, and sterile solutions. They assemble both sterile and nonsterile equipment, as well as adjust and check it to ensure it is working properly. Technologists also get patients ready for surgery by washing, shaving, and disinfecting incision sites. They transport patients to the operating room, help position them on the operating table, and cover them with sterile surgical "drapes." Technologists also observe patients' vital signs, check charts, and assist the surgical team with putting on sterile gowns and gloves.

During surgery, technologists pass instruments and other sterile supplies to surgeons and surgeon assistants. They may hold retractors, cut sutures, and help count sponges, needles, supplies, and instruments. Surgical technologists help prepare, care for, and dispose of specimens taken for laboratory analysis and help apply dressings. Some operate sterilizers, lights, or suction machines, and help operate diagnostic equipment.

After an operation, surgical technologists may help transfer patients to the recovery room and clean and restock the operating room.

Working Conditions

Surgical technologists work in clean, well-lighted, cool environments. They must stand for long periods and remain alert during operations. At times they may be exposed to communicable diseases and unpleasant sights, odors, and materials.

Most surgical technologists work a regular 40-hour week, although they may be on call or work nights, weekends and holidays on a rotating basis.

Employment

Surgical technologists held about 71,000 jobs in 2000. Almost three-quarters are employed by hospitals, mainly in operating and delivery rooms. Others are employed in clinics and surgical centers, and in the offices of physicians and dentists who perform outpatient surgery. A few, known as private scrubs, are employed directly by surgeons who have special surgical teams, like those for liver transplants.

Training, Other Qualifications, and Advancement

Surgical technologists receive their training in formal programs offered by community and junior colleges, vocational schools, universities, hospitals, and the military. In 2001, the Commission on Accreditation of Allied Health Education Programs (CAAHEP) recognized 350 accredited programs. High school graduation normally is required for admission. Programs last 9 to 24 months and lead to a certificate, diploma, or associate degree.

Programs provide classroom education and supervised clinical experience. Students take courses in anatomy, physiology, microbiology, pharmacology, professional ethics, and medical terminology. Other studies cover the care and safety of patients during surgery, aseptic techniques, and surgical procedures. Students also learn to sterilize instruments; prevent and control infection; and handle special drugs, solutions, supplies, and equipment.

Technologists may obtain voluntary professional certification from the Liaison Council on Certification for the Surgical Technologist by graduating from a CAAHEP-accredited program and passing a national certification examination. They may then use the designation Certified Surgical Technologist, or CST. Continuing education or reexamination is required to maintain certification, which must be renewed every 6

years. Certification may also be obtained from the National Center for Competency Testing. To qualify to take the exam, candidates follow one of three paths: complete an accredited training program, undergo a 2-year hospital on-the-job training program, or acquire seven years experience working in the field. After passing the exam, individuals may use the designation National Certified Technician O.R. This certification may be renewed every 5 years through either continuing education or reexamination. Most employers prefer to hire certified technologists.

Surgical technologists need manual dexterity to handle instruments quickly. They also must be conscientious, orderly, and emotionally stable to handle the demands of the operating room environment. Technologists must respond quickly and know procedures well to have instruments ready for surgeons without having to be told. They are expected to keep abreast of new developments in the field. Recommended high school courses include health, biology, chemistry, and mathematics.

Technologists advance by specializing in a particular area of surgery, such as neurosurgery or open heart surgery. They also may work as circulating technologists. A circulating technologist is the "unsterile" member of the surgical team who prepares patients; helps with anesthesia; obtains and opens packages for the "sterile" persons to remove the sterile contents during the procedure; interviews the patient before surgery; keeps a written account of the surgical procedure; and answers the surgeon's questions about the patient during the surgery. With additional training, some technologists advance to first assistants, who help with retracting, sponging, suturing, cauterizing bleeders, and closing and treating wounds. Some surgical technologists manage central supply departments in hospitals, or take positions with insurance companies, sterile supply services, and operating equipment firms.

Job Outlook

Employment of surgical technologists is expected to grow faster than the average for all occupations through the year 2010 as the volume of surgery increases. The number of surgical procedures is expected to rise as the population grows and ages. As the "baby boom" generation enters retirement age, the over 50 population will account for a larger portion of the general population. Older people require more surgical procedures. Technological advances, such as fiber optics and laser technology, will also permit new surgical procedures to be performed.

Hospitals will continue to be the primary employer of surgical technologists, although much faster employment growth is expected in offices and clinics of physicians, including ambulatory surgical centers.

Earnings

Median annual earnings of surgical technologists were $29,020 in 2000. The middle 50 percent earned between $24,490 and $34,160. The lowest 10 percent earned less than $20,490, and the highest 10 percent earned more than $40,310. Median annual earnings of surgical technologists in 2000 were $31,190 in offices and clinics of medical doctors and $28,340 in hospitals.

Related Occupations

Other health occupations requiring approximately 1 year of training after high school include dental assistants, licensed practical and licensed vocational nurses, medical and clinical laboratory technicians, medical assistants, and respiratory therapy technicians.

Sources of Additional Information

For additional information on a career as a surgical technologist and a list of CAAHEP-accredited programs, contact:

- Association of Surgical Technologists, 7108-C South Alton Way, Englewood, CO 80112. Internet: http://www.ast.org

For information on becoming a Certified Surgical Technologist, contact:

- Liaison Council on Certification for the Surgical Technologist, 7790 East Arapahoe Rd., Suite 240, Englewood, CO 80112-1274. Internet: http://www.lcc-st.org/index_ie.htm

For information on becoming a National Certified Technician O.R., contact:

- National Center for Competency Testing, 7007 College Blvd., Suite 250, Overland Park, KS 66211. Internet: http://www.ncctinc.com

Surveyors, Cartographers, Photogrammetrists, and Surveying Technicians

O*NET 17-1021.00, 17-1022.00, 17-3031.01, 17-3031.02

Significant Points

- Four out of five are employed in engineering services and in government.

- Computer skills enhance employment opportunities.

Nature of the Work

Measuring and mapping the earth's surface are the responsibilities of several different types of workers. Traditional *land surveyors* establish official land, air space, and water boundaries. They write descriptions of land for deeds, leases, and other legal documents; define air space for airports; and measure construction and mineral sites. Other surveyors provide data relevant to the shape, contour, location, elevation, or dimension of land or land features. *Cartographers* compile geographic, political, and cultural information and prepare maps of large areas. *Photogrammetrists* measure and analyze aerial photographs to prepare detailed maps and drawings. *Surveying technicians* assist land surveyors by operating survey instruments and collecting information in the field, and by performing computations and computer-aided drafting in offices. *Mapping technicians* calculate mapmaking information from field notes. They also draw topographical maps and verify their accuracy.

Land surveyors manage survey parties who measure distances, directions, and angles between points and elevations of points, lines, and contours on, above, and below the earth's surface. They plan the fieldwork, select known survey reference points, and determine the precise location of important features in the survey area. Surveyors research legal records, look for evidence of previous boundaries, and analyze the

data to determine the location of boundary lines. They also record the results of the survey, verify the accuracy of data, and prepare plots, maps, and reports. Surveyors who establish boundaries must be licensed by the state in which they work; they are known as professional land surveyors. Professional land surveyors are sometimes called to provide expert testimony in court cases concerning surveying matters.

A survey party gathers the information needed by the land surveyor. A typical survey party consists of a party chief and one or more surveying technicians and helpers. The party chief, who may be either a land surveyor or a senior surveying technician, leads day-to-day work activities. Surveying technicians assist the party chief by adjusting and operating surveying instruments, such as the theodolite (used to measure horizontal and vertical angles) and electronic distance-measuring equipment. Surveying technicians or assistants position and hold the vertical rods, or targets, that the theodolite operator sights on to measure angles, distances, or elevations. They also may hold measuring tapes, if electronic distance-measuring equipment is not used. Surveying technicians compile notes, make sketches, and enter the data obtained from surveying instruments into computers. Survey parties may include laborers or helpers who perform less-skilled duties, such as clearing brush from sight lines, driving stakes, or carrying equipment.

New technology is changing the nature of the work of surveyors and surveying technicians. For larger projects, surveyors are increasingly using the Global Positioning System (GPS), a satellite system that precisely locates points on the earth by using radio signals transmitted via satellites. To use this system, a surveyor places a satellite signal receiver—a small instrument mounted on a tripod—on a desired point. The receiver simultaneously collects information from several satellites to establish a precise position. The receiver also can be placed in a vehicle for tracing out road systems. Because receivers now come in different sizes and shapes and the cost of the receivers has fallen, much more surveying work is being done using GPS. Surveyors then must interpret and check the results produced by the new technology.

Cartographers measure, map, and chart the earth's surface, which involves everything from geographical research and data compilation to actual map production. They collect, analyze, and interpret both spatial data—such as latitude, longitude, elevation, and distance—and nonspatial data—such as population density, land use patterns, annual precipitation levels, and demographic characteristics. Cartographers prepare maps in either digital or graphic form, using information provided by geodetic surveys, aerial photographs, and satellite data. *Photogrammetrists* prepare detailed maps and drawings from aerial photographs, usually of areas that are inaccessible, difficult, or less cost-efficient to survey by other methods. *Map editors* develop and verify map contents from aerial photographs and other reference sources. Some states require photogrammetrists to be licensed as professional land surveyors.

Some surveyors perform specialized functions that are closer to those of a cartographer than to those of a traditional surveyor. For example, *geodetic surveyors* use high-accuracy techniques, including satellite observations (remote sensing), to measure large areas of the earth's surface. *Geophysical prospecting surveyors* mark sites for subsurface exploration, usually petroleum related. *Marine or hydrographic surveyors* survey harbors, rivers, and other bodies of water to determine shorelines, topography of the bottom, water depth, and other features.

The work of surveyors and cartographers is changing because of advancements in technology. These advancements include not only the GPS, but also new earth resources data satellites, improved aerial photography, and geographic information systems (GIS)—which are computerized data banks of spatial data. From the older specialties of photogrammetrist and cartographer, a new type of mapping scientist is emerging. The *geographic information specialist* combines the functions of mapping science and surveying into a broader field concerned with the collection and analysis of geographic information.

Working Conditions

Surveyors usually work an 8-hour day, 5 days a week, and may spend a lot of time outdoors. Sometimes they work longer hours during the summer, when weather and light conditions are most suitable for fieldwork. Seasonal demands for longer hours are related to demand for specific surveying services. Home purchases are traditionally related to the start and end of the school year. Construction is related to the materials to be used (concrete and asphalt are restricted by outside temperatures, unlike wood framing). Aerial photography is most effective when the leaves are off the trees.

Land surveyors and technicians engage in active, and sometimes strenuous, work. They often stand for long periods, walk considerable distances, and climb hills with heavy packs of instruments and other equipment. They can also be exposed to all types of weather. Traveling often is part of the job; they may commute long distances, stay overnight, or temporarily relocate near a survey site.

While surveyors can spend considerable time indoors planning surveys, analyzing data, and preparing reports and maps, cartographers spend virtually all of their time in offices and seldom visit the sites they are mapping.

Employment

Surveyors, cartographers, photogrammetrists, and surveying technicians held about 121,000 jobs in 2000. Engineering and architectural services firms employed about 63 percent of these workers. Federal, state, and local governmental agencies employed an additional 16 percent. Major federal government employers are the U.S. Geological Survey (USGS), the Bureau of Land Management (BLM), the Army Corps of Engineers, the Forest Service (USFS), the National Oceanic and Atmospheric Administration (NOAA), the National Imagery and Mapping Agency (NIMA), and the Federal Emergency Management Agency (FEMA). Most surveyors in state and local government work for highway departments and urban planning and redevelopment agencies. Construction firms, mining and oil and gas extraction companies, and public utilities also employ surveyors, cartographers, photogrammetrists, and surveying technicians. About 5,000 were self-employed in 2000.

Training, Other Qualifications, and Advancement

Most people prepare for a career as a licensed surveyor by combining postsecondary school courses in surveying with extensive on-the-job training. However, as technology advances, a 4-year college degree is becoming more of a prerequisite. About 25 universities now offer 4-year programs leading to a BS degree in surveying. Junior and community colleges, technical institutes, and vocational schools offer 1-, 2-, and 3-year programs in both surveying and surveying technology.

All 50 states and all U.S. territories (Puerto Rico, Guam, Marianna Islands, and Virgin Islands) license land surveyors. For licensure, most

state licensing boards require that individuals pass a written examination given by the National Council of Examiners for Engineering and Surveying. Most states also require that surveyors pass a written examination prepared by the state licensing board. In addition, they must meet varying standards of formal education and work experience in the field. In the past, many individuals started as members of survey crews and worked their way up to become licensed surveyors with little formal training in surveying. However, because of advancing technology and rising licensing standards, formal education requirements are increasing. At present, most states require some formal post-high school coursework and 10 to 12 years of surveying experience to gain licensure. However, requirements vary among states. Generally, the quickest route to licensure is a combination of 4 years of college, 2 to 4 years of experience (a few states do not require any), and passing the licensing examinations. An increasing number of states require a bachelor's degree in surveying or in a closely related field, such as civil engineering or forestry (with courses in surveying), regardless of the number of years of experience.

High school students interested in surveying should take courses in algebra, geometry, trigonometry, drafting, mechanical drawing, and computer science. High school graduates with no formal training in surveying usually start as apprentices. Beginners with postsecondary school training in surveying usually can start as technicians or assistants. With on-the-job experience and formal training in surveying—either in an institutional program or from a correspondence school—workers may advance to senior survey technician, then to party chief, and in some cases, to licensed surveyor (depending on state licensing requirements).

The National Society of Professional Surveyors, a member organization of the American Congress on Surveying and Mapping, has a voluntary certification program for surveying technicians. Technicians are certified at four levels requiring progressive amounts of experience, in addition to the passing of written examinations. Although not required for state licensure, many employers require certification for promotion to positions with greater responsibilities.

Surveyors should have the ability to visualize objects, distances, sizes, and abstract forms. They must work with precision and accuracy because mistakes can be costly. Members of a survey party must be in good physical condition because they work outdoors and often carry equipment over difficult terrain. They need good eyesight, coordination, and hearing to communicate verbally and manually (using hand signals). Surveying is a cooperative process, so good interpersonal skills and the ability to work as part of a team are important. Good office skills are also essential. Surveyors must be able to research old deeds and other legal documents and prepare reports that document their work.

Cartographers and photogrammetrists usually have a bachelor's degree in a field such as engineering, forestry, geography, or a physical science. Although it is possible to enter these positions through previous experience as a photogrammetric or cartographic technician, most cartographic and photogrammetric technicians now have had some specialized postsecondary school training. With the development of GIS, cartographers and photogrammetrists need additional education and stronger technical skills—including more experience with computers—than in the past.

The American Society for Photogrammetry and Remote Sensing has a voluntary certification program for photogrammetrists. To qualify for this professional distinction, individuals must meet work experience standards and pass an oral or written examination.

Job Outlook

Overall employment of surveyors, cartographers, photogrammetrists, and surveying technicians is expected to grow about as fast as the average for all occupations through the year 2010. The widespread availability and use of advanced technologies, such as GPS, GIS, and remote sensing, are increasing both the accuracy and productivity of survey, photogrammetric, and mapping work. However, job openings will continue to result from the need to replace workers who transfer to other occupations or leave the labor force altogether.

Prospects will be best for surveying and mapping technicians, whose numbers are expected to grow slightly faster than the average for all occupations through 2010. The short training period needed to learn to operate the equipment, the current lack of any formal testing or licensing, and the relatively lower wages all make for a healthy demand for these technicians, as well as for a readily available supply.

As technologies become more complex, opportunities will be best for surveyors, cartographers, and photogrammetrists who have at least a bachelor's degree and strong technical skills. Increasing demand for geographic data, as opposed to traditional surveying services, will mean better opportunities for cartographers and photogrammetrists involved in the development and use of geographic and land information systems. New technologies, such as GPS and GIS, also may enhance employment opportunities for surveyors and surveying technicians who have the educational background enabling them to use these systems, but upgraded licensing requirements will continue to limit opportunities for professional advancement for those with less education.

Opportunities for surveyors, cartographers, and photogrammetrists should remain concentrated in engineering, architectural, and surveying services firms. However, nontraditional areas such as urban planning and natural resource exploration and mapping also should provide areas of employment growth, particularly with regard to producing maps for management of natural emergencies and updating maps with the newly available technology. Continued growth in construction through 2010 should require surveyors to lay out streets, shopping centers, housing developments, factories, office buildings, and recreation areas, while setting aside flood plains, wetlands, wildlife habitats and environmentally sensitive areas for protection. However, employment may fluctuate from year to year along with construction activity, or mapping needs for land and resource management.

Earnings

Median annual earnings of surveyors were $36,700 in 2000. The middle 50 percent earned between $26,480 and $49,030. The lowest 10 percent earned less than $19,570, and the highest 10 percent earned more than $62,980.

Median annual earnings of cartographers and photogrammetrists were $39,410 in 2000. The middle 50 percent earned between $29,200 and $51,930. The lowest 10 percent earned less than $23,560 and the highest 10 percent earned more than $64,780.

Median hourly earnings of surveying and mapping technicians were $13.48 in 2000. The middle 50 percent of all surveying technicians earned between $10.46 and $17.81 in 2000. The lowest 10 percent earned less than $8.45, and the highest 10 percent earned more than $22.40. Median hourly earnings of surveying and mapping technicians employed in engineering and architectural services were $12.39 in 2000, while those employed by local governments had median hourly earnings of $15.77.

In 2001, land surveyors in nonsupervisory, supervisory, and managerial positions in the federal government earned an average salary of $57,416; cartographers, $62,369; geodetic technicians, $53,143; surveying technicians, $34,623; and cartographic technicians, $40,775.

Related Occupations

Surveying is related to the work of civil engineers, architects, and landscape architects, because an accurate survey is the first step in land development and construction projects. Cartography and geodetic surveying are related to the work of environmental scientists and geoscientists, who study the earth's internal composition, surface, and atmosphere. Cartography also is related to the work of geographers and urban and regional planners, who study and decide how the earth's surface is to be used.

Sources of Additional Information

Information about career opportunities, licensure requirements, and the surveying technician certification program is available from:

- National Society of Professional Surveyors, Suite #403, 6 Montgomery Village Ave., Gaithersburg, MD 20879. Internet: http://www.acsm.net/nsps/index.html

Information on a career as a geodetic surveyor is available from:

- American Association of Geodetic Surveying (AAGS), Suite #403, 6 Montgomery Village Ave., Gaithersburg, MD 20879. Internet: http://www.acsm.net

General information on careers in photogrammetry and remote sensing is available from:

- ASPRS: The Imaging and Geospatial Information Society, 5410 Grosvenor Lane, Suite 210, Bethesda, MD 20814-2160. Internet: http://www.asprs.org

Systems Analysts, Computer Scientists, and Database Administrators

O*NET 15-1011.00, 15-1051.00, 15-1061.00, 15-1081.00

Significant Points

- As computer applications expand, systems analysts, computer scientists, and database administrators are projected to be the among the fastest growing occupations.

- Relevant work experience and a bachelor's degree are prerequisites for many jobs; for more complex jobs, a graduate degree is preferred.

Nature of the Work

The rapid spread of computers and information technology has generated a need for highly trained workers to design and develop new hardware and software systems and to incorporate new technologies. These workers—computer systems analysts, computer scientists, and database administrators—include a wide range of computer specialists. Job tasks and occupational titles used to describe these workers evolve rapidly, reflecting new areas of specialization or changes in technology, as well as the preferences and practices of employers.

Systems analysts solve computer problems and enable computer technology to meet individual needs of an organization. They help an organization realize the maximum benefit from its investment in equipment, personnel, and business processes. This process may include planning and developing new computer systems or devising ways to apply existing systems' resources to additional operations. Systems analysts may design new systems, including both hardware and software, or add a new software application to harness more of the computer's power. Most systems analysts work with a specific type of system that varies with the type of organization they work for—for example, business, accounting, or financial systems, or scientific and engineering systems. Some systems analysts also are referred to as *systems developers* or *systems architects*.

Analysts begin an assignment by discussing the systems problem with managers and users to determine its exact nature. They define the goals of the system and divide the solutions into individual steps and separate procedures. Analysts use techniques such as structured analysis, data modeling, information engineering, mathematical model building, sampling, and cost accounting to plan the system. They specify the inputs to be accessed by the system, design the processing steps, and format the output to meet the users' needs. They also may prepare cost-benefit and return-on-investment analyses to help management decide whether implementing the proposed system will be financially feasible.

When a system is accepted, analysts determine what computer hardware and software will be needed to set it up. They coordinate tests and observe initial use of the system to ensure it performs as planned. They prepare specifications, work diagrams, and structure charts for computer programmers to follow and then work with them to "debug," or eliminate errors from, the system. Analysts, who do more in-depth testing of products, may be referred to as *software quality assurance analysts*. In addition to running tests, these individuals diagnose problems, recommend solutions, and determine if program requirements have been met.

In some organizations, *programmer-analysts* design and update the software that runs a computer. Because they are responsible for both programming and systems analysis, these workers must be proficient in both areas. As this becomes more commonplace, these analysts increasingly work with object-oriented programming languages, as well as client/server applications development, and multimedia and Internet technology.

One obstacle associated with expanding computer use is the need for different computer systems to communicate with each other. Because of the importance of maintaining up-to-date information—accounting records, sales figures, or budget projections, for example—systems analysts work on making the computer systems within an organization compatible so that information can be shared. Many systems analysts are involved with "networking," connecting all the computers internally—in an individual office, department, or establishment—or externally, because many organizations now rely on e-mail or the Internet. A primary goal of networking is to allow users to retrieve data and information from a mainframe computer or a server and use it on their machine. Analysts must design the hardware and software to allow free exchange of data, custom applications, and the computer power to process it all.

Networks come in many variations and *network systems and data communications analysts* analyze, design, test, and evaluate systems such as local area networks (LAN), wide area networks (WAN), Internet, Intranets, and other data communications systems. These analysts perform network modeling, analysis and planning; they also may research related products and make necessary hardware and software recommendations. *Telecommunications specialists* focus on the interaction between computer and communications equipment.

The growth of the Internet and expansion of the World Wide Web, the graphical portion of the Internet, have generated a variety of occupations related to design, development, and maintenance of Web sites and their servers. For example, *webmasters* are responsible for all technical aspects of a Web site, including performance issues such as speed of access, and for approving site content. *Internet developers* or *web developers*, also called *Web designers*, are responsible for day-to-day site design and creation.

Computer scientists work as theorists, researchers, or inventors. Their jobs are distinguished by the higher level of theoretical expertise and innovation they apply to complex problems and the creation or application of new technology. Those employed by academic institutions work in areas ranging from complexity theory, to hardware, to programming language design. Some work on multidisciplinary projects, such as developing and advancing uses of virtual reality, in human-computer interaction, or in robotics. Their counterparts in private industry work in areas such as applying theory, developing specialized languages or information technologies, or designing programming tools, knowledge-based systems, or even computer games.

With the Internet and electronic business creating tremendous volumes of data, there is growing need to be able to store, manage, and extract data effectively. *Database administrators* work with database management systems software and determine ways to organize and store data. They determine user requirements, set up computer databases, and test and coordinate changes. It is the responsibility of an organization's database administrator to ensure performance, understand the platform the database runs on, and add new users. Because they also may design and implement system security, database administrators often plan and coordinate security measures. With the volume of sensitive data generated every second growing rapidly, data integrity, backup, and keeping databases secure have become an increasingly important aspect of the job for database administrators.

Working Conditions

Systems analysts, computer scientists, and database administrators normally work in offices or laboratories in comfortable surroundings. They usually work about 40 hours a week—the same as many other professional or office workers. However, evening or weekend work may be necessary to meet deadlines or solve specific problems. Given the technology available today, telecommuting is common for computer professionals. As networks expand, more work can be done from remote locations using modems, laptops, electronic mail, and the Internet.

Like other workers who spend long periods in front of a computer terminal typing on a keyboard, they are susceptible to eye strain, back discomfort, and hand and wrist problems such as carpal tunnel syndrome or cumulative trauma disorder.

Employment

Systems analysts, computer scientists, and database administrators held about 887,000 jobs in 2000, including about 71,000 who were self-employed. Employment was distributed among the following detailed occupations:

Computer system analysts 431,000
Network systems and data communications analysts 119,000
Database administrators 106,000
Computer and information scientists, research 28,000
All other computer specialists 203,000

Although they are increasingly employed in every sector of the economy, the greatest concentration of these workers is in the computer and data processing services industry. Firms in this industry provide nearly every service related to commercial computer use on a contract basis. Services include systems integration, networking, and reengineering; data processing and preparation; information retrieval, including on-line databases and Internet; onsite computer facilities management; development and management of databases; and a variety of specialized consulting. Many systems analysts, computer scientists, and database administrators work for other employers, such as government, manufacturers of computer and related electronic equipment, insurance companies, financial institutions, and universities.

A growing number of computer specialists, such as systems analysts and network and data communications analysts, are employed on a temporary or contract basis—many of whom are self-employed, working independently as contractors or self-employed consultants. For example, a company installing a new computer system may need the services of several systems analysts just to get the system running. Because not all of them would be needed once the system is functioning, the company might contract with systems analysts or a temporary help agency or consulting firm. Such jobs may last from several months up to 2 years or more. This growing practice enables companies to bring in people with the exact skills they need to complete a particular project, rather than having to spend time or money training or retraining existing workers. Often, experienced consultants then train a company's in-house staff as a project develops.

Training, Other Qualifications, and Advancement

Rapidly changing technology means an increasing level of skill and education demanded by employers. Companies are looking for professionals with a broader background and range of skills, including not only technical knowledge, but also communication and other interpersonal skills. This shift from requiring workers to possess solely sound technical knowledge emphasizes workers who can handle various responsibilities. While there is no universally accepted way to prepare for a job as a systems analyst, computer scientist, or database administrator, most employers place a premium on some formal college education. A bachelor's degree is a prerequisite for many jobs; however, some jobs may require only a 2-year degree. Relevant work experience also is very

important. For more technically complex jobs, persons with graduate degrees are preferred.

For systems analyst, programmer-analyst, as well as database administrator positions, many employers seek applicants who have a bachelor's degree in computer science, information science, or management information systems (MIS). MIS programs usually are part of the business school or college. These programs differ considerably from computer science programs, emphasizing business and management-oriented coursework and business computing courses. Many employers increasingly seek individuals with a master's degree in business administration (MBA) with a concentration in information systems, as more firms move their business to the Internet. For some networks systems and data communication analysts, such as webmasters, an associate degree or certificate generally is sufficient, although ore advanced positions might require a computer-related bachelor's degree. For computer and information scientists, a doctoral degree generally is required due to the highly technical nature of their work.

Despite the preference towards technical degrees, persons with degrees in a variety of majors find employment in these computer occupations. The level of education and type of training employers require depend on their needs. One factor affecting these needs is changes in technology. As demonstrated by the current demand for workers with skills related to the Internet, employers often scramble to find workers capable of implementing "hot" new technologies. Another factor driving employers' needs is the time frame in which a project must be completed.

Most community colleges and many independent technical institutes and proprietary schools offer an associate degree in computer science or a related information technology field. Many of these programs may be more geared toward meeting the needs of local businesses and are more occupation-specific than those designed for a 4-year degree. Some jobs may be better suited to the level of training these programs offer. Employers usually look for people who have broad knowledge and experience related to computer systems and technologies, strong problem-solving and analytical skills, and good interpersonal skills. Courses in computer science or systems design offer good preparation for a job in these computer occupations. For jobs in a business environment, employers usually want systems analysts to have business management or closely related skills, while a background in the physical sciences, applied mathematics, or engineering is preferred for work in scientifically oriented organizations. Art or graphic design skills may be desirable for webmasters or Web developers.

Job seekers can enhance their employment opportunities by participating in internship or co-op programs offered through their schools. Because many people develop advanced computer skills in one occupation and then transfer those skills into a computer occupation, a related background in the industry in which the job is located, such as financial services, banking, or accounting, can be important. Others have taken computer science courses to supplement their study in fields such as accounting, inventory control, or other business areas. For example, a financial analyst proficient in computers might become a systems analyst or computer support specialist in financial systems development, while a computer programmer might move into a systems analyst job.

Systems analysts, computer scientists, and database administrators must be able to think logically and have good communication skills. They often deal with a number of tasks simultaneously; the ability to concentrate and pay close attention to detail is important. Although these computer specialists sometimes work independently, they often work in teams on large projects. They must be able to communicate effectively with computer personnel, such as programmers and managers, as well as with users or other staff who may have no technical computer background.

Computer scientists employed in private industry may advance into managerial or project leadership positions. Those employed in academic institutions can become heads of research departments or published authorities in their field. Systems analysts may be promoted to senior or lead systems analyst. Those who show leadership ability also can become project managers or advance into management positions such as manager of information systems or chief information officer. Database administrators also may advance into managerial positions such as chief technology officer, based on their experience managing data and enforcing security. Computer specialists with work experience and considerable expertise in a particular subject area or application may find lucrative opportunities as independent consultants or choose to start their own computer consulting firms.

Technological advances come so rapidly in the computer field that continuous study is necessary to keep skills up to date. Employers, hardware and software vendors, colleges and universities, and private training institutions offer continuing education. Additional training may come from professional development seminars offered by professional computing societies.

Technical or professional certification is a way to demonstrate a level of competency or quality in a particular field. Product vendors or software firms also offer certification and may require professionals who work with their products to be certified. Many employers regard these certifications as the industry standard. For example, one method of acquiring enough knowledge to get a job as a database administrator is to become certified in a specific type of database management. Voluntary certification also is available through other organizations. Professional certification may provide a job seeker a competitive advantage.

Job Outlook

Systems analysts, computers scientists, and database administrators are expected to be the among the fastest growing occupations through 2010. Employment of these computer specialists is expected to increase much faster than the average for all occupations as organizations continue to adopt and integrate increasingly sophisticated technologies. Growth will be driven by very rapid growth in computer and data processing services, which is projected to be the fastest growing industry in the U.S. economy. In addition, many job openings will arise annually from the need to replace workers who move into managerial positions or other occupations or who leave the labor force.

The demand for networking to facilitate the sharing of information, the expansion of client/server environments, and the need for computer specialists to use their knowledge and skills in a problem-solving capacity will be major factors in the rising demand for systems analysts, computer scientists, and database administrators. Moreover, falling prices of computer hardware and software should continue to induce more businesses to expand computerized operations and integrate new technologies. In order to maintain a competitive edge and operate more efficiently, firms will continue to demand computer specialists who are knowledgeable about the latest technologies and are able to apply them to meet the needs of businesses.

Increasingly, more sophisticated and complex technology is being implemented across all organizations, which should fuel the demand for these computer occupations. There is a growing demand for system analysts to allow firms to be maximize their efficiency by using available technology. The explosive growth in electronic commerce—doing business on the Internet—and the continuing need to build and maintain databases that store critical information on customers, inventory, and projects is fueling demand for database administrators familiar with the latest technology.

The development of new technologies usually leads to demand for various workers. The expanding integration of Internet technologies by businesses, for example, has resulted in a growing need for specialists who can develop and support Internet and intranet applications. The growth of electronic commerce means more establishments use the Internet to conduct their business online. This translates into a need for information technology professionals who can help organizations use technology to communicate with employees, clients, and consumers. Explosive growth in these areas also is expected to fuel demand for specialists knowledgeable about network, data, and communications security.

As technology becomes more sophisticated and complex, employers demand a higher level of skill and expertise. Individuals with an advanced degree in computer science, computer engineering, or an MBA with a concentration in information systems should enjoy very favorable employment prospects. College graduates with a bachelor's degree in computer science, computer engineering, information science, or management information systems also should enjoy favorable prospects for employment, particularly if they have supplemented their formal education with practical experience. Because employers continue to seek computer specialists who can combine strong technical skills with good interpersonal and business skills, graduates with non-computer science degrees but who have had courses in computer programming, systems analysis, and other information technology areas, also should continue to find jobs in these computer fields. In fact, individuals with the right experience and training can work in these computer occupations regardless of their college major or level of formal education.

Earnings

Median annual earnings of computer systems analysts were $59,330 in 2000. The middle 50 percent earned between $46,980 and $73,210 a year. The lowest 10 percent earned less than $37,460, and the highest 10 percent earned more than $89,040. Median annual earnings in the industries employing the largest numbers of computer systems analysts in 2000 were:

Computer and data processing services	$64,110
Professional and commercial equipment	63,530
Federal government	59,470
Local government	52,490
State government	51,230

Median annual earnings of database administrators were $51,990 in 2000. The middle 50 percent earned between $38,210 and $71,440. The lowest 10 percent earned less than $29,400, and the highest 10 percent earned more than $89,320. In 2000, median annual earnings of database administrators employed in computer and data processing services were $63,710, and in telephone communication, $52,230.

Median annual earnings of network systems and data communication analysts were $54,510 in 2000. The middle 50 percent earned between $42,310 and $69,970. The lowest 10 percent earned less than $33,360, and the highest 10 percent earned more than $88,620. Median annual earnings in the industries employing the largest numbers of network systems and data communications analysts in 2000 were:

Management and public relations	$60,260
Commercial banks	59,910
Computer and data processing services	59,160
Telephone communications	51,780
State government	42,000

Median annual earnings of computer and information scientists, research, were $70,590 in 2000. The middle 50 percent earned between $54,700 and $89,990. The lowest 10 percent earned less than $41,390, and the highest 10 percent earned more than $113,510. Median annual earnings of computer and information scientists employed in computer and data processing services in 2000 were $71,940.

Median annual earnings of all other computer specialists were $50,590 in 2000. Median annual earnings of all other computer specialists employed in computer and data processing services were $51,970, and in professional and commercial equipment, $80,270 in 2000.

According to the National Association of Colleges and Employers, starting offers for graduates with a master's degree in computer science averaged $61,453 in 2001. Starting offers for graduates with a bachelor's degree in computer science averaged $52,723; in computer programming, $48,602; in computer systems analysis, $45,643; in information sciences and systems, $45,182; and in management information systems, $45,585.

According to Robert Half International, starting salaries in 2001 ranged from $72,500 to $105,750 for database administrators. Salaries for Internet-related occupations ranged from $60,500 to $84,250 for security administrators; $58,000 to $82,500 for webmasters; and $56,250 to $76,750 for Internet/Intranet developers.

Related Occupations

Other workers who use logic, and creativity to solve business and technical problems are computer programmers, computer software engineers, computer and information systems managers, financial analysts and personal financial advisors, urban and regional planners, engineers, mathematicians, statisticians, operations research analysts, management analysts, and actuaries.

Sources of Additional Information

Further information about computer careers is available from:

- Association for Computing Machinery (ACM), 1515 Broadway, New York, NY 10036. Internet: http://www.acm.org

- IEEE Computer Society, Headquarters Office, 1730 Massachusetts Ave. NW., Washington, DC 20036-1992. Internet: http://www.computer.org

- National Workforce Center for Emerging Technologies, 3000 Landerholm Circle SE., Bellevue, WA 98007. Internet: http://www.nwcet.org

Information about becoming a Certified Computing Professional is available from:

- Institute for Certification of Computing Professionals (ICCP), 2350 East Devon Ave., Suite 115, Des Plaines, IL 60018. Internet: http://www.iccp.org

Taxi Drivers and Chauffeurs

O*NET 53-3041.00

Significant Points

- Taxi drivers and chauffeurs can work all schedules, including full-time, part-time, night, evening, and weekend work.

- Job opportunities will be good; many people work in these jobs for short periods, so replacement needs are high.

- Many taxi drivers and chauffeurs like the independent, unsupervised work of driving their automobile.

Nature of the Work

Anyone who has been in a large city knows the importance of taxi and limousine service. *Taxi drivers*, also known as *cab drivers*, help passengers get to and from their homes, workplaces, and recreational pursuits such as dining, entertainment, and shopping. They also help out-of-town business people and tourists get around in new surroundings.

At the start of their driving shift, taxi drivers usually report to a taxicab service or garage where they are assigned a vehicle, most frequently a large, conventional automobile modified for commercial passenger transport. They record their name, work date, and cab identification number on a trip sheet. Drivers check the cab's fuel and oil levels, and make sure the lights, brakes, and windshield wipers are in good working order. Drivers adjust rear and side mirrors and their seat for comfort. Any equipment or part not in good working order is reported to the dispatcher or company mechanic.

Taxi drivers pick up passengers in one of three ways: cruising the streets to pick up random passengers; prearranged pickups; and pickups from taxi stands established in highly trafficked areas. In urban areas, the majority of passengers hail or "wave down" drivers cruising the streets. Customers may also prearrange a pickup by calling a cab company and giving a location, approximate pick up time, and destination. The cab company dispatcher then relays the information to a driver by two-way radio, cellular telephone, or on-board computer. Outside of urban areas, the majority of trips are dispatched in this manner. Drivers also pick up passengers waiting at cab stands or in taxi lines at airports, train stations, hotels, and other places where people frequently seek taxis.

Some drivers transport individuals with special needs, such as those with disabilities and the elderly. These drivers, also known as *paratransit drivers*, operate specially equipped vehicles designed to accommodate a variety of needs in non-emergency situations. Although special certification is not necessary, some additional training on the equipment and passenger needs may be required.

Drivers should be familiar with streets in the areas they serve so they can use the most efficient route to destinations. They should know the locations of frequently requested destinations, such as airports, bus and railroad terminals, convention centers, hotels, and other points of interest. In case of emergency, the driver should also know the location of fire and police stations and hospitals.

Upon reaching the destination, drivers determine the fare and announce it to the rider. Fares often consist of many parts. In many cabs, a taximeter measures the fare based on the length of the trip and the amount of time the trip took. Drivers turn the taximeter on when passengers enter the cab and turn it off when they reach the final destination. The fare also may include a surcharge for additional passengers, a fee for handling luggage, or a drop charge—an additional flat fee added for the use of the cab. In some cases, fares are determined by a system of zones through which the taxi passes during a trip. Each jurisdiction determines the rate and structure of the fare system covering licensed taxis. Passengers generally add a tip or gratuity to the fare. The amount of the gratuity depends on the passengers' satisfaction with the quality and efficiency of the ride and courtesy of the driver. Drivers issue receipts upon request from the passenger. They enter onto the trip sheet all information regarding the trip, including the place and time of pick-up and drop-off and the total fee. These logs help check the driver's activity and efficiency. Drivers also must fill out accident reports when necessary.

Chauffeurs operate limousines, vans, and private cars for limousine companies, private businesses, government agencies, and wealthy individuals. This service differs from taxi service in that all trips are prearranged. Many chauffeurs transport customers in large vans between hotels and airports, bus, or train terminals. Others drive luxury automobiles, such as limousines, to business events, entertainment venues, and social events. Still others provide full-time personal transportation for wealthy families and private companies.

At the start of the workday, chauffeurs ready their automobiles or vans for use. They inspect the vehicle for cleanliness and, when needed, vacuum the interior and wash the exterior body, windows, and mirrors. They check fuel and oil levels and make sure the lights, tires, brakes, and windshield wipers work. Chauffeurs may perform routine maintenance and make minor repairs, such as changing tires or adding oil and other fluids when needed. If a vehicle requires more complicated repair, they take it to a professional mechanic.

Chauffeurs cater to passengers with attentive customer service and a special regard for detail. They help riders into the car by holding open doors, holding umbrellas when raining, and loading packages and luggage into the trunk of the car. They may perform errands for their employers such as delivering packages or picking up clients arriving at airports. Many chauffeurs offer conveniences and luxuries in their limousines to insure a pleasurable ride, such as newspapers, magazines, music, drinks, televisions, and telephones. A growing number of chauffeurs work as full-service executive assistants, simultaneously acting as driver, secretary, and itinerary-planner.

Working Conditions

Taxi drivers and chauffeurs occasionally have to load and unload heavy luggage and packages. Driving for long periods can be tiring and uncomfortable, especially in densely populated urban areas. Drivers must be alert to conditions on the road, especially in heavy and congested traffic or in bad weather. They must take precautions to prevent accidents and avoid sudden stops, turns, and other driving maneuvers that would jar passengers. Taxi drivers also risk robbery because they work alone and often carry large amounts of cash.

Work hours of taxi drivers and chauffeurs vary greatly. Some jobs offer full-time or part-time employment with work hours that can change from day to day or remain the same every day. It is often necessary for drivers to report to work on short notice. Chauffeurs who work for a single employer may be on call much of the time. Evening and weekend work are common for limousine and taxicab services.

The needs of the client or employer dictate the work schedule for chauffeurs. The work of taxi drivers is much less structured. Working free from supervision, they may break for a meal or a rest whenever their vehicle is unoccupied. This occupation is attractive to individuals seeking flexible work schedules, such as college and postgraduate students. Similarly, other service workers such as ambulance drivers and police officers often consider moonlighting as taxi drivers and chauffeurs.

Full-time taxi drivers usually work one shift a day, which may last from 8 to 12 hours. Part-time drivers may work half a shift each day, or work a full shift once or twice a week. Drivers may work shifts at all times of the day and night, because most taxi companies offer services 24 hours a day. Early morning and late night shifts are common. Drivers work long hours during holidays, weekends, and other special events that support heavier demand for their services. Independent drivers, however, often set their own hours and schedules.

Design improvements in newer cabs have reduced stress and increased the comfort and efficiency of drivers. Many regulators require standard amenities such as air conditioning and general upkeep of the vehicles. Modern taxicabs also are sometimes equipped with sophisticated tracking devices, fare meters, and dispatching equipment. Satellites and tracking systems link many of these state-of-the-art vehicles with company headquarters. In a matter of seconds, dispatchers can deliver directions, traffic advisories, weather reports, and other important communications to drivers anywhere in the transporting area. The satellite link-up also allows dispatchers to track vehicle location, fuel consumption, and engine performance. Drivers can easily communicate with dispatchers to discuss delivery schedules and courses of action should there be mechanical problems. For instance, automated dispatch systems help dispatchers locate the closest driver to a customer in order to maximize efficiency and quality of service. When threatened with crime or violence, drivers may have special "trouble lights" to alert authorities of emergencies and guarantee that help arrives quickly.

Taxi drivers and chauffeurs meet many different types of people. Dealing with rude customers and waiting for passengers requires patience. Many municipalities and taxicab and chauffeur companies require taxi drivers to wear clean and neat clothes. Many chauffeurs wear formal attire such as a tuxedo, a coat and tie, a dress, or a uniform and cap.

Employment

Taxi drivers and chauffeurs held about 176,000 jobs in 2000. Almost one-third worked for local and suburban passenger transportation and taxicab companies. Others worked for service oriented companies such as automotive dealers, automotive rental agencies, hotels, healthcare facilities, and social services agencies. About 27 percent were self-employed.

Training, Other Qualifications, and Advancement

Local governments set license standards and requirements for taxi drivers and chauffeurs that include minimum qualifications for driving experience and training. Many taxi and limousine companies set higher standards than required by law. It is common for companies to review applicants' medical, credit, criminal, and driving records. In addition, many companies require a higher minimum age and prefer that drivers be high school graduates.

Persons interested in driving a limousine or taxicab must first have a regular automobile driver's license. They also must acquire a chauffeur or taxi driver's license, commonly called a "hack" license. Local authorities generally require applicants for a hack license to pass a written exam or complete a training program that may include up to 80 hours of classroom instruction. To qualify through either an exam or a training program, applicants must know local geography, motor vehicle laws, safe driving practices, regulations governing taxicabs, and display some aptitude for customer service. Many training programs include a test on English proficiency, usually in the form of listening comprehension; applicants who do not pass the English exam must take an English course along with the formal driving program. In addition, some classroom instruction includes route management, map reading, and service for passengers with disabilities. Many taxicab or limousine companies sponsor applicants and give them a temporary permit that allows them to drive, although they may not yet have finished the training program or passed the test. However, some jurisdictions, such as New York City, have discontinued this practice and now require driver applicants to complete the licensing process before operating a taxi or limousine.

Some taxi and limousine companies give new drivers on-the-job training. They show drivers how to operate the taximeter and communications equipment, and how to complete paperwork. Other topics covered may include driver safety and popular sightseeing and entertainment destinations. Many companies have contracts with social service agencies and transportation services to transport elderly and disabled citizens in non-emergency situations. To support these services, new drivers may get special training on how to handle wheelchair lifts and other mechanical devices.

Taxi drivers and chauffeurs should be able to get along with many different types of people. They must be patient when waiting for passengers or when dealing with rude customers. It is also helpful for drivers to be tolerant and have even tempers when driving in heavy and congested traffic. Drivers should be dependable because passengers rely on them to be picked up at a prearranged time and taken to the correct destination. To be successful, drivers must be responsible and self-motivated because they work with little supervision. Increasingly, companies encourage drivers to develop their own loyal customer base to improve their businesses.

The majority of taxi drivers and chauffeurs are called "lease drivers." Lease drivers pay a daily, weekly, or monthly fee to the company allowing them to lease their vehicle. In the case of limousines, leasing also allows the driver access to the company's dispatch system. The fee may also include a charge for vehicle maintenance, insurance, and a deposit on the vehicle. Lease drivers may take their cars home with them when they are not on duty.

Opportunities for advancement are limited for taxi drivers and chauffeurs. Experienced drivers may obtain preferred routes or shifts. Some advance to dispatcher or manager jobs; others may start their own limousine company. On the other hand, many drivers like the independent, unsupervised work of driving their automobile.

In small and medium-size communities, drivers are sometimes able to buy their taxi, limousine, or other type of automobile and go into business for themselves. These independent owner-drivers require an additional permit allowing them to operate their vehicle as a company. Some big cities limit the number of operating permits. In these cities, drivers become owner-drivers by buying permits from owner-drivers who leave the business. Although many owner-drivers are successful, some fail to cover expenses and eventually lose their permit and automobile. Good business sense and courses in accounting, business, and business arithmetic can help an owner-driver become successful. Knowledge of mechanics enables owner-drivers to perform routine maintenance and minor repairs to cut expenses.

Job Outlook

Persons seeking jobs as taxi drivers and chauffeurs should encounter good opportunities. Many job openings will occur each year as drivers transfer to other occupations or leave the labor force. However, opportunities for drivers vary greatly in terms of earnings, work hours, and working conditions, depending on economic and regulatory conditions. Opportunities should be best for persons with good driving records and the ability to work flexible schedules.

Employment of taxi drivers and chauffeurs is expected to grow faster than the average for all occupations through the year 2010, as local and suburban travel increases with population growth. Employment growth will also stem from federal legislation requiring increased services for persons with disabilities. Opportunities should be best in rapidly growing metropolitan areas.

Job opportunities can fluctuate from season to season and from month to month. Extra drivers may be hired during holiday seasons and peak travel and tourist times. During economic slowdowns, drivers are seldom laid off but they may have to increase their working hours, and earnings may decline somewhat. In economic upturns, job openings are numerous as drivers leave the occupation for other opportunities.

Earnings

Earnings of taxi drivers and chauffeurs vary greatly, depending on the number of hours worked, customers' tips, and other factors. Median hourly earnings of salaried taxi drivers and chauffeurs, including tips, were $8.19 in 2000. The middle 50 percent earned between $6.68 and $10.46 an hour. The lowest 10 percent earned less than $5.86, and the highest 10 percent earned more than $13.47 an hour. Median hourly earnings in the industries employing the largest numbers of taxi drivers and chauffeurs in 2000 were as follows:

Local and suburban transportation	$8.58
Taxicabs	8.34
Automotive rentals, no drivers	7.93
Hotels and motels	7.51
Personnel supply services	6.63

According to limited information available, the majority of self-employed taxi owner-drivers earned from about $20,000 to $30,000 annually, including tips. However, professional drivers with a regular clientele often earn more. Many chauffeurs who worked full time earned from about $25,000 to $50,000, including tips. Earnings were generally higher in urban areas.

Related Occupations

Other workers who have similar jobs include ambulance drivers, except emergency medical technicians; busdrivers; and truckdrivers and driver/sales workers.

Sources of Additional Information

Information on licensing and registration of taxi drivers and chauffeurs is available from offices of local governments regulating taxicabs. For information about work opportunities as a taxi driver or chauffeur, contact local taxi or limousine companies or state employment service offices.

For general information about the work of taxi drivers and the taxi industry, contact:

- Taxi, Limousine, and Paratransit Association, 3849 Farragut Ave., Kensington, MD 20895

For general information about the work of limousine drivers, contact:

- National Limousine Association, 2365 Harrodsburg Rd., Suite A325, Lexington, KY 40504. Telephone (toll free): 800-652-7007

Teacher Assistants

O*NET 25-9041.00

Significant Points

- Approximately 4 in 10 teacher assistants work part-time.

- Educational requirements range from a high school diploma to some college training.

- A growing special education population, among other factors, is expected to cause faster-than-average employment growth.

Nature of the Work

Teacher assistants provide instructional and clerical support for classroom teachers, allowing teachers more time for lesson planning and teaching. Teacher assistants tutor and assist children in learning class material using the teacher's lesson plans, providing students with individualized attention. Teacher assistants also supervise students in the cafeteria, schoolyard, school discipline center, or on field trips. They record grades, set up equipment, and help prepare materials for instruction. Teacher assistants are also called teacher aides or instructional aides. Some refer to themselves as paraeducators.

Some teacher assistants perform exclusively noninstructional or clerical tasks, such as monitoring nonacademic settings. Playground and lunchroom attendants are examples of such assistants. Most teacher assistants, however, perform a combination of instructional and clerical duties. They generally instruct children, under the direction and guidance of teachers. They work with students individually or in small groups—listening while students read, reviewing or reinforcing classwork, or helping them find information for reports. At the secondary school level, teacher assistants often specialize in a certain subject, such as math or science. Teacher assistants often take charge of special projects and prepare equipment or exhibits, such as for a science demonstration. Some assistants work in computer laboratories, helping students using computers and educational software programs.

In addition to instructing, assisting, and supervising students, teacher assistants grade tests and papers, check homework, keep health and attendance records, type, file, and duplicate materials. They also stock supplies, operate audiovisual equipment, and keep classroom equipment in order.

Many teacher assistants work extensively with special education students. As schools become more inclusive, integrating special education students into general education classrooms, teacher assistants in general education and special education classrooms increasingly assist students with disabilities. Teacher assistants attend to a disabled student's physical needs, including feeding, teaching good grooming habits, or assisting students riding the school bus. They also provide personal attention to students with other special needs, such as those whose families live in poverty, or students who speak English as a second language, or who need remedial education. Teacher assistants help assess a student's progress by observing performance and recording relevant data.

Teacher assistants also work with infants and toddlers who are disabled or developmentally delayed. Under the guidance of a teacher or therapist, teacher assistants perform exercises or play games to help the child develop physically and behaviorally. Some teacher assistants work with young adults helping them obtain a job or apply for community services for the disabled.

Working Conditions

Approximately 4 in 10 teacher assistants work part-time. However, even among full-time workers, nearly half work less than 8 hours per day. Most assistants who provide educational instruction work the traditional 9- to 10-month school year. Teacher assistants work in a variety of settings, including private homes, preschools, or in local government offices working with young adults. But most work in classrooms in elementary, middle, and secondary schools. They also work outdoors supervising recess when weather allows, and they spend much of their time standing, walking, or kneeling.

Seeing students develop and gain appreciation of the joy of learning can be very rewarding. However, working closely with students can be both physically and emotionally tiring. Teacher assistants who work with special education students often perform more strenuous tasks, including lifting, as they help students with their daily routine. Those who perform clerical work may tire of administrative duties, such as copying materials or typing.

Employment

Teacher assistants held almost 1.3 million jobs in 2000. About 80 percent worked in public and private education, mostly in the elementary grades. Approximately half assisted Special Education Teachers in working with children with disabilities. Most of the others worked in child daycare centers and religious organizations.

Training, Other Qualifications, and Advancement

Educational requirements for teacher assistants range from a high school diploma to some college training. Teacher assistants with instructional responsibilities usually require more training than those who do not perform teaching tasks. Increasingly, employers prefer teacher assistants who have some college training. Some teacher assistants are aspiring teachers who are working towards their degree while gaining experience. Many schools require previous experience in working with children. Schools often require a valid driver's license and perform a background check on applicants.

A number of 2-year and community colleges offer associate degree programs that prepare graduates to work as teacher assistants. However, most teacher assistants receive on-the-job training. Those who tutor and review lessons with students must have a thorough understanding of class materials and instructional methods, and should be familiar with the organization and operation of a school. Teacher assistants also must know how to operate audiovisual equipment, keep records, and prepare instructional materials, as well as have adequate computer skills.

Teacher assistants should enjoy working with children from a wide range of cultural backgrounds, and be able to handle classroom situations with fairness and patience. Teacher assistants also must demonstrate initiative and a willingness to follow a teacher's directions. They must have good writing skills and be able to communicate effectively with students and teachers. Teacher assistants who speak a second language, especially Spanish, are in great demand to communicate with growing numbers of students and parents whose primary language is not English.

About one third of all states have established guidelines or minimum educational standards for the hiring and training of teacher assistants, and an increasing number of states are in the process of implementing them. Although requirements vary by state, most require an individual to have at least a high school diploma or general equivalency degree (GED), or some college training. In states that have not established guidelines or minimum educational standards, local school districts determine hiring requirements.

Advancement for teacher assistants, usually in the form of higher earnings or increased responsibility, comes primarily with experience or additional education. Some school districts provide time away from the job or tuition reimbursement so that teacher assistants can earn their bachelor's degrees and pursue licensed teaching positions. In return for tuition reimbursement, assistants are often required to teach a certain length of time for the school district.

Job Outlook

Employment of teacher assistants is expected to grow faster than the average for all occupations through 2010. Many school districts report shortages of teachers. If schools continue to experience problems hiring teachers, the demand for teacher assistants to assist and monitor students and provide teachers with clerical assistance will grow. In addition, despite projections of only moderate increases in overall student enrollments, the number of special education students and those who speak English as a second language are expected to grow more rapidly. Because teacher assistants play a large role in helping students with special needs, the rising number of these students will create additional demand for teacher assistants. In addition to jobs stemming from employment growth, numerous job openings will arise as workers transfer to other occupations, leave the labor force to assume family responsibilities, return to school, or leave for other reasons—characteristic of occupations that require limited formal education and offer relatively low pay.

The number and size of special education programs are growing in response to increasing enrollments of students with disabilities. Federal legislation mandates appropriate education for all children, and emphasizes placing children with disabilities into regular school settings, when possible. Children with special needs require much personal attention, and special education teachers, as well as general education teachers with special education students, rely heavily on teacher assistants.

School reforms that call for more individual instruction should further enhance employment opportunities for teacher assistants. As schools strive to meet new standards, they are hiring more teacher assistants to provide students with the personal instruction and remedial education they need. An increasing number of after-school programs and summer programs also will create new opportunities for teacher assistants.

Demand is expected to vary by region of the country. Where population growth is fastest, such as in areas of the south and west, school enrollments are also rising quickly, resulting in stronger demand for teacher assistants. Teacher assistants, particularly those that can speak a foreign language, are in demand in school systems with large numbers of immigrants.

Earnings

Median annual earnings of teacher assistants in 2000 were $17,350. The middle 50 percent earned between $13,930 and $22,080. The lowest 10 percent earned less than $12,260, and the highest 10 percent earned more than $27,550.

Teacher assistants who work part-time ordinarily do not receive benefits. Full-time workers usually receive health coverage and other benefits.

About 4 out of 10 teacher assistants belonged to unions in 2000—mainly the American Federation of Teachers and the National Education Association—which bargain with school systems over wages, hours, and the terms and conditions of employment.

Related Occupations

Teacher assistants who instruct children have duties similar to those of preschool, kindergarten, elementary, middle, and secondary school teachers, special education teachers, and school librarians. However, teacher assistants do not have the same level of responsibility or training. The support activities of teacher assistants and their educational backgrounds are similar to those of childcare workers, library technicians, and library assistants. Teacher assistants who work with children with disabilities perform many of the same functions as occupational therapy assistants and aides.

Sources of Additional Information

For information on teacher assistants, including training and certification, contact:

- American Federation of Teachers, Paraprofessional and School Related Personnel Division, 555 New Jersey Ave. NW, Washington, DC 20001. Internet: http://www.aft.org/psrp

For information on a career as a teacher assistant, contact:

- National Resource Center for Paraprofessionals in Education and Related Services, 6526 Old Main Hill, Utah State University, Logan, UT 84322. Internet: http://www.nrcpara.org

School superintendents and state departments of education can provide details about employment requirements.

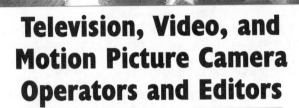

Television, Video, and Motion Picture Camera Operators and Editors

O*NET 27-4031.00, 27-4032.00

Significant Points

- Technical expertise, a "good eye," imagination, and creativity are essential.

- Keen competition for job openings is expected, because many talented peopled are attracted to the field.

- About one-fourth of camera operators are self-employed.

Nature of the Work

Television, video, and motion picture camera operators produce images that tell a story, inform or entertain an audience, or record an event. *Film and video editors* edit soundtracks, film, and video for the motion picture, cable, and broadcast television industries. Some camera operators do their own editing.

Making commercial quality movies and video programs requires technical expertise and creativity. Producing successful images requires choosing and presenting interesting material, selecting appropriate equipment, and applying a good eye and steady hand to assure smooth natural movement of the camera.

Camera operators use television, video, or motion picture cameras to shoot a wide range of subjects, including television series, studio programs, news and sporting events, music videos, motion pictures, documentaries, and training sessions. Some film or videotape private ceremonies and special events. Those who record images on videotape are often called *videographers*. Many are employed by independent television stations, local affiliates, large cable and television networks, or smaller, independent production companies. *Studio camera operators* work in a broadcast studio and usually videotape their subjects from a fixed position. *News camera operators*, also called *electronic news gathering (ENG) operators*, work as part of a reporting team, following newsworthy events as they unfold. To capture live events, they must anticipate the action and act quickly. ENG operators may need to edit raw footage on the spot for relay to a television affiliate for broadcast.

Camera operators employed in the entertainment field use motion picture cameras to film movies, television programs, and commercials. Those who film motion pictures are also known as *cinematographers*. Some specialize in filming cartoons or special effects. They may be an integral part of the action, using cameras in any of several different camera mounts. For example, the camera operator can be stationary and shoot whatever passes in front of the lens, or the camera can be mounted on a track, with the camera operator responsible for shooting the scene from different angles or directions. Other camera operators sit on cranes and follow the action, while crane operators move them into position. *Steadicam operators* mount a harness and carry the camera on their shoulders to provide a more solid picture while they move about the action. Camera operators who work in the entertainment field often meet with directors, actors, editors, and camera assistants to discuss ways of filming, editing, and improving scenes.

Working Conditions

Working conditions for camera operators and editors vary considerably. Those employed in government, television and cable networks, and advertising agencies usually work a 5-day, 40-hour week. On the other hand, ENG operators often work long, irregular hours and must be available to work on short notice. Camera operators and editors working in motion picture production also may work long, irregular hours.

ENG operators and those who cover major events, such as conventions or sporting events, frequently travel locally, stay overnight on assignments, or travel to distant places for longer periods. Camera operators filming television programs or motion pictures may travel to film on location.

Some camera operators work in uncomfortable or even dangerous surroundings, especially ENG operators covering accidents, natural disasters, civil unrest, or military conflicts. Many camera operators must wait long hours in all kinds of weather for an event to take place and stand or walk for long periods while carrying heavy equipment. ENG operators often work under strict deadlines.

Employment

Television, video, and motion picture camera operators held about 27,000 jobs in 2000; and film and video editors held about 16,000. One-fourth of camera operators were self-employed. Some self-employed camera operators contracted with television networks, documentary or independent filmmakers, advertising agencies, or trade show or convention sponsors to do individual projects for a predetermined fee, often at a daily rate.

Most salaried camera operators were employed by television broadcasting stations or motion picture studios. Half of the salaried film and video editors worked for motion picture studios. Most camera operators and editors worked in metropolitan areas.

Training, Other Qualifications, and Advancement

Employers usually seek applicants with a "good eye," imagination, and creativity, as well as a good technical understanding of camera operation. Camera operators and editors usually acquire their skills through on-the-job training or formal postsecondary training at vocational schools, colleges, universities, or photographic institutes. Formal education may be required for some positions.

Many universities, community and junior colleges, vocational-technical institutes, and private trade and technical schools offer courses in camera operation and videography. Basic courses cover equipment, processes, and techniques. Bachelor's degree programs, especially those including business courses, provide a well-rounded education.

Individuals interested in camera operations should subscribe to videographic newsletters and magazines, join clubs, and seek summer or part-time employment in cable and television networks, motion picture studios, or camera and video stores.

Camera operators in entry-level jobs learn to set up lights, cameras, and other equipment. They may receive routine assignments requiring camera adjustments or decisions on what subject matter to capture. Camera operators in the film and television industries usually are hired for a project based on recommendations from individuals such as producers, directors of photography, and camera assistants from previous projects, or through interviews with the producer. ENG and studio camera operators who work for television affiliates usually start in small markets to gain experience.

Camera operators need good eyesight, artistic ability, and hand-eye coordination. They should be patient, accurate, and detail-oriented. Camera operators also should have good communication skills, and, if needed, the ability to hold a camera by hand for extended periods.

Camera operators who operate their own businesses, or freelance, need business skills as well as talent. These individuals must know how to submit bids; write contracts; get permission to shoot on locations that normally are not open to the public; obtain releases to use film or tape of people; price their services; secure copyright protection for their work; and keep financial records.

With increased experience, operators may advance to more demanding assignments or positions with larger or network television stations. Advancement for ENG operators may mean moving to larger media markets. Other camera operators and editors may become directors of photography for movie studios, advertising agencies, or television programs. Some teach at technical schools, film schools, or universities.

Job Outlook

Camera operators and editors can expect keen competition for job openings because the work is attractive to many people. The number of individuals interested in positions as videographers and movie camera operators usually is much greater than the number of openings. Those who succeed in landing a salaried job or attracting enough work to earn a living by freelancing are likely to be the most creative, highly motivated, able to adapt to rapidly changing technologies, and adept at operating a business. Related work experience or job-related training also is beneficial to prospective camera operators.

Employment of camera operators and editors is expected to grow faster than the average for all occupations through 2010. Rapid expansion of the entertainment market, especially motion picture production and distribution, will spur growth of camera operators. In addition, computer and Internet services provide new outlets for interactive productions. Camera operators will be needed to film made-for-the-Internet broadcasts such as live music videos, digital movies, sports, and general information or entertainment programming. These images can be de-

livered directly into the home either on compact discs or over the Internet. Modest growth also is expected in radio and television broadcasting.

Earnings

Median annual earnings for television, video, and motion picture camera operators were $27,870 in 2000. The middle 50 percent earned between $19,230 and $44,150. The lowest 10 percent earned less than $14,130, and the highest 10 percent earned more than $63,690. Median annual earnings were $31,560 in motion picture production and services and $23,470 in radio and television broadcasting.

Median annual earnings for film and video editors were $34,160 in 2000. The middle 50 percent earned between $24,800 and $52,000. The lowest 10 percent earned less than $18,970, and the highest 10 percent earned more than $71,280. Median annual earnings were $36,770 in motion picture production and services, the industry employing the largest numbers of film and video editors.

Many camera operators who work in film or video are freelancers; their earnings tend to fluctuate each year. Because most freelance camera operators purchase their own equipment, they incur considerable expense acquiring and maintaining cameras and accessories.

Related Occupations

Related arts and media occupations include artists and related workers, broadcast and sound engineering technicians and radio operators, designers, and photographers.

Sources of Additional Information

Information about career and employment opportunities for camera operators and film and video editors is available from local offices of state employment service agencies, local offices of the relevant trade unions, and local television and film production companies who employ these workers.

Tellers

O*NET 43-3071.00

Significant Points

- Most jobs require only a high school diploma.
- Numerous job opportunities should arise due to high turnover.
- Slower-than-average growth is expected in overall employment, reflecting the spread of computers and other office automation as well as organizational restructuring.

Nature of the Work

The teller is the person most people associate with a bank. Tellers make up 25 percent of bank employees, and conduct most of a bank's routine transactions. Among their responsibilities are cashing checks, accepting deposits and loan payments, and processing withdrawals. They also may sell savings bonds, accept payment for customers' utility bills and charge cards, process necessary paperwork for certificates of deposit, and sell travelers' checks. Some tellers specialize in handling foreign currencies or commercial or business accounts.

Being a teller requires a great deal of attention to detail. Before cashing a check, a teller must verify the date, bank name, identification of the person to receive payment, and legality of the document. They also must make sure that written and numerical amounts agree and that the account has sufficient funds to cover the check. The teller then must carefully count cash to avoid errors. Sometimes a customer withdraws money in the form of a cashier's check, which the teller prepares and verifies. When accepting a deposit, tellers must check the accuracy of the deposit slip before processing the transaction.

Prior to starting their shift, tellers receive and count an amount of working cash for their drawer. A supervisor, usually the head teller, verifies this amount. Tellers use this cash for payments during the day and are responsible for its safe and accurate handling. Before leaving, tellers count cash on hand, list the currency-received tickets on a balance sheet, make sure the accounts balance, and sort checks and deposit slips. Over the course of a workday, tellers also may process numerous mail transactions. Some tellers replenish cash drawers and corroborate deposits and payments to automated teller machines (ATMs).

In most banks, head tellers are responsible for the teller line. They set work schedules, ensure that the proper procedures are adhered to, and act as a mentor to less experienced tellers. In addition, head tellers may perform the typical duties of a teller as needed and deal with the more difficult customer problems. They may access the vault, ensure the correct cash balance is in the vault, and oversee large cash transactions. Technology continues to play a large role in the job duties of all tellers. In most banks, for example, tellers use computer terminals to record deposits and withdrawals. These terminals often give tellers quick access to detailed information on customer accounts. Tellers can use this information to tailor services to fit a customer's needs or to recommend an appropriate bank product or service.

As banks begin to offer more and increasingly complex financial services, tellers are being trained to identify potential sales opportunities. This requires them to learn about the various financial products and services the bank offers so they can briefly explain them to customers and refer interested customers to appropriate specialized sales personnel. In addition, tellers in many banks are being cross-trained to perform some of the functions of customer service representatives.

Working Conditions

Tellers typically are employed in an office environment.

Because the majority of tellers use computers on a daily basis, these workers may experience eye and muscle strain, backaches, headaches, and repetitive motion injuries. Also, tellers who review detailed data may have to sit for extended periods of time.

Most tellers work regular business hours, plus some evenings and Saturday mornings.

Employment

Tellers held about 499,000 jobs in 2000; about 1 out of 4 worked part-time. The overwhelming majority worked in commercial banks, savings institutions, or credit unions. The remainder were employed in a variety of other financial service companies.

Training, Other Qualifications, and Advancement

Most tellers are required to have at least a high school diploma. However, having some college is becoming increasingly important. Although a degree is rarely required, many graduates accept entry-level clerical positions to get into a particular company or to enter the finance field with the hope of being promoted to professional or managerial positions. Some companies have a set plan of advancement that tracks college graduates from entry-level clerical jobs into managerial positions. Workers with bachelor's degrees are likely to start at higher salaries and advance more easily than those without degrees do.

Experience in a related job also is recommended. For example, cash-handling experience is important for tellers. Experience working in an office environment or in customer service is always beneficial. Regardless of the type of work, most employers prefer workers with good communication skills who are computer-literate; knowledge of word processing and spreadsheet software is especially valuable.

Once hired, tellers usually receive on-the-job training. Under the guidance of a supervisor or other senior worker, new employees learn company procedures. Some formal classroom training also may be necessary, such as training in specific computer software. Tellers must be careful, orderly, and detail-oriented in order to avoid making errors and recognize errors made by others. These workers also should be discreet and trustworthy because they frequently come in contact with confidential material. Additionally, all tellers should have a strong aptitude for numbers.

Tellers can prepare for better jobs by taking courses offered or accredited by the American Institute of Banking (an educational affiliate of the American Bankers Association) or the Institute of Financial Education (an affiliate of the Bank Administration Institute). These organizations have several hundred chapters in cities across the country and numerous study groups in small communities.

Tellers usually advance by taking on more duties in the same occupation for higher pay or by transferring to a closely related occupation. Most companies fill office and administrative support supervisory and managerial positions by promoting individuals from within their organization, so tellers who acquire additional skills, experience, and training improve their advancement opportunities.

Job Outlook

Employment of tellers is expected to decline through 2010. Nevertheless, many job openings will arise from replacement needs because turnover is high—a characteristic typical of large occupations that normally require little formal education and offer relatively low pay.

The banking industry will continue to undergo many changes that will impact employment of traditional tellers, who perform only routine transactions. Principal among these are technology and changing employment needs. For example, ATMs and the increased use of direct deposit of paychecks and benefit checks have reduced the need for bank customers to interact with tellers for routine transactions. In addition, electronic banking is spreading rapidly throughout the banking industry. This type of banking, conducted over the telephone or the Internet, also will reduce the number of tellers over the long run.

Teller employment also is being impacted by the increasing use of 24-hour phone centers by many large banks. These telephone centers allow a customer to interact with a bank representative at a distant location, either by telephone or video terminal. Such centers usually are staffed by customer service representatives, who can handle a wider variety of transactions than tellers, including loan applications and credit card issuance.

Even though some banks have streamlined their branches, the total number of bank branches is expected to increase to meet the needs of a growing population. Branches are being added in nontraditional locations, such as grocery stores, malls, and mobile trailers designed to reach people who do not have easy access to banks. Often, these branches are open longer hours and offer greater customer convenience. Many of these nontraditional branch offices are small and are staffed by tellers who also have customer service training. As a result, tellers who can provide a variety of financial services will be in greater demand in the future.

Earnings

Salaries of tellers vary considerably. The region of the country, size of city, and type and size of establishment all influence salary levels. Also, the level of expertise required and the complexity and uniqueness of a teller's responsibilities also may affect earnings. Median hourly earnings of full-time tellers in 2000 were $9.21.

Related Occupations

Tellers enter data into a computer, handle cash, and keep track of business and other financial transactions. Other occupations that perform these duties include brokerage clerks; cashiers; credit authorizers, checkers, and clerks; loan interviewers and clerks; new accounts clerks; order clerks; and secretaries and administrative assistants.

Sources of Additional Information

Information on employment opportunities for tellers is available from local offices of the state employment service.

Textile, Apparel, and Furnishings Occupations

O*NET 51-6011.01, 51-6011.02, 51-6011.03, 51-6021.01, 51-6021.02, 51-6021.03, 51-6031.01, 51-6031.02, 51-6041.00, 51-6042.00, 51-6051.00, 51-6052.01, 51-6052.02, 51-6061.00, 51-6062.00, 51-6063.00, 51-6064.00, 51-6091.01, 51-6092.00, 51-6093.00, 51-6099.99

Significant Points

● Most workers learn through on-the-job training.

● Employment is expected to decline for most occupations, primarily due to increased imports, laborsaving machinery, and offshore assembly.

● Earnings of most workers are low.

Nature of the Work

Textiles and leather clothe our bodies, cover our furniture, and adorn our homes. Textile, apparel, and furnishings workers produce these materials and fashion them into a wide range of products that we use in our daily lives. Jobs range from those that employ computers, to those that operate large industrial machinery and smaller power equipment, to those that involve substantial handwork.

Textile machine operators. Textile machinery operators run machines that make textile products from fibers. Textiles are the basis of towels, bed linens, hosiery and socks, and nearly all clothing, but they also are a key ingredient of products ranging from roofing to tires. The first step in manufacturing textiles is preparing the natural or synthetic fibers. *Extruding and forming machine operators, synthetic and glass fibers* set up and operate machines that extrude—or force—liquid synthetic material such as rayon, fiberglass, or liquid polymers out through small holes and draw out filaments. Other operators put natural fibers such as cotton, wool, flax, or hemp through carding and combing machines that clean and align them into short lengths called "sliver." When sliver is produced, different types of natural fibers and synthetics filaments may be combined to give the product a desired texture, durability, or other characteristics. *Textile winding, twisting, and drawing out machine operators* take the sliver and draw out, twist, and wind it to produce yarn, taking care to repair any breaks.

Textile bleaching and dyeing machine operators control machines that wash, bleach, or dye either yarn or finished fabrics and other products. *Textile knitting and weaving machine operators* put the yarn on machines that weave, knit, loop, or tuft it into a product. Woven fabrics are used to make apparel and other goods, while some knitted products—such as hosiery—and tufted products—such as carpeting—emerge in near finished form. Different types of machines are used for these processes, but operators perform similar tasks. They repair breaks in the yarn and monitor the yarn supply, while tending many machines at once. *Textile cutting machine operators* trim the fabric into various widths and lengths, depending on its intended use.

Apparel workers. Apparel workers cut fabric and other materials and sew it into clothing and related products. Workers in a variety of occupations fall under the heading of apparel workers. *Tailors, dressmakers, and sewers* make custom clothing and alter and repair garments for individuals. However, workers in most apparel occupations are found in manufacturing where they perform specialized tasks in the production of large numbers of garments that are shipped to retail establishments for sale to the public.

Fabric and apparel patternmakers convert a clothing designer's original model of a garment into a pattern of separate parts that can be laid out on a length of fabric. After discussing the item with the designer, these skilled workers usually use a computer to outline the parts and draw in details to indicate the position of pleats, buttonholes, and other features. In the past, patternmakers laid out the parts on paper using pencils and drafting instruments, such as rulers. Patternmakers then alter the size of the pieces in the pattern to produce garments of various sizes, and may "mark" the fabric showing the best layout of pattern pieces to minimize waste of material.

Once an item's pattern has been made and marked, mass production of the garment begins. Cutters and trimmers take the patterns and cut out material. They must pay close attention to their work because mistakes are costly. They place multiple layers of material on the cutting table and use an electric knife or other cutting tools to cut out the various pieces of the garment following the outline of the pattern; delicate materials may be cut by hand. In some companies, computer-controlled machines do the cutting.

Sewing machine operators join the parts together, reinforce seams, and attach buttons, hooks, zippers, and accessories to produce clothing. After the product is sewn, other workers remove lint and loose threads and inspect and package the garments.

Shoe and leather workers. Shoe and leather workers are employed either in manufacturing or in personal services. In shoe manufacturing, *shoe machine operators and tenders* operate a variety of specialized machines that perform cutting, joining, and finishing functions. In personal services, *shoe and leather workers and repairers* perform a variety of repairs and custom leatherwork for members of the general public. The construct, decorate, or repair shoes, belts, purses, saddles, luggage, and other leather products. They also may repair some products made of canvas or plastic. When making custom shoes or modifying existing footwear for people with foot problems or special needs, they cut pieces of leather, shape them over a form shaped like a foot, and sew them together. They then attach soles and heels using sewing machines or cement and nails. They also dye and polish the items using a buffing wheel for a smooth surface and lustrous shine. When making luggage, they fasten leather to a frame and attach handles and other hardware. They also cut and secure linings inside the frames and sew or stamp designs onto the luggage exterior. In addition to the steps listed above, saddle makers often apply leather dyes and liquid topcoats to produce a gloss finish on a saddle. They may also decorate the saddle surface by hand stitching or by stamping the leather with decorative patterns and designs. Shoe and leather workers and repairers who own their own shops keep records and supervise other workers.

Upholsterers. *Upholsterers* make, fix, and restore furniture that is covered with fabric. Upholsterers who restore furniture remove old fabric and stuffing to get back down to the springs and wooden frame. They use hammers and tack pullers to remove the old parts. They reglue loose sections of the frame and refinish exposed wood. The springs sit on a cloth mat, called webbing, that is attached to the frame. Upholsterers replace torn webbing and examine the springs and replace broken or bent ones.

Upholsterers who make new furniture start with a bare wooden frame. First, they install webbing, tacking it to one side of the frame, stretching it tight, and tacking it to the other side. Then, they tie each spring to the webbing and to its neighboring springs. Upholsterers next cover the springs with filler, such as foam or a polyester batt or similar fibrous batting material, to form a smooth, rounded surface. They then measure and cut fabric for the arms, backs, seats, sides, and other surfaces, leaving as little waste as possible. They sew the fabric pieces together and attach them to the frame using tacks, staples, or glue. Lastly, they attach any ornaments, such as fringes, buttons, or rivets.

Laundry and drycleaning workers. *Laundry and drycleaning workers* clean cloth garments, linens, draperies, blankets, and other articles. They also may clean leather, suede, furs, and rugs. When necessary, they treat spots and stains on articles before laundering or drycleaning. They tend machines during cleaning and ensure that items are not lost or misplaced with those of another customer. *Pressers, textile, garment, and related materials* shape and remove wrinkles from items after cleaning by steam pressing or ironing by hand. Workers then assemble each customer's items, box or bag them, and prepare an itemized bill for the customer.

Working Conditions

Most persons in textile, apparel and furnishings occupations work a standard 5-day, 35- to 40-hour week. Evenings and weekend work is common for shoe and leather workers, laundry and drycleaning workers, and tailors, dressmakers, sewers employed in retail stores. In manufacturing, some employers add second shifts to justify the expense of new machinery. Many textile and fiber mills often use rotating schedules of shifts so that employees do not continuously work nights or days. But these rotating shifts sometimes cause workers to have sleep disorders and stress-related problems.

While much of the work in apparel manufacturing still is based on a piecework system that allows for little interpersonal contact, some apparel firms are placing more emphasis on teamwork and cooperation. Under this new system, individuals work closely with one another and each team or module often governs itself, increasing the overall responsibility of each operator.

Working conditions vary by establishment and by occupation. In manufacturing, machinery in textile mills often is noisy, as are areas in which sewing and pressing are performed in apparel factories; patternmaking and spreading areas tend to be much quieter. Many older factories are cluttered, hot, and poorly lit and ventilated, but more-modern facilities usually have more workspace and are well-lit and ventilated. Textile machinery operators use protective glasses and masks that cover their noses and mouths to protect against airborne materials. Many machines operate at high speeds, and textile machinery workers must be careful not to wear clothing or jewelry that could get caught in moving parts. In addition, extruding and forming machine operators wear protective shoes and clothing when working with certain chemical compounds.

Work in apparel production can be physically demanding. Some workers sit for long periods, and others spend many hours on their feet, leaning over tables and operating machinery. Operators must be attentive while running equipment such as sewing machines, pressers, and automated cutters. A few workers wear protective devices such as gloves. In some instances, new machinery and production techniques have decreased the physical demands upon workers. For example, newer pressing machines now are operated by foot pedals or computer controls, and do not require much strength to operate.

Laundries and drycleaning establishments often are hot and noisy; but those in retail stores tend to be less noisy and more comfortable. Areas in which shoe and leather workers make or repair shoes and other leather items can be noisy and odors from leather dyes and stains often are present. Workers need to pay close attention when working with machines to avoid punctures, lacerations, and abrasions.

Upholstery work is not dangerous, but upholsterers usually wear protective gloves and clothing when using sharp tools and lifting and handling furniture or springs. Upholsterers stand most of the workday and may do a lot of bending and heavy lifting. They also may work in awkward positions for short periods.

Employment

Textile, apparel, and furnishings workers held over 1.3 million jobs in 2000. Employment in the detailed occupations that make up this group was distributed as follows:

Sewing machine operators	399,000
Laundry and drycleaning workers	236,000
Pressers, textile, garment, and related materials	110,000
Tailors, dressmakers, and sewers	101,000
All other textile, apparel, and furnishings workers	95,000
Textile winding, twisting, and drawing out machine setters, operators, and tenders	90,000
Textile knitting and weaving machine setters, operators, and tenders	70,000
Upholsterers	58,000
Extruding and forming machine setters, operators, and tenders, synthetic and glass fibers	41,000
Textile cutting machine setters, operators, and tenders	38,000
Textile bleaching and dyeing machine operators and tenders	37,000
Shoe and leather workers and repairers	19,000
Fabric and apparel patternmakers	15,000
Shoe machine operators and tenders	9,100

Manufacturing jobs are concentrated in California, New York, North Carolina, Pennsylvania, Tennessee, and Georgia. Jobs in reupholstery, shoe repair and custom leather work, and laundry and drycleaning establishments are found in cities and towns throughout the nation. Only about 7 percent of all workers in textile, apparel, and furnishings occupations were self-employed, as compared with more than one-third of tailors, dressmakers, and sewers and more than one-quarter of upholsterers.

Training, Other Qualifications, and Advancement

Most employers prefer to hire high school graduates for jobs in textile, apparel, and furnishings occupations. Entrants with postsecondary vocational training or previous work experience in apparel production usually have a better chance of getting a job and advancing to a supervisory position. Regardless of setting, workers usually begin by performing simple tasks.

In manufacturing, textile and apparel workers need good hand-eye coordination, manual dexterity, physical stamina, and the ability to perform repetitive tasks for long periods. Machine operators usually are trained on the job by more-experienced employees or by machinery manufacturers' representatives. As they gain experience, they are assigned more difficult operations. Further advancement is limited, however. Some production workers may become first-line supervisors, but most can advance only to more-skilled operator jobs. As machinery in the industry continues to become more complex, knowledge of the basics of computers and electronics will increasingly be an asset. In addition, the trends toward cross-training of operators and working in teams will increase the time needed to become fully trained on all machines and require interpersonal skills to work effectively with others.

Retailers prefer to hire custom tailors, dressmakers, and sewers with previous experience in apparel manufacture, design, or alteration. Knowledge of fabrics, design, and construction is very important. Some experienced custom tailors open their own tailoring shop. Custom tailoring is a very competitive field, however, and training in small-business operations can mean the difference between success and failure. Although laundries and drycleaners prefer entrants with previous work experience, they routinely hire inexperienced workers.

Precision shoe and leather workers and repairers generally learn their skills on the job. Manual dexterity and the mechanical aptitude to work with handtools and machines are important in shoe repair and leather working. Shoe and leather workers who produce custom goods should have artistic ability as well. Beginners start as helpers for experienced workers but, in manufacturing, they may attend more-formal in-house training programs. Trainees generally become fully skilled in 6 months to 2 years. Shoe repairers need to keep their skills up-to-date to work with the rapidly changing footwear styles and materials. Some do this by attending trade shows, while others attend specialized training seminars and workshops in custom shoe making, shoe repair, and other leather work sponsored by associations. Skilled workers who produce and modify prescription footwear may become certified as *pedorthists* by the Pedorthic Footwear Association after completing 120 hours of training and passing an examination. Some in the shoe and leather working occupations begin as workers or repairers and advance to salaried supervisory and managerial positions. Some open their own shop, but knowledge of business practices and management and a pleasant manner when dealing with customers are needed to stay in business.

Most upholsterers learn their skills on the job, but a few learn their skills through apprenticeships. Inexperienced persons also may take training in basic upholstery in vocational schools and some community colleges. Upholsterers should have manual dexterity, good coordination, and the strength needed to lift heavy furniture. An eye for detail, a flair for color, and the ability to use fabrics creatively also are helpful. It takes about 3 years of on-the-job training for beginners hired as helpers to become fully skilled upholsterers. The primary forms of advancement for upholsterers are opening their own shop or moving into management. The upholstery business is very competitive, so operating a shop successfully is difficult. In large shops and factories, experienced or highly skilled upholsterers may become supervisors or sample makers.

Job Outlook

Employment of textile, apparel, and furnishings workers is expected to decline through 2010. Apparel workers have been among the most rapidly declining occupational groups in the economy, and increasing imports, the use of offshore assembly, and greater productivity through new automation will contribute to additional job losses. Because of the large size of this occupation, however, many thousands of job openings will arise each year from the need to replace persons who transfer to other occupations, retire, or leave the occupation for other reasons.

Employment in the domestic textile and apparel industries has declined in recent years as foreign producers have gained a greater share of the U.S. market. Imports are expected to continue to increase, and domestic output and employment decrease, as the U.S. market is opened further by the North American Free Trade Agreement (NAFTA), the Agreement on Textiles and Clothing (ATC) of the World Trade Organization, and the Caribbean Basin Initiative. NAFTA and the Caribbean Basin Initiative allow most apparel produced in Mexico, Canada, and many other Western Hemisphere countries to be imported duty-free to the United States. The ATC, as it is phased in, will result in the elimination of quotas and a reduction in tariffs for many apparel products produced in additional countries. Domestic production—especially of apparel—will continue to move abroad and imports to the U.S. market will increase. Declines in U.S. apparel production will cause declines in domestic textile production because the apparel industry is the largest consumer of American-made textiles.

Domestic apparel manufacturers are developing the ability to take advantage of their close proximity to the U.S. market by responding more quickly to changes in market demand. U.S. producers use computers and electronic data interchange with retailers to closely monitor the sales of the items that they produce and to replenish diminishing inventories quickly. They are, therefore, able to keep retailers stocked with the most popular items and to cut back production of apparel that is not selling well.

Fierce competition in the market for apparel will keep domestic apparel and textile firms under intense pressure to cut costs and produce more with fewer workers. The textile industry already is highly automated but it will continue to seek to increase worker productivity through the introduction of laborsaving machinery. Employment is expected to decline as textile firms invest in new equipment, reorganize work practices, and consolidate. New machinery, such as faster air jet looms and computer-integrated manufacturing technology, will allow each operator to monitor a larger number of machines. Many factories are also reorganizing production floors to give workers additional responsibility, further increasing productivity. Also, textile firms are merging to take advantage of economies of scale and to pool resources for investment in new equipment. These practices will make the textile industry increasingly competitive, but they will decrease employment of many machine operator occupations. Persons with technical skills and some computer training will have the best opportunities.

Despite advances in technology, the apparel industry has had difficulty employing automated equipment extensively due to the soft properties of textile products. The industry produces a wide variety of apparel items that change frequently with changes in style and season. Adapting existing technology to the production of apparel is time consuming and expensive, and each change could require retooling. However, some larger firms and those that produce standardized items that change infrequently have automated presewing functions, material handling, and some simple sewing procedures. Technological developments, such as computer-aided marking and grading, computer-controlled cutters, semi-automatic sewing and pressing machines, and automated material handling systems have increased output while reducing the need for some workers in larger firms. Assembly and sewing continues to be the most labor-intensive step in the production of apparel, and increasing numbers of sewing machine operator jobs are expected to be lost to lower-wage workers abroad. But productivity improvements will allow many of the presewing functions of design, patternmaking, marking, and cutting to continue be done domestically, and employment of workers who perform these functions will not be as adversely affected. However, as the domestic apparel industry continues to restructure and consolidate, more of the smaller, less-efficient producers will lose market share to larger U.S. firms and foreign producers.

Tailors, dressmakers, and sewers, the most skilled apparel workers, also are expected to experience declining employment. Demand for their services will continue to lessen as consumers are increasingly likely to buy new, mass-produced apparel instead of purchasing custom-made apparel or having clothes altered or repaired.

Employment of shoe and leather workers is expected to decline through 2010 due to growing imports of less-expensive shoes and leather goods, increasing productivity of U.S. manufacturers, and the more frequent tendency to buy new shoes rather than repair damaged ones. However, declines are expected to be somewhat offset as more people invest in expensive leather shoes that they will want repaired. Also, as the population continues to age, more people will need custom shoes for health reasons.

Employment of upholsterers is expected to decline through 2010 as firms manufacturing new furniture and automotive seats use more-durable coverings and continue to become more automated and efficient. Demand for the reupholstery of furniture also is expected to decline as the increasing manufacture of new, relatively inexpensive upholstered furniture causes many people to simply replace old, worn furniture. However, demand will continue steady for upholsterers to restore very valuable furniture. Most reupholstery work is labor-intensive and not easily automated. Job opportunities for experienced upholsterers should be good because few young people enter the occupation and few shops offer training.

Earnings

Earnings of textile, apparel, and furnishings workers vary by occupation. Because many production workers in apparel manufacturing are paid according to the number of acceptable pieces they or their group produce, their total earnings depend on skill, speed, and accuracy. Workers covered by union contracts tend to have higher earnings. Median hourly earnings by occupation in 2000 were as follows:

Extruding and forming machine setters, operators, and tenders, synthetic and glass fibers	$12.66
Fabric and apparel patternmakers	11.57
Upholsterers	11.42
Textile knitting and weaving machine setters, operators, and tenders	10.32
Tailors, dressmakers, and custom sewers	10.14
Textile winding, twisting, and drawing out machine setters, operators, and tenders	9.89
Textile bleaching and dyeing machine operators and tenders	9.42
All other textile, apparel, and furnishings workers	9.25
Textile cutting machine setters, operators, and tenders	9.23
Shoe machine operators and tenders	8.89
Shoe and leather workers and repairers	8.32
Sewers, hand	8.09
Sewing machine operators	7.80
Pressers, textile, garment, and related materials	7.77
Laundry and drycleaning workers	7.59

Benefits also vary. A few large employers, for example, include childcare in their benefits package. Apparel workers in retail trade also may receive a discount on their purchases from the company for which they work. In addition, some of the larger manufacturers operate company stores, from which employees can purchase apparel products at significant discounts. Some small firms, however, offer only limited benefits.

Related Occupations

Textile, apparel, and furnishings workers apply their knowledge of textiles and leathers to fashion products using hand tools and machinery.

Other occupations that produce products using hand tools, machines, and their knowledge of the materials with which they work include assemblers and fabricators, dental laboratory technicians, food processing workers, jewelers and precious stone and metal workers, and woodworkers.

Sources of Additional Information

Information about job opportunities in textile, apparel, and furnishings occupations is available from local employers and local offices of the state employment service.

For general information on careers, technology, and trade regulations in the textile industry, contact:

- American Textile Manufacturers Institute, Inc., 1130 Connecticut Ave. NW., Suite 1200, Washington, DC 20036-3954

- Institute of Textile Technology, 2551 Ivy Rd., Charlottesville, NC 22903-4614. Internet: http://www.itt.edu

For general information on the apparel industry, contact:

- American Apparel Manufacturers Association, 2500 Wilson Blvd., Suite 301, Arlington, VA 22201

For information about the custom-made prescription shoe business and training opportunities in this field, contact:

- Pedorthic Footwear Association, 7150 Columbia Gateway Dr., Suite G, Columbia, MD 21046. Internet: http://www.pedorthics.org

To receive a list of technical schools with accredited programs in upholstery, contact:

- Accrediting Commission of Career Schools and Colleges of Technology, 2101 Wilson Blvd., Suite 302, Arlington, VA 22201. Internet: http://www.accsct.org

Tool and Die Makers

O*NET 51-4111.00

Significant Points

- Most tool and die makers train for 4 or 5 years in apprenticeships or postsecondary programs; employers typically recommend apprenticeship training.

- Job seekers with the appropriate skills and background should enjoy excellent opportunities.

Nature of the Work

Tool and die makers are among the most highly skilled production workers in the economy. These workers produce tools, dies, and special guiding and holding devices that enable machines to manufacture a variety of products we use daily—from clothing and furniture to heavy equipment and parts for aircraft.

Toolmakers craft precision tools that are used to cut, shape, and form metal and other materials. They also produce jigs and fixtures (devices that hold metal while it is bored, stamped, or drilled) and gauges and other measuring devices. Die makers construct metal forms (dies) that are used to shape metal in stamping and forging operations. They also make metal molds for diecasting and for molding plastics, ceramics, and composite materials. In addition to developing, designing and producing new tools and dies, these workers also may repair worn or damaged tools, dies, gauges, jigs, and fixtures.

To perform these functions, tool and die makers employ many types of machine tools and precision measuring instruments. They also must be familiar with the machining properties, such as hardness and heat tolerance, of a wide variety of common metals and alloys. As a result, tool and die makers are knowledgeable in machining operations, mathematics, and blueprint reading. In fact, tool and die makers often are considered highly specialized machinists.

Working from blueprints, tool and die makers first must plan the sequence of operations necessary to manufacture the tool or die. Next, they measure and mark the pieces of metal that will be cut to form parts of the final product. At this point, tool and die makers cut, drill, or bore the part as required, checking to ensure that the final product meets specifications. Finally, these workers assemble the parts and perform finishing jobs such as filing, grinding, and polishing surfaces.

Modern technology is changing the ways in which tool and die makers perform their jobs. Today, for example, these workers often use computer-aided design (CAD) to develop products and parts. Specifications entered into computer programs can be used to electronically develop drawings for the required tools and dies. Numerical tool and process control programmers use computer-aided manufacturing (CAM) programs to convert electronic drawings into computer programs that contain a sequence of cutting tool operations. Once these programs are developed, computer numerically controlled (CNC) machines follow the set of instructions contained in the program to produce the part. (Computer-controlled machine tool operators or machinists normally operate CNC machines; however, tool and die makers are trained in both operating CNC machines and writing CNC programs, and they may perform either task. CNC programs are stored electronically for future use, saving time and increasing worker productivity.) Next, tool and die makers assemble the different parts into a functioning machine. They file, grind, shim, and adjust the different parts to properly fit them together. Finally, the tool and die makers set up a test run using the tools or dies they have made to make sure that the manufactured parts meet specifications. If problems occur, tool and die makers compensate by adjusting the tools or dies.

Working Conditions

Tool and die makers usually work in toolrooms. These areas are quieter than the production floor because there are fewer machines in use at one time. They also are generally clean and cool to minimize heat-related expansion of metal workpieces and to accommodate the growing number of computer-operated machines. To minimize the exposure of workers to moving parts, machines have guards and shields. Many computer-controlled machines are totally enclosed, minimizing the exposure of workers to noise, dust, and the lubricants used to cool workpieces during machining. Tool and die makers also must follow safety rules and wear protective equipment, such as safety glasses to shield against bits of flying metal, earplugs to protect against noise, and gloves and masks to reduce exposure to hazardous lubricants and cleaners. These workers also need stamina because they often spend much of the day on their feet and may do moderately heavy lifting.

Companies employing tool and die makers have traditionally operated only one shift per day. Overtime and weekend work are common, especially during peak production periods.

Employment

Tool and die makers held about 130,000 jobs in 2000. Most worked in industries that manufacture metalworking machinery and equipment, metal forgings and stampings, motor vehicles, miscellaneous plastics products, and aircraft and parts. Although they are found throughout the country, jobs are most plentiful in the midwest, northeast, and west, where many of the metalworking industries are located.

Training, Other Qualifications, and Advancement

Most tool and die makers learn their trade through 4 or 5 years of education and training in formal apprenticeships or postsecondary programs. The best way to learn all aspects of tool and die making, according to most employers, is a formal apprenticeship program that combines classroom instruction and job experience. A growing number of tool and die makers receive most of their formal classroom training from community and technical colleges, sometimes in conjunction with an apprenticeship program.

Tool and die maker trainees learn to operate milling machines, lathes, grinders, spindles, and other machine tools. They also learn to use handtools for fitting and assembling gauges, and other mechanical and metal-forming equipment. In addition, they study metalworking processes, such as heat treating and plating. Classroom training usually consists of mechanical drawing, tool designing, tool programming, blueprint reading, and mathematics courses, including algebra, geometry, trigonometry, and basic statistics. Tool and die makers increasingly must have good computer skills to work with CAD technology and CNC machine tools.

Workers who become tool and die makers without completing formal apprenticeships generally acquire their skills through a combination of informal on-the-job training and classroom instruction at a vocational school or community college. They often begin as machine operators and gradually take on more difficult assignments. Many machinists become tool and die makers.

Because tools and dies must meet strict specifications—precision to one ten-thousandth of an inch is common—the work of tool and die makers requires a high degree of patience and attention to detail. Good eyesight is essential. Persons entering this occupation also should be mechanically inclined, able to work and solve problems independently, and capable of doing work that requires concentration and physical effort.

There are several ways for skilled workers to advance. Some move into supervisory and administrative positions in their firms; many obtain their college degree and go into engineering or tool design Some may start their own shops.

Job Outlook

Applicants with the appropriate skills and background should enjoy excellent opportunities for tool and die maker jobs. The number of workers receiving training in this occupation is expected to continue to be fewer than the number of openings created each year by tool and die makers who retire or transfer to other occupations. As more of these highly skilled workers retire, employers in certain parts of the country report difficulty attracting well-trained applicants. A major factor limiting the number of people entering the occupation is that many young people who have the educational and personal qualifications necessary to learn tool and die making may prefer to attend college or may not wish to enter production-related occupations.

Despite expected excellent employment opportunities, little or no change in employment of tool and die makers is projected over the 2000–2010 period because advancements in automation, including CNC machine tools and computer-aided design, should improve worker productivity, thus limiting employment. On the other hand, tool and die makers play a key role in the operation of many firms. As firms invest in new equipment, modify production techniques, and implement product design changes more rapidly, they will continue to rely heavily on skilled tool and die makers for retooling.

Earnings

Median hourly earnings of tool and die makers were $19.76 in 2000. The middle 50 percent earned between $15.67 and $24.45. The lowest 10 percent had earnings of less than $12.44, while the top 10 percent earned more than $28.88. Median hourly earnings in the manufacturing industries employing the largest number of tool and die makers in 2000 are shown in the following table:

Motor vehicles and equipment	$25.76
Aircraft and parts	22.17
Metal forgings and stampings	21.52
Metalworking machinery	18.99
Miscellaneous plastics products, not elsewhere classified	18.92

Related Occupations

The occupations most closely related to the work of tool and die makers are other machining occupations. These include machinists; computer-control programmers and operators; and machine setters, operators, and tenders—metal and plastic.

Another occupation that requires precision and skill in working with metal is welding, soldering, and brazing workers.

Sources of Additional Information

For information about careers in tool and die making, contact:

- Precision Machine Products Association, 6700 West Snowville Rd., Brecksville, OH 44141-3292. Internet: http://www.pmpa.org

- National Tooling and Metalworking Association, 9300 Livingston Rd., Ft. Washington, MD 20744. Internet: http://www.ntma.org

- PMA Educational Foundation, 6363 Oak Tree Blvd., Independence, OH 44131-2500. Internet: http://www.pmaef.org

Travel Agents

O*NET 41-3041.00

Significant Points

- Travel benefits, such as reduced rates for transportation and accommodations, attract many people to this occupation.

- Training at a postsecondary vocational school or college or university is increasingly important for getting a job.

- New developments in Internet technology, allowing people to access travel information from their personal computers and make their own travel arrangements, will limit the need for travel agents in the future.

Nature of the Work

Constantly changing airfares and schedules, thousands of available vacation packages, and a vast amount of travel information on the Internet can make travel planning frustrating and time-consuming. To sort out the many travel options, tourists and business people often turn to travel agents, who assess their needs and help them make the best possible travel arrangements. Also, many major cruiselines, resorts, and specialty travel groups use travel agents to promote travel packages to millions of people every year.

In general, travel agents give advice on destinations and make arrangements for transportation, hotel accommodations, car rentals, tours, and recreation. They also may advise on weather conditions, restaurants, tourist attractions, and recreation. For international travel, agents also provide information on customs regulations, required papers (passports, visas, and certificates of vaccination), and currency exchange rates.

Travel agents consult a variety of published and computer-based sources for information on departure and arrival times, fares, and hotel ratings and accommodations. They may visit hotels, resorts, and restaurants to evaluate their comfort, cleanliness, and the quality of food and service so that they can base recommendations on their own travel experiences or those of colleagues or clients.

Travel agents also promote their services, using telemarketing, direct mail, and the Internet. They make presentations to social and special-interest groups, arrange advertising displays, and suggest company-sponsored trips to business managers. Depending on the size of the travel agency, an agent may specialize by type of travel, such as leisure or business, or destination, such as Europe or Africa.

Working Conditions

Travel agents spend most of their time behind a desk conferring with clients, completing paperwork, contacting airlines and hotels for travel arrangements, and promoting group tours. During vacation seasons and holiday periods, they may be under a great deal of pressure. Many agents, especially those who are self-employed, frequently work long hours. With advanced computer systems and telecommunication networks, some travel agents are able to work at home.

Employment

Travel agents held about 135,000 jobs in 2000 and are found in every part of the country. More than 8 out of 10 salaried agents worked for travel agencies. Many of the remainder worked for membership organizations.

Training, Other Qualifications, and Advancement

The minimum requirement for those interested in becoming a travel agent is a high school diploma or equivalent. Technology and computerization are having a profound effect on the work of travel agents, however, and formal or specialized training is increasingly important. Many vocational schools offer 6- to 12-week full-time travel agent programs, as well as evening and weekend programs. Travel agent courses also are offered in public adult-education programs and in community and 4-year colleges. A few colleges offer bachelor's or master's degrees in travel and tourism. Although few college courses relate directly to the travel industry, a college education sometimes is desired by employers to establish a background in fields such as computer science, geography, communication, foreign languages, and world history. Courses in accounting and business management also are important, especially for those who expect to manage or start their own travel agencies.

The American Society of Travel Agents (ASTA) offers a correspondence course that provides a basic understanding of the travel industry. Travel agencies also provide on-the-job training for their employees, a significant part of which consists of computer instruction. Computer skills are required by all employers to operate airline and centralized reservation systems.

Experienced travel agents can take advanced self or group study courses from the Institute of Certified Travel Agents (ICTA) that lead to the designation of Certified Travel Counselor (CTC). The ICTA also offers marketing and sales skills development programs and destination specialist programs, which provide a detailed knowledge of regions such as North America, western Europe, the Caribbean, and the Pacific Rim.

Travel experience is an asset since personal knowledge about a city or foreign country often helps to influence clients' travel plans, as is experience as an airline reservation agent. Patience and the ability to gain the confidence of clients also are useful qualities. Travel agents must be well organized, accurate, and meticulous to compile information from various sources and plan and organize their clients' travel itineraries. Other desirable qualifications include good writing, computer, and sales skills.

Some employees start as reservation clerks or receptionists in travel agencies. With experience and some formal training, they can take on greater responsibilities and eventually assume travel agent duties. In agencies with many offices, travel agents may advance to office manager or to other managerial positions.

Those who start their own agencies generally have had experience in an established agency. Before they can receive commissions, these agents usually must gain formal approval from suppliers or corporations, such as airlines, shiplines, or raillines. The Airlines Reporting Corporation and the International Airlines Travel Agency Network, for example, are the approving bodies for airlines. To gain approval, an agency must be financially sound and employ at least one experienced manager or travel agent.

There are no federal licensing requirements for travel agents. However, nine states—California, Florida, Hawaii, Illinois, Iowa, Ohio, Oregon, Rhode Island, and Washington—require some form of registration or certification of retail sellers of travel services. More information may be obtained by contacting the office of the attorney general or department of commerce for each state.

Job Outlook

Employment of travel agents is expected to grow more slowly than the average for all occupations through 2010. Some job openings will arise as new agencies open and existing agencies expand, but most openings will occur as experienced agents transfer to other occupations or leave the labor force.

New developments will continue to limit the need for travel agents. The Internet increasingly allows people to access travel information from their personal computers, enabling them to research and plan their own trips, make their own reservations and travel arrangements, and purchase their own tickets. Further, suppliers of travel services now are able to make their services available through other means, such as electronic ticketing machines and remote ticket printers. Also, airline companies have put a limit on the amount of commissions they will pay to travel agencies, reducing revenues. However, many consumers still will prefer to use a professional travel agent to ensure reliability, to save time, and, in some cases, money.

Projected employment growth stems from increased spending on tourism and business travel over the next decade. With rising household incomes, smaller families, and an increasing number of older people who are more likely to travel, more people are expected to travel on vacation—and to do so more frequently—than in the past. Business travel also should grow as business activity expands. Further, professional and related workers, who are projected to be the fastest growing occupational group, do a significant amount of business travel.

Several other factors also will lead to more business for travel agents. For example, charter flights and larger, more efficient planes have brought air transportation within the budgets of more people, and the easing of federal regulation of air fares and routes has fostered greater competition among airlines, resulting in more affordable service. In addition, American travel agents now organize more tours for the growing number of foreign visitors. Also, travel agents often are able to offer various travel packages at a substantial discount.

The travel business is sensitive to economic downturns and international political crises, when travel plans are likely to be deferred. Therefore, the number of job opportunities for travel agents fluctuates.

Earnings

Experience, sales ability, and the size and location of the agency determine the salary of a travel agent. Median annual earnings of travel agents were $25,150 in 2000. The middle 50 percent earned between $19,890 and $31,820. The bottom 10 percent of travel agents earned less than $15,900, while the top 10 percent earned over $39,300.

Salaried agents usually enjoy standard benefits that self-employed agents must provide for themselves. Among agencies, those focusing on corporate sales pay higher salaries and provide more extensive benefits, on average, than those who focus on leisure sales. When they travel for personal reasons, agents usually get reduced rates for transportation and accommodations. In addition, agents sometimes take "familiarization" trips, at no cost to themselves, to learn about various vacation sites. These benefits attract many people to this occupation.

Earnings of travel agents who own their agencies depend mainly on commissions from airlines and other carriers, cruise lines, tour operators, and lodging places. Commissions for domestic travel arrangements,

cruises, hotels, sightseeing tours, and car rentals are about 7–10 percent of the total sale, and for international travel, about 10 percent. Travel agents also may charge clients a service fee for the time and expense involved in planning a trip.

During the first year of business or while awaiting corporation approval, self-employed travel agents often have low earnings. Their income usually is limited to commissions from hotels, cruises, and tour operators and to nominal fees for making complicated arrangements. Established agents may have lower earnings during economic downturns.

Related Occupations

Travel agents organize and schedule business, educational, or recreational travel or activities. Other workers with similar responsibilities include tour and travel guides, and reservation and transportation ticket agents and travel clerks.

Sources of Additional

For further information on training opportunities, contact:

- American Society of Travel Agents, Education Department, 1101 King St., Alexandria, VA 22314

For information on certification qualifications, contact:

- The Institute of Certified Travel Agents, 148 Linden St., P.O. Box 812059, Wellesley, MA 02181-0012

Truckdrivers and Driver/Sales Workers

O*NET 53-3031.00, 53-3032.01, 53-3032.02, 53-3033.00

Significant Points

- Opportunities should be good, because this occupation has among the greatest number of job openings each year.

- Competition is expected for jobs offering the highest earnings or most favorable work schedules.

- A commercial driver's license is required to operate most larger trucks.

Nature of the Work

Truckdrivers are a constant presence on the nation's highways and interstates, delivering everything from automobiles to canned foods. Firms of all kinds rely on trucks for pickup and delivery of goods because no other form of transportation can deliver goods from doorstep to doorstep. Even if goods travel in part by ship, train, or airplane, trucks carry nearly all goods at some point in their journey from producer to consumer.

Before leaving the terminal or warehouse, truckdrivers check the fuel level and oil in their trucks. They also inspect the trucks to make sure the brakes, windshield wipers, and lights are working and that a fire extinguisher, flares, and other safety equipment are aboard and in working order. Drivers make sure their cargo is secure and adjust their mirrors so that both sides of the truck are visible from the driver's seat. Drivers report equipment that is inoperable, missing, or loaded improperly to the dispatcher.

Once under way, drivers must be alert to prevent accidents. Drivers can see farther down the road, because large tractor-trailers sit higher than cars, pickups, and vans. This allows drivers to seek traffic lanes that allow for a steady speed, while keeping sight of varying road conditions.

The length of deliveries varies according to the type of merchandise and its final destination. Local drivers may provide daily service for a specific route, while other drivers make intercity and interstate deliveries that take longer and may vary from job to job. The driver's responsibilities and assignments change according to the time spent on the road, the type of payloads transported, and vehicle size.

Heavy truck and tractor-trailer drivers drive trucks or vans with a capacity of at least 26,000 Gross Vehicle Weight (GVW). They transport goods including cars, livestock, and other materials in liquid, loose, or packaged form. Many routes are from city to city and cover long distances. Some companies use two drivers on very long runs—one drives while the other sleeps in a berth behind the cab. "Sleeper" runs may last for days, or even weeks, usually with the truck stopping only for fuel, food, loading, and unloading.

Some heavy truck and tractor-trailer drivers who have regular runs transport freight to the same city on a regular basis. Other drivers perform unscheduled runs because shippers request varying service to different cities every day. Dispatchers tell these drivers when to report for work and where to haul the freight. Increasingly, trucking companies use automated routing equipment to track goods during shipment.

After these truckdrivers reach their destination or complete their operating shift, the U.S. Department of Transportation requires that they complete reports detailing the trip, the condition of the truck, and the circumstances of any accidents. In addition, federal regulations require employers to subject drivers to random alcohol and drug tests while they are on duty.

Long-distance heavy truck and tractor-trailer drivers spend most of their working time behind the wheel, but may load or unload their cargo after arriving at the final destination. This is especially common when drivers haul specialty cargo, because they may be the only one at the destination familiar with procedures or certified to handle the materials. Auto-transport drivers, for example, drive and position cars on the trailers and head ramps at the manufacturing plant and remove them at the dealerships. When picking up or delivering furniture, drivers of long-distance moving vans hire local workers to help them load or unload.

Light or delivery services truckdrivers drive trucks or vans with a capacity under 26,000 GVW. They deliver or pick up merchandise and packages within a specific area. This may include short "turnarounds" to deliver a shipment to a nearby city, pick up another loaded truck or van, and drive it back to their home base the same day. These services may require use of delivery tracking or location software to track the whereabouts of the merchandise or packages. Light or delivery services truckdrivers usually load or unload the merchandise at the customer's place of business. They may have helpers if there are many deliveries to make during the day, or if the load requires heavy moving. Typically, before the driver arrives for work, material handlers load the trucks and

arrange items in order of delivery to minimize handling of the merchandise. Customers must sign receipts for goods and pay drivers the balance due on the merchandise if there is a cash-on-delivery arrangement. At the end of the day, drivers turn in receipts, money, records of deliveries made, and any reports on mechanical problems with their trucks.

Some local truckdrivers have sales and customer service responsibilities. The primary responsibility of *driver/sales workers*, or *route drivers*, is to deliver and sell their firm's products over established routes or within an established territory. They sell goods such as food products, including restaurant takeout items, or pick up and deliver items such as laundry. Their response to customer complaints and requests can make the difference between a large order and a lost customer. Route drivers may also take orders and collect payments.

The duties of driver/sales workers vary according to their industry, the policies of their particular company, and the emphasis placed on their sales responsibility. Most have wholesale routes that deliver to businesses and stores, rather than to homes. For example, wholesale bakery driver/sales workers deliver and arrange bread, cakes, rolls, and other baked goods on display racks in grocery stores. They estimate the amount and variety of baked goods to stock by paying close attention to the items that sell well and to those left sitting on the shelves. They may recommend changes in a store's order or encourage the manager to stock new bakery products. Driver/sales workers employed by laundries that rent linens, towels, work clothes, and other items visit businesses regularly to replace soiled laundry. From time to time, they solicit new orders from businesses along their route.

After completing their route, driver/sales workers order items for the next delivery based on product sales trends, weather, and customer requests.

Working Conditions

Truckdriving has become less physically demanding because most trucks now have more comfortable seats, better ventilation, and improved, ergonomically designed cabs. Although these changes make the work environment more attractive, driving for many hours at a stretch, unloading cargo, and making many deliveries can be tiring. Local truckdrivers, unlike long-distance drivers, usually return home in the evening. Some self-employed long-distance truckdrivers who own and operate their trucks spend most of the year away from home.

Design improvements in newer trucks reduce stress and increase the efficiency of long-distance drivers. Many of the newer trucks are virtual miniapartments on wheels, equipped with refrigerators, televisions, and bunks. Satellites and Global Positioning Systems (GPS) link many of these state-of-the-art vehicles with company headquarters. Troubleshooting information, directions, weather reports, and other important communications can be delivered to the truck anywhere in the country within seconds. Drivers can easily communicate with the dispatcher to discuss delivery schedules and courses of action in the event of mechanical problems. The satellite linkup also allows the dispatcher to track the truck's location, fuel consumption, and engine performance.

Many drivers must also work with computerized inventory tracking equipment. It is important for the producer, warehouse, and customer to know the product's location at all times, in order to keep costs low and the quality of service high. For example, voice recognition software has replaced bar code readers in some freezer and refrigerator trucks, reducing error rates and improving function in cold conditions. Drivers must be able to adapt to an increasingly technology-driven workplace.

The U.S. Department of Transportation governs work hours and other working conditions of truckdrivers engaged in interstate commerce. A long-distance driver cannot work more than 60 hours in any 7-day period. Federal regulations also require that truckers rest 8 hours for every 10 hours of driving. Many drivers, particularly on long runs, work close to the maximum time permitted because they typically are compensated according to the number of miles or hours they drive. Drivers on long runs may face boredom, loneliness, and fatigue. Drivers frequently travel at night, on holidays, and weekends to avoid traffic delays and deliver cargo on time.

Local truckdrivers frequently work 50 or more hours a week. Drivers who handle food for chain grocery stores, produce markets, or bakeries typically work long hours, starting late at night or early in the morning. Although most drivers have regular routes, some have different routes each day. Many local truckdrivers, particularly driver/sales workers, load and unload their own trucks. This requires considerable lifting, carrying, and walking each day.

Employment

Truckdrivers and driver/sales workers held about 3.3 million jobs in 2000. Most truckdrivers find employment in large metropolitan areas along major interstate roadways where major trucking, retail, and wholesale companies have distribution outlets. Some drivers work in rural areas, providing specialized services such as delivering newspapers to customers or coal to a railroad.

Trucking companies employed about 28 percent of all truckdrivers in the United States. Almost 32 percent worked for companies engaged in wholesale or retail trade, such as auto parts stores, oil companies, lumber yards, restaurants, or distributors of food and grocery products. The remaining truckdrivers were distributed across many industries, including construction, manufacturing, and services.

Fewer than 1 out of 10 truckdrivers were self-employed. Of these, a significant number were owner-operators, who either served a variety of businesses independently or leased their services and trucks to a trucking company.

Training, Other Qualifications, and Advancement

State and federal regulations govern the qualifications and standards for truckdrivers. All drivers must comply with federal regulations and any state regulations that are stricter than federal requirements. Truckdrivers must have a driver's license issued by the state in which they live, and most employers require a clean driving record. Drivers of trucks designed to carry at least 26,000 pounds—including most tractor-trailers, as well as bigger straight trucks—must obtain a commercial driver's license (CDL) from the state in which they live. All truckdrivers who operate trucks transporting hazardous materials must obtain a CDL, regardless of truck size. Federal regulations governing the CDL exempt certain groups, including farmers, emergency medical technicians, firefighters, some military drivers, and snow and ice removers. In many states, a regular driver's license is sufficient for driving light trucks and vans.

To qualify for a commercial driver's license, applicants must pass a written test on rules and regulations, and then demonstrate that they can operate a commercial truck safely. A national databank permanently records all driving violations incurred by persons who hold commercial licenses. A state will check these records and deny a commercial driver's license to a driver who already has a license suspended or revoked in another state. Licensed drivers must accompany trainees until the trainees get their own CDL. Information on how to apply for a commercial driver's license may be obtained from state motor vehicle administrations.

While many states allow those who are at least 18 years old to drive trucks within state borders, the U.S. Department of Transportation establishes minimum qualifications for truckdrivers engaged in interstate commerce. Federal Motor Carrier Safety Regulations require drivers to be at least 21 years old and to pass a physical examination once every 2 years. The main physical requirements include good hearing, at least 20/40 vision with glasses or corrective lenses, and a 70-degree field of vision in each eye. Drivers can not be colorblind. Drivers must be able to hear a forced whisper in one ear at not less than 5 feet, with a hearing aide if needed. Drivers must have normal use of arms and legs and normal blood pressure. Drivers can not use any controlled substances, unless prescribed by a licensed physician. Persons with epilepsy or diabetes controlled by insulin are not permitted to be interstate truckdrivers. Federal regulations also require employers to test their drivers for alcohol and drug use as a condition of employment, and require periodic random tests of the drivers while they are on duty. In addition, a driver must not have been convicted of a felony involving the use of a motor vehicle; a crime using drugs; driving under the influence of drugs or alcohol; or hit-and-run driving that resulted in injury or death. All drivers must be able to read and speak English well enough to read road signs, prepare reports, and communicate with law enforcement officers and the public. Also, drivers must take a written examination on the Motor Carrier Safety Regulations of the U.S. Department of Transportation.

Many trucking operations have higher standards than those described. Many firms require that drivers be at least 22 years old, be able to lift heavy objects, and have driven trucks for 3 to 5 years. Many prefer to hire high school graduates and require annual physical examinations. Companies have an economic incentive to hire less-risky drivers because good drivers can increase fuel economy with their driving skills and decrease liability costs for the company.

Taking driver-training courses is a desirable method of preparing for truckdriving jobs and for obtaining a commercial driver's license. High school courses in driver-training and automotive mechanics also may be helpful. Many private and public vocational-technical schools offer tractor-trailer driver training programs. Students learn to maneuver large vehicles on crowded streets and in highway traffic. They also learn to inspect trucks and freight for compliance with federal, state, and local regulations. Some programs provide only a limited amount of actual driving experience, and completion of a program does not guarantee a job. Persons interested in attending a driving school should check with local trucking companies to make sure the school's training is acceptable.

Some states require prospective drivers to complete a training course in basic truckdriving before being issued their CDL. In Maine, for example, prospective applicants must complete an 8-week course at a school certified by the Professional Truck Drivers Institute (PTDI). PTDI-certified schools provide training that meets Federal Highway Administration guidelines for training tractor-trailer drivers.

Drivers must get along well with people because they often deal directly with customers. Employers seek driver/sales workers who speak well and have self-confidence, initiative, tact, and a neat appearance. Employers also look for responsible, self-motivated individuals able to work with little supervision.

Training given to new drivers by employers is usually informal, and may consist of only a few hours of instruction from an experienced driver, sometimes on the new employee's own time. New drivers may also ride with and observe experienced drivers before assignment of their own runs. Drivers receive additional training to drive special types of trucks or handle hazardous materials. Some companies give 1 to 2 days of classroom instruction covering general duties, the operation and loading of a truck, company policies, and the preparation of delivery forms and company records. Driver/sales workers also receive training on the various types of products they carry, so that they will be effective sales workers.

Very few people enter truckdriving professions directly out of school; most truckdrivers previously held jobs in other occupations. Driving experience in the armed forces can be an asset. In some cases, a person may also start as a truckdriver's helper, driving part of the day and helping to load and unload freight. Senior helpers receive promotion when driving vacancies occur.

Although most new truckdrivers are assigned immediately to regular driving jobs, some start as extra drivers, substituting for regular drivers who are ill or on vacation. They receive a regular assignment when an opening occurs.

New drivers sometimes start on panel trucks or other small straight trucks. As they gain experience and show competent driving skills, they may advance to larger and heavier trucks, and finally to tractor-trailers.

Advancement of truckdrivers generally is limited to driving runs that provide increased earnings or preferred schedules and working conditions. For the most part, a local truckdriver may advance to driving heavy or special types of trucks, or transfer to long-distance truckdriving. Working for companies that also employ long-distance drivers is the best way to advance to these positions. A few truckdrivers may advance to dispatcher, manager, or traffic work—for example, planning delivery schedules.

Some long-distance truckdrivers purchase a truck and go into business for themselves. Although many of these owner-operators are successful, some fail to cover expenses and eventually go out of business. Owner-operators should have good business sense as well as truckdriving experience. Courses in accounting, business, and business mathematics are helpful, and knowledge of truck mechanics can enable owner-operators to perform their own routine maintenance and minor repairs.

Job Outlook

Opportunities should be favorable for persons interested in truckdriving. This occupation has among the largest number of job openings each year. Although growth in demand for truckdrivers will create thousands of openings, many openings also will occur as experienced drivers transfer to other fields of work, retire, or leave the labor force for other reasons. Jobs vary greatly in terms of earnings, weekly work hours, number of nights spent on the road, and quality of equipment operated. Competition is expected for jobs with the most attractive earnings and working conditions, because truckdriving does not require education beyond high school.

Employment of truckdrivers is expected to increase about as fast as the average for all occupations through the year 2010, as the economy grows and the amount of freight carried by truck increases. The increased use of rail, air, and ship transportation requires truckdrivers to pick up and deliver shipments. Growth in the number of long-distance drivers will remain strong because these drivers transport perishable and time-sensitive goods more efficiently than do alternative modes of transportation, such as railroads.

Average growth of light and heavy truck driver employment will outweigh slow growth in driver/sales worker jobs. The number of truckdrivers with sales responsibilities is expected to increase more slowly than the average for all other occupations because companies are increasingly shifting sales, ordering, and customer service tasks to sales and office staffs, and using regular truckdrivers to make deliveries to customers.

Job opportunities may vary from year to year, because the strength of the economy dictates the amount of freight moved by trucks. Companies tend to hire more drivers when the economy is strong and deliveries are in high demand. Consequently, when the economy slows, employers hire fewer drivers, or even lay off drivers. Independent owner-operators are particularly vulnerable to slowdowns. Industries least likely to be affected by economic fluctuation tend to be the most stable places for employment.

Earnings

Median hourly earnings of heavy truck and tractor-trailer drivers were $15.25 in 2000. The middle 50 percent earned between $11.97 and $19.12 an hour. The lowest 10 percent earned less than $9.58, and the highest 10 percent earned more than $22.50 an hour. Median hourly earnings in the industries employing the largest numbers of heavy truck and tractor-trailer drivers in 2000 were as follows:

Trucking and courier services, except air $16.35
Personnel supply services 15.93
Groceries and related products 15.39
Miscellaneous special trade contractors 13.50
Concrete, gypsum, and plaster products 13.22

Median hourly earnings of light or delivery services truckdrivers were $10.74 in 2000. The middle 50 percent earned between $8.19 and $14.48 an hour. The lowest 10 percent earned less than $6.57, and the highest 10 percent earned more than $19.25 an hour. Median hourly earnings in the industries employing the largest numbers of light or delivery services truckdrivers in 2000 were as follows:

Air transportation, scheduled $16.61
Trucking and courier services, except air 12.60
Groceries and related products 11.34
Motor vehicles, parts, and supplies 8.19
Eating and drinking places 6.56

Median hourly earnings of driver/sales workers, including commission, were $9.79 in 2000. The middle 50 percent earned between $6.70 and $14.28 an hour. The lowest 10 percent earned less than $5.88, and the highest 10 percent earned more than $18.77 an hour. Median hourly earnings in the industries employing the largest numbers of driver/sales workers in 2000 were as follows:

Beer, wine, and distilled beverages	$14.49
Laundry, cleaning, and garment services	13.79
Groceries and related products	12.27
Nonstore retailers	11.05
Eating and drinking places	6.41

As a general rule, local truckdrivers receive an hourly wage and extra pay for working overtime, usually after 40 hours. Employers pay long-distance drivers primarily by the mile. Their rate per mile can vary greatly from employer to employer and may even depend on the type of cargo. Typically, earnings increase with mileage driven, seniority, and the size and type of truck driven. Most driver/sales workers receive a commission based on their sales in addition to an hourly wage.

Most self-employed truckdrivers are primarily engaged in long-distance hauling. After deducting their living expenses and the costs associated with operating their trucks, they commonly have earnings of $20,000 to $25,000 a year.

Many truckdrivers are members of the International Brotherhood of Teamsters. Some truckdrivers employed by companies outside the trucking industry are members of unions representing the plant workers of the companies for which they work.

Related Occupations

Other driving occupations include ambulance drivers and attendants, except emergency medical technicians; busdrivers; and taxi drivers and chauffeurs.

Sources of Additional Information

Information on truckdriver employment opportunities is available from local trucking companies and local offices of the state employment service.

Information on career opportunities in truckdriving may be obtained from:

- American Trucking Associations, Inc., 2200 Mill Rd., Alexandria, VA 22314

- American Trucking Association Foundation, 2200 Mill Rd., Alexandria, VA 22314

The Professional Truck Driver Institute, a nonprofit organization established by the trucking industry, manufacturers, and others, certifies truckdriver training courses meeting industry standards. A free list of certified tractor-trailer driver training courses may be obtained from:

- Professional Truck Driver Institute, 2200 Mill Rd., Alexandria, VA 22314. Internet: http://www.ptdi.org

Water and Liquid Waste Treatment Plant and System Operators

O*NET 51-8031.00

Significant Points

- Employment is concentrated in local government and private water supply and sanitary services companies.

- Postsecondary training is increasingly an asset as the number of regulated contaminants grows and treatment plants become more complex.

- Operators must pass exams certifying that they are capable of overseeing various treatment processes.

Nature of the Work

Clean water is essential for everyday life. *Water treatment plant and system operators* treat water so that it is safe to drink. *Liquid waste treatment plant and system operators*, also known as wastewater treatment plant and system operators, remove harmful pollutants from domestic and industrial liquid waste so that it is safe to return to the environment.

Water is pumped from wells, rivers, and streams to water treatment plants, where it is treated and distributed to customers. Liquid waste travels through customers' sewer pipes to liquid waste treatment plants, where it is treated and returned to streams, rivers, and oceans, or reused for irrigation and landscaping. Operators in both types of plants control processes and equipment to remove or destroy harmful materials, chemical compounds, and microorganisms from the water. They also control pumps, valves, and other processing equipment to move the water or liquid waste through the various treatment processes, and dispose of the removed waste materials.

Operators read, interpret, and adjust meters and gauges to make sure plant equipment and processes are working properly. They operate chemical-feeding devices, take samples of the water or liquid waste, perform chemical and biological laboratory analyses, and adjust the amount of chemicals, such as chlorine, in the water. They use a variety of instruments to sample and measure water quality, and common hand and power tools to make repairs. Operators also make minor repairs to valves, pumps, and other equipment.

Water and liquid waste treatment plant and system operators increasingly rely on computers to help monitor equipment, store sampling results, make process-control decisions, schedule and record maintenance activities, and produce reports. When problems occur, operators may use their computers to determine the cause of the malfunction and its solution.

Occasionally operators must work under emergency conditions. A heavy rainstorm, for example, may cause large amounts of liquid waste to flow into sewers, exceeding a plant's treatment capacity. Emergencies also can be caused by conditions inside a plant, such as chlorine gas leaks or oxygen deficiencies. To handle these conditions, operators are trained to make an emergency management response and use special safety equipment and procedures to protect public health and the facility. During these periods, operators may work under extreme pressure to correct problems as quickly as possible. These periods may create dangerous working conditions, and operators must be extremely cautious.

The specific duties of plant operators depend on the type and size of plant. In smaller plants, one operator may control all machinery, perform tests, keep records, handle complaints, and do repairs and maintenance. A few operators may handle both a water treatment and a liquid waste treatment plant. In larger plants with many employees, operators may be more specialized and only monitor one process. The staff also may include chemists, engineers, laboratory technicians, mechanics, helpers, supervisors, and a superintendent.

Water pollution standards have become increasingly stringent since adoption of two major federal environmental statutes: the Clean Water Act of 1972, which implemented a national system of regulation on the discharge of pollutants; and the Safe Drinking Water Act of 1974, which established standards for drinking water. Industrial facilities sending their wastes to municipal treatment plants must meet certain minimum standards to ensure that the wastes have been adequately pretreated and will not damage municipal treatment facilities. Municipal water treatment plants also must meet stringent drinking water standards. The list of contaminants regulated by these statutes has grown over time. For example, the 1996 Safe Drinking Water Act Amendments include standards for the monitoring of cryptosporidium and giardia, two biological organisms that cause health problems. Operators must be familiar with the guidelines established by federal regulations and how they affect their plant. In addition to federal regulations, operators also must be aware of any guidelines imposed by the state or locality in which the plant operates.

Working Conditions

Water and liquid waste treatment plant and system operators work both indoors and outdoors, and may be exposed to noise from machinery and unpleasant odors. Operators' work is physically demanding and often is performed in unclean locations. They must pay close attention to safety procedures for they may be confronted with hazardous conditions, such as slippery walkways, dangerous gases, and malfunctioning equipment. Plants operate 24 hours a day, 7 days a week; therefore, operators work one of three 8-hour shifts, including weekends and holidays, on a rotational basis. Operators may be required to work overtime.

Employment

Water and liquid waste treatment plant and system operators held about 88,000 jobs in 2000. Most worked for local governments. Some worked for private water supply and sanitary services companies, which increasingly provide operation and management services to local governments on a contract basis.

Water and liquid waste treatment plant and system operators are employed throughout the country, but most jobs are in larger towns and cities. Although nearly all work full time, those who work in small towns may only work part-time at the treatment plant. The remainder of their time may be spent handling other municipal duties.

Training, Other Qualifications, and Advancement

A high school diploma usually is required to become a water or liquid waste treatment plant operator. Operators need mechanical aptitude and should be competent in basic mathematics, chemistry, and biology. They must have the ability to apply data to formulas of treatment requirements, flow levels, and concentration levels. Some basic familiarity with computers also is necessary because of the trend toward computer-controlled equipment and more sophisticated instrumentation. Certain positions, particularly in larger cities and towns, are covered by civil

service regulations. Applicants for these positions may be required to pass a written examination testing mathematics skills, mechanical aptitude, and general intelligence.

Completion of an associate degree or 1-year certificate program in water quality and liquid waste treatment technology increases an applicant's chances for employment and promotion because plants are becoming more complex. Offered throughout the country, these programs provide a good general knowledge of water and liquid waste treatment processes, as well as basic preparation for becoming an operator.

Trainees usually start as attendants or operators-in-training and learn their skills on the job under the direction of an experienced operator. They learn by observing and doing routine tasks such as recording meter readings; taking samples of liquid waste and sludge; and performing simple maintenance and repair work on pumps, electric motors, valves, and other plant equipment. Larger treatment plants generally combine this on-the-job training with formal classroom or self-paced study programs.

The Safe Drinking Water Act Amendments of 1996, enforced by the U.S. Environmental Protection Agency, specify national minimum standards for certification and recertification of operators of community and nontransient, noncommunity water systems. As a result, operators must pass an examination to certify that they are capable of overseeing liquid waste treatment plant operations. There are different levels of certification depending on the operator's experience and training. Higher certification levels qualify the operator for a wider variety of treatment processes. Certification requirements vary by state and by size of treatment plants. Although relocation may mean having to become certified in a new location, many states accept other states' certifications.

Most state drinking water and water pollution control agencies offer training courses to improve operators' skills and knowledge. These courses cover principles of treatment processes and process control, laboratory procedures, maintenance, management skills, collection systems, safety, chlorination, sedimentation, biological treatment, sludge treatment and disposal, and flow measurements. Some operators take correspondence courses on subjects related to water and liquid waste treatment, and some employers pay part of the tuition for related college courses in science or engineering.

As operators are promoted, they become responsible for more complex treatment processes. Some operators are promoted to plant supervisor or superintendent; others advance by transferring to a larger facility. Postsecondary training in water and liquid waste treatment, coupled with increasingly responsible experience as an operator, may be sufficient to qualify for superintendent of a small plant, where a superintendent also serves as an operator. However, educational requirements are rising as larger, more complex treatment plants are built to meet new drinking water and water pollution control standards. With each promotion, the operator must have greater knowledge of federal, state, and local regulations. Superintendents of large plants generally need an engineering or science degree.

A few operators get jobs with state drinking water or water pollution control agencies as technicians, who monitor and provide technical assistance to plants throughout the state. Vocational-technical school or community college training generally is preferred for technician jobs. Experienced operators may transfer to related jobs with industrial liquid waste treatment plants, water or liquid waste treatment equipment and chemical companies, engineering consulting firms, or vocational-technical schools.

Job Outlook

Employment of water and liquid waste treatment plant and system operators is expected to grow as fast as the average for all occupations through the year 2010. Because the number of applicants in this field is normally low, job prospects will be good for qualified applicants.

The increasing population and growth of the economy are expected to boost demand for essential water and liquid waste treatment services. As new plants are constructed to meet this demand, employment of water and liquid waste treatment plant and system operators will increase. In addition, many job openings will occur as experienced operators transfer to other occupations or leave the labor force.

Local governments are the largest employers of water and liquid waste treatment plant and system operators. However, federal certification requirements have increased reliance on private firms specializing in the operation and management of water and liquid waste treatment facilities. As a result, employment in privately owned facilities will grow faster than the average. Increased pretreatment activity by manufacturing firms also will create new job opportunities.

Earnings

Median annual earnings of water and liquid waste treatment plant and system operators were $31,380 in 2000. The middle 50 percent earned between $24,390 and $39,530. The lowest 10 percent earned less than $19,120, and the highest 10 percent earned more than $47,370. Median annual earnings of water and liquid waste treatment plant and systems operators in 2000 were $31,120 in local government and $29,810 in water supply.

In addition to their annual salaries, water and liquid waste treatment plant and system operators usually receive benefits that may include health and life insurance, a retirement plan, and educational reimbursement for job-related courses.

Related Occupations

Other workers whose main activity consists of operating a system of machinery to process or produce materials include chemical plant and system operators; gas plant operators; petroleum pump system operators, refinery operators, and gaugers; power plant operators, distributors, and dispatchers; and stationary engineers and boiler operators.

Sources of Additional Information

For information on employment opportunities, contact state or local water pollution control agencies, state water and liquid waste operator associations, state environmental training centers, or local offices of the state employment service.

For information on certification, contact:

- Association of Boards of Certification, 208 Fifth St., Ames, IA 50010-6259. Internet: http://www.abccert.org

For educational information related to a career as a water or liquid waste treatment plant and system operator, contact:

- American Water Works Association, 6666 West Quincy Ave., Denver, CO 80235

- Water Environment Federation, 601 Wythe St., Alexandria, VA 22314-1994. Internet: http://www.wef.org

Water Transportation Occupations

O*NET 53-5011.01, 53-5011.02, 53-5021.01, 53-5021.02, 53-5021.03, 53-5022.00, 53-5031.00

Significant Points

- Many jobs in water transportation occupations require a merchant mariner's document or a license from the U.S. Coast Guard.

- Merchant mariners on ocean-going ships are hired for periods ranging from a single voyage to several continuous voyages and may be away from home continuously for months.

- Jobs aboard ocean-going vessels have high pay but competition for them remains keen, and merchant mariners might have to wait months between work opportunities.

Nature of the Work

Movement of huge amounts of cargo, as well as passengers, between nations and within our nation depends on workers in water transportation occupations. They operate and maintain deep-sea merchant ships, tugboats, towboats, ferries, dredges, excursion vessels, and other waterborne craft on the oceans, the Great Lakes, rivers and canals, other waterways, and in harbors.

Captains, mates, and pilots of water vessels command or supervise the operations of ships and water vessels, both within domestic waterways and on the deep sea. *Captains* or *masters* are in overall command of the operation of a vessel, and they supervise the work of any other officers and crew. They determine the course and speed, maneuver to avoid hazards, and continuously monitor the vessel's position using charts and navigational aides. Captains either direct or oversee crew members who steer the vessel, determine its location, operate engines, communicate to other vessels, perform maintenance, handle lines, or operate vessel equipment. Captains and their department heads ensure that proper procedures and safety practices are followed, check that machinery and equipment are in good working order, and oversee the loading and discharging of cargo or passengers. They also maintain logs and other records tracking the ships' movements, efforts at controlling pollution, and cargo/passenger carrying records.

Deck officers or *mates* perform the work for captains on vessels when they are on watch. Mates also supervise and coordinate activities of the crew aboard the ship. They inspect the cargo holds during loading to ensure the load is stowed according to specifications and regulations. Mates supervise crew members engaged in maintenance and the primary up-keep of the vessel. All mates stand watch for specified periods, usually 4 hours on and 8 hours off. However, on smaller vessels, there may be only one mate (called a *pilot* on some inland towing vessels) who alternates watches with the captain. The mate would assume command of the ship if the captain became incapacitated. When more than one mate is necessary aboard a ship, they typically are designated Chief Mate or First Mate, Second Mate, and Third Mate.

Pilots guide ships in and out of harbors, through straits, and on rivers and other confined waterways where a familiarity with local water depths, winds, tides, currents, and hazards such as reefs and shoals are of prime importance. Pilots on river and canal vessels are usually regular crew members, like mates. Harbor pilots are generally independent contractors, who accompany vessels while they enter or leave port. They may pilot many ships in a single day. *Motorboat operators* operate small, motor-driven boats to carry passengers and freight. They also take depth soundings in turning basins, and serve as liaisons between ships, between ship and shore, harbor and beach, or area patrol.

Ship engineers operate, maintain, and repair propulsion engines, boilers, generators, pumps, and other machinery. Merchant marine vessels usually have four engineering officers: a chief engineer, and a first, second, and third assistant engineer. Assistant engineers stand periodic watches, overseeing the safe operation of engines and machinery.

Marine oilers and more experienced *qualified members of the engine department*, or QMEDs, maintain the proper running order of their vessels in the engine spaces below decks under the direction of the ship's engineering officers. They lubricate gears, shafts, bearings, and other moving parts of engines and motors; read pressure and temperature gauges and record data; and may assist with repairs and adjust machinery.

Sailors operate the vessel and its deck equipment under the direction of the ship's officers, and keep the non-engineering areas in good condition. They stand watch, looking out for other vessels and obstructions in the ship's path and navigational aids such as buoys and lighthouses. They also steer the ship, measure water depth in shallow water, and maintain and operate deck equipment such as lifeboats, anchors, and cargo-handling gear. On vessels handling liquid cargo, sailors hook up hoses, operate pumps, and clean tanks, while on tugboats or tow vessels, they tie barges together into tow units, inspect them periodically, and disconnect them when the destination is reached. When docking or departing, they handle lines. They also perform routine maintenance chores such as repairing lines, chipping rust, and painting and cleaning decks or other areas. Experienced sailors are designated *able seamen* on ocean-going vessels, but may just be called deckhands on inland waters; larger vessels usually have a *boatswain*, or head seaman.

A typical deep-sea merchant ship has a captain, three deck officers or mates, a chief engineer and three assistant engineers, a radio operator, plus six or more non-officers, such as deck seamen, oilers and QMEDs, and cooks or foodhandlers. The size and service of the ship determine the number of crew for a particular voyage. Small vessels operating in harbors, rivers, or along the coast may have a crew comprised only of a captain and one deckhand. The cooking responsibilities usually fall under the deckhands' duties.

On larger coastal ships, the crew may include a captain, a mate or pilot, an engineer, and seven or eight seamen. Non-licensed positions on a large ship may include a full-time cook, an electrician, and machinery mechanics. On cruise ships, which also may be considered coastal ships, *bedroom stewards* keep passengers' quarters clean and comfortable.

Working Conditions

Merchant mariners spend extended periods at sea. Most deep-sea mariners are hired for one or more voyages that last for several months,

although there is no job security after that voyage. Many are unemployed for weeks or months before they have another opportunity to join another ship's crew.

The rate of unionization for these workers is almost 75 percent, much higher than the average for all occupations. Consequently, merchant marine officers and seamen, both veterans and beginners, are hired for voyages through union hiring halls or directly by shipping companies. Hiring halls prioritize the candidates by the length of time the person has been out of work, and fill open slots accordingly. Hiring halls are typically found in major seaports.

At sea, these workers usually stand watch for 4 hours and are off for 8 hours, 7 days a week. Those employed on Great Lakes ships work 60 days and have 30 days off, but do not work in the winter when the lakes are frozen. Workers on rivers, canals, and in harbors are more likely to have year-round work. Some work 8- or 12-hour shifts and go home every day. Others work steadily for a week or month and then have an extended period off. When working, they are usually on duty for 6 or 12 hours and are off for 6 or 12 hours. Those on smaller vessels are normally assigned to one vessel and have steady employment.

People in water transportation occupations work in all weather conditions. Although merchant mariners try to avoid severe storms while at sea, working in damp and cold conditions is often inevitable. While it is uncommon nowadays for vessels to suffer sea disasters such as fire, explosion, or a sinking, workers face the possibility that they may have to abandon their craft on short notice if it collides with other vessels or runs aground. They also risk injury or death from falling overboard, and hazards associated with working with machinery, heavy loads, and dangerous cargo.

Most newer vessels are air-conditioned, soundproofed from noisy machinery, and equipped with comfortable living quarters. Nevertheless, some mariners dislike the long periods away from home and the confinement aboard ship, and consequently leave the industry.

Employment

Water transportation workers held about 70,000 jobs in 2000. The total number who worked at some point in the year was somewhat higher because many merchant marine officers and seamen worked only part of the year. The following table shows employment in the occupations that make up this group:

Sailors and marine oilers	32,000
Ship and boat captains and operators	25,000
Ship engineers	8,600
All other water transportation workers	4,900

More than 75 percent of these workers were employed in water transportation services. Of these, about 39 percent worked in establishments related to marine cargo handling, towing and tugboat services, marinas, or boat cleaning and marine salvaging. About 25 percent worked in the transportation of freight on the oceans or the Great Lakes, while about 13 percent were employed in the water transportation of passengers on the deep seas, ferries, or sightseeing boats. The federal government employed approximately 10 percent of all water transportation workers.

Training, Other Qualifications, and Advancement

Entry, training, and educational requirements for most water transportation occupations are established and regulated by the U.S. Coast Guard, an agency of the U.S. Department of Transportation. All officers and operators of watercraft must be licensed by the Coast Guard, which offers various kinds of licenses, depending on the position and type of craft.

There are two ways to qualify for a deck or engineering officer's license: Applicants must either accumulate sea time and meet regulatory requirements or graduate from the U.S. Merchant Marine Academy or one of the six state maritime academies. In both cases, applicants must pass a written examination. Federal regulations also require that an applicant pass a physical examination, a drug screening, and a National Driver Register Check before being considered. Persons without formal training can be licensed if they pass the written exam and possess sea service appropriate to the license for which they are applying. However, it is difficult to pass the examination without substantial formal schooling or independent study. Also, because seamen may work 6 months a year or less, it can take 5 to 8 years to accumulate the necessary experience. The academies offer 4-year academic programs leading to a bachelor of science degree or a license as a third mate (deck officer) or third assistant engineer (engineering officer) , issued by the Coast Guard. Qualified academy graduates can earn a commission as ensign in the U.S. Naval Reserve, Merchant Marine Reserve, or the Coast Guard Reserve. With experience and additional training, third officers may qualify for higher rank.

Sailors and unlicensed engineers working on U.S. flagged deep-sea and Great Lakes vessels must hold a Coast Guard-issued document. Additionally, they must hold certification when working aboard liquid-carrying vessels. Able seamen also must hold government-issued certification. For employment in the merchant marine as an unlicensed seaman, a merchant mariner's document issued by the Coast Guard is needed. Most of the jobs must be filled by U.S. citizens. However, a small percentage of applicants for merchant mariner documents do not need to be U.S. citizens, but must at least be aliens legally admitted into the United States and holding a green card. A medical certificate of excellent health attesting to vision, color perception, and general physical condition is required for higher level deckhands and unlicensed engineers. While no experience or formal schooling is required, training at a union-operated school is the best source. Beginners are classified as ordinary seamen and may be assigned to any of the three unlicensed departments: deck, engine, or steward. With experience at sea, and perhaps union-sponsored training, an ordinary seaman can pass the able seaman exam and move up with 3 years of service.

No special training or experience is needed to become a seaman or deckhand on vessels operating in harbors or on rivers or other waterways. Newly hired workers are generally given a short introductory course and then learn skills on the job. After sufficient experience, they are eligible to take a Coast Guard exam to qualify as a mate, pilot, or captain. Substantial knowledge gained through experience, courses taught at approved schools, and independent study are needed to pass the exam.

Harbor pilot training is usually an extended apprenticeship with a towing company or a pilot association. Entrants may be able seamen or licensed officers.

Job Outlook

Keen competition is expected to continue for jobs in water transportation occupations. Overall, employment in water transportation occupations is projected to grow more slowly than the average for all occupations through the year 2010. Opportunities will vary by sector.

Employment in deep-sea shipping for American mariners is expected to stabilize after several years of decline. New international regulations have raised shipping standards with respect to safety, training, and working conditions. Consequently, competition from ships that sail under foreign *flags of convenience* (FOCs) should lessen as insurance rates rise for ships that do not meet the new standards. Insuring ships under industrialized countries' flags, including that of the United States, should become less expensive, increasing the amount of international cargo carried by U.S. ships. A fleet of deep-sea U.S. flagged ships is considered to be vital to the nation's defense, so some receive federal support through a maritime security subsidy and other provisions in laws limit certain federal cargoes to ships that fly the U.S. flag.

Newer ships are designed to be operated safely by much smaller crews. Innovations include automated controls and computerized monitoring systems in navigation, engine control, watchkeeping, ship management, and cargo handling. As older vessels are replaced, computer skills will become more important for crews. Possible future developments include "fast ships," ocean-going cargo vessels that use jet propulsion, which would decrease ocean-crossing times significantly. If such plans are successful, the industry will benefit in terms of increased business and employment.

Vessels on rivers and canals and on the Great Lakes carry mostly bulk products such as coal, iron ore, petroleum, sand and gravel, grain, and chemicals. Although shipments of these products are expected to grow through the year 2010, current imports of steel are dampening employment on the Lakes. Employment in water transportation services is likely to rise, however.

Growth also is expected in the cruiseline industry within U.S. waters. Vessels that operate between U.S. ports are required by law to be U.S. flagged vessels. The building and staffing of several new cruise ships over the next 3 to 4 years will create new opportunities for employment at sea in the cruise line industry, which is composed mostly of foreign flagged ships.

Nevertheless, openings within the traditional water transportation sector for mariners, though expanding slightly, will remain tight. Some experienced merchant mariners may continue to go for periods of time without work. However, this situation appears to be changing, as the demand for licensed and non-licensed personnel has been on the rise. Maritime academy graduates who have not found licensed shipboard jobs in the U.S. merchant marine find jobs in related industries. Because they are commissioned as ensigns in the Naval or Coast Guard Reserve, some are selected for active duty in the Navy or Coast Guard. Some find jobs as seamen on U.S. flagged or foreign flagged vessels, tugboats, other watercraft, or enter civilian jobs with the U.S. Navy or Coast Guard. Some take land-based jobs with shipping companies, marine insurance companies, manufacturers of boilers or related machinery, or other related jobs.

Earnings

Earnings vary widely depending on the particular water transportation position and experience, ranging from the minimum wage in some beginning seamen or mate positions to more than $33.77 an hour for some experienced ship engineers. Median hourly earnings in 2000 of water transportation occupations were as follows:

Ship engineers $22.85
Ship and boat captains and operators 21.62
Sailors and marine oilers 13.52
All other water transportation workers 11.70

Annual pay for captains of larger vessels, such as container ships, oil tankers, or passenger ships, may exceed $100,000, but only after many years of experience. Similarly, captains of tugboats often earn more than the median reported here, with earnings dependent on the port and the nature of the cargo.

Related Occupations

Workers in other occupations who make their living on the seas and coastal waters include fishers and fishing vessel operators and some members of branches of the armed forces.

Sources of Additional Information

Information on merchant marine careers, training, and licensing requirements is available from:

- Maritime Administration, U.S. Department of Transportation, 400 7th St. SW., Room 7302, Washington, DC 20590. Internet: http://www.marad.dot.gov

- Seafarers' International Union, 5201 Auth Way, Camp Springs, MD 20746

- Paul Hall Center for Maritime Training and Education, P.O. Box 75, Piney Point, MD 20674-0075. Internet: http://www.seafarers.org/phc

- International Organization of Masters, Mates, and Pilots, 700 Maritime Boulevard, Linthicum Heights, MD 21090-1941

- U.S. Coast Guard National Maritime Center, Licensing and Evaluation Branch, 4200 Wilson Blvd., Suite 630, Arlington, VA 22203-1804. Internet: http://www.uscg.mil/stcw/m-pers.htm

Individuals interested in attending the merchant marine academy should contact:

- Admissions Office, U.S. Merchant Marine Academy, Steamboat Rd., Kings Point, NY 11024-1699

Weighers, Measurers, Checkers, and Samplers, Recordkeeping

O*NET 43-5111.00

Significant Points

- Many jobs for weighers, measurers, checkers, and samplers are entry level and do not require more than a high school diploma.

- Workers develop the necessary skills through on-the-job training lasting from several days to a few months.

- Automation should not have a significant effect on employment in this occupation because most of its duties need to be done manually.

- Numerous job openings will arise each year from the need to replace workers who leave this very large occupational group.

Nature of the Work

Weighers, measurers, checkers, and samplers weigh, measure, and check materials, supplies, and equipment in order to keep relevant records. Most of their duties are clerical. They verify quantity, quality, and overall value and condition of items purchased, sold, or produced against records, bills, invoices, or receipts. Weighers, measurers, checkers, and samplers check and document items using either manual or automated data processing systems. They check the items to ensure accuracy of the recorded data. They prepare reports on warehouse inventory levels and use of parts. Weighers, measurers, checkers, and samplers also check for any defects in the items and record the severity of the defects.

These workers use weight scales, counting devices, tally sheets, and calculators to properly record information about the products. They usually move objects to and from the scales using a handtruck or forklift. They issue receipts for the products when needed or requested.

Working Conditions

Weighers, measurers, checkers, and samplers work in a wide variety of businesses, institutions, and industries. Some work in warehouses, stockrooms, or shipping and receiving rooms that may not be temperature controlled. Others may spend time in cold storage rooms or outside on loading platforms, where they are exposed to the weather.

The typical work week is Monday through Friday.

Employment

Weighers, measurers, checkers, and samplers held about 83,000 jobs in 2000. Their employment is spread across most industries. Department stores and air carriers accounted for about 16 percent of these jobs. Wholesale trade and services comprised 28 percent of employment.

Training, Other Qualifications, and Advancement

Many weighers, measurers, checkers, and sampler jobs are entry level and do not require more than a high school diploma. Employers, however, prefer to hire those who are familiar with computers and other electronic office and business equipment. Those who have taken business courses or have previous business, dispatching, or specific job-related experience may be preferred. Because communication with other people is an integral part of these jobs, good oral and written communications skills are essential. Typing, filing, recordkeeping, and other clerical skills also are important.

Weighers, measurers, checkers, and samplers usually learn the job by doing routine tasks under close supervision. They learn how to count and mark stock, and then start keeping records and taking inventory.

Strength, stamina, good eyesight, and an ability to work at repetitive tasks, sometimes under pressure, are important characteristics.

Advancement opportunities for weighers, measurers, checkers, and samplers vary with the place of employment.

Job Outlook

Employment of weighers, measurers, checkers, and samplers is expected to grow about as fast as the average for all occupations through 2010. The emphasis on accurate and nondefective materials, as well as the use of records for verifying information, is an increasingly important responsibility for companies that will increase the need for weighers, measurers, checkers, and samplers. Furthermore, automation should not have a significant effect on employment in this occupation because most of its duties need to be done manually. In addition to those resulting from job growth, openings should arise from the need to replace workers who leave the labor force or transfer to other occupations.

Earnings

Median hourly earnings in 2000 for weighers, measurers, checkers, and samplers were $11.36.

Weighers, measurers, checkers, and samplers usually receive the same benefits as most other workers. If uniforms are required, employers usually provide either the uniforms or an allowance to purchase them.

Related Occupations

Other workers who determine and document characteristics of materials or equipment include cargo and freight agents; production, planning, and expediting clerks; shipping, receiving, and traffic clerks; stock clerks and order fillers; and procurement clerks.

Sources of Additional Information

Information about job opportunities may be obtained from local employers and local offices of the state employment service.

Welding, Soldering, and Brazing Workers

O*NET 51-4121.01, 51-4121.02, 51-4121.03, 51-4121.04, 51-4121.05, 51-4122.01, 51-4122.02, 51-4122.03, 51-4122.04

Significant Points

- Job prospects should be excellent.

- Training ranges from a few weeks of school or on-the-job training for low-skilled positions to several years of combined school and on-the-job training for highly skilled jobs.

Nature of the Work

Welding is the most common way of permanently joining metal parts. In this process, heat is applied to metal pieces, melting and fusing them to form a permanent bond. Because of its strength, welding is used in shipbuilding, automobile manufacturing and repair, aerospace applications, and thousands of other manufacturing activities. Welding also is used to join beams when constructing buildings, bridges, and other structures, and to join pipes in pipelines, power plants, and refineries.

Welders use many types of welding equipment set up in a variety of positions, such as flat, vertical, horizontal, and overhead. They may perform manual welding, in which the work is entirely controlled by the welder, or semiautomatic welding, in which the welder uses machinery, such as a wire feeder, to help in performing welding tasks.

Arc welding is the most common type of welding. Standard arc welding involves two large metal alligator clips that are carrying a strong electrical current. One clip is attached to any part of the workpiece being welded. The second clip is connected to a thin welding rod. When the rod touches the workpiece, a powerful electrical circuit is created. The massive heat created by the electrical current causes both the workpiece and the steel core of the rod to melt together, cooling quickly to form a solid bond. During welding, the flux that surrounds the rod's core vaporizes, forming an inert gas that serves to protect the weld from atmospheric elements that might weaken it. Two common advanced types of arc welding are Gas Tungsten Arc (TIG) and Gas Metal Arc (MIG) welding. Instead of welding rods, these welding systems use a spool of continuously fed wire, which allows the welder to weld longer stretches without stopping to replace the rod. Instead of using gas flux surrounding the rod, TIG and MIG protect the initial weld from the environment by blowing inert gas onto the weld.

Like arc welding, soldering and brazing use metal to join two pieces of metal. However, the metal added during the process has melting point lower than that of the workpiece, so only the added metal is melted, not the workpiece. Soldering uses metals with a melting point below 800 degrees Fahrenheit; brazing uses metals with a melting point above 800 degrees Fahrenheit. Because soldering and brazing do not melt the workpiece, these processes normally do not create distortions or weaknesses in the workpiece that can occur with welding. Soldering commonly is used to join electrical, electronic, and other small metal parts. Brazing produces a stronger joint than does soldering, and often is used to join metals other than steel, such as brass parts.

Skilled welding, soldering, and brazing workers generally plan work from drawings or specifications or use their knowledge of fluxes and base metals to analyze parts. These workers then select and set up welding equipment and examine welds, to ensure that they meet standards or specifications. Some welders have more limited duties, however. They perform routine jobs that already have been planned and laid out and do not require extensive knowledge of welding techniques.

Automated welding is used in an increasing number of production processes. In these instances, a machine or robot performs the welding tasks while monitored by a welding machine operator. Welding, soldering, and brazing machine setters, operators, and tenders follow specified layouts, work orders, or blueprints. Operators must load parts correctly and constantly monitor the machine to ensure that it produces the desired bond.

The work of arc, plasma, and oxy-gas cutters is closely related to that of welders. However, instead of joining metals, cutters use the heat from an electric arc, a stream of ionized gas, or burning gases to cut and trim metal objects to specific dimensions. Cutters also dismantle large objects, such as ships, railroad cars, automobiles, buildings, or aircraft. Some operate and monitor cutting machines similar to those used by welding machine operators. Plasma cutting has been increasing in popularity because, unlike other methods, it can cut a wide variety of metals, including stainless steel, aluminum, and titanium.

Working Conditions

Welding, soldering, and brazing workers often are exposed to a number of potential hazards, including the intense light created by the arc, hazardous fumes, and burns. In the interests of safety, they wear safety shoes, goggles, hoods with protective lenses, and other devices designed to prevent burns and eye injuries and to protect them from falling objects. They normally work in well-ventilated areas to limit their exposure to fumes. Automated welding, soldering, and brazing machine operators are not exposed to as many dangers, however, and a face shield or goggles usually provide adequate protection for these workers.

Welders and cutters may work outdoors, often in inclement weather, or indoors, sometimes in a confining area designed to contain sparks and glare. When outdoors, they may work on a scaffold or platform high off the ground. In addition, they may be required to lift heavy objects and work in a variety of awkward positions, having to make welds while bending, stooping, or working overhead.

Although about half of welders, solderers, and brazers work a 40-hour week, overtime is common, and some welders work up to 70 hours per week. Welders also may work in shifts as long as 12 hours. Some welders, solderers, brazers, and machine operators work in factories that operate around-the-clock.

Employment

Welding, soldering, and brazing workers held about 521,000 jobs in 2000. Of these jobs, 3 of every 4 were found in manufacturing and services. Most manufacturing jobs were in the transportation equipment, industrial machinery and equipment, or fabricated metal products industries. Services industry jobs were mainly in repair shops and personnel supply agencies. Most jobs for welding, soldering, and brazing machine setters, operators, and tenders were found in manufacturing industries, primarily those producing fabricated metal products, motor vehicles, and construction and related machinery.

Training, Other Qualifications, and Advancement

Training for welding, soldering, and brazing workers can range from a few weeks of school or on-the-job training for low-skilled positions to several years of combined school and on-the-job training for highly skilled jobs. Formal training is available in high schools, vocational schools, and postsecondary institutions, such as vocational-technical institutes, community colleges, and private welding schools. The armed forces operate welding schools as well. Some employers provide training. Courses in blueprint reading, shop mathematics, mechanical drawing, physics, chemistry, and metallurgy are helpful. Knowledge of computers is gaining in importance, especially for welding, soldering,

and brazing machine operators, who are becoming responsible for the programming of computer-controlled machines, including robots.

Some welders become certified, a process whereby the employer sends a worker to an institution, such as an independent testing lab or technical school, to weld a test specimen to specific codes and standards required by the employer. Testing procedures are based on the standards and codes set by one of several industry associations with which the employer may be affiliated. If the welding inspector at the examining institution determines that the worker has performed according to the employer's guidelines, the inspector will then certify the welder being tested as able to work with a particular welding procedure.

Welding, soldering, and brazing workers need good eyesight, hand-eye coordination, and manual dexterity. They should be able to concentrate on detailed work for long periods and be able to bend, stoop, and work in awkward positions. In addition, welders increasingly need to be willing to receive training and perform tasks in other production jobs.

Welders can advance to more skilled welding jobs with additional training and experience. For example, they may become welding technicians, supervisors, inspectors, or instructors. Some experienced welders open their own repair shops.

Job Outlook

Job prospects should be excellent for skilled candidates, as many potential entrants who have the educational and personal qualifications to acquire the necessary skills may prefer to attend college or may prefer work that has more comfortable working conditions. Employment of welding, soldering, and brazing workers is expected to grow about as fast as the average for all occupations over the 2000–2010 period. In addition, many openings will arise as workers retire or leave the occupation for other reasons.

The major factor affecting employment of welders is the health of the industries in which they work. Because almost every manufacturing industry uses welding at some stage of manufacturing or in the repair and maintenance of equipment, a strong economy will keep demand for welders high. A downturn affecting industries such as auto manufacturing, construction, or petroleum, however, would have a negative impact on the employment of welders in those areas, and could cause some layoffs. Levels of government funding for infrastructure repairs and improvements also are expected to be an important determinant of the future number of welding jobs.

Regardless of the state of the economy, the pressures to improve productivity and hold down labor costs are leading many companies to invest more in automation, especially computer-controlled and robotically-controlled welding machinery. This may affect the demand for low-skilled manual welding, soldering, and brazing workers because the jobs that are currently being automated are the simple, repetitive ones. The growing use of automation, however, should increase demand for highly skilled welding, soldering, and brazing machine setters, operators, and tenders. Welders working on construction projects or in equipment repair will not be affected by technology change to the same extent that other welders are, because their jobs are not as easily automated.

Technology is helping to improve welding, creating more uses for welding in the workplace and expanding employment opportunities. For example, new ways are being developed to bond dissimilar materials and nonmetallic materials, such as plastics, composites, and new alloys.

Also, laser beam and electron beam welding, new fluxes, and other new technologies and techniques are improving the results of welding, making it applicable to a wider assortment of jobs. Improvements in technology also have boosted welding productivity, making it more competitive with other methods of joining metals.

Earnings

Median hourly earnings of welders, cutters, solderers, and brazers were $13.13 in 2000. The middle 50 percent earned between $10.74 and $16.37. The lowest 10 percent had earnings of less than $8.86, while the top 10 percent earned over $20.74. Median hourly earnings in the industries employing the largest numbers of welders, cutters, solderers, and brazers in 2000 were as follows:

Construction and related machinery $13.51
Motor vehicles and equipment 13.43
Fabricated structural metal products.......................................12.91
Miscellaneous repair shops...12.33
Personnel supply services 10.55

Median hourly earnings of welding, soldering, and brazing machine setters, operators, and tenders were $13.09 in 2000. The middle 50 percent earned between $10.41 and $16.83. The lowest 10 percent had earnings of less than $8.64, while the top 10 percent earned over $23.32. Median hourly earnings in the industries employing the largest numbers of welding machine operators in 2000 were as follows:

Motor vehicles and equipment $16.16
Construction and related machinery 13.72
Fabricated structural metal products.......................................12.77

Many welders belong to unions. Among these are the International Association of Machinists and Aerospace Workers; the International Brotherhood of Boilermakers, Iron Ship Builders, Blacksmiths, Forgers and Helpers; the International Union, United Automobile, Aerospace and Agricultural Implement Workers of America; the United Association of Journeymen and Apprentices of the Plumbing and Pipe Fitting Industry of the United States and Canada; and the United Electrical, Radio, and Machine Workers of America.

Related Occupations

Welding, soldering, and brazing workers are skilled metal workers. Other metal workers include machinists; machine setters, operators, and tenders—metal and plastic; computer-control programmers and operators; tool and die makers; sheet metal workers; and boilermakers.

Sources of Additional Information

For information on training opportunities and jobs for welding, soldering, and brazing workers, contact local employers, the local office of the state employment service, or schools providing welding, soldering, or brazing training.

Information on careers in welding is available from:

● American Welding Society, 550 N.W. Lejeune Rd., Miami, FL 33126-5699. Internet: http://www.aws.org

Woodworkers

O*NET 51-7011.00, 51-7021.00, 51-7031.00, 51-7032.00, 51-7041.01, 51-7041.02, 51-7042.01, 51-7042.02, 51-7099.99

Significant Points

● Most woodworkers are trained on the job; basic machine operations may be learned in a few months, but becoming a skilled woodworker often requires 2 or more years.

● Employment is expected to grow more slowly than average, reflecting relatively slow growth among lesser skilled woodworkers.

● Job prospects will be best for highly skilled workers and those with knowledge of computerized numerical control machine tool operation.

Nature of the Work

In spite of the development of sophisticated plastics and other materials, the demand for wood products continues unabated. Helping to meet this demand are woodworkers. Woodworkers are found in industries that produce wood, such as sawmills and plywood mills; in industries that use wood to produce furniture, kitchen cabinets, musical instruments, and other fabricated wood products; or in small shops that make architectural woodwork, furniture, and many other specialty items.

All woodworkers are employed at some stage of the process through which logs of wood are transformed into finished products. Some of these workers produce the structural elements of buildings; others mill hardwood and softwood lumber; still others assemble finished wood products. They operate machines that cut, shape, assemble, and finish raw wood to make the doors, windows, cabinets, trusses, plywood, flooring, paneling, molding, and trim that are components of most homes. Others may fashion home accessories, such as beds, sofas, tables, dressers, and chairs. In addition to these household goods, woodworkers also make sporting goods, including baseball bats, racquets, and oars, as well as musical instruments, toys, caskets, tool handles, and thousands of other wooden items.

Production woodworkers set up, operate, and tend woodworking machines such as power saws, planers, sanders, lathes, jointers, and routers that cut and shape components from lumber, plywood, and other wood products. In sawmills, *sawing machine operators and tenders* set up, operate, or tend wood sawing machines that cut logs into planks, timbers, or boards. In plants manufacturing wood products, woodworkers first determine the best method of shaping and assembling parts working from blueprints, supervisors' instructions, or shop drawings that woodworkers themselves produce. Before cutting, they often must measure and mark the materials. They verify dimensions and may trim parts using hand tools such as planes, chisels, wood files, or sanders to insure a tight fit. *Woodworking machine operators and tenders* set up, operate, or tend a specific woodworking machine such as drill presses, lathes, shapers, routers, sanders, planers, and wood-nailing machines. Lower skilled operators may merely press a switch on a woodworking machine and monitor the automatic operation whereas more highly skilled operators set up equipment, cut and shape wooden parts, and verify dimensions using a template, caliper, or rule.

The next step in the manufacturing process is the production of subassemblies using fasteners and adhesives. The pieces then are brought together to form a complete unit. The product is then finish sanded, stained, and, if necessary, coated with a sealer, such as lacquer or varnish. Woodworkers may perform this work in teams or be assisted by a helper.

Woodworkers have been greatly affected by the introduction of computer-controlled machinery. This technology has raised worker productivity by allowing one operator to simultaneously tend a greater number of machines. With computerized numerical controls (CNC), an operator can program a machine to perform a sequence of operations automatically, resulting in greater precision and reliability. The integration of computers with equipment has improved production speeds and capabilities, simplified setup and maintenance requirements, and increased the demand for workers with computer skills.

While this costly equipment has had a great impact on workers in the largest, most efficient firms, precision or custom woodworkers—who generally work in smaller firms—have continued to employ the same production techniques they have used for many years. Workers such as *cabinetmakers and bench carpenters; model makers and patternmakers;* and *furniture finishers* work on a customized basis, often building one-of-a-kind items. These highly skilled precision woodworkers usually perform a complete cycle of tasks, cutting, shaping, preparing surfaces, and assembling prepared parts of complex wood components into a finished wood product. For this reason, these workers normally need substantial training and an ability to work from detailed instructions and specifications. In addition, they often are required to exercise independent judgment when undertaking an assignment.

Working Conditions

Working conditions vary by industry and specific job duties. In primary industries, such as logging and sawmills, working conditions are physically demanding, due to the handling of heavy, bulky material. Workers in these industries also may encounter excessive noise and dust and other air pollutants. However, the use of earplugs and respirators may partially alleviate these problems. Also, rigid adherence to safety precautions minimizes risk of injury from contact with rough wood stock, sharp tools, and power equipment. The risk of injury also is lowered by the installation of computer-controlled equipment, which reduces the physical labor and hands-on contact with machinery.

In secondary industries, such as furniture and kitchen cabinet manufacturing, working conditions also depend on the industry and the particular job. Employees who operate machinery often must wear ear and eye protection, follow operating safety instructions, and use safety shields or guards to prevent accidents. Those who work in the finishing area must either be provided with an appropriate dust or vapor mask, a complete protective safety suit, or work in a finishing environment that removes all vapors and particulate matter from the atmosphere. Prolonged standing, lifting, and fitting heavy objects are common characteristics of the job.

Employment

Woodworkers held about 409,000 jobs in 2000. Self-employed woodworkers, mostly cabinetmakers and furniture finishers, accounted for

10 percent of these jobs. Employment among detailed woodworking occupations was distributed as follows:

Cabinetmakers and bench carpenters	159,000
Woodworking machine setters, operators, and tenders, except sawing	103,000
Sawing machine setters, operators, and tenders, wood	57,000
Furniture finishers	45,000
All other woodworkers	35,000
Model makers and patternmakers, wood	10,000

More than 7 out of 10 woodworkers were employed in manufacturing industries. Among these woodworkers, 27 percent were found in establishments fabricating household and office furniture and fixtures and 40 percent worked in lumber and wood products, manufacturing a variety of raw, intermediate, and finished wood stock. Wholesale and retail lumber dealers, furniture stores, reupholstery and furniture repair shops, and construction firms also employ woodworkers.

Woodworking jobs are found throughout the country. However, production jobs are concentrated in the south and northwest, close to the supply of wood, whereas furniture makers are more prevalent in the east. Custom shops can be found everywhere, but generally are concentrated in or near highly populated areas.

Training, Other Qualifications, and Advancement

Most woodworkers are trained on the job, picking up skills informally from experienced workers. Some acquire skills through vocational education or by working as carpenters on construction jobs. Others may attend colleges or universities that offer training in areas including wood technology, furniture manufacturing, wood engineering, and production management. These programs prepare students for positions in production, supervision, engineering, and management.

Beginners usually observe and help experienced machine operators. They may supply material to or remove fabricated products from machines. Trainees also do simple machine operating jobs, while at first closely supervised by experienced workers. As beginners gain experience, they perform more complex jobs with less supervision. Some may learn to read blueprints, set up machines, and plan the sequence of the work. Most woodworkers learn basic machine operations and job tasks in a few months, but becoming a skilled woodworker often requires 2 or more years.

Employers increasingly seek applicants with a high school diploma or the equivalent, because of the growing sophistication of machinery and the constant need for retraining. Persons seeking woodworking jobs can enhance their employment and advancement prospects by completing high school and receiving training in mathematics, science, and computer applications. Other important qualities for entrants in this occupation include mechanical ability, manual dexterity, and the ability to pay attention to detail.

Advancement opportunities often are limited and depend upon availability, seniority, and a worker's skills and initiative. Sometimes experienced woodworkers become inspectors or supervisors responsible for the work of a group of woodworkers. Production workers often can advance into these positions by assuming additional responsibilities and by attending workshops, seminars, or college programs. Those who are highly skilled may set up their own woodworking shops.

Job Outlook

Overall employment of woodworkers is expected to grow more slowly than the average for all occupations through the year 2010—reflecting relatively slow growth among lesser-skilled woodworking machine setters, operators, and tenders, except sawing, and furniture finishers. On the other hand, employment of higher-skilled woodworkers—including model makers and patternmakers, wood; sawing machine setters, operators, and tenders, wood; and cabinetmakers and bench carpenters—is expected to grow about as fast as the average for all occupations. In addition, thousands of openings will arise each year because of the need to replace experienced woodworkers who transfer to other occupations or leave the labor force.

Demand for woodworkers will stem from increases in population, personal income, and business expenditures, in addition to the continuing need for repair and renovation of residential and commercial properties. Therefore, opportunities should be particularly good for woodworkers who specialize in such items as moldings, cabinets, stairs, and windows. Due to increasingly automated manufacturing processes, prospects will be best for highly skilled woodworkers with knowledge of CNC machine tool operation.

Several factors may limit the growth of woodworking occupations. Technological advances, like robots and CNC machinery, will continue to increase productivity among woodworkers, preventing employment from rising as fast as the demand for wood products, particularly in the mills and manufacturing plants where many processes can be automated. In addition, some jobs in the United States will be lost as imports continue to grow and as U.S. firms move some production to other countries. Also, the demand for wood may be reduced somewhat, as materials such as metal, plastic, and fiberglass continue to be used in many products as alternatives to wood. Environmental measures designed to control various pollutants used in, or generated by, woodworking processes also may adversely impact employment.

Employment in all woodworking specialties is highly sensitive to economic cycles. During economic downturns, workers are subject to layoffs or a reduction in hours.

Earnings

Median hourly earnings of cabinetmakers and bench carpenters were $10.83 in 2000. The middle 50 percent earned between $8.69 and $13.72. The lowest 10 percent earned less than $7.24, and the highest 10 percent earned more than $17.21. Median hourly earnings in the industries employing the largest numbers of cabinetmakers and bench carpenters in 2000 are shown in the following table:

Partitions and fixtures	$12.24
Furniture and homefurnishings stores	11.15
Millwork, plywood, and structural members	10.75
Household furniture	9.83

Median hourly earnings of sawing machine setters, operators, and tenders, wood were $10.23 in 2000. The middle 50 percent earned between $8.40 and $12.60. The lowest 10 percent earned less than $7.12, and the highest 10 percent earned more than $15.36. Median hourly earnings in the industries employing the largest numbers of sawing machine setters, operators, and tenders, wood in 2000 are shown in the following table:

Sawmills and planing mills	$10.56
Millwork, plywood, and structural members	10.36
Household furniture	9.88

Median hourly earnings of woodworking machine setters, operators, and tenders, except sawing were $10.00 in 2000. The middle 50 percent earned between $8.19 and $12.32. The lowest 10 percent earned less than $6.95, and the highest 10 percent earned more than $14.88. Median hourly earnings in the industries employing the largest numbers of woodworking machine setters, operators, and tenders, except sawing in 2000 are shown in the following table:

Millwork, plywood and structural members	$10.36
Household furniture	10.05
Sawmills and planing mills	9.83
Miscellaneous wood products	9.37
Wood containers	8.30

In 2000, median hourly earnings were $10.34 for furniture finishers and $9.48 for all other woodworkers.

Some woodworkers, such as those in logging or sawmills who are engaged in processing primary wood and building materials, are members of the International Association of Machinists. Others belong to the United Brotherhood of Carpenters and Joiners of America.

Related Occupations

Carpenters also work with wood. In addition, many woodworkers follow blueprints and drawings and use machines to shape and form raw wood into a final product. Workers who perform similar functions working with other materials include sheet metal workers, structural and reinforcing iron and metal workers, computer control programmers and operators, machinists, and tool and die makers.

Sources of Additional Information

For information about woodworking occupations, contact local furniture manufacturers, sawmills and planing mills, cabinetmaking or millwork firms, lumber dealers, a local of one of the unions mentioned above, or the nearest office of the state employment service.

Writers and Editors

O*NET 27-3041.00, 27-3042.00, 27-3043.01, 27-3043.02, 27-3043.04

Significant Points

- Most jobs require a college degree either in the liberal arts—communications, journalism, and English are preferred—or a technical subject for technical writing positions.

- Competition is expected to be less for lower paying, entry-level jobs at small daily and weekly newspapers, trade publications, and radio and television broadcasting stations in small markets.

● Persons who fail to gain better paying jobs or earn enough as independent writers usually are able to transfer readily to communications-related jobs in other occupations.

Nature of the Work

Writers and editors communicate through the written word. Writers and editors generally fall into one of three categories. *Writers and authors* develop original fiction and nonfiction for books, magazines and trade journals, newspapers, online publications, company newsletters, radio and television broadcasts, motion pictures, and advertisements. *Technical writers* develop scientific or technical materials, such as scientific and medical reports, equipment manuals, appendices, or operating and maintenance instructions. They also may assist in layout work. *Editors* select and prepare material for publication or broadcast and review and prepare a writer's work for publication or dissemination.

Nonfiction writers either select a topic or are assigned one, often by an editor or publisher. Then, they gather information through personal observation, library and Internet research, and interviews. Writers select the material they want to use, organize it, and use the written word to express ideas and convey information. Writers also revise or rewrite sections, searching for the best organization or the right phrasing.

Creative writers, poets, and lyricists, including novelists, playwrights, and screenwriters, create original works (such as prose, poems, plays, and song lyrics) for publication or performance. Some works may be commissioned (at the request of a sponsor); others may be written for hire (based on completion of a draft or an outline). *Copy writers* prepare advertising copy for use by publication or broadcast media, or to promote the sale of goods and services. *Newsletter writers* produce information for distribution to association members, corporate employees, organizational clients, or the public. Writers and authors also construct crossword puzzles and prepare speeches.

Technical writers put scientific and technical information into easily understandable language. They prepare scientific and technical reports, operating and maintenance manuals, catalogs, parts lists, assembly instructions, sales promotion materials, and project proposals. They also plan and edit technical reports and oversee preparation of illustrations, photographs, diagrams, and charts. *Science and medical writers* prepare a range of formal documents presenting detailed information on the physical or medical sciences. They impart research findings for scientific or medical professions, organize information for advertising or public relations needs, and interpret data and other information for a general readership.

Many writers prepare material directly for the Internet. For example, they may write for electronic newspapers or magazines, create short fiction, or produce technical documentation only available online. Also, they may write the text of Web sites. These writers should be knowledgeable about graphic design, page layout and desktop publishing software. Additionally, they should be familiar with interactive technologies of the Web so they can blend text, graphics, and sound together.

Freelance writers sell their work to publishers, publication enterprises, manufacturing firms, public relations departments, or advertising agencies. Sometimes, they contract with publishers to write a book or article. Others may be hired on a job-basis to complete specific assignments such as writing about a new product or technique.

Editors review, rewrite, and edit the work of writers. They may also do original writing. An editor's responsibilities vary depending on the employer and type and level of editorial position held. In the publishing industry, an editor's primary duties are to plan the contents of books, technical journals, trade magazines, and other general interest publications. Editors decide what material will appeal to readers, review and edit drafts of books and articles, offer comments to improve the work, and suggest possible titles. Additionally, they oversee the production of the publications.

Major newspapers and newsmagazines usually employ several types of editors. The *executive editor* oversees *assistant editors* who have responsibility for particular subjects, such as local news, international news, feature stories, or sports. Executive editors generally have the final say about what stories are published and how they are covered. The *managing editor* usually is responsible for the daily operation of the news department. *Assignment editors* determine which reporters will cover a given story. *Copy editors* mostly review and edit a reporter's copy for accuracy, content, grammar, and style.

In smaller organizations, like small daily or weekly newspapers or membership newsletter departments, a single editor may do everything or share responsibility with only a few other people. Executive and managing editors typically hire writers, reporters, or other employees. They also plan budgets and negotiate contracts with freelance writers, sometimes called "stringers" in the news industry. In broadcasting companies, *program directors* have similar responsibilities.

Editors and program directors often have assistants. Many assistants, such as copy editors or *production assistants*, hold entry-level jobs. They review copy for errors in grammar, punctuation, and spelling, and check copy for readability, style, and agreement with editorial policy. They suggest revisions, such as changing words or rearranging sentences to improve clarity or accuracy. They also do research for writers and verify facts, dates, and statistics. Production assistants arrange page layouts of articles, photographs, and advertising; compose headlines; and prepare copy for printing. *Publication assistants* who work for publishing houses may read and evaluate manuscripts submitted by freelance writers, proofread printers' galleys, or answer letters about published material. Production assistants on small papers or in radio stations compile articles available from wire services or the Internet, answer phones, and make photocopies.

Most writers and editors use personal computers or word processors. Many use desktop or electronic publishing systems, scanners, and other electronic communications equipment.

Working Conditions

Some writers and editors work in comfortable, private offices; others work in noisy rooms filled with the sound of keyboards and computer printers as well as the voices of other writers tracking down information over the telephone. The search for information sometimes requires travel to diverse workplaces, such as factories, offices, or laboratories, but many have to be content with telephone interviews, the library, and the Internet.

For some writers, the typical work week runs 35 to 40 hours. However, writers occasionally may work overtime to meet production deadlines. Those who prepare morning or weekend publications and broadcasts work some nights and weekends. Freelance writers generally work more flexible hours, but their schedules must conform to the needs of the client. Deadlines and erratic work hours, often part of the daily routine for these jobs, may cause stress, fatigue, or burnout.

Changes in technology and electronic communications also affect a writer's work environment. For example, laptops allow writers to work from home or while on the road. Writers and editors who use computers for extended periods may experience back pain, eyestrain, or fatigue.

Employment

Writers and editors held about 305,000 jobs in 2000. About 126,000 jobs were for writers and authors; 57,000 were for technical writers; and 122,000 were for editors. Nearly one-fourth of jobs for writers and editors were salaried positions with newspapers, magazines, and book publishers. Substantial numbers, mostly technical writers, work for computer software firms. Other salaried writers and editors work in educational facilities, advertising agencies, radio and television broadcasting studios, public relations firms, and business and nonprofit organizations, such as professional associations, labor unions, and religious organizations. Some develop publications and technical materials for government agencies or write for motion picture companies.

Jobs with major book publishers, magazines, broadcasting companies, advertising agencies, and public relations firms are concentrated in New York, Chicago, Los Angeles, Boston, Philadelphia, and San Francisco. Jobs with newspapers, business and professional journals, and technical and trade magazines are more widely dispersed throughout the country.

Thousands of other individuals work as freelance writers, earning some income from their articles, books, and less commonly, television and movie scripts. Most support themselves with income derived from other sources.

Training, Other Qualifications, and Advancement

A college degree generally is required for a position as a writer or editor. Although some employers look for a broad liberal arts background, most prefer to hire people with degrees in communications, journalism, or English. For those who specialize in a particular area, such as fashion, business, or legal issues, additional background in the chosen field is expected. Knowledge of a second language is helpful for some positions.

Technical writing requires a degree in, or some knowledge about, a specialized field—engineering, business, or one of the sciences, for example. In many cases, people with good writing skills can learn specialized knowledge on the job. Some transfer from jobs as technicians, scientists, or engineers. Others begin as research assistants, or trainees in a technical information department, develop technical communication skills, and then assume writing duties.

Writers and editors must be able to express ideas clearly and logically and should love to write. Creativity, curiosity, a broad range of knowledge, self-motivation, and perseverance also are valuable. Writers and editors must demonstrate good judgment and a strong sense of ethics in deciding what material to publish. Editors also need tact and the ability to guide and encourage others in their work.

For some jobs, the ability to concentrate amid confusion and to work under pressure is essential. Familiarity with electronic publishing, graph-

ics, and video production equipment increasingly is needed. Online newspapers and magazines require knowledge of computer software used to combine online text with graphics, audio, video, and 3-D animation.

High school and college newspapers, literary magazines, community newspapers, and radio and television stations all provide valuable, but sometimes unpaid, practical writing experience. Many magazines, newspapers, and broadcast stations have internships for students. Interns write short pieces, conduct research and interviews, and learn about the publishing or broadcasting business.

In small firms, beginning writers and editors hired as assistants may actually begin writing or editing material right away. Opportunities for advancement can be limited, however. In larger businesses, jobs usually are more formally structured. Beginners generally do research, fact-checking, or copy editing. They take on full-scale writing or editing duties less rapidly than do the employees of small companies. Advancement often is more predictable, although it comes with the assignment of more important articles.

Job Outlook

Employment of writers and editors is expected to increase faster than the average for all occupations through the year 2010. Employment of salaried writers and editors for newspapers, periodicals, book publishers, and nonprofit organizations is expected to increase as demand grows for their publications. Magazines and other periodicals increasingly are developing market niches, appealing to readers with special interests. Also, online publications and services are growing in number and sophistication, spurring the demand for writers and editors. Businesses and organizations are developing newsletters and Internet Web sites and more companies are experimenting with publishing materials directly for the Internet. Advertising and public relations agencies, which also are growing, should be another source of new jobs. Demand for technical writers and writers with expertise in specialty areas, such as law, medicine, or economics, is expected to increase because of the continuing expansion of scientific and technical information and the need to communicate it to others.

In addition to job openings created by employment growth, many openings will occur as experienced workers retire, transfer to other occupations, or leave the labor force. Replacement needs are relatively high in this occupation; many freelancers leave because they cannot earn enough money.

Despite projections of fast employment growth and numerous replacement needs, the outlook for most writing and editing jobs is expected to be competitive. Many people with writing or journalism training are attracted to the occupation. Opportunities should be best for technical writers and those with training in a specialized field. Rapid growth and change in the high technology and electronics industries result in a greater need for people to write users' guides, instruction manuals, and training materials. Developments and discoveries in the law, science, and technology generate demand for people to interpret technical information for a more general audience. This work requires people who are not only technically skilled as writers, but also familiar with the subject area. Also, individuals with the technical skills for working on the Internet may have an advantage finding a job as a writer or editor.

Opportunities for editing positions on small daily and weekly newspapers and in small radio and television stations, where the pay is low, should be better than those in larger media markets. Some small publications hire freelance copy editors as backup for staff editors or as additional help with special projects. Aspiring writers and editors benefit from academic preparation in another discipline as well, either to qualify them as writers specializing in that discipline or as a career alternative if they are unable to get a job in writing.

Earnings

Median annual earnings for salaried writers and authors were $42,270 in 2000. The middle 50 percent earned between $29,090 and $57,330. The lowest 10 percent earned less than $20,290, and the highest 10 percent earned more than $81,370. Median annual earnings were $26,470 in the newspaper industry.

Median annual earnings for salaried technical writers were $47,790 in 2000. The middle 50 percent earned between $37,280 and $60,000. The lowest 10 percent earned less than $28,890, and the highest 10 percent earned more than $74,360. Median annual earnings in computer and data processing services were $51,220.

Median annual earnings for salaried editors were $39,370 in 2000. The middle 50 percent earned between $28,880 and $54,320. The lowest 10 percent earned less than $22,460, and the highest 10 percent earned more than $73,330. Median annual earnings in the industries employing the largest numbers of editors were as follows:

Computer and data processing services	$45,800
Periodicals	42,560
Newspapers	37,560
Books	37,550

Related Occupations

Writers and editors communicate ideas and information. Other communications occupations include announcers; interpreters and translators; news analysts, reporters, and correspondents; and public relations specialists.

Sources of Additional Information

For information on careers in technical writing, contact:

- Society for Technical Communication, Inc., 901 N. Stuart St., Suite 904, Arlington, VA 22203. Internet: http://www.stc.org

For information on union wage rates for newspaper and magazine editors, contact:

- The Newspaper Guild-CWA, Research and Information Department, 501 Third St. NW, Suite 250, Washington, DC 20001

THE QUICK JOB SEARCH

Seven Steps to Getting a Good Job in Less Time

The Complete Text of a Results-Oriented Booklet by Michael Farr

Millions of job seekers have found better jobs faster using the techniques in The Quick Job Search. So can you! The Quick Job Search covers the essential steps proven to cut job search time in half and is used widely by job search programs throughout North America. Topics include how to identify your key skills, define and research your ideal job, write a great resume, use the most effective job search methods, get more interviews, answer tough interview questions, and much more. While it is a section in this book, The Quick Job Search is available as a separate booklet and in an expanded form as Seven Steps to Getting a Job Fast. At the end of this section, I've included several professionally written resumes for you to use as examples when writing your resume. These resumes would be suitable for use when applying for some of America's top jobs for People Without a Four-Year Degree.

The Quick Job Search Is Short, But It May Be All You Need

While *The Quick Job Search* is short, it covers the basics on how to explore career options and conduct an effective job search. While these topics can seem complex, I have found some simple truths about job searches:

★ If you are going to work, you might as well define what you really want to do and are good at.

★ If you are looking for a job, you might as well use techniques that will reduce the time it takes to find one—and that help you get a better job than you might otherwise.

That's what I emphasize in this little book.

Trust Me—Do the Worksheets. I know you will resist completing the worksheets. But trust me, they are worth your time. Doing them will give you a better sense of what you are good at, what you want to do, and how to go about getting it. You will also most likely get more interviews and present yourself better. Is this worth giving up a night of TV? Yes, I think so. Once you finish this minibook and its activities, you will have spent more time planning your career and will know more about finding a job than most people do.

Why Such a Short Book? I've taught job seeking skills for many years, and I've written longer and more detailed books than this one. Yet I have often been asked to tell someone, in a few minutes or hours, the most important things they should do in their career planning or job search. Instructors and counselors also ask the same question because they have only a short time to spend with folks they're trying to help. I've given this a lot of thought, and the seven topics in this minibook are the ones I think are most important to know.

This minibook is short enough to scan in a morning and conduct a more effective job search that afternoon. Doing all the activities would take more time but would prepare you far better. Of course, you can learn more about all of the topics it covers, but this little book may be all you need.

You can't just read about getting a job. The best way to get a job is to go out and get interviews! And the best way to get interviews is to make a job out of getting a job.

After many years of experience, I have identified just seven basic things you need to do that make a big difference in your job search. Each will be covered and expanded on in this minibook.

1. Identify your key skills.

2. Define your ideal job.

3. Learn the two most effective job search methods.

4. Write a superior resume.

5. Organize your time to get two interviews a day.

6. Dramatically improve your interviewing skills.

7. Follow up on all leads.

We all have thousands of skills. Consider the many skills required to do even a simple thing like ride a bike or bake a cake. But, of all the skills you have, employers want to know those key skills you have for the job they need done. You must clearly identify these key skills, and then emphasize them in interviews.

Step 1

Identify Your Key Skills and Develop a "Skills Language" to Describe Yourself

One employer survey found that about 90 percent of the people interviewed by the employers did not present the skills they had to do the job they sought. They could not answer the basic question "Why should I hire you?"

Knowing and describing your skills are essential to doing well in interviews. This same knowledge is important in deciding what type of job you will enjoy and do well. For these reasons, I consider identifying your skills a necessary part of a successful career plan or job search.

The Three Types of Skills

Most people think of their "skills" as job-related skills, such as using a computer. But we all have other types of skills that are important for success on a job—and that are important to employers. The triangle at right presents skills in three groups, and I think that this is a very useful way to consider skills for our purposes.

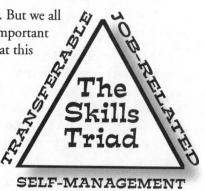

The Skills Triad

Let's review these three types of skills—self-management, transferable, and job-related—and identify those that are most important to you.

Self-Management Skills

Write down three things about yourself that you think make you a good worker.

YOUR "GOOD WORKER" TRAITS

1. _____

2. _____

3. _____

You just wrote down the most important things for an employer to know about you! They describe your basic personality and your ability to adapt to new environments. They are some of the most important skills to emphasize in interviews, yet most job seekers don't realize their importance—and don't mention them.

Review the Self-Management Skills Checklist that follows and put a check mark beside any skills you have. The key self-management skills listed first cover abilities that employers find particularly important. If one or more of the key self-management skills apply to you, mentioning them in interviews can help you greatly.

SELF-MANAGEMENT SKILLS CHECKLIST

Check Your Key Self-Management Skills—Employers Value These Highly

_____ accept supervision	_____ good attendance	_____ productive
_____ get along with coworkers	_____ hard worker	_____ punctual
_____ get things done on time	_____ honest	

Check Your Other Self-Management Skills

_____ able to coordinate	_____ enthusiastic	_____ learn quickly
_____ ambitious	_____ expressive	_____ loyal
_____ assertive	_____ flexible	_____ mature
_____ capable	_____ formal	_____ methodical
_____ cheerful	_____ friendly	_____ modest
_____ competent	_____ good-natured	_____ motivated
_____ complete assignments	_____ helpful	_____ natural
_____ conscientious	_____ humble	_____ open-minded
_____ creative	_____ imaginative	_____ optimistic
_____ dependable	_____ independent	_____ original
_____ discreet	_____ industrious	_____ patient
_____ eager	_____ informal	_____ persistent
_____ efficient	_____ intelligent	_____ physically strong
_____ energetic	_____ intuitive	_____ practice new skills

(continues)

_____ reliable	_____ solve problems	_____ thrifty
_____ resourceful	_____ spontaneous	_____ trustworthy
_____ responsible	_____ steady	_____ versatile
_____ self-confident	_____ tactful	_____ well-organized
_____ sense of humor	_____ take pride in work	
_____ sincere	_____ tenacious	

List Your Other Self-Management Skills

_____

_____

After you are done with the list, circle the five skills you feel are most important and list them in the box that follows.

YOUR TOP FIVE SELF-MANAGEMENT SKILLS

1. _____
2. _____
3. _____
4. _____
5. _____

Note

When thinking about their skills, some people find it helpful to complete the Essential Job Search Data Worksheet that starts on page 462. It organizes skills and accomplishments from previous jobs and other life experiences. Take a look at it and decide whether to complete it now or later.

Transferable Skills

We all have skills that can transfer from one job or career to another. For example, the ability to organize events could be used in a variety of jobs and may be essential for success in certain occupations. Your mission is to find a job that requires the skills you have and enjoy using.

In the following list, put a check mark beside the skills you have. You may have used them in a previous job or in some non-work setting.

Quip

It's not bragging if it's true. Using your new skills language may be uncomfortable at first, but employers need to learn about your skills. So practice saying positive things about the skills you have for the job. If you don't, who will?

TRANSFERABLE SKILLS CHECKLIST

Check Your Key Transferable Skills—Employers Value These Highly

_____ instruct others	_____ manage people	_____ organize/manage projects
_____ negotiate	_____ meet deadlines	_____ public speaking
_____ manage money, budgets	_____ meet the public	_____ written communication

Check Your Skills for Working with Things

_____ assemble things	_____ good with hands	_____ use complex equipment
_____ build things	_____ observe/inspect things	_____ use computers
_____ construct/repair things	_____ operate tools, machines	
_____ drive, operate vehicles	_____ repair things	

Check Your Skills for Working with Data

_____ analyze data	_____ compile	_____ manage money
_____ audit records	_____ count	_____ observe/inspect
_____ budget	_____ detail-oriented	_____ record facts
_____ calculate/compute	_____ evaluate	_____ research
_____ check for accuracy	_____ investigate	_____ synthesize
_____ classify things	_____ keep financial records	_____ take inventory
_____ compare	_____ locate information	

Check Your Skills for Working with People

_____ administer	_____ instruct	_____ pleasant
_____ advise	_____ interview people	_____ sensitive
_____ care for	_____ kind	_____ sociable
_____ coach	_____ listen	_____ supervise
_____ confront others	_____ negotiate	_____ tactful
_____ counsel people	_____ outgoing	_____ tolerant
_____ demonstrate	_____ patient	_____ tough
_____ diplomatic	_____ perceptive	_____ trusting
_____ help others	_____ persuade	_____ understanding

(continues)

Check Your Skills for Working with Words/Ideas

_____ articulate	_____ edit	_____ public speaking
_____ communicate verbally	_____ ingenious	_____ remember information
_____ correspond with others	_____ inventive	_____ write clearly
_____ create new ideas	_____ library research	
_____ design	_____ logical	

Check Your Leadership Skills

_____ arrange social functions	_____ initiate new tasks	_____ results-oriented
_____ competitive	_____ make decisions	_____ risk-taker
_____ decisive	_____ manage or direct others	_____ run meetings
_____ delegate	_____ mediate problems	_____ self-confident
_____ direct others	_____ motivate people	_____ self-motivate
_____ explain things to others	_____ negotiate agreements	_____ solve problems
_____ influence others	_____ plan events	

Check Your Creative/Artistic Skills

_____ artistic	_____ drawing, art	_____ perform, act
_____ dance, body movement	_____ expressive	_____ present artistic ideas

List Your Other Transferable Skills

_____

_____

When you are finished, circle the five transferable skills you feel are most important for you to use in your next job and list them in the box below.

YOUR TOP FIVE TRANSFERABLE SKILLS

1. _____
2. _____
3. _____
4. _____
5. _____

Job-Related Skills

Job content or job-related skills are those you need to do a particular occupation. A carpenter, for example, needs to know how to use various tools. Before you select job-related skills to emphasize, you must first have a clear idea of the jobs you want. So let's put off developing your job-related skills list until you have defined the job you want. That topic is covered next.

Note

Complete the worksheet that follows after you have read "Step 2: Define Your Ideal Job."

YOUR TOP FIVE JOB-RELATED SKILLS

1. _____

2. _____

3. _____

4. _____

5. _____

Quip

It's a hassle, but... Completing the Essential Job Search Data Worksheet that starts on page 462 will help you define what you are good at—and remember examples of when you did things well. This information will help you define your ideal job and will be of great value in interviews. Look at the worksheet now, and promise to do it tonight.

Step 2

Define Your Ideal Job (You Can Compromise on It Later If Needed)

Too many people look for a job without clearly knowing what they are looking for. Before you go out seeking *a* job, I suggest that you first define exactly what you want—*the* job.

Most people think that a job objective is the same as a job title, but it isn't. You need to consider other elements of what makes a job satisfying for you. Then, later, you can decide what that job is called and what industry it might be in.

EIGHT FACTORS TO CONSIDER IN DEFINING YOUR IDEAL JOB

As you try to define your ideal job, consider the following eight important questions. Once you know what you want, your task then becomes finding a position that is as close to your ideal job as possible.

1. **What skills do you want to use?** From the skills lists in Step 1, select the top five skills that you enjoy using and most want to use in your next job. _____

_____

_____

(continues)

(continued)

2. **What type of special knowledge do you have?** Perhaps you know how to fix radios, keep accounting records, or cook food. Write down the things you know from schooling, training, hobbies, family experiences, and other sources. One or more of these knowledges could make you a very special applicant in the right setting. _____

_____

_____

3. **With what types of people do you prefer to work?** Do you like to work in competition with others, or do you prefer hardworking folks, creative personalities, or some other types? _____

_____

_____

4. **What type of work environment do you prefer?** Do you want to work inside, outside, in a quiet place, a busy place, a clean place, or have a window with a nice view? List the types of things that are most important to you. _____

_____

_____

5. **Where do you want your next job to be located—in what city or region?** Near a bus line? Close to a childcare center? If you are open to living and working anywhere, what would your ideal community be like? _____

_____

_____

6. **How much money do you hope to make in your next job?** Many people will take less money if they like a job in other ways—or if they quickly need a job to survive. Think about the minimum you would take as well as what you would eventually like to earn. Your next job will probably pay somewhere in between. _____

_____

_____

7. **How much responsibility are you willing to accept?** Usually, the more money you want to make, the more responsibility you must accept. Do you want to work by yourself, be part of a group, or be in charge? If so, at what level? _____

_____

_____

8. **What things are important or have meaning to you?** Do you have important values you would prefer to include as a basis of the work you do? For example, some people want to work to help others, clean up our environment, build things, make machines work, gain power or prestige, or care for animals or plants. Think about what is important to you and how you might include this in your next job.

_____

_____

Is It Possible to Find Your Ideal Job?

Can you find a job that meets all the criteria you just defined? Perhaps. Some people do. The harder you look, the more likely you are to find it. But you will likely need to compromise, so it is useful to know what is *most* important to include in your next job. Go back over your responses to the eight factors and mark those few things that you would most like to have or include in your ideal job. Then write a brief outline of this ideal job below. Don't worry about a job title, or whether you have the experience, or other practical matters yet.

My Ideal Job Would Be

_____

_____

_____

_____

_____

Explore Specific Job Titles and Industries

You might find your ideal job in an occupation you haven't considered yet. And, even if you are sure of the occupation you want, it may be in an industry that's not familiar to you. This combination of occupation and industry forms the basis for your job search, and you should consider a variety of options.

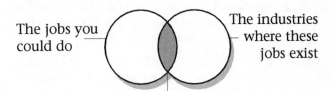

The jobs you could do — The industries where these jobs exist

Your ideal job exists in the overlap of those jobs that interest you most *and* of those industries that best meet your needs and interests!

Review the Top Jobs in the Workforce

There are thousands of job titles, and many jobs are highly specialized, employing just a few people. While one of these more specialized jobs may be just what you want, most work falls within more general job titles that employ large numbers of people.

The list of job titles that follows was developed by the U.S. Department of Labor. It contains approximately 260 major jobs that employ about 85 percent of the U.S. workforce.

The job titles are organized within 14 major groupings called interest areas, presented in all capital letters and bold type. These groupings will help you quickly identify fields most likely to interest you. Job titles are presented in regular type within these groupings.

(continues)

(continued)

Begin with the interest areas that appeal to you most, and underline any job title that interests you. (Don't worry for now about whether you have the experience or credentials to do these jobs.) Then quickly review the remaining interest areas, underlining any job titles there that interest you. Note that some job titles are listed more than once because they fit into more than one interest area. When you have gone through all 14 interest areas, go back and circle the 5 to 10 job titles that interest you most. These are the ones you will want to research in more detail.

1. **ARTS, ENTERTAINMENT, AND MEDIA**—Actors, Producers, and Directors; Announcers; Artists and Related Workers; Athletes, Coaches, Umpires, and Related Workers; Broadcast and Sound Engineering Technicians and Radio Operators; Dancers and Choreographers; Designers; Desktop Publishers; Musicians, Singers, and Related Workers; News Analysts, Reporters, and Correspondents; Photographers; Public Relations Specialists; Television, Video, and Motion Picture Camera Operators and Editors; Writers and Editors

2. **SCIENCE, MATH, AND ENGINEERING**—Actuaries; Aerospace Engineers; Agricultural and Food Scientists; Agricultural Engineers; Architects, Except Landscape and Naval; Atmospheric Scientists; Biological and Medical Scientists; Biomedical Engineers; Chemical Engineers; Chemists and Materials Scientists; Civil Engineers; Computer and Information Systems Managers; Computer-Control Programmers and Operators; Computer Hardware Engineers; Computer Programmers; Computer Software Engineers; Computer Support Specialists and Systems Administrators; Conservation Scientists and Foresters; Construction and Building Inspectors; Drafters; Economists and Market and Survey Researchers; Electrical and Electronics Engineers; Engineering and Natural Sciences Managers; Engineering Technicians; Engineers; Environmental Engineers; Environmental Scientists and Geoscientists; Industrial Engineers, Including Health and Safety; Landscape Architects; Materials Engineers; Mathematicians; Mechanical Engineers; Mining and Geological Engineers, Including Mining Safety Engineers; Nuclear Engineers; Operations Research Analysts; Petroleum Engineers; Physicists and Astronomers; Psychologists; Sales Engineers; Science Technicians; Social Scientists, Other; Statisticians; Surveyors, Cartographers, Photogrammetrists, and Surveying Technicians; Systems Analysts, Computer Scientists, and Database Administrators; Urban and Regional Planners

3. **PLANTS AND ANIMALS**—Agricultural Workers; Animal Care and Service Workers; Farmers, Ranchers, and Agricultural Managers; Fishers and Fishing Vessel Operators; Forest, Conservation, and Logging Workers; Grounds Maintenance Workers; Pest Control Workers; Veterinarians

4. **LAW, LAW ENFORCEMENT, AND PUBLIC SAFETY**—Correctional Officers; Emergency Medical Technicians and Paramedics; Firefighting Occupations; Job Opportunities in the Armed Forces; Judges, Magistrates, and Other Judicial Workers; Lawyers; Occupational Health and Safety Specialists and Technicians; Paralegals and Legal Assistants; Police and Detectives; Private Detectives and Investigators; Security Guards and Gaming Surveillance Officers

5. **MECHANICS, INSTALLERS, AND REPAIRERS**—Aircraft and Avionics Equipment Mechanics and Service Technicians; Automotive Body and Related Repairers; Automotive Service Technicians and Mechanics; Coin, Vending, and Amusement Machine Servicers and Repairers; Computer, Automated Teller, and Office Machine Repairers; Diesel Service Technicians and Mechanics; Electrical and Electronics Installers and Repairers; Electronic Home Entertainment Equipment Installers and Repairers; Elevator Installers and Repairers; Heating, Air-Conditioning, and Refrigeration Mechanics and Installers; Heavy Vehicle and Mobile Equipment Service Technicians and Mechanics; Home Appliance Repairers; Industrial Machinery Installation, Repair, and Maintenance Workers; Line Installers and Repairers; Precision Instrument and Equipment Repairers; Radio and Telecommunications Equipment Installers and Repairers; Small Engine Mechanics

6. **CONSTRUCTION, MINING, AND DRILLING**—Boilermakers; Brickmasons, Blockmasons, and Stonemasons; Carpenters; Carpet, Floor, and Tile Installers and Finishers; Cement Masons, Concrete Finishers, Segmental Pavers, and Terrazzo Workers; Construction Equipment Operators; Construction Laborers; Construction Managers; Drywall Installers, Ceiling Tile Installers, and Tapers; Electricians; Glaziers; Hazardous Materials Removal

Workers; Insulation Workers; Painters and Paperhangers; Pipelayers, Plumbers, Pipefitters, and Steamfitters; Plasterers and Stucco Masons; Roofers; Sheet Metal Workers; Structural and Reinforcing Iron and Metal Workers

7. **TRANSPORTATION**—Air Traffic Controllers; Aircraft Pilots and Flight Engineers; Busdrivers; Rail Transportation Occupations; Taxi Drivers and Chauffeurs; Truckdrivers and Driver/Sales Workers; Water Transportation Occupations

8. **INDUSTRIAL PRODUCTION**—Assemblers and Fabricators; Bookbinders and Bindery Workers; Dental Laboratory Technicians; Food Processing Occupations; Industrial Production Managers; Inspectors, Testers, Sorters, Samplers, and Weighers; Jewelers and Precious Stone and Metal Workers; Machine Setters, Operators, and Tenders—Metal and Plastic; Machinists; Material Moving Occupations; Ophthalmic Laboratory Technicians; Painting and Coating Workers, Except Construction and Maintenance; Photographic Process Workers and Processing Machine Operators; Power Plant Operators, Distributors, and Dispatchers; Prepress Technicians and Workers; Printing Machine Operators; Semiconductor Processors; Stationary Engineers and Boiler Operators; Tool and Die Makers; Water and Liquid Waste Treatment Plant and System Operators; Welding, Soldering, and Brazing Workers; Woodworkers

9. **BUSINESS DETAIL**—Administrative Services Managers; Bill and Account Collectors; Billing and Posting Clerks and Machine Operators; Bookkeeping, Accounting, and Auditing Clerks; Brokerage Clerks; Cargo and Freight Agents; Cashiers; Communications Equipment Operators; Computer Operators; Counter and Rental Clerks; Couriers and Messengers; Court Reporters; Credit Authorizers, Checkers, and Clerks; Customer Service Representatives; Data Entry and Information Processing Workers; Dispatchers; File Clerks; Financial Clerks; Gaming Cage Workers; Human Resources Assistants, Except Payroll and Timekeeping; Information and Record Clerks; Interviewers; Material Recording, Scheduling, Dispatching, and Distributing Occupations, Except Postal Workers; Medical Records and Health Information Technicians; Medical Transcriptionists; Meter Readers, Utilities; Office and Administrative Support Worker Supervisors and Managers; Office Clerks, General; Order Clerks; Payroll and Timekeeping Clerks; Postal Service Workers; Procurement Clerks; Production, Planning, and Expediting Clerks; Receptionists and Information Clerks; Secretaries and Administrative Assistants; Shipping, Receiving, and Traffic Clerks; Stock Clerks and Order Fillers; Tellers; Weighers, Measurers, Checkers, and Samplers, Recordkeeping

10. **SALES AND MARKETING**—Advertising, Marketing, Promotions, Public Relations, and Sales Managers; Demonstrators, Product Promoters, and Models; Insurance Sales Agents; Real Estate Brokers and Sales Agents; Retail Salespersons; Sales Representatives, Wholesale and Manufacturing; Sales Worker Supervisors; Securities, Commodities, and Financial Services Sales Agents; Travel Agents

11. **RECREATION, TRAVEL, AND OTHER PERSONAL SERVICE**—Barbers, Cosmetologists, and Other Personal Appearance Workers; Building Cleaning Workers; Chefs, Cooks, and Food Preparation Workers; Flight Attendants; Food and Beverage Serving and Related Workers; Food Service Managers; Gaming Services Occupations; Hotel, Motel, and Resort Desk Clerks; Lodging Managers; Personal and Home Care Aides; Recreation and Fitness Workers; Reservation and Transportation Ticket Agents and Travel Clerks; Textile, Apparel, and Furnishings Occupations

12. **EDUCATION AND SOCIAL SERVICE**—Archivists, Curators, and Museum Technicians; Childcare Workers; Counselors; Education Administrators; Instructional Coordinators; Library Assistants, Clerical; Library Technicians; Probational Officers and Correctional Treatment Specialists; Protestant Ministers; Rabbis; Roman Catholic Priests; Social and Human Service Assistants; Social Workers; Teacher Assistants; Teachers—Adult Literacy and Remedial and Self-Enrichment Education; Teachers—Postsecondary; Teachers—Preschool, Kindergarten, Elementary, Middle, and Secondary; Teachers—Special Education

13. **GENERAL MANAGEMENT AND SUPPORT**—Accountants and Auditors; Budget Analysts; Claims Adjusters, Appraisers, Examiners, and Investigators; Cost Estimators; Financial Analysts and Personal Financial Advisors; Financial Managers; Funeral Directors; Human Resources, Training, and Labor Relations Managers and Specialists;

(continues)

(continued)

Insurance Underwriters; Loan Officers and Counselors; Management Analysts; Property, Real Estate, and Community Association Managers; Purchasing Managers, Buyers, and Purchasing Agents; Tax Examiners, Collectors, and Revenue Agents; Top Executives

14. **MEDICAL AND HEALTH SERVICES**—Cardiovascular Technologists and Technicians; Chiropractors; Clinical Laboratory Technologists and Technicians; Dental Assistants; Dental Hygienists; Dentists; Diagnostic Medical Sonographers; Dietitians and Nutritionists; Licensed Practical and Licensed Vocational Nurses; Medical and Health Services Managers; Medical Assistants; Nuclear Medicine Technologists; Nursing, Psychiatric, and Home Health Aides; Occupational Therapist Assistants and Aides; Occupational Therapists; Opticians, Dispensing; Optometrists; Pharmacists; Pharmacy Aides; Pharmacy Technicians; Physical Therapist Assistants and Aides; Physical Therapists; Physician Assistants; Physicians and Surgeons; Podiatrists; Radiologic Technologists and Technicians; Recreational Therapists; Registered Nurses; Respiratory Therapists; Speech-Language Pathologists and Audiologists; Surgical Technologists

Note

Thorough descriptions for many of the job titles in the preceding list can be found in this book. You can also find job descriptions on the Internet at http://www.bls.gov/oco/.

The Guide for Occupational Exploration, *Third Edition, provides more information on the interest areas used in the list. This book is published by JIST Works and also describes about 1,000 major jobs, arranged within groupings of related jobs.*

Finally, "A Short List of Additional Resources" at the end of this minibook will give you resources for more job information.

CONSIDER MAJOR INDUSTRIES

The *Career Guide to Industries,* another book by the U.S. Department of Labor, gives very helpful reviews for the major industries mentioned in the list below. Organized in groups of related industries, this list covers about 75 percent of the nation's workforce. Many libraries and bookstores carry the *Career Guide to Industries,* or you can find the information on the Internet at http://www.bls.gov/oco/cg/.

Underline industries that interest you, and then learn more about the opportunities they present. Note that some industries pay more than others, often for the same skills or jobs, so you should explore a variety of industry options.

GOODS-PRODUCING INDUSTRIES—Agriculture, Mining, and Construction: agricultural production; agricultural services; construction; mining and quarrying; oil and gas extraction. **Manufacturing:** aerospace manufacturing; apparel and other textile products; chemical manufacturing, except drugs; drug manufacturing; electronic equipment manufacturing; food processing; motor vehicle and equipment manufacturing; printing and publishing; steel manufacturing; textile mill products.

SERVICE-PRODUCING INDUSTRIES—Transportation, Communications, and Public Utilities: air transportation; cable and other pay television services; public utilities; radio and television broadcasting; telecommunications; trucking and warehousing. **Wholesale and Retail Trade:** department, clothing, and accessory stores; eating and drinking places; grocery stores; motor vehicle dealers; wholesale trade. **Finance and Insurance:** banking; insurance; securities and commodities. **Services:** advertising; amusement and recreation services; childcare services; computer and data processing services; educational services; health services; hotels and other lodging places; management and public relations services; motion picture production and distribution; personnel supply services; social services, except child care. **Government:** federal government; state and local government, except education and health.

YOUR TOP JOBS AND INDUSTRIES WORKSHEET

Go back over the lists of job titles and industries. For items 1 and 2 below, list the jobs that interest you most. Then select the industries that interest you most, and list them below in item 3. These are the jobs and industries you should research most carefully. Your ideal job is likely to be found in some combination of these jobs and industries, or in more specialized but related jobs and industries.

1. The 5 job titles that interest you most _____

_____

_____

_____

_____

2. The 5 next most interesting job titles _____

_____

_____

_____

_____

3. The industries that interest you most _____

_____

_____

_____

_____

_____

And, Now, We Return to Job-Related Skills

Back on page 431, I suggested that you should first define the job you want, and then identify key job-related skills you have that support your ability to do it. These are the job-related skills to emphasize in interviews.

So, now that you have determined your ideal job, you can pinpoint the job-related skills it requires. If you haven't done so, complete the Essential Job Search Data Worksheet on pages 462–466. It will give you specific skills and accomplishments to highlight.

Yes, completing that worksheet requires time, but doing so will help you clearly define key skills to emphasize in interviews, when what you say matters so much. People who complete that worksheet will do better in their interviews than those who don't.

After you complete the Essential Job Search Data Worksheet, go back to page 431 and write in Your Top Five Job-Related Skills. Include there the job-related skills you have that you would most like to use in your next job.

Use the Most Effective Methods to Reduce Your Job Search Time

Employer surveys found that most employers don't advertise their job openings. They hire people they know, people who find out about the jobs through word of mouth, and people who happen to be in the right place at the right time. While luck plays a part, you can increase your "luck" in finding job openings.

Let's look at the job search methods that people use. The U.S. Department of Labor conducts a regular survey of unemployed people actively looking for work. The survey results are presented below.

Percentage of Unemployed Using Various Job Search Methods

- ◆ Contacted employer directly: 64.5%
- ◆ Sent out resumes/filled out applications: 48.3%
- ◆ Contacted public employment agency: 20.4%
- ◆ Placed or answered help wanted ads: 14.5%
- ◆ Contacted friends or relatives: 13.5%

- ◆ Contacted private employment agency: 6.6%
- ◆ Used other active search methods: 4.4%
- ◆ Contacted school employment center: 2.3%
- ◆ Checked union or professional registers: 1.5%

Source: U.S. Department of Labor, Current Population Survey

Note: This section covers a number of job search methods. Most of the material is presented as information, with a few interactive activities. While each topic is short and reasonably interesting, taking a break now and then will help you absorb it all.

What Job Search Methods Work Best?

The survey shows that most people use more than one job search technique. For example, one person might read want ads, fill out applications, and ask friends for job leads. Others might send out resumes, contact everyone they know from professional contacts, and sign up at employment agencies.

But the survey covered only nine job search methods and, on those, asked only whether the job seeker did or did not use each method. The survey did not cover the Internet, nor did it ask whether a method worked in getting job offers.

Unfortunately, there hasn't been much recent research on the effectiveness of various job search methods. Most of what we know is based on older research and the observations of people who work with job seekers. I'll share what we do know about the effectiveness of job search methods in the content that follows.

Getting the Most Out of Less-Effective Job Search Methods

The truth is that every job search method works for some people. But experience and research show that some methods are more effective than others are. Your task in the job search is to spend more of your time using more effective methods—and increase the effectiveness of all the methods you use.

Quip

Your job search objective. Almost everyone finds a job eventually, so your objective should be to find a good job in less time. The job search methods I emphasize in this minibook will help you do just that.

So let's start by looking at some traditional job search methods and how you can increase their effectiveness. Only about one-third of all job seekers get their jobs using one of these methods, but you should consider using them.

Help Wanted Ads

Most jobs are never advertised, and only about 15 percent of all people get their jobs through the want ads. Everyone who reads the paper knows about these openings, so competition is fierce. The Internet also lists many job openings. But, as with want ads, enormous numbers of people view these postings. Some people do get jobs this way, so go ahead and apply. Just be sure to spend most of your time using more effective methods.

Filling Out Applications

Most employers require job seekers to complete an application form. But applications are designed to collect negative information—and employers use applications to screen people out. If, for example, your training or work history is not the best, you will often never get an interview, even if you can do the job.

Completing applications is a more effective approach for young job seekers than for adults. The reason is that there is a shortage of workers for the relatively low-paying and entry-level jobs youth typically seek. As a result, employers are more willing to accept a lack of experience or lack of job skills in youth. Even so, you will get better results by filling out the application if asked to do so and then requesting an interview with the person in charge.

When you complete an application, make it neat and error-free, and do not include anything that could get you screened out. If necessary, leave a problem section blank. It can always be explained after you get an interview.

Employment Agencies

There are three types of employment agencies. One is operated by the government and is free. The others are run as for-profit businesses and charge a fee to either you or an employer. There are advantages and disadvantages to using each.

The government employment service and one-stop centers. Each state has a network of local offices to pay unemployment compensation, provide job leads, and offer other services—at no charge to you or to employers. The service's name varies by state, and it may be called "Job Service," "Department of Labor," "Unemployment Office," "Workforce Development," or another name. Many states have "One-Stop Centers" that provide employment counseling, reference books, computerized career information, job listings, and other resources.

An Internet site at www.doleta.gov/uses will give you information on the programs provided by the government employment service, plus links to other useful sites. Another Internet site, called America's Job Bank at www.ajb.dni.us, allows visitors to see all jobs listed with the government employment service and to search for jobs by region and other criteria.

The government employment service lists only 5 to 10 percent of the available openings nationally, and only about 6 percent of all job seekers get their jobs there. Even so, visit your local office early in your job search. Find out if you qualify for unemployment compensation and learn more about its services. Look into it—the price is right.

Private employment agencies. Private employment agencies are businesses that charge a fee either to you or to the employer who hires you. You will often see their ads in the help wanted section of the newspaper, and many have Web sites. Fees can be from less than one month's pay to 15 percent or more of your annual salary.

Be careful about using fee-based employment agencies. Recent research indicates that more people use and benefit from fee-based agencies than in the past. But realize that relatively few people who register with private agencies get a job through them.

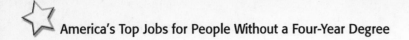

If you use them, ask for interviews where the employer pays the fee. Do not sign an exclusive agreement or be pressured into accepting a job, and continue to actively look for your own leads. You can find these agencies in the phone book's yellow pages, and a government-run Web site at www.ajb.dni.us lists many of them as well.

Temporary agencies. Temporary agencies offer jobs lasting from several days to many months. They charge the employer a bit more than your salary, and then pay you and keep the difference. You pay no direct fee to the agency. Many private employment agencies now provide temporary jobs as well.

Temp agencies have grown rapidly for good reason. They provide employers with short-term help, and employers often use them to find people they may want to hire later. Temp agencies can help you survive between jobs and get experience in different work settings; working for a temp agency may lead to a regular job. They provide a very good option while you look for long-term work, and you may get a job offer while working in a temp job.

School and Employment Services

Contacting a school employment center is one of the job search methods included in the survey presented earlier. Only a small percentage of respondents said they used this option. This is probably because few had the service available.

If you are a student or graduate, find out about these services. Some schools provide free career counseling, resume-writing help, referrals to job openings, career interest tests, reference materials, and other services. Special career programs work with veterans, people with disabilities, welfare recipients, union members, professional groups, and many others. So check out these services and consider using them.

Mailing Resumes and Posting Them on the Internet

Many job search "experts" used to suggest that sending out lots of resumes was a great technique. That advice probably helped sell their resume books, but mailing resumes to people you do not know was never an effective approach. Every so often this would work, but a 95-percent failure rate and few interviews were the more common outcomes, and still are.

While mailing your resume to strangers doesn't make much sense, posting it on the Internet might because

1. It doesn't take much time.

2. Many employers have the potential of finding your resume.

But job searching on the Internet also has its limitations, just like other methods. I'll cover resumes in more detail later and provide tips on using the Internet throughout this minibook.

The Two Job Search Methods That Work Best

The fact is that most jobs are not advertised, so how do *you* find them? The same way that about two-thirds of all job seekers do: networking with people you know (which I call warm contacts), and making direct contacts with an employer (which I call cold contacts). Both of these methods are based on the most important job search rule of all:

THE MOST IMPORTANT JOB SEARCH RULE
DON'T WAIT UNTIL THE JOB OPENS BEFORE CONTACTING THE EMPLOYER!

Employers fill most jobs with people they have met before jobs formally "open." So the trick is to meet people who can hire you before a job is available! Instead of saying, "Do you have any jobs open?" say, "I realize you may not have any openings now, but I would still like to talk to you about the possibility of future openings."

Method 1: Develop a Network of Contacts in Five Easy Stages

One study found that 40 percent of all people located their jobs through a lead provided by a friend, a relative, or an acquaintance. That makes people you know the number one source of job leads—more effective than all the traditional methods combined!

Developing and using your contacts is called "networking," and here's how it works:

1. **Make lists of people you know.** Make a thorough list of anyone you are friendly with. Then make a separate list of all your relatives. These two lists alone often add up to 25 to 100 people or more. Next, think of other groups of people that you have something in common with, such as former coworkers or classmates, members of your social or sports groups, members of your professional association, former employers, and members of your religious group. You may not know many of these people personally or well, but most will help you if you ask them.

2. **Contact them in a systematic way.** Next, contact each of these people. Obviously, some people will be more helpful than others, but any one of them might help you find a job lead.

3. **Present yourself well.** Begin with your friends and relatives. Call and tell them you are looking for a job and need their help. Be as clear as possible about the type of employment you want and the skills and qualifications you have. Look at the sample JIST Cards and phone script on pages 442–443 for good presentation ideas.

4. **Ask them for leads.** It is possible that your contacts will know of a job opening that might interest you. If so, get the details and get right on it! More likely, however, they will not, so you should ask each person these three questions:

◆

The Three Magic Networking Questions

- ◆ *Do you know of any openings for a person with my skills?* If the answer is no (which it usually is), then ask…
- ◆ *Do you know of someone else who might know of such an opening?* If your contact does, get that name and ask for another one. If he or she doesn't, ask…
- ◆ *Do you know of anyone who might know of someone else who might know?* Another good way to ask this is "Do you know someone who knows lots of people?" If all else fails, this will usually get you a name.

◆

5. **Contact these referrals and ask them the same questions.** With each original contact, you can extend your network of acquaintances by hundreds of people. Eventually, one of these people will hire you or refer you to someone who will!

If you are persistent in following these five steps, networking may be the only job search method you need. It works.

Method 2: Contact Employers Directly

It takes more courage, but making direct contact with employers is a very effective job search technique. I call these "cold contacts" because people you don't know in advance will need to "warm up" to your inquiries. Two basic techniques for making cold contacts follow.

Use the yellow pages to find potential employers. Begin by looking at the index in your phone book's yellow pages. For each entry, ask yourself, "Would an organization of this kind need a person with my skills?" If you answer yes, then that organization or business type is a possible target. You can also rate "yes" entries based on your interest, writing an A next to those that seem very interesting, a B next to those that you are not sure of, and a C next to those that aren't interesting at all.

Next, select a type of organization that got a "yes" response, such as "hotels," and turn to that section of the yellow pages. Call each hotel listed and ask to speak to the person who is most likely to hire or supervise you. The sample telephone script on the following page gives you ideas about what to say.

You can easily adapt this approach to the Internet by using sites like www. yellowpages.com to get contacts anywhere in the world.

Drop in without an appointment. You can also walk into a business or organization that interests you and ask to speak to the person in charge. Particularly effective in small businesses, dropping in also works surprisingly well in larger ones. Remember to ask for an interview even if there are no openings now. If your timing is inconvenient, ask for a better time to come back for an interview.

> ### Quip
>
> *The phone book is the most complete, up-to-date source of job search targets. The index for the yellow pages organizes potential employers into categories that are ideal for job seekers. Find a listing that interests you, and then contact employers listed there. All it takes is a 30-second phone call to get the name of the hiring authority!*

Most Jobs Are with Small Employers

Businesses and organizations with 250 or fewer employees employ about 70 percent of all U.S. workers. They are also the source for as much as 80 percent of the new jobs created each year. They are simply too important to overlook in your job search! Many of them don't have personnel departments, making direct contacts even easier and more effective.

JIST Cards®—An Effective Mini Resume

Look at the sample cards that follow—they are JIST Cards, and they get results. Computer printed or even neatly written on a 3-by-5–inch card, JIST Cards include the essential information employers want to know.

JIST Cards have been used by thousands of job search programs and millions of people. Employers like their direct and timesaving format, and they have been proven as an effective tool to get job leads. Attach one to your resume. Give them to friends, relatives, and other contacts and ask them to pass them along to others who might know of an opening. Enclose them in thank-you notes after an interview. Leave one with employers as a business card. However you get them in circulation, you may be surprised at how well they work.

Sandra Zaremba

Home phone: (219) 232-7608
E-mail: SKZ1128@aol.com

Position: General Office/Clerical

Over two years' work experience, plus one year of training in office practices. Familiar with a variety of computer programs, including word processing, spreadsheets, accounting, and some database and graphic design programs. Am Internet literate and word-process 70 wpm accurately. Can post general ledger and handle payables, receivables, and most accounting tasks. Responsible for daily deposits averaging more than $200,000 monthly. Good interpersonal skills. Can meet strict deadlines and handle pressure well.

Willing to work any hours.

Organized, honest, reliable, and hard working.

```
                    Jonathan McLaughlin
            Answering machine: (509) 674-8736
                 Cell phone: (509) 541-0981

Objective: Electronics—installation, maintenance, and sales

Skills: Four years of work experience, plus two years advanced
training in electronics. AS degree in Electronics Engineering
Technology. Managed a $500,000/year business while going to
school full time, with grades in the top 25%. Familiar with all
major electronics diagnostic and repair equipment. Hands-on
experience with medical, consumer, communications, business,
and industrial electronics equipment and applications. Good
problem-solving and communication skills. Customer service
oriented.

Willing to do what it takes to get the job done.

Self-motivated, dependable, learn quickly.
```

You can easily create JIST Cards on a computer and print them on card stock you can buy at any office supply store. Or have a few hundred printed cheaply by a local quick print shop. While they are often done as 3-by-5 cards, they can be printed in any size or format.

Use the Phone to Get Job Leads

Once you have created your JIST Card, you can use it as the basis for a phone "script" to make warm or cold calls. Revise your JIST Card content so that it sounds natural when spoken, and then edit it until you can read it out loud in about 30 seconds. Use the sample phone script that follows to help you write your own.

"Hello, my name is Pam Nykanen. I am interested in a position in hotel management. I have four years' experience in sales, catering, and accounting with a 300-room hotel. I also have an associate degree in hotel management, plus one year of experience with the Bradey Culinary Institute. During my employment, I helped double revenues from meetings and conferences and increased bar revenues by 46 percent. I have good problem-solving skills and am good with people. I am also well-organized, hard working, and detail-oriented. When may I come in for an interview?"

Once you have your script, make some practice calls to warm or cold contacts. If making cold calls, contact the person most likely to supervise you. Then present your script just as you practiced it, without stopping.

While it doesn't work every time, most people, with practice, can get one or more interviews in an hour by making such calls.

While the sample script assumes you are calling someone you don't know, it can be changed for warm contacts and referrals. Making cold calls takes courage—but works very well for many who are willing to do it.

Quip

Dialing for dollars. The phone can get you more interviews per hour than any other job search tool. But it won't work unless you use it actively.

Quip

Overcome phone phobia! Making cold calls takes guts, but job search programs find that most people can get one or more interviews an hour using cold calls. Start by calling people you know and people they refer you to. Then try calls to businesses that don't sound very interesting. As you get better, call more desirable targets.

Using the Internet in Your Job Search

I provide Internet-related tips throughout this minibook, but the Internet deserves a separate section, so here it is.

The Internet has limitations as a job search tool. While many have used it to get job leads, it has not worked well for far more. Too many assume they can simply add their resume to resume databases, and employers will line up to hire them. Just like the older approach of sending out lots of resumes, good things sometimes happen, but not often.

I recommend two points that apply to all job search methods, including using the Internet:

◆ It is unwise to rely on just one or two methods in conducting your job search.

◆ It is essential that you use an active rather than a passive approach in your job search.

Tips to Increase Your Internet Effectiveness

I encourage you to use the Internet in your job search but suggest you use it along with other techniques, including direct contacts with employers. The following suggestions can increase the effectiveness of using the Internet in your job search.

Be as specific as possible in the job you seek. This is important in using any job search method and even more so in using the Internet. The Internet is enormous, so it is essential to be as focused as possible in what you are looking for. Narrow your job title or titles to be as specific as possible. Limit your search to specific industries or areas of specialization.

Have reasonable expectations. Success on the Internet is more likely if you understand its limitations. For example, employers trying to find someone with skills in high demand, such as network engineers or nurses, are more likely to use the Internet to recruit job candidates.

> **Quip**
>
> *If the Internet is new to you,* I recommend a book titled Cyberspace Job Search Kit *by* Mary Nemnich and Fred Jandt. *It covers the basics plus lots of advice on using the Internet for career planning and job seeking.*

Limit your geographic options. If you don't want to move, or would move but only to certain areas, state this preference on your resume and restrict your search to those areas. Many Internet sites allow you to view only those jobs that meet your location criteria.

Create an electronic resume. With few exceptions, resumes submitted on the Internet end up as simple text files with no graphic elements. Employers search databases of many resumes for those that include key words or meet other searchable criteria. So create a simple text resume for Internet use and include on it words likely to be used by employers searching for someone with your abilities. See the resume on page 454 for an example.

Get your resume into the major resume databases. Most Internet employment sites let you add your resume for free, and then charge employers to advertise openings or to search for candidates. These easy-to-use sites often provide all sorts of useful information for job seekers.

Make direct contacts. Visit Web sites of organizations that interest you and learn more about them. Some will post openings, allow you to apply online, or even provide access to staff who can answer your questions. Even if they don't, you can always e-mail a request for the name of the person in charge of the area that interests you and then communicate with that person directly.

Network. You can network online, too, to get names and e-mail addresses of potential employer contacts or other people who might know of someone with a job opening. Look at interest groups, professional association sites, alumni sites, chat rooms, and employer sites—just some of the many creative ways to network with and to interact with people via the Internet.

Useful Internet Sites

Thousands of Internet sites provide information on careers or education. Many have links to other sites that they recommend. Service providers such as America Online (www.aol.com) and the Microsoft Network (www.msn.com) have career information and job listings plus links to other sites. Larger portal sites offer links to recommended career-related sites—AltaVista (www.altavista.com), Lycos (www.lycos.com), and Yahoo (www.yahoo.com) are just a few of these portals. These major career-specific sites can get you started:

- The Riley Guide at www.rileyguide.com
- America's Job Bank at www.ajb.dni.us
- CareerPath.com at www.careerpath.com
- Monster.com at www.monster.com
- The JIST site at www.jist.com

Step 4

Write a Simple Resume Now and a Better One Later

Sending out resumes and waiting for responses is not an effective job-seeking technique. But, many employers *will* ask you for one, and a resume can be a useful tool in your job search. I suggest that you begin with a simple resume you can complete quickly. I've seen too many people spend weeks working on their resume when they could have been out getting interviews instead. If you want a "better" resume, you can work on it on weekends and evenings. So let's begin with the basics.

Tips for Creating a Superior Resume

The following tips make sense for any resume format:

Write it yourself. It's okay to look at other resumes for ideas, but write yours yourself. It will force you to organize your thoughts and background.

Make it error-free. One spelling or grammar error will create a negative impressionist (see what I mean?). Get someone else to review your final draft for any errors. Then review it again because these rascals have a way of slipping in.

Make it look good. Poor copy quality, cheap paper, bad type quality, or anything else that creates a poor appearance will turn off employers to even the best resume content. Get professional help with design and printing if necessary. Many professional resume writers and even print shops offer writing and desktop design services if you need help.

Be brief, be relevant. Many good resumes fit on one page, and few justify more than two. Include only the most important points. Use short sentences and action words. If it doesn't relate to and support the job objective, cut it!

> **Quip**
>
> *Most jobs are never advertised because employers don't need to advertise or don't want to. Employers trust people referred to them by someone they know far more than they trust strangers. And most jobs are filled by referrals and people that the employer knows, eliminating the need to advertise. So, your job search must involve more than looking at ads.*

Be honest. Don't overstate your qualifications. If you end up getting a job you can't handle, who does it help? And a lie can result in your being fired later.

Be positive. Emphasize your accomplishments and results. A resume is no place to be too humble or to display your faults.

Be specific. Instead of saying, "I am good with people," say, "I supervised four people in the warehouse and increased productivity by 30 percent." Use numbers whenever possible, such as the number of people served, percent sales increase, or dollars saved.

You should also know that everyone feels that he or she is a resume expert. Whatever you do, someone will tell you that it's wrong. Remember that a resume is simply a job search tool. You should never delay or slow down your job search because your resume is not "good enough." The best approach is to create a simple and acceptable resume as quickly as possible and then use it. As time permits, create a better one if you feel you must.

> **Quip**
>
> *Avoid the resume pile.* Resume experts often suggest that a "dynamite" resume will jump out of the pile. This is old-fashioned advice. It assumes that you are applying to large organizations and for advertised jobs. Today, most jobs are with small employers and are not advertised. My advice is to avoid joining that stack of resumes in the first place, by looking for openings that others overlook.

Chronological Resumes

Most resumes use a chronological format where the most recent experience is listed first, followed by each previous job. This arrangement works fine for someone with work experience in several similar jobs, but not as well for those with limited experience or for career changers.

Look at the two resumes for Judith Jones that follow. Both use the chronological approach. The first resume would work fine for most job search needs—and it could be completed in about an hour. Notice that the second one includes some improvements. The first resume is good, but most employers would like the additional positive information in the improved resume.

Basic Chronological Resume Example

Judith J. Jones

115 South Hawthorne Avenue
Chicago, Illinois 66204
(312) 653-9217 (home)
email: jj@earthlink.com

Leaves lots of options open by not using one job title.

JOB OBJECTIVE

Desire a position in the office management, accounting, or administrative assistant area. Prefer a position requiring responsibility and a variety of tasks.

EDUCATION AND TRAINING

Acme Business College, Lincoln, Illinois
Graduate of a one-year business program.

U.S. Army
Financial procedures, accounting functions.

John Adams High School, South Bend, Indiana
Diploma, business education.

Other: Continuing education classes and workshops in business communication, computer spreadsheet and database programs, scheduling systems, and customer relations.

Emphasis on all related education is important, because it helps overcome her lack of "work" experience.

Everything supports her job objective

EXPERIENCE

2001-present—Claims Processor, Blue Spear Insurance Co., Wilmette, Illinois. Handle customer medical claims, develop management reports based on spreadsheets I created, exceed productivity goals.

2000-2001—Returned to school to upgrade my business and computer skills. Took courses in advanced accounting, spreadsheet and database programs, office management, human relations, and new office techniques.

1998-2000—E4, U.S. Army. Assigned to various stations as a specialist in finance operations. Promoted prior to honorable discharge.

1996-1998—Sandy's Boutique, Wilmette, Illinois. Responsible for counter sales, display design, cash register and other tasks.

1994-1996—Held part-time and summer jobs throughout high school.

Uses her education in this section to add credentials

PERSONAL

I am reliable, hard working, and good with people.

Improved Chronological Resume Example

Adds lots of details to reinforce skills throughout.

More details here.

Judith J. Jones

115 South Hawthorne Avenue • Chicago, Illinois 66204
(312) 653-9217 (home)
email: jj@earthlink.com

JOB OBJECTIVE

Seeking position requiring excellent business management skills in an office environment. Position should require a variety of tasks, including office management, word processing, and spreadsheet and database program use.

EDUCATION AND TRAINING

Acme Business College, Lincoln, Illinois.
Completed one-year program in Professional Office Management. Grades in top 30 percent of my class. Courses included word processing, accounting theory and systems, advanced spreadsheet and database programs, time management, and basic supervision.

John Adams High School, South Bend, Indiana.
Graduated with emphasis on business courses. Excellent grades in all business topics and won top award for word-processing speed and accuracy.

Other: Continuing education programs at my own expense, including business communications, customer relations, computer applications, sales techniques, and others.

Uses numbers to reinforce results.

EXPERIENCE

2001-present—Claims Processor, Blue Spear Insurance Company, Wilmette, Illinois. Handle 50 complex medical insurance claims per day, almost 20 percent above department average. Created a spreadsheet report process that decreased department labor costs by over $30,000 a year (one position). Received two merit raises for performance.

2000-2001—Returned to business school to gain advanced skills in accounting, office management, sales and human resources. Computer courses included word processing and graphics design, accounting and spreadsheet software, and database and networking applications. Grades in top 30 percent of class.

1998-2000—Finance Specialist (E4), U.S. Army. Responsible for the systematic processing of over 200 invoices per day from commercial vendors. Trained and supervised eight employees. Devised internal system allowing 15 percent increase in invoices processed with a decrease in personnel. Managed department with a budget equivalent of over $350,000 a year. Honorable discharge.

1996-1998—Sales Associate promoted to Assistant Manager, Sandy's Boutique, Wilmette, Illinois. Made direct sales and supervised four employees. Managed daily cash balances and deposits, made purchasing and inventory decisions, and handled all management functions during owner's absence. Sales increased 26 percent and profits doubled during my tenure.

1994-1996—Held various part-time and summer jobs through high school while maintaining good grades. Earned enough to pay all personal expenses, including car and car insurance. Learned to deal with customers, meet deadlines, work hard, handle multiple priorities, and develop other skills.

SPECIAL SKILLS AND ABILITIES

Quickly learn new computer applications and am experienced with a number of business software applications. Have excellent interpersonal, written, and oral communication and math skills. Accept supervision well, am able to supervise others, and work well as a team member. Like to get things done and have an excellent attendance record.

Tips for Writing a Simple Chronological Resume

Follow these tips for writing a basic chronological resume.

Name. Use your formal name rather than a nickname if it sounds more professional.

Address and contact information. Avoid abbreviations in your address and include your ZIP code. If you may move, use a friend's address or include a forwarding address. Most employers will not write to you, so you must provide reliable phone numbers and other contact options. Always include your area code in your phone number because you never know where your resume might travel. If you don't have an answering machine, get one—and leave it on whenever you leave home. Make sure your voice message presents you in a professional way. Include alternative ways to reach you, like a cell phone, beeper, and e-mail address.

Job objective. You should almost always have one, even if it is general. In the sample resumes, notice how Judy keeps her options open with her broad job objective. Writing "secretary" or "clerical" might limit her from being considered for jobs she might take.

Education and training. Include any training or education you've had that supports your job objective. If you did not finish a formal degree or program, list what you did complete and emphasize accomplishments. If your experience is not strong, add details here like related courses and extracurricular activities. In the two examples, Judy puts her business schooling in both the education and experience sections. Doing this fills a job gap and allows her to present her training as equal to work experience.

Previous experience. Include the basics like employer name, job title, dates employed, and responsibilities—but emphasize things like specific skills, results, accomplishments, and superior performance.

Personal data. Do not include irrelevant details like height, weight, and marital status—doing so is considered very old-fashioned. But you can include information like hobbies or leisure activities in a special section that directly supports your job objective. The first sample includes a "Personal" section in which Judy lists some of her strengths, which are often not included in a resume.

References. You do not need to list references since employers will ask for them if they want them. If your references are particularly good, you can mention this somewhere—the last section is often a good place. List your references on a separate page and give it to employers who ask. Ask your references what they will say about you and, if positive, if they would write you a letter of recommendation to give to employers.

Tips for an Improved Chronological Resume

Once you have a simple, errorless, and eye-pleasing resume, get on with your job search. There is no reason to delay! If you want to create a better resume in your spare time (evenings or weekends), try these additional tips.

Job objective. A poorly written job objective can limit the jobs an employer might consider you for. Think of the skills you have and the types of jobs you want to do; describe them in general terms. Instead of using a narrow job title like "restaurant manager," you might write "manage a small to mid-sized business."

> ## Quip
> *Skip the negatives.* Remember that a resume can get you screened out, but it is up to you to get the interview and the job. So, cut out anything negative in your resume!

Education and training. New graduates should emphasize their recent training and education more than those with a few years of related work experience would. A more detailed education and training section might include specific courses you took, and activities or accomplishments that support your job objective or reinforce your key skills. Include other details that reflect how hard you work, such as working your way through school or handling family responsibilities.

Skills and accomplishments. Include things that support your ability to do well in the job you seek now. Even small things count. Maybe your attendance was perfect, you met a tight deadline, or you did the work of others during vacations. Be specific and include numbers—even if you have to estimate them. The improved chronological resume example features a "Special Skills and Abilities" section and more accomplishments and skills. Notice the impact of the numbers to reinforce results.

Job titles. Past job titles may not accurately reflect what you did. For example, your job title may have been "cashier," but you also opened the store, trained new staff, and covered for the boss on vacations. Perhaps "head cashier and assistant manager" would be more accurate. Check with your previous employer if you are not sure.

Promotions. If you were promoted or got good evaluations, say so—"cashier, promoted to assistant manager," for example. A promotion to a more responsible job can be handled as a separate job if doing so results in a stronger resume.

Gaps in employment and other problem areas. Employee turnover is expensive, so few employers want to hire people who won't stay or who won't work out. Gaps in employment, jobs held for short periods, or a lack of direction in the jobs you've held are all things that concern employers. So consider your situation and try to give an explanation of a problem area. Here are a few examples:

2000—Continued my education at…

2002—Traveled extensively throughout the United States.

2000 to present—Self-employed barn painter and widget maker.

2001—Had first child, took year off before returning to work.

Use entire years to avoid displaying an employment gap you can't explain easily. For example "2001 to 2002" can cover a few months of unemployment at the beginning of 2001.

Skills and Combination Resumes

The functional or "skills" resume emphasizes your most important skills, supported by specific examples of how you have used them. This approach allows you to use any part of your life history to support your ability to do the job you want.

While a skills resume can be very effective, it requires more work to create one. And some employers don't like them because they can hide a job seeker's faults (such as job gaps, lack of formal education, or little related work experience) better than a chronological resume. Still, a skills resume may make sense for you.

Look over the sample resumes that follow for ideas. Notice that one resume includes elements of a skills *and* a chronological resume. This so-called "combination" resume makes sense if your previous job history or education and training are positive.

More Resume Examples

Find resume layout and presentation ideas in the four samples that follow.

The chronological resume sample on page 451 focuses on accomplishments through the use of numbers. While Maria's resume does not say so, it is obvious that she works hard and that she gets results.

The skills resume on page 452 is for a recent high school graduate whose only paid work experience was at a fast-food place!

The combination resume on page 453 emphasizes Mary Beth's relevant education and transferable skills because she has no work experience in the field. The resume was submitted by professional resume writer Janet L. Beckstrom of Flint, Michigan (e-mail wordcrafter@voyager.net).

The electronic resume on page 454 is appropriate for scanning or e-mail submission. It has a plain format that is easily read by scanners. It also has lots of key words that increase its chances of being selected when an employer searches a database. The resume is based on one from *Cyberspace Resume Kit* by Mary Nemnich and Fred Jandt and published by JIST Works.

> **Quip**
>
> A resume is not the most effective tool for getting interviews. A better approach is to make direct contact with those who hire or supervise people with your skills and ask them for an interview, even if no openings exist now. Then send a resume.

Chronological Resume Emphasizes Results

A simple chronological format with few but carefully chosen words. It has an effective summary at the beginning, and every word supports her job objective.

She emphasizes results!

Maria Marquez

4141 Beachway Road
Redondo Beach, California 90277

Messages: (213) 432-2279
E-mail: mmarq@msn.net

Objective: Management Position in a Major Hotel

Summary of Experience: Four years' experience in sales, catering, banquet services, and guest relations in 300-room hotel. Doubled sales revenues from conferences and meetings. Increased dining room and bar revenues by 44%. Won prestigious national and local awards for increased productivity and services.

Experience: Park Regency Hotel, Los Angeles, California
Assistant Manager
1999 to Present

- Oversee a staff of 36 including dining room and bar, housekeeping, and public relations operations.
- Introduced new menus and increased dining room revenues by 44% Gourmet America awarded us their first place Hotel Haute Cuisine award as a result of my efforts.
- Attracted 28% more diners with the first revival of Big Band Cocktail Dances in the Los Angeles area.

Notice her use of numbers to increase impact of statements

Kingsmont Hotel, Redondo Beach, California
Sales and Public Relations
1997 to 1999

- Doubled revenues per month from conferences and meetings.
- Redecorated meeting rooms and updated sound and visual media equipment. Careful scheduling resulted in no lost revenue during this time.
- Instituted staff reward program, which resulted in an upgrade from B- to AAA+ in the *Car and Travel Handbook*.

Bullets here and above increase readability and emphasis.

Education: Associate Degree in Hotel Management from Henfield College of San Francisco. One-year certification program with the Boileau Culinary Institute, where I won the Grand Prize Scholarship.

While Maria had only a few years of related work experience, she used this resume to help her land a very responsible job in a large resort hotel.

Skills Resume for Someone with Limited Work Experience

A skills resume where each skill directly supports the job objective of this recent high school graduate with very limited work experience.

Lisa M. Rhodes
813 Lava Court • Denver, Colorado 81613
Home: (413) 643-2173 (leave message)
Cell phone: (413) 442-1659
Email: lrhodes@netcom.net

Position Desired

Sales-oriented position in a retail sales or distribution business.

Support for the skills comes from all life activities: school, clubs, part-time jobs.

Key skills →

Skills and Abilities ✓

Communications   Good written and verbal presentation skills. Use proper grammar and have a good speaking voice.

Interpersonal   Able to get along well with coworkers and accept supervision. Received positive evaluations from previous supervisors.

← Good emphasis on adaptive skills.

Flexible   Willing to try new things and am interested in improving efficiency on assigned tasks.

Attention to Detail   Concerned with quality. My work is typically orderly and attractive. Like to see things completed correctly and on time.

Hard Working   Throughout high school, worked long hours in strenuous activities while attending school full-time. Often handled as many as 65 hours a week in school and other structured activities, while maintaining above-average grades.

Very strong statement.

Customer Contacts   Routinely handled as many as 500 customer contacts a day (10,000 per month) in a busy retail outlet. Averaged lower than a .001% complaint rate and was given the "Employee of the Month" award in my second month of employment. Received two merit increases. Never absent or late.

Good use of numbers

Cash Sales   Handled over $2,000 a day ($40,000 a month) in cash sales. Balanced register and prepared daily sales summary and deposits.

Reliable   Excellent attendance record, trusted to deliver daily cash deposits totaling over $40,000 a month.

Education

Franklin High School. Took advanced English and other classes. Member of award-winning band. Excellent attendance record. Superior communication skills. Graduated in top 30% of class.

Other

Active gymnastics competitor for four years. This taught me discipline, teamwork, how to follow instructions, and hard work. I am ambitious, outgoing, reliable, and willing to work.

Lisa's resume makes it clear that she is talented and hard working.

Combination Resume for a Career Changer

Writer's comments: This client was finishing computer programming school and had no work experience in the field. After listing the topics covered in the course, I summarized her employment experience, specifying that she earned promotions quickly. This **Mary Beth Kurzak** *would be attractive to any employer.*

2188 Huron River Drive • Ann Arbor, MI 48104 • 734-555-4912

Profile
➤ Strong educational preparation with practical applications in computer/internet programming.
➤ Highly motivated to excel in new career.
➤ A fast learner, as evidenced by success in accelerated training program.
➤ Self-directed, independent worker with proven ability to meet deadlines and work under pressure.
➤ Maintain team perspective with ability to build positive working relationships and foster open communication.

Education/Training
ADVANCED TECHNOLOGY CENTER • Dearborn, MI   xxxx-Present
Pursuing Certification in **Internet/Information Technology**   *Anticipated completion:* Aug. xxxx
An accelerated program focusing on computer and internet programming.
Highlights of Training:

- Networking Concepts	- Client Server	- UNIX
- Programming Concepts	- Visual Basic	- IIS
- Programming in Java/Java Script	- C/C++	- VB/ASP
- Web Authoring Using HTML	- Oracle	- CGI
- Photoshop	- DHTML, XML	- Perl

Important to include specific things learned

Highlights of Experience and Abilities

Customer Service
➤ Determined member eligibility and verified policy benefits.
➤ Responded to customer questions; interpreted and explained complex insurance concepts.
➤ Collaborated with health care providers regarding billing and claim procedures.

Experiences selected to support job objective

Leadership
➤ Creatively supervised 30 employees, many of whom were significantly older.
➤ Motivated employees and improved working conditions, resulting in greater camaraderie.
➤ Trained coworkers in various technical and nontechnical processes.

Analytical/Troubleshooting
➤ Investigated and resolved computer system errors.
➤ Researched discrepancies in claims and identified appropriate actions.
➤ Compiled and analyzed claims statistics.

Administrative Support and Accounting
➤ Managed and processed medical, mental health and substance abuse claims.
➤ Oversaw accounts receivable; reconciled receipts and prepared bank deposits.
➤ Coordinated 50+ line switchboard; routed calls as appropriate.

Employment History
MEDICAL SERVICES PLUS [Contracted by Health Solutions - Southfield, MI]   xxxx-xxxx
Promoted within eight months of hire.
Claims Supervisor / Claims Adjudicator

HANSEN AGENCY OF MICHIGAN • Ann Arbor, MI   xxxx-xxxx
Earned two promotions in one year.
Claims Adjudicator / Accounting Clerk / Receptionist

FORD WILLOW RUN TRANSMISSION PLANT • Ypsilanti, MI   Summer xxxx
Temporary Production Worker

PEARL HARBOR MEMORIAL MUSEUM • Pearl Harbor, HI   xxxx-xxxx
Assistant Crew Manager

References available on request

Submitted by Janet L. Beckstrom

Electronic Resume

RICHARD JONES

3456 Generic Street

Potomac MD 11721

Phone messages: (301) 927-1189

E-mail: richj@riverview.com

Format to be scanned or e-mailed. No bold, bullets, or italics.

SUMMARY OF SKILLS

Lots of key words to help get selected by computer searches by employers.

Rigger, maintenance mechanic (carpentry, electrical, plumbing, painting), work leader. Read schematic diagrams. Flooring (wood, linoleum, carpet, ceramic and vinyl tile). Plumbing (pipes, fixtures, fire systems). Certified crane and forklift operator, work planner, inspector.

++

EXPERIENCE *Includes results statements and numbers below*

Total of nine years in the trades—apprentice to work leader.

* MAINTENANCE MECHANIC LEADER, Smithsonian Institution, Washington, DC, April 2001 to present: Promoted to supervise nine staff in all trades, including plumbing, painting, electrical, carpentry, drywall, flooring. Prioritize and schedule work, inspect and approve completed jobs. Responsible for annual budget of $750,000 and assuring that all work done to museum standards and building codes.

* RIGGER / MAINTENANCE MECHANIC, Smithsonian Institution, February 1998 to April 2001: Built and set up exhibits. Operated cranes, rollers, forklifts, and rigged mechanical and hydraulic systems to safely move huge, priceless museum exhibits. Worked with other trades in carpentry, plumbing, painting, electrical and flooring to construct exhibits.

* RIGGER APPRENTICE, Portsmouth Naval Shipyard, Portsmouth, NH, August 1996 to January 1998: Qualified signalman for cranes. Moved and positioned heavy machines and structural parts for shipbuilding. Responsible for safe operation of over $2,000,000 of equipment on a daily basis, with no injury or accidents. Used cranes, skids, rollers, jacks, forklifts and other equipment.

+++

TRAINING AND EDUCATION

HS graduate, top 50% of class.

Additional training in residential electricity, drywall, HV/AC, and refrigeration systems. Certified in heavy crane operation, forklift, regulated waste disposal, industrial blueprints.

Use the information from your completed Essential Job Search Data Worksheet to write your resume.

Redefine What Counts As an Interview, Then Get 2 a Day

The average job seeker gets about 5 interviews a month—fewer than 2 a week. Yet many job seekers use the methods in this minibook to get 2 interviews a day. Getting 2 interviews a day equals 10 a week and 40 a month. That's 800 percent more interviews than the average job seeker gets. Who do you think will get a job offer quicker?

But getting 2 interviews a day is nearly impossible unless you redefine what counts as an interview. If you define an interview in a different way, getting 2 a day is quite possible.

THE NEW DEFINITION OF AN INTERVIEW
AN INTERVIEW IS ANY FACE-TO-FACE CONTACT WITH SOMEONE
WHO HAS THE AUTHORITY TO HIRE OR SUPERVISE A PERSON WITH
YOUR SKILLS—EVEN IF NO OPENING EXISTS AT THE TIME YOU INTERVIEW.

If you use this new definition, it becomes *much* easier to get interviews. You can now interview with all sorts of potential employers, not just those who have job openings now. While most other job seekers look for advertised or actual openings, you can get interviews before a job opens up or before it is advertised and widely known. You will be considered for jobs that may soon be created but that others will not know about. And, of course, you can also interview for existing openings like everyone else does.

Spending as much time as possible on your job search and setting a job search schedule are important parts of this step.

Make Your Search a Full-Time Job

Job seekers average fewer than 15 hours a week looking for work. On average, unemployment lasts three or more months, with some people out of work far longer (older workers and higher earners, for example). My many years of experience with job seekers indicate that the more time you spend on your job search each week, the less time you will likely remain unemployed.

Of course, using the more effective job search methods presented in this minibook also helps. Many job search programs that teach job seekers my basic approach of using more effective methods and spending more time looking have proven to cut in half the average time needed to find a job. More importantly, many job seekers also find better jobs using these methods.

So, if you are unemployed and looking for a full-time job, you should plan to look on a full-time basis. It just makes sense to do so, although many do not, or they start out well but quickly get discouraged. Most job seekers simply don't have a structured plan—they have no idea what they are going to do next Thursday. The plan that follows will show you how to structure your job search like a job.

Decide How Much Time You Will Spend Looking for Work Each Week and Day

First and most importantly, decide how many hours you are willing to spend each week on your job search. You should spend a minimum of 25 hours a week on hard-core job search activities with no goofing around. Let me walk you through a simple but effective process to set a job search schedule for each week.

PLAN YOUR JOB SEARCH WEEK

1. How many hours are you willing to spend each week looking for a job? _____

2. Which days of the week will you spend looking for a job? _____

    _____

3. How many hours will you look each day? _____

4. At what times will you begin and end your job search on each of these days? _____

    _____

Create a Specific Daily Job Search Schedule

Having a specific daily schedule is essential because most job seekers find it hard to stay productive each day. The sample daily schedule that follows is the result of years of research into what schedule gets the best results. I tested many schedules in job search programs I ran, and this particular schedule worked best. So use the sample daily schedule for ideas on creating your own, but I urge you to consider using one like this. Why? Because it works.

A Sample Daily Schedule That Works

Time	Activity
7 a.m.	Get up, shower, dress, eat breakfast.
8–8:15 a.m.	Organize work space, review schedule for today's interviews and promised follow-ups, update schedule as needed.
8:15–9 a.m.	Review old leads for follow-up needed today; develop new leads from want ads, yellow pages, the Internet, warm contact lists, and other sources; complete daily contact list.
9–10 a.m.	Make phone calls and set up interviews.
10–10:15 a.m.	Take a break.
10:15–11 a.m.	Make more phone calls, set up more interviews.
11 a.m.–Noon	Send follow-up notes and do other "office" activities as needed.
Noon–1 p.m.	Lunch break, relax.
1–3 p.m.	Go on interviews, make cold contacts in the field.
Evening	Read job search books, make calls to warm contacts not reachable during the day, work on a "better" resume, spend time with friends and family, exercise, relax.

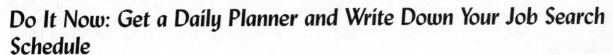

Do It Now: Get a Daily Planner and Write Down Your Job Search Schedule

This is important: If you are not accustomed to using a daily schedule book or electronic planner, promise yourself to get a good one tomorrow. Choose one that allows plenty of space for each day's plan on an hourly basis, plus room for daily to-do listings. Write in your daily schedule in advance; then add interviews as they come. Get used to carrying it with you and use it!

Step 6

Dramatically Improve Your Interviewing Skills

Interviews are where the job search action is. You have to get them; then you have to do well in them. According to surveys of employers, most job seekers do not effectively present the skills they have to do the job. Even worse, most job seekers can't answer one or more problem questions.

This lack of performance in interviews is one reason why employers will often hire a job seeker who does well in the interview over someone with better credentials. The good news is that you can do simple things to dramatically improve your interviewing skills. This section will emphasize interviewing tips and techniques that make the most difference.

Your First Impression May Be the Only One You Make

Some research suggests that if the interviewer forms a negative impression in the first five minutes of an interview, your chances of getting a job offer approach zero. But I know from experience that many job seekers can create a lasting negative impression in seconds. Since a positive first impression is so important, here are some suggestions to help you get off to a good start.

Dress and groom like the interviewer is likely to be dressed—but cleaner! Employer surveys find that almost half of all people's dress or grooming creates an initial negative impression. So this is a big problem. If necessary, get advice on your interviewing outfits from someone who dresses well. Pay close attention to your grooming too—little things do count.

Be early. Leave in plenty of time to be a few minutes early to an interview.

Be friendly and respectful with the receptionist. Doing otherwise will often get back to the interviewer and result in a quick rejection.

Follow the interviewer's lead in the first few minutes. It's often informal small talk but very important for that person to see how you interact. This is a good time to make a positive comment on the organization or even something you see in the office.

Do some homework on the organization before you go. You can often get information on a business and on industry trends from the Internet or a library.

Make a good impression before you arrive. Your resume, e-mails, applications, and other written correspondence create an impression before the interview, so make them professional and error-free.

A Traditional Interview Is Not a Friendly Exchange

In a traditional interview situation, there is a job opening, and you will be one of several applicants for it. In this setting, the employer's task is to eliminate all applicants but one. The interviewer's questions are designed to elicit information that can be used to screen you out. And your objective is to avoid getting screened out. It's hardly an open and honest interaction, is it?

This illustrates yet another advantage of setting up interviews before an opening exists. This eliminates the stress of a traditional interview. Employers are not trying to screen you out, and you are not trying to keep them from finding out stuff about you.

Having said that, knowing how to answer questions that might be asked in a traditional interview is good preparation for any interview you face.

How to Answer Tough Interview Questions

Your answers to a few key problem questions may determine if you get a job offer. There are simply too many possible interview questions to cover one by one. Instead, the 10 basic questions below cover variations of most other interview questions. So, if you can learn to answer these 10 questions well, you will know how to answer most others.

Top 10 Problem Interview Questions

1. Why should I hire you?

2. Why don't you tell me about yourself?

3. What are your major strengths?

4. What are your major weaknesses?

5. What sort of pay do you expect to receive?

6. How does your previous experience relate to the jobs we have here?

7. What are your plans for the future?

8. What will your former employer (or references) say about you?

9. Why are you looking for this type of position, and why here?

10. Why don't you tell me about your personal situation?

The Three-Step Process for Answering Interview Questions

I know this might seem too simple, but the three-step process is easy to remember and can help you create a good answer to most interview questions. The technique has worked for thousands of people, so consider trying it. The three steps are

1. Understand what is really being asked.

2. Answer the question briefly.

3. Answer the real concern.

Step 1. Understand what is really being asked. Most questions are designed to find out about your self-management skills and personality, but interviewers are rarely this blunt. The employer's *real* question is often one or more of the following:

- ◆ Can I depend on you?

- ◆ Are you easy to get along with?

- ◆ Are you a good worker?

- ◆ Do you have the experience and training to do the job if we hire you?

- ◆ Are you likely to stay on the job for a reasonable period of time and be productive?

Ultimately, if you don't convince the employer that you will stay and be a good worker, it won't matter if you have the best credentials—he or she won't hire you.

Step 2. Answer the question briefly. Present the facts of your particular work experience, but…

♦ Present them as advantages, not disadvantages.

Many interview questions encourage you to provide negative information. One classic question I included in my list of Top 10 Problem Interview Questions was "What are your major weaknesses?" This is obviously a trick question, and many people are just not prepared for it.

A good response is to mention something that is not very damaging, such as *"I have been told that I am a perfectionist, sometimes not delegating as effectively as I might."* But your answer is not complete until you continue with Step 3.

Step 3. Answer the real concern by presenting your related skills.

♦ Base your answer on the key skills you have that support the job, and give examples to support these skills.

For example, an employer might say to a recent graduate, "We were looking for someone with more experience in this field. Why should we consider you?" Here is one possible answer:

"I'm sure there are people who have more experience, but I do have more than six years of work experience, including three years of advanced training and hands-on experience using the latest methods and techniques. Because my training is recent, I am open to new ideas and am used to working hard and learning quickly."

In the previous example (about your need to delegate), a good skills statement might be

"I've been working on this problem and have learned to let my staff do more, making sure that they have good training and supervision. I've found that their performance improves, and it frees me up to do other things."

Whatever your situation, learn to answer questions that present you well. It's essential to communicate your skills during an interview, and the three-step process can help you answer problem questions and dramatically improve your responses. It works!

The Most Important Interview Question of All: "Why Should I Hire You?"

This is the most important question of all to answer well. Do you have a convincing argument why someone should hire you over someone else? If you don't, you probably won't get that job you really want. So think carefully about why someone *should* hire you and practice your response. Then, make sure you communicate this in the interview, even if the interviewer never asks the question in a clear way.

Tips on Negotiating Pay—How to Earn a Thousand Dollars a Minute

Remember these few essential ideas when it comes time to negotiate your pay.

THE ONLY TIME TO NEGOTIATE IS AFTER YOU HAVE BEEN OFFERED THE JOB.

Employers want to know how much you want to be paid so that they can eliminate you from consideration. They figure if you want too much, you won't be happy with their job and won't stay. And if you will take too little, they may think you don't have enough experience. So *never* discuss your salary expectations until an employer offers you the job.

IF PRESSED, SPEAK IN TERMS OF WIDE PAY RANGES.

If you are pushed to reveal your pay expectations early in an interview, ask the interviewer what the normal pay range is for this job. Interviewers will often tell you, and you can say that you would consider offers in this range.

If you are forced to be more specific, speak in terms of a wide pay range. For example, if you figure that the company will likely pay from $20,000 to $25,000 a year, say that you would consider "any fair offer in the low to mid-twenties." This statement covers the employer's range *and goes a bit higher*. If all else fails, tell the interviewer that you would consider any reasonable offer.

For this to work, you must know in advance what the job is likely to pay. You can get this information by asking people who do similar work, or from a variety of books and Internet sources of career information.

SALARY NEGOTIATION RULE
THE ONE WHO NAMES A SPECIFIC NUMBER FIRST, LOSES.

Don't Say "No" Too Quickly

Never, ever turn down a job offer during an interview! Instead, thank the interviewer for the offer and ask to consider the offer overnight. You can turn it down tomorrow, saying how much you appreciate the offer and asking to be considered for other jobs that pay better or whatever.

But this is no time to be playing games. If you want the job, you should say so. And it is okay to ask for additional pay or other concessions. But if you simply can't accept the offer, say why and ask the interviewer to keep you in mind for future opportunities. You just never know.

Step 7

Follow Up on All Contacts

It's a fact: People who follow up with potential employers and with others in their network get jobs faster than those who do not. Here are a few rules to guide you in your job search.

Rules for Effective Follow-Up

- Send a thank-you note or e-mail to every person who helps you in your job search.
- Send the note within 24 hours after speaking with the person.
- Enclose JIST Cards with thank-you notes and all other correspondence.
- Develop a system to keep following up with good contacts.

Thank-You Notes Make a Difference

While thank-you notes can be e-mailed, most people appreciate and are more impressed by a mailed note. Here are some tips about mailed thank-you notes that you can easily adapt to e-mail use.

Thank-you notes can be handwritten or typed on quality paper and matching envelopes. Keep them simple, neat, and error-free. And make sure to include a few copies of your JIST Cards. Here is an example of a simple thank-you note.

2244 Riverwood Avenue
Philadelphia, PA 17963
April 16, XXXX

Ms. Helen A. Colcord
Henderson & Associates, Inc.
1801 Washington Blvd., Suite 1201
Philadelphia, PA 17993

Dear Ms. Colcord:

Thank you for sharing your time with me so generously today. I really appreciated seeing your state-of-the-art computer equipment.

Your advice has already proved helpful. I have an appointment to meet with Mr. Robert Hopper on Friday. As you anticipated, he does intend to add more computer operators in the next few months.

In case you think of someone else who might need a person like me, I'm enclosing another JIST Card. I will let you know how the interview with Mr. Hopper goes.

Sincerely,

William Henderson

William Henderson

Use Job Lead Cards to Help Organize Follow-Ups

If you use contact management software, use it to schedule follow-up activities. But the simple paper system I describe here can work very well or can be adapted for setting up your contact management software.

Use a simple 3-by-5–inch card to record essential information about each person in your network. Buy a 3-by-5–inch card file box and tabs for each day of the month. File the cards under the date you want to contact the person, and the rest is easy.

I've found that staying in touch with a good contact every other week can pay off big. Here's a sample card to give you ideas about creating your own.

> Organization: **Mutual Health Insurance**
> Contact person: **Anna Tomey**
> Phone number: **(555) 555-2211**
> Source of lead: **Aunt Ruth**
> Notes: **4/10 called. Anna on vacation. Call back 4/15. 4/15 Interview set 4/20 at 1:30. 4/20 Anna showed me around. They use the same computers we used in school. Sent thank-you note and JIST Card. Call back 5/1. 5/1 Second interview 5/8 at 9 a.m.**

In Closing

You won't get a job offer because someone knocks on your door and offers one. Job seeking does involve luck, but you are more likely to get lucky if you are out getting interviews.

I'll close this minibook with a few final tips:

- Approach your job search as if it were a job itself. Create and stick to a daily schedule, and spend at least 25 hours a week looking.

- Follow up on each lead you generate and ask each one for referrals.

- Set out each day to schedule at least two interviews, and use the new definition of an interview, which includes talking to businesses that don't have an opening now.

- Send out lots of thank-you notes and JIST Cards.

- When you want the job, tell the employer that you want it and why the company should hire you over someone else.

Don't get discouraged. There are lots of jobs out there, and someone needs an employee with your skills—your job is to find that someone.

I wish you luck in your job search and your life.

ESSENTIAL JOB SEARCH DATA WORKSHEET

Take some time to complete this worksheet carefully. It will help you write your resume and answer interview questions. You can also photocopy it and take it with you to help complete applications and as a reference throughout your job search. Use an erasable pen or pencil to allow for corrections. Whenever possible, emphasize skills and accomplishments that support your ability to do the job you want. Use extra sheets as needed.

Your name _____

Date completed _____

Job objective _____

Key Accomplishments

List three accomplishments that best prove your ability to do the kind of job you want.

1. _____
2. _____
3. _____

Education and Training

Name of high school(s); years attended _____

_____

Subjects related to job objective _____

_____

Related extracurricular activities/hobbies/leisure activities _____

_____

Accomplishments/things you did well _____

_____

Specific things you can do as a result _____

_____

Schools you attended after high school; years attended; degrees/certificates earned _____

_____

Courses related to job objective _____

_____

Related extracurricular activities/hobbies/leisure activities _____

_____

Accomplishments/things you did well _____

_____

Specific things you can do as a result _____

_____

Other Training

Include formal or informal learning, workshops, military training, things you learned on-the-job or from hobbies—anything that will help support your job objective. Include specific dates, certificates earned, or other details as needed. _____

_____

_____

_____

Work and Volunteer History

List your most recent job first, followed by each previous job. Military experience, unpaid or volunteer work, and work in a family business should be included here, too. If needed, use additional sheets to cover *all* significant paid or unpaid work experiences. Emphasize details that will help support your new job objective! Include numbers to support what you did: the number of people served over one or more years,

(continues)

the number of transactions processed, percentage of sales increased, total inventory value you were responsible for, payroll of the staff you supervised, total budget responsible for, and so on. Emphasize results you achieved, using numbers to support them whenever possible. Mentioning these things on your resume and in an interview will help you get the job you want!

Job 1

Dates employed _____

Name of organization _____

Supervisor's name and job title _____

Address _____

_____

Phone number/e-mail address/Web site _____

_____

What did you accomplish and do well? _____

_____

Things you learned, skills you developed or used _____

_____

Raises, promotions, positive evaluations, awards _____

_____

Computer software, hardware, and other equipment you used _____

_____

Other details that might support your job objective _____

_____

Job 2

Dates employed _____

Name of organization _____

Supervisor's name and job title _____

Address _____

_____

Phone number/e-mail address/Web site _____

_____

What did you accomplish and do well? _____

_____

Things you learned, skills you developed or used _____

_____

Raises, promotions, positive evaluations, awards _____

_____

Computer software, hardware, and other equipment you used _____

_____

Other details that might support your job objective _____

_____

Job 3

Dates employed _____

Name of organization _____

Supervisor's name and job title _____

Address _____

_____

Phone number/e-mail address/Web site _____

_____

What did you accomplish and do well? _____

_____

Things you learned, skills you developed or used _____

_____

Raises, promotions, positive evaluations, awards _____

_____

Computer software, hardware, and other equipment you used _____

_____

Other details that might support your job objective _____

_____

References

Think of people who know your work well and will say positive things about your work and character. Past supervisors are best. Contact them and tell them what type of job you want and your qualifications, and ask what they will say about you if contacted by a potential employer. Some employers will not provide references by phone, so ask them for a letter of reference for you in advance. If a past employer may say negative things, negotiate what they will say or get written references from others you worked with there.

(continues)

(continued)

Reference name _____

Position or title _____

Relationship to you _____

Contact information (complete address, phone number, e-mail address) _____

_____

_____

Reference name _____

Position or title _____

Relationship to you _____

Contact information (complete address, phone number, e-mail address) _____

_____

_____

Reference name _____

Position or title _____

Relationship to you _____

Contact information (complete address, phone number, e-mail address) _____

_____

_____

A Short List of Additional Resources

Thousands of books and uncounted Internet sites provide information on career subjects. Space limitations do not permit me to describe the many good resources available, so I list here some of the most useful ones. Because this is my list, I've included books I've written or that JIST publishes. You should be able to find these and many other resources at libraries, bookstores, and Web book-selling sites, such as Amazon.com.

Resumes and Cover Letter Books

My books. I'm told that *The Quick Resume & Cover Letter Book* is now one of the top-selling resume books at various large bookstore chains. It is very simple to follow, is inexpensive, has good design, and has good sample resumes written by professional resume writers. *America's Top Resumes for America's Top Jobs* includes a wonderfully diverse collection of resumes covering most major jobs and life situations, plus brief but helpful resume-writing advice.

Other books published by JIST. The following titles include many sample resumes written by professional resume writers, as well as good advice: *Cover Letter Magic,* by Enelow and Kursmark; *Cyberspace Resume Kit,* Nemnich and Jandt; *The Edge Resume & Job Search Strategy,* Corbin and Wright; *The Federal Resume Guidebook,* Troutman; *Expert Resumes for Computer and Web Jobs,* Enelow and Kursmark; *Expert Resumes for Teachers and Educators,* Enelow and Kursmark; *Gallery of Best Cover Letters,* Noble; *Gallery of Best Resumes,* Noble; and *Resume Magic*, Whitcomb.

Job Search Books

My books. *The Very Quick Job Search—Get a Better Job in Half the Time* is a thorough book with detailed advice and a "quick" section of key tips you can finish in a few hours. *The Quick Interview & Salary Negotiation Book* also has a section of quick tips likely to make the biggest difference in your job search, as well as sections with more detailed information on problem questions and other topics. *Getting the Job You Really Want* includes many in-the-book activities and good career decision-making and job search advice.

Other books published by JIST. Titles include *Career Success Is Color Blind*, Stevenson; *Cyberspace Job Search Kit*, Nemnich and Jandt; *Inside Secrets to Finding a Teaching Job*, Warner and Bryan; and *Job Search Handbook for People with Disabilities*, Ryan.

Books with Information on Jobs

Primary references. The *Occupational Outlook Handbook* is the source of job titles listed in this minibook. Published by the U.S. Department of Labor and updated every other year, the *OOH* covers about 85 percent of the workforce. A book titled the *O*NET Dictionary of Occupational Titles* has descriptions for over 1,000 jobs based on the O*NET (for Occupational Information Network) database developed by the Department of Labor. The *Enhanced Occupational Outlook Handbook* includes the *OOH* descriptions plus more than 2,000 additional descriptions of related jobs from the O*NET and other sources. The *Guide for Occupational Exploration*, Third Edition, allows you to explore major jobs based on your interests. All of these books are available from JIST.

Other books published by JIST. Here are a few good books that include job descriptions and helpful details on career options: *America's Fastest Growing Jobs; America's Top Jobs for College Graduates; America's Top Jobs for People Without a Four-Year Degree; America's Top Computer and Technical Jobs; America's Top Medical, Education & Human Services Jobs; America's Top White-Collar Jobs; Best Jobs for the 21st Century* (plus versions for people with and without degrees); *Career Guide to America's Top Industries;* and *Guide to America's Federal Jobs.*

Internet Resources

If the Internet is new to you, I recommend a book titled *Cyberspace Job Search Kit* by Mary Nemnich and Fred Jandt. It covers the basics plus offers advice on using the Internet for career planning and job seeking. The *Quick Internet Guide to Career and Education Information* by Anne Wolfinger gives excellent reviews of the most helpful sites and ideas on how to use them. The *Occupational Outlook Handbook's* job descriptions also include Internet addresses. And www.jist.com lists recommended sites for career, education, and related topics, along with comments on each.

Be aware that some sites provide poor advice, so ask your librarian, instructor, or counselor for suggestions on those best for your needs.

Other Resources

Libraries. Most libraries have the books mentioned here, as well as many other resources. Many also provide Internet access so that you can research online information. Ask the librarian for help finding what you need.

People. People who hold the jobs that interest you are one of the best career information sources. Ask them what they like and don't like about their work, how they got started, and the education or training needed. Most people are helpful and will give advice you can't get any other way.

Career counseling. A good vocational counselor can help you explore career options. Take advantage of this service if it is available to you! Also consider a career-planning course or program, which will encourage you to be more thorough in your thinking.

Sample Resumes for Some of America's Top Jobs for People Without a Four-Year Degree

If you read the previous information in this section, you know that I believe resumes are an over-rated job search tool. Even so, you will probably need one, and you should have a good one.

Unlike some career authors, I do not preach that there is one right way to do a resume. I encourage you to be an individual and to do what you think will work well for you. But, I also know that some resumes are clearly better than others. The following pages contain several resumes that you can use as examples when preparing your resume. All these resumes are from my book *America's Top Resumes for America's Top Jobs,* available through JIST Publishing.

The resumes have these points in common:

- Each is for an occupation described in this book. The resumes are arranged in alphabetic order by job title.

- Each is particularly good in some way. Notes on the resumes point out their features.

- Each was written by a professional resume writer who is a member of one or more professional associations, including the Professional Association of Resume Writers (www.parw.com) or the National Resumes Writers' Association (www.nrwa.com). These writers are highly qualified and hold various credentials. Most are willing to provide help (for a fee) and welcome your contacting them (although this is not a personal endorsement). Contact information for the resume writers appears on page 484.

Automotive Service Technicians and Mechanics

This concise, dynamic resume has been very successful for John. Each time he faxes it to someone, he gets called for an interview within minutes!

JOHN C. TAYLER

Phone: 801-892-6299 • Pager: 801-892-6380 • 2463 Elm Avenue, Salt Lake City, UT 84109 • JCTayler@hotmail.com

The reader can see immediately how qualified John is within the industry.

ASE CERTIFIED MASTER TECHNICIAN
STATE INSPECTIONS CERTIFIED / COUNTY EMISSIONS CERTIFIED

Master Technician with 20+ years' experience in all phases of Automotive Technology. Proven leader in the industry possessing **expert diagnostic ability.** Proficient in **heavy equipment repair.** Highly motivated team player dedicated to producing outstanding results and increased profitability.

SPECIALIZED TRAINING

- **Advanced Automotive Climate Control,** Auto Parts Plus — 2001
- **Advanced Automotive Tune-up and Electrical Troubleshooting,** Federal Mogul/Champion — 2000
- **Advanced Hydrostatic Drive Diagnostics and Repair,** Bombardier Recreational Product — 2000
- **Advanced Applied Emissions Technical Training,** Salt Lake Community College — 1995
- **Utah Safety Inspection Training,** SLC Emissions Testing — 1995
- **ASE Certifications,** Salt Lake Community College — 1994

AUTOMOTIVE TECHNICAL EXPERTISE

- Full Service Automotive Excellence, providing **Bumper-to-Bumper Expert Diagnostics and Repair.**

- Specializing in major and minor repair for **ALL MAKES and MODELS:**
  Japanese, European and Domestic vehicles, 4x4s, Trucks, RVs, Dump Trucks, Caterpillars, Tractors, Tractor-Trailers, Snow Cats, Diesel, and other heavy equipment.

- Brakes — Clutches — Water Pumps — P/S Pumps — Rack & Pinion Steering — Shocks & Struts
- Front-end Work — 4 x 4 Front-end Work — Precision Engine Rebuilding — Engine Overhaul
- Cooling and Heating Systems — Batteries — Mufflers — Carburetors — CV Joints — Differentials
- Radiators — Alternators — Starters — Fuel Injection Systems — Wiring Repair and Replacement

PROFESSIONAL EXPERIENCE

- Tayler Mobile Automotive, **Owner/Manager,** present
- McNeil's Automotive, **Lead Automotive Technician,** 1996–present
- Snowbird Ski Resort, **Lead Heavy Line Technician,** 1992–1996
- Marathon Automotive, **Lead Automotive Technician,** 1991–1992
- Courtesy Car Company, **Service Manager,** 1985–1991
- Kmart (presently Penske Automotive), **Acting Service Manager,** 1980–1985

Barbers, Cosmetologists, and Other Personal Appearance Workers

Fonts and graphics were carefully chosen to create a stylish resume for applying for jobs in upscale Los Angeles hair salons.

LaTonya Jefferson
500 Maple Street, Apt. 103
Kansas City, Missouri 64134
(816) 555-1212
LaTonyaJefferson@email.com

LaTonya's resume was a hit with everyone who saw it !

Hair Stylist / Cosmetologist

Accomplished professional dedicated to enhancing client appearance in areas of universal hair care. Proven skills in execution of perfect hair-coloring techniques. Builder of "totally satisfied" customer relationships. Peer mentor and public educator in all facets of cosmetology. Licensed in Kansas and Missouri. PC-competent in MS Word, Excel and the Internet. World traveler fluent in Spanish and French.

Experience

HAIR COLOR SPECIALIST, Spectacular Salon and Day Spa, Mission, KS (6/99 to Present)
Serve 18 clients per day from diverse cultural backgrounds. Participate in hair-show demonstrations.

➢ Acknowledged for highest level of salon retail sales among 10 stylists.

➢ Achieved rank of Head Colorist after only two-year employment period.

ASSISTANT MAKEUP ARTIST, Monique's Boutique Fashion Show, Kansas City, MO (9/99)

➢ Performed makeup and color services for 30 models in this annual event.

Education

INSTRUCTOR TRAINING, Superior School of Hair Styling, Leawood, KS (1999 to 2000)

➢ Completed 300 of the 350 hours required for certification.

CERTIFICATE OF COMPLETION, Midwest College of Cosmetology, Blue Springs, MO (7/98)

➢ Pivot Point Curriculum

➢ Sales Woman of the Month — awarded seven times

➢ Perfect Attendance

➢ Selected courses: Hair Chemistry; Advanced Color; Production Makeup Artist

PROFESSIONAL TRAINING, Heartland College of Beauty Arts, Kansas City, MO (1995 to 1996)

➢ Outstanding Work Award — received three times

➢ Selected courses: Ethnic Hair Care; Hair Weaving and Extensions; Hair Color

She recently landed the job of her dreams and moved west.

Carpenters

A well-written resume where every point supports his job objective.

Michael Dillan
25 M Street
Pertherly, New Jersey 08256
(888) 258-6663
ifihadahammer@hotmail.com

Objective

To obtain a **carpentry** position in the **building and maintenance industry** that will utilize my experience in residential and commercial construction.

Summary

Broad-based experience in areas including
- Carpentry/framing/construction
- Cost estimating
- Blueprint drawing and design
- Interior and exterior finishing

Profile

Conscientious, responsible worker who gets the job done in a timely manner, pays close attention to detail and technical specifications, and possesses the ability to supervise all aspects of construction and maintenance, with excellent communication skills with both management and tradespeople.

Good emphasis on his adaptive skills.

Experience

Bulleted items present his many skills in various trades.

1997–Present

CJA Remodeling, Jacobs, NJ
Carpenter
- Work on new residential and commercial buildings.
- Provide accurate cost estimates.
- Interpret blueprints to specification.
- Frame and install siding and roofing materials.
- Install cabinets in bathrooms and kitchens.
- Complete installations throughout the building and handle all maintenance of completed projects.

1996–1997

J. G. Carpentry, Piscataway, NJ
Carpenter
- Constructed and maintained residential construction sites.
- Installed all doors and windows.
- Installed sheet rock and countertops throughout the buildings.
- Completed custom ceilings.
- In charge of maintenance after construction.

1995–1997

Carpentry Workers International, Penthington, NJ
Carpenter• Local 835
- Worked as a carpenter apprentice.
- Installed cabinets.

Education

Diploma, Mountaintown County Vocational Technical High School, 1989
Special Courses:
- Carpentry and Cabinet Making
- Architectural and Mechanical Drawing and Drafting
- Cost Estimation

Emphasizes related courses.

Awards

- National Builders Association, First Place, 1988 and 1989
- Honorary Excellence Award, New Jersey Builders' Association, 1989
- Mountaintown County Carpentry Exhibition, Second Place, 1988–1989

Computer Operators

Bradley was aiming for a senior operator position in his current company.

BRADLEY CUMMINGS

90 Parkway Road
Croton, NY 10566
(914) 772-9866
irwcu45@compuserv.com

Profile

These sections highlight his staff leadership and training experience and his technical expertise.

Computer Operations Professional

- Skilled technical professional with 6 years of computer operations experience in mainframe systems, as well as leading and training staff.
- Desktop support includes installation and troubleshooting of PC hardware, operating systems and software applications.
- Recognized by management for dedication, strong service orientation and consistent record of quality performance.

Technical Skills

Hardware/Operating Systems: IBM 3083 and ES/9000; IBM 3880 disk drives; IBM 3203 printers; IBM-PC compatibles; Windows 95, 97 and 2000.

Software: MVS, JES2, IDMS, CICS, PANVALET, TSO, DOS, MS Office (Word, Excel, PowerPoint, Access).

Programming Languages: JCL, COBOL.

Experience

His resume presents a very well-rounded picture of his capabilities.

HARTWELL INDUSTRIES, White Plains, NY   1990–present
Computer Operator (1998–present)

Promoted to computer operator in Information Systems with oversight of 3 other operators on IBM ES/9000 mainframe system, using MVS, JES2, IDMS, CICS, PANVALET and TSO. Generate timely reports to all departments; perform daily and weekly system backups.

- Provide first-level technical support to internal users and monitor hardware to ensure effective operations.
- Selected to lead a continuous improvement team to enhance computer operations efficiency.
- Train and develop new operators in system procedures and processes.
- Support users on PC hardware, operating systems (Windows 2000) and software (MS Office products) installation and troubleshooting.

Tape Librarian (1990–1998)

Performed all tape library functions to support daily computer operations in a timely manner.

- Monitored and filed tape media for mid-range operations; scanned tapes for vaulting.
- Assisted with disaster recovery and media handling for backup/recovery operations.
- Maintained up-to-date documentation of tape and library operations.
- Supported customer requests for off-site storage or other needs.

Education

A.S. in Computer Technology/Programming, 1995
Dutchess Community College, Poughkeepsie, NY

Bradley faced a very competitive interview process, but he landed the job even though another person had more years of experience.

Construction and Building Inspectors

GEORGE INSPECTOR, JR.
707 SOUTH ROOFTOP LANE ✶ TREMONT, MICHIGAN 48812 ✶ 616-555-5555 ✶ EYEINSPECT@JUNO.NET

Emphasizes important adaptive skills first.

PROFILE

Professionalism
* Highly experienced and detail-minded construction inspector with a broad base of knowledge in all aspects of construction.
* Reputable qualities include courtesy to the public and responding to inquiries on a timely basis with a friendly, pleasant disposition and helpful attitude.
* Noted for cooperation, fairness, and respect toward all levels of management, lenders, coworkers, government officials, and customers.

Organization
* Complete reports in an efficient and timely manner by developing and following an appointment schedule.
* Knowledgeable in maintaining records and submitting all necessary government inspection forms for all departments including FMHA, HUD, FHA, and Fannie Mae.
* Prepare construction activity reports on progress, review bids, pay estimates, read plans and specifications, and assist in preparing construction appraisals to meet all state and local business building safety codes.

Expertise
* Perform on-site inspection during all phases of construction projects including commercial, single- and multi-family developments, water towers, plants, and wastewater treatment facilities, migrant camps, fire stations, and other community facilities.
* Coordinate and act as liaison between various government officials, departments, private contractors and engineers, and lending institutions.
* Ensure adherence to plans and specifications and an acceptable level of workmanship.
* Make recommendations on appropriate actions for problems with existing and new construction projects, resolving differences and approving minor design changes not involving additional cost or alteration of basic design.
* Check materials, work methods, safety measures, installation of electric and plumbing hardware, and all other aspects of projects to determine contract compliance.

PROFESSIONAL EXPERIENCE

Construction Inspector   7/1992–Present
    Farmers Home Administration USDA, Grant, Michigan

Construction Inspector   5/1984–7/1992
    City of Houston, Houston, Texas

Salesman   6/1987–5/1990
    Boise Cascade, Houston, Texas

Field Engineer   5/1981–4/1984
    Townsend and Bottom Inc., St. Clair, Michigan

Surveyor's Assistant   1/1981–5/1981
    Dunn Construction Engineering, Inc., Port Huron, Michigan

Note that this resume does not include educational credentials as this person's strength.

Cost Estimators

Four bulleted statements highlight this individual's most-important qualifications.

John Carpenter

40 Watertown Street
Binghamton, New York 13747

(607) 666-9999
hammertime@aol.com

Chief Estimator/Project Manager

Qualifications

- **Five years of experience as Chief Estimator and Project Manager.**

- **Fifteen-plus years of local engineering, design and construction expertise** in the upstate New York building industry, preparing bid estimates and managing $300,000 to $3 million construction projects.

- **Senior construction generalist with a diverse skills.** Excel within small construction companies that require "wearing many hats." Proven expertise in business development; project management for both fieldwork and administrative projects; estimating via computer applications; drafting and architectural drawing; and management of shop, carpentry and millworking operations.

- **Innovative information manager.** Repeatedly automated bidding and construction processes for past employers, increasing production and decreasing overhead. Advanced user:

  AutoCAD version 10, Generic CAD version 6, Construction Management Systems estimating software, Super Project, Varco Pruden, VP Command building design and drafting program, Novell Networking, Access, Excel, Lotus 1-2-3, Microsoft Office, GTCO digitizer tablets and HP Draft Pro Plotter.

Education and Credentials

A.A.S. Degree, Construction Technology: State University of New York, Canton College, 1984
Certified Engineer Technician: A.S.C.E.T. Professional Engineering Society.

Estimating Experience

Estimator and Project Manager   1999 – present
JAMES SMITH AND SONS CONTRACTING COMPANY, Vestal, New York
Utilize in-depth knowledge of project costs, purchasing, construction techniques and technology, and local construction services market to estimate and manage large construction projects.

- Bid and supported 4 major contract wins in FY2001, cumulatively valued at $6 million.
- Manage estimating projects that generated over $10,000 per month in gross sales FY2001.
- As chief estimator, identify upcoming opportunities and generate 3–4 project estimates a month.
- Win 1 of every 3 estimates the company decides to submit.
- Manage a millwork shop generating $400,000 in annual gross sales with 30% net profits.

Accomplishment statements are brief yet powerful.

Chief Estimator and Project Manager   1994 – 1999
ARCHER AND SONS, Binghamton, New York
Prepared estimates, assisted proposal and business development team, and managed major construction projects throughout New York State.

- Projects included: The Marriott Hotel, Cornell University; The Law School Renovation Project, Cornell University; various Taco Time Restaurants; and school building upgrades in upstate New York.
- All projects came in on time, within 10% of originally prepared cost estimates.

Estimator/AutoCAD Drafter   1985 – 1993
WAY-LAN CONSTRUCTION COMPANY, INC., Binghamton, New York

Credit Authorizers, Checkers, and Clerks

During a 5-year career with a credit organization, Carole had 5 great accomplishments, most notably in the area of improving operational processes.

Her areas of expertise are highlighted in the "Value Offered" section.

CAROLE MORGAN-LOWE

2525 Kiesewetter Drive, Loveland, OH 45140
(513) 555-0050 • morganlowe@cinci.rr.com

VALUE OFFERED

Credit Authorization Expertise: Five years' experience in credit approval marked by steady advancement and record of accomplishments in training, team leadership, fraud prevention, and problem resolution.

Process Improvement: Increased efficiency, reduced staff time, eliminated fraud, and drastically cut numbers of problem calls by analyzing and improving operational processes.

Training: Trained new associates in all facets of credit authorization; earned consistently excellent training evaluations.

Personal Attributes: Rapidly productive in new positions and new environments. Dedicated to continuous learning and performance improvement. Focused and capable under pressure and time constraints.

EXPERIENCE AND ACCOMPLISHMENTS

FACS GROUP, Mason, Ohio (Credit services facility for Federated Department Stores)   1997–2002
Lead Associate, Credit Authorization Unit, 1999–2002

Promoted to manage call center of 8 to 20 associates involved in opening new accounts, granting credit, and approving credit increases. Served as liaison to nationwide credit bureaus. Developed weekly, quarterly, biennial, and annual reports and statistical analyses of associate performance.

- Successfully met performance standards for call response time and customer satisfaction while contending with high staff turnover and supporting a rapidly growing organization.

- On own initiative, aggressively addressed fraudulent accounts. Analyzed account activity, identified trends, and developed process to identify potential fraud and shut down the account before a loss occurred.

- Eliminated 350,000 problem calls annually by analyzing nature and volume of calls, then developing a proactive reporting system to identify potential problem accounts before they resulted in calls to the call center.

- Dramatically improved the efficiency of management reporting processes. Created spreadsheets that automated numerous processes for multiple reporting requirements and saved at least 40 management hours monthly; spreadsheets adopted for use throughout the department.

- Personally handled all escalated customer calls, striving to maintain customer satisfaction while enforcing company policies and good credit practices.

Credit Authorization Trainer, 1998–1999

In a rapid-growth environment, trained new hires in credit fundamentals, credit authorization, and computer system use in fast-paced 6-week training courses.

- Averaged 2.8 (of maximum 3.0) on post-training student surveys for communication style, effectiveness of training methods, and classroom management.

Authorization Associate, 1997–1998

Assessed customer information and granted or denied credit extensions.

EDUCATION

University of Cincinnati: Completed 2 years toward B.S. in Business Administration.

Flight Attendants

This resume was very effective for Stacey, despite the fact that she had no experience as a flight attendant.

STACEY HERD

3382 Collier Road
Acampo, California 95220
home: (209) 334-9685   cell: (209) 327-2673
(luv2fly@msn.com)

The airline she applied to was impressed by her resume and commented positively on the e-mail address, which she created for this position.

FLIGHT ATTENDANT

KEY QUALIFICATIONS

Her qualifications include solid people skills and the ability to handle stress.

- Over 6 years of successful experience in customer service and customer response operations.
- Strong desire to work in a fun-filled, high-energy, customer-focused environment, or contribute to making it that way.
- Excellent people skills and understanding of human behavior, combined with coursework in General Psychology.
- Proven ability to adjust to changing situations; utilize good judgment during unexpected emergency situations.
- Genuine team player committed to positive performance and efficient operations.
- Demonstrate leadership and problem-solving ... meeting day-to-day challenges, juggling multiple responsibilities.
- Build relationships with customers through attention to detail and providing service and solutions.

RELATED EXPERIENCE

EQUESTRIAN SERVICES, Acampo, CA
Manager/Business Owner (1996 to Present)
Successfully maintain overall operations of active equestrian business. Assist trainers and support staff. Acquire confidence and customer satisfaction of a highly professional customer base.
- Establish outstanding customer relationships, acquiring a business reputation for strengths in service quality, customer needs assessment, and knowledge.
- Investigate, listen, and problem-solve customer complaints to mutual satisfaction.
- Track expenditures within budget; maintain inventory and billing functions.

STALLION STATION, Porterville, CA
Office Manager (January 2000 to July 2000)   Supervisor: Jeff Davis, Business Owner
As Office Manager, significantly improved accuracy and timeliness of A/R, monthly billing, purchasing, and inventory.
- Served effectively as team player in a team of 10.
- Member of the customer service team charged with entire customer relationship management for 300+ customer base.
- Performed data, file management, and order fulfillment functions.

UNION BANK, Stockton, CA
Merchant Teller (1995 to 2000)   Supervisor: Donna Schmidt, Vice President
- Organized and coordinated multiple tasks including cash transactions, balancing, and customer service.
- Named "Employee of the Month"... maintained high standards for job performance and initiated work process improvements when necessary.

HONORS & AWARDS

Recipient of 6 awards for outstanding efforts and performance in improving productivity and increasing sales.

EDUCATION

San Joaquin Delta College, Stockton, CA —Dean's List
- Undergraduate Studies in General Psychology (45 Units): Principles of Sociology, Social Psychology, Human Behavior, Child Development, Abnormal Psychology, General Psychology
Graduate, Johnson High School, Sacramento, CA

She was hired within two weeks!

Funeral Directors

CONFIDENTIAL

This resume is targeted to a particular organization.

M. HOWARD CRANSTON, JR.

6109 Cook Drive, Apt. H   Montgomery, Alabama 36100   mhc11@yahoo.com   ✆ 334.555.5555

WHAT I CAN BRING TO THE FAITH CHAPEL AS A FUNERAL DIRECTOR AND EMBALMER

These three specific attributes correspond to the unique needs of the profession and this employer.

o **Compassion** to anticipate our families' needs

o **Skill** to preserve the living image of the deceased

o **Dedication** to make each burial a seamless integration of details

RECENT WORK HISTORY

o **Licensed Funeral Director** and **Embalmer**, Prattville Memorial Chapel and Memory Gardens, Prattville, Alabama, February 01 – Present

I perform the full line of services for Prattville Memorial Chapel. The organization is a six-year-old, family-owned operation that services about 160 calls each year from the five counties it serves.

o **Forensic Technician**, Alabama Department of Forensic Science, Office of the Medical Examiner, Montgomery, Alabama, November 98 – January 01

I helped perform autopsies on those who died of suspicious causes and gathered fingerprints and evidence in cases of homicide, suicide, and accidental deaths. I was bound by the stringent standards that bind all information submitted to courts of law.

o **Licensed Funeral Director** and **Embalmer** *and later also* **Merchandising Manager** *promoted to* **Assistant Manager** of White Chapel (a corporate division of Leak-Memory Chapel) *promoted to* **Manager** of White Chapel *promoted to* **Manager**, Leak-Memory Chapel Operations, Leak-Memory Chapel, Montgomery, Alabama , January 70 – October 98

Leak-Memory is the capital city's most well-respected and oldest funeral home.

LICENSES

o Embalmer's license number 0000; Funeral Director's license number 11111. Both expire October 1, 2002. (Alabama enjoys full reciprocity with Florida.)

SERVICE TO MY COMMUNITY

o One of the first in the industry to volunteer to remove and transport eye tissue to eye banks up to 90 miles away.

EDUCATION

o Diploma, John A. Gupton College of Mortuary Science, Nashville, Tennessee

COMPUTER LITERACY

o Fully proficient in FALCON (SCI's proprietary program developed for the funeral industry to generate contracts, help with bookkeeping, and store personal data about the deceased).

o Working knowledge of Internet search protocols, Windows 98.

CONFIDENTIAL

Line Installers and Repairers

JEFFREY K. KNOWLES

1823 Lakeshore Road ▪ South Orange, NJ 07079 ▪ (973) 585-7835
jkknowles@optonline.net

Special qualifications are emphasized with bold type.

PROFILE

Telecommunications Specialist with an extensive 18-year background in all phases of **cable splicing for the largest U.S. communications provider.** Special talent for identifying, troubleshooting, repairing and maintaining aerial, underground, and buried copper and fiber-optic cable. Progressive experience in new construction, upgrade installations, and emergency cable failures. Read and interpret work prints, circuit diagrams, and plat books. Strong work ethic; will do what it takes to get the job done and meet deadlines. **Hazmat Certified. OSHA familiarity. Hook qualified. Member of Local 2245, Communication Workers of America (CWA).**

PROFESSIONAL EXPERIENCE

VERIZON COMMUNICATIONS, INC. • Newark, NJ   **4/69 to Present**
(Largest U.S Communications Provider • Formerly Bell Atlantic Corp.)
Cable Splicer

Locate, troubleshoot, and clear analog and digital cable problems and leaks in pressurized cable. Identify the conditioning of cable pairs for special circuits.

- Read and interpret service orders, circuit diagrams, plat book, blueprints, and schematics.
- Work on energized circuits to avoid interruption of service. Climb utility poles/towers, utilizing truck-mounted lift bucket. Descend into sewers/underground vaults to locate cables.
- Cut lead sheath from installed cable to gain access to defective cable connections.
- Test (trace/phase-out) each conductor to identify corresponding conductors in adjoining cable sections, according to electrical diagrams and specifications.
- Prevent incorrect connections between individual communication circuits and electric power circuits, using test lamp or bell system.
- Fireproof and insulate materials.

Accomplishments are set apart & italicized.

  ~ *Accountable for troubleshooting over 100 major cable failures and restoring service to over 1,500 customer subscriber lines per failure in the wake of Hurricanes Gloria and Bob; and performed major repairs through ice storms of 1976 and 1977.*
  ~ *Instrumental in completing Generic 5E7 project.*
  ~ *Recipient of numerous awards for safety and perfect attendance.*

TECHNICAL EQUIPMENT

Safety Equipment: Blowers / Explosive Meters / Cone & Signs / Ladders / Slings / Ladder Steps Block & Step Ladders ▪ **Locating Equipment:** 965 Dynatel Cable Analyzer / Breakdown Set / Heath Kit / Buried Cable Locator / Sidekick Meter / Digital Multi-Meter ▪ **Hand Tools:** Cable Dresser / Siemen Case & Flats Side Cutters / Dikes / Can Wrenches / Electric & Air Powered Tools

INDUSTRY EQUIPMENT & SERVICE

ISDNs / DSLs / Frame Relays / Enterprises / T3 & T1 / DDS II (DSO) / Trunks / DIDs / Centrex & Analog Lines / Superpaths / Pots / Flexpaths / Switchways / TKNAs / Muxes / Multi-Plexers / Alarms

PROFESSIONAL DEVELOPMENT COURSES

ALTEC AT-2000 / TELSTA – A-28C/A-28D / Defensive Driving (Distance Learning) / Code of Business Conduct / IFAS DO I&M NY / CMC 386 Overview / Telecommunications Act Training / Asbestos Safety Awareness for Outside Field Techs / CAT for Customer Services / HAZCOM-Generic/Job Specific / D.O.T Motor Carrier Safety Regulations / Area HAZCOM Manager Training / First Aid/CPR / Ribbon Optic Cable Splicing / Siecor Optical Cable Fusion Splicing / SLC-96

These three final sections of the resume contain many relevant keywords.

Payroll and Timekeeping Clerks

Katrina was an office/billing clerk who wanted to return to her prior occupation as a payroll clerk.

KATRINA LARSON

7889 Forester Avenue • Huntington Beach, CA 92647 • (714) 847-3362 • katlarson@juno.com

A functional-style resume with an objective is used so her payroll experience leads and is emphasized to prospective employers.

OBJECTIVE: Payroll Clerk

SUMMARY OF QUALIFICATIONS

- Well organized and detail oriented with experience in payroll, office support, data entry and billing. Computer skills include MS Word, Excel and various proprietary software programs.

- Self-motivated employee who performs diligently to accomplish business goals. Able to learn new skills quickly and effectively.

- Adept in customer relations with the ability to handle and resolve issues. Team-oriented; thrive in fast-paced environments. Record of dependability.

EXPERIENCE

Payroll / Billing

- ◆ Maintaining up-to-date payroll data and records, including entering changes in exemptions, insurance coverage, savings deductions, job title and department transfers.

- ◆ Compiling summaries of earnings, taxes, deductions, leave, disability and nontaxable wages for report preparation.

- ◆ Calculating employee federal and state income and social security taxes and employer's social security, unemployment and workers' compensation payments.

- ◆ Researching and resolving payroll discrepancies in a timely manner.

- ◆ Maintaining accurate customer billing information and preparing invoices in an efficient, timely manner.

Reception / Customer Service

- ◆ Greeting visitors; answering busy multiline telephone systems; screening and transferring calls while handling general inquiries.

- ◆ Addressing customer concerns, researching and resolving problems to ensure service satisfaction; extensive interface with all levels of internal personnel.

Administrative Support

- ◆ Performing diverse administrative duties such as word-processing correspondence, creating presentations and maintaining confidential files/records.

- ◆ Scheduling and coordinating meetings and appointments; ordering department supplies.

This resume was very effective for her and successfully averted the issue of noncurrent payroll experience.

EMPLOYMENT HISTORY

This section is placed at the end, so the fact that her current position is not in payroll becomes less important.

SULLIVAN CORP., Huntington Beach, CA
Office/Billing Clerk (1996–present)

JENSEN INC., Long Beach, CA
Payroll Clerk (1994–1996)

FINLANDIA INC., Long Beach, CA
Payroll Clerk (1992–1994)

WARNER PACKAGING, Westfield, MA
Receptionist/Accounting Clerk (1989–1992)

EDUCATION

Accounting courses — Fullerton Community College, Fullerton, CA

Printing Machine Operators

Since Kathy has no formal education beyond high school, no education is included. Her resume emphasizes her management skills to keep that option open.

KATHY McWILLIAMS
10875 Barker Road
Greenville, North Carolina 47124
24-hour answering service: 225-243-9872
katemcw1013@earthlink.net

Objective

Responsible position in a full-service printing and bindery operation.

Summary

Over 13 years of experience in all phases of printing and bindery operations. Excellent attendance record and a stable work history. Willing to accept responsibility and have supervisory experience. Self-motivated, with a work history of superior production and performance. Good "people" skills and interested in learning new techniques.

Technical Skills

Over 13 years of experience in a variety of custom and high-volume printing operations. I can operate and maintain all standard printing and bindery equipment, including

- Stahl and O&M Folders
- Thermograph machines
- Heidelberg SORKZ
- Heidelberg KORD
- Solna 125 and 225
- Davidson 702 Perfector
- Plate making

- Polar & Challenger Papercutters
- Stitchers, drillers, and all bindery operations
- ATF 2217 Super Chief
- 1250 Multilith
- AB Dicks with T-51 head
- Stripping to 4-color process
- Camera experience

Related Skills

I have substantial work experience in the printing and bindery industries and am able to do most things needed, including:

- Repair most printing equipment, including total reconditioning.
- Certified forklift driver, familiar with warehouse operations.
- Have supervised as many as 12 press and bindery workers.
- Complete all necessary paperwork, including narrative report.
- Good customer contact and problem-solving skills.

These "extra" skills are listed separately.

Work Experience

Excellent references are available from

Shoney Newsweek	**Head Pressman/Foreman**	11/96 to Present
Minute Press	**Head Pressman**	11/89 to 11/96

This tells the reader that Kathy has a good work history.

Security Guards and Gaming Surveillance Officers

The functional style works well here to avoid repetition of duties.

ROBERT SMITH

❖

1235 Main Street, Berkeley, California 94703
robtsmith@netzero.com
(510) 684-5624

Experienced security guard available for a challenging opportunity utilizing my expertise in loss prevention, administration, and customer service.

Highlights qualifications in three key areas.

Areas of Expertise

Security ———————————————————————————

Committed to establishing a secure and safe environment for both staff and customers.

♦ Observe buildings for property damage and security breaches. Screen visitors for proper identification. Prepare work space for next shift of workers; responsibly open and close office while taking security measures.

♦ Monitor vehicles to prevent illegal parking. Maintain records of vehicles cited for parking violations. Arrange ground transportation for customers.

Customer Service ———————————————————————

Dedicated to offering friendly, professional, and resourceful customer service to diverse groups of people in a timely manner.

♦ Quick to answer customer questions and complaints; repeatedly solicit customer feedback, all to ensure high-quality service.

♦ Experience selling products and services directly to customers over the phone and in person.

Administration ———————————————————————

Execute indispensable clerical support for busy management teams.

♦ Skilled in answering multi-line phones and routing calls to appropriate party with expedience and ease.

♦ Accurately completed reports of daily income after handling cash transactions.

Work Experience

1992–2002	**Security Manager**	ABC Security — Berkeley, CA
1987–1992	**Security Guard**	Burns Security — Oakland, CA
1980–1987	**Night Manager**	Kmart — El Cerrito, CA

❖ ❖ ❖

Welding, Soldering, and Brazing Workers

The specific skill section and the "Certifications" section, combined with his obvious desire to enhance his abilities through education, stood out to hiring authorities.

LEONARD BAKER

10 Blackbird Lane • Bridgeville, Pennsylvania 16666

(412) 645-3219   lbaker@hotmail.com

MACHINIST • WELDER • FITTER

- Proficient and skilled in technical specialty. Recognized for dedicated work ethic and productivity. Capable of doing work that requires concentration, high degree of patience and attention to detail. Mechanically inclined. Able to work independently.
- Thrive in a team and deadline-oriented environment. Exceptional organizational skills; capable of prioritizing, scheduling and managing heavy workflow.
- Proficient in technical skills/machine operations/equipment processes, including:

specific skills

✓ MIG	✓ Fluxcore	✓ Computer Numeric Control
✓ TIG	✓ Submerged Arc	✓ Gantry Crane
✓ Stick	✓ Inner shield	✓ Tolerancing
✓ Pulse	✓ Drill Press	✓ Forklift Operator
✓ Aluminum	✓ Technical Math	✓ Machine Print Reading
✓ Blueprint Reading	✓ Applied Math	✓ Lathes and Milling Machines

PROFESSIONAL EXPERIENCE

His longevity in his current position and "Perfect attendance" reference under "Education" show there is little risk to the employer in hiring this person.

WELDER A, Forker Industries — *Bridgetown, Pennsylvania*   *1988 – Present*
- Fit and weld boxcars with Fluxcore and Submerged Arc welding. Examine welds to ensure they meet specifications.
- Instrumental on shift that slashed project hours from 11 (by another shift) to 8, while maintaining quality of workmanship.

WELDER ASSEMBLER, Sun Engineering — *Walton, Texas*   *1987 – 1988*
- Used spray-arc welding equipment. Assembled dock levelers and functioned as a saw operator, forklift driver, truck driver and member of installation crew.

WELDER FITTER, Perfection Metal Products — *Hazen, Texas*   *1986 – 1987*
- Fitted and welded frames for the electronic industry using MIG and TIG welding. Recognized for outstanding workmanship by lead man.

LABORER, City of Wilding — *Wilding, Texas*   *1985 – 1986*
- Received commendation from mayor for exemplary service to the citizens of Wilding by working 96+ hours during a winter storm to repair water main leaks.

CERTIFICATIONS

• Arc Welding	• Flat, 3/8" Dia. Plug Weld	• 7018 AWS Structural
• 1/8" LH	• AWS SMAW 3/8" Butt Weld	• Code D1.1
• Plumbing and Pipefitting Fundamentals	• Gas Metal Arc Welding, Advanced	• Flat and Vertical, Inside Corner Filler
• Vertical Outside Corner	• AWS D1	• GMAW AWS D7.7
• Vertical, T-Butt Weld	• 75-Fillet Vertical and Overhead Positions	• 86 GMAW, Spray Arc Single V Groove w/ Backing 1G-Flat

shows his desire to enhance his abilities

EDUCATION

A.S., Machine Technology, November 2001
***Dean's Certificates*; 3.94 GPA; *Perfect Attendance*; Class President**
Capitol School of Trades — *Weathersfield, Pennsylvania*

note reference to his perfect attendance

Writers and Editors

Targeting a specific organization and opportunity, this resume is able to highlight the exact capabilities that will be of most value.

Alex Duart

P. O. Box 125 ❖ Prattville, Alabama 36000 ❖ duarta@hotmail.com ❖ 334.555.5555

Value to Variety Press International

As a **writer and editor**, I can translate your vision into written words that are read, remembered, and acted upon.

Capabilities you can use now:

- ❖ **Seasoned writer** who gets the best stories
- ❖ **Organized editor** who meets tight deadlines
- ❖ **"Turnaround" specialist** with solid track record

Work history with selected examples of success:

Business Owner, Champion Products, Montgomery, Alabama (99–Present)

- ❖ Found and served specialty markets, met customer needs, developed promotion plans, and controlled costs.

Editorial Director, Norpress Publishers, Montgomery, Alabama (89–91, 92–98)
One of the first employees of industry leader in natural resource magazines. Helped this aggressive company build a national circulation of 200,000.

- ❖ Transformed unfocused collection of promotional literature into major resource book. Found and wrote the stories, did most of the editing. Handled promotion. *Results:* Sold nearly 30,000 copies of this $25 technical manual. **Won $50,000 advertising packages.**
- ❖ Helped build five magazines. Did it all, from hiring writers to setting details of layout. Spun off full-color, slick magazine from tabloid. *Results:* **Advertising up. Successfully converted free publication to paid publication.**
- ❖ Convinced nation's expert to let me do in-depth story on his one-of-a-kind system. *Results:* Although other competitors had tried and failed, I got *all* the information. Expert impressed. Our **25,000 audited readers very happy.**

Results are included for each achievement.

Editorial Director, The Colophon Press, Atlanta Branch, San Francisco, California (86–89)
Key contributor to two magazines this 100-year old house publishes.

- ❖ Major contributor and key researcher for flagship publications. *Results:* **Exceeded** corporate goals by **at least 15% every year for six years.**
- ❖ Developed and followed up on list of key decision makers in readers' markets. *Results:* **Always got the story. Manufacturers asked my opinion of their newest products.**

Computer literacy:

- ❖ Expert in Word for Windows 2000 and WordPerfect
- ❖ Working knowledge of Excel, Lotus 1-2-3, Quicken, Peachtree Accounting, Windows

Skills that help build your productivity:

- ❖ Accomplished photographer comfortable with 35 mm and 2¼ x 2¼ formats
- ❖ Complete knowledge of paste-up procedures

Education:

- ❖ Attended Waller State University, Waller, Alabama: 30 semester hours in English

Contact Information for Resume Contributors

The following professional resume writers contributed resumes to this section. Their names are listed in alphabetical order. Each entry indicates which resume that person contributed.

Beverly Baskin, EdS, MA, NCCC, CPRW LPC
BBCS Counseling Services
6 Alberta Dr.
Marlboro, NJ 07746
Toll-free phone: (800) 300-4079
Fax (732) 972-8846
E-mail: bbcs@att.net
www.baskincareer.com
Resume on page 471

Donna Farrise
President, Dynamic Resumes of Long Island, Inc.
300 Motor Pkwy., Ste. 200
Hauppauge, NY 11788
Phone: (631) 951-4120
Fax: (631) 952-1817
E-mail: donna@dynamicresumes.com
www.dynamicresumes.com
Resume on page 478

Louise Garver, MA, JCTC, CMP, CPRW, MCDP
President, Career Directions, LLC
P.O. Box 587
Broad Brook, CT 06016
Phone: (860) 623-9476
Fax: (860) 623-9473
E-mail: TheCareerPro@aol.com
www.resumeimpact.com
Resumes on page 472 and 479

Alice Hanson, CPRW
President, Aim Resumes
P.O. Box 75054
Seattle, WA 98125
Phone: (206) 527-3100
Fax: (206) 527-3101
E-mail: alice@aimresume.com
www.aimresume.com
Resume on page 474

Leatha Jones, CPRW, CEIP
2124 Kittredge St. #78
Berkeley, CA 94704
E-mail: Leatha517J@aol.com
Resume on page 481

Louise Kursmark, CPRW, JCTC, CCM, CEIP
President, Best Impression Career Services, Inc.
Cincinnati, OH 45242
Toll-free phone: (888) 792-0030
Fax: (513) 792-0961
E-mail: LK@yourbestimpression.com
www.yourbestimpression.com
Resume on page 475

Diana C. LeGere
President, Executive Final Copy
P.O. Box 171311
Salt Lake City, UT 84117
Toll-free phone: (866) 754-5465
Phone: (801) 550-5697
Fax: (626) 602-8715
E-mail: executiveresumes@yahoo.com
www.executivefinalcopy.com
Resume on page 469

Meg Montford, CCM, CPRW
President, Abilities Enhanced
P.O. Box 9667
Kansas City, MO 64134
Phone: (816) 767-1196
Fax: (801) 650-8529
E-mail: meg@abilitiesenhanced.com
www.abilitiesenhanced.com
Resume on page 470

Patricia L. Nieboer, CPS, CPRW
Fremont, MI
(No additional contact information available)
Resume on page 473

Don Orlando, MBA, CPRW, JCTC, CCM
President, The McLean Group
640 S. McDonough St.
Montgomery, AL 36104
Phone: (334) 264-2020
Fax: (334) 264-9227
E-mail: yourcareercoach@aol.com
Resumes on pages 477 and 483

Dede Penick
Indianapolis, IN
(No additional contact information available)
Resume on page 480

Anita Radosevich, CPRW, JCTC, CEIP
President, Anita's Business & Career Services
315 W. Pine St., Ste. #5
Lodi, CA 95240
Phone: (209) 368-4444
Fax: (209) 368-2438
E-mail: anita@abcresumes.com
www.abcresumes.com
Resume on page 476

Jane Roqueplot, Certified Behavioral Consultant
President, JaneCo's Sensible Solutions
194 N. Oakland Ave.
Sharon, PA 16146
Phone: (724) 342-0100
Fax: (724) 346-5263
E-mail: janeir@janecos.com
www.janecos.com
Resume on page 482

Section Three

IMPORTANT TRENDS IN JOBS AND INDUSTRIES

In putting this section together, my objective was to give you a quick review of major labor market trends. To accomplish that, I chose two excellent articles that originally appeared in U.S. Department of Labor publications.

The first article is "Tomorrow's Jobs." It provides a superb—and short—review of the major trends that *will* affect your career in the years to come. Read it for ideas on selecting a career path for the long term.

The second article is "Employment Trends in Major Industries." While you may not have thought much about it, the industry you work in is just as important as your occupational choice. This great article will help you learn about the major trends affecting various industries.

Tomorrow's Jobs

Population

Comments

This article, with minor changes, comes from the *Occupational Outlook Handbook* and was written by the U.S. Department of Labor staff. The material provides a good review of major labor market trends, including trends for broad types of occupations and industries.

Much of this article uses 2000 data, the most recent available at press time. By the time it is carefully collected and analyzed, the data used by the Department of Labor is typically several years old. Since labor market trends tend to be gradual, this delay does not affect the material's usefulness.

You may notice that some job titles in this article differ from those used elsewhere in *America's Top Jobs for People Without a Four-Year Degree*. This is not an error. The material that follows uses a different set of occupations than I used in choosing this book's described jobs.

Making informed career decisions requires reliable information about opportunities in the future. Opportunities result from the relationships between the populations, labor force, and the demand for goods and services.

Population ultimately limits the size of the labor force—individuals working or looking for work—which constrains how much can be produced. Demand for various goods and services determines employment in the industries providing them. Occupational employment opportunities, in turn, result from skills needed within specific industries. For example, opportunities for computer engineers and other computer-related occupations have surged in response to rapid growth in demand for computer services.

Examining the past and projecting changes in these relationships is the foundation of the Occupational Outlook Program. The following article presents highlights of Bureau of Labor Statistics projections of the labor force and occupational and industry employment that can help guide your career plans.

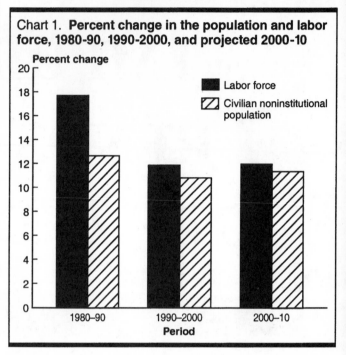

Chart 1. **Percent change in the population and labor force, 1980-90, 1990-2000, and projected 2000-10**

Population trends affect employment opportunities in a number of ways. Changes in population influence the demand for goods and services. For example, a growing and aging population has increased the demand for health services. Equally important, population changes produce corresponding changes in the size and demographic composition of the labor force.

The U.S. population is expected to increase by 24 million over the 2000–2010 period, at a slightly faster rate of growth than during the 1990–2000 period but slower than over the 1980–1990 period (chart 1). Continued growth will mean more consumers of goods and services, spurring demand for workers in a wide range of occupations and industries. The effects of population growth on various occupations will differ. The differences are partially accounted for by the age distribution of the future population.

The youth population, aged 16 to 24, will grow more rapidly than the overall population, a turnaround that began in the mid-1990s. As the baby boomers continue to age, the group aged 55 to 64 will increase by 11 million persons over the 2000–2010 period—more than any other group. Those aged 35 to 44 will be the only group to decrease in size, reflecting the birth dearth following the baby boom.

Minorities and immigrants will constitute a larger share of the U.S. population in 2010 than they do today. Minority groups that have grown the fastest in the recent past—Hispanics and Asians and others—are projected to continue to grow much faster than white, non-Hispanics.

Labor Force

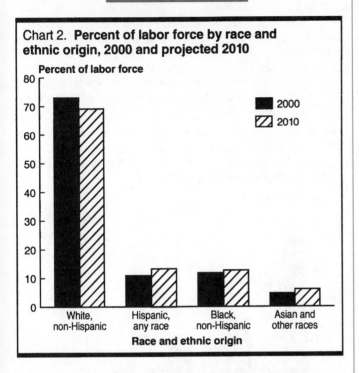

Chart 2. Percent of labor force by race and ethnic origin, 2000 and projected 2010

Percent of labor force

Legend: ■ 2000 ▨ 2010

Race and ethnic origin: White, non-Hispanic / Hispanic, any race / Black, non-Hispanic / Asian and other races

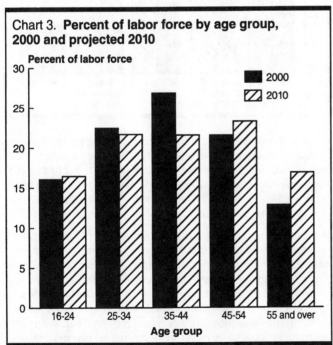

Chart 3. Percent of labor force by age group, 2000 and projected 2010

Percent of labor force

Legend: ■ 2000 ▨ 2010

Age group: 16-24 / 25-34 / 35-44 / 45-54 / 55 and over

Population is the single most important factor in determining the size and composition of the labor force—comprising people who are either working or looking for work. The civilian labor force is projected to increase by 17 million, or 12 percent, to 158 million over the 2000–2010 period.

The U.S. workforce will become more diverse by 2010. White, non-Hispanic persons will continue to make up a decreasing share of the labor force, falling from 73.1 percent in 2000 to 69.2 percent in 2010 (chart 2). However, despite relatively slow growth, white, non-Hispanics will have the largest numerical growth in the labor force between 2000 and 2010, reflecting the large size of this group. Hispanics, non-Hispanic blacks, and Asian and other ethnic groups are projected to account for an increasing share of the labor force by 2010, growing from 10.9 to 13.3 percent, 11.8 to 12.7 percent, and 4.7 to 6.1 percent, respectively. By 2010, for the first time, Hispanics will constitute a greater share of the labor force than will blacks. Asians and others continue to have the fastest growth rates, but still are expected to remain the smallest of the four labor force groups.

The numbers of men and women in the labor force will grow, but the number of men will grow at a slower rate than the number of women. The male labor force is projected to grow by 9.3 percent from 2000 to 2010, compared with 15.1 percent for women. As a result, men's share of the labor force is expected to decrease from 53.4 to 52.1 percent, while women's share is expected to increase from 46.6 to 47.9 percent.

The youth labor force, aged 16 to 24, is expected to increase its share of the labor force to 16.5 percent by 2010, growing more rapidly than the overall labor force. The large group 25 to 54 years old, who made up 71 percent of the labor force in 2000, is projected to decline to 66.6 percent of the labor force by 2010. Workers 55 and older, on the other hand, are projected to increase from 12.9 percent to 16.9 percent of the labor force between 2000 and 2010, due to the aging of the baby-boom generation (chart 3).

Education and Training

Projected job growth varies widely by education and training requirements. All seven of the education and training categories projected to have faster-than-average employment growth require a postsecondary vocational or academic award (chart 4). These seven categories will account for two-fifths of all employment growth over the 2000–2010 period.

Employment in occupations requiring at least a bachelor's degree is expected to grow 21.6 percent and account for five out of the six fastest growing education or training categories. Two categories—jobs requiring an associate degree (projected to grow 32 percent over the 2000–2010 period, faster than any other category) and jobs requiring a postsecondary vocational award—together will grow 24.1 percent. The four categories of occupations requiring work-related training are projected to increase 12.4 percent, compared with 15.2 percent for all occupations combined.

Education is essential in getting a high-paying job. In fact, all but two of the 50 highest paying occupations require a college degree. Air traffic controllers and nuclear power reactor operators are the only occupations of the 50 highest paying that do not require a college degree.

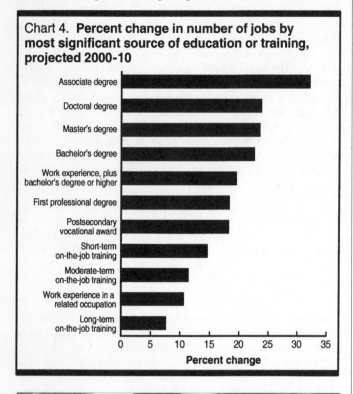

Chart 4. **Percent change in number of jobs by most significant source of education or training, projected 2000-10**

Employment

Total employment is expected to increase from 146 million in 2000 to 168 million in 2010, or by 15.2 percent. The 22 million jobs that will be added by 2010 will not be evenly distributed across major industrial and occupational groups. Changes in consumer demand, technology, and many other factors will contribute to the continually changing employment structure in the U.S. economy.

The following two sections examine projected employment change from both industrial and occupational perspectives. The industrial profile is discussed in terms of primary wage and salary employment. Primary employment excludes secondary jobs for those who hold multiple jobs. The exception is employment in agriculture, which includes self-employed and unpaid family workers in addition to wage and salary workers.

The occupational profile is viewed in terms of total employment—including primary and secondary jobs for wage and salary, self-employed, and unpaid family workers. Of the nearly 146 million jobs in the U.S. economy in 2000, wage and salary workers accounted for 134 million; self-employed workers accounted for 11.5 million; and unpaid family workers accounted for about 169,000. Secondary employment accounted for 1.8 million of all jobs. Self-employed workers held 9 out of 10 secondary jobs; wage and salary workers held most of the remainder.

Industry

The long-term shift from goods-producing to service-producing employment is expected to continue (chart 5). *Service-producing industries*—including finance, insurance, and real estate; government; services; transportation, communications, and utilities; and wholesale and retail trade—are expected to account for approximately 20.2 million of the 22.0 million new wage and salary jobs generated over the 2000–2010 period. The services and retail trade industry divisions will account for nearly three-fourths of total wage and salary job growth, a continuation of the employment growth pattern of the 1990–2000 period.

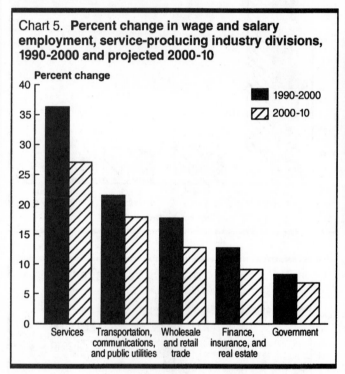

Chart 5. **Percent change in wage and salary employment, service-producing industry divisions, 1990-2000 and projected 2000-10**

Services. This is the largest and fastest growing major industry group and is expected to add 13.7 million new jobs by 2010, accounting for 3 out of every 5 new jobs created in the U.S. economy. Over two-thirds of this projected job growth is concentrated in three sectors of services industries—business, health, and social services.

Business services—including personnel supply services and computer and data processing services, among other detailed industries—will add 5.1 million jobs. The personnel supply services industry, consisting of employment agencies and temporary-staffing services, is projected to be the largest source of numerical employment growth in the economy, adding 1.9 million new jobs. However, employment in computer and data processing services—which provides prepackaged and specialized software, data and computer systems design and management, and computer-related consulting services—is projected to grow by 86 percent between 2000 and 2010, ranking as the fastest growing industry in the economy.

Health services—including home healthcare services, hospitals, and offices of health practitioners—will add 2.8 million new jobs as demand for healthcare increases because of an aging population and longer life expectancies.

Social services—including child daycare and residential care services—will add 1.2 million jobs. As more women enter the labor force, demand for childcare services is expected to grow, leading to the creation of 300,000 jobs. An elderly population seeking alternatives to nursing homes and hospital care will boost employment in residential care services, which is projected to grow 63.5 percent and add 512,000 jobs by 2010.

Transportation, communications, and utilities. Overall employment is expected to increase by 1.3 million jobs, or by 17.9 percent. Employment in the transportation sector is expected to increase by 20.7 percent, from 4.5 million to 5.5 million jobs. Trucking and warehousing will provide the most new jobs in the transportation sector, adding 407,000 jobs by 2010. Due to population growth and urban sprawl, local and interurban passenger transit is expected to increase 31 percent over the 2000–2010 period, the fastest growth among all the transportation sectors.

Employment in the communications sector is expected to increase by 16.9 percent, adding 277,000 jobs by 2010. Half of these new jobs—139,000—will be in the telephone communications industry; however, cable and other pay television will be the fastest growing segment of the sector over the next decade, with employment expanding by 50.6 percent. Increased demand for residential and business wireline and wireless services, cable service, and high-speed Internet connections will fuel the growth in communications industries.

Employment in the utilities sector is projected to increase by only 4.9 percent through 2010. Despite increased output, employment in electric services, gas production and distribution, and combination utility services is expected to decline through 2010 due to improved technology that increases worker productivity. The growth in the utilities sector will be driven by water supply and sanitary services, in which employment is expected to increase 45.1 percent by 2010. Jobs are not easily eliminated by technological gains in this industry because water treatment and waste disposal are very labor-intensive activities.

Wholesale and retail trade. Employment is expected to increase by 11.1 percent and 13.3 percent, respectively, growing from 7 million to 7.8 million in wholesale trade and from 23.3 million to 26.4 million in retail trade. Increases in population, personal income, and leisure time will contribute to employment growth in these industries as consumers demand more goods. With the addition of 1.5 million jobs, the eating and drinking places segment of the retail trade industry is projected to have the largest numerical increase in employment within the trade industry group.

Finance, insurance, and real estate. Overall employment is expected to increase by 687,000 jobs, or 9.1 percent, by 2010. The finance sector of the industry—including depository and nondepository institutions and securities and commodity brokers—will account for one-third of these jobs. Security and commodity brokers and dealers are expected to grow the fastest among the finance segments; the projected 20.3 percent employment increase by 2010 reflects the increased number

of baby boomers in their peak savings years, the growth of tax-favorable retirement plans, and the globalization of the securities markets. However, employment in depository institutions should continue to decline due to an increase in the use of Internet banking, ATM machines, and debit cards.

The insurance sector—including insurance carriers and insurance agents and brokers—is expected to add 152,000 new jobs by 2010. The majority of job growth in the insurance carriers segment will be attributable to medical service and health insurance, in which employment is projected to increase by 16 percent. The number of jobs with insurance agents and brokers is expected to grow about 14.3 percent by 2010, as many insurance carriers downsize their sales staffs and as agents set up their own businesses.

The real estate sector is expected to add the most jobs out of the three sectors—272,000 by 2010. As the population grows, demand for housing also will grow.

Government. Between 2000 and 2010, government employment, excluding public education and hospitals, is expected to increase by 6.9 percent, from 10.2 million to 10.9 million jobs. Growth in government employment will be fueled by growth at the state and local levels, in which the number of jobs will increase by 12.2 and 11.2 percent, respectively, through 2010. Growth at these levels is due mainly to an increased demand for services and the shift of responsibilities from the federal government to the state and local governments. Federal government employment is expected to decline by 7.6 percent as the federal government continues to contract out many government jobs to private companies.

Employment in the *goods-producing industries* has been relatively stagnant since the early 1980s. Overall, this sector is expected to grow 6.3 percent over the 2000–2010 period. Although employment is expected to increase more slowly than

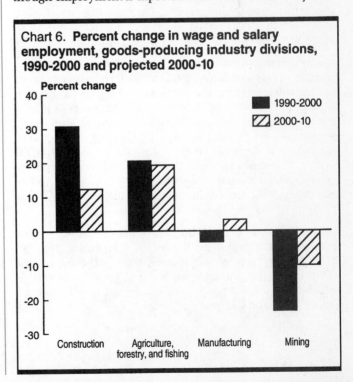

Chart 6. **Percent change in wage and salary employment, goods-producing industry divisions, 1990-2000 and projected 2000-10**

in the service-producing industries, projected growth within the goods-producing sector varies considerably (chart 6).

Construction. Employment in construction is expected to increase by 12.3 percent, from 6.7 million to 7.5 million. Demand for new housing and an increase in road, bridge, and tunnel construction will account for the bulk of job growth in this industry.

Agriculture, forestry, and fishing. Overall employment in agriculture, forestry, and fishing is expected to increase by 19.3 percent, from 2.2 million to 2.6 million. Three-fourths of this growth will come from veterinary services and landscape and horticultural services, which will add 96,000 and 229,000 jobs, respectively. Employment in crops, livestock, and livestock products is expected to continue to decline due to advancements in technology. The numbers of jobs in forestry and in fishing, hunting, and trapping are expected to grow only 1.9 percent by 2010.

Manufacturing. Rebounding from the 1990–2000 decline of 607,000 manufacturing jobs, employment in this sector is expected to grow modestly, by 3.1 percent, by 2010, adding 577,000 jobs. The projected employment growth is attributable mainly to the industries that manufacture durable goods. Durable goods manufacturing is expected to grow 5.7 percent, to 11.8 million jobs, over the next decade. Despite gains in productivity, the growing demand for computers, electronic components, motor vehicles, and communications equipment will contribute to this employment growth.

Nondurable manufacturing, on the other hand, is expected to decline by less than 1 percent, shedding 64,000 jobs overall. The majority of employment declines are expected to be in apparel and other textile products and leather and leather products industries, which together are expected to shed 131,000 jobs by 2010 because of increased job automation and international competition. On the other hand, drug manufacturing is expected to grow 23.8 percent due to an aging population and increasing life expectancies.

Mining. Employment in mining is expected to decrease 10.1 percent, or by some 55,000 jobs, by 2010. The majority of the decline will come from coal mining, in which employment is expected to decrease by 30 percent. The numbers of jobs in metal mining and nonmetallic mineral mining also are expected to decline by 13.8 and 3.2 percent, respectively. Employment decreases in these industries are attributable mainly to technology gains that boost worker productivity, growing international competition, restricted access to federal lands, and strict environmental regulations that require cleaning of burning fuels.

Oil and gas field services is the only mining industry in which employment is projected to grow, by 3.7 percent, through 2010. Employment growth is due chiefly to the downsizing of the crude petroleum, natural gas, and gas liquids industry, which contracts out production and extraction jobs to companies in oil and gas field services.

Occupation

Expansion of the service-producing sector is expected to continue, creating demand for many occupations. However, projected job growth varies among major occupational groups (chart 7).

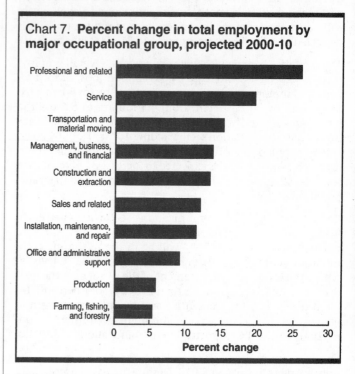

Chart 7. **Percent change in total employment by major occupational group, projected 2000-10**

Professional and related occupations. Professional and related occupations will grow the fastest and add more new jobs than any other major occupational group. Over the 2000–2010 period, a 26-percent increase in the number of professional and related jobs is projected, a gain of 6.9 million. Professional and related workers perform a wide variety of duties and are employed throughout private industry and government. Nearly three-quarters of the job growth will come from three groups of professional occupations—computer and mathematical occupations; healthcare practitioners and technical occupations; and education, training, and library occupations—which will add 5.2 million jobs combined.

Service occupations. Service workers perform services for the public. Employment in service occupations is projected to increase by 5.1 million, or 19.5 percent, the second-largest numerical gain and second-highest rate of growth among the major occupational groups. Food preparation and serving-related occupations are expected to add the most jobs among the service occupations, 1.6 million by 2010. However, healthcare support occupations are expected to grow the fastest, 33.4 percent, adding 1.1 million new jobs.

Transportation and material moving occupations. Transportation and material moving workers transport and transfer people and materials by land, sea, or air. These occupations should grow 15.2 percent and add 1.5 million jobs by 2010. Among transportation occupations, motor vehicle operators will add the most jobs—745,000. Rail transportation occupations are the only group in which employment is projected to decline, by 18.6 percent, through 2010. Material moving occupations will grow 14 percent and will add 681,000 jobs.

Management, business, and financial occupations. Workers in management, business, and financial occupations plan and direct the activities of business, government, and other organizations. Employment is expected to increase by 2.1 million, or 13.6 percent, by 2010. Among managers, the numbers of computer and information systems managers and of public relations managers will grow the fastest, by 47.9 and 36.3 percent, respectively. General and operations managers will add the most new jobs—363,000 by 2010. Agricultural managers and purchasing managers are the only workers in this group whose numbers are expected to decline, losing 325,000 jobs combined. Among business and financial occupations, accountants and auditors and management analysts will add the most jobs—326,000 combined. Management analysts also will be one of the fastest growing occupations in this group, along with personal financial advisors, with job increases of 28.9 and 34 percent, respectively.

Construction and extraction occupations. Construction and extraction workers construct new residential and commercial buildings and also work in mines, quarries, and oil and gas fields. Employment of these workers is expected to grow 13.3 percent, adding 989,000 new jobs. Construction trades and related workers will account for the majority of these new jobs—862,000 by 2010. Most extraction jobs will decline, reflecting overall employment losses in the mining and oil and gas extraction industries.

Sales and related occupations. Sales and related workers transfer goods and services among businesses and consumers. Sales and related occupations are expected to add 1.9 million new jobs by 2010, growing by 11.9 percent. The majority of these jobs will be among retail salespersons and cashiers, occupations that will add almost 1 million jobs combined.

Installation, maintenance, and repair occupations. Workers in installation, maintenance, and repair occupations install new equipment and maintain and repair older equipment. These occupations will add 662,000 jobs by 2010, growing by 11.4 percent. Automotive service technicians and general maintenance and repair workers will account for 3 in 10 new installation, maintenance, and repair jobs. The fastest growth rate will be among telecommunications line installers and repairers, an occupation that is expected to grow 27.6 percent over the 2000–2010 period.

Office and administrative support occupations. Office and administrative support workers perform the day-to-day activities of the office, such as preparing and filing documents, dealing with the public, and distributing information. Employment in these occupations is expected to grow by 9.1 percent, adding 2.2 million new jobs by 2010. Customer service representatives will add the most new jobs—631,000. Desktop publishers will be among the fastest growing occupations, growing 66.7 percent over the decade. Order clerks, tellers, and insurance claims and policy processing clerks will be among the jobs with the largest employment losses.

Production occupations. Production workers are employed mainly in manufacturing, assembling goods, and operating plants. Production occupations will grow 5.8 percent and add 750,000 jobs by 2010. Metal and plastics workers and assemblers and fabricators will add the most production jobs—249,000 and 171,000, respectively. Textile, apparel, and furnishings occupations will account for much of the job losses among production occupations.

Farming, fishing, and forestry occupations. Farming, fishing, and forestry workers cultivate plants, breed and raise livestock, and catch animals. These occupations will have the slowest job growth among the major occupational groups—5.3 percent, adding 74,000 new jobs by 2010. Farm workers account for nearly 3 out of 4 new jobs in this group. The numbers of both fishing and logging workers are expected to decline, by 12.2 and 3.5 percent, respectively.

Computer occupations are expected to grow the fastest over the projection period (chart 8). In fact, these jobs account for 8 out of the 20 fastest growing occupations in the economy. In addition to high growth rates, these eight occupations combined will add more than 1.9 million new jobs to the economy.

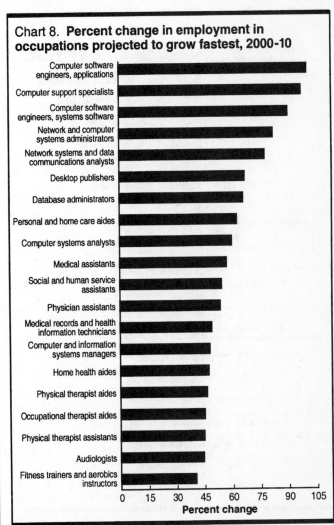

Chart 8. **Percent change in employment in occupations projected to grow fastest, 2000-10**

Health occupations comprise most of the remaining fastest growing occupations. High growth rates among computer and health occupations reflect projected faster-than-average growth in the computer and data processing and health services industries.

The 20 occupations listed in chart 9 will account for more than one-third of all new jobs, 8 million combined, over the 2000–2010 period. The occupations with the largest numerical increases cover a wider range of occupational categories than those occupations with the fastest growth rates. Computer and health occupations will account for some of these increases in employment, as will occupations in education, sales, transportation, office and administrative support, and food service. Many of these occupations are very large and will create more new jobs than those with high growth rates. Only 4 out of the 20 fastest growing occupations—computer software engineers, applications; computer software engineers, systems software; computer support specialists; and home health aides—also are projected to be among the 20 occupations with the largest numerical increases in employment.

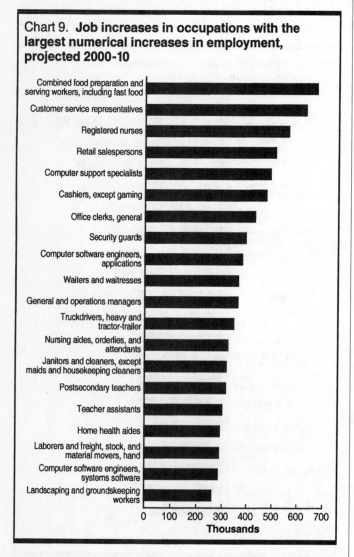

Chart 9. **Job increases in occupations with the largest numerical increases in employment, projected 2000-10**

Declining occupational employment stems from declining industry employment, technological advancements, changes in business practices, and other factors. For example, increased productivity and farm consolidations are expected to result

in a decline of 328,000 farmers over the 2000–2010 period (chart 10). The majority of the 20 occupations with the largest numerical decreases are office and administrative support and production occupations, which are affected by increasing automation and the implementation of office technology that reduces the need for these workers. For example, the increased use of ATM machines and Internet banking will reduce the number of tellers.

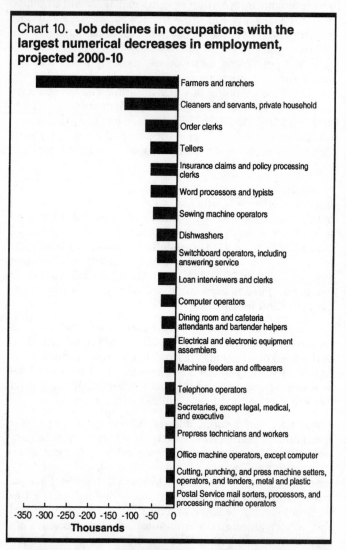

Chart 10. **Job declines in occupations with the largest numerical decreases in employment, projected 2000-10**

Total Job Openings

Job openings stem from both employment growth and replacement needs (chart 11). Replacement needs arise as workers leave occupations. Some transfer to other occupations while others retire, return to school, or quit to assume household responsibilities. Replacement needs are projected to account for 60 percent of the approximately 58 million job openings between 2000 and 2010. Thus, even occupations with little or no change in employment still may offer many job openings.

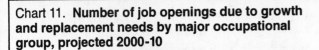

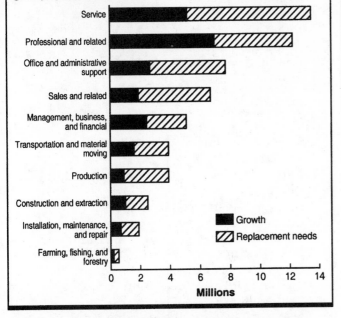

Chart 11. **Number of job openings due to growth and replacement needs by major occupational group, projected 2000-10**

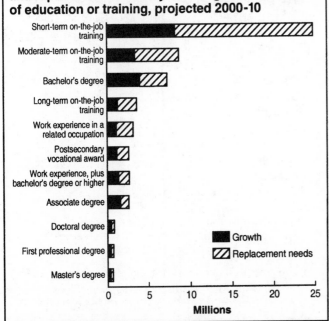

Chart 12. **Number of job openings due to growth and replacement needs by most significant source of education or training, projected 2000-10**

projected to generate more openings from job growth than from replacement needs.

Due to high replacement needs, service occupations are projected to have the largest number of total job openings, 13.5 million. A large number of replacements are expected to arise as young workers leave food preparation and service occupations. Replacement needs generally are greatest in the largest occupations and in those with relatively low pay or limited training requirements.

Office automation will significantly affect many individual office and administrative support occupations. Overall, these occupations are projected to grow more slowly than the average, while some are projected to decline. Office and administrative support occupations are projected to create 7.7 million job openings over the 2000–2010 period, ranking third behind service and professional and related occupations.

Agriculture, forestry, and fishing occupations are projected to have the fewest job openings, approximately 500,000. Because job growth is expected to be slow, and levels of retirement and job turnover high, more than 80 percent of these projected job openings are due to replacement needs.

Employment in occupations requiring an associate degree is projected to increase 32 percent, faster than any other occupational group categorized by education or training. However, this category ranks only eighth among the 11 education and training categories in terms of job openings. The largest number of job openings will be among occupations requiring short-term on-the-job training (chart 12).

Almost two-thirds of the projected job openings over the 2000–2010 period will be in occupations that require on-the-job training and arise mostly from replacement needs. These jobs will account for 37.3 million of the projected 57.9 million total job openings through 2010. However, many of these jobs typically offer low pay and benefits; this is more true of jobs requiring only short-term on-the-job training, which will account for 24.8 million openings, than of the occupations in any other education or training category.

Jobs requiring a bachelor's degree, and which usually offer higher pay and benefits, will account for about 7.3 million job openings through 2010. Most of these openings will result from job growth.

Professional and related occupations are projected to grow faster and add more jobs than any other major occupational group, with 7 million new jobs by 2010. Three-fourths of this job growth is expected among computer and mathematical occupations; healthcare practitioners and technical occupations; and education, training, and library occupations. With 5.2 million job openings due to replacement needs, professional and related occupations are the only major group

Employment Trends in Major Industries

Comments

While hundreds of specialized industries exist, about 75 percent of all workers are employed in just 42 major ones. Space limitations do not allow us to provide you with detailed information on all industries; however, the following article presents a good overview of trends within industry types. It gives you important facts to consider in making your career plans. The article comes, with minor changes, from a U.S. Department of Labor publication titled *Career Guide to Industries.*

While you may not have thought much about it, the industry you work in will often be as important as the career you choose. For example, some industries pay significantly higher wages than others. So, if you found your way back to this article, read it over carefully and consider the possibilities.

For more information on a specific industry, look for the *Career Guide to Industries* in your library. A more widely available version of the same book is published by JIST under the title *Career Guide to America's Top Industries*. It is available through bookstores and many libraries. Here are the industries covered in the *Career Guide to Industries:*

Agriculture, Mining, and Construction
Agricultural Production
Agricultural Services
Construction
Mining and Quarrying
Oil and Gas Extraction
Manufacturing
Aerospace Manufacturing
Apparel and Other Textile Products
Chemical Manufacturing, Except Drugs
Drug Manufacturing
Electronic Equipment Manufacturing
Food Processing
Motor Vehicle and Equipment Manufacturing
Printing and Publishing
Steel Manufacturing
Textile Mill Products
Transportation, Communications, and Public Utilities
Air Transportation
Cable and Other Pay Television Services
Public Utilities
Radio and Television Broadcasting
Telecommunications
Trucking and Warehousing
Wholesale and Retail Trade
Department, Clothing, and Accessory Stores
Eating and Drinking Places
Grocery Stores
Motor Vehicle Dealers
Wholesale Trade
Finance and Insurance
Banking
Insurance
Securities and Commodities
Services
Advertising
Amusement and Recreation Services
Childcare Services
Computer and Data Processing Services
Educational Services
Health Services
Hotels and Other Lodging Places
Management and Public Relations Services
Motion Picture Production and Distribution
Personnel Supply Services
Social Services, Except Childcare
Government
Federal Government, Excluding the Postal Service
State and Local Government, Excluding Education and Hospitals

Overview

The U.S. economy is made up of industries with diverse characteristics. For each industry covered in the Department of Labor's publication *Career Guide to Industries*, detailed information is provided about specific characteristics: the nature of the industry, working conditions, employment, occupations in the industry, training and advancement, earnings, and outlook. This article provides an overview of these characteristics for the economy as a whole.

Nature of the Industry

Industries are defined by the goods and services they provide. Because workers in the United States produce such a wide variety of products and services, the types of industries in the U.S. economy range widely, from aerospace manufacturing to motion picture production. Although many of these industries are related, each industry has a unique combination of occupations, production techniques, inputs and outputs, and business characteristics. Understanding the nature of the industry is important, because it is this unique combination that determines working conditions, educational requirements, and the job outlook for the industry.

Industries are comprised of many different places of work, called *establishments*, which range from large factories and office complexes employing thousands of workers to small businesses employing only a few workers. Not to be confused with companies, which are legal entities, establishments are physical locations where people work, such as the branch office of a bank. Establishments that produce similar goods or services are grouped together into *industries*. Industries that produce related types of goods or services are, in turn, grouped together into *major industry divisions*. These are further grouped into the *goods-producing sector* (agriculture, mining, and construction; and manufacturing) or the *service-producing sector* (transportation, communications, and public utilities; wholesale and retail trade; finance and insurance; services; and government).

Distinctions within industries are also varied. Each industry is comprised of a number of subdivisions, which are determined largely by differences in production processes. An easily recognized example of these distinctions is in the food processing industry, which is made up of subdivisions that produce meat products, preserved fruits and vegetables, bakery items, beverages, and dairy products, among others. Each of these subdivisions requires workers with varying skills and employs unique production techniques. Another example of these distinctions is in public utilities, which employs workers in establishments that provide electricity, sanitary services, water, and natural gas. Working conditions and establishment characteristics often differ widely in each of these smaller subdivisions.

There were more than 7 million business establishments in the United States in 1999. The average size of these establishments varies widely across industries. Among industry divisions, manufacturing included many industries having among the highest employment per establishment in 1999. For example, the aerospace and steel manufacturing industries each averaged 200 or more employees per establishment.

Most establishments in the wholesale trade, retail trade, finance, and services industries are small, averaging fewer than 20 employees per establishment. Exceptions are the scheduled air transportation industry with 166.8 employees, and colleges, universities, and professional schools with 433.4. In addition, wide differences within industries can exist. Hospitals, for example, employ an average of 717.5 workers, while doctors' offices employ an average of 8.7. Similarly, although there is an average of 13 employees per establishment for all of retail trade, department stores employ an average of 164.3 people.

Establishments in the United States are predominantly small; 54.2 percent of all establishments employed fewer than 5 workers in 1999. The medium-sized to large establishments employ a greater proportion of all workers. For example, establishments that employed 50 or more workers accounted for only 5.4 percent of all establishments, yet employed 59 percent of all workers. The large establishments—those with more than 500 workers—accounted for only 0.3 percent of all establishments, but employed 20.3 percent of all workers. Table 1 presents the percent distribution of employment according to establishment size.

Establishment size can play a role in the characteristics of each job. Large establishments generally offer workers greater occupational mobility and advancement potential, whereas small establishments may provide their employees with broader experience by requiring them to assume a wider range of responsibilities. Also, small establishments are distributed throughout the nation; every locality has a few small businesses. Large establishments, in contrast, employ more workers and are less common, but they play a much more prominent role in the economies of the areas in which they are located.

TABLE 1

Percent Distribution of Establishments and Employment in All Industries by Establishment Size, 1999

Establishment Size (Number of Workers)	Establishments	Employment
Total	100.0	100.0
1–4	54.2	5.9
5–9	19.4	8.1
10–19	12.5	10.7
20–49	8.5	16.3
50–99	2.9	12.8
100–249	1.7	16.4
250–499	0.4	9.6
500–999	0.2	7.2
1,000 or more	0.1	13.2

SOURCE: Department of Commerce, County Business Patterns, 1999

Working Conditions

Just as the goods and services of each industry are different, working conditions in industries can vary significantly. In some industries, the work setting is quiet, temperature-controlled, and virtually hazard free. Other industries are characterized by noisy, uncomfortable, and sometimes dangerous work environments. Some industries require long workweeks and shift work; in many industries, standard 35- to 40-hour workweeks are common. Still other industries can be seasonal, requiring long hours during busy periods and abbreviated schedules during slower months. These varying conditions usually are determined by production processes, establishment size, and the physical location of work.

One of the most telling indicators of working conditions is an industry's injury and illness rate. Among the most common incidents causing work-related injury or illness are overexertion, being struck by an object, and falling on the same level. In 1999, approximately 5.7 million nonfatal injuries and illnesses were reported throughout private industry. Among major industry divisions, manufacturing had the highest rate of injury and illness—9.2 cases for every 100 full-time workers. Finance, insurance, and real estate had the lowest rate—1.8 cases. About 5,900 work-related fatalities were reported in 2000. Transportation incidents, contact with objects and equipment, assaults and violent acts, and falls were the most common events resulting in fatal injuries. Table 2 presents industries with the highest and lowest rates of nonfatal injury and illness.

TABLE 2

Nonfatal Injury and Illness Rates of Selected Industries, 2000

Industry	Cases Per 100 Full-Time Employees
All industries	6.3
High rates	
Transportation equipment	13.7
Transportation by air	13.3
Lumber and wood products	13.0
Primary metal	12.9
Food and kindred products	12.7
Fabricated metal products	12.6
Low rates	
Insurance carriers	1.9
Engineering and management	1.7
Depository institutions	1.5
Legal services	1.0
Insurance agents and brokers	0.9
Securities and commodities	0.6

Work schedules are another important reflection of working conditions, and the operational requirements of each industry lead to large differences in hours worked and in part-time versus full-time status. In retail trade, 28.9 percent of employees worked part time in 2000, compared with only 4.4 percent in manufacturing. Table 3 presents industries having relatively high and low percentages of part-time workers.

TABLE 3

Percent of Part-Time Workers in Selected Industries, 2000

Industry	Percent Part-Time
All industries	15.3
Many part-time workers	
Eating and drinking places	37.8
Department, clothing, and accessory stores	31.3
Grocery stores	30.4
Amusement and recreation services	29.3
Child-care services	28.2
Motion picture production and distribution	23.0
Educational services	21.9
Social services	20.9
Few part-time workers	
Public utilities	3.2
Chemical manufacturing, except drugs	3.0
Drug manufacturing	2.6
Electronic equipment manufacturing	2.4
Mining and quarrying	1.9
Aerospace manufacturing	1.8
Steel manufacturing	1.5
Motor vehicle and equipment manufacturing	1.5

The low proportion of part-time workers in some manufacturing industries often reflects the continuous nature of the production processes that makes it difficult to adapt the volume of production to short-term fluctuations in product demand. Once begun, it is costly to halt these processes; machinery must be tended and materials must be moved continuously. For example, the chemical manufacturing industry produces many different chemical products through controlled chemical reactions. These processes require chemical operators to monitor and adjust the flow of materials into and out of the line of production. Because production may continue 24 hours a day, 7 days a week, under the watchful eyes of chemical operators who work in shifts, full-time workers are more likely to be employed.

Retail trade and service industries, on the other hand, have seasonal cycles marked by various events, such as school openings or important holidays, that affect the hours worked. During busy times of the year, longer hours are common, whereas slack periods lead to cutbacks and shorter workweeks. Jobs in these industries are generally appealing to students and others who desire flexible, part-time schedules.

Employment

The total number of jobs in the United States in 2000 was 145.6 million. This included 11.5 million self-employed workers, 169,000 unpaid workers in family businesses, and more than 133.9 million wage and salary workers—including primary and secondary job holders. The total number of jobs is projected to increase to 167.8 million by 2010, and wage and salary jobs are projected to account for more than 155.9 million of them.

As shown in Table 4, although wage and salary jobs are the vast majority of all jobs, they are not evenly divided among the various industries. The services major industry division is the largest source of employment, with more than 50 million workers, followed by the wholesale and retail trade and manufacturing major industry divisions. Wage and salary employment ranged from only 216,000 in cable and other pay television services to 11.8 million in educational services. Three industries—educational services, health services, and eating and drinking places—together accounted for almost 31 million jobs, or nearly a quarter of the nation's employment.

TABLE 4

Wage and Salary Employment in Selected Industries, 2000, and Projected Change, 2000 to 2010

Industry	2000 Employment (in 1000s)	2000 Percent Distribution	2010 Employment (in 1000s)	2010 Percent Distribution	2000–2010 Percent Change	2000–2010 Employment Change
All industries	133,896	100.0	155,872	100.0	16.4	21,977
Goods-producing industries	27,984	20.9	29,728	19.1	6.2	1,745
Agriculture, mining, and construction	9,514	7.1	10,682	0.0	12.3	1,167
Agricultural production	1,120	0.8	1,092	0.7	–2.5	–28
Agricultural services	1,099	0.8	1,524	1.0	38.6	425
Construction	6,698	5.0	7,522	4.8	12.3	825
Mining and quarrying	231	0.2	199	0.1	–14.0	–32
Oil and gas extraction	311	0.2	289	0.2	–7.3	–23
Manufacturing	18,469	13.8	19,047	12.2	3.1	577
Aerospace manufacturing	551	0.4	655	0.4	18.9	104
Apparel and other textile products	633	0.5	530	0.3	–16.3	–103
Chemical manufacturing, except drugs	723	0.5	691	0.4	–4.5	–32
Drug manufacturing	315	0.2	390	0.3	23.8	75
Electronic equipment manufacturing	1,554	1.2	1,657	1.1	6.6	103
Food processing	1,684	1.3	1,634	1.0	–3.0	–50
Motor vehicle and equipment manufacturing	1,013	0.8	1,100	0.7	8.6	87
Printing and publishing	1,547	1.2	1,545	1.0	–0.2	–3
Steel manufacturing	225	0.2	176	0.1	–21.6	–49
Textile mill products	529	0.4	500	0.3	–5.4	–29
Service-producing industries	105,912	79.1	126,144	80.9	19.1	20,232
Transportation, communications, and public utilities	7,019	5.2	8,274	5.3	17.9	1,255
Air transportation	1,281	1.0	1,600	1.0	24.9	319
Cable and other pay television services	216	0.2	325	0.2	50.6	109
Public utilities	851	0.6	893	0.6	4.9	42
Radio and television broadcasting	255	0.2	280	0.2	9.7	25
Telecommunications	1,168	0.9	1,311	0.8	12.2	143
Trucking and warehousing	1,856	1.4	2,262	1.5	21.9	407
Wholesale and retail trade	30,331	22.7	34,200	21.9	12.8	3,869
Department, clothing, and accessory stores	4,030	3.0	4,198	2.7	4.2	168
Eating and drinking places	8,114	6.1	9,600	6.2	18.3	1,486
Grocery stores	3,107	2.3	3,281	2.1	5.6	174
Motor vehicle dealers	1,221	0.9	1,366	0.9	11.9	145
Wholesale trade	7,024	5.2	7,800	5.0	11.1	776
Finance, insurance, and real estate	7,560	5.6	8,247	5.3	9.1	687
Banking	2,029	1.5	1,999	1.3	–1.5	–31
Insurance	2,346	1.8	2,497	1.6	6.4	151
Securities and commodities	748	0.6	900	0.6	20.3	152
Services	50,764	37.9	64,483	41.4	27.0	13,719
Advertising	302	0.2	400	0.3	32.5	98
Amusement and recreation services	1,728	1.3	2,325	1.5	34.5	597
Childcare services	712	0.5	1,010	0.6	41.9	298
Computer and data processing services	2,095	1.6	3,900	2.5	86.2	1,805
Educational services	11,797	8.8	13,400	8.6	13.6	1,603
Health services	11,065	8.3	13,882	8.9	25.5	2,817
Hotels and other lodging places	1,912	1.4	2,167	1.4	13.3	255
Management and public relations services	1,090	0.8	1,550	1.0	42.2	460
Motion picture production and distribution	287	0.2	369	0.2	28.7	82
Personnel supply services	3,887	2.9	5,800	3.7	49.2	1,913
Social services, except childcare	2,191	1.6	3,118	2.0	42.3	927
Government	10,238	7.6	10,940	7.0	6.9	702
Federal government	1,917	1.4	1,772	1.1	–7.6	–145
State and local government	7,461	5.6	8,318	5.3	11.5	856

Although workers of all ages are employed in each industry, certain industries tend to employ workers of distinct age groups. For the reasons mentioned previously, retail trade employs a relatively high proportion of younger workers to fill part-time and temporary positions. The manufacturing sector, on the other hand, has a relatively high median age because many jobs in the sector require a number of years to learn and perfect skills that do not easily transfer to other firms. Also, manufacturing employment has been declining, providing fewer opportunities for younger workers to get jobs. As a result, almost one-third of the workers in retail trade were 24 years of age or younger in 2000, compared with only 10 percent of workers in manufacturing. Table 5 contrasts the age distribution of workers in all industries with the distributions in five very different industries.

TABLE 5

Percent Distribution of Wage and Salary Workers by Age Group, Selected Industries, 2000

Industry	Age Group			
	16 to 24	25 to 44	45 to 64	65 to 90
All industries	15	50	32	3
Textile mill products manufacturing	9	47	41	3
Public utilities	5	51	42	1
Eating and drinking places	45	39	15	2
Computer and data processing services	11	67	22	1
Educational services	11	43	43	3

Employment in some industries is concentrated in one region of the country, and job opportunities in these industries should be best in the states in which their establishments are located. Such industries are often located near a source of raw materials upon which the industries rely. For example, oil and gas extraction jobs are concentrated in Texas, Louisiana, and Oklahoma; many textile mill products manufacturing jobs are found in North Carolina, Georgia, and South Carolina; and a significant proportion of motor vehicle and equipment manufacturing jobs are located in Michigan. On the other hand, some industries such as grocery stores and educational services have jobs distributed throughout the nation, reflecting population density in different areas.

Occupations in the Industry

As mentioned above, the occupations found in each industry depend on the types of services provided or goods produced. For example, construction companies require skilled trades workers to build and renovate buildings, so these companies employ a large number of carpenters, electricians, plumbers, painters, and sheet metal workers. Other occupations common to the construction sector include construction equipment operators and mechanics, installers, and repairers. Retail trade, on the other hand, displays and sells manufactured goods to consumers, so this sector hires numerous sales clerks and other workers, including nearly 5 out of 6 cashiers. Table 6 shows the major industry divisions and the occupational groups which predominate in the division.

The nation's occupational distribution clearly is influenced by its industrial structure, yet there are many occupations, such as general manager or secretary, which are found in all industries. In fact, some of the largest occupations in the U.S. economy are dispersed across many industries. Because nearly every industry relies on administrative support, for example, this occupational group is the largest in the nation (see Table 7). Other large occupational groups include service occupations, professional specialty workers, and operators, fabricators, and laborers.

TABLE 6

Industry Divisions and Largest Occupational Concentration, 2000

Industry Division	Largest Occupational Group	Percent of Wage and Salary Jobs
Agriculture, forestry, and fishing	Farming, forestry, and fishing	45.5
Mining	Construction and extraction	33.6
Construction	Construction and extraction	67.6
Manufacturing	Production	51.7
Transportation, communications, and public utilities	Transportation and material moving	36.0
Wholesale and retail trade	Sales and related	32.4
Finance, insurance, and real estate	Office and administrative support	45.3
Services	Professional and related	36.9
Government	Office and administrative support	26.8

TABLE 7

Total Employment in Broad Occupational Groups, 2000, and Projected Change, 2000–2010 (Employment in Thousands)

Occupational Group	Employment, 2000	Percent Change, 2000–2010
Total, all occupations	145,571	15.2
Management, business, and financial	15,519	13.6
Professional and related	26,758	26.0
Service	26,075	19.5
Sales and related	15,513	11.9
Office and administrative support	23,882	9.1
Farming, fishing, and forestry	1,406	5.3
Construction and extraction	7,451	13.3
Installation, maintenance, and repair	5,820	11.4
Production	13,060	5.8
Transportation and material moving	10,088	15.2

Training and Advancement

Workers prepare for employment in many ways, but the most fundamental form of job training in the United States is a high school education. Fully 87.5 percent of the nation's workforce possessed a high school diploma or its equivalent in 2000. As the premium placed on education in today's economy increases, workers are responding by pursuing additional training. In 2000, 28.8 percent of the nation's workforce had some college or an associate degree, while an additional 27.5 percent continued in their studies and attained a bachelor's degree or higher. In addition to these types of formal education, other sources of qualifying training include formal company training, informal on-the-job training, correspondence courses, the Armed Forces, and friends, relatives, and other nonwork-related training.

The unique combination of training required to succeed in each industry is determined largely by the industry's occupational composition. For example, machine operators in manufacturing generally need little formal education after high school, but sometimes complete considerable on-the-job training. These requirements by major industry division are clearly demonstrated in Table 8.

TABLE 8

Percent Distribution of Highest Grade Completed or Degree Received by Industry Division, 2000

Industry Division	Bachelor's Degree or Higher	Some College or Associate Degree	High School Graduate or Equivalent	Less than 12 Years or No Diploma
Agriculture, forestry, and fishing	14	22	34	30
Mining	17	26	45	12
Construction	10	25	44	21
Manufacturing	21	26	39	15
Transportation, communications, and public utilities	21	35	37	8
Wholesale trade	25	31	34	11
Retail trade	14	30	36	21
Finance, insurance, and real estate	37	33	25	4
Business and repair services	29	29	29	12
Personal services	13	28	38	22
Entertainment and recreation services	25	30	28	17
Professional and related services	48	27	20	5
Government	36	36	25	3

Persons with no more than a high school diploma accounted for about 63.8 percent of all workers in agriculture, forestry, and fishing; 64.7 percent in construction; 53.4 percent in manufacturing; 44.8 percent in wholesale trade; and 57.4 in retail trade. On the other hand, workers who had acquired at least some training at the college level accounted for 72.4 percent of all workers in government; 71.4 percent in finance, insurance, and real estate; and 75.1 percent in professional and related services.

Education and training are also important factors in the variety of advancement paths found in different industries. In general, workers who complete additional on-the-job training or education increase their chances of being promoted. In much of the manufacturing sector, for example, production workers who receive training in management and computer skills increase their likelihood of being promoted to supervisors. Other factors which affect advancement opportunities include the size of the establishment or company, institutionalized career tracks, and the skills and aptitude of each worker. Each industry has some unique advancement paths, so persons who seek jobs in particular industries should be aware of how these paths may later shape their careers.

Earnings

As with other characteristics, earnings differ from industry to industry, the result of a highly complicated process that relies on a number of factors. For example, earnings may vary due to the occupations in the industry, average hours worked, geographical location, industry profits, union affiliation, and educational requirements. In general, wages are highest in metropolitan areas to compensate for the higher cost of living. And, as would be expected, industries that employ relatively few unskilled minimum-wage or part-time workers tend to have higher earnings.

A good illustration of these differences is shown by the earnings of all wage and salary workers in petroleum refining, which averaged $1,099 a week in 2000, and those in eating and drinking places, where the weekly average was $177. These differences are so large because petroleum-refining establishments employ more highly skilled, full-time workers, while eating and drinking places employ many lower skilled, part-time workers. In addition, many workers in eating and drinking places are able to supplement their low wages with money they receive as tips, which is not included in the industry wages data. Table 9 highlights the industries with the highest and lowest average weekly earnings.

TABLE 9

Average Weekly Earnings of Production or Nonsupervisory Workers on Private Nonfarm Payrolls in Selected Industries, 2000

Industry	Earnings
All industries	$474
Industries with high earnings	
Petroleum refining	1,099
Pipelines, except natural gas	956
Aircraft and parts	901
Computer and data processing services	897
Electric, gas, and sanitary services	895
Coal mining	871
Blast furnaces and basic steel products	870
Securities and commodities brokers	841
Engineering and architectural services	821
Motion picture production and services	811
Industries with low earnings	
Agricultural services	379
Nursing and personal care facilities	349
Apparel and other textile products manufacturing	338
Drug stores and proprietary stores	323
Hotels and motels	298
Food stores	281
Department stores	278
Amusement and recreation services	262
Child daycare services	258
Eating and drinking places	177

Employee benefits, once a minor addition to wages and salaries, continue to grow in diversity and cost. In addition to traditional benefits—including paid vacations, life and health insurance, and pensions—many employers now offer various benefits to accommodate the needs of a changing labor force. Such benefits are child care; employee assistance programs that provide counseling for personal problems; and wellness programs that encourage exercise, stress management, and self-improvement. Benefits vary among occupational groups, full- and part-time workers, public and private sector workers, regions, unionized and nonunionized workers, and small and large establishments. Data indicate that full-time workers and those in medium-size and large establishments—those with 100 or more workers—receive better benefits than part-time workers and those in smaller establishments.

Union penetration of the workforce varies widely by industry, and it also may play a role in earnings and benefits. In 2000, about 15 percent of workers throughout the nation were union members or were covered by union contracts. As Table 10 demonstrates, union affiliation of workers varies widely by industry. Approximately one-third of the workers in government and transportation, communications, and public utilities are union members or are covered by union contracts, compared with fewer than 4 percent in business and repair services; agriculture, forestry, and fishing; and finance, insurance, and real estate.

TABLE 10

Union Members and Other Workers Covered by Union Contracts as a Percent of Total Employment in Major Industry Divisions, 2000

Industry Division	Union Members or Covered by Union Contracts
Total, all industries	14.9
Government	35.7
Transportation, communications, and public utilities	31.9
Construction	20.4
Manufacturing	15.7
Mining	11.6
Entertainment and recreation services	10.5
Personal services	9.8
Wholesale trade	5.6
Retail trade	5.2
Professional and related services	5.2
Business and repair services	3.8
Agriculture, forestry, and fishing	3.3
Finance, insurance, and real estate	2.8

Outlook

Total employment in the United States is projected to increase by about 15 percent over the 2000–2010 period. Employment growth, however, is only one source of job openings; the total number of openings in any industry also depends on the industry's current employment level and its need to replace workers who leave their jobs. Throughout the economy, in fact, replacement needs will create more job openings than will employment growth. Employment size is a major determinant of job openings—larger industries generally provide more openings. The occupational composition of an industry is another factor. Industries with high concentrations of professional, technical, and other jobs that require more formal education—occupations in which workers tend to leave their jobs less frequently—generally have fewer openings resulting from replacement needs. On the other hand, more replacement openings generally occur in industries with high concentrations of service, labor, and other jobs that require little formal education and have lower wages, because workers in these jobs are more likely to leave their occupations.

Employment growth is determined largely by changes in the demand for the goods and services produced by an industry, worker productivity, and foreign competition. Each industry is affected by a different set of variables that impacts the number and composition of jobs that will be available. Even within an industry, employment in different occupations may grow at different rates. For example, changes in technology, production methods, and business practices in an industry might eliminate some jobs while creating others. Some industries may be growing rapidly overall, yet opportunities for workers in occupations that are adversely affected by technological change could be stagnant. Similarly, employment of some occupations may be declining in the economy as a whole yet may be increasing in a rapidly growing industry.

As shown in Table 4, employment growth rates over the next decade will vary widely among industries. Employment in goods-producing industries is expected to increase as growth in agricultural services, construction, and manufacturing is partially offset by declining employment in agricultural production and mining and quarrying. Rapid growth in agricultural services will be driven by its landscaping and veterinary services components. Growth in construction employment will stem from new factory construction as existing facilities are modernized; from new school construction, reflecting growth in the school-age population; and from infrastructure improvements such as road and bridge construction. Employment in agricultural production and mining and quarrying is expected to decline due to laborsaving technology. Reliance on foreign sources of energy also is expected to play a role in employment declines in mining and in oil and gas extraction.

Manufacturing employment will increase slightly, as strong demand continues for high-technology electrical goods and pharmaceuticals despite improvements in production technology and rising imports. Apparel manufacturing is projected to lose about 103,000 jobs over the 2000–2010 period—more than any other manufacturing industry—due primarily to increasing imports. But other manufacturing industries with strong domestic markets and export potential are expected to experience increases in employment. The drug manufacturing and aerospace manufacturing industries are two examples. Sales of drugs are expected to increase with growth in the

population, particularly among the elderly, and the introduction of new drugs to the market. An increase in air traffic, coupled with the need to replace aging aircraft will generate strong sales for commercial aircraft. Both drug and aerospace manufacturing also have large export markets.

Growth in overall employment will result primarily from growth in service-producing industries over the 2000–2010 period, almost all of which are expected to have increasing employment. Rising employment in these industries will be driven by services industries, the largest and fastest-growing major industry group, which are projected to provide almost 2 out of 3 new jobs across the nation. Health, education, and personnel supply services will account for 6.3 million of these new jobs. In addition, employment in the nation's fastest-growing industry—computer and data processing services—is expected to nearly double, adding another 1.8 million jobs. Job growth in the services sector will result from overall population growth, the rise in the elderly and school-age populations, and the trend toward contracting out for computer, personnel, and other business services.

Wholesale and retail trade is expected to add 3.9 million jobs over the coming decade. More than 776,000 of these jobs will arise in wholesale trade, reflecting growth both in trade and in the overall economy. Retail trade is expected to add 3.1 million jobs over the 2000–2010 period, the result of increases in both population and personal income. Although most retail stores are expected to add employees, nonstore retailers will experience the fastest growth rate—35 percent—as electronic commerce and mail-order sales account for an increasing portion of retail sales. Eating and drinking places will have the largest number of new jobs, nearly 1.5 million.

Employment in transportation, communications, and public utilities is projected to increase by nearly 1.26 million new jobs. The trucking and warehousing industry will have the biggest increase—407,000 jobs. Trucking industry growth will be fueled by growth in the volume of goods that need to be shipped as the economy expands. Air transportation is expected to generate nearly 319,000 jobs. Air transportation will expand as consumer and business demand increases, reflecting a growing population and increased business activity. Demand for new telecommunications services, such as Internet and wireless communications, will lead to an expansion of the telecommunications infrastructure. Employment growth is projected to add 143,000 jobs. While radio and television broadcasting will show average growth due to consolidations in the industry, employment of cable and other pay-television companies will increase by 51 percent as they upgrade their systems to deliver a wider array of communication and programming services.

Overall employment growth in finance, insurance, and real estate is expected to be around 9 percent, with close to 687,000 jobs added by 2010. Securities and commodities will be the fastest-growing industry in this group, adding more than 152,000 jobs. A growing interest in investing and the popularity of 401(k) and other pension plans are fueling increases in this industry. In contrast, employment in the largest industry in this group, banking, will decrease by 1.5 percent, or –31,000 jobs, as technological advances and the increasing use of electronic banking reduce the need for large administrative support staffs. Nondepository institutions—including personal and business credit institutions, as well as mortgage banks—are expected to grow as fast as the average, adding 111,800 jobs. Insurance carriers will grow more slowly than average, increasing by only 42,600 jobs.

All 702,000 new government jobs are expected to arise in state and local government, reflecting growth in the population and its demand for public services. In contrast, the federal government is expected to lose more than 145,000 jobs over the 2000–2010 period, as efforts continue to cut costs by contracting out services and giving states more responsibility for administering federally funded programs.

In sum, recent changes in the economy are having far-reaching and complex effects on employment in all industries. Jobseekers should be aware of these changes, keeping alert for developments that affect job opportunities in each industry and the variety of occupations in each industry.

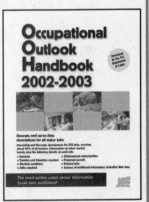
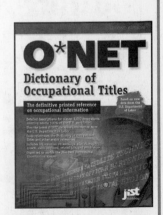

Enhanced Occupational Outlook Handbook,
Fourth Edition

Based on data from the U.S. Department of Labor
Compiled by Editors at JIST

This award-winning book combines the best features of America's three most authoritative occupational references—the *Occupational Outlook Handbook,* the *Dictiona~~~~~7~~~~ ~~~~~~~~~~~artment of Labor's Occup~~~~~ ~~~~~ence with over 2,000 job ~~~~ ~~~~~nterest and then ob~~~~ ~~~~ecialized jobs related to~~~~~

~~~~.95 Softcover
~~~~.95 Hardcover

Gallery of B~~~~~~~~~~~~ple
Without a F~~~~~~~~~~~~ Edition

A ~~~~~~~~~~~~~~~~~~~~~~~~~ **essional Resume**
W~~~~~~~~~~~~~~~~~~~~~~~~
Da~~~~~~~~~~~~~~~~~~~~~~

Sa~~~~~~~~~~~~~~~~~~~~~ ange of styles, formats,
oc~~~~~~~~~~~~~~~~~~~~~~ groups and written by
pro~~~~~~~~~~~~~~~~~~~~~~st resume tips on
de~~~~~~~~~~~~~~~~~

~~~55 / **$16.95**

America's T~~~~~~~~~~~~~~~~ica's
Top Jobs, Se~~~~~

M~~~~~~~~~

T~~~~~~~~~~~~~~~~~~~~~~~~~~~~~~~~~~ resumes for major
oc~~~~~~~~~~~~~~~~~~~~~~~~~~~~~~~~~uthors present nearly 400
outstanding resumes—all written and submitted by professional resume writers. The resumes are arranged by occupational groups and are designed for jobs at all levels of education, training, and experience. Handwritten annotations on the resumes highlight their unique points and strengths.

The book also provides valuable career planning and job search advice, including tips for writing and using your resume.

ISBN 1-56370-856-6 / Order Code LP-J8566 / **$19.95**